Iraq, 1990–2006
A Diplomatic History through Documents

Volume II

The revelatory volumes of *Iraq, 1990–2006: A Diplomatic History through Documents* detail the diplomatic saga involving Iraq and the international community from 1990 to 2006. Volume I covers the start of the Gulf War to the eve of the September 11 attacks. Volume II takes the reader from the shock of 9/11 to the prelude to the Iraq War. Volume III stretches from March 20, 2003, the first day of the Iraq War, to the formation of the Iraqi government in April 2006. Compiled over the span of more than fifteen years, the diverse set of speeches, statements, transcripts, letters, resolutions, and other primary source documents that comprise this 4,000-plus-page collection includes Iraqi, other Arab, and European documents that are usually overlooked in the English-language press. Insightful introductions to the three volumes are authored by David Kay, former U.N. arms inspector and head of the Iraq Survey Group; Andrew M. Parasiliti, former foreign policy adviser to Senator Chuck Hagel; and noted Mideast expert Kenneth M. Pollack.

Philip Auerswald is an associate professor at the School of Public Policy, George Mason University, and a research associate at the Belfer Center for Science and International Affairs, Kennedy School of Government, Harvard University. He is co-editor of *Seeds of Disaster, Roots of Response: How Private Action Can Reduce Public Vulnerability* (2006), *Clinton's Foreign Policy: A Documentary Record* (2003), and *The Kosovo Conflict: A Diplomatic History through Documents* (2000). Auerswald was a founding co-editor of the *Foreign Policy Bulletin: The Documentary Record of U.S. Foreign Policy*.

Iraq, 1990–2006

A Diplomatic History through Documents

Volume II

Edited by

Philip Auerswald

George Mason University

CAMBRIDGE
UNIVERSITY PRESS

CAMBRIDGE UNIVERSITY PRESS
Cambridge, New York, Melbourne, Madrid, Cape Town, Singapore, São Paulo, Delhi

Cambridge University Press
32 Avenue of the Americas, New York, NY 10013-2473, USA

www.cambridge.org
Information on this title: www.cambridge.org/9780521853811

First published 2009

Printed in the United States of America

A catalog record for this publication is available from the British Library.

Library of Congress Cataloging in Publication data
Iraq, 1990–2006 : a diplomatic history through documents / edited by
Philip Auerswald.
    p. cm.
Includes bibliographical references and index.
ISBN 978-0-521-85380-4 (hardback : v. 1) – ISBN 978-0-521-85381-1 (hardback : v. 2) –
ISBN 978-0-521-76765-1 (hardback : v. 3) – ISBN 978-0-521-76776-7 (packaged set)
1. Iraq – History – 1991–2003 – Sources.   2. Iraq – History – 2003 – Sources.
3. United States – Foreign relations – Iraq – Sources.   4. Iraq – Foreign relations –
United States – Sources.   5. Persian Gulf War, 1991 – Sources.   6. Iraq War, 2003 – Sources.
7. United Nations – Iraq – Sources.   8. Disarmament – On-site inspection – Iraq – Sources.
9. Weapons of mass destruction – Iraq – Sources.   I. Auerswald, Philip E.   II. Title.
DS79.75.I728   2009
956.7044'3–dc22   2009016386

ISBN   978-0-521-85381-1 hardback

Contents

Volume II

Volume I

Volume III

Introduction ▬▬▬▬▬▬▬▬▬▬▬▬▬▬▬▬▬▬▬▬▬▬

By Andrew Parasiliti

The documents in this volume provide primary source material for the period from the September 11, 2001, terrorist attacks on the United States through March 19, 2003, the eve of Operation Iraqi Freedom.

The decision to invade Iraq can only be understood in the context of the 9/11 attacks. The recasting of Iraq as the central front in a global war on terrorism came with some controversy. While President Bush gained congressional backing for the use of force in Iraq, his efforts to win the support of the U.N. Security Council and build an international coalition were less than successful. The absence of U.N. Security Council support for military action is widely cited as one of many reasons for the difficulties the United States has faced in postwar Iraq.

Links

In the months following 9/11, the United States waged war against those responsible for the attacks—the Al-Qaeda group led by Osama bin Laden, and the Taliban-led government in Afghanistan that had harbored Al-Qaeda. But that campaign was only the first phase in what became a "Global War on Terrorism." While Afghanistan had been a state sponsor of Al-Qaeda, it was a weak if not failing state. The Bush administration became preoccupied with the threat from those state sponsors of terrorism that either possessed or sought to develop or acquire nuclear, biological, radiological, or chemical weapons— weapons of mass destruction, or WMD. The possibility of a terrorist attack against the United States involving WMD motivated President George W. Bush to undertake an offensive strategy in the Global War on Terrorism and to look at other potential threats to the United States—including from Saddam Hussein's Iraq.

On September 12, 2001, President Bush tasked Richard Clarke, then National Coordinator for Security, Infrastructure Protection, and Counterterrorism, with determining whether Iraq might have played a role in the 9/11 attacks. Clarke found no "compelling case" for Iraq's involvement. Deputy Secretary of Defense Paul Wolfowitz, among others, argued within the administration for action against Iraq, even if the probability was low that Iraq had been involved in 9/11. Although President Bush decided on September 15 to proceed with military action only against Afghanistan, he also directed the Pentagon to prepare contingencies for military operations against Iraq in the event that the latter had acted against the United States.[1] On November 21, 2001, Bush asked Secretary of Defense Donald Rumsfeld to begin drafting a war plan for Iraq.[2]

The Bush administration's public redirecting or linking of Iraq to the war on terrorism began markedly with the President's State of the Union address on January 29, 2002. In the speech, Bush referred to Iran, North Korea, and Iraq—"states like these and their terrorist allies"—as constituting an "axis of evil, arming to threaten the peace of the world." Bush said that he would be "deliberate, yet time is not on our side. I will not wait on events, while dangers gather. I will not stand by, as peril draws closer and closer. The United States of America will not permit the world's most dangerous regimes to threaten us with the world's most destructive weapons" (p. 41).

The President's January 2002 speech signaled a new direction in U.S. national security strategy. In what came to be known as the Bush Doctrine, the United States would now use military force preemptively to prevent the United States and its allies from being threatened with WMD.[3] Iraq became the first test case for the Bush Doctrine of "preemption." Prior to 9/11, the prevailing view had been that Iraq was a difficult though manageable threat. Saddam Hussein's regional ambitions were contained through economic sanctions and no-fly zones over northern and southern Iraq. His WMD programs, while worrisome, were more or less in check and did not have the capability to threaten the U.S. homeland. Early in 2001, the Bush administration had even sought to implement a more narrow containment strategy toward Iraq—one that focused on "smart" sanctions—in order to reverse a perceived erosion of international support for multilateral sanctions against Iraq because of the toll that sanctions were taking on Iraq's population.

There was also an existing policy of "regime change" in Iraq, the result of the Iraq Liberation Act passed by the U.S. Congress in 1998, but it was neither the focus nor the direction of U.S. policy before 9/11. After the 2002 State of the Union address, however, dealing with Iraq, which was now designated as one of the "world's most dangerous regimes," acquired a heightened sense of urgency and priority in the U.S. Global War on Terrorism.

The Congress

In the spring and summer of 2002, Bush administration officials spoke more frequently about the potential threat from Iraq. Concerned about the increasing possibility of war, the Senate Foreign Relations Committee held two days of hearings on Iraq, July 31-August 1, 2002. By August, the administration realized that it needed a political strategy to win congressional and popular backing for a potential U.S. attack on Iraq, and a diplomatic strategy for an international coalition to support America's policies toward Iraq.

There are many important speeches, testimony, and remarks reproduced in this volume, but two are especially noteworthy with regard to the recasting of the Iraqi threat in the context of the war on terrorism.

On August 26, 2002, Vice President Dick Cheney spoke to the National Convention of the Veterans of Foreign Wars and declared, "We now know that Saddam has resumed his efforts to acquire nuclear weapons." Cheney expressed "no doubt that Saddam Hussein now has weapons of mass destruction... no doubt that he is amassing them to use against our friends, against our allies, and against us... and no doubt that his aggressive regional ambitions will lead him to future confrontations with his neighbors." The vice president cautioned that a "return of inspectors would provide no assurance whatsoever of his compliance with U.N. resolutions" (p. 223).

On October 7, President Bush himself linked Iraq more directly than ever to a potential terrorist threat to the United States—including the prospect of nuclear terrorism. Bush said that "Iraq has trained al-Qaeda members in bomb-making and poisons and deadly gases" and "the evidence indicates that Iraq is reconstituting its nuclear weapons programs." Bush continued: "America must not ignore the threat gathering against us. Facing clear evidence of peril, we cannot wait for the final proof—the smoking gun—that could come in the form of a mushroom cloud" (p. 399).

The administration's case for a "clear evidence of peril" from Iraq set the tone for the October 2002 congressional debate over authorizing the use of force against Iraq. There was also a general consensus at the time that Iraq had not fully accounted for its WMD programs, and that something had to be done in response to Iraq's flouting of U.N. Security Council resolutions.

On October 11, 2002, a joint resolution calling for the "Authorization for the Use of Military Force in Iraq" passed in Congress by a vote of 296–133 in the House of Representatives and 77–23 in the Senate. It authorized the president "to use the Armed Forces of the United States as he determines to be necessary and appropriate to

1. defend the national security of the United States against the continuing threat posed by Iraq; and
2. enforce all relevant United Nations Security Council resolutions regarding Iraq" (p. 474).

The overwhelming vote in favor of the resolution may have obscured an uneasiness and uncertainty about a possible war with Iraq. The vote took place a little more than one year after the 9/11 attacks and just one month before the 2002 congressional elections. The sense of vulnerability and urgency that America felt in the immediate aftermath of the 9/11 attacks resonates in many of the speeches and remarks by administration officials and members of Congress included in this volume.

The legislation also required a "presidential determination" that "diplomatic or other peaceful means alone" would not be adequate to meet the objectives above before force could be authorized. President Bush submitted this determination to Congress on March 18, 2003. Many in Congress later questioned whether the administration's determination was based on a biased standard in favor of using force.

The Security Council

Increasingly concerned about the likelihood of war with Iraq, Secretary of State Colin Powell requested a meeting with President Bush, and on August 5, 2002, over two hours of dinner conversation, Powell convinced the president of the need to build an international coalition to deal with Iraq.[4] On September 12, 2002, President Bush told the U.N. General Assembly, "We will work with the U.N. Security Council for the necessary resolutions" and that "Security Council resolutions will be enforced... or action will be unavoidable" (p. 269). On November 8, the U.N. Security Council unanimously passed Resolution 1441, declaring Iraq in "material breach of its obligations under relevant resolutions" and calling on Iraq to provide unrestricted access to U.N. weapons inspectors (p. 601), which Iraq agreed to do five days later.

Resolution 1441 proved to be the high-water mark of U.S. diplomatic efforts against Iraq. On December 19, 2002, Secretary Powell said that Iraq's formal declaration of its WMD programs that month "totally fails to meet the resolution's [1441] requirements" and included "material omissions that, in our view, constitute another material breach" (p. 761). A gap soon developed between the United States and other members of the Security Council about the urgency of the Iraqi threat. Although there was agreement on the need for Iraq to respect U.N. Security Council resolutions and to allow U.N. weapons inspections, the United States could not persuade other Council members that the use of force might be required to enforce Iraqi compliance, especially while inspections were taking place. There was also a debate, both initially within the administration and also among members of the Security Council, about whether a second Security Council resolution would be necessary if force were to be used against Iraq. Some delegates—pointing to the progress made by the enhanced inspections conducted by the United Nations Monitoring, Verification, and Inspection Commission and the International Atomic Energy Agency (IAEA)—insisted that more time was needed for inspections and that force should only be considered as a last resort.

On February 5, 2003, Secretary Powell presented to the U.N. Security Council the best case he could make based on U.S. intelligence sources that Iraq was both concealing and reconstituting its WMD programs (pp. 945–968). The evidence presented in Powell's speech has been much discussed and analyzed elsewhere, and thus need not be reviewed in detail here. Nevertheless, it is also worth reading the reaction of the other members of the Security Council to Powell's speech. While not taking the evidence at face value, other Security Council members replied that Powell's presentation was reason for continued U.N. inspections in Iraq, but not for war. Russian foreign minister Igor

Ivanov, for example, said, "The information provided today by the United States Secretary of State once again convincingly indicates that the activities of the international inspectors in Iraq must continue" (p. 972). French Foreign Minister Dominique Galouzeau de Villepin also argued for further inspections and said the "use of force can only be a final recourse" (p. 974).

Throughout the debate in the Security Council, IAEA director Mohamed El Baradei challenged some of the administration's most alarming and worrisome assumptions about Iraq's nuclear programs. On January 27, 2003, El Baradei said flatly, "To conclude, we have to date found no evidence that Iraq has revived its nuclear weapons program since the elimination of the program in the 1990s" (p. 905). El Baradei's conclusion, repeated in each of his reports to the Security Council, directly contradicted the Bush administration's "no doubt" that Saddam Hussein had sought to reconstitute his nuclear weapons programs.

In the weeks leading up to the war, the gap between the U.S. and U.N. assessments of the threat from Iraq grew. For example, in his report to the Security Council on March 7, El Baradei reported on the IAEA's "thorough investigation" of the assertion by Secretary Powell, in his February 5 speech to the Security Council, and President Bush, in his January 28, 2003, State of the Union Address (p. 912), that Iraq had attempted to purchase high-strength aluminum tubes for nuclear weapons production. El Baradei "concluded that Iraq's efforts to import those aluminum tubes were not likely to have been related to the manufacture of centrifuges and, moreover, that it was highly unlikely the Iraq could have achieved the considerable re-design needed to use them in a revived centrifuge program" (p. 1219).

Transformation

While the overwhelming focus of the case for war was on the potential threat from Iraq's WMD programs, the administration also presented an ideological rationale, namely, that regime change in Iraq would be a first step toward changing the strategic landscape of the Middle East. "Neoconservatives" within and outside of the administration considered the toppling of Saddam Hussein's regime as an opportunity to begin a democratic transformation of the Middle East and, perhaps, as the completion of the unfinished business of the 1991 Gulf War.

I will cite two examples here, although there are many in this volume. In his speech on August 26, 2002, Vice President Cheney said, "Regime change in Iraq would bring about a number of benefits to the region. When the gravest threats are eliminated, the freedom-loving peoples of the region will have a chance to promote the values that can bring lasting peace" (p. 225). On February 26, 2003, President Bush said, "A liberated Iraq can show the power of freedom to transform that vital region, by bringing peace and progress into the lives of millions" (p. 1147).

Conclusion

Soon after 9/11, Iraq had moved to the center of U.S. global strategy in the war on terrorism. There were allegations of the potential dual threat of terrorism and WMD from Saddam Hussein's regime. And there was a sense of opportunity, if not excitement, projected by those who believed Iraq could be the first step in the transformation of the Middle East. The U.S. rush to war in Iraq meant bypassing the U.N. Security Council, once it became clear (in March 2003) that it would not be possible to obtain a second resolution that would have effectively authorized the use of force against Iraq (pp. 1211–1212). The lack of international support for the war handicapped the postwar transition in Iraq.

The documents in this volume provide the raw material for further study and reflection on the causes and rationale of the U.S. decision to invade Iraq, and the implications of that decision for the United States, Iraq, and the Middle East.

Andrew Parasiliti is vice president of BGR International. From 2001 to 2005, he served as foreign policy advisor to U.S. Senator Chuck Hagel (R-NE), a member of the Senate Foreign Relations Committee.

---

1. National Commission on Terrorist Attacks Upon the United States, *The 9/11 Commission Report: Final Report of the National Commission on Terrorist Attacks Upon the United States, Authorized* (First) Edition, (New York: Norton), pp. 334–36.
2. Bob Woodward, *Plan of Attack* (New York: Simon & Schuster, 2004), pp. 1–4.
3. George W. Bush et al., *The National Security Strategy of the United States of America*, September 2002.
4. Bob Woodward, *Bush at War* (New York: Simon & Schuster, 2002), pp. 331–34.

Chapter 1

September 11–December 17, 2001
The September 11 Attacks and Their Immediate Aftermath

Remarks by President Bush, September 11, 2001

President Bush delivered his remarks at 9:30 A.M. at the Emma E. Booker Elementary School in Sarasota, Florida, where he had been discussing education.

Ladies and gentlemen, this is a difficult moment for America. I, unfortunately, will be going back to Washington after my remarks. Secretary Rod Paige and the Lt. Governor will take the podium and discuss education. I do want to thank the folks here at Booker Elementary School for their hospitality.

Today we've had a national tragedy. Two airplanes have crashed into the World Trade Center in an apparent terrorist attack on our country. I have spoken to the Vice President, to the Governor of New York, to the Director of the FBI, and have ordered that the full resources of the federal government go to help the victims and their families, and to conduct a full-scale investigation to hunt down and to find those folks who committed this act.

Terrorism against our nation will not stand.

And now if you would join me in a moment of silence. May God bless the victims, their families, and America. Thank you very much.

Remarks by President Bush, September 11, 2001

President Bush delivered his remarks upon arriving at Barksdale Air Force Base in Louisiana, in transit to an undisclosed, secure location.

I want to reassure the American people that the full resources of the federal government are working to assist local authorities to save lives and to help the victims of these attacks. Make no mistake: The United States will hunt down and punish those responsible for these cowardly acts.

I've been in regular contact with the Vice President, the Secretary of Defense, the national security team and my Cabinet. We have taken all appropriate security precautions to protect the American people. Our military at home and around the world is on high alert status, and we have taken the necessary security precautions to continue the functions of your government.

We have been in touch with the leaders of Congress and with world leaders to assure them that we will do whatever is necessary to protect America and Americans.

I ask the American people to join me in saying a thanks for all the folks who have been fighting hard to rescue our fellow citizens and to join me in saying a prayer for the victims and their families.

The resolve of our great nation is being tested. But make no mistake: We will show the world that we will pass this test. God bless.

Statement by President Bush, September 11, 2001

President Bush delivered the following address to the nation at 8:30 P.M.

Today, our fellow citizens, our way of life, our very freedom came under attack in a series of deliberate and deadly terrorist acts. The victims were in airplanes, or in their offices; secretaries, businessmen and women, military and federal workers; moms and dads, friends and neighbors. Thousands of lives were suddenly ended by evil, despicable acts of terror.

The pictures of airplanes flying into buildings, fires burning, huge structures collapsing, have filled us with disbelief, terrible sadness, and a quiet, unyielding anger. These acts of mass murder were intended to frighten our nation into chaos and retreat. But they have failed; our country is strong.

A great people has been moved to defend a great nation. Terrorist attacks can shake the foundations of our biggest buildings, but they cannot touch the foundation of America. These acts shattered steel, but they cannot dent the steel of American resolve.

America was targeted for attack because we're the brightest beacon for freedom and opportunity in the world. And no one will keep that light from shining.

Today, our nation saw evil, the very worst of human nature. And we responded with the best of America—with the daring of our rescue workers, with the caring for strangers and neighbors who came to give blood and help in any way they could.

Immediately following the first attack, I implemented our government's emergency response plans. Our military is powerful, and it's prepared. Our emergency teams are working in New York City and Washington, D.C. to help with local rescue efforts.

Our first priority is to get help to those who have been injured, and to take every precaution to protect our citizens at home and around the world from further attacks.

The functions of our government continue without interruption. Federal agencies in Washington which had to be evacuated today are reopening for essential personnel tonight, and will be open for business tomorrow. Our financial institutions remain strong, and the American economy will be open for business, as well.

The search is underway for those who are behind these evil acts. I've directed the full resources of our intelligence and law enforcement communities to find those responsible and to bring them to justice. We will make no distinction between the terrorists who committed these acts and those who harbor them.

I appreciate so very much the members of Congress who have joined me in strongly condemning these attacks. And on behalf of the American people, I thank the many world leaders who have called to offer their condolences and assistance.

America and our friends and allies join with all those who want peace and security in the world, and we stand together to win the war against terrorism. Tonight, I ask for your prayers for all those who grieve, for the children whose worlds have been shattered, for all whose sense of safety and security has been threatened. And I pray they will be comforted by a power greater than any of us, spoken through the ages in Psalm 23: "Even though I walk through the valley of the shadow of death, I fear no evil, for You are with me."

This is a day when all Americans from every walk of life unite in our resolve for justice and peace. America has stood down enemies before, and we will do so this time. None of us will ever forget this day. Yet, we go forward to defend freedom and all that is good and just in our world.

Thank you. Good night, and God bless America.

Open Letter from Iraqi President Hussein to the Government and People of America and other Western Nations, September 12, 2001

In the name of God, Most Gracious, Most merciful

Once again, we would like to comment on what happened in America on September 11, 2001, and its consequences. The comments we made on the next day of the event represent the essence of our position regarding this event and other events, but the aftermath of what happened in America, in the West in particular and in the world in general, makes it important for every leader to understand the meaning of responsibility toward his people, his nation, and humanity in general to follow up the development of the situation, to understand the meaning of what is going on, and hence to elaborate his country's and people's position so as not to restrict oneself to only following the event.

When the event took place Arab rulers and the rulers of countries whose religion of their people is Islam, rushed to condemn the event. The Westerners rushed within hours to make statements and adopt resolutions, some of which are dangerous ones, in solidarity with America and against terrorism.

Even before being sure, western governments decided to join their forces to the America even if that meant declaring war on the party that will be proved to have been involved in what happened.

It is only normal to say that by the explanation of the present situation, as it has been said or by comparison to the action previously taken by America against specific countries, it could be enough for some of the executors of the operation to have come from a country named by America or said to have instigated the operation, for the American military retaliation on what they call an aggression. We don't know if they would do the same thing whether any of the planners and executors of the operation were found, to have lived or held the nationality of a Western country or whether the intention and the designs are already made against an Islamic party.

It is most probable from the beating of media war drums that America and some Western governments are targeting a party who won't be but Muslim.

The event that took place in America is an extraordinary event. It is not a simple one. According to figures announced by official American sources or by what has been spread by the media, the number of victims is great. Nobody has any doubts, or denies that America and the West have the capabilities to mobilize force and use it, to inflict destruction on others on the basis of simple doubts or even whimsically, and can send their American missiles and the NATO fighters to where ever they want to destroy and harm whoever America decides to harm in a fit of anger, by greed, or by being pushed by Zionism.

Many countries of the world have suffered from America's technological might, and many peoples do recognize that America had killed thousands or even millions of human beings in their countries.

The event that took place in America was an extraordinary one. It is not a simple event.

It is the first time that someone crosses to America to unleash the fire of his anger inside it, as indicated by what was said by the media, on the hypothesis that the executors of this act came from abroad.

Since this event is unprecedented, is it wise to deal with it by precedent methods that can be used by whoever has the technical and scientific capacities of America and the West!?

If the target and the aim is one or more Islamic countries, as it has been said by the media and the intelligence services of some Western countries, this would only fall in the same direction that America and the West have always taken by targeting their fire on wherever they want to experiment a new weapon on.

We ask again: America's targeting the fire of its weapons on specific targets, and harming it or destroying it with the support of Western governments and of a fabricated story would it solve the problem? Would this bring security to America and the world? Or Isn't the use by America and some Western governments of their fire against others in the world including, or in the forefront of whom the Arabs and the Muslims, is one of the most important reasons of the lack of stability in the world at the present time?

Isn't the evil inflicted on America in the act of September 11, 2001, and nothing else is a result of this and other acts? This is the main question and this is what the American administration along with of the Western governments or the Western public opinion should answer in the first place with serenity and responsibility, without emotional reaction and without the use of the same old methods that America used against the world.

On September 12, 2001, we said that no one crossed the Atlantic to America carrying weapons before this event, except the Westerners who established the United States of America. America is the one who crossed the Atlantic carrying arms of destruction and death against the world. Here we want to ask a question: wasn't the use of American weapons, including the nuclear weapon against Japan, enough before September 11, 2001, for America to prepare to use it in a heavier and a stronger way? Or isn't using it in an irresponsible way, and without justification as does any oppressive force in the world, is what made America the most hated country in the world, starting from the Third World, to the Medium World and passing to the civilized world, as is the world divided by the West and America?

The national security of America and the security of the world could be attained if the American leaders and those who beat the drums for them among the rulers of the present time in the West or outside the West become rational, if America disengages itself from its evil alliance with Zionism, which has been scheming to exploit the world and plunge it in blood and darkness, by using America and some Western countries.

What the American peoples need mostly is someone who tells them the truth, courageously and honestly as it is. They don't need fanfares and cheerleaders, if they want to take a lesson from the event so as to reach a real awakening, in spite of the enormity of the event that hit America. But the world, including the rulers of America, should say all this to the American peoples, so as to have the courage to tell the truth and act according to what is right and not what to is wrong and unjust, to undertake their responsibilities in fairness and justice, and by recourse to reason, passion, according to the spirit of chance and capability.

In addition, we say to the American peoples, what happened on September 11, 2001 should be compared to what their government and their armies are doing in the world, for example, the international agencies have stated that more than one million and a half Iraqis have died because of the blockade imposed by America and some Western countries, in addition to the tens of thousands who died or are injured in the military action perpetrated by America along with those who allied with it against Iraq. Hundreds of bridges, churches, mosques, colleges, schools, factories, palaces, hotels, and thousands of private houses were destroyed or damaged by the American and Western bombardment, which is ongoing even today against Iraq. If you replay the images of the footage taken by the western media itself of this destruction, you will see that they are not different from the images of the two buildings hit by the Boeing airplanes, if not more atrocious, especially when they are mixed with the remains of men, women, and children. There is, however, one difference, namely that those who direct their missiles and bombs to the targets, whether Americans or from another Western country, are mostly targeting by remote controls, that is why they do so as if they were playing an amusing game. As for those who acted on September 11, 2001, they did it from a close range, and with, I imagine, giving their lives willingly, with an irrevocable determination.

For this reason also, the Americans, and the world with them, should understand the argument that made those people give their lives in sacrifice, and what they sacrificed themselves for, in that way.

When one million and a half Iraqi human beings die, according to Western documents, from a population of twenty five million, because of the American blockade and aggression, it means that Iraq has lost about one twenty-fifth of its population. And just as your beautiful skyscrapers were destroyed and caused your grief, beautiful buildings and precious homes crumbled over their owners in Lebanon, Palestine and Iraq by American weapons used by the Zionists. In only one place, which was a civilian shelter, which is the Ameriyah Shelter, more than four hundred human beings, children, young and old men and women, died in Iraq by American bombs.

In the same day, the 11th of September, one of their aggressive military airplanes was shot down over Iraq. And on the same day of the event in America on 11th September, and American jetfighter was perpetration aggression against Iraq and was shot down.

As for what is going on in Palestine, if Zionist let you see on your TVs the bodies of children, women and men who are daily killed by American weapons, and with American backing to the Zionist entity, the pain you are feeling would be appeased.

Americans should feel the pain they have inflicted on other peoples of the world, so as when they suffer, they will find the right solution and the right path.

All that has been inflicted on the Arabs and Muslims by America and the West, didn't push Muslims to become racists and harass the Westerners who walk in the streets of Baghdad, Damascus, Tunis, Cairo and other Arab capitals, even when the Westerners, and especially Americans insulted the holy sites of Muslim and Arabs by what is almost an occupation of Saudi Arabia in order to launch their evil fires against Baghdad, and when the American carriers roam the Arab Gulf, and their fighters daily roam the sky to throw tons of bombs and missiles over Iraq, so that about two hundred thousand tons of bombs have been used against Iraq, in addition to using depleted uranium!! All these are facts that are very well known not only to Arabs and Muslims, but to the whole world also. But because of only one incident that happened in America in one day, and upon an unconfirmed accusations so far, Arabs and Muslims, including some who hold the American citizenship, are being harassed openly and publicly in America and some Western countries. Some western countries are preparing themselves to participate in an American military action, against an Islamic country as the indications point out. In this case, who is being fanatic?

Isn't this solidarity, and this in-advance approval by some Western leaders, of a military aggression against an Islamic country, the most flagrant form of the new Crusades, fanaticism. It reminds Arabs and Muslims of those Crusade wars launched by the West and NATO against Iraq?

Finally, if you, rulers respect and cherish the blood of your peoples, why do you find it easy to shed the blood of others including the blood of Arabs and Muslims? If you respect your values, why don't you respect the values of Arabs and Muslims?

America needs wisdom, not power. It has used power, along with the West, to its extreme extent, only to find out latter that it doesn't achieve what they wanted. Will the rulers of America try wisdom just for once so that their people can live in security and stability?

In the name of God, Most Gracious, Most merciful,

Invite all to the way of thy Lord with the wisdom and beautiful preaching, and argue with them in ways that are best and most gracious, for the lord knoweth best who have strayed from His path and who receive guidance.

Open Letter from Iraqi President Hussein to the People and Government of the United States and other Western Countries, September 17, 2001

In the name of God, the most Compassionate, the most Merciful.

Once again, we make a return to comment on the incidence that took place in America on September 11, not for its significance as such, but for the implications surrounding it and its ramifications in terms of results on the level of the world of which we are part or rather a special case as a nation known as it is with the basis and uniqueness of its faith.

On previous occasions, we have already said that the United States needs to try wisdom after it has tried force over the last fifty years or even more. We still see that this is the most important thing the world must advise the U.S. about if there is anybody who wants to say something or adopt an attitude towards this incidence, and who is concerned about world peace and stability. This is the case if the U.S. and the world are convinced with the dictum and the verdict, namely that what has happened came to America from without, not within.

It is among the indisputables in the law or general norms, in dealings, in social life, and even political life, that any charge should be based on evidence if the one who makes the accusation is keen to convince others or has respect to that who listens to the accusation or is concerned with it as part of the minimal obligation of his duty. But the U.S. has made the charge before verification, even before possessing the minimum evidence about such a charge. It has even not availed itself the opportunity to verify things, first and foremost. It started a drive of incitement and threat, or said something irresponsible by broadening the base of charges to include states, circles and individuals.

American officials set about making charges or giving the guided media, the Zionist media and its symbols within the authority and outside it a free hand in order to prepare the public mind for the charge.. What does this mean?

In a nutshell, it means that the U.S. gives no heed to the law or rely on it. It has no concern for the counter viewpoint in line with its dangerous policy towards this issue or others. That is why we find that it takes no pain to secure evidence. Therefore, it needs no evidence to pass its verdict. It is content with saying something, passing verdicts, whether people other than the American officials are convinced or not. This means, in keeping with the policy it has pursued since 1990, that it has no regard to the viewpoint of the peoples and governments in the world in it entirety. It gives it no weight or heed despite the fact that it claims to be the democratic state (number one) in the world. The basic meaning of democracy even by the standards of its initial emergence in the Western world, that facts should lay bare before the people so that the people would assume their responsibility with full awareness. Our description of the U.S. attitude vis-á-vis this incidence is a practical description. It means that American officials do not respect even their own people's viewpoint, let alone the world's. In this conduct, the American officials behave as though they are deluding the peoples, beating up the misleading media drums to do the job of mobilizing them against enemy or enemies against whom no evidence about their accountability for the action they are accused of has been furnished. All the officials there seek to achieve is to foment the hostility of the peoples of the U.S. against whoever they assumed to be an enemy before the incidence has occurred. The tax-payer would be in a position where he is prepared to accept the blackmail trap arms manufacturers have laid for him in addition to the wrangled interests on the level of senior military and civil officials in the U.S..

One might argue that political verdicts do not always emanate from the same bases, procedures or courses adopted by the judiciary or criminal courts. Rather, precedents and backgrounds could suffice to arrive at a conclusion which may prove right. Even if, for the sake of argument, we go along this notion, just to keep the debate uninterrupted, we say that this could be true about the media and statements which are of media and propaganda nature, even political statements. In this instance, the error could not be necessarily fatal.

But is this permissible in war?

Once more, we say that war is not an ordinary case. Neither is it procedural in the life of nations and peoples. It is a case of unavoidable exception. Evidence based on conclusion is not enough, even if it is solid to make a charge against a given party or several parties, a state or several states to the extent that the one who makes the charge declares war at the party or parties against which charges were made and bears the responsibility of whatever harm might be sustained by his own people and the others including death, the destruction of possessions and the ensuing serious repercussions. It was only the U.S. administration that has made the charge against a certain religion, not just a given nationality.

Let us also accept the interventions of those who contend that the U.S. has not said this, through its senior officials and within this limitation. In fact, some officials have denied that their policy is one of making the charge against a given religion. However, we believe that the lack of evidence to make a charge, the disrespect to the golden sound rule of proper accusation which leads to the declaration of war and restricts the charge to a certain nation, states, designations and individuals, can only be understood as a premeditated charge without evidence that the action was carried out by Moslems. This is complemented by free reins for the media to float it, to prepare the public opinion to accept it or to be tuned to it so that anything opposed to it would sound like a discord.

Below is the list: Afghanistan. Osama bin Laden—the Islamic Qa'ida (base) party or organization. Syria. Yemen-Algeria. Iraq-Lebanon-Palestine.

The list may be curtailed or enlarged according to the pretexts of the policy of power, which has found its opportunity or the power that is looking for its opportunity to declare war. Whether the items of the list are increased or cut down, would all this mean anything but the accusation of Moslems, including, or rather in the forefront of whom Arabs? Why should this cross the minds of U.S. officials unless they have basically assumed themselves and their policy to be enemies of Arabs and Moslems?

Could this charge mean anything other than the desire to settle old scores, all based on the assumption that their foreign policies are incompatible with the American policy, or they do not give in to the U.S.-Zionist policy vis-á-vis the world and Palestine?

Consider statements by the U.S. officials who say the war would be long because it is aimed at several states. Notice the blackmail or better, the terrorism they mean and which was designed to include several states and parties on a list that could be longer or shorter in accordance with a policy of sheer terrorism and blackmail, first and foremost, the illusion that Arabs and Moslems and the people of Palestine would leave the arena for the aggression of the Zionist entity and its vile imperialism.

These charges which were made without consideration and in an instantaneous way mean that the mentality of the U.S. administration has been pre-loaded, prior to the incidence, even if we apply the norms of today and not the norms of the law. It has made assumption tantamount to conclusive verdict, namely that Islam, with Arabs in the lead of Moslems are enemies of the U.S.. More precisely, the U.S. on the level of its rulers has taken it as a final verdict that it is the enemy of Arabs and Moslems. In so doing, they have stored the final verdict in their minds. On this basis, they built their preparation in advance. On this basis too, they prepared (the mind) of the computer, which was programmed on this assumption, which has taken the form of a conclusive verdict. This reminds us of the free reins given to political writers, the so-called thinkers, including past heads of state and ministers who the Zionist policy wanted, over the last ten or fifteen years to assume that faith based on the religion of Islam with the ensuing implication is the new enemy of the U.S. and the West and it is the backdrop against which American rulers act, with the participation of some Western rulers who came under the pressure and interpretations of Zionist thought and scheming.

Obviously, this assumption is no longer a pure assumption for the purpose of scrutiny testing and examination. It has become part and parcel of conclusive verdicts. That is why the verdict was instantaneous, without consideration or waiting for the evidence to have a basis, evidence on which the pre-supposition is based in order to be a conclusive one. The charge has not only been made against all governments in Islamic or Arab states but also against all Islamic peoples, including the Arab nation and to all designations, parties, states and governments whose policies do not please the U.S., whose policies and positions are not palatable to the U.S. in particular or because they call for the liberation of Palestine and a halt to the U.S. aggression on Iraq, and adherence to their independence and their nations' heritage.

Any one who is surprised by this practical conclusion, allowing courteous words to be said on the margin of verdicts to replace it, has to contemplate our verdict:

The U.S. has declared it is at war. It is gearing up for war since the early moments in the wake of the incidence, as though it were the opportunity those concerned have been waiting for. It has allocated the necessary funds for the war, or part of them. Have you ever heard or read in the near on far history, of a state declaring war before even defining who its enemy is? The opportunity to declare the state of war came with the incidence that befell it. It is not yet known whether it was carried out by a foreign enemy or from inside. Thus, the war declared by America would cease to be a reason for the incidence. Rather, it is the incidence that has availed the opportunity to launch the war, which has not been a result of the incidence under any circumstances!

One might contend it is the nature of the incidence, the scale of pain the American officials felt as a result of what their peoples suffered, the embarrassment they felt due to the sufferings that hit the people there, that prompted American rulers to rush to declare war. The suffering of the people is not caused by the incidence alone, but by the failure of the authorities concerned which have been preoccupied by hatching conspiracies abroad, assassination and sabotage operations against world states and freedom-loving people. They rushed to declare war and name the parties so that they would leave no option but to launch the war. Once again, we say, could this be a reason and ground to facilitate the charge and the subsequent resolutions, why should not it be a ground for others as well?

If the fall in the whirlwind of rage, not the pre-meditated planning, results into war resolutions on their senior level inside the U.S., why should not you expect someone to direct his fire to it under the pressure of similar considerations or danger?

Once again we say that the U.S. administration and those in the West who allied themselves with it against Arabs and Moslems, now and in the past, or rather against the world, in all the arenas that witnessed the scourges of the alliance, are in need to take recourse to wisdom after they have had power at their disposal and deployed it to such an extent that it ceased to frighten those who experienced it. Dignity, the sovereignty of the homeland and the freedom of the sincere man is a sacred case, along with other sacred things which real Moslems uphold, including Arabs who are in the lead.

If this is the practical description of the pre-mediated intentions that decided war against Arabs and Moslems, while the party that took the decision waits for a cover to declare a war, and may launch it against those whom it has been biding time, could there be anyone who could avert it other than God, the Almighty? Anyone other than the will of the peoples, when they become fully aware, after they know and fear God, after they have believed in Him.

"For us Allah sufficeth, and He is the best disposer of affairs." (Holy Quran)

Once again we say that the peoples do not believe any more the slogans of the United States, accept those whom it intends evil against. Even when it says it is against terrorism, the United States doesn't apply this to the World, and according to the International Law. But according to its will to impose what it wants on the World and refuse what it thinks might be harmful to it only, and export the other kinds of it to the World. To certify this, could the United States tell its peoples how many organizations working against their own countries are existing in the United States? And how many of those, the term terrorism could be applied to if one standard is used and not the double standards? And how many are those it finances overtly and covertly? How many are those accused with killing and theft in other countries are now in the United States? If the United States presents such inventory to its peoples and to the World, and initiated implementing one standard and one norm on its agents and those it calls friends. And if it starts the same storm against the killers in the Zionist entity responsible of killing Palestinians in occupied Palestine and in Tunis and Lebanon. And if it charges its own secret services with what they committed of special actions and assassinations they brag to publish in the form of stories. Only then one can believe the new American slogans that America is trying to make them believe. Only then it becomes legitimate to ask the World to do what it believes is useful for its security and the security of the World.

It is a chance to air an opinion whose time has come. It is also addressed to the peoples of the U.S. and the Western people in general. Zionism has been planning for the domination of the world since its well-known conference it convened in Basle in 1897. Ever since, it has been working in this direction. It has scored successes you can feel by controlling finance, media and commerce centers in your countries and whoever rules in your name, here and there, in decision-making centers. But its domination is not yet fulfilled to have its will absolute and final. This could only be feasible when two heavenly faiths upheld by the biggest bloc in the world are thrown into conflict. Otherwise, Zionism would be denied the accomplishment of all its ambitions. The masterminds of Zionism are, therefore, working for a clash between Christianity and Islam on the assumption that this, and only this, could secure the chance to dominate the world, when new opportunities open up for their domination. Could there be any better situation than that when the stealing dog finds his household pre-occupied by a grief so that it could win the thing it has set its eye on, the thing that whetted its mouth? Would the sensible men in the West be aware of that? Or would Zionism outsmart them to attain its aims?

Address by President Bush, September 20, 2001

President Bush delivered the following address to a Joint Session of Congress and the American People.

Mr. Speaker, Mr. President Pro Tempore, members of Congress, and fellow Americans:

In the normal course of events, Presidents come to this chamber to report on the state of the Union. Tonight, no such report is needed. It has already been delivered by the American people.

We have seen it in the courage of passengers, who rushed terrorists to save others on the ground—passengers like an exceptional man named Todd Beamer. And would you please help me to welcome his wife, Lisa Beamer, here tonight.

We have seen the state of our Union in the endurance of rescuers, working past exhaustion. We have seen the unfurling of flags, the lighting of candles, the giving of blood, the saying of prayers—in English, Hebrew, and Arabic. We have seen the decency of a loving and giving people who have made the grief of strangers their own.

My fellow citizens, for the last nine days, the entire world has seen for itself the state of our Union—and it is strong.

Tonight we are a country awakened to danger and called to defend freedom. Our grief has turned to anger, and anger to resolution. Whether we bring our enemies to justice, or bring justice to our enemies, justice will be done.

I thank the Congress for its leadership at such an important time. All of America was touched on the evening of the tragedy to see Republicans and Democrats joined together on the steps of this Capitol, singing "God Bless America." And you did more than sing; you acted, by delivering $40 billion to rebuild our communities and meet the needs of our military.

Speaker Hastert, Minority Leader Gephardt, Majority Leader Daschle and Senator Lott, I thank you for your friendship, for your leadership and for your service to our country.

And on behalf of the American people, I thank the world for its outpouring of support. America will never forget the sounds of our National Anthem playing at Buckingham Palace, on the streets of Paris, and at Berlin's Brandenburg Gate.

We will not forget South Korean children gathering to pray outside our embassy in Seoul, or the prayers of sympathy offered at a mosque in Cairo. We will not forget moments of silence and days of mourning in Australia and Africa and Latin America.

Nor will we forget the citizens of 80 other nations who died with our own: dozens of Pakistanis; more than 130 Israelis; more than 250 citizens of India; men and women from El Salvador, Iran, Mexico and Japan; and hundreds of British citizens. America has no truer friend than Great Britain. Once again, we are joined together in a great cause—so honored the British Prime Minister has crossed an ocean to show his unity of purpose with America. Thank you for coming, friend.

On September the 11th, enemies of freedom committed an act of war against our country. Americans have known wars—but for the past 136 years, they have been wars on foreign soil, except for one Sunday in 1941. Americans have known the casualties of war—but not at the center of a great city on a peaceful morning. Americans have known surprise attacks—but never before on thousands of civilians. All of this was brought upon us in a single day—and night fell on a different world, a world where freedom itself is under attack.

Americans have many questions tonight. Americans are asking: Who attacked our country? The evidence we have gathered all points to a collection of loosely affiliated terrorist organizations known as al Qaeda. They are the same murderers indicted for bombing American embassies in Tanzania and Kenya, and responsible for bombing the USS Cole.

Al Qaeda is to terror what the mafia is to crime. But its goal is not making money; its goal is remaking the world—and imposing its radical beliefs on people everywhere.

The terrorists practice a fringe form of Islamic extremism that has been rejected by Muslim scholars and the vast majority of Muslim clerics—a fringe movement that perverts the peaceful teachings of Islam. The terrorists' directive commands them to kill Christians and Jews, to kill all Americans, and make no distinction among military and civilians, including women and children.

This group and its leader—a person named Osama bin Laden—are linked to many other organizations in different countries, including the Egyptian Islamic Jihad and the Islamic Movement of Uzbekistan. There are thousands of these terrorists in more than 60 countries. They are recruited from their own nations and neighborhoods and brought to camps in places like Afghanistan, where they are trained in the tactics of terror. They are sent back to their homes or sent to hide in countries around the world to plot evil and destruction.

The leadership of al Qaeda has great influence in Afghanistan and supports the Taliban regime in controlling most of that country. In Afghanistan, we see al Qaeda's vision for the world.

Afghanistan's people have been brutalized—many are starving and many have fled. Women are not allowed to attend school. You can be jailed for owning a television. Religion can be practiced only as their leaders dictate. A man can be jailed in Afghanistan if his beard is not long enough.

The United States respects the people of Afghanistan—after all, we are currently its largest source of humanitarian aid—but we condemn the Taliban regime. It is not only repressing its own people, it is threatening people everywhere by sponsoring and sheltering and supplying terrorists. By aiding and abetting murder, the Taliban regime is committing murder.

And tonight, the United States of America makes the following demands on the Taliban: Deliver to United States authorities all the leaders of al Qaeda who hide in your land. Release all foreign nationals, including American citizens, you have unjustly imprisoned. Protect foreign journalists, diplomats and aid workers in your country. Close immediately and permanently every terrorist training camp in Afghanistan, and hand over every terrorist, and every person in their support structure, to appropriate authorities. Give the United States full access to terrorist training camps, so we can make sure they are no longer operating.

These demands are not open to negotiation or discussion. The Taliban must act, and act immediately. They will hand over the terrorists, or they will share in their fate.

I also want to speak tonight directly to Muslims throughout the world. We respect your faith. It's practiced freely by many millions of Americans, and by millions more in countries that America counts as friends. Its teachings are good and peaceful, and those who commit evil in the name of Allah blaspheme the name of Allah. The terrorists are traitors to their own faith, trying, in effect, to hijack Islam itself. The enemy of America is not our many Muslim friends; it is not our many Arab friends. Our enemy is a radical network of terrorists, and every government that supports them.

Our war on terror begins with al Qaeda, but it does not end there. It will not end until every terrorist group of global reach has been found, stopped and defeated.

Americans are asking, why do they hate us? They hate what we see right here in this chamber—a democratically elected government. Their leaders are self-appointed. They hate our freedoms—our freedom of religion, our freedom of speech, our freedom to vote and assemble and disagree with each other.

They want to overthrow existing governments in many Muslim countries, such as Egypt, Saudi Arabia, and Jordan. They want to drive Israel out of the Middle East. They want to drive Christians and Jews out of vast regions of Asia and Africa.

These terrorists kill not merely to end lives, but to disrupt and end a way of life. With every atrocity, they hope that America grows fearful, retreating from the world and forsaking our friends. They stand against us, because we stand in their way.

We are not deceived by their pretenses to piety. We have seen their kind before. They are the heirs of all the murderous ideologies of the 20th century. By sacrificing human life to serve their radical visions—by abandoning every value except the will to power—they follow in the path of fascism, and Nazism, and totalitarianism. And they will follow that path all the way, to where it ends: in history's unmarked grave of discarded lies.

Americans are asking: How will we fight and win this war? We will direct every resource at our command—every means of diplomacy, every tool of intelligence, every instrument of law enforcement, every financial influence, and every necessary weapon of war—to the disruption and to the defeat of the global terror network.

This war will not be like the war against Iraq a decade ago, with a decisive liberation of territory and a swift conclusion. It will not look like the air war above Kosovo two years ago, where no ground troops were used and not a single American was lost in combat.

Our response involves far more than instant retaliation and isolated strikes. Americans should not expect one battle, but a lengthy campaign, unlike any other we have ever seen. It may include dramatic strikes, visible on TV, and covert operations, secret even in success. We will starve terrorists of funding, turn them one against another, drive them from place to place, until there is no refuge or no rest. And we will pursue nations that provide aid or safe haven to terrorism. Every nation, in every region, now has a decision to make. Either you are with us, or you are with the terrorists. From this day forward, any nation that continues to harbor or support terrorism will be regarded by the United States as a hostile regime.

Our nation has been put on notice: We are not immune from attack. We will take defensive measures against terrorism to protect Americans. Today, dozens of federal departments and agencies, as well as state and local governments, have responsibilities affecting homeland security. These efforts must be coordinated at the highest level. So tonight I announce the creation of a Cabinet-level position reporting directly to me—the Office of Homeland Security.

And tonight I also announce a distinguished American to lead this effort, to strengthen American security: a military veteran, an effective governor, a true patriot, a trusted friend—Pennsylvania's Tom Ridge. He will lead, oversee and coordinate a comprehensive national strategy to safeguard our country against terrorism, and respond to any attacks that may come.

These measures are essential. But the only way to defeat terrorism as a threat to our way of life is to stop it, eliminate it, and destroy it where it grows.

Many will be involved in this effort, from FBI agents to intelligence operatives to the reservists we have called to active duty. All deserve our thanks, and all have our prayers. And tonight, a few miles from the damaged Pentagon, I have a message for our military: Be ready. I've called the Armed Forces to alert, and there is a reason. The hour is coming when America will act, and you will make us proud.

This is not, however, just America's fight. And what is at stake is not just America's freedom. This is the world's fight. This is civilization's fight. This is the fight of all who believe in progress and pluralism, tolerance and freedom.

We ask every nation to join us. We will ask, and we will need, the help of police forces, intelligence services, and banking systems around the world. The United States is grateful that many nations and many international organizations have already responded—with sympathy and with support. Nations from Latin America, to Asia, to Africa, to Europe, to the Islamic world. Perhaps the NATO Charter reflects best the attitude of the world: An attack on one is an attack on all.

The civilized world is rallying to America's side. They understand that if this terror goes unpunished, their own cities, their own citizens may be next. Terror, unanswered, can not only bring down buildings, it can threaten the stability of legitimate governments. And you know what—we're not going to allow it.

Americans are asking: What is expected of us? I ask you to live your lives, and hug your children. I know many citizens have fears tonight, and I ask you to be calm and resolute, even in the face of a continuing threat.

I ask you to uphold the values of America, and remember why so many have come here. We are in a fight for our principles, and our first responsibility is to live by them. No one should be singled out for unfair treatment or unkind words because of their ethnic background or religious faith.

I ask you to continue to support the victims of this tragedy with your contributions. Those who want to give can go to a central source of information, libertyunites.org, to find the names of groups providing direct help in New York, Pennsylvania, and Virginia.

The thousands of FBI agents who are now at work in this investigation may need your cooperation, and I ask you to give it.

I ask for your patience, with the delays and inconveniences that may accompany tighter security; and for your patience in what will be a long struggle.

I ask your continued participation and confidence in the American economy. Terrorists attacked a symbol of American prosperity. They did not touch its source. America is successful because of the hard work, and creativity, and enterprise of our people. These were the true strengths of our economy before September 11th, and they are our strengths today.

And, finally, please continue praying for the victims of terror and their families, for those in uniform, and for our great country. Prayer has comforted us in sorrow, and will help strengthen us for the journey ahead.

Tonight I thank my fellow Americans for what you have already done and for what you will do. And ladies and gentlemen of the Congress, I thank you, their representatives, for what you have already done and for what we will do together.

Tonight, we face new and sudden national challenges. We will come together to improve air safety, to dramatically expand the number of air marshals on domestic flights, and take new measures to prevent hijacking. We will come together to promote stability and keep our airlines flying, with direct assistance during this emergency.

We will come together to give law enforcement the additional tools it needs to track down terror here at home. We will come together to strengthen our intelligence capabilities to know the plans of terrorists before they act, and find them before they strike.

We will come together to take active steps that strengthen America's economy, and put our people back to work.

Tonight we welcome two leaders who embody the extraordinary spirit of all New Yorkers: Governor George Pataki, and Mayor Rudolph Giuliani. As a symbol of America's resolve, my administration will work with Congress, and these two leaders, to show the world that we will rebuild New York City.

After all that has just passed—all the lives taken, and all the possibilities and hopes that died with them—it is natural to wonder if America's future is one of fear. Some speak of an age of terror. I know there are struggles ahead, and dangers to face. But this country will define our times, not be defined by them. As long as the United States of America is determined and strong, this will not be an age of terror; this will be an age of liberty, here and across the world.

Great harm has been done to us. We have suffered great loss. And in our grief and anger we have found our mission and our moment. Freedom and fear are at war. The advance of human freedom—the great achievement of our time, and the great hope of every time—now depends on us. Our nation—this generation—will lift a dark threat of violence from our people and our future. We will rally the world to this cause by our efforts, by our courage. We will not tire, we will not falter, and we will not fail.

It is my hope that in the months and years ahead, life will return almost to normal. We'll go back to our lives and routines, and that is good. Even grief recedes with time and grace. But our resolve must not pass. Each of us will remember what happened that day, and to whom it happened. We'll remember the moment the news came—where we were and what we were doing. Some will remember an image of a fire, or a story of rescue. Some will carry memories of a face and a voice gone forever.

And I will carry this: It is the police shield of a man named George Howard, who died at the World Trade Center trying to save others. It was given to me by his mom, Arlene, as a proud memorial to her son. This is my reminder of lives that ended, and a task that does not end.

I will not forget this wound to our country or those who inflicted it. I will not yield; I will not rest; I will not relent in waging this struggle for freedom and security for the American people.

The course of this conflict is not known, yet its outcome is certain. Freedom and fear, justice and cruelty, have always been at war, and we know that God is not neutral between them.

Fellow citizens, we'll meet violence with patient justice—assured of the rightness of our cause, and confident of the victories to come. In all that lies before us, may God grant us wisdom, and may He watch over the United States of America.

Executive Order, September 24, 2001

By the authority vested in me as President by the Constitution and the laws of the United States of America, including the International Emergency Economic Powers Act (50 U.S.C. 1701 et seq.)(IEEPA), the National Emergencies Act (50 U.S.C. 1601 et seq.), section 5 of the United Nations Participation Act of 1945, as amended (22 U.S.C. 287c) (UNPA), and section 301 of title 3, United States Code, and in view of United Nations Security Council Resolution (UNSCR) 1214 of December 8, 1998, UNSCR 1267 of October 15, 1999, UNSCR 1333 of December 19, 2000, and the multilateral sanctions contained therein, and UNSCR 1363 of July 30, 2001, establishing a mechanism to monitor the implementation of UNSCR 1333,

I, GEORGE W. BUSH, President of the United States of America, find that grave acts of terrorism and threats of terrorism committed by foreign terrorists, including the terrorist attacks in New York, Pennsylvania, and the Pentagon committed on September 11, 2001, acts recognized and condemned in UNSCR 1368 of September 12, 2001, and UNSCR 1269 of October 19, 1999, and the continuing and immediate threat of further attacks on United States nationals or the United States constitute an unusual and extraordinary threat to the national security, foreign policy, and economy of the United States, and in furtherance of my proclamation of September 14, 2001, Declaration of National Emergency by Reason of Certain Terrorist Attacks, hereby declare a national emergency to deal with that threat. I also find that because of the pervasiveness and expansiveness of the financial foundation of foreign terrorists, financial sanctions may be appropriate for those foreign persons that support or otherwise associate with these foreign terrorists. I also find that a need exists for further consultation and cooperation with, and sharing of information by, United States and foreign financial institutions as an additional tool to enable the United States to combat the financing of terrorism.

I hereby order:

Section 1. Except to the extent required by section 203(b) of IEEPA (50 U.S.C. 1702(b)), or provided in regulations, orders, directives, or licenses that may be issued pursuant to this order, and notwithstanding any contract entered into or any license or permit granted prior to the effective date of this order, all property and interests in property of the following persons that are in the United States or that hereafter come within the United States, or that hereafter come within the possession or control of United States persons are blocked:

(a) foreign persons listed in the Annex to this order;

(b) foreign persons determined by the Secretary of State, in consultation with the Secretary of the Treasury and the Attorney General, to have committed, or to pose a significant risk of committing, acts of terrorism that threaten the security of U.S. nationals or the national security, foreign policy, or economy of the United States;

(c) persons determined by the Secretary of the Treasury, in consultation with the Secretary of State and the Attorney General, to be owned or controlled by, or to act for or on behalf of those persons listed in the Annex to this order or those persons determined to be subject to subsection 1(b), 1(c), or 1(d)(i) of this order;

(d) except as provided in section 5 of this order and after such consultation, if any, with foreign authorities as the Secretary of State, in consultation with the Secretary of the Treasury and the Attorney General, deems appropriate in the exercise of his discretion, persons determined by the Secretary of the Treasury, in consultation with the Secretary of State and the Attorney General;

(i) to assist in, sponsor, or provide financial, material, or technological support for, or financial or other services to or in support of, such acts of terrorism or those persons listed in the Annex to this order or determined to be subject to this order; or

(ii) to be otherwise associated with those persons listed in the Annex to this order or those persons determined to be subject to subsection 1(b), 1(c), or 1(d)(i) of this order.

Sec. 2. Except to the extent required by section 203(b) of IEEPA (50 U.S.C. 1702(b)), or provided in regulations, orders, directives, or licenses that may be issued pursuant to this order, and notwithstanding any contract entered into or any license or permit granted prior to the effective date:

(a) any transaction or dealing by United States persons or within the United States in property or interests in property blocked pursuant to this order is prohibited, including but not limited to the making or receiving of any contribution of funds, goods, or services to or for the benefit of those persons listed in the Annex to this order or determined to be subject to this order;

(b) any transaction by any United States person or within the United States that evades or avoids, or has the purpose of evading or avoiding, or attempts to violate, any of the prohibitions set forth in this order is prohibited; and

(c) any conspiracy formed to violate any of the prohibitions set forth in this order is prohibited.

Sec. 3. For purposes of this order:

(a) the term "person" means an individual or entity;

(b) the term "entity" means a partnership, association, corporation, or other organization, group, or subgroup;

(c) the term "United States person" means any United States citizen, permanent resident alien, entity organized under the laws of the United States (including foreign branches), or any person in the United States; and

(d) the term "terrorism" means an activity that—

(i) involves a violent act or an act dangerous to human life, property, or infrastructure; and

(ii) appears to be intended—

(A) to intimidate or coerce a civilian population;

(B) to influence the policy of a government by intimidation or coercion; or

(C) to affect the conduct of a government by mass destruction, assassination, kidnapping, or hostage-taking.

Sec. 4. I hereby determine that the making of donations of the type specified in section 203(b)(2) of IEEPA (50 U.S.C. 1702(b)(2)) by United States persons to persons determined to be subject to this order would seriously impair my ability to deal with the national emergency declared in this order, and would endanger Armed Forces of the United States that are in a situation where imminent involvement in hostilities is clearly indicated by the circumstances, and hereby prohibit such donations as provided by section 1 of this order. Furthermore, I hereby determine that the Trade Sanctions Reform and Export Enhancement Act of 2000 (title IX, Public Law 106-387) shall not affect the imposition or the continuation of the imposition of any unilateral agricultural sanction or unilateral medical sanction on any person determined to be subject to this order because imminent involvement of the Armed Forces of the United States in hostilities is clearly indicated by the circumstances.

Sec. 5. With respect to those persons designated pursuant to subsection 1(d) of this order, the Secretary of the Treasury, in the exercise of his discretion and in consultation with the Secretary of State and the Attorney General, may take such other actions than the complete blocking of property or interests in property as the President is authorized to take under IEEPA and UNPA if the Secretary of the Treasury, in consultation with the Secretary of State and the Attorney General, deems such other actions to be consistent with the national interests of the United States, considering such factors as he deems appropriate.

Sec. 6. The Secretary of State, the Secretary of the Treasury, and other appropriate agencies shall make all relevant efforts to cooperate and coordinate with other countries, including through technical assistance, as well as bilateral and multilateral agreements and arrangements, to achieve the objectives of this order, including the prevention and suppression of acts of terrorism, the denial of financing and financial services to terrorists and terrorist organizations, and the sharing of intelligence about funding activities in support of terrorism.

Sec. 7. The Secretary of the Treasury, in consultation with the Secretary of State and the Attorney General, is hereby authorized to take such actions, including the promulgation of rules and regulations, and to employ all powers granted to the President by IEEPA and UNPA as may be necessary to carry out the purposes of this order. The Secretary of the Treasury may redelegate any of these functions to other officers and agencies of the United States Government. All agencies of the United States Government are hereby directed to take all appropriate measures within their authority to carry out the provisions of this order.

Sec. 8. Nothing in this order is intended to affect the continued effectiveness of any rules, regulations, orders, licenses, or other forms of administrative action issued, taken, or continued in effect heretofore or hereafter under 31 C.F.R. chapter V, except as expressly terminated, modified, or suspended by or pursuant to this order.

Sec. 9. Nothing contained in this order is intended to create, nor does it create, any right, benefit, or privilege, substantive or procedural, enforceable at law by a party against the United States, its agencies, officers, employees or any other person.

Sec. 10. For those persons listed in the Annex to this order or determined to be subject to this order who might have a constitutional presence in the United States, I find that because of the ability to transfer funds or assets instantaneously, prior notice to such persons of measures to be taken pursuant to this order would render these measures ineffectual. I therefore determine that for these measures to be effective in addressing the national emergency declared in this order, there need be no prior notice of a listing or determination made pursuant to this order.

Sec. 11. (a) This order is effective at 12:01 a.m. eastern daylight time on September 24, 2001.

(b) This order shall be transmitted to the Congress and published in the Federal Register.

ANNEX
Al Qaida/Islamic Army
Abu Sayyaf Group
Armed Islamic Group (GIA)
Harakat ul-Mujahidin (HUM)
Al-Jihad (Egyptian Islamic Jihad)
Islamic Movement of Uzbekistan (IMU)
Asbat al-Ansar
Salafist Group for Call and Combat (GSPC)
Libyan Islamic Fighting Group
Al-Itihaad al-Islamiya (AIAI)
Islamic Army of Aden
Osama bin Laden
Muhammad Atif (aka, Subhi Abu Sitta,
Abu Hafs Al Masri)
Sayf al-Adl
Shaykh Sai'id (aka, Mustafa Muhammad Ahmad)
Abu Hafs the Mauritanian (aka, Mahfouz Ould al-Walid, Khalid Al-Shanqiti)
Ibn Al-Shaykh al-Libi
Abu Zubaydah (aka, Zayn al-Abidin Muhammad Husayn, Tariq)
Abd al-Hadi al-Iraqi (aka, Abu Abdallah)
Ayman al-Zawahiri
Thirwat Salah Shihata
Tariq Anwar al-Sayyid Ahmad (aka, Fathi, Amr al-Fatih)
Muhammad Salah (aka, Nasr Fahmi Nasr Hasanayn)
Makhtab Al-Khidamat/Al Kifah
Wafa Humanitarian Organization
Al Rashid Trust
Mamoun Darkazanli Import-Export Company

United Nations Security Council Resolution 1373, September 28, 2001

The Security Council,
   Reaffirming its resolutions 1269 (1999) of 19 October 1999 and 1368 (2001) of 12 September 2001,
   Reaffirming also its unequivocal condemnation of the terrorist attacks which took place in New York, Washington, D.C., and Pennsylvania on 11 September 2001, and expressing its determination to prevent all such acts,
   Reaffirming further that such acts, like any act of international terrorism, constitute a threat to international peace and security,

Reaffirming the inherent right of individual or collective self- defense as recognized by the Charter of the United Nations as reiterated in resolution 1368 (2001),

Reaffirming the need to combat by all means, in accordance with the Charter of the United Nations, threats to international peace and security caused by terrorist acts,

Deeply concerned by the increase, in various regions of the world, of acts of terrorism motivated by intolerance or extremism,

Calling on States to work together urgently to prevent and suppress terrorist acts, including through increased cooperation and full implementation of the relevant international conventions relating to terrorism,

Recognizing the need for States to complement international cooperation by taking additional measures to prevent and suppress, in their territories through all lawful means, the financing and preparation of any acts of terrorism,

Reaffirming the principle established by the General Assembly in its declaration of October 1970 (resolution 2625 (XXV)) and reiterated by the Security Council in its resolution 1189 (1998) of 13 August 1998, namely that every State has the duty to refrain from organizing, instigating, assisting or participating in terrorist acts in another State or acquiescing in organized activities within its territory directed towards the commission of such acts,

Acting under Chapter VII of the Charter of the United Nations,

1. Decides that all States shall:

(a) Prevent and suppress the financing of terrorist acts;

(b) Criminalize the wilful provision or collection, by any means, directly or indirectly, of funds by their nationals or in their territories with the intention that the funds should be used, or in the knowledge that they are to be used, in order to carry out terrorist acts;

(c) Freeze without delay funds and other financial assets or economic resources of persons who commit, or attempt to commit, terrorist acts or participate in or facilitate the commission of terrorist acts; of entities owned or controlled directly or indirectly by such persons; and of persons and entities acting on behalf of, or at the direction of such persons and entities, including funds derived or generated from property owned or controlled directly or indirectly by such persons and associated persons and entities;

(d) Prohibit their nationals or any persons and entities within their territories from making any funds, financial assets or economic resources or financial or other related services available, directly or indirectly, for the benefit of persons who commit or attempt to commit or facilitate or participate in the commission of terrorist acts, of entities owned or controlled, directly or indirectly, by such persons and of persons and entities acting on behalf of or at the direction of such persons;

2. Decides also that all States shall:

(a) Refrain from providing any form of support, active or passive, to entities or persons involved in terrorist acts, including by suppressing recruitment of members of terrorist groups and eliminating the supply of weapons to terrorists;

(b) Take the necessary steps to prevent the commission of terrorist acts, including by provision of early warning to other States by exchange of information;

(c) Deny safe haven to those who finance, plan, support, or commit terrorist acts, or provide safe havens;

(d) Prevent those who finance, plan, facilitate or commit terrorist acts from using their respective territories for those purposes against other States or their citizens;

(e) Ensure that any person who participates in the financing, planning, preparation or perpetration of terrorist acts or in supporting terrorist acts is brought to justice and ensure that, in addition to any other measures against them, such terrorist acts are established as serious criminal offenses in domestic laws and regulations and that the punishment duly reflects the seriousness of such terrorist acts;

(f) Afford one another the greatest measure of assistance in connection with criminal investigations or criminal proceedings relating to the financing or support of terrorist acts, including assistance in obtaining evidence in their possession necessary for the proceedings;

(g) Prevent the movement of terrorists or terrorist groups by effective border controls and controls on issuance of identity papers and travel documents, and through measures for preventing counterfeiting, forgery or fraudulent use of identity papers and travel documents;

3. Calls upon all States to:

(a) Find ways of intensifying and accelerating the exchange of operational information, especially regarding actions or movements of terrorist persons or networks; forged or falsified travel documents; traffic in arms, explosives or sensitive materials; use of communications technologies by terrorist groups; and the threat posed by the possession of weapons of mass destruction by terrorist groups;

(b) Exchange information in accordance with international and domestic law and cooperate on administrative and judicial matters to prevent the commission of terrorist acts;

(c) Cooperate, particularly through bilateral and multilateral arrangements and agreements, to prevent and suppress terrorist attacks and take action against perpetrators of such acts;

(d) Become parties as soon as possible to the relevant international conventions and protocols relating to terrorism, including the International Convention for the Suppression of the Financing of Terrorism of 9 December 1999;

(e) Increase cooperation and fully implement the relevant international conventions and protocols relating to terrorism and Security Council resolutions 1269 (1999) and 1368 (2001);

(f) Take appropriate measures in conformity with the relevant provisions of national and international law, including international standards of human rights, before granting refugee status, for the purpose of ensuring that the asylum seeker has not planned, facilitated or participated in the commission of terrorist acts;

(g) Ensure, in conformity with international law, that refugee status is not abused by the perpetrators, organizers or facilitators of terrorist acts, and that claims of political motivation are not recognized as grounds for refusing requests for the extradition of alleged terrorists;

4. Notes with concern the close connection between international terrorism and transnational organized crime, illicit drugs, money-laundering, illegal arms-trafficking, and illegal movement of nuclear, chemical, biological and other potentially deadly materials, and in this regard emphasizes the need to enhance coordination of efforts on national, subregional, regional and international levels in order to strengthen a

global response to this serious challenge and threat to international security;

5. Declares that acts, methods, and practices of terrorism are contrary to the purposes and principles of the United Nations and that knowingly financing, planning and inciting terrorist acts are also contrary to the purposes and principles of the United Nations;

6. Decides to establish, in accordance with rule 28 of its provisional rules of procedure, a Committee of the Security Council, consisting of all the members of the Council, to monitor implementation of this resolution, with the assistance of appropriate expertise, and calls upon all States to report to the Committee, no later than 90 days from the date of adoption of this resolution and thereafter according to a timetable to be proposed by the Committee, on the steps they have taken to implement this resolution;

7. Directs the Committee to delineate its tasks, submit a work program within 30 days of the adoption of this resolution, and to consider the support it requires, in consultation with the Secretary-General;

8. Expresses its determination to take all necessary steps in order to ensure the full implementation of this resolution, in accordance with its responsibilities under the Charter;

9. Decides to remain seized of this matter.

Statement by Osama bin Laden, Released October 7, 2001

The following message was first broadcast on the Arabic television station Al Jazeera.

We seek refuge with the Lord of our bad and evildoing. He whom God guides is rightly guided but he whom God leaves to stray, for him wilt thou find no protector to lead him to the right way.

I witness that there is no God but God and Mohammed is His slave and Prophet.

God Almighty hit the United States at its most vulnerable spot. He destroyed its greatest buildings.

Praise be to God.

Here is the United States. It was filled with terror from its north to its south and from its east to its west.

Praise be to God.

What the United States tastes today is a very small thing compared to what we have tasted for tens of years.

Our nation has been tasting this humiliation and contempt for more than 80 years.

Its sons are being killed, its blood is being shed, its holy places are being attacked, and it is not being ruled according to what God has decreed.

Despite this, nobody cares.

When Almighty God rendered successful a convoy of Muslims, the vanguards of Islam, He allowed them to destroy the United States.

I ask God Almighty to elevate their status and grant them Paradise. He is the one who is capable to do so.

When these defended their oppressed sons, brothers, and sisters in Palestine and in many Islamic countries, the world at large shouted. The infidels shouted, followed by the hypocrites.

One million Iraqi children have thus far died in Iraq although they did not do anything wrong.

Despite this, we heard no denunciation by anyone in the world or a fatwa by the rulers' ulema [body of Muslim scholars].

Israeli tanks and tracked vehicles also enter to wreak havoc in Palestine, in Jenin, Ramallah, Rafah, Beit Jala, and other Islamic areas and we hear no voices raised or moves made.

But if the sword falls on the United States after 80 years, hypocrisy raises its head lamenting the deaths of these killers. who tampered with the blood, honor, and holy places of the Muslims.

The least that one can describe these people is that they are morally depraved.

They champion falsehood, support the butcher against the victim, the oppressor against the innocent child.

May God mete them the punishment they deserve.

I say that the matter is clear and explicit.

In the aftermath of this event and now that senior U.S. officials have spoken, beginning with Bush, the head of the world's infidels, and whoever supports him, every Muslim should rush to defend his religion.

They came out in arrogance with their men and horses and instigated even those countries that belong to Islam against us.

They came out to fight this group of people who declared their faith in God and refused to abandon their religion.

They came out to fight Islam in the name of terrorism.

Hundreds of thousands of people, young and old, were killed in the farthest point on earth in Japan.

[For them] this is not a crime, but rather a debatable issue.

They bombed Iraq and considered that a debatable issue.

But when a dozen people of them were killed in Nairobi and Dar es Salaam, Afghanistan and Iraq were bombed and all hypocrite ones stood behind the head of the world's infidelity—behind the Hubal [an idol worshipped by pagans before the advent of Islam] of the age—namely, America and its supporters.

These incidents divided the entire world into two regions—one of faith where there is no hypocrisy and another of infidelity, from which we hope God will protect us.

The winds of faith and change have blown to remove falsehood from the [Arabian] peninsula of Prophet Mohammed, may God's prayers be upon him.

As for the United States, I tell it and its people these few words: I swear by Almighty God who raised the heavens without pillars that neither the United States nor he who lives in the United States will enjoy security before we can see it as a reality in Palestine and before all the infidel armies leave the land of Mohammed, may God's peace and blessing be upon him.

God is great and glory to Islam.

May God's peace, mercy, and blessings be upon you.

Letter from Iraqi President Hussein to Western Nations and Governments, October 29, 2001

In the name of God the Merciful, the Compassionate,

Once again we address a letter to all the peoples and governments of the West, including the United States.

Peace be upon those who expect a greeting of peace from us, or upon those who answer it by saying : and peace be upon you too (wa Alaikum Asalam).

The world focused its full attention on the analysis and follow up of the events of last September, but those who made an in-depth analysis may have not been the majority of the people. Nevertheless, it seems to us that they have, now, increased in number. The number of officials in power who are looking into the depth of what happened, its motives or reasons, and its results and effects, has also increased. Their number and way of conduct, at the time of the event, was deplorable for those who are not aware that not everyone is capable of a deep contemplation of major events or complex circumstances, just as not many people are capable of dreaming of what is better.

Now that the emotions have relatively calmed down in the heart and spirit of those who applauded the event, or those who condemned it, I say that, the role of leaders should be played, with their people's support, on the basis of the description and the role of their responsibilities. One of the most important qualities of any leader is saving other from death not by marking the dark ditches on the road, but also by preventing those who do not see the marks from falling into the abyss. Then comes the quality of exaltation, or ascendancy of the people he is in charge of, along with their potential thought and action. The danger that may threaten any people or nation, does not call upon the people in charge to lead the way against this danger only, but also to analyze its reasons in view of abating them, or treating those reasons radically, to eliminate them so that they would never surge again.

I am sorry to say that the general approach in this direction is still weak, so far. Western governments are the first in this phenomena of weakness. Some voices have risen on the part of some peoples, journalists, writers, and, in a very restricted way, the voices of those who are preparing themselves, in the shadow, to replace the rulers there. Nevertheless, the latter are still hesitant voices that deal with the situation in the light of the balance of interests of the posts they expect to occupy, and of the influence of the centers of power. As for the United States, the hope in the awareness of its people is greater than it is in its Administrations, if the people could see the facts as they are, unless these Administrations are set free from the conclusive influence of Zionism, and other centers of influence which serve their own interests that are associated with their well-known goals.

The events of September 11, and the following reaction of people in rage, or those who took advantage of the situation, including waging the aggression on Afghanistan on the basis of suspicions, and the accompanying insinuations and statements by the media or by American, and non-American leaders, have shown that this vast world can be set on fire by a spark coming from the West, even if that spark comes all the way from across the Atlantic. Naturally, setting something on fire is easier than extinguishing it, and because deeds of virtue exalt the soul and the being, while evil deeds downgrade them, the latter become easier to commit for those who are tempted to do so.

On the basis of this realistic image, the entire world needs to be saved from the deep abyss it is being push into by the U.S., and the likes of the U.S., whether they are states, individuals, or organizations. In fact, now that we know the limits of how American rulers conduct themselves in crisis, the U.S. itself needs to be saved by the world while it is saving itself. Otherwise, the world will be pulled down by the weight of the U.S. while falling down to the bottom of a deep pit from which it will not be able to come out until that pit is filled with blood and tragedies, not to mention those who will suffocate because they cannot swim.

As we said before to those who launched aggressions on us, including the U.S., in and before Um-Almarik (the mother of the battles), the world, like Iraq and its Arab nation, needs steadfastness to face the aggression, make it miss its targets. It must not allow the U.S. to be victorious. The victory of the U.S. and its allies over Iraq would conceal the opposing attitude and analysis, and would not allow it to emerge again for a long time. In fact, the U.S. is in no need for additional vanity and arrogance, but if it ever defeated Iraq, God forbid, it would acquire an additional vanity that would push it to a higher level of vanity, which would bring it closer to not farther from the abyss.

Yes, vanity needs to be confronted, and the oppressor needs to be confronted, just as those who find it easy to commit evil deeds and throw embers at people, need to be confronted. On the basis of what we said about Iraq while confronting aggressions, the world now needs to abort the U.S. aggressive schemes, including its aggression on the Afghan people, which must stop.

Again we say that when someone feels that he is unjustly treated, and no one is repulsing or stopping the injustice inflicted on him, he personally seeks ways and means for lifting that justice. Of course, not everyone is capable of finding the best way for lifting the injustice inflicted on him. People resort to what they think is the best way according to their own ideas, and they are not all capable of reaching out for what is beyond what is available to arrive to the best idea or means.

To find the best way, after having found their way to God and His rights, those who are inflicted by injustice need not to be isolated from their natural milieu, or be ignored deliberately, or as a result of mis-appreciation, by the officials in this milieu. They should, rather, be reassured and helped to save themselves, and their surroundings. It is only normal to say that punishment is a necessity in our world, because what is a necessity in the other world must also be necessary in our world on Earth. But, the punishment in the other world is fair and just, and the prophets and messengers of God (peace be upon them all) conducted punishment and called for it in justice, and not on the basis of suspicions and whims. Hence, any punishment conducted by man must be just and convincing. I think, that you, often criticize those whom you criticize in order to weaken them, by saying that they use emergency laws, and what emergency laws, by western standards, cannot be a general rule. But now, unlike what you used to say about those whom you accuse of being dictators and despots, we see dozens of emergency laws and measures adopted by the governments of the West, with the U.S. in the forefront, after facing one painful event.

Do you know how many painful events, larger and more dangerous than that of

September 11 in U.S., were inflicted upon countries and peoples whom you used to accuse of being non-democratic?! This fact alone, is an example that should be pondered upon by the governments and peoples of the West, but it is not our main subject here.

Once again, we say that, injustice and the pressure that results from it on people lead to explosions. As explosions are not always organized, it is to be expected that they may harm those who make them and others. The events of September 11, should be seen on this basis, and on the basis of imbalanced reactions, on the part of governments accused of being democratic, if the Americans are sure that these were carried out by people from abroad.

To concentrate not on what is important, but rather on what is the most important, we say again that after having seen that the flames of any fire can expand to cover all the world, it first and foremost, needs justice based on fairness. The best and most sublime expression of this is in what we have learned from what God the Al Mighty ordered to be, or not to be. If we disagree in the essence of this, then our criticism should be, that we should not prevent others from getting or enjoying what we want for ourselves, and that we should not adopt double standards, by giving others what we do not want or refuse for ourselves. Everybody must be aware that no one who has a fortune can be safe in the middle of a society of hungry people. His problem would be greater if he had made his fortune by exploiting those hungry people, and at their expense. The second Caliph in the state of Islam, Umar Ibin Alkhatab (God be pleased with him) ordered the suspension of the punishment of cutting the hand of a thief in the year of Remada (drought) despite the fact that this punishment in clearly stipulated in the Holy Quran. He did so, because he was aware, by his sense of a believer, the correct standards of Faith may be shaken when a man or his family are hungry, and also because he believed that hunger is more aggressive than the act of stealing, and that saving a man's life was more important than saving somebody's property. Hence, he froze a holy rule (Sharia). Have the people of our present time learned this lesson, so that they can live in peace and security? Or do the parties concerned think that the security they want for themselves, will be achieved by amplifying the killing, intimidation, and starvation of others?!

We have heard in the news, recently, that American officials think that the source of anthrax is probably the U.S. itself. Is this conclusion or information just a tactic to divert the attention of those who were terrorized to hear that Bin Laden is the source of anthrax, and to hear insinuations to other accusations, that many Americans think that they should not persist in harming the people he cares for, because that would push him to a stronger reaction in this way or by other means? Or have they done this to divert attention from the incompetence of American official bodies in the events of September 11, and they find now that they have achieved their goal and consequently, the act and the actors should be buried?!

Anyhow, this and other things show that weapons of mass destruction become a burden on their owners and on humanity, if they were not absolutely necessary for self-defense and defending their countries.

Hence, instead of getting themselves and the world busy with the so-called anti-missiles shield so that they drain their budget, and the budgets of other nations, as well as the pockets of American tax-payers, they should be busy in eliminating the weapons of mass destruction in the U.S. first, and then or at the same time, in other parts of the world. It goes without saying, that the West, including the U.S., are the ones who first built the weapons of mass destruction i.e. nuclear, biological, and chemical weapons. It was the West, and the U.S. in the first place, who used these weapons. The events of September, and the what Americans themselves said that the anthrax came from the U.S., clearly show the importance of world co-operation, on the basis of a binding agreement to get rid of the burden and the threat of the weapons of mass destruction, as a first step that might stimulate other steps, if injustice and aggression contracted. The utmost threat to humanity, and to the peoples of the U.S., is the American weapons of mass destruction, along with the similar weapons of the Zionist entity, and along or after it, the similar weapons of other countries.

As the U.S. is across the Atlantic, it is the first country to be asked to make such an initiative in order to confirm its credibility. And because the Zionist entity usurps and occupies Arab territories, and holy places, oppresses the Arabs and injures their human feelings, and as blunders are expected from it, and the reaction of the oppressed people is to be expected, it becomes necessary to disarm the Zionist entity of these weapons.

At that moment, and when the U.S. is really willing to disarm itself of these weapons, we do not think that anyone of a sound mind would stay out of the framework of such a practical plan.

It is then, that the U.S. will adopt a balanced attitude toward the world, and will find the path of wisdom. The world will deal with it in respect and love, when they see love and respect in Americans relations with them. The world, including U.S., will live in peace, and not on the brink of an abyss. The surveillance of the prevailing security, will be based on a sort of real solidarity: the solidarity of brave and just men, and not the solidarity based on intimidation and fear of the powerful, or which serves interests or creates opportunities.

I pray to God the Al-Mighty that I have conveyed the message, and let God be my witness.

God is the greatest.

God is the greatest.

Statement by Osama Bin Laden, Released November 3, 2001

The following statement by Osama Bin Laden was originally broadcast on Al-Jazeera television.

We praise God, seek His help, and ask for His forgiveness.

We seek refuge in God from the evils of our souls and our bad deeds.

A person who is guided by God will never be misguided by anyone and a person who is misguided by God can never be guided by anyone.

I bear witness that there is no God but Allah alone, Who has no partner.

Amid the huge developments and in the wake of the great strikes that hit the United States in its most important locations in New York and Washington, a huge media clamor has been raised.

This clamor is unprecedented. It conveyed the opinions of people on these events.

People were divided into two parts. The first part supported these strikes against U.S. tyranny, while the second denounced them.

Afterward, when the United States launched the unjust campaign against the Islamic Emirate in Afghanistan, people also split into two parties.

The first supported these campaigns, while the second denounced and rejected them.

These tremendous incidents, which have split people into two parties, are of great interest to the Muslims, since many of the rulings pertain to them.

These rulings are closely related to Islam and the acts that corrupt a person's Islam.

Therefore, the Muslims must understand the nature and truth of this conflict so that it will be easy for them to determine where they stand.

While talking about the truth of the conflict, opinion polls in the world have shown that a little more than 80 per cent of Westerners, of Christians in the United States and elsewhere, have been saddened by the strikes that hit the United States.

The polls showed that the vast majority of the sons of the Islamic world were happy about these strikes because they believe that the strikes were in reaction to the huge criminality practiced by Israel and the United States in Palestine and other Muslim countries.

After the strikes on Afghanistan began, these groups changed positions.

Those who were happy about striking the United States felt sad when Afghanistan was hit, and those who felt sad when the United States was hit were happy when Afghanistan was hit. These groups comprise millions of people.

The entire West, with the exception of a few countries, supports this unfair, barbaric campaign, although there is no evidence of the involvement of the people of Afghanistan in what happened in America.

The people of Afghanistan had nothing to do with this matter. The campaign, however, continues to unjustly annihilate the villagers and civilians, children, women, and innocent people.

The positions of the two sides are very clear. Mass demonstrations have spread from the farthest point in the eastern part of the Islamic world to the farthest point in the western part of the Islamic world, and from Indonesia, Philippines, Bangladesh, India, Pakistan to the Arab world and Nigeria and Mauritania.

This clearly indicates the nature of this war. This war is fundamentally religious. The people of the East are Muslims. They sympathized with Muslims against the people of the West, who are the crusaders.

Those who try to cover this crystal clear fact, which the entire world has admitted, are deceiving the Islamic nation.

They are trying to deflect the attention of the Islamic nation from the truth of this conflict.

This fact is proven in the book of God Almighty and in the teachings of our messenger, may God's peace and blessings be upon him.

Under no circumstances should we forget this enmity between us and the infidels. For, the enmity is based on creed.

We must be loyal to the believers and those who believe that there is no God but Allah.

We should also renounce the atheists and infidels. It suffices me to seek God's help against them.

God says: "Never will the Jews or the Christians be satisfied with thee unless thou follow their form of religion."

It is a question of faith, not a war against terrorism, as Bush and Blair try to depict it.

Many thieves belonging to this nation were captured in the past. But, nobody moved.

The masses which moved in the East and West have not done so for the sake of Osama.

Rather, they moved for the sake of their religion. This is because they know that they are right and that they resist the most ferocious, serious, and violent Crusade campaign against Islam ever since the message was revealed to Muhammad, may God's peace and blessings be upon.

After this has become clear, the Muslim must know and learn where he is standing vis-a-vis this war.

After the U.S. politicians spoke and after the U.S. newspapers and television channels became full of clear crusading hatred in this campaign that aims at mobilizing the West against Islam and Muslims, Bush left no room for doubts or the opinions of journalists, but he openly and clearly said that this war is a crusader war. He said this before the whole world to emphasize this fact.

What can those who allege that this is a war against terrorism say? What terrorism are they speaking about at a time when the Islamic nation has been slaughtered for tens of years without hearing their voices and without seeing any action by them?

But when the victim starts to take revenge for those innocent children in Palestine, Iraq, southern Sudan, Somalia, Kashmir and the Philippines, the rulers' ulema (Islamic leaders) and the hypocrites come to defend the clear blasphemy. It suffices me to seek God's help against them.

The common people have understood the issue, but there are those who continue to flatter those who colluded with the unbelievers to anesthetized the Islamic nation to prevent it from carrying out the duty of jihad so that the word of God will be above all words.

The unequivocal truth is that Bush has carried the cross and raised its banner high and stood at the front of the queue.

Anyone who lines up behind Bush in this campaign has committed one of the 10 actions that sully one's Islam.

Muslim scholars are unanimous that allegiance to the infidels and support for them against the believers is one of the major acts that sully Islam.

There is no power but in God. Let us investigate whether this war against Afghanistan that broke out a few days ago is a single and unique one or if it is a link to a long series of crusader wars against the Islamic world.

Following World War I, which ended more than 83 years ago, the whole Islamic world fell under the crusader banner—under the British, French, and Italian governments.

They divided the whole world, and Palestine was occupied by the British.

Since then, and for more than 83 years, our brothers, sons, and sisters in Palestine have been badly tortured.

Hundreds of thousands of them have been killed, and hundreds of thousands of them have been imprisoned or maimed.

Let us examine the recent developments. Take for example the Chechens.

They are a Muslim people who have been attacked by the Russian bear which embraces the Christian Orthodox faith.

Russians have annihilated the Chechen people in their entirety and forced them to flee to the mountains where they were assaulted by snow and poverty and diseases.

Nonetheless, nobody moved to support them. There is no strength but in God.

This was followed by a war of genocide in Bosnia in sight and hearing of the entire world in the heart of Europe.

For several years our brothers have been killed, our women have been raped, and our children have been massacred in the safe havens of the United Nations and with its knowledge and cooperation.

Those who refer our tragedies today to the United Nations so that they can be resolved are hypocrites who deceive God, His Prophet and the believers.

Are not our tragedies but caused by the United Nations? Who issued the Partition Resolution on Palestine in 1947 and surrendered the land of Muslims to the Jews? It was the United Nations in its resolution in 1947.

Those who claim that they are the leaders of the Arabs and continue to appeal to the United Nations have disavowed what was revealed to Prophet Muhammad, God's peace and blessings be upon him.

Those who refer things to the international legitimacy have disavowed the legitimacy of the Holy Book and the tradition of Prophet Muhammad, God's peace and blessings be upon him.

This is the United Nations from which we have suffered greatly. Under no circumstances should any Muslim or sane person resort to the United Nations. The United Nations is nothing but a tool of crime.

We are being massacred everyday, while the United Nations continues to sit idly by.

Our brothers in Kashmir have been subjected to the worst forms of torture for over 50 years. They have been massacred, killed, and raped. Their blood has been shed and their houses have been trespassed upon.

Still, the United Nations continues to sit idly by.

Today, and without any evidence, the United Nations passes resolutions supporting unjust and tyrannical America, which oppresses these helpless people who have emerged from a merciless war at the hands of the Soviet Union.

Let us look at the second war in Chechnya, which is still underway. The entire Chechen people are being embattled once again by this Russian bear.

The humanitarian agencies, even the U.S. ones, demanded that President Clinton should stop supporting Russia.

However, Clinton said that stopping support for Russia did not serve U.S. interests.

A year ago, Putin demanded that the cross and the Jews should stand by him. He told them: You must support us and thank us because we are waging a war against Muslim fundamentalism.

The enemies are speaking very clearly. While this is taking place, the leaders of the region hide and are ashamed to support their brothers.

Let us examine the stand of the West and the United Nations in the developments in Indonesia when they moved to divide the largest country in the Islamic world in terms of population.

We should view events not as separate links, but as links in a long series of conspiracies, a war of annihilation. This criminal, Kofi Annan, was speaking publicly and putting pressure on the Indonesian government, telling it: You have 24 hours to divide and separate East Timor from Indonesia.

Otherwise, we will be forced to send in military forces to separate it by force.

The crusader Australian forces were on Indonesian shores, and in fact they landed to separate East Timor, which is part of the Islamic world.

Therefore, we should view events not as separate links, but as links in a long series of conspiracies, a war of annihilation in the true sense of the word.

In Somalia, on the excuse of restoring hope, 13,000 of our brothers were killed. In southern Sudan, hundreds of thousands were killed.

But when we move to Palestine and Iraq, there can be no bounds to what can be said.

Over one million children were killed in Iraq. The killing is continuing.

As for what is taking place in Palestine these days, I can only say we have no one but God to complain to.

What is taking place cannot be tolerated by any nation. I do not say from the nations of the human race, but from other creatures, from the animals. They would not tolerate what is taking place.

A confidant of mine told me that he saw a butcher slaughtering a camel in front of another camel.

The other camel got agitated while seeing the blood coming out of the other camel. Thus, it burst out with rage and bit the hand of the man and broke it.

How can the weak mothers in Palestine endure the killing of their children in front of their eyes by the unjust Jewish executioners with U.S. support and with U.S. aircraft and tanks?

Those who distinguish between America and Israel are the real enemies of the nation. They are traitors who betrayed God and His prophet, and who betrayed their nation and the trust placed in them. They anesthetize the nation.

These battles cannot be viewed in any case whatsoever as isolated battles, but rather, as part of a chain of the long, fierce, and ugly crusader war.

Every Muslim must stand under the banner of There is no God but Allah and Muhammad is God's Prophet.

I remind you of what our Prophet, may God's peace and blessings upon him, told Ibn Abbas, may God be pleased with him.

He told him: Boy, I am going to teach you a few words. Obey God, He will protect you. Obey Him, you will find Him on your side. If you ask for something, ask God. If you seek help, seek the help of God.

You should know that if all people come together to help you, they will only help you with something that God has already preordained for you.

And if they assemble to harm you, they will only harm you with something that

God has already preordained for you. God wrote man's fate and it will never change.

I Tell the Muslims who did their utmost during these weeks: You must continue along the same march.

Your support for us will make us stronger and will further support your brothers in Afghanistan.

Exert more efforts in combating this unprecedented war crime.

Fear God, O Muslims and rise to support your religion. Islam is calling on you: O Muslims, O Muslims, O Muslims.

God bear witness that I have conveyed the message. God bear witness that I have conveyed the message. God bear witness that I have conveyed the message.

God's peace and blessings be upon you.

United Nations Security Council Resolution 1382, November 29, 2001

The Security Council,

Recalling its previous relevant resolutions, including its resolutions 986 (1995) of 14 April 1995, 1284 (1999) of 17 December 1999, 1352 (2001) of 1 June 2001 and 1360 (2001) of 3 July 2001, as they relate to the improvement of the humanitarian programme for Iraq,

Convinced of the need as a temporary measure to continue to provide for the civilian needs of the Iraqi people until the fulfillment by the Government of Iraq of the relevant resolutions, including notably resolutions 687 (1991) on 3 April 1991 and 1284 (1999), allows the Council to take further action with regard to the prohibitions referred to in resolution 661 (1990) of 6 August 1990 in accordance with the provisions of these resolutions,

Determined to improve the humanitarian situation in Iraq,

Reaffirming the commitment of all Member States to the sovereignty and territorial integrity of Iraq,

Acting under Chapter VII of the Charter of the United Nations,

1. *Decides* that the provisions of resolution 986 (1995), except those contained in paragraphs 4, 11 and 12 and subject to paragraph 15 of resolution 1284 (1999), and the provisions of paragraphs 2, 3 and 5 to 13 of 1360 (2001) shall remain in force for a new period of 180 days beginning at 0001 hours, Eastern Standard Time, on 1 December 2001;

2. *Notes* the proposed Goods Review List (as contained in Annex 1 to this resolution) and the procedures for its application (as contained in Annex 2 to this resolution) and decides that it will adopt the List and the procedures, subject to any refinements to them agreed by the Council in light of further consultations, for implementation beginning on 30 May 2002;

3. *Reaffirms* the obligation of all States, pursuant to resolution 661 (1990) and subsequent relevant resolutions, to prevent the sale or supply to Iraq of any commodities or products, including weapons or any other military equipment, and to prevent the making available to Iraq of any funds or any other financial or economic resources, except as authorized by existing resolutions;

4. *Stresses* the obligation of Iraq to cooperate with the implementation of this resolution and other applicable resolutions, including by respecting the security and safety of all persons directly involved in their implementation;

5. *Appeals* to all States to continue to cooperate in the timely submission of technically complete applications and the expeditious issuing of export licenses, and to take all other appropriate measures within their competence in order to ensure that urgently needed humanitarian supplies reach the Iraqi population as rapidly as possible;

6. *Reaffirms* its commitment to a comprehensive settlement on the basis of the relevant resolutions of the Security Council, including any clarification necessary for the implementation of resolution 1284 (1999);

7. *Decides* that, for the purposes of this resolution, references in resolution 1360 (2001) to the 150-day period established by that resolution shall be interpreted to refer to the 180-day period established pursuant to paragraph 1 above;

8. *Decides* to remain seized of the matter.

Annex 1: Proposed Goods Review List (GRL), 06/29/01

(Note: Arms and munitions are prohibited under UNSCR 687, para. 24 and thus are not included on the review list.)

A. Items subject to the provisions of UNSCR 1051 (1996).

B. The List contained in document S/2001/1120, annex (to the extent, if any, the items on these lists are not covered by UNSCR 687, para. 24). The list includes the following general categories and includes clarifying notes and statements of understanding: (1) advanced materials; (2) materials processing; (3) electronics; (4) computers; (5) telecommunications and information security; (6) sensors and lasers; (7) navigation and avionics; (8) marine; and (9) propulsion.

C. The following individual items, as further described in the annex:

Command, Control, Communication and Simulation

1. Specific advanced telecommunications equipment.
    2. Information security equipment.

Sensors, Electronic Warfare, and Night Vision

3. Specialized electronic instrumentation and test equipment.
    4. Image intensifier night vision systems, tubes, and components.

Aircraft and Related Items

5. Specialized radar equipment.
    6. Non-civil certified aircraft; all aero gas turbine engines; unmanned aerial vehicles; and parts and components.
    7. Non-xray explosive detection equipment.

Naval-related Items

8. Air independent propulsion (AIP) engines and fuel cells specially designed for underwater vehicles, and specially designed components therefor.

   9. Marine acoustic equipment.

Explosives

10. Charges and devices specially designed for civil projects, and containing small quantities of energetic materials.

Missile-Related Items

11. Specialized vibration test equipment.

Conventional Weapons Manufacturing

12. Specialized semiconductor manufacturing equipment. Heavy Military Transport

   13. Low-bed trailers/loaders with a carrying capacity greater than 30 metric tonnes and width equal to or greater than 3 meters.

Biological Weapons Equipment

14. Certain Biological Equipment.

Remarks by President Bush, December 17, 2001

We want to thank you for coming to the White House to celebrate Eid. It's so nice of you to be here. It reminds us how much we all have in common, how similar boys and girls are, no matter what their religion may be. So thanks for being here today. We're really thrilled you're here.

Eid is a time of joy, after a season of fasting and prayer and reflection. Each year, the end of Ramadan means celebration and thanksgiving for millions of Americans. And your joy during this season enriches the life of our great country. This year, Eid is celebrated at the same time as Hanukkah and Advent. So it's a good time for people of these great faiths, Islam, Judaism and Christianity, to remember how much we have in common: devotion to family, a commitment to care for those in need, a belief in God and His justice, and the hope for peace on earth.

We also share a custom I know all of you are excited about, and that's giving gifts to children. And after this is over, I have a little gift for you, from the White House. This season is meant to be a time of rejoicing, as well as a time of generosity. I'm proud that our country, during Eid, is helping the people of Afghanistan. And I'm proud that the children of America, through America's Fund for Afghan Children, are giving food and clothes and toys to the children of Afghanistan.

The people of Afghanistan have suffered so much, and we're committed to helping them in their time of hardship and in their time of need. These are challenging days for our nation, but holidays like this one remind us about how much we have to be thankful for, and that God delights in joy and generosity of men and women and children. People of every faith are welcome here in the people's house. People of every background are welcome to come here to the White House.

I want to thank you all for coming, and I'd like to go read, if you don't mind, read from a book to you. Is that okay? How about that. Let's go do that, and then we'll go back over here. We've got a special gift for you.

Thank you all for coming. We're getting ready to leave. I may answer a few questions if you have some. Stretch, and then Ron.

Q. Mr. President, have you—with the campaign against the Taliban winding down to a very small area of Afghanistan, will you consider this operation a success if Osama bin Laden is at large?

President Bush. Osama bin Laden is going to be brought to justice. It may happen tomorrow, it may happen in a month, it may happen in a year. But he is going to be brought to justice. He's on the run. He thinks he can hide, but he can't. We've been at this operation now for about two and a half months, and we've made incredible progress. And one of the objectives I've said, in this theater, in all theaters for that matter, is that we want al Qaeda killers brought to justice. And we'll bring him to justice.

Q. What do you know, sir, about whether he's still in Afghanistan? And have you spoken to the Pakistani government about helping you to track him down if, in fact, he has fled across the border?

President Bush. Well, the Pakistanis will help us, and they are helping us look for not only one—Osama bin Laden, but for all the al Qaeda murderers and killers. They will be brought to justice. And it's just a matter of time, as far as I'm concerned. We've got all kinds of reports that he's in a cave, that he's not in a cave, that he's escaped, that he hasn't escaped. And there's all kinds of speculation.

But when the dust clears, we'll find out where he is, and he'll be brought to justice.

Q. Will you order a military tribunal for him?

President Bush. You know, one thing at a time, Ron. I do have the option of military tribunals, because I think it's going to be a way to protect national security matters. But I'll make that judgment when we bring him to justice.

Q. On another matter, sir, have investigators concluded the anthrax used in the mailings have a domestic source? Are you looking for—

President Bush. Well, we're still looking on that. We've all got different feelings about it. I—and we're gathering as much information. And as soon as we make definitive conclusions, we'll share it with the American people.

Q.—what the next steps might be in fighting terrorism in other countries or regions?

President Bush. Yes, we're looking. I mean, any time there is somebody harboring a killer or a terrorist, we will work with them to bring those people to justice. And one of the things I won't do, of course, is tell the enemy what our next move will be. I'm working to build—to keep our coalition strong.

Colin Powell and myself and others in the administration are constantly talking to world leaders to encourage them to cut off money, or disrupt killer cells that might be hiding in their countries. We've made great progress. We've arrested over—I think it's over 300 now. We're beginning to shut down financial institutions around the world.

Not every operation needs to be a military operation to be successful against the terrorist networks. And I'm pleased to tell you that the coalition is working cooperatively. And we're sharing a lot of intelligence between nations, and it's having an effect.

Q. So might Iraq be next, probably?

President Bush. Oh, no, I'm not going to tell the enemy what's next. They just need to know that so long as they plan, and have got plans to murder innocent people, America will be breathing down their neck.

Q. Mr. President, what are you learning about John Walker's involvement in the Taliban or al Qaeda, and should he face the death penalty if he's found to be a—

President Bush. I'm going to let the appropriate law enforcement agencies make recommendations to me. He has been questioned, properly questioned by the U.S. government. I have yet to see the transcript myself. But we'll make the decision on what to do with Mr. Walker. He is a U.S. citizen. Obviously, I've said that U.S. citizens will not go into military tribunals. And so we'll make the determination whether or not he stays within the military system or comes into the civil justice system, the civil system in America.

Chapter 2

January 23–August 21, 2002
Bush Administration Redirects Focus of "War on Terrorism" Towards Iraq

CHRONOLOGY

2002

January 29. In his State of the Union address, President George W. Bush characterizes Iraq, Iran, North Korea as an "axis of evil," threatening world peace with weapons of mass destruction.

April. Baghdad suspends oil exports to protest against Israeli incursions into Palestinian territories. Despite calls by Saddam Hussein, no other Arab countries follow suit. Exports resume after 30 days.

May 14. The United Nations Security Council passes Resolution 1409, which reaffirms U.N. members' commitment to maintaining the territorial integrity of Iraq.

July 5. Iraq once again rejects new U.N. weapons inspections proposals.

August 2. In a letter to the U.N. Secretary General, Iraq invites Hans Blix to visit the country to discuss disarmament issues.

August 19. The U.N. Secretary General rejects Iraq's August 2 proposal as the "wrong work program", but recommends that Iraq allow the return of weapons inspectors in accordance with UNSC resolution 1284, passed in 1999.

August. According to U.S. Intelligence, China, with help from France and Syria, secretly sells Iraq the prohibited chemical hydroxy-terminated polybutadiene, or HTPB, which is used in making solid fuel for long-range missiles. France denies that the sale took place. U.S. intelligence traces the sale back to China's Qilu Chemicals company in Shandong province. The chemical sale involves a French company known as CIS Paris, which helped broker the sale of 20 tons of HTPB. The chemicals were then reportedly shipped from China to Iraq via the Syrian port of Tartus.

Sources: Chronology entries are drawn from www.abc.com, www.bbc.com, www.nytimes.com, www.reuters.com, www.washingtonpost.com, www.wikipedia.com, and staff research.

DOCUMENTS

Remarks by President Bush, January 23, 2002

President Bush delivered his remarks at a Reserve Officers Association luncheon in Washington, D.C.

[*Introductory remarks omitted.*]

Next week I will go before Congress to lay out my priorities for the coming year. There will be no room for misunderstanding. The most basic commitment of our government will be the security of our country. We will win this war; we will protect our people; and we will work to renew the strength of our economy.

Our first priority is the military. The highest calling to protect the people is to strengthen our military. And that will be the priority of the budget I submit to the United States Congress. Those who review our budget must understand that we're asking a lot of our men and women in uniform, and we'll be asking more of them in the future. In return, they deserve every resource, every weapon needed to achieve the final and full victory.

My '03 budget calls for more than $48 billion in new defense spending. This will be the largest increase in defense spending in the last 20 years, and it includes another pay raise for the men and women who wear the uniform.

We will invest in more precision weapons, in missile defenses, in unmanned vehicles, in high-tech equipment for soldiers on the ground. The tools of modern warfare are effective. They are expensive. But in order to win this war against terror, they are essential. Buying these tools may put a strain on the budget, but we will not cut corners when it comes to the defense of our great land.

Another priority is to protect our people from future terrorist attacks. And so the second priority in my budget will be a major new increase in spending for homeland security. The federal government has already acted quickly to increase the number of sky marshals, to support the largest criminal investigation in U.S. history, to acquire antibiotics for large-scale treatment of anthrax, to deploy hundreds of Coast Guard cutters and aircraft and small boats to patrol ports, and to station 8,000 National Guardsmen in the nation's airports.

All this came in response to a sudden emergency. Now we must undertake a sustained strategy for homeland defense. In our next budget, we move forward to complete the hiring of 30,000 new federal airport security workers. We will hire an additional 300 FBI agents to help fight the war on terror. We'll purchase new equipment to improve the safety of the mail, and protect the men and women who deliver our mail. We'll begin a major program of research to combat the threat of bioterrorism. We'll modernize public health labs throughout the country, improving their capacity to detect and treat outbreaks of disease. We will ensure that state and local firemen and police and rescue workers are prepared for terrorism. And we will do more to secure our borders.

The American people are on watch against future attacks. And so will their government. The truth of the matter is, though, in order to fully secure America and our allies, those of us who love and defend freedom, in order to make sure we're safe in the long run, we must find the terrorists wherever they think they can hide, and, as I like to say, get 'em.

Excerpts from the President's State of the Union Address, January 29, 2002

Mr. Speaker, Vice President Cheney, members of Congress, distinguished guests, fellow citizens: As we gather tonight, our nation is at war, our economy is in recession, and the civilized world faces unprecedented dangers. Yet the state of our Union has never been stronger.

We last met in an hour of shock and suffering. In four short months, our nation has comforted the victims, begun to rebuild New York and the Pentagon, rallied a great coalition, captured, arrested, and rid the world of thousands of terrorists, destroyed Afghanistan's terrorist training camps, saved a people from starvation, and freed a country from brutal oppression.

The American flag flies again over our embassy in Kabul. Terrorists who once occupied Afghanistan now occupy cells at Guantanamo Bay. And terrorist leaders who urged followers to sacrifice their lives are running for their own.

America and Afghanistan are now allies against terror. We'll be partners in rebuilding that country. And this evening we welcome the distinguished interim leader of a liberated Afghanistan: Chairman Hamid Karzai.

The last time we met in this chamber, the mothers and daughters of Afghanistan were captives in their own homes, forbidden from working or going to school. Today women are free, and are part of Afghanistan's new government. And we welcome the new Minister of Women's Affairs, Doctor Sima Samar.

Our progress is a tribute to the spirit of the Afghan people, to the resolve of our coalition, and to the might of the United States military. When I called our troops into action, I did so with complete confidence in their courage and skill. And tonight, thanks to them, we are winning the war on terror. The man and women of our Armed Forces have delivered a message now clear to every enemy of the United States: Even 7,000 miles away, across oceans and continents, on mountaintops and in caves—you will not escape the justice of this nation.

For many Americans, these four months have brought sorrow, and pain that will never completely go away. Every day a retired firefighter returns to Ground Zero, to feel closer to his two sons who died there. At a memorial in New York, a little boy left his football with a note for his lost father: Dear Daddy, please take this to heaven. I don't want to play football until I can play with you again some day.

Last month, at the grave of her husband, Michael, a CIA officer and Marine who died in Mazur-e-Sharif, Shannon Spann said these words of farewell: "Semper Fi, my love." Shannon is with us tonight.

Shannon, I assure you and all who have lost a loved one that our cause is just, and our country will never forget the debt we owe Michael and all who gave their lives for freedom.

Our cause is just, and it continues. Our discoveries in Afghanistan confirmed our worst fears, and showed us the true scope of the task ahead. We have seen the depth of our enemies' hatred in videos, where they laugh about the loss of innocent life. And the depth of their hatred is equaled by the madness of the destruction they design. We have found diagrams of American nuclear power plants and public water facilities, detailed instructions for making chemical weapons, surveillance maps of American cities, and thorough descriptions of landmarks in America and throughout the world.

What we have found in Afghanistan confirms that, far from ending there, our war against terror is only beginning. Most of the 19 men who hijacked planes on September the 11th were trained in Afghanistan's camps, and so were tens of thousands of others. Thousands of dangerous killers, schooled in the methods of murder, often supported by outlaw regimes, are now spread throughout the world like ticking time bombs, set to go off without warning.

Thanks to the work of our law enforcement officials and coalition partners, hundreds of terrorists have been arrested. Yet, tens of thousands of trained terrorists are still at large. These enemies view the entire world as a battlefield, and we must pursue them wherever they are. So long as training camps operate, so long as nations harbor terrorists, freedom is at risk. And America and our allies must not, and will not, allow it.

Our nation will continue to be steadfast and patient and persistent in the pursuit of two great objectives. First, we will shut down terrorist camps, disrupt terrorist plans, and bring terrorists to justice. And, second, we must prevent the terrorists and regimes who seek chemical, biological or nuclear weapons from threatening the United States and the world.

Our military has put the terror training camps of Afghanistan out of business, yet camps still exist in at least a dozen countries. A terrorist underworld—including groups like Hamas, Hezbollah, Islamic Jihad, Jaish-i-Mohammed—operates in remote jungles and deserts, and hides in the centers of large cities.

While the most visible military action is in Afghanistan, America is acting elsewhere. We now have troops in the Philippines, helping to train that country's armed forces to go after terrorist cells that have executed an American, and still hold hostages. Our soldiers, working with the Bosnian government, seized terrorists who were plotting to bomb our embassy. Our Navy is patrolling the coast of Africa to block the shipment of weapons and the establishment of terrorist camps in Somalia.

My hope is that all nations will heed our call, and eliminate the terrorist parasites who threaten their countries and our own. Many nations are acting forcefully. Pakistan is now cracking down on terror, and I admire the strong leadership of President Musharraf.

But some governments will be timid in the face of terror. And make no mistake about it: If they do not act, America will.

Our second goal is to prevent regimes that sponsor terror from threatening America or our friends and allies with weapons of mass destruction. Some of these regimes have been pretty quiet since September the 11th. But we know their true nature. North Korea is a regime arming with missiles and weapons of mass destruction, while starving its citizens.

Iran aggressively pursues these weapons and exports terror, while an unelected few repress the Iranian people's hope for freedom.

Iraq continues to flaunt its hostility toward America and to support terror. The Iraqi regime has plotted to develop anthrax, and nerve gas, and nuclear weapons for over a decade. This is a regime that has already used poison gas to murder thousands of its own citizens—leaving the bodies of mothers huddled over their dead children. This is a regime that agreed to international inspections—then kicked out the inspectors. This is a regime that has something to hide from the civilized world.

States like these, and their terrorist allies, constitute an axis of evil, arming to threaten the peace of the world. By seeking weapons of mass destruction, these regimes pose a grave and growing danger. They could provide these arms to terrorists, giving them the means to match their hatred. They could attack our allies or attempt to blackmail the United States. In any of these cases, the price of indifference would be catastrophic.

We will work closely with our coalition to deny terrorists and their state sponsors the materials, technology, and expertise to make and deliver weapons of mass destruction. We will develop and deploy effective missile defenses to protect America and our allies from sudden attack. And all nations should know: America will do what is necessary to ensure our nation's security.

We'll be deliberate, yet time is not on our side. I will not wait on events, while dangers gather. I will not stand by, as peril draws closer and closer. The United States of America will not permit the world's most dangerous regimes to threaten us with the world's most destructive weapons.

Our war on terror is well begun, but it is only begun. This campaign may not be finished on our watch—yet it must be and it will be waged on our watch.

We can't stop short. If we stop now—leaving terror camps intact and terror states unchecked—our sense of security would be false and temporary. History has called America and our allies to action, and it is both our responsibility and our privilege to fight freedom's fight.

Our first priority must always be the security of our nation, and that will be reflected in the budget I send to Congress. My budget supports three great goals for America: We will win this war; we'll protect our homeland; and we will revive our economy.

September the 11th brought out the best in America, and the best in this Congress. And I join the American people in applauding your unity and resolve. Now Americans deserve to have this same spirit directed toward addressing problems here at home. I'm a proud member of my party—yet as we act to win the war, protect our people, and create jobs in America, we must act, first and foremost, not as Republicans, not as Democrats, but as Americans.

It costs a lot to fight this war. We have spent more than a billion dollars a month—over $30 million a day—and we must be prepared for future operations. Afghanistan proved that expensive precision weapons defeat the enemy and spare innocent lives, and we need more of them. We need to replace aging aircraft and make our military more agile, to put our troops anywhere in the world quickly and safely. Our men and women in uniform deserve the best weapons, the best equipment, the best training—and they also deserve another pay raise.

My budget includes the largest increase in defense spending in two decades—because while the price of freedom and security is high, it is never too high. Whatever it costs to defend our country, we will pay.

The next priority of my budget is to do everything possible to protect our citizens and strengthen our nation against the ongoing threat of another attack. Time and distance from the events of September the 11th will not make us safer unless we act on its lessons. America is no longer protected by vast oceans. We are protected from attack only by vigorous action abroad, and increased vigilance at home.

My budget nearly doubles funding for a sustained strategy of homeland security, focused on four key areas: bioterrorism, emergency response, airport and border security, and improved intelligence. We will develop vaccines to fight anthrax and other deadly diseases. We'll increase funding to help states and communities train and equip our heroic police and firefighters. We will improve intelligence collection and sharing, expand patrols at our borders, strengthen the security of air travel, and use technology to track the arrivals and departures of visitors to the United States.

Homeland security will make America not only stronger, but, in many ways, better. Knowledge gained from bioterrorism research will improve public health. Stronger police and fire departments will mean safer neighborhoods. Stricter border enforcement will help combat illegal drugs. And as government works to better secure our homeland, America will continue to depend on the eyes and ears of alert citizens.

A few days before Christmas, an airline flight attendant spotted a passenger lighting a match. The crew and passengers quickly subdued the man, who had been trained by al Qaeda and was armed with explosives. The people on that plane were alert and, as a result, likely saved nearly 200 lives. And tonight we welcome and thank flight attendants Hermis Moutardier and Christina Jones.

Once we have funded our national security and our homeland security, the final great priority of my budget is economic security for the American people. To achieve these great national objectives—to win the war, protect the homeland, and revitalize our economy—our budget will run a deficit that will be small and short-term, so long as Congress restrains spending and acts in a fiscally responsible manner. We have clear priorities and we must act at home with the same purpose and resolve we have shown overseas: We'll prevail in the war, and we will defeat this recession.

* * * *

During these last few months, I've been humbled and privileged to see the true character of this country in a time of testing. Our enemies believed America was weak and materialistic, that we would splinter in fear and selfishness. They were as wrong as they are evil.

The American people have responded magnificently, with courage and compassion, strength and resolve. As I have met the heroes, hugged the families, and looked into the tired faces of rescuers, I have stood in awe of the American people.

And I hope you will join me—I hope you will join me in expressing thanks to one American for the strength and calm and comfort she brings to our nation in crisis, our First Lady, Laura Bush.

None of us would ever wish the evil that was done on September the 11th. Yet after America was attacked, it was as if our entire country looked into a mirror and saw our better selves. We were reminded that we are citizens, with obligations to each other, to our country, and to history. We began to think less of the goods we can accumulate, and more about the good we can do.

For too long our culture has said, "If it feels good, do it." Now America is embracing a new ethic and a new creed: "Let's roll." In the sacrifice of soldiers, the fierce brotherhood of firefighters, and the bravery and generosity of ordinary citizens, we have glimpsed what a new culture of responsibility could look like. We want to be a nation that serves goals larger than self. We've been offered a unique opportunity, and we must not let this moment pass.

My call tonight is for every American to commit at least two years—4,000 hours over the rest of your lifetime—to the service of your neighbors and your nation. Many are already serving, and I thank you. If you aren't sure how to help, I've got a good place to start. To sustain and extend the best that has emerged in America, I invite you to join the new USA Freedom Corps. The Freedom Corps will focus on three areas of need: responding in case of crisis at home; rebuilding our communities; and extending American compassion throughout the world.

One purpose of the USA Freedom Corps will be homeland security. America needs retired doctors and nurses who can be mobilized in major emergencies; volunteers to help police and fire departments; transportation and utility workers well-trained in spotting danger.

Our country also needs citizens working to rebuild our communities. We need mentors to love children, especially children whose parents are in prison. And we need more talented teachers in troubled schools. USA Freedom Corps will expand and improve the good efforts of AmeriCorps and Senior Corps to recruit more than 200,000 new volunteers.

And America needs citizens to extend the compassion of our country to every part of the world. So we will renew the promise of the Peace Corps, double its volunteers over the next five years; and ask it to join a new effort to encourage development and education and opportunity in the Islamic world.

This time of adversity offers a unique moment of opportunity—a moment we must seize to change our culture. Through the gathering momentum of millions of acts of service and decency and kindness, I know we can overcome evil with greater good. And we have a great opportunity during this time of war to lead the world toward the values that will bring lasting peace.

All fathers and mothers, in all societies, want their children to be educated, and live free from poverty and violence. No people on Earth yearn to be oppressed, or aspire to servitude, or eagerly await the midnight knock of the secret police.

If anyone doubts this, let them look to Afghanistan, where the Islamic "street" greeted the fall of tyranny with song and celebration. Let the skeptics look to Islam's own rich history, with its centuries of learning, and tolerance and progress. America will lead by defending liberty and justice because they are right and true and unchanging for all people everywhere.

No nation owns these aspirations, and no nation is exempt from them. We have no intention of imposing our culture. But America will always stand firm for the non-negotiable demands of human dignity: the rule of law; limits on the power of the state; respect for women; private property; free speech; equal justice; and religious tolerance.

America will take the side of brave men and women who advocate these values around the world, including the Islamic world, because we have a greater objective than eliminating threats and containing resentment. We seek a just and peaceful world beyond the war on terror.

In this moment of opportunity, a common danger is erasing old rivalries. America is working with Russia and China and India, in ways we have never before, to achieve peace and prosperity. In every region, free markets and free trade and free societies are proving their power to lift lives. Together with friends and allies from Europe to Asia, and Africa to Latin America, we will demonstrate that the forces of terror cannot stop the momentum of freedom.

The last time I spoke here, I expressed the hope that life would return to normal. In some ways, it has. In others, it never will. Those of us who have lived through these challenging times have been changed by them. We've come to know truths that we will never question: evil is real, and it must be opposed. Beyond all differences of race or creed, we are one country, mourning together and facing danger together. Deep in the American character, there is honor, and it is stronger than cynicism. And many have discovered again that even in tragedy—especially in tragedy—God is near.

In a single instant, we realized that this will be a decisive decade in the history of liberty, that we've been called to a unique role in human events. Rarely has the world faced a choice more clear or consequential.

Our enemies send other people's children on missions of suicide and murder. They embrace tyranny and death as a cause and a creed. We stand for a different choice, made long ago, on the day of our founding. We affirm it again today. We choose freedom and the dignity of every life.

Steadfast in our purpose, we now press on. We have known freedom's price. We have shown freedom's power. And in this great conflict, my fellow Americans, we will see freedom's victory.

Thank you all. May God bless.

Address by Secretary of Defense Rumsfeld, January 31, 2002

Secretary Donald Rumsfeld delivered his address at the National Defense University, Fort McNair, Washington DC.

[*Introductory remarks omitted.*]

Just before Christmas I traveled to Afghanistan and the neighboring countries, where I had an opportunity to spend time with our troops in the field. They are remarkable. They're brave, they're dedicated, they voluntarily risk their lives in a dangerous corner of the world to defend our freedom and our way of life, and I was grateful to be able to personally tell them that.

Among the many, I met with an extraordinary group of men, the Special Forces who'd been involved in the attack on Mazar-e Sharif. Now I've said on a number of occasions that the war on terrorism would likely be unlike any war we had fought before. These men surprised us all with their early requests for supplies. They asked for boots, ammunition—and horse feed.

From the moment they landed in Afghanistan, they began adapting to the circumstances on the ground. They sported beards and traditional scarves. They rode horses—horses that had been trained to run into machine-gun fire, atop saddles that had been fashioned from wood and saddle bags that had been crafted from Afghan carpets. They used pack mules to transport equipment along some of the roughest terrain in the world, riding at night, in darkness, often near mine fields and along narrow mountain trails with drops so sheer that, as one soldier put it, it took him a week to ease the death-grip on his saddle. Many had never been on horseback before.

As they linked up and trained with anti-Taliban forces, they learned from their new allies about the realities of war on Afghan soil, and they assisted the Afghans with weapons, with supplies, with food, with tactics and training. And they helped plan the attack on Mazar.

On the appointed day, one of their teams slipped in and hid well behind the lines, ready to call in airstrikes, and the bomb blasts would be the signal for others to charge. When the moment came, they signaled their targets to the coalition aircraft and looked at their watches. Two minutes and 15 seconds, 10 seconds—and then, out of nowhere, precision-guided bombs began to land on Taliban and al-Qaeda positions. The explosions were deafening, and the timing so precise that, as the soldiers described it, hundreds of Afghan horsemen literally came riding out of the smoke, coming down on the enemy in clouds of dust and flying shrapnel. A few carried RPGs. Some had as little as 10 rounds for their weapons. And they rode boldly—Americans, Afghans, towards the Taliban and al Qacda fighters. It was the first cavalry attack of the 21st century.

After the battle one soldier described how he was called over by one of the Afghans who'd been with him, started to pull up his pant leg, and he thought he was going to see a wound. Instead, he looked down and saw a prosthetic limb. The Afghan had ridden into battle with only one good leg.

Now, what won the battle for Mazar and set in motion the Taliban's fall from power was a combination of ingenuity of the Special Forces, the most advanced precision-guided munitions in the U.S. arsenal delivered by U.S. Navy, Air Force and Marine crews, and the courage of the Afghan fighters, some with one leg. That day on the plains of Afghanistan, the 19th century met the 21st century, and they defeated a dangerous and determined adversary, a remarkable achievement.

When President Bush called me back to the Pentagon after a quarter of a century, he asked me to come up with a new defense strategy to work with the Department of Defense and the senior military to fashion a new approach. He knew I was an old-timer, but I'll bet he never imagined for a second that we'd bring back the cavalry.

But really, this is precisely what transformation is about. Here we are in the year 2002, fighting the first war of the 21st century, and the horse cavalry was back and being used, but being used in previously unimaginable ways. It showed that a revolution in military affairs is about more than building new high tech weapons, though that is certainly part of it. It's also about new ways of thinking, and new ways of fighting.

In World War II, the German blitzkrieg revolutionized warfare. But it was accomplished by a German military that was really only about 10 or 15 percent transformed. The Germans saw that the future of war lay not with massive armies and protracted trench warfare, but rather with its small, high quality, mobile shock forces supported by air power and coordinated with air power, capable of pulling off lightning strikes against the enemy. They developed the lethal combination of fast-moving tanks, mobilized infantry and artillery supported by dive bombers, all concentrated on one part of the enemy line. The effect was devastating on their adversary's capabilities, on their morale, and it was, for a period, on the cause of freedom in the world.

What was revolutionary and unprecedented about the blitzkrieg was not the new capabilities the Germans employed, but rather the unprecedented and revolutionary way that they mixed new and existing capabilities.

In a similar way, the battle for Mazar was a transformational battle. Coalition forces took existing military capabilities from the most advanced laser-guided weapons to antique, 40-year-old B-52s—actually, 40 years old doesn't sound antique to me—but the B-52s had been updated with modern electronics—and also to the most rudimentary, a man on horseback. And they used them together in unprecedented ways, with devastating effect on enemy positions, on enemy morale, and this time, on the cause of evil in the world.

Preparing for the future will require us to think differently and develop the kinds of forces and capabilities that can adapt quickly to new challenges and to unexpected circumstances. An ability to adapt will be critical in a world where surprise and uncertainty are the defining characteristics of our new security environment. During the Cold War, we faced a fairly predictable set of threats. We came to know a great deal about our adversary, because it was the same one for a long period. We knew many of the capabilities they possessed, and we fashioned strategies and capabilities that we believed we needed to deter them. And they were successful. It worked.

For almost a half a century, that mix of strategy, forces and capabilities allowed us to keep the peace and to defend freedom. But the Cold War is over. The Soviet Union is gone, and with it, the familiar security environment to which our nation had grown accustomed.

As we painfully learned on September 11th, the challenges of a new century are not nearly as predictable as they were during the Cold War. Who would have imagined only a few months ago that terrorists would take commercial airliners, turn them into missiles and use them to strike the Pentagon and the World Trade Towers, killing thousands? But it happened.

And let there be no doubt, in the years ahead, it is likely that we will be surprised again by new adversaries who may also strike in unexpected ways.

And as they gain access to weapons of increasing power—and let there be no doubt but that they are—these attacks will grow vastly more deadly than those we suffered several months ago.

Our challenge in this new century is a difficult one. It's really to prepare to defend our nation against the unknown, the uncertain and what we have to understand will be the unexpected. That may seem on the face of it an impossible task, but it is not. But to accomplish it, we have to put aside the comfortable ways of thinking and planning, take risks and try new things so that we can prepare our forces to deter and defeat adversaries that have not yet emerged to challenges.

Well before September 11th, the senior civilian and military leaders of the Department of Defense were in the process of doing just that. With the Quadrennial Defense Review, we took a long, hard look at the emerging security environment and we came to the conclusion that a new defense strategy was appropriate. We decided to move away from the "two major theater war" construct for sizing our forces, an approach that called for maintaining two massive occupation forces capable of marching on and occupying capitals of two aggressors at the same time and changing their regimes. This approach served us well in the immediate post-Cold War period, but it really threatened to leave us reasonably prepared for two specific conflicts and under-prepared for the unexpected contingencies of the 21st century.

To ensure we have the resources to prepare for the future, and to address the emerging challenges to homeland security, we needed a more realistic and balanced assessment of our near-term warfighting needs. Instead of maintaining two occupation forces, we will place greater emphasis on deterrence in four critical theaters, backed by the ability to swiftly defeat two aggressors at the same time, while preserving the option for one massive counter-offensive to occupy an aggressor's capital and replace the regime. Since neither aggressor would know which the president would choose for a regime change, the deterrent is undiminished. But by removing the requirement to maintain a second occupation force, as we did under the old strategy, we can free up resources for the future and the various lesser contingencies which we face, have faced, are facing and will most certainly face in the period ahead.

To prepare for the future, we also decided to move away from the so-called threat-based strategy that had dominated our country's defense planning for nearly a half-century and adopt what we characterized as a capability-based strategy, one that focuses less on who might threaten us or where we might be threatened, and more on how we might be threatened and what we need to do to deter and defend against such threats. Instead of building our armed forces around plans to fight this or that country, we need to examine our vulnerabilities, asking ourselves, as Frederick the Great did in his great General Principles of War, what design would I be forming if I were the enemy, and then fashioning our forces as necessary to deter and defeat those threats.

For example, we know that because the U.S. has unparalleled land, sea and air power, it makes little sense for potential adversaries to try to build up forces to compete with those strengths. They learned from the Gulf War that challenging our armed forces head-on is foolhardy. So rather than building competing armies, navies and air forces, they will likely seek to challenge us asymmetrically, by looking at our vulnerabilities and building capabilities with which they can, or at least hope, to exploit them.

They know, for example, that an open society is vulnerable to new forms of terrorism. They suspect that U.S. space assets and information networks, critical to our security and our economy, are somewhat vulnerable. And they are. They see that our ability to project force into the distant corners of the world where they live depends in some cases on vulnerable foreign bases. And they know we have no defense against ballistic missiles on our cities, our people, our forces, or our friends, creating incentives for the development of weapons of mass destruction and the means to deliver them.

Our job is to close off as many of those avenues of potential attack as is possible. We need to prepare for new forms of terrorism, to be sure, but also attacks on U.S. space assets, cyber attacks on our information networks, cruise missiles, ballistic missiles, nuclear, chemical and biological weapons. At the same time, we must work to build up our own areas of advantage, such as our ability to project military power over long distances, precision strike weapons, and our space, intelligence and undersea warfare capabilities.

Before the terrorist attacks on New York and Washington we had decided that to keep the peace and defend freedom in the 21st century our defense strategy and force structure must be focused on achieving six transformational goals:

First, to protect the U.S. homeland and our bases overseas.

Second, to project and sustain power in distant theaters.

Third, to deny our enemies sanctuary, making sure they know that no corner of the world is remote enough, no mountain high enough, no cave or bunker deep enough, no SUV fast enough to protect them from our reach.

Fourth, to protect our information networks from attack.

Fifth, to use information technology to link up different kinds of U.S. forces so that they can in fact fight jointly.

And sixth, to maintain unhindered access to space and protect our space capabilities from enemy attack.

Our experience on September 11th, and indeed in the Afghan campaign, have served to reinforce the importance of moving the U.S. defense posture in these directions. Our challenge in the 21st century is to defend our cities and our infrastructure from new forms of attack while projecting force over long distances to fight new and perhaps distant adversaries.

To do this, we need rapidly deployable, fully integrated joint forces capable of reaching distant theaters quickly and working with our air and sea forces to strike adversaries swiftly, successfully, and with devastating effect. We need improved intelligence, long-range precision strikes, sea-based platforms to help counter the access denial capabilities of adversaries.

Our goal is not simply to fight and win wars, it is to try to prevent wars. To do so, we need to find ways to influence the decision-makers of potential adversaries, to deter them not only from using existing weapons, but to the extent possible, try to dissuade them from building dangerous new capabilities in the first place.

Just as the existence of the U.S. Navy dissuades others from investing in competing navies—because it would truly cost a fortune and would not succeed in providing a margin of military advantage—we must develop new capabilities that merely by our possessing them will dissuade adversaries from trying to compete.

For example, deployment of effective missile defenses may dissuade others from spending to obtain ballistic missiles when they cannot provide them what they want, which is really the power to hold the United States and our allies' cities hostage to, in effect, nuclear blackmail.

Hardening U.S. space systems and building capabilities to defend our space assets could dissuade adversaries from developing and using small killer satellites to attack and cripple U.S. satellite networks. New earth-penetrating and thermobaric weapons could make obsolete the deep underground facilities where today terrorists hide and terrorist states conceal their weapons of mass destruction capabilities.

In addition to new capabilities, transformation also requires rebalancing existing forces and existing capabilities by adding more of what the Pentagon has come to call low-density, high-demand assets, which is really a euphemism, in plain English, for "our priorities were wrong, and we didn't buy enough of what we need."

For example, the experience in Afghanistan showed the effectiveness of unmanned aircraft. But it also revealed how few we have and what their weaknesses are. The department has known for some time that it does not have enough manned recon-naissance and surveillance aircraft, command-and-control aircraft, air-defense capa-bilities, chemical and biological defense units, as well as certain types of special oper-ations forces.

But in spite of the shortages of these and other scarce systems, the United States postponed the needed investment while continuing to fund what were, in retrospect, less valuable programs. That needs to change.

Moreover, as we change investment priorities, we have to begin shifting the balance in our arsenal between manned and unmanned capabilities between short- and long-range systems, stealthy and non-stealthy systems, between shooters and sensors, and between vulnerable and hardened systems. And we need to make the leap into the information age, which is the critical foundation of our transformation efforts.

As we deployed forces and capabilities to defend U.S. territory after September 11th, we found that our new responsibilities in homeland defense have exacerbated these shortages. No U.S. president should be placed in the position where he must choose between protecting our citizens at home and protecting our interests and our forces overseas. We, as a country, must be able to do both.

The notion that we could transform while cutting the defense budget over the past decade was seductive, but false.

Of course, while transformation requires building new capabilities and expanding our arsenal, it also means reducing stocks of weapons that are no longer necessary for the defense of our country. Just as we no longer need a massive, heavy force designed to repel a Soviet tank invasion, we also no longer need many thousands of offensive nuclear warheads we amassed during the Cold war to deter a Soviet nuclear attack.

During the Cold War, U.S. security demanded our having a nuclear force large enough and diverse enough to survive and to retaliate after a Soviet first strike. Today our adversaries have changed. The terrorists who struck us on September 11th were clearly not deterred by doing so from the massive U.S. nuclear arsenal. In the 21st cen-tury, we need to find new ways to deter new adversaries that will most assuredly arise. That's why President Bush is taking a new approach to strategic deterrence, one that will combine deep reductions in offensive nuclear forces with improved conventional capabilities and the development and deployment of missile defenses capable of pro-tecting the U.S. and our friends and forces deployed from limited missile attacks.

At the same time as we reduce the number of weapons in our nuclear arsenal, we must also refashion the arsenal, developing new conventional offensive and defensive systems more appropriate for deterring the potential adversaries that we now face. And we must ensure the safety and reliability of our nuclear arsenal. No country that has nuclear weapons, as we do, can do anything other than be very respectful of the power, the lethality of those weapons and see that they are safe and reliable, and kept that way.

Taken together, this new triad of reduced offensive nuclear forces, advanced con-ventional capabilities and a range of new defenses are all part of a new approach to deterrence and to defense, but we cannot get here from there without a new approach to balancing the various risks that our country faced.

In the past, the threat-based approach focused attention on near-term war risks, and it had the effect of crowding out investments in the critical areas of people, modernization and transformation. If we are to have a 21st century military, we must balance all of those risks as we allocate defense dollars. It's not an easy thing to do. We're quite good a balancing one war risk against another war risk. But comparing a war risk against the benefit of transformation five years down the road, or balancing it against modernization, or balancing it against the importance of people and the critical element that people are in our defense structure is a much more difficult task. We have to see that we do not cheat the future or the people who risk their lives to secure that future for us. We believe the new approach that we've fashioned will help to do just that.

And we must transform not only our armed forces, but also the Department that serves them by encouraging a culture of creativity and intelligent risk taking. We must promote a more entrepreneurial approach to developing military capabilities, one that encourages people, all people, to be proactive and not reactive, to behave somewhat less like bureaucrats and more like venture capitalists; one that does not wait for threats to emerge and be "validated," but rather anticipates them before they emerge and develops new capabilities that can dissuade and deter those nascent threats.

We need to change not only the capabilities at our disposal, but also how we think about war. All the high-tech weapons in the world will not transform U.S. armed forces unless we also transform the way we think, the way we train, the way we exercise and the way we fight.

Some believe that, with the U.S. in the midst of a dangerous war on terrorism, now is not the time to transform our armed forces. I believe that quite the opposite is true. Now is precisely the time to make changes. The impetus and the urgency added by the events of September 11th powerfully make the case for action.

Every day, we are faced with urgent near-term requirements that create pressure to push the future off the table. But September 11th taught us that the future holds many unknown dangers and that we fail to prepare for them at our peril.

Our challenge is to make certain that, as time passes and the shock of what befell us that day wears off, we do not simply go back to doing things the way we did them before. The war on terrorism is a transformational event that cries out for us to rethink our activities, each of us to rethink our activities, and put that new thinking into action.

Almost every day in meetings, I am confronted by people who come to me with approaches and recommendations and suggestions and requests that reflect a mindset that is exactly the same as before September 11th. They understand that September 11th occurred, but the power of this institution to continue what is is so great that we all need to be reminded and indeed jarred to realize the urgency that exists.

I will say this: The Department of Defense, in my judgment, is up to the task. If you just look at what has been accomplished in the last year—in one year—the year 2001, we adopted a new defense strategy; we replaced the decade-old Two Major Regional War construct for troop sizing with a new approach that is considerably more appropriate to our new world; we adopted a new approach to balancing risks, the near-term war risks, the people risks; the transformation risks and the modernization risks, and we reorganized and revitalized our missile defense research and testing program, free of the constraints of the ABM Treaty; we reorganized the Department to better focus on space capabilities. Through the Nuclear Posture Review, we adopted a new approach to strategic deterrence that increases our security while reducing the numbers of strategic nuclear weapons. And within a week or so, we will be briefing the president on a new Unified Command Structure. And all this was accomplished while fighting a war on terrorism. Not a bad start for a department that has a reputation and is also criticized for being incapable of changing and resistant to change.

Of course, as we transform, we must not make the mistake of assuming that our experience in Afghanistan presents us with a model for the next military campaign.

Preparing to re-fight the last war is a mistake repeated throughout much of military history, and one we must avoid, and will. But we can glean important lessons from recent experiences that apply to the future. Here are a few worth considering:

First, wars in the 21st century will increasingly require all elements of national power: economic, diplomatic, financial, legal, law enforcement, intelligence, as well as overt and covert military operations. Clausewitz said "war is the continuation of politics by other means." In this new century, many of those means may not be military.

Second, the ability of forces to communicate and operate seamlessly on the battlefield will be critical to our success. In Afghanistan, we saw composite teams of U.S. special forces on the ground, working with Navy, Air Force and Marine pilots in the sky, to identify targets, communicate targeting information and coordinate the timing of strikes with devastating consequences for the enemy. The change between what we were able to do before U.S. forces, special forces, were on the ground and after they were on the ground was absolutely dramatic.

The lesson of this war is that effectiveness in combat will depend heavily on "jointness," how well the different branches of our military can communicate and coordinate their efforts on the battlefield. And achieving jointness in wartime requires building that jointness in peacetime. We need to train like we fight and fight like we train, and too often, we don't.

Third, our policy in this war of accepting help from any country on a basis that is comfortable for them and allowing them to characterize what it is they doing to help us instead of our characterizing if for them or our saying that we won't have a country participate unless they could participate in every single respect of this effort, is enabling us to maximize both their cooperation and our effectiveness against the enemy.

Fourth, wars can benefit from coalitions of the willing, to be sure. But they should not be fought by committee. The mission must determine the coalition, and the coalition must not determine the mission. If it does, the mission will be dumbed down to the lowest common denominator, and we can't afford that.

Fifth, defending the U.S. requires prevention, self-defense and sometimes preemption. It is not possible to defend against every conceivable kind of attack in every conceivable location at every minute of the day or night. Defending against terrorism and other emerging 21st century threats may well require that we take the war to the enemy. The best, and in some cases, the only defense, is a good offense.

Sixth, rule out nothing, including ground forces. The enemy must understand that we will use every means at our disposal to defeat them, and that we are prepared to make whatever sacrifices are necessary to achieve victory. To the extent the United States is seen as leaning back, we weaken the deterrent, we encourage people to engage in acts to our detriment. We need to be leaning forward as a country.

Seventh, getting U.S. special forces on the ground early dramatically increased the effectiveness of the air campaign. In Afghanistan, precision-guided bombs from the sky did not achieve their effectiveness until we had boots, and eyes, on the ground to tell the bombers exactly where to aim.

And finally, we need to be straight with the American people. We need to tell them the truth. And when you can't tell them something, we need to tell them that we can't tell them something. The American people understand what we're trying to accomplish, what is needed to get the job done, that it's not easy and that there will be casualties. And they must know that, good news or bad, we will tell it to them straight. Broad bipartisan public support must be rooted in a bond of trust, of understanding and of common purpose.

There is a great deal we can learn from this first war of the 21st century. But we cannot, and must not, make the mistake of assuming that terrorism is the only threat. The next threat we face may indeed be from terrorists, but it could also be a cyber-war, a traditional, state-on-state conflict or something entirely different.

And that's why, even as we prosecute this war on terrorism, we must be preparing for the next war. We need to transform our forces for new and unexpected challenges. We must be prepared for surprise. We must learn to live with little or no warning.

And as we do so, much will change about our armed forces—about the way they will think and fight in this new century.

But there are some things that will remain ever the same through the course of this century and beyond.

In 1962, during a similar time of upheaval and transformation, as our forces prepared to meet the new challenges of the Cold War, General MacArthur addressed the cadets at West Point, and he said, "Through all this welter of change, your mission remains fixed, determined, inviolable: It is to win wars."

The mission of the armed forces remains equally fixed today, equally determined and inviolable. But we must recognize, that earlier generation did, that we will accomplish it only if we have the wisdom, and the courage and the will to change.

Our men and women in uniform are doing a brilliant job in the war on terrorism. We're grateful to them. We're proud. And the best way that we can show our appreciation is to make sure that they have the resources, the capabilities and the innovative culture they need not only to win today's war, but to deter and, if necessary, defeat the aggressors we will surely face in the dangerous century ahead.

We are truly fortunate to have each of you—dedicated, determined and devoted—in the service of our great nation. We look across the globe at the young men and women and what they're doing, and no one can go visit them and not some away with just enormous pride and confidence in the armed services of the United States.

Thank you very much.

* * * *

Q. Yes, sir. National missile defense has been a priority for your administration since the first day. The president reaffirmed that priority in the State of the Union address. How has that priority, role, and mission changed, if it has, since the events of 9-11?

Secretary Rumsfeld. Oh, I don't know that it has. If you think about it, when I was in my confirmation hearing, I was asked about the range of things that concern me, and it was really two things. One was our intelligence-gathering capability, given the complexity of the world and the fact that we don't have one or two targets, we've got a great many targets, and the fact that denial and deception is so advanced today in the world that it's a very difficult thing to do to actually have actionable intelligence. I don't know how many times General Franks and I sat there and worried through the question of actionable intelligence in the past several months, but it was a great many days.

And we talked about the asymmetric threats, and it was never one over the others, because it moves along the spectrum. To the extent it's not advantageous to tackle armies and navies and air forces, it becomes quite advantageous to look at areas of weakness, including, obviously, terrorist attacks, cruise missiles, ballistic missiles, cyberattacks, attacks on space assets and communications assets.

So I think that that missile defense issue remains. It's something we've—we were inhibited by the ballistic missile treaty, the ABM Treaty. In a few months, that will be behind us. We've been not doing tests that would be in violation, because our country doesn't violate treaties. The president's now given the six-month notice.

At the end of that time, we'll be able to actually execute a robust R&D program to see the best, most cost-effective way to provide defenses that will dissuade people from thinking that they can hold our country and our forces and our friends and allies hostage.

Q. Sir, Lieutenant Colonel Pete Maunz, ICAF. In regard to the war on terrorism, how do we know when we've won the war? What indicators are you looking for?

Secretary Rumsfeld. I'll let you know. No, that's not fair. It's a tough question. There will not be a signing ceremony on the USS Missouri—for several reasons, but.... The reality is that our goal is to be able to live as free people and to be able to get up in the morning and go out and know that our children can go to school and they'll come home safely, and that we don't have to carry weapons and hide and live underground and be fearful and acquiesce and give up our freedoms because some other group of people have imposed their will on us.

Now, what does that mean? It means that we have to go after the terrorist networks. It means that we have to deal with countries that harbor terrorists. And you are never going to solve every terrorist act. I mean, some people in Chicago terrorize their neighbors. But that's not what we're talking about here. We're talking about global terrorism. And I think we can do an effective job on that problem. I think it will take a period of years. It's not something that will be quick. It's not something that at the end of that that it will be over and then you can relax, because there will always be people who will attempt to work their will against their neighbors and against the United States.

But I think we'll know when we have been successful in for the most part dealing with the most serious global network threats and the countries that are harboring those. The real—the real concern at the present time is the nexus between terrorist networks and terrorist states that have weapons of mass destruction. And let there be no doubt, there is that nexus, and it must force people all across this globe to realize that what we're dealing with here is something that is totally different than existed in previous periods, and it poses risks of not thousands of lives, but hundreds of thousands of lives, when one thinks of the power and lethality of those weapons.

* * * *

Q. Joanne Callahan, Central Intelligence Agency. Mr. Secretary, you have alluded to the fact that you need actionable intelligence and that there has to be a lot more flexibility, interoperability, elimination of stovepipes, and that sort of thing.

Since you are undergoing a period of transformation, one could argue that the intelligence community, in order to continue to provide relevant support, also has to change. I'm wondering if you can talk about briefly the type of intelligence that has worked for you and—without getting into specifics, of course—and what you might like to see, what you're looking for from the intelligence community in the future. Thank you.

Secretary Rumsfeld. We have developed a very close relationship between the CIA and the Department of Defense in the last 12 months. I think I probably have lunch with George Tenet about once a week, and I'm probably with him once a day, on the phone or in person. And I know Tom Franks has got—in fact, I'm going to have you come up here and comment on this, because here's a real-life example that's happening, where we have tried to connect and fuse the relationship between DOD and the agency. It's never perfect, but it has gotten better every single day since September 11th, I think it's fair to say.

Remarks by National Security Advisor Rice, February 1, 2002

National Security Advisor Condoleezza Rice delivered her remarks to the Conservative Political Action Conference in Arlington, Virginia.

Imagine for a moment that someone had sat you down on September 10th, placed a tape in your VCR and told you that, here's what the President's next State of the Union Address is going to sound like. Each of us placed in those circumstances would have reacted in two ways, both at the same time. As we heard him, and as we viewed the window through which we had just climbed, our stomachs would have churned with the knowledge that our nation and the world had suffered such a great catastrophe. And behind our veil of ignorance, we would have been driven and, in fact, reluctant at the same time to ask the questions, who and what and where and particularly why September 11th.

But second, our hearts would have been filled with enormous pride, knowing that a great nation once again had set its sights on great causes, that our defense of liberty is unabashed and unafraid and morally clear.

On September 10th, we could not have known that America would prove itself so stalwart in the face of such a great challenge. We could not have known that there could be so many countless acts of selflessness and outpouring to ease the suffering of our fellow citizens, and a renewed appreciation of the duties, the responsibilities and the privileges of citizenship. And we could barely have imagined the seismic shifts that were about to occur in international politics.

One of the most important and one of the most immediate shifts has been a renewed appreciation of American national power. Specifically, the importance of a powerful military used responsibly in the service of our values.

If you go back just a little while, there was a lot of speculation that the future of the American armed forces actually lay largely in so-called operations other than war, in policing civil and ethnic conflicts and in humanitarian missions. Well, I don't hear anybody saying that any more.

The fact is that there are real threats out there. Freedom still faces ruthless enemies. And America and its allies have to deter and, if necessary, defeat them.

Our military has done extraordinary things in the past four months. It has shown its power and its precision. It has fought an enemy unlike any we have faced in our history, and we've helped liberate a nation. It has really been extraordinary to witness from the inside, as those of you who have been watching from without have seen, what this military can do.

When we woke up on September 12th and began planning our response, I can tell you that the American military didn't exactly have an operational plan on the shelf, a template that said "Afghanistan Campaign." We especially didn't have a template on the shelf that said, your ground forces are going to be on horseback—your 19th century ground forces with your 21st century air power.

And the President was making clear to those who were planning the campaign every day that he wanted the use of American military force to be meaningful and effective. He was not going to use pinpricks to deal with the circumstances in which we found ourselves.

He understood immediately that only the decisive use of American military power maintains our credibility. But he also told people that we weren't going to respond rashly or do something just for the sake of doing something.

In a very short time frame, we did have a campaign plan for Afghanistan. It was a plan that was daring in conception and difficult in execution. It was truly outside the box, and eventually it was successful. It was successful because the way was paved by strong diplomacy. It was successful because we had a President who was determined and focused and patient. It was successful because we had a commander-in-chief who let his military do the job.

And it was successful because our military forces are the strongest and best equipped and most professional in the history of the world.

Tuesday night, the world saw the President resolve to ensure that our forces remain without peer. He will ask in his budget for an additional $48 billion for our armed forces, the single largest increase since Ronald Reagan was President. And, as President

Bush said Tuesday night, while the price of freedom and security is high, it is never too high. Whatever it costs to defend our nation, we will pay it.

As a result of our resolve, the Taliban regime has been routed and all that remains of it is remnant. Afghanistan is no longer a terrorist-sponsored state but, rather, a state that is trying to make its way to a better future for its people.

But al Qaeda is far from finished. It operates in dozens of countries around the world and it threatens many more. And the President has made clear that we and our allies will not rest until the threat from al Qaeda and the network itself is no more.

We will pursue its members by every means at our disposal. We will disrupt its plans, destroy its bases, arrest its members, break up its cells and choke off its finances. And our enemy is not just al Qaeda, but every terrorist group of global reach. This is not just our struggle; it is the struggle of the civilized world.

The United States has made clear to leaders on every continent that there is no such thing as a good terrorist and a bad terrorist. You cannot condemn al Qaeda and hug Hamas.

The United States draws no distinction between the terrorists and the regimes that feed, train, supply and harbor them. Simply put, harboring terrorists isn't a very good business to be in right now.

Now, many nations are trying hard to do the right thing, to improve their border security, to enforce their laws, to improve their ability to track terrorists in their movements and finances. And the United States is actively helping countries to improve their immune systems against terrorism.

On the other hand, there are some who, shall we say, are not moving with alacrity to shut down terror within their borders. They have been put on notice.

The President also put the world on notice on Tuesday night, that our nation will do everything in its power to deny the world's most dangerous powers the world's most dangerous weapons. It is a stubborn and extremely troubling fact that the list of states that sponsor terror and the lists that are seeking to acquire weapons of mass destruction happens to overlap substantially. And we know that if an al Qaeda type organization were to come into possession of a weapon of mass destruction, they would have no hesitation to use it.

In his State of the Union, the President was crystal clear about the growing danger posed by such states as North Korea, Iran and Iraq that pursue weapons of mass destruction. The President is calling on the world, on our friends and our allies, to join us in preventing these regimes from developing and deploying these weapons, either directly or through stateless terrorist surrogates. This is a serious matter and it requires a serious response.

North Korea is now the world's number one merchant for ballistic missiles, open for business with anyone, no matter how malign the buyer's intentions.

The United States has offered a roadmap for reciprocal steps that would enable North Korea to take a better course. We've had no serious response from Pyongyang.

Iraq continues to threaten its neighbors, the neighborhood, and its own people, and it continues to flaunt obligations that it undertook in 1991. And that can mean only one thing: It remains a dangerous regime, and it remains a regime determined to acquire these terrible weapons.

And Iran. Iran's direct support of regional and global terrorism and its aggressive efforts to acquire weapons of mass destruction belie any good intentions it displayed in the days after the world's worst terrorist attacks in history.

All of these nations have a choice to make—to abandon the course they now pursue. Unfortunately, these terrible regimes have shown no inclination to do so. But the United States and the world have only one choice, and that is to act with determination and resolve.

As the President said, we must not and we will not wait on events while dangers gather, and we will use every tool at our disposal to meet this grave global threat. We will work to strengthen nonproliferation regimes and export controls. We will use our new and budding relationship with Russia to redouble our efforts to prevent the leakage of dangerous materials and technologies. And we will move ahead with a missile defense system that can do the job, unconstrained by the Anti-Ballistic Missile Treaty.

This President is determined and committed to protecting America, our forces, our allies and our friends from terror that comes packaged atop a missile. And the United States is unequivocal in its resolve to do what we must to insure ourselves. As the President said, the price of indifference would be catastrophic.

But even as we address today's multiple challenges, even as we recognize that the war on terrorism is one that will have to be fought for a long time to come, we can look ahead to tremendous opportunities that are before us. We want to leave this world not just safer, but better. We are committed to a world of greater trade, of greater democracy and greater human rights for all the world's people wherever they live. September 11th makes this commitment more important, not less. Because, ladies and gentlemen, you know that America stands for something real. It stands for rights that are inalienable and truths that are self-evident. It stands for compassion and hope.

September 11th reintroduced America to a part of itself that some had forgotten or that some thought we no longer had. And we will carry this better part of ourselves out into the wider world.

We are a generous people. President Bush and the United States of America are committed to channeling our noble energies into an effort to encourage development and education and opportunity throughout the world, including the Muslim world. On every continent, in every land, this President, the education President at home, wants to press the goal of education for all abroad. Because there is one remarkable thing about education. It allows you to remake yourself into something new. It opens up to you the full range of possibilities of what you can be.

You know, I am, of course, a professor at Stanford University. And I can tell you that one of the most heartening things about being a professor in a great university is the students that you meet. You look out at your student body and you recognize that at this elite university, there may be one student who's a fourth generation Stanford legatee, but sitting right next to that student is a kid whose parents might be migrant farm workers, or a kid from rural America who is the first to go to school in his or her family. And you think, that's what this country is about, it's a belief that it really doesn't matter where you came from; it matters where you're going.

Terrorism, the kind of hatred and the kind of hopelessness that gets foisted on people around the world, cannot stand in a world in which people have that kind of hope. And that's why education in practical skills, rather than education in hatred is so important to peace and stability in the long run.

We are moving quickly, with places like Pakistan, to help them improve their educational systems. We have a teacher training initiative with Central America to improve the state of teaching in those countries. And we are putting millions of dollars into textbooks and into teacher training for new schools in Afghanistan where, for the first time in years, young girls will have that opportunity as well.

America is a remarkable country. One that finds its unity of purpose not in common blood but in common values. It is a country that rewards creativity and entrepreneurship and tries to bring opportunity through education for all. But in our hour of need, we found a country that has been renewed in those values and a country that looked to honor and family and to faith to get us through. There is a lot to do ahead of us. But renewed in who we are, renewed in our common purpose and our values, we will succeed. Thank you very much.

Remarks by Secretary of Defense Rumsfeld, February 3, 2002

Secretary Donald H. Rumsfeld was interviewed by Sam Donaldson of ABC News.

Q. Let's move on to the president's speech last Tuesday night. He singled out Iran, Iraq and North Korea, calling them an "axis of evil." And then he said something I think that is as tough as we've ever heard a president in modern times say, actually without going to war. Here it was: "I will not wait on events while dangers gather. I will not stand by as peril draws closer and closer. The United States of America will not permit the world's most dangerous regimes to threaten us with the world's most destructive weapons."

"I will not wait. I will not stand by. The United States will not permit." At what point, if these three countries continue to try to acquire weapons of mass destruction, will the United States make good on that promise?

Secretary Rumsfeld. Well, first, I think the applause that followed the president's remarks is an indication that there is a growing realization, a broad realization today that we are living in a different time. With weapons of mass destruction more readily available to a number of nations and potentially to terrorist networks. We have to think about this problem in a dramatically different way than we did previously.

And the president's point, I think, was sound. And I've been impressed, looking at comments around the world and comments in the United States and in the Congress in support of the president's statement, that in fact these three countries have engaged in activities with respect to their own people, as well as their neighbors, that have to be described as "evil." And that we do know of certain knowledge that each of those three countries is engaged in active weapons of mass destruction programs. And we do know that those countries have relationships with terrorist networks.

It's that nexus between weapons of mass destruction and terrorist networks that the president was citing as being different for today and something that we really have to think very carefully about what we do as a people, and as a world, and as a society, given that nexus.

Q. When do we do it? If they continue to try to acquire the weapons, do we do it in the middle of their effort to acquire? Do we wait till they have acquired? Do we wait until they're poised to use them? I think Americans would certainly want the president or any administration to prevent an enemy from using weapons of mass destruction. But at what point does he say "I will not stand idly by?" Where's the line?

Secretary Rumsfeld. Well, those are difficult calls and those are calls that presidents make. And he will. He'll make his own judgment. And he will watch and take the appropriate steps to provide for the protection of the American people and our deployed forces, and our friends and allies.

* * * *

Q. Well, you made a judgment the other day which you expressed and I think you scared a lot of people. Let me just take a look at some of your words and see what you meant. "As they gain access to weapons of increasing power, and let there be no doubt but that they are, these attacks will grow vastly more deadly than those we suffered several months ago." Attacks on the United States. How do you know this?

Secretary Rumsfeld. Well, anyone who looks at the techniques of taking American airliners filled with Americans and taking box openers and capturing crews and turning those airplanes into missiles and driving them into buildings and killing thousands of people, we know roughly the effect of that. It was thousands. We also know that biological weapons, for example, or nuclear weapons, or radiation weapons, or chemical weapons can kill tens of thousands and hundreds of thousands, not simply thousands.

Q. But you seem to be predicting not that it's possible, but that it's going to happen.

Secretary Rumsfeld. No, no. I'm—what I'm saying, very directly, is that we have a series of countries on the terrorist list. Any number of them are active, developing weapons of mass destruction, and that they have relations with terrorist networks. And we must not sit idly by as a country, as a world, and accept that outcome, that eventually, if we wait long enough, eventually it's reasonable to expect that terrorist nations will provide weapons of mass destruction to terrorist networks. We know the al-Qaeda were actively seeking chemical and biological weapons. There's evidence galore to that effect. We have to face that. It isn't a matter of scaring anybody, it's exactly what President Bush said. We need to consider the world we're living in and live with a sense of heightened awareness. And we can live in this world. We can do that.

* * * *

Q. Let me just say that you were requesting, and the president, a 48-billion-dollar increase in the defense budget for the next fiscal year and over a five-year period up to 451 billion dollars, that's where it would be. That's a 120-billion-dollar increase. Now, the old question of guns versus butter then arises.

Let me just show you a chart of some of the cuts we understand the president is asking in domestic programs: Nine billion dollars cut in highway programs; a freeze in the Army Corps of Engineers projects; a cut of 180 million from a youth job program. Perhaps a cut of an addition 620 million in state grants for training and education. And the critics will say "all to pay for the expanded defense budget."

Secretary Rumsfeld. The reality is that the United States is now spending about three percent of our gross national product on defense. Back in the Kennedy and Eisenhower period, it was closer to 10 percent. In the Ford period, it was around five percent of our gross national product. Today, it's about three percent. It is certainly a percentage that our country can afford.

Second, if one thinks about it, we all got up today and went about our business, people going to church, people going to the Superbowl, people coming in to meet with you—

Q. And we appreciate it.

Secretary Rumsfeld. Thank you. And we did it because we can enjoy our freedom. Because we live in a world that's underpinned by peace and stability, for the most part. And it is our national security, the United States of America, at this time in history, that is able to contribute to peace and stability in the world. And without peace and stability, we can't have prosperity, we can't be able to enjoy our freedoms, we can't have economic opportunity. That's so central. You've been in war zones. You've been to Beirut. You've been to Kabul. You know what they look like. People are not on the streets. They're off the streets. The buildings are pock-marked. Roads are blown up.

Q. But isn't it a fact that the American people will have to be told that in order to do the things that you argue we need to do are going to have to give up a lot of the butter?

Secretary Rumsfeld. In President Truman's presidency, they made a decision during the Korean War to moderate the growth in non-defense spending. That's what President Bush has done. He's kept the growth in non-defense spending to about one or two or three percent, which is a very responsible thing to do. And he's said that the American people need to have an increase in the defense budget and in the homeland security budget.

Q. All I'm suggesting, sir, is you may have to say "you can't have it all" to the American people. Because at one time, President Bush—

Secretary Rumsfeld. Well, the American people know that. They establish priorities in their daily lives everyday. The American people aren't unrealistic. I've got a lot of confidence in the American people. They get up and they look at their budgets, they know that they can have this, but not that. And that's the way it is for our country.

Remarks by Secretary of State Powell, February 3, 2002

Secretary Colin Powell was interviewed by Bob Schieffer and Gloria Borger on CBS's Face the Nation.

Q. Okay, let's shift now to the President's speech on Tuesday. The President talked about the "axis of evil"—Iran, Iraq, North Korea. I would ask you first, did you sign off on that speech?

Secretary Powell. Yes, I saw the speech before it was delivered. I commented on it a week before. And I fully supported that line. It's a good, powerful, strong line that makes the case that these three nations are representative of a group of nations that continue to act in ways that are just inconsistent with the expectations of the 21st century and are hindering our campaign against terrorism.

Q. At the outset of this administration, though, Mr. Secretary, you were somebody who wanted to open up talks, for example, with North Korea. Isn't that almost impossible now, given what the President has said?

Secretary Powell. No, the President has made it very clear that we are dissatisfied with the actions of North Korea, that they continue to develop missiles, they continue to develop missiles that could carry weapons of mass destruction, and they sell them. But the President has also said we are prepared to talk to the North Koreans, to negotiate with them, any time, any place, any where, without any preconditions. He made that decision last summer. I presented that decision to the North Koreans through my associates in the State Department. We presented that to the South Koreans. That remains our policy. We are prepared to talk to the North Koreans. They have a Get Out of Jail card.

If they don't want to be condemned this way as members of this group of nations that the President so identified, they should change their policies. It is a country that people are starving in. We are providing most of the food that keeps these people alive. We are not designating those people as evil; we are saying the regimes are evil. And the North Koreans could turn that around very quickly if they would enter into positive discussions with the South Koreans and with the United States and with the other nations in the region if they would stop developing these kinds of weapons.

Q. Well, let's talk about Iran. Why was Iran listed as one of the three? Republican Senator Chuck Hagel, member of the Foreign Relations Committee, said he was a little surprised because he thought the Iranians had been actually helping us behind the scenes.

Secretary Powell. We have always identified Iran as a state sponsor of terrorism. They continue to sponsor terrorist activities. It is quite true that there is a debate, a battle taking place, within Iran between those individuals who we could call more moderate in their approach and may want to be seeking ways to reach out to the rest of the world, and the fundamentals who are against those kinds of outreach efforts.

And so, for example, in Afghanistan we saw the Iranians play a helpful role at the

Bonn conference in setting up the Interim Authority for the new government of Afghanistan, and they played a helpful role in Japan a couple of weeks ago. At the reconstruction conference they made a significant contribution.

But we also see them doing some unhelpful things with respect to Afghanistan and revolutionary guard elements trying to gain undue influence in western Afghanistan and taking other actions that we don't find that satisfactory.

Q. Such as?

Secretary Powell. Well, trying to exert influence in western Afghanistan and trying to exert influence in Kabul. And so what we are saying to them is this is the time to be part of this campaign, this coalition moving forward. This is the time to stop supporting terrorist organizations such as Hezbollah. This is the time to stop developing weapons of mass destruction. This is the time to stop trying to develop nuclear weapons. And this is the time for nations in the neighborhood to stop assisting them in developing weapons of mass destruction.

So what we are saying to them is don't be a part of this category of nations; come on out, join this campaign, stop it.

* * * *

Q. Well, let's go back to this whole business of the "axis of evil." Are we on the brink of war with these people, with these countries?

Secretary Powell. I didn't hear the President announce any new policies in the State of the Union Address, and I didn't hear him declare war on anybody. What he said, in a very straightforward direct manner, is that as we go forward in this campaign against terrorism and after we go after terrorists, we have to go after and identify those nations that are assisting terrorists or are developing weapons of mass destruction that can get into the hands of terrorists.

And so he spoke in a very clear, direct way. And all of the people who are sort of reacting to this should not be reacting to what the President said; they ought to be reacting to those nations who are not acting in a proper way, who are giving evidence that that they are pursuing evil ends.

Q. Well, was he, in fact, warning that there could be preemptory action by the United States, that if we find out that somebody is helping a terrorist, if somebody is making one of these weapons, that we will reserve the right to go in and take out that weapon before they are able to use it or before they are able to—

Secretary Powell. We reserve the right to do whatever is necessary to protect ourselves and to protect our friends and allies. And as the President also said in his speech, he will be consulting with our friends and allies as we move forward, just as he has been consulting with our friends and allies before he gave the speech the other evening. The fact of the matter is that President Bush speaks directly. He speaks from the heart and speaks with passion. And he wanted to get everybody's attention that as we go forward in this campaign against terrorism, we cannot take our eye off these kinds of regimes that are part and parcel of this whole problem that we have.

Q. Well, Russia, for example, challenged this "axis of evil" attack, saying that there was not evidence that Iran, for example, had a connection to terrorist organizations. So what message are you sending to a country like Russia?

Secretary Powell. The message we are giving to Russia is we disagree with them on this. We have designated Iran as a state that sponsors terrorism. They sponsor Hezbollah and other organizations, and I don't think that is much in dispute by anybody.

Q. So where do you draw the line?

Secretary Powell. We draw the line quite clearly. If you want to be part of a 21st century that is founded on democracy and freedom and moving forward and non-aggressive behavior, then you should not be developing weapons of mass destruction that you plan to have as a way to threaten your neighbors or intimidate your neighbors, or, worse, attack your neighbors.

You should not be developing the kinds of missiles that can deliver such weapons. You should not be supporting terrorists. You should be using the resources you have in your country, the kinds of resources that Iran has in the form of oil. You should be dealing with the real problems you have, such as in North Korea where you're starving to death as a population, and not be investing what little treasure you have in that society to develop weapons of mass destruction and missiles, and then sell them to other regimes that are along the "axis of evil," if I may say so.

Q. Is there anything, let's say in the last six months, has Iran increased its capability in any way? Is there any additional evidence over the recent months that Iran is any further along to building weapons of mass destruction?

Secretary Powell. Iran continues to try to import to obtain weapons, conventional weapons, and they are trying to improve their ability to fire and use and develop and make ballistic missiles. And there is no question they are continuing efforts to see if they can develop a nuclear capability. And there is no question that North Korea is continuing to sell missiles. And the same day the President was giving the speech, I happened to come across more intelligence information suggesting that the North Koreans have not stopped in the slightest; in fact, they are trying to increase the capability of some of the systems that they make available for export. This is dangerous. The President spoke to it.

Q. And what about Iraq?

Secretary Powell. With respect to Iraq, the problem is quite simple. We suspect they are developing weapons of mass destruction. We more than suspect it. We know it. There is an easy way for them to demonstrate that they are not. And that is, as the President has said, let the inspectors in. What the President has been saying continuously is there are U.N. resolutions with respect to weapons of mass destruction in Iraq; let the inspectors in. They threw them out in 1998. They ought to be allowed back in. If Iraq is not a member of the "axis of evil" club, let the inspectors in to establish it and prove it.

The burden should not be on the President; it should not be on us; and it should not be on the State of the Union Address which clearly pointed out these problems. The burden and all of the counter-rhetoric we are hearing is misdirected. It ought to be directed at these nations that are pursuing these kinds of capabilities. And the President called it the way it is.

Q. Mr. Secretary, one more question on the "axis of evil" club, as you have sort of termed it this morning. And that is, what if these countries do continue to develop weapons of mass destruction? What if we do find out that they are going against the advice that the President laid down Tuesday night? What happens then?

Secretary Powell. Well, the President has all the options available to him: political means, diplomatic means, economic means and military means. And I know the President will consult with our friends and allies in the world because it is not just a danger to the United States; it is a danger to the whole world, to the civilized world. And then we'll see what might be necessary to persuade them, convince them or force them to act in ways that are more responsible. We prefer diplomatic ways, political solutions. We're not looking for a war. We are trying to avoid war. But we will not resist the challenge that these nations present to us.

Q. Is this a signal that we would act unilaterally, though?

Secretary Powell. We're not trying to give a signal that we are going to act unilaterally. If it's necessary, we can, and we will if we have to. But it is much better to operate within a framework of like-minded nations, and that is the President's policy. He has spent an enormous amount of time just in the past week talking to foreign leaders. King Abdullah was in the Oval Office on Friday. Chancellor Schroeder was in for dinner on Thursday night.

I won't even count for you how many heads of state and foreign ministers I've spoken to in the last five days. This is not a matter of us going off alone all by ourselves. We keep in touch with all of our friends and allies. It's just an incorrect charge, a false charge, to say that we do not consult with our friends and allies. That is what I spent most of my days doing.

Remarks by Senator Biden, February 4, 2002

Senator Joseph Biden (D-DE), Chairman of the Senate Foreign Relations Committee, delivered his remarks at the Center for Strategic and International Studies in Washington, D.C.

As the shock of 9-11 begins to wear off, one unanticipated consequence now emerging is a fuller appreciation of why foreign policy matters. Before 9-11, few Americans believed that what happens beyond our borders affects their lives. We were a nation focused on ourselves, constantly looking in the mirror, but rarely out the window.

But on September 11, our perspective abruptly changed. Suddenly foreign policy became something that affected our economic security as well as our personal security. Before September 11, only a few of us were discussing the real threats we face, and how to defend against them. Even fewer were discussing anything even remotely resembling a multi-year, multi-billion dollar commitment to homeland defense. A few weeks later, a half dozen letters made threats of biological or chemical weapons, or a deadly vial in a backpack, much more real.

We were forced to come face to face with our worst fears. We saw the kind of death and destruction that could be wielded by religious fundamentalism, anti-Americanism and terrorists fueled by blind hatred.

And we learned that we should not leap forward with answers before we're sure we've asked the right questions—like whether or not to invest in missile defense when a more imminent threat was transnational terrorism.

Now we are faced with the hard choices about what we need to do and how to do it.

The good news is we are the world's only superpower. The bad news is we're the world's only superpower. All too often nations expect us to make their problems our highest priority.

So, while we can't be all things to all people, we should not shrink back from our unavoidable responsibility to bear the burden of international leadership. If 9-11 was a wake-up call to the American people, it was also a wake-up call to the unilateralists in the Bush Administration.

George Bush came into office disdainful of engagement with the world. He spoke of "nation-building" as an unacceptable option.

When he became President he pulled back from treaties on nuclear testing, on germ warfare, on environmental protection, and announced his intention to withdraw unilaterally from the ABM Treaty.

Less than a year after he was elected, when the first plane hit the World Trade Center, the notion of unilateralism was put to the test. To his credit, he realized it was time to reach out to allies and embrace new partners.

I commend him for this. Epiphanies, I believe, are veto-proof. We can only hope they're permanent as well.

The response has been positive. NATO soldiers flew surveillance flights over the eastern seaboard of the United States.

Musharraf made the strategic decision to align Pakistan with the West.

Putin provided us with intelligence on Afghanistan. He helped secure our presence in the Central Asian republics, and countries around the world joined with common purpose in a common struggle.

Today we must ask if President Bush is going to maximize the strategic opportunities we now have to shape the next fifty years as the Cold War shaped the last fifty, and make long-term engagement one of the strategic weapons in his diplomatic arsenal.

U.S. foreign policy must recognize that many of the new threats we face will require multilateral responses.

But no one, least of all the enemies of the United States, should have any doubt that another attack on this nation would lead to our use of overwhelming force, in concert with others or alone, and with the full weight of American power and resolve.

But more and more, from law enforcement to intelligence, we have to work closely with international partners. The reason is obvious: Al Qaeda is neither limited nor deterred by national boundaries.

Isolation is not an option. Unilateralism is not an option.

We must be engaged—the question is how.

Let me be clear. I don't believe engagement is simply supporting treaties on biological weapons, or the environment, or even the ABM Treaty, although these are important, if not critical, symbols of our intentions.

America's engagement around the world is a long-term investment in our security, and should be at the core of our foreign policy.

The first real test of post-9-11 engagement is to stay the course in Afghanistan.

After twenty-three years of almost constant war, the country is in total chaos. Food and water are scarce. Kabul is a moonscape. Devastated. Destroyed.

Not, primarily, by American bombs but by years of war, failed regimes and struggles among armed warlords.

Our military personnel call it: "the other end of ground zero..."

And yet after four days in Kabul, I was surprised at the deep pool of goodwill from a nation so often portrayed as bitterly resentful of any foreign presence.

The Afghan people want us to stay. They need our help. They need security. They know the difference between those who come as enemies and those who come as liberators.

Let me share with you a story Hamid Karzai told me just a couple weeks ago in Kabul.

Let me give you two more examples of what I mean. I met with the Minister of Education and asked him what he needed most urgently. I expected to hear about rebuilding shattered schoolhouses, or the need for desks, books, pencils, and so on. But he looked me in the eye and said, "Security. Without it, nothing can be built."

When we went to the old Soviet Embassy, we met with some of the 20,000 refugees from the Shomali Plain living in absolute squalor with little water, little food, and no hope.

But even the prospect of escaping those conditions to return home could not overcome their fear. The Shomali plain, a vast and fertile agricultural area just north of Kabul, was the breadbasket of the nation before the Taliban turned it into an arid sea of dust.

All they wanted was to go back to their farms, but the refugees told us they couldn't because they had no assurance their families would be safe if they tried to return.

Security is the basic issue in Afghanistan.

If Chairman Karzai is to govern effectively, the first things he needs are a military, a police force, and an infusion of economic assistance. And he needs them now.

Tokyo was a start, but more will have to be done, and the United States will have to take the lead. If we don't, no one else will.

And like it or not, our leadership role must include soldiers on the ground. If others step forward, fine, but whatever it takes, we should do it. History will judge us harshly if we allow the hope of a liberated Afghanistan to evaporate because we failed to stay the course.

A robust multi-national force helping the nascent Afghan government extend authority to all its borders is a wise investment by the West and our regional allies in Central Asia.

President Bush's aversion to even the rudimentary elements of establishing order and stability—because it might put him on the road to "nation building"—must be outweighed by our national security need to prevent Afghanistan from backsliding into a lawless safe haven for anti-American terrorists.

This means a continued engagement in Afghanistan until we can transition from a multi-national to an Afghan force. But first things first.

Pockets of Al Qaeda and Taliban still need to be rooted out. Incidents of firefights and even major battles continue throughout the country.

Just last week the Kabul government suffered a setback with the reversal at Gardez.

At a Kandahar hospital there was a shootout where Taliban with grenades strapped to their chests had been holed up for six weeks.

Their leader, Mullah Omar, is still at large. No one knows where Osama bin Laden is hiding, if he's alive. Their top lieutenants are still on the run. Others have been killed or fled to other countries. And we have to finish the job before we talk about what comes next.

But we can't seem to talk about what comes next without talking about Iraq. It's obvious we must end the reign of Saddam Hussein. It would be unrealistic, if not downright foolish, to believe we can claim victory in the war on terrorism if Saddam is still in power.

But rather than talking about it now, let me in the interest of time, save my thoughts about Saddam for the Q&A at the end of my remarks.

Clearly, whatever strategic decision we make on what comes next—it will require hard choices.

Engagement in Afghanistan, engagement with allies and friends around the world, waging war on terrorism, and homeland defense will take more than our will and resolve. It will take a huge increase in the level of spending. But most of all it will require us to prioritize, something many in elected office find it hard to do. Our job in Washington is to debate what comes first, to determine priorities.

Some people are calling the new budget a "guns and butter" budget, while this morning's Post calls it a "War Budget". Either way, without the squandered 400 billion dollar surplus we were projected to have by 2004, we've got more than a numbers problem. We've got a priorities problem.

Let me focus for a few moments just on the guns side of the equation. I agree with the President, and have argued for some time, that an increase in conventional military spending is necessary to prepare the nation for the next generation of challenges.

Let's look at the top six modernization programs. The cost estimates today begin at a minimum of 350 billion dollars.

339 F-22s to replace an aging F-15 fleet will cost $ 62 billion. 2912 Joint Strike Fighters to replace aging F-16s, A-10s, and F-14s will cost about $223 billion. 30 new C-17s will cost $6 billion.

A thousand Advanced Amphibious Assault Vehicles to move Marines from water to land at high speed will cost $14.9 billion. And one more aircraft carrier will have a price tag of about $6.5 to $7.5 billion.

And let's not forget about national missile defense estimates by the Congressional Budget Office that an effective mid-course intercept system alone would cost more than $50 billion. And that estimate leaves out the cost of defending our allies, which the President insists he also wants to do.

With today's budget release calling for $7.8 billion for missile defense for FY '03, the Administration is well on its way towards an expenditure in the hundreds of billions.

We haven't even gotten into President Bush's promise of pay raises for our men and women in uniform and other high ticket items to enhance the quality of life for military families.

And we haven't gotten into what demands we'll encounter in combating the so-called Axis of Evil, three very bad actors, for whom we must devise very different approaches.

Today, with delivery of the President's little blue budget book, it's not too soon to begin prioritizing the most pressing threats to our security. In my book, not to mention that of the Joint Chiefs and the National Intelligence Estimate, terrorism with weapons of mass destruction—but without ICBMs—is the greatest threat we face.

There are many sources for these weapons, and it takes years to get or build them. But there's a shortcut, a place that has it all. It's "the candy store." Other people call it "Russia."

A year ago, Howard Baker and Lloyd Cutler issued a report on the state of Russia's nuclear materials. Baker testified to the Foreign Relations Committee regarding "the enormity of this danger." He said: "And the fact that we have not blown ourselves up so far is no guarantee that we could not still; or that some rogue nation or rogue group has not yet successfully stolen a nuclear weapon does not mean that they cannot still do it if all you have is a padlock out there."

How shall we meet that threat, along with the threat that chemical or biological weapons might find their way from Russia to the rogues?

Senator Richard Lugar and I believe one way is to reduce Russia's Soviet-era debt, in return for Russia investing the proceeds in non-proliferation programs. We hold over $3 billion in such debt, and our allies hold several times that. Debt reduction could help Russia secure its sensitive materials and technology—and avoid an expected payment crunch next year.

Baker and Cutler proposed spending 30 billion dollars over 8-to-10 years to secure Russia's nuclear materials and technology.

I would add another $10 billion for our share of chemical weapons destruction in Russia, a few billion dollars to keep their chemical and biological weapons experts out of harm's way, and some more to track down and secure their missing radioactive materials that could be used to make a radiological "dirty bomb." That adds up to roughly $ 45 billion—which is still less than the price of that mid-course intercept system to defend us against ICBM's. Does anyone doubt that our first priority must be to close Russia's candy store?

By the way, we haven't begun talking about things the American people believe ought to be very high priorities: Social Security, Medicare and a real prescription drug program.

Ladies and gentlemen, I hope I'm not dating myself too much by recalling former Senator Everett McKinley Dirksen's famous words: "A billion here, a billion there...before you know it, you're talking about real money. I may not be a mathematician, folks, but this budget doesn't add up. You just can't fit ten pounds into a five pound bag.

No one could have imagined the tragedy of September 11, or the associated financial costs we're still incurring. But when our nation is challenged, that's when we're at our best. And our best means we must have the will to make the hard choices.

Now we need to prioritize, to determine how best to secure America's future. In my capacity as Chairman, I want the Foreign Relations Committee to reclaim its highest function and shine a bright light on the issues of the day. To discuss with experts how our national security concerns abroad are indivisible from the physical and economic security of the American people here at home.

Starting tomorrow with Secretary of State Colin Powell we hope to lay out for the American people the difficult but inevitable choices we must make to ensure our continued well-being and prosperity.

We will be looking at a broad range of issues: How do we protect ourselves from weapons of mass destruction? What about nonproliferation? How do we take advantage of new opportunities to enhance key bilateral relationships?

What's next in the war on terrorism? What do we do about infectious disease, democratization, human rights?

Folks, in a twist of fate, we may be able to turn recent calamity into good luck. History may have given us the best chance we've had since the end of World War II to build a new framework for international affairs.

So far, the American people have been served well by the President and his Administration in the prosecution of the war on international terrorism, but the war is only five months old and the new patterns of cooperation and support are young and fragile. We should nourish them and help them flourish.

Today the doors to international cooperation and American leadership have opened, but if we slam them shut too often we will lose our chance to realign forces for decades to come—and we will be condemned to repeat our wars rather than move beyond them.

Remarks by Senator Biden, Senator Helms, and Secretary of State Powell, February 5, 2002

Senator Joseph Biden (D-DE), Senator Jesse Helms (R-NC), and Secretary Colin Powell delivered their remarks during a hearing of the Senate Foreign Relations Committee.

Senator Biden. Today the Committee on Foreign Relations begins a series of hearings to review American foreign policy in the wake of the attacks on the United States last September. The essential objectives of the hearings are two-fold: to highlight the serious national security challenges facing this country and to ensure that we are allocating our resources properly to meet those challenges.

We begin with Secretary of State Powell, who has done a first-rate job in guiding American foreign policy, particularly since the attacks of September 11. The Administration has skillfully assembled and led an international coalition to wage the war against al-Qaeda and the Taliban, and to attack the threat of terrorism across all fronts—military, diplomatic, legal and financial. Mr. Secretary, we welcome you back to the Committee.

Out of the destruction of September 11 can come seeds of opportunity. The challenge for the United States is to ensure that we seize the opportunity to build a new framework for international affairs for the 21st century.

In that regard, we will be interested in hearing from the Secretary, today and in the months ahead, on several key issues. Let me just highlight a handful:

First, are we doing enough to secure our victory in Afghanistan? America's armed forces have waged a brilliant campaign to end the tyrannical rule of the Taliban. But having spent four days in Kabul last month, it is clear that much remains to be done:

• al-Qaeda and Taliban elements remain active in many parts of the country;

• security is inadequate—not only in the countryside, but in Kabul itself;

• and the task of reconstruction of a nation devastated by two decades of war is immense.

We must complete the job in Afghanistan

• militarily against terrorist and Taliban operatives, and through U.S. participation in a multi-national security force,

• and economically, in partnership with other nations, to rebuild the country.

Second, what are the implications of the President's declaration last week that North Korea, Iran, and Iraq comprise an "axis of evil?" Was this merely a rhetorical device, designed to lump together three nations we have long considered dangerous rogue states, or does it indicate a significant shift in U.S. policy toward these nations?

I agree with the President that each nation poses a security threat—to the United States and to the civilized world. But they are hardly identical or allied with each other, and our policies toward them have involved different strategies. For example, working with our partners in South Korea and Japan, we have until now embraced a policy of engagement with North Korea so as to achieve an agreement for a verifiable end to that country's long-range missile programs and sales. Does the President intend to abandon this approach?

Third, what is the current state of U.S. strategic and non-proliferation policy? Since the Secretary was last before us, there have been several significant events:

• the Administration announced that the United States will withdraw from the ABM Treaty;

• the Administration concluded, after a lengthy review, that most ongoing non-proliferation programs with Russia and other Eurasian states should be sustained;

• and the new National Intelligence Estimate affirmed that the United States remains at greater risk from a non-missile delivery of a weapon of mass destruction than from delivery by a ballistic missile.

I hope the Secretary can update us on the Administration's discussions with Russia on mutual arms reductions, particularly on the question of whether the Administration intends to reach agreement on a binding treaty that would be submitted to Senate.

Any understanding with Russia on the future of our respective nuclear arsenals must, in my view, rest on more than a handshake. Let me make clear my view: any formal agreement on mutual force reductions should be in the form of a treaty. The Senate did not allow the previous administration to do an end run around it on arms control, and I don't believe we will allow this one to do so, either.

I also believe the events of September 11—and the subsequent discovery of information about al-Qaeda's efforts to obtain weapons of mass destruction, combined with the National Intelligence Estimate—make it imperative that we focus more resources on what should be our highest national security priority: preventing the proliferation of nuclear, chemical or biological weapons.

Finally, is the President's budget for international affairs adequate to protect our national security? The President's request of $25.4 billion is less than the amount provided in Fiscal 2002, after including the emergency funds provided after September 11.

True, as compared against the regular appropriations contemplated before September 11, the budget contains a 5.9 percent increase in nominal terms.

But these are not regular times—as the President has correctly emphasized. And the budget this year should be measured against the total spending for last year. By that standard, the budget for Fiscal 2003 appears to assume that we can return to the status quo ante.

Aside from the promised expansion for the Peace Corps—a development that I welcome—and the continuation of the Secretary's proposal to address the personnel shortfall in the Department, there appear to be few significant initiatives or increases in the foreign affairs budget that reflect the changed world in which we now live.

The President's budget provides for a significant increase for the Department of Defense and homeland security, but appears to fall short in providing enough resources for our first line of defense—our diplomatic corps.

Let me turn now to my friend, Senator Helms, who is beginning his final year in the Senate, for any comments he may have. Then we will hear from the Secretary.

Senator Helms. Mr. Secretary, I think you are aware that all of us are delighted when you visit the Foreign Relations Committee. You always attract many visitors to our Committee meetings.

First, Mr. Secretary, I am confident that you agree that the President's State of the Union address reminded a lot of us of President Reagan's appearances. Both came at times when great challenges confronted our nation and both set out to overcome them—and in the process give renewed confidence to the American people.

President Reagan defeated communism, President Bush, no doubt about it, will defeat terrorism.

America's enemies never obey the laws of war or, for that matter, any other laws. Their twisted and evil methods are intended to put at risk every innocent American every man, woman and child. That is a challenge we must face up to.

That is why, Mr. Secretary, I applaud your clear understanding that the terrorists being held at Guantanamo Bay absolutely are not prisoners of war—and, in no way, merit any legal protections of the Geneva Conventions. There is an important higher truth, which you have grasped, sir—to be in the custody of the United States is to enjoy the rights conferred by a decent people.

Our military forces—the world has never known finer—have restored civilization to Afghanistan, but our country's greatest challenges lie ahead. We must finish the business of Afghanistan and bin Laden before we undertake new military commitments.

Then, Mr. Secretary, Saddam must go! He is anathema to the well-being of the people of the Middle East, as well as to our own national security. There's no doubt that the people of Iraq will happily get rid of the scourge known by the entire world as Saddam Hussein; but it needs to be known that U.S. policy, and if necessary, U.S. air power, support them.

Similarly, the dictatorships of Iran and North Korea must be made to confront a choice: to live in peace with the world, or to join Mullah Omar, and his like, on the ash heap of history's tyrants. The President warned the "axis of evil"—Iran, Iraq, North Korea—that he will not "wait on events while dangers gather."

Mr. Secretary, you and the President have the full support of the Congress and the American people whenever and wherever you back up that statement.

Mr. Secretary, this is my final year in the Senate, and I do not intend that it be an idle one. Several other issues besides the war on terrorism merit the immediate attention, in my judgment, of both Congress and the Administration.

First, the next round of NATO expansion should begin at the Prague Summit in November. I see no reason why the most successful alliance in history should not incorporate the Baltic nations and other countries that share our values, goals and interests. We also must put aside the notion that Russia may soon have a veto over NATO decisions (as Lord Robertson, the NATO Secretary General, foolishly suggested).

Our new strategic relationship with Russia must be conducted in a manner to advance our national interest while promoting real democratic change in Russia.

Today, Russia is selling missiles and nuclear technology to Iran, a charter member of the "axis of evil" and a country that poses, to quote President Bush, "a grave and growing danger" to the United States.

Russia's war on the innocent people of Chechnya and Moscow's refusal to seek a negotiated settlement have resulted in more casualties than the Soviet Union's war in Afghanistan. The lawless environment of Chechnya is certain to become a breeding ground for terrorists.

Third, we must move beyond those outdated relics of the Cold War—such as the ABM Treaty—that in now way advance U.S. security interests; we must stand firmly behind our intention to build and deploy ballistic missile defenses. The attacks of September 11 were devastating enough—we must do everything possible to make certain that any further attack will not be a nuclear one.

Fourth, we cannot forget our commitment to democracy and the rule of law around the world—particularly in our own Western Hemisphere. In Latin America, the mistakes of nearly a decade of inattention are now apparent.

Finally, Mr. Secretary, I do hope that we can complete work on the State Department Authorization bill consistent with the budget that the President put forward yesterday, a bill containing reform of the Foreign Service, revamping U.S. broadcasting programs while continuing to enhance security at all of our overseas facilities.

Secretary Powell. Let me take this opportunity, sir, to thank you for all the support that you have provided to the Department, especially to our diplomats who are out there on the front line of offense, as I like to call it. And also, sir, if I can drift back to my earlier days, thank you for all the support you have provided to the men and women in uniform, our GI's who serve us so well. And Mr. Chairman, thank you for the personal support that you have given me going on some 15 years. I deeply appreciate it, sir. Thank you so much.

Mr. Chairman, I do have a statement that will go beyond just the crises of the day and try to lay out for you some of the opportunities that are out there. You captured it perfectly, Senator Biden, when you said there are seeds of opportunity. There are a lot of great things happening in the world right now. There are a lot of new opportunities that have been provided to us out of the crisis of the 11th of September and other things that were going on before then that shows the impact that President Bush's leadership is having on the international environment. And as I go through my presentation and talk about some of these opportunities, I will marry them up with the crises of the day as well.

I want to say a word, though, about something Senator Helms said and that was the "axis of evil." And it does have a familiar ring, Senator Helms—it occurred to me as well—it's the old evil empire of the Ronald Reagan days. And the fact of the matter is Ronald Reagan was right, and the fact of the matter is George Bush is right. And as I go through my presentation, I hope that I will be able to demonstrate why these nations that he identified, and there are others in this category, I would submit, are deserving of this kind of designation.

But at the same time, it does not mean that we are ready to invade anyone or that we are not willing to engage in dialogue; quite the contrary. But because we are willing to engage in dialogue, and we are quite willing to work with friends and allies around the world to deal with these kinds of regime is no reason for us not to identify them for what they are, regimes that are inherently evil. Their people are not evil, but the governments that lead them are evil. And the clearer we make this statement and the more sure we are of our judgments, the better able we will be to lead the international coalition, lead nations who are like-minded in pursuit of changes in the policies of these nations, and it will make for a better and safer world for all of us. So I thank you for that comparison.

I might touch on something you mentioned also, Senator Helms, which is not in my prepared statement or in my reading statement, and that is the detainees at Guantanamo Bay and other detainees held in Afghanistan who may be heading toward Guantanamo Bay. You are quite right, all of us in the administration are united in the view that they are not deserving of prisoner of war status.

There is a question that we are examining, and it is a difficult question, and that is the legal application of the Geneva Convention. This is a new kind of conflict. It is a new world, but at the same time, we want to make sure that everybody understands we are a nation of law, abiding by our international obligations. And so we are examining very carefully and have been for a number of days now, the exact applicability or lack of applicability to the Geneva Convention to the detainees.

And this is a decision the President will be making in the very near future. Whether he finds one way or the other on this issue, the reality is that they will be treated humanely in accordance with the precepts of the convention, because that's the kind of people we are. We treat people well. We treat people humanely. And you can be sure that's what is happening with the detainees at Guantanamo, and all others who are in the custody of the United States Armed Forces, or other parts of the United States Government.

* * * *

Mr. Chairman, I now want to talk about foreign policy, and I'll talk about it in the usual terms, in the regional setting, in talking about specific countries. But I hope as I do this, you will see it in a broader tapestry, a tapestry of the growth of democracy around the world, the impact that market economic principles are having around the world as more and more nations understand that this is the direction in which they must move.

I hope you will see it in terms of how more and more nations, notwithstanding the terrible crises that still exist and the horrible regimes that are still in place, nevertheless more and more nations are understanding the power of the individual. When you empower individual man and woman with the opportunity to reach the heights of possibility limited only by their unwillingness to work and ambition and not by the political system in which they are trapped or in which they are living, so many wonderful things have happened. So as I get into the "eaches,*" let's not forget the power of the whole, the power of democracy and the power of the free enterprise system.

Let me begin, sir, by talking about Russia. One of the major items on my agenda almost every single day has to do with Russia. President Bush, in his conduct of our foreign policy with Russia, has defied some of our critics, and he has structured a very strong relationship. The meetings that he has had with President Putin and the dialogue that has taken place between Russian Foreign Minister Ivanov and me and between Secretary Rumsfeld and his counterpart and at a variety of other levels have positioned the United States for a strengthened relationship with Russia, the land of 11 time zones.

The way that Russia responded to the events of September 11th was reflective of this positive relationship. Russia has been a key member of the anti-terrorist coalition. It has played a crucial role in our success in Afghanistan while providing intelligence, bolstering the Northern Alliance, and assisting our entry into Central Asia. As a result, we have seriously eroded the capabilities of the terrorist network that posed a direct threat to both of our countries.

Just as an illustration of how things have changed, a year or so ago when I first came into office, there was a bit of tension between me and my Russian colleagues over what the United States might or might not be doing in Central Asia. After September 11th, after we coordinated with one another, after we had such a successful nine or ten months of dialogue, of building trusts between the two administrations, things changed so radically. So much so that when my colleague, Foreign Minister Ivanov, a few weeks ago was asked on television, "Igor, why are you cooperating with the Americans in Central Asia? They are the enemy, aren't they?" Foreign Minister Ivanov said, "No, you're wrong. The enemy is terrorism. The enemy is smuggling. The enemy is extremism. The enemy are all these other transnational threats. We are now allied with the United States in fighting these kinds of enemies, and we will find a way to move forward in cooperation."

It is this kind of most dramatic change that I think is one of the seeds of opportunity that Senator Biden talked about. And as we go forward in this next year, we're not going to let this seed be trampled out. We're going to continue working with Russia and with the countries in the region to structure a new relationship that will bring stability to the region and provide opportunities for peace and democracy and economic reform.

Similarly, the way we agreed with Russia to disagree on the ABM Treaty reflects the intense dialogue we had over the 11 months before we made that decision. A dialogue in which we told the Russians where we were headed. We said to them clearly, we are going forward to achieve missile defense. We are going to have missile defense. And we can work together. And if we can't work together, then we'll have to agree to disagree. We didn't just pull out of the treaty on a whim, we spent time exploring opportunities with them, exploring options with them. We made it clear where we were going. And we asked them, is there a way we can do this together to go forward.

At the end of the day, we agreed to disagree, and we notified Russia that we were going to withdraw from the ABM Treaty. I notified Foreign Minister Ivanov that we were going to make this decision. I went to Moscow and sat in the Kremlin with President Putin and described to him how we would unfold this decision so that he was ready for it and he could respond in an appropriate way in accordance with his national interest. President Bush talked to President Putin about it.

And then at the end of the day, we made our announcement. To the surprise of, I would say a number of people, an arms race has not broken out, and there is not a crisis in U.S.-Russia relations. In fact, their response was we disagree with you, we think you made the wrong choice, but you have made that choice and now that disagreement is behind us. Our strategic relationship is still important. It is vital, and we will continue to move forward. And I think this is an indication of a mature relationship with Russia and especially a positive relationship between the two Presidents, President Bush and President Putin.

Both Presidents pledged to reduce further a number of their offensive nuclear weapons, and we are hard at work on an agreement to record these mutual commitments. This is all part of the new strategic framework with Russia.

To your point, Senator Biden, Mr. Chairman, we do expect that as we codify this framework, there will be something that will be legally binding, and we are examining different ways in which this can happen. It can be an executive agreement that both houses of Congress might wish to speak on, or it might be a treaty. And we are exploring with Russia, and we are discussing within the administration, the best way to make this a legally binding or codified agreement in some way.

We even managed to come to an agreement on how we're going to work through NATO. We are now developing mechanisms for pursuing joint Russia-NATO consultations and actions of 20 on a number of concrete issues. Our aim is to have these mechanisms in place for the foreign ministers' ministerial meeting in Reykjavik in

May. And as we head for the NATO summit in Prague in November, where expansion of the alliance will be considered, I believe we will find the environment for the continued expansion of NATO a great deal calmer than we might have expected.

And Senator Helms, I just might mention that as we talk about NATO at 20, and as we talk about the expansion of the alliance, it will all be done without Russia having any veto about what NATO might do at 19, or what the alliance will do in determining who should be allowed into the alliance. Russians understand this perfectly, but at the same time, we are responsive to their concerns. And we are trying to meet those concerns. That's what you would expect to do with somebody you are now calling a partner and not an enemy.

We will defend our interests, and we will defend the interests of our alliance, but we want to work with our new partner, the Russians, who increasingly want to be drawn and/or attracted, and want to be integrated in the West in a way that fits the mutual interest of both sides.

I believe the way we handle the war on terrorism, the ABM Treaty, nuclear reduction and NATO is reflective of the way we will be working together with Russia in the future. Building on the progress we have already made will require energy, good will and creativity on both sides as we seek to resolve some of the tough issues on our agenda. We have not forgotten about Russian abuse of human rights, and we raise issues with them. We raise Chechnya at every opportunity. We raise freedom of the press at every opportunity. We raise proliferation activities to countries such as Iran, or Russian intransigence with respect to the sanctions policy for Iraq. And there has been considerable progress on that issue, and we can discuss that in greater detail when we get to the question and answer period, with respect to moving to smart sanctions.

Neither have we neglected to consider what the situation in Afghanistan has made plain for all of us to see. How do we achieve that more stable security situation in Central Asia? In fact, the way we are approaching Central Asia is symbolic of the way we are approaching the relationship between us and Russia as a whole, and the growing trust between our two countries. Issues that used to be sources of contention are now sources of cooperation, and we will continue to work with the Russians, as I indicated earlier, to make sure that the seeds that Senator Biden alluded to are landed in fertile ground, get the nutrition they need, and blossom in a positive direction.

Mr. Chairman, we have also made significant progress in our relationship with China. We moved from what was a very volatile situation in April, when the reconnaissance plane was shot down over Hainan Island, and people were concerned that this would be such an obstacle that we wouldn't be able to go forward, and things would not work out.

As it turned out, things did work out. We were able to recover our crew rather quickly, and the plane came back not too long after that. And both countries were interested in getting this incident behind us. And I think you saw, as a result of the trip I took to China in the summer, but most importantly President Bush's trip to the APEC meeting in Shanghai in October, and the subsequent meeting between President Jiang Zemin and President Bush at that APEC Summit, showed that the relationship is back on an improving track.

Because there are certain shared interests that we have with China, and we have emphasized those shared interests. They are regional and global interests, such as

China's accession to the WTO, stability on the Korean Peninsula, and combating the scourge of HIV/AIDS. On such issues, we can talk, and we can roduce constructive outcomes. There are other interests where we decidedly do not see eye to eye, such as on arms sales to Taiwan, human rights, religious freedom, missile proliferation. On such issues, we can have a dialogue and try to make progress.

But we do not want the issues where we differ to constrain us from pursuing those where we share common goals, and that is the basis upon which our relations are going rather smoothly at present, that and counter-terrorism.

President Jiang Zemin was one of the first world leaders to call President Bush and offer his sorrow and condolences for the tragic events of September 11th, and in the almost five months since that day, China has helped in the war against terrorism. Beijing has also helped in the reconstruction of Afghanistan and we hope will help even more in the future.

Moreover, China has played a constructive role in helping us manage over these past few weeks the very dangerous situation in South Asia between India and Pakistan. When I could call the Foreign Minister of China, Mr. Tang, and have a good discussion, making sure that our policies were known and understood, it made for a more reasoned approach to what was a volatile situation between India and Pakistan. As a result, China supported the approach that the rest of the international community had taken. Beijing was not trying to be a spoiler but, instead, was trying to help us alleviate tensions and convince the two parties to scale down their dangerous confrontation, which now appears they are trying very hard to do.

So it is a case where this so-called coalition that has been formed has utility far beyond terrorism in Afghanistan. We are just talking to each other a lot more; we are finding other areas in which we can cooperate, and the India-Pakistan crisis was one of them.

All of this cooperation, however, came as a result of our careful efforts to build the relationship over the months since the reconnaissance plane incident. We never walked away from our commitment to human rights, to nonproliferation or religious freedom, and we never walked away from the position that we don't think the Chinese—that we think the Chinese political system is the right one for the 21st century. We don't. But we, at the same time, are anxious to engage and we continue to tell the Chinese that if their economic development continues apace and the Chinese people see the benefits of being part of a world that rests on the rule of law, we can continue to work together constructively. A candid, constructive and cooperative relationship is what we are building with China: candid where we disagree; constructive where we can see some daylight; and cooperative where we have common regional, global or economic interests. These are the principles that President Bush will take with him to Beijing later this month when he meets again with President Jiang Zemin.

As we improved our relations with China, we also reinvigorated our bilateral alliance with Japan, Korea and Australia. Nowhere has this been more visible than the war on terrorism, where cooperation has been solid and helpful from all of our Pacific and Asian allies and friends. Prime Minister Koizumi of Japan immediately offered Japan's strong support within the confines of its constitution, and he is working carefully to enhance Japan's capability to contribute to such global and regional actions in the future. Always the linchpin of our security strategy in East Asia, the U.S.-Japan security alliance now is as strong a bond between our two countries as it has been in the half century of its existence. Our shared interests, values and concerns, plus the dictates of regional security, make it imperative that we sustain this renewed vigor in our key Pacific alliance, and we will.

With respect to the Peninsula, our alliance with the Republic of Korea has also been strengthened by Korea's response to the war on terrorism and by our careful analysis of and our consultations with the South Koreans on where we needed to take the dialogue with North Korea. President Bush has made it clear that we are dissatisfied with the actions of North Korea, that they continue to develop and sell missiles that could carry weapons of mass destruction, but both we and the Republic of Korea are ready to resume dialogue with Pyongyang on this or any other matter at any time the North Koreans decide to come back to the table. The ball is in their court. We conducted our review last year. When that review was finished in the summer, I communicated to the North Koreans and communicated to our South Korean friends that the United States was ready to talk any time, any place, anywhere, without any preconditions with North Korea. North Korea has chosen not to respond. North Korea has chosen to continue to develop missiles, although they comply with the moratorium that they placed upon themselves, and they stay with in the KEDO Agreement, as we do. But nevertheless, their actions have not been responsible and their people are still starving, and we are helping to feed those people.

So while we are open to dialogue, I see no reason that we should not call it the way it is and refer to them by the terms that are appropriate to their conduct and to their behavior. And those of us who are in the business of dealing with North Korea realize it is a very, very difficult account; but, at the same time, we are waiting for them to come out and realize that a better world awaits them if only they would put this hard past behind them.

Other friends in the region have also been forward-leaning, and I could list all of them, but just let me say that our Australian friends in particular have been forward-leaning in their efforts to support the war on terrorism. Heavily committed in East Timor already, Australia nonetheless offered its help immediately, and we have been grateful for that help. The people of Australia are indeed some of America's truest and most trusted friends.

As I look across the Pacific to East Asia, I see a much improved security scene, and I believe that President Bush and his interests in Asia and the Pacific region deserves a great deal of the credit for this success.

Let me turn for a moment, Mr. Chairman and members of the committee, to Europe, where I think there has been a great deal of success in our relations over the last year. In waging war together on terrorism, our cooperation with Europe has grown stronger. NATO invoked Article 5 for the first time ever on September 12th, the day after the events of September 11. Since then, the European Union has moved swiftly to round up terrorists, close down terrorist financing networks, and improve law enforcement and aviation security cooperation. President Bush has made it clear that even as we fight the war on terrorism, we will not be deterred from achieving the goal that we share with the Europeans of a Europe whole, free and at peace. We continue to work toward this goal with our allies and partners in Europe.

While in the Balkans there remain several challenges to achieving this goal, we believe we are meeting those challenges. We have seized war criminals, helped bring about significant changes in governments in Croatia and Yugoslavia. And our military forces are partnered with European forces in Kosovo and Bosnia to help bring stability and self-governance, while European-led action fosters a settlement in Macedonia. We need to finish the job in the Balkans, and we will. And we went in together, and we will come out together.

I also believe we have been successful in bringing the Europeans to a calmer level of maturing with respect to what many had labeled in Europe as "unbridled U.S. unilateralism." Notwithstanding the reaction we have seen to the President's State of the Union speech last week, I still believe that is the case. We spend an enormous amount of our time consulting with our European and other friends. It is a priority for the President. He met with Chancellor Schroeder. I don't even want to count the number of European ministers I have been in touch with over the last week or so.

But beyond Europe, we have been in constant touch with foreign ministers around the world, defense ministers around the world. The President is readily available for the leaders who come to this country. We believe in consultation, but we also believe in leading. We believe in multilateralism, but we also believe in sticking up for what we believe is right, and not sacrificing it up just on the altar of multilateralism for the sake of multilateralism. Leadership is staking out what you believe in and coalition-leading means leading, and that is what this President does. And I think he does it very, very well. And he demonstrated it in Europe last year, beginning with his speech in Warsaw, talking about a Europe whole and free; his participation in G-8 meetings; and the U.S.-European Summit, and the European Summit; our extensive consultations with respect to the new strategic framework with Russia; and culminating in the brilliant way in which the President pulled together the coalition against terrorism. I believe we have demonstrated to the world that we can be decisively cooperative when it serves our interests and the interests of the world. We have also demonstrated that when it is a matter of principle, we will stand on that principle whether it is universally applauded or not.

I think we have been very successful. Let me note also that this sort of principled approach characterizes our determined effort to reduce the threat of weapons of mass destruction, an effort well under way before the tragic events of September 11th added even greater urgency. We and the Russians will reduce our deployed nuclear weapons; in the meantime, along with our friends and allies, we're going to go after proliferation. We are going to make sure that we do everything possible to cut off the kinds of technologies that rogue nations are using to threaten the world.

The principled approach that we take does not equate to no cooperation; quite the contrary. We are ready to cooperate, not just with our European friends, but our Asian friends, and we are quite prepared to cooperate and anxious to cooperate in even broader form. We are looking forward to the World Summit on Sustainable Development in Johannesburg later this year. There we will have an opportunity to talk about all kinds of transnational issues, good governance, protection of our oceans, fisheries and forests, and how best to narrow the gap between the rich countries and the poor countries of the world.

And that also allows me then to turn to Africa, where this summit will be held next September. We have crafted a new and more, I think, effective approach to Africa, the success of which was most dramatically demonstrated in the WTO deliberations in Doha last November, that led to the launching of a new trade round.

The United States found its position in these deliberations, being strongly supported by the developing countries, most notably those from Africa. You may have some idea of how proud that makes me as American Secretary of State, proud of my country and proud of this Congress, for its deliberate work to make this possible. The Congress laid the foundation for our efforts with the African Growth and Opportunity Act, an historic piece of legislation with respect to the struggling economies in Africa.

In the first year of implementation of this act, we have seen substantial increases in trade with several countries: South Africa by 11 percent; Kenya, 21 percent; Lesotho, 51 percent; and Madagascar a whopping 117 percent, all based on the first three quarters of 2001 compared to the same period in 2000. Likewise, we are very pleased with the excellent success we had with the first U.S. Sub-Saharan Africa Trade and Economic Cooperation Forum, which was held last October.

A large part of our approach to Africa and to other developing regions and countries as well will be a renewed and strengthened concern with progress toward good governance as a prerequisite for development assistance. Where conditions are favorable, where the rule of law is in place, where there is transparency in their economic and financial systems, then we will encourage investment. We will encourage companies to take a look at those nations that are moving in the right direction. Agriculture, of course, is the background of Africa's economies, and we are working with them to revitalize their agricultural sector in an open system in order to reduce hunger and lift the rural majority out of poverty. Fighting corruption, good governance, getting rid of debt, getting rid of those despotic regimes and individuals who hold their people back, all of this is part of our agenda.

The people of Africa know that in many cases their governments do not deliver the healthcare, transportation and other systems that they need to be successful in the 21st Century. And our policies toward these countries will be to put them on the right path, move them in the right direction, and allow their people to enjoy the benefits that come from democracy and economic freedom.

We also know that especially in Africa none of this potential economic success is possible if we don't do something about HIV/AIDS. It is destroying families, destroying societies, destroying nations. That is why I am pleased to report that pledges to the global fund to fight AIDS, tuberculosis and malaria now exceed $1.7 billion and continues to grow. Soon the fund is expected to accept proposals and begin disbursing money. And we will continue to support that with additional contributions.

Mr. Chairman, we have also I think had some success here in our own hemisphere with the President's warm relationship with Mexico's President Fox, to the Summit of the Americas in Quebec last spring, to the signing of the Inter-American Democratic Charter in Lima, Peru, to our ongoing efforts to create a free trade area of the Americas. All of this suggests to me that we are moving in the right direction in our own hemisphere even though there are difficult problems in Argentina, Colombia, Venezuela and other places that are of concern to us.

We need to keep democracy and market economics on the march in Latin America, and we need to do everything we can to help our friends dispel some of the dark clouds that are there.

Our Andean counter-drug initiative is aimed at fighting the illicit drugs problem while promoting economic development, human rights and democratic institutions in Colombia and among its Andean neighbors.

For our Caribbean neighbors, the situation has gotten worse as a result of September 11th. Lower growth, decreased tourism, increased unemployment, decreased tax revenue and decreased external financial flows. This economic decline is also affected by increasing rates of HIV/AIDS. I will be going to the Caribbean later this week to meet with the foreign ministers of the Caribbean to talk about these problems and to also talk about these problems and to also talk about President Bush's Third Border Initiative which seeks to broaden our engagement with our Caribbean neighbors based on recommendations of the regions' leaders on the areas most critical to their economic and social development.

The Third Border Initiative is centered on economic capacity building and on leveraging public-private partnerships to help meet the region's pressing needs. At the end of the day, it is typical to exaggerate what we have at stake in our own hemisphere. Political and economic stability in our own hemisphere and in our own neighborhood reduces the scale of illegal immigration coming to the United States, drug trafficking, terrorism and economic turmoil. It also promotes the expansion of trade and investment. So we must remain engaged in our own hemisphere.

I touched on some of the dark clouds that are on our foreign policy horizon, but let me focus on one or two areas that are especially distressing. The Middle East, of course, is the one that is upper most on my mind and the minds of most of us here in the room. With respect to the tragic confrontation between Israel and the Palestinians, I want you to know that we will continue to try and focus the parties on the need to walk back from violence, to find a political solution. Our priorities have been and will remain clear, ending the violence and terror, the establishment of an enduring cease fire, and then move forward along the path outlined in the Tenet Security Work Plan and the Mitchell Report recommendations. Agreed to by both sides and supported by the international community, this forward movement will ultimately lead to negotiations on all of the issues but must be resolved between the two parties.

Israelis and Palestinians share a common dream: to live side by side in genuine, lasting security and peace in two states, Israel and Palestine, with internationally recognized borders. We share that vision. The President spoke to that vision in his speech to the U.N. last fall, and I gave more form to that vision in the speech I gave at Louisville. Even though things have not gone well in the recent weeks, we cannot walk away from it. We must not become frustrated or yield to those who would have us turn away from this conflict or from this critical region.

As the President has said, the United States has too many vital interests at stake to take such a step, and one of those vital is the security of Israel. A positive vision will not be realized, however, as long as violence and terror continue. The President and I and General Zinni have been unequivocal with Chairman Arafat. The Palestinian people will never see their aspirations achieved through violence. Chairman Arafat must act decisively to confront the sources of terror and choose once and for all the option of peace over violence. He cannot have it both ways. He cannot engage with us and others in the pursuit of peace and at the same time permit or tolerate continued violence and terror. I have made it clear to Chairman Arafat and to his associates that the smuggling of arms by the Palestinian Authority by Iran and Hezbollah aboard the Karine A is absolutely unacceptable. Chairman Arafat must ensure that no further activities of this kind ever take place and he must take swift action against all Palestinian officials who were involved.

He knows what he must do. Actions are required, not just words, if we are to be able to move forward. Israel must act as well. Prime Minister Sharon has spoken of his desire to improve the situation of life for Palestinian civilians confronted with a disastrous economic situation and suffering daily. We have urged the Israeli government to act in ways that help ease these hardships and avoid further escalation or complicate efforts to reduce violence.

Difficult as the present circumstances are, the United States will remain engaged. But, in the end, Israel and the Palestinians must make the hard decisions necessary to resume progress toward peace.

With regard to another trouble spot that occupies much of our attention—Iraq— that country remains a significant threat to the regions' stability. We are working at the U.N. and elsewhere to strengthen international controls. We stopped the free fall of the sanctions regime. We got the Security Council back together. We are working hard to come up with the smart sanctions that we think are appropriate and we will not stop in that effort. And I am confident, very confident, that by the end of this six month sanctions period we will be able to implement smart sanctions in a way that all members of the Security Council will be able to abide with.

There was reporting this morning that the Iraqi regime has asked the U.N. to have a discussion. It should be a very short discussion. The inspectors have to go back in under our terms, under no one else's terms. Under the terms of the Security Council resolution, the burden is upon this evil regime to demonstrate to the world that they are not doing the kinds of things we suspect them of. And if they aren't doing these things, then it is beyond me why they do not want the inspectors in to do whatever is necessary to establish that such activities are not taking place.

With regard to Iran, we have a longstanding list of grievances, but at the same time, we have been in conversation with Iran. We take note of the positive role they played in the campaign against al-Qaida and the Taliban. We take note of the contribution they have made to Afghanistan's reconstruction efforts. But we also have to take note of their efforts with respect to the ship, the Karine A. We have to take note of some of the things some parts of the Iranian Government are doing in Afghanistan, which are not as helpful as what other parts of the Iranian Government are doing. We have to take note of the fact that they are still a state sponsor of terrorism.

And so we are ready to talk, but we will not ignore the reality that is before our eyes. And those who got so distressed about the President's strong statement, ought to not be looking in our direction; they ought to be looking in the direction of regimes such as Iran, which conduct themselves in this way.

I might just touch very briefly, Mr. Chairman, on the standoff between India and Pakistan. It's of concern to us, but I'm pleased that both nations remain committed to finding a peaceful solution to this crisis, and we will continue to work with them. I visited there a few weeks ago and had positive discussions with both sides, and both sides have made it clear to me then and in their actions since that they are trying to move forward and find a diplomatic solution.

President Musharraf gave a very powerful speech that put his country on the right path, and I hope he will continue to take action to reduce incidents over the Line of Control, and round up terrorist organizations and do it in a way that will give India confidence that they are both united in a campaign against terrorism, and not let it degenerate into a campaign against each other.

Mr. Chairman, I think you are aware of what we have been doing in Afghanistan. I don't need to belabor the point. We should be so proud of our men and women in uniform who fought that campaign with such skill and efficiency. And now the task before us is to make sure that we help the people of Afghanistan and the new authority of Afghanistan get the financial wherewithal they need to start building hope for the people of Afghanistan, and to bring reality to that hope.

I was pleased that, as one of the co-chairs of the Tokyo Reconstruction Conference, the conference was able to come up with $4.5 billion to be disbursed over a period of five years, which will get the country started. The big challenge facing Mr. Karzai and his colleagues, the challenge of security, providing a secure environment throughout the country so that the reconstruction effort can begin.

With respect to our continued campaign against terrorism, I think the President has spoken clearly. We will continue to pursue terrorism. We will pursue al-Qaida around the world. We will go after other terrorist organizations, and we will deal with those nations that provide a haven or a harbor for terrorists, and we will not shrink from this. We have the patience for it; we have the persistence for it; we have the leadership for it.

Mr. Chairman, in my prepared statement, you have the various details of budget items, and since I've gone on quite a bit, I don't want to belabor it any longer. But I just wanted to take the time that I did to show that there is a lot more going on than just what we read about in the daily papers on a particular crisis. We have forged good relations with Russia and China. We have solid relations with the Europeans. We have solid relations with our allies in the Pacific-Asia region. We are working the problems of Africa and our own hemisphere.

There is no part of the world that we are not interested in. We are a country of countries. We are touched by every country, and we touch every country. And we have a values-based foreign policy that rests on principle, and it is principle that is founded in our value system of democracy, the free enterprise system, the individual rights of men and women. We seek no enemies; we seek only friends. But we will confront our enemies, and we will do it under what I believe is the solid, dedicated, persistent leadership of the man who heads the foreign policy of the United States, President George W. Bush.

Excerpt from the "Beirut Declaration" Issued by the Arab League, March 28, 2002

The Arab League issued the following "final communique" following its summit meeting in Beirut, Lebanon.

We, the kings, presidents, and emirs of the Arab states meeting in the Council of the Arab League Summit in Beirut, capital of Lebanon... have conducted a thorough assessment of the developments and challenges... relating to the Arab region and, more specifically, to the occupied Palestinian territory.

* * * *

Iraq

The Council welcomes the assurances by the Republic of Iraq that it will respect the independence, sovereignty, and security of the state of Kuwait and safeguard its territorial integrity.

Within the same framework, the leaders emphasize the importance of suspending media campaigns and negative statements to create a positive atmosphere....

The Council calls for respecting Iraq's independence, sovereignty, security, territorial integrity, and regional safety.

The Council calls on Iraq to cooperate in seeking a... definitive solution to the issue of the Kuwaiti prisoners and detainees and returning [Kuwaiti] properties.

The Council also calls on Kuwait to cooperate with what Iraq offers with respect to its nationals who are reported as missing through the International Committee of the Red Cross.

The Council welcomes the resumption of the dialogue between Iraq and the United Nations....

The Council calls for lifting the sanctions on Iraq and ending the tribulation of the fraternal Iraqi people....

The Council rejects threats of aggression against some Arab states, particularly Iraq, and reiterates categorical rejection of attacking Iraq.

The Council denounces international terrorism, including the terrorist attack on the United States on 11 September 2001, as well as the Israeli Government's exploitation of this attack.

The Council emphasizes the distinction between international terrorism and the peoples' legitimate right to resist foreign occupation, and stresses the need to reach an international agreement within the framework of the United Nations.

Remarks by Secretary of Defense Rumsfeld, April 1, 2002

It is important, I think, that all of us keep in mind that the September 11th attack on America was not just an attack on our country but, indeed, an attack on free people everywhere, and that terrorism was not a crime perpetrated by alleged criminals but really, it was an act of war waged by enemies who need to be tracked down, found and defeated wherever they hide, where they train, where they operate, no matter how long it takes. Unless and until that occurs, terrorism will not just continue but expand and will intensify in its power and scope.

Murderers are not martyrs. Targeting civilians is immoral, whatever the excuse. Terrorists have declared war on civilization, and states like Iran, Iraq and Syria are inspiring and financing a culture of political murder and suicide bombing. The president has declared war on terrorism. It's a war unlike any other America has ever fought—not only in the nature of the battle and the weapons and tactics employed, which will undoubtedly change from place to place, but in this conflict, the battlefield is but one front of many.

Not only are we attacking the enemies arrayed against us, but we're going after the sources of their funding. We're seeking to disrupt their operations and to deny them their havens. We're working to make it clear that sponsors and supporters of terrorists that being a friend to terrorists and by implication an adversary of the United States is not in their best interest. When I'm asked how long we can continue the war on terrorism, when will it end and how will we know when we've achieved victory, it seems to me there is only one answer. The question boils down to this: How long will we keep doing what we're doing to protect the American people from attack from weapons of mass destruction and from terrorism of the type we witnessed on September 11th, and the answer is, as long as it takes. And we'll produce whatever is necessary to win, and go wherever it is necessary to win.

As the president has repeatedly said, this nation will defend freedom. The American people, and the men and women who are fighting to defend them, understand very clearly and are patient and are determined to prevail.

* * * *

Q. Mr. Secretary, has the United States, namely, the United States military, now got control of Abu Zubaydah, who is believed to be a top associate of Osama bin Laden? I believe he was captured, or a man suspected to be him was captured last week in Pakistan and wounded in trying to flee.

Secretary Rumsfeld. I don't think there's any doubt but a man named Abu Zubaydah is a close associate of UBL's, and if not the number two, very close to the number two person in the organization. I think that's well established.

I have absolutely to say about the subject, however.

Q. You mean you won't say whether the United States is holding him, or whether he's been turned over to the United States, or whether you suspect that he was among those captured?

Secretary Rumsfeld. No.

Q. Could I ask why, sir?

Secretary Rumsfeld. Well, I don't know that it's—I've thought about it, and I can't find that at this stage that it would be useful.

Q. Why not—

Secretary Rumsfeld. And I can imagine how it could conceivably be unuseful to begin the process of describing each person that the United States may or may not have one form of access to or another. And it just—if you start down that road, it just seems to me it tells other people much more than one would want to tell them.

Q. But if the United States had him, he would certainly be the most senior person held by the United States. Wouldn't that be an important event?

Secretary Rumsfeld. I think that as the United States proceeds in this task to try to get access to additional information, obviously we have been and continue to go after the senior al Qaeda and Taliban leadership. And as individuals in that category are— as we gain access to them, clearly it's helpful from an intelligence-gathering standpoint and that type of thing. The fact that it's an important event doesn't mean necessarily that it's something that it's useful for the United States to get into. Therefore, I've tried to think about this over a period of time. And there's been speculation, is Osama bin Laden dead or alive and one thing and another, and I just can't quite bring myself, at this stage, anyway, to think that discussing it's helpful.

Q. Is that true also in the case of Osama bin Laden; that if he had been captured, you wouldn't confirm that either?

Secretary Rumsfeld. I wouldn't say that. I just don't know what the situation would be. I think the test is, if our interest is in defending the American people in this country and overseas and American interests, if that is in fact our interest, which it is, then what we have to do is make a calibration as to how we can best do that. And as we have said repeatedly, one of the single most important things we can do is to gather intelligence information. And when one's gathering information and then piecing things together, it is helpful to be able to do that in an environment that not everyone in the world knows precisely what kind of information you may have.

So, while I don't—you know, there may be some point where someone in this government decides that it's a good thing to say, "Gee, X or Y or Z is in this location or another," at the moment I have not been able to find my way to a conclusion that suggests that it would be helpful to us.

Q. Mr. Secretary, you have some experience in overseeing the campaign against terrorism. Do you think the sort of operation that Israel is mounting now has the potential to reduce the terrorist threat in the region? And in the context of a peace settlement, would it be conceivable that American forces might have a peacekeeping role in the Middle East?

Secretary Rumsfeld. Well, I guess—first of all, I'd prefer to have not a lot of voices talking about sensitive, difficult subjects, and this clearly is for the most part an issue that the secretary of State, Colin Powell, is deeply immersed in and the president of the United States. The Pentagon at this stage is not.

Now, I happen to be in an awful lot of meetings on the subject, and needless to say,

I have thoughts. But there's no question but that it is a difficult situation and that the president and the secretary are working with the problem, in my view, in a very constructive way, attempting to be helpful.

As far as a U.S. peacekeeping role, let me say this; I read some speculation that somebody had talked to somebody and discussed the possibility of U.S. military personnel. I can say that I don't believe that's the case; that I don't know of anything like that, nor does Secretary Powell. And the only thing either one of us can think of is that in the past there had been some discussion that if Tenet and Mitchell both happened to go into play or force or activity or—that some monitors of some type might be— some relatively small number of monitors, not military people and not peacekeepers, but I believe the phrase was "monitors" conceivably could be desirable. And I don't think there was any indication of what country they might come from, to my knowledge. And to my knowledge, they would not be military people.

* * * *

Q. Mr. Secretary, what do you mean when you say that Iran and Iraq and Syria are inspiring a culture of murder? Could you explain?

Secretary Rumsfeld. Sure, I'd be happy to.

Q. And also, why today? Why do you bring this up today?

Secretary Rumsfeld. Well, as I'm sure you've read, the Iraqis, Saddam Hussein, have announced that they're offering stipends to families of people—of suicide bombers. They've decided that that's a good thing to do, so they're running around encouraging people to be suicide bombers and offering—I think I saw something like $10,000 per family. I would not consider that a very constructive move. Indeed, I would suggest that that is very actively trying to kill innocent men, women and children. And that's exactly what the Iraqis intend to be doing by doing that. There's no question but that the Iranians were deeply involved in Karine A—ship that was captured by the Israelis that had tons of equipment that was being sent down into the occupied areas of that part of the world for the purpose of conducting terrorist attacks. There's no question but that the Iranians work with the Syrians and send folks into Damascus and down the Beirut—Damascus-Beirut Road and then into South Lebanon so that they can conduct terrorist attacks. This is all well known. These countries are not only trying to kill people outside their countries, but they are repressing their own people. They have an active program of denying the rights of the people in those three countries, that is vicious, repressive and, unfortunately, successful.

Q. Is the United States going to do something about that?

Secretary Rumsfeld. Well, I think that—you know, that's not for me to say. That's for the president—for the president, and when he talked about those countries, and I think properly so, is attempting to point the world attention on what's taking place in those countries. Those people in those countries are being badly treated. Look at the—

any independent organization's assessment of—or what the life—what life is like in those three countries. And it is not a happy situation. So they are simultaneously repressing their own people and denying them their rights and simultaneously going outside their country and attempting to finance and encourage and arm and equip people to go kill people in neighboring countries. Now that is uncivilized behavior.

Q. And Syria? You did Iraq and Iran and Syria—[*inaudible*]

Secretary Rumsfeld. Oh, Iran is closely cooperating with Syria, and they're sending their folks right into Damascus and down into the Bekaa and then down into Southern Lebanon and committing terrorist acts. Iran was involved in the Karine A.

Q. Mr. Secretary, there is more than just those three countries that are contributing and supporting to some of the activities that have led to terrorism around the area surrounding Israel. Do you have messages to some of the other countries that happen to be good friends of the United States that are funneling money to those very same groups?

Secretary Rumsfeld. Well, I think, of course, any minor segment of that religion where it is taught that it is a good thing to kill innocent people and to strap weapons and bombs and plastics around your body and go into shopping malls and restaurants and synagogues and kill people, that people who fund that are in fact contributing to the problem of terrorism. And needless to say, people who don't condemn it are not being helpful; people who—whether it's in this country or Western Europe or the Middle East—no matter where. I think that people have to tell the truth, and the truth is that a whole generation of young people are being taught something that is totally inconsistent with that religion, and they're being encouraged to go out and kill themselves, and as they kill other innocent people—as they kill innocent people in other countries. And it seems to me it's important for every country in the world, and people in the world who don't think that's a good idea, to stand up and say so.

Q. So this includes important American friends like Saudi Arabia, Egypt, Jordan, many very important American friends in the region?

Secretary Rumsfeld. I would think that that would be a rather broad statement on your part. It isn't countries that do this, in the case of those countries, or in our country or Egypt or other countries, it's individuals, and it's an individual mullah, and it's an individual financier who decides they want to send their money and help out those folks. And I think that's wrong, and I think it's dangerous, and I think it's like feeding an alligator hoping it eats you last.

Q. Can you see those countries standing up in the way that you've just described?

Secretary Rumsfeld. Well, I hope so. I hope so.

Q. Mr. Secretary, those countries, the leaders of those countries have said repeat-

edly in the last few weeks that because the U.S. is not doing enough to tap down violence in the Middle East, in Israel, they would not support strikes on Iraq, should it come to that.

From a military standpoint, do we need those—I mean, do we need those nations' support if, in fact, the Pentagon was tasked to attack Iraq or Iran, to do something about those nations you just talked about—you just discussed? Does it complicate the task?

Secretary Rumsfeld. Well, the task hasn't been assigned. And that's kind of a triple hypothetical.

My personal view is that there are—the situation in the Middle East ebbs and flows; it has throughout my adult life. I suspect it will going forward. And the important thing to do is try to stop terrorist acts and to stop the fact that innocent people are being killed, and see if some process like Tenet or Mitchell can't get back into play.

Remarks by Secretary of Defense Rumsfeld, April 3, 2002

There's been some speculation on Abu Zubaydah. And let me just be very precise so that some of the misinformation and misunderstanding that's sweeping the air waves in the last 24 hours is put to rest.

We, the United States government, have made a conscious decision not to release his location, as a matter of security.

Second, the United States is providing him appropriate medical attention. We have every interest in seeing that he remains alive and has an opportunity to discuss a variety of things with us that conceivably could be helpful to the global war on terrorism.

Third, the United States is responsible for his detention, and any speculation to the contrary is inaccurate.

Next, I'd like to elaborate modestly on a point I made the other day to the effect that Saddam Hussein and the regime in Iraq are offering $10,000 per family if they're able to persuade a family to have their teenager strap explosives on them and go out and kill themselves and kill innocent men, women, and children. It turns out that he has raised that amount, and it's $25,000 per family, not $10,000 per family.

Think of it. Here is an individual who is the head of a country, Iraq, who has proudly, publicly made a decision to go out and actively promote and finance human sacrifice for families that will have their youngsters kill innocent men, women, and children. That is an example of what it is we're dealing with.

* * * *

Q. Mr. Secretary, how do you know that he's—Saddam Hussein has raised the ante, as you say, from $10,000, $25,000?

Secretary Rumsfeld. It is being said publicly.

Q. How is this getting out? I mean, is he spreading leaflets, is it by radio, is it word of mouth? And to your knowledge, is this money being paid in cash or what?

Secretary Rumsfeld. He is pleased with his idea and is promoting it in the region. It is a matter of public record.

Q. Mr. Secretary, can I ask you to respond to complaints from private humanitarian aid groups about the practice of U.S. military personnel operating in a humanitarian role, out of uniform, that they feel this adds to the risk for the civilian humanitarian workers? In Afghanistan, I mean.

Secretary Rumsfeld. It is a serious issue, and General Myers is addressing it and will comment in a moment. I do think, however, it ought to be remembered that humanitarian workers had been driven out of Afghanistan during the Taliban and al Qaeda rule. The people of Afghanistan were suffering, being deprived of food and medical care, and were being repressed by the government. The only reason that humanitarian workers are today back in Afghanistan is because of the U.S. military, and I think it's important to get that into perspective.

And one of the great advantages of the fact that the al Qaeda and the Taliban have been driven out of positions of power in that country is that in fact internally displaced people have been able to go home, roads have been opened, refugees are beginning to return, and humanitarian workers from all countries in the world are able to return. It is also true that U.S. military people have delivered a great amount of food, have provided, through their civil action and civil assistance programs, a great deal of assistance themselves.

* * * *

Q. Mr. Secretary, on that subject, as you know, there's a great deal of uproar in the Arab world about what's going on between the Israelis and the Palestinians right now. To what extent is that complicating any work that may need to be done, and political work that may need to be done to prepare for possible military operations against Iraq? Assuming you don't want to do that unilaterally, you will need the support of some of those countries in the region. Is that a complicating factor?

Secretary Rumsfeld. Look. What's happening in the Middle East is terrible. It is a tragedy. It is terrorism. Innocent people are being killed—men, women and children of all religions and—you know, you go in and you blow up a supermarket or a restaurant or a pizza parlor, you don't know who's in there. Israel's a country that has Arab citizens, as well as Israeli—Jewish citizens. And same thing with the World Trade tower. There were people of every religion, every nation, killed in the World Trade Center.

We don't talk about future plans we might have, so I'm not inclined to talk about complications to future plans that might or might not exist or—at all. I can just say that standing alone, the situation there is most unfortunate and the president and the secretary of State and, indeed, others have done a good deal to work with the leadership there on a continuing basis, and they are doing so as we meet here today.

Remarks by Secretary of State Powell, April 3, 2002

Secretary Colin Powell was interviewed on CBS's 60 Minutes II by Scott Pelley. The transcript is of the interview as it was recorded; excerpts were aired on the program.

Q. Mr. Secretary, one of the principal foreign policy goals of this nation is to oust Saddam Hussein from Iraq. How do you do that when every Arab nation is aligned against us with regard to Israel and Palestine?

Secretary Powell. Well, we continue to examine what options are available to the international community and to the United States. In the first instance, we're working multilaterally within the U.N. to make sure the sanctions remain on the Iraqi regime, and we had some success in recent days working with other members of the Security Council.

What we have said to our Arab friends is you may not see Saddam Hussein the same way we do, but you ought to, because those weapons of mass destruction that he is developing—chemical, biological, nuclear—they're more likely than not directed at one of you than us. He'll have a harder time getting it to us. And he has demonstrated in the past he will use it. He has gassed Iranians. He has gassed his own people. He invaded Kuwait.

So there may be a little bit of patience with him on the part of the Arab nations right now, but I'm quite sure that not one of them would really wring their hands or cry too long if the regime was overthrown.

Q. But doesn't our support for Israel, in the present circumstances, make it virtually impossible to move against Iraq, with no Arab support on our side?

Secretary Powell. Well, nothing is impossible. We have enormous capabilities available to us. But obviously I would not be forthcoming, I would not be straight with you, if I said the situation in the Middle East between the Israelis and the Palestinians does not affect our situation throughout the region. We understand that.

But at the same time, we cannot let Saddam Hussein, or the authorities in Tehran, in Iran or the authorities in Syria conduct terrorist activities and support terrorist organizations, using the Middle East conflict as an excuse for those terrorist organizations. To some extent, their support for that kind of terrorist activity is fueling the crisis in the Middle East. So rather than saying we've got to solve that in order to deal with them, they are the ones who are contributing to this problem.

And what the President said in his remarks after September 11th is it's time to stop that. If you really want to get serious and you want to join a world that is moving forward, it's time to stop that kind of support for terrorist activity. And the President will continue to point out the nature of these regimes, and why we view them in such a light.

Remarks by President Bush and British Prime Minister Blair, April 6, 2002

President Bush and Prime Minister Tony Blair delivered their remarks at a press conference during the Prime Minister's visit to President Bush's ranch in Crawford, Texas.

President Bush. It is always a pleasure for any American President to welcome the Prime Minister of Great Britain, because ours is a special and unique relationship. And our relationship is strong because of my respect for the Prime Minister. I appreciate his advice, I appreciate his counsel and I appreciate his friendship.

* * * *

No nation has been stronger in fighting global terrorism than Great Britain. I'm extremely grateful for the Prime Minister's courageous leadership since September the 11th. And the world is grateful for all that Great Britain has contributed in the war against terror—everything from special forces to ground forces to naval forces to peacekeepers.

The Prime Minister and I both understand that defeating global terror requires a broad based, long-term strategy. We understand the importance of denying terrorists weapons of mass destruction. And we understand the importance of adapting NATO to meet new threats, even as NATO prepares to take on new members and forges a new relationship with Russia.

The Prime Minister and I also agree that, even as we work to make the world safer, we must also work to make the world better. Our countries will continue to work closely to bring greater hope and opportunity to developing nations.

We also had extensive conversations about the situation in the Middle East. Both our nations are strongly committed to finding a just settlement. Both of us agree on the fundamental elements that a just settlement must include. We share a vision of two states, Israel and Palestine, living side by side in peace and in security.

* * * *

Prime Minister Blair. We discussed, of course, the issues of international terrorism and weapons of mass destruction. I would like to pay a particular tribute to the President for his courage and for his leadership in the aftermath of the 11th of September. And I think that it is worth reflecting that over these past few months, although very much still remains to be done, we have accomplished, nonetheless, a very great deal in Afghanistan and in the pursuit of those responsible for that terrible event on the 11th of September. And we will continue to work in any way we can in order to make sure that this scourge of international terrorism is defeated.

We also agreed and made it very clear, as well, that the issue of weapons of mass destruction cannot be ducked, it is a threat, it is a danger to our world and we must heed that threat and act to prevent it being realized.

In addition, I was grateful for the President's kind words about the contribution

Britain has made in Afghanistan. We made that willingly, because we believe it is important not just that we root out the last remnants of the al Qaeda terrorist network in Afghanistan, but also that we help that country to go from being a failed state, failing its region and its people, to a state that offers some hope of stability and prosperity for the future.

* * * *

Q. Thank you. Mr. President, you have yet to build an international coalition for military action against Iraq. Has the violence in the Middle East thwarted your efforts? And Prime Minister Blair, has Bush convinced you on the need for a military action against Iraq?

President Bush. Adam, the Prime Minister and I, of course, talked about Iraq. We both recognize the danger of a man who's willing to kill his own people harboring and developing weapons of mass destruction. This guy, Saddam Hussein, is a leader who gasses his own people, goes after people in his own neighborhood with weapons of— chemical weapons. He's a man who obviously has something to hide.

He told the world that he would show us that he would not develop weapons of mass destruction and yet, over the past decade, he has refused to do so. And the Prime Minister and I both agree that he needs to prove that he isn't developing weapons of mass destruction.

I explained to the Prime Minister that the policy of my government is the removal of Saddam and that all options are on the table.

Prime Minister Blair. I can say that any sensible person looking at the position of Saddam Hussein and asking the question, would the region, the world, and not least the ordinary Iraqi people be better off without the regime of Saddam Hussein, the only answer anyone could give to that question would be, yes.

Now, how we approach this, this is a matter for discussion. This is a matter for considering all the options. But a situation where he continues to be in breach of all the United Nations resolutions, refusing to allow us to assess, as the international community have demanded, whether and how he is developing these weapons of mass destruction. Doing nothing in those circumstances is not an option, so we consider all the options available.

But the President is right to draw attention to the threat of weapons of mass destruction. That threat is real. How we deal with it, that's a matter we discuss. But that the threat exists and we have to deal with it, that seems to me a matter of plain common sense.

Q. Prime Minister, we've heard the President say what his policy is directly about Saddam Hussein, which is to remove him. That is the policy of the American administration. Can I ask you whether that is now the policy of the British government? And can I ask you both if it is now your policy to target Saddam Hussein, what has happened to the doctrine of not targeting heads of states and leaving countries to decide who their leaders should be, which is one of the principles which applied during the Gulf War?

Prime Minister Blair. Well, John, you know it has always been our policy that Iraq would be a better place without Saddam Hussein. I don't think anyone can be in any doubt about that, for all the reasons I gave earlier. And you know reasons to do with weapons of mass destruction also deal with the appalling brutality and repression of his own people. But how we now proceed in this situation, how we make sure that this threat that is posed by weapons of mass destruction is dealt with, that is a matter that is open. And when the time comes for taking those decisions, we will tell people about those decisions.

But you cannot have a situation in which he carries on being in breach of the U.N. resolutions, and refusing to allow us the capability of assessing how that weapons of mass destruction capability is being advanced, even though the international community has made it absolutely clear that he should do so.

Now, as I say, how we then proceed from there, that is a matter that is open for us.

President Bush. Maybe I should be a little less direct and be a little more nuanced, and say we support regime change.

Q. That's a change though, isn't it, a change in policy?

President Bush. No, it's really not. Regime change was the policy of my predecessor, as well.

Q. And your father?

President Bush. You know, I can't remember that far back. It's certainly the policy of my administration. I think regime change sounds a lot more civil, doesn't it? The world would be better off without him. Let me put it that way, though. And so will the future.

See, the worst thing that can happen is to allow this man to abrogate his promise, and hook up with a terrorist network. And then all of a sudden you've got one of these shadowy terrorist networks that have got an arsenal at their disposal, which could create a situation in which nations down the road get blackmailed. We can't let it happen, we just can't let it happen. And, obviously, the Prime Minister is somebody who understands this clearly. And that's why I appreciate dealing with him on the issue. And we've got close consultations going on, and we talk about it all the time. And he's got very good advice on the subject, and I appreciate that.

Q. And I'm not sure necessarily whether the Prime Minister would agree with you on Yasser Arafat. But can I ask you, I think what Europeans have a problem with about expanding any war on terror to Iraq is linkage. They can see a linkage between al Qaeda and Afghanistan. They can't see a direct linkage to Saddam Hussein.

Would you accept that there isn't a direct linkage and how, therefore—

President Bush. First of all, I wouldn't accept that. But can't they see linkage between somebody who's willing to murder his own people and the danger of him possessing weapons of mass destruction, which he said he would not develop? I see the linkage between somebody who is willing to go into his own neighborhood and use chemical weapons in order to keep himself in power, and at the same time develop a weapon that could be aimed at Europe, aimed at Israel, aimed anywhere, in order to affect foreign policy through his—you know, I can't imagine people not seeing the threat and not holding Saddam Hussein accountable for what he said he would do, and we're going to do that.

History has called us into action. The thing I admire about this Prime Minister is he doesn't need a poll or a focus group to convince him the difference between right and wrong. And it's refreshing to see leaders speak with moral clarity when it comes to the defense of freedom.

I intend to speak with clarity when it comes to freedom, and I know Prime Minister Tony Blair does, as well. And we will hold Saddam Hussein accountable for broken promises. And that's what a lot of our discussion over there on Prairie Chapel Ranch has been about. And, other than eating lunch, which we're fixing to go do, we're going to continue our discussions.

Prime Minister Blair. You talked about no linkage there. There is a reason why United Nations resolutions were passed, nine of them, calling upon him to stop developing weapons of mass destruction. I mean, there is a reason why weapons inspectors went in there, and that is because we know he has been developing these weapons.

We know that those weapons constitute a threat. Three days after the 11th of September when I made my first statement to the House of Commons in Britain, I specifically said then this issue of weapons of mass destruction has got to be dealt with. And the reason for that is that what happened on the 11th of September was a call to us to make sure that we didn't repeat the mistake of allowing groups to develop destructive capability and hope that, at some point in time, they weren't going to use it. They develop that destructive capability for a reason.

Now, we've made it very clear to you how we then proceed and how we deal with this. All the options are open. And I think after the 11th of September, this President showed that he proceeds in a calm and a measured and a sensible, but in a firm way. Now, that is precisely what we need in this situation, too.

And, as I say to you, never forget he knows perfectly well what the international community has demanded of him over these past years, and he's never done it.

Remarks by Secretary of State Powell, April 7, 2002

Q. The Arab League passed a resolution unanimously saying the United States should not attack Iraq; in fact went further, saying an attack on Iraq would be an attack on all the Arab nations. Kuwait—Kuwait, who you led the war to defend—voted for that resolution in favor of Iraq. Saudi Arabia. How do you feel ten years later that those countries that you protected and defended against Saddam Hussein are now aligning themselves with him?

Secretary Powell. I don't think any one of them would shed many tears if suddenly there was a new leader in Baghdad, notwithstanding any resolution that might come out of these kinds of meetings.

Q. Saudi Arabia will allow us to use their military bases to attack Saddam Hussein?

Secretary Powell. We have not asked Saudi Arabia for the use of their military bases to attack Saddam Hussein because the President has not yet decided upon any particular option with respect to how to deal with Saddam Hussein. At the moment, we're working within the United Nations to get in place the smart sanctions, which we will get in place within the next several weeks, and to demand, as the President has demanded previously, that the inspectors be allowed back in.

Q. The Saudis have not said the United States must get peace in the Middle East or you'll never use our bases?

Secretary Powell. I have heard no such conversation with the Saudis.

Remarks by Secretary of Defense Rumsfeld, April 12, 2002

Secretary Rumsfeld was interviewed by Lester Holt of MSNBC.

Q. We just passed the six-month point in the U.S. war in Afghanistan. Operation Anaconda, was that the last major combat we're going to see over there?

Secretary Rumsfeld. No. No, I think there will be more. There's no question but that there are still Al-Qaeda and Taliban in the country. They're in the mountains, they're in the villages, they're also over the borders, and attempting to regroup from time to time. We intend to find those pockets as they assemble, and go after them and capture them to the extent we're successful. I think that there will be additional operations that will take place in Afghanistan in the period ahead.

Q. I recall—I don't recall his exact words, but I recall at the outset of the war the president was clear there were some things that would have to be kept secret during this war. That's a given. Can you at least tell me, have you been successful in secret, in covert operations? Are there successes that you wish you could be shouting from that podium over there?

Secretary Rumsfeld. Sure. The complexity of this war is that unlike World War II or Korea, there is not a line and the good guys are on one side and the bad guys are on the other side where everyone can see how you're doing and see the progress. Our effort is worldwide, and it involves all elements of national power. It involves shutting down bank accounts, arresting people, law enforcement, maritime intercept of ships as a deterrent to see that they don't transfer terrorists or terrorist capabilities.

* * * *

Q. I know you have been very careful to try to downplay making this war personal. Osama bin Laden, we know, has not been captured, his whereabouts are unknown. Has there been a point over the last six months where you thought you had him, you thought you either had him cornered or you thought he was dead?

Secretary Rumsfeld. No. There have been times when other people in the government have thought we had him, I have not. I'm—my attitude about it is, we're going to keep after him. I think we'll eventually find him. But we haven't, and until you have, you don't have him.

Q. Right now, we don't know if he's dead. So he's not a martyr. He's not issuing videotapes right now.

Secretary Rumsfeld. That's interesting.

Q. It's interesting. Do you kind of like him right there right now, where he is a nothing at this point? No factor.

Secretary Rumsfeld. Well, I think my first choice would be to have him in custody. But, if you don't have him in custody, you certainly want him feeling the pressure, and there's no question but that he and his associates recognize that we're putting a lot of pressure on him. We're looking hard, and they've got to be very careful about, if they're moving around, they've got to move around frequently. They have to watch out who they deal with so that someone doesn't turn them in. There are rewards out for those folks. And he's a mass murderer. He's a dangerous person. We would prefer to have him. But we're going to keep the pressure on until we find him.

Q. Mr. Secretary, if I had a dime for every pundit I've interviewed over the last several months talking about Iraq, should the U.S. attack, should the U.S. not attack, I'd be a rich man. The fact is, this administration has continued to talk about the threat that Iraq poses weapons of mass destruction, a threat to its neighbors. Assuming that all that is true how can you not attack, how can you not respond militarily?

Secretary Rumsfeld. Well, you know, it's a big world, and there are six, seven countries on the terrorist list, North Korea is, Cuba is, Syria is, Libya, Iraq, Iran. And they have had a past where they have engaged in terrorist acts, or assisted terrorist organizations, or harbored and provided sanctuary for terrorists. The ones that are developing weapons of mass destruction are clearly of particular concern. To the extent those weapons get in the hands of terrorists, there is no question but that they would use them, just as they flew airplanes into buildings.

Q. And Saddam Hussein is on your list?

Secretary Rumsfeld. And that being the case, it seems to me that the world, not just the United States, but the world has to recognize that we have a very modest margin for error. We simply have to be very aggressive and attentive to those countries, and do everything humanly possible. There's lots of ways you can put pressure on people. You can do it diplomatically; you can do it from an economic standpoint.

Q. But that hasn't worked.

Secretary Rumsfeld. They have not used those weapons.

Q. Well, certainly there's been economic and embargoes, and United Nations inspectors have been expelled for the last three years.

Secretary Rumsfeld. There's no question but that the economic has not worked in Iran—correction, in Iraq. They are continuing to be able to get in military capabilities that make them more powerful.

Q. Is it a matter of when or if the U.S. goes?

Secretary Rumsfeld. Well, first of all, it's a matter for the president and the country and for other countries to consider the situation that the world is in. If, in fact, weapons of mass destruction are used by terrorists, or by terrorist states, we're not talking about a few thousand people; we're talking about hundreds and hundreds of thousands of people who could die from a biological attack, or a nuclear attack. So this is something that people have to take aboard, they have to consider, they have to weigh in their minds, and as that happens, as people begin to understand the enormous size of that thought of weapons of mass destruction in the hands of people who flew their airplanes into the Pentagon here, people have to recognize and I think it's going to take a lot of countries coming to that conclusion.

Remarks by United Nations Secretary-General Annan, April 12, 2002

Secretary-General Kofi Annan delivered his remarks before the U.N. Commission on Human Rights in Geneva.

This session of the Commission on Human Rights must be one of the most important it has ever held.

We meet under the shadow of the desperate situation in Israel and the occupied Palestinian territory, which has become an affront to the conscience of mankind. I shall have more to say about that at the end of my address.

But we also meet in the shadow of what happened in the United States on the 11th of September last year, and of what has happened in many countries since then, as a direct or indirect consequence.

On that day, several thousand human beings were brutally deprived of the most fundamental of all human rights—the right to life—by a premeditated act of terror, which many have called a crime against humanity.

That abominable act expressed a state of mind in which human rights cease to have any meaning. We still do not know—and we may never know—the precise motives of those who committed it. All we know is that, for whatever reason, they had reached a point where human life—their own and other people's—had ceased to count. They were prepared to use any means, no matter how callous, cruel or destructive, to achieve their political objective.

That is what we are up against. That is the sickness we have to confront and combat, wherever we may meet it.

It follows that we cannot achieve security by sacrificing human rights. To try and do so would hand the terrorists a victory beyond their dreams.

On the contrary, I am convinced that greater respect for human rights, along with democracy and social justice, will in the long term prove the only effective prophylactic against terror.

We must continue the struggle to give everyone on this planet a reason to value their own rights, and to respect those of others. At the same time, we must constantly reaffirm the primacy of the rule of law, and the principle that certain acts are so evil that no cause, however noble, can justify their use.

The end does not justify the means. Instead, the means tarnish, and may pervert, the end.

No doubt there is a hard core of terrorists whose minds are already beyond our reach, and against whom we have no choice but to defend ourselves physically—with great vigilance at all times, with exemplary justice when they fall into our hands, and, when necessary, with military force.

But let us do all these things in accordance with the law. And let us be careful, in defending ourselves, not to play into the enemy's hands, or to act as his recruiting sergeant.

Vigilance is essential—but in exercising it, let us not lose sight of such fundamental principles as the presumption of innocence until guilt is proved. Nor must we forget that even the guilty retain certain basic rights, such as those laid down in the Universal Declaration of Human Rights and the International Covenant on Civil and Political Rights: "No one shall be subjected to torture or to cruel, inhuman or degrading treatment or punishment."

Let us beware of falling, in our turn, into the trap of thinking our aim is so vital that even the worst of means can be used to reach it. That way, instead of preventing terrorism, I fear we would encourage it.

Instead, let us ensure that our security measures are firmly founded in law. In defending the rule of law, we must ourselves be bound by law.

As for justice, it must indeed be both the means and the end of our struggle against terrorism.

Mass murderers must no longer go unpunished, whether they are terrorists, warlords or dictators.

That is why I so much welcome the historic milestone that was passed yesterday, when we achieved the threshold of 60 ratifications of the Statute of the International Criminal Court. The Statute will now come into force on the first of July, and by next year the Court should be operational.

This will not detract from the responsibility of States to prosecute and punish war crimes and crimes against humanity committed by their citizens or within their jurisdiction. Nor will it undermine their ability to do so.

On the contrary, it will give all States a strong incentive to improve their standards in this respect, since the Court will have jurisdiction only where the State primarily concerned is either unable or unwilling to proceed.

Over time, I believe the practice and procedures of the Court will provide a benchmark of international justice, against which the standards of States can be measured.

It is a well known principle that justice must not only be done, but also be clearly seen to be done. When criminals are punished, no fair-minded person should be in doubt of the justice of either conviction or sentence.

And justice does not mean only punishment of the guilty. It must also mean fair treatment of the innocent.

Let us, therefore, be careful not to place whole communities under suspicion, and subject them to harassment, because of acts committed by some of their members. Nor must we allow the struggle against terrorism to become a pretext for the suppression of legitimate opposition or dissent.

When I spoke to this Commission in 1999, I said that "no government has the right to hide behind national sovereignty in order to violate the human rights or fundamental freedoms of its peoples".

That point is, I believe, more widely accepted now than it was then. A good example of this is found in the recent report on the responsibility to protect, by the Independent Commission which addressed all aspects of the problem. After broad consultations conducted in all regions of the world, the Commission concluded that there is a wide understanding that States have a responsibility to uphold and protect the human rights of their citizens. When they fail, or when they themselves become the threat from which the citizens need to be protected, then the responsibility falls on the international community.

Terrorism is one of the threats against which States must protect their citizens. They have not only the right, but also the duty to do so. But States must also take the greatest care to ensure that counter-terrorism does not, any more than sovereignty, become an all-embracing concept that is used to cloak, or justify, violations of human rights.

Any sacrifice of fundamental freedoms in the struggle against terror is not only wrong in itself, but will ultimately be self-defeating.

The greatest effort is needed to ensure fair treatment for those most exposed to prejudice, such as religious and other minorities, as well as migrants. Never has the need for tolerance been greater.

Let us remember that diversity is what gives the human species its splendour, and has enabled it to make progress, as peoples of different experience and culture have constantly learnt from one another. Whenever we fail to respect each other's right to different beliefs and forms of worship, or to form different communities with their own ways of life, our humanity is diminished.

What we cannot and must not tolerate is the use of violence by members of one community against another. All attacks on mosques, churches, synagogues and other centers of communal life must stop.

These issues were already on your agenda before the 11th of September. Indeed, the very week before that, we were discussing them at the World Conference against Racism, Racial Discrimination, Xenophobia and Related Forms of Intolerance in South Africa.

My point is to stress that what happened on the 11th of September has not diminished the importance of your agenda, but, if anything, increased it. The need for effective mechanisms to protect minorities and other vulnerable groups is as great now as it has ever been.

The Commission on Human Rights itself has a vital role to play in devising and overseeing such mechanisms. And in the struggle against terrorism, its role must be complementary to that of the Security Council.

Of course, the Council and its Counter-Terrorism Committee must themselves be sensitive to human rights as they pursue their vital work. But while the Council has primary responsibility for the maintenance of international peace and security, this Commission has a particular responsibility to promote the international implementation of human rights. Therefore, it must make every effort to protect those threatened by violations of human rights, whether these violations result directly from terrorism or are committed in the name of counter-terrorism.

And in this context, I note that you have decided to send a mission led by Mary Robinson to the Middle East.

The political and the human rights bodies must clearly understand that their tasks are complementary, and make a real effort to work coherently together. Only so can we hope for an adequate response to the challenges we now face.

And finally, let me turn to the use of military force.

This may be necessary, in certain cases, to defend us against terrorism, as against other forms of assault. But let us be careful to use it only in self-defense, or in accordance with decisions of the Security Council.

And when we do use it, let us be careful to use it within the law—the international law of war. Targeting civilians and disproportionate use of force beyond legitimate military objectives are violations of international humanitarian law, and must be rejected.

Moral clarity and intellectual accuracy are needed in every judgement on the use of force by States. But the same must apply when we judge the actions of armed resistance movements. The killing of innocent civilians violates international law, and undermines the legitimacy of the cause it purports to serve. That, of course, applies also to suicide bombings aimed at civilians, which are as indiscriminate and morally repugnant as they are politically harmful.

Needless to say, this is where I think especially of what is now happening in the Middle East, where international norms of human rights and humanitarian law are being violated on a massive scale.

We must all be deeply upset by the spectacle of so many unnecessary deaths; so much destruction and distress; so much erosion of restraints and coarsening of moral sensibility. I have already made my position clear in the Security Council and in direct contacts with the leaders of both sides.

The parties are now locked in the logic of war. In order to move them to the logic of peace, bring peace and security again within their reach, we must address the core issues: occupation; violence, including terrorism; and the economic plight of the

Palestinians. We must also remember that one cause of the current situation has been the persistent denial of fundamental human rights.

The task of the international community, and of this Commission, is to help bring both parties back to civilized standards of conduct; to insist on respect for human rights and humanitarian law; and to demand access for humanitarian organizations, as well as respect for freedom of expression.

A start would be for the leaders of both sides to make an immediate declaration of commitment to respect basic norms of human rights and humanitarian law. I solemnly call on them to take this step forthwith.

One of the lessons of the history of the United Nations is that it cannot afford to be neutral in the face of great moral challenges. We are faced with such a moral challenge today. Wanton disregard for human rights and humanitarian law is something we cannot accept. We must let those responsible know that they face the verdict of history.

I plead, once again, for the respect of international law, including international humanitarian law, whenever force is used—whether by States or by resistance movements. In particular, we need to ensure respect for the four Geneva Conventions. Their purpose is crystal clear, and their wording is broad enough to apply to all armed conflicts, no matter what the specific circumstances.

There is no need to reinterpret them. What is vital is that, from now on, they should be obeyed.

Remarks by Secretary of Defense Rumsfeld, April 15, 2002

Q. There is a report in the Washington Post today that Secretary Wolfowitz had asked for a report from the CIA on the capabilities of the U.N. inspection team to do a reasonable assessment of Iraq's ability to create weapons of mass destruction. Can you confirm that that report was carried out at DOD request and give us your opinion of whether the U.N. is up to this task, provided they're allowed back in, inspecting—

Secretary Rumsfeld. Let me think how I want to respond to that. First of all, what an official of government asks of another official of government on a classified matter is obviously no business of anyone else's, one would think.

The article I saw characterized something as having been requested—something of a kind with an investigation. That, I know, is not the case. And to what extent somebody may have asked somebody about this, that or the other thing, I probably ask different intelligence elements, as I'm sure Dick Myers does, every single day, probably eight, 10, 12, 15 questions, asking people to look into this, amplify on that, please undertake a study of this—and I'm sure it's 12 or 15 a day of one or more intelligence agencies. I'm sure the other senior people in the department do as well.

Q. The inspection—do you have an opinion on the inspection, the ability of the U.N. to conduct reasonable inspections of Iraq?

Secretary Rumsfeld. The answer is that there were inspectors in that country for a long time, and they did a lot of looking around and they found some things. But for the most part, anything they found was a result of having been cued to something as a result of a defector giving them a heads up that they ought to do this, that or the other thing.

There now has been a long period of years without inspectors in there. The inspection regime that existed originally, which was not able to find much, other than what defectors mentioned and cued them to, coupled with the long period without inspectors, coupled with the enormous amount of dual-use equipment that's been going in there, enabling them to become more mobile, enabling them to go underground to a greater extent than they had been previously, suggests to the reasonable person, one would think, that it would have to be an enormously intrusive inspection regime for anyone—any reasonable person to have confidence that it could in fact find, locate and identify the government of Iraq's very aggressive weapons of mass destruction program, which has been going on for years.

Q. So you're fairly unoptimistic about it?

Secretary Rumsfeld. I just can't quite picture how intrusive something would have to be that it could offset the ease with which they had previously been able to deny and deceive, and which today one would think they would be vastly more skillful, having had all this time without inspectors there. So it's hard for me to—you know, what one would want is an inspection regime that could give the rest of the world reasonable confidence that in fact Saddam Hussein was not doing that which everyone knows he has been trying to do; that is to say, develop nuclear capability and continue to enhance his other weapons of mass destruction, meaning biological and chemical weapons.

Q. When you said underground, did you mean physical underground or a clandestine—

Secretary Rumsfeld. Both.

Remarks by President Bush, April 17, 2002

President Bush delivered his remarks at the George C. Marshall ROTC Award Ceremony at the Virginia Military Institute.

In the days just after September the 11th, I told the American people that this would be a different war, fought on many fronts. Today, around the world, we make progress on the many fronts. In some cases, we use military force. In others, we're fighting through diplomacy, financial pressure, or special operations. In every case, we will defeat the threats against our country and the civilized world.

Our progress—our progress is measured day by day, terrorist by terrorist. We recently apprehended one of al Qaeda's top leaders, a man named Abu Zabaydah. He was spending a lot of time as one of the top operating officials of al Qaeda, plotting and planning murder. He's not plotting and he's not planning anymore. He's under lock and key, and we're going to give him some company. We're hunting down the killers one by one.

We're learning a lot about al Qaeda operations and their plans. As our enemies have fled their hideouts in Afghanistan, they left some things behind. We found laptop computers, drawings and maps. And through them, we're gaining a clearer picture of the terrorist targets and their methods.

Our international coalition against these killers is strong and united and acting. European nations have frozen almost $50 million in suspected terrorist assets, and that's important. Many European states are taking aggressive and effective law enforcement action to join us in rounding up these terrorists and their cells. We're making good progress.

Yet, it's important for Americans to know this war will not be quick and this war will not be easy. The first phase of our military operation was in Afghanistan, where our armed forces continue to perform with bravery and with skill. You've got to understand that as we routed out the Taliban, they weren't sent in to conquer; they were sent in to liberate. And they succeeded. And our military makes us proud.

The battles in Afghanistan are not over. American and allied troops are taking risks today in what we call Operation Mountain Lion—hunting down the al Qaeda and Taliban forces, and keeping them on the run. Coalition naval forces, in the largest combined flotilla since World War II, are patrolling escape routes and intercepting ships to search for terrorists and their supplies.

As the spring thaw comes, we expect cells of trained killers to try to regroup, to murder, create mayhem and try to undermine Afghanistan's efforts to build a lasting peace. We know this from not only intelligence, but from the history of military conflict in Afghanistan. It's been one of initial success, followed by long years of floundering and ultimate failure. We're not going to repeat that mistake.

In the United States of America, the terrorists have chosen a foe unlike they have any—they have never faced before. They've never faced a country like ours before: we're tough, we're determined, we're relentless. We will stay until the mission is done.

We know that true peace will only be achieved when we give the Afghan people the means to achieve their own aspirations. Peace—peace will be achieved by helping Afghanistan develop its own stable government. Peace will be achieved by helping Afghanistan train and develop its own national army. And peace will be achieved through an education system for boys and girls which works.

We're working hard in Afghanistan. We're clearing minefields. We're rebuilding roads. We're improving medical care. And we will work to help Afghanistan to develop an economy that can feed its people without feeding the world's demand for drugs.

And we help the Afghan people recover from the Taliban rule. And as we do so, we find mounting horror, evidence of horror. In the Hazarajat region, the Red Cross has found signs of massacres committed by the Taliban last year, victims who lie in mass graves. This is the legacy of the first regime to fall in the war against terror. These mass graves are a reminder of the kind of enemy we have fought and have defeated. And they are the kind of evil we continue to fight.

By helping to build an Afghanistan that is free from this evil and is a better place in which to live, we are working in the best traditions of George Marshall. Marshall knew that our military victory against enemies in World War II had to be followed by a moral victory that resulted in better lives for individual human beings.

After 1945, the United States of America was the only nation in the world strong enough to help rebuild a Europe and a Japan that had been decimated by World War II. Today, our former enemies are our friends. And Europe and Japan are strong partners in the rebuilding of Afghanistan.

This transformation is a powerful testimony to the success of Marshall's vision, and a beacon to light the path that we, too, must follow.

In the second phase of the war on terror, our military and law enforcement intelligence officers are helping countries around the world in their efforts to crack down on terror within their borders. Global terrorism will be defeated only by global response. We must prevent al Qaeda from moving its operations to other countries. We must deny terrorists the funds they need to operate. We must deny them safe havens to plan new horrors and indoctrinate new recruits.

We're working with Yemen's government to prevent terrorists from reassembling there. We sent troops to help train local forces in the Philippines, to help them defeat terrorists trying to establish a militant regime. And in the Republic of Georgia, we provide temporary help to its military, as it routes out a terrorist cell near the Russian border. Wherever global terror threatens the civilized world, we and our friends and our allies will respond and will respond decisively.

Every nation that joins our cause is welcome. Every nation that needs our help will have it. And no nation can be neutral. Around the world, the nations must choose. They are with us, or they're with the terrorists.

And in the Middle East, where acts of terror have triggered mounting violence, all parties have a choice to make. Every leader, every state must choose between two separate paths: the path of peace or the path of terror. In the stricken faces of mothers, Palestinian mothers and Israeli mothers, the entire world is witnessing the agonizing cost of this conflict. Now, every nation and every leader in the region must work to end terror.

All parties have responsibilities. These responsibilities are not easy, but they're clear. And Secretary of State Powell is helping make them clear. I want to thank Secretary Powell for his hard work at a difficult task. He returns home having made progress towards peace.

We're confronting hatred that is centuries old, disputes that have lingered for decades. But I want you to know, I will continue to lead toward a vision of peace.

We will continue to remind folks they have responsibilities in the short run to defuse the current crisis. The Palestinian Authority must act, must act on its words of condemnation against terror. Israel must continue its withdrawals. And all Arab states must step up to their responsibilities.

The Egyptians and Jordanians and Saudis have helped in the wider war on terrorism. And they must help confront terrorism in the Middle East. All parties have a responsibility to stop funding or inciting terror. And all parties must say clearly that a murderer is not a martyr; he or she is just a murderer.

And all parties must realize that the only vision for a long-term solution is for two states—Israel, Palestine—to live side by side in security and in peace. That will require hard choices and leadership by Israelis, Palestinians, and their Arab neighbors. The time is now for all to make the choice for peace.

And, finally, the civilized world faces a grave threat from weapons of mass destruction. A small number of outlaw regimes today possess and are developing chemical and biological and nuclear weapons. They're building missiles to deliver them, and at the same time cultivating ties to terrorist groups. In their threat to peace, in their mad ambitions, in their destructive potential and in the repression of their own people, these regimes constitute an axis of evil and the world must confront them.

America, along with other nations, will oppose the proliferation of dangerous weapons and technologies. We will proceed with missile defenses to protect the American people, our troops and our friends and allies. And America will take the necessary action to oppose emerging threats.

We'll be deliberate and we will work with our friends and allies. And, as we do so, we will uphold our duty to defend freedom. We will fight against terrorist organizations in different ways, with different tactics, in different places. And we will fight the threat from weapons of mass destruction in different ways, with different tactics, in different places.

Yet, our objective is always the same: we will defeat global terror, and we will not allow the world's most dangerous regimes to threaten us with the world's most dangerous weapons.

America has a much greater purpose than just eliminating threats and containing resentment, because we believe in the dignity and value of every individual. America seeks hope and opportunity for all people in all cultures. And that is why we're helping to rebuild Afghanistan. And that is why we've launched a new compact for development for the Millennium Challenge Account. And that is why we work for free trade, to lift people out of poverty throughout the world.

A better world can seem very distant when children are sent to kill other children, and old hatreds are stoked and carefully passed from one generation to another, and a violent few love death more than life. Yet hatred, fanaticism are not the way of the future, because the hopes of humanity are always stronger than its hatreds.

And these hopes are universal in every country and in every country—in every culture. Men and women everywhere want to live in dignity to create and build and own, to raise their children in peace and security.

The way to a peaceful future can be found in the non-negotiable demands of human dignity. Dignity requires the rule of law, limits on the power of the state, respect for women, private property, equal justice, religious tolerance. No nation owns these principles. No nation is exempt from them.

Sixty years ago, few would have predicted the triumph of these values in Germany and Japan. Fifteen years ago, few would have predicted the advance of these values in Russia. Yet, Americans are not surprised. We know that the demands of human dignity are written in every heart.

The demands have a power and momentum of their own, defying all pessimism. And they are destined to change lives and nations on every continent. America has acted on these hopes throughout our history. General George Marshall is admired for the war he fought, yet best remembered for the peace he secured.

The Marshall Plan, rebuilding Europe and lifting up former enemies, showed that America is not content with military victory alone. Americans always see a greater hope and a better day. And America sees a just and hopeful world beyond the war on terror.

Many of you will help achieve this better world. At a young age, you've taken up a great calling. You'll serve your country and our values. You'll protect your fellow citizens. And, by your effort and example, you will advance the cause of freedom around the world. And so I'm here to thank you for your commitment and congratulate you on the high honor you have received.

White House Press Briefing, May 1, 2002

Q. What is the President's rational for invading Iraq? I've been reading stories every day of preparations, no set plan yet I admit, but anyway, all of the senior administration officials talk all the time, including the President, about a change of regime. What is the rational for that?

Mr. Fleischer. Well, Helen, the President does believe that the people of Iraq, as well as the region, would be better off without Saddam Hussein in charge of Iraq.

Q. A lot of people would be better off in a lot of places.

Mr. Fleischer. Can I continue? And if you recall, Helen, the Congress passed last year—or in a previous administration—legislation that made regime change the official policy of the government. And that was signed into law by President Clinton. So President Bush is continuing—

Q. What law was that?

Mr. Fleischer. It's called the Iraqi Liberation Act, signed—passed by—

Q. Did it say we were going to overturn—

Mr. Fleischer.—passed by the House and the Senate, signed into law by President Clinton. Regime change, in whatever form it takes, is the policy of the United States government, under President Clinton, continued under President Bush.

Q. So what is President Bush's rationale for that?

Mr. Fleischer. As I indicated, that the President believes that the people of Iraq, as well as the region, will be more peaceful, better off without Saddam Hussein in charge of Iraq, given the fact that Saddam Hussein has invaded two of his neighbors.

Remarks by Saudi Foreign Affairs Advisor Al-Jubeir, May 6, 2002

Saudi Foreign Affairs Advisor Adel Al-Jubeir was interviewed in the National Journal by Lee Michael Katz.

Q. You've also been very careful about your image in the United States after September 11. Is Saudi Arabia trying to compete with Israel in influencing Congress?

Mr. Al-Jubeir. After September 11, we made an effort to reach out to members and explain to them what Saudi Arabia is doing in the war on terrorism, because there were a lot of misrepresentations in the American media.

Our dealings with Congress are not an attempt to compete with anyone. Our dealings are an attempt to explain the nature of the bilateral relationship and its importance to both countries. Members of Congress in general are reasonable and willing to listen. A lot of the shock that people had in the fall has dissipated to a large extent.

Q. The fact remains that 15 of 19 of the September 11 hijackers had Saudi ties. Many people say that religious schools nurtured by Saudi money in Pakistan, in Afghanistan, around the world-even here-preach hate against the United States. What has Saudi Arabia done about that?

Mr. Al-Jubeir. On the issue of the Saudis on the planes, Osama bin Laden's Al Qaeda organization has membership from 60 different countries. He could have put any number of nationalities on those planes. He intentionally chose Saudis to give the operation a Saudi face in order to drive a wedge between the U.S. and Saudi Arabia. You know what? He almost succeeded, but it didn't work. With regard to the funding of schools, it's unfortunate that when it comes to Saudi Arabia, oftentimes charges are treated as facts. They're not investigated. We have not been able to get anyone to name one school—one school—preaching hatred of the West that is funded by Saudi Arabia.

* * * *

Q. Would Saudi Arabia support a U.S. decision to go to war to remove Saddam Hussein from Iraq and would it allow the United States to use its Prince Sultan Air Base command center?

Mr. Al-Jubeir. We believe that the Iraq situation is an arms control problem and not a terrorism problem. The inspectors should be returned to Iraq and economic sanctions eased so the Iraqi people can enjoy a better standard of living.

Our view is the use of force at this time would not serve America's interests, or the interests of the region. Saudi Arabia is not a theater for individual initiatives designed for any purpose that does not serve our interests.

Remarks by National Security Advisor Rice, May 16, 2002

I'm going to give you a chronology of the events that occurred during the spring and summer of 2001. But I want to start with a little definitional work. When we talk about threats, they come in many varieties. Very often we have uncorroborated information; sometimes we have corroborated but very general information. But I can tell you that it is almost never the case that we have information that is specific as to time, place, or method of attack.

In the period starting in December 2000, the intelligence community started reporting increase in traffic concerning terrorist activities. In the April-May time frame, there was specific threat reporting about al Qaeda attacks against U.S. targets or interest that might be in the works.

Now, there was a clear concern that something was up, that something was coming, but it was principally focused overseas. The areas of those concern were the Middle East, the Arabian Peninsula, and Europe.

In the June time frame, arrests for the Millennium plot, there was testimony by the participants in the Millennium plot that Abu Zabeda had said that there might be interest in attacking the United States. And this comes out of testimony that was there as a result of the Millennium plot. And then in June—on June 26th, there was a threat spike, and as a result, again focusing overseas, the State Department issued a worldwide caution. Again, that was June 26th, and you probably remember that caution.

Now, the FAA was also concerned of threats to U.S. citizens such as airline hijackings, and therefore, issued an information circular—and an information circular goes out the private carriers from law enforcement—saying that we have a concern. That was a June 22nd information circular.

At the end of June, there was a status of threat and action meeting that the—what we call the Counterterrorism Security Group—it is a group that is interagency that meets on the direction of an NSC Special Assistant, Dick Clarke at that time. There was a meeting of that, and Dick Clarke reported to me that steps were being taken by the CSG.

On July 2nd, as a result of some of that work, the FBI released a message saying that there are threats to be worried about overseas, but we cannot—while we cannot foresee attacks domestically, we cannot rule them out. This is an inlet, and again, an inlet goes out to law enforcement from the FBI.

On July 2nd, the FAA issued another IC, saying that Ressam—again associated with the Millennium plot—said that there was an intention of using explosives in an airport terminal. This was a very specific IC.

On July 5th, the threat reporting had become sufficiently robust, though not, again, very specific, but sufficiently robust, there was a lot of chatter in the system, that in his morning meeting the President asked me to go back and to see what was being done about all of the chatter that was there. Andy Card and I met that afternoon with Dick Clarke, and Dick Clarke informed us that he had already had a meeting of the CSG core group and that he was holding another meeting that afternoon that would be focused on threats, and that would bring the domestic agencies into the CSG.

On July 6th, the CSG core players met again because there was concern about—very high concern about potential attacks in Paris, Turkey, Rome, and they acted to go so far as to suspend non-essential travel of U.S. counterterrorism staff. So this is a period in which, again, attacks—potential attacks overseas were heightened enough that there was almost daily meeting now, sometimes twice a day, of either the CSG or its subgroups. Contingency planning was done on how to deal with multiple, simultaneous attacks around the world.

The period in mid-July was a point of another major threat spike, and it all related to the G-8 summit that was coming up. And in fact, there was specific threat information about the President. There was a lot of work done with liaison services abroad; in fact, the CIA went on what I think you would call a full-court press to try and deal with these potential attacks, and indeed, managed through these intelligence activities and liaison activities to disrupt attacks in Paris, Turkey and Rome.

On July 18th, the FAA issued another IC, saying that there were ongoing terrorist threats overseas, and that although there were no specific threats directed at civil aviation, they told the airlines, "we urge you to use the highest level of caution."

On July 18th also, the FBI issued another inlet on the Millennium plot conviction, reiterating its July 2nd message saying we're concerned about threats as a result of the Millennium plot conviction.

At the end of July, the FAA issued another IC, which said, there's no specific target, no credible info of attack to U.S. civil aviation interests, but terror groups are known to be planning and training for hijackings, and we ask you, therefore, to urge—to use caution.

Throughout July and August, several times a week, there were meetings of the CSG, reviewing information at hand. There was no specific new information that came in in that period of time after the end of July and sort of in August, leading up to September. But the agencies were still at a heightened state of alert. Particularly overseas. I think the military actually had dropped its state of alert, but everybody was still on a heightened state of alert.

On August 1st, the FBI issued another inlet on the upcoming third East Africa bombing anniversary, and again reiterated the message that had been in the July 2nd inlet.

Now, on August 6th, the President received a presidential daily briefing which was not a warning briefing, but an analytic report. This analytic report, which did not have warning information in it of the kind that said, they are talking about an attack against so forth or so on, it was an analytic report that talked about UBL's methods of operation, talked about what he had done historically, in 1997, in 1998. It mentioned hijacking, but hijacking in the traditional sense, and in a sense, said that the most important and most likely thing was that they would take over an airliner, holding passengers and demand the release of one of their operatives. And the blind sheikh was mentioned by name as—even though he's not an operative of al Qaeda, but as somebody who might be bargained in this way.

I want to reiterate, it was not a warning. There was no specific time, place or method mentioned. What you have seen in the run-up that I've talked about is that the FAA was reacting to the same kind of generalized information about a potential hijacking as a method that al Qaeda might employ, but no specific information saying that they were planning such an attack at a particular time.

There is one other FAA IC in this period, issued on August 16th, where the FAA issued an IC on disguised weapons. They were concerned about some reports that the terrorists had made breakthroughs in cell phones, key chains and pens as weapons.

There are a number of other ICs that were also issued; we don't think they were germane to this, but I'm sure you can get the full record of all of the ICs that were released from Transportation.

I want to reiterate that during this time, the overwhelming bulk of the evidence was that this was an attack that was likely to take place overseas. The State Department, the Defense Department were on very high states of alert. The embassies were—have very clear protocols on how to button up; so does the military. That was done. But at home, while there was much less reporting or chatter at home, people were thinking about the U.S. and the FBI was involved in a number of investigations of potential al Qaeda personnel operating in the United States.

And that's my opening, and I'll take questions.

Q. Why didn't the American public know about these facts before they got on planes in the summer and fall of last year?

Dr. Rice. It is always, as you've learned since September 11th, a question of how good the information is and whether or not putting the information out is a responsible thing to do. I've emphasized that this was the most generalized kind of information. There was no time, there was no place, there was no method of attack. It simply said, these are people who train and seem to talk possibly about hijackings—that you would have risked shutting down the American civil aviation system with such generalized information. I think you would have had to think five, six, seven times about that very, very hard.

Steps were taken, and I'm sure security steps were taken. But you have to realize that when you're dealing with something this general, there's a limit to the amount that you can do.

Q. What security steps—

Dr. Rice. Again, the FAA asked security personnel, ground personnel to have a heightened state of alert because there were tensions in the Middle East—

Q.—in any security—

Dr. Rice. There were tensions in the Middle East that were leading to terrorists who had sympathies with those Middle East events. There were various trials going on, and it was the association with all that was going on that said, look, these are people who talk from time to time about—and train for hijacking; you should take a look at your security procedures and try to respond. But this was very generalized information.

Q. Specifically, after this August 6th analytic report briefing that the President had, what did he do? What did other people in the administration do? What did he make of it? What action was taken? And why didn't he ever tell the American people about it?

Dr. Rice. Well, the action was being taken, because, if you notice, what is briefed to him in kind of a summary way—and I should say, he had said to his briefer, I'd like you from time to time to give me summaries of what you know about potential attacks. And this was an analytic piece that tried to bring together several threads—in 1997, they talked about this; in 1998, they talked about that; it's been known that maybe they want to try and release the blind Sheikh—I mean, that was the character of it. And so the actions were being taken in response to the generalized information that was being reported here, too. And the President was aware that there were ongoing efforts that were being taken.

Q.—any specific information just prior to August 6th that raised concerns about hijacking of U.S. planes?

Dr. Rice. Again, this was generalized information that put together the fact that there were terrorist groups who were unhappy about things that were going on in the Middle East, as well as al Qaeda operatives, which we'd been watching for a long time—that there was more chatter than usual, and that we knew that they were people who might try a hijacking. But, you know, again, that terrorism and hijacking might be associated is not rocket science.

Q. Why shouldn't this be seen as an intelligence failure, that you were unable to predict something happening here?

Dr. Rice. Steve, I don't think anybody could have predicted that these people would take an airplane and slam it into the World Trade Center, take another one and slam it into the Pentagon; that they would try to use an airplane as a missile, a hijacked airplane as a missile. All of this reporting about hijacking was about traditional hijacking. You take a plane—people were worried they might blow one up, but they were mostly worried that they might try to take a plane and use it for release of the blind Sheikh or some of their own people.

But I think that there's always a fine balance, but even in retrospect, even in hindsight, there was nothing in what was briefed to the President that would suggest that you would go out and say to the American people, look, I just read that terrorists might hijack and aircraft. They talk about hijacking an aircraft once in a while, but have no specifics about when, where, under what circumstances.

Q. Condi, this analytic report that the President received sounds like it wasn't his ordinary morning brief. Was it something that he had requested because of the various elements that had come up? Was it something you had requested? And just to follow up on Terry's point here, was the hijacking mentioned here based on any new intelligence that had been developed between these meetings that you mentioned in the July 5th-6th time frame, or was it simply—did it come out of the Philippines experience?

Dr. Rice. It was actually summarizing the kind of intelligence that they'd been acting on. I think it's a little strong to actually call it intelligence—the interpretation that was there that these were people who might try hijacking.

It was—very often as a part of his normal brief, David, he will get things that have been prepared for him because he's asked for a specific kind of document. And as I said, he frequently says, you know, I'd like to see everything you know about X; or I'd like you to summarize—because, as you can imagine, you get intelligence in little snippets, it's helpful from time to time to put it together.

Q. And did this also include then the unified FBI findings? Of course, the Phoenix memo had been through the FBI in July—did it include concerns about Moussaoui? And how much did this bring in the other agencies?

Dr. Rice. This did not include the issues that you just talked about, it did not.

Q. Was that a failure to your mind? Should it have?

Dr. Rice. Look, let me just speak to the Moussaoui and the so-called Phoenix memorandum. As you might imagine, a lot of things are prepared within agencies; they're distributed internally, they're worked internally. It's unusual that anything like that would get to the President. He doesn't recall seeing anything, I don't recall seeing anything of this kind.

Q. On Phoenix or on Moussaoui—

Dr. Rice. On either. Prior to September 11th. But I've asked George Tenet and I've asked Bob Mueller and I've asked my own people to spend some time really going in depth and seeing whether or not it was possible that it got to the President.

Q. Condi, officials who are familiar with the President's briefing have suggested that the information about hijackings was so vague and so general that you could read it from the podium without any danger to sources and methods. Could you read us those couple of lines about hijackings?

Dr. Rice. I'm not going to read you the couple of lines, but I will tell you, Jim, that it was very vague. The one piece that had any texture at all was that it might be for the purpose of freeing an operative like the blind Sheikh.

But again, most of what people were acting on was these were terrorist groups who were dissatisfied. We had reasons to believe that there was more chatter, more talk of attacks. Hijackings seemed one possibility. They train and seemed to be interested in that, but nothing more specific than that.

Q. I've been led to believe that hijacking was actually a minor part of that briefing. You're suggesting it was an analytical look at all of the kinds of things that al Qaeda was considering and working on?

Dr. Rice. I would say that most of it was actually historical. It was not a catalogue of, they might use this, they might use this, they might use this, they might use that. That was not the character. But it was mostly historical, going back to things that happened in '97, things that happened in '98, kind of methods of operation in the embassy bombings, might they return to some of those methods. It was that kind of thing.

Q. So, two questions. No discussion at all then in this analytical briefing about either the information during the investigation in the Philippines about possibly flying a plane into the CIA building, or the investigation overseas about possibly flying a plane into the Eiffel Tower? No analytical information discussing those options at all?

And, B, you know that you would not be here today if it weren't eight months after the attack we hear for the first time that, even in a general sense, the word "hijacking" and "al Qaeda" was before the President prior to September 11th. Why is it that in all the questioning of administration officials—the President, the Vice President, yourself and others, did you have any hint, did you have any clue, that nobody simply said, you know, we didn't; there was this general talk once of hijacking, but we looked into it, it had nothing to do with this, there was no connection?

Dr. Rice. John, this all came out as a result of our preparations to help the committees on the Hill that are getting ready to review the events. It wasn't—frankly, it didn't pop to the front of people's minds, because it's one report among very, very many that you get.

And so it's out of that review that it became clear that this was there. I will say that, again, hijacking before 9/11 and hijacking after 9/11 do mean two very, very different things. And so focusing on it before 9/11—perhaps it's clear that after 9/11 you would have looked at this differently, but certainly not before 9/11.

Q. And no discussion in this briefing, or any others, about the possibility of al Qaeda hijacking, and the fact that there have been active investigations into the possibility of a CIA building plot, or an Eiffel Tower plot. Never came up?

Dr. Rice. It did not come up.

Q. Was that an intelligence failure, that nobody said, you know, there has been talk about doing this elsewhere?

Dr. Rice. We knew that there were—that there were discussions of hijacking. We knew that there were—that they had thought about hijackings in a number of places. But, again, the information that was there in the PDB, which is the reference point here, was not about those activities.

Q. When did the White House hear about the Phoenix memorandum? You said it was before—not before September 11th. When did you finally hear about the Phoenix memorandum?

Dr. Rice. No, what I said—let me be very clear, because we're going to be certain of our facts here. And as you might imagine, it takes a little time to make sure of the facts. Neither the President, nor I have recollection of ever hearing about the Phoenix memo in the time prior to September 11th. We've asked FBI, CIA, our own people, to go back and see whether or not it's possible that it somehow came to him. I personally became aware of it just recently.

Q. And the second question, Dr. Rice. Many members of Congress, of both parties, are expressing some anger or saying they weren't informed about these briefings, or intelligence readings, or whatever was being held in the White House in August and September. Was that a valid point in July and August?

Dr. Rice. Well, the general threat information of the kind that I've been talking about—heightened sense of alert, concerns that al Qaeda might be plotting something, particularly, overseas—it is my understanding that on a regular basis, the intelligence committees were told about the concerns of the intelligence agencies about these kinds of activities.

Again, this is principally—these were all principally pretty general, with the exception I think of the overseas threat that had to do with the G-8, which was more specific than anything else that we had.

Q. Dr. Rice, can you tell us whether you had conversations with Mr. Clarke expressly about what the potential impact on American commercial aviation would be in the event of a hijacking and the taking of hostages? You said earlier that the impact could have been extraordinary. Could you elaborate? And what did you and Mr. Clarke discuss as to—

Dr. Rice. I'm sorry, that it could have been extraordinary?

Q. That you'd considered issuing a warning.

Dr. Rice. No, I didn't say that. I said, you always have to consider whether or not from some incredibly general information you want to try and issue a warning, because this was very, very general information. I don't think we ever thought a warning made sense in this context. It was not like post 9/11, when even then people have said, well, you issued a really general warning, what are people supposed to do?

In the pre 9/11 period, we really never even considered issuing a warning. I was saying that if it had been considered, you would have had to consider very carefully what kind of impact you would have. But it was actually never considered. What was done was to get the FAA in the room so that they could do the things that they thought appropriate under these circumstances.

Q. Did you meet directly with—

Dr. Rice. I did not.

Q. Going back to the August 6th briefing that he had, that's the very first time that the President hears both the term hijacking and UBL together. Did he respond at all? And secondly, were those two linked in any way in briefings that he got after that, until September 11th?

Dr. Rice. Well, there are a couple of other times that hijacking and terrorism are mentioned in this—

Q. How many?

Dr. Rice. I think a couple. I mean, it's not—it doesn't feature prominently in the reporting, because again, it was not based on information that they were planning a particular hijacking at a particular point in time. Certainly nothing like we were looking at that there might be attacks against the G-8 leadership, there might be attacks against the President. It might be in Rome. A lot of chatter around Rome. Nothing like that. This was an analytic piece about methods that they had available to them.

Q. As a follow-up to that, between August 6th and September 11th, this was somehow kept on the President's plate, in front of the President a bit. Was it kept on your plate, as well?

Dr. Rice. Certainly what was—first of all, kept on the plate of the agencies was that a number of these ICs were still in force. So there was a continued alert level. As I've said, the one place where I think we've determined that there was a lowering of alert level was the military came down kind of one-half level. As you know, it's very hard for them to stay on extremely high alert.

We continued to monitor and follow this. There are threat conferences, threat warning conferences, meetings of the CSG, civets, as we call them, by teleconference several times a week. And that continued in this period. But there was no new information that suggested something more was afoot.

Q. Dr. Rice, there are a lot of widows and widowers and family members of the victims of September 11th who are listening to this, and thinking today that the government let them down, that there were intelligence failures. As the person who is supposed to connect the dots with the NSC for the President, what would you like to say to them today?

Dr. Rice. This government did everything that it could in a period in which the information was very generalized, in which there was nothing specific to which to react. And had this President known of something more specific, or known that a plane was going to be used as a missile, he would have acted on it. But the fact is, this, in retrospect even, looks hard to put together. At the time, we were looking at something very different. To the degree that hijacking was an issue, it was traditional hijacking.

The threats—al Qaeda—you know, you did have the FBI actively pursuing leads and trying to run this down. You did get the disruption of attacks in Rome and Paris and in Turkey. But this President, who takes extremely seriously the security of the

United States, was doing everything that he could in this period, as were the rest of the public servants in this government.

Q. Dr. Rice, I'd like to know a little bit more about the August 6th meeting. It was at the ranch. Were you there? And was the analytic report the only subject discussed in the briefing? Was it an oral presentation, was it a document? How lengthy was the document? Was there only one mention of hijacking in that document?

Dr. Rice. It is a document, Judy. There were other things briefed that day. I don't actually know what they were. The President's daily briefing is usually several briefings on various subjects. I was here in Washington, not in Crawford, but I did talk with the—I always talk to the President immediately after his briefings.

The President and I talked all the time during this period of time about al Qaeda. He was particularly concerned not just about threats to—that they might be threatening us, but how we went after them. And so there was a lot of work going on in this entire period also to try and put together a strategy to bring them down.

Q. How long was the document, and was there, in fact, only one sentence that mentioned hijacking?

Dr. Rice. The word, "hijacking" is mentioned once in the specific way that I've talked about and one other time kind of in summary. It's a page and a half document.

Q. You said that all of this came out as you prepared documents for upcoming committee hearings. Was this a document that you had intended would get out in the public forum of committee hearings, or had you asked them to keep it classified?

Dr. Rice. We had not made any determination as to what documents were going forward, the nature of that. We're working with the committee right now to try to make sure that they have access to the information. I mean, after all, it is important that the full story get out there. The American people deserve that; the administration wants that. And we are working with the committee on these documents.

Q. Had this document actually gone to Capitol Hill?

Dr. Rice. I don't know the answer to that, John. I don't think so—no, this document had not.

Q. Dr. Rice, when the information was passed on from the FAA to the airline carriers, did any of that information include specifically a reference to al Qaeda or Osama bin Laden? Because terrorists are terrorists, but this group obviously was viewed even by the government as a more serious threat. Did those warnings—were they specific enough to say, not just worry about hijacks, or worry about terrorist hijacking, but did they say bin Laden?

Dr. Rice. We were worried about al Qaeda, and al Qaeda was clearly at the top of the heap. But there were other terrorist organizations that we were also worried about in this period of time. The EIJ, for instance, because it was—the blind Sheikh's organization was that organization. So I think that what you saw was that the concern about terrorism, or about terrorists, was actually broader than just al Qaeda. Al Qaeda was one of organization that might use this particular method. So it said "terrorist."

Q. Dr. Rice, forgive me, this page and a half document on August 6th, I know you say it was non-specific, and I know you say it's a compendium and an analytical report—how can you say it wasn't a warning? Are you not telling the President that there's danger ahead?

Dr. Rice. No. A warning—there was nothing that said this is going to happen, or this might happen. It said, this is a method that these people might be considering. That was the nature of this. And it was very non-specific. In the sense that—you know, if—going again, comparing it to what we were seeing, for instance, on the G-8, this was an analytic piece that looked at methods that they might use.

Everybody knew that terrorists and hijacking have been associated—for time immemorial. And how many hijackings have there been by terrorists? In that sense, there was nothing really new here. And in fact, since it was mentioned a couple of other times that there might be hijackings—again, non-specific—I think it would be very hard to characterize this as a warning.

Q. Dr. Rice, are you aware of the reports at the time that—was in Washington on September 11th, and on September 10th, $100,000 was wired to Pakistan to this group here in this area? While he was here meeting with you or anybody in the administration?

Dr. Rice. I have not seen that report, and he was certainly not meeting with me.

Q. Dr. Rice, on the issue of connecting the dots, you talked about a number of things here—the possibility of a CIA building, the Eiffel Tower, Moussaoui, Phoenix, all those other dots that are out there. Where do you think those dots should have come together? Should the briefer who prepared the document for the President have known about all those things? Is there a place where this should have come together?

Dr. Rice. Well, I think that one of the important questions is how we go forward, organizationally, to deal with some scenes. And I thought Director Mueller's testimony yesterday to this effect, that called for reorganization that would cause great fusion of intelligence from different sources, and particularly from domestic and foreign sources, is probably right.

But let me just say, we've already begun to make some of those changes. There is an Office of Homeland Security. And I think that's an important change. Secondly, every day now, in the morning, the President sits with the Vice President, with Andy Card, with me, with George Tenet, with Bob Mueller, and with Tom Ridge—and often with John Ashcroft—and there's a kind of fusion going on at the top. And the challenge is going to be to build down into the system that same kind of bringing together of information. And I think that's what Bob Mueller and George Tenet and others are looking at. And it's one reason that we have every reason to want to look at—fully at what happened.

Q. On the G-8 plot—could you just say something more about the G-8 plot? Wasn't that an airplane filled with explosives? Wasn't that plane—

Dr. Rice. There were many different potential methods described concerning the G-8. Many. The most troubling was not a specific method with a specific place, but specific targets, like the President.

Q.—want to ask about, was there any link to bin Laden in those threats? And how serious did you take them? How specific were they?

Dr. Rice. We took the threats very seriously, because they were somewhat more specific. Again, when I say more specific, it didn't say, on July this date, at this place, at this time, so- and-so will happen. But there was greater texture, there was certainly more information. It's one reason that George Tenet went out of his way to, I would say, tell the agency to go to the ramparts out in the field, to really stir up our liaison services. And I think it was successful, because there were several disruptions.

Campbell, you have got the last question.

Q. I just want to go back to the issue of hijacking. You said the FAA in July did issue a kind of warning or an alert of sorts to the
airlines, saying that terror groups were planning or training for hijacking, did you not—at the end of July? You were taking us through the time line. I just want to be clear that, isn't it unusual that you would make the decision to bring the FAA into this? That there was enough concern that hijackings would be a problem that you would say, you need to let the airlines know and—

Dr. Rice. The FAA was one of only—only one of the domestic agencies brought in. Customs was brought in; INS was brought in. So this was an effort to bring in domestic agencies that might have potential vulnerabilities. But, again, let me read it, because it's extremely important, because, again, they were acting on general information, and therefore, the IC is very general.

And it says, "The target is not clear"—this is July 31—"The target is not clear. The FAA has no credible info to attack U.S. civil aviation interests. Nevertheless, some of the current active groups are known to plan and train for hijackings. FAA encourages all U.S. carriers to exercise prudence and demonstrate a high degree of alertness."

So, again, the operative words here, that "some of the current active groups are known to plan and train for," not, they're planning a particular hijacking.

Q. But you went through a list of these. I mean, is it possible—how do you get the airlines to pay attention to them, if you're putting them out periodically, and if it is something general like this, what do you really expect them to do?

Dr. Rice. Well, the problem, as I was explaining when somebody asked me, why didn't we go public with some of these alerts—or some of this information—is that when you're dealing with very general information, all you can do is tell people it's very general. And I—you would have to refer to the Transportation Department and the FAA to get a better sense for what protocols are followed, or how this is all done. But the FAA issued these ICs that, again, were based on very general information and were intended just to alert people that these were organizations that were angry, there was a lot of threat reporting about them, and hijacking was considered to be one of their methods. And that was the extent of it.

White House Press Briefing, May 16, 2002

I want to make a statement about another matter. Throughout the summer, the administration received heightened reporting on threats on U.S. interests and territories, most of it focused on threats abroad. As a result, several actions were taken to button down security. All appropriate action was taken based on the threat information that the United States government received.

The possibility of a traditional hijacking, in the pre-September 11th sense, has long been a concern of the government, dating back decades. The President did not—not—receive information about the use of airplanes as missiles by suicide bombers. This was a new type of attack that had not been foreseen. As a result, a series of changes and improvements have been made to the way the United States deals with a terrorist threat. And I'll be happy to talk about those during the briefing.

Q. Can you tell us specifically what date the President was briefed that there was a threat of hijacking, where he was when he got the briefing, who he gave—a couple more—who gave him the briefing, what agencies were warned about the threat, and what did those agencies do in response to that?

Mr. Fleischer. Okay. Ron, as the President has said, throughout the summer, beginning in May, the President received, as I indicated, reporting on threats and intelligence hits throughout the summer, mainly focused on overseas. In August, the President, as you know, was at his ranch in Crawford. As part of his morning daily intelligence briefing from the CIA, he received that generalized information that I've talked about, vis a vis hijacking.

Q. Wasn't Tenet—

Mr. Fleischer. No, the Director did not personally deliver that briefing.

Q. What date?

Mr. Fleischer. It was early August.

Q. So before the arrest of Zacharias Moussaoui?

Mr. Fleischer. Early August. I know it was the first week of August.

Q. If you can get us the exact day. And then what happened with that threat? What agent—what law enforcement or federal agencies were told about it, and what did they do in response? And the threats—just for clarification—were related to al Qaeda and Osama bin Laden, right?

Mr. Fleischer. Throughout the summer, they received numerous threat warnings, as I indicated. In fact, as the President—let me cite you the President's words, as he described the information that was available to him. This was what the President himself said on December 20th, 2001, to The Washington Post in an interview he gave them.

"We also had been getting some intelligence hits throughout the summer—mainly focused overseas, by the way—and there had been a series of responses that we took to harden embassies. But it was clear that bin Laden felt emboldened and didn't feel threatened by the United States."

As a result of the information that came in beginning in that May period and throughout the summer, embassies were hardened throughout the world, military installations went through their normal procedures to harden against potential terrorist attacks. Those are a series of concrete actions that are taken by the embassies and by installations.

Domestically, through normal security channels, the Department of Transportation and the Federal Aviation Administration were made aware of general information that, while mentioning hijackings, did not include specific and detailed warnings. This information, as with all sensitive security information, was passed on to the carriers through a series of briefings and notifications. It is important to note that this was non-specific threat that mentioned hijacking.

Q. Well, I'm confused. Is that in response to the information that started coming on May 5th, or in response to the briefing he got the first week of August?

Mr. Fleischer. As I indicated this morning, keep in mind exactly the process of how information flows to the President when it comes to these type of briefings. When the information comes to the President, it's because the agencies have developed in a period of time prior to the briefing. So this information developed earlier in the course of the summer, beginning in May. It was shared with the President in August in the sense of what I have described to you. So throughout this period, this information was conveyed to these agencies, throughout the summer period.

Q. The agencies were warned before the President of the United States was?

Mr. Fleischer. Well, of course, as the agencies get this information—they have it. The FBI, CIA, they get the information. They, of course, by definition, have it prior to the President. That's how they can brief the President on it.

* * * *

Q. But, Ari, post-9/11, when hijacking had taken on that word, new context, new meaning, several administration officials, including as you just pointed out, the President of the United States himself, was asked about what did the White House know, and the President, when asked, said we had intelligence hits. He didn't say, and you know, we had a warning about hijackings. Why not? Why didn't he level with the American people about what he knew?

Mr. Fleischer. The President did level with the American people, and so did Director Tenet, so did all people that I have seen—I have several statements from government officials exactly about what the government knew and what was said prior to September 11th, and let—

Q. But none of them used the word "hijacking," though. Vice President Cheney, when he spoke on Meet The Press on the 16th of September, said—

Mr. Fleischer. Again, Terry, I think it's a fair point that you raise. But the simple answer is that you are using the post-September 11th knowledge of what a hijacking could be and applying it to August, prior to September 11th, and changing what was then the traditional understanding of what a hijacking represented. It was a total—it was a total sea change.

Q. These questions were asked after September 11th. These questions were asked after September 11th of the President, of the Vice President, of you, yourself. And no one in the White House said, yes, the information had come in that al Qaeda was planning hijackings.

Mr. Fleischer. Because that information, as I indicated at the top of the briefing, that information is so generalized it did not contain any information specific to using airplanes as weapons, exactly what took place on September 11th. That was the generalized nature of the information, which puts it in a totally different category. And again, the sense, pre-9/11, of what a hijacking represented was how that information was heard and understood.

Q. Will the White House cooperate with any congressional investigation into these matters?

Mr. Fleischer. Yes, the White House will, of course. The White House is working with the congressional committees that are investigating this matter, and we will continue to do so.

White House Press Briefing, May 17, 2002

Q. Two questions. First, Dr. Rice laid out yesterday what the administration was hearing and concluding about threats to U.S. and U.S. interests overseas during the course of last summer, and it seems there was a lot of urgency within the administration.

Granted that hindsight is 20/20, does the President believe that he and his administration communicated to the American public effectively enough the kind of urgency that Dr. Rice described was in the administration during the weeks leading up to September 11th?

Mr. Fleischer. Let me draw your attention to a series of things that the President said publicly, and actions that the President took. In fact, you can begin by going back to the President's speech as a candidate, at the Citadel on February 23rd, 1999. If you recall, that's a speech that the White House handed out to you in the aftermath of September 11th, because in many ways, it showed the priority that this President was bringing to office about the need to fight terrorism. And he said in that speech at the Citadel, "And there is more to be done preparing here at home. I will put a high priority on detecting and responding to terrorism on our soil."

In March, on March 4th, 2001, when the President went to participate in the christening of the Ronald Reagan, in Newport News, Virginia, the President said, "Our present dangers are less concentrated, and more varied. They come from rogue nations, from terrorism." And he went on.

And finally, the President on May 8th, in a statement that you all have, issued a statement about domestic preparedness against weapons of mass destruction. And that was a warning from the President about protecting America's homeland and citizens from the threats of weapons of mass destruction, as one of our nation's most important national security challenges.

Beyond that, Terry, in the realm of action, this is why—one of the reasons why once our nation was hit in this attack on September 11th, we were able to respond so quickly. In the events leading up to September 11th, and over the course of the first year, or the first nine months of this President's administration, the President came to Washington determined to do something more fundamental about terrorism, because of the threats that it poses to our interests abroad, as well as to Americans here at home.

And as a result of a process that involved the CIA, the Department of Defense, the Department of State, the National Security Council, a national security presidential directive was developed and prepared throughout 2001, that was approved by what's called the principals committee, which is essentially Cabinet level officers involved in national security, on September 4th, 2001.

That document was then finalized on September 10th. It had not yet gone to the President. That national security presidential directive was a comprehensive, multi-front plan to dismantle the al Qaeda. It involved a direction to the Pentagon to develop military options for the dismantling of al Qaeda. It involved action on the financial front to dry up their resources. And it also involved working with our—with the Northern Alliance, in an attempt to dismantle the al Qaeda.

The President was aware that bin Laden, of course, as previous administrations it's been well-known that bin Laden was determined to strike the United States. In fact, the label on the President's—the PDB was, "bin Laden determined to strike the United States." And in another piece of this, it was just something that has been well-known to you all, is that the creation of the Office of Homeland Security was something that was planned even before September 11th, as Senator Feinstein has reminded her colleagues.

Remarks by Secretary of Defense Rumsfeld, May 17, 2002

Secretary Donald Rumsfeld was interviewed by Katie Couric on NBC's Today Show.

Q. Certainly you've heard about all the controversy, with Dick Gephardt asking what the president knew and when he knew it. Many newspapers across the country are focused on this story. What is your reaction that the Bush administration perhaps did not act quickly enough or efficaciously enough when it came to warnings that some kind of terrorist attack might occur on this country?

Secretary Rumsfeld. Well, I think, when all the dust settles, the American people will know the truth. And the truth is that every day there are numerous threat warnings—the walk-ins off the street, pieces or scraps of intelligence collected by the FBI, pieces of information that are gathered by the Central Intelligence Agency in one way or another. And they are then looked at and sorted and sifted.

And what has to be done is to recognize that when you're all through sifting all of those, some, a very small number, prove to be actionable. That is to say, there's sufficiently specific information that someone can do something about it.

And, needless to say, when that happens, someone does do something about it and they make an effort to either alert people, which we do in the Pentagon—for example, if we have a threat warning in the Middle East, we alert the combatant commander there, and he then puts his forces on a different alert level. And there are procedures for that taking place.

The vast majority of the reports and scraps of information that come in tend to be eventually discounted as not being valid or, at the minimum, not being actionable.

Q. But there's some feeling, Mr. Secretary, that some warnings were not properly heeded by the powers that be; for example, the FBI memo that was written or the FBI agent who warned about people training at U.S. flight schools, about foreigners doing that back in July. There were other memos and sort of more generic CIA briefings. Should these things have been taken in toto, and should more have been done as a result of these things?

Secretary Rumsfeld. Well, I wasn't aware of the FBI information that you mentioned until it showed up in the press very recently, so I can't speak to how valid it might have been at that time. But it seems to me that the information is collected, it is collated, and judgments are made and warnings are issued.

And a great many events that would otherwise have occurred, terrorist activities, are, in fact, stopped; one very recently. We gathered some information in Afghanistan in a building that ended up stopping a terrorist act in Singapore within a matter of days thereafter, where the terrorists had planned to attack a U.S. ship, a U.S. building and a Singapore facility, and it was stopped. So there are a great many things that are stopped.

The advantage a terrorist has is a terrorist can attack at any time at any place using any conceivable technique, and it is not physically possible to defend in every place, at every moment of the day or night, against every conceivable technique. So—

Q. But is it possible, Mr. Secretary, to have better coordination among all the agencies who might be getting these bits and pieces and scraps of information so they can join forces and prevent something like this happening in the future?

Secretary Rumsfeld. Well—

Q. It's pretty disconcerting and unsettling that some of these warnings, albeit disparate, were surfacing prior to September 11th.

Secretary Rumsfeld. Well, you can be certain—the American people can be certain, which is what's important, that the changes that have taken place over the past year or two—as the threats have increased, the warnings have increased—have been substantial and that the caution and the heightened awareness and the steps that have been taken at airports, the steps that have been taken by the FBI and the CIA, all are contributing to a safer circumstance for the American people.

But even that does not suggest that there cannot be a terrorist event somewhere, someplace in the world. And I suspect there will be. That's just the nature of the world we live in. That's why President Bush is focusing on the right thing, and that is to go after the global terrorist networks where they are and to go after the countries that are harboring those terrorists. That is really the only way to defend against terrorism.

Remarks by Secretary of Defense Rumsfeld, May 20, 2002

Secretary Donald Rumsfeld was interviewed by Alan Murray on CNBC.

Q. Mr. Secretary, we want to talk about the transformation of the American military but before we do that let me ask you about the news of the day. The Vice President was on TV on Sunday and said, "I think that the prospects of a future attack on the U.S. are almost a certainty. It could happen tomorrow, it could happen next week, it could happen next year, but they will keep trying and we have to be prepared."
Is he talking about new information there, about imminent attacks?

Secretary Rumsfeld. We get new information all the time. Some of it is valid and some of it proves not to be valid. There is no question but that the Vice President is exactly right. We have to know that there are hundreds and hundreds of these people trained in terrorist training camps. They had massive a fundraising activity base, very well trained, and they have been disbursed all across the world including the United States of America. It is only realistic to expect that there will be another attack, and we do have to be prepared. Although I would rephrase that slightly.

The only way to deal with terrorists is to go after them. You can't defend every place at every time. Even if you know there is going to be an attack, it's almost impossible.

You simply have to go find them where they are and dry up their money and arrest them and capture or kill them.

Q. But we have been doing that since September 11th. Have we reduced the risk? Is the risk lesser today than it was on September 12th?

Secretary Rumsfeld. Oh, my goodness, yes. We have reduced it in several ways. One is we've taken a whole host of steps here in the United States. The American people are on a state of heightened awareness. We are obviously; if you go to an airport you can see the changes that have been made. We are much more careful at our border and our ports. We have combat air patrols flying sometimes over the United States and sometimes on strip alert in various parts of the country. We've done a series of things that make, that have improved our ability to discover and deal with and mitigate if one occurs, a terrorist attack.

In addition we have gone out to find them. We've been drying up their money, we've been arresting a lot of them, we've been interrogating hundreds and hundreds of them and piecing together all of this information. There is no question but that we've done a great deal since September 11th, and indeed before September 11th in particular.

Q. So the best defense is a good offense?

Secretary Rumsfeld. It is really critical that you go after them.

When you think about it, when you're walking down the street a terrorist could go after a person or a building or anything using any conceivable technique at any time of the day or night and you can't defend in every place at every time against every thing. It's not possible. Realism forces us to accept that fact. Therefore we have to go after them.

Q. So if I knew what you know, if I had access to all the information that you have access to, how should I feel about my safety as an American living life in America? Should I feel safe?

Secretary Rumsfeld. Well, when you know there are terrorists out there who are determined to kill innocent people, that's what a terrorist does. They kill innocent people—men, women and children. Clearly we have to be aware of that. Should that alter our lives? Answer, not noticeably. We ought to get up and go about our business just like we all do. But do we have to be realistic and say my goodness, that is a very clear possibility, it's not a probability that there will be additional attacks? There will be.

Q. Were you surprised at the level of outcry over the news of the last week that there was going to be more attacks and, I guess really what I'm asking is has America gone back to sleep too quickly? Have things gone back to normal too quickly?

Secretary Rumsfeld. I guess I don't know that there was such an outcry and I don't think people have gone back to sleep. I think the American people are fully aware of the risks that exist. There has been a great deal of discussion about it, a great deal of analysis, and the fact is there are a number of global terrorist organizations and a number of states that are harboring them and a number of people that are financing them and the American people know that.

Q. We now know that on August 6th President Bush got a briefing at the ranch raising the possibility of al Qaeda being involved in hijacks. We now know there was an FBI agent in the Phoenix office who sent in a memo saying hey, watch out for these flight schools, al Qaeda could be doing things there, we need to keep an eye on it.

In retrospect, do you think anyone dropped the ball there? Do you think that information should have been responded to in a better way than it was?

Secretary Rumsfeld. Oh, goodness. I'm not going to get into that. The law enforcement agencies and intelligence-gathering agencies gather all kinds of information. A lot of it is supplied to the Pentagon so that we can, for example, and the State Department, so we can be sensitive about risks to embassies, our U.S. military forces overseas, our ships, planes, and we have various threat alerts that we put out.

But if you took a year and looked at all the press information that arrives in one command, say General Franks' Central Command, there is so much—It's just mountainous.

Q. And you can't respond on high alert to every single one of them.

Secretary Rumsfeld. Well you can't, or else the terrorists have won. What you have to do is go find the terrorists because if they can jerk you around—

The other thing they do is they will put out a threat to see how you're going to react to it. They go to school on it. They'll issue a threat, make sure we hear it, watch what our reaction is, then they know what the reaction is. So you have to make sure that what you're doing does not inform them and assist them in what they're trying to do, namely to harm.

Q. Let's turn the topic here a little bit if we can. You've been talking a lot about transforming the American military. Can you tell us in concise terms what you mean by transforming the military. From what to what?

Secretary Rumsfeld. Sure. First of all, it is not from something to something. It is a process. It is a procedure. You never start from an untransformed state to a transformed state and then go back. If you do, you're in an untransformed state.

Transformation really can be almost anything. It can be a new satellite, for example, that gives you a capability that didn't exist before, and in a significant way it transforms how we function, how you deal with something.

It can be old platforms, exactly the same one, but by providing interconnectivity and improved real time communication or better situational awareness as to what's taking place on a battlefield, within a battle space, that can be transformation.

I've also gone to the point of saying that probably the most transformational thing of all is finding people who think right, who are not stuck in the past, who are willing to look at things [inaudible], and who don't believe that simply because something has always been done that way that it must be done that way. So I think it's a culture, almost, in a sense. I should say in addition to the other things it's a culture.

Q. How do you talk to the military about transformation? Is it like when you were running a company, when you were running Searle or General Instruments, you were by reputation a turn-around guy. Is this like that? How do you change the mindset?

Secretary Rumsfeld. What we do is we go in that room next door, the senior military and the senior civilian leadership, and we must have had eight meetings of two, two and a half, three hours each, talking about what transformation is so that we had a common understanding of it. We went through a whole briefing.

If we were to brief the President, if we were to brief the Congress, if we were going to brief our troops about what this thing called transformation is, what would we say? How would we say it? How would we get from where we are to where we think we need to be? We did that. We ended up with everyone in the room, all the senior military and senior civilians, coming away with an understanding of what it's about and what it means to their service, what it means to their function here in the office of the Secretary of Defense. It's hard work and it is not simple. There's no bumper sticker for it.

Q. What kind of conflict are we preparing for? Obviously in the '50s and the '60s we knew who the adversary was, we knew where they were, we knew how they might or might not come at us. What kind of conflict are we preparing for now?

Secretary Rumsfeld. We have switched our strategy from a threat-based strategy, described in what you just mentioned, the old Soviet Union, to what we call a capabilities-based threat.

We can't know exactly where a threat is going to come from and we cannot know who will bring that threat necessarily. Nor can we know exactly what kind of capabilities will be used.

What we can know is we have vulnerabilities. We know that. We know what we have strength in and what we have weaknesses in, and we know that the people who don't wish us well look at that and say to themselves there's no point in developing a big army, navy and air force trying to go up against the United States. So they look for asymmetrical ways they can go about it, and certainly about as asymmetrical as you can get is flying an American airliner into this building. But things like ballistic missiles, cruise missiles, cyber attacks, terrorist attacks, weapons of mass destruction, chemical, biological, nuclear, radiation weapons. All of those things have the advantage of an asymmetrical approach to it. So when we say capabilities based we can imagine the kinds of things people can do to us and the kinds of capabilities we need to deal with those potential threats.

White House Press Briefing, May 21, 2002

Q. Ari, Secretary Rumsfeld said today, terrorists are certain to acquire eventually

nuclear, chemical and biological weapons. What do you say to Americans who are alarmed by this increasingly troubling information?

Mr. Fleischer. Well, the President has warned that that is terrorists' goal. As you've heard the President say, that one of the things he worries about is terrorists mating up with existing nations that sponsor terrorism, such as Iraq, and getting their hands on weapons of mass destruction.

One of the things that everybody saw on September 11th is our enemies will not hesitate to hit us if they have the means to do so. And that is why we're in the midst of a very important war, not only in Afghanistan, but to deny terrorists a base of operations to regroup—to diminish their abilities to harm us.

Q. Any words of comfort for Americans, in terms of the effort domestically to block such an attack here?

Mr. Fleischer. Well, I think that the American people have seen a nation wake up on September 11th and mobilize. The American people themselves understand the vulnerabilities our nation faces. But, Scott, the fundamental fact of the matter is, we're a target because we're free. And because we're free, we're also strong. And that's been the history of our country.

This is not the first time we've had enemies who have sought to bring harm to us. As time moves forward and technology evolves, the risk is that it's a different kind of war, as the President has said, that it's a new type of war. It's no longer the type of war where a satellite can pick up a fleet leaving a port. It's a war now where you have terrorists, just—ones, twos—just small numbers of them, who have the means and have the desire to try to strike us. But every time there's ever been a threat to our country, our country has led the world in preserving freedom and in fighting. And we are in the midst of a struggle now.

Q. On the August 6th memo or analysis report that the President received, is the reason that he doesn't want to release that to congressional investigators is that that he fears that Democrats will use the other secret contents of that report for political purposes, in an attempt to embarrass him?

Mr. Fleischer. David, I don't really think it's anything, per se, about that memo, in and of itself, on the 6th as much as it is the overall principle about the President's daily brief, which is shared with such an extraordinarily small number of people who are in a need-to-know situation, a need-to-know position, so they can use that information to protect the country, to prevent the next possible attack.

I think that's what the President is concerned with. He's also concerned with the fact that if the presidential daily brief, which is a highly sensitized—the most highly sensitized classified document in the government—if that document were to be at risk of public reporting, public release, the people who prepare it will hold back and not give the President of the United States, the person who needs most of the—the most information, they will be inclined to give him less, rather than more, because they fear it will get made public and that could compromise sources or methods.

* * * *

Q. Ari, I was just wondering, just going back to Scott's question here, the President said in the Rose Garden a while ago that he would do everything in his power to prevent terrorists from acquiring weapons of mass destruction—nuclear, biological and chemical. Did the Secretary of Defense's statement this morning that they're certain to acquire them kind of say, despite our best efforts and the efforts of the President, we're bound to lose this battle?

Mr. Fleischer. Well, let me take a look at the Secretary's exact words. I haven't heard them until I walked out here. So let me take a look at precisely how he said it, because the Secretary knows what the President knows—and that is that we're in a middle of a war to protect the country and to diminish the ability of any people who would do us harm from getting their hands on such weapons.

Q. Is there some sort of heightened campaign on the part of the administration—valid or not—to raise the awareness? I mean, you have Cheney speaking on Sunday, someone else yesterday. Now we have Rumsfeld. And so is this to arouse the American people to a new danger? Do you have some new information?

Mr. Fleischer. What you have is a consistent approach where the President has said—and you've heard him say this many times—that every day he begins his day with a review of what's called the threat matrix, which is a compilation of intelligence information about potential attacks on the United States, our allies or our interests abroad. The President begins his day looking at that information, then talks to his security team about the credibility of it, whether or not it's something that we can have any actionable steps taken to prevent it from happening.

So the President referred to this for a considerable period of time. Many people in government have. Governor Ridge, for example, has often talked about, in various forms with the public and with the press, the need for continued scrutiny, the alert system we have set up where we remain on yellow or elevated alert, thanks to the collaborative effort Governor Ridge put together.

Q. There seems to be some sort of—

Mr. Fleischer. Well, I'm getting to that. All of these are the background for what you have now heard in some greater detail over the course of the weekend.

I think, Helen, it was just more as a result of all the controversy that took place last week, just an effort by people who were on the shows to answer questions, because they're reflecting things about the generalized level of alert and concern we have that's been out there. And, of course, there has been a recent increase in the chatter that we've heard in the system, and that was reflected in what they have said. So I think they're doing their level best to answer questions that people have.

Remarks by President Bush and German Chancellor Schroeder, May 23, 2002

President Bush and Chancellor Schroeder delivered their remarks at a press conference in Berlin, Germany.

Q. Should the American people conclude there were some intelligence lapses before September 11th? And can you please explain why you oppose a commission to look into the matter, and why you won't release the August 6th memo?

And quickly to you, sir, do you think there should be regime change in Iraq?

President Bush. Well, first of all, I've got great confidence in our CIA and FBI. I know what's taken place since the attacks on September the 11th. Our communications between the two agencies is much better than ever before. We've got a much better—doing a much better job of sharing intelligence.

I, of course, want the Congress to take a look at what took place prior to September the 11th. But since it deals with such sensitive information, in my judgment, it's best for the ongoing war against terror that the investigation be done in the intelligence committee. There are committees set up with both Republicans and Democrats who understand the obligations of upholding our secrets and our sources and methods of collecting intelligence. And therefore, I think it's the best place for Congress to take a good look at the events leading up to September the 11th.

Q. The August 6th memo—

President Bush. Oh, yes. Well, one of the things that is very important, Ron, is that the information given to the President be protected, because we don't want to give away sources and uses and methodology of intelligence-gathering. And one of the things that we're learning is in order to win this war on terror, we've got to have the best intelligence-gathering possible. And not only have we got to share intelligence between friends—which we do—but we're still at war, we've still got threats to the homeland that we've got to deal with. And it's very important for us to not hamper our ability to wage that war. And so there are ways to gather information, to help improve the system without jeopardizing the capacity for us to gather intelligence, and those are the ways I support.

Chancellor Schroeder. Saddam Hussein is a dictator, there can be no doubt, nothing else. And he does act without looking after his people whatsoever. We're agreed when it comes to that. And we're also agreed to the fact that it is up to the international community of states to go in and exercise a lot of political pressure in the most—possible way. The United Nations have decided to do so, as well. We need to pressurize him so that international arms inspectors can get into the country to find out what weapons of mass destruction can be found in his hands. I mean, there is no difference there between President Bush and myself when it comes to the assessment of this situation.

We then obviously also talked about the question as to what should happen in the future, what could happen in the future. I have taken notice of the fact that His Excellency, the President, does think about all possible alternatives. But despite what people occasionally present here in rumors, there are no concrete military plans of attack on Iraq. And that is why, for me, there is no reason whatsoever to speculate about when and if and how. I think such speculation should be forbidden. That, certainly, is not the right thing for a Chancellor. And I am in this position.

We will be called upon to take our decision if and when, after consultations—and we've been assured that such consultations are going to be happening—and then we'll take a decision. And before that, I think we should not speculate about serious questions like this one.

Q. Mr. President, Chancellor, looking beyond Iraq, given the fact that Syria, too, in U.S. terminology, is a state sponsor of terrorism, given the fact that Saudi Arabia is anything but a democratic pluralistic society, how do both of you want to have this whole region, the Middle East, look like once the fight against terror is over?

President Bush. Yes, it's a great question. Would you care to go first, Mr. Chancellor—I'll be glad to answer it, if you like.

First, you need to know that in order for the region to be peaceful and hopeful, there must be a resolution to the Palestinian-Israeli conflict. I believe that strongly. And that's why my government and I feel strongly that we've got to work toward a vision of peace that includes two states living side by side.

And the positive news is that many Arab leaders understand that they have got to be a part of the process now. We spent a great deal of time talking to the Saudis, for example—you mentioned the Saudis. They must be a party to the process. They have—sometimes in the past the process has not gone forward because there hasn't been, as we say in America, the buy-in by the parties; they haven't been a party to the process.

And I'm pleased to report, as you can probably see in your newspapers, they are now, they're involved. I think one of our—and the reason I mention that is because I think their involvement to a process that I'm optimistic will succeed will then enable us to continue to more likely have an effect on promoting values that we hold dear—values of rule of law and democracy and minority rights.

The institutions of change are more likely to be effective with our ability to achieve a peace in the Middle East. And so much of the ability to promote reform—which we're for—hinges on our abilities and capacities to get something done. And it's going to take a while, I believe, but, nevertheless, we are making progress. And my administration spends a great deal of time on the Middle East, because we understand that it is a linchpin for convincing regimes to adopt the habits of freedom that sometimes we take for granted in our respective countries.

Chancellor Schroeder. Well, I don't think I've got to add a lot to what's been said—possibly so much. I think there cannot be peace in the Middle East without the United States of America and without them being active in this field. And it was not without reason that I pointed to the tremendously important speech of the President. It's very important. And that is why we support the efforts towards peace undertaken by the United States, but also by all other members of the so-called Quartet. We are supporting this in the framework of the European Union, but we're also doing it from bilateral channels. And my impression is—and here yet again, I fully agree with the President that a certain degree of progress is visible in this process.

Now, obviously, we cannot be satisfied with the degree of progress, but still we have moved a little bit and there is no alternative to the way that the President just described. There is no such thing as a magic formula to solve this tremendously difficult problem. Nobody has such a formula. And that is why I think the task that the President just described is certainly one that needs to be seriously supported by the European Union and by us, bilaterally.

Q. You meet with President Putin tomorrow. How are you going to talk him into ending nuclear cooperation with Iran?

President Bush. Well, that's a—that's going to be a topic. One way to make the case is that if you arm Iran, you're liable to get the weapons pointed at you; that you've got to be careful in dealing with a country like Iran.

This is a country that doesn't—it's not transparent, it's not open. It's run by a group of extremists who fund terrorist activity, who clearly hate our mutual friend, Israel. And, you know, it's very unpredictable. And, therefore, Russia needs to be concerned about proliferation into a country that might view them as an enemy at some point in time. And if Iran gets a weapon of mass destruction, deliverable by a missile, that's going to be a problem. That's going to be a problem for all of us, including Russia.

So that's how I'm going to make the case. We've got a lot of work to do with Russia. I will continue to make the case. As you know, Steve, I have brought that subject up ever since I've started meeting with Vladimir Putin.

The good news is, we're—our relationship is a friendly relationship; that I view President Putin as a friend, I view Russia as a friend, not as an enemy. And therefore, it's much easier to solve these difficult issues, and issue like proliferation, amongst friends.

And I want to appreciate the Chancellor's kind words about tomorrow's treaty signing. It's going to be a positive development for America, and I believe a positive development for Europe. And then, of course, we're going to Rome afterwards, and that, too, will be a positive development for Europe and America. And it is within the—it's in this positive relationship and positive atmosphere that we're more likely to be able to achieve satisfaction on non-proliferation.

Q. Mr. President, the Chancellor just said that your government does not seem to be very specific right now when it comes to plans to attack Iraq. Is that true, sir? And could you, nevertheless, try to explain to the German people what your goals are when it comes to Iraq?

And secondly, by German standards, Germany has already shouldered a huge burden in military terms of the fight against terrorism. Are you satisfied with that, or do you want Germany to do more?

President Bush. Look, I mean, he knows my position, and the world knows my position about Saddam Hussein. He's a dangerous man. He's a dictator who gassed his own people. He's had a history of incredible human rights violations. And he is a—it's dangerous to think of a scenario in which a country like Iraq would team up with an al Qaeda type organization, particularly if and when they have the capacity, had the capacity, or when they have the capacity to deliver weapons of mass destruction via ballistic missile. And that's a threat. It's a threat to Germany, it's a threat to America, it's a threat to civilization itself. And we've got to deal with it. We can play like it's not there, we can hope it goes away. But that's not going to work. That's not going to make us safer.

And I told the Chancellor that I have no war plans on my desk, which is the truth, and that we've got to use all means at our disposal to deal with Saddam Hussein. And I appreciate the German Chancellor's understanding of the threats of weapons of mass destruction. And they're real.

Now, I know some would play like they're not real. I'm telling you, they're real. And if you love freedom, it's a threat to freedom. And so we're going to deal with it, and we'll deal with it in a respectful way. The Chancellor said that I promised consultations. I will say it again: I promise consultations with our close friend and ally. We will exert a unified diplomatic pressure. We will share intelligence. We love freedom, and so does the Chancellor, and we cannot allow these weapons to be in a position that will affect history.

Listen, history has called us to action. I don't want to be in a position where we look back, and say, why didn't they lead, where were they when it came to our basic freedoms? And we are going to lead.

What was the other part of your question? That's what you get for asking long questions, or what I get for answering long answers.

Q. That's perfectly all right. The second question was, sir, that Germany has already shouldered a huge burden in military terms, and do you expect more—

President Bush. Germany has shouldered a significant burden. And we are very grateful for that. The Chancellor and I talked about how to make sure we complete the task in Afghanistan—which is to continue chasing down the killers, by the way, and to find them before they hit us—but, as well, is to leave institutions behind so that Afghanistan can run herself, so Afghanistan can be a peaceful nation, so Afghanistan can function. And we both recognize that our presence is just going to have to be there for a—for quite a while. And the Chancellor made that commitment, and I appreciate that. I'm very satisfied with the commitment of the German government.

Q. Thank you, sir. On the subject of weapons of mass destruction, the strategic arms agreement you'll sign in Moscow does not address what many people say is now the greatest threat posed by the Russian arsenal of weapons of mass destruction, that's proliferation to terrorists or rogue states because of insufficient security. What specific plan do you have to address that issue with President Putin? Do you believe the Russian government is doing a good job securing those weapons? And what do you say to critics of this arms deal who say that by taking the material off the war-

heads, you provide more opportunities for terrorists to get them?

President Bush. Well, I guess I'll start with the critics. I say, would you rather have them on the launchers? Would you rather have the warheads pointed at people? I would think not. Secondly, this issue about the so-called loose nuke issue has been around for quite a while. This isn't anything new. This is a problem that we are jointly working on. As you know, Terry—and others may not know—we've got what's called Nunn-Lugar, which is a significant expenditure of taxpayers' money to help Russia dispose of and dismantle nuclear warheads, which we're willing to do. As a matter of fact, the '03 budget is nearly a billion dollars toward that end.

We're working with Chancellor Schroeder on what's called 10-plus-10-over-10: $10 billion from the U.S., $10 billion from other members of the G7 over a 10-year period, to help Russia securitize the dismantling—the dismantled nuclear warheads.

And President Putin understands that. He understands the need to work closely with all of us. And he understands that a loose nuke could affect his security as it affects somebody else's security. He's a wise man, he's aware of the issues that we confront. That's why he's one of the best partners we have on the war against terror. He understands the implications and consequences of terror. And he also recognizes that a nightmare scenario is a dirty bomb, or some kind of nuclear bomb in the hands of a—in the hands of any kind of terrorist organization.

Remarks by Secretary of Defense Rumsfeld, May 23, 2002

Secretary Donald Rumsfeld was interviewed by Wolf Blitzer of CNN.

Q. You caused some alarm bells on Tuesday when you spoke out about the notion that the terrorists were going to get chemical, biological, perhaps even nuclear weapons. It was inevitable, you said. Was that based on a hunch or some hard new intelligence information that you have?

Secretary Rumsfeld. Wolf, I didn't set off any alarm bells. The press did. I was asked in a Senate hearing to respond to a question by Senator Inouye. I did. And I said exactly what I have been saying for six, eight, ten, twelve months. Nothing new, nothing notable, other than the truth, which is extremely important. And that is that there are a series of terrorist states that everyone knows which ones they are that have weapons of mass destruction. They have chemical weapons. They have biological weapons, for the most part. Some have or shortly will have nuclear weapons. And they have close relationships with terrorist states. It doesn't take a genius to figure out that because of those relationships and that nexus, that connection, that we have to expect that global terrorist networks that we know are trying to get these weapons will, in fact, be successful at some point in the future. That's all I said.

Q. Is there some new information, though, that's come to you—

Secretary Rumsfeld. There's new information every day. We see all kinds of intelligence information, and there's no question but that exactly what I said is correct, that we do have evidence that they have been trying to get these kinds of capabilities, particularly chemical and biological, and that the countries that they have relationship with do have these capabilities.

Q. And let's review those countries, Iran being one of them.

Secretary Rumsfeld. Certainly Iran. Certainly Iraq.

Q. Which groups are the Iranians supporting?

Secretary Rumsfeld. Certainly North Korea. Syria has chemical and biological weapons. Libya has been on the terrorist list as another country, another example. Cuba's been on the terrorist list.

* * * *

Q. But it's still alarming to hear the Secretary of Defense say that it's only a matter of time before people who hate the United States, terrorists who've shown no reluctance in the past to kill as many Americans as possible, that they might get their hands on chemical, biological, or even nuclear weapons.

Secretary Rumsfeld. But it should come as no more newsworthy today than it did three, six, eight, nine months ago.

* * * *

Q. Let me ask you this. The kind of suicide bombings, the soft targets, the restaurants, the coffee shops, the malls, what we've seen in Israel: are you concerned that could happen here?

Secretary Rumsfeld. I think that when you have terrorists that are working for ways to attack a country like the United States, they're not likely to go against our armies, navies or air forces. They're likely to go after asymmetrical advantages that they can achieve. And that includes ballistic missiles. It includes cruise missiles It includes cyber attacks. It includes the kinds of things we saw on September 11th. It includes suicide bombings. All of those things are the kinds of things that they can do because we are a free people, because the terrorists can attack any place at any time using any technique. And you can't defend everywhere every time. Which is why President Bush's approach is so sound and so solid and so important. We simply have to go after the global terrorists where they are and root them out and deal with countries that are harboring those terrorists.

Q. And, remember, the President said the United States will not differentiate between terrorists and those states that harbor terrorists. But you're suggesting that states like Iran and Syria are harboring and supporting terrorists, Iraq, to a certain degree, of course, as well. What are you doing about that?

Secretary Rumsfeld. Well, there's a full spectrum of things one can do, ranging from diplomatic and economic. If you want me to take Iraq, what we're doing—the Congress has passed a law suggesting that they believe that a regime change is the proper thing for Iraq. Saddam Hussein's regime—it's so clear, the way they repress their people. It's so clear that they're developing weapons of mass destruction.

Now, how do you do that? Well, there's lots of things one does. There're diplomatic steps. There's economic steps. We're using these northern and southern no-fly zones now to keep them constrained and try to reduce their ability to be successful in their quest for nuclear weapons.

Q. There doesn't seem to be a whole lot of support among the allies in Europe or the moderate Arab states for another U.S. military strike at Iraq with the aim of regime change or getting rid of Saddam Hussein. Can you go it alone?

Secretary Rumsfeld. I'm not going to get into that. You can be sure that the United States isn't going to do anything that it's not capable of doing. And if we do something, we'll be capable of doing it. But it's not for me to make those judgments.

Q. You saw the story in today's *USA Today* on the front page suggesting that your military chiefs are not enthusiastic about going after Iraq right now, that the military might be stretched too thin already in Afghanistan.

Secretary Rumsfeld. I glanced at it; I didn't read it. I meet with those folks all the time. I have no reason to give credence to that.

Q. Obviously there's no specific authorization from the President yet to take military action against the Iraqis. But you probably noticed in the last few days alone—what?—there were several incidents that the U.S. was shot at by Iraqi ground fire in the no-fly zones, and the U.S. shot right back.
Is that situation heating up right now?

Secretary Rumsfeld. No. Our aircraft and the coalition aircraft—the British fly those missions as well, and we get shot at from time to time, and in almost every instance find an opportunity to go back and attempt to destroy the surface-to-air missiles or the anti-aircraft or the radars that were coordinating the ground fire. It happens, you know, once or twice a week.

There has not been any noticeable change in the recent period with respect to the frequency.

Q. The dispute between the Israelis and the Palestinians: how much of a setback has that been in your planning for the possible resumption of military strikes against Iraq?

Secretary Rumsfeld. Well, that question is premised on a set of assumptions about Iraq that seems to me are, you know, not on the table. I would say that it is unfortunate that Israel and the Palestinians are engaged in a process which is killing lots of people, and another suicide bombing in Israel recently, which is a terrorist act. But it isn't affecting anything other than causing great harm to the people in the region.

Q. Let's talk about the war in Afghanistan. Some critics now—and you know there's always going to be some critics—they're coming out and suggesting the U.S. is getting bogged down. Operation Anaconda becomes Operation Mountain Lion, becomes Operation Condor, and that you're not really engaged in significant military action against al Qaeda and Taliban forces recently.

Secretary Rumsfeld. Well, of course, the press is impatient. They're constantly wanting high drama and bombs dropping, flares going up and lights and sound. The fact of the matter is we're doing what we said we were going to do on September 10th and 11th—September 11th and 12th and 13th. We're using all elements of national power to put pressure on terrorists. Some of it is visible; some of it is not visible. We're drying up bank accounts. We're making it more difficult to transfer money. We're making it more difficult for them to recruit. We've changed the government in Afghanistan from the Taliban terrorists harboring a collection of thugs to an interim government headed by Mr. Karzai that is attempting to move it towards a transitional government. Every time, in every place, we see concentrations of al Qaeda or Taliban or global terrorists, we will go and attack them. They know that. And every place there were concentrations, we went and attacked them, and we killed a lot of them, and we captured a lot of them. They don't get into concentrations any more. Now they're hiding in caves and they're hiding in tunnels and they're in small groups, and they're much more difficult to find. They're less of a military task now than a law enforcement and an intelligence gathering task.

Q. And you're still working on the assumption that Osama bin Laden is alive.

Secretary Rumsfeld. I don't have to have an assumption. I don't know if he is or isn't. We've not heard a sound from him since last December.

Q. Are these recent videotapes that have surfaced old stuff?

Secretary Rumsfeld. That's what everyone seems to conclude. I haven't bothered to look at them. But it doesn't make a lot of difference in this sense. If he's alive, he's clearly having a tough time running his organization. There's so much pressure on him. If he's not alive, there are four, five, six, eight people who can step right in and run the organization. They know where the bank accounts are, they know where the weapons are hidden, they know the training manuals, they can set up a training camp somewhere else. There're lots of places in the world that are not being governed, if you will, where they could set up training camps. And if they do, we'll find them and we'll go after them.

United Nations Security Council Resolution 1413, May 23, 2002

The Security Council,

Reaffirming its previous resolutions on Afghanistan, in particular its resolution 1386 (2001) of 20 December 2001,

Reaffirming also its strong commitment to the sovereignty, independence, territorial integrity and national unity of Afghanistan,

Supporting international efforts to root out terrorism, in keeping with the Charter of the United Nations, and reaffirming also its resolutions 1368 (2001) of 12 September 2001 and 1373 (2001) of 28 September 2001,

Recognizing that the responsibility for providing security and law and order throughout the country resides with the Afghans themselves, and welcoming in this respect the cooperation of the Afghan Interim Authority with the International Security Assistance Force,

Expressing its appreciation to the United Kingdom of Great Britain and Northern Ireland for taking the lead in organizing and commanding the International Security Assistance Force and recognizing with gratitude the contributions of many nations to the International Security Assistance Force,

Welcoming the letter from the Foreign Minister of Turkey to the Secretary- General of 7 May 2002 (S/2002/568), and taking note of Turkey's offer contained therein to assume the lead in commanding the International Security Assistance Force,

Recalling the letter dated 19 December 2001 from Dr. Abdullah Abdullah to the President of the Security Council (S/2001/1223),

Determining that the situation in Afghanistan still constitutes a threat to international peace and security,

Determined to ensure the full implementation of the mandate of the International Security Assistance Force, in consultation with the Afghan Interim Authority and its successors established by the Bonn Agreement,

Acting for these reasons under Chapter VII of the Charter of the United Nations,

1. Decides to extend the authorization, for a period of six months beyond 20 June 2002, of the International Security Assistance Force, as defined in resolution 1386 (2001);

2. Authorizes the Member States participating in the International Security Assistance Force to take all necessary measures to fulfil the mandate of the International Security Assistance Force;

3. Calls upon Member States to contribute personnel, equipment and other resources to the International Security Assistance Force, and to make contributions to the Trust Fund established pursuant to resolution 1386 (2001);

4. Requests the leadership of the International Security Assistance Force to provide monthly reports on implementation of its mandate, through the Secretary- General;

5. Decides to remain actively seized of the matter.

Remarks by President Bush and Russian President Putin, May 24, 2002

President Bush and President Putin delivered their remarks at the Kremlin.

Q. The Bush team says that your sales of nuclear technology and sophisticated military technology to Iran are the world's single biggest proliferation problem right now. Do you agree with that assessment, and did you make any specific promises today in your meeting with President Bush?

President Bush. Well, first, we spent a lot of time on this subject. And as I said yesterday in Germany, I worry about Iran and I'm confident Vladimir Putin worries about Iran, and that was confirmed today. He understands terrorist threats, just like we understand terrorist threats. And he understands that weapons of mass destruction are dangerous to Russia, just as they are to America. And he's explained that point himself, of course, now, he standing here.

But we spoke very frankly and honestly about the need to make sure that a non-transparent government run by radical clerics doesn't get their hands on weapons of mass destruction. It could be harmful to us and harmful to Russia. And the President can speak for himself. And he gave me some assurances that I think will be very comforting for you to listen to. And I'm confident we can work together on this issue. This is in both our countries' mutual interest that we solve this problem.

President Putin. I will confirm what Mr. Bush has just said, and I agree with your evaluation of threats in this regard. Generally speaking, I believe that the problem of nonproliferation is one of the key problems as regards ensuring international security.

Incidentally, this happened to be one of the main motivating and underpinning logical stimuluses to work in Russia-NATO framework together on non-proliferation on nuclear arms.

At the same time, I'd like to point out that cooperation between Iran and Russia is not all a character which would undermine the process on non-proliferation. Our cooperation is exclusively, as regards energy sector, focused on the problems of economic nature. I'd like to point out also that the U.S. has taken a commitment upon themselves to build similar nuclear power plant in North Korea, similar to Russia.

And in addition to Iran, I think, we also need to think about other countries here. For example, we have some questions concerning development of missile programs in Taiwan, in some other countries where we've been witnessing active work of producing mass destruction weapons and their carriers. All of that should be a subject of our in-depth discussion both bilaterally and in the frameworks of NATO-Russia agreement. That's one of the key issues of the modern times, I believe.

It would seem to me that in order to be efficient, in this sense, like in other areas, we need to address the main task, to upgrade confidence mutually. And today I mentioned to President Bush here, that as regards Iran and some other countries, according to our data, the missile programs of those countries, nuclear programs, are built largely on the basis of the technologies and with the support of the Western companies. We do have such info, and we stand ready to share it with our American partners. So if we pursued that way, not dealing with generalities, then we'll get results with respect to this very complicated and very important for our two countries track.

Joint Statement by President Bush and Russian President Putin, May 24, 2002

Reaffirming our commitment expressed on October 21, 2001 to fight terrorism in all its forms wherever it may occur, we commend the efforts of the worldwide coalition against terrorism since the tragic events of September 11, 2001. The member nations of the coalition must continue their concerted action to deny safe haven to terrorists; to destroy their financial, logistical, communications, and other operational networks; and to bring terrorists to justice. We note with satisfaction that U.S.-Russia counterterrorism cooperation is making an important contribution to the global coalition against terrorism.

A successful campaign against terrorism must be conducted by nations through bilateral, regional, and multilateral cooperation, and requires a multifaceted approach that employs law enforcement, intelligence, diplomatic, political, and economic actions. We stress that initiatives against terrorism must be conducted in an atmosphere of rule of law and with respect for universal human rights.

Recognizing the importance of multilateral counterterrorism efforts, such as those under the auspices of the United Nations, the Group of Eight, the European Union, the OSCE, the "Six Plus Two" group, and NATO-Russia, we encourage the further development of regional counterterrorism initiatives, including within the framework of the Shanghai Cooperation Organization and its cooperation with the United States, that improve information-sharing, law enforcement cooperation, and border security. Of these institutions, we note that the U.N. Security Council Counterterrorism Committee plays a key coordinating role in the struggle against international terrorism. In support of regional cooperation, the United States is sponsoring a counterterrorism conference in June 2002 to include participation from the Central Asian and Caucasus states, Afghanistan, Turkey, China, and Russia.

We call upon all nations to implement fully the provisions of U.N. Security Council resolutions, including resolutions 1368, 1373, 1377 and 1390, directed against terrorism, the Taliban, and al-Qaida, and to become parties at the earliest opportunity to the twelve international antiterrorism conventions, including the Convention for the Suppression of the Financing of Terrorism. The United States supports conclusion of the Russian-proposed nuclear terrorism convention, and joins Russia in urging other nations to enlist in the efforts to resolve the outstanding issues related to the text. We call upon all nations to take steps to comply with the Financial Action Task Force (FATF) recommendations on money laundering and terrorist financing. We shall work to block the financial assets of named terrorists and their organizations without delay.

We underscore the need to bring to a logical conclusion efforts to eliminate the terrorist infrastructure in Afghanistan related to Usama Bin Laden, the al-Qaida organization, and the Taliban. Afghanistan should never again be a haven for terrorism. Reaffirming our support for the important role of the U.N. in efforts to implement successfully the Bonn Agreement, including the upcoming Loya Jirga, we share a vision of a stable, independent Afghanistan at peace with its neighbors and the rest of the world and on the road to a more prosperous future.

We recognize the links between illegal drug trafficking and terrorism and stress the importance of U.S.-Russia cooperation on counternarcotics. Both our countries are dedicated to continuing their support for regional initiatives, such as those of the "Six Plus Two" Working Group on Drugs, to encourage cooperation among member countries and to strengthen their counternarcotics capabilities. We both strongly support the Afghan Interim Authority's plan to implement its poppy ban.

Believing that the sovereignty, long-term stability, prosperity, and further democratic development of the states of Central Asia serve the strategic interests of the United States and Russia, we pledge transparency and cooperation in our relations with the states of Central Asia. An important step for ensuring their security is to eradicate terrorist activities in Afghanistan once and for all and to assist in the prevention of their reoccurrence.

We reaffirm our commitment to working with the Government of Georgia on counterterrorism issues, while upholding Georgian sovereignty, and hope that the presence of terrorists in this country will be eliminated. As members of the Friends of the U.N. Secretary-General on Georgia, the United States and Russia remain committed to advancing a peaceful, political resolution of the conflicts in Abkhazia and South Ossetia. We pledge to work closely with all relevant parties to these conflicts to reduce military tensions, address civilians' security concerns, and foster a lasting political settlement that preserves Georgia's territorial integrity and protects the rights of all of those involved in the conflicts. We highly appreciate the contribution of the U.N. Security Council, concerned states, and international mechanisms which participate in peaceful efforts toward resolution of these conflicts.

We note with satisfaction the entry into force of the Treaty on Mutual Legal Assistance in Criminal Matters between the United States of America and the Russian Federation, which will facilitate joint efforts on criminal and terrorist cases.

We will work to strengthen the exchange of professional know-how and experience in such areas as transportation security, hostage takeover, and airplane hijacking, among others.

We will work to strengthen national, bilateral, and multilateral measures to prevent the proliferation of weapons of mass destruction, related technologies, and delivery means as an essential element of the fight against international terrorism and all those who support it.

An important step in our joint cooperation will be a meeting of our scientists in June. We will seek to develop jointly new technology to detect nuclear material that can be used to manufacture weapons for purposes of terrorism.

The U.S.-Russia Working Group on Afghanistan has proven a successful vehicle for joint efforts between the United States and Russia to counter terrorism emanating from Afghanistan. Recognizing the increased threat of terrorism originating in other regions of the world, we have directed that the Working Group's agenda be broadened, and that it be renamed the U.S.-Russia Working Group on Counterterrorism. Among other issues, this Working Group will address the threats posed by nuclear, biological, and chemical terrorism. The next meeting of the Working Group will take place in the Washington area in July 2002.

Remarks by Secretary of State Powell, May 25, 2002

Secretary Colin Powell delivered his remarks in St. Petersburg, Russia during the President's trip to Russia.

Q. Secretary Powell, on yesterday's meetings with President Putin, can you be a little more specific about what kind of commitments he made in relation to the exports to Iran? And also what your assessment is, now that you've had a chance to talk with him, about how much loose nuclear material remains unsecured in Russia, the degree to which that is an existing concern. We know you set up a commission, so there has to be some concern. But we don't really have a quantitative sense of what you think is out there.

Secretary Powell. With respect to Iran, I would answer the question this way. Both nations are agreed that we don't want to contribute to proliferation of nuclear weapons technology, and that includes nuclear weapons technology to Iran. Both nations are committed to the proposition that this would not be a good thing for any one of them to be involved in.

There is a disagreement between we and the Russians about the nature of some of their activities. It's a disagreement that's gone on for some time. We believe that some of the activities they are participating in can be seen as helping Iran in the direction of proliferation. They disagree with our assessment. They say that they are as sensitive to this issue as we are, they are closer to Iran than we are and, therefore, that's why they are more sensitive, and that their activities do not assist Iran in that direction.

We disagree with that, and the groups that have been set up, plus our continuing bilateral dialogue that's been going on for quite a while will continue to explore this. There are some areas that I look forward to taking up with Foreign Minister Ivanov to see if he can assure me, or I can convince him who has the right side of this argument. The good news is that we've had candid discussions about this, and I hope we'll be able to solve this going forward, just as we have solved some of the other difficult issues that we have faced over the past year.

With respect to fissile material, I can't tell you how much is unaccounted for, if any. I just don't have that data. That's why we're working with them, and we're investing in our comprehensive threat reduction efforts. And we want to have a broader dialogue with them, to get a better understanding of what they have done over the years, what they have produced over the years, how can we be more effective in capturing that material, recycling it to be used as fuel, or for other purposes, or getting it under solid accountability, so that the whole world can be more comfortable with the knowledge that it is under solid accountability.

Q. Have they been reluctant to give you that data?

Secretary Powell. We have not gotten all the intimation on not just that type of technology, but other technology—chemical activities, biological activities that they've had ongoing over the years. And the group that has been set up consisting of the four ministers—the two Ivanovs, Rumsfeld and Powell, these are some of the areas we'll be exploring with them.

* * * *

Q. Mr. Secretary, can you talk about Russia's role as an ally in the war against terrorism, and how that has changed the dynamic of the relationship?

Secretary Powell. Well, after 9/11, President Putin gave a very powerful statement that aligned Russia fully with the campaign against terrorism. And he has acted on his—the commitments he made that day. And they have become a strong partner in the campaign against terrorism. They have supported our efforts in Afghanistan, as the President noted yesterday. They have been very forthcoming in a number of other areas.

And we have been operating in Central Asia in close coordination and cooperation with the Russians in a way that would have been unthinkable just a year, year and a half ago. And so we are very pleased with the support we have gotten and we also want to operate in Central Asia in a way that is mindful of their interest in the region, as well.

Remarks by Secretary of State Powell, May 26, 2002

Secretary Colin Powell was interviewed by Wolf Blitzer of CNN in St. Petersburg, Russia during the President's trip to Russia.

Q. Mr. Secretary, the Russians have rejected your request to stop exporting nuclear technology to Iran, a founding member of the President's "axis of evil." What else can we do about this?

Secretary Powell. We will continue to discuss this issue with the Russians. There was agreement between the two presidents that we don't want to see Iran develop a nuclear weapon or weapons of mass destruction. That is destabilizing for the region, and it is more of a danger to the Russians, who are in the region, than it is for the United States. So we have a common objective.

We have a disagreement about what it is the Russians are providing them that would help them achieve that goal. The Russians say that they are not providing that kind of technology or equipment to the Iranians, and we have some evidence that they are. So we talk about these issues candidly, and I look forward to continuing this discussion with Foreign Minister Ivanov, and I know that Secretary Rumsfeld will have similar discussions with Defense Minister Ivanov.

So it's an area of disagreement with respect to what they are doing, but there is no disagreement with respect to our overall goal not to see this kind of capability in the hands of the Iranians.

Q. And no immediate solution on the horizon, right?

Secretary Powell. Well, there are a number of ideas we are exploring with the Russians that might lead to a solution, and that is why we created this committee consisting of the four ministers—the defense ministers and foreign ministers of the Russian Federation and the United States—and we'll be working together to find a way forward.

Q. On the Iraq situation, I listened very carefully to what President Bush said the other day in Germany with the German Chancellor Schroeder. I want you to listen precisely to what the President said, and then I'll have a question. Listen to this: "I told the Chancellor that I had no war plans on my desk, which is the truth, and that we have got to use all means at our disposal to deal with Saddam Hussein."
Does that mean you—the U.S. Government is ratcheting back from the potential of another Desert Storm-like invasion involving hundreds of thousands of troops?

Secretary Powell. I don't know that we had ratcheted up. What the President said is what he has been saying repeatedly and what I have been saying regularly, as has Don Rumsfeld and National Security Advisor Condi Rice: The President has no war plans on his desk; his advisors have not provided him a recommendation for military action against Iraq.
And what the President specifically referred to is we're looking at all options available to us. We have been working within the United Nations to get the inspectors back in. We have gotten the goods review list finished now within the Security Council of the United Nations to control the technology and the equipment and the consumer goods that go into Iraq in a more effective way. And obviously we are also exploring political options as well as military options. But the President does not have a recommendation before him for the simple reason that his advisors—and I am one of those advisors—have not provided him one.

Q. The goal is still, though, what you call regime change in Baghdad, getting rid of Saddam Hussein one way or another; is that right?

Secretary Powell. Yes, that remains the United States' goal. And there is an international goal of getting the inspectors in to make sure that he complies with the obligations he entered into ten years ago to not have any weapons of mass destruction. And that is what the inspectors are all about, and that is what the Oil-for-Food program is all about and the goods review list that we just completed with the Security Council.
But we believe, as a United States position, that the region and the people of Iraq would be better off with another leader, another regime.

Remarks by Secretary of State Powell, May 31, 2002

Secretary Colin Powell was interviewed by Jon Leyne of BBC News.

Q. On Iraq, we keep hearing there are no plans on the President's desk to invade Iraq. What does that mean?

Secretary Powell. It seems to me a rather clear declaratory sentence: There are no plans on the President's desk. He has received no recommendation from his advisors to undertake a military operation against Iraq. There is no question however that we believe the regime should be changed. So we're working with the international community, with the U.N. to put smart sanctions in place, and we've succeeded with a great deal of help, and frankly leadership on the part of the British Government. And now we are trying to get the inspectors back in. The President has called for the inspectors to go back in repeatedly.

And at the same time, outside these multilateral efforts, the President believes, we all believe—I certainly believe—I've been watching this fellow for a number of years—that the people of Iraq and the people of the region would be better off if there was a change in regime. And we are constantly reviewing options and plans that people come up with as to how this might be accomplished—politically, diplomatically, and yes of course we examine military options as well. But as the President has said repeatedly, and in recent days again, he has no war plan on his desk and his advisors have not provided one. All speculation to the contrary is nothing but speculation to the contrary.

Remarks by Secretary of Defense Rumsfeld, June 3, 2002

Secretary Donald Rumsfeld was interviewed by the Washington Post Editorial Board.

Q. Do you have any better sense now than you did a few months ago of how many al Qaeda people have left not just the tribal areas, but have gone into Pakistan cities or other countries since last fall?

Secretary Rumsfeld. I guess I don't. I've heard so many numbers as to how many were killed, and we know we've got some handfuls of hundreds, and we know that a lot got away. And we don't know if when they got away they decided they didn't want to do anything anymore, or if they are still active cadre that are waiting to find someone to tell them what to do.

But we know they're in enough countries and have enough money and have enough leadership that you've got to expect they in fact are going to act again.

You kind of walk through what you know. You know there is proliferation of weapons of mass destruction. You know those six or seven terrorist states are testing chemical, biological and actively seeking some of the nuclear and radiation capabilities. And you know there's a linkage between the terrorist organizations and the terrorist states. Therefore it seems to me that reasonable people have got to say to themselves that if left to their own devices they are going to get their hands on weapons of mass destruction.

You can't know whether that's going to happen within a week or a month or a year or two years. But you have to know that it isn't a question of whether it will happen but that it will happen.

I was sitting here having breakfast with congressmen when the plane went into the World Trade Center, and we were talking about surprise and warning and events that would occur in the world.

The way I try to think of it is, for myself, one ought—assuming that's correct, and it seems to me it's not debatable that terrorists may have those things, they have relationships with global terrorist organizations. We have lots of evidence that the global terrorist networks want weapons of mass destruction. Therefore one has to say they're going to get them at some point unless they're stopped.

The question to provide the sense of urgency for yourself, if you say to yourself, say it's a week, a month, a year or two years, what is it that I wish I had done now, today, starting today, between now and when that happens, that would help improve our ability to prevent it from happening, and you've got to assume it's not a single event, but it's multiple events as we know, it's the way these things work.

And second, what could one do to mitigate the effect if and when it does happen? Because it's not possible to defend every place at every time against every conceivable technique. Therefore you've got to assume something's going to get through the net because you can't stop everything.

So you have to say what ought everyone—federal, state, local, public, private— ought we to be doing and how ought we to be getting ourselves arranged so that we can prevent as many of those types of things, given the fact that if it is a weapon of mass destruction, some type of biological weapon, for example, and it's contagious, for example you're not talking about thousands of people, you're talking about tens of thousands of people.

So all of us in and out of government have to have that sense of urgency with respect to this set of problems. They're distinctly different from earlier periods. You could be wrong on a conventional attack of some kind and it's harmful and people die. If you're wrong on something that's less than conventional or other than conventional it is not—It is something multiples of that.

* * * *

Q. You spoke about our disrupting al Qaeda and impacts of weapons of mass destruction. To what degree do you think the administration is getting distracted from that central task by these other crises that come up? The very fact that you're going to this conflict; George Tenet is in Israel. Is there a danger of the focus being lost that you need on the al Qaeda problem?

Secretary Rumsfeld. I don't think so. We've got a lot of people who can worry about things and a lot of people who do. It's hard. Most of these folks are working long hours and long weeks. Long months. But the global war on terrorism and the threat that I see and that all of us are reminded of every day as you feel through intelligence scraps and try to sort through, helps to keep the mind focused.

You're right, Colin and the president and now George have spent a pile of time on the Middle East and still are. Afghanistan takes a lot of time. It's a big world. It's a complicated world. It's a dangerous world. It's an untidy world. It's an imperfect world.

White House Press Briefing, June 4, 2002

Q. Ari, on the intelligence investigation, the President said a couple of things today. One, he said it's clear that the agencies were not communicating properly prior to the 9/11 attacks. He also said that now they are, that there's been a cultural shift that he's pleased about. Does that mean that he believes the joint intelligence briefings on the Hill now are pointless? And secondly, on what basis does he believe that there's been a cultural shift that means that the intelligence agencies, the FBI and the CIA, would be able to do a better job than they did before?

Mr. Fleischer. You essentially have two major events going on in Washington. One is the current fight against terrorism, making certain America is not hit again. And that is where the changes that were made have taken place in the FBI and in the CIA—those changes are ongoing. And it was a reflection, as the President has pointed out many times about the mission of the FBI used to be going after kidnappers, going after spies, et cetera, and now it's a shift focused on preventing a next potential terrorist attack.

That's much the focus of the administration. Congress is also doing its part to protect the nation. Congress is taking a look back. Congress is reviewing events leading up to September 11th, investigating the agencies that were involved and how they received information. And the President looks at what Congress is doing as something that can be potentially very constructive if Congress takes it seriously and if Congress approaches it not in a way of finger-pointing or second-guessing, but in a way of what can we learn to help continue to protect America. So those are the two events really that are going on. And they should be perfectly consistent with each other.

Q. But that doesn't speak to the cultural changes. I mean, the Justice Department and the FBI have had major counterterrorism units going back years. Just because this administration says after 9/11 that that's going to become the sole focus, does he believe that that just makes it so?

Mr. Fleischer. No. But I think what does give it the greatest likelihood of making it so is the fact that our nation got attacked and the people who work in these agencies recognize we've gone from a culture which was a peacetime culture of prosecution of crime to a wartime culture that is protecting America from the next potential attack. And it's often the case in our history that it takes momentous developments to force change in people and in systems in the government and throughout society.

I think people in government are going through something very much that people in America are going through, recognizing that much did change on September 11th, that the way things were done can no longer be done the way it was. And frankly, I think, what you really have in this government is people like Bob Mueller and George

Tenet who were the leading reformers in making those changes, within their own agencies. And it's not always easy, but they are the ones who are making that effort, and it's going to continue.

Q. Just to button this up, one other thing on this. The President believes this change has already occurred—is that how we're to interpret his remarks?

Mr. Fleischer. I think he's saying it's occurring. I can walk you through, I'd be happy to, many of the specific things that have already been done. But these changes don't take place overnight, they take time. You have people, as the President today referred to as number threes, fours, fives burrowed deep into agencies that are sometimes the slower ones to change. But there's no mistaking the fact that the leadership, the people at the top, have brought changes to their agencies, and are working very well together as part of those changes.

White House Press Briefing, June 4, 2002

Q. Ari, on the intelligence investigation, the President said a couple of things today. One, he said it's clear that the agencies were not communicating properly prior to the 9/11 attacks. He also said that now they are, that there's been a cultural shift that he's pleased about. Does that mean that he believes the joint intelligence briefings on the Hill now are pointless? And secondly, on what basis does he believe that there's been a cultural shift that means that the intelligence agencies, the FBI and the CIA, would be able to do a better job than they did before?

Mr. Fleischer. You essentially have two major events going on in Washington. One is the current fight against terrorism, making certain America is not hit again. And that is where the changes that were made have taken place in the FBI and in the CIA—those changes are ongoing. And it was a reflection, as the President has pointed out many times about the mission of the FBI used to be going after kidnappers, going after spies, et cetera, and now it's a shift focused on preventing a next potential terrorist attack.

That's much the focus of the administration. Congress is also doing its part to protect the nation. Congress is taking a look back. Congress is reviewing events leading up to September 11th, investigating the agencies that were involved and how they received information. And the President looks at what Congress is doing as something that can be potentially very constructive if Congress takes it seriously and if Congress approaches it not in a way of finger-pointing or second-guessing, but in a way of what can we learn to help continue to protect America. So those are the two events really that are going on. And they should be perfectly consistent with each other.

Q. But that doesn't speak to the cultural changes. I mean, the Justice Department and the FBI have had major counterterrorism units going back years. Just because this administration says after 9/11 that that's going to become the sole focus, does he believe that that just makes it so?

Mr. Fleischer. No. But I think what does give it the greatest likelihood of making it so is the fact that our nation got attacked and the people who work in these agencies recognize we've gone from a culture which was a peacetime culture of prosecution of crime to a wartime culture that is protecting America from the next potential attack. And it's often the case in our history that it takes momentous developments to force change in people and in systems in the government and throughout society.

I think people in government are going through something very much that people in America are going through, recognizing that much did change on September 11th, that the way things were done can no longer be done the way it was. And frankly, I think, what you really have in this government is people like Bob Mueller and George Tenet who were the leading reformers in making those changes, within their own agencies. And it's not always easy, but they are the ones who are making that effort, and it's going to continue.

Q. Just to button this up, one other thing on this. The President believes this change has already occurred—is that how we're to interpret his remarks?

Mr. Fleischer. I think he's saying it's occurring. I can walk you through, I'd be happy to, many of the specific things that have already been done. But these changes don't take place overnight, they take time. You have people, as the President today referred to as number threes, fours, fives burrowed deep into agencies that are sometimes the slower ones to change. But there's no mistaking the fact that the leadership, the people at the top, have brought changes to their agencies, and are working very well together as part of those changes.

Remarks by President Bush, June 6, 2002

President Bush delivered the following address to the nation.

Good evening. During the next few minutes, I want to update you on the progress we are making in our war against terror, and to propose sweeping changes that will strengthen our homeland against the ongoing threat of terrorist attacks.

Nearly nine months have passed since the day that forever changed our country. Debris from what was once the World Trade Center has been cleared away in a hundred thousand truckloads. The west side of the Pentagon looks almost as it did on September the 10th. And as children finish school and families prepare for summer vacations, for many, life seems almost normal.

Yet we are a different nation today—sadder and stronger, less innocent and more courageous, more appreciative of life, and for many who serve our country, more willing to risk life in a great cause. For those who have lost family and friends, the pain will never go away—and neither will the responsibilities that day thrust upon all of us. America is leading the civilized world in a titanic struggle against terror. Freedom and fear are at war—and freedom is winning.

Tonight over 60,000 American troops are deployed around the world in the war against terror—more than 7,000 in Afghanistan; others in the Philippines, Yemen, and the Republic of Georgia, to train local forces. Next week Afghanistan will begin selecting a representative government, even as American troops, along with our allies, still continuously raid remote al Qaeda hiding places.

Among those we have captured is a man named Abu Zabedah, al Qaeda's chief of operations. From him, and from hundreds of others, we are learning more about how the terrorists plan and operate; information crucial in anticipating and preventing future attacks.

Our coalition is strong. More than 90 nations have arrested or detained over 2,400 terrorists and their supporters. More than 180 countries have offered or are providing assistance in the war on terrorism. And our military is strong and prepared to oppose any emerging threat to the American people.

Every day in this war will not bring the drama of liberating a country. Yet every day brings new information, a tip or arrest, another step, or two, or three in a relentless march to bring security to our nation and justice to our enemies.

Every day I review a document called the threat assessment. It summarizes what our intelligence services and key law enforcement agencies have picked up about ter- rorist activity. Sometimes the information is very general—vague talk, bragging about future attacks. Sometimes the information is more specific, as in a recent case when an al Qaeda detainee said attacks were planned against financial institutions.

When credible intelligence warrants, appropriate law enforcement and local offi- cials are alerted. These warnings are, unfortunately, a new reality in American life— and we have recently seen an increase in the volume of general threats. Americans should continue to do what you're doing—go about your lives, but pay attention to your surroundings. Add your eyes and ears to the protection of our homeland.

In protecting our country, we depend on the skill of our people—the troops we send to battle, intelligence operatives who risk their lives for bits of information, law enforcement officers who sift for clues and search for suspects. We are now learning that before September the 11th, the suspicions and insights of some of our front-line agents did not get enough attention.

My administration supports the important work of the intelligence committees in Congress to review the activities of law enforcement and intelligence agencies. We need to know when warnings were missed or signs unheeded—not to point the finger of blame, but to make sure we correct any problems, and prevent them from happen- ing again.

Based on everything I've seen, I do not believe anyone could have prevented the horror of September the 11th. Yet we now know that thousands of trained killers are plotting to attack us, and this terrible knowledge requires us to act differently.

If you're a front-line worker for the FBI, the CIA, some other law enforcement or intelligence agency, and you see something that raises suspicions, I want you to report it immediately. I expect your supervisors to treat it with the seriousness it deserves. Information must be fully shared, so we can follow every lead to find the one that may prevent tragedy.

I applaud the leaders and employees at the FBI and CIA for beginning essential reforms. They must continue to think and act differently to defeat the enemy.

The first and best way to secure America's homeland is to attack the enemy where he hides and plans, and we're doing just that. We're also taking significant steps to strengthen our homeland protections—securing cockpits, tightening our borders, stockpiling vaccines, increasing security at water treatment and nuclear power plants.

After September the 11th, we needed to move quickly, and so I appointed Tom Ridge as my Homeland Security Advisor. As Governor Ridge has worked with all levels of government to prepare a national strategy, and as we have learned more about the plans and capabilities of the terrorist network, we have concluded that our government must be reorganized to deal more effectively with the new threats of the 21st century. So tonight, I ask the Congress to join me in creating a single, permanent department with an overriding and urgent mission: securing the homeland of America, and protecting the American people.

Right now, as many as a hundred different government agencies have some responsibilities for homeland security, and no one has final accountability. For example, the Coast Guard has several missions, from search and rescue to maritime treaty enforcement. It reports to the Transportation Department, whose primary responsibilities are roads, rails, bridges and the airways. The Customs Service, among other duties, collects tariffs and prevents smuggling—and it is part of the Treasury Department, whose primary responsibility is fiscal policy, not security.

Tonight, I propose a permanent Cabinet-level Department of Homeland Security to unite essential agencies that must work more closely together: Among them, the Coast Guard, the Border Patrol, the Customs Service, Immigration officials, the Transportation Security Administration, and the Federal Emergency Management Agency. Employees of this new agency will come to work every morning knowing their most important job is to protect their fellow citizens. The Department of Homeland Security will be charged with—

The Department of Homeland Security will be charged with four primary tasks. This new agency will control our borders and prevent terrorists and explosives from entering our country. It will work with state and local authorities to respond quickly and effectively to emergencies. It will bring together our best scientists to develop technologies that detect biological, chemical, and nuclear weapons, and to discover the drugs and treatments to best protect our citizens. And this new department will review intelligence and law enforcement information from all agencies of government, and produce a single daily picture of threats against our homeland. Analysts will be responsible for imagining the worst, and planning to counter it.

The reason to create this department is not to create the size of government, but to increase its focus and effectiveness. The staff of this new department will be largely drawn from the agencies we are combining. By ending duplication and overlap, we will spend less on overhead, and more on protecting America. This reorganization will give the good people of our government their best opportunity to succeed by organizing our resources in a way that is thorough and unified.

What I am proposing tonight is the most extensive reorganization of the federal government since the 1940s. During his presidency, Harry Truman recognized that our nation's fragmented defenses had to be reorganized to win the Cold War. He proposed uniting our military forces under a single Department of Defense, and creating the National Security Council to bring together defense, intelligence, and diplomacy. Truman's reforms are still helping us to fight terror abroad, and now we need similar dramatic reforms to secure our people at home.

Only the United States Congress can create a new department of government. So tonight, I ask for your help in encouraging your representatives to support my plan. We face an urgent need, and we must move quickly, this year, before the end of the congressional session. All in our government have learned a great deal since September the 11th, and we must act on every lesson. We are stronger and better prepared tonight than we were on that terrible morning—and with your help, and the support of Congress, we will be stronger still.

History has called our nation into action. History has placed a great challenge before us: Will America—with our unique position and power—blink in the face of terror, or will we lead to a freer, more civilized world? There's only one answer: This great country will lead the world to safety, security, peace and freedom.

Thank you for listening. Good night, and may God bless America.

Remarks by Secretary of Defense Rumsfeld, June 6, 2002

Secretary Donald Rumsfeld delivered his remarks at NATO Headquarters in Brussels, Belgium.

It is a pleasure to be back in Brussels and at NATO. We had good meetings today. Among other things I thanked our allies for their broad and prompt and effective support in the Global War on Terrorism.

I would say it has been a particularly productive NATO meeting in that we agreed that at Prague our leaders will decide on specific new military capabilities to meet the new military threats that face us.

From the decision to invoke Article 5 for the first time in Alliance history to the NATO AWACS crews that patrolled the U.S. skies after September 11th to the forces of NATO nations that are at this moment serving on the seas and in the air and on the ground in the Afghanistan theater, the NATO Alliance has been critical to our success in the war thus far. Indeed tomorrow I will visit with some of the NATO AWACS crews in Germany to personally thank them for their wonderful assistance in helping to defend the United States these past many months.

Operation Enduring Freedom is being facilitated greatly by our relationships in NATO. Our coalition activities in Afghanistan and in other regions in the world today are really made possible, in major part, by the decades of joint planning and joint training that have taken place within NATO.

Today we discussed the way ahead in the War on Terrorism and how the Alliance must further transform to meet the threat facing all of our countries in the 21st century—the spread of weapons of mass destruction into the hands terrorist states. This threat is not theoretical; it is real. It is dangerous. If we do not prepare promptly to counter it, we could well experience attacks in our countries that could make the events of September 11 seem modest by comparison.

President Bush recently said in Berlin that "those who despise human freedom will attack it on every continent. Those who seek missiles and terrible weapons are also familiar with the map of Europe." That is why dealing with these threats in the 21st Century must be central to the NATO Alliance, just as dealing with the Soviet threat was central in the 20th Century.

Ministers have tasked the NATO military authorities to identify a specific set of capabilities that the allies will commit to fulfill. As we look to the Prague summit, where undoubtedly some new members will be invited to join the alliance, we discussed the idea of asking new members—in addition to maintaining certain core military capabilities—to choose areas of special emphasis for their militaries to take on and to be responsible for delivering those capabilities for the alliance.

We also discussed reform of the NATO command, military command structure and the force structures. Finally, we discussed the NATO planned reductions in SFOR and KFOR. These reductions are a sign not of retreat in our view but of success. And we're very pleased with the progress that's being shown.

I should add that I've had a number of bilateral meetings during my visit here. Besides the secretary general, and I've met with the minister for Defense of France and I will shortly meet with the minister of Defense of Ukraine.

It has also been a pleasure to see the Minister of Defense of the Russian Federation Sergei Ivanov. This is the first time we have had a bilateral meeting among our many bilateral meetings that we haven't spent most the time talking about arms control. So that is a, I think, a reflection of the change in that relationship.

We discussed the way ahead in the war on terrorism. I thanked the minister for their continuing contributions to Operation Enduring Freedom. We visited about the situation in South Asia, which is a concern of course to both of our countries, and indeed all the countries of the world. Mr. Ivanov is going to meet with me again shortly after the NATO at 20 meeting where he will provide me with a debriefing of the meetings that President Putin had with both the leaders, Pakistan as well as India. And we certainly agreed on the need for both of our countries to stay in close touch as we both continue to work with India and Pakistan and encourage them in their efforts to find a peaceful solution.

Finally, I should make a—well, just a personal comment. The last time I was here, six months ago in December, I visited Andre Destark who had been the Belgian Ambassador to NATO when I was Ambassador to NATO back in 1973 and 4. And within days thereafter Andre died and he was the—one of the founding ambassadors to the alliance—he served, I think, longer than any permanent representative to NATO has ever served, some 22 or 3 years—I think it was 23—and was the dean of the North Atlantic Council. He wrote probably the best book on NATO and was someone who really made significant contributions in how this alliance has evolved over the decades.

And with that I would be happy to respond to questions.

Q. Regarding terrorism and weapons of mass destruction, you said something to the effect that the real situation is worse than the facts show. I wonder if you could tell us what is worse than is generally understood.

Secretary Rumsfeld. Sure. All of us in this business read intelligence information. And we read it daily and we think about it and it becomes, in our minds, essentially what exists. And that's wrong. It is not what exists.

I say that because I have had experiences where I have gone back and done a great deal of work and analysis on intelligence information and looked at important countries, target countries, looked at important subject matters with respect to those target countries and asked, probed deeper and deeper and kept probing until I found out what it is we knew, and when we learned it, and when it actually had existed. And I found that, not to my surprise, but I think anytime you look at it that way what you find is that there are very important pieces of intelligence information that countries, that spend a lot of money, and a lot of time with a lot of wonderful people trying to learn more about what's going in the world, did not know some significant event for two years after it happened, for four years after it happened, for six years after it happened, in some cases 11 and 12 and 13 years after it happened.

Now what is the message there? The message is that there are no "knowns." There are thing we know that we know. There are known unknowns. That is to say there are things that we now know we don't know. But there are also unknown unknowns. There are things we don't know we don't know. So when we do the best we can and we pull all this information together, and we then say well that's basically what we see as the situation, that is really only the known knowns and the known unknowns. And each year, we discover a few more of those unknown unknowns.

It sounds like a riddle. It isn't a riddle. It is a very serious, important matter.

There's another way to phrase that and that is that the absence of evidence is not evidence of absence. It is basically saying the same thing in a different way. Simply because you do not have evidence that something exists does not mean that you have evidence that it doesn't exist. And yet almost always, when we make our threat assessments, when we look at the world, we end up basing it on the first two pieces of that puzzle, rather than all three.

Q. Secretary Rumsfeld, how confident are you that your European partners will deliver on the capabilities front in Prague? And what is the consequence for NATO as an alliance if they don't deliver?

Secretary Rumsfeld. I must say I have confidence that reasonable people find their way to reasonably right decisions. Sometimes it takes time. Sometimes there are circumstances that require some countries to take somewhat longer than another. But personally, I think that if reasonable people, publics, if publics look at the world and look at the proliferation of weapons of mass destruction, which is pervasive—people who want those weapons can get them. The terrorist states have them—one or more of the various types of weapons of mass destruction. The terrorist states have intimate relationships with terrorist networks—global networks. We all know that. They're all public. You know this. It does not take a genius to figure out that global terrorist networks are going to have their hands on weapons of mass destruction in the period ahead. No one can say if it's a week, or a month, or a year, or two years. All we do know of certain knowledge is that they are aggressively trying to get them.

That says to me that—let's take a number. I forget what the NATO number is. Two percent, two and a half percent of gross national product as a reasonable number for defense investment. In the United States we're at about 3.3 percent, I think, for this year as a budget proposal by the president.

There isn't a doubt in my mind but that the publics of the NATO nations, when confronted with the possibility of weapons of mass destruction in the hands of the kinds of people who flew those airplanes, passenger airplanes, into the World Trade Center and into the Pentagon, who obviously would be perfectly willing to use weapons of mass destruction, let there be no doubt, that the publics of the NATO countries would willingly provide a relatively modest fraction of our gross domestic products to provide the kinds of investments that will enable the NATO countries, individually and collectively, to contribute to peace and stability in the world, and to provide a degree of safety for their people which they clearly will need. We are in a new security environment as a people. And I have every confidence that political leadership can persuade people of that fact.

So I don't look at what it would mean for the alliance, because I think the alliance has demonstrated impressive durability over a period of decades in notably different security environments. And I suspect that the alliance will do so again.

Q. Mr. Secretary, you said we are in a new security environment. So the present world is very much different from the world in which the Washington Treaty, on which NATO is based, was signed directly after the second World War. Is NATO not in need for an update of the Washington Treaty?

Secretary Rumsfeld. Goodness. I shouldn't say I don't think so, although that's what I think. What I should say is that I haven't thought about that carefully. I should do some research and see if I think it might be in need of an update. But I doubt that I'll do it.

My impression is that changing some words might or might not be useful. What really needs to be done is for the people in this alliance to recognize how enormously valuable it is in the world, that there are such common values and common interests on the part of the nations in the North Atlantic Treaty Organization. We are countries that have no interest in taking over other peoples' real estate. We are countries that have an abiding interest in peace and prosperity. We are countries that want to above all be capable of and smart enough to invest so that we can contribute to peace and stability in the world and that our people or populations or citizens can have the benefits of free political and free economic systems.

Those fundamental values and those common interests are critically important to this alliance. We have a lot at stake; all of us do, each member of this Alliance. Our publics have a lot at stake in the success of the alliance.

Q. In light of the short warning time that you have with weapons of mass destruction, should NATO be prepared to take preemptive military action against terrorist states that have weapons of mass destruction and that have indicated that they're ready to use them?

Secretary Rumsfeld. That's a good question. Let me answer it slightly off to the side. What NATO ought to have is really up to all the NATO countries and not this one individual.

I will say this—I think that every country that is living in this period, this new security environment, has to recognize that historically we have organized and trained and equipped ourselves to contest aggressive, hostile armies, navies and air forces. The situation today is that opponents of free people—terrorists who go around killing innocent men, women and children regardless of race or religion or nationality—are not competing against our armies, navies and air forces.

They are using so-called asymmetrical techniques: terrorist attacks, weapons of mass destruction potentially, cyber-attacks potentially, cruise missiles to be sure, ballistic missiles to be sure. And it is our task to see that we acknowledge that change that has taken place and transform not just the United States military, as we're trying to do, but the NATO institution and the NATO militaries, as well.

Because if we're not able to use, for example, precision guided munitions, and are stuck with dumb bombs—dumb bombs are fine when you're dealing with armies, navies and air forces. They're not fine when you've got the much more difficult task of trying to track down and deal with terrorist networks and nations that harbor terrorists, as one example of the difference.

Second, as you pointed out we do have to be a much more readily deployable—our capabilities do. Ours do and other NATO nations do. So there are things we've got to do to get ourselves rearranged. And we're hard at it.

Q. Sir, if I could just follow up on that previous question. In his last statement, Lord Robertson said that in its nature, NATO remains a defensive alliance and that we're not going out looking for problems to solve. But on that point, how can these new threats be addressed if you don't necessarily take either preemptive or offensive action, in order to deal with weapons of mass destruction and not just be reacting to things after they happen?

Secretary Rumsfeld. Sure. Well that ties in, of course, to Jim's question. Let me go back and worry that a bit.

If a terrorist can attack at any time, in any place, and using any technique, and it's physically impossible to defend in every place, at every time against every technique, then one needs to calibrate the definition of "defensive." Because literally, the only way to defend against individuals or groups or organizations or countries that have weapons of mass destruction and are bent on using them against you, for example—and you know you can't defend at every place at every time against every technique—then the only defense is to take the effort to find those global networks and to deal with them as the United States did in Afghanistan.

Now is that defensive or is it offensive? I personally think of it as defensive. We had no interest in doing anything in Afghanistan. It was not on the radarscope. And the terrorists that had been trained there in that global network attacked the United States.

All one has to do is read the intelligence information to know that there are a good number of people who have been well trained. They are well financed. They are located in 40 or 50 countries. And they are determined to attack the values and the interests and the peace and the way of life of the people that are represented in the North Atlantic Treaty Organization nations.

I don't find this task notably different. It's different in the sense that we're not dealing armies, navies and air forces. But, clearly, every nation has the right of self-defense and this is the only, only conceivable way for us to defend ourselves against those kinds of threats.

Q. Sir, due to the military capabilities the technological gap is always mentioned and the U.S. and European companies are always complaining about the U.S. Customs restrictions. How far is the U.S. government now worked to minimize this restriction in the kind of better cooperation?

Secretary Rumsfeld. Well we've got a high degree of cooperation on technological matters with most NATO countries.

It seems to me the issue on technology is a gap of investment as the basic problem. The United States has been investing in technologies and a number of countries have invested less in technologies. That is part of the problem.

The degree of interaction from a technological standpoint is extensive. The gap in military capabilities between some countries and other countries however, it seems to me, is in the first instance a gap of investment, and in the second instance it is a set of—a relationship of teeth to tail—how much support and how much overhead do we have relative to how many people you would characterize as the teeth part of the teeth-to-tail effort. And third, I would say it is—I don't know quite how to put this—there have been a number of ministers today who have, I think quite properly, pointed up the importance of recognizing that not every country in the alliance is the same size or has the same security needs or is likely to want to have exactly the same kind of military. And therefore, it makes a lot of sense to do as some ministers are already doing and have indicated that they plan to do, and that is to look at a specific area, and develop a high degree of competence in that either as an individual nation or with one, two, three or four nations, or in the case of AWACS with the entire alliance.

It is that kind of rational approach to expensive businesses like defense with the serious threats that need to be dealt that reflect to me a very forward looking, rational, sensible way to approach the problem.

We'll make this the next to the last question and that's the last question.

Q. I am just wondering if you the opportunity today to talk with NATO defense ministers about Iraq, specifically about Iraq?

Secretary Rumsfeld. Did I talk with whom?

Q. With all the defense ministry, the ministers of defense.

Secretary Rumsfeld. The subject of Iraq came up. It came up in the context that I brought it up here—as one of those states that's a terrorist state—it's on the terrorist list, everyone knows that, it's all public. It's one of those states that has had relationships with terrorist networks, and it is a state that has had an enormous aggressive appetite for weapons of mass destruction.

In fact, it has liked that subject so much that it actually used chemical weapons on their own people. They have had a very serious nuclear weapons effort underway, goodness, going back what, of certain knowledge a decade and a half or two decades. They have without question a biological weapon program. But so did several other terrorist states come up and it tended to be in that context.

Remarks by President Bush, June 8, 2002

President Bush delivered the following radio address to the nation.

Good morning. Nearly nine months have passed since September the 11th, and America is leading the world in a titanic struggle against terror. The first and best way to secure America's homeland is to attack the enemy where he hides and plans, and we are doing just that.

We have also concluded that our government must be reorganized to deal most effectively with the new threats of the 21st century. So I have asked the Congress to join me in creating a single, permanent Cabinet-level Department of Homeland Security, with an overriding and urgent mission: securing the American homeland, and protecting the American people.

President Discusses Homeland Security Department President Meets with Congressional Leaders on Homeland Security Remarks by the President in Address to the Nation The Department of Homeland Security will unite essential agencies that must work more closely together, among them the Coast Guard and the Border Patrol, the Customs Service, Immigration officials, the Transportation Security Administration, and the Federal Emergency Management Agency. Employees of this new agency will come to work every morning knowing that their most important job is to protect their fellow citizens.

The Department of Homeland Security will be charged with four primary tasks. This new agency will control our borders and prevent terrorists and explosives from entering our country. It will work with state and local authorities to respond quickly and effectively to emergencies. It will bring together our best scientists to develop technologies that detect biological, chemical, and nuclear weapons, and to discover the drugs and treatments to best protect our citizens. And this new department will review intelligence and law enforcement information from all agencies of government, and produce a single daily picture of threats against our homeland. Analysts will be responsible for imagining the worst, and planning to counter it.

What I am proposing is the most extensive reorganization of the federal government since the 1940s. During his presidency, Harry Truman recognized that our nation's fragmented defenses had to be reorganized to win the Cold War. He proposed uniting our military forces under a single Department of Defense, and creating the National Security Council to bring together defense, intelligence, and diplomacy. President Truman's reforms are still helping us to fight terror abroad, and now we need similar dramatic reforms to secure our people at home.

Only the United States Congress can create a new department of government, so I'm asking for your help in encouraging your representatives to support my plan. We face an urgent need, and we must move quickly, this year, before the end of the congressional session.

All in our government have learned a great deal since September the 11th, and we must act on every lesson. We are stronger and better prepared today than we were on that terrible morning. And with your help, and the support of the Congress, we will be stronger still.

Remarks by Secretary of Defense Rumsfeld, June 9, 2002

Secretary Donald Rumsfeld delivered his remarks upon arriving in Kuwait during his trip to Europe, the Middle East, and South Asia.

Q. With the presence of thousands of American troops in Kuwait and tens of thousands in the general area, what does Kuwait and the smaller countries have to fear from Iraq?

Secretary Rumsfeld. Well I suppose you'd have to ask Kuwait that question. There is no question but that the record that Iraq has in this area is one of aggression, externally and internally.

* * * *

Q. Will you be sounding about on possible action against Iraq in the months to come?

Secretary Rumsfeld. If I were I wouldn't discuss it.

Q. Sir, this spring during the Arab Summit, Kuwait and Iraq had a very formal reconciliation. I'm wondering if you are concerned that Kuwait is moving closer to Saddam Hussein's [*inaudible*]?

Secretary Rumsfeld. Not at all.

* * * *

Q. Mr. Secretary, if I could follow up on that question about the Arab League Summit? It was more than a reconciliation. They passed a resolution that in exchange for Iraq's recognition of Kuwait sovereignty, all the Arab states said they would view an attack on Iraq as an attack on any of them. Given that resolution should the decision be made to move against Iraq given evidence of weapons of mass destruction? Can you count on the support of these important allies?

Secretary Rumsfeld. Well first, I'm not going to get into the subject of an attack on Iraq. That's not why I'm here. That's not a subject that's appropriate for me, that's appropriate for presidents and leaders of countries. The cooperation we have been receiving, we are currently receiving, and I have every reason to say we will be receiving from the nations—these countries in the region that we're going to be visiting today and tomorrow—has been terrific and we have a very close relationship that is as strong today as it was yesterday and I suspect it will be the same tomorrow.

Q. Mr. Hoon said the other day that he saw very aggressive postures—the Brits have—in recent weeks from the Iraqi's. Painting their aircraft is what he meant. Does the U.S. share that assessment—a much more aggressive Iraq in the last few weeks?

Secretary Rumsfeld. As I answered, it's not clear to me I could calibrate a difference in the last few weeks. There's no question but that Iraq continues to be aggressively attempting to not be constrained by the U.N. Resolutions and by the northern and southern no fly zones.

Q. He said that they've been improving their technology or their capabilities. Is that primarily through duel use technology or...?

Secretary Rumsfeld. Well there's an awful lot that comes in illegally as well.

Q. What is your message going to be to these Gulf countries?

Secretary Rumsfeld. Well, these are countries that are very close to the United States. We have excellent relationships with them. We have a lot of folks in the region. With Kuwait obviously you will see the relationship there. In Bahrain, we've had a relationship for 50 years, we have had ships located there and in Qatar we've got a very good relationship as well. So I'm looking forward to being here and it's been too long for me as Secretary of Defense to not have been here. I've just been so busy with other things but I'm very pleased that I can be here now.

Remarks by Secretary of Defense Rumsfeld, June 10, 2002

Secretary Donald Rumsfeld delivered his remarks in Kuwait City.

Good morning. It is a pleasure for me to be back in Kuwait after a good number of years and to have an opportunity to thank His Highness the Amir and the national security team, the Minister of Defense, for Kuwait's friendship and very strong support in so many ways.

Our relationship, of course, from a military to military stand point dates back to the Gulf War conflict and in more recent times, obviously, with respect to Operation Enduring Freedom. Kuwait has provided strong support for coalition forces involved in the war on terrorism. It's helping us in a variety of other ways as well, including the support for the U.N. resolutions with respect to Iraq. The American people appreciate the strong support as well as the wonderfully cooperative relationships between our two countries.

It's now been over a decade since the Gulf War, when a broad coalition came together to repel Iraqi aggression against Kuwait and to defeat the forces that occupied this country and visited such terrible destruction upon it. Today, the United States has suffered acts of aggression, and again a broad coalition has come together, including the State of Kuwait, to defeat that aggression.

In my meetings, we had good discussions about the way ahead with respect to the global war on terrorism. We discussed the stability in the Gulf region and certainly, the continuing violations of U.N. resolutions by Iraq. But I am very pleased to be here and to have had this chance to discuss so many matters of mutual interest, and I would be happy to respond to questions.

Q. What do you make of the statement made by the Iraqi government yesterday that Iraq has no weapons of mass destruction and is not developing any?

Secretary Rumsfeld. They are lying. Next.

Q. There was a sort of a draw down during the war in Afghanistan on some of the stocks you had in the region, especially cruise missiles. Have you replenished most of your stocks back in the region, the stuff you have stored for the deterrence against Iraq? When are you supposed to complete such an operation?

Secretary Rumsfeld. Two things happen when you have an engagement such as Afghanistan. Before you go in you have stocks that you believe are appropriate for what you might need in the region, and then you actually engage in the campaign and you find that the usage is different than you had anticipated.

So when you replenish, you replenish to fill not the old requirements but the new ones that you've learned you very likely will have to have. It may be less of some things and more of other things, but the short answer to your question is yes; as the conflict began in October in Afghanistan, we began monitoring those things and seeing that we began the process of replenishing stocks in ways that would be appropriate, including here, and we're very much in that mode right now.

We have two ways we can do that. One way is to actually see that production lines are open and new stocks, new munitions, are being manufactured. The other way to do it is on an interim basis to level out across the world. We can take from one region and move to another region depending on what our assessment is and then replenish that region with stocks as the manufacturing line produces them.

Q. Did you get commitments from Kuwait that they would take part in any new effort to contain Iraq if it comes to military might?

Secretary Rumsfeld. I wouldn't put it that way. Kuwait has been obviously very cooperative in all aspects of supporting the U.N. resolutions and the world community's effort to see that Iraq does not develop weapons of mass destruction, and that it does not entertain acts of aggression against its neighbors. We had a variety of discussions along that line.

* * * *

Q. A lot of people in this country say that they're tired of the Iraqi threats toward their country. Would it mean any military might in the near future that will end up in toppling the regime in Iraq, and would you increase your troops in the region?

Secretary Rumsfeld. The United States government, for a number of years now, has believed that the solution in Iraq would be regime change. That is to say that their current regime has, by its behavior, its repression of its own people, by its invasion of Kuwait, by its development of weapons of mass destruction, by its continued violations of the no-fly zones, by its unwillingness to release prisoners from Kuwait, by its unwillingness to return archives and records that were stolen, by a whole host of acts and indications of behavior that are harmful to the region.

So the U.S. policy favoring regime change is something that for a number of years has been the policy and the conviction of successive governments in our country. Towards that end, obviously, we have been participating with coalition forces in attempting to enforce the no-fly zone. We have been working with Kuwait and other countries, with respect to other aspects of the U.N. resolutions, sanctions and so forth. What might take place prospectively is not something that is for me to be talking about. But clearly, if you want the policy of our country, it is that the regime of Saddam Hussein is a destabilizing factor of the region.

Q. When you say that Iraq is lying. That story mentioned having weapons—

Secretary Rumsfeld. Sometimes I understate for emphasis.

Q. I don't think I missed the point. But it was a two part thing, that were not developing and that they did not have any. Were they lying about one, or both?

Secretary Rumsfeld. No. They have them and they continue to develop them and they have weaponized chemical weapons, we know that. They've had an active program to develop nuclear weapons. It's also clear that they are actively developing biological weapons. I don't know what other kinds of weapons would fall under the rubric of weapons of mass destruction, but if there are more, I suspect they're working on them as well, even though I don't happen to know what they are. It is just false, not true, inaccurate and typical.

Q. During your tenure do you expect to see regime change in Iraq?

Secretary Rumsfeld. Oh, I would certainly hope so. I would think most of the people in the region and in the world recognize that the world would be a better place without that regime. That regime threatens its neighbors repeatedly; it is listed on the terrorist list for the world that every one knows. They are not a model of good behavior.

Q. I want to ask about the Kuwaiti detainees in Guantanamo Bay and what's coming up concerning them? Did you discuss this issue with the Kuwaitis you met here?

Secretary Rumsfeld. We did indeed. It came up on several occasions. We have invited representatives from the Kuwaiti government to visit and to meet with the individuals who we captured in Afghanistan during the conflict. The purpose of the visit clearly would be to assist in intelligence gathering and second, to determine the extent to which there may be any law enforcement interests with respect to those individuals.

What we are doing in Guantanamo Bay, Cuba, is we have taken there a number of people from Afghanistan that were captured from a variety of different nationalities, and have people from our country and from other countries meeting with them and asking questions to try to gather intelligence so that we can prevent additional attacks on our country, our forces, and our friends and our allies. To the extent that when we gather that intelligence, we then provide it to the countries involved so that they too can have foreknowledge, to the extent possible, of attacks that were being planned.

We take that information from these hundreds of people and mesh it with the information we get when we capture a safe house for example, and take it from a computer, or a pager, or a cell phone, and papers, materials, and go through all of that and try to fit together a picture of what the plans are and who the other people may be who might be connected, and who is providing the money for them and who is helping them, who's facilitating their movement between countries with illegal passports and how they operate. We have found training manuals that show that they are very skillful in denying and deceiving interrogators as to who they are, and they constantly change their stories.

So it is a process that takes some time, and it's moving along, it's moving along well and we know of certain knowledge that by virtue of the coalition forces' efforts in capturing people and then interrogating them, by virtue of the materials that have been captured in caves and tunnels, and safe houses and compounds, by virtue of the people who have been arrested in other countries and interrogated, that is all that information comes together and the world that is together in trying to stop global terrorism is better informed, better able to stop those types of things.

Now, what we do with the detainees in the Guantanamo Bay is recognize that because of their skill in avoiding interrogation and how well they've been trained to do that, that it takes some months, and takes time and we have to be patient and wait until they decide that suddenly it is in their interest to talk. We've had some people who have been captured for a different purpose, and for a whole year they wouldn't say much, and after a year they would. With respect to the specifics of the Kuwaiti detainees, I think there is twelve or thirteen, I can't remember. Twelve? The representatives of the government will be meeting with them and we'll be discussing their disposition with them.

* * * *

Q. When Vice President Cheney came to the region several months ago, we heard from many Arab leaders that no action against Iraq should be taken until the conflict between Israel and the Palestinians had calmed down somewhat. Did you get a similar message from the Kuwaiti officials that you met?

Secretary Rumsfeld. First of all, I don't want to, by answering, agree with the premise of your question that that is what happened during Vice President Cheney's visit.

Q. But there were many public statements made.

Secretary Rumsfeld. Well, I've set it aside. So in my answer I will not indicate that I think that that's an accurate representation of his trip. Second I would say, I am trying to think if it has come up at all in that context, in this visit. If it did, and I don't recall it, it must have been off to the side as an issue. I guess I don't think it did come up that way. But in answering it that way, I'm kind of saying what the representatives of Kuwait have said, and it's not my business to do that. But it certainly was not a subject of considerable discussion. Third, I would point out that the Arab and Israeli issues, the Palestinian issues with Israel, have been going on all of my adult life.

It is a very complicated set of issues between Israel and the Palestinians, and it is important that the international community work with both sides to try to solve it. Goodness knows President Bush and Secretary Powell, as well as leaders from other countries—Crown Prince Abdullah of Saudi Arabia, and President Mubarak, who is in the United States at the present time, King Abdullah of Jordan, so many world leaders—have been making efforts to assist with that problem. But if anyone thinks that it is going to, within some near time frame, be resolved, I think that is high hopes.

We ought to work on it, we've got to find first a way to get a more secure situation so that the conditions for a peace process would be improved, but I think that the cast of your question is something that is unrealistic.

Remarks by Secretary of State Powell, June 12, 2002

Secretary Colin Powell delivered his remarks after the meeting of G-8 Foreign Ministers in Whistler, Canada.

Good afternoon, ladies and gentlemen. We just finished a, I think, very useful set of discussions among the G-8 foreign ministers. We talked about, as you know, counterterrorism, we talked about Afghanistan, we talked about the situation in India and Pakistan.

With respect to the counter-terrorism discussions, I'm quite pleased at the seriousness with which my G-8 colleagues continue to take the campaign against terrorism, and I'm pleased with the commitments that they continue to make on what they will do internally, what they will do to help nations that need their capability to be enhanced to be more effective members of the campaign against terrorism, especially implementing the requirements of U.N. Resolution 1373 on financial assault against the terrorist financial infrastructure. I sensed a clear commitment that we all have to help other nations who may not have the same technical ability and financial ability as we have to go after that.

So I think I can say that the coalition remains united and we have had a chance, I hope, or will have a chance shortly, to see the statement that we put out. The coalition remains united in this campaign against terrorism.

On Afghanistan, we had a good discussion. We are pleased at the progress we have made over the last seven or eight months, pleased that the loya jirga is underway, and we wait for the results of that meeting. We recognize, at the same time, that despite the progress that has been made, there is much more work we have to do. I encouraged all of my colleagues to make sure that the financial commitments that were made are lived up to. I take note of the fact that the United States committed itself to some $300 million in the first year, and we have already provided somewhere in the neighborhood of $360 million, so we are oversubscribed. The need is real, the need is great. We were all pleased at the progress that has been made. We will continue to follow the situation closely, stay in close touch with one another, as we help the Afghan authority expand its control from Kabul out to the rest of the country, and as we make sure that the money that goes into the central government is used in a most effective way. So a lot has been done; a lot remains to be done.

We note that the Turkish government will be taking over the Turkish armed forces; the ISAF mission beginning at the beginning of next month. And, of course, in due course, at the end of the year we'll have to identify another nation to pick up that responsibility, and we'll begin that dialogue in the weeks ahead.

Then, finally, on India/Pakistan and the situation there, I thank all my colleagues for the work they have done along side of us in talking to the Pakistanis and the Indians to impress upon them the need to find a political solution, and we're all gratified that in the last several days we have seen some steps to diffuse this crisis; some beginning steps. The tension is still there, the danger is still there, but the assurances that President Musharraf gave to us and, in turn, passed on to the Indian government, conveyed earlier by the administration and this past weekend reaffirmed by Deputy Secretary Armitage, that these would be permanent changes, permanent ending of the line of control, infiltration and crossings, and I think we now are moving in the right direction with the reciprocal steps that the Indians have taken.

Secretary Rumsfeld did meetings in New Delhi and is now in Islamabad where he'll meet with Pakistani officials, and I look forward to getting reports from Don of those conversations.

So with that, I will take your questions for a few moments. Todd?

Q. Can you say anything—I'm not asking you to be undiplomatic at this gathering, but is there anything that can be said about which nations might not have been as forthcoming as they might have been in commitment to Afghanistan, and was there any frank discussion today about how that could be done or—

Secretary Powell. We didn't go over a list of nations and what they committed to and how much they paid to this point. I think the nations that were in the room have made very strong commitments to Afghanistan and they're all going to their different parliaments and legislatures to come up with the money, and then convert commitments into actual funds. So I have no doubt that they will honor all of the commitments they have made. I'm just encouraging them to do it as quickly as possible because the need is great. We've got to make sure we keep a cash flow going to the authority.

Q. Are all the nations here in agreement that ISAF should remain in Kabul, or do some of the other countries think that should be expanded throughout the country?

Secretary Powell. Nobody specifically asked for an extension, although there was a discussion of that possibility, and we went through the history of ISAF and how it came out of the Bonn conference and initially it was to go to Kabul. Over the course of the last several months, we've examined the security situation throughout the country. It isn't as unstable as it was believed to be, and we believe the proper investment now is not to try to find forces from expanded ISAF but to concentrate on building up the Afghan army, the Afghan police force, and using them, along with the extension of central power, out to the regions to bring under control those regional leaders or warlords, as some of them might be called, to extend political control over them, use the financial tools available to help with that, and ultimately build up the Afghan army and police force so they can police their own country. And that really is the right solution, as opposed to additional foreign forces going in at this time. None of my colleagues made a recommendation to expand ISAF. We kind of reviewed the history of ISAF.

Q. Did you encounter questions or skepticism about the President's strike force policy?

Secretary Powell. It didn't come up. We didn't have a discussion about it, but, you know, we'll have discussions tonight and more discussions tomorrow. It didn't come up, but I don't think it will be a neuralgic subject for discussion.

Statement by United Nations Secretary General Annan, June 13, 2002

The Secretary-General warmly congratulates Hamid Karzai on his election by the Loya Jirga as the head of the Afghan Transitional Authority. The Secretary-General has been following closely the proceedings of the Loya Jirga. He welcomes the enthusiastic embrace of this democratic process by the Afghan people and their leaders. Today's election constitutes an important step towards peace and stability in Afghanistan, following the path set out in the Bonn Agreement.

The Secretary-General urges delegates to continue to use the peaceful forum of the Loya Jirga to pursue national reconciliation and to create a representative Government. He looks forward to the successful completion of the Loya Jirga's work and the inauguration of the new Transitional Authority.

Remarks by Secretary of Defense Rumsfeld and Pakistani Foreign Minister Sattar, June 13, 2002

Secretary Donald Rumsfeld and Minister Abdul Sattar delivered their remarks in Islamabad, Pakistan.

Q. Mr. Minister, what is Pakistan's perception of al Qaeda cells being inside this country, and would Pakistan allow U.S. troops to go after those cells potentially on their own?

Foreign Minister Sattar. Pakistani authorities are doing all that we can in order to locate and identify any al Qaeda cells or individuals in our country. We are very grateful to the United States for the assistance that U.S. agencies have provided to us in the form of locating these people, their addresses and so on. All the operations against these people have been conducted by Pakistani forces. Police, paramilitary forces have conducted these operations, and while I can't presume to speak for the secretary, my general perception is that the U.S. is satisfied with the work that our own forces have been doing in order to take action against al Qaeda individuals and cells who manage to enter Pakistan.

Q. Do you believe that it's a significant number here?

Foreign Minister Sattar. Well, as you know, only a few weeks ago, with the help of the U.S. agencies, we were able to locate quite a few people in Faisalabad and in Lahore. And I am very glad to say that our forces conducted a most efficient operation overnight and were able to apprehend and arrest these people for further action. And we continue to welcome such assistance from the United States.

Secretary Rumsfeld. Let me—may I just comment on it briefly? The cooperation we have received from this government has been truly wonderful. We have received— every reasonable approach has been responded to in a responsible and a constructive and a prompt way. The cross-border operation is a difficult situation. If people can move across the border in remote locations, it is a complication, it's a scene in a difficult effort to track down people. Even there, if you think about it, this government, despite the tension on their eastern border, has kept large numbers of troops on their western border, on their Afghanistan border, enabling us to do work on the Afghan side of the border that has been very, very helpful.

So I would also add that the government here has arrested—I don't know how many people, but a very large number of al Qaeda and Taliban. We have benefited from that by intelligence gathering information that has helped the United States and other countries all across the globe in gathering information and intelligence that enables us to work to prevent additional terrorist attacks. We've got to keep in mind what this is about: this is about people who go around the world killing innocent men women and children, and our task is to gather information so we can stop those attacks from happening.

Remarks by Secretary of State Powell, June 20, 2002

Secretary Colin Powell delivered his remarks at a World Refugee Day event.

To look into the face of a refugee woman is to peer into the very eyes of the exodus. Mirrored in them are memories of fear and flight, of devastation and despair. But when those extraordinary eyes look back at your, they are also the eyes of hope, and surely they are the eyes of a heroine.

Of the 22 million refugees and others under the care of UNHCR in the world today, 18 million are women and children. We have seen it again and again, from Cambodia to Colombia, from Kosovo to Congo, from Liberia to Bosnia, from Sierra Leone to East Timor to Afghanistan. Wherever tyranny and terror, conflict and chaos, force families to flee their homelands, it is the women—it is the women—who become the most vulnerable to the worst kind of violence. And is it also the women who play the most vital roles in their families' survival.

For them, every new day brings life or death, burdens and dangers. Most often it falls to refugee women to provide the family's income and to provide an education for the children. It is most often up to them to search for fuel, food, water, medicine—the very bare essentials of life. They risk bullets, land mines and rape to provide the little that their families need just to survive.

The strengths refugee women bring are also critical to the functioning of the refugee camps, and when safe returns are possible, their contributions have proven crucial to the recovery and reconstruction of their home countries.

Afghanistan has been much in the headlines, and we are privileged indeed to welcome today Safia Jahed, an Afghan refugee woman. In a few moments, you will hear her story. After a harrowing journey out of Afghanistan, she and her family lived as refugees in Pakistan. They have resettled in the United States and now live in Virginia.

Safia is only one of the five million Afghans who were driven from their country during more than two decades of invasion, civil war, and most recently Taliban oppression. And each of them, every single one of them, has a compelling story to tell.

Yet I know Safia would be the first to remind us that there are refugees in need of protection and assistance not just in Afghanistan, but in every continent. This is a worldwide challenge, and meeting it requires a strong, sustained commitment from the entire world.

As President Bush has so strongly stated, the United States will continue to be a global leader on behalf of refugees. Decade after decade, ordinary Americans throughout our country have generously supported worldwide refugee relief efforts, and communities across America also have opened their hearts and their homes to refugees in need.

And here I want to single out the outstanding young winners of UNHCR's poster competition. These youngsters represent hometowns all across our great country. Now their artistry is on display here in the nation's capital, and we are all so proud of these young people.

It is often said that America is a nation of immigrants. We are also a nation of refugees. And as President Bush said in his statement, refugees who have settled here in the United States have given back so much in return, contributing to America's great vibrancy and our great diversity. America's commitment to refugees is enduring. It is about who we are as a people.

The Bush Administration will not permit the attacks of September 11th and the continuing threat from terrorism to shake our nation's commitment to refugees. That commitment speaks to our most fundamental values—values of compassion, tolerance and humanity; values that are the antithesis of everything that terrorists stand for. We will continue to afford refugees the full range of protection and assistance, and we will continue to be the world's leader in refugee resettlement.

The United States will maintain our support to UNHCR and other international agencies and their partners, the many private voluntary organizations that are devoted to easing the plight of refugees. These dedicated humanitarians often risk their own lives to bring relief to the suffering. It is noble work, indeed.

And America will continue to be a champion of refugee women. We will promote programs to protect them from sexual and gender-based violence. We will foster their economic self-reliance. We will work to ensure their participation in the management of refugee camps, and we will help improve their access and that of their children to health care and education.

The powerful photographs here on display at Union Station and the wonderful refugee groups who are performing over the next week will give tens of thousands of visitors a chance to look into the faces of the world's refugees; faces of different colors, from a great variety of cultures—all children of the same creator; faces that tell stories of strength, stories of courage, and above all stories of hope. Today, with caring people all around the globe, we renew our pledge to keep that precious hope alive, now and forever.

Statement by United Nations Secretary-General Annan, June 12, 2002

The following statement was delivered on behalf of Secretary-General Kofi Annan by Assistant Secretary-General for Political Affairs Danilo Turk to the Organization for Security and Cooperation in Europe (OSCE) High-level Conference on Preventing and Combating Terrorism in Lisbon, Portugal.

The scale of the terrorist attacks that took place on 11 September last year has prompted an unprecedented international effort to coordinate action in the fight against terrorism.

International and regional organizations have responded swiftly to this new challenge, and have placed terrorism clearly on their agendas. Now, the challenge is to make international efforts effective.

The spread of terrorism is a threat to the very foundations of the United Nations, and to the spirit of its Charter. Over the years, the Organization has played an important role in establishing a legal framework for the eradication of terrorism through one of its basic roles: the codification of international law—more specifically through 12 United Nations anti-terrorist conventions and protocols. These conventions must be strictly observed and effectively implemented if terrorism is to be defeated.

More recently, and especially since 1999, the Security Council has emphasized that international terrorism constitutes a threat to international peace and security. In its resolution 1373, the Security Council underscored the need to fight terrorists and those who aid, harbour or support them. The Council established a Counter-Terrorism Committee that is currently reviewing the measures taken by United Nations Member States to implement that resolution. The international community should ensure that appropriate assistance will be made available to States in need of help in implementing resolution 1373.

While the international community must be resolute in countering terrorism, it must be scrupulous in the ways in which this effort is pursued. The fight against terrorism should not lead to the adoption of measures that are incompatible with human rights standards. Such a development would hand a victory to those who so blatantly disregard human rights in their use of terror. Greater respect for human rights, accompanied by democracy and social justice, will in the long term prove effective measures against terror. The design and enforcement of means to fight terrorism should, therefore, be carried out in strict adherence with international human rights obligations.

Nor should the current focus on counter-terrorism obscure the wider work of the United Nations and other international organizations. Indeed, key areas of work of the Organization's global mission, such as disarmament, controls over weapons of mass destruction, and crime prevention, are directly related to the fight against terrorism.

This conference is an important contribution to the efforts of the international community to rise to this challenge in a spirit of cooperation. I wish you all success in your deliberations.

Remarks by Secretary of State Powell, June 13, 2002

Secretary of State Powell was interviewed by CTV news in Whistler, Canada during the G-8 Foreign Ministers Conference.

Q. I know the United States has also given advice to Canada on improving its security as a result of September 11th. There is a perception in the U.S. that Canada is a gateway for terrorists, and I'd like your thoughts on that.

Secretary Powell. Well, Canada is a marvelous gateway into the United States, and we treasure that. We want to have an open relationship with Canada and, frankly, with the nations around the world. We are a nation of immigrants. We are a nation that welcomes people to come to our shores, to resettle in the United States, to go to school, to get healthcare, to visit our country. One of the ways to get there is through Canada. At the same time, we, in light of 9/11, have to do a better job of knowing who is coming, and do we know enough about them? Have we checked them to make sure they are coming to behave properly in our country and, once in our country, will we know when it is time for them to leave our country because a visa has expired or it's, for other reasons, time for them to go?

So, working with Canada, we are trying to do a better job of remaining an open society, but a society that also protects itself and defends itself. The first obligation of any government is to protect its citizens. Canada has the same challenge. So I am very pleased that the collaboration that has taken place between Minister Manley and Senator Tom Ridge, working on homeland security issues and with my department, the State Department, and the Ministry of Foreign Affairs working on those areas that are within their purview. So Canada understands this as well. They understand that they are not only protecting us, but protecting Canada and Canadian citizens, and I am very pleased at the level of cooperation.

Q. At this moment, then, you feel confident that Canada isn't, as we've been hearing, a haven for terrorist organizations.

Secretary Powell. No, I never would have said that. There is no doubt that there are terrorists in Canada; there are terrorists in the United States. We discovered that on 9/11. None of us is free from that scourge. What we have to do is work closely together with intelligence exchange, law-enforcement exchange, cooperation, how to defend our borders going back and forth, how to do a better job of getting into their financial network to see how they're financing all of this activity in order to protect ourselves.

Nobody is immune. And to the extent that there are terrorists, Canada, the one thing I'm sure of in the Canadian authority is that every level and every ministry are doing everything they can to find them and bring them to justice.

Q. I want to also talk about Iraq on this, because certainly since September 11th, it seems, even again here, that the—Canada and the EU are looking for more assurances that there was some kind of role by Iraq in those attacks before they would agree to any kind of military action. Was that at all part of your mission here to convince them of taking military action?

Secretary Powell. No, that was not a subject for the G-8 ministerial meeting. Essentially, we talked about a number of issues preparing our respective governments before the head of state, head of government meeting that will take place in Kananaskis. Obviously, we did talk about proliferation activities in Iraq. There is no dispute among the ministers that Iraq has been pursuing weapons of mass destruction and the means to deliver them. This is of concern to all of us. We all work together within the United Nations to keep sanctions in place and to keep pushing to get inspectors back into Iraq.

Now, as a separate U.S. policy, we believe that Iraq would be better served with another regime, new leadership. That is a goal of U.S. policy. But we discussed with our friends around the world, through all of the ministers here from the G-8, why we think that is important. But, at the moment, the President does not have a military plan on his desk and he is not ready to make any decisions beyond those decisions that are now to our friends. The President has assured all of them that as he starts to move forward, if and when he does, he will consult with our friends. So I was not sent here to put together any combat operations.

Q. You think people get nervous as a result of—

Secretary Powell. People should be nervous about the fact that there is a country such as Iraq with all that wealth available to it through oil, that is using that wealth to develop chemical, biological and even nuclear weapons, if they could get their hands on them, in order to threaten innocent people throughout the Persian Gulf region, and in due course perhaps even threaten us here, this far away. That capability might well fall in the hands of terrorists. So, while people focus on will the United States take military action or not, and that causes them to be agitated, they're going to be more agitated about what's going on in Iraq and the nature of that regime.

Q. Why doesn't the United States then stop using the oil from Iraq?

Secretary Powell. Oil is a fungible commodity that goes into the world market. What we have been able to do—and then it's available. What we have been able to do, though, is control the funds going into Iraq, for the most part through the oil-for-food program. There's still about two to three billion dollars a year that gets out through smuggling activities from outlying states. But the United States, working with its Security Council colleagues, we have been, I think, quite successful in the past year in putting in place a "smart sanctions" regime, as we call it, which the U.N. approved last month, that will continue to control the money that goes to the regime and will control it in a way that that money, when it comes to the oil-for-food program, will go for goods that help people, that help the economy. We're not against the people of Iraq, just the regime. But the money will not go for any technology or any equipment that might be used for the development of a weapon of mass destruction.

Q. When we talk about the global good, then, certainly the term "unilateralists" has been hurled at the United States, saying that they won't participate in any international treaties, Kyoto land mines, war crimes, this kind of thing; that it's sort of a "my way or the doorway" concept. I wonder if that perception matters to you.

Secretary Powell. It's a perception that does matter to us, but it's not a perception that's based in reality. It's an easy claim to make and it's an easy charge to throw when somebody disagrees with us on a particular position we might have taken with respect to, say, Kyoto or the international criminal court when we have a disagreement with our friends. But having a disagreement with our friends doesn't mean we're unilateralist, "my way or the doorway". It means that we have failed to persuade you of a principle position that we hold. We've failed to persuade our friends. But the amount of consultation that we do: President Bush's recent trip to Europe, President Bush signing a treaty in Moscow, reducing the number of nuclear weapons both the United States and Russia will have, President Bush signing a political declaration in Moscow with President Putin on a way focusing to bring Russia to the west, President Bush then going to Rome and, with his NATO colleagues, initialing another agreement that creates a NATO/Russia council, President Bush's summit meeting with the European Union, the amount of time he spends with foreign leaders and, if I may humbly say, the amount of time I spend looking in the multilateral community, suggests, to me anyway, that we are all doing all we can to consult with our friends. But when we disagree on an issue that we have strong feelings about, an issue of principle, because we don't join the consensus doesn't mean that we don't respect the consensus and respect the views of others. But if we feel strongly about something, then we feel we have to move in that direction. And sometimes we turn out not to have been wrong.

Last year there was a huge outcry, and my Canadian colleagues particularly were pretty scathing, some of them, in their criticism of the fact that the United States might leave the ABM Treaty. It was going to create an arms race, it was going to destabilize the world, it was going to break up relations with Russia, and we were being unilateralists and it was the wrong thing to do. Well, today, the 13th of June, the ABM Treaty went out of existence, and we have signed new agreements with Moscow, there is no arms race, and we are now permitted to develop technology to protect us from rogue states developing weapons of mass destruction and delivering them in missiles.

So sometimes the positions we take are seen as unilateral and are going to be so destructive turn out not to be destructive and turn out, perhaps, to have been the right answer.

Q. You know, in a couple of weeks, the leaders are coming here for the full G-8 session, and the priority or the focus of the Canada Prime Minister has been on Africa.

And I wonder if you feel that that should be a secondary position based on the war on terrorism, or if you think they should alter the agenda.

Secretary Powell. I'm sure the Prime Minister will come up with an agenda that will reflect what the G-8 leaders want to talk about. Clearly, we will have to talk about the campaign against terrorism, and clearly we will have to talk about how to help developing nations, and Africa is an area of special concern because of poverty, because of economic distress, especially in sub-Saharan Africa, and because of the added problem of HIV/AIDS. You can be sure that the United States will be interested in participating in that.

We've been doing a lot with respect to Africa, the African Growth and Opportunity Act which makes it easier for Africans to sell products in the United States, and the Millennium Challenge Account which President Bush announced a couple of months ago that is adding five billion dollars a year of additional funding going to those nations that are committed to democracy and economic reform, and to help them develop the infrastructure to attract both aid and trade. A lot of that money will be going to African states. But we believe that with this particular account, we have to also make it available to other nations. [*Inaudible*] has great needs, and I'm pleased that the Prime Minister is focusing on those needs. There are other areas in the world that have great needs as well. You can be sure that the United States will be more than willing to participate in an extended dialogue on Africa, along with Prime Minister Chretien, so we'll make the case that there are other nations in the world.

United Nations Security Council Resolution 1419, June 26, 2002

The Security Council,

Reaffirming its previous resolutions on Afghanistan, in particular its resolution 1383 (2001) of 6 December 2001,

Reaffirming also its strong commitment to the sovereignty, independence, territorial integrity and national unity of Afghanistan,

Reaffirming also its strong commitment to help the people of Afghanistan to bring to an end the tragic conflicts in Afghanistan and promote lasting peace, stability, and respect for human rights,

Reaffirming also its strong support for international efforts to root out terrorism, in keeping with the Charter of the United Nations, and reaffirming also its resolutions 1368 (2001) of 12 September 2001 and 1373 (2001) of 28 September 2001,

Reiterating its endorsement of the Agreement on Provisional Arrangements in Afghanistan Pending the Re-establishment of Permanent Government Institutions, signed in Bonn on 5 December 2001 (S/2001/1154) (the Bonn Agreement), and welcoming initial steps for its implementation, including the establishment of the Human Rights and Judicial Commissions,

1. Welcomes the successful and peaceful holding, from 11 June to 19 June, of the Emergency Loya Jirga opened by former King Mohammed Zaher, the "Father of the

Nation," and notes with particular satisfaction the large participation of women, as well as the representation of all ethnic and religious communities;

2. Commends the Afghan people for the success of the Emergency Loya Jirga and encourages them to continue to exercise their inalienable right to determine freely their own political future;

3. Welcomes the election, by the Emergency Loya Jirga, of the Head of State, President Hamid Karzai, and the establishment of the Transitional Authority;

4. Reiterates its strong support for the Transitional Authority in the full implementation of the Bonn Agreement, including the establishment of a Constitutional Commission, and in strengthening the central government, building a S/RES/1419 (2002) national army and police force, implementing demobilization/reintegration activities and improving the security situation throughout Afghanistan, combating illicit drug trafficking, ensuring respect for human rights, implementing judicial sector reform, establishing the basis for a sound economy and reconstructing productive capacity and infrastructure;

5. Calls on all Afghan groups, in this regard, to cooperate fully with the Transitional Authority in order to complete the process according to the Bonn Agreement and to implement the decisions of the Emergency Loya Jirga;

6. Urges the Transitional Authority to build on efforts of the Interim Administration to eradicate the annual poppy crop;

7. Urges also the Transitional Authority to build further on efforts of the Interim Administration to promote the welfare and interests of Afghan women and children and to provide education to boys and girls;

8. Commends the role of the United Nations system in support of efforts by the Afghans, reiterates its strong support for the Special Representative of the Secretary-General, Mr. Lakhdar Brahimi, and the staff of the United Nations Assistance Mission in Afghanistan (UNAMA), and reaffirms its endorsement of the full authority of the Special Representative of the Secretary-General, in accordance with its relevant resolutions, over the planning and conduct of all United Nations activities in Afghanistan;

9. Commends also the contribution of the International Security Assistance Force (ISAF) in providing a secure environment for the Emergency Loya Jirga;

10. Stresses once again the importance of continued international support to complete the process according to the Bonn Agreement, calls upon donor countries that pledged financial aid at the Tokyo conference to fulfil their commitments promptly and calls upon all Member States to support the Transitional Authority and to provide long-term assistance, as well as current budget support, for the current expenses of the Transitional Authority, and for the social and economic reconstruction and rehabilitation of Afghanistan as a whole;

11. Calls for significantly greater and more rapid international assistance to the vast number of Afghan refugees and internally displaced persons to facilitate their orderly return and effective reintegration into society in order to contribute to the stability of the entire country;

12. Calls upon all Afghan groups to support full and unimpeded access by humanitarian organizations to people in need and to ensure the safety and security of humanitarian workers;

13. Decides to remain actively seized of the matter.

Remarks by Secretary of State Powell, June 30, 2002

Secretary Colin Powell was interviewed on Fox News by Tony Snow.

Q. Al Gore gave a speech last night. I want to show you part of the speech because he is criticizing your administration's handling of affairs in the Middle East and also the war on terror:

"President Bush, unfortunately, has allowed his political team to use the war as a political wedge to divide Americans. They haven't gotten Osama bin Laden or the al-Qaida operation and they have refused to allow enough troops from the international community to be put into Afghanistan to keep it from sliding back under control of the warlords."

Your reaction?

Secretary Powell. With all due respect to former Vice President Gore, that's patent nonsense. We have a good situation in Afghanistan. We have gotten rid of the Taliban. Al-Qaida is on the run, and we'll chase them down. It's time-consuming. I notice the previous administration didn't even make a serious try at it.

And we have just seen a Loya Jirga which continued the authority in Kabul under President Karzai, and we have 12,000 troops there under Operation Enduring Freedom going after the Taliban remnants and al-Qaida, and we have an International Security Assistance Force in Kabul and we are constantly reviewing the security situation in the region. Hundreds of millions of dollars are going into the reconstruction of the Afghan society. We have pulled together a very effective international coalition to help the people of Afghanistan achieve a better future.

Q. There were reports today that there's a handwritten note from Usama bin Laden to one of his lieutenants after the Tora Bora bombings, indicating that he certainly survived that. In addition, there's an op-ed piece today in The Washington Post by Monsoor Ijaz and also a former American ambassador to Sudan arguing that the Sudanese had offered—here, just read part of it. It's from Tim Carney and Monsoor Ijaz and here's a quote:

"Three months later, after offering to hand bin Laden over to U.S. authorities, Sudan expelled him. Sudan gave U.S. authorities permission to photograph two terror camps. Washington failed to follow up. In August, Sudan"—this is back in the '90s—"sent an olive branch letter to President Clinton through Ijaz. There was no reply."

Secretary Powell. Well, perhaps that's what Vice President Gore should have been talking about, what happened on their watch, as opposed to the progress we've made on our watch, not only in Afghanistan, but I would also submit in Sudan. We recently sent as a presidential emissary to Sudan Senator Jack Danforth. He had very successful trips there. We now have a policy with respect to Sudan that will start to move them in the direction of cooperating with us in the campaign against terrorism, and to move forward to find a peaceful solution to that terrible crisis in the Sudan.

* * * *

Q. It was interesting. In the President's speech he did not mention Saudi Arabia. The Israeli Defense Forces have come up with this series of documents—I have them here and I'm told that they've been sent to the State Department—that indicate that there have been large sums of moneys transferred from Saudi Arabia to a number of terrorist organizations.

We are showing on the screen right now a translation of one of them. It lists a number of suicide bombers, the dates on which—the dates and locations on which their acts took place, and then the family payments, which are in Saudi riyals.

Are you persuaded that the Saudi Government is doing everything it can to stop financing terror and stop Saudi citizens from doing so?

Secretary Powell. Well, first of all, with respect to references to Saudi Arabia in the President's speech, there was not a specific reference but I think as you know, Tony, we have been very appreciative of the role that Saudi Arabia has played, and especially Crown Prince Abdullah, in putting forward a vision for the Palestinian people of how we can find a solution to this crisis.

With respect to payments to organizations such as Hamas and similar organizations, we have spoken to our Arab friends, and the President has made reference to this in his speech, that this kind of payment should stop. I haven't seen that specific piece of paper, but from what I see of what you put on the screen, the Saudis would say that they are not giving it to an organization, they are giving it to individuals in need. Nevertheless, I think it's a real problem when you incentivize in any way suicide bombings.

Remarks by President Bush, July 8, 2002

Q. We continue to see reports on the state of planning to get rid of Saddam Hussein in Iraq. I know it's unlikely that you'll share any details with us, though we'd be delighted to hear them, sir—

President Bush. Somebody else thinks they are, evidently.

Q. But I wonder, Mr. President, regardless of when or how, is it your firm intention to get rid of Saddam Hussein in Iraq—

President Bush. Yes.

Q. —and how hard to you think it will be?

President Bush. It's the stated policy of this government to have a regime change. And it hasn't changed. And we'll use all tools at our disposal to do so.

I actually didn't read the whole story about somebody down there at level five flexing some "know-how" muscle, but there's all kind—listen, I recognize there's speculation out there. But people shouldn't speculate about the desire of the government to have a regime change. And there's ways, different ways to do it.

Q. How involved are you in the planning, sir? We know that you meet with General Franks, you meet with Rumsfeld to talk about this. How involved are you?

President Bush. I'm involved. I mean, I'm involved in the military planning, diplomatic planning, financial planning, all aspects of—reviewing all the tools at my disposal. And—but in my remarks to American people, I remind them I'm a patient person and there's a—but I do firmly believe that the world will be safer and more peaceful if there's a regime change in that government.

* * * *

Q. Does your promise on—or your goal of catching Osama bin Laden dead or alive, does that still stand?

President Bush. I don't know if he is dead or alive, for starters—so I'm going to answer your question with a hypothetical. Osama bin Laden, he may be alive. If he is, we'll get him. If he's not alive, we got him.

But the issue is bigger than one person. That's what I keep trying to explain to the American people. We're talking about networks that need to be disrupted, plans that need to be stopped. These people are cold-blooded killers. They're interested in killing innocent Americans, still. And, therefore, we will continue to pursue them.

And I understand the frustrations of this war. Everybody wants to be a war correspondent. They want to go out there and see the tanks moving across the plains or the airplanes flying in formation and—but that's not the way this war is going to be fought all the time. There's a lot of actions that take place that you'll never see. And there's—and some of it, hopefully, will continue to take place as a result of the actions of our friends, such as that which took place in the Philippines—Abu Sayyaf, the leader evidently was killed by Philippine troops. And that's positive. That's a positive development.

We're constantly working with nations that might become havens for terrorists, to make sure that there's no place for them to bunch up or train or to—and it's—and we're making progress. But it's a long journey, and that's what people have got to know.

White House Press Briefing, July 10, 2002

Q. Does the President see any contradiction between saying at his news conference, telling us that the war on terrorism didn't depend on the fate of bin Laden, depending on one man, at the same time he's planning to use 250,000 Americans to go after one man in Iraq, Saddam Hussein?

Mr. Fleischer. Well, one, I don't see a connection between the two, other—

Q. You don't? One man?

Mr. Fleischer.—than the United States is involved in a war against terror. And two, vis-á-vis Iraq, as you know, I'm not going to comment on anything that is or is not a potential military plan. But the President—

Q. There is no plan? Every day we read there is a plan.

Mr. Fleischer. The President has indicated that he's made no decisions, and he's dismissed some of the recent speculation by people who are not in a position to know what he knows.

Remarks by Secretary of Defense Rumsfeld, July 15, 2002

Secretary Donald Rumsfeld was interviewed on CNBC by Brian Williams.

Q. Every major American newspaper and newscast has had details of various war plans in Iraq that are in front of this President, or near this President, that he will be looking at. Why telegraph U.S. options militarily on the ground in Iraq?

Secretary Rumsfeld. Well, first of all, we're not telegraphing U.S. options on the ground. The United States government is not. The President has properly pointed out the repressiveness of that regime, and the fact that that regime is developing weapons of mass destruction that pose a real threat to the people of Iraq, to the people that live in the region, as well as to the people across the globe. This is a very dangerous regime. The President said that.

We have always had war plans and contingency plans and operation plans in this building. We had them 25 years ago, when I was Secretary of Defense, and we have them today. I've recently issued contingency guidance that has required that we review all of those plans, and there are dozens of them, for a whole host of both combatant contingencies, as well as non-combatant contingencies, such as evacuations, and that type of thing. We're reviewing all of them, and updating them. And we're elevating the risks, so that they can be judged, and they can be brought up to an appropriate level of potential value.

Every once in a while, there are people in the United States government who decide that they want to break Federal criminal law, and release classified information, and they ought to be imprisoned. And if we find out who they are, they will be imprisoned. It is putting peoples' lives at risk. It is making more difficult the task of finding ter-rorists across the globe. It is a serious violation of Federal criminal law. Why people do it, I do not know. They obviously want to make themselves look important, and they have favorite reporters and press people that they think they can curry favor with. And they go to them, and hand them things that ought not to be given to the public, and those—they then appear in a public press.

It happens that the piece that you're referring to, that was on the front page of The New York Times, is not something that was at a high level. It was apparently some-thing—we do—we don't know what it is. I've never seen it; General Franks has never seen it. Goodness knows, the President's never seen it. It was something that was done down at a lower level, either at somebody's request, or not at somebody's request, and it has no official blessing by anybody up at any reasonable level in the government of the United States. But nonetheless, it obviously goes out, and it represents what somebody who advises somebody at a lower level, thought was a good idea. So, they took that piece of paper, and gave it to a reporter.

I would dearly like to find them. I think that people who know who those people are would do the country a service if they'd let me know who those people are. And I'd like to see them behind bars.

Q. You seem quite angered by this particular leak, even though the President, at some point, will have to let the American people in on American plans in Iraq.

Secretary Rumsfeld. Wrong, you do not let anybody in on war plans.

Q. If you're committing a Desert Storm, Part Two? At some point—

Secretary Rumsfeld. If you have plans as to how one is going to conduct an operation, you do not let anybody know what those are, because the enemy knows what they are. The enemy is then able to take steps that will cause greater loss of life on the part of Americans, and coalition forces, and clearly, make more difficult the accomplishment of the task.

Q. Let me come at it this way. Saddam Hussein is in power, despite an American war against him. It is widely said that, even with 2, 300, 400,000 American troops, and all the technology this country has to bring to bear in that region, it will take, as an assist, an uprising from within to help to topple that regime, a stated and sworn enemy of the United States. Do you think the dissention is there inside Iraq?

Secretary Rumsfeld. Well, you never know. I think that to go back to Desert Storm, it's instructive that hundreds of Iraqi military people surrendered to privates and corporals in the United States Army; that tens of thousands, 70, 80,000 troops surrendered, within a matter of days. The regime of Saddam Hussein is so vicious, and killed so many of their own people, and used chemical weapons against their own people, and denies those people opportunities—the ability to travel, the ability to speak out. It is a—one of the most vicious regimes on the face of the earth.

Now, people that live in a regime like that don't like it. It is not the kind of thing that you can overthrow readily, but because it's so vicious, and there's so many people in prison, and so many people that have been shot and murdered by the Saddam Hussein regime. But any idea that the Iraqi people want to live like that would be just nonsensical, because people don't want to have to live like that.

* * * *

Q. Is the American stomach there for a two-front war, right now?

Secretary Rumsfeld. The American stomach is there to do what's right for the world, and for our country, and for the American people. And I guess in this instance, if one looks at the terrorist states that are developing weapons of mass destruction—

not just Iraq, but clearly, Iran and Syria and Libya and North Korea, and others—one has to say, "What is the responsibility of a government, if we know of reasonably certain knowledge, that within X number of months or years, one or more of those countries is going to have chemical, biological, and nuclear weapons that they have the ability to impose on the rest of the world. Is it better to wait until they do it, and have a perfect excuse, or reason for acting, and you act, after 500,000 or a million people are dead? Or is it better to do something beforehand, and save the lives of hundreds of thousands, or potentially millions, of people?"

That is the issue that our society, and our friends and allies around the world, and the American people, and our President, have to address. And it is the nexus between weapons of mass destruction, and terrorist organizations, and terrorist states. So, it's a big issue for our time.

Remarks by Deputy Secretary of Defense Wolfowitz, July 14, 2002

Deputy Secretary Paul Wolfowitz was interviewed on Turkish television by Mithat Bereket.

Q. Welcome to Turkey, to Istanbul, sir.

Yes, I mean it is nice to see you here and thanks a lot for sharing your time and let's start with a direct question. Nowadays, everybody is wondering about this. I mean two simple questions actually. "When" and "how" about the operation in Iraq? Very simple but very important questions. I mean, what is going on?

Deputy Secretary Wolfowitz. First of all, let me say something, which is that this is a visit that was actually planned back in last December but we had to postpone it two times. We finally got it on. And it is to discuss a whole range of U.S.-Turkish issues. We've got such a close relationship; even just in the defense field alone there are six or seven major things to discuss, from participation in Joint Strike Fighter to our peacekeeping operations in the Balkans to our work together in Afghanistan. And, of course, Iraq is one of those issues, but I think a lot of people are assuming that the United States has made a whole lot of decisions. The truth is, the President has stated very clearly a problem and he has presented that problem to his own government to think about solutions and he is interested in discussing with close friends, especially friends like Turkey, what the solutions are. And I am really here more to listen than to tell people we have decided this, this, and this, because we haven't. Turkey has some unique perspectives on this part of the world and it has some very substantial national interest in this part of the world, and I am really here to understand those better and to go back and help people in Washington understand those better.

Q. A lot of discussion is going at the moment about the possible operation on Iraq in the American press as well. I mean, in your opinion, what sort of an operation do you believe must be organized to topple Saddam Hussein?

Deputy Secretary Wolfowitz. There is a lot of discussion in press. Some of it is well informed and some of it isn't. There is a lot of discussion in the Administration. There is a recognition that this is a major issue, that there aren't simple answers, that it is very important to think it through, to think through not only how we achieve that result but how to make sure that when we achieve that result that the outcome is something that is good for everybody. And those issues that I don't have answers to, I have ideas; I am here to learn about Turkish ideas and be able to communicate some of those ideas back to my colleagues in Washington.

Q. So to sum this up, can we say that there is no decision taken yet in this Administration vis-á-vis an operation, a possible operation on Iraq?

Deputy Secretary Wolfowitz. That is a fair conclusion, and what again, I repeat, the President has said very clearly there is a problem there that we can't continue to live with indefinitely but we are open to all kinds of suggestions about what is the best way to deal with that problem. We have not made any decision, any final decisions yet.

Q. You mentioned briefly, but could you please elaborate: in your meetings in Ankara, what will you tell Turkish officials, I mean, what is the purpose of your visit?

Deputy Secretary Wolfowitz. The purpose of my visit, most of all, is to listen, to learn, to try to get a good feeling of the range of issues that exist between us, and obviously most importantly those that are in the defense area. But I shouldn't say most important—from my perspective the ones that I am most responsible for are in the defense area. Most important probably is if I can improve my understanding of Turkey's current economic situation and the things that Turkey would like to see from the United States by way of help. I am not an economist. I am not from the Treasury Department, but I can go back and give my perspective on what Turkey needs. And it is very important. Turkey's economic success is very important to the United States, because Turkey is a wonderful partner and a strong partner is what you want to have.

Q. Where do you place Turkey in this region? I mean, where does the American Administration place Turkey in this region: in the Middle East, or vis-á-vis Iraq, for example? I mean, what will be the expectations or what are the expectations from Turkey?

Deputy Secretary Wolfowitz. Well, for one thing we don't place Turkey in this region, we place Turkey in both straddling Europe and Asia, which gives Turkey a unique importance. And, frankly, for many years, I personally have understood Turkey's unique importance in the whole Muslim world. I was the American Ambassador for three years in Indonesia, which has the largest Muslim population of any country in the world. And I believe Indonesia and Turkey are the only two countries with Muslim majorities where Islam is not the state religion. As Americans, who believe in the importance of separating church and state, we think those examples are very valuable examples and we would like to see those become models of success for other countries. So we think of Turkey in many respects, but obviously in this region

Turkey is one of the strongest countries in this region, one of the biggest countries in this region, one of the most economically important countries in this region, and, of all of our allies, one of those most affected by what takes place in this region. So we have a lot to talk to Turkey about.

Q. And coming back to Iraq again, one of the biggest, let's say, worries or reservations of Turkey, vis-á-vis the Iraqi possible scenarios, is the integrity of Iraq. I mean, it seems that the Kurds in northern Iraq are eager for, at least, an autonomous northern Iraq, or maybe a federal state, after the toppling of Saddam Hussein. Now, I mean, what is your position on that and what will you tell Turkish government to convince the Turkish government on the integrity of Iraq?

Deputy Secretary Wolfowitz. Well, our position is very clear that we have to maintain a territorial integrity of Iraq, and there cannot be a separate Kurdish state and our position is influenced very strongly by understanding the Turkish interests, because we do not want an outcome in Iraq which causes problems for Turkey. We want an outcome in Iraq that helps Turkey, which creates a prosperous Iraq that becomes a valuable trading partner for Turkey. And we believe that, in fact, that is an outcome that is achievable. But one of the things I am very interested in learning during this visit is what ideas Turkish officials have about how best to ensure that that positive outcome is the result and what things we need to think about ahead of time to make sure that the negative outcomes don't happen. But, I think Turkey and the United States are the two countries with greatest capabilities to influence the outcome. So, it is very important for us to coordinate our thinking.

Q. For a long period of time, I mean, it was a situation like with or without you when you think about Saddam in Iraq. I mean, it seems that everybody, including the United States, preferred the weak Saddam and a weak Iraq, but the integrity of Iraq, than to an Iraq without a Saddam, but a disintegrated Iraq. Now what sort of a future do you wish to see in Iraq? Will it be a federal state, for example?

Deputy Secretary Wolfowitz. I think that the reality is that Iraq is disintegrating under Saddam. I think that anyone who thinks that he maintains the territorial integrity of Iraq should visit northern Iraq today. That is not the answer, clearly isn't the answer. What the answer is, exactly, is hard to say as long as he is there suppressing real opinion in Iraq. But I do believe that the more the international community insists that the territorial integrity of Iraq must be an outcome, the more we will influence the various people who influence that outcome to understand that that's the direction we have to go.

Remarks by Secretary of State Powell, July 15, 2002

Secretary Colin Powell was interviewed on ABC's Nightline by Ted Koppel.

Q. Let's start getting specific. If indeed—in fact, maybe I should begin with a question. We've had conflicting stories coming out of this building over the last week or two suggesting, first of all, that there is a plan already being formulated for an attack against Iraq; more recently, a story in USA Today saying no, we're only going to do it if indeed the Iraqis give us sufficient provocation.

Is that story true?

Secretary Powell. Well, you haven't had any conflicting reports out of this Department over the last week or two.

Q. I'm saying we're the ones making the conflicting reports.

Secretary Powell. What we have consistently said is that the President has no plan on his desk to invade Iraq at the moment, nor has one been presented to him, nor have his advisors come together to put a plan to him. He is in the most intense consultations with his friends and allies around the world. He has discussed this issue with his friends at the G-8 meeting in Canada recently. A steady stream of Arab leaders have been through the Oval Office in recent weeks, and the President has spoken to them.

He is aware of the feelings of our friends with respect to Iraq. He is working very hard within the United Nations. I spent a year on his behalf putting in place "smart sanctions" so that we're not hurting the Iraqi people; we're just constraining the ability of the Iraqi Government to develop weapons of mass destruction. That was multilateral, not unilateral. He has called for the inspectors to go in as part of the U.N. regime. That is multilateral, not unilateral.

But he also believes—and perhaps no one else agrees with him, but I think most people do; they just are a little reluctant to how to get to this end—that the Iraqi people would be better served with a different regime, not with a regime that gasses its own people, gasses its neighbors, and are developing the worst kinds of weapons that will be more of a threat to its neighbors and regional stability than it will be to the United States.

The United States could stand back and say we're going to ignore it. We can't ignore it, because we are concerned about our friends and allies and our interests around the world, and because we are the leader of a world that wants to be free.

Q. When you talk about the consultation with Arab states, with our friends in Europe, with the G-8, no question there's been consultation, but from what we're hearing from them and from their representatives, the consultation has tended to involve disagreement on their part, frustration on their part. They sense that the United States should not do this, should not move militarily against Iraq.

Any reason to believe that they're going to change their minds on that?

Secretary Powell. Well, we'll see what their minds are when the President finally puts in front of them something that might suggest military action. So far, he has not. He is interested in their perspective. He has listened carefully to them. He has made it clear to all of our friends and allies, and to those who are not friends and allies of us, that he believes regime change is the right way to go.

When we talk to our friends, that's being multilateral. It doesn't necessarily mean we will get them all to agree with us or that we are at the mercy of their agreement and their consensus.

Sometimes we have strong disagreements—the International Criminal Court is one—where we believe we have a principled position. It is an isolated position. Most of the rest of the world believes that the International Criminal Court is no threat to any U.S. serviceperson or U.S. political official. We have a different point of view.

And when we send our young volunteers around the world, in numbers that no other nation sends its young people around the world, we have worldwide responsibilities. We're glad to meet those responsibilities, but we want those young men and women to be subject to the constitutional processes of the United States Government and our Constitution, and that's how—that's why their parents entrusted them to our care.

And so it is a real issue for us, and we tried to find a solution within the U.N. over the last couple of weeks. We found a temporary bridge for a year or so, and we'll be working with our friends to make the case to them that we should receive some special understanding of our concerns, just as we are listening to their concerns.

When you have a principled position, you should fight for it, you should try to present the case, and when they have a principled position, we should listen to them. But we shouldn't go along with the consensus just because it is the consensus if we believe it is inconsistent with our principled position.

Remarks by Deputy Secretary of Defense Wolfowitz, July 17, 2002

Deputy Secretary Paul Wolfowitz delivered his remarks upon departing from his visit to Ankara, Turkey.

This was a long-planned visit, which I was looking forward to for quite some time. I'm very glad that we came.

We came to review a very broad range of issues that concern both our countries. The United States and Turkey have a true strategic partnership. It's a partnership of countries that have very large common interests. Countries that have important perspectives to share with one another. Perhaps most of all it's two great democracies. And I think at this time of challenge in a world where there are people to whom democracy and freedom are anathema, it is wonderful to have an ally like Turkey, who is a model of democracy for Muslims in the rest of the world.

We appreciate very much the graciousness and hospitality of the Turkish Government, the Turkish officials to receive us at a time when obviously there were other things on their mind besides our visit.

But I must say in all of our meetings, including the Prime Minister, it was impressive how much attention was given to the issues in our relationship, both bilateral and regional and larger strategic issues. We've discussed a very broad range of subjects. One of the things that characterizes this as a strategic partnership, is that issues that would normally be exclusively of concern to trade negotiators, for example, become issues of concern to [the department of] defense. So, among the many things we discussed, qualified industrial zones was on the list as well.

Obviously we discussed regional issues, including Iraq. But I'd like to emphasize, because of [speculation in the media], we didn't come here asking any decisions of the Turkish Government. We came here to gain benefit of Turkish perspectives, to be able to go back to Washington better informed about how Turkey views its interests and what Turkey's views are.

Q. Can the United States carry out an attack against Iraq without Turkish cooperation?

Deputy Secretary Wolfowitz. I've said it many times and I'm happy to say it again. The President of the United States has said one thing and he said it very clearly. Which is that a regime like the one in Iraq, that is hostile to United States, that supports terrorism and that has weapons of mass destruction and is developing more weapons of mass destruction, is a danger that we can't afford to live with indefinitely. What we do about it, how we solve that problem, involves a whole range of decisions which only the President can make and he hasn't made them yet. In fact, for making those decisions it's very important to him to have the benefit of key countries, and key parties, and Turkey is as important as any country in figuring out how to grapple with this issue. What I think there is no question about is that when there is a democratic Iraq, and that is our goal, an Iraq that preserves the territorial integrity of that country, that does not lead to an [independent Kurdish state]—we are opposed to that—as the Turkish Government is opposed to [it]. An Iraq that truly cares for the welfare of its own people. It won't be only the people of Iraq that benefit from that; it will be the whole world and very much this region. Turkey stands to benefit enormously [*inaudible*].

Q. Mr. Wolfowitz, what kind of a role do you expect Turkey to play in a time of operation [*inaudible*] plus how do you plan [*inaudible*]?

Deputy Secretary Wolfowitz. Let me repeat. We didn't come here with an idea of what Turkey's role should be or with a decision about an operation. We came here as part of the process of informing our President about the decisions he has to confront in order to deal with that problem which he has identified so clearly. They are difficult decisions for us and we need the benefit of Turkey's perspectives [*inaudible*].

Q. Turkey fears any possible strikes could damage its economic recovery. One thing that has been cited is the tourism sector. Are there any assurances that a strike might take the timing, take tourism into account when setting a timing?

Deputy Secretary Wolfowitz. Turkey's economic situation simply is of great concern to the United States. We've been working closely with Turkey for over a year now I believe and we've discussed this with the IMF. Again, I mentioned these are not normally the subjects a deputy secretary of defense gets involved with, but when it comes to Turkey, it does, although it's the secretary of treasury who has a leading role in it.

Turkey's economic health is hugely important and obviously, the current political crisis puts extra strains on it. One of the benefits of this visit to me was to have a clear understanding of exactly what kinds of worries Turkey has—of near term and immediate term. Long term, I don't think we are talking about worries long term. The prospects for this economy are very good.

Q. Mr. Wolfowitz, in any of the talks in Ankara or in Istanbul, did you put forward a choice for this coalition to be in office during a possible U.S. land attack on Iraq?

Deputy Secretary Wolfowitz. I admire your persistence. But let me say over again, we didn't come here putting choices before anyone. We came here to learn, to understand, to have as good an appreciation of Turkish perspectives as we could develop. Something that impressed me about this country, about the officials, about the government, about the Prime Minister, is their ability, even at a time of political crisis, or certainly great political uncertainty, to be able to talk clearly and dispassionately and with quite impressive analysis of the many issues that we have to face. We did not come here asking for decisions. We haven't made our own decisions ourselves.

Remarks by Secretary of Defense Rumsfeld, July 22, 2002

Q. And over the past couple of weeks, there's been a lot of speculation, at home and abroad, and Deputy Secretary Wolfowitz was travelling in that region and stopped in Turkey, in which apparently there were talks about a possible U.S. military attack of some kind on Iraq. Besides the U.S. government's position that there should be a regime change in Iraq, what would the justification be for a U.S. military attack or invasion of Iraq?

Secretary Rumsfeld. Your question was particularized to a country. My answer is a concept or a generic answer, which I think is a useful way to look at it before anyone goes down to any particular country.

During the 20th century, we were dealing for the most part with conventional weapons, and they tended to kill hundreds or thousands of people. In the 21st century, we're dealing with weapons of mass destruction—chemical, biological, nuclear, radiation—that can kill not just hundreds or thousands, but they can kill hundreds of thousands or millions of people in the case of, for example, contagious biological agent. In the 20th century, our margin for error had a penalty of X. In the 21st century, the margin for error or penalty has a penalty that is many, many multiples of X.

That means that the people of the country, the people in parliaments around the world, the press, academic institutions, have to look at our circumstance in the 21st century, and say, "Fair enough. We're living—we lived in the old world with conventional capabilities and their proliferation. Now we're living in a world with weapons of mass destruction proliferating rather rapidly to a variety of nations, a variety of non-state entities potentially that have already indicated their appetite for the weapon. They've indicated their willingness to kill as many innocent men, women and children through terrorist acts as they can."

So the world—the academic institutions, the parliaments, the press, the governments of the world—democratic governments—you know, dictatorial regimes, repressive regimes do violence to their neighbors frequently, and democratic regimes tend not to. But they have to ask question, what is the responsible course of action? If that's the circumstance, if I've accurately characterized it, it means that we have to say to ourselves, on the one hand, are we—is it incumbent upon us to wait until there is a Pearl Harbor—wait until there is an attack that has killed several thousand people or—and risk not several thousand but several hundreds of thousands of people or millions? Is that—is that the responsibility of free people today in the 21st century? Or conversely, is it the responsibility of free people to look at the world and take people at their word and watch the progress of the acquisition of weapons of mass destruction and see the risk that poses to hundreds of thousands of people or potentially millions of people in your country and in your friends' and allies' countries and in deployed forces and take a step that would prevent that in your own self-defense?

And that, it seems to me, is an issue that ought to be discussed. It ought to be considered. It ought to be elevated—not in a particularized situation of one country or another, but it is a serious, important concept that the—our country ought to consider. And I think that you're increasingly seeing that happen. I think you're finding people starting to think about it, starting to talk about it, starting to recognize what the benefits and what the burdens are of different courses of action.

Q. You mentioned specifically contagious biological agents. Is there evidence—

Secretary Rumsfeld. They worry me.

Q. Is there evidence that Iraq is, in fact, developing contagious biological agents and is willing to use them in conjunction with terrorists of any ilk?

Secretary Rumsfeld. Now you're asking me to, first of all, define what I would consider to be a proper cause of action—a fact pattern that would be sufficient to cause one to have to have to face that dilemma that I elevated and constructed. And I'd prefer not to do that, so I'll take the next question.

* * * *

Q. Does the concept that you've outlined include at some point going to the public and going to Congress and getting them on board, signing them for an attack like this? Or is it something you would do—

Secretary Rumsfeld. Those are issues for the president, as I said.

Q. How do you characterize—you said you want to see the nation engage in the sort of debate of that question that you put before us today in your answer to Mick's question. How would you characterize what the current state of debate is? What is the current way of viewing this that you think needs to be changed or looked at or readdressed?

Secretary Rumsfeld. Yes. I think what we're doing is we're migrating over in the direction that I've outlined. I think that to the extent one particularizes it to a specific country, the debate and discussion and national dialogue, indeed international dialogue, loses something important, because what's important is that the national security environment in the world has changed. We are dealing with a different margin for error.

We're dealing with different penalties that will result from our decisions. Whichever decision we make, the penalties will be notably different than they were in the last century. And it is that that has to get up on the table so that people will develop a comfort with the circumstance we're in, and that that issue has been talked about and thought about and rolled around in our heads to the point where people become satisfied that we have a good sense of where we are as a people and where other countries are.

Q. Okay.

Secretary Rumsfeld. Did I give you—

Q. On that point, Mr. Secretary, was President Bush premature when he named Iraq, Iran and North Korea as an axis of evil?

Secretary Rumsfeld. No. I think indeed it was—if one—if one a year from now, two years from now, three years from now looks back and something good happens in any one of those three countries, I think you'll find that it was the axis-of-evil speech that started ferment in those countries and a dialogue and a focus on the tragedy that exists for the people in North Korea, the starvation, the enormous numbers, thousands and thousands of human beings who are political prisoners in camps that are the size of major cities, the repression that takes place.

If one thinks of what's happening in Iran, you can't help but be encouraged to see the fact that the young people and women and the people who understand. These are intelligent people. These are industrious people. These are people that understand the world, and they see what their lives are like and what's being imposed on them by the clerics. And anyone who knows anything about Iraq knows that it just ranks right up there as one of the most vicious regimes in the world.

And I think that that speech will be seen as having said to the world: Let's look at what's taking place. We've got these three countries—call them the "axis of evil," call them what you want—but they are doing perfectly terrible things to their people. They have weapons of mass destruction. Their appetite for additional weapons is enormous. They are bringing things in like a vacuum cleaner to enhance and develop and move beyond their current WMD capabilities. And they are countries that don't wish their neighbors well. Now that's a good thing for a leader to point at. So it's not only not a mistake; I think history will say it was a very, very useful thing to have done.

Remarks by Senator Biden, July 28, 2002

Chairman of the Senate Foreign Relations Committee Joseph Biden (D-DE) was interviewed on ABC's This Week by Cokie Roberts.

Q. While the attention of the country has been focused on the stock market, the next step in the war on terrorism occupies much of official Washington. Is President Bush planning to attack Iraq soon? With reports of American troops massing on the Iraqi borders, some in Congress are insisting that invasion plans should be debated before they're implemented. The Senate Foreign Relations Committee will begin hearings on Iraq policy this week. The chairman of that committee, Delaware Democrat Joseph Biden, joins us now. Thanks for being with us, Senator Biden.

Senator Biden. Hi, Cokie. Happy to be here.

Q. We're seeing reports in today's Washington Post that the military, members of the military are opposed to an invasion of Iraq, saying that the policy of containment and sanctions is working. And yet we see other reports that the president's poised to go in. What's happening?

Senator Biden. Well, Cokie, let me begin by saying that this is not the Democrats looking at this, this is Senator Lugar, Senator Hagel and myself, Republicans. We've been thinking about having these hearings. I've had long discussions with Condoleezza Rice, the national security advisor, and with the president on this. So this is not at odds with the president. This is just beginning to raise the issue, what's at stake here, what's the nature of the threat when we go in and if we go in and take out Saddam Hussein? How long will we have to stay? Will it require tens of thousands of troops to be there for three, four, five years? These are questions the American public has a right to have some knowledge about what the alternatives are, what the debate is about. And as you've indicated, there's clear division within the administration, not only the uniform personnel and the civilian personnel over at the Defense Department, but among the civilian personnel within the administration. And so the administration supports these hearings, and I don't expect we're going to see any action on Iraq, in terms of military action, absent serious provocation by Iraq anywhere in the near term. Meaning between now and November, I'd be very surprised.

Q. You would be very surprised? Because there are certainly...

Senator Biden. I would be very surprised.

Q. ... commentaries and such that this is a "wag the dog" scenario, that the president might be bringing up Iraq to take attention away from the economy, going into this election.

Senator Biden. Well, I'm assuming, and I mean this sincerely, the president will be considerably more responsible than that, and the vast majority of the members of the administration, I think, want to do this by the numbers. The important part is not whether or not we think Saddam should go, but how he should go. And one of the things we have to consider here, Cokie, is there's no doubt the American military can go in and take down Saddam Hussein. But you have to pre-position an awful lot of forces, and if it's not going to be pre-positioning tens of thousands of forces—and that would take time, it would take 60 to 90 days to do that—what about these quick-hit scenarios you hear about, and what are the consequences of that? Will Saddam Hussein use the chemical weapons I believe and we believe he has, with the Scud missiles, Scud Bs [ph] he has, to attack Israel and widen the war? What are the options available? What will our allies do? Will they come in after the fact and help us keep that country and split it into three chaotic regions? I mean, these are important questions. I'm convinced, from my discussions with the president, he's taking it seriously. I believe he has not made a final decision yet, and I think—I am not expecting any wild, precipitous action by anyone.

Q. This morning the king of Jordan, King Abdullah, was asked about this. He said that the only solution is dialogue with Iraq, and he then went on to say that the Arab-Israeli conflict should be solved. Let me show you exactly what he said: "The problem is trying to take on the question of Iraq with the lack of positive movement on the Israeli-Palestinian, Israeli-Arab track seems, at this point, somewhat ludicrous," his words. Do you agree with that?

Senator Biden. Well, no. First of all, dialogue with Saddam is useless, in my view. The question is whether or not containing him and building the consensus to go after him physically is a better way to do that in the near term, or to go in full bore now. But I am—it is clear, it is a fact that the failure of progress and escalation in the Middle East, as it relates to Israel and the Palestinian question, really raises the ante here. That's why some of us believe that Saddam's interest would be to, if he's attacked now, to widen the war to a Middle East war. That is, attack Israel and force Israel to respond, and then we have everything out of kilter. So there is some—there are some very reasonable people we're going to hear from in the committee who suggest that there need be some progress made on the Israeli- Palestinian front before an all-out effort moved against Iraq. But the flip side of that is, there are those who believe if you went in and took down Saddam Hussein now, we would have a salutary impact on the entire region and would, in fact, help the situation in the Middle East. And we're going to hear from all those people—not administration officials, because I don't want to force them to have to make a decision. I'm not trying to find out operational plans. We just want—Senator Lugar, myself and others want to make sure we have begun a real serious discussion about the options and about the consequences.

Q. And then should that serious discussion carry over to a resolution, a congressional resolution, to authorize war, as there was in the Persian Gulf War?

Senator Biden. Well, in my view, that should come at the request of the president of the United States. I'm of the view that the president does not have the constitutional authority to invade Iraq without clear proof that they participated in 9/11 with Al Qaida and/or that we're under threat of imminent attack. I do believe if the president laid out his plan—not in detail, the plan—laid out his rationale, indicated what we were going to do after the fact, once we take down Saddam Hussein, and then ask for support from the Congress, I believe he would get that. But I...

Q. Would you vote for that?

Senator Biden. ... think we're far from there. Well, it depends on what he laid out. If he decides he's going to stay the course, he has the Europeans in there to help us not win the war, but win the peace, then I'd be very inclined. I think if Saddam's around in five years, we have a problem. But I look at Afghanistan, Cokie, and I begin to wonder. We're not really quite staying the course in Afghanistan, in my view. We're not extending the international security force. I'm very concerned that what is not—it would be an exaggeration to say lack of resolve, but I think Afghanistan is far from finished yet. So it matters a lot. And when the president asked me—he always kids me and says, "Senator"—or he calls me Mr. Chairman—"Mr. Chairman," he said, "you think he should come down. Why don't you think I should go quickly?" And I said, "Mr. President"—or something to that effect. And I said, "Mr. President, I remind you, there's a reason why your father stopped and didn't go to Baghdad."

Q. Well, you've told that story before, and what's his answer to that?

Senator Biden. And he does not give an answer. He says that's being considered. And the end of the story is, I say there's a reason he stopped, he didn't want to stay for five years. There's not a single informed voice that suggests we're not going to have to make a long-term commitment if we go in and take down Saddam to in fact stabilize that country. And the American people should be aware what that cost is. I'm ready to pay that cost if it's laid out clearly.

Q. Senator, just very quickly on another subject in your hat on the Judiciary Committee, Priscilla Owens, up for federal judgeship. Are you going to vote for her?

Senator Biden. I don't know. I am looking at the entire record right now. I was unable to attend the hearing because I was conducting a hearing in the Foreign Relations Committee on this subject. And we may, I'm told, vote for or against her as early as this week. I am worried that she seems to have—and in fairness to her, I've not read the record, my staff has prepared it—she seems to have found a way to go beyond what the law calls for, in several cases, in order to impose her own view. But I'm not certain of that yet. I've only voted no 11 times over a thousand votes for the court. I'll look at it very closely.

Remarks by Secretary of Defense Rumsfeld, July 29, 2002

Q. Mr. Secretary, over the weekend, yesterday, U.S. and British warplanes bombed a communications site in Iraq. I understand that six times there's been some sort of skirmish in Iraq in the last month alone. What do you attribute to the step-up in hostilities there? And moreover, we keep seeing this war plan and that war plan; what's the future hold? What's next?

Secretary Rumsfeld. I do not believe—I'd have to go back and check, but I do not believe that there have been a notable pickup in the number of response firings that the Northern and Southern no-fly-zone watches have been engaged in the last two, three, four weeks. What they are there for, those U.S. and British aircraft flying out of the region, is that Saddam Hussein had several U.N. resolutions where he agreed not to have weapons of mass destruction, where he agreed to not fly in certain areas, where he agreed to not reinforce his troops down south, where he agreed not to attempt to intimidate his neighbors, the Kurds or the Shia or others, and to not increase his military capability in certain ways.

What's been taking place is they have been firing at coalition aircraft, U.S. and British, from time to time, and when they do, we fire back. And we fire back at those things we can find which seem appropriate. And clearly one of the things that's appropriate are communications systems, because it's the communications and the fiber optics that they've been putting in that enable them to cue a variety of radars and have a better success rate of tracking our aircraft.

So you can expect that there will be, on a weekly basis, these exchanges. And our purpose would be to punish and destroy things that are of military value to him, that are in many ways inconsistent with the U.N. resolutions that we're enforcing.

* * * *

Q. If I can follow. There's this concern about weapons of mass destruction in Iraq. Why not just go hit them? Why wait for something—for the future?

Secretary Rumsfeld. The Iraqis have a great deal of what they do deeply buried. The Iraqis have benefited from American spies defecting to the Soviet Union or Russia and providing information as to how we do things, and then they proliferate that information on how another country can best achieve denial and deception and avoid having the location, precise location, actionable locations of things known.

Third, there is enormous flow of things across the Iraqi border. They've got billions of dollars from their oil for food. Instead of buying food for the children, they're buying weapons. They're buying dual-use capability. A biological laboratory can be on wheels in a trailer and make a lot of bad stuff, and it's movable, and it looks like most any other trailer. So the idea that it's easy to simply go do what you suggested ought to be done from the air, the implication being from the air, is a misunderstanding of the situation. They have chemical weapons. They have biological weapons. They have an enormous appetite for nuclear weapons. They were within a year or two of having them when the—Desert Storm got on the ground and found enough information to know how advanced their program was. They've kept their nuclear physicists and scientists together in a kluge, and they're continuing to work. So it is a bigger task than that suggests.

White House Press Briefing, July 30, 2002

Q. Ari, what does the President think of the widespread perception that he would, at a terrible human toll, attack Iraq to avenge his father? You hear that everywhere.

Mr. Fleischer. Nowhere I've heard, Helen. I think that—

Q. You've never heard it?

Mr. Fleischer. The President focuses on protecting our country, and protecting our country from whatever the source may be. And particularly in the case of Iraq, the President has, in his State of the Union, referred to Iraq as part of the axis of evil, and for good reason, given the behavior of Iraq toward its neighbors, its belligerent manner, the way it's attacked Kuwait, the war it fought with Iran, its use of chemical weapons against its own people. And that's why the President has, with the support of the American people, said—

Q. So that has no validity at all? Never?

Mr. Fleischer. Of course not. This is about protecting our country.

Q. And what right does the President have to take the United States into an attack on a country which has not provoked it? I mean, you're going back a long way to find some reasons. And I don't think they're accepted by the American people, because you haven't explained it.

Mr. Fleischer. Well, I'm not going to accept the premise that the President is going to attack Iraq.

Q. You're not?

Mr. Fleischer. The President has not given any such indication. The President has said he will protect the American people. But I think that your read of the American people is not where the country is when it comes to wanting action to protect themselves against the dangers that Iraq poses.

Q. So he's going to really explain his reasons if he does attack Iraq?

Mr. Fleischer. I'm not going to go too far down this hypothetical line of reasoning. But I will refer you to the speeches the President has given on it, and you can hear for yourself.

Remarks by Senators Biden, Lugar and Wellstone, July 31, 2002

Senators Joseph Biden (D-DE, Chairman), Richard Lugar (R-IN), and Paul Wellstone (D-MN) delivered their remarks at the opening of two days of hearings by the Senate Foreign Relations Committee on Iraq.

Senator Biden. Welcome, everyone, here this morning to what is the beginning of, I hope, for lack of a better phrase, a national dialog on a very important question. There are some very difficult decisions for the President and for the Congress, and we think it's important, the members of this committee, that we begin to discuss what is being discussed all over, but not here in the Congress so far.

The attacks of 9/11 have forever transformed how Americans see the world. Through tragedy and pain, we have learned that we cannot be complacent about events abroad. We cannot be complacent about those who espouse hatred for us. We must confront clear danger with a new sense of urgency and resolve.

Saddam Hussein's pursuit of weapons of mass destruction, in my view, is one of those clear dangers. Even if the right response to his pursuit is not so crystal clear, one thing is clear. These weapons must be dislodged from Saddam Hussein, or Saddam Hussein must be dislodged from power. President Bush has stated his determination to remove Saddam from power, a view many in Congress share. If that course is pursued, in my view, it matters profoundly how we do it and what we do after we succeed.

The decision to go to war can never be taken lightly. I believe that a foreign policy, especially one that involves the use of force, cannot be sustained in America without the informed consent of the American people. And so just as we have done in other important junctures in our history, the Foreign Relations Committee today begins what I hope will be a national dialog on Iraq that sheds more light than heat and helps inform the American people so that we can have a more informed basis upon which they can draw their own conclusions.

I'm very pleased and grateful for the close cooperation of my Republican colleagues, Senator Helms, in absentia, and his staff, in particular Senator Lugar and Senator Hagel, in putting these hearings together. This is a bipartisan effort. It reminds me of the way that things used to work in this committee when I joined it in 1973.

I want to say a word now about what the hearings are not about, from my perspective. They are not designed to prejudice any particular course of action. They are not intended to short- circuit the debate taking place within the administration. I know I speak for all members of the committee in saying at the outset that we recognize our responsibility as we conduct these hearings to do so in a way that reflects the magnitude of the decisions the administration is wrestling with and the Congress will have to deal with.

We've coordinated these hearings closely with the White House. We're honoring the administration's desire not to testify at this time. We expect, at some later date, to convene hearings at which the administration would send representatives to explain their thinking once it has been clarified and determined. We do not expect this week's hearings to exhaust all aspects of this issue. They are a beginning. But over the next 2 days, we hope to address several fundamental questions.

First, what is the threat from Iraq? Obviously, to fully answer this question will require us to have additional and closed hearings on top of hearings in S-407 and discussions we've already had with the intelligence community. Second, depending on our assessment of the threat—or depending on one's assessment of the threat, what is the appropriate response? And, third, how do Iraq's neighbors, other countries in the region, and our allies see the, "Iraqi problem"? And, fourth, and maybe most important, if we participate in Saddam's departure, what are our responsibilities the day after?

In my judgment, President Bush is right to be concerned about Saddam Hussein's relentless pursuit of weapons of mass destruction and the possibility that he may use them or share them with terrorists. Other regimes hostile to the United States and our allies already have or seek to acquire weapons of mass destruction. What distinguishes Saddam is that he has used them against his own people and against Iran. And for nearly 4 years now Iraq has blocked the return of U.N. weapons inspectors.

We want to explore Saddam's track record in acquiring, making, and using weapons of mass destruction and the likelihood, in the opinion of the experts that will come before us in the next 2 days—the likelihood that he would share them with terrorists.

We want to know what capabilities Saddam has been able to rebuild since the inspectors were forced out of Iraq and what he now has or might soon acquire. We want to understand his conventional military strength and what dangers he poses to his neighbors as well as to our forces, should they intervene.

Once we have established a better understanding of the threat, we want to look at the possible responses. The containment strategy pursued since the end of the gulf war and apparently supported by some in our military has kept Saddam boxed in. Some advocates for continuing this strategy believe it's exceeded their expectations. And some others advocate the continuation coupled with tough, unfettered weapons inspection. How practical is that? Others believe that containment raises the risks Saddam will continue to play cat and mouse with the inspectors, build more weapons of mass destruction and share them with those who wouldn't hesitate to use them against us. In this view, if we wait for the danger to become clear and present, it could become too late. It could be too late. Acting to change the regime, in this view, may be a better course.

But a military response also raises questions. Some fear that attacking Saddam Hussein would precipitate the very thing we're trying to prevent, his last resort to weapons of mass destruction. We also have to ask whether resources can be shifted to a major military enterprise in Iraq without compromising the war on terror in other parts of the world.

My father has an expression, God love him. He says, "If everything's equally important to you, Joe, nothing is important." How do we prioritize? What is the relative value? What are the costs?

We have to inquire about the cost of a major military campaign and the impact on our economy. As pointed out yesterday in one of the major newspapers in America, in today's dollars, the cost of the gulf war was about $75 billion. Our allies paid 80 percent of that, including the Japanese. If we go it alone, does it matter? Will we encompass and take on the whole responsibility? What impact will that have on American security and the economy? We have to consider what support we're likely to get from our key allies in the Middle East and Europe, and we must examine whether there are any consequences if we move for regional stability.

Finally, the least explored, in my view, but in many ways the most critical question relates to our responsibilities, if any, for the day after Saddam is taken down, if taken down by the use of the U.S. military. This is not a theoretical exercise. In Afghanistan, the war was prosecuted exceptionally well, in my view, but the follow-through commitment to Afghanistan security and reconstruction has, in my judgment, fallen short.

It would be a tragedy if we removed a tyrant in Iraq, only to leave chaos in its wake. The long suffering Iraqi people need to know a regime change would benefit them. So do Iraq's neighbors. We need a better understanding of what it would take to secure Iraq and rebuild it economically and politically. Answering these questions could improve the prospects for military success by demonstrating to Iraqis that we are committed to staying for the long haul.

These are just some of the questions we hope to address today and tomorrow and in future hearings and, no doubt, in the fall. In short, we need to weigh the risks of action versus the risks of inaction.

To reiterate my key point, if we expect the American people to support their government over the long haul when it makes a difficult decision, if the possibility exists that we may ask hundreds of thousands of our young men and women in uniform to put themselves in harm's way, if it is the consensus or a decision reached by the administration that thousands or tens of thousands of troops would be required to remain behind for an extended period of time, if those measures are required, then we must gain, in my view, the informed consent of the American people.

I welcome our witnesses today. We have a group of extremely competent people, one of whom got on a plane in Sydney and traveled 24 hours straight to be here for this hearing, and others who have come from long distances, as well. These are men and women of stature, background knowledge, academic and practical understanding of the region and the country, and we're anxious to hear from them.

I would now ask Senator Lugar if he would like to make an opening statement. And although we usually reserve opening statements just to the ranking member and the chairman, I would, since we only have a few members here at the moment, invite my other three colleagues if they would like to make a, "short"—not as long as the chairman's—short statement.

When you get to be chairman, you can make long statements.

Senator Lugar.

Senator Lugar. Well, thank you very much, Mr. Chairman, for your leadership in organizing these hearings and for a comprehensive statement that really does set forward the major issues we must discuss.

I was an outspoken advocate for United States military action against Iraq that culminated in Desert Shield and Desert Storm. I urged President Bush at a very early date to seek congressional authorization for deployment of troops and the use of force in the Persian Gulf. At the time, many in and out of the administration feared the possibility of losing that vote. I believed all along the votes would be there, but had the votes for authorization not been there, it would have been far better to have known this at the beginning rather than to be surprised down the road that the Nation was not behind the President. A few weeks later, the House and Senate did vote to authorize President Bush to use military force against Iraq, and the administration benefited immensely from this overt decision of the American people.

If President Bush determines that large-scale offensive military action is necessary against Iraq, I hope that he will follow the lead established by the previous Bush administration and seek congressional authorization. The administration must be assured of the commitment of the American people in pursuing policies and actions in Iraq after focused and vigorous discussion and debate. It is unfortunate that today, some 10 years after the gulf war, we still face threats posed by Saddam Hussein. This did not necessarily have to be the case.

On April 18, 1991, I wrote to President Bush urging him to send our forces to Baghdad and to complete the job. He was gracious enough to receive me in the White House to discuss that letter. I believe that while we had the forces present, we should end the regime of Saddam Hussein and build a democratic Iraq. And, for a number of reasons, our President chose instead to pursue a policy of containment. Those important reasons for that decision, then and now, include our plans for the future of a post-Saddam-Hussein Iraq and future stability of Iraq's neighbors.

We must estimate soberly the human and economic costs of war plans and post-war plans. I am under no illusion that this will be an easy task. The President and the administration will have to make the case to the American people regarding the threat posed to the United States security by Saddam Hussein and the weapons of mass destruction he appears intent on producing and potentially utilizing against Americans and other targets.

But the President will also have to make a persuasive case to our friends and allies, particularly those in the region. Simply put, Saddam Hussein remains a threat to the United States, allied, and regional security. However, the situation on the ground in the region has changed since 1991, and it is not at all clear that the tactics of that campaign should be re-employed today.

Ten years ago, the United States had done the military and diplomatic spade work in the region. We had developed a war plan. Allies in the region permitted the United States forces to launch attacks from their territory. We had collected a coalition of willing and able allies. Our allies were willing to pay for $48 billion of the $61 billion cost. We were prepared to utilize the force necessary to defeat Iraqi forces. And, most importantly, we had the support of the American people. We have not yet determined if these same conditions are present today. They might be, but we have not yet engaged all the parties necessary to ensure a successful outcome.

At the end of the Persian Gulf war, the agreements surrounding the cease-fire included an Iraqi commitment to destroy a stockpile of nuclear, chemical, and biological weapons and the ability to produce them in the future. I fully supported this endeavor. Iraq's possession of weapons of mass destruction represents a potential threat the world cannot ignore. On several occasions since the end of the war, the United States and our allies have resorted to the use of military force to counter the threat Iraq poses to its neighbors and to the United States' vital national-security interests. Saddam Hussein has demonstrated his ability and willingness to use weapons of mass destruction and spread instability through military force against his own people and neighbors.

Unfortunately, the overriding priority of his regime has been the maintenance of his own power. These hearings seek to shed light on our policy alternatives. The administration understands that ultimately it will have to make a case for its policy decisions. This is not an action that can be sprung on the American people. Leaks of military plans are dangerous to our security. But public debate over policy is important to the construction of strong public support for actions that will require great sacrifices from the American people.

I look forward to working closely with the chairman to lead this debate and to lay some of the foundation of the coalescing of administration and congressional thinking and support that will be essential for a campaign against Saddam Hussein.

* * * *

Senator Wellstone. For months now, high-ranking administration officials have openly discussed launching a military attack on Iraq to overthrow Saddam Hussein. Until very recently, however, serious public discussion on the nature and urgency of Iraq's threat, the range of possible U.S. policy responses, and the consequences of a possible U.S. or allied military attack has been in short supply. I believe a free-ranging and open discussion of the policy options facing us on Iraq is long overdue, and wish to thank Senator Biden for scheduling this hearing today, and those which are to follow. By initiating these hearings, the committee is taking an important and historic first step in meeting its constitutional obligations to ensure that the representatives of the people have a chance to thoroughly assess these profoundly important questions before any action is taken.

From all that I have seen, I do not believe the administration has yet made a case for taking military action against Iraq. Before any decisions about major changes in U.S. policy in the region are made—including possible military or other action—our country and our people need to learn as much as we can about the available choices on Iraq and their likely consequences.

Among other things, we must know the impact of a U.S. pre- emptive attack on the international coalition effort to combat terrorism, our nation's number one national security priority. With few exceptions, our coalition partners and regional friends oppose military action. We need to take a hard look at whether taking military action against Iraq would be worth jeopardizing the steady progress we are now making with scores of other nations in actually preventing terrorists from acquiring the resources to attack us again as they did on September 11.

We also must know the nature and urgency of the threat from Iraq, the range of possible American policy responses beyond the use of force, the legal authority for U.S. or concerted international action there, the impact on our economy and on the world economy, and the human toll of any such conflict.

We must also have some clearer idea of our policy goals. Should the goal of U.S. policy be to overthrow the regime and install a regime less hostile to U.S. interests, to compel Iraq finally to agree with unfettered U.N.-sponsored weapons inspections, to destroy suspected weapons of mass destruction production facilities, or some combination of these? What is the precedent for the U.S. to launch a major military operation in the absence of direct provocation by the target country? Should U.S. action be targeted and covert, or overwhelming and overt? What would we expect the casualties among U.S. service personnel to be in a potential war on Iraq, and would it be higher, as most experts agree, than in the current war in Afghanistan? Are Americans ready to shoulder that burden now? What would the death toll be among ordinary, innocent Iraqi civilians? Why is the U.N.-sponsored sanctions process, recently overhauled and more narrowly targeted, continuing to erode, and what can be done about that? All of these questions and more must be answered in this process.

The most recent leaked military plan for invading Iraq calls for a heavy reliance on air strikes, focusing first and primarily on Baghdad. What is never mentioned in this report is the fact that Baghdad is also a crowded city of four to five million people, and it would be virtually impossible to take measures sufficient to prevent innocent non-combatants from being harmed.

We must also consider the major responsibilities likely to flow from any military victory. What would it take to secure Iraq and to rebuild it economically and politically? How many U.S. forces would be required to go in, to secure the country and restore some semblance of democratic rule, and for how long would they stay? Would the American people be willing to shoulder the cost of billions of dollars needed for this effort, billions of dollars also urgently needed back here at home? In short, after a military victory has been declared, will the U.S. stay committed for the long haul? In Afghanistan, we won the war, but the follow-through commitment to secure Afghanistan's peace through security and reconstruction has fallen short. That fact, probably as much an any other, has had a chilling effect on regional support for U.S. action on Iraq.

No one here disagrees that the world would be a much better place without the brutal dictatorship of Saddam Hussein. He has preyed on his neighbors, has used chemical weapons on his own people, and continues to be one of the world's worst violators of human rights. However, if a decision to take military action is made, it should only be made after the administration has engaged in a serious and thoughtful sustained public discussion on Iraq with the American people, and only after all diplomatic and other peaceful options have been exhausted. Further, if the administration decides to move, it must come back to Congress and seek war powers authorization before engaging in a large scale escalation of hostilities.

I believe these hearings are an important first step in beginning a serious and thoughtful discussion of U.S. policy toward Iraq, one which has been sorely needed, and I look forward to the testimony of the witnesses before us.

White House Press Briefing, July 31, 2002

Q. Ari, the leaders of France and Germany say that if there is a problem, and there obviously is one, with Iraq, that it should be handled by the United Nations. It's a U.N. problem, it's a defiance of U.N., violation of U.N. resolutions. Why does the United States, and why does President Bush, think it's a unilateral problem that the United States should handle alone and is preparing for a war, apparently?

Mr. Fleischer. One, the President does not think it's a unilateral problem. The President thinks that Iraq presents a worldwide problem to peace.

Q. Then why doesn't he go through the U.N.?

Mr. Fleischer. And the President, in many of his meetings, as you know—when he was in Germany—he said so publicly at the time—the United States will continue to consult with our allies about what, if any, action needs to be taken, whether that action is diplomatic, political, financial, military—all of that is part and parcel of America's ongoing consultations with nations around the world.

Q. Well, why doesn't he go through the U.N.?

Mr. Fleischer. He is continuing—

Q. That's a real forum that's been set up since practically World War II.

Mr. Fleischer. And as you know, the President is working through the United Nations in the passage of the smart sanctions program, which now has been agreed to by Russia and was voted on by the United Nations earlier this summer, to apply sanctions to Iraqi products in an effort to make Iraq live up to the terms that it pledged when it signed a cease-fire that ended the Persian Gulf War. In addition, we're working through the United Nations on the arms inspectors program, a program which Iraq has thumbed its nose at the United Nations.

* * * *

Q. Ari, the Defense Secretary Rumsfeld seems to be ruling out all options against Iraq except for military ones. I know you won't discuss details, but has the administration decided on what course of action to take against Saddam Hussein? And that includes what the scope of military action will be?

Mr. Fleischer. Well, the President has not made any decisions. The President remains committed, however, to America's bipartisan policy of regime change through whatever means that would take, whether that's political, whether it's diplomatic, whether it's financial, whether it's military. But he's made no decisions.

But he does feel deeply, as the President has said in numerous speeches—I'll cite for you the President gave when he visited Germany for example, where he said, "If we ignore this threat we invite certain blackmail and place millions of our citizens in grave danger." The President at West Point also said, "We cannot defend America and our friends by hoping for the best. We cannot put our faith in the words of tyrants who solemnly sign nonproliferation treaties and then systematically break them. If we wait for the threats to fully materialize, we have waited too long."

* * * *

Q. Back on Iraq. What is the President's level of skepticism that Saddam Hussein will eventually comply with a thorough weapons inspection effort?

Mr. Fleischer. Well, it's high. The President's level of skepticism is high. Saddam Hussein has entered into agreements before that he has immediately violated. Saddam Hussein has told the world that he would allow weapons inspectors in, that he would comply with their weapons inspections, that he would open all his plants and facilities to the weapons inspectors. And as history has shown, even while the weapons inspectors were there, he did not keep his word. He violated his agreements.

So the President begins this with the point of view, what's most important is the result of a weapons inspection, not so much the process—the result being for the world to be assured that Iraq is not pursuing the development of weapons of mass destruction. Because Saddam Hussein has already shown that when he has weapons, he is willing to use them, and use them against his own people, even if they're chemical weapons of mass destruction.

Remarks by President Bush and Jordanian King Abdullah, August 1, 2002

President Bush and King Abdullah delivered their remarks at the White House.

Q. Mr. President, you seem to—the two of you seem to disagree on Iraq. Are you going to discuss those disagreements? And could you maybe elucidate on those disagreements?

President Bush. Well, I appreciate that, John. The policy of my government, our government, of this administration is regime change. For a reason. Saddam Hussein is a man who poisons his own people, who threatens his neighbors, who develops weapons of mass destruction. And I will assure His Majesty, like I have in the past, we're looking at all options, the use of all tools. I'm a patient man. But I haven't changed my opinion since the last time he was in the Oval Office. And one of the things we will do is consult with our friends. But he just needs to know how I feel. He knows how I feel, I had the opportunity and the honor of explaining that to him before and he'll find out I haven't changed my mind.

King Abdullah. All I'd like to say is that, again, what I found from day one with the President is he understands the bigger picture and that at the end of the day, peace and stability for the Middle East has been at the forefront of his mind. And so we have many areas where we find common base to be able to move the region forward.

Remarks by Secretary of Defense Rumsfeld, August 5, 2002

Q. Mr. Secretary, if Iraq is such a threat why is it that the countries that are so close to it geographically speaking do not seem to share the desire for an immediate, at least, regime change. And to go beyond the notion of taking out the specific threat of whatever weapons they might have, what kind of commitment do you think it would take for American troops to actually see, to follow through with a regime change?

Secretary Rumsfeld. I would really prefer not to spend the entire time we have on Iraq. The reason I say that is it simply feeds the frenzy that seems to be seizing the media today in the United States and I don't think that's a particularly useful thing to do. I'll answer this question on Iraq and then I'd much prefer to discuss a host of other subjects, all of which are interesting.

The premise of your question is probably wrong. If the behavior of Iraq is as characterized, why wouldn't other countries be concerned about it. I think if you sat down with the leadership of any country over there that you'd find they have a very low regard for that fellow. You'd also find they're much smaller countries and they're much weaker. When you have a neighbor that is that big and has that big an army and has chemical weapons and has used them on its neighbors, the Iranians; they have used them on its own people; an active biological weapons program; an aggressive nuclear weapons program, then it's like the little guy in the neighborhood's fairly careful about what he says publicly.

But I think that if you think that regime would win a popularity contest in the region, you're just wrong.

Q. No, I just wonder if they would support an attempt to overthrow that regime.

Secretary Rumsfeld. Well, they did the last time, and we'll see if the decision's made to do something at some point down the road or if the sanctions issues come up again or if there's a major diplomatic effort that's embarked on, why I think you'd find that countries would find a way publicly or privately to be supportive.

I don't know of anyone I've talked to out in the region who would walk across the street to shake Saddam Hussein's hand.

Remarks by Secretary of Defense Rumsfeld and Chairman of the Joint Chiefs of Staff Myers, August 7, 2002

Secretary Rumsfeld. Turning to Iraq for just a second, in just the last week Iraq has fired at coalition aircraft five times in Operation Northern Watch and five times during Operation Southern Watch. We responded most recently on Sunday with three precision- guided munitions against air-defense facilities about 145 miles southwest of Baghdad.

And in Iraq maritime intercept operations, we have diverted 36 vessels in the last one-week period, ending on Monday. The number is a little higher than usual because the Iraqis are using these smaller ships and vessels, these dhows, to try to circumvent their—the U.N. sanctions there.

* * * *

Q. And might I ask you regarding today's report in the Washington Times, have the chiefs—have the chiefs—are you now convinced that in the final analysis, it's going to take a military operation to remove Saddam Hussein, and have you-all signed on to that, that idea?

General Myers. Well, can I talk about the articles that have been in—probably the last three or four weeks I guess there have been a series of articles. From where I sit and the people that I talk to on a daily basis, meaning the Joint Chiefs of Staff, other senior military officials, the things that are said and portrayed in the articles simply aren't said or said to me—they are not accurate portrayals of what I see on a daily basis and what I hear.

And beyond that, the kind of advice that the military provides to Secretary Rumsfeld and the president and the rest of the National Security Council is certainly privileged communications and I'm not going to share that with you here.

Q. Well, do you think these leaks—Mr. Secretary, do these leaks represent some kind of political jockeying from all sides in town trying to get the upper hand on what they perceive should be done to remove Saddam?

Secretary Rumsfeld. I don't have any idea what motivates people. The—I mean, I've been kind of struck by the articles being so inconsistent one with another. One day it says that the chiefs are totally out of the loop and not being consulted and they're unhappy, another says they are consulted but they don't agree, another says they're consulted and they do agree. I think it's all kind of mischievous and—but it's not for me to speculate as to why people do things.

Q. Mr. Secretary, I talked to Senator Levin last week, and on the record he said he's talked to a number of top military people and they have significant cautions and concerns about going into Iraq and that the civilian leadership in the building is not giving them due consideration. And I asked him, did you follow this up—did you check this after these articles came out, and he said no, this was a long time ago after talking to a number of people, uniformed officials.

General Myers, is there a reservoir of concern within the building—

General Myers. I think I just answered that.

Q. Well, this is on the record from a top senator, though. I mean—

General Myers. I'm just—I'm just saying that if—I mean the way things are portrayed in these articles simply haven't occurred in front of me, okay? And I can't talk about our operational plans or what our advice is, and so forth. But you can imagine if we were planning an operation against the moon, that we would have a lot of discussion about how best to do that and so forth. So there's obviously going to be discussion about how we go against the moon—

Q. What about the perception that the civilian leadership isn't giving adequate consideration to the military views? I mean, what's your take on the process by which—

General Myers. I'll give you my take on the process—and this is not Iraq-specific—but my take on the process, I don't think—in my time in uniform, in my time in this building, doing what I've been doing as the vice chair—assistant chairman, the vice chairman and the chairman, we are permitted to give our views frequently and regularly and continuously. And we're asked for our views. And, I mean, there's never been a better exchange, in my opinion.

And so I don't know where these things get started. I don't know who's—I mean, like I said, it is not consistent—those articles are not consistent with what I see and what I observe and what I hear.

* * * *

Q. Mr. Secretary, today in an interview with the Associated Press, Saudi Foreign Minister Prince Saud said that the U.S. military would not be able to use Prince Sultan Air Base for any attack on Iraq. Number one, have you seen those comments? And your reaction to that statement.

Secretary Rumsfeld. I have not seen the comments. I have been told that such a statement was made.

You asked what my reaction is. The president has not proposed such a thing. Therefore, I don't find it really something that has been engaged as such.

State Department Press Briefing, August 8, 2002

Q. So, do you have any reaction to Saddam Hussein's speech today warning the U.S. against any military attack against his country?

Mr. Reeker. Well, I think some comments have come from other corners of our government, but it's obvious once again that Saddam's comments are a bluster from an internationally isolated dictator, demonstrative yet again that this regime shows no intention to live up to its obligations under U.N. Security Council resolutions. Those obligations are about disarmament.

The President and the Secretary have been quite clear. We continue to leave all our options available regarding Iraq. Saddam Hussein's regime remains a serious threat to the Iraqi people, to the people of the region, to the neighbors of Iraq, and to international peace and stability. And as the President underscored in his State of the Union Address earlier this year, the regime not only pursues weapons of mass destruction and missiles, but it has shown no reluctance to use weapons even against its own people, as we have seen so vividly in the past.

So we are going to continue working closely with our allies, with the international community, to secure Iraq's full compliance with all U.N. Security Council resolutions, the obligations that Iraq undertook, including the unconditional acceptance and full cooperation with the U.N. weapons inspectors to verify the disarmament that Iraq is required to undertake.

Q. Can you confirm that you've gotten positive replies from everybody who was invited to the meeting tomorrow, everyone whose names you gave us are expected to be there?

Mr. Reeker. Which meeting are we talking about?

Q. The Iraqi oppositions meeting. Sorry.

Mr. Reeker. Yes, as I discussed yesterday, I believe we expect—let me find here what I have on that. Well, we talked about it yesterday—expect representatives of the six groups— that have been invited to Washington for this meeting co-hosted by Under Secretary of State for Political Affairs Grossman and Under Secretary of Defense Feith. It will take place at the Department, that is tomorrow, August 9th.

So there were six groups representing Iraqi oppositionists, and we expect to have representatives from all six of those groups.

Q. I'm asking about the names of the people that you gave us. Are those all the people who will be here, not just the groups?

Mr. Reeker. I'm not sure of the exact things. You might want to check with the groups particularly to see exactly who is going to make it in terms of who may or may not represent the individual leaders of those groups that we invited. I can check back on that and we'll see as we approach the meeting tomorrow, since the meeting is tomorrow.

This obviously is a meeting that is designed to discuss next steps in coordinating our work with the Iraqi opposition. We think it's important to have this coordination and cooperation among those groups, and that is what our meeting will encourage.

* * * *

Q. Back to the Iraqi opposition. How much confidence does the United States have at this point that these six groups can actually work together in a cohesive manner? And also, how do you view them in terms of viability as a serious opposition to Saddam?

Mr. Reeker. I think our goal has been to work with as broad an array of Iraqi opposition as possible. As you know, that has been something we've done for some time. We are trying to establish a process to give a voice to Iraqi experts. We have been doing that not only with the contacts that we've had, with the meeting that we'll have tomorrow hosted by Under Secretary Grossman, but also with the working group meetings that we've had with a variety of experts who can look at the future of Iraq, because obviously there will be a post-Saddam era and there are many that want to look at how to shape Iraq for that era when they are pulled out of the darkness that they have lived under with Saddam Hussein and his cronies.

So we want to work with these groups. We have extensive contacts with them. We want them to work together for common goals which will benefit the people of Iraq and the region and the peace and security of the whole world. And that is what our meetings are about. That is what we're going to talk to these representatives about when we meet with them tomorrow. And we will continue to discuss next steps and how we can coordinate with them and how they can cooperate among themselves.

State Department Press Briefing, August 13, 2002

Q. Mr. Talibani, one of the Kurdish opposition leaders that was in town this week, said in an interview today that the Kurdish factions have offered to the United States for U.S. forces to land or be based in Kurdish territory should the U.S. attack Iraq. Can you confirm that? What do you think of these public comments? And I have a follow-up.

Mr. Reeker. I can't particularly confirm that. I wasn't in those meetings, nor have I found anybody that had that specific reference made, but I saw the public comments on television a short while ago. Obviously it is a hypothetical discussion because, as you know, the President has himself made clear, Secretary Powell and other senior officials have reiterated, the President has taken no decision on any military action vis-á-vis Iraq. You know our views on that. It is quite clear. The Secretary reiterated that, and those were views we shared with the Iraqi opposition groups that were here over the past few days, including in the meeting the Secretary dropped by on Friday, other meetings they've had with other departments here in Washington.

So that's something in terms of our focus, as the Secretary said, working with these groups to see, measure the effectiveness of the opposition elements, how they interact with each other, and the focus of course being on the future of Iraq, having a representative form of government to reflect, as Secretary Powell said, the best of 21st century values in the 21st century world, and not the criminal values of the current regime in Baghdad.

Q. Do you see—this is—it sounds as if this the first time that these groups have made such public offerings to the United States. Do you see this as a—that the U.S. could increase its cooperation with the Kurdish groups? And in addition to that, Mr. Talibani also said that the Kurdish groups have asked the U.S. for protective gear for assurances—and assurances that should Saddam Hussein go into Kurdish territory that they would want to be protected by the U.S.. And I know that you've spoken about the no-fly zones, but in addition to that, has the United States given the Kurdish groups any assurances that if Saddam Hussein were to go into Kurdish territory that they would be protected?

Mr. Reeker. With respect to the security issue, certainly free Iraqis like those in the north run risks. I mean, the record of Saddam Hussein's regime in oppressing and murdering its own people is all too clear, whether we think back to the terror of Halabja or various incursions into other areas, the suppression of people seeking freedom in the south. So we're very conscious of the nature of Saddam Hussein's regime and the risks that those who oppose it run. That's why we have in place Operation Northern Watch and Operation Southern Watch, the no-fly zones, and it's why we have made clear that should Saddam move against the Kurds we would respond.

Q. There was another group that was here that was based in Tehran, one of the six groups, and the leader of that group [*inaudible*] said today in Tehran that he opposed any U.S. invasion of Iraq. Do you feel that—that those comments in any way undermine the assurances that you got when the representatives were here with the other six?

Mr. Reeker. Ben, I just can't add anything more to making very clear what our policy is about Iraq, the discussions we've had with Iraqi opposition groups, and the fact that the President has taken no decisions, has kept all his options on the table. When we have anything more to say about it to respond to your various hypothetical statements and commentary that abounds, then I'll be happy to try to share it with you. But there's just nothing more I can add now.

Remarks by Secretary of Defense Rumsfeld, August 13, 2002

Q. What can you tell us about any high-level meetings with Iraqi opposition?

Secretary Rumsfeld. Well, they were in town for several days and may still be. They had meetings with the State Department, with Marc Grossman, Doug Feith and others—Secretary Powell. And they had apparently a videoconference with Vice President Cheney. And Dick Myers and I visited with them; I think it was Saturday morning. They had views to express and had questions to ask. They were, I thought, really useful and constructive meetings. They've, of course, been involved in various activities for a good many years now. And it was interesting for me for the first time to meet many of them; I'd met several but not all.

* * * *

Q. Do you still believe that even a vigorous weapons inspection program would not be able to find the weapons Saddam Hussein has had four years to hide?

Secretary Rumsfeld. The—it seems to me, and I'm no weapons inspector, so I'm no expert on the subject, but the biggest successes that were achieved by inspectors when inspectors were permitted in were achieved as a result of information that came from defectors. And they were then able to use that information, go into areas and find some things. And when they found some things, Iraq admitted that they were the things that they said they were: chemical, biological weapons of various types.

It is a big country. They've had years to do what they want to do. They have done a great deal of underground tunneling. They have things that are mobile. It makes it very difficult for inspectors under the best of circumstances to find things.

And I just think that a regime—an inspection regime would have to be so intrusive; it'd have to be any time, any place. You'd have to be undoubtedly able to talk to anyone. You'd have to be able to sometimes talk to people outside of the country, with their families with them, because, as you may recall, the defector who went out, when he returned to Iraq, was killed by Saddam Hussein—two of them. I believe they were sons-in-laws of Saddam Hussein.

So if you can't get access to people to get information and access on a basis that they feel safe and that their families feel safe, it would seem to me it would be very difficult.

But we're not anywhere near close that—close to that. I mean, they haven't agreed to any inspectors on any basis, let alone on a basis that would be sufficiently intrusive that reasonable people could expect to learn what they might need to learn.

Letter from Iraqi Foreign Affairs Minister Sabri to United Nations Secretary-General Annan, August 15, 2002

I wish to thank you for your letter of 6 August 2002 in reply to our proposal on the holding of a series of technical discussions between Iraqi experts and those of the United Nations Monitoring, Verification and Inspection Commission (UNMOVIC) with a view to reviewing the progress made in disarmament between May 1991 and December 1998 and to determining how the remaining questions may be settled. I also wish to thank you for your willingness to maintain the dialogue between the United Nations and Iraq for the purpose of resolving outstanding problems between the two parties in accordance with principles of international legitimacy and Security Council resolutions.

Relations between Iraq and the Security Council underwent a serious crisis after the large-scale military aggression launched by the United States and the United Kingdom against Iraq on 16 December 1998, at a time when the Council was in session to consider how to implement your proposal concerning a comprehensive review of the obligations fulfilled by Iraq. Iraq and many other countries were hoping that that review would attain its objectives and would lead to the fulfillment by the Council of the obligations set forth in its resolutions on Iraq, including the lifting of the iniquitous embargo imposed against Iraq in August 1990, the cessation of the persistent acts of aggression against Iraq, and the establishment in the Middle East of a zone free from weapons of mass destruction.

In spite of the condemnation and protests of the international community at that cowardly act of aggression, in whose organization the former United Nations Special Commission (UNSCOM) and its Chairman, Richard Butler, participated, the United States not only prevented the Security Council from taking any measure but even induced it to adopt resolution 1284 (1999). This reformulation of resolution 687 (1991) imposed new conditions, thereby enabling the Council to evade more easily its obligations with regard to Iraq. In its resolution 1382 (2001) of 29 November 2001, the Council itself admitted the non-applicability of resolution 1284 (1999), when it acknowledged that this resolution called for certain clarifications.

By preventing the Security Council from discharging its obligations towards Iraq, the United States added to the sufferings of the Iraqi people by virtue of the maintenance of the embargo, which, by 11 August 2002, had caused the deaths of 1,732,151 Iraqis, most of them children. It also prevented the limited and provisional "oil-for-food" program from meeting the most elementary needs of the Iraqi people, since, by

1 August 2002, it had put on hold 2,170 contracts, totalling $5.3 billion, and it recently imposed a retroactive oil-price-setting mechanism, which has led to a sharp decline in Iraqi oil exports and a steep reduction in the income received under the program.

Since 1991, the United States and the United Kingdom have regularly violated the sovereignty, independence and territorial integrity of Iraq in the illegally imposed no-fly zones. They have committed military acts of aggression on a daily basis since the end of 1998. They launched five large-scale military attacks against Iraq in 1993, 1996, 1998 and 2001. They apply an official policy of interference in the internal affairs of Iraq and are attempting by every means to invade Iraq with a view to installing a puppet regime there, in flagrant violation of international law, the Charter of the United Nations and the relevant resolutions of the Security Council. For its part, the Security Council has never adopted any official measure in this regard.

In order to find a way out of the crisis in the relations between Iraq and the United Nations, the Iraqi Government replied favorably to your proposal concerning the initiation of a dialogue, without conditions, with a flexible timetable, the goal being to arrive at a balanced and equitable implementation of relevant Security Council resolutions which reflects international law and the Charter of the United Nations. In the course of the first series of discussions, held in February 2002, we presented our views on the crisis. The dialogue resumed in March 2002 after being frozen by the United States for more than a year.

In March 2002 you agreed with us that the dialogue between the two parties should be based on international law, the Charter of the United Nations and the resolutions of the Security Council, and not on the political agenda of any State. We said that this dialogue must be dissociated from the political agenda of the United States, which has used, and intends to continue using, the United Nations as an instrument of their foreign policy, which is hostile to Iraq.

During this series of discussions we put 19 questions (see attachment) and requested a response from the Security Council. In these questions, we asked the Council to address the matter of its obligations towards Iraq, as set down in its own resolutions with respect to the lifting of the iniquitous embargo imposed pursuant to paragraphs 21 and 22 of resolution 687 (1991), the establishment in the Middle East of a zone free from weapons of mass destruction as required by paragraph 14 of the same resolution, the cessation of the attacks launched by the United States and the United Kingdom inside and outside the no-fly zones, in violation of all the Council resolutions calling for respect for the sovereignty, independence and territorial integrity of Iraq, the restoration of the economic, cultural, health and social infrastructure of Iraq, after the severe damage caused by the United States-British attacks, the reparation of the moral and psychological harm done to the Iraqi people in violation of international law and international humanitarian law, the recognition of Iraq's right to defend itself under Article 51 of the Charter of the United Nations, and the adoption of decisions regarding the arbitrary Security Council measures preventing Iraq from exercising its right of self defense.

During this series of discussions, we informed you that responses by the Security Council to our questions were necessary in order to provide the Iraqi leaders with sufficient information to enable them to take appropriate decisions concerning the vital interests, security, sovereignty and independence of Iraq. The Iraqi leaders cannot take appropriate decisions on these extremely important questions without knowing the Council's position regarding its obligations towards Iraq under the provisions of its own resolutions. The situation is even more confused because we have to deal with ambiguous texts that can be interpreted in various ways, as the Security Council itself acknowledged in paragraph 6 of resolution 1382 (2001).

In your reply, you indicated that Iraq's questions were legitimate and that you would transmit them to the Security Council for a response. You said that the presence at the discussions of the Executive Chairman of UNMOVIC, Mr. Hans Blix, was an important advance, and you expressed the hope that the technical discussions would take place in parallel with the political discussions, with a view to reaching a comprehensive settlement.

During this series of discussions, Mr. Hans Blix tried to demonstrate that UNMOVIC was different from the former UNSCOM, the mandate of the latter having been marked by scandals, espionage operations and the proven participation of the United States information services, which were directing the work of the Special Commission. All of this led to the cessation of UNSCOM activities and the expulsion of its Chairman. For your part, you reassured the Iraqi party as to the intentions and conduct of Mr. Blix.

These affirmations gave us hope. Accordingly, we sent to the following series of discussions, held in May 2002, a high-level technical delegation composed of the best Iraqi disarmament and inspection experts. Iraq's technical team was headed by two consultants of ministerial rank who discharged the most senior functions in disarmament and inspection. The Iraqi team also included the most senior official of the Iraqi National Surveillance Service and a number of Iraqi experts and scientists specialized in missiles and nuclear, chemical and biological questions.

During the series of discussions held in May 2002, we were surprised to find that the Security Council had not replied to any of our questions and that Mr. Blix refused to hold detailed technical discussions with the Iraqi technical team concerning evaluation modalities during the period elapsed and how to deal with the questions which UNMOVIC considered to be outstanding since this period.

We next participated in the series of discussions held on 4 and 5 July 2002 in Vienna, accompanied by a high-level technical team, with a view to obtaining replies from the Security Council to our questions, studying the elements of a final settlement and engaging in technical discussions with UNMOVIC to determine how to evaluate the progress achieved in disarmament between May 1991 and December 1998 and how to settle the remaining questions.

In the discussions held in Vienna, progress was made with respect to the restitution of Kuwaiti documents, since we agreed with you on a mechanism for the restitution of the Kuwaiti archives and other documents. We also made progress in our technical discussions with the International Atomic Energy Agency. The Agency was of the view that no disarmament question was still outstanding and that the three remaining questions could be settled within the framework of a continuing inspection operation. For your part, you informed us, again, that you had not obtained replies from the Security Council to our questions, despite the legitimacy of our request.

During this series of discussions, we reaffirmed that the only way out of the crisis in the relations between Iraq and the United Nations, caused by the conduct of the

United States, was to resolve all the elements of the problem, in other words to lift the comprehensive and inhumane embargo imposed for 12 years on the Iraqi people; to respect the security and territorial integrity of Iraq; to deal with the problem of the destruction caused by the United States-British military attacks and the comprehensive embargo; and for both parties to establish a transparent mechanism which would enable the United Nations to verify United States allegations regarding the possession and development by Iraq of weapons of mass destruction, including nuclear, chemical and biological weapons.

In this context, we stated that the experience of the past 11 years had demonstrated without any shadow of a doubt that no purpose was served when the Security Council, under the pressure of the United States, concentrated on a single element (weapons inspection and monitoring) and neglected the links between this element and the other requirements specified in Council resolutions. Here, an important and revealing fact needs to be stated: when it returned to Iraq, the inspection team carried out 427 inspections between mid-November and mid-December 1998, and the Chairman of UNSCOM, Richard Butler, noted that Iraq had failed to cooperate in five, or 1 per cent, of these inspections. This means that, even in the opinion of intransigent and suspicious persons like Butler, Iraq cooperated in 99 per cent of the cases, a point which the Security Council should bear in mind in fulfilling its obligations. Yet, between 16 and 20 December 1998, Iraq was rewarded for this very high level of cooperation with the launching by the United States and the United Kingdom of 460 Cruise missiles and thousands of aerial bombs and missiles.

We have reaffirmed that the Iraqi request concerning a comprehensive settlement was based on international law and resolutions of the Security Council, which in the most recent of those resolutions, namely resolution 1382 (2001), requested that a comprehensive settlement should be reached.

To move forward the technical discussions, the Iraqi delegation attending the discussions in Vienna made a proposal aimed at advancing the dialogue on weapons inspection. It suggested the holding of an expanded technical meeting to take stock of the preceding period (May 1991-December 1998), and more precisely to determine what had been accomplished in the way of disarmament tasks specified in Security Council resolutions and to find a way of settling the remaining disarmament questions which the former UNSCOM had listed at the end of 1998 and which Mr. Amorim mentioned in his report at the beginning of 1999, the goal being to lay jointly and clearly the basis for any future inspection operation. At the end of this series of discussions, you told us that you would endeavor to obtain the Council's replies to our questions and our appeal for a comprehensive settlement, and that you hoped that the discussions would continue with the Iraqi delegation, including at the technical level.

In order to continue the contacts with you, in both the political and technical fields, I sent you a letter dated 1 August 2002 proposing the holding of a series of technical discussions between the two parties, in implementation of the proposal that you had made during the Vienna discussions.

To our great regret, we learned through the press (the daily newspaper Al-Hayat of 4 August 2002) of the speedy, direct and negative reaction by Mr. Blix to the proposals made in our letter, and this was even before you met with the Security Council on 5 August to consider these proposals. The position taken by Mr. Blix reminds us of the bitter experience that we, along with the United Nations, had with Mr. Richard Butler, Chairman of the former Special Commission (UNSCOM), who, through his acts, statements and decisions, exceeded the powers of the United Nations Secretariat and the Security Council.

Mr. Blix's comments to the effect that paragraph 7 of Security Council resolution 1284 (1999) prohibits him from discussing with the Iraqi party the technical aspects of the method for resolving in the future the outstanding questions do not square with the facts and realities and ignore the obscure and inapplicable nature of that resolution, which justifies our opposition to the text and is confirmed by three permanent members as well as Security Council resolution 1382 (2001) itself, paragraph 7 of which refers to a list of basic outstanding questions in the field of disarmament to be drawn up by UNMOVIC after its return to Iraq. In the proposal set forth in our letter, we are not asking that this list (which, contrary to what UNMOVIC claims, does not exist) be discussed, but rather that we take stock of the disarmament tasks which have been carried out and that we reach agreement on the way to resolve the tasks which the former Special Commission listed as not having been completed as of 15 December 1998, as they were defined by the former Special Commission at that time and set forth in the report that Ambassador Amorim submitted to the Security Council on 30 March 1999.

The technical dialogue that we have proposed is designed to avoid the differences of views and the crises which marked the work of the inspectors during the period from 1991 to 1998 and to lay a solid foundation on which future cooperation would be built. If the outstanding questions from the earlier period are not resolved, it will be difficult to begin a new period that would be based on professional cooperation aimed at settling the remaining disarmament questions insofar as we would find ourselves again in a minefield and only a few weeks would pass before the new monitoring regime once again would lead to differences of views and crises and the inspectors would again withdraw after having raised further demands for updated information in such a way as to cause further harmful effects and provide the United States and those who support it with a pretext for attacking Iraq again, as had occurred throughout the period from 1991 to 1998.

With regard to the chronology for implementing the measures set forth in resolution 1284 (1999), I should like to reaffirm that we are not requesting a discussion of the key disarmament tasks that remain to be carried out under paragraph 7 of that resolution in order to raise the question of the chronology for implementing those measures. Therefore, the chronology for implementing the measures set forth in the Security Council resolutions can also be considered in a comprehensive manner, that is to say, within the context of the implementation of all the measures set out in the Council resolutions, according to their merit and without selectively giving preference to one or another issue or resolution. From this point of view, the first necessary measure to be carried out urgently is that contained in the eighth preambular paragraph of resolution 686 (1991), which reaffirms the commitment of all Member States to the independence, sovereignty and territorial integrity of Iraq. The United States and the United Kingdom should also immediately put an end to the illegal so-called air exclusion zones and all other acts which violate Iraq's sovereignty, independence and territorial integrity. Then there is the implementation of paragraphs 14, 21 and 22 of resolution 687 (1991) and the reconsideration of the arbitrary compensation imposed on Iraq, through judicious application of paragraph 19 of resolution 687 (1991) and paragraph 3 of resolution 705 (1991), before proceeding to the other applicable provisions.

I should like to reaffirm, in this regard, that the proposal for a technical meeting that we put forward during the Vienna discussions and in the preceding letter that we addressed to you is in accordance with and complements your own proposal of September 1998 aimed at undertaking a comprehensive consideration of the disarmament phase since, according to the document that you submitted to the Security Council on 5 October 1998, the direct goal of the first phase of comprehensive consideration was to reach agreement on a method of work and a timetable which, if they were respected, would make it possible to meet speedily the disarmament requirements set forth in section C of resolution 687 (1991).

The proposal set forth in our letter therefore constitutes a very important step towards a comprehensive solution that would ensure that all the requirements of the relevant Security Council resolutions are satisfied in a synchronized manner.

The statement of the facts provided below is designed to demonstrate the scope of the injustice and the harm done to Iraq by the United States, which is using Security Council resolutions to cover illegal activities violating international law, the Charter of the United Nations and the Security Council resolutions concerning Iraq. These activities on the part of the United States have, furthermore, seriously harmed the credibility of the United Nations and represent a flagrant example of double standards. The brazen interference by the United States in the work of the Organization and its acts of aggression against Iraq since 1991, in violation of the Charter of the United Nations, have never stopped us from hoping that this bitter experience will be overcome and that the United Nations will assume even more effectively its role of saving future generations from the scourge of war, ensuring respect for basic human rights, affirming the equal rights of all nations, small or large, and promoting social progress and the establishment of better living conditions in greater freedom.

We have thus committed ourselves to continuing the dialogue with the United Nations Secretariat in spite of all the difficulties in order to ensure the complete implementation of all the Security Council resolutions, in accordance with the Charter of the United Nations. On the basis of this principle, we reaffirm our offer of a further series of technical discussions in order to evaluate what was accomplished in the preceding phase and to consider how to deal with the issues which had not yet been settled when the inspectors voluntarily withdrew in 1998, on the basis of the outstanding questions referred to in Ambassador Amorim's report. At the same time, the United Nations technical delegation will be entirely free to raise all the issues that it deems necessary in order to make progress in the discussion and establish rules making it possible to lay a common foundation for the following phase of monitoring and inspection activities, including consideration of the practical arrangements for establishing the monitoring regime in the future, and lay the groundwork for progress towards reaching a comprehensive settlement under which all the requirements of the relevant Security Council resolutions would be satisfied in a synchronized manner.

Looking forward to a positive response, I should like to convey to you the assurances of my highest consideration.

Attachment

Questions which Iraq's Foreign Minister presented to the United Nations Secretary-General in the session of talks on 7 March 2002 and to which he requested answers from the Security Council

1. What is your vision and assessment of what we have achieved after seven years and seven months of Iraq's cooperation with the Special Committee and the International Atomic Energy Agency? How can this cooperation be built on?

2. If one or two of the Security Council's permanent members say that they are not assured of Iraq's disarmament, we want to know what they want to be assured of. What are they looking for? What is the necessary time frame to complete this? We also ought to be satisfied, not just the Security Council, in order to go on cooperating with it. If they have any doubts about a certain site or activity, we ought to know about it.

3. How do you explain the stance of a permanent member of the Security Council which officially calls for the invasion of Iraq and the imposition of an agent regime on its people by force, in clear violation of the Security Council resolutions themselves, which clearly state that Iraq's sovereignty, independence and territorial integrity and the rules of international law and the United Nations Charter must be respected? At the same time, it demands that Iraq implement the Security Council's resolutions.

4. Is the Security Council seriously adhering to its mandate and the resolutions which it adopted, in particular, resolution 687 (1991), and to the fair, legal reading of this resolution? Or is the Security Council subject to the United States explanation of the resolutions and to the unilateral decisions of the United States concerning Iraq?

5. How could normal relations between Iraq and the Security Council be achieved under the current declared United States policy of seeking to invade Iraq and change by force its patriotic political regime?

6. The United States continuously declares that the economic sanctions imposed on Iraq will remain as long as the patriotic political regime in Iraq stays. What is the Security Council's position on this policy, which violates the relevant Security Council resolutions?

7. What guarantees could the United Nations offer to prevent interference between Iraq's relations with the United Nations and the United States agenda?

8. The concept of synchronicity in implementing the reciprocal obligations set forth in the Security Council resolutions related to Iraq is necessary and essential to rebuild confidence between Iraq and the Security Council. What are your views on the obligations related to Iraq's rights, first and foremost the lifting of sanctions, respect for Iraq's sovereignty, independence and territorial integrity and making the Middle East region free of weapons of mass destruction. What are the obligations the Security Council ought to implement to open up a new page of cooperation between Iraq and the United Nations? How could we set up a mechanism that secures the synchronized implementation of the two sides' obligations?

9. Is it fair to ask Iraq to implement Security Council resolutions and the same not be demanded of a permanent member of the Security Council which continues to vio-

late those resolutions, especially those related to respecting Iraq's sovereignty, independence and territorial integrity, and officially vows that its policy aims to invade the Republic of Iraq and overthrow its regime?

10. After disclosure of the espionage activities of former UNSCOM inspectors and the International Atomic Energy Agency according to confessions made by some members of the Special Committee and statements issued by United States sources and some Security Council permanent members and to what was acknowledged by the Secretariat, is it fair that inspectors return to Iraq who could be used to spy against Iraq and its leadership and to update information about Iraq's vital economic installations so as to bomb them in a coming aggression?

11. Could the United Nations ensure that those coming to Iraq are not spies and will not commit espionage activities?

12. Could the United Nations guarantee the elimination of the two no-fly zones? Could the United Nations guarantee that the upcoming inspection would not be a prelude to an aggression against Iraq as in 1998? Could the United Nations guarantee that the United States would not attack Iraq during the inspection operations, as throughout the seven and a half years from May 1991 to December 1998?

13. What is the Secretary-General's view about the time required for the inspection teams to make sure that Iraq does not have weapons of mass destruction and to inform the Security Council of this fact? What methods is the United Nations thinking of using in this respect and how far are they in keeping with the related international accords?

14. How would inspectors from States which are declaring their intention to threaten Iraq's national security, invade it and change its regime, apply their international, unbiased mandate on Iraq or respect the Security Council's resolutions and their duties under the Charter? The presence of United States and British inspectors on the Special Committee and the International Atomic Energy Agency helped the United States and the United Kingdom collect intelligence data and specify locations that were targeted in their aggression. All locations which had been visited by the inspection teams were exposed in the 1998 aggression, including the presidential sites, despite the inspectors' statement that there were no weapons of mass destruction. The United States and the United Kingdom also bombed all the industrial sites according to inspection data while they were under continuous monitoring.

15. What is the Secretary-General's view of the structure of UNMOVIC? Is it plausible to approve individuals who violated their unbiased mandate and duties, in addition to the reputation of the Organization, when they spied on Iraq?

16. What is the mandate of UNMOVIC? The United Nations statements and documents released up to now are ambiguous. What is the authority of its Head? What is the authority of its College of Commissioners? What is the form of the Secretary-General's supervision of its functioning? What are the guarantees that the Commission and its chief would not abuse their authority? What are the guarantees that the Commission would not violate Iraq's sovereign rights?

17. The dropping of 120,000 tons of bombs, including 800 tons of depleted uranium, on Iraq during the 1991 aggression and the aggressions that followed, in addition to the all-out, 12-year blockade, has led to the semi-demolition of the economic, health, education and services infrastructure. Iraq will need to utilize all its resources

when sanctions are lifted to rebuild its basic installations. The question of compensation and its high rates poses a big obstacle to this. What does the Secretary-General envisage to correct this situation? Does he intend to send expert teams to Iraq to discuss the question of reconstruction and its costs and to prepare the requirements to urge the Security Council to reconsider the question of compensation?

18. The blockade and the military aggressions launched by the United States and Britain against Iraq since 1991 have caused huge material and human losses in Iraq. What are the possibilities of considering, within a comprehensive solution based on justice, compensating Iraq for the human, material and psychological damage and losses that its people have suffered on the same basis adopted by the Security Council for compensation?

19. Iraq has a firm right to self-defense under Article 15 of the Charter. The Security Council did not abide by its commitments concerning Iraq's sovereignty and territorial integrity, thus encouraging regional parties to violate Iraq's national security. How do you see the question of Iraq's right to self-defense and its right under international law and the Charter to possess defense weapons?

Remarks by General Franks, August 15, 2002

General Tom Franks, combatant commander of the U.S. Central Command, delivered his remarks at a Department of Defense briefing.

Q. May I ask General Franks a question about Iraq, the situation on the ground in Iraq. Do you see any evidence that the Iraqis are dispersing elements of their military capability, whether it may be conventional or otherwise?

General Franks. We do not see evidence of some magnitude of shift that would sort of go probably in the direction that you're trying to go. As you know, because of Operation Southern Watch, we pay attention to what's going on there. You know, we have an obligation under Security Council resolutions to continue to do our intel, surveillance and reconnaissance activities inside these so-called no-fly zones, and so we watch that. And the specifics of, I guess, what we see when we look at that, I wouldn't want to get into, and I think you'd probably understand that.

Q. General Franks, three of the most repeated words in news accounts in the last three months have talked about "leaked war plans." To what extent at your level do these numerous stories compromise your ability to craft options, recommend courses of action to policymakers or not? I mean, do these represent things that are actually bubbling up from CENTCOM or just things you haven't even been able to track that have little or no relevance to your process, whatever the process ends up being?

General Franks. Let me give you an answer that's too clever by half, by saying on the day that we permit what we read in our media to affect what we try to do as part of the Department of Defense on behalf of the nation, that would be a sad day. And so probably that's the most direct answer that I can give you.

I think the secretary, and I think perhaps others, have said that the intentional leaking of any sort of activity that carries a classification by anyone is wrong. And so we take that as a given, but we continue to do the work that the president and secretary ask us to do in CENTCOM.

Q. The point, though, is a lot of the press is being seen as, you know, traitors, fellow travelers, for putting this stuff out. You're the chief planner. Have any of the stories, to date, actually resulted in national security compromises as you, as the tactical military commander would understand—

General Franks. I think we probably want to be careful to either confirm or deny something that could be helpful to a potential adversary. And so I really can't—I really can't give you a good answer to it.

We're going to continue our work. I'll say that.

Remarks by President Bush and Secretary of Defense Rumsfeld, August 21, 2002

President Bush and Secretary Donald Rumsfeld delivered their remarks after meeting at the President's ranch in Crawford, Texas.

Q. Sir, after you've studied today the military capabilities of the United States and looking ahead to future threats, one thing that has to factor in is the growing number of U.S. allies, Russia, Germany, Bahrain, now Canada, who say that if you go to war with Saddam, you're going to go alone.

Does the American military have the capability to prosecute this war alone?

President Bush. Well, look, if you're asking—are you asking about Iraq? The subject didn't come up in this meeting.

But, having said that, we take all threats seriously and we will continue to consult with our friends and allies.

I know there is this kind of intense speculation that seems to be going on, a kind of a—I don't know how you would describe it. It's kind of a churning—

Secretary Rumsfeld. Frenzy.

President Bush. Frenzy is how the Secretary would describe it. But the subject didn't come up.

We will obviously continue to consult with our friends and allies. Your question makes certain assumptions that may or may not be true. But we will continue to talk with our—with the people concerned about peace and how to secure the peace, and those are needed consultations.

Not only will we consult with friends and allies, we'll consult with members of Congress.

Secretary Rumsfeld. Could I just add a comment there, Mr. President? I think it's worth noting on that particular subject, that the President of the United States and the

Secretary of State and our country has put together a coalition that stretches across the entire globe that is addressing the problem of the global war on terrorism. It is 80 or 90 countries. There are 37 or 38 down in Tampa, Florida, with liaison officers. We have, at any given time, 18, 20, a couple dozen of countries involved in Afghanistan participating.

The coalition that is working on the global war on terrorism that the President and the Secretary have put together is broad, it's deep, it's impressive, and it is in fact what is helping the forward progress that we're achieving, the traction that we're getting with respect to dealing with the terrible, terribly difficult problem of global terrorist networks.

* * * *

Q. [General Franks today] has said that he is drawing up war plans to provide you with credible options. Now, should the American people conclude from that that you're reaching some critical point, that a decision is imminent?

President Bush. First of all, in the midst of the frenzy I want you to note that General Franks is not here. General Franks is doing his job. And one of the jobs that the Secretary of Defense has tasked to members of his general staff is to prepare for all contingencies, whether it be in the particular country that you seem to be riveted on, or any other country, for that matter.

We face a—the world is not stable. The world changes. There are—this terrorist network is global in nature and they may strike anywhere. And, therefore, we've got to be prepared to use our military and all the other assets at our disposal in a way to keep the peace. So General Franks is doing what the Secretary has asked.

Would you like to comment on that?

Secretary Rumsfeld. I would. As the President indicated, one of the things we discussed here today was the contingency planning guidance that he signed. I then meet with all of the combatant commanders for every area of responsibility across the globe. I do it on a regular basis. We go over all the conceivable contingencies that could occur.

So General Franks, as well as every other combatant commander—I met, I think, within the last 30 days with at least three of them on various types of contingency plans in totally different parts of the world. That's my job. That's their job, is to see that we have the ability to protect the American people and deal effectively on behalf of our friends and our allies and our deployed forces.

So it is their task to work with me and ultimately with the President as the chain of command goes from the Commander-in-Chief, the President of the United States, to me, to the combatant commanders. And they're doing exactly what I've asked them to do and what the President has asked me to do.

* * * *

Q. Considering how much discussion has been going on recently about Saddam, do you feel a need to get out there and make a case for toppling him? And, if so, do you feel a need to do it before Election Day?

President Bush. What I need to do is to continue to, as we call it, consult with people who share our interests to make the world a safer place, and I will do so. The American people know my position, and that is, is that regime change is in the interests of the world. How we achieve that is a matter of consultation and deliberative—deliberation, which I do, I'm a deliberate person.

I say it in my speeches, which you fortunately don't have to cover, that I'm a patient man. And when I say I'm a patient man, I mean I'm a patient man, and that we will look at all options and we will consider all technologies available to us and diplomacy and intelligence.

But one thing is for certain, is that this administration agrees that Saddam Hussein is a threat and he will be—that's a part of our thinking. And that hasn't changed.

Nothing he has done has convinced me—I'm confident the Secretary of Defense—that he is the kind of fellow that is willing to forgo weapons of mass destruction, is willing to be a peaceful neighbor, that is—will honor the people—the Iraqi people of all stripes, will—values human life. He hasn't convinced me, nor has he convinced my administration.

August 26–October 10, 2002
"The Danger to Our Country is Grave...":
The Bush Administration Presses Congress to Authorize Use of Force in Iraq

CHRONOLOGY

2002

September 12. In an address to the United Nations General Assembly, President Bush challenges the U.N. to confront the "grave and gathering danger" of Iraq or stand aside as the United States and likeminded nations act. The U.N. Security Council begins discussion on drafting a new resolution to encourage Iraq to comply with the previous 16 U.N. resolutions.

September 24. British Prime Minister Tony Blair announces the publication of a dossier on Iraq's military capability.

September 26. Secretary of Defense Donald Rumsfeld accuses Iraq of harboring al Qaeda terrorists and aiding their quest for weapons of mass destruction.

Sources: Chronology entries are drawn from www.abc.com, www.bbc.com, www.nytimes.com, www.reuters.com, www.washingtonpost.com, www.wikipedia.com, and staff research.

DOCUMENTS

Remarks by Vice President Cheney, August 26, 2002

Vice President Dick Cheney delivered his remarks at the National Convention of the VFW.

[T]he challenges to our country involve more than just tracking down a single person or one small group. Nine-eleven and its aftermath awakened this nation to danger, to the true ambitions of the global terror network, and to the reality that weapons of mass destruction are being sought by determined enemies who would not hesitate to use them against us.

It is a certainty that the al Qaeda network is pursuing such weapons, and has succeeded in acquiring at least a crude capability to use them. We found evidence of their efforts in the ruins of al Qaeda hideouts in Afghanistan. And we've seen in recent days additional confirmation in videos recently shown on CNN—pictures of al Qaeda members training to commit acts of terror, and testing chemical weapons on dogs. Those terrorists who remain at large are determined to use these capabilities against the United States and our friends and allies around the world.

As we face this prospect, old doctrines of security do not apply. In the days of the Cold War, we were able to manage the threat with strategies of deterrence and containment. But it's a lot tougher to deter enemies who have no country to defend. And containment is not possible when dictators obtain weapons of mass destruction, and are prepared to share them with terrorists who intend to inflict catastrophic casualties on the United States.

The case of Saddam Hussein, a sworn enemy of our country, requires a candid appraisal of the facts. After his defeat in the Gulf War in 1991, Saddam agreed under to U.N. Security Council Resolution 687 to cease all development of weapons of mass destruction. He agreed to end his nuclear weapons program. He agreed to destroy his chemical and his biological weapons. He further agreed to admit U.N. inspection teams into his country to ensure that he was in fact complying with these terms.

In the past decade, Saddam has systematically broken each of these agreements. The Iraqi regime has in fact been very busy enhancing its capabilities in the field of chemical and biological agents. And they continue to pursue the nuclear program they began so many years ago. These are not weapons for the purpose of defending Iraq; these are offensive weapons for the purpose of inflicting death on a massive scale, developed so that Saddam can hold the threat over the head of anyone he chooses, in his own region or beyond.

On the nuclear question, many of you will recall that Saddam's nuclear ambitions suffered a severe setback in 1981 when the Israelis bombed the Osirak reactor. They suffered another major blow in Desert Storm and its aftermath.

But we now know that Saddam has resumed his efforts to acquire nuclear weapons. Among other sources, we've gotten this from the firsthand testimony of defectors—including Saddam's own son-in- law, who was subsequently murdered at Saddam's direction. Many of us are convinced that Saddam will acquire nuclear weapons fairly soon.

Just how soon, we cannot really gauge. Intelligence is an uncertain business, even in the best of circumstances. This is especially the case when you are dealing with a totalitarian regime that has made a science out of deceiving the international community. Let me give you just one example of what I mean. Prior to the Gulf War, America's top intelligence analysts would come to my office in the Defense Department and tell me that Saddam Hussein was at least five or perhaps even 10 years away from having a nuclear weapon. After the war we learned that he had been much closer than that, perhaps within a year of acquiring such a weapon.

Saddam also devised an elaborate program to conceal his active efforts to build chemical and biological weapons. And one must keep in mind the history of U.N. inspection teams in Iraq. Even as they were conducting the most intrusive system of arms control in history, the inspectors missed a great deal. Before being barred from the country, the inspectors found and destroyed thousands of chemical weapons, and hundreds of tons of mustard gas and other nerve agents.

Yet Saddam Hussein had sought to frustrate and deceive them at every turn, and was often successful in doing so. I'll cite one instance. During the spring of 1995, the inspectors were actually on the verge of declaring that Saddam's programs to develop chemical weapons and longer-range ballistic missiles had been fully accounted for and shut down. Then Saddam's son-in-law suddenly defected and began sharing information. Within days the inspectors were led to an Iraqi chicken farm. Hidden there were boxes of documents and lots of evidence regarding Iraq's most secret weapons programs. That should serve as a reminder to all that we often learned more as the result of defections than we learned from the inspection regime itself.

To the dismay of the inspectors, they in time discovered that Saddam had kept them largely in the dark about the extent of his program to mass produce VX, one of the deadliest chemicals known to man. And far from having shut down Iraq's prohibited missile programs, the inspectors found that Saddam had continued to test such missiles, almost literally under the noses of the U.N. inspectors.

Against that background, a person would be right to question any suggestion that we should just get inspectors back into Iraq, and then our worries will be over. Saddam has perfected the game of cheat and retreat, and is very skilled in the art of denial and deception. A return of inspectors would provide no assurance whatsoever of his compliance with U.N. resolutions. On the contrary, there is a great danger that it would provide false comfort that Saddam was somehow "back in his box."

Meanwhile, he would continue to plot. Nothing in the last dozen years has stopped him—not his agreements; not the discoveries of the inspectors; not the revelations by defectors; not criticism or ostracism by the international community; and not four days of bombings by the U.S. in 1998. What he wants is time and more time to husband his resources, to invest in his ongoing chemical and biological weapons programs, and to gain possession of nuclear arms.

Should all his ambitions be realized, the implications would be enormous for the Middle East, for the United States, and for the peace of the world. The whole range of weapons of mass destruction then would rest in the hands of a dictator who has already shown his willingness to use such weapons, and has done so, both in his war with Iran and against his own people. Armed with an arsenal of these weapons of terror, and seated atop ten percent of the world's oil reserves, Saddam Hussein could then be expected to seek domination of the entire Middle East, take control of a great portion of the world's energy supplies, directly threaten America's friends throughout the region, and subject the United States or any other nation to nuclear blackmail.

Simply stated, there is no doubt that Saddam Hussein now has weapons of mass destruction. There is no doubt he is amassing them to use against our friends, against our allies, and against us. And there is no doubt that his aggressive regional ambitions will lead him into future confrontations with his neighbors—confrontations that will involve both the weapons he has today, and the ones he will continue to develop with his oil wealth.

Ladies and gentlemen, there is no basis in Saddam Hussein's conduct or history to discount any of the concerns that I am raising this morning. We are, after all, dealing with the same dictator who shoots at American and British pilots in the no-fly zone, on a regular basis, the same dictator who dispatched a team of assassins to murder former President Bush as he traveled abroad, the same dictator who invaded Iran and Kuwait, and has fired ballistic missiles at Iran, Saudi Arabia, and Israel, the same dictator who has been on the State Department's list of state sponsors of terrorism for the better part of two decades.

In the face of such a threat, we must proceed with care, deliberation, and consultation with our allies. I know our president very well. I've worked beside him as he directed our response to the events of 9/11. I know that he will proceed cautiously and deliberately to consider all possible options to deal with the threat that an Iraq ruled by Saddam Hussein represents. And I am confident that he will, as he has said he would, consult widely with the Congress and with our friends and allies before deciding upon a course of action. He welcomes the debate that has now been joined here at home, and he has made it clear to his national security team that he wants us to participate fully in the hearings that will be held in Congress next month on this vitally important issue.

We will profit as well from a review of our own history. There are a lot of World War II veterans in the hall today. For the United States, that war began on December 7, 1941, with the attack on Pearl Harbor and the near-total destruction of our Pacific Fleet. Only then did we recognize the magnitude of the danger to our country. Only then did the Axis powers fully declare their intentions against us. By that point, many countries had fallen. Many millions had died. And our nation was plunged into a two-front war resulting in more than a million American casualties. To this day, historians continue to analyze that war, speculating on how we might have prevented Pearl Harbor, and asking what actions might have averted the tragedies that rate among the worst in human history.

America in the year 2002 must ask careful questions, not merely about our past, but also about our future. The elected leaders of this country have a responsibility to consider all of the available options. And we are doing so. What we must not do in the face of a mortal threat is give in to wishful thinking or willful blindness. We will not simply look away, hope for the best, and leave the matter for some future administration to resolve. As President Bush has said, time is not on our side. Deliverable weapons of mass destruction in the hands of a terror network, or a murderous dictator, or the two working together, constitutes as grave a threat as can be imagined. The risks of inaction are far greater than the risk of action.

Now and in the future, the United States will work closely with the global coalition to deny terrorists and their state sponsors the materials, technology, and expertise to make and deliver weapons of mass destruction. We will develop and deploy effective missile defenses to protect America and our allies from sudden attack. And the entire world must know that we will take whatever action is necessary to defend our freedom and our security.

As former Secretary of State Kissinger recently stated: "The imminence of proliferation of weapons of mass destruction, the huge dangers it involves, the rejection of a viable inspection system, and the demonstrated hostility of Saddam Hussein combine to produce an imperative for preemptive action." If the United States could have preempted 9/11, we would have, no question. Should we be able to prevent another, much more devastating attack, we will, no question. This nation will not live at the mercy of terrorists or terror regimes.

I am familiar with the arguments against taking action in the case of Saddam Hussein. Some concede that Saddam is evil, power- hungry, and a menace—but that, until he crosses the threshold of actually possessing nuclear weapons, we should rule out any preemptive action. That logic seems to me to be deeply flawed. The argument comes down to this: yes, Saddam is as dangerous as we say he is, we just need to let him get stronger before we do anything about it.

Yet if we did wait until that moment, Saddam would simply be emboldened, and it would become even harder for us to gather friends and allies to oppose him. As one of those who worked to assemble the Gulf War coalition, I can tell you that our job then would have been infinitely more difficult in the face of a nuclear-armed Saddam Hussein. And many of those who now argue that we should act only if he gets a nuclear weapon, would then turn around and say that we cannot act because he has a nuclear weapon. At bottom, that argument counsels a course of inaction that itself could have devastating consequences for many countries, including our own.

Another argument holds that opposing Saddam Hussein would cause even greater troubles in that part of the world, and interfere with the larger war against terror. I believe the opposite is true. Regime change in Iraq would bring about a number of benefits to the region. When the gravest of threats are eliminated, the freedom-loving peoples of the region will have a chance to promote the values that can bring lasting peace. As for the reaction of the Arab "street," the Middle East expert Professor Fouad Ajami predicts that after liberation, the streets in Basra and Baghdad are "sure to erupt in joy in the same way the throngs in Kabul greeted the Americans." Extremists in the region would have to rethink their strategy of Jihad. Moderates throughout the region would take heart. And our ability to advance the Israeli-Palestinian peace process would be enhanced, just as it was following the liberation of Kuwait in 1991.

The reality is that these times bring not only dangers but also opportunities. In the Middle East, where so many have known only poverty and oppression, terror and tyranny, we look to the day when people can live in freedom and dignity and the young can grow up free of the conditions that breed despair, hatred, and violence.

In other times the world saw how the United States defeated fierce enemies, then helped rebuild their countries, forming strong bonds between our peoples and our governments. Today in Afghanistan, the world is seeing that America acts not to conquer but to liberate, and remains in friendship to help the people build a future of stability, self-determination, and peace.

We would act in that same spirit after a regime change in Iraq. With our help, a liberated Iraq can be a great nation once again. Iraq is rich in natural resources and human talent, and has unlimited potential for a peaceful, prosperous future. Our goal would be an Iraq that has territorial integrity, a government that is democratic and pluralistic, a nation where the human rights of every ethnic and religious group are recognized and protected. In that troubled land all who seek justice, and dignity, and the chance to live their own lives, can know they have a friend and ally in the United States of America.

Great decisions and challenges lie ahead of us. Yet we can and we will build a safer and better world beyond the war on terror. Over the past year, millions here and abroad have been inspired once again by the bravery and the selflessness of the American armed forces. For my part, I have been reminded on a daily basis, as I was during my years at the Pentagon, of what a privilege it is to work with the people of our military. In whatever branch, at whatever rank, these are men and women who live by a code, who give America the best years of their lives, and who show the world the finest qualities of our country.

As veterans, each of you has a place in the long, unbroken line of Americans who came to the defense of freedom. Having served in foreign wars, you bore that duty in some of our nation's most difficult hours. And I know that when you come together, your thoughts inevitably turn to those who never lived to be called veterans. In a book about his Army years, Andy Rooney tells the story of his childhood friend Obie Slingerland—a decent, good-hearted, promising boy who was captain of the high school football team. Obie later went on to be the quarterback at Amherst before entering the Navy and becoming a pilot. Still a young man in his early 20s, he was killed while flying a combat mission off the carrier Saratoga. Andy Rooney writes: "I have awakened in the middle of the night a thousand times and thought about the life I had that Obie never got to have."

Many of you have known that experience. The entire nation joins you in honoring the memory of your friends, and all who have died for our freedom. And the American people will always respect each one of you for your standing ready to make that same sacrifice. On the nation's behalf, and for myself and President Bush, I thank you for the service you gave to your fellow citizens, for the loyalty you have shown to each other and for the great honor you have brought to your uniform, to our flag, and to our country.

Remarks by Secretary of Defense Rumsfeld and Chairman of the Joint Chiefs of Staff Myers, September 3, 2002

Q. Mr. Secretary, much has been said and reported about alleged differences between you and the vice president, on one hand, and Secretary Powell on the other, on a possible preemptive invasion of Iraq to remove Saddam Hussein from power. Secretary Powell indicated over the weekend that he is willing to—in fact, wants inspectors to go back into Iraq. Do you think that there's anything that inspectors in Iraq could do to change this administration's policy to remove Saddam Hussein from power for a regime change?

Secretary Rumsfeld. Well, with respect to the first part of the question, I came to this town in 1957 to work up on Capitol Hill, and I don't suppose there's been a year in the period since that that there haven't been stories just like the ones you're citing here that there are differences of opinions. The truth of the matter is that the president's national security team meets together frequently. We do so in person, we do so on the phone. We have excellent discussions and it is a very friendly, professional and constructive set of discussions that take place in that process.

I don't know of differences that—there are always differences of perspective, there are differences of—institutional differences from time to time. But the president is the president. He is the one who ran for that office and was elected to that office. He's the one who makes decisions and calibrations and guidance, and he does it very well. I don't know quite why it is that it seems so much easier for folks to personalize things rather than to go to substance.

The subject you raised second, with respect to inspections, is clearly a complicated set of issues. And my understanding—and I hate to even talk about this because someone will contrast it with something that somebody else said that I haven't read or seen and attempt to find a seam between what I'm going to say and what somebody else may have said. But it obviously has been the position of this administration to favor inspections. It is the Iraqis that ended the inspections. That we all know. We protested when the Iraqis threw the inspectors out.

The Iraqis made a conscious decision to tell the international community that the arrangement that they had entered into at the end of the Gulf War involving inspections, and the other undertakings with respect to not developing weapons of mass destruction and the like—they made a conscious decision at various points to negate those agreements, to tell the international community that they no longer would abide by them. And so the offense, if there is one, is committed against the United Nations and the international community.

Would it be nice if they had not thrown the inspectors out? Yes, that would have been preferable. Would it be preferable for inspectors to be able to have any-time/any-place access so that at least some additional knowledge could be gained? Sure it would. Are the Iraqis—do they have a pattern of denying that? Yes, they do.

Q. Do you think it's possible for inspectors to go in there—you've repeatedly said you don't— do you think it's possible for inspectors to go in there and somehow change this administration's push for a regime change in Baghdad? Do you think it's possible?

Secretary Rumsfeld. I just simply don't know. Those are judgments that the president will have to make. First of all, I think that the intrusiveness of any inspection regime that would be sufficiently permissive to enable the rest of the world to know that in fact the U.N. resolutions were being fulfilled and lived up to would be such that it's unlikely for the folks there to agree to it. And I haven't seen any inclination on their part to agree to anything except as a ploy from time to time to muse over the possibility we might do this or we might do that and kind of play the international community and the U.N. process like a guitar, plucking the right string at the right moment to delay something. But it would clearly have to be a—for—to fulfill the import of the U.N. resolutions and the understandings that were agreed upon, it would require an inspection regime of such intrusiveness that it—at least thus far, it's unlikely, I think, that those folks would be inclined to agree to even half of it.

Q. Mr. Secretary, if I could just follow up on—the other thing that Colin Powell said in that BBC interview over the weekend—

Secretary Rumsfeld. I must confess, I did not see the full interview. I saw a snippet on television and therefore am purposely not commenting on his statement, because I haven't had a chance to read it. I'm just stating what the president has said and what our policy has been and what I see to be our current policy. And anyone who goes out of here thinking that there's some difference between anything I'm saying and what Colin said I think is—would be a total misunderstanding of the situation.

Q. I'm not trying to draw a distinction between what you said, but I just want to point—

Secretary Rumsfeld. Well, but I want to make sure everyone understood that.

Q. I want to point to something he said and then ask you what flows from that, which is, in answer to the question from David Frost about whether the rest of the world agreed that Saddam Hussein was, in fact, a clear and present threat, Powell said, "I think the world has to be presented with the information, with the intelligence that's available, that debate is needed within the international community so that everybody can make a judgment about this." And my question is, when might we see some of this intelligence, some of the hard evidence about the threat from Saddam Hussein, other than the general statements that have already been made?

Secretary Rumsfeld. Well, needless to say, I agree with what Colin said in the quote you just indicated. I think those are decisions that the president will make. I believe very strongly that we are living in a new security environment. The president believes that and has said so. It is notably different; it's different in a variety of different ways.

And the debate and discussion that's taking place in the world I think is a healthy one and a good thing. And I think it'll be taking place—it's taking place here in Washington. It's taking place in other capitals. It very likely will take place in the Congress, when Congress returns and begins to have the hearings that they have indicated that they may very well have. And I know the president has indicated that he wants to be cooperative and have administrative—

Q. But—but he—

Secretary Rumsfeld.—witnesses participate in those. And one would think that it would be in that context that the discussions about what the fact patterns are would be most appropriately presented.

Q. Well, let me just ask you, is there hard evidence, are there—I don't know—intelligence, are there photographs, is there other intelligence, are you assembling that kind of information so that when the appropriate time comes the president will be able to make the case and convince the world?

Secretary Rumsfeld. Well, you're suggesting the president wants to make a particular case. But what the president wants to do is to—and will do, in his own time, is to provide information that he feels is important with respect to any judgment he decides to make. And he has not decided what judgments he may make. But he certainly would underpin those judgments with factual information.

Q. Tariq Aziz said this morning—he characterized you and several other people in the Bush administration as warmongers, as using the issue of inspections as a pretext to try to topple the regime. And he said he is willing to sit down and talk about all of the issues involving Iraq. Do you take that to be a serious offer? Do you take that to be further maneuvering, as you indicated earlier?

Secretary Rumsfeld. Well, I have met with Tariq Aziz a number of times, both in Baghdad and in Washington and elsewhere. And clearly, he does the bidding of his master, Saddam Hussein. They have over a good many years demonstrated a wonderful talent and skill at manipulating the media. And they—and international organizations, and other countries. When it's the right moment to lean forward, they lean forward. When it's the right moment to lean back, they lean back. And it's a dance. It's a dance they engage in. They will go week after week after week stiffing the international community, the U.N. and others. They then will find that things are going in a way that they're uncomfortable with, and then they will throw out an opportunity of one sort or another and get people—hopeful people leaning forward, saying, "See, there's our opportunity. We do have a chance to work with those people. All we need to do is be more accommodating to them." And therefore they'll swing the discussion and the debate that way. There might be inspections. The inspections might be this, that or the other thing. And then you'll find at the last moment they'll withdraw that carrot or that opportunity and go back into their other mode of thumbing their nose at the international community.

Where they'll be at any given moment is, of course, something that's entirely up to them. But at least thus far we do know certain facts. We know that they have rejected inspections. We know they have not lived up to their obligations under the U.N. resolutions and the agreements that they signed at the conclusion of the Gulf War.

Q. In your view, what would be the merit of inspections if they in fact verified disarmament and left Saddam Hussein in power? It would not seem to achieve your goal or the administration's policy goal of removing him.

Secretary Rumsfeld. Again, that's a call for the president, really; it's not for me. The policy of our government has been regime change. It's been regime change by the Congress, by the successive executive branch over the past two administrations. And it was rooted in several things. It was rooted in the conviction that the world would be a better place if there were a government in that part of the world that was not developing weapons of mass destruction, was not on the terrorist list, did not pose threats to its neighbors, did not repress its people and subject its minorities to abuses and did not have any development of weapons of mass destruction. Therefore, inspections have a role with respect of one of those elements, and obviously the world would be a better place if those folks were not developing weapons of mass destruction. But the other elements of the problem would remain.

Q. Along that line, Mr. Secretary, Vice President Cheney said last week that Iraq was once close to producing or obtaining nuclear weapons, and said that they're getting close again. What evidence does the U.S. have that Iraq, Saddam Hussein, may be getting close again to obtaining a nuclear weapon?

Secretary Rumsfeld. Oh, I think I'll leave that for the coming days and weeks. I mean, we know the obvious. We know that they were a lot closer than any of the experts had estimated they would be with respect to a nuclear weapon, and that was discovered during the post-1991 period by actually seeing what was there. To the extent inspectors have been out now for a number of years, we know that we don't know what's taken place during those period of years. To the extent that they have kept their nuclear scientists together and working on these efforts, one has to assume they have not been playing tiddly-winks, that they have been focusing on nuclear weapons. And so we know what we know.

We know that they have an enormous appetite, that they were very close, within a short period of time, to having a weapon. We know that our estimate had been that it was multiples of years compared to what it actually was; and therefore, we know we weren't very good at what we were supposedly doing—that is to say, estimating that. And we also know that since the end of the Cold War, that the proliferation of these technologies has been pervasive. And we know that they have porous borders. And we know some other things, but those are the kinds of things that would come out if and when the president decides that he thinks it's appropriate.

Q. If I could follow up, when you said you'd leave that for the coming days and weeks, does that mean the administration intends to in the coming weeks reveal some of this evidence that maybe—

Secretary Rumsfeld. Those are judgments that have to be made down the road depending what the president decides he wants to do.

Q. Mr. Secretary, about the vice president's speech, twice last week he said that the consequences of inaction against Saddam Hussein far outweigh the consequences of some preemptive strike. Yet we repeatedly hear from the president that he has not made a decision and that he's a patient man. In your assessment, is there a mixed message here, or are we just reading it wrong?

Secretary Rumsfeld. Well, you know, any time four, five, six, seven people all talk and they talk about these subjects and they are asked specific questions by people that are cast in a certain way and the question contains a reference to something that someone else said, not the full context of it, not the whole text, but some blurb or piece that happened to appear on television or happened to appear in the newspaper, and then somebody responds to that, why, it is—there's no question but that if every—someone wanted to take all the column inches or all the minutes on television by the top people in any government at any given time on the same subjects and ignore how the question was asked and ignore the context of the quote, that you could end up juxtaposing things in ways that would sell newspapers, by saying, "Aha! There's a disagreement there. He said this; she said that. What about this? What about that?"

That's baloney! These people meet together all the time. They know what each other thinks. Do they sometimes say things one way, and someone else might have said it some other, different way? Sure they do. But what's important is what the president says. And what's important is what the president decides. And what's important is the documentation that's provided at some point, if he decides that he feels that's appropriate.

And I think also what's important is that people lift their eyes up off their shoelaces and go back to the fundamental and the fundamental issue is that we live in a different world today. We live in the 21st century. We're not back in the 20th century, where the principal focus is conventional weapons. We're in the 21st century, where the principal focus must be weapons—unconventional weapons—weapons potentially that could involve killing not hundreds of people but tens of thousands of people—chemical weapons, biological weapons, potentially nuclear weapons.

And that means that we have to take that aboard as a people, and we have to talk about it, and we have to consider it. What does it mean? How does it conceivably affect our behavior? There are clearly risks to acting in any instance. But there are also risks to not acting. And those have to be weighed. People have to talk about them intelligently. These are important subjects for Congress, for the press, for the academic institutions, for the world community. And that's what this process is.

And I keep hearing people say, "Oh, Europe's unhappy with this" or "Somebody doesn't agree with that" or "Some general said this" or "Some civilian said that." I think what's important is the substance of this discussion. And I see too little attention to it and too much attention to the personality aspects of it, if you will, and to the trying to juxtapose what one person said against what somebody else said for the personality aspect of it, rather than for the substance of it. And if you think about our circumstance, when the penalty for not acting is September 11th, if you will, or a Pearl Harbor, where hundreds and a few thousand people are killed, that is a very serious thing. You've made a conscious decision not to act. And the penalty with that, for those people, it's a hundred percent. It's not one thousand or two thousand, it's that person is gone. If, on the other hand, the penalty for not acting is not a conventional or a terrorist attack of that magnitude, but one of many multiples of that, it forces people to stop and have the kind of debate we're having. What ought we to be thinking about? How ought we, if at all, to be changing our behavior? How ought we to live in this new 21st century world? What does it mean that tens of thousands of human beings can be killed in a biological attack if we allow it to happen as a society? Are we comfortable with that? Is that something that we've decided that it's so disadvantageous to take an action without proof that you could go into a court of law and prove beyond a reasonable doubt that something was going to happen, that the capabilities existed for— of absolute certain knowledge, and that the intent to use those was imminent and clear, and you don't—you may not have the type of certain knowledge. You may want that kind of knowledge in a law enforcement case, where we're interested in protecting the rights of the accused. You may have a different conclusion if you're talking about the death of tens of thousands or hundreds of thousands of innocent men, women and children. We're not talking about combatants here, we're talking about the kinds of people who were killed on September 11th. So it is that construct that needs to be considered. And it ought to be—it ought to be talked about and well read through and thought about, it seems to me.

Q. You—you said just now that one of the reasons Saddam is so dangerous is because he's threatening his neighbors. Now the very neighbors say that they don't feel threatened today because of containment and they oppose a military intervention. So what do you say to them?

Secretary Rumsfeld. Well, I suppose—first of all, it depends on who you're talking to, and it depends on when you're talking to them, and it depends on whether you're talking in public or in private. All anyone has to do is go back and read the statements that Saddam Hussein has made about the "illegitimacy", quote- unquote, the alleged "illegitimacy" of his neighboring regimes, and the hostility he feels towards them. So it seems to me the truth is self-evident.

Q. Mr. Secretary, you mentioned Congress several times, as you already have said, that's coming back today and tomorrow. And of course you and the president have also said that you believe Congress should be consulted. But do you think it's prudent that you should seek the consent of Congress? Do you think it's a wise idea for Congress to approve an action before it might be decided?

Secretary Rumsfeld. The—under our Constitution, Article 1 is the Congress of the United States, the people's branch. They're there for a reason, and there is no question but that they have a role. What that role is, is a subject for lawyers; how they want to execute it is a subject for Congress; how the president wants to interact with them is a subject for the executive branch. And that will all play out over the coming days and weeks. But there's no question but that the Congress has an important role, in my view.

Q. General Myers, General Zinni, about 10 days ago, made a speech in which he said that the people who are most enthusiastic about taking action in Iraq have not themselves been in combat, or something to that effect, and that generals, as a group, tend to see it differently. And he even listed a few, most of them retired, actually.

Do you have any thoughts about—I'm sure you've seen what he said. Do you have any thoughts about what he said?

General Myers. I've only seen what was reported that he said in the paper. I've not seen his actual remarks. And so it's hard to comment. He delivered his remarks—I think I've stood up here before and talked about the Joint Chiefs of Staff and others involved in all our processes in this war on terrorism, and that I don't think—I think people tend to read things into statements that really don't reflect the true nature of the deliberations and advice we're providing.

But, I don't know what else to say about it. Everybody's entitled to their opinion.

Q. But do the responsibilities of—you know, for military officers mean that they have any different perspective in this instance than civilian leadership might have?

General Myers. Well, I think in some cases it may be slightly different, but not different than the civilian leadership of the department. I don't know anybody that cares more passionately about the people of this department than the secretary and the deputy secretary and those civilian leaders. So in one sense, no, and in another sense, in terms of just pure military expertise, I think the military brings something to the equation that's valuable, and we do so in a very unconstrained way.

Q. General Myers, a couple of days ago there was a story reporting that many military officers in the Pentagon are concerned that if we mounted a military operation against Iraq, it would be a huge distraction and drain on resources from the search for al Qaeda and the greater war on terrorism. Is that an issue that you and other members of the Joint Chiefs of Staff are discussing? Is that a serious issue?

General Myers. An issue that we discuss and that the staff works almost continuously is how U.S. armed forces are used around the world. For those parts of the force that are under particular stress, what steps can we take to mitigate it? If we're asked to do something else, whatever that is, are we prepared to do that? Do we have the logistics? Do we have the command and control structure? Do we have the people? Do we have the right skill sets? And if not, then how do we—that's something we talk about all the time. We talk about that with the secretary. We don't just talk about it, but the secretary probes us to respond to lots of those types of questions. So that is not unusual—that that goes on. It goes on—it went on before September 11th. It's—it'll go on as we continue this war.

Q. Well, but would a major regional conflict be a serious drain on the resources that are being devoted to the war on terrorism, or is the war on terrorism using so few of those resources that there are plenty left?

General Myers. Let me just say it this way: that if you go back to the Quadrennial Defense Review, in the defense strategy that was laid out in that review, it says we want our forces to be able to do a series of things. And in that series of things, we cover the cases that you just mentioned—the war on terrorism, another major regional conflict, and we think we can do that. And we've looked at that several times, and I've stood up here and I've said that we have the resources to do—now does that—to do what we need to do.

Does that mean we're not going to have to prioritize, that there won't be certain resources that will be—could possibly be in scarce demand, given different scenarios? Well, sure. But that's what we do. We do that even today. So—

Secretary Rumsfeld. Plus homeland security, which Dick might have mentioned, plus some other, lesser contingencies, such as Bosnia and the other things we're doing.

General Myers. Yeah. It's not just a war on terrorism; it is—as the secretary said, it's—if you go back and read the QDR and take the—I don't want to go through that now. But if you take the defense strategy out of that, which does include homeland security for the first time as a mission that we need to put resources towards and which we're doing in a fairly major way that we have not done in the past, at least accounted for them—we put forces toward it, but we never accounted for them—I think we have a great strategy with a very good way to account for how busy people are going to be.

Q. Mr. Secretary, could I just ask you quickly, would you feel that you have failed in your job if you left office and Saddam Hussein was still in power?

Secretary Rumsfeld. No. Look it is an interesting question. I haven't thought about it that way. But there is a constitution, and the president is the president, and the president and the Congress make those kinds of judgments; secretaries of Defense do not.

I have a set of statutory responsibilities. And I have obligations to the president, and I have obligations to the Congress under their statute, and I have various international responsibilities. And to the extent I do them in a manner that is consistent with the best interests of our country, then I'm happy and feel that I've been successful. And to the extent that I ever felt that something was being done in a way that I did not feel in the best interests of the country, it would be my obligation to step aside. But that— I don't feel that way at all. I feel we've got a very orderly process that is benefiting from 24 hour, seven day a week examination by everybody in the world, to look for flaws and little things on it that might be questioned or elaborated on. And that's fine, too. That's all part of the Constitution, too.

Q. Following the heightened sensitivity to the threat since September 11th and linear and perhaps logical inferences about Saddam Hussein's pursuit of weapons of mass destruction, is there any concrete difference in the threat posed by Saddam Hussein in Iraq today than there was, say, one year ago today?

Secretary Rumsfeld. Well, without putting an adjective to it, the short answer is yes, there is a difference today from a year ago. When you're dealing with any entity— let's call it the moon—that—give credit—give credit where's credit's due—where there—where you know of certain knowledge that the moon has in the past had weapons of mass destruction capabilities and that the moon has been continuing free of inspections and with relatively open borders, with a great deal of dual use capabilities, has been proceeding aggressively to further develop those capabilities and make them more mature, more robust, with greater lethality, greater distances and greater variety, then one has to say that the situation has changed, and not for the better.

Remarks by President Bush, September 4, 2002

President Bush made the following remarks at the White House after meeting with Congressional Leaders.

Thank you all for coming. It's been my honor to welcome the leadership of the United States Congress here, to welcome them back from the August recess. We talked about a variety of issues—talked about the defense appropriations bill, and terrorism insurance, and an energy bill. Spent most of our time talking about a serious threat to the United States, a serious threat to the world, and that's Saddam Hussein.

One of the things I made very clear to the members here is that doing nothing about that serious threat is not an option for the United States. I also made it very clear that we look forward to a open dialogue with Congress and the American people about the threat, and that not only will we consult with the United States Congress—

we, being the administration—but that my administration will fully participate in any hearings that the Congress wishes to have on this subject, on the subject about how to make America a more secure country, how to best protect the American families in our country.

At the appropriate time, this administration will go to the Congress to seek approval for—necessary to deal with the threat. At the same time, I will work with our friends in the world. I've invited Prime Minister Blair to come to Camp David on Saturday, and he'll—he's coming. I've looked forward to talking with him about our mutual concerns about how to make the world more secure and safe.

I will see Jean Chretien on Monday, as we—we'll talk about how to make our borders work better, but, at the same time, I'll talk to him about this subject. I'll be on the phone to leaders of the—China and Russia and France, and then I'll be giving the speech at the United Nations.

Saddam Hussein is a serious threat. He is a significant problem. And it's something that this country must deal with. And today the process starts about how to have an open dialogue with the elected officials and, therefore, the American people about our future and how best to deal with it.

Let me answer a couple of questions. Steve Holland, Fournier, and then Gregory, and that's it.

Q. Mr. President, what's your opinion on putting U.N. weapons inspectors back in Iraq? Will you ask the U.N. to do that? Is that a viable option?

President Bush. First of all, I'll be giving a speech on Tuesday—or the 12th—and you can come and listen to it. But let me say to you that the issue is not inspectors, the issue is disarmament. This is a man who said he would not arm up. This is a man who told the world that he would not harbor weapons of mass destruction. That's the primary issue. And I'll be discussing ways to make sure that that is the case.

Q. So you will be—you will be discussing ways to make sure that he disarms? Are you talking about having inspectors back in?

President Bush. I will first remind the United Nations that for 11 long years, Saddam Hussein has side-stepped, crawfished, wheedled out of any agreement he had made not to harbor—not to develop weapons of mass destruction, agreements he's made to treat the people within his country with respect. And so I'm going to call upon the world to recognize that he is stiffing the world. And I will lay out and I will talk about ways to make sure that he fulfills his obligations.

Q. Let me just follow up on your opening statement. When you say you're going to seek congressional approval, does that mean, in effect, Congress will have veto authority over your plan to oust Saddam Hussein?

President Bush. I'm confident we will be able to—I'll be able to work with Congress to deal with this threat to the American people. And that's what I meant.

Q. Mr. President, you talked about Saddam Hussein stiffing the world. In your mind, has the time come to issue the Iraqi leader an ultimatum similar to that that you issued to the Taliban?

President Bush. I am going to state clearly to the United Nations what I think. And I think that he has not fulfilled any of the obligations that he made to the world. And I believe it's important for the world to deal with this man. And I believe it's really important for the United States Congress to have an open dialogue about how to deal with this threat.

We are in a new era; the first battle of the—the first war of the 21st century took place in Afghanistan. The United States is under threats. We are—we spent a lot of time, people around this table, good-hearted people who care deeply about America spent a lot of time thinking about how best to secure our homeland even further. And this is a debate the American people must hear, must understand. And the world must understand, as well, that its credibility is at stake.

Remarks by Secretary of State Powell, September 4, 2002

Secretary Colin Powell was interviewed while attending the World Summit on Sustainable Development in Johannesburg, South Africa.

The President spoke to this very clearly today. He said that he is beginning an intensive process of consultation with the American Congress, he's going to talk to the American people, he's talking to the world. He'll be talking to a number of foreign leaders over the next several days and he'll be talking at the United Nations next week on the threat posed to not just the United States but to the whole world by Iraq.

Q. Will he present the evidence—

Secretary Powell. Here's the evidence. First, Iraq has violated all the resolutions that were placed upon it requiring it to get rid of its weapons of mass destruction. There's no debate about this. It is absolutely a fact that Iraq has not complied with these resolutions to get rid of weapons of mass destruction.

Second fact: The Iraqis are pursuing still, after all these years, they are still pursuing these weapons, and they are still pursuing this technology. And when Tariq Aziz, the Deputy Prime Minister, comes and says they are not, it's a lie and everybody knows it's a lie. And he's trying to con us. One day he says no inspectors, the next day he says maybe inspectors. It's all a con.

Now, what the United Nations has to do is to look at these facts and make a judgment as to what they should do about the fact that this regime has been thwarting the will of the international community for all these years. And the United States is willing to point this out to the world and make the case to the world. The President will make it clear to the allies in the days ahead, he'll make it clear at the United Nations next week. He has also said he has made no decisions with respect to what options he might choose to pursue, either within the multilateral environment or what we might have to do as a nation unilaterally.

Q. Is there any difference—

Secretary Powell. And the thing that is clear about all of this is that doing nothing is not an option, as the President said.

Q. Right. But is there any difference of opinion between you and other members of the administration on the advice that the President is being given?

Secretary Powell. The President benefits from all the advice that we give him as a group, and a lot of the chatter about all of the disagreements that take place within the administration is mostly that: chatter. We talk to each other in an open, candid environment. We're all old friends. There are no wars going on within the administration; there's good debate. And that debate and that discussion and the advice that we give to the President has only one purpose, and that's to make sure that the President understands all the issues with respect to any particular problem that is before him.

And with respect to Iraq, it's a very serious matter and we have to make sure he gets the best advice. And I'm confident that I, Secretary Rumsfeld and Vice President Cheney, my former Secretary Cheney, and Condi Rice and George Tenet of the CIA and all of our colleagues are doing everything we can to make to sure the President gets the best advice, and we are unified together and we are behind him.

Remarks by Secretary of State Powell, September 4, 2002

Secretary Colin Powell delivered his remarks while attending the World Summit on Sustainable Development in Johannesburg, South Africa.

Q. Could you identify what progress, if any, you've made towards the Iraqi question—you've had discussions—to have untrammeled [*inaudible*] this the key issue for you now?

Secretary Powell. We were pushing for the international community to recognize that the situation could not continue the way it has been for the past four years since inspectors left. But the issue, I said to all of them, is not inspectors; the issue is disarmament. The President made that point again in his statement to the Congress, and I'm sure he'll be making it again in the future. One way toward achieving that goal of disarmament is perhaps with inspectors playing that role. That remains to be seen. Iraq has frustrated previous efforts of inspectors and created conditions which caused the inspectors to leave in 1998. So we'll see.

Regime change is another way to deal with the question of weapons of mass destruction, and that's why it has been a policy of the United States for the last roughly four-plus years. So, as the President said to Congressional leaders today and said in his statement and the letter that he has sent to Congressional leaders, he plans to consult widely with members of Congress, with the American people; he plans to consult with a number of foreign leaders over the next several days, and then consult with many more when he is up at the United Nations General Assembly next week. Then he will present a message to the General Assembly of the direction in which he believes we ought to move.

Inspections will be an issue, but they are not the primary issue. The primary issue is how do we get Iraq to comply with its obligations under these various U.N. resolutions. For Tariq Aziz to come here and issue the same sort of vapid statements that he has issued in the past about "we have no weapons of mass destruction and we will never let inspectors in'" but then the next day he gives a wink and a nod, that "maybe we will let the weapons inspectors in", well, that's not good enough anymore. We can't let the international community be frustrated in that way. We cannot allow this regime with this leader to simply ignore the multilateral views of the international community as reflected in those many U.N. resolutions. I got a solid expression of support from everybody I spoke to on that basic premise, that this challenge must be dealt with, and as the President said today, doing nothing is not an option.

Q. Have you discussed at all during the day the alleged proposal of [*inaudible*] backed by forcible entry to specific targeted facilities if the Iraqis don't comply with these requirements, and do you have any views on such a proposal?

Secretary Powell. Well, I'm not sure where the proposal comes from and if it is a proposal. It's certainly an idea that is out there and some commentators have mentioned it, but it did not come up in any of my discussions today. We were focusing on the obligations that Iraq has; we were focusing on weapons of mass destruction, the threat that they present to the civilized world; and what was the civilized world, in the form of the United Nations and the rest of the international community, going to do about it.

Q. Mr Secretary, you used the word multilateral views as expressed in the United Nations Security Council, and after some of your meetings today, some of your counterparts came out and said that they do not support U.S. unilateral action, but would support some kind of multilateral approach to deal with the problem of Iraq. As you talk about multilateral views, do you think that the Bush administration will take a multilateral approach in dealing with the Iraqi problem, such as the U.N. or any other international body?

Secretary Powell. The President made it clear today that he has every intention of consulting widely with Congress, with the American people of course, and with our friends and allies and with the U.N.. He at the same time made it clear that we preserve all of our options to do what we believe is necessary to deal with this problem. I think to pigeonhole it as multilateral or unilateral—what we're trying to do now is to make sure that the world understands the threat as clearly as we believe it should understand this threat, because it is a real one. We cannot allow the international community to be thwarted in this effort to require Iraq to comply with the obligations it entered into at the end of the Gulf War and for a number of years thereafter.

Q. Mr Secretary, I'm still a little a confused, and perhaps that's deliberate in terms of the inspections. Given the record of the last 11 years—the cat and mouse game

that you've just described—is there sort of scenario or any plan that you can see that the inspectors could get back in there and actually do their job?

Secretary Powell. As you know, the United States' position has been that the inspectors should go back in. That's the President's position. But they cannot go back in and be dealt with the way they were dealt with say, in 1996/7/8. So they will have to go back in, if they go back in, with a clear understanding that they have to be able to do their job, and that means that they have to be able to go wherever they believe it is necessary to go, whenever they feel it is appropriate to go, and see whoever they have to see to get to the bottom of this. Now, I think Dr. Blix has made this clear to the Iraqis, I think the Secretary General has made this clear to the Iraqis, and we'll just see what the next step is with respect to inspection regime—whether there is going to be one or not. I don't want to prejudge it at this time.

Our position has been clear: inspectors should go back in. The President said so, reaffirmed that yesterday in his press conference when he was discussing this issue. But we also understand that they have been frustrated in the past. They accomplished quite a bit for a number of years, and slowly obstacles were put in their way so that they could not continue with their work. We cannot send them back in under the conditions that existed at the time they came out. But this is a matter for further discussion with the United Nations.

Q. I just want to clarify—what is the nature of the threat right now [*inaudible*] that it is different from a year ago? Is there some information that the government has that it hasn't yet felt the need to disclose to the public [*inaudible*] in the sense that people don't understand what makes the situation new and different at this moment?

Secretary Powell. The first thing I would say is that what brings it center-stage is that we see this regime that continues to move in this direction of developing weapons of mass destruction. This is not in dispute—we have never abandoned it, and the intelligence case is clear that they have weapons of mass destruction of one kind or another, and they are trying to develop more, and develop those that they do not yet have an operational capability for. That intention is clear. I think when the intelligence information is presented, everybody can see that they have not abandoned this, and they are continuing to pursue it with even greater vigor, and that should get our attention.

And this other point I would make before getting to the specifics of your question is that there is a fundamental problem with a regime such as Iraq, which entered into all of these obligations, which said they would not have any weapons of mass destructions or capability, and then claim they do not, when it is obvious they do. This is not something you can just turn your head and forget about or look away, and this President has made it clear at the very beginning of his administration that he would not look away. And so we have been examining this; we have had many meetings, we have had many discussions and we now believe it is time to take the case to the international community.

With respect to timeliness and with respect to the quality of the intelligence, Don Rumsfeld will be briefing some senators today, I believe, in Washington, and in the course of the weeks ahead in our testimony, and in both classified and unclassified ways, we will be presenting all the information we have, and allow the world to make its own judgment as to the nature of this regime and what this regime has been up to. And as you heard from Prime Minister Blair yesterday, they too plan to make available all the information they have.

Q. I'm interested in the whole question of regime change, and particularly what happens after the fact. How much thought have you given to how you would ensure a democratic and stable government in an area that has no history of anything like that, and how long are you willing to stay in, given that it has turned out to be a little more complicated than you thought in Afghanistan?

Secretary Powell. Well, the President has not made any decision to go in, go anywhere, do anything yet. What he is doing now is consulting. But obviously, when one starts down a road such as this, you have to think through all the consequences, and you have to consider what would be required, and what the day after would look like. And it is not a simple matter.

There is not a tradition of democracy [there], but there are lots of places in the world today where there was no tradition of democracy ten years ago, but suddenly there is democracy; so it does not mean because it has not existed before, it cannot exist in the future. It can, and that has been demonstrated on a regular basis. The tradition that the Iraqi people have been suffering under for all these years is a tradition they will be willing to see pass into their history books, and let's see what democracy is all about.

But the President has not reached any conclusions or made any decisions yet that would trigger a more specific answer than that.

Q. Mr Secretary, I am still a little confused by what the Administration [*inaudible*] on the U.N. inspection [*inaudible*] and what Vice President Cheney [*inaudible*].

Secretary Powell. The President's [*inaudible*] and he said inspectors should go back in. It's been his policy ever since—I think he first articulated that directly in January, and he has continued with it. There is no question that one should be skeptical about any inspection regime, and I think I have expressed skepticism about it. Although I think it is a step that the U.N. will have to consider—whether or not they could get them back in—as a way of getting the U.N. to coalesce around any subsequent action if the inspectors don't get back in. I think both Secretary Rumsfeld and Vice President Cheney have expressed their skepticism—as I said yesterday—with great vividness. It is an open question as to whether or not an inspection regime could work or could really find everything that's happening within that society.

So what we have all been saying, both Vice President Cheney and Secretary Rumsfeld and myself, is that we should not see inspections standing alone, if we can get some acceptable regime going, as the be-all and end-all of the problem. We will have to make a judgment that goes well beyond what inspectors [*inaudible*] as to whether or not this regime, or the successor regime of Saddam Hussein, has complied with the obligations Iraq has under the various resolutions.

Q. Secretary Powell, can you envision a situation at this point where Iraq would allow unfettered inspections and use of force would not be possible, and he would live up to his U.N. obligations? Under what scenario do you see that happening?

Secretary Powell. I am not going to [*inaudible*] the course of action that the Iraqis might take—I am not going to speculate on their behalf. I think they should be sitting there recognizing that things are changing, that the whole world is now seized with this problem. It's been the only story for the past several weeks, if not longer. The whole world is seized with this problem. The President of the United States said today he is taking it to the American people, taking it to the Congress, taking it to the international community, taking it to the United Nations, and every meeting, every grouping that takes place now discusses this issue. I think what we have done is make it clear that we cannot continue in this manner; that it is no longer an option to do nothing about the criminal actions of this government, this regime; for the Iraqi regime not to comply with the U.N. resolutions or to satisfy its obligations under those resolutions. Now what they are going to do about it remains to be seen, and I don't want to speculate on what they might or might not do and what the community might do in response.

Q. When you talk about all the options remaining on the table, I've been hearing a chorus from other leaders that the United States should look at some sort of multinational approach in leading with Iraq or going through the U.N.. Are you saying that the United States still reserves its right to unilateral action toward Iraq regardless —

Secretary Powell. Yes, the United States reserves its right to do whatever it feels it has to do to protect its security and to protect the American people. At the same time, the President has said he is a patient person and he is consulting widely with the Congress, with the American people, and with the international community as to what we should do; because this is an affront, not just against the United States, but against the whole civilized world, that in this day and age a man like that, and a regime like that— which has been placed under these restrictions by the United Nations over a period of years—has not complied with them and believes that it can do so with impunity. That is something that is of concern to us unilaterally, and we believe it should be of concern to all of the international community multilaterally.

Q. Could you address the criticism raised that the United States isn't really serious about inspections because whether or not they go forward and whether or not they find anything, regime change will remain the bottom line principal goal of the Bush administration?

Secretary Powell. First things first. The President has said "let the inspectors back in". We believe that regime change would benefit the Iraqi people, benefit the region, benefit the world. That was a policy that was decided upon as United States government policy in late 1997-98 because of Iraq's demonstrated unwillingness to comply with the resolutions. And now it is four years later and we continue to have that policy. That would be the quickest, cleanest solution, if the regime were to be changed. But there is an international community out there and there are these resolutions that are still present, and the United States will be consulting with our friends and allies about how best to move forward.

Remarks by President Bush and British Prime Minister Blair, September 7, 2002

President Bush and British Prime Minister Blair delivered their remarks during their meeting at Camp David, Maryland.

President Bush. Its my honor to welcome the Prime Minister back to Camp David. I look forward to spending a good three hours talking to our friend about how to keep the peace. This world faces some serious threat—and threats—and we're going to talk about it. We're going to talk about how to promote freedom around the world. We're going to talk about our shared values of—recognizes the worth of every individual.

And I'm looking forward to this time. It's awfully thoughtful of Tony to come over here. It's an important meeting, because he's an important ally, an important friend.

Prime Minister Blair. I'm looking very much forward, obviously, to discussing the issues that are preoccupying us at the moment with the President. And I thank him for his kind invitation to come here and his welcome.

The point that I would emphasize to you is that the threat from Saddam Hussein and weapons of mass destruction, chemical, biological, potentially nuclear weapons capability, that threat is real. We only need to look at the report from the International Atomic Agency this morning showing what has been going on at the former nuclear weapons sites to realize that. And the policy of inaction is not a policy we can responsibly subscribe to. So the purpose of our discussion today is to work out the right strategy for dealing with this, because deal with it we must.

Q. Mr. President, can you tell us what conclusive evidence of any nuclear—new evidence you have of nuclear weapons capabilities of Saddam Hussein?

President Bush. We just heard the Prime Minister talk about the new report. I would remind you that when the inspectors first went into Iraq and were denied—finally denied access, a report came out of the Atomic—the IAEA that they were six months away from developing a weapon. I don't know what more evidence we need.

Prime Minister Blair. Absolutely right. And what we—what we know from what has been going on there for a long period of time is not just the chemical, biological weapons capability, but we know that they were trying to develop nuclear weapons capability. And the importance of this morning's report is it yet again it shows that there is a real issue that has to be tackled here.

I mean, I was just reading coming over here the catalog of attempts by Iraq to conceal its weapons of mass destruction, not to tell the truth about it over—not just over a period of months, but over a period of years. Now, that's why the issue is important. And, of course, it's an issue not just for America, not just for Britain, it's an issue for the whole of the international community. But it is an issue we have to deal with. And that's why I say to you that the policy of inaction, doing nothing about it, is not something we can responsibly adhere to.

Q. A question for the President and the Prime Minister. Will you, Mr. President, seek a U.N. resolution prior to any action against Iraq?

And for the Prime Minister, would you sanction any action against Iraq before— without a U.N. resolution?

President Bush. Well, first, I'm going to give a speech next Thursday, and I'd like you to tune in.

Prime Minister Blair. As I said to you I think at the press conference we gave earlier in the week, this is an issue for the whole of the international community. But the U.N. has got to be the way of dealing with this issue, not the way of avoiding dealing with it. Now, of course, as we showed before in relation to Afghanistan, we want the broadest possible international support, but it's got to be on the basis of actually making sure that the threat that we've outlined is properly adhered to.

Because the point that I would emphasize to you is it's not us, it's not Britain or America that's in breach of United Nations resolutions. It's Saddam Hussein and Iraq. And therefore, this issue is there for the international community to deal with. And we've got to make sure that it is a way of dealing with it.

Q.—what is your actual target in Iraq? Is it weapons of mass destruction, or Saddam Hussein? And if the Prime Minister could answer, too.

President Bush. Well, as you know, our government in 1998—action that my administration has embraced—decided that this regime was not going to honor its commitments to get rid of weapons of mass destruction. The Clinton administration supported regime change. Many members of the United States Senate supported regime change. My administration still supports regime change. There's all kinds of ways to change regimes.

This man is a man who said he was going to get rid of weapons of mass destruction. And for 11 long years, he has not fulfilled his promise. And we're going to talk about what to do about it. We owe it to future generations to deal with this problem, and that's what these discussions are all about.

Q. Do you have any support from any other countries in the world, apart from Britain? And Mr. Blair, too.

President Bush. Yes. A lot of people understand that this man has defied every U.N. resolution—16 U.S. resolutions he's ignored. A lot of people understand he holds weapons of mass destruction. A lot of people understand he has invaded two countries. A lot of people understand he's gassed his own people. A lot of people understand he is unstable. So we've got a lot of support. A lot of people understand the danger.

Prime Minister Blair. Yes, and I can tell you from the discussions I've had with people, of course, there are people asking perfectly reasonable questions about this, but the one thing that no one can deny is that Saddam Hussein is in breach of the United Nations resolutions on weapons of mass destruction—that is, chemical, biological, nuclear weapons; that that poses a threat not just to the region, because there is no way, if those weapons were used, that the threat would simply stay in the region.

People understand that. Now, we've got to make sure that we work out a way forward that, of course, mobilizes the maximum support, but does so on the basis of removing a threat that the United Nations itself has determined is a threat to the whole of the world.

Remarks by Secretary of State Powell, September 8, 2002

Secretary Colin Powell was interviewed by Tony Snow and Brit Hume on Fox News Sunday.

Q. Here to help us assess Saddam Hussein's capabilities and sketch out potential allied response is Secretary of State Colin Powell. Easy for me to say. Let us take a look at Saddam's capabilities first. There seems to be a lot of controversy. He possesses significant chemical and biological stocks, correct?

Secretary Powell. There is no doubt that he has chemical weapons stocks. We destroyed some after the Gulf War with the inspection regime, but there is no doubt in our mind that he still has chemical weapons stocks and he has the capacity to produce more chemical weapons.

With respect to biological weapons, we are confident that he has some stocks of those weapons and he is probably continuing to try to develop more. And biological weapons are very dangerous because they can be produced just about in any kind of pharmaceutical facility.

With respect to nuclear weapons, we are quite confident that he continues to try to purse the technology that would allow him to develop a nuclear weapon. Whether he could do it in one, five, six or seven, eight years is something that people can debate about. But what nobody can debate about is the fact that he still has the incentive, he still intends to develop those kinds of weapons. And as we saw in reporting just this morning, he is still trying to acquire, for example, some of the specialized aluminum tubing one needs to develop centrifuges that would give you an enrichment capability.

So there's no question that he has these weapons. But even more importantly, he is striving to do even more, to get even more. That's why he won't let the inspectors back in. That's why he has frustrated the will of the international community and that's why he has been violating all of these resolutions for all these years.

Q. I want to get to all that, but still a couple more questions on his capabilities. If

he were able to deploy right now his chemical and biological stocks, how many people could he kill?

Secretary Powell. I don't know. It depends on how he deployed them, where he deployed them. Chemical weapons are different from biological weapons. And let's just recognize the fact that he has them, he has used them before, and he has killed thousands of people in their use.

Q. Has he, since inspectors left, improved his technology for disseminating those kinds of weapons?

Secretary Powell. We know that he has been working hard on developing a means to disseminate those weapons. He had artillery, he had rockets, and I'm sure he is looking at other technologies. We have evidence that he has been looking at aerial vehicles.

Q. Drones?

Secretary Powell. Drones. He is looking for ways to disseminate it because just having it in a stockpile doesn't do you any good; you have to have a means of delivering it. And that's what concerns us. We know he's working on the means to deliver it against his neighbors certainly, and I have no doubt that he is probably trying to figure out if he could develop ways to deliver it against us. And that's why we have to be concerned.

Q. Agreements at the end of the Gulf War limited the range of missiles that can employ to 150 kilometers. Has he extended the range of his missiles?

Secretary Powell. We believe that he has some scuds left over from the war. How many, we can't be sure, but we're quite sure he has some scuds that have greater range than the 150 kilometers permitted by the United Nations. And we also know that on some occasions in recent years he has tested missiles that went beyond the 150-kilometer range limit of the United Nations. And we also know that he has people around the world trying to determine whether or not they can bring into Iraq weapons that have greater capability and greater range.

Q. All right. Scott Ritter is in Baghdad today. He addressed the Iraqi parliament, such as it is. I want to play a quote from him and then get your response:
"The rhetoric of fear that is disseminated by my government and others has not to date been backed up by hard facts that substantiate any allegations that Iraq is today in possession of weapons of mass destruction or has links to terror groups responsible for attacking the United States. Void of such facts, all we have is speculation."

Secretary Powell. We have facts, not speculation. Scott is certainly entitled to his opinion, but I'm afraid that I would not place the security of my nation and the security of our friends in the region on that kind of an assertion by somebody who is not in the intelligence chain any longer. There is no doubt in my mind that he does have capacity and he is trying to improve that capability and build upon that capability.

And it's debatable as to how much and where it is and all sorts of questions can be raised, and they should be raised and should be debated. This is an important issue. But there can be no debate about the fact that he is in violation of the obligations he entered into at the end of the Gulf War. And if Scott is right, then why are they keeping the inspectors out? If Scott is right, why don't they say: "Anytime, anyplace, anywhere, bring them in. Everybody come in. We are clean"?

The reason is they're not clean. And we have to find out what they have and what we're going to do about it. And that's why it's been the policy of this government to insist that Iraq be disarmed in accordance with the terms of the relevant U.N. resolutions, and we believe the best way to do that is with a regime change. And that's why that has been U.S. policy, even though it's not United Nations policy.

Q. All right. Now one more question on that and then I want to get into regime change and U.N. resolutions and so on. Saddam has all this stuff. How determined is he to use them and how much of a danger is he to American interests right now?

Secretary Powell. I think he is a danger to American interests right now, our interests in the region, and in due course interests elsewhere as he develops the capability to deliver this kind of weapon at greater ranges. But I don't think we should just sit around and wait to see whether he does it or not. He has certainly indicated over the years that he wants to move in this direction and believes it will make him a bigger power than the tin pot dictator he is now. And I don't think, as the President has said and as Prime Minister Blair said yesterday, doing nothing is no longer an option.

Q. You would like to see Saddam out of power?

Secretary Powell. Of course. Who wouldn't? There isn't anybody in the whole world, frankly, any civilized leader of the world, who would not like to see a change in regime. There is concern about how it happens. There is concern about what would happen after. But even those who are speaking out most boldly about let's not do anything certainly would breathe a sigh of relief if Saddam Hussein was no longer in Baghdad.

Q. Help us out now in deciphering what administration policy is. The President says he'd like to get inspectors in. But it's also clear, as you've pointed out in multiple interviews, that there have been nine U.N. resolutions since the end of the Gulf War; Saddam has violated every one of them. Why on earth do we give him a tenth chance?

Secretary Powell. There's a number of reasons that one should at least consider this, and that's what the administration is doing. We are committed to the disarmament of Iraq so that they don't have these kinds of weapons. It's what they agreed to.

The issue is not inspectors or inspections. That is a tool. It is a means, a first step. But disarmament is the issue. And we will stay focused on that and we believe that regime change is the surest way to make sure that it's disarmed, that you would not get another leader in Baghdad who would be as committed as Saddam Hussein.

But the United Nations has an inspection regime standing by ready to go in. We have been part of the support of that inspection regime. Everybody should be suspicious about inspections, as to whether they can do the whole job for you, and some of the debates you've been hearing within the government have to do with the degree of effectiveness that such inspections could really bring to the table.

So you should have a skeptical attitude as to how much inspections can do, particularly in the presence of a regime that's going to do everything they can to hide things from inspectors. But we are going to discuss all of this with our friends and colleagues and the President will make a statement with his conclusions as to what he thinks we should do to move forward as a community, as an international community.

It's important for me to make this point now, Tony: Saddam Hussein is not just offending the United States; Saddam Hussein and the Iraqi regime, by their inaction, by their violation of these resolutions over these many years, is affronting the international community, is violating the will of the international community, violating the will of the multilateral United Nations.

Q. When the President goes to the United Nations General Assembly, is he going to say, as many suspect: You've put together all these resolutions regarding Iraq; we are still technically at a state of war but there's a ceasefire, and he's even violated the provisions of that; you need to enforce your own resolutions; if not, we may have to take action?

Secretary Powell. Well, I think I'll wait and let the President make his statement before I tell you what might be in that statement. The President has spent a great deal of time in recent days talking to his advisors. We were all up at Camp David Friday night and Saturday. He met with Prime Minister Blair, talked to a number of leaders, and he is putting his message together.

One thing I will confirm is that he will certainly point out in his speech that Saddam Hussein has been in violation of all of these resolutions and the conditions within these resolutions, conditions in resolutions that were passed by the United Nations, by the Security Council of the United Nations, over a long period of time, and therefore the United Nations should feel offended, the United Nations should feel that something has to be done.

Q. Well, the United Nations probably should have felt offended the last four years, but it hasn't done anything.

Secretary Powell. Well, the President will, no doubt, give them a strong message that it's time to do something.

Q. All right. There have also been reports, including and probably today, from a former mistress of Saddam Hussein that the Iraqi Government has had regular contact over the last 15 years or so with Osama bin Laden and al-Qaida. Have there been Iraqi/al-Qaida links preceding last September 11th?

Secretary Powell. There have been reports of such links and it wouldn't surprise me that such links existed. I mean, who knows who's speaking to whom over a long period of time? So I would not dismiss the fact that there may have been contacts. I can't confirm anything about this previous mistress's statement, whoever she is.

Q. Fair enough. On the other hand, the graver concern is: Is it possible that Iraq has been working with and supporting al-Qaida in its mission to kill Americans?

Secretary Powell. We cannot yet make a definitive conclusion that such a thing has occurred. We know that there is some al-Qaida presence in Iraq but we cannot come up with the kind of evidence and smoking gun case that some people would like to see. But I can assure you we're devoting a large amount of our intelligence and other assets to determining whether or not there are any such links.

Q. There has been a lot of talk, as you know, about possibly military action against Iraq, and many people have many scenarios. I want to present a few to you. First, former Secretary of State James Baker. He has said, and we'll provide a quote here, he has some suspicions that if the United States goes in militarily, it's going to lead to a long commitment. Let's look at the quote from Secretary Baker. It says:
"The only realistic way to effect regime change in Iraq is through the application of military force, including sufficient ground troops to occupy the country [including Baghdad], depose the current leadership and install a successor government. Anyone who thinks we can effect regime change in Iraq with anything less than this is simply not realistic."
Also in there is the implication that it would require some occupying force for a period of time. Do you think that would be correct?

Secretary Powell. Well, let me answer it this way, and I certainly have enormous respect for my colleague and dear friend Jim Baker. He lays out a scenario that has to be thought through carefully. If you start to think about the requirement that might exist—and no decision has been made by the President—but a requirement that might exist in the future for military action, you have to think it all the way through. How would you do it? What would the after look like and how would you deal with the after? How would you put together a better system than that which you are replacing?

The President is considering all of these things and we spend a great deal of time talking about the political options, the diplomatic options and the military options. And as the President has said to the nation just a few weeks ago, he is patient. He knows what needs to be done. He has spoken clearly about that. But he is patient as he thinks through the options that are available to him, and his national security advisors are spending a great deal of time with him in this process of looking at the options and making sure we understand the advantages and disadvantages as he focuses on what he wants to do and the decisions he has to make.

Q. Brent Scowcroft, with whom you and I both worked in the first Bush administration, has some thoughts about the after. Let's take a look at something that appeared in an op-ed piece he wrote not so long ago:

"An attack on Iraq at this time would seriously jeopardize, if not destroy, the global counter terrorist campaign we have undertaken."

Is action against Saddam Hussein directly at odds with the war on terror?

Secretary Powell. No, I think that consideration of what to do about Saddam Hussein is very consistent with the war against terror. There is no question that in addition to developing weapons of mass destruction Saddam Hussein has also supported terrorist activity over the years and in fact was responsible for a terrorist attack against President George Herbert Walker Bush, Bush 41, as we call him. And so for us to continue our campaign against terrorism, it's absolutely correct for us to be looking at Saddam Hussein and his regime as well.

And what makes this so difficult is that he does have a proclivity toward terrorist activity and he is developing weapons of mass destruction that he might use or perhaps could make available to other terrorist organizations. So I don't think it goes against the campaign against terror; it's very consistent with the campaign against terror.

And what we have to do is talk to our friends and allies. That's why we're spending so much time on it. That's why it's important for the President to hear from other leaders in the world. And that's why I think Brent Scowcroft has made a useful contribution to the debate, because all of these things have to be thought through. And that's why the President is showing the patience that is characteristic of him.

Q. If Saddam Hussein does not permit inspectors or does not permit them in the way that we think fulfills United Nations resolutions, would it then be appropriate for the United States to take preemptive, or what you have in the past called protective, action directly against Iraq?

Secretary Powell. I think it is always an option for the United States, and for that matter, it's an option for the United Nations. Preemption or prevention is a concept that's been with us all along. It is not anything that's new and revolutionary. I think it has risen in the hierarchy of thinking these days because it's a different world after 9/11. It's a different world where you don't have state actors coming at you and you can see their armies forming and you know what's going to happen. But when you can intercept a terrorist act that is heading your way or you can deal with a regime or a situation before it comes to a crisis level and threatens you, then it is an option that you should keep in mind and on the table.

Q. Do U.N. resolutions and congressional resolutions as well grant the President the authority to do that right now if he deems necessary?

Secretary Powell. I think there is a sound legal argument that the President, if he felt it was necessary to do something now, can find the authority within existing U.N. resolutions. But I'm not saying that that's the way he would go. I think what the President conveyed to the American people last week was that he wants to consult with the Congress, and as he said, he will go to the Congress for what he thinks he may need. And I am confident that he will be speaking to not only the U.N. General Assembly, but many other leaders in New York this week, and discuss with them what the options are.

Q. Mr. Secretary, Members of Congress have already expressed misgivings or doubts that Saddam Hussein threatens the United States. You hear this from Senator Levin, Chairman of the Armed Services Committee, for example. When you say that he threatens us, do you mean that he threatens us on our mainland directly or he threatens us, our interests or our allies, what?

Secretary Powell. I think he certainly threatens our interests in the region and he threatens our allies, and he has demonstrated that previously by invading Kuwait. And we also saw during the Iraq-Iran War that he was quite willing to use chemical weapons against Iran. Now, we weren't a party to that one. And we also saw that in order to control his own population he was willing to use chemical weapons.

And so if he's willing to use weapons in this way, should we say, well, we're too far away for us to worry about this? Or should we assume that with this kind of individual and with this kind of capability, he may eventually find a way to deliver it to the United States mainland? Now, this I think is one of the concerns we have and it's what's driving the President and all of us on this issue.

Q. The argument is made that if he ever were to achieve the ability to have a nuclear weapon that he would most likely not use it for a first strike attack on a nation like ours because he would be annihilated if he did, which creates a setting in which it is argued that the only circumstance under which he would ever use such a weapon is if he were attacked, so that's a very good reason not to attack him, ever apparently.

What's your answer to that?

Secretary Powell. My answer is that we don't want to face this decision tree that you just laid out with a person like Saddam Hussein. He has not acted rationally in the past and we should not expect him to act rationally in the future. It is better that Saddam Hussein and the Iraqi regime not be allowed to acquire nuclear weapons.

Q. It sounds as if from what you're saying here and what other administration officials have been saying is if inspections of some kind are going to be given or may be given one last chance. Vice President Cheney was fairly emphatic in his comments about inspectors. He said, you know, that that they not only were unsuccessful the last time they were in there, as we later found out from defectors and others, but that they create a sense of security that may be false and thereby make them dangerous.

Do you disagree with that?

Secretary Powell. I think what the Vice President was doing was expressing a great deal of skepticism with respect to inspectors, and it's well-deserved skepticism. They did quite a bit of good work, but we also discovered that once defectors came out they told us more information that the inspectors never had found. But with that additional information, inspectors were able to do more.

But we shouldn't rest our total policy and give full confidence to any inspection regime, and no inspection regime would be of any use, based on our experience, unless it's anywhere, anytime, anyplace, anybody. And any regime, if somebody were to put up an inspection regime to go in, if there was some way to do that, it would have to be with something far more robust and aggressive than we saw last time. But right now, all of these issues are under consideration.

Q. Let's assume for a moment that such an inspections regime were proposed and the United Nations was prepared to send it in there, perhaps one like the one that was talked about this week from the Carnegie Endowment where it would be backed by a very large and capable military force. The United States policy remains one of regime change. The question that is raised about that, sir: Therefore, what incentive does Saddam Hussein have for allowing intrusive inspections of that kind when the greatest superpower in the history of the world remains bent on his removal?

Secretary Powell. The incentive he has is to come into compliance and perhaps start to lead his country in a new direction. We don't believe that he is the person to lead his country in a new direction. That's why we continue to believe that regime change is appropriate. But the United Nations policy is not regime change.

Keep in mind that we came to a policy of regime change in the previous administration, supported by the way, by the Congress. Many of the Congress Members who now are nervous about regime change were all for it when the law was passed some years ago. And the reason that the previous administration came to that conclusion and we support that conclusion is because we think the best way to achieve the disarmament that everybody has been looking for is with a new regime.

Q. Secretary Powell, I want to revisit just briefly the whole notion of urgency here. Vice President Cheney has said time is not on our side. He wants Congress to act before it leaves town. Do you think that's important?

Secretary Powell. I think it would be useful for Congress, if the President asks them to act, I think it would be useful for them to act as quickly as possible after he has made a specific request of them.

Q. But is it essential? Is the timeline with Saddam Hussein so constricted that if there is not action by the end of the year, there could be terrible consequences for us or our allies?

Secretary Powell. I can't answer that. I can't say that there would or there would not be. I just know that time is not on our side. It is not in our interest to let this issue linger indefinitely, as it has lingered for the last several years. Congress—the President will be addressing this issue in greater detail with Congress after he has spoken to the United Nations, and at that point we will make a judgment and you'll see what the sense of urgency is that we believe is appropriate, and will ask Congress to act in accordance with that sense of urgency.

Q. Do you expect the President then to make an appeal to Congress before the end of the year?

Secretary Powell. I don't want to speak for the President now, but I would be surprised if we have not indicated to the Congress before the end of the year what it is we will need from them in order to pursue whatever policy choice the President settles upon.

Q. You and the national security team met with the President, as you pointed out, Friday and yesterday, then Tony Blair came. He is reported to be putting together another dossier, this time on Saddam Hussein. When our allies see that dossier—the French who have been somewhat skeptical, the Germans who have been openly skeptical—do you think they're going to change their tune?

Secretary Powell. I can't answer that. I haven't seen the final British dossier and—

Q. But you've seen the intelligence.

Secretary Powell. I've seen the intelligence and I think the intelligence is persuasive. And the French have their own intelligence systems and means, as do all of the others. They know what we know. We've shared with them over the years. It is no secret—

Q. Do they know all we know?

Secretary Powell. Probably not. I don't think—I hope nobody ever knows all we know. But I think they know enough to come to the same conclusion that he has this capability and he continues to develop it. I don't think you'll find any of these leaders who will say to you right now that Saddam Hussein is not a threat, he doesn't have any of these weapons, we don't have to worry. What they're saying is he may have these weapons, we don't know how much, we don't know how urgent it is, and let's find a way short of conflict to solve the problem. That's what they're all saying.

The question is: What are we going to do in the immediate future to deal with this real threat? And we're putting cards—we're putting the cards on the table for our friends and allies. This is the time to deal with a problem that's been there for years—violation of international law, violation of the will of the international community.

And the United States, often accused of being unilateral, is now bringing the problem back to its original source, the United Nations, and saying here is the case. They have violated all these resolutions, all of these conditions within the resolutions, and we can no longer turn away. It is no longer an option, as the President has said and as Prime Minister Blair said; it is no longer an option to simply ignore this and do nothing.

Q. We have seen in recent days the dissemination of satellite photos that indicate action that a phosphorous plant, which can be used to extract uranium, as well a nuclear plant where there's new construction, it's expected that that possibly can be linked to the construction of nuclear weapons.

Can we rule out right now Saddam's having a nuclear weapon?

Secretary Powell. I would not want to give you an intelligence judgment on that. Our best information right now is that he is working hard on it, but we cannot confirm that he has one. But we are absolutely certain that he continues to try to develop one or obtain one.

Q. Now, you suggest here that the President and the administration are going to say to the United Nations this is a man who lives by violation of resolution after resolution, it is time for something to be done, and in a sense put the ball in the court of the United Nations.

Does the administration have a goal in mind, a policy in mind, an approach in mind, that it would like to see the United Nations take? And what would that be?

Secretary Powell. I am sure that the President will describe the approach that he has in mind to the United Nations on Thursday. But it is not just a matter of saying it's a ball in your court and we therefore lose our option to do what we might think is appropriate to do. Even though the United States, the President, when he goes to the General Assembly will be presenting this case to them as a violation of their resolutions, the President will retain all of his authority and options to act in a way that may be appropriate for us to act unilaterally to defend ourselves.

Q. We've talked a fair amount about the international community. There's a widespread expectation, as reflected this week, Amra Moussa of the Arab League saying that the "gates of hell" would open if there were military action. We've had statements from the Prime Minister of Turkey and elsewhere. A number of people seem to have the expectation that the United States is going to use force or is in one way, shape or form going to remove Saddam Hussein.

You know the Middle East well. If we do not do that, do we lose respect among allies as well as enemies?

Secretary Powell. I think it is important for the United States to speak clearly about its goals and objectives and then to act on them. And what we have said clearly is that this is a regime that must not be allowed to retain weapons of mass destruction. This is a regime, at least the United States believes, should be changed. Our friends in the Arab world know it. The leaders in Turkey know it. I met with the President of Turkey earlier this week. They are all anxious to see whether or not the U.N. will be involved in this. There is a desire for the international community to act.

And I think it's important for us to stick to our principles and stick to the policy objectives that we have out there. And it may not be the gates of hell opening; it may be the gates of promise opening when Saddam Hussein finally leaves the scene.

Q. Is the Iraqi opposition capable of putting together a functioning democratic government?

Secretary Powell. We believe that in due course the Iraqi opposition, plus individuals within Iraq, both those outside and those inside, with the support of the international community, after the departure from the scene of Mr. Hussein, have the potential and the promise of putting together a better system of government that reflects the will of all the people of Iraq and is based on some concept, a solid concept, of democracy. Sure, why not?

Q. How do you rate George W. Bush as Commander-in-Chief?

Secretary Powell. He's an excellent Commander-in-Chief. I enjoy working with him. We saw his determination and his decisiveness after 9/11. What is very pleasing to me with respect to working with the President is that he listens to all the options, he allows us to debate the pros and cons of all the options, and then he makes his decision.

Q. So we've heard.

Secretary Powell. Well, that's the way it should be. That's the way it should be. We're dealing with serious issues. We're dealing with matters of life and death and the security of this nation. And it is our obligation as national security officials and cabinet officers to make sure that the President gets all of the options presented to him, the tone and the tint, the color, the sharp edges. This isn't any problem within an administration; it's what the administration hoped for. And I'm pleased that President Bush encourages it, welcomes it, and then he makes his decision and we execute it.

Q. It's reported that Saddam Hussein is more afraid of this President than he was of the first President Bush. Should he be?

Secretary Powell. I have no idea what Saddam Hussein thinks, but the answer is he should be afraid of this one, just as he should have been more afraid of the first one.

Q. All right. There have been a lot of rumors—you know—that you're going to leave. Have you told anybody that you would leave?

Secretary Powell. No, of course not. This, you know, this is late August media hysteria of the kind I have seldom seen before in all my career. I'm minding my own business, trying to enjoy a week's vacation in Long Island, and you would think the whole government had collapsed. This is nonsense.

Q. The implication, too, is that you're the kind of guy who, if you lose an argument—we don't even know if you have—that you just go off and quit in a huff.

Secretary Powell. That's ridiculous. What have I ever quit?

Remarks by Secretary of Defense Rumsfeld, September 8, 2002

Secretary Donald Rumsfeld was interviewed by Bob Schieffer on CBS's "Face the Nation."

Q. Let's talk about now. How close are we to war with Iraq?

Secretary Rumsfeld. Well, the president has, I think, put it exactly right. He has said that the one choice we don't have is to do nothing. He has decided to go to the Congress and to the United Nations later this week and make the case of what Iraq has done for 11 years. It has invaded its neighbors. It's violated almost every single U.N. resolution that relates to Iraq, and has, against the agreement they had to disarm; they proceeded to develop weapons of mass destruction—chemical, biological, and nuclear. And they—they create a problem for the international community that's— that's significant. And the president has initiated a discussion, a dialogue, a debate, which I think is a—is a good thing. And there are a variety of ways that the world might approach it, but not acting, I think, probably—not recognizing the seriousness of the problem, as the president said, is the one thing we can't do.

Q. Well, let me ask you, then, tell me about the seriousness of the problem. We read in the New York Times today a story that says that Saddam Hussein is closer to acquiring nuclear weapons. Does he have nuclear weapons? Is there a smoking gun here?

Secretary Rumsfeld. "Smoking gun" is an interesting phrase. It implies that what we're doing here is law enforcement, that what we're looking for is a case that we can take into a court of law and prove beyond a reasonable doubt. The problem with that is the way one gains absolutely certainty as to whether a dictator like Saddam Hussein has a nuclear weapon is if he uses it—

Q. Uh-huh.

Secretary Rumsfeld.—and that's a little late. It's not late if you're interested in protecting rights of the defendant in a court of law, but it's a quite different thing, if one thinks about it.

I was musing over the fact that there are so many books that have been written— "Why England Slept," Pearl Harbor, what happened, why didn't we know? Right now on Capitol Hill, the members of the House and the Senate are trying to—are looking, having investigations on September 11th of last year, and trying to connect the dots, as they say, trying to piece together what might have been known, and why didn't we know it, and why weren't we able to connect the dots? What the president is saying very simply to the world is let's look at the dots today. Our task is not to connect— connect the dots as to why England slept, or what happened with Pearl Harbor, or what happened on September 11th only. Our task is to connect the dots before the fact, and—and see if we can't behave in a way that there won't be books written about why we slept, or what happened.

Q. Well, is there information, sensitive information that the administration has that it has not yet shared with the public that makes you take this more seriously than say some people on the outside take it at this point?

Secretary Rumsfeld. Well, I have found over the years being in and out of government that I think the way our system is such an open system that probably, you know, 80 some odd percent of what is knowable inside the government—what is known inside the government is probably known outside the government in one way or another, if not with hard facts.

The problem we have, of course, is a real one. Intelligence—we spend billions of dollars gathering intelligence, and to do it you have to have methods of doing [it] and sources from whom you get this information. And to the extent you take that intelligence and spread it out in the public record, what you do is you put people's lives at risk, the sources of that information, because people can connect the dots there and say "Well, who knew that?" And then they go out and they stop people from helping us learn that type of information. Or, if it's a source, a satellite or some other thing, to the extent that we reveal the information and show our capability, we then lose that capability because they find ways to deceive and deny us from gaining access to it. So, there's a very good reason for not taking all the information. And the short answer is of course there's information inside the government that's not been spread before the public, and there has to be, and there should be.

Q. Will some of that information become known in the weeks to come?

Secretary Rumsfeld. I'm sure some of it will; I'm sure some of it won't.

Now, there's a second thing about this. We know of certain knowledge that we know these things—we know them. We also know there's a category of things we don't know. And, then we don't even know a category of things that we don't know.

Q. Uh-huh.

Secretary Rumsfeld. Now, what happens is that if you go back and take a piece of intelligence when you have it, and then I assert to you "this is a fact." Then you ask the intel people, "Well, when did we learn it?" And they say, "Well, we learned it this year." Then we say, "Well, when did it happen?" It may have happened two, six, eight years before, and we didn't know it. After the Iran -Iraq war, Desert Storm, after they invaded Kuwait and did what they did, all the damage, we went in and were able to find out that they were within six months to a year of having a nuclear weapon. The best intelligence estimates at that time, from any country in the world, estimated somewhere between two or three to six years before they would have a weapon.

Now, until you're down on the ground, you can't know precisely, so the intelligence we have is clearly sufficient for the president to say that he believes the world has to recognize that the Iraqis have violated these—repeatedly violated these U.N. resolutions. They've told the international community they have no respect for the U.N., no respect for their resolutions, and no respect for the agreements they signed, and—and that they are proceeding to do things that they agreed not to do.

Q. Well, do we have any alternative now—I mean, does the administration consider this threat so serious at this point that there is no alternative to removing Saddam Hussein?

Secretary Rumsfeld. I think that what we'll find is that the president will—will go before the United Nations and lay out a speech and make what he believes to be is a recommendation to the international community and to the world, and he'll do that later this week, and I think that will answer your question.

Q. **Would the United States go it alone if the others choose not to go with us?**

Secretary Rumsfeld. Well, that's a tough question. Obviously, your first choice in life is to have everyone agree with you. The reality is that that's seldom the case. And, of course, that's what leadership is about—is deciding what's right, what's important, what's the best course of action, and then providing leadership, going out and telling the Congress, as the president has decided to do, going out and telling the international community what he believes.

The fact that there is not unanimity today should be no surprise. He's not made the case. The case is now—he said this week, this is the first step, the meeting with the congressional leadership. And it is—it was the first step. And—and the case will be made by administration officials testifying before the Congress in the weeks ahead. The case will be made before the United Nations. He met with Prime Minister Blair this week.

The coalition we have today on the global war on terrorism involves more than half the nations of the globe, 90-plus nations. Imagine, it is—it is the biggest coalition that I can ever—have ever imagined in my lifetime. That coalition wasn't there on September 11th of last year. That had to be built. It was built one country at a time over a long period of time. And why? Because if you're right, if you provide leadership, and you—you stake out a direction, people, over time, find a way to support that—that leadership.

Q. **But let me ask you this. I am told—the Washington Post says, reports that you had prepared a long article for today's op ed page in the Washington Post in which you lay out the argument for unilateral preemptive action should that become necessary. We're now told that that article was withdrawn. Have they muzzled Don Rumsfeld? What's happened here?**

Secretary Rumsfeld. No. Come on, Bob. You know better than that. I'm not muzzle-able, if there is such a word. I wrote an article and—and they were discussing it, my staff were discussing it with the Washington Post, and it's a good article. My guess is we'll use it in some period ahead, but I have not finished editing it. And after thinking about it and—and considering it, I decided that the president was meeting with Prime Minister Blair—it seemed to me that that was the message that the world ought to be seeing, not some op ed piece by me, and that the president was going to be speaking on Tuesday, and I suspect I'll probably publish that later this week or next week if it still seems to be appropriate and relevant. It's a good article.

Q. If the United States, with or without allies, goes into Iraq, takes out Saddam Hussein, there is a regime change, what happens after that? Are we prepared to stay for a while? Would we have to stay for a while?

Secretary Rumsfeld. Well, you know, for me to talk about that presumes that the president will decide to do that and he hasn't. So, I think that it would be kind of like the op ed piece that I hadn't decided to publish. And so then the question will be "Well, why didn't it happen?"

Q. Uh-huh.

Secretary Rumsfeld. And I think that if you want to depersonalize it and not talk about Iraq, I think that—go to Afghanistan. You bet—I mean, there's no question but that if you—if you take it upon yourself and with your allies, coalition partners, to go into Afghanistan and—and take the Taliban out, and run the al Qaeda out, and stop it from being a terrorist training camp, and liberate the Afghanistan people, you can't then just walk away. You—you have to, with the world community, work in that country to see that—that something better replaces it. I mean, here you—in—you had a repressive regime in that country, and we're working with a government that was elected, the Karzai government, through the loya jirga process, and attempting to see that those people are able to go to school, and humanitarian workers are able to be there, and it's been a wonderful thing that's happened in Afghanistan.

Q. Back now with the secretary of defense, Donald Rumsfeld. Mr. Secretary, let me ask you this question. What would Saddam have—Hussein—have to do to satisfy you?

Secretary Rumsfeld. Well, of course, what's important is not satisfying me, it's—

Q. Yes, I understand that, but let's say the United States.

Secretary Rumsfeld.—it's—it's—or the world.

Q. Yes.

Secretary Rumsfeld. I mean, the—the reality is that he agreed at the end of the Gulf War to—to turn over all of his weapons of mass destruction and discontinue developing them. He didn't do the turnover, and he has continued aggressively to develop them, as you pointed out, from one of the articles today. There were a series—I think 27, 28, 29 resolutions and stipulations that he would adhere to. He's violated all but two or three, consistently.

Now, what does that mean? It means that the United Nations, the world community, involved itself in this matter, came to some conclusions, and a single dictator in that country decided that he would toy with them—agree one day, violate the next day, lie, cheat, put things underground—consistently for 11 years.

Now, does that matter? Well, I think it's probably not a good thing for the United Nations to be laughed at, and sneered at, and disobeyed, and—and made to be—to not be significant enough that a country like Iraq would be willing to—to adhere to it. And for the United Nations to acquiesce in that, it seems to me, is an unfortunate thing.

Q. So he needs to give up the weapons he has?

Secretary Rumsfeld. Well, the purpose is disarmament. I mean, clearly, here's a terrorist state, on the terrorist list, who threatens his neighbors, who is continuing to develop weapons of mass destruction, has not disarmed as they agreed to, represses his own people viciously. And so one says, "Well, what would one have to do?" I suppose it depends on who you're talking to. The Congress decided that regime change was the appropriate thing and passed legislation, and it became the policy of the United States government. President Clinton signed the legislation, and that's been our policy of this country for a number of years now.

Q. Let me—let me ask you about the whole idea of inspections. I hear some people in the administration say we need to make one more try to get the inspectors in there. I have heard others who have said "I'm not sure inspections make much difference any more." What's the situation on inspections? Do—

Secretary Rumsfeld. Well you probably hear the same people say both of those things.

Q. Perhaps.

Secretary Rumsfeld. I mean, the president's going to make a judgment about that, obviously, and I'm sure there'll be a—

Q. Do you think they're worth anything any more? Can we really learn anything from inspections at this point?

Secretary Rumsfeld. Well, inspections would have to be in—sufficiently intrusive that one could come away and have confidence that you could say yes—you see, the purpose is not inspections, the purpose is disarmament. So, the question is would—would—is there such a thing as an inspection regime that would be sufficiently intrusive, and how—what would it look like—that you could at the end of that period say to yourself, "Well, fair enough, he's disarmed. All of these things have been regurgitated and there they are, they've been destroyed. And isn't—isn't that a good thing."

Now, is that possible? Anyone's guess is as good as anyone else. But he has resisted the—the much less intrusive inspection regimes repeatedly, and indeed, finally threw the inspectors out completely. So, I don't know the answer to the question. And I think what the president very likely will do is he'll go before the United Nations and give his best judgment on that question.

Q. What is it that we fear most from Saddam Hussein? Is it that he poses a direct threat himself, or that he becomes sort of the wholesaler and has an entire government to develop these weapons which he can then sell or give to the retailers, the people—the little mom and pop terrorists around the country—to distribute? What is it that—that bothers us most about him?

Secretary Rumsfeld. It's the aggregation of all of those things. It is the fact that Iraq is a terrorist state, on the terrorist list. It is a state that is developing and has developed, and possessed, and in fact used weapons of mass destruction already. It's one of the few countries in the world that—where the leadership still is in power that have used weapons of mass destruction against their neighbors.

Q. You know, that's an interesting thing, though—he's never used them against us.
Secretary Rumsfeld. No, he has not. And he has used them against his own people. He's used them against his neighbors. And we would prefer he not use them against us.

Q. Let me just—

Secretary Rumsfeld. Is—is—that comment, of course, suggests ought we to wait until he—

Q. Until he does—

Secretary Rumsfeld.—uses them against us. Is that—is that the implication of that question? If you go back to September 11th, we lost three thousand innocent men, women and children. Well, if—if you think that's a problem, imagine—imagine a September 11th with weapons of mass destruction.

Q. Let me just—

Secretary Rumsfeld. It's not three thousand, it's tens of thousands of innocent men, women and children.

Q. Sure. Let me, just for the sake of argument, give you the argument that some people have made to me. I was on vacation last week and out in Australia, and one of the things that concerns people there is they say they recognize there's the threat, but they say let's suppose the United States decides to take preemptive action against Iraq and we're tied up with Iraq and China then decides "Well, perhaps we've got a little threat down here from Taiwan, maybe we ought to go ahead and take care of that right now." What would you say to them in response to that? Is that a possibility?

Secretary Rumsfeld. I would say to them what we've said to the world, that the United States has fashioned a defense strategy, last year, which has asserted that we will have, and do have a capability in the United States to provide for homeland defense, to undertake a major regional conflict and win decisively, including occupying a country and changing the regime if necessary, and simultaneously swiftly defeat another aggressor in another theater, and in addition have the capability of conducting a number of lesser contingencies such as Bosnia or Kosovo.

Remarks by Secretary of Defense Rumsfeld, September 8, 2002

Q. Mr. Secretary if the U.N. does not support United States actions to get rid of Saddam Hussein, should the United States go it alone?

Secretary Rumsfeld. The President has not proposed any particular action to the U.N. He is going to be speaking there on the 12th. He will be pointing out the truth, and the truth is that Iraq stands in violation of most of the resolutions of the United Nations related to Iraq—some 26 or 27 instances of violations.

The resolutions of the U.N. are not U.S. standards, they're world standards. They're international community standards, and I think what the U.N. is going to have to address is how it feels about that. How does it—What does the United Nations feel it's appropriate to do when they come together, pass resolutions of that type, where Saddam Hussein sits down and agrees to disarm and no longer engage in weapon of mass destruction activities, and then proceed basically over an 11 year period but certainly over the last four or five years in flagrant violation of all of those resolutions, what does the international community think about that?

And as the President said when he met with the congressional leadership this week, we're at the beginning of that process. The case will be presented as to the extent to which Iraq is in violation of those resolutions, and at that point they will proceed—he will proceed—with the Congress and with the United Nations in discussing and having a dialogue on that subject.

Q. So, sir, is it your view that the United States should try to help shape a U.N. policy in reaction to Saddam Hussein? Or should the United States go it alone?

Secretary Rumsfeld. Those are questions that the President and Secretary Powell will be addressing in the days ahead as they meet with the Congress and the international community up at the U.N. General Assembly.

The word evidence is an interesting thing. It tends to suggest like a court of law in the United States that what we're engaged in here is a law enforcement process where you're looking to get all the evidence, take your time, protect the rights of the accused, have witnesses argue the case, and then beyond a reasonable doubt have a jury of the peers, make a judgment and a decision.

In the international world it isn't a court of law. It is not a matter of beyond a reasonable doubt. It's a question of what ought the international community to do? What ought individual countries to do? And it is quite a different thing.

The other part of the problem with it is that in intelligence gathering, and billions of dollars are spent on intelligence gathering, it is a fact that to the extent you take intelligence information and make it available to the general public, it all comes from a source or it comes from a method of intelligence gathering. And to the extent you make it available you run the risk, indeed the certainty in some cases of exposing the source that it came from and risking that person's life or at the minimum eliminating the value of that source because they no longer can provide the information. The same thing with the method. If you have a technique of intelligence gathering and you reveal it, reveal the information, it can be known then what that method is.

So protection of sources and methods is important and that is why it is necessary in our world if you're going to spend billions and billions of dollars a year trying to develop intelligence information, to be somewhat careful about the extent to which it is provided to the general public.

Q. Mr. Secretary, do you have any concerns about going the route of the U.N.?

Secretary Rumsfeld. The concern of the President and the United States is that we see with the end of the Cold War, the relaxation of tension in the world and the proliferation of all of these technologies across the globe. To the extent that happens, if you think back to September 11th which is coming up this year, a year ago, we lost over 3,000 innocent men, women and children. To the extent weapons of mass destruction are used in an attack of that type, it's not 3,000 but it's tens of thousands of people who could be lost. And it is a fact that proliferation of weapons of mass destruction technology is pervasive in the world. North Korea for example is selling ballistic missile technologies to any number of countries. There are networks that exist in the world that are assisting countries with chemical and biological weapons.

Q. What about [*inaudible*]?

Secretary Rumsfeld. I don't really care to discuss specific countries or their specific programs. Most of those countries, along with several others, are on the terrorist state, and almost every country on the terrorist list as terrorist states are engaged in chemical, biological and/or nuclear development programs, and testing programs in the case of chemical and biological.

Q. Mr. Secretary, if the United States took the route of going through the U.N., beyond the speech of the President, what concerns do you have that that might delay the whole process for months in the event of whatever action is decided against Iraq?

Secretary Rumsfeld. Well of course those are judgments that the President and ultimately the Congress and the United Nations have to make. They have to weigh the advantages and disadvantages and the certainties and uncertainties.

The one thing the President has said, it seems to me, is that there are a variety of ways to approach these problems but the one thing that's not acceptable is to do nothing because the risks of doing nothing are real, and the second thing he said which I think is important to keep in mind is when you have knowledge of weapons of mass destruction, chemical, biological and nuclear weapons programs in countries that are terrorist states and that have relations with terrorist networks, that time is not on your side because every day that goes by, given the availability of these technologies and the availability of technicians to assist people with those programs, as every week or months or a year go by, they are moving down the field and developing more lethal capabilities.

The second thing you have to keep in mind with a situation like this is enormously important. As much as we spend and as good as we are at intelligence gathering, it is absolutely crystal clear in retrospect, that at any given moment there are an enormous number of things we do not know where our assessments are wrong, and they're always wrong on the short side. That is to say after another year or two passes we will look back on this year, this moment, and find that there were things happening in the world that we did not know. We know that because we can go back and find important weapons of mass destruction events that occurred in terrorist states that we didn't know for two, four, six, eight, ten years. Now if that's true, that means that at this moment there are things we do not know and we can know that we do not know them.

Q. One of the arguments for going to the U.N. is to increase international support. How important do you think it is in your judgment to have allies with the United States in the event of action? Apart from Britain, that is.

Secretary Rumsfeld. It's always your preference to have support. In a perfect world, one would like unanimity, but that's why we elect leaders is to help provide direction and help provide leadership and to be persuasive with other countries and to— Think what President Bush has done and Secretary Powell in fashioning a 90-country coalition in the global war on terrorism. Now that coalition did not exist last September 11th. That was built one country at a time over months. Today it's the biggest coalition in the history of the world.

If capable leaders provide capable leadership and direction, countries over time nod and say that's right, that is the right way we should be going.

Q. Mr. Secretary, there's a new CBS poll that says that American support for invading Iraq is fading. How does the Administration convince the American people that we are right to attack?

Secretary Rumsfeld. First of all, public opinion polls go up and down, they spin like weather vanes. They're interesting, I suppose. I don't happen to look at them. What Presidents do is they decide what they believe is—They're elected to do this. They're elected to decide what they believe is in the best interest of the country and then to make the case and provide leadership in that direction. My guess is that's what we'll be seeing in the weeks ahead.

Remarks by Secretary of Defense Rumsfeld, September 9, 2002

Secretary Donald Rumsfeld was interviewed by Charlie Gibson on ABC's Good Morning America.

Q. There is an argument that goes that we give up our leverage against [Saddam Hussein] if we go to war against him. Our leverage being you export any weapons you have, you use any weapons you have, and effectively you're toast. But if we go in there now, preemptively, don't we give up that leverage to keep him from using them or exploiting those weapons?

Secretary Rumsfeld. Well, it's interesting. First of all the President is going before the Congress and the United Nations and will lay down his case on September 12th to the world. It seems to me it's best to wait and see what he proposes. He's not proposed going to war with Iraq. Your questions have buried in them the assumption that that decision's been made. That decision has not been made.

What the President has said is the one thing that's not acceptable is to do nothing.

Q. Why not under the criteria earlier established, go after Iran? They, we know, have weapons of mass destruction. They, we know, have taken care and harbored terrorists. Why not go after them?

Secretary Rumsfeld. Well, it's interesting. That could be said about a number of terrorist states.

The situation with Iran is, in my view, different. I think you've got a population there that is in ferment. I think the young people and women are putting pressure on the clerics that are controlling that country. I think if we go back in time and recall how rapidly it switched from the Shah of Iran to the Ayatollah, I have a feeling it could switch back. I think it could. That's a country where that's a possibility.

The regime in Iraq is so repressive. There isn't any likelihood that it could be done from within.

Q. So is the goal to disarm Saddam Hussein or is it regime change?

Secretary Rumsfeld. The goal is what the President has said, and that is the Congress passed a regime change piece of legislation a number of years ago in a prior Administration, and regime change has been the policy of the United States government. The question of disarmament is clearly what the task is.

Q. So if inspectors went in tomorrow and somehow found all of his weapons development programs and were able to magically make them go away, that wouldn't be enough?

Secretary Rumsfeld. The Congress' regime change legislation would still stand, and obviously when one thinks about the extent to which the people there were oppressed, and the conventional threat Saddam Hussein poses to its neighbors, those problems would still be there but the world would be a lot safer place if, as you say, it all magically happened. But I don't know why a hypothetical question like that is terribly useful because it isn't going to happen.

Q. With all due respect, isn't it a bit ingenuous to say that we haven't made the decision whether or not to go to war yet because absent our going in there and kicking him out to get the regime change, we don't expect him to step aside.

Secretary Rumsfeld. Well, you never know. There are a lot of dictators living in various countries around the world in quiet splendor and you don't hear much about them, but they're there. Maybe Dr. Valier is floating around somewhere and Idi Amin is floating around somewhere, and certainly the world would be a better place if he decided that it was in his best interest to take his family and leave.

Remarks by President Bush, September 12, 2002

President Bush delivered his remarks before the United Nations General Assembly.

Mr. Secretary General, Mr. President, distinguished delegates, and ladies and gentlemen: We meet one year and one day after a terrorist attack brought grief to my country, and brought grief to many citizens of our world. Yesterday, we remembered the innocent lives taken that terrible morning. Today, we turn to the urgent duty of protecting other lives, without illusion and without fear.

We've accomplished much in the last year—in Afghanistan and beyond. We have much yet to do—in Afghanistan and beyond. Many nations represented here have joined in the fight against global terror, and the people of the United States are grateful.

The United Nations was born in the hope that survived a world war—the hope of a world moving toward justice, escaping old patterns of conflict and fear. The founding members resolved that the peace of the world must never again be destroyed by the will and wickedness of any man. We created the United Nations Security Council, so that, unlike the League of Nations, our deliberations would be more than talk, our resolutions would be more than wishes. After generations of deceitful dictators and broken treaties and squandered lives, we dedicated ourselves to standards of human dignity shared by all, and to a system of security defended by all.

Today, these standards, and this security, are challenged. Our commitment to human dignity is challenged by persistent poverty and raging disease. The suffering is great, and our responsibilities are clear. The United States is joining with the world to supply aid where it reaches people and lifts up lives, to extend trade and the prosperity it brings, and to bring medical care where it is desperately needed.

As a symbol of our commitment to human dignity, the United States will return to UNESCO. This organization has been reformed and America will participate fully in its mission to advance human rights and tolerance and learning.

Our common security is challenged by regional conflicts—ethnic and religious strife that is ancient, but not inevitable. In the Middle East, there can be no peace for either side without freedom for both sides. America stands committed to an independent and democratic Palestine, living side by side with Israel in peace and security. Like all other people, Palestinians deserve a government that serves their interests and listens to their voices. My nation will continue to encourage all parties to step up to their responsibilities as we seek a just and comprehensive settlement to the conflict.

Above all, our principles and our security are challenged today by outlaw groups and regimes that accept no law of morality and have no limit to their violent ambitions. In the attacks on America a year ago, we saw the destructive intentions of our enemies. This threat hides within many nations, including my own. In cells and camps, terrorists are plotting further destruction, and building new bases for their war against civilization. And our greatest fear is that terrorists will find a shortcut to their mad ambitions when an outlaw regime supplies them with the technologies to kill on a massive scale.

In one place—in one regime—we find all these dangers, in their most lethal and aggressive forms, exactly the kind of aggressive threat the United Nations was born to confront.

Twelve years ago, Iraq invaded Kuwait without provocation. And the regime's forces were poised to continue their march to seize other countries and their resources. Had Saddam Hussein been appeased instead of stopped, he would have endangered the peace and stability of the world. Yet this aggression was stopped—by the might of coalition forces and the will of the United Nations.

To suspend hostilities, to spare himself, Iraq's dictator accepted a series of commitments. The terms were clear, to him and to all. And he agreed to prove he is complying with every one of those obligations.

He has proven instead only his contempt for the United Nations, and for all his pledges. By breaking every pledge—by his deceptions, and by his cruelties—Saddam Hussein has made the case against himself.

In 1991, Security Council Resolution 688 demanded that the Iraqi regime cease at once the repression of its own people, including the systematic repression of minorities—which the Council said, threatened international peace and security in the region. This demand goes ignored.

Last year, the U.N. Commission on Human Rights found that Iraq continues to commit extremely grave violations of human rights, and that the regime's repression is all pervasive. Tens of thousands of political opponents and ordinary citizens have been subjected to arbitrary arrest and imprisonment, summary execution, and torture by beating and burning, electric shock, starvation, mutilation, and rape. Wives are tortured in front of their husbands, children in the presence of their parents—and all of these horrors concealed from the world by the apparatus of a totalitarian state.

In 1991, the U.N. Security Council, through Resolutions 686 and 687, demanded that Iraq return all prisoners from Kuwait and other lands. Iraq's regime agreed. It broke its promise. Last year the Secretary General's high-level coordinator for this issue reported that Kuwait, Saudi, Indian, Syrian, Lebanese, Iranian, Egyptian, Bahraini, and Omani nationals remain unaccounted for—more than 600 people. One American pilot is among them.

In 1991, the U.N. Security Council, through Resolution 687, demanded that Iraq renounce all involvement with terrorism, and permit no terrorist organizations to operate in Iraq. Iraq's regime agreed. It broke this promise. In violation of Security Council Resolution 1373, Iraq continues to shelter and support terrorist organizations that direct violence against Iran, Israel, and Western governments. Iraqi dissidents abroad are targeted for murder. In 1993, Iraq attempted to assassinate the Emir of Kuwait and a former American President. Iraq's government openly praised the attacks of September the 11th. And al Qaeda terrorists escaped from Afghanistan and are known to be in Iraq.

In 1991, the Iraqi regime agreed to destroy and stop developing all weapons of mass destruction and long-range missiles, and to prove to the world it has done so by complying with rigorous inspections. Iraq has broken every aspect of this fundamental pledge.

From 1991 to 1995, the Iraqi regime said it had no biological weapons. After a senior official in its weapons program defected and exposed this lie, the regime admitted to producing tens of thousands of liters of anthrax and other deadly biological agents for use with Scud warheads, aerial bombs, and aircraft spray tanks. U.N. inspectors believe Iraq has produced two to four times the amount of biological agents it declared, and has failed to account for more than three metric tons of material that could be used to produce biological weapons. Right now, Iraq is expanding and improving facilities that were used for the production of biological weapons.

United Nations' inspections also revealed that Iraq likely maintains stockpiles of VX, mustard and other chemical agents, and that the regime is rebuilding and expanding facilities capable of producing chemical weapons.

And in 1995, after four years of deception, Iraq finally admitted it had a crash nuclear weapons program prior to the Gulf War. We know now, were it not for that war, the regime in Iraq would likely have possessed a nuclear weapon no later than 1993.

Today, Iraq continues to withhold important information about its nuclear program—weapons design, procurement logs, experiment data, an accounting of nuclear materials and documentation of foreign assistance. Iraq employs capable nuclear scientists and technicians. It retains physical infrastructure needed to build a nuclear weapon. Iraq has made several attempts to buy high- strength aluminum tubes used to enrich uranium for a nuclear weapon. Should Iraq acquire fissile material, it would be able to build a nuclear weapon within a year. And Iraq's state-controlled media has reported numerous meetings between Saddam Hussein and his nuclear scientists, leaving little doubt about his continued appetite for these weapons.

Iraq also possesses a force of Scud-type missiles with ranges beyond the 150 kilometers permitted by the U.N. Work at testing and production facilities shows that Iraq is building more long- range missiles that it can inflict mass death throughout the region.

In 1990, after Iraq's invasion of Kuwait, the world imposed economic sanctions on Iraq. Those sanctions were maintained after the war to compel the regime's compliance with Security Council resolutions. In time, Iraq was allowed to use oil revenues to buy food. Saddam Hussein has subverted this program, working around the sanctions to buy missile technology and military materials. He blames the suffering of Iraq's people on the United Nations, even as he uses his oil wealth to build lavish palaces for himself, and to buy arms for his country. By refusing to comply with his own agreements, he bears full guilt for the hunger and misery of innocent Iraqi citizens.

In 1991, Iraq promised U.N. inspectors immediate and unrestricted access to verify Iraq's commitment to rid itself of weapons of mass destruction and long-range missiles. Iraq broke this promise, spending seven years deceiving, evading, and harassing U.N. inspectors before ceasing cooperation entirely. Just months after the 1991 cease-fire, the Security Council twice renewed its demand that the Iraqi regime cooperate fully with inspectors, condemning Iraq's serious violations of its obligations. The Security Council again renewed that demand in 1994, and twice more in 1996, deploring Iraq's clear violations of its obligations. The Security Council renewed its demand three more times in 1997, citing flagrant violations; and three more times in 1998, calling Iraq's behavior totally unacceptable. And in 1999, the demand was renewed yet again.

As we meet today, it's been almost four years since the last U.N. inspectors set foot in Iraq, four years for the Iraqi regime to plan, and to build, and to test behind the cloak of secrecy.

We know that Saddam Hussein pursued weapons of mass murder even when inspectors were in his country. Are we to assume that he stopped when they left? The history, the logic, and the facts lead to one conclusion: Saddam Hussein's regime is a grave and gathering danger. To suggest otherwise is to hope against the evidence. To assume this regime's good faith is to bet the lives of millions and the peace of the world in a reckless gamble. And this is a risk we must not take.

Delegates to the General Assembly, we have been more than patient. We've tried sanctions. We've tried the carrot of oil for food, and the stick of coalition military strikes. But Saddam Hussein has defied all these efforts and continues to develop weapons of mass destruction. The first time we may be completely certain he has a— nuclear weapons is when, God forbids, he uses one. We owe it to all our citizens to do everything in our power to prevent that day from coming.

The conduct of the Iraqi regime is a threat to the authority of the United Nations, and a threat to peace. Iraq has answered a decade of U.N. demands with a decade of defiance. All the world now faces a test, and the United Nations a difficult and defining moment. Are Security Council resolutions to be honored and enforced, or cast aside without consequence? Will the United Nations serve the purpose of its founding, or will it be irrelevant?

The United States helped found the United Nations. We want the United Nations to be effective, and respectful, and successful. We want the resolutions of the world's most important multilateral body to be enforced. And right now those resolutions are being unilaterally subverted by the Iraqi regime. Our partnership of nations can meet the test before us, by making clear what we now expect of the Iraqi regime.

If the Iraqi regime wishes peace, it will immediately and unconditionally forswear, disclose, and remove or destroy all weapons of mass destruction, long-range missiles, and all related material.

If the Iraqi regime wishes peace, it will immediately end all support for terrorism and act to suppress it, as all states are required to do by U.N. Security Council resolutions.

If the Iraqi regime wishes peace, it will cease persecution of its civilian population, including Shi'a, Sunnis, Kurds, Turkomans, and others, again as required by Security Council resolutions.

If the Iraqi regime wishes peace, it will release or account for all Gulf War personnel whose fate is still unknown. It will return the remains of any who are deceased, return stolen property, accept liability for losses resulting from the invasion of Kuwait, and fully cooperate with international efforts to resolve these issues, as required by Security Council resolutions.

If the Iraqi regime wishes peace, it will immediately end all illicit trade outside the oil-for-food program. It will accept U.N. administration of funds from that program, to ensure that the money is used fairly and promptly for the benefit of the Iraqi people.

If all these steps are taken, it will signal a new openness and accountability in Iraq. And it could open the prospect of the United Nations helping to build a government that represents all Iraqis—a government based on respect for human rights, economic liberty, and internationally supervised elections.

The United States has no quarrel with the Iraqi people; they've suffered too long in silent captivity. Liberty for the Iraqi people is a great moral cause, and a great strategic goal. The people of Iraq deserve it; the security of all nations requires it. Free societies do not intimidate through cruelty and conquest, and open societies do not threaten the world with mass murder. The United States supports political and economic liberty in a unified Iraq.

We can harbor no illusions—and that's important today to remember. Saddam Hussein attacked Iran in 1980 and Kuwait in 1990. He's fired ballistic missiles at Iran and Saudi Arabia, Bahrain, and Israel. His regime once ordered the killing of every person between the ages of 15 and 70 in certain Kurdish villages in northern Iraq. He has gassed many Iranians, and 40 Iraqi villages.

My nation will work with the U.N. Security Council to meet our common challenge. If Iraq's regime defies us again, the world must move deliberately, decisively to hold Iraq to account. We will work with the U.N. Security Council for the necessary resolutions. But the purposes of the United States should not be doubted. The Security Council resolutions will be enforced—the just demands of peace and security will be met—or action will be unavoidable. And a regime that has lost its legitimacy will also lose its power.

Events can turn in one of two ways: If we fail to act in the face of danger, the people of Iraq will continue to live in brutal submission. The regime will have new power to bully and dominate and conquer its neighbors, condemning the Middle East to more years of bloodshed and fear. The regime will remain unstable—the region will remain unstable, with little hope of freedom, and isolated from the progress of our times. With every step the Iraqi regime takes toward gaining and deploying the most terrible weapons, our own options to confront that regime will narrow. And if an emboldened regime were to supply these weapons to terrorist allies, then the attacks of September the 11th would be a prelude to far greater horrors.

If we meet our responsibilities, if we overcome this danger, we can arrive at a very different future. The people of Iraq can shake off their captivity. They can one day join a democratic Afghanistan and a democratic Palestine, inspiring reforms throughout the Muslim world. These nations can show by their example that honest government, and respect for women, and the great Islamic tradition of learning can triumph in the Middle East and beyond. And we will show that the promise of the United Nations can be fulfilled in our time.

Neither of these outcomes is certain. Both have been set before us. We must choose between a world of fear and a world of progress. We cannot stand by and do nothing while dangers gather. We must stand up for our security, and for the permanent rights and the hopes of mankind. By heritage and by choice, the United States of America will make that stand. And, delegates to the United Nations, you have the power to make that stand, as well.

Remarks by President Bush, September 13, 2002

President Bush delivered delivered his remarks at a press conference held the following press conference in New York a day after addressing the United Nations General Assembly.

Q. Thank you, sir. Knowing what you know about Saddam, what are the odds that he's going to meet all your demands and avoid confrontation?

President Bush. I am highly doubtful that he'll meet our demands. I hope he does, but I'm highly doubtful. The reason I'm doubtful is he's had 11 years to meet the demands. For 11 long years he has basically told the United Nations and the world he doesn't care. And so, therefore, I am doubtful, but nevertheless, made the decision to move forward to work with the world community. And I hope the world community knows that we're extremely serious about what I said yesterday, and we expect quick resolution to the issue. And that's starting with quick action on a resolution.

Q. Yes, sir, how soon are you expecting the resolution from the United Nations? In a week, month, days?

President Bush. As soon as possible.

Q. And how—what kind of deadline would you perceive within that resolution?

President Bush. Well, there will be deadlines within the resolution. Our chief negotiator for the United States, our Secretary of State, understands that we must have deadlines. And we're talking days and weeks, not months and years. And that's essential for the security of the world. This man has had 11 years to comply. For 11 long years, he's ignored world opinion. And he's put the credibility of the United Nations on line.

As I said yesterday, we'll determine—how we deal with this problem will help determine the fate of multilateral body, which has been unilaterally ignored by Saddam Hussein. Will this body be able to keep the peace and deal with the true threats, including threats to security in Central African and other parts of the world, or will it be irrelevant?

Q. Mr. President, thank you. Are you concerned that Democrats in Congress don't want a vote there until after U.N. action? And secondly, have you spoken with President Putin since your speech yesterday?

President Bush. I have not spoken to President Putin since my speech. I did speak to his Foreign Minister, as did Colin Powell. I'll speak to President Putin, I'm confident, soon. I'll have—I think we've got a scheduled phone call, actually.

And the first part of the question was, Democrats waiting for the U.N. to act? I can't imagine an elected United States—elected member of the United States Senate or House of Representatives saying, I think I'm going to wait for the United Nations to make a decision. It seems like to me that if you're representing the United States, you ought to be making a decision on what's best for the United States. If I were running for office, I'm not sure how I'd explain to the American people—say, vote for me, and, oh, by the way, on a matter of national security, I think I'm going to wait for somebody else to act.

And so I—we'll see. My answer to the Congress is, they need to debate this issue and consult with us, and get the issue done as quickly as possible. It's in our national interests that we do so. I don't imagine Saddam Hussein sitting around, saying, gosh, I think I'm going to wait for some resolution. He's a threat that we must deal with as quickly as possible.

Remarks by Secretary of State Powell, September 13, 2002

Secretary Colin Powell was interviewd by Paula Zahn on CNN's American Morning.

Q. Do you think war is inevitable?

Secretary Powell. War is never inevitable, and the President did not come to the United Nations yesterday to declare war. We came to the United Nations to lay out a case against a regime and an individual leading that regime that for ten years has violated U.N. instructions, has violated international law. And everybody has been suggesting that the United States should present its case to the world community, and that's what the President did today: He put the problem square where the problem belongs, before the United Nations Security Council.

Q. If you are able to get a resolution together that will get inspectors back into Iraq, do you think Saddam Hussein might surprise the world and comply?

Secretary Powell. I gave up predicting what Saddam Hussein might or might not do many, many years ago. And we are not focusing on the inspectors at this point. We want to talk to members of the Security Council this morning, my colleagues from the 14 other countries of the Security Council, make sure they understood the President's speech, the determination and the power behind his speech, and see how they would like to proceed. I think we need resolutions that record this indictment against Saddam Hussein and talks about actions that would be required of the Iraqi regime and what actions the international community might take in the event that he continues to violate yet another resolution.

But this resolution, or resolutions if it turns out to be more than one, they have to be tough, they have to have deadlines on them, and they cannot be resolutions of the kind we've had in the past that the Iraqis can simply walk away from with impunity.

Q. So are you saying these initial resolutions will not then set any sort of timetable for inspectors to go back in?

Secretary Powell. Well, we'll see what they set. But they have some ideas that go beyond just the issues of inspectors, and I'll be presenting those ideas to my colleagues in the Security Council.

Q. Let's talk, though, about what you might have to face down the road, and that is the issue of inspections. Vice President Cheney has said he thinks inspections are dangerous, he thinks they would provide a false comfort. How much faith do you have in restoring the concept of legitimate inspections, if that's the way this resolution reads over time?

Secretary Powell. I think it's very accurate, as the Vice President noted, to view inspections with some skepticism. The first seven years of the inspection regime, they found out quite a bit. They destroyed a lot of material. But they didn't find out everything, and it was only later we discovered some of the other things that Saddam Hussein was doing. So inspections in and of themselves won't solve the problem entirely, but they are a tool that can be used and I think the Vice President was correct in saying we have to be skeptical and we should not think that just because you got inspectors back in this problem is solved. It's just one tool that could be used.

But the issue of inspectors is not uppermost in our mind here in New York this morning with the Security Council. The nature of the indictment that's been laid before the international body on what Saddam Hussein has been doing for the last ten years and to try to achieve consensus within the Security Council on what we should do about it and how we can put a deadline on our actions so that he cannot continue to just walk away from these obligations and to treat the United Nations with this kind of disrespect.

Q. So as you're trying to achieve this consensus, can you explain to us this morning why you think the U.N. has allowed for Iraq to violate more than 16 longstanding resolutions?

Secretary Powell. Because in the course of this 11- or 12-year period when these violations occurred, the United Nations was not prepared to take action against the violations. President Clinton in 1998 executed air strikes against Iraq, but that didn't solve the problem, and the U.N. did not have sufficient inclination or strength, I guess, political strength at that time, to take any more aggressive action.

This time, President Bush feels very, very strongly that you cannot just look away, you cannot allow Iraq to flout the will of the international community. And we must come together to deal with this crisis or it tends to make the United Nations somewhat irrelevant. We can't have an irrelevant United Nations. It's a powerful, important international organization. It has a mandate from its founding charter that instructs it to deal with issues like this. And that is the point that President Bush was making yesterday.

Q. We have 20 seconds left. Do you believe that the U.N. has the inclination this time around to make these resolutions stick?

Secretary Powell. I think that the U.N. will take it much more seriously this time around because of the determination shown by President Bush to make sure we do something this time and not let Saddam Hussein walk away. And I'll be testing that proposition in the course of today and in the days and weeks ahead as we structure these resolutions.

Remarks by Secretary of State Powell, September 13, 2002

Secretary Colin Powell delivered his remarks at U.N. Headquarters in New York City.

Well, good afternoon ladies and gentlemen. We've had a very busy day here at the U.N., but I think a very productive day. There've been a number of meetings with the 6 + 2 Group in an extended forum where we got a chance to review the progress in our work in Afghanistan.

As you know, I had meetings with the EU ministers, a number of other bilateral meetings with the President, with Central African leaders, and we also had a meeting with President Bush and President Kabila and President Kagame of Rwanda and the DRC, along with President Mbeki [South Africa] and the progress we're making to resolve the conflict within the Democratic Republic of the Congo. And then I had what I felt were very productive meetings with the permanent members at the ministerial level of the Security Council, and I also met with the ten elected members of the Security Council.

So I'm fortunate they had met with all 15 members and I'm pleased at the response that I received from the President's speech yesterday. I think all the members of the Council are now seized with the issue to recognize the challenge that Iraq does present to international law and to the mandate of the Security Council, and they understand that we cannot continue in this manner; and I promised them that the United States would be engaged with each one of the 15 members of the Security Council in the days and weeks ahead, in order to come up with appropriate resolutions or one resolution to deal with this. That remains an open question.

I'm pleased with the response. I think we're off to a good start with respect to dialogue and with respect to tabling language in the not too distant future on the specific elements that might be in such a resolution. I'm prepared to take one or two questions.

Q. Could you discuss how long does President Saddam Hussein have now? What did you talk about this morning at the GCC meetings, please?

Secretary Powell. Have for what?

Q. To comply with whatever resolutions the Security Council —

Secretary Powell. Well, we haven't written a resolution and we haven't come to a judgment on what would be in a resolution yet, so it's not possible for me to answer that question. But the one thing I'm reasonably sure of, that whatever resolution we do come up with must have a deadline to it. It cannot be a resolution such as the resolutions in the past where they were issued and there was no subsequent action to comply or be made to comply in terms of the resolution.

* * * *

Q. [*Inaudible*], if you could tell me what their general view is of taking action in the Council against Saddam Hussein?

Secretary Powell. Within the Gulf Cooperation Council I found understanding and support for the President's speech. I think they are also anxious to see Iraq comply with previous resolutions, and I suspect they will be in touch with the Iraqi leadership. They also did point out to me the position of the GCC and the Arab League that we should not be at conflict in the region. President Bush came here to lay out the challenge to the United Nations and I think he did that very effectively and they recognized that and expressed their appreciations of the President's position. And we will be in close contact with the GCC as we move forward.

Q. Mr. Secretary, what have the Russians told you about their view towards Iraq and what you're trying to do?

Secretary Powell. We had a good discussion with Foreign Minister Ivanov and he also understood the dimensions of the problem, but I think I'll let him speak to what his position is before I comment on it.

Q. Mr. Secretary, you say that you all understand the need to take action and a deadline. Are you all clear in the Security Council on what Iraq needs to do to comply with the U.N. resolutions and how long they need to do it?

Secretary Powell. What they need to do they have, they have known that for the last 11 years. We will now work with our friends in the Security Council to see what elements should be in a new resolution. But this is the beginning of a dialogue, we did not table specific language, I didn't get the outline of what I thought was appropriate as a way of moving forward and that's what we're pursuing in the days ahead. And all of the ministers have to have time now to consult with their governments at cabinet level or with their prime ministers and presidents, and I would expect that next week, under the leadership of Ambassador Negroponte, our permanent representative here, we'll be talking to all the permanent representatives here in New York and they'll be consulting back to their cabinet ministers and to their governments as we start to actually put down language and see what the Security Council will agree upon.

Remarks by Secretary of Defense Rumsfeld, September 13, 2002

Secretary Donald Rumsfeld delivered his remarks at a media roundtable with reporters from the BBC and Voice of America.

Q. Can I just ask one question on the subject of Iraq? President Bush has been speaking this morning about the timetable he has in mind. He says he's talking about days and weeks rather than months and years. There have been various reports suggesting a quiet military buildup going on in the Gulf perhaps preparatory to something. Could you comment on that? Is that what we're seeing?

Secretary Rumsfeld. I didn't hear the President's comments so I can't comment on them.

The only thing I would add on the Afghanistan situation however, is that we do take very seriously the responsibility that the international community has to contribute to the reconstruction effort in that country and to work with the Karzai government to see that his position and his administration's position is strengthened in the country so that they will be able to begin to provide for their own security and their own future, and we're serious about all the things we're doing, and we've done a great deal and we intend to continue to do a great deal and we're hopeful that the international community will step forward and fulfill their pledges.

* * * *

Q. If I may move to Iraq, Mr. Secretary. The President two days ago at the United Nations made a case how the United Nations failed so far to prevent Saddam from keeping or acquiring weapons of mass destruction. And in 1996 it took a defector, not an inspector, to discover what Saddam is up to.

Why do we have to go and pursue another Security Council Resolution?

Secretary Rumsfeld. Well, I don't know that we do or don't. I think what the President's decided, that the breach of those resolutions is an offense not to the United States but to the United Nations and to the nation in the United Nations who have taken it upon themselves repeatedly, I don't know what number it is. Fifteen, 16, something like that, resolutions. An enormous number. Sixteen? Yeah. And the nations in the United Nations have said in strident language that Saddam Hussein must do this, must do that, shall not do this. To the extent he has broken I believe all but one, and probably has broken that as well and we just don't know it, failed to live up to those resolutions, one would think that the President did exactly the right thing by very forcefully going to the United Nations and noting for them what they seem to have not registered fully. That is that the Iraqi regime stands in material breach of all of those resolutions.

Now he did not say therefore you must do this or you should do that, the President. He said how do you feel about that? Don't you think you ought to take that aboard? And unless—If you want this institution to be relevant, if you want this institution to have a role in the world, oughtn't the institution take aboard the fact that they have passed all of these resolutions and they have all been broken? He has not offered a specific resolution to the United Nations that I know of. I know Secretary Powell is going to be working with the countries. There is any number of things the United Nations might decide to do. The easiest would be to simply say that's right and have a finding, again, an additional finding on the part of the United Nations that in fact they have broken all of those resolutions. There are any numbers of other gradations of that. I don't know what they'll end up deciding to do.

Q. We have a policy of the Iraq Liberation Act which was passed by Congress and at the same time we have obligations towards the United Nations and the Security Council. Do you see any contradiction between pursuing a regime change publicly and internationally, in the Security Council, not dealing with this kind of issue? How can the United States kind of merge the two policies together?

Secretary Rumsfeld. Well, I guess that's a question for the President, but there certainly isn't any reason that any country in the United Nations can't support the United Nations resolutions which do not involve regime change and simultaneously have a national position which is their sovereign right as the Congress demonstrated, to have a policy that expresses the view that regime change is really the appropriate solution.

The U.S. policy, I'd have to go back and read it, but I don't believe it specifies a specific method of achieving regime change. I think it probably talks about political, economic, as well as the military activity with respect to the Northern No-Fly Zone and the Southern No-Fly Zone. So that has been the policy for a number of years of the United States. I don't find that in conflict. And to what extent it would be merged is of course a judgment for the United Nations and for the President either in agreement or not.

Q. I have a follow-up on the Iraqi issue, if I may. You said once that the mission dictates the coalition and not that the coalition dictates the mission.

Secretary Rumsfeld. Uh huh.

Q. What is the mission today vis-á-vis Iraq and what kind of coalition would you envision?

Secretary Rumsfeld. I do believe that the mission ought to determine the coalition. To the extent a coalition is fashioned without a mission, it's kind of like a coalition in a government. They get together and they take the things they see and know and come to an agreement and then they agree to govern. And the next day or week or month a new issue comes along and they haven't addressed that, they haven't agreed on that. So pretty soon the government falls.

What we decided was, a year ago, that countries are different. They have different histories, they have different circumstances, they have different opinions among their populations, and that what we ought to do is recognize the urgent thing was to be able to conduct the global war on terrorism was to get people to help and we ought to take their help on any basis that they want to give it.

So if a country's willing to share intelligence but it doesn't have a navy or an army or an air force or it is afraid to say so publicly because the population is very divided on that issue and they want to give us intelligence, my attitude is we'll take it. And the coalition's goal was to find the terrorists and to capture or kill them and stop them, and to stop nations from harboring and providing safe haven for terrorists. And we now have over 90 countries that are helping in one way or another and they're helping in totally different ways. The reason the coalition is so powerful and so broad and so deep is because we aren't asking every country to do exactly the same thing. We aren't asking every country to do everything publicly as opposed to privately. We're not asking them all to freeze bank accounts. We'd like them to, but if they're willing to share intelligence and they're willing to do some other things but they're not willing to freeze bank accounts of terrorists, we can live with that and that's what we do.

You can't answer your question with respect to Iraq until someone makes a decision as to what precisely they think ought to be done with respect to Iraq, and that's obviously not been concluded at this stage. The President's in the process of going to the Congress and going to the world community and saying here's what we believe is the situation and we want to talk with you about it and see what you think about it in a very deliberative way.

Q. On Iraq, sir, one of the things our partners in the international community are apparently interested in is evidence of Iraq's intentions, particularly with weapons of mass destruction. Before they make a decision as to what they might or might not do, do you have fresh evidence that you can make public now on Iraq's intentions with weapons of mass destruction? There have been suggestions that you have some new indications of their plan.

Secretary Rumsfeld. I thought the President laid out the case, the public case very very well. He listed a whole series of breaches in behavior. He pointed out that they do have these capabilities. He pointed out that they've already used them against their own people and their neighbors.

When I hear the word evidence it conjures up a couple of things for me. One is that somebody is misguided and is looking for the kind of information that you could take into a court of law and prove beyond a reasonable doubt and that's one mindset kind of under Article 3 of our Constitution in the criminal justice system where the goal is to punish a person, which of course the goal is not here to punish anybody. The goal is to learn information and to have them disarm themselves of their weapons of mass destruction capabilities. There's no debate in the world as to whether they have those weapons. There's no debate in the world as to whether they're continuing to develop and acquire them. There's no debate in the world as to whether or not he's used them. There's no debate in the world as to whether or not he's consistently threatening his neighbors with them. We all know that. A trained ape knows that. All you have to do is read the newspaper.

Now the other reason for asking for more evidence, of course, is to delay it and to not do anything. That's fine. That's a legitimate opinion. These are tough issues. These aren't simple. People ought to have different views and they ought to discuss them and debate them. I've got no problem with people having different opinions on this. I think that's just fine. But to have an insatiable appetite for new, fresh evidence when the landscape is littered with evidence in multiple languages, it strikes me that it would be a mistake to run around in circles trying to do that.

Second, intelligence information is gathered. It's gathered from sources or it's gathered by using methods, as you know well. To the extent you take everything you're able to learn and you disgorge it trying to persuade the last soul on earth that Saddam Hussein has weapons of mass destruction and has used them and is continuing to develop and build up his capabilities and is continuing to threaten his neighbors, what do you do?

All you do is you absolutely certainly put people's lives at risk if they're the sources of the information. And you almost absolutely deny yourself the future use of those methods of gathering intelligence.

Now that is not a very smart thing to do. In fact it would be a mindless thing to do. Furthermore, if you did it to that person who is seeking that last piece of smoking gun, the last shred of possible thing that we could find, if you gave them that, they'd still want another.

So my view of it is that we ought to make a case. The President's doing that. He did a wonderful job at the United Nations. The Central Intelligence Agency and the Director of Central Intelligence will be making the intelligence case. There is a policy case, which Secretary Powell will be making before the Congress and before the United Nations Security Council. My view on it is that—You know in life it would be wonderful if everyone agreed with everybody but these are tough issues. These are important issues. And everyone's not going to agree and that's okay. That's the way life is.

Q. How did 9/11 and the Iraqi conflict change the approach to the Iraqi issue? Would you have made that case if 9/11 hadn't taken place?

Secretary Rumsfeld. Well, the United Nations has made it repeatedly over a period of a decade, eleven years. We're still flying Operation Northern Watch and Southern Watch trying to restrain his ability to attack his neighbors and to repress his minorities. Legislation was passed years before.

You know what's going on is very interesting if you think about it. You think of the books that have been written after major wars like "Why England Slept" or "Pearl Harbor, What Happened?" Then all the analysts go back and they try to connect the dots. They try to figure out what scraps of information were known and why weren't they able to piece it all together and behave in a way and provide the leadership in a way that would have prevented that from happening?

Right now in the Congress of the United States as we sit here, there are hearings going on about September 11th of last year. They are trying to connect the dots. They are trying to find—We have disgorged thousands of pieces of paper up to the Congress and they have people, dozens of people pouring over these pieces of paper trying to find out who knew what when and how that might have connected and how somebody might have been able to stop something. They call it connecting the dots.

What we're trying to do is help people connect the dots before that happens the next time. That's hard. We don't have thousands of pages of documentation we can disgorge. But what we're trying to do is say to the world and what the President did so eloquently up at the United Nations was to say to the world look, it's a different security environment, it's a dangerous world, the regime is doing what it's doing, and the implications of it in a world of weapons of mass destruction are notably different than they were with respect to September 11th or with respect to Pearl Harbor. It's a different security environment and let's try to connect the dots before the fact.

Now is it possible to connect the dots even after the fact perfectly? No. That makes it 20 times harder to connect the dots before the fact. That's what leadership's about, that's what it's called.

Q. It sounds to me like you're saying the evidence is there, it's time for action.

Secretary Rumsfeld. I'm not saying anything like that. That's not my job. That's the President's job. That's the United Nations' job. That's the Congress' job. My job as Defense Secretary is not that at all. I'm just trying to add a little conceptual underpinning to the debate that's taking place.

Q. You said, "those who are asking for more evidence, are trying to delay it?" What is it? And, Who are those people?

Secretary Rumsfeld. No. I said there are various reasons for wanting more evidence. First of all, it's human nature. We all would like perfection. We'd like all the dots connected for us with a ribbon wrapped around it.

Second is that people, at least in our country, have a tendency to think of the court of law where you want evidence beyond a reasonable doubt. You want to be able to be certain that you know before anyone's punished. My point is, this isn't punishment. We've got the wrong model in our minds if we're thinking about punishment. We're not. This isn't retaliation or retribution. That isn't what the United States of America is about.

Then I said that some people then, even if they had all of that, would still they'd like more simply because it's human nature and it would delay it and help you not have to make a tough decision.

Q. You said that it's the President's decision as to what action to take.

Secretary Rumsfeld. And the United Nations and the Congress, yeah.

Q. Mr. Bush seemed to be saying at the United Nations that it's up to the United Nations to act, but if it doesn't the United States is prepared to. Is that how you interpreted it?

Secretary Rumsfeld. I think I'll let his words stand. He's the President.

Q. You have spoken about your skepticism or your concerns about reintroducing an inspection regime because of the level of assurances that you need in terms of seeking out new weapons of mass destruction and what Saddam Hussein might or might not have.
Do you believe that faced with the initiative by Mr. Bush that Saddam Hussein now will be prepared to accept the kind of inspection regime that you would be assured with?

Secretary Rumsfeld. Oh, I have no idea.

Q. And Mr. Secretary, what would a regime change in Iraq [mean] for the whole Middle East region? A, to the Arab-Israeli conflict and B, to the democratization of the [inaudible]?

Secretary Rumsfeld. I suppose beauty is in the eye of the beholder, but it's hard to believe you could have a regime that would be worse. The views that the President has expressed and others around the world is the belief that an Iraq that is in one piece, an entire country, an Iraq that does not have weapons of mass destruction, an Iraq that is not a threat to its neighbors, an Iraq that is not a threat to its own people and has respect for minorities and has a system which allows them to have a voice in what takes place in their country would be the model that, the general model that one would want. It would be up to the Iraqi people to figure out what template within those reasonable constraints seemed appropriate.

What would that mean to the Iraqi people? It would mean that fewer of them would get killed every year; fewer Iraqi people would be repressed. Iraq would become a part of the world community and economic—The Iraqi people are very intelligent, they're well educated, they're industrious. The energy that would flow into that country from an economic standpoint within a reasonable period of time—It's a wealthy country. I mean they've got oil revenues for one thing, but they also have a good population, a well-educated population.

So how do you measure that? Think of the faces in Afghanistan when the people were liberated, when they moved out in the streets and they started singing and flying kites and women went to school and people were able to function and other countries were able to start interacting with them. That's what would happen in Iraq. It's a pariah state today.

What would it mean to its neighbors? It would mean they were no longer threatened. It would mean they no longer had a neighbor with weapons of mass destruction that were trying to blackmail them and impose their will on them. It would transform that part of the world significantly it seems to me in terms of—Think of the benefits that would accrue in Jordan, in Turkey, in the neighboring countries because of economic activity and the like. Everyone would be better off except a small clique.

Q. Mr. Secretary, you have to help me out here, and help us out because every day now there's a new report that comes out. General Franks is here, he's meeting with officials, he meets the President, and they're talking plans for Iraq. The next day—

Secretary Rumsfeld. That's the press saying that. That isn't General Franks saying that.

Q. Agreed. The next day you have CENTCOM is having an exercise and they're dispatching some of their staff to Qatar. You had a report about equipment being propositioned in Kuwait. It all makes it sound like it's a question of the next 24 hours we're going in.

How do you deal with this sense of imminence? Can you put it in some kind of perspective?

Secretary Rumsfeld. Well, I don't know quite how to answer the question. First of all, the President is a straightforward person. He has said what he has said. He's taken folks up to the Congress; he's going to the United Nations. He's not made a decision as to what he believes is the appropriate course.

We have—General Franks has been wanting to move portions of his headquarters from Tampa, Florida over there ever since I've known him a year and a half plus ago. The headquarters for Europe's in Europe; the headquarters in the Pacific is in the Pacific; our headquarters for Central Command is in Tampa.

So if you start trying to read those tea leaves I think you'll have trouble.

How do I deal with it? Very comfortably.

Remarks by President Bush, September 14, 2002

President Bush delivered the following radio address to the nation.

Good morning. Today I'm meeting with Italian Prime Minister Silvio Berlusconi about the growing danger posed by Saddam Hussein's regime in Iraq, and the unique opportunity the U.N. Security Council has to confront it.

I appreciate the Prime Minister's public support for effective international action to deal with this danger. The Italian Prime Minister joins other concerned world leaders who have called on the world to act. Among them, Prime Minister Blair of Great Britain, Prime Minister Aznar of Spain, President Kwasniewski of Poland. These leaders have reached the same conclusion I have—that Saddam Hussein has made the case against himself.

He has broken every pledge he made to the United Nations and the world since his invasion of Kuwait was rolled back in 1991. Sixteen times the United Nations Security Council has passed resolutions designed to ensure that Iraq does not pose a threat to international peace and security. Saddam Hussein has violated every one of these 16 resolutions—not once, but many times.

Saddam Hussein's regime continues to support terrorist groups and to oppress its civilian population. It refuses to account for missing Gulf War personnel, or to end illicit trade outside the U.N.'s oil-for-food program. And although the regime agreed in 1991 to destroy and stop developing all weapons of mass destruction and long-range missiles, it has broken every aspect of this fundamental pledge.

Today this regime likely maintains stockpiles of chemical and biological agents, and is improving and expanding facilities capable of producing chemical and biological weapons. Today Saddam Hussein has the scientists and infrastructure for a nuclear weapons program, and has illicitly sought to purchase the equipment needed to enrich uranium for a nuclear weapon. Should his regime acquire fissile material, it would be able to build a nuclear weapon within a year.

The former head of the U.N. team investigating Iraq's weapons of mass destruction program, Richard Butler, reached this conclusion after years of experience: "The fundamental problem with Iraq remains the nature of the regime itself. Saddam Hussein is a homicidal dictator who is addicted to weapons of mass destruction."

By supporting terrorist groups, repressing its own people and pursuing weapons of mass destruction in defiance of a decade of U.N. resolutions, Saddam Hussein's regime has proven itself a grave and gathering danger. To suggest otherwise is to hope against the evidence. To assume this regime's good faith is to bet the lives of millions and the peace of the world in a reckless gamble. And this is a risk we must not take.

Saddam Hussein's defiance has confronted the United Nations with a difficult and defining moment: Are Security Council resolutions to be honored and enforced, or cast aside without consequence? Will the United Nations serve the purposes of its founding, or will it be irrelevant?

As the United Nations prepares an effective response to Iraq's defense, I also welcome next week's congressional hearings on the threats Saddam Hussein's brutal regime poses to our country and the entire world. Congress must make it unmistakably clear that when it comes to confronting the growing danger posed by Iraq's efforts to develop or acquire weapons of mass destruction, the status quo is totally unacceptable.

The issue is straightforward: We must choose between a world of fear, or a world of progress. We must stand up for our security and for the demands of human dignity. By heritage and choice, the United States will make that stand. The world community must do so, as well.

Remarks by Secretary of State Powell, September 15, 2002

Secretary Colin Powell was interviewed by Tim Russert on NBC's Meet the Press.

Q. Will the United Nations Security Council adopt a resolution which puts the inspectors back into Iraq, guaranteed unfettered access; if it's denied by Saddam Hussein, followed by all necessary means, including military action?

Secretary Powell. Well, we'll have to see; but you've certainly laid out the elements that I think have to be in a resolution. One, a clear recognition that Saddam Hussein is in material breach of all the obligations that he entered into as a result of these many U.N. resolutions. The second element of any resolution has to be action that he must take in order to try to deal with this breach. And then I believe a third element of any resolution or combination of resolutions has to be what the U.N. will do, what the international community will do, if he does not act in the way that has been demanded by the United Nations.

So this is a test for the United Nations, as the President has said. Everybody said, take it to the international community; and that's exactly what President Bush did last Thursday.

Q. You said "combination of resolutions." Wouldn't it be better to have just one resolution, do it or else? If you divide it into two resolutions, you could have politicking, negotiating, he could say no to the inspectors, and you couldn't get a subsequent resolution demanding military action.

Secretary Powell. You're absolutely right. It would be easier to do it in one resolution. But the Security Council is a group of 15 nations that come together, five Permanent Members and then 10 elected members; and what we have to do is get a sense of what all of those members think is the right way to go. So the President used the word "resolutions" in his speech in order to show that we want to hear from our friends and colleagues.

Now, the President gave his speech on Thursday. We had a large number of meetings on Friday with members of the Security Council, other leaders; and we want to give them time to get back to their capitals, consider what the President said, and come back with instructions this week so we can actually begin the work on resolutions, I hope, no later than the end of the coming week.

Q. That was a last minute change in the President's speech to add that "s"? It was very intentional?

Secretary Powell. The President knew what he was doing when he used the word "resolutions."

Q. Jim Baker, the former Secretary of State under former President Bush, has a piece this morning in the papers which says that it is absolutely not acceptable to have any more than just one resolution.

Secretary Powell. Well, we'll see what the Security Council thinks is acceptable or not acceptable. A case can be made that perhaps two resolutions—I'm not making that case, but there are others in the Security Council who I want to hear from in greater detail who believe that there is a case for two resolutions. It has all the dangers you indicated, Tim; you get into a debate, you get into a discussion. What I've said to my Security Council colleagues: don't vote for the first resolution; if you want two resolutions, don't vote for the first one at the same time you know you will not vote for the second one. That's not what we're talking about. We're talking about a solution this time where the Iraqis are required to act; and if they do not act, then the U.N. must act and not just say let's come back next year and examine this again.

Q. Would it help us in the United Nations in terms of negotiations if the U.S. paid the $250 million we still owe to the U.N.?

Secretary Powell. Oh, absolutely. But I think everybody in the U.N. recognizes that the United States fully intends to meet all of its outstanding obligations. It's just a matter of getting some legislation passed and also getting the cap lifted, a little technical element—the cap lifted on the amount we owe toward peacekeeping operations from 25% to 27%, then we'll be cleared up with the U.N.. That's going to happen.

Q. The key members of the Security Council, the Permanent Members—the United States, Great Britain firmly on board. The French?

Secretary Powell. The French are considering everything that they heard in the President's speech, and I had very good conversations with my French colleague, Foreign Minister Dominique de Villepin, and I am sure he will be consulting with President Chirac.

President Chirac made a statement last week indicating that they would prefer two resolutions, and that's what Foreign Minister de Villepin said to me also. And we will be discussing that next week with his Permanent Representative in New York.

Q. The Chinese?

Secretary Powell. The Chinese listened carefully. They understand the seriousness of this matter. They too believe that Iraq should come into compliance with the resolutions, and they have not expressed any further opinion yet. I would expect to hear from them next week, as well.

Q. The Russians—former President Yeltsin of Russia said this morning, "Iraq is not spreading terrorism. I do not see any danger from Saddam Hussein."

Secretary Powell. Well, I certainly appreciate former President Yeltsin's position; but I think President Putin and my colleague, Foreign Minister Igor Ivanov, do believe that Iraq does present a danger and that Iraq should comply with all of the U.N. resolutions. Now, how far Russia is willing to go with respect to the action Iraq should now take and what action the United Nations should take in the absence of Iraqi action remains to be seen.

The purpose of our meetings on Friday and the President's speech on Thursday was not to lay out a resolution but to begin a political dialogue for several days to a week—let everybody think about it, reflect about it, and come back, then we'll begin the work on the resolution and we'll see what we're able to accomplish. But I can assure you that the United States is going into this discussion on a resolution or resolutions with a very firm position that Iraq is in material breach. We'll see what action the Security Council wants to place upon Iraq to perform; but it has to be tough, it has to be something that is not going to be debated and negotiated with the Iraqis, and there has to be a time deadline to it, there has to be some time dimension to this or we're just kicking the football further down the field.

And then the third element will be, of course, what the U.N. is willing to say now with respect to the actions it will take in the absence of Iraqi compliance. We have to remember that what the President did is exactly what so many people were asking for the President to do: consult with our friends and allies, bring it to the international community. These are U.N. resolutions that have been violated, not an issue with the United States alone, but the entire international community. And that's exactly what the President did. Frankly, I think in that speech the President has changed the entire political environment in which this matter is being considered.

Q. By challenging the U.N. to prove their relevancy?

Secretary Powell. By challenging the U.N. to prove its relevance. In 16 resolutions, multiple conditions have not been met. Deputy Prime Minister Tariq Aziz saying one thing one day, something else the other day, essentially humiliating the U.N. by the way in which Iraq has responded to the demands of the United Nations. And what the

President said, if the U.N. is to be relevant, especially in a case like this, the U.N. has to meet its responsibilities, step up to the challenge that has been presented to it by Iraqi intransigence and violation of all these resolutions.

Q. How much time are you giving the United Nations Security Council to act? A few weeks?

Secretary Powell. I think it's a matter of weeks and not months, otherwise we'll just be dribbling this along. So it's a matter of weeks. Now, I don't want to be more precise than that because drafting U.N. resolutions is not one of the easiest things in the world to do, and then get the necessary votes for it.

Q. And in the resolution, how much time would Saddam Hussein have to comply with the demand to readmit inspectors?

Secretary Powell. This is something we'll have to discuss within the Security Council, but it too will be a relatively short timeline.

Q. Weeks?

Secretary Powell. Well, we'll see. I don't want to nail myself down yet. But you can be sure that we will go in with a negotiating position that it should be a very short period of time. There isn't a need for a long period of time. The Iraqi regime, Saddam Hussein, knows what he has to do. It's been out there for years. So we don't need to give him a lot of time because we're not entering into a negotiation. What we're really looking for, more than anything else: Are the Iraqis going to make a strategic choice right now to do something other than what they have been doing? The issue isn't so much inspectors, no inspectors, ultimatums, no ultimatums. The question is, are the Iraqis finally going to obey international law? And if they are, it's one issue. If they're not, then the U.N. has to be prepared to act, in our judgment.

Q. If and when the inspectors get back in, no negotiations on the ground—

Secretary Powell. There can be no further negotiations, and it can't be an inspection regime of the kind we saw run aground in 1998. Dr. Hans Blix, who is the head of UNMOVIC, the inspection team, has made it clear that he does not want to go back in and start negotiating at different sites and palaces and all that kind of nonsense. All of that has to be cleaned up. It has to be anytime, anyplace, with any person who might have knowledge of these weapons of mass destruction activities, if we get back to an inspection regime. I don't know if we will or we won't. But it has to be tough and it cannot be some sort of haggling operation with the Iraqis. They've had their chance, and we see what happens when they are allowed to participate in that kind of negotiation.

Q. Do you believe Saddam Hussein would bring the inspectors back?

Secretary Powell. I don't know. I'm not going to predict. I don't know. The U.N. should test that proposition and be prepared to act if he says no.

Q. If, in fact, he did allow the inspectors to come back in and he did cooperate, could we have disarmament without regime change?

Secretary Powell. The fundamental issue that got us to the regime change policy was not—disarmament certainly was number one, but there are a number of other elements in these U.N. resolutions: oppression of minorities, returning of Kuwaiti prisoners and other prisoners to include accounting for an American pilot who was lost. There are many other conditions that would also have to be looked at, and that might be the subject of yet another resolution.

But I think if we got to that point where reasonable people could say we're disarmed—and I'm not sure it's just inspectors alone that can make that determination—we'll have to see where we are at that point.

Q. So Saddam Hussein could save himself by disarming?

Secretary Powell. I am not going to go that far. Our policy remains regime change. Why? Because we saw in 1997 and 1998 under the previous administration that Saddam Hussein was essentially disregarding the instructions of the United Nations, disregarding his obligations, and it seemed the only way to make sure that the U.N. would be obeyed would be regime change, to change the regime. That still remains U.S. policy, and we will see what the U.N. effort is able to do. The President retains all of his options to act in a way that he believes is appropriate to defend U.S. interests and the interests of our friends and allies. So even though we are now working closely with the U.N., the President went up there to deliver a declaration of purpose, not a declaration of war; but at the same time, he retains all of his options as President of the United States to do what he thinks is necessary to defend us.

Q. Many Democrats are asking, why has this issue been focused on so dramatically just 60 days before the mid-term elections? Why not six months ago? Why not six months from now? What is the clear and present and imminent danger that Saddam Hussein poses toward the United States that demands that it be raised now?

Secretary Powell. We didn't just raise it now. We have been working on this issue since this administration came into office. One of the first things we set about doing was to keep the sanctions regime from falling apart. When we came into office, that sanctions regime that was providing some level of containment on the Iraqi regime was falling apart. We worked for a year, saved the sanctions and made it a more sensible system that does not punish the Iraqi people. So we have been working this for a long time. It has no relationship to any mid-term election coming up.

What makes it imminent, as opposed to next year being more imminent or last year perhaps being imminent? The fact of the matter is what has not changed is his intention, his intention to continue moving in the direction of enhancing his ability to acquire and use weapons of mass destruction. Waiting for another year will not cause that intention to be any greater or less. The intention is there. He has demonstrated it.

Q. And we can afford a war in Afghanistan and a war in Iraq?

Secretary Powell. Well, we are not talking about a war yet. The President has reserved all his options; but I am confident that, should it be necessary to undertake military action elsewhere in the world, we can do it at the same time that we are continuing the campaign in Afghanistan.

Q. And if we toppled Saddam Hussein, who would run Iraq?

Secretary Powell. If the Iraqi regime were to leave the scene in one manner or another, then that would be a major issue for the international community: how the international community could help the people of Iraq put in place a government that is more representative of the people than the current government is, and at the same time keep the country intact. This is a country that has many, many benefits and has many advantages compared to other developing countries. It has oil. It has an educated population. There is a great deal of potential. If only the wealth of this country had been used for good purposes rather than evil purposes over the last 20 years, Iraq could have been an island of stability in rather a destabilized area. And let's hope that might be the outcome regardless of how Saddam Hussein ultimately passes from the scene.

Q. On September 11, former President Clinton appeared on the David Letterman show and offered some words of advice—let me show you what they were—about the war: "You're looking at a couple of weeks of bombing, and then I'd be astonished if this campaign took more than a week. Astonished."
Do you agree with that?

Secretary Powell. Oh, I'm not going to comment on that. I will let our military authorities and Secretary Rumsfeld in due course comment on what the nature of any campaign might be. We're not talking about war right now. We're talking about the declaration of purpose that the President put before the United Nations the other day. He retains his options, and I can assure you that my colleagues in the Pentagon—whom I know very well and I know exactly what they are doing right now—will put together a plan, if it ever comes to a war, that will try to resolve it as quickly and as decisively as possible.

Q. Ken Adelman, who worked in a former Republican administration, said it would be a "cakewalk."

Secretary Powell. You know, there are a lot of people who think combat is going to be a cakewalk; but it seems to me you'd better let the military leaders who have to actually run this campaign decide how to conduct such a campaign, if such a campaign is necessary.

Q. One concern that was raised is if we begin to build up for a military operation, would Saddam Hussein try his own preemptive strike? Again, here's President Clinton:

"But if he's got these stocks of chemical and biological weapons, and if he knows he's toast, don't you think he'll use what he can and give away what he can't to people who will be using them on us for years to come so he can have the last laugh?"

Would we, in effect, put Saddam in a position where he would use his chemical and biological weapons before we had a chance to be ready?

Secretary Powell. These are all hypotheticals, which are charming to talk about in late night talk shows; but I think that in the serious shows, like this morning, we should not just wildly speculate about what he might or might not do. We know what capability he has, and you can be sure that all that has been factored into whatever planning we are doing now.

Q. But in the Persian Gulf war, which you were very much involved in, Israel was patient. Even though SCUD missiles went into Israel, they held back. Will you expect Prime Minister Sharon to withstand an Iraqi attack and not join in the war effort?

Secretary Powell. Right now, there is not a war underway, and the President has not decided whether or not military action—unilaterally on the part of the United States or with other willing nations—will be required or not. But I can assure you that if we ever start down this road, we will be in the closest consultation with all of our friends in the region, to include Israel.

Q. Senator Bob Graham, Chairman of the Intelligence Committee, said something last week that caught a lot of attention. Let me show you:

"We have recently let Saddam Hussein know what the consequences of his use of weapons of mass destruction—chemical, biological, or, if and when he acquires it, nuclear—against any of his neighbors, and that would be annihilation. That is what has been conveyed to Baghdad. And that, according to our best information, is what Saddam Hussein expects if he were to use a weapon of mass destruction."

Can you confirm that?

Secretary Powell. I have no idea what the Senator is referring to. I'll have to chat with him about it.

Q. Do you believe and agree with something that Brent Scowcroft said way back in August? And I'll show you: "Let's suppose we launch an attack on Saddam Hussein tomorrow. I think we could have an explosion in the Middle East, and thus destroy the war on terrorism."

Secretary Powell. I don't think it will destroy the war on terrorism if it was necessary to act in Iraq. I think that the Middle East region is quite volatile right now and obviously we would have to take into consideration the impact of a conflict in Iraq.

But there is another way of looking at it as well; and that is if you were able to get rid of this regime, if this regime were to go, you might find all kinds of new possibilities and opportunities in the Middle East as a result of a more stable, non-threatening regime in Baghdad.

Q. There were reports, however, that you called General Scowcroft after those comments and thanked him for them.

Secretary Powell. I talk to General Scowcroft constantly; he is a good friend of mine. And I talk to many other people on a regular basis. I try to keep as informed about the different points of view out there as I can. I think it's the duty of a former National Security Advisor, as well as a sitting Secretary of State, to talk to former National Security Advisors and former Secretaries of State of all persuasions.

Q. That was very diplomatic.

Secretary Powell. Thank you.

Q. Let me turn to Iran and North Korea. Why aren't they also targets of the United States—either resolutions to get rid of weapons of mass destruction, with a threat of military action if need be?

Secretary Powell. The President has clearly stated that there are problems with both of these regimes, and they are all on what he defined as the "Axis of Evil." And we are working both accounts in different ways. We don't think they present quite the real and present danger, and neither one of them is in flagrant disregard of 10 years' worth of U.N. resolutions. We have to remember Iraq invaded Iran in 1980, Iraq invaded Kuwait in 1990, Iraq used chemical weapons against Iran, Iraq used chemical weapons against its own people. I think this regime really stands in first place with respect to something that has to be dealt with.

We are in contact with the North Koreans. They understand the issues that we have with them. The President also said we're willing to talk to you anytime, anyplace, to see if it's not possible to change the nature of this regime. And frankly, our strong diplomatic position, our hard position, seems to be having some effect because we have seen some changes in North Korean attitudes and behavior recently, some other things that are not so encouraging. So we'll just keep pursuing that.

And we also sense that there is a churning taking place in Iran. There seem to be different factions debating what the future of that nation should be, the nature of its political system in the future, the nature of its economic system and whether they get a whole lot out of trying to develop weapons of mass destruction, or whether that just continues to push them in a corner of being a pariah on the face of the earth. So the Iranians are going through a bit of dialogue over this, and we'll watch it and see how it develops.

Q. But we know the Iranians are harboring al-Qaida terrorists, and the President said we would not allow that. North Korea—your Under Secretary of State John

Bolton went to Korea and said North Korea is armed to the teeth, including weapons of mass destruction and ballistic missiles; they're the foremost vendor of missile technology in the world.

Secretary Powell. Yes, and that's why they will have to change those attitudes or change those policies, or they will continue to sink deeper and deeper into a swamp out of which they won't be able to get. They can't feed their own people, they don't have an economy that's functioning, and they are slowly falling apart. That's why I think they're starting to find new ways to engage with us. And we'll see whether there is seriousness of purpose in their efforts and whether or not there is a way to get them out of this business of weapons proliferation. We'll just have to wait and see; but that's why the President put them on the "Axis of Evil," because they are pursuing these sorts of things.

Q. Where in international law does it provide that the United States of America has the right to change the government or topple the government of an independent sovereign country?

Secretary Powell. I think we can find in international law on the inherent right of self-defense within the U.N. Charter authority, if such authority is needed. The President has a responsibility to defend the people of the United States under our Constitution. It's one of the principal responsibilities of a Commander-in-Chief and of the President of the United States.

Q. Are you concerned that a country like China would say, well, Taiwan represents a terrorist threat; we're going to take it out?

Secretary Powell. I don't see that as a link or that anything that might happen in Iraq would necessarily drive a similar situation elsewhere in the world. Obviously we would have to watch that. What makes this different are these resolutions. What makes this different is 11 years of violation. And the U.N. every year notes these violations and doesn't do anything about it. So how relevant can the U.N. be if it does not take some kind of action in the face of this kind of violation and intransigence?

Q. Someone you know well, General Anthony Zinni, who works as a special assistant, special envoy, for you sometimes, had this to say: "It's pretty interesting that all the generals see a possible war with Iraq the same way, and all the others who have never fired a shot are hot to go to war, see it another way."

Secretary Powell. No sensible person wants to go to war if war can be avoided. I'll never step back from that statement and that position. But sometimes war cannot be avoided, and when it cannot be avoided, then do it and do it well. I think that's what Tony was saying, and Tony is one of the great heroes in my book. He is one heck of a Marine. He's done a great job for his nation over many years, and he speaks straight and candidly and has strong feelings about this.

Q. Is there reluctance at the Pentagon to go to war with Iraq?

Secretary Powell. I won't comment on the Pentagon. My interaction with the Chairman of the Joint Chiefs of Staff and the Vice Chairman of the Joint Chiefs of Staff and with General Tommy Franks and all of our meetings suggests to me that they are doing the right kind of military planning, the kind of planning one would expect them to be doing. You can be sure that whatever they are doing, they are presenting the President all of his options; and they are prepared to execute the spirit of the President's decision, whatever they are called upon to do.

Q. There are some in the administration who argue that it was not necessary to go to Congress for authorization, it was not necessary to go to the United Nations for a Security Council resolution, it was not necessary to seek inspections to return one more time. It appears the President has now adopted those three positions. Is that a victory for Colin Powell within the administration?

Secretary Powell. Colin Powell doesn't worry about victories and losses. All I care about is do I give the President my best advice and the best information upon which he can make a decision.

In this instance, he weighed all the advice he was getting, he looked at all of the options available to him; and he decided that whether he needed the legal authority or not, it was the right thing to do, the correct thing to do, to bring the Congress of the United States into this in consultation and ask them to pass a resolution in due course. And it'll be in the near future. The President believes strongly that we ought to try to get a resolution from Congress before they adjourn. And that's the right way to do it. The President saw that clearly.

The President also recognized, and we had a number of conversations about this, all of the President's advisors discussing this issue, that because this was a clear violation of U.N. resolutions—and nobody can argue about this. You can argue about whether he is one day or one year away from having a nuclear weapon, but you cannot argue about the fact that he has the intention of acquiring such technology, and you cannot argue about the fact that he is in violation of these resolutions. This is not arguable. And so the President decided it was the right thing to do to take this problem back to the international community from where it originated. That's exactly what he has done. I think it was a very "statesman" speech that he gave the other day, and all of us were solidly behind everything that was in that speech.

Remarks by Secretary of State Powell, September 16, 2002

Secretary Colin Powell delivered his remarks at the United Nations Headquarters in New York.

Well, I don't know. We'll have to wait and see what comes out of Baghdad. But the one thing I'm absolutely sure about is that we're going to continue to move forward within the Security Council on a new resolution. And I'm very pleased at the response that the President's speech has generated. I've had quite a number of bilateral meetings and

I think that the political dynamic has changed, and there is a great deal of pressure now being placed upon Iraq to come into compliance with the U.N. mandates of the last 12 years.

But it's going to be on the new terms in the resolution that I hope we'll be able to complete in the not too distant future, and we're hard at work working with our Security Council colleagues. And it will have to be a strong resolution, and if any conditions are placed, they'll be conditions that are placed by the United Nations on Iraq, and not conditions that Iraq is going to place on the United Nations.

Q. Mr. Secretary, the Saudi Foreign Minister said over the weekend that it would have some U.S. reviews on assets in Saudi Arabia and airspace and things like that for a potential attack on Iraq if the United States—

Secretary Powell. I think what I heard him say was that all members of the United Nations are bound by Security Council resolutions, and I think that was a forthcoming statement. We're not talking about attacks or bases right now, so I will let his statement stand without further comment.

Q. Mr. Powell, if there are signs that Iraq might let the inspectors in because of international pressure, if they do, will there be honest implementation of all resolutions vis-á-vis Iraq, including the guarantees of sovereignty?

Secretary Powell. We have always intended—[interrupted by public address announcement]. We have always wanted full implementation of all United Nations resolutions. And there will be, in the not too distant future I hope, a new resolution from the United Nations that I think will capture all the violations of the last 11 years. And we'll see whether or not Iraq understands the seriousness of the position that it is in and whether it will respond to this collection from the Security Council.

Q. Mr. Secretary, have you got indication yet that you're going to get the sort of consequences named in that resolution for Iraq that you've been asking for?

Secretary Powell. Well, we've just begun our consultations, and I'm encouraged by what I've heard so far from the Security Council representatives that I've spoken to. But as I say, this is a consultation, it is a negotiation, and we're just now starting to look at language, so I would not want to prejudge what my Council colleagues might agree to.

Remarks by Secretary of Defense Rumsfeld, September 16, 2002

Last Thursday, the President of the United States told the United Nations that the regime in Iraq is a grave and gathering danger to the world. He asked that the United Nations enforce the Security Council sanctions that Saddam Hussein had violated and ignored for a little over a decade. Iraq, of course, has refused to remove or destroy its weapons of mass destruction and long- range missiles, and Iraq continues to repress its own people.

The President's speech reminded the world that the 21st century has brought a dangerous new national security environment. Our coalition forces have had good success against terrorists in Afghanistan, but global terrorists remain a threat, possibly with still more lethal weapons. In the last century, free nations of the world were dealing essentially with conventional weapons. The potential casualties in a surprise attack were those that are logical with a conventional attack. Going back to Pearl Harbor, the loss was something like 2,400 people, a lot of people, mainly military combatants. As grievous as that loss was, however, it would be considered small in comparison to the weapons of mass destruction that the terrorists could unleash in this 21st century. With chemical, biological, radiation and nuclear weapons, the risk is not of losing additional thousands of people, but possibly tens of thousands, and very likely civilians, innocent men, women and children, as opposed to combatants.

The United States since September 11th of last year has crafted a coalition of some 90 countries, close to half of the nations of the world, in the global war on terrorism. The work of those countries is being seen almost every day. The sharing of intelligence, the pressure that's been put on terrorists, the people that have been scooped up in a variety of raids in more than one continent, the intelligence information that's been gathered as a result of those raids all is helping to achieve the effort. And you'll recall I've talked about the fact that it's like an iceberg in that a great deal of what's taking place in the world is below the surface of the sea. And it is because of that wonderful coalition and the cooperation that exists that we're seeing such important progress take place.

Last week, the President set forth at the United Nations the pattern of Iraqi defiance. The U.N. is now considering what to do about that pattern. The Congress addressed the matter back in 1998 when it passed a joint resolution that declared, quote, "That the government of Iraq is in material and unacceptable breach of its international obligations. And therefore, the President is urged to take appropriate action to bring Iraq into compliance with its international obligations." That was 1998 in a joint resolution that was approved by Congress.

In the coming days, the administration will take the President's case to the Congress. As the options are considered and as the President considers his course of action, many will be asking some obvious questions: Why Iraq? Why now? Can we afford it? Why not wait? What are the risks? And these are not inappropriate questions. Some are useful. And certainly they will be commented on by the administration witnesses who will be testifying before the Congress.

When I testify before the House and Senate Armed Services Committee later this week, it will not be an intel briefing. Intel briefings will be generally supplied by the director of Central Intelligence and his deputy. It will not be a play by play as to what the goal is in the United Nations with respect to resolutions and that type of thing. That will be what Secretary Powell will be—who's working on that—will be testifying to. It will be a—an elaboration on the case that the President made to the world. And it will, in the case of the Senate, involve an open session and then a closed session.

It's interesting that as we go through this week and next week, the House and Senate intelligence committees are up there poring over literally thousands, probably tens of thousands, of pages of documentation attempting to connect the dots with respect to what happened on September 11th. The—this has been going on for months. And the executive agencies have been disgorging documentation at their request by the bucket.

But what will be taking place in the next few weeks in the Congress will be attempting to connect the dots before a tragedy happens, not after a tragedy happens. The goal will be to try to take the pieces and help people understand that it isn't simple—that there isn't a single smoking gun that everyone nods and says "A-ha! That's it." If we wait for a smoking gun in this instance, it obviously would be after the fact. You'd find it after the fact. You'd find it after lethal weapons were used against the United States, our friends and allies. And that's a little late when you're dealing with capabilities of the lethality that represent these capabilities.

Q. Mr. Secretary, Saudi Arabia, with many U.S. attack planes on base, said previously it would not allow any invasion of Iraq from its territory. Now the Saudis are saying yes, they will, if such an invasion would be sanctioned by the United Nations. Number one, how do you feel about such a caveat? And number two, does this raise pressure on Baghdad to allow unfettered searches?

Secretary Rumsfeld. Well, I've been reading for weeks that the United States is all alone, and oughtn't that to tell us something? First of all, the President has not made a decision to do anything with respect to Iraq, except to make the case to the Congress and to make the case to the United Nations that the United Nations resolutions are being defied and have the effect of damaging that institution's relevance and standing in the world, and that they ought to address that.

Throughout the period of weeks when I read these articles that we're all alone, I have also been in touch with a number of countries, as have Secretary Powell and the President, and the articles have not been accurate. There are any number of countries that are, in one or more ways, in agreement with what the President has been saying.

The truth is, when countries are engaged in elections, people say things that they think they should say. And when countries live close to somebody, like Saddam Hussein, that has threatened their neighbors, threatened their regimes, invaded, used weapons—chemical weapons against them, they're careful about what they say publicly. And that's fine.

So all I would say is that the impression I've gotten as to the degree of support for the United States and the President with respect to his words and his interests and his hopes and goals is not consistent with what we are seeing privately and—

Q. Well—

Secretary Rumsfeld. Now how do I feel about it? Sure, any country that feels it's in their interest—think back to the global war on terrorism. I've said, "Look, we'll take help any way we can get it, and if someone wants to make it private, that's fine. If someone wants to make it public, that's nice." And it's obvious that help that's private is helpful. And it's—we've benefited enormously in the global war on terrorism from the intelligence sharing by countries that are ostensibly not helping us.

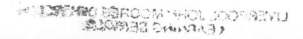

In addition, any country that does decide to step forward and say that they will help in—on this basis or that basis, or for this reason or that reason, or in this circumstance or that circumstances, or in any circumstance whatsoever that anyone can imagine, that's all helpful, because it tells the rest of the world that they have some political cover, if you want to use the current phrase. And so we're always pleased when a country steps forward and says something like that.

Q. Does this increase the pressure on Baghdad to perhaps allow—

Secretary Rumsfeld. Yes. No question. To the extent the Congress and members of the U.N. step up and acknowledge what the President has said as a fact, which it clearly puts greater pressure on Saddam Hussein, and it puts greater pressure on the Iraqi regime.

Q. But you mentioned the Congress. How about Saudi Arabia?

Secretary Rumsfeld. Sure.

Q. Does this move by Saudi Arabian increase pressure on Iraq?

Secretary Rumsfeld. I said when a country does or when the Congress does—people of the Congress and—or people around the world of distinction—I mean, I see articles by former secretaries of State and so forth, and when they are supportive of what the President is doing and what we're trying to achieve in the Congress and the United Nations, that's helpful.

Q. Mr. Secretary, do you understand the Saudi comments to represent that they will now allow U.S. ground troops to be stationed in Saudi and participate in a ground invasion of Iraq if the President decides that and to launch offensive strikes from Saudi Arabia?

Secretary Rumsfeld. The President has not made a decision like that, and—

Q. Can you talk about the Saudi foreign minister's comments—

Secretary Rumsfeld. The last thing in the world I will do is interpret any foreign minister's views. We have said from the beginning, they ought to say what they want to say in the way they want to say it, in a way that makes them comfortable. And that's what they're doing. And it's not for me to interpret the minister or the prime minister of any country on the face of the earth. And I tend not to do it unless they specifically ask me to.

Q. Mr. Secretary, two months ago I asked you if the United States would consider a preemptive strike against North Korea because North Korea was obtaining weapons of mass destruction, and you said at that time, quote: "You gotta be kidding," unquote. In other words, no way. And yet the United States is considering—under-

line "considering"—a preemptive strike against Iraq. What's the difference? And should we, perhaps, also consider taking action against North Korea and Iran, since they were mentioned in the State of the Union?

Secretary Rumsfeld. Well, as you know well, the President's remarks to the United Nations and to the country did not address the subject of North Korea or Iran. He did, properly, in my view, characterize those three countries, those two plus Iraq, as the axis of evil. And I think that what's taken place since that speech has been an indication of how useful that speech was because you can clearly see stirrings in various countries, including one or more of those, taking place, and also in some of the other countries in the terrorist list. So it's been—that speech has been a good thing.

I see distinctive differences in the three myself, as does the President. And the case against Saddam Hussein is encompassed in the President's remarks to the United Nations. He stands in violation of—16 times, I think the President said—resolutions of the world community.

Iran is clearly a country that is harboring al Qaeda. It says it isn't, but it is. It is a country that is developing—aggressively developing nuclear capabilities and increasingly longer-range ballistic missiles and other weapons of mass destruction. It is also a country, however, that has a population that is in ferment. And there's no question in my mind but that the young people and the women in that country, particularly, as well as others, who are uncomfortable with this tight control by a small clique of clerics that they try to impose on the people of that country—is increasingly difficult for them to do.

And I have no—I think most of the world was dumbfounded at how quickly that country turned from the shah to the ayatollahs. I think it's possible that we could be dumbfounded someday to see it turn away from this clique of clerics, because clearly, they're not managing their affairs in a way that's in the interest of the Iranian people.

North Korea is quite a different situation. It is—all one has to do is look at it compared to South Korea and it just wrings your heart out to see what's happening to those people. They're starving. They're being repressed. They're being treated terribly. There's large numbers in concentration camps and fleeing the country.

I don't know what's going to happen in North Korea, except that we do know that they are one of the world's worst proliferators, particularly with ballistic missile technologies. We know they're a country that has been aggressively developing nuclear weapons and has nuclear weapons. {"The IC judged in the mid-1990s that North Korea had produced one, possibly two nuclear weapons," according to the December 2001 Unclassified Summary of a National Intelligence Estimate.} And we know they're a danger first and foremost to their own people, and second, they're a threat principally because of their proliferating activities, as opposed to being a threat to South Korea.

So I see a different situation, and I think the President's approaching it properly.

Q. Will you be moving additional forces to the region as these diplomatic efforts proceed at the United Nations?

Secretary Rumsfeld. Well, we move forces all around the world all the time. People come, people go. We don't talk about deployments; they happen. All I can say is that I don't know what the President will decide or what the Congress, the U.N. will decide, but whatever they decide, this department will be capable of doing that which it might be asked. But we're not going to talk about deployments, obviously.

Q. What about moving CENTCOM headquarters?

Secretary Rumsfeld. CENTCOM headquarters, Tom Franks has been after me to do that ever since I arrived in the department, and there's a certain logic to it. The European Command is in Europe, the Pacific Command's in the Pacific, and the Central Command is in Tampa. You think, my goodness, why is that? Well, it's just history. And it's clearly difficult to deal in those time zones if your team of people dealing in that time zone is physically in Tampa as opposed to in the time zone, in the area of responsibility of the Central Command. So what he's doing is looking at different ways, alternatives of doing things. And what will eventually happen, I think, remains to be seen. But he clearly is developing some capability in that part of the world.

* * * *

Q. Well, this one is—[*inaudible*]—as we turn up pressure on Saddam Hussein and perhaps the U.N. takes action, that we see a desperation play by him—perhaps handing off some of his weapons of mass destruction—his chemical, his biological—to others who would do this country harm? And doesn't that necessitate a need to move quickly?

Secretary Rumsfeld. Well, you know, it seems to me what you have to do is, you have to move in a manner and at a pace that reflects the reality that every day, every week, every month that goes by, he gets—his weapons of mass destruction programs are more fully developed, more mature, are closer to their goal and their establishing whatever it is his different goals may be with respect to those capabilities. Every day that goes by gives him other opportunities to connect with terrorist networks and, as you suggest, either activate Iraqi sleeper cells around the world or connect with networks that have sleeper capabilities in multiple countries, including this one. So that is, on the one hand, one of the things one has to consider. And time, as the President indicated, is not on our side. Time is on the side of those that are attempting to acquire those capabilities. And we have to have that in mind.

Q. How concerned are people in this building about that desperation-play scenario?

Secretary Rumsfeld. The people in this building, uniformed and civilian, are systematically thinking through all of the kinds of things that you're raising and dozens and dozens of others—pages of them—things that can go wrong; things that can be a problem; things that can threaten our country; things that can threaten our interests, our people, our fiends, our allies; things that can happen that aren't intuitive. And they have been—it is their job—our job to do that, to think those things through—what conceivably can happen? You have to think of specific things, like you've cited one, of which there are dozens. But you also have to think not about specific threats or locations of threats or a specific country or a network, but you have to think through, given the kinds of capabilities that exist in the world, where might they come from that have no connection to anything else, or seemingly no connection, and how might capabilities be used that could surprise people? For example, the use of aircraft into this building was not anything that was on the threat matrix as a likely thing to happen. So the new century forces us to think anew, and we are and our people are.

Q. May I just follow one more time? How likely do you see it that Saddam Hussein would do something like that? I guess that's the real question. How he would do it is another matter. But given the fact that we continue to turn up pressure on Saddam Hussein, how likely do you think it that he would so something like that?

Secretary Rumsfeld. Well, I think your question suggests a truth, and the truth is that in Desert Storm, the Gulf War, the stated purpose was not to change the regime. Therefore, that issue was demystified for him. He could pretty much feel that when it was over, he might win or lose, but he'd still be around.

Clearly, if the President goes forward, which he has not decided to do, and if the Congress or the U.N., or whoever else decides there are things that ought to be done, at this stage, there's still the question about regime change in his mind, not whether or not the Congress has spoken on that, not whether or not the President's spoken on that, but it's an open question.

I think that you have to think of that question in this way. The regime is small; it's his family, it's a handful of generals and people who may very well be simpatico with him. It's hard to believe that people are, but let's pretend they are. There are a large number of people in that country who are hostages to him. They do not agree with him, they do not support him. They're frightened to death of him. And he kills numbers of them every year just so he can maintain that level of fear. Those are the folks who would have to implement his wishes. He is who he is. But to be successful in executing the kinds of things that might be done will require that he use other people. And I would think that other people would be very, very careful about their roles in the use of weapons of mass destruction or their relationship with terrorist networks because they would be nominating themselves as part of the regime that ought to get special attention.

Q. The British government is to release next week a dossier or white paper on Iraq. And according to reports in the British press, it's said to include some of the first really definitive evidence that Saddam Hussein trained at least two of bin Laden's top lieutenants. It also purportedly says that Iraq is rebuilding three chem/bio laboratories. My question is, are you aware of any such evidence?

And next week I guess you'll be going to a NATO meeting. Will you be sharing evidence like this, or more evidence with your NATO counterparts as you continue to make the case against Iraq?

Secretary Rumsfeld. I am aware of a lot of intelligence information. I have no idea what is in the paper that you've characterized, that might or might not come out of the U.K.

And the answer to the last part of the question is yes, we will be meeting with our NATO friends in the middle of next week, I believe—yeah, the middle of next week. And there very likely will be an intelligence briefing of some sort that would take place there.

Q. Do you believe, though, that Saddam Hussein has trained top lieutenants to Osama bin Laden?

Secretary Rumsfeld. Oh, I don't want to get into that.

Letter from Iraqi Foreign Affairs Minister Sabri to United Nations Secretary-General Annan, September 17, 2002

Dear Secretary-General,

I have the honor to refer to the series of discussions held between Your Excellency and the Government of the Republic of Iraq on the implementation of relevant Security Council resolutions on the question of Iraq which took place in New York on 7 March and 2 May and in Vienna on 4 July 2002, as well as the talks which were held in your office in New York on 14 and 15 September 2002, with the participation of the Secretary-General of the League of Arab States.

I am pleased to inform you of the decision of the Government of the Republic of Iraq to allow the return of the United Nations weapons inspectors to Iraq without conditions.

The Government of the Republic of Iraq has responded, by this decision, to your appeal, to the appeal of the Secretary-General of the League of Arab States, as well as those of Arab, Islamic and other friendly countries.

The Government of the Republic of Iraq has based its decision concerning the return of inspectors on its desire to complete the implementation of the relevant Security Council resolutions and to remove any doubts that Iraq still possesses weapons of mass destruction. This decision is also based on your statement to the General Assembly on 12 September 2002 that the decision by the Government of the Republic of Iraq is the indispensable first step towards an assurance that Iraq no longer possesses weapons of mass destruction and, equally importantly, towards a comprehensive solution that includes the lifting of sanctions imposed in Iraq and the timely implementation of other provisions of the relevant Security Council resolutions, including resolution 687(1991). To this end, the Government of the Republic of Iraq is ready to discuss the practical arrangements necessary for the immediate resumption of inspections.

In this context, the Government of the Republic of Iraq reiterates the importance of the commitment of all Member States of the Security Council and the United Nations to respect the sovereignty, territorial integrity and political independence of Iraq, as stipulated in the relevant Security Council resolutions and article (II) of the Charter of the United Nations.

I would be grateful if you would bring this letter to the attention of the Security Council members.

Please accept, Mr. Secretary-General the assurances of my highest consideration.

Remarks by President Bush, September 18, 2002

President Bush delivered his remarks after meeting with Congressional Leaders in the White House.

Listen, I want to thank the Vice President and the leadership of the Congress for coming down for breakfast today. We had a really good discussion about our common concerns. The leadership is committed to moving important legislation forward, legislation that will help expand our job base. We talked about the energy bill; we talked about terrorism insurance; we talked about the defense appropriations; we talked about the appropriations process.

We also talked about Iraq. We talked about the fact that Saddam Hussein has stiffed the United Nations for 11 long years, and that, once again, he said—made some kind of statement, trying to take the pressure off of himself. This statement about unconditional inspections was something he's made in the past. He deceives, he delays, he denies. And the United States, and I'm convinced, the world community, aren't going to fall for that kind of rhetoric on—by him again.

We talked about a resolution out of Congress and how it was important for us to work with Congress to pass a strong resolution. I told the members that within the next couple of days this administration will develop language as—that we think is necessary. And we look forward to working with both Republicans and Democrats to get a resolution passed.

I want to thank the leadership for its commitment to get a resolution done before members go home for the election break. I think it's an important signal. It's an important signal for the country, but as importantly, it's an important signal for the world to see that this country is united in our resolve to deal with threats that we face.

And so, thank you all for coming. I'll take a couple of questions. Fournier, Kyle.

Q. Like it or not, is it accurate to say that Saddam playing his move has made the allies go—

President Bush. Do what now?

Q. Has Saddam's latest move helped make the allies go wobbly on it?

President Bush. Oh, all they've got to do is look at the record. It's his latest ploy, his latest attempt not to be held accountable for defying the United Nations. He's not going to fool anybody. I mean, he is—we've seen him before. And we'll remind the world that by defying the United Nations he is becoming more and more threat to world peace. And I'm convinced that the world understands the ploy. And one of the jobs the United States has is to remind people about not only the threat, but the fact that his defiance has weakened the United Nations. And the United Nations, in order for the world to be a more peaceful place, must rise up and deal with this threat and hold him to account. And that's what we expect out of the Security Council.

Q. Mr. President, a follow on Ron's question. Do you think that you'll be able to persuade France and Russia to go along with us on whatever it is you and the Congress decide to do? And frankly, sir, is that necessary? Are you prepared to go it alone?

President Bush. Listen, we're speculating about what nations are going to do. I'm convinced that when we continue to make the case about his defiance, his deception, his—the fact that time and time again, dozens of times, he has told the world, oh, I will comply, and he never does—that the nations which long for peace and care about the validity of the United Nations will join us.

And so we're going to work hard to continue to make the case. I think reasonable people understand this man is unreasonable. And reasonable people understand that this is just a ploy, this is a tactic, this is a way to try to say to the world, oh, I'm a wonderful, peaceful fellow, when, in fact, he not only kills his own people, he's terrorized his neighborhood and he's developing weapons of mass destruction. We must deal with him.

Statement by Secretary of Defense Rumsfeld, September 18, 2002

The following is the prepared testimony of Secretary Donald Rumsfeld which he delivered before the House and Senate Armed Services Committees on September 18 and 19.

Last week, we commemorated the one-year anniversary of the most devastating attack our nation has ever experienced—more than 3,000 innocent people killed in a single day.

Today, I want to discuss the task of preventing even more devastating attacks— attacks that could kill not thousands, but potentially tens of thousands of our fellow citizens.

As we meet, state sponsors of terror across the world are working to develop and acquire weapons of mass destruction. As we speak, chemists, biologists, and nuclear scientists are toiling in weapons labs and underground bunkers, working to give the world's most dangerous dictators weapons of unprecedented power and lethality.

The threat posed by those regimes is real. It is dangerous. And it is growing with each passing day. We cannot wish it away.

We have entered a new security environment, one that is dramatically different than the one we grew accustomed to over the past half-century. We have entered a world in which terrorist movements and terrorists states are developing the capacity to cause unprecedented destruction.

Today, our margin of error is notably different. In the 20th century, we were dealing, for the most part, with conventional weapons-weapons that could kill hundreds or thousands of people, generally combatants. In the 21st century, we are dealing with weapons of mass destruction that can kill potentially tens of thousands of people— innocent men, women and children.

Further, because of the nature of these new threats, we are in an age of little or no warning, when threats can emerge suddenly—at any place or time—to surprise us. Terrorist states have enormous appetite for these powerful weapons—and active programs to develop them. They are finding ways to gain access to these capabilities. This is not a possibility—it is a certainty. In word and deed, they have demonstrated a willingness to use those capabilities.

Moreover, after September 11th, they have discovered a new means of delivering these weapons—terrorist networks. To the extent that they might transfer WMD to terrorist groups, they could conceal their responsibility for attacks. And if they believe they can conceal their responsibility for an attack, then they would likely not be deterred.

We are on notice. Let there be no doubt: an attack will be attempted. The only question is when and by what technique. It could be months, a year, or several years. But it will happen. It is in our future. Each of us needs to pause, and think about that for a moment—about what it would mean for our country, for our families—and indeed for the world.

If the worst were to happen, not one of us here today will be able to honestly say it was a surprise. Because it will not be a surprise. We have connected the dots as much as it is humanly possible—before the fact. Only by waiting until after the event could we have proof positive. The dots are there for all to see. The dots are there for all to connect. If they aren't good enough, rest assured they will only be good enough after another disaster—a disaster of still greater proportions. And by then it will be too late.

The question facing us is this: what is the responsible course of action for our country? Do you believe it is our responsibility to wait for a nuclear, chemical or biological 9/11? Or is it the responsibility of free people to do something now—to take steps to deal with the threat before we are attacked?

The President has made his position clear: the one thing that is not an option is doing nothing.

There are a number of terrorist states pursuing weapons of mass destruction—Iran, Libya, North Korea, Syria, to name but a few. But no terrorist state poses a greater and more immediate threat to the security of our people, and the stability of the world, than the regime of Saddam Hussein in Iraq.

No living dictator has shown the murderous combination of intent and capability—of aggression against his neighbors; oppression of his own people; genocide; support of terrorism; pursuit of weapons of mass destruction; the use of weapons of mass destruction; and the most threatening hostility to its neighbors and to the United States, than Saddam Hussein and his regime.

Mr. Chairman, these facts about Saddam Hussein's regime should be part of this record and of our country's considerations:

Saddam Hussein has openly praised the attacks of September 11th. Last week, on the anniversary of 9-11, his state-run press called the attacks "God's punishment." He has repeatedly threatened the U.S. and its allies with terror—once declaring that "every Iraqi [can] become a missile." He has ordered the use of chemical weapons—Sarin, Tabun, VX, and mustard agents—against his own people, in one case killing 5,000 innocent civilians in a single day. His regime has invaded two of its neighbors, and threatened others. In 1980, they invaded Iran, and used chemical weapons against

Iranian forces. In 1990, they invaded Kuwait and are responsible for thousands of documented cases of torture, rape and murder of Kuwaiti civilians during their occupation. In 1991, they were poised to march on and occupy other nations—and would have done so, had they not been stopped by the U.S. led coalition forces. His regime has launched ballistic missiles at four of their neighbors—Israel, Iran, Saudi Arabia and Bahrain. His regime plays host to terrorist networks, and has directly ordered acts of terror on foreign soil. His regime assassinates its opponents, both in Iraq and abroad, and has attempted to assassinate the former Israeli Ambassador to Great Britain, and a former U.S. President. He has executed members of their cabinet, including the Minister of Health, whom he personally shot and killed. His regime has committed genocide and ethnic cleansing in Northern Iraq, ordering the extermination of between 50,000 and 100,000 people and the destruction of over 4,000 villages. His attacks on the Kurds drove 2 million refugees into Turkey, Syria and Iran. His regime has brought the Marsh Arabs in Southern Iraq to the point of extinction, drying up the Iraqi marsh lands in order to move against their villages—one of the worst environmental crimes ever committed. His regime is responsible for catastrophic environmental damage, setting fire to over 1,100 Kuwaiti oil wells. His regime beat and tortured American POWs during the 1991 Persian Gulf War, and used them as "human shields." His regime has still failed to account for hundreds of POWs, including Kuwaiti, Saudi, Indian, Syrian, Lebanese, Iranian, Egyptian, Bahraini and Omani nationals—and an American pilot shot down over Iraq during the Gulf War. His regime on almost a daily basis continues to fire missiles and artillery at U.S. and coalition aircraft patrolling the no-fly zones in Northern and Southern Iraq, and has made clear its objective of shooting down coalition pilots enforcing U.N. resolutions—it is the only place in the world where U.S. forces are shot at with impunity. His regime has subjected tens of thousands of political prisoners and ordinary Iraqis to arbitrary arrest and imprisonment, summary execution, torture, beatings, burnings, electric shocks, starvation and mutilation. He has ordered doctors to surgically remove the ears of military deserters, and the gang rape of Iraqi women, including political prisoners, the wives and daughters of their opposition and members of the regime suspected of disloyalty. His regime is actively pursuing weapons of mass destruction, and willing to pay a high price to get them—giving up tens of billions in oil revenue under economic sanctions by refusing inspections to preserve his WMD programs. His regime has amassed large, clandestine stockpiles of biological weapons—including anthrax and botulism toxin, and possibly smallpox. His regime has amassed large, clandestine stockpiles of chemical weapons—including VX, sarin, cyclosarin and mustard gas. His regime has an active program to acquire and develop nuclear weapons. They have the knowledge of how to produce nuclear weapons, and designs for at least two different nuclear devices. They have a team of scientists, technicians and engineers in place, as well as the infrastructure needed to build a weapon. Very likely all they need to complete a weapon is fissile material—and they are, at this moment, seeking that material—both from foreign sources and the capability to produce it indigenously. His regime has dozens of ballistic missiles, and is working to extend their range in violation of U.N. restrictions. His regime is pursuing pilotless aircraft as a means of delivering chemical and biological weapons. His regime agreed after the Gulf War to give up weapons of mass destruction and submit to international inspections—then lied, cheated and hid their WMD programs for more than a decade. His regime has in place an elaborate, organized system of denial and deception to frustrate both inspectors and outside intelligence efforts. His regime has violated U.N. economic sanctions, using illicit oil revenues to fuel their WMD aspirations. His regime has diverted funds from the U.N.'s "oil for food" program—funds intended to help feed starving Iraqi civilians—to fund WMD programs. His regime violated 16 U.N. resolutions, repeatedly defying the will of the international community without cost or consequence. And his regime is determined to acquire the means to strike the U.S., its friends and allies with weapons of mass destruction, acquire the territory of their neighbors, and impose their control over the Persian Gulf region. As the President warned the United Nations last week, "Saddam Hussein's regime is a grave and gathering danger." It is a danger to its neighbors, to the United States, to the Middle East, and to international peace and stability. It is a danger we do not have the option to ignore.

The world has acquiesced in Saddam Hussein's aggression, abuses and defiance for more than a decade.

In his U.N. address, the President explained why we should not allow the Iraqi regime to acquire weapons of mass destruction—and issued a challenge to the international community: to enforce the numerous resolutions the U.N. has passed and Saddam Hussein has defied; to show that Security Council's decisions will not to be cast aside without cost or consequence; to show that the U.N. is up to the challenge of dealing with a dictator like Saddam Hussein; to show that the U.N. is determined not to become irrelevant.

President Bush has made clear that the United States wants to work with the U.N. Security Council to deal with the threat posed by the Iraqi regime. But he made clear the consequences of Iraq's continued defiance: "The purposes of the United States should not be doubted. The Security Council resolutions will be enforced, or action will be unavoidable. And a regime that has lost its legitimacy will also lose its power."

The President has asked the Members of the House and the Senate to support the actions that may be necessary to deliver on that pledge. He urged that the Congress act before the Congressional recess. He asked that you send a clear signal—to the world community and the Iraqi regime—that our country is united in purpose and ready to act. Only certainty of U.S. and U.N. purposefulness can have even the prospect of affecting the Iraqi regime.

It is important that Congress send that message as soon as possible—before the U.N. Security Council votes. The Security Council must act soon, and it is important that the U.S. Congress signal the world where the U.S. stands before the U.N. vote takes place. Delaying a vote in the Congress would send a message that the U.S. may be unprepared to take a stand, just as we are asking the international community to take a stand, and as Iraq will be considering its options.

Delay would signal the Iraqi regime that they can continue their violations of the U.N. resolutions. It serves no U.S. or U.N. purpose to give Saddam Hussein excuses for further delay. His regime should recognize that the U.S. and the U.N. are purposeful.

It was Congress that changed the objective of U.S. policy from containment to regime change, by the passage of the Iraq Liberation Act in 1998. The President is now asking Congress to support that policy.

A decision to use military force is never easy. No one with any sense considers war a first choice—it is the last thing that any rational person wants to do. And it is important that the issues surrounding this decision be discussed and debated.

In recent weeks, a number of questions have been surfaced by Senators, Members of Congress and former government officials. Some of the arguments raised are important. Just as there are risks in acting, so too there are risks in not acting.

Those risks need to be balanced, and to do so it is critical to address a number of the issues that have been raised:

Some have asked whether an attack on Iraq would disrupt and distract the U.S. from the Global War on Terror.

The answer to that is: Iraq is a part of the Global War on Terror—stopping terrorist regimes from acquiring weapons of mass destruction is a key objective of that war. We can fight all elements of this war simultaneously.

Our principal goal in the war on terror is to stop another 9/11—or a WMD attack that could make 9/11 seem modest by comparison—before it happens. Whether that threat comes from a terrorist regime or a terrorist network is beside the point. Our objective is to stop them, regardless of the source.

In his State of the Union address last January, President Bush made our objectives clear. He said: "by seeking weapons of mass destruction, these regimes pose a grave and growing danger. They could provide these arms to terrorists, giving them the means to match their hatred. They could attack our allies or attempt to blackmail the United States. In any of these cases the price of indifference would be catastrophic." Ultimately, history will judge us all by what we do now to deal with this danger.

Another question that has been asked is this: The Administration argues Saddam Hussein poses a grave and growing danger. Where is the "smoking gun?"

Mr. Chairman, the last thing we want is a smoking gun. A gun smokes after it has been fired. The goal must be to stop Saddam Hussein before he fires a weapon of mass destruction against our people. As the President told the United Nations last week, "The first time we may be completely certain he has nuclear weapons is when, God forbid, he uses one. We owe it to our citizens to do everything in our power to prevent that day from coming." If the Congress or the world wait for a so-called "smoking gun," it is certain that we will have waited too long.

But the question raises an issue that it is useful to discuss—about the kind of evidence we consider to be appropriate to act in the 21st century.

In our country, it has been customary to seek evidence that would prove guilt "beyond a reasonable doubt" in a court of law. That approach is appropriate when the objective is to protect the rights of the accused. But in the age of WMD, the objective is not to protect the "rights" of dictators like Saddam Hussein—it is to protect the lives of our citizens. And when there is that risk, and we are trying to defend against the closed societies and shadowy networks that threaten us in the 21st century, expecting to find that standard of evidence, from thousands of miles away, and to do so before such a weapon has been used, is not realistic. And, after such weapons have been used it is too late.

I suggest that any who insist on perfect evidence are back in the 20th century and still thinking in pre-9/11 terms. On September 11th, we were awakened to the fact that America is now vulnerable to unprecedented destruction. That awareness ought to be sufficient to change the way we think about our security, how we defend our country—and the type of certainty and evidence we consider appropriate.

In the 20th century, when we were dealing largely with conventional weapons, we could wait for perfect evidence. If we miscalculated, we could absorb an attack, recover, take a breath, mobilize, and go out and defeat our attackers. In the 21st century, that is no longer the case, unless we are willing and comfortable accepting the loss not of thousands of lives, but potentially tens of thousands of lives—a high price indeed.

We have not, will not, and cannot know everything that is going on in the world. Over the years, even our best efforts, intelligence has repeatedly underestimated the weapons capabilities of a variety of countries of major concern to us. We have had numerous gaps of two, four, six or eight years between the time a country of concern first developed a WMD capability and the time we finally learned about it.

We do know that the Iraqi regime has chemical and biological weapons of mass destruction and is pursuing nuclear weapons; that they have a proven willingness to use the weapons at their disposal; that they have proven aspirations to seize the territory of, and threaten, their neighbors; proven support for and cooperation with terrorist networks; and proven record of declared hostility and venomous rhetoric against the United States. Those threats should be clear to all.

In his U.N. address, the President said "we know that Saddam Hussein pursued weapons of mass murder even when inspectors were in his country. Are we to assume that he stopped when they left?" To the contrary, knowing what we know about Iraq's history, no conclusion is possible except that they have and are accelerating their WMD programs.

Now, do we have perfect evidence that can tell us precisely the date Iraq will have a deliverable nuclear device, or when and where he might try to use it? That is not knowable. But it is strange that some seem to want to put the burden of proof on us—the burden of proof ought to be on him—to prove he has disarmed; to prove he no longer poses a threat to peace and security. And that he cannot do.

Committees of Congress currently are asking hundreds of questions about what happened on September 11th—pouring over thousands of pages of documents, and asking who knew what, when and why they didn't prevent that tragedy. I suspect, that in retrospect, most of those investigating 9/11 would have supported preventive action to pre-empt that threat, if it had been possible to see it coming.

Well, if one were to compare the scraps of information the government had before September 11th to the volumes of information the government has today about Iraq's pursuit of WMD, his use of those weapons, his record of aggression and his consistent hostility toward the United States—and then factor in our country's demonstrated vulnerability after September 11th—the case the President made should be clear.

As the President said, time is not on our side. If more time passes, and the attacks we are concerned about come to pass, I would not want to have ignored all the warning signs and then be required to explain why our country failed to protect our fellow citizens.

We cannot go back in time to stop the September 11th attack. But we can take actions now to prevent some future threats.

Some have argued that the nuclear threat from Iraq is not imminent—that Saddam is at least 5-7 years away from having nuclear weapons.

I would not be so certain. Before Operation Desert Storm in 1991, the best intelligence estimates were that Iraq was at least 5-7 years away from having nuclear weapons. The experts were flat wrong. When the U.S. got on the ground, it found the Iraqi's were probably six months to a year away from having a nuclear weapon—not 5 to 7 years.

We do not know today precisely how close he is to having a deliverable nuclear weapon. What we do know is that he has a sizable appetite for them, that he has been actively and persistently pursuing them for more than 20 years, and that we allow him to get them at our peril. Moreover, let's say he is 5-7 years from a deliverable nuclear weapon. That raises the question: 5-7 years from when? From today? From 1998, when he kicked out the inspectors? Or from earlier, when inspectors were still in country? There is no way of knowing except from the ground, unless one believes what Saddam Hussein says.

But those who raise questions about the nuclear threat need to focus on the immediate threat from biological weapons. From 1991 to 1995, Iraq repeatedly insisted it did not have biological weapons. Then, in 1995, Saddam's son-in-law defected and told the inspectors some of the details of Iraq's biological weapons program. Only then did Iraq admit it had produced tens of thousands of liters of anthrax and other biological weapons. But even then, they did not come clean. U.N. inspectors believe Iraq had in fact produced two to four-times the amount of biological agents it had declared. Those biological agents were never found. Iraq also refused to account for some three tons of materials that could be used to produce biological weapons.

Iraq has these weapons. They are much simpler to deliver than nuclear weapons, and even more readily transferred to terrorist networks, who could allow Iraq to deliver them without fingerprints.

If you want an idea of the devastation Iraq could wreak on our country with a biological attack, consider the recent "Dark Winter" exercise conducted by Johns Hopkins University. It simulated a biological WMD attack in which terrorists released smallpox in three separate locations in the U.S. Within 22 days, it is estimated it would have spread to 26 states, with an estimated 6000 new infections occurring daily. Within two months, the worst-case estimate indicated one million people could be dead and another 2 million infected. Not a nice picture.

The point is this: we know Iraq possesses biological weapons, and chemical weapons, and is expanding and improving their capabilities to produce them. That should be of every bit as much concern as Iraq's potential nuclear capability.

Some have argued that even if Iraq has these weapons, Saddam Hussein does not intend to use WMD against the U.S. because he is a survivor, not a suicide bomber— that he would be unlikely to take actions that could lead to his own destruction.

Then why is Iraq pursuing WMD so aggressively? Why are they willing to pay such a high price for them—to suffer a decade of economic sanctions that have cost them tens of billions in oil revenues—sanctions they could get lifted simply by an agreement to disarm?

One answer is that, as some critics have conceded, "he seeks weapons of mass destruction to deter us from intervening to block his aggressive designs." This is no doubt a motivation. But consider the consequences if they were allowed to succeed.

Imagine for a moment that Iraq demonstrated the capacity to attack U.S. or European populations centers with nuclear, chemical or biological weapons. Then imagine you are the President of the United States, trying to put together an international coalition to stop their aggression, after Iraq had demonstrated that capability. It would be a daunting task. His regime believes that simply by possessing the capacity to deliver WMD to Western capitals, he will be able to prevent—terrorize—the free world from projecting force to stop his aggression—driving the West into a policy of forced isolationism.

That said, it is far from clear that he would not necessarily restrain from taking actions that could result in his destruction. For example, that logic did not stop the Taliban from supporting and harboring al-Qaeda as they planned and executed repeated attacks on the U.S. And their miscalculation resulted in the destruction of their regime. Regimes without checks and balances are prone to grave miscalculations. Saddam Hussein has no checks whatsoever on his decision-making authority. Who among us really believes it would be wise or prudent for us to base our security on the hope that Saddam Hussein, or his sons who might succeed him, could not make the same fatal miscalculations as Mullah Omar and the Taliban?

It is my view that we would be ill advised to stake our people's lives on Saddam Hussein's supposed "survival instinct."

Some have argued Iraq is unlikely to use WMD against us because, unlike terrorist networks, Saddam has a "return address."

Mr. Chairman, there is no reason for confidence that if Iraq launched a WMD attack on the U.S. it would necessarily have an obvious "return address." There are ways Iraq could easily conceal responsibility for a WMD attack. They could deploy "sleeper cells" armed with biological weapons to attack us from within—and then deny any knowledge or connection to the attacks. Or they could put a WMD-tipped missile on a "commercial" shipping vessel, sail it within range of our coast, fire it, and then melt back into the commercial shipping traffic before we knew what hit us. Finding that ship would be like searching for a needle in a haystack—a bit like locating a single terrorist. Or they could recruit and utilize a terrorist network with similar views and objectives, and pass on weapons of mass destruction to them. It is this nexus between a terrorist state like Iraq with WMD and terrorist networks that has so significantly changed the U.S. security environment.

We still do not know with certainty who was behind the 1996 bombing the Khobar Towers in Saudi Arabia—an attack that killed 19 American service members. We still do not know who is responsible for last year's anthrax attacks. The nature of terrorist attacks is that it is often very difficult to identify who is ultimately responsible. Indeed, our consistent failure over the past two decades to trace terrorist attacks to their ultimate source gives terrorist states the lesson that using terrorist networks as proxies is an effective way of attacking the U.S. with impunity.

Some have opined there is scant evidence of Iraq's ties to terrorists, and he has little incentive to make common cause with them.

That is not correct. Iraq's ties to terrorist networks are long-standing. It is no coincidence that Abu Nidal was in Baghdad, when he died under mysterious circumstances. Iraq has also reportedly provided safe haven to Abdul Rahman Yasin, one of the FBI's most wanted terrorists, who was a key participant in the first World Trade Center bombing. We know that al-Qaeda is operating in Iraq today, and that little happens in Iraq without the knowledge of the Saddam Hussein regime. We also know that there have been a number of contacts between Iraq and al-Qaeda over the years. We know Saddam has ordered acts of terror himself, including the attempted assassination of a former U.S. President.

He has incentives to make common cause with terrorists. He shares many common objectives with groups like al-Qaeda, including an antipathy for the Saudi royal family and a desire to drive the U.S. out of the Persian Gulf region. Moreover, if he decided it was in his interest to conceal his responsibility for an attack on the U.S., providing WMD to terrorists would be an effective way of doing so.

Some have said that they would support action to remove Saddam if the U.S. could prove a connection to the attacks of September 11th—but there is no such proof.

The question implies that the U.S. should have to prove that Iraq has already attacked us in order to deal with that threat. The objective is to stop him before he attacks us and kills thousands of our citizens.

The case against Iraq does not depend on an Iraqi link to 9/11. The issue for the U.S. is not vengeance, retribution or retaliation—it is whether the Iraqi regime poses a growing danger to the safety and security of our people, and of the world. There is no question but that it does.

Some argue that North Korea and Iran are more immediate threats than Iraq. North Korea almost certainly has nuclear weapons, and is developing missiles that will be able to reach most of the continental United States. Iran has stockpiles of chemical weapons, is developing ballistic missiles of increasing range, and is aggressively pursuing nuclear weapons. The question is asked: why not deal with them first?

Iran and North Korea are indeed threats—problems we take seriously. That is why President Bush named them specifically, when he spoke about an "Axis of Evil." And we have policies to address both.

But Iraq is unique. No other living dictator matches Saddam Hussein's record of waging aggressive war against his neighbors; pursuing weapons of mass destruction; using WMD against his own people and other nations; launching ballistic missiles at his neighbors; brutalizing and torturing his own citizens; harboring terrorist networks; engaging in terrorist acts, including the attempted assassination of foreign officials; violating his international commitments; lying, cheating and hiding his WMD programs; deceiving and defying the express will of the United Nations over and over again.

As the President told the U.N., "in one place—in one regime—we find all these dangers in their most lethal and aggressive forms."

Some respond by saying, OK, Iraq poses a threat we will eventually have to deal with—but now is not the time to do so.

To that, I would ask: when? Will it be a better time when his regime is stronger? When its WMD programs are still further advanced? After he further builds his forces, which are stronger and deadlier with each passing day? Yes, there are risks in acting. The President understands those risks. But there are also risks in further delay. As the President has said: "I will not wait on events, while dangers gather. I will not stand by, as peril draws closer and closer. The United States of America will not permit the world's most dangerous regimes to threaten us with the world's most destructive weapons."

Others say that overthrowing the regime should be the last step, not the first.

I would respond that for more than a decade now, the international community has tried every other step. They have tried diplomacy; they have tried sanctions and embargoes; they have tried positive inducements, such as the "oil for food" program; they have tried inspections; they have tried limited military strikes. Together, all these approaches have failed to accomplish the U.N. goals.

If the President were to decide to take military action to overthrow the regime, it would be not the first step, it would be the last step, after a decade of failed diplomatic and economic steps to stop his drive for WMD.

Some have asked: why not just contain him? The West lived for 40 years with the Soviet threat, and never felt the need to take pre-emptive action. If containment worked on the Soviet Union, why not Iraq?

First, it's clear from the Iraqi regimes 11 years of defiance that containment has not led to their compliance. To the contrary, containment is breaking down—the regime continues to receive funds from illegal oil sales and procure military hardware necessary to develop weapons of mass murder. So not only has containment failed to reduce the threat, it has allowed the threat to grow.

Second, with the Soviet Union we faced an adversary that already possessed nuclear weapons—thousands of them. Our goal with Iraq is to prevent them from getting nuclear weapons. We are not interested in establishing a balance of terror with the likes of Iraq, like the one that existed with the Soviet Union. We are interested in stopping a balance of terror from forming.

Third, with the Soviet Union, we believed that time was on our side—and we were correct. With Iraq, the opposite is true—time is not our side. Every month that goes by, his WMD programs are progressing and he moves closer to his goal of possessing the capability to strike our population, and our allies, and hold them hostage to blackmail.

Finally, while containment worked in the long run, the Soviet Union's nuclear arsenal prevented the West from responding when they invaded their neighbor, Afghanistan. Does anyone really want Saddam to have that same deterrent, so he can invade his neighbors with impunity?

Some ask: Why does he have to be overthrown? Can't we just take out the capabilities he has that threaten us?

While the President has not made that decision, the problem with doing it piecemeal is this: First, we do not know where all of Iraq's WMD facilities are. We do know where a fraction of them are. Second, of the facilities we do know, not all are vulnerable to attack from the air. Some are underground. Some are mobile. Others are purposely located near population centers—schools, mosques, hospitals, etc.—where an air strike could kill large numbers of innocent people. The Iraq problem cannot be solved with air strikes alone.

Some have argued that, if we do have to go to war, the U.S. should first layout details of a truly comprehensive inspections regime, which, if Iraq failed to comply, would provide a casus belli.

I would respond this way: if failure to comply with WMD inspections is a casus belli, the U.N. already has it—Iraq's non- compliance with U.N. inspection regimes has been going on for more than a decade. What else can one ask for?

The U.S. is not close to inspections as an element of an effective response. But the goal is not inspections—it is disarmament. Any inspections would have to be notably different from the past. Given the history of this regime, the world community has every right to be skeptical that it would be. And that is why, in 1998, the U.S. began to speak of regime change.

Our goal is disarmament. The only purpose of any inspections would be to prove that Iraq has disarmed, which would require Iraq to reverse its decades-long policy of pursuing these weapons. Something they are unlikely to do.

There are serious concerns about whether an inspections regime could be effective. Even the most intrusive inspection regime would have difficulty getting at all his weapons of mass destruction. Many of his WMD capabilities are mobile and can be hidden to evade inspectors. He has vast underground networks and facilities to hide WMD, and sophisticated denial and deception techniques. It is simply impossible to "spot check" a country the size of Iraq. Unless we have people inside the Iraqi program who are willing to tell us what they have and where they have it—as we did in 1995 with the defection of Saddam's son in law, Hussein Kamel—it is easy for the Iraqi regime to hide its capabilities from us.

Indeed, Hans Blix, the chief U.N. Weapons inspector, said as much in an interview with the *New York Times* last week. According to the Times, " [Mr. Blix] acknowledged that there were some limitations to what his team could accomplish even if it was allowed to return. Mr. Blix said his inspectors might not be able to detect mobile laboratories for producing biological weapons materials, or underground storehouses for weapons substances, if the inspectors did not have information about such sites from the last time they were in Iraq or have not seen traces of them in satellite surveillance photography."

When UNSCOM inspectors were on the ground, they did an admirable job of uncovering many of Iraq's violations—which is undoubtedly why Iraq had them expelled. But despite the U.N.'s best efforts, from 1991-1995 Saddam was able to conceal some of his nuclear program and his biological weapons program. Some aspects were uncovered after his son-in-law defected and provided information that allowed inspectors to find them. And even then, Iraq was able to hide many of those activities from inspectors—capabilities he most likely still has today, in addition to what he has developed in recent years.

There is a place in this world for inspections. They tend to be effective if the target nation is cooperating—if they are actually willing to disarm and want to prove to the world that they are doing so. They tend not be as effective in uncovering deceptions and violations when the target is determined not to disarm. Iraq's record of the past decade shows the regime is not interested in disarming or cooperating. Their behavior demonstrates they want weapons of mass destruction and are determined to continue developing them.

Some ask: now that Iraq has agreed to "unconditional inspections," why does Congress need to act?

Iraq has demonstrated great skill at playing the international community. When it's the right moment to lean forward, they lean forward. When it's a time to lean back, they lean back. It's a dance. They can go on for months or years jerking the U.N. around. When they find that things are not going their way, they throw out a proposal like this. And hopeful people say: "There's our opportunity. They are finally being reasonable. Seize the moment. Let's give them another chance." And then we repeatedly find, at the last moment, that Iraq withdraws that carrot and goes back into their mode of rejecting the international community. And the dance starts all over again.

The issue is not inspections. The issue is disarmament. The issue is compliance. As the President made clear in his U.N. address, we require Iraq's compliance with all 16 U.N. resolutions that they have defied over the past decade. And, as the President said, the U.N. Security Council—not the Iraqi regime—needs to decide how to enforce its own resolutions. Congress's support for the President is what is needed to further generate international support.

Some have asked whether military intervention in Iraq means the U.S. would have to go to war with every terrorist state that is pursuing WMD?

The answer is: no. Taking military action in Iraq does not mean that it would be necessary or appropriate to take military action against other states that possess or are pursuing WMD. For one thing, preventive action in one situation may very well produce a deterrent effect on other states. After driving the Taliban from power in Afghanistan, we have already seen a change in behavior in certain regimes.

Moreover, dealing with some states may not require military action. In some cases, such as Iran, change could conceivably come from within. The young people and the women in Iran are increasingly fed up with the tight clique of Mullahs—they want change, and may well rise up to change their leadership at some point.

Some say that there is no international consensus behind ousting Saddam—and most of our key allies are opposed.

First, the fact is that there are a number of countries that want Saddam Hussein gone. Some are reluctant to say publicly just yet. But, if the U.S. waited for a consensus before acting, we would never do anything. Obviously, one's first choice in life is to have everyone agree with you at the outset. In reality, that is seldom the case. It takes time, leadership and persuasion. Leadership is about deciding what is right, and then going out and persuading others.

The coalition we have fashioned in the global war on terror today includes some 90 nations—literally half the world. It is the greatest coalition ever assembled in the annals of human history. It was not there on September 11th. It was built, one country at a time, over a long period of time. If we had waited for consensus, the Taliban would still be in power in Afghanistan today. The worldwide coalition was formed by leadership.

During the Persian Gulf War, the coalition eventually included 36 nations. But they were not there on August 2, 1990 when Saddam invaded Kuwait. They were not there on August 5th, when the President George H. W. Bush announced to the world that Saddam's aggression "will not stand." That coalition was built over a period of many months.

With his U.N. speech, President George W. Bush began the process of building international support for dealing with Iraq. The reaction has been positive. We will continue to state our case, as the President is doing, and I suspect that as he does so, you will find that other countries in increasing numbers will cooperate and participate. Will it be unanimous? No. Does anyone expect it to be unanimous? No. Does it matter that it will not be unanimous? No. But does the U.S. want all the support possible—you bet. Just as we have in the coalition supporting the Global War on Terrorism.

The point is: if our nation's leaders do the right thing, others will follow and support the just cause—just they have in the global war against terror.

Some say that our European allies may reluctantly go along in the end, but that U.S. intervention in Iraq would spark concern in the Arab world—that not one country in that regions supports us, and many are vocally opposed.

That is not so. Saddam's neighbors are deathly afraid of him—and understandably so. He has invaded his neighbors, used weapons of mass destruction against them, and launched ballistic missiles at them. He aspires to dominate the region. The nations of the region would be greatly relieved to have him gone, and that if Saddam Hussein is removed from power, the reaction in the region will be not outrage, but great relief. And the reaction of the Iraqi people will most certainly be jubilation.

Some ask, but will they help us? Will they give us access to bases and territory and airspace we need to conduct a military operation?

The answer is that the President has not decided to take military action, but, if he does, we will have all the support we need to get the job done. You can be certain of it.

Another argument is that military action in Iraq will be expensive, and will have high costs for the global economy.

That may be true. But there are also dollar costs to not acting—and those costs could well be far greater. Consider: the New York City Comptroller estimates that the economic costs of the Sept. 11 attacks to New York alone were between $83 and $95 billion. He further estimated that New York lost 83,000 existing jobs and some 63,000 jobs the city estimates would have been created had the attacks not happened. One institute puts the cost to the national economy at $191 billion—including 1.64 million jobs lost as a direct result of the 9/11 attacks. Other estimates are higher—as much as $250 billion in lost productivity, sales, jobs, advertising, airline revenue and the like. And that is not to mention the cost in human lives, and the suffering of those who lost fathers and mothers, sons and daughters, sisters and brothers that day.

And we must not forget that the costs of a nuclear, chemical or biological weapons attack would be far worse. The price in lives would be not thousands, but tens of thousands. And the economic costs could make September 11th pale by comparison. Those are the costs that also must be weighed carefully. And this is not mention the cost to one's conscience of being wrong.

Some have suggested that if the U.S. were to act it might provoke Saddam Hussein's use of WMD. Last time, the argument goes, he didn't use chemical weapons on U.S. troops and allies because he saw our goal was not to oust him, but to push back his aggression. This time, the argument goes, the opposite would be true, and he would have nothing to lose by using WMD.

That is an important point. And the President made clear on March 13, 2002 the consequences of such an attack. He said: "we've got all options on the table because we want to make it very clear to nations that you will not threaten the United States or use weapons of mass destruction against us, our allies, or our friends."

There are ways to mitigate the risk of a chem-bio attack, but it cannot be entirely eliminated—it is true that could be a risk of military action. But consider the consequences if the world were to allow that risk to deter us from acting. We would then have sent a message to the world about the value of weapons of mass destruction that we would deeply regret having sent. A country thinking about acquiring WMD would conclude that the U.S. had been deterred by Iraq's chemical and biological weapons capabilities, and they could then resolve to pursue those weapons to assure their impunity. The message the world should want to send is the exact opposite. The message should be that Iraq's pursuit of WMD has not only not made it more secure, it has made it less secure—that by pursuing those weapons, they have attracted undesired attention to themselves.

But if he is that dangerous, then that only makes the case for action stronger—because the longer we wait, the more deadly his regime becomes. If the world community were to be deterred from acting today by the threat that Iraq might use chemical or biological weapons, how will the U.N. feel when one day, when Iraq demonstrates it has a deliverable nuclear weapon? The risks will only grow worse. If we are deterred today, we could be deterred forever—and Iraq will have achieved its objective. Or will the world community be deterred until Iraq uses a weapon of mass destruction, and only then decide it is time to act.

But I would suggest that even if Saddam Hussein were to issue an order for the use chemical or biological weapons, that does not mean his orders would necessarily be carried out. Saddam Hussein might not have anything to lose, but those beneath him in the chain of command most certainly would have a great deal to lose—let there be no doubt. He has maintained power by instilling fear in his subordinates. If he is on the verge of losing power, he may also lose his ability to impose that fear—and, thus, the blind obedience of those around him. Wise Iraqis will not obey orders to use WMD.

If President Bush were to decide to take military action, the U.S. will execute his order and finish the job professionally—Saddam Hussein and his regime would be removed from power. Therefore, with that certain knowledge, those in the Iraqi military will need to think hard about whether it would be in their interest to follow his instructions to commit war crimes by using WMD—and then pay a severe price for that action. The United States will make clear at the outset that those who are not guilty of atrocities can play a role in the new Iraq. But if WMD is used all bets are off.

I believe many in the Iraqi Armed Forces despise Saddam Hussein, and want to see him go as much as the rest of the world does. Those who may not despise him, but decide they would prefer to survive, may desert and try to blend into the civilian population or escape the country. This is what happened in Panama, when it became clear that Noriega was certain to be on his way out.

Some say that Saddam might succeed in provoking an Israeli response this time — possibly a nuclear response—and that this would set the Middle East aflame.

We are concerned about the Iraqi regime attacking a number of its neighbors, and with good reason: Saddam Hussein has a history of doing so. Iraq has attacked Bahrain, Iran, Israel, Jordan, Kuwait and Saudi Arabia. Iraq is a threat to its neighbors. We will consult with all of our allies and friends in the region on how to deal with this threat.

But the fact that they have blackmailed their neighbors makes the case for action stronger. If we do nothing, that blackmail will eventually become blackmail with weapons of mass destruction—with significantly new consequences for the world.

Some have said the U.S. could get bogged down in a long-term military occupation, and want to know what the plan is for a post-Saddam Iraq?

That is a fair question. It is likely that international forces would have to be in Iraq for a period of time, to help a new transitional Iraqi government get on its feet and create conditions where the Iraqi people would be able to choose a new government and achieve self-determination. But that burden is a small one, when balanced against the risks of not acting.

In Afghanistan, our approach was that Afghanistan belongs to the Afghans—we did not and do not aspire to own it or run it. The same would be true of Iraq.

In Afghanistan, the U.S. and coalition countries helped create conditions so that the Afghan people could exercise their right of self-government. Throughout the Bonn process and the Loya Jirga process, a new president was chosen, a new cabinet sworn-in, and a transitional government, representative of the Afghan people, was established to lead the nation.

If the President were to make the decision to liberate Iraq, with coalition partners, it would help the Iraqi people establish a government that would be a single country, that did not threaten its neighbors, the United States, or the world with aggression and weapons of mass destruction, and that would respect the rights of its diverse population.

Iraq has an educated population that has been brutally and viciously repressed by Saddam Hussein's regime. He has kept power not by building loyalty, but by instilling fear—in his people, his military and the government bureaucracy. I suspect that there would be substantial defections once it became clear that Saddam Hussein was finished. Moreover, there are numerous free Iraqi leaders—both inside Iraq and abroad—who would play a role in establishing that new free Iraqi government. So there is no shortage of talent available to lead and rehabilitate a free Iraq.

In terms of economic rehabilitation, Iraq has an advantage over Afghanistan. A free Iraq would be less dependent on international assistance, and could conceivably get back on its feet faster, because Iraq has a marketable commodity—oil.

Some have raised concerns that other countries elsewhere in the world might take advantage of the fact that the U.S. in tied up in Iraq, and use that as an opportunity to invade neighbors or cause other mischief.

There is certainly a risk that some countries might underestimate our capability to handle Iraq and stop their aggression at the same time. But let there be no doubt: we have that capability.

Last year, we fashioned a new defense strategy, which established that we will and do have the capability to near simultaneously:

Defend the U.S. homeland; Undertake a major regional conflict and win decisively—including occupying a country and changing their regime; If necessary, swiftly defeat another aggressor in another theater; and Simultaneously conduct a number of lesser contingencies—such as Bosnia, Kosovo and Afghanistan. The United States can do the above, if called upon to do so.

Another argument is that acting without provocation by Iraq would violate international law.

That is untrue. The right to self-defense is a part of the U.N. Charter. Customary international law has long provided for the right of anticipatory self-defense—to stop an attack before it happens. In addition, he is in violation of multiple U.N. Security Council resolutions. Those concerned about the integrity of international law should focus on their attention his brazen defiance of the U.N..

Some ask: What has changed to warrant action now?

What has changed is our experience on September 11th. What has changed is our appreciation of our vulnerability—and the risks the U.S. faces from terrorist networks and terrorist states armed with weapons of mass destruction.

What has not changed is Saddam Hussein's drive to acquire these weapons. Every approach the U.N. has taken to stop Iraq's drive for WMD has failed. In 1998, after Iraq had again kicked out U.N. inspectors, President Clinton came to the Pentagon and said:

"If [Saddam] fails to comply, and we fail to act, or we take some ambiguous third route which gives him yet more opportunities to develop his weapons of mass destruction and continue to ignore the solemn commitment he made. He will conclude that the international community has lost its will. He will conclude that he can go right on and do more to rebuild an arsenal of devastating destruction. The stakes could not be higher. Some day, some way, I guarantee you, he'll use that arsenal."

At the time, the U.S. massed forces in the Persian Gulf, ready to strike. At the last minute, Iraq relented and allowed U.N. inspectors to return. But predictably, they kicked them out again ten months later. They have not been allowed to return since. He has not only paid a price for that defiance, he has been rewarded for his defiance of the U.N. by increased trade from a large group of U.N. member nations.

If, in 1998, Saddam Hussein posed the grave threat that President Clinton correctly described, then he most certainly poses a vastly greater danger today, after four years without inspectors on the ground to challenge his WMD procurement and development efforts. To those who still ask—that is what has changed!

Some have asked what are the incentives for Iraq to comply—is there is anything the Iraqi regime could do to forestall military action? Or is he finished either way?

Our objective is gaining Iraq's compliance. Our objective is an Iraq that does not menace its neighbors, does not pursue WMD, does not oppress its people or threaten the United States. The President set forth in his speech what an Iraqi regime that wanted peace would do. Everything we know about the character and record of the current Iraqi regime indicates that it is highly unlikely to do the things the President has said it must do. So long as Saddam Hussein is leading that country, to expect otherwise is, as the President put it, to "hope against the evidence." If Saddam Hussein is in a corner, it is because he has put himself there. One choice he has is to take his family and key leaders and seek asylum elsewhere. Surely one of the one hundred and eighty plus counties would take his regime—possibly Belarus.

Some ask does the U.S. needs U.N. support?

The President has asked the U.N. Security Council to act because it is the U.N. Security Council that is being defied, disobeyed and made less relevant by the Iraqi regime's defiance. There have already been 16 U.N. resolutions, every one of which Saddam Hussein has ignored. There is no shortage of U.N. resolutions. What there is is a shortage of consequences for Saddam's ongoing defiance of those 16 U.N. resolutions. The President has made the case that it is dangerous for the United Nations to be made irrelevant by the Iraqi regime.

As the President put it in his address last week, "All the world now faces a test, and the United Nations a difficult and defining moment. Are Security Council resolutions to be honored and enforced, or cast aside without consequence? Will the United Nations serve the purpose of its founding, or will it be irrelevant?"

But the President has also been clear that all options are on the table. The only option President Bush has ruled out is to do nothing.

Mr. Chairman, as the President has made clear, this is a critical moment—for our country and for the world. Our resolve is being put to the test. It is a test that, unfortunately, the world's free nations have failed before in recent history—with terrible consequences.

Long before the Second World War, Hitler wrote in Mein Kampf indicating what he intended to do. But the hope was that maybe he would not do what he said. Between 35 and 60 million people died because of a series of fatal miscalculations. He might have been stopped early—at a minimal cost of lives—had the vast majority of the world's leaders not decided at the time that the risks of acting were greater than the risks of not acting.

Today, we must decide whether the risks of acting are greater than the risks of not acting. Saddam Hussein has made his intentions clear. He has used weapons of mass destruction against his own people and his neighbors. He has demonstrated an intention to take the territory of his neighbors. He has launched ballistic missiles against U.S. allies and others in the region. He plays host to terrorist networks. He pays rewards to the families of suicide bombers in Israel—like those who killed five Americans at the Hebrew University earlier this year. He is hostile to the United States, because we have denied him the ability he has sought to impose his will on his neighbors. He has said, in no uncertain terms, that he would use weapons of mass destruction against the United States. He has, at this moment, stockpiles chemical and biological weapons, and is pursuing nuclear weapons. If he demonstrates the capability to deliver them to our shores, the world would be changed. Our people would be at great risk. Our willingness to be engaged in the world, our willingness to project power to stop aggression, our ability to forge coalitions for multilateral action, could all be under question. And many lives could be lost.

We need to decide as a people how we feel about that. Do the risks of taking action to stop that threat outweigh these risks of living in the world we see? Or is the risk of doing nothing greater than the risk of acting? That is the question President Bush has posed to the Congress, to the American people and to the world community.

The question comes down to this: how will the history of this era be recorded? When we look back on previous periods of our history, we see there have been many books written about threats and attacks that were not anticipated:

"At Dawn We Slept: The Untold Story of Pearl Harbor" "December 7, 1941: The Day the Admirals Slept Late" "Pearl Harbor: Final Judgment" "From Munich to Pearl Harbor" "While England Slept" "The Cost of Failure" The list of such books is endless. And, unfortunately, in the past year, historians have added to that body of literature—there are already books out on the September 11th attacks and why they were not prevented. As we meet today, Congressional committees are trying to determine why that tragic event was not prevented.

Each is an attempt by the authors to "connect the dots"—to determine what happened, and why it was not possible to figure out that it was going to happen.

Our job today—the President's, the Congress' and the U.N.'s is to connect the dots before the fact—to anticipate vastly more lethal attacks before they happens—and to make the right decision as to whether we should take preventive action— before it is too late.

We are on notice—each of us. Each has a solemn responsibility to do everything in our power to ensure that, when the history of this period is written, the books won't ask why we slept—to ensure that history will instead record that on September 11th the American people were awakened to the impending dangers—and that those entrusted with the safety of the American people made the right decisions and saved our nation, and the world, from 21st century threats.

President Bush is determined to do just that.

Remarks by Secretary of Defense Rumsfeld, September 18, 2002

Secretary Donald Rumsfeld was interviewed by PBS's Jim Lehrer.

Q. Forty-eight hours later, how does Iraq's offer to let inspectors back in look to you?

Secretary Rumsfeld. Well, it looks a lot like earlier ploys and plays and moves that Iraq has taken. It's very clear that even within the letter it has contradictions. It in one place talks about without any constraints or conditions, and then later in the letter it talks about beginning negotiations and discussions about how it would be done.

Second, it's interesting that here's a letter that purports to say that, fair enough, we're willing to work with the U.N. and allow inspectors in, and within the last 48 hours they've fired on American aircraft six times in Northern and Southern Iraq.

Q. I assume that's the no fly zone?

Secretary Rumsfeld. In the no fly zones that the coalition forces, the United States and Great Britain and men and women in uniform from our two countries have been flying over those zones, implementing the U.N. resolutions, and they fired from the ground artillery and rockets at these aircraft six times since that letter was delivered. If that isn't a signal as to what they have in mind, I don't know what it is.

Q. So, this letter should be ignored by the United States and the U.N.?

Secretary Rumsfeld. Oh, it's a letter not to the United States, it's a letter to the United Nations. And that's for the president and Secretary Powell to work with. I'm just really repeating what Secretary Powell has said with respect to the letter. It's pretty clear that it is not what it seems to be.

Q. But in terms of inspections, you said—you told the Congress today that this isn't about inspections this is about disarmament. Is inspections not a step toward disarmament?

Secretary Rumsfeld. That is what was hoped years ago, after the Gulf War. The hope was that Iraq would become a country that would disarm as they signed and agreed to do at the end of the war. The U.N. resolutions said that the way to implement that disarmament was to have inspectors in. And clearly that's one way to do it. Inspectors have the benefit of working pretty well, if they're working with a country that wants to disarm, and has agreed to disarm. And then they invite inspectors in so that the world can know that they, in fact, did do it. It only works if you have a cooperative partner. You can't go in and inspect a country that's resisting those inspections and expect to find very much, because so much of it is mobile, so much of it is underground. So, there clearly is a role in our world for inspections, but it tends to be with a cooperative partner, and we've seen the situation with Iraq where they've violated some 16 U.N. resolutions, and finally threw the inspectors out.

Q. Do you see, based on everything that you know, do you see any scenario that could disarm Iraq the way the United States wants it to be disarmed short of military action?

Secretary Rumsfeld. I don't think it's the United States that wants Iraq to be disarmed, it was the world community, the international.

Q. The world community.

Secretary Rumsfeld. The United Nations voted repeatedly, over and over, and over, that that is what Iraq agreed to do that.

Q. But I mean now, that was years ago now, and we're in this situation now, and the president of the United States says, no more, action has to be taken, this has to end. Do you see a scenario short of military action that's going to get what the president and the world community wants to get, which is a disarmed Iraq?

Secretary Rumsfeld. Well, one would certainly hope so. That is to say that, no one with any sense would want to go to war, war is a last result, not a first result. We've gone through 11 years of violating these U.N. resolutions. We've gone through 11 years where—recent years, four years, where they threw the inspectors out, and there's been no one there. And their progress on weapons of mass destruction, chemical, biological and nuclear have gone forward. Now, if Saddam Hussein and his family decided that the game was up, and we'll go live in some foreign country, like other leaders have done, clearly the Shah of Iran left, Idi Amin left, Baby Doc Duvalier left, any number of leaders who have departed their countries recognizing that the game was up, that it was over, that they'd run their term. So that could happen. It's entirely possible that the people in that country, a lot of wonderful people who are hostages, they're hostages to a very vicious regime, they could decide that it was time, the time was up, and change the regime from inside. It's a very repressive regime. It would be a very difficult thing to do. But, clearly, the overwhelming majority of people, even in the army don't want Saddam Hussein there. Look what he's done to the country. He's a pariah.

He's threatening his neighbors. He's listed on the terrorist state. Their economy should be a booming economy with those oil revenues. And those people would want to be liberated.

Q. As Secretary of Defense, let's say that all those possibilities do not pan out, and let's say some kind of military action is required down the road, whenever. As Secretary of Defense, what would you say to the young men and women of America and their families as to why this is in the vital interest of this country to a point where they have to risk their lives for it?

Secretary Rumsfeld. Well, you know, it's interesting in your opening remarks you were talking about the congressional hearings on September 11th, and the fact that they've spent months pouring over all kinds of documentation and trying to connect the dots. What happened, what did people know, and how might they have figured it out sooner so that we could have prevented 3,000 innocent men, women and children from being killed on September 11th of last year. What we're trying to do—that's difficult, and they are having a dickens of a time trying to figure out that. We're trying to connect the dots before there is another September 11th. We're trying to connect the dots not only before there's another September 11th on our country, but before there's a September 11th that involves weapons of mass destruction, biological or chemical, or a nuclear weapon. That is a serious responsibility that the government has. It's not an easy thing to do. It is a difficult thing to do. Indeed, it's more difficult than trying to connect the dots after it's happened. But if we wait until after it's happened, we're not talking about 3,000 people being killed when this happened on September 11th, we're talking about potentially tens of thousands of people being killed.

Q. But what do you say—

Secretary Rumsfeld. And you say to them, you say to the American people, the first responsibility of government is to provide for the common defense. That is what the central government is there for, very essentially. That's it's principal task. And as one looks at the world and sees this new security environment and sees the nexus between weapons of mass destruction, terrorist states, and terrorist networks, and reflects on last September 11th, reflects on our vulnerability as free people, and how many people can come into our country and do things in our country, and how available today biological weapons and chemical weapons, and, indeed, elements of nuclear weapons are today, what one would say is, if we want to live in a more peaceful world, if we want to avoid that kind of a catastrophe, our country has to recognize that new security environment, and recognize that absorbing that blow, waiting for it and absorbing it, and then having an investigation afterward is not a preferred option.

Q. What would you say to an American people, or to a member of a family of somebody in the military who says, fine, I hear you, Mr. Secretary, how do you know that Saddam Hussein and the people of Iraq would use these weapons against the United States in a way that jeopardizes my life, or my families lives?

Secretary Rumsfeld. First of all, the truth has a wonderful virtue, one can't know what can happen in the future. What you can do is try to connect the dots. You have a vicious dictator, who has already weaponized chemical and biological weapons, and already used them on their neighbors, and on their own people. They have killed thousands of their own people with chemical weapons, and they have used them against the Iranians. So, we know we have a leader who is a dictator, he's got the programs, who has a perfect willingness to use them. And then one looks at their rhetoric, what are they saying about their neighbors, what are they saying about the United States, why are they offering $20,000 bonuses to the families of suicide bombers who blow up people in other countries in shopping malls and discotheque, and pizza parlors. Why do they do those things? Well, what kind of a threat does that pose?

If you were talking about a conventional capability, your standard of evidence would be one thing, you say, well, we can absorb that. If you're talking about an unconventional capability, one has to be very careful about saying you're going to absorb it.

Q. But then somebody can come back to you and say, wait a minute, we had a deterrence thing with the Soviet Union for many, many years, and we had the capability of blowing them to smithereens, and they were doing the same to us, a lot more so than Saddam Hussein in Iraq, and it worked. We never took a preemptive strike against the Soviet Union.

Secretary Rumsfeld. Right. And that balance of terror, or mutual assured destruction did, in fact, work with the Soviet Union for a variety of different reasons. It did not work for everything. It did not stop the Soviet Union from invading other countries, like Afghanistan. If we had a balance of terror, if you will, with Saddam Hussein, which is not our first choice. Our first choice is to prevent that, but if you had one, it wouldn't stop them from invading Kuwait again, or invading Saudi Arabia, which they were ready to do, or getting in another war with Iran, or attacking their other neighbors, or destroying Israel as they talk about every day in their rhetoric. It wouldn't stop them from that.

Furthermore, a balance of mutual assured destruction with the Soviet Union didn't stop the Korean War, it didn't stop the Vietnam War, it didn't stop a whole host of other things in the world. It was a limited deterrent effect. It was a limited constraint or containment policy, but it was never perfect.

Furthermore, the nexus between terrorist networks and a terrorist state with weapons of mass destruction, it's perfectly possible for Saddam Hussein to work with a terrorist network, arrange for them to have the biological weapons. They have sleeper cells around the world, and to use them without a return address. Suicide bombers are not deterred, they're proud. They think they're going to heaven. So the deterrent argument would be wonderful if there were something like that that worked. But it's so obviously fallacious.

Q. No way to deter Saddam Hussein from using what he may or may not have?

Secretary Rumsfeld. Well, you know, one of the concerns about a conflict with Saddam Hussein is that he would use those weapons. The problem is, he can't do it himself. He needs others to do it, and I would think that the Iraqi military and the linkages he has to those weapons ought to be very, very careful about thinking about using them. The concern of the United States is those weapons. The concern of the United States is the regime at the top. And clearly people who would use those weapons are not going to have a happy future if, in fact, they do them.

Q. A man asked me today while I was on an airplane coming back from Colorado, and a man said to me, wait a minute, we know about the Al-Qaeda terrorists, they've already killed Americans. Why don't we get rid of them first and then worry about the guy who might do something to us, Saddam Hussein. What would you say to him?

Secretary Rumsfeld. Well, the global war on terrorism is important, and this is a part of it. It is the nexus between an Al-Qaeda type network and other terrorist network and a terrorist state like Saddam Hussein who has those weapons of mass destruction. As we sit here, there are senior Al-Qaeda in Iraq. They are there. They are also in Iran. They are also in other countries. They're in Pakistan.

Q. That can't separate them out is what you're saying, right?

Secretary Rumsfeld. Not from the air.

Q. But, what I mean is going after Saddam Hussein is also going after Al-Qaeda, in a way?

Secretary Rumsfeld. It is clearly, if one deals with that problem in whatever way the president may decide, and he has not made a decision, except he said the choice we don't have is to do nothing, because time is on their side. With the Soviet Union time was on our side, going back to that deterrent analogy, we could wait, their economy was getting weaker and weaker, and weaker, and they were isolated, and finally it imploded. Time is not on our side here. He's got the oil revenues, he's buying additional weapons, he's moving his weapons of mass destruction programs forward, he's dealing with terrorists. And every week month and year that go on he's going to be more of a threat not less of a threat.

Q. Speaking of time, there have been several stories in the last few days in the newspapers that you and your colleagues in the military are concerned about a military action against Iraq, because of the weather. It has to be before January of February, because things start to get too hot after that. Is that legit? Is that a problem?

Secretary Rumsfeld. I don't know that I want to get into that. Obviously there's lots of things that are more favorable at one moment than at another moment. There are so many considerations that go into it, certainly weather is one. But, I don't know that I'd want to differentiate among them particularly.

Q. But, in terms of what's going on with the U.N. now, would you concede that at

least what that letter did, we'll go back to where we started, the letter from Iraq, has slowed a process, or the process down. Does the inspector thing now have to be played out some way?

Secretary Rumsfeld. I don't know that it will prove to have slowed things down. I was with the president and Secretary Powell this morning when Colin briefed the National Security Council on what's taking place in the United Nations. And I didn't get the sense that either one of them were in a relaxed mode. They clearly are going to be moving forward with short timetables in the United Nations.

Q. What about the diplomatic thing here? Do we, meaning the big we, the Western world or the world that's upset about all of this, not just the United States, have to call Iraq's bluff? If you think this is not real, and other people think this isn't real, does this bluff have to be called, and does that take time, does it slow things down, is that a legitimate course to take?

Secretary Rumsfeld. It depends on what credence one gives the moves that Iraq makes. I mean, here is a country that's violated every U.N. resolution that relates to it. It has lied, it has thrown the inspectors out. The idea that they're likely to be credible with respect to one more opportunity is, I think, debatable. And I think the problem the U.N. has is they have issued very tough resolutions year after year, after year, and they have never been implemented. Now, at some point an institution has to ask how does it feel about that, does it want to be irrelevant as an institution? Does it want to have relevance, or is it willing to simply keep making resolutions and having a dictator like Iraq tell the world community not to worry, you're irrelevant. I think the U.N. is facing an issue here, and I think the president put it very, very well before that institution. It is not a U.S. issue for the U.N., it's a U.N. resolution, it's a U.N. issue.

Q. You don't think the offer of Iraq to readmit the inspectors kind of takes a little steam out of all of that? The French, several Arab nations, the Russians have already said, we don't think we need to do anything right now, no new resolutions, let's play this thing out with the inspectors. That's not a problem?

Secretary Rumsfeld. I don't doubt for a minute that Iraq and maybe some other countries would like to rope a dope it along, and just keep delaying things and putting it off. That's always the case. There's never unanimity on anything that I've seen, at least rarely. But, I think most countries are pretty wise and perceptive. The truth is that Saddam Hussein has been about four times as clever as the United States, the U.N., and the Western world in managing public opinion. They're just masters at manipulating the press, and putting out disinformation. They're already moving military units and elements next to mosques, and next to hospitals, and next to schools. So that—

Secretary Rumsfeld. Exactly, so they can claim that the coalition has done all these terrible things. It's an old pattern. I don't know what credence it will be given up in the U.N. Only time will tell. I know that Colin is working with the other countries, and a lot of them have been very forthright, and understand what's taking place.

Q. Meanwhile, and finally, to your responsibilities as Secretary of Defense. Whenever a decision is made, whatever the decision is made by the president to do something, is the United States military ready to do anything on that scale of everything that's been discussed?

Secretary Rumsfeld. Absolutely.

Q. Without question?

Secretary Rumsfeld. Without question.

Q. We can do that and still keep going after Al-Qaeda, and do all of our other responsibilities?

Secretary Rumsfeld. Absolutely. The military leaders and the combatant commanders, and the services and I have all met repeatedly. We have a force sizing construct and a strategy that enables the United States of America to engage in two major conflicts, near simultaneously, to win decisively in one and occupy the country, to swiftly defeat in the other case and hold, and to simultaneously provide for homeland defense, and a series of lesser contingencies, such as Bosnia or Kosovo. And we have the capability to pursue the global war on terrorism, and certainly the problems of Iraq are part of the global war on terrorism as we've been doing.

Q. So whatever the president decides, if it's a military decision on Iraq, you're prepared to do it, and do it whatever it is?

Secretary Rumsfeld. There is just no question about it. The United States military will be prepared to do whatever the president orders, and do it well.

Remarks by Secretary of State Powell, September 19, 2002

Secretary Colin Powell delivered the following testimony before the House Committee on International Relations.

Mr. Chairman, Congressman Lantos, and other members of the committee, you and I have been discussing Iraq for many years. In fact, many of the committee members go back to the days before the Gulf war when I came up and testified on so many occasions about what we were doing in that buildup of Desert Shield.

We all remember vividly that in 1990, Saddam Hussein's forces, as both of you have noted, invaded Kuwait, brutalized that population, and at that time rejected the international community's ultimatum to withdraw.

The United States built a world-wide coalition—we got the whole international community involved at that time—with the clear political purpose of liberating Kuwait. And the military instrument of that coalition, led by America, had an equally clear military objective that flowed directly from the political purpose, and that was to eject the Iraqi army out of Kuwait.

The United Nations Security Council endorsed this purpose and objective, and the international community responded with unprecedented political backing, financial support, and military forces. And as a result, we not only accomplished our mission in the Gulf War, the way in which we did it was a model of American leadership and a model of international cooperation.

When the war ended, the Security Council of the United Nations agreed to take measures to ensure that Iraq did not threaten any of its neighbors again. Saddam Hussein, as you all both have noted and all will note, was a man after all who had sent his armies against Iran in 1980 and then against Kuwait in 1990, who had fired ballistic missiles at neighboring countries, and who had used chemical weapons in the war with Iran and even against his own people. The United States and the international community at that time were strongly determined to prevent any future aggression.

So United Nations Security Council Resolution 687 of 3 April 1991 fixed the terms of the ceasefire in the Gulf. And the fundamental purpose of this resolution and many more that followed was restoration of regional peace and security by way of a series of stringent demands on Iraq, particularly its disarmament with respect to weapons of mass destruction and possession of ballistic missiles with ranges greater than 150 kilometers. Desert Storm had dramatically reduced Iraq's more conventional military capability while at the same time not leaving Iraq so prostrate that it could not defend itself against Iran. It just had finished a war with Iran and we did not want to give Iran an opportunity to start that war up again from a position of superiority. The focus of 687 was on weapons of mass destruction, and the resolutions that followed focused on that and other problems with Iraq that I will touch on in a moment.

Mr. Chairman, members of the committee, you know the rest of the story. You heard the President relate it at the United Nations seven days ago today. Iraq has defied the United Nations and refused to comply completely with any of the United Nations Security Council Resolutions that were passed. Moreover, since December of 1998 when the United Nations inspection teams left Iraq because of the regime's flagrant defiance of the U.N., the Iraqi regime, Saddam Hussein, has been free to pursue weapons of mass destruction.

Meanwhile, the world has changed dramatically.

Since September 11, 2001, the world is a different place, a more dangerous place than the place that existed before September 11 or a few years ago when the inspectors were last in. As a consequence of the terrorist attacks on that day and of the war on terrorism that those attacks made necessary, a new reality was born: the world had to recognize that the potential connection between terrorists and weapons of mass destruction moved terrorism to a new level of threat, a threat that could not be deterred, as has been noted; a threat that we could not allow to grow because of this connection between states developing weapons of mass destruction and terrorist organizations willing to use them without any compunction and in an undeterrable fashion. In fact, that nexus became the overriding security concern of our nation. It still is and will continue to be so for years to come.

We now see that a proven menace like Saddam Hussein, in possession of weapons of mass destruction, could empower a few terrorists to threaten millions of innocent people.

President Bush is fully determined to deal with this threat. This Administration is determined to defeat it. I believe the American people would have us do no less.

President Bush is also aware of the need to engage the international community. Just as an earlier President Bush did some 12 years ago, he understands perfectly how powerful a strong and unified international community can be, as we have seen so well-demonstrated in the war on terrorism in Afghanistan and elsewhere, a war on terrorism that is each day producing new successes, one step, one arrest, one apprehension at a time.

The need to engage the international community is why the President took his message on the grave and gathering danger of Iraq to the United Nations last week. Moreover, it is the United Nations that is the offended party, not Iraq, as some people might claim. Not just the United States, it is the international community that should be offended.

It is a combination of United Nations resolutions that have been systematically and brutally ignored and violated for these past 12 years. It was United Nations inspectors who found it impossible to do their job and had to leave the work unfinished.

The President's challenge to the United Nations General Assembly was a direct one and it was a very simple one: if you would remain relevant, you must act. You must not look away from this challenge.

The President's speech was powerful. I was there. I listened to it. I knew what he was going to say, and I could see the energy in the room as he delivered it. It energized the United Nations General Assembly and it energized the debate taking place at this 57th meeting of the United Nations General Assembly. It changed the political landscape on which this issue was being discussed. It made it clear that Iraq is the problem. Iraq is the one that is in material breach of the demands placed on it by this multilateral organization, the United Nations.

The President made clear what was expected of Iraq was to repair this breach if they could. He made it clear that the issue, however, was more than just disarming Iraq by eliminating its weapons of mass destruction and by constraining its mid and long range missile capability. The U.N. resolutions also spoke of terrorism, human rights, the return of prisoners, the return of property, and the proper use of the Oil-for-Food program. And the indictment that the President laid out didn't need much discussion or debate. Everybody sitting in that chamber last Thursday new that Iraq stood guilty of the charges. It convicted itself by its action over these past 12 years. There can be no question that Iraq is in material breach of its obligations.

Over the past weekend while I worked the aftermath of the President's speech, I saw the pressure build on Iraq as the Arab League, the Secretary General and so many other nations pressed Iraq on the need to take action because it stood guilty and nobody could deny the guilt.

And four days ago, on Monday, Iraq responded not with a serious offer but with a familiar, tactical ploy to try to get out of the box, to try to get out of the corner once more. The Iraqi Foreign Minister said Iraq would let the inspectors in "without conditions." And this morning, in a speech at the United Nations he challenged President Bush's September 12th speech. He even called for a discussion of the issue of inspection teams in accordance "with international law." he said. He is already walking back.

He is already stepping away from the without condition statement they made on Monday. But he is not deceiving anybody. It is a ploy we have seen before. We have seen it on many occasions. And on each occasion, once inspectors began to operate, Iraq continued to do everything to frustrate their work.

Mr. Chairman, I will call your attention and the members' attention to the written statement that I have submitted, and I ask that it be put in the record, where I record a dozen examples of Iraq's defiance of the U.N. mandate. Cited in that longer statement is everything from intimidation at gunpoint to holding up inspectors while all the incriminating evidence was removed from the site to be inspected. It is a litany of defiance, unscrupulous behavior and every sort of attempt at noncompliance. And by no means have I listed everything, only a sampling.

The Iraqi regime is infamous for its ploys, stalling tactics, its demands on inspectors, sometimes at the point of a gun, and its general and consistent defiance of the mandate of the United Nations Security Council. There is absolutely no reason to expect that Iraq has changed, that this latest effort of theirs to welcome inspectors without conditions is not just another ploy.

Let's be absolutely clear about the reason for their announcement Monday and what their Foreign Minister said today. They did not suddenly see the error of their ways. They did not suddenly want to clear up the problems of the past 12 years. They were responding to the heat and the pressure generated by the international community after President Bush's speech.

The United States has made it clear to our Security Council colleagues that we will not fall for this ploy. This is the time not to welcome what they said and become giddy, as some have done. This is the time to apply even more pressure. We must not relent. We must not believe that inspectors going in under the same conditions that caused their withdrawal four years ago is in any way acceptable or will bring us to a solution to this problem. These four years have been more than enough for Iraq to procure, develop, and hide proscribed items well beyond the reach of the kinds of inspections that were subject to Saddam's cheat and retreat approach from 1991 to 1998.

If inspectors do go back in because the U.N. feels it is appropriate for them to do so, they must go back in under a new regime with new rules, without any conditions and without any opportunity for Iraq to frustrate their efforts.

It is up now to the United Nations Security Council to decide what action is required of Iraq to deal with this material breach of the United Nations mandate. If part of that solution that the Security Council comes to involves an inspection regime, it must be a regime that goes in with the authority of a new resolution that removes the weaknesses of the present regime and which will not tolerate any Iraqi disobedience. It cannot be a resolution that will be negotiated with Iraq. The resolution must be strong enough and comprehensive enough that it produces disarmament, and not just inspections.

Many United Nation members, including some on the Security Council, want to take Iraq at its word and send inspectors back in without any new resolution or new authority. It's a recipe for failure, and we will not support that. The debate we have begun to have within the Council is on the need for and the wording of a resolution. Our position is clear: we must face the facts and find Iraq in material breach, then we must specify the actions we demand of Iraq, which President Bush has already laid out in his speech last week.

And then here's the key element. Here's what will make it different from what we did in the past, and this must be an essential element of any road going forward, any plan to go forward from the Security Council. We must determine what consequences this time will flow from Iraq's failure to take action. That is what makes this different. This time, unlike any time over the previous 12 years of Iraqi defiance, there must be hard consequences. This time Iraq must comply with the U.N. mandate or there will be decisive action to compel compliance.

We will listen to other points of view and we'll try to reach agreement within the Council. It will be a difficult debate. We will also preserve at all times the President of the United States' authority and ability to defend our nation and our interest, as he sees fit—do it with our friends, do it with the United Nations, or do it alone. But the President has made it clear that this is a problem that must be solved and will be solved.

Some have suggested that there is a conflict in this approach, that U.S. interests should be our total concern. But Mr. Chairman, both of these issues, both multilateral and unilateral, are important. We are a member of the United Nations Security Council. We are a member of the United Nations. It is a multilateral institution whose resolutions have been violated. But the United States, as a separate matter, believes that its interests are threatened even if the United Nations has not continued to come to that conclusion.

We are trying to solve this problem through the United Nations and in a multilateral way. The President took the case to the U.N. because it is the body that should deal with such matters as Iraq. It was created to deal with such matters. President Bush is hoping that the U.N. will act in a decisive way. But at the same time, as he has made clear, and my other colleagues in the Administration have made clear and I make clear today, if the United Nations is not able to act and act decisively—and I think that would be a terrible indictment of the U.N.—then the United States will have to make its own decision as to whether the danger posed by Iraq is such that we have to act in order to defend our country and to defend our interests.

And Mr. Chairman, our diplomatic efforts at the United Nations would be helped by a strong, strong congressional resolution authorizing President Bush to take action. The President should be authorized to use all means he determines appropriate, including military force, to enforce the United Nations Security Council resolutions that Iraq is defying and to defend the United States and its interests against the threat Iraq poses and to restore international peace and security to the region.

I know that the Administration has provided language to the Congress. I ask that the Congress consider it carefully and quickly, and I ask for immediate action on such a resolution to show the world that the United States is united in this effort. To help the United Nations understand the seriousness of this issue, it would be important for all of us to speak as a nation, as a country, and to give this powerful signal to our diplomatic efforts in the United Nations.

Mr. Chairman, my colleagues in the intelligence community and my colleague, Secretary Rumsfeld, are giving the Congress additional information with respect to military ideas and options, with respect to the intelligence supporting the conclusions we have come to. So I will not take any time to do that here today, but I am prepared to answer any questions in these areas that you think I might be competent and qualified to answer.

But let me say this about the Iraq threat before I stop and allow the greater part of our time available for your important questions to be answered. We can have debates, discussions and disagreements about the size and nature of the Iraqi stockpile of weapons of mass destruction, and we can discuss whether they are or are not violating the range constraints on the missiles that they have. But no one can doubt the record of Iraqi violations of United Nations Security Council resolutions. That is not debatable. It's a fact. It's a stated fact.

And no one can doubt Iraq's intention to continue to try to get these weapons of mass destruction unless they are stopped, and that is also not debatable. And I hope that will help to shape our debate and our discussions and the important decisions that we may have to make as a nation. These two realities—their intention and their continued violations over time—are indisputable.

With that, Mr. Chairman, I will stop and look forward to the questions from the committee. And once again, I ask that my full statement be put in the record.

Remarks by President Bush, September 19, 2002

President Bush delivered his remarks after meeting at the White House with Secretary of State Powell and National Security Advisor Rice.

At the United Nations Security Council it is very important that the members understand that the credibility of the United Nations is at stake, that the Security Council must be firm in its resolve to deal with a truth threat to world peace, and that is Saddam Hussein. That the United Nations Security Council must work with the United States and Britain and other concerned parties to send a clear message that we expect Saddam to disarm. And if the United Nations Security Council won't deal with the problem, the United States and some of our friends will.

That's the message the Secretary of State has delivered forcefully. That's the message that he will continue to carry.

* * * *

Q. How many of our friends are willing to join the United States in this effort?

President Bush. Ron, I think time will tell. I think you're going to see a lot of nations—that a lot of nations love freedom. They understand the threat. They understand that the credibility of the United Nations is at stake. They heard me loud and clear when I said, either you can be the United Nations, a capable body, a body able to keep the peace, or you can be the League of Nations. And we're confident that people will follow our lead.

Q. Sir, the chief weapons inspector is going to be briefing the U.N. Security Council today, and there have already been some reports that, in his talks with the Iraqis, that they're limiting access to certain sites. Are those reports true? And do you think

they're trying to—

President Bush. Well, I haven't gotten a report from what he intends to say. But let me give you just some general observations. First of all, there are no negotiations to be held with Iraq. They have nothing to negotiate. They're the people who said that they would not have weapons of mass destruction. The negotiations are over. It is up to the U.N. Security Council to lay out resolutions that confirms what Iraq has already agreed to, see.

Secondly, I don't trust Iraq, and neither should the free world. For 11 years, they have deceived the world. They have said, we'll conform to resolutions. They've never conformed to resolutions. They've never conformed to the agreement that they laid out 11 years ago. Sixteen times they've defied Security resolutions.

And so, they—the burden of proof is—must be place squarely on their shoulders. But there's no negotiations about whether or not they've been telling the truth or not.

Let's see here—Mark.

Q. Mr. President, are you going to send Congress your proposed resolution today? And are you asking for a blank check, sir?

President Bush. I am sending suggested language for a resolution. I want—I've asked for Congress' support to enable the administration to keep the peace. And we look forward to a good, constructive debate in Congress. I appreciate the fact that the leadership recognizes we've got to move before the elections. I appreciate the strong support we're getting from both Republicans and Democrats, and look forward to working with them.

Q. Mr. President, how important is it that that resolution give you an authorization of the use of force?

President Bush. That will be part of the resolution, the authorization to use force. If you want to keep the peace, you've got to have the authorization to use force. But it's—this will be—this is a chance for Congress to indicate support. It's a chance for Congress to say, we support the administration's ability to keep the peace. That's what this is all about.

Q. Will regime change be part of it?

President Bush. Yes. That's the policy of the government.

Remarks by Secretary of Defense Rumsfeld, September 21, 2002

Secretary Donald Rumsfeld was interviewed by Jamie McIntyre on CNN.

Q. Let me start off with the news from Baghdad today. Iraq said today that it will not cooperate with any new U.N. Security Council resolutions that run contrary to an agreement that it believes it reached with the U.N. Secretary General Kofi Annan. Your reaction to that?

Secretary Rumsfeld. Well, I don't know that I have a reaction. Certainly, one can't be surprised. Anyone that has watched the past decade has seen the Iraqi government defy some 16 U.N. resolutions and change their position depending on what they thought was tactically advantageous to them, and have jerked the United Nations around. So, it is no surprise at all.

Q. By taking that tact, does Iraq effectively play into your hands, into the United States' hands by giving you justification for moving ahead with possible military action?

Secretary Rumsfeld. Well, of course, those are judgments that the president will make after talking to Colin Powell and others who are working the U.N. piece of the puzzle. But, it is not the U.N. and Iraq, I mean the United States and Iraq, it's Iraq and the United Nations. So, they couldn't be playing into our hands in any sense. They are doing what they have done to the United Nations over a period of many, many years, and that's to defy them.

Remarks by Secretary of Defense Rumsfeld, September 21, 2002

Secretary Donald Rumsfeld was interviewed by Tony Allen-Mills of the Sunday Times London.

Q. The point has been repeatedly made in various countries that that cooperation is potentially jeopardized if the United States goes it alone on Iraq. Even in Britain there is a strong undercurrent of doubt that an attack on Iraq is currently justified by the evidence that's been presented so far. What is most important to the United States, that it defend itself in the manner that it sees fit or that it preserves these international alliances that is it has very painstakingly built?

Secretary Rumsfeld. I find it fascinating to listen to the loose language that politicians and the media use, "go it alone". That is precisely what you said is what you hear and read all over the world. The global war on terrorism has 90 countries participating. Does that sound unilateralist? Not to me. Not to you, I'm sure. It's a breathtakingly broad and deep coalition. It is a current, modern, visible manifestation of the fact that the United States recognizes the value of cooperating with other countries and yet it has become so fashionable, particularly in Europe, to want to stick a stick in people's eye and say call it unilateralist. It's utter nonsense. With respect to your question, my assumption is that sovereign states act for good and valid reasons that they believe are in their interest. The global war on terrorism exists. It will be a long one. A lot of people on the globe are vulnerable to terrorist acts. To suggest that if any one of the sovereign nations of the 90 in the global war on terrorism did something that one or another of the other 90 nations didn't agree with that they would then penalize themselves by not cooperating in the global war on terror and shoot themselves on the foot, if you will as a figure of speech—I don't know if you use that in England but...

Q. Yes, we do.

Secretary Rumsfeld. ...we do in Chicago—would be mindless. The allegation on its face is ridiculous. Second, it seems that at the moment just as it was fashionable at the beginning of the global war on terrorism to suggest that the United States was unilateralist, it's fashionable today with respect to Iraq. Now, the fact of the matter is it's false. We have any number of countries who have agreed to cooperate with respect to Iraq. So, the "go-it-alone" is more a statement by a person in a single country who personally, as opposed to their country, may or may not agree with what the media is saying the president is thinking. How is that? Is that sufficiently clear and direct?

They read something in the press and say oh my goodness, isn't that terrible, the president is not going to go to Congress and ask for their help, the president is not going to go to the United Nations and ask for their help, president is going to, quote, "go it alone". The United States Government has been talking to dozens and dozens and dozens and dozens of countries all over the world and any number have agreed to help in one way or another. And any number have said they would prefer that this happened or prefer that that happen or if this doesn't happen they may not be able to help in that way but they could help this some other way. So to prejudge the outcome of, at the very beginning of that process—as president said when he spoke to the United Nations, this is the first step—to prejudge it negatively, about him and about the United States, and then repeat it mindlessly day after day after day is unimpressive.

Q. I gather that you did many years ago once encounter Saddam Hussein during a visit to Iraq. I'm just wondering if you have any particular recollections of that meeting.

Secretary Rumsfeld. Vivid.

Q. How was he?

Secretary Rumsfeld. He is a survivor. He took over by the use of force. He maintains his position by the use of force, vicious force. It is clearly kind of one of the last Cold War, authoritarian regimes. The damage that he has done to the people of that country who are intelligent and like most people one would think freedom loving but been denied that freedom, the number of expatriates around the world who have gone on to do wonderful things and talented things is a reflection of the energy and the vitality of those people. But if you read what the international organizations that look at human rights, I'm just floored at all of the people in the world who normally would be concerned about human rights who when it comes to Saddam Hussein turn a blind eye, seem not to be concerned about what he has done to those human beings. It is a tragic, terrible story. And yet people who one would think would be concerned seem not concerned, selective.

Remarks by Senators Biden and Shelby, September 22, 2002

Senators Joseph Biden (D-DE) and Richard Shelby (R-AL) were interviewed on CBS's Face the Nation by Bob Schieffer and Gloria Borger.

Q. Senator Biden, are we going to war with Iraq?

Senator Biden. Well, the president hasn't made that clear yet. I think we are making it clear, the president is, that if the U.N. doesn't act, he reserves the right to act and enforce the U.N. resolutions, and my guess is he'll intend to do that, and that wouldn't be probably till some time after the first of the year. But that's the—that's the course we're on, Bob.

Q. You're—you're saying that you think that we're going to do this, in other words.

Senator Biden. Well, let me put it this way. I think it depends a great deal on what happens at the U.N., not in terms of our sovereignty and us deciding to go it alone. We should reserve the right to move alone regardless of what the U.N. does. But I think it will matter to the president when and how and if he uses force, depending on what kind of support he has around the world. For example, if the Turks don't sign on, this is a very difficult military undertaking, not able to use Turkey or fly over Turkey. If the Saudis don't sign on, it's a very—it's not impossible, but it makes it very, very different. And so I think the president will be working—regardless of what happens in the U.N. resolution, the president will be working feverishly and hopefully effectively during the months of November—October, November and December gathering international support for whatever effort he decides is most needed to deal with the situation in Iraq.

Q. Senator Shelby, if you had to make a prediction right now, do you think we'll be going into Iraq?

Senator Shelby. I believe we will, unless he does a total 180- degree turn. It's going to be a few months, but first, Bob, I believe that the Bush resolution's going to pass the Senate and the House by overwhelming numbers.

Q. Really?

Senator Shelby. Big-time, and there are going to be a lot of Democrats support it. They—they might be tinkering around the edges of the resolution, but the substance of the Bush resolution—as I would call it, the resolution to deal with Iraq—is going to pass, I predict, and—and what will happen in the U.N., I don't know. This could drive the U.N., but we're going to find out who our friends are in the world in the next few months.

Q. Senator Biden, speaking of this war, there are—there are reports today that unlike the Gulf War, Israel is now saying that it will retaliate if attacked. What can we do, or can we do anything to say to them, 'No, don't'? Or this all right?

Senator Biden. You know, Gloria, this is the reason why how we do this and our justification for using force, if we use it, is so important. We're going to lay down a precedent here. Dr. Kissinger, former secretary of State, is talking about how dangerous it is to enunciate the rationale for going into Iraq as a doctrine of preemption or for a regime change. If we make that the premise for our action, then, in fact, what— what denies—what pressure can we put on Israel not to do something that could make this an overall Middle East war? What pressure can we put on India not to attack Pakistan? So the details matter here a great deal, and that's why I think that the president started this off the right way. He went to the U.N.. He's made the case by the U.N. standards as to why the U.N. should act.

Now what the president should be doing, in my view, is going to the American public, making a statement to the United States public, go on air and say 'This is why I believe we will have to act,' if we do, and the rationale for it, and what we're in for, because I think we're ready to support the president, but there can be no foreign policy that succeeds without the informed consent of the American people. The American people have no idea what the president knows, and that is he's going to have to stay in Iraq with thousands and thousands of troops, as many as—estimated, of course— as many as 75,000 troops for up to four or five years. Whether that's true or not, it's clear there's thousands of troops, billions of dollars. And I think that the president now, having made the case at the U.N., has to begin to make the case to the American people about not only the—the doability of this, but the commitment we're going to be making as a nation, and I think it's important that it be done in terms of weapons of mass destruction. That should be our international rationale for moving, if we move...

Q. I—I...

Senator Biden. ...not this new doctrine of preemption and this doctrine of regime change...

Q. I...

Senator Biden. ...because then what do you tell the Israelis?

Q. I—I think you bring up a very interesting point. And, in fact, I want to get back to that. But I want to go back to this business about Israel. Let me just ask you the other side—and I want to get both of your views on this. Senator Shelby, the president's talking about building a coalition to go against Iraq. What's the downside of Israel going in militarily if we go into Iraq or if they're attacked? Sen.

Senator Shelby. Well, I—I think we all recognize there is a downside; that—that the Israelis go in—it could just be a widespread w—war in the Middle—Middle East. And also we'd be perceived—we'd be fighting side by side with the Israeli against all the Arab interests, and the war could spread. I think that's some of the concerns. But having said that, any nation has a right to defend its own interests, and Israel would be no—no different. I believe Senator Biden was talking about staying in Iraq, you know, and all of this. I don't believe that we will have to stay there that long. I don't believe that—that we're going to need that many troops. I'll leave that up to the military planners. But at the same time, we heard all those horror story—stories in '90 and '91. None of it came about.

Q. Well, let me go back to Senator Biden, because I want to ask you why you believe that. But, Senator Biden, what is the downside of—of Israel joining in the fight here?

Senator Biden. Well, the downside is what Dick just—what Richard just said, which is that it becomes a—a I—Arab-Israeli war. And you f—you—you would find probably every embassy in the Middle East burned to the ground before it went too far. It would not be perceived as what—it should stay on focus. The re—what makes Saddam Hussein different is he invaded a country; he lost a war; the terms of surrender were specific requirements made and commitments made to the United Nations that he has violated. And—and—and that's—that's what it's about now. And that's what it should stay about. And the moment that Israel, for example, strikes—and they will not do it lightly, if they do it—strikes back at—at Iraq, what happens then to the ability of any Muslim nation to continue to support even subrosa our efforts? And so, again, it's a chance we may have to take. I'm not just suggesting we rule that out.

And by the way, where I got those figures were from military planners who testified before my committee—a—a colonel whose whole job is to plan in the aftermath of a war. And you—you know what's going on in Afghanistan right now, Bob. We—we—we are now changing positions. The Defense Department saying we should expand the international security force because we're worried we may lose the fight. The American people are grown up. You tell them what we need to do, tell them the threat and they will back the president. But we haven't told them all the story yet.

Q. Senator Shelby, I—I know you want to talk about this for one second, so go ahead.

Senator Shelby. You—I—I was just going to say in regard to what Senator Biden just said. I believe the American people are a lot smarter than some people give them credit for.

Senator Biden. I agree.

Senator Shelby. They're a lot better informed than a lot of people give them credit for. You can see the polls in the last week. You can see the dynamic change in America toward—toward the war since President Bush went before the United Nations. They understand what's going on. They see these hearings that we're—we've been having in the joint committee. They're concerned about safety.

Q. But let's—let's back up for a moment and talk about inspections...

Senator Shelby. OK.

Q. ...before we talk about war. And last week Iraq said, 'Yes, we're going to allow the weapons inspectors in.' Over the weekend they said, 'Well, wait a minute. We want to do it under the old resolutions. We don't want to tie it to the use of force.' What does that mean? What can we do? We want one vote, and we want to tie it to the use of force.

Senator Shelby. Well, I think that we need to back the Bush resolution as—as it's come up, the substance of it. And—and gone—Saddam Hussein is going to put all kind of restrictions on any kind of inspections. He's played that game a long time. He knows how to play it. The clock is ticking. Time's on his side. He has no real intention—intentions of ever having meaningful inspections. That is just a trick.

Q. Sen—Senator Biden, is—wait, is the president, though, locked into some kind of inspections now, do you think?

Senator Biden. No. I don't think he's locked into that. I—I met with Foreign Minister Ivanov with Senator Lugar and myself for an hour, so—I think it was Thursday. Ivanov and others are the—the Russians are prepared to have a new resolution relating to the nature of the regime—I mean, excuse me, the—the inspection regime, and so it has to be a different inspection regime than under the old resolution for it to have any—any possibility of determining what he is doing and how much he's done. And if, in fact, the U.N. rejects that, then I think the president has every right—and we would support his right—to—to use force to enforce a genuine inspection regime that could tell us something about what he is doing.

But the details matter, Gloria. The draft resolution sent up by the president was just a draft for discussion. It sets out all of the U.N. resolutions and says, 'I want authority to go to war if, in fact, w—he does not live up to them.' I don't think there's a single American that's ready to go to war over whether or not Bahraini prisoners are returned. I do think Americans may be ready to go to war to dislodge weapons of mass destruction from Saddam Hussein. So there—there is this—detail matters for historical purposes, and it matters for the rationale we offer the world as to why we're moving. And we can offer a compelling rationale, in my view. And that's what we should be about doing now.

Remarks by President Bush, September 26, 2002

President Bush delivered his remarks following a meeting with Congressional Leaders at the White House.

Good morning. We've just concluded a really good meeting with both Democrats and Republicans—members of the United States Congress—to discuss our national security and discuss how best to keep the peace. The security of our country is the commitment of both political parties and the responsibility of both elected branches of government.

We are engaged in a deliberate and civil and thorough discussion. We are moving toward a strong resolution. And all of us, and many others in Congress, are united in our determination to confront an urgent threat to America. And by passing this resolution we'll send a clear message to the world and to the Iraqi regime: the demands of the U.N. Security Council must be followed. The Iraqi dictator must be disarmed. These requirements will be met, or they will be enforced.

The danger to our country is grave. The danger to our country is growing. The Iraqi regime possesses biological and chemical weapons. The Iraqi regime is building the facilities necessary to make more biological and chemical weapons. And according to the British government, the Iraqi regime could launch a biological or chemical attack in as little as 45 minutes after the order were given.

The regime has long-standing and continuing ties to terrorist organizations. And there are al Qaeda terrorists inside Iraq. The regime is seeking a nuclear bomb, and with fissile material, could build one within a year. Iraq has already used weapons of mass death against—against other countries and against her own citizens. The Iraqi regime practices the rape of women as a method of intimidation; and the torture of dissenters and their children.

For more than a decade, the regime has answered Security Council resolutions with defiance, bad faith and deception. We know that the Iraqi regime is led by a dangerous and brutal man. We know he's actively seeking the destructive technologies to match is hatred. We know he must be stopped. The dangers we face will only worsen from month to month and from year to year. To ignore these threats is to encourage them. And when they have fully materialized it may be too late to protect ourselves and our friends and our allies. By then the Iraqi dictator would have the means to terrorize and dominate the region. Each passing day could be the one on which the Iraqi regime gives anthrax or VX—nerve gas—or some day a nuclear weapon to a terrorist ally. We refuse to live in this future of fear. Democrats and Republicans refuse to live in a future of fear. We're determined to build a future of security. All of us long for peace, peace for ourselves, peace for the world.

Members here this morning are committed to American leadership for the good of all nations. I appreciate their spirit. I appreciate their love for country. The resolution we are producing will be an instrument of that leadership. I appreciate the spirit in which members of Congress are considering this vital issue. Congress will have an important debate, a meaningful debate, an historic debate. It will be conducted will all civility. It will be conducted in a manner that will make Americans proud, and Americans to understand the threats to our future. We're making progress, we're near an agreement. And soon, we will speak with one voice.

Thank you all for being here. God bless America.

Remarks by Secretary of State Powell, September 26, 2002

Secretary Colin Powell delivered the following testimony before the Senate Foreign Relations Committee.

We have talked about Iraq a number a times over the years, and I always have to go back to 1990 when Saddam Hussein's forces invaded Kuwait when I was Chairman of the Joint Chiefs of Staff and they brutalized the population and rejected at that time the international community's ultimatum to withdraw.

At that time, we build a worldwide coalition with the clear political purpose of liberating Kuwait, and the military instrument of that coalition, led by America, had an equally clear military objective that flowed directly from the political purpose, and that was to eject the Iraqi army from Kuwait.

The United Nations Security Council endorsed this purpose and objective, and the international community responded with unprecedented political backing, financial support and military forces. As a result, we not only accomplished our mission in the Gulf War, we did it in a way that I think was a model of American international leadership and international cooperation.

When that war ended, the United Nations Security Council agreed to take measures to ensure that Iraq did not threaten any of its neighbors again. Saddam Hussein, we knew, was a man who, after all, had sent his armies against Iran in 1980 and than against Kuwait in 1990. We knew he was a man who had fired ballistic missiles at neighboring countries and who had used chemical weapons in the war with Iran, and even against his own people.

The United States and the international community were strongly determined to prevent any future aggression, so United Nations Security Council Resolution 687 of April 1991 fixed the terms of the ceasefire in the Gulf. And the fundamental purpose of this resolution, and many more that followed, was restoration of regional peace and security by way of a series of stringent demands on Iraq, particularly its disarmament with respect to weapons of mass destruction and ballistic missiles with ranges greater than 150 kilometers.

Desert Storm had dramatically reduced Iraq's more conventional military capability while at the same time—and we did this deliberately—not leaving Iraq so prostrate that it could not defend itself against Iran, its former enemy.

Mr. Chairman, members of the committee, you know the rest of the story. You heard the President relate it at the United Nations two weeks ago today. Iraq has defied the United Nations and refused to comply completely with any of the United Nations Security Council resolutions. Moreover, since December of 1998 when the U.N. inspections teams left Iraq because of the regime's flagrant defiance of the United Nations, the Iraqi regime has been free to pursue the development of weapons of mass destruction.

Meanwhile, the world has changed dramatically. Since September 11th, 2001, the world is a different place. As a consequence of the terrorist attacks on that day and of the war on terrorism that those attacks made necessary, a new reality was born. The world had to recognize that the potential connection between terrorists and weapons of mass destruction moved terrorism to a new level of threat. In fact, that nexus became the overriding security concern of our nation. It still is and it will continue to be our overriding concern for some years to come.

We now see that a proven menace like Saddam Hussein in possession of weapons of mass destruction could empower a few terrorists with those weapons to threaten millions of innocent people. President Bush is fully determined to deal with this threat. His administration is determined to defeat it. I believe the American people would have us do no less. President Bush is also aware of the need to engage the international community. He understands how powerful a strong and unified international community can be, as we have seen so well demonstrated in the war on terrorism in Afghanistan and elsewhere.

The need to engage the international community is why the President took his message on the grave and gathering danger of Iraq to the United Nations on the 12th of September. Moreover, it is the United Nations that is the offended party, not Iraq, as some would have us believe or might even claim. It was the United Nations resolutions that were systematically and brutally ignored and violated for these past 12 years. It was United Nations inspectors who found it impossible to do their job and had to leave the work unfinished.

The President's challenge therefore to the United Nations General Assembly, and through them to the Security Council, was a direct one and it was a very simple one: If you would remain relevant, then you must act in the face of these repeated violations.

I was there that day and the President's speech was a powerful one and it energized the entire meeting hall. It changed the political landscape on which this issue was being discussed—that one speech—and it made it clear that Iraq is the problem, Iraq is the one who is in material breach of the demands placed upon it by the United Nations. It is not the United States that is in the dock, it is not the United Nations that is in the dock, it is not the Security Council that is in the dock, it is not France or Britain or Russia or the United Kingdom or all the other members of the Security Council. It is Iraq that is in the dock and we must not lose sight of that simple, clear fact.

The President in his speech then went on to make it clear what was expected of Iraq to repair this material breach. He made it clear that the issue was more than disarming Iraq by eliminating its weapons of mass destruction and its mid- and long-range missile programs. The United Nations resolutions also spoke of terrorism, of human rights, the return of prisoners and property. Iraq stands guilty. It convicts itself by its actions. There can be no question that it is in material breach of its obligations. All of these demands on Iraq are spelled out in the 16 Security Council resolutions levied against that country since 1991.

Over the weekend following the President's speech at the U.N., I watched the reaction. I watched the pressure build on the Iraqi regime as the Arab League, the Secretary General and so many others pressed Iraq on their need to take action. They essentially told Iraq the jig was up, nobody was going to listen to these phony excuses anymore, and the pressure built to an enormous level.

On Monday of that week, the next week, Iraq responded with a familiar tactical ploy. The Iraqi Foreign Minister said Iraq would let the inspectors back in without conditions. And later in the week in a speech at the United Nations, their Foreign Minister challenged President Bush's September 12th speech. He even called for a discussion of the issues of inspection teams in accordance with international law, already qualifying his Monday offer of inspections without conditions.

Now two days ago, we have an Iraqi presidential advisor telling the press in Baghdad that weapons inspectors would be allowed to go wherever they want. But these people are not deceiving anyone. It is a ploy we have seen before on many occasions, and on each occasion, each of these occasions, once inspectors began to operate, Iraq continued to do everything to frustrate their work.

Mr. Chairman, I will just call your and the members' attention to the written statement that I have provided where I record a dozen examples of Iraq's defiance of these resolutions and of the U.N. mandate. Cited in my longer statement is everything from intimidation at gunpoint to holding up inspectors while all the incriminating evidence was removed. It is a litany of defiance and unscrupulous behavior and every sort of attempt at noncompliance. And I by no means in my longer statement have listed everything, only a sampling.

The regime is infamous for its ploys, its stalling tactics, its demand on inspectors, sometimes at the point of a gun, and its general and consistent defiance of the mandate of the United Nations Security Council. There is absolutely no reason at all to expect that Iraq has changed. At least they haven't given us any indications to suspect that they have changed. And this latest effort to welcome inspectors without conditions is another ploy. Let's be clear about the reason for their suddenly being willing after several years to accept inspectors. The Iraqis did not suddenly see the error of their ways. They were responding to the heat and pressure generated by the international community after President Bush's speech at the U.N.. We must keep that pressure on.

The United States has made it clear to our Security Council colleagues that we will not fall for this ploy. This is the time to apply more pressure, not to relent. We must not believe that inspectors going in on the same conditions and under the same terms that they went in on so many occasions earlier will be acceptable now. We won't fall for that. These four years have been more than enough time for Iraq to procure, develop, hide proscribed items well beyond the reach of the kinds of inspections that were subject to Saddam's cheat and retreat approach from 1991 to '98.

It is up to the United Nations Security Council to decide what action is now required of Iraq to deal with this material breach of the U.N.'s mandate. If part of the solution involves an inspection regime, it must be a regime that goes in with the authority of a new resolution that removes the weaknesses of the present regime and which will not tolerate any Iraqi disobedience. It cannot be a resolution that we are going to negotiate with Iraq. The resolution or resolutions must be strong enough and comprehensive enough so that they produce disarmament and not just inspections.

Many U.N. members, including some on the Security Council, want to take Iraq at its word and send inspectors back in right now without any new resolution or new authority. And we believe that this would be a recipe for failure.

The debate we are having within the Security Council now is on the need for and the wording of a resolution or, some feel, more than one resolution. Our position is clear. We must face the facts and find Iraq in material breach. Then we must specify the actions we demand of Iraq. And President Bush has already discussed what he believes is appropriate.

And then there's a third element. We must determine what consequences will flow from Iraq's failure to take action. Just laying out a new inspection regime and declaring them in material breach isn't enough. The Security Council must face up to their responsibility to take action or allow action to be taken in the face of continued Iraqi violation. That is what makes it different this time. This time, unlike any time over the previous 12 years of Iraqi defiance, there must be hard consequences. This time, Iraq must comply with the U.N. mandate or there will be decisive action to compel compliance.

We are listening to other points of view and we are working to reach agreement within the Security Council. It is a difficult debate. There are strong views one way or the other. As you may have noticed in some of the press reporting in the last 24 hours, we have come into agreement with the United Kingdom on what the elements of a resolution should look like. I am sending a senior official from my department to Paris this evening, and then on to Moscow to discuss with the French and the Russians what we believe should be in such a resolution. We are briefing representatives of the Chinese Government here in Washington today. And so far in the last 12 hours I've spoken to my French colleague, Foreign Minister de Villepin, my Russian colleague Foreign Minister Ivanov, my Chinese colleague Foreign Minister Tang, and Secretary General Kofi Annan, describing the progress we have made with the British and the fact that we are now expanding the circle of consultation.

We are a long way from getting agreement, but we're working hard. And there are many points where we are in agreement, and there are some outstanding issues that have to be dealt with.

Some have suggested that there is a conflict in this approach, that U.S. interests should be our total concern. We are a member of the U.N. Security Council; we are a member of the United Nations. It is a multilateral institution whose resolutions have been violated. So I think it is quite appropriate for the President to seek action by the United Nations through its Security Council. But the United States, as an entirely separate matter, believes that its interest is threatened. We believe that we are at risk and our interests in different parts of the world are at risk by Iraqi development of weapons of mass destruction and by the nature of this regime.

We are trying to solve this problem through the United Nations and in a multilateral way.

But at the same time, if the United Nations is not able to act and to act decisively, and I think that would be a terrible indictment of the United Nations, then the United States will have to make its own decision as to whether the danger posed by Iraq is such that we have to act in order to defend our country and our interests.

I believe strongly, Mr. Chairman and members of the committee, that our diplomatic efforts at the United Nations would be helped enormously by a strong congressional resolution authorizing President Bush to take necessary and appropriate action. Language has been proposed by the President, and I know it's a subject of intense discussion in both bodies and with the White House and various members of the President's National Security Team. But I hope it is not too prolonged, and I ask for your action in the very near future to provide the President such a resolution to show the world that we are united in this effort.

Mr. Chairman, my colleagues in the intelligence community and the Department of Defense are giving the Congress the information that it will need with respect to the details of our intelligence assessment and military contingency planning that Secretary Rumsfeld is conducting, and I will leave those issues to them. But let me just make two points before I end this presentation.

We can have debates about the size and nature of the Iraqi stockpile. We can have debates about how long it will take them to reach this level of readiness or that level of readiness with respect to these weapons. But no one can doubt two things. One, they are in violation of these resolutions. There is no debate about that. And secondly, they have not lost the intent to develop these weapons of mass destruction, whether they are one day, five days, one year, or seven years from any particular weapon, whether their stockpile is small, medium or large, what has not been lost is the intent to have such weapons of mass destruction.

The challenge before us is to see whether or not the Iraqi regime makes a sea change in its behavior because of this international presence. And they'll only make this kind of change if they sense there will be consequences for not having made such a change. The President is determined that we cannot look away again, and I can assure you that this issue is receiving the highest attention within the State Department, Defense Department, and all the other institutions of government.

If I just may close with one other observation, because I know it came up earlier in the hearing, this comment about new doctrine of preemption. If you would go to the new national security strategy that the President issued not too long ago and look at the specific section which talks about our strategy and doctrine, you will find that we have not abandoned containment, we have not abandoned deterrence. We still have thousands of nuclear weapons. We still have a magnificent military force that can deter. We haven't abandoned these time-honored methods of using our national power. But what that chapter specifically says, there is a new threat out there now. There is a threat that doesn't respond the way older threats did to deterrence, that does not respond to theories of containment. These are terrorists. These are people who are willing to ignore that's going to happen to them. They are suicidal. They believe in evil concepts. And they're going to come at us. And so, a doctrine of preemption, or an element of preemption in our strategy is appropriate. It's not a new doctrine. It's been around for as long as warfare has been around. I can give you example after example in our own history of preemptive actions. In fact, I might even suggest that when President Clinton thought it necessary to attack that chemical plant in Sudan not too long ago, one might say that was a preemptive act, or an act of prevention. When you have this kind of new threat, this kind new enemy, then this doctrine of preemption should rise a little higher in your consideration, because this kind of enemy will not be deterred or contained the way, perhaps, the Soviet Union might have been and was contained and deterred in the past.

So see it as elevation of one of the many tools that we've always had, but don't see it as a new doctrine that excludes or eliminates all the other tools of national security and military power.

Remarks by Secretary of Defense Rumsfeld and Chairman of the Joint Chiefs of Staff Myers, September 30, 2002

Secretary Rumsfeld. Two weeks ago, Iraq sent a letter to the U.N. promising to, quote, "allow the return of United Nations weapons inspectors to Iraq without conditions," unquote. The letter declared that Iraq, quote, "based its decision concerning the return of inspectors on its desire to complete the implementation of the relevant Security

Council resolutions and to remove any doubts that Iraq still possesses weapons of mass destruction," unquote.

Hopeful people around the world found solace in those words. Unfortunately, Iraq's behavior over the past decade requires that thoughtful people measure Iraq by its actions, as opposed to its words.

Within hours of the arrival of that letter, Iraq was again firing at U.S. and coalition aircraft patrolling the northern and southern no-fly zones. Within hours of promising to fulfill the relevant Security Council resolutions and to do so, quote, "without conditions," unquote, Iraq was trying to shoot down and kill coalition pilots, U.S. and U.K., who are implementing those relevant U.N. Security Council resolutions. One would think that that would be taken as a powerful signal. Since the Iraqi letter arrived two weeks ago, they have fired on coalition aircraft 67 times, including 14 times this past weekend. That ought to tell reasonable people something.

For close observers of the Iraqi regime, their conduct cannot be a surprise. Since the Persian Gulf War, Iraq has agreed to a series of U.N commitments and failed to fulfill each one.

Three resolutions in particular are relevant. In April 1991 the Security Council passed Resolution 688. It stipulated that Iraq must stop at once repression of its own people, including the repression of minorities. Soon after accepting the resolution, Iraq began to systematically attack the Shi'as and the marsh Arabs of southern Iraq and the Kurds in northern Iraq, from 1991 through 1992.

To halt that outrage and protect Iraqi citizens from further bombing and helicopter attacks, in August 1992 coalition nations, including Britain and the U.S., came together to establish the no-fly zones over those regions, to enforce U.N. Resolution 688. Almost as soon as these zones were created, pilots enforcing them were being fired on with missiles and artillery by Iraq. And that Iraqi aggression against those aircraft continues to this day.

Another U.N. Security Council resolution, 687, established ceasefire conditions that included ending Iraq's weapons of mass destruction programs and providing for U.N. inspections to determine Iraq's compliance with the ban on weapons of mass destruction. The inspections included a ground component and air components called Operations Northern and Southern Watch. The ground component came to an abrupt end in December of 1998, when the inspectors informed the United Nations that after eight years of Iraqi threats and broken promises, they could not perform their missions. Aerial inspections, however, continued. As coalition aircraft attempt to enforce the no-fly zones, they conduct aerial surveillance to help determine compliance with U.N. resolutions 688 and 687, which bans nuclear, chemical and biological weapons.

In October 1994, Iraq defied terms of the cease-fire, moving Republican Guard armored divisions near the Iraqi-Kuwaiti border and threatening to expel U.N. weapons inspectors. U.S. troops moved into the area to turn back the aggression, and the U.N. Security Council passed resolution 949, ordering Iraq to stop threatening its neighbors and establishing no-drive zones which Iraqi ground forces were no longer allowed to enter. Coalition pilots of Operation Southern Watch risk heir lives every day to enforce those U.N. resolutions.

Iraqi weapons continue to fire on U.S. and U.K. coalition pilots as they enforce these resolutions. With each missile launched at our air crews, Iraq expresses its contempt for the U.N. resolutions—a fact that must be kept in mind as their latest inspection offers are evaluated.

That offer has already been subject to Iraqi revisionism. Three days after September 16th letter was delivered promising to accept inspectors, quote, "without condition," unquote, Iraq's foreign minister gave a speech to the U.N. in which he placed conditions on any future inspections. He declared in part that Iraq rejects any transgression at the expense of its right to sovereignty, security and independence that is a contradiction with the principles of the U.N. charter and international law. He then declared that the U.N. resolutions were, quote, "unjust and at odds with the U.N. charter and international law." He further declared, quote, "Iraq demands that its inalienable rights are met, including respect for its sovereignty, security and the lifting of the blockade imposed on it."

Over the years, the Iraqi regime has shown a great deal of cleverness in playing the international community and the world's media. When it's useful to lean forward, they do so. And many in the international community applaud. But when Iraq wishes to lean back, and many in the international community have been inclined to ignore, temporize or acquiesce, undoubtedly because it wasn't convenient to do otherwise.

The U.S. is interested in compliance with the U.N. resolutions and the disarmament of Iraq. This is the only place in the world where U.S. and British pilots are regularly fired at in an attempt to shoot down U.S. and British airplanes and the aircrews who are enforcing these U.N. resolutions. The president has challenged the United Nations to enforce its resolutions. It's an important moment for the credibility of the members of the United Nations.

Remarks by President Bush, September 19, 2002

I appreciate our Secretary of State coming by to brief the Vice President and me and Condoleezza Rice about our progress in working with the United Nations, convincing the United Nations Security Council to firmly deal with a threat to world peace.

Before we talk about that, I do want to express our condolences to those who lost their lives in Israel. It's been back-to-back suicide bombings. We strongly condemn terror. We strongly condemn violence. And we continue to send our message to the good people of that region that if you're interested in peace, that if you want people to be able to grow up in a peaceful world, all parties must do everything they can to reject and stop violence.

At the United Nations Security Council it is very important that the members understand that the credibility of the United Nations is at stake, that the Security Council must be firm in its resolve to deal with a truth threat to world peace, and that is Saddam Hussein. That the United Nations Security Council must work with the United States and Britain and other concerned parties to send a clear message that we expect Saddam to disarm. And if the United Nations Security Council won't deal with the problem, the United States and some of our friends will.

That's the message the Secretary of State has delivered forcefully. That's the message that he will continue to carry. And, Mr. Secretary, I appreciate your hard work. You're doing a fine job.

Secretary Powell. Thank you, Mr. President.

President Bush. And we're proud of your efforts.

Secretary Powell. Thank you, sir.

President Bush. I'll be glad to answer a few calls—answers, starting with Ron.

Q. How many of our friends are willing to join the United States in this effort?

President Bush. Ron, I think time will tell. I think you're going to see a lot of nations—that a lot of nations love freedom. They understand the threat. They understand that the credibility of the United Nations is at stake. They heard me loud and clear when I said, either you can be the United Nations, a capable body, a body able to keep the peace, or you can be the League of Nations. And we're confident that people will follow our lead.

Q. Sir, the chief weapons inspector is going to be briefing the U.N. Security Council today, and there have already been some reports that, in his talks with the Iraqis, that they're limiting access to certain sites. Are those reports true? And do you think they're trying to—

President Bush. Well, I haven't gotten a report from what he intends to say. But let me give you just some general observations. First of all, there are no negotiations to be held with Iraq. They have nothing to negotiate. They're the people who said that they would not have weapons of mass destruction. The negotiations are over. It is up to the U.N. Security Council to lay out resolutions that confirms what Iraq has already agreed to, see. Secondly, I don't trust Iraq, and neither should the free world. For 11 years, they have deceived the world. They have said, we'll conform to resolutions. They've never conformed to resolutions. They've never conformed to the agreement that they laid out 11 years ago. Sixteen times they've defied Security resolutions. And so, they—the burden of proof is—must be place squarely on their shoulders. But there's no negotiations about whether or not they've been telling the truth or not. Let's see here—Mark.

Q. Mr. President, are you going to send Congress your proposed resolution today? And are you asking for a blank check, sir?

President Bush. I am sending suggested language for a resolution. I want—I've asked for Congress' support to enable the administration to keep the peace. And we look forward to a good, constructive debate in Congress. I appreciate the fact that the leadership recognizes we've got to move before the elections. I appreciate the strong support we're getting from both Republicans and Democrats, and look forward to working with them.

Q. Mr. President, how important is it that that resolution give you an authorization of the use of force?

President Bush. That will be part of the resolution, the authorization to use force. If you want to keep the peace, you've got to have the authorization to use force. But it's—this will be—this is a chance for Congress to indicate support. It's a chance for Congress to say, we support the administration's ability to keep the peace. That's what this is all about.

Q. Will regime change be part of it?

President Bush. Yes. That's the policy of the government.

White House Draft of Potential Congressional Joint Resolution Authorizing Use of Force in Iraq, September 19, 2002

Whereas Congress in 1998 concluded that Iraq was then in material and unacceptable breach of its international obligations and thereby threatened the vital interests of the United States and international peace and security, stated the reasons for that conclusion, and urged the president to take appropriate action to bring Iraq into compliance with its international obligations (Public Law 105-235);

Whereas Iraq remains in material and unacceptable breach of its international obligations by, among other things, continuing to possess and develop a significant chemical and biological weapons capability, actively seeking a nuclear weapons capability, and supporting and harboring terrorist organizations, thereby continuing to threaten the national security interests of the United States and international peace and security;

Whereas Iraq persists in violating resolutions of the United Nations Security Council by continuing to engage in brutal repression of its civilian population, including the Kurdish peoples, thereby threatening international peace and security in the region, by refusing to release, repatriate, or account for non-Iraqi citizens wrongfully detained by Iraq, and by failing to return property wrongfully seized by Iraq from Kuwait;

Whereas the current Iraqi regime has demonstrated its capability and willingness to use weapons of mass destruction against other nations and its own people;

Whereas the current Iraqi regime has demonstrated its continuing hostility toward, and willingness to attack, the United States, including by attempting in 1993 to assassinate former President Bush and by firing on many thousands of occasions on United States and Coalition Armed Forces engaged in enforcing the resolutions of the United Nations Security Council;

Whereas members of al-Qaida, an organization bearing responsibility for attacks on the United States, its citizens, and interests, including the attacks that occurred on Sept. 11, 2001, are known to be in Iraq;

Whereas Iraq continues to aid and harbor other international terrorist organizations, including organizations that threaten the lives and safety of American citizens;

Whereas the attacks on the United States of Sept. 11, 2001. underscored the gravity of the threat that Iraq will transfer weapons of mass destruction to international terrorist organizations;

Whereas the United States has the inherent right, as acknowledged in the United Nations Charter, to use force in order to defend itself;

Whereas Iraq's demonstrated capability and willingness to use weapons of mass destruction, the high risk that the current Iraqi regime will either employ those weapons to launch a surprise attack against the United States or its armed forces or provide them to international terrorists who would do so, and the extreme magnitude of harm that would result to the United States and its citizens from such an attack, combine to justify the use of force by the United States in order to defend itself;

Whereas Iraq is in material breach of its disarmament and other obligations under United Nations Security Council Resolution 687, to cease repression of its civilian population that threatens international peace and security under United Nations Security Council Resolution 688, and to cease threatening its neighbors of United Nations operations in Iraq under United Nations Security Council Resolution 949, and United Nations Security Council Resolution 678 authorizes use of all necessary means to compel Iraq to comply with these "subsequent relevant resolutions;

Whereas Congress in the Authorization for Use of Military Force Against Iraq Resolution (Public Law 102-1) has authorized the president to use the Armed Forces of the United States to achieve full implementation of Security Council Resolutions 660, 661, 662, 664, 665, 666, 667, 669, 670, 674, and 677, pursuant to Security Council Resolution 678;

Whereas Congress in section 1095 of Public Law 102-190 has stated that it "supports the use of all necessary means to achieve the goals of Security Council Resolution 687 as being consistent with the Authorization for Use of Military Force Against Iraq (Public Law 102-1)," that Iraq's repression of its civilian population violates United Nations Security Council Resolution 688 and "constitutes a continuing threat to the peace, security, and stability of the Persian Gulf region," and that Congress "supports the use of all necessary means to achieve the goals of Resolution 688";

Whereas Congress in the Iraq Liberation Act (Public Law 105-338) has expressed its sense that it should be the policy of the United States to support efforts to remove from power the current Iraqi regime and promote the emergence of a democratic government to replace that regime;

Whereas the president has authority under the Constitution to take action in order to deter and prevent acts of international terrorism against the United States, as Congress recognized in the joint resolution on Authorization for Use of Military Force (Public Law 107-40); and

Whereas the president has authority under the Constitution to use force in order to defend the national security interests of the United States;

Now, therefore, be it resolved by the Senate and House of Representatives of the United States of America in Congress assembled,

SECTION 1. SHORT TITLE.

This joint resolution may be cited as the "Further Resolution on Iraq."

SECTION 2. AUTHORIZATION FOR USE OF UNITED STATES ARMS FORCES.

The president is authorized to use all means that he determines to be appropriate, including force, in order to enforce the United Nations Security Council resolutions referenced above, defend the national security interests of the United States against the threat posed by Iraq, and restore international peace and security in the region.

Remarks by U.K. Prime Minister Blair, September 24, 2002

Prime Minister Tony Blair addressed the Parliament, announcing the publication of a dossier on Iraq and Weapons of Mass Destruction.

Mr. Speaker, thank you for recalling Parliament to debate the best way to deal with the issue of the present leadership of Iraq and Weapons of Mass Destruction.

Today we published a 50 page dossier detailing the history of Iraq's WMD, its breach of U.N. resolutions and the current attempts to rebuild the illegal WMD programme. I have placed a copy in the Library of the House.

At the end of the Gulf War, the full extent of Saddam's chemical, biological and nuclear weapons programmes became clear. As a result, the U.N. passed a series of resolutions demanding Iraq disarm itself of such weapons and establishing a regime of weapons inspection and monitoring to do the task. They were to be given unconditional and unrestricted access to all and any Iraqi sites.

All this is accepted fact. In addition, it is fact, documented by U.N. inspectors, that Iraq almost immediately began to obstruct the inspections. Visits were delayed; on occasions, inspectors threatened; materiel was moved; special sites, shut to the inspectors, were unilaterally designated by Iraq.

The work of the inspectors continued but against a background of increasing obstruction and non-compliance. Indeed, Iraq denied its biological weapons programme existed until forced to acknowledge it after high ranking defectors disclosed it in 1995.

Eventually in 1997, the U.N. inspectors declared they were unable to fulfil their task. A year of negotiation and further obstruction occurred until finally in late 1998, the U.N. team were forced to withdraw. As the dossier sets out, we estimate on the basis of the U.N.'s work that there were: up to 360 tonnes of bulk chemical warfare agents, including one and a half tonnes of VX nerve agent; up to 3,000 tonnes of precursor chemicals; growth media sufficient to produce 26,000 litres of anthrax spores; and over 30,000 special munitions for delivery of chemical and biological agents.

All of this was missing or unaccounted for.

Military action by the U.S. and U.K. followed and a certain amount of infrastructure for Iraq's WMD and missile capability was destroyed, setting the Iraqi programme back, but not ending it.

From late 1998 onwards, the sole inhibition on Saddam's WMD programme was the sanctions regime. Iraq was forbidden to use the revenue from its oil except for certain specified non-military purposes. The sanctions regime, however, was also subject to illegal trading and abuse. Because of concerns about its inadequacy—and the impact on the Iraqi people—we made several attempts to refine it, culminating in a new U.N. resolution in May of this year. But it was only partially effective. Around $3bn of money is illegally taken by Saddam every year now, double the figure for 2000. Self-evidently there is no proper accounting for this money.

Because of concerns that a containment policy based on sanctions alone could not sufficiently inhibit Saddam's weapons programme, negotiations continued after 1998 to gain re-admission for the U.N. inspectors. In 1999 a new U.N. resolution demanding their re-entry was passed and ignored. Further negotiations continued. Finally, after several months of discussion with Saddam's regime this year, Kofi Annan, the U.N. Secretary General, concluded that Saddam was not serious about re-admitting the inspectors and ended the negotiations. That was in July.

All of this is established fact. I set out the history in some detail because occasionally debate on this issue seems to treat it almost as if it had suddenly arisen, coming out of nowhere on a whim, in the last few months of 2002. It is an 11 year history: a history of U.N. will flouted, lies told by Saddam about existence of his chemical, biological and nuclear weapons programmes, obstruction, defiance and denial. There is one common consistent theme, however: the total determination of Saddam to maintain the programme; to risk war, international ostracism, sanctions, the isolation of the Iraqi economy, in order to keep it. At any time, he could have let the inspectors back in and put the world to proof. At any time he could have co-operated with the U.N.. Ten days ago he made the offer unconditionally, under threat of war. He could have done it at any time in the last eleven years. But he didn't. Why? The dossier we publish gives the answer. The reason is because his chemical, biological and nuclear weapons programme is not an historic leftover from 1998. The inspectors aren't needed to clean up the old remains. His WMD programme is active, detailed and growing. The policy of containment is not working. The WMD programme is not shut down. It is up and running.

The dossier is based on the work of the British Joint Intelligence Committee. For over 60 years, beginning just prior to WWII, the JIC has provided intelligence assessments to British Prime Ministers. Normally its work is secret. Unusually, because it is important we explain our concerns over Saddam to the British people, we have decided to disclose these assessments. I am aware, of course, that people are going to have to take elements of this on the good faith of our intelligence services. But this is what they are telling me the British Prime Minister and my senior colleagues. The intelligence picture they paint is one accumulated over the past four years. It is extensive, detailed and authoritative.

It concludes that Iraq has chemical and biological weapons, that Saddam has continued to produce them, that he has existing and active military plans for the use of chemical and biological weapons, which could be activated within 45 minutes, including against his own Shia population; and that he is actively trying to acquire nuclear weapons capability.

On chemical weapons, the dossier shows that Iraq continues to produce chemical agent for chemical weapons; has rebuilt previously destroyed production plants across Iraq; has bought dual-use chemical facilities; has retained the key personnel formerly engaged in the chemical weapons programme; and has a serious ongoing research programme into weapons production, all of it well funded.

In respect of biological weapons, again production of biological agents has continued; facilities formerly used for biological weapons have been rebuilt; equipment has been purchased for such a programme; and again Saddam has retained the personnel who worked on it, pre 1991. In particular, the U.N. inspection regime discovered that Iraq was trying to acquire mobile biological weapons facilities which are easier to conceal. Present intelligence confirms they have now got such facilities. The biological agents we believe Iraq can produce include anthrax, botulinum, toxin, aflatoxin and ricin. All eventually result in excruciatingly painful death. As for nuclear weapons, Saddam's previous nuclear weapons programme was shut down by the inspectors, following disclosure by defectors of the full, but hidden, nature of it. That programme was based on gas centrifuge uranium enrichment. The known remaining stocks of uranium are now held under supervision by the International Atomic Energy Agency.

But we now know the following. Since the departure of the inspectors in 1998, Saddam has bought or attempted to buy: specialized vacuum pumps of the design needed for the gas centrifuge cascade to enrich uranium; an entire magnet production line of the specification for use in the motors and top bearings of gas centrifuges; dual use products such as Anhydrous Hydrogen Fluoride and fluoride gas, which can be used both in petrochemicals but also in gas centrifuge cascades; a filament winding machine, which can be used to manufacture carbon fibre gas centrifuge rotors; and has attempted, covertly, to acquire 60,000 or more specialized aluminum tubes, which are subject to strict controls due to their potential use in the construction of gas centrifuges.

In addition, we know Saddam has been trying to buy significant quantities of uranium from Africa, though we do not know whether he has been successful. Again key personnel who used to work on the nuclear weapons programme are back in harness. Iraq may claim that this is for a civil nuclear power programme but it has no nuclear power plants.

That is the position in respect of weapons. But, of course, the weapons require ballistic missile capability. This is again subject to U.N. disarmament resolutions. Iraq is supposed only to have missile capability up to 150 km for conventional weaponry. Pages 27-31 of the dossier detail the evidence on this issue. It is clear both that a significant number of longer-range missiles were effectively concealed from the previous inspectors and remain, including up to 20 extended range Scud missiles; that in mid 2001, there was a step change in the programme and by this year, Iraq's development of weapons with a range over 1,000 kms was well underway; that hundreds of key people are employed on this programme; facilities are being built; and equipment procured, usually clandestinely. Sanctions and import controls have hindered this programme but only slowed its progress. The capability being developed is for multi-purpose use, including with WMD warheads.

Now, that is the assessment to me from the JIC. In addition, we have well-founded intelligence to tell us that Saddam sees his WMD programme as vital to his survival, as a demonstration of his power and his influence in the region.

There will be some who dismiss all this. Intelligence is not always right. For some of this material there may be innocent explanations.

There will be others who say, rightly, that, for example, on present going, it could be several years before he acquires a usable nuclear weapon. Though, if he were able to purchase fissile materiel illegally, it would only be a year or two.

But let me put it at its simplest: on this 11 year history; with this man, Saddam; with this accumulated, detailed intelligence available; with what we know and what we can reasonably speculate: would the world be wise to leave the present situation undisturbed; to say, despite 14 separate U.N. demands on this issue, all of which Saddam is in breach of, we should do nothing; to conclude that we should trust not to the good faith of the U.N. weapons inspectors but to the good faith of the current Iraqi regime? Our case is simply this: not that we take military action, come what may; but that the case for ensuring Iraqi disarmament (as the U.N. has stipulated) is overwhelming. I defy anyone on the basis of this evidence to say that is an unreasonable demand for the international community to make when, after all, it is only the same demand that we have made for 11 years and he has rejected.

People say: but why Saddam? I don't in the least dispute there are other causes of concern on WMD. I said as much in this House on 14 September last year. But two things about Saddam stand out. He has used these weapons, thousands dying in chemical weapons attacks in Iraq itself. He used them in the Iran-Iraq war, started by him, in which one million people died. And his is a regime with no moderate elements to appeal to. Read the chapter on Saddam and human rights. Read not just about the one million dead in the war with Iran, not just about the 100,000 Kurds brutally murdered in northern Iraq; not just the 200,000 Shia Muslims driven from the marshlands in southern Iraq; not just the attempt to subjugate and brutalize the Kuwaitis in 1990 which led to the Gulf War. Read about the routine butchering of political opponents; the prison "cleansing" regimes in which thousands die; the torture chambers and hideous penalties supervised by him and his family and detailed by Amnesty International. Read it all and again I defy anyone to say that this cruel and sadistic dictator should be allowed any possibility of getting his hands on more chemical, biological or even nuclear weapons.

Why now? People ask. I agree I cannot say that this month or next, even this year or next, that he will use his weapons. But I can say that if the international community having made the call for his disarmament, now, at this moment, at the point of decision, shrugs its shoulders and walks away, he will draw the conclusion dictators faced with a weakening will, always draw. That the international community will talk but not act; will use diplomacy but not force; and we know, again from our history, that diplomacy, not backed by the threat of force, has never worked with dictators and never will work. If we take this course, he will carry on, his efforts will intensify, his confidence grow and at some point, in a future not too distant, the threat will turn into reality. The threat therefore is not imagined. The history of Saddam and WMD is not American or British propaganda. The history and the present threat are real. And if people say: why should Britain care? I answer: because there is no way that this man, in this region above all regions, could begin a conflict using such weapons and the consequences not engulf the whole world.

That, after all, is the reason the U.N. passed its resolutions. That is why it is right the U.N. Security Council again makes its will and its unity clear and lays down a strong new U.N. resolution and mandate. Then Saddam will have the choice: comply willingly or be forced to comply. That is why alongside the diplomacy, there must be genuine preparedness and planning to take action if diplomacy fails.

Let me be plain about our purpose.

Of course there is no doubt that Iraq, the region and the whole world would be better off without Saddam. They deserve to be led by someone who can abide by international law, not a murderous dictator.

Someone who can bring Iraq back into the international community where it belongs, not languishing as a pariah.

Someone who can make the country rich and successful, not impoverished by Saddam's personal greed.

Someone who can lead a government more representative of the country as a whole, while maintaining absolutely Iraq's territorial integrity.

We have no quarrel with the Iraqi people. Liberated from Saddam, they could make Iraq prosperous and a force for good in the Middle East.

So the ending of regime would be the cause of regret for no-one other than Saddam. But our purpose is disarmament. No-one wants military conflict. The whole purpose of putting this before the U.N. is to demonstrate the united determination of the international community to resolve this in the way it should have been resolved years ago: through a proper process of disarmament under the U.N..

Disarmament of all WMD is the demand. One way or another it must be acceded to.

There are two other issues with a bearing on this question which I will deal with. First, Afghanistan is a country now freed from the Taliban, but still suffering. This is a regime we changed, rightly. I want to make it clear, once again, we are entirely committed to its re-construction. We will not desert the Afghan people. We will stick with them until the job is done.

Secondly, I have no doubt the Arab world knows it would be better off without Saddam. Equally, I know there is genuine resentment at the state of the Middle East Peace Process, which people want to see the international community pursue with the same vigour. Israel will defend its people against these savage acts of terrorism. But the very purpose of this terrorism is to prevent any chance for peace. Meanwhile the Palestinians are suffering in the most appalling and unacceptable way. We need urgent action to build a security infrastructure that gives both Israelis and Palestinians confidence and stops the next suicide bomb closing down the prospects of progress. We need political reform for the Palestinian Authority. And we need a new Conference on the Middle East Peace Process based on the twin principles of a secure Israel and a viable Palestinian state. We can condemn the terrorism and the reaction to it. But frankly, that gets us nowhere. What we need is a firm commitment to action and a massive mobilization of energy to get the peace process moving again; and we will play our part in any way we can.

Finally, there are many acts of this drama still to be played out. I have always said that Parliament should be kept in touch with all developments, in particular those that would lead us to military action. That remains the case. To those who doubt it, I say: look at Kosovo and Afghanistan. We proceeded with care, with full debate in this House and when we took military action, did so as a last resort. We shall act in the same way now. But I hope we can do so, secure in the knowledge that should Saddam continue to defy the will of the international community, this House, as it has in our history so many times before, will not shrink from doing what is necessary and right.

Executive Summary from U.K. Government Report on Iraq's Weapons of Mass Destruction, September 24, 2002

The report from the Government of Prime Minister Tony Blair was titled "Iraq's Weapons of Mass Destruction: The Assessment of the British Government."

Executive Summary

1. Under Saddam Hussein, Iraq developed chemical and biological weapons, acquired missiles allowing it to attack neighboring countries with these weapons, and persistently tried to develop a nuclear bomb. Saddam has used chemical weapons, both against Iran and against his own people. Following the Gulf War, Iraq had to admit to all this. And in the ceasefire of 1991 Saddam agreed unconditionally to give up his weapons of mass destruction.

2. Much information about Iraq's mass destruction weaponry is already in the public domain from U.N. reports and from Iraqi defectors. This points clearly to Iraq's continuing possession, after 1991, of chemical and biological agents and weapons produced before the Gulf War. It shows that Iraq has refurbished sites formerly associated with the production of chemical and biological agents. And it indicates that Iraq remains able to manufacture these agents, and to use bombs, shells, artillery rockets and ballistic missiles to deliver them.

3. An independent and well researched overview of this public evidence was provided by the International Institute for Strategic Studies (IISS) on 9 September. The IISS report also suggested that Iraq could assemble nuclear weapons within months of obtaining fissile material from foreign sources.

4. As well as the public evidence, however, significant additional information is available to the government from secret intelligence sources, described in more detail in this paper. This intelligence cannot tell us about everything. However, it provides a fuller picture of Iraqi plans and capabilities. It shows that Saddam Hussein attaches great importance to possessing weapons of mass destruction which he regards as the basis for Iraq's regional power. It shows that he does not regard them only as weapons of last resort. He is ready to use them, including against his own population, and is determined to retain them, in breach of United Nations Security Council Resolutions.

5. Intelligence also shows that Iraq is preparing plans to conceal evidence of these weapons, including incriminating documents, from renewed inspections. And it confirms that despite sanctions and the policy of containment, Saddam has continued to make progress with his illicit weapons programmes.

6. As a result of the intelligence we judge that Iraq has:
   • continued to produce chemical and biological agents;
   • military plans for the use of chemical and biological weapons, including against its own Shia population. Some of these weapons are deployable within 45 minutes of an order to use them. command and control arrangements in place to use chemical and biological weapons. Authority ultimately resides with Saddam Hussein. (There is intelligence that he may have delegated this authority to his son Qusai);
   • developed mobile laboratories for military use, corroborating earlier reports about the mobile production of biological warfare agents;
   • pursued illegal programmes to procure controlled materials of potential use in

the production of chemical and biological weapons programmes;

• tried covertly to acquire technology and materials which could be used in the production of nuclear weapons;

• sought significant quantities of uranium from Africa, despite having no active civil nuclear power programme that could require it;

• recalled specialists to work on its nuclear programme;

• illegally retained up to 20 Al Hussein missiles, with a range of 650km, capable of carrying chemical or biological warheads;

• started deploying its Al-Samoud liquid propellant missile, and has used the absence of weapons inspectors to work on extending its range to at least 200km, which is beyond the limit of 150km imposed by the United Nations;

• started producing the solid-propellant Ababil-100, and is making efforts to extend its range to at least 200km, which is beyond the limit of 150km imposed by the United Nations;

• constructed a new engine test stand for the development of missiles capable of reaching the U.K. Sovereign Base Areas in Cyprus and NATO members (Greece and Turkey), as well as all Iraq's Gulf neighbors and Israel;

• pursued illegal programmes to procure materials for use in its illegal development of long range missiles;

• learnt lessons from previous U.N. weapons inspections and has already begun to conceal sensitive equipment and documentation in advance of the return of inspectors.

7. These judgements reflect the views of the Joint Intelligence Committee (JIC). More details on the judgements, and on the development of the JIC's assessments since 1998, are set out in Part 1 of this paper.

8. Iraq's weapons of mass destruction are in breach of international law. Under a series of United Nations Security Council Resolutions Iraq is obliged to destroy its holdings of these weapons under the supervision of U.N. inspectors. Part 2 of the paper sets out the key U.N. Security Council Resolutions. It also summarizes the history of the U.N. inspection regime and Iraq's history of deception, intimidation and concealment in its dealings with the U.N. inspectors.

9. But the threat from Iraq does not depend solely on the capabilities we have described. It arises also because of the violent and aggressive nature of Saddam Hussein's regime. His record of internal repression and external aggression gives rise to unique concerns about the threat he poses. The paper briefly outlines in Part 3 Saddam's rise to power, the nature of his regime and his history of regional aggression. Saddam's human rights abuses are also catalogued, including his record of torture, mass arrests and summary executions.

10. The paper briefly sets out how Iraq is able to finance its weapons programme. Drawing on illicit earnings generated outside U.N. control, Iraq generated illegal income of some $3 billion in 2001.

Remarks by President Bush, September 24, 2002

President Bush spoke with reporters during a photo opportunity with the Cabinet at the White House.

We just had a very productive Cabinet meeting. We realize there's little time left in— before the Senate and the House goes home, but we're optimistic a lot can get done before now and then. Congress must act now to pass a resolution which will hold Saddam Hussein to account for a decade of defiance.

It's time to get a homeland security bill done, one which will allow this President and this administration, and future Presidents—give us the tools necessary to protect the homeland. And we're working as hard as we can with Phil Gramm and Zell Miller to get this bill moving. It's a good bill. It's a bill that both Republicans and Democrats can and should support.

My message, of course, is that, to the senators up here that are more interested in special interests, you better pay attention to the overall interests of protecting the American people.

We can get budget going. I need a defense bill. The Senate needs to get, and the House needs to get, their differences reconciled and get a defense bill to my desk before they go home. That's a very important signal to send. And at the same time, since there is no budget in the Senate, they've got to be mindful of over-spending.

Very important for those up there who keep talking about budget—balanced budget, and all that, to not over-spend. If they're truly that concerned about the deficit, then one way they can help is to be fiscally sound with the people's money.

We talked about the need to get pension reform and an energy bill, terrorism insurance. There's time to get all this done, and we look forward to working with the members of Congress to get it done.

I'll answer a couple of questions, starting with Fournier of the AP.

Q. Thank you, Mr. President. Can I have your reaction to two recent assessments on the situation in Iraq? First, Tony Blair said today that Saddam has tried to acquire significant quantities of uranium and can quickly deploy chemical and biological weapons. But there seems to be little new information in the dossier. Secondly, former Vice President Al Gore—

President Bush. He explained why.

Q. Pardon me, sir?

President Bush. Explained why he didn't put new information—to protect sources. Go ahead.

Q. The Vice President yesterday said that you've managed to replace the world's sympathy on Iraq with fear, anxiety and uncertainty. And you're using the issue to steer attention away from the inability to get Osama bin Laden.

President Bush. I'm confident a lot of Democrats here in Washington, D.C. will understand that Saddam is a true threat to America. And I look forward to working with them to get a strong resolution passed.

Prime Minister Blair, first of all, is a very strong leader, and I admire his willingness to tell the truth and to lead. Secondly, he has—continues to make the case, like we make the case, that Saddam Hussein is a threat to peace; that for 11 years he has deceived the world. For 11 years, he's ignored the United Nations, and for 11 years he has stockpiled weapons. And we shouldn't deceive ourselves about this man. He has poisoned his people before. He has poisoned his neighborhood. He is willing to use weapons of mass destruction. And the Prime Minister continues to make the case, and so will I.

And I again call for the United Nations to pass a strong resolution holding this man to account. And if they're unable to do so, the United States and our friends will act, because we believe in peace; we want to keep the peace. We don't trust this man—and that's what the Blair report showed today.

The reason why it wasn't specific is because—I understand why—he's not going to reveal sources and methods of collection of sensitive information. Those sources and methods may be—will be used later on, I'm confident, as we gather more information about how this man has deceived the world.

Q. Sir, do you want to specifically respond, please, to Al Gore, instead of just generally about Democrats? What did you think about his—

President Bush. About his response—I mean, there's a lot of Democrats in Washington, D.C. who understand that Saddam Hussein is a true threat, and that we must hold him to account. And I believe you'll see, as we work to get a strong resolution out of the Congress, that a lot of Democrats are willing to take the lead when it comes to keeping the peace.

Q. Sir, Arab leaders are warning the terrorism coalition and your efforts in Iraq are at risk because of the Arafat siege. Why didn't U.S. support last night's U.N. resolution, and what can you say to get to Israel to end the siege?

President Bush. What we do support is this, Steve—and our abstention should have sent a message that we hope that all parties stay on the path to peace. And I laid out what the path to peace—what the path to peace was here at the—in the Rose Garden: First of all, we all have got to fight terror. But as we fight terror, particularly in the Middle East, they've got to build the institution necessary for a Palestinian state to emerge; that we've got to promote the leadership that is willing to condemn terror and, at the same time, work toward the embetterment of the lives of the Palestinian people. There are a lot of suffering people there and we've got to help end the suffering.

And I thought the actions Israelis take—Israelis took were not helpful in terms of the establishment and development of the institutions necessary for a Palestinian state to emerge. We will continue to work with all parties in the region, Israel and everybody else who wants to fight off terror, we'll do that.

In order for there to be peace we must battle terror. But at the same time, we must have a hopeful response. And the most hopeful response of all for the Palestinian people is for—to work for a state to emerge. And that is possible; I believe strongly it can happen. I believe it's—I believe in peace in the Middle East. And I would urge all governments to work toward that peace.

And we're making progress, and that's what's important for the world to know. We're making progress on the security front, we're making progress on the political reform front. We're making progress to make it clear that if there is to be a peaceful settlement, that the Palestinians must be given the opportunity to bring forth leadership which is willing to work toward peace. And it was not helpful what happened recently.

Excerpt from Remarks by Senate Majority Leader Daschle, September 25, 2002

Senator Tom Daschle delivered his remarks on the Senate Floor.

I am very saddened by the fact that we have debated homeland security now for 4 weeks. I have noted on several occasions that there is no reason, on a bipartisan basis, this body cannot work together to overcome our differences and to pass a meaningful and substantive bill dealing with homeland security.

Some have suggested that the delay has been politically motivated, and I have said: I am not willing to believe that. In fact, yesterday I said: We intend to give the President the benefit of the doubt.

Over the course of the last several weeks, as we have debated national security, the issue of war in Iraq has become more and more prominent. And again, as I go back to my experience in 1991 and 1992, during a similar period—the fall and winter prior and after an election—I expressed the concern that our politics in this climate could easily create a politicized environment and, in so doing, diminish, minimize, degrade the debate on an issue as grave as war.

No one here needs to be reminded of the consequences of war. No one here should have to be admonished about politicizing the debate about war. But, Mr. President, increasingly, over the course of the last several weeks, reports have surfaced which have led me to believe that indeed there are those who would politicize this war.

I was given a report about a recommendation made by Matthew Dowd, the pollster for the White House and the Republican National Committee. He told a victory dinner not long ago—I quote—"The No. 1 driver for our base motivationally is this war."

Dowd said war could be beneficial to the GOP in the 2002 elections. And then I quote: "When an issue dominates the landscape like this one will dominate the landscape, I think through this election and probably for a long time to come, it puts Republicans on a very good footing."

I thought: Well, perhaps that is a pollster. Perhaps pollsters are paid to say what is best regardless of what other considerations ought to be made. Pollsters are paid to tell you about the politics of issues. And were it left with pollsters, perhaps I would not be as concerned.

But then I read that Andy Card was asked: Well, why did this issue come before

Washington and the country now? Why are we debating it in September? Where were we last year? Where were we last spring? And Mr. Card's answer was: "From a marketing point of view, you don't introduce new products in August."

New products? War?

And then I listen to reports of the Vice President. The Vice President comes to fundraisers, as he did just recently in Kansas. The headline written in the paper the next day about the speech he gave to that fundraiser was: Cheney talks about war: electing Taff would aid war effort.

And then we find a diskette discovered in Lafayette Park, a computer diskette that was lost somewhere between a Republican strategy meeting in the White House and the White House.

Advice was given by Karl Rove, and the quote on the disk was: "Focus on war."

I guess, right from the beginning, I thought: Well, first it was pollsters, and then it was White House staff, and then it was the Vice President. And all along I was asked: Are you concerned about whether or not this war is politicized? And my answer, on every occasion, was: Yes. And then the followup question is: Is the White House politicizing the war? And I said: Without question, I can't bring myself to believe that it is. I can't believe any President or any administration would politicize the war. But then I read in the paper this morning, now even the President—the President is quoted in the Washington Post this morning as saying that the Democratic-controlled Senate is "not interested in the security of the American people."

Not interested in the security of the American people?

You tell Senator Inouye he is not interested in the security of the American people. You tell those who fought in Vietnam and in World War II they are not interested in the security of the American people.

That is outrageous—outrageous.

The President ought to apologize to Senator Inouye and every veteran who has fought in every war who is a Democrat in the Senate. He ought to apologize to the American people.

That is wrong. We ought not politicize this war. We ought not politicize the rhetoric about war and life and death.

I was in Normandy just last year. I have been in national cemeteries all over this country. And I have never seen anything but stars—the Star of David and crosses on those markers. I have never seen "Republican" and "Democrat."

This has to end, Mr. President. We have to get on with the business of our country. We have to rise to a higher level.

Our Founding Fathers would be embarrassed by what they are seeing going on right now.

We have to do better than this. Our standard of deportment ought to be better. Those who died gave their lives for better than what we are giving now.

So, Mr. President, it is not too late to end this politicization. It is not too late to forget the pollsters, forget the campaign fundraisers, forget making accusations about how interested in national security Democrats are; and let's get this job done right.

Let's rise to the occasion. That is what the American people are expecting. And we ought to give them no less.

Excerpt from Remarks by Senate Majority Leader Daschle, September 25, 2002

Senator Tom Daschle delivered his remarks on the Senate Floor.

Mr. President, the other matter I wanted to come to the floor to discuss is the reaction to some of the comments that I made this morning.

A number of our colleagues have come to the floor and, as I understand it, the administration has stated that if I had understood the context in which the President made those remarks—the remarks that Senate Democrats are not concerned about national security—that I probably would not have been so critical. In fact, they criticized me for having criticized the President.

Mr. President, what context is there that legitimizes an accusation of that kind? I don't care whether you are talking about homeland security , I don't think you can talk about Iraq, you can't talk about war, you can't talk about any context that justifies a political comment like that.

This is politicization, pure and simple. I meant it this morning and I mean it now. I don't know what may have motivated those in the White House to make the decision to politicize this debate, but it has to stop. There is no context within which anybody can make that accusation about people on this side of the aisle on an issue relating to homeland security, or Iraq, or defense, or anything else.

So let's get that straight. I would hope that we can finally bring this debate to a level that it deserves.

I can recall in 1991 and 1992—especially in 1992—when President Bush made the decision he did. I can recall several of my staff coming to me, suggesting that we say this or that. But never once did I have someone on my staff, someone here in the Senate, refer to the politics of the war with Iraq.

I remember sitting at my desk, handwriting my speech, explaining to my people in South Dakota, and to whomever else might be listening, why I made the decision I did. I did not make that decision for political reasons. And I don't think there is a person in this Chamber who did.

We need that same level of debate this time if we are going to have a debate, if we are going to do it this close to an election.

So I want all the apologies at the other side of Pennsylvania Avenue, all of these explanations about "context" to be taken for what they are worth. They are not worth the paper they are printed on.

The time has come for us to quit the explanations, to quit the rationalizations, to quit the politicization, and do what we should do as Americans: Make our statement, make our judgment, have a debate, and send as clear a message to Saddam Hussein as we can.

We are not going to tolerate his actions. And we, as a country, will build on a coalition to do the right thing.

I hope this will be the last word. I look forward to talking directly with those in the White House, those on this side of the aisle, as we fashion our response, as we take this matter as seriously as we should, as we do it in a way that lives up to the expectations of the American people.

Remarks by President Bush, September 26, 2002

President Bush delivered his remarks following a meeting with Congressional Leaders at the White House.

Good morning. We've just concluded a really good meeting with both Democrats and Republicans—members of the United States Congress—to discuss our national security and discuss how best to keep the peace. The security of our country is the commitment of both political parties and the responsibility of both elected branches of government.

We are engaged in a deliberate and civil and thorough discussion. We are moving toward a strong resolution. And all of us, and many others in Congress, are united in our determination to confront an urgent threat to America. And by passing this resolution we'll send a clear message to the world and to the Iraqi regime: the demands of the U.N. Security Council must be followed. The Iraqi dictator must be disarmed. These requirements will be met, or they will be enforced.

The danger to our country is grave. The danger to our country is growing. The Iraqi regime possesses biological and chemical weapons. The Iraqi regime is building the facilities necessary to make more biological and chemical weapons. And according to the British government, the Iraqi regime could launch a biological or chemical attack in as little as 45 minutes after the order were given.

The regime has long-standing and continuing ties to terrorist organizations. And there are al Qaeda terrorists inside Iraq. The regime is seeking a nuclear bomb, and with fissile material, could build one within a year. Iraq has already used weapons of mass death against—against other countries and against her own citizens. The Iraqi regime practices the rape of women as a method of intimidation; and the torture of dissenters and their children.

For more than a decade, the regime has answered Security Council resolutions with defiance, bad faith and deception. We know that the Iraqi regime is led by a dangerous and brutal man. We know he's actively seeking the destructive technologies to match is hatred. We know he must be stopped. The dangers we face will only worsen from month to month and from year to year. To ignore these threats is to encourage them. And when they have fully materialized it may be too late to protect ourselves and our friends and our allies. By then the Iraqi dictator would have the means to terrorize and dominate the region. Each passing day could be the one on which the Iraqi regime gives anthrax or VX—nerve gas—or some day a nuclear weapon to a terrorist ally. We refuse to live in this future of fear. Democrats and Republicans refuse to live in a future of fear. We're determined to build a future of security. All of us long for peace, peace for ourselves, peace for the world.

Members here this morning are committed to American leadership for the good of all nations. I appreciate their spirit. I appreciate their love for country. The resolution we are producing will be an instrument of that leadership. I appreciate the spirit in which members of Congress are considering this vital issue. Congress will have an important debate, a meaningful debate, an historic debate. It will be conducted will all civility. It will be conducted in a manner that will make Americans proud, and Americans to understand the threats to our future. We're making progress, we're near an agreement. And soon, we will speak with one voice.

Thank you all for being here. God bless America.

White House Draft of Potential Congressional Joint Resolution Authorizing Use of Force in Iraq, September 26, 2002

Whereas in 1990 in response to Iraq's war of aggression against and illegal occupation of Kuwait, the United States forged a coalition of nations to liberate Kuwait and its people in order to defend the national security interests of the United States and enforce United Nations Security Council resolutions relating to Iraq;

Whereas after the liberation of Kuwait in 1991, Iraq entered into a United Nations sponsored cease-fire agreement pursuant to which Iraq unequivocally agreed, among other things, to eliminate its nuclear, biological and chemical weapons programs and the means to deliver and develop them, and to end its support for international terrorism;

Whereas the efforts of international weapons inspectors, United States intelligence agencies and Iraqi defectors led to the discovery that Iraq had large stockpiles of chemical weapons and a large-scale biological weapons program, and that Iraq had an advanced nuclear weapons development program that was much closer to producing a nuclear weapon than intelligence reporting had previously indicated;

Whereas Iraq, in direct and flagrant violation of the cease-fire, attempted to thwart the efforts of weapons inspectors to identify and destroy Iraq's weapons of mass destruction stockpiles and development capabilities, which finally resulted in the withdrawal of inspectors from Iraq on Oct. 31, 1998;

Whereas in 1998 Congress concluded that Iraq's continuing weapons of mass destruction programs threatened vital United States interests and international peace and security, declared Iraq to be in "material and unacceptable breach of its international obligations," and urged the president "to take appropriate action, in accordance with the Constitution and relevant laws of the United States, to bring Iraq into compliance with its international obligations" (Public Law 105-235);

Whereas Iraq remains in material and unacceptable breach of its international obligations by, among other things, continuing to possess and develop a significant chemical and biological weapons capability, actively seeking a nuclear weapons capability, and supporting and harboring terrorist organizations, thereby continuing to threaten the national security interests of the United States and international peace and security;

Whereas Iraq persists in violating resolutions of the United Nations Security Council by continuing to engage in brutal repression of its civilian population, including the Kurdish peoples, thereby threatening international peace and security in the region, by refusing to release, repatriate or account for non-Iraqi citizens wrongfully detained by Iraq, including an American serviceman, and by failing to return property wrongfully seized by Iraq from Kuwait;

Whereas the current Iraqi regime has demonstrated its capability and willingness to use weapons of mass destruction against other nations and its own people;

Whereas the current Iraqi regime has demonstrated its continuing hostility toward, and willingness to attack the United States, including by attempting in 1993 to assassinate former President Bush and by firing on many thousands of occasions on United States and Coalition Armed Forces engaged in enforcing the resolutions of the United Nations Security Council;

Whereas members of Al Qaeda, an organization bearing responsibility for attacks on the United States, its citizens and interests, including the attacks that occurred on Sept. 11, 2001, are known to be in Iraq;

Whereas Iraq continues to aid and harbor other international terrorist organizations, including organizations that threaten the lives and safety of American citizens;

Whereas the attacks on the United States of Sept. 11, 2001, underscored the gravity of the threat posed by the acquisition of weapons of mass destruction by international terrorist organizations;

Whereas Iraq's demonstrated capability and willingness to use weapons of mass destruction, the risk that the current Iraqi regime will either employ those weapons to launch a surprise attack against the United States or its Armed Forces or provide them to international terrorists who would do so, and the extreme magnitude of harm that would result to the United States and its citizens from such an attack, combine to justify action by the United States to defend itself;

Whereas United Nations Security Council Resolution 678 authorizes the use of all necessary means to enforce United Nations Security Council Resolution 660 and subsequent relevant resolutions, and to compel Iraq to cease certain activities that threaten international peace and security, including the development of weapons of mass destruction and refusal or obstruction of United Nations weapons inspections in violation of United Nations Security Council Resolution 687, repression of its civilian population in violation of United Nations Security Council Resolution 688, and threatening its neighbors or United Nations operations in Iraq in violation of United Nations Security Council Resolution 949;

Whereas Congress in the Authorization for Use of Military Force Against Iraq Resolution (Public Law 102-1) has authorized the President "to use United States Armed Forces pursuant to United Nations Security Council Resolution 678 (1990) in order to achieve implementation of Security Council Resolutions 660, 661, 662, 664, 665, 666, 667, 669, 670, 674, and 677";

Whereas in December 1991, Congress expressed its sense that it "supports the use of all necessary means to achieve the goals of United Nations Security Council Resolution 687 as being consistent with the Authorization of Use of Military Force Against Iraq Resolution (Public Law 102-I)," that Iraq's repression of its civilian population violates United Nations Security Council Resolution 688 and "constitutes a continuing threat to the peace, security, and stability of the Persian Gulf region," and that Congress, "supports the use of all necessary means to achieve the goals of United Nations Security Council Resolution 688";

Whereas the Iraq Liberation Act (Public Law 105-338) expressed the sense of Congress that it should be the policy of the United States to support efforts to remove from power the current Iraqi regime and promote the emergence of a democratic government to replace that regime;

Whereas on Sept. 12, 2002, President Bush committed the United States to work with the United Nations Security Council to meet our common challenge "posed by Iraq and to work for the necessary resolutions," while also making clear that the Security Council resolutions will be enforced, and the just demands of peace and security will be met, or action will be unavoidable;

Whereas Congress supports the efforts by the President to enforce through the Security Council the United Nations Security Council resolutions referenced above;

Whereas Congress urges the Security Council to act promptly and decisively to ensure that Iraq compiles with the Security Council resolutions referenced above;

Whereas the president and Congress agree on the need to pursue vigorously the war on terrorism and that Iraq's ongoing support for international terrorist groups combined with its development of weapons of mass destruction in direct violation of its obligations under the 1991 cease-fire and other United Nations Security Council resolutions make clear that it is in the national security interests of the United States and in furtherance of the war on terrorism that the United Nations Security Council resolutions referenced above be enforced, including through the use of force if necessary;

Whereas the president has authority under the Constitution to take action in order to deter and prevent acts of international terrorism against the United States, as Congress recognized in the joint resolution on Authorization for Use of Military Force (Public Law 107-40); and,

Whereas it is in the national security interests of the United States to restore international peace and security to the Persian Gulf region;

Now, therefore, be it

Resolved by the Senate and House of Representatives of the United States of America in Congress assembled,

SECTION 1. SHORT TITLE.

This joint resolution may be cited as the "Authorization for the Use of Military Force Against Iraq."

SECTION 2. AUTHORIZATION FOR USE OF UNITED STATES ARMED FORCES.

(a) AUTHORIZATION. The president is authorized to use the Armed Forces of the United States as he determines to be necessary and appropriate in order to

(1) defend the national security interests of the United States against the threat posed by Iraq and

(2) enforce the United Nations Security Council Resolutions referenced above.

(b) DETERMINATION. In connection with the exercise of the authority granted in subsection (a) to use force, the president shall, prior to such exercise or as soon thereafter as may be feasible, make available to the speaker of the House of Representatives and the president pro tempore of the Senate his determination that

(1) such use of force is necessary and appropriate to defend the national security interests of the United States against the threat posed by Iraq or enforce the United Nations Security Council resolutions referenced above) and

(2) reliance by the United States on further diplomatic means alone either (A) will not adequately protect the national security interests of the United States against the

threat posed by Iraq or (B) is not likely to lead to enforcement of the United Nations Security Council solutions referenced above.

(c) WAR POWERS RESOLUTION REQUIREMENTS.

(1) SPECIFIC STATUTORY AUTHORIZATION. Consistent with section 8(a)(l) of the War Powers Resolution, the Congress declares that this section is intended to constitute specific statutory authorization within the meaning of section 5(b) of the War Powers Resolution.

(2) APPLICABILITY OF OTHER REQUIREMENTS. Nothing in this resolution supersedes any requirement of the War Powers Resolution.

SECTION 3. REPORTS TO CONGRESS

(a) The president shall, at least once every 90 days, submit to the Congress a report on matters relevant to this joint resolution.

(b) Reports submitted in accordance with the War Powers Resolution or Public Law 102-1 will satisfy the requirements of subsection (a).

Remarks by President Bush, October 1, 2002

Q. Mr. President, the Permanent Five of the Security Council are meeting as you speak, and France is holding fast to its position of wanting a two-stage resolution. Are you willing to modify your position, sir, and come in line with France's position, in the spirit of cooperation, to achieve a tough U.N. resolution?

President Bush. What I won't accept is something that allows Saddam Hussein to continue to lie, deceive the world. He's been doing that for 11 years. For 11 years, he's told the United Nations Security Council, don't worry, I accept your resolution; then he doesn't follow through. And I'm just not going to accept something that is weak. It is not worth it. It's—the United Nations must show its backbone. And we will work with members of the Security Council to put a little calcium there, put calcium in the backbone, so this organization is able to more likely keep the peace as we go down the road.

Q. Are you suggesting the French proposal is weak?

President Bush. I'm suggesting that the same old stuff isn't going to work, John. And we won't accept the status quo. There needs to be a strong new resolution in order for us to make it clear to the world—and to Saddam Hussein, more importantly—that you must disarm.

And I look forward to looking at all their proposals. Just like we're dealing with everybody concerned, we will listen to points of view. But the final bottom line has got to be a very strong resolution, so that we don't fall into the same trap we have done for the last 11 years, which is nothing happens.

Saddam Hussein has thumbed his nose at the world. He's a threat to the neighborhood. He's a threat to Israel. He's a threat to the United States of America. And we're just going to have to deal with him. And the best way to deal with him is for the world to rise up and say, you disarm, and we'll disarm you. And if not—if, at the very end of the day, nothing happens—the United States, along with others, will act.

White House Press Briefing, October 1, 2002

Q. Yes, Ari, I have two questions for you. The first one has to do with the U.N. Russia, China and France continue to publicly say through high officials that they don't want military action, they want diplomatic steps to be taken. What happens—and I hope it's not a hypothetical. But if the U.N. does not give the President the resolution he and Tony Blair are asking for, does the President feel the resolutions already existing are enough for the United States to take unilateral military action?

Mr. Fleischer. Well, the President feels that the resolutions that currently exist have been ignored, and if the United Nations were to pass just a warmed-up version of the existing resolutions, then the United Nations is going to be proven to not take Saddam Hussein seriously, and that the United Nations is at risk of being considered the League of Nations.

They've tried it for 10 years and it hasn't worked, and the President believes deeply that it is time for the United Nations to speak differently, to speak effectively, and not to repeat the mistakes that have been made for a decade that have only seen Saddam Hussein continue to build up his weapons. And so that's where the President's focus is.

Now, as to where matters stand with China and France and Russia, the dialogue is continuing. There are still conversations taking place at various diplomatic levels, and I think you're going to see those conversations continue for the time-being.

* * * *

Q. Ari, is there concern here at the White House that the meetings taking place in Vienna between the weapons inspectors and representatives of the Iraqi government are undermining the President's efforts to get a single resolution out of the U.N.?

Mr. Fleischer. No, I have not heard that. I think there are some people who have had different thoughts about whether it should be one or two resolutions, people in other countries, with or without what's happening with Hans Blix in the meetings in Vienna. And those conversations will continue. But the President, again, thinks it's very important for the United Nations to act differently and not just repeat the mistakes that have been made for 10 years, that have allowed Saddam Hussein to think that he can act with impunity as he builds up his arms. And so the United States position remains that the best resolution—and what we are seeking—is one resolution.

* * * *

Q. Isn't it true the State Department is crafting behind the scenes a compromise that would have a two-stage resolution with a trigger—the second resolution with military force would kick in if Iraq doesn't comply with the first one?

Mr. Fleischer. The President has said clearly that he wants to see a one-resolution solution. He does not think that we need to send any signs of weakness to Saddam Hussein; that Saddam Hussein will exploit any opportunity he sees that gives him a signal that the world is not united, that the world is not speaking as one, and that the world is willing to give Saddam Hussein more time. Because more time for Saddam Hussein means more development of more weapons.

* * * *

Q. If I could do one more on a separate thing. Just going back to the subject of the congressional resolution, the President and you all have talked about the focus is disarming Saddam Hussein, disarming Iraq. Why then shouldn't the President solely have military force used for that focus, to disarm Saddam Hussein?

Mr. Fleischer. If you're saying, why should the United States retreat from the previous positions taken by the United Nations and the United States Congress, it's because retreating in the face of Saddam Hussein's threat is not an option.

Q. But it's unfair to really compare it, because the previous resolutions didn't authorize the use of force. You're talking about authorizing the use of military force. And my question is, if—

Mr. Fleischer. You know, that supposes that the people who passed regime change didn't mean it, or they thought that Saddam Hussein would term-limit himself. And when they passed regime change in 1998, you have to assume that they meant it. And they cited all those reasons in there about the Iraqi violations of the oil-for-food program, which by the way, he uses to build up his arms. So therefore, it's important to mention it, not to leave it unsaid. That's how he's getting his money for arms. They cited his support for terror, his repression of people, his hostility toward his neighbors. All of these were cited in 1998 by the Congress as why regime change is necessary.

Q. But they didn't authorize the use of force to bring about regime change.

Mr. Fleischer. Well, that's why I said, unless they didn't mean what they voted for in 1998—and I don't think Congress indicated that—or unless they thought Saddam Hussein was into term limits, they remain important criteria today.

Q. Ari, the CBO has new estimates that the war in Iraq would cost between $9 billion and $13 billion. Does the White House think that's too low?

Mr. Fleischer. Again, the President has not made any decisions about military action or what military option he might pursue. And so I think it's impossible to speculate. I can only say that the cost of a one-way ticket is substantially less than that. The cost of one bullet, if the Iraqi people take it on themselves, is substantially less than that. The cost of war is more than that. But there are many options that the President hopes the world and people of Iraq will exercise themselves of that gets rid of the threat. But it's impossible to say what the President options are militarily from a price tag, because he's made no decisions.

* * * *

Q. Is the White House advocating assassination as a possible option for Saddam Hussein?

Mr. Fleischer. I think that it's fair to say that the Iraqi regime is not satisfied with Saddam Hussein, that Saddam Hussein has created a great many enemies inside Iraq. And it is impossible to last forever as a brutal dictator who suppresses his own people, who tortures his own people, who deliberately brings women in public to be raped, so it can be witnessed by their families. He has not exactly created goodwill among the Iraqi people.

Q. If I could follow on that, would the White House like to see Saddam Hussein dead?

Mr. Fleischer. The policy is regime change. And that remains—and that remains the American position. Clearly, in the event that there is any type of military operation, command and control would, of course, be issues that would come up.

Q. Is the hope, though, that he ends up dead in all this?

Mr. Fleischer. Regime change is the policy, in whatever form it takes.

Q. I just want to re-ask again then, the question I've been asking for several weeks. Is the administration about to rescind the executive order prohibiting assassination of foreign leaders, and claim that he's an international terrorist, and in fact, put out a hit on him?

Mr. Fleischer. No. The policy remains in place, per the law.

Q. Why is there no consideration to rescinding that executive order?

Mr. Fleischer. It's just—because it's not come up as matter that I've heard discussed, Connie. And so I can't tell you why something doesn't get discussed.

Q. Could you ask?

Mr. Fleischer. I don't really think it's an issue. The policy remains regime change, as expressed by the Congress.

* * * *

Q. What is the administration's position on what kind of access inspectors should have to presidential palaces in Iraq?

Mr. Fleischer. Unfettered access, unconditional access, anybody, anywhere.

Q. And that means no prior notice, no—not a requirement that they be accompanied by diplomats?

Mr. Fleischer. I can only express it as plain as that. Unfettered, unconditional, any time, and anywhere.

Q. Current U.N. resolutions embraced—a 1998 resolution embraced an agreement between Secretary General Kofi Annan and Saddam Hussein that told them they would give prior notice and they would be accompanied by inspectors. Is that one of the reasons that you have to have a new U.N. resolution?

Mr. Fleischer. Absolutely. This is one of the reasons that the existing inspection regime has not worked. Keep in mind, when the Western ear hears "presidential palace," you tend to think of a place in which a leader sleeps—rather a legitimate purpose. That's not what's going on here. These are places that Saddam Hussein doesn't even go to. These are government facilities, government property, where who knows what is going on, and there's a good reason Saddam Hussein does not want people to go there and take a look at these facilities, even if he never sleeps there.

And that's why the existing regime has been a regime that, for 10 years, Saddam Hussein has been able to play cat-and-mouse with the world. And the President thinks the time has come now for the United Nations to do something different, to act differently, so that we don't repeat those same mistakes.

Q. So a new U.N. resolution, the one the U.S. favors, would clear away all the old underbrush and say simply that inspectors have the right to go anywhere, anytime, get at anyplace, no prior notice, no accompaniment by diplomats?

Mr. Fleischer. Here are the three criteria the United States is seeking in a new resolution that would be tough and effective and different. One, it would make plain for the world to see what Saddam Hussein has violated. Two, it would call on Saddam Hussein to cease his violations of those provisions. And, three, it would make clear what will happen if Saddam Hussein fails to cease his violations.

* * * *

Q. Ari, back on Saddam's travel plans and his retirement plans, what steps has the administration taken to encourage other nations to sort of arrange an easy out for this situation?

Mr. Fleischer. Well, I think this is something that Secretary Rumsfeld has talked about before. My point being, never underestimate the yearning of people to stop being tortured, to stop being suppressed. Don't overestimate the support there is for Saddam Hussein within Iraq. Don't take this as a prediction of things to come, because I can't possibly make predictions of things to come. But don't overestimate Saddam Hussein's support from his own people.

Events will go where events will go. The point the President makes is that the free world needs to be prepared to deal with somebody who has such a history of developing weapons for the purpose of using weapons, and in the process, he has separated himself from the country. And that's why Congress called it the Iraqi Liberation Act.

* * * *

Q. Ari, could I just clarify the one bullet line—is the White House from this podium advocating the assassination of Saddam Hussein by his own people, by his military?

Mr. Fleischer. No, the question was about potential costs and different scenarios for costs. And I just cited the fact that Saddam Hussein has survived as a result of the repression and suppression of his own people, and that's a reality about what life is like inside Iraq.

Q. But I'm not asking you a question about costs. I'm asking you if you intend to advocate from that podium that some Iraqis, person put a bullet in his head?

Mr. Fleischer. Regime change is welcome in whatever form that it takes.

Q. So the answer is, yes?

Mr. Fleischer. Thank you. Regime change is welcome in whatever form it takes.

Remarks by Secretary of State Powell, October 1, 2002

Good evening, ladies and gentlemen. I wanted to say a few words about the developments in Vienna today. Let me begin by saying that let there be no doubt in anyone's mind that the United States will continue to pursue a new U.N. resolution with the Security Council. We believe strongly that we have to keep moving in this direction because, as we have seen in the last several weeks, pressure works, and we have to keep the pressure up.

A new U.N. resolution will give Dr. Blix and the UNMOVIC team and the IAEA the most rigid procedures, the highest standards for Iraq to meet in order to satisfy the international community that they do not have or are not developing weapons of mass destruction and that which they do have can be destroyed by UNMOVIC. We will not be satisfied with Iraqi half-truths or Iraqi compromises or Iraqi efforts to get us back into the same swamp that they took the United Nations into back in 1998.

Pressure works. We're going to keep it up. We're going to work with our partners in the Security Council to put in place a new resolution, a new resolution that also has to have associated with it consequences for failure on the part of the Iraqis to act and to respond to the requirements of the international community. That's what makes this situation different and that's why we need a new resolution, so that we can have consequences associated with failure to perform on the part of the Iraqi Government.

We look forward to receiving a briefing from Dr. Blix, as a member of the Security Council, when he briefs the Security Council later this week. Dr. Blix is doing a fine job, but he needs to be in receipt of additional guidance and instructions from the Security Council in the form of new resolution language. And so we will continue to work with our Security Council colleagues to come up with such language in the form of a resolution.

We have to be mindful of what we have seen over the last several weeks: a firm position taken by the President of the United States, firm resolve on the part of the international community that we will not turn away from Iraq's continued violation of existing resolutions. And the way to make sure that that is the case is to put down a new, strong, tough resolution of what we want, not what Iraq wants, but what the international community must have to deal with this issue of weapons of mass destruction. And we must link in with that resolution consequences if there is continued violation of earlier resolutions on all sorts of subjects, as well as any violation of this new resolution.

So we will continue to drive forward on the track that we started on the 12th of September when President Bush gave his very, very important and vital speech before the United Nations General Assembly.

Q. Mr. Secretary, about ten days ago you said that if the U.N. inspectors prepared to go back without a U.N. resolution, the United States would try to thwart that. Could you elaborate on what you meant by "thwart" and does that remain U.S. policy?

Secretary Powell. The inspection team, UNMOVIC, is an agent of the Security Council. We are a member of the Security Council. Our position right now is that UNMOVIC cannot simply go back in under the former terms of reference. We can even see today that there were still places that are off limits, that were not talked about, that were not dealt with. There are still issues in debate. And so we don't want to get into a negotiating situation with the Iraqis under these old terms. That's why we need a new resolution with clear terms, tough terms, high standards, because we are determined to solve this problem once and for all.

And therefore, within the Security Council, I hope we will have discussions over the next couple of weeks—beginning today, frankly, we had discussions in New York today on the elements of a resolution—with different points of view being heard. But I hope that as a result of that process we will come up with strong new instructions for Dr. Blix, and Dr. Blix, as an agent of the Security Council, will carry out what the Security Council instructs him to do. And that's exactly what Dr. Blix has said and that's what he said in his press conference today and what he told the Iraqis. He was discussing modalities of inspection today, but he also made it clear that he is waiting to see whether or not he gets new instructions from the Security Council. And our position is that he should get such new instructions in the form of a new resolution.

Q. Mr. Secretary, could the discussions with the Iraqis have come after the approval of a new resolution?

Secretary Powell. It was up to Dr. Blix to work out certain technical details and modalities, which is what he did. But as Dr. Blix made it clear, the only discussions he could have was on the basis of the old resolutions. But we have made it clear that those old resolutions are what got us in trouble in the first place.

So we believe that Dr. Blix, in order to do his job well, is deserving of new instructions, strong instructions, and the strongest support possible from the Security Council in the form of a new Security Council resolution that is not going to be negotiated with the Iraqi Government but will be debated among the Security Council members, and I hope will be agreed to. And that will be the instructions that Dr. Blix will carry out, and the AIEA.

Q. Mr. Secretary, if it doesn't go your way, is the State Department planning to draft or in the process of drafting a backup resolution, a second resolution, if it comes to that?

Secretary Powell. We have a resolution before our colleagues in the Security Council. We haven't tabled it. Informal discussions are taking place. And as you have heard me say on many occasions before, it's a resolution that talks about the violations that Iraq has committed over the years; two, what Iraq must do in terms of an inspection regime, a tough inspection regime, not negotiated with them but imposed upon them, as it should be; and finally, we believe in that resolution there should be a statement of the consequences that might flow from continued violation.

As you know, there are other members of the Security Council who would prefer to deal with that consequences issue in a separate resolution, and they are entitled to their view and we will discuss their view within the Council. But we have our position and it's the position we're holding to.

Q. Mr. Secretary, there were some countries, of course France and Russia, that didn't want a resolution and wanted to see what comes out of these inspections. How much progress have you made on convincing them that there should be a resolution at all? Do you have the agreement of Russia, France and China that there should be a resolution with new, stronger standards, including full access also to presidential sites? Do you have that already?

Secretary Powell. We have made some progress and we have heard some strong views coming back from some of our partners, and we will work all this out in the course of our negotiations. What I think everybody understands is that this is not something we can turn away from.

Secondly, the old regime did not work. The old inspection regime did not work. They tied it up in knots. And before we declare that everything is okay today because of two days' worth of discussions on technical modalities, not one inspector has stepped foot in Iraq and not one thing has changed since 1998. And we are absolutely convinced that we can make the case that a new resolution with tough standards is appropriate, with consequences associated with further violation so that we're not back here a year from now talking about this all over again.

I think there's a common understanding among the Security Council members of these elements. There are discussions taking place and there are debates and different points of view as to how these elements should be packaged and what further referral should be made to the Security Council. And that's what the debate revolves around and what the elements should be in the inspection regime, and there is discussion and debate about that.

Q. Is there a difference of view about presidential sites being fully open?

Secretary Powell. All sites. The Iraqis are the ones who said without conditions. The Iraqis are the ones who said unfettered. But they're always shaving. They're always shaping what they said yesterday the next day. And so this is what we cannot allow to have happen this time, where they are able to pick and choose and say one thing one day, something else the next day. What we have to do is speak with a loud, clear, coherent voice from the United Nations Security Council, and that is what Iraq will have to do and those are the instructions that will be given to Dr. Blix, and we will see what happens after that.

So I think there's an understanding that we have to deal with this now and not next year, and to deal with it now you need to have the strongest resolution we can come up with and we have to have consequences associated with continued violation, and especially violation, obviously, of a new resolution.

One more.

Q. Mr. Secretary, what Dr. Blix did today, or what he said he did, was to secure Iraq's commitment on cooperation under the old rules, the already existing resolutions. After the adoption of the new resolution, do you think that Mr. Blix's team will have to talk again with the Iraqis to make sure that they will agree to these new terms? And if so, then wasn't today's meeting in Vienna useless?

Secretary Powell. Dr. Blix has done an excellent job and he cleared out quite a bit of the underbrush that existed with the old resolutions and might give us something to work with on the new resolutions. The Iraqis made some concessions, but they made—in other areas they made no concessions. It was the same old—the same old stuff. And so we want to have a fuller discussion with Dr. Blix to see what he thinks was accomplished, but we have made it clear that we do not believe the inspection regime that existed previously is adequate to the demands of the day and adequate to the challenge we're facing right now with continued Iraqi intransigence.

Q. Mr. Secretary, I just want to clarify something, if I can. Will the United States work to prevent the return of inspectors until a new resolution is passed? And also, is it now a nonstarter for the—is a two-resolution solution a no-go for the United States?

Secretary Powell. What I've said is that we're pressing forward on a one-resolution solution. We think it's best. We think we've got a convincing case of that, and so do our United Kingdom colleagues. Other nations have a different point of view. That's why you have consultations. That's why you have a negotiation. We want to hear those points of view and we want to see what can be achieved and we will see which argument prevails.

With respect to the inspectors going back in, there is nothing—there is no magic calendar as to when they have to go in. They should go in when they have the authority to do their job. And we believe that Dr. Blix and his team of professionals are deserving of the strongest possible authority and the ability to do their job and to do it right, and that will only come from a new resolution that keeps the pressure up on Iraq and a new resolution that has linked to it consequences so that we can get to the bottom of this once and for all.

Q. Are you prepared to prevent the return—their return?

Secretary Powell. I've really answered your question. We do not believe that they should go back in under the old set of resolutions and under the old inspection regime, and therefore we do not believe they should go in until they have new instructions in the form of a new resolution. Thank you.

Remarks by President Bush, Representative Hastert (R-IL), Representative Gephardt (D-MO), Senator Warner (R-VA), Senator Lieberman (D-CT) and Senator McCain (R-AZ), October 2, 2002

The following remarks were made at the White House upon introduction of a Resolution in the House and Senate authorizing the use of force in Iraq.

Thank you all for coming. Today I'm joined by leaders of the House and the Senate from both political parties to show our unity of purpose in confronting a gathering threat to the security of America and to the future of peace.

I want to thank in particular Speaker Hastert, and Leader Gephardt, Leader Lott, for the tremendous work in building bipartisan support on this vital issue. I also want to thank Senators Warner, Lieberman, McCain, and Bayh for introducing this resolution which we've agreed to on the floor of the Senate this morning.

The text of our bipartisan resolution is clear and it is strong. The statement of support from the Congress will show to friend and enemy alike the resolve of the United

States. In Baghdad, the regime will know that full compliance with all U.N. Security demands is the only choice, and that time remaining for that choice is limited.

On its present course, the Iraqi regime is a threat of unique urgency. We know the treacherous history of the regime. It has waged a war against its neighbors; it has sponsored and sheltered terrorists; it has developed weapons of mass death; it has used them against innocent men, women and children. We know the designs of the Iraqi regime. In defiance of pledges to the U.N., it has stockpiled biological and chemical weapons. It is rebuilding the facilities used to make those weapons.

U.N. inspectors believe that Iraq could have produce enough biological and chemical agent to kill millions of people. The regime has the scientists and facilities to build nuclear weapons, and is seeking the materials needed to do so.

We know the methods of this regime. They buy time with hollow promises. They move incriminating evidence to stay ahead of inspectors. They concede just enough to escape—to escape punishment, and then violate every pledge when the attention of the world is turned away.

We also know the nature of Iraq's dictator. On his orders, opponents have been decapitated and their heads displayed outside their homes. Women have been systematically raped as a method of intimidation. Political prisoners are made to watch their own children being tortured. The dictator is a student of Stalin, using murder as a tool of terror and control within his own cabinet, within his own army, even within his own family. We will not leave the future of peace and the security of America in the hands of this cruel and dangerous man.

None of us here today desire to see military conflict, because we know the awful nature of war. Our country values life, and never seeks war unless it is essential to security and to justice. America's leadership and willingness to use force, confirmed by the Congress, is the best way to ensure compliance and avoid conflict. Saddam must disarm, period. If, however, he chooses to do otherwise, if he persists in his defiance, the use of force may become unavoidable.

The course of action may bring many sacrifices. Yet delay, indecision and inaction could lead to a massive and sudden horror. By timely and resolute action, we can defend ourselves and shape a peaceful future. Together with the Congress, I will do everything necessary to protect and defend our country.

In accepting this responsibility, we also serve the interests and the hopes of the Iraqi people. They are a great and gifted people, with an ancient and admirable culture, and they would not choose to be ruled by violence and terror. The people of Iraq are the daily victims of Saddam Hussein's oppression. They will be the first to benefit when the world's demands are met. Americans believe all men and women deserve to be free. And as we saw in the fall of the Taliban, men and women celebrate freedom's arrival.

The United States will work with other nations. We'll work with other nations to bring Saddam to account. We'll work with other nations to help the Iraqi people form a just government and a unified country. And should force be required, the United States will help rebuild a liberated Iraq.

Countering Iraq's threat is also a central commitment on the war on terror. We know Saddam Hussein has longstanding and ongoing ties to international terrorists. With the support and shelter of a regime, terror groups become far more lethal. Aided by a terrorist network, an outlaw regime can launch attacks while concealing its involvement. Even a dictator is not suicidal, but he can make use of men who are. We must confront both terror cells and terror states, because they are different faces of the same evil.

I brought this issue to the attention of the world, and many, many countries share our determination to confront this threat. We're not alone. The issue is now before the United States Congress. This debate will be closely watched by the American people, and this debate will be remembered in history. We didn't ask for this challenge as a country, but we will face it, and we will face it together.

As the vote nears, I urge all members of Congress to consider this resolution with the greatest of care. The choice before them could not be more consequential. I'm confident that members of both parties will choose wisely.

I appreciate members of Congress who are willing to address you all, starting with the Speaker of the House, Denny Hastert.

Representative Hastert. Thank you, Mr. President. This is a bipartisan agreement. The White House deserves credit for working with Republicans and Democrats to achieve this historic resolution. The resolution does not tie the President's hands, it gives him flexibility he needs to get the job done. This resolution does not require the President to get United Nations approval before proceeding. It supports the President's effort to work with the United Nations, but it doesn't require him to seek U.N. approval first. If the President determines that he has to act unilaterally to protect American people, he can, and he has the ability to do that.

I think the bottom line for all of us here is, we've been through this process, we've been through September 11th. We visited Ground Zero. We've been at the Pentagon the day after. And we don't want that type of tragedy to happen in this country again. And we will do everything in our power to prevent it from happening again.

Representative Gephardt. Good afternoon. Let me begin by saying that the most important issue the President and the Congress ever address is that of life and death. The first responsibility of our government is to protect the security of our nation and our citizens.

In our view, Iraq's use and continuing development of weapons of mass destruction, combined with efforts of terrorists to acquire such weapons, pose a unique and dangerous threat to our national security. Many of us believe that we need to deal with this threat diplomatically if we can, militarily if we must.

Every member of Congress must make their own decision on the level of threat posed by Iraq and what to do to respond to that threat. I've said many times to my caucus that each member should be guided by his or her own conscience, free from others trying to politicize the issue or questioning others' motives.

In response to the President's desire for congressional support and, in keeping with our constitutional responsibilities, I have worked to draft a resolution that reflects the views of a large bipartisan segment of Congress. My underlying goal in this process has been to ensure that Iraq is disarmed, and to lessen the likelihood that weapons of mass destruction can be passed to terrorists.

Over the past several days, I have solicited views from all the members of my caucus and have negotiated with the administration to secure a number of important improvements that reflect these views. These improvements include: support for and prioritization of U.S. diplomatic efforts at the United Nations; limitations on the scope of the authorization; presidential determinations to Congress before our Armed Forces may be used against Iraq. These include assurances by the President that he has exhausted diplomatic means to address this threat, and that any military action against Iraq will not undermine our ongoing efforts in the war against terrorism. Regular consultations with, and reporting to Congress on the administration's efforts to address this threat and post-conflict contingencies in Iraq.

You all know that we have a lot of differences on many issues. We disagree on many domestic issues. But this is the most important thing that we do. This should not be about politics. We have to do what is right for the security of our nation and the safety of all Americans.

We're about to begin a great debate in the United States Congress. Part of the majesty of our democratic achievement of a democratic governance is that on issues of war and peace, life and death, we have entrusted those decisions not just to the President, but to the Congress as a co-equal branch of this government. We now take that solemn obligation, and I believe that when the debate is finished, we will have discharged that responsibility in the highest tradition of this country and our great people.

Senator Warner. Mr. President, colleagues, America has always led in the cause of freedom. And now, in this century, this resolution marks, I think, the most significant step in fulfilling America's history in carrying out our responsibilities.

Mr. President, to you, and to Prime Minister Blair who has joined you, great, great gratitude is owed not only by the people of the United States, but by the people of the world, for your efforts to bring to the forefront this issue, and to put it squarely on the United Nations to fulfill their responsibilities, and to call upon the Congress for their support.

We do that here today, Mr. President. And I'm very privileged to stand here with leaders—Senator Lott, Senator Lieberman, Senator McCain—that led the '91 effort in that resolution. Mr. President, we delivered for your father. We will deliver for you. And I predict, while the vote was a margin of five in '91, it will be a stronger bipartisan margin this time.

And as the Congress closed the ranks behind that historic debate in '91, so will the Congress close its ranks such that this nation can speak with one voice, the Congress and our President united. Thank you, sir.

Senator Lieberman. There is no more fateful, important, or difficult responsibility that the Constitution gives members of Congress than to decide when, whether, and how to authorize the President as Commander-in-Chief to go to war. Mr. President, in your eloquent, powerful, and convincing statement this morning, you have reminded us, and I believe the American people, about why this is such a circumstance.

I have felt for more than a decade now that every additional day that Saddam Hussein is in power in Iraq is an additional day of danger for the Iraqi people, for his neighbors in the region, particularly for the people and military of the United States of America, and indeed for the people of the world. And that is why I am grateful for the opportunity to stand with my colleagues from both parties, and both Houses, and with you, Mr. President, in offering this resolution to authorize you to take military action to protect the region and the world from Iraq under Saddam Hussein, and to enforce the resolutions that are relevant of the United Nations.

There are those who say that this represents hurried or precipitous action, that we should give Saddam and the Iraqi government another chance. The record shows that for the last 10 years, we have tried—the world has tried—in just about every way— diplomatic, economic and otherwise, except military, in the end—to convince Saddam Hussein to live by the rules of international law and civilization. They've not worked.

The moment of truth has arrived. For Saddam Hussein, this is his last chance, and the best chance for the international community to come together behind the rule of law, and to show that resolutions of the United Nations are worth more than the paper that they are written on.

I am truly hopeful that the broad bipartisan support that I see here today behind you, Mr. President, as our Commander-in-Chief, will strengthen the work of your Secretary of State and your administration at the United Nations. I am convinced, as impressive as this group is here today, though there will be a serious debate ahead in both Houses of Congress, and amendments will certainly be offered in the Senate—as is the right and responsibility of those who disagree with this amendment—that in the end, those who disagree with this resolution—in the end, this resolution will pass in the Senate with a very large, bipartisan majority.

And that, today, is the best hope for a stronger America and for a life for the American people that is safer.

Senator McCain. I'd like to thank the President for his leadership in addressing a challenge that many of us believe should have been addressed at least four years ago. I'd like to thank Speaker Hastert, Leader Gephardt, Senator Lott for their leadership and the efforts they've made to bring this issue to the Congress and to the American people.

I'd like to also thank my friends, Senator Lieberman, Senator Warner, and Senator Bayh. Because of their efforts, there's now identical resolutions in both Houses of Congress. They will be debated, they will be discussed, and I believe the American people and the Congress will be enlightened, educated, and better off for having a debate that I know will be respectful of the views of all members of Congress.

The Constitution of the United States designates the President of the United States as Commander-in-Chief. The Congress of the United States plays a role, and I believe that this process we are about to embark on is the appropriate role that Congress should carry out its responsibilities. But at the end of the day, the final, most serious responsibility of sending young American men and women into harm's way rests with the President of the United States. And I am convinced that an overwhelming, significant majority of both Houses of Congress, speaking for their constituents, will provide the President of the United States with the endorsement and the support that he needs, if necessary, as a last resort, to preserve America's security by a regime change in Iraq. I thank him for his leadership.

Remarks by Vice President Cheney, October 2, 2002

For every bit of progress that we've achieved all of us appreciate that we're still closer to the beginning of this conflict than we are to its end. The President and I start every day with a briefing on the threats facing our country. There can be no doubt that our enemies are determined to do further significant harm to the American people. Nine-eleven and its aftermath have given us a clear picture of the true ambitions of the global terror network, as well as the growing danger of weapons of mass destruction. In that changing environment, as always, we must take the facts as they are and think anew about the requirements of national security.

In the days of the Cold War we were able to manage the threat with strategies of deterrence and containment. But it's a lot tougher to deter enemies who have no country to defend. And containment is not possible when dictators obtain weapons of mass destruction and are prepared to share them with terrorists.

For this new century it's very clear what our national security strategy must be. We must maintain a military second to none, and when necessary we must preempt grave threats to America before they materialize.

We've already found confirmation that the Al Qaeda terrorists are pursuing weapons of mass destruction. At the same time there's a danger of terror groups joining together with the regimes that have or are seeking to build such weapons. In Iraq, we know that Saddam Hussein is pressing forward with these capabilities. He has used weapons of mass destruction both in his war against Iran and against his own people.

The government of the United States will not look the other way as threats gather against the American people. We will continue working closely with members of Congress on both sides of the aisle to build a strong bipartisan resolution. And, of course, just this afternoon the President was able to announce—with a bipartisan leadership—that we had, in fact, reached agreement on a resolution that will be introduced in both Houses, sponsored by a cross-section of members of both parties in Congress. We're confident that when Congress passes that, friends and enemies alike will understand the unity and the determination of our country.

We're also consulting with the leaders of many nations. In his speech to the United Nations General Assembly, President Bush made clear to the international community the kinds of challenges we must face together. He reminded the U.N. that Saddam Hussein made a series of commitments after his defeat in Desert Storm and that he has broken every single one of them.

Saddam agreed to cease at once the repression of his people, yet the systematic violation of human rights continues in Iraq to this day. He agreed to return all prisoners from Kuwait and other lands, yet more than 600 are still unaccounted for, including one American pilot. Saddam Hussein agreed to renounce all involvement with terrorism and to permit no terrorist organizations to operate in Iraq, yet Iraq continues to shelter and support terrorist organizations. Dissidents abroad are targeted for murder. The Iraqi regime has attempted to assassinate the Emir of Kuwait and a former President of the United States.

Saddam Hussein promised the United Nations that he would destroy and cease further development of weapons of mass destruction and long-range missiles, and that he would submit to unrestricted inspections. He has flatly broken these pledges, producing chemical and biological weapons and aggressively pursuing a nuclear weapons program while also working to develop long-range missiles.

Empty words from the Iraqi regime will not cause us to ignore history or reality. Saddam Hussein has spent more than a decade in complete defiance of all the demands of the United Nations. The question for the international community is whether Security Counsel resolutions will be enforced or disregarded without consequence—whether the United Nations will be effective or irrelevant.

As for the United States, the President has made our position very clear: we will work with the United Nations to meet our common challenge; the Security Council resolutions are to be enforced or action will be unavoidable. We must and we will defend our freedom and our security.

Remarks by United Nations Secretary-General Annan, October 2, 2002

Q. Just a quick question about Iraq, if I might. Some of the permanent five countries of the Security Council want to put presidential sites, nullify all of the agreements that were made on presidential sites, and put that back on the table for clear and unfettered access. What is your feeling about that Sir?

Secretary-General Annan. I think the [Security] Council has a resolution before it and they are all reviewing it, and I think we should wait to see what the Council eventually comes up with. But until the Council comes up with new guidelines, Mr. Blix is guided by existing resolutions, and it is on that basis that he has been dealing with the Iraqis.

Q. Has anyone from the permanent five delegations or from the Iraqi delegation contacted you about that matter?

Secretary-General Annan. I think it is really an issue for the Council, I mean, the Council endorsed the arrangements that were made and it is up to the Council—as a master of its own deliberations—and they can decide what they want to do.

Q. Do you think that talk about assassination—putting a bullet in the head of a leader—as speculated by the White House spokesman is helpful to the dialogue that's going on now?

Secretary-General Annan. Well, we at the U.N. don't get involved with that, and we don't operate on that basis.

Remarks by President Bush, October 3, 2002

We'll determine whether or not the U.N. Security Council wants to live up to its obligations. After all, for 11 long years the dictator in Iraq, the man who has gassed his own people, gassed people in his neighborhood, the man who's expressly—expressed his hatred for America and our friends and allies—we'll see whether or not the United Nations will be the United Nations or the League of Nations when it comes to dealing with this man who for 11 years has thumbed his nose at resolution after resolution after resolution after resolution.

My intent, of course, is for the United Nations to do its job. I think it'll make it easier for us to keep the peace. My intent is for the world to understand that the obligation is up to Saddam Hussein to disarm like he said he would do. My intent is to put together a vast coalition of countries who understand the threat of Saddam Hussein.

The military option is my last choice, not my first. It's my last choice. But Saddam has got to understand, the United Nations must know, that the will of this country is strong.

Yesterday, I had the honor of standing on the steps of the White House, at the Rose Garden. Republican leader and Democrat leader alike—Speaker Hastert and Leader Gephardt, Trent Lott and Joe Lieberman, John McCain and Evan Bayh, member after member—who have committed to join with the administration to send a clear signal that when it comes to defending our freedom, the United States of America will stand united and stand strong.

The choice is up to the United Nations to show its resolve. The choice is up to Saddam Hussein to fulfill its word—his word. And if neither of them acts, the United States, in deliberate fashion, will lead a coalition to take away the world's worst weapons from one of the world's worst leaders. (Applause.)

I say that because I have a deep desire for peace, peace in America, peace in the Middle East. I believe peace is possible. I believe that out of the evil done to America can come some really—some good. And one of the good is international peace, I believe that.

And, therefore, I will continue to speak clearly about good and evil, continue to renounce terrorism in any form, continue to lead the world toward peace, peace not only for ourselves, but because we value all human life, peace in parts of the world that have given up on peace.

Remarks by Illinois State Senator Obama, October 02, 2002

State Senator Barack Obama delivered his remarks in Chicago, IL.

Good afternoon. Let me begin by saying that although this has been billed as an anti-war rally, I stand before you as someone who is not opposed to war in all circumstances. The Civil War was one of the bloodiest in history, and yet it was only through the crucible of the sword, the sacrifice of multitudes, that we could begin to perfect this union, and drive the scourge of slavery from our soil. I don't oppose all wars.

My grandfather signed up for a war the day after Pearl Harbor was bombed, fought in Patton's army. He saw the dead and dying across the fields of Europe; he heard the stories of fellow troops who first entered Auschwitz and Treblinka. He fought in the name of a larger freedom, part of that arsenal of democracy that triumphed over evil, and he did not fight in vain. I don't oppose all wars.

After September 11th, after witnessing the carnage and destruction, the dust and the tears, I supported this administration's pledge to hunt down and root out those who would slaughter innocents in the name of intolerance, and I would willingly take up arms myself to prevent such tragedy from happening again. I don't oppose all wars. And I know that in this crowd today, there is no shortage of patriots, or of patriotism.

What I am opposed to is a dumb war. What I am opposed to is a rash war. What I am opposed to is the cynical attempt by Richard Perle and Paul Wolfowitz and other armchair, weekend warriors in this administration to shove their own ideological agendas down our throats, irrespective of the costs in lives lost and in hardships borne.

What I am opposed to is the attempt by political hacks like Karl Rove to distract us from a rise in the uninsured, a rise in the poverty rate, a drop in the median income - to distract us from corporate scandals and a stock market that has just gone through the worst month since the Great Depression. That's what I'm opposed to. A dumb war. A rash war. A war based not on reason but on passion, not on principle but on politics. Now let me be clear—I suffer no illusions about Saddam Hussein. He is a brutal man. A ruthless man. A man who butchers his own people to secure his own power. He has repeatedly defied U.N. resolutions, thwarted U.N. inspection teams, developed chemical and biological weapons, and coveted nuclear capacity. He's a bad guy. The world, and the Iraqi people, would be better off without him.

But I also know that Saddam poses no imminent and direct threat to the United States, or to his neighbors, that the Iraqi economy is in shambles, that the Iraqi military a fraction of its former strength, and that in concert with the international community he can be contained until, in the way of all petty dictators, he falls away into the dustbin of history. I know that even a successful war against Iraq will require a U.S. occupation of undetermined length, at undetermined cost, with undetermined consequences. I know that an invasion of Iraq without a clear rationale and without strong international support will only fan the flames of the Middle East, and encourage the worst, rather than best, impulses of the Arab world, and strengthen the recruitment arm of Al Qaeda. I am not opposed to all wars. I'm opposed to dumb wars.

So for those of us who seek a more just and secure world for our children, let us send a clear message to the President today. You want a fight, President Bush? Let's finish the fight with Bin Laden and Al Qaeda, through effective, coordinated intelligence, and a shutting down of the financial networks that support terrorism, and a homeland security program that involves more than color-coded warnings. You want a fight, President Bush?

Let's fight to make sure that the U.N. inspectors can do their work, and that we vigorously enforce a non-proliferation treaty, and that former enemies and current allies like Russia safeguard and ultimately eliminate their stores of nuclear material, and that nations like Pakistan and India never use the terrible weapons already in their possession, and that the arms merchants in our own country stop feeding the countless wars that rage across the globe. You want a fight, President Bush?

Let's fight to make sure our so-called allies in the Middle East, the Saudis and the Egyptians, stop oppressing their own people, and suppressing dissent, and tolerating corruption and inequality, and mismanaging their economies so that their youth grow up without education, without prospects, without hope, the ready recruits of terrorist cells. You want a fight, President Bush? Let's fight to wean ourselves off Middle East oil, through an energy policy that doesn't simply serve the interests of Exxon and Mobil. Those are the battles that we need to fight. Those are the battles that we willingly join. The battles against ignorance and intolerance. Corruption and greed. Poverty and despair.

The consequences of war are dire, the sacrifices immeasurable. We may have occasion in our lifetime to once again rise up in defense of our freedom, and pay the wages of war. But we ought not—we will not—travel down that hellish path blindly. Nor should we allow those who would march off and pay the ultimate sacrifice, who would prove the full measure of devotion with their blood, to make such an awful sacrifice in vain.

White House Press Briefing, October 3, 2002

Q. Ari, the word has gone out that the President is getting increasingly impatient with the pace of progress, or the lack of progress at the United Nations Security Council on a single resolution. Yesterday, French President Jacques Chirac declared that he is "totally hostile" to the idea of a resolution that would automatically authorize the use of force. What's the President's message to the French President today?

Mr. Fleischer. Well, in regard to the first part, I noticed there was a report on the news last night that didn't cite anybody that made that case, that the White House is impatient or the White House—I'll just cite what Secretary Powell said this morning. Secretary Powell said that he's optimistic that we'll be able to get an agreement from the United Nations Security Council. And the President believes that it is vital for the Security Council to act and speak differently than it has over the last 10 years, and that he believes, as a result of the diplomatic efforts that are underway, that indeed will be the result. The President just could not imagine that the United Nations Security Council would become irrelevant by letting the status quo remain.

So the diplomatic conversations are going to continue with our allies—with China, with Russia, with France and other members of the Security Council. And I think what you're seeing is, diplomacy unfold. And in the end, the President remains optimistic the outcome will be solid.

Q. The art of diplomacy suggests that everyone has to move a little bit. The President has shown no sign of that so far.

Mr. Fleischer. How do you know that?

Q. Is he willing to move toward the French position?

Mr. Fleischer. How do you know the President has not moved?

Q. Because he hasn't signed on to France's idea of a two-step resolution.

Mr. Fleischer. I submit to you that much of these negotiations are, as you would expect, diplomatic conversations that take place in private. And as you know, the President said—has a resolution that he's been working on with the British. And of course, we are amenable to working with other nations on the exact wording in the resolution.

But the point the President made in his speech to the United Nations is that it is imperative for the United Nations to act so that Saddam Hussein knows that he needs to disarm.

Q. Ari, did the President say today that he knows war, in one of the speeches, or he's been a part of a war?

Mr. Fleischer. No, what the President has said, Helen, the only thing I could think of that you may have picked up, is the President in his meetings with congressional members and other, has said, with a lot of sadness, that he is the one, as Commander-in-Chief and as President, who in the course of the war in Afghanistan, has hugged the widows of those whose lives were lost in Afghanistan. And it's a role that he does not relish. It's one of the deepest burdens of the job.

Q. But he didn't say that he was involved in any war?

Mr. Fleischer. I've never heard him say that, Helen. He has talked about those who lost their lives in the war, and what it's like for the President to meet with the survivors, the families of people who have been killed in combat, and how difficult it is, how emotional it is, and that he doesn't look forward to ever having to do it again. But he also then—

Q. Well, why is he preaching a war with Iraq if he doesn't want to do it again?

Mr. Fleischer. Then he states how resolute he is to protect American lives.

Q. Does he have any idea of how many people would die in this war that he—

Mr. Fleischer. Helen, I don't know that anybody can tell you. Perhaps everything can be averted if—

Q. We don't even know how many died in Afghanistan. There's no casualty figures.

Mr. Fleischer. I think what the President is worried about is how many Americans will die if Saddam Hussein is successful in acquiring the nuclear weapons and weapons of mass destruction that he seeks, because he has a history of using the ones he gets.

* * * *

Q. Ari, why isn't the President impatient at the pace of progress at the U.N.? It's been three weeks since he gave his speech—

Mr. Fleischer. Because I think the President understands how the U.N. works. And when the President went up there he said that this would be a matter of days and weeks, not months. And it is not a matter of months. And so the President understands that diplomacy is a painstaking task and an important one. It's a serious task, and that's what you see going on up at the United Nations now.

* * * *

Q. Do you have a sense, though, of how many countries are lined up behind the President now—when the President talks about a "vast coalition", how many countries he has behind him?

Mr. Fleischer. I just will refer to the way the President has said it, and the President has said he'll be joined by many.

Q. And I just have two other follows, sorry. At the U.N., give us any sense of how close you all are to getting an agreement?

Mr. Fleischer. Let me try to give you a report about the U.N. Of course, there is a meeting underway, the United Nations Security Council, as we speak, and Hans Blix is reporting to the United Nations Security Council. Hans Blix will also be in Washington tomorrow at the State Department, and we welcome his visit to the State Department. The conversations with him are important.

At the Security Council, I think it's fair to say that there are a lot of loose ends that are being discussed. Secretary Annan said earlier today, "the Council is discussing whether or not the regime should not be"—the inspection regime—should not be tightened or strengthened—"should or should not be tightened or strengthened, to ensure that we don't repeat the weaknesses of the past." Those are Kofi Annan's words this morning.

There is widespread recognition in the Security Council that the existing regime failed to do the job—it failed to disarm Saddam Hussein, and it has left a threat in place. They are meeting now with Hans Blix to discuss what to do about these weaknesses in the past, as Kofi Annan called them. And we welcome this discussion, it's an important one. Tomorrow, the discussion will continue when Hans Blix comes to the State Department. And the United States thinks it's vital that if the inspectors are to return, they have the means and the ability and the will of the world to do their job.

Q. Final—and I have to ask—the Iraqi Vice President has said a way to resolve this would be a duel between President Bush and Saddam Hussein.

Mr. Fleischer. Yes, there can be no serious response to an irresponsible statement like that. I just want to point out that in the past, when Iraq had disputes, it invaded its neighbors. There were no duels; there were invasions. There was use of weapons of mass destruction and the military. That's how Iraq settles its disputes.

* * * *

Q. Ari, earlier with John, you said that you asked him—how do you know that the President hasn't shifted. And I understand that no White House Press Secretary ever

likes to talk about a shift in policy, but isn't the increasing use of "disarmament" as opposed to "regime change", isn't that—isn't that, in and of itself, a shift on the part of the President? And secondly—

Mr. Fleischer. Disarmament was the first statement the President made to the United Nations in New York. So I fail to see how something can be a shift when it's a repeat of a core message that the President has delivered to the world.

* * * *

Q. Yes, Ari, two-part question. First one has to do—you've been using the word "regime change" continually. Now the word "effective disarmament" is also popping up. Secretary Powell I think gave an interview to USA Today to which—correct me if I'm wrong—one of the implications was that if Saddam Hussein disarms himself in a way which the United States considers totally disarmament, he might remain in power. Is that a possibility?

Mr. Fleischer. That's not what the Secretary said. I think that's rather a stretch to think that's what the Secretary said. The Secretary basically repeated what the President said when he went up to New York at the United Nations. If you remember, the President, in his speech to the United Nations had, I think it was six paragraphs that began with the word "if," all describing that if the Iraqis wish peace, they will—and the President went through the list of the things they need to do—destroy weapons in support for terror, release and account for the POWs, and their illicit program that gets around their obligations in the Oil-For-Food Program.

The President said if that happens, it would signify a new openness and accountability from Iraq. But nothing that Secretary Powell said would give anybody the indication that Saddam Hussein has shown any willingness to conduct himself in a way that would do all of those things. If he did, he really wouldn't be the dictator that he has been. And I don't think anybody thinks that Saddam Hussein is changing.

* * * *

Q. Even if you acknowledge that the existing rules would only lead to additional mistakes being repeated, is there not a benefit to be gained from having inspectors looking around there now to see what they can find?

Mr. Fleischer. There's a real risk that would be taken in doing that, and showing Saddam Hussein that he's in charge, that he can run people around again, and that the world will not act. After he's done it for so long, this would be akin to the world saying, we don't mean what we say, you can do it again. You can give the visitors the runaround, and the world will do nothing. The President thinks that has happened for too long already.

Q. You've spoken of the need for diplomacy to take some time. Why wait for it? Why not get the inspectors back in?

Mr. Fleischer. The President thinks they should go in under the new auspices, so they can do their job. If they go in under the current regime, it is—it is a fool's errand to call them inspectors. They would be nothing more than tourists who get a runaround.

* * * *

Q. Given what we were just talking about, are you still expecting support from the Russians in the Security Council?

Mr. Fleischer. The President is optimistic, as Secretary Powell said he is optimistic, that at the end of the day the world will see the issue as he laid it out in New York, because the President cannot imagine the United Nations wants to make itself irrelevant.

Q. Is he going to be talking to Mr. Putin again?

Mr. Fleischer. Well, the conversations are continuing at many levels and I always do my best to try to report to you on the calls. Now, he hasn't spoken to him since the last time I reported it to you. But there are many conversations going on through the United Nations, through other diplomatic levels, through the State Department, as you would expect.

Q. Thank you. In the U.N. or any other coalition you would form, are you asking for financial and military support, as well as just verbal support? And also, if there is regime change, would you expect that oil contracts with other countries are canceled by Iraq at that point in time?

Mr. Fleischer. I can't speculate about any outcomes with that type of specificity. And I would say that the President has made it clear that it is important for the United Nations to act, through the Security Council. If they don't, the President has made perfectly plain that the United States and Britain and others will be part of a wide-ranging coalition that will help protect the world, and will do so in many ways. I can't go into a delineation of all of them. And we'll see what the events develop.

Q. In the administration's view, are there any circumstances under which Saddam Hussein could remain in power?

Mr. Fleischer. I think that anybody who thinks that the conditions that the President laid out in New York, which are the conditions that the world must honor in order to protect the peace, are actions that Saddam Hussein has shown any willingness to engage in over the last ten years. So unless somebody thinks that all of a sudden Saddam Hussein would change his ways, would become a reformer, would become a person who believes in freedom, who would cease his militaristic approach, I think they're going down a path that no one in the world agrees with.

Q. You're saying it's not likely that he would do what is necessary to remain in power, but—

Mr. Fleischer. I don't know—I don't know of a single person who has come to any type of judgment that Saddam Hussein would do that. And that is why the world faces such a threat from this man.

Q. But the administration's policy, if I understand it, has been that regime change is necessary because that is the only way, or the surest way, to make him disarm. But that there are other ways, as you pointed out in the President's "if" statements in his U.N. speech, that there are other ways that disarmament could be accomplished.

Mr. Fleischer. Well, you have two issues going on at the same time. You have the issues before the United Nations Security Council, which involve the world coming together and saying that the resolutions that passed that focus on disarmament, focus on abandonment of hostility as a way to handle relations with neighbors, cessation of repression of people within Iraq—all those issues—weapons of mass destruction development—need to be addressed per those U.N. Security Council resolutions.

Separately and apart, but equally important, you have the United States Congress' statement from 1998, which is likely to be echoed shortly in a big bipartisan vote in the House and Senate in the next week or so, saying that it should be the policy of the United States to support efforts to remove the regime headed by Saddam Hussein from power in Iraq and to promote the emergence of a democratic government to replace that regime. That, verbatim, are the words of the Congress, signed by President Clinton in 1998.

Q. So quite apart from efforts to disarm and whether or not they succeed, regime change is still in place—regardless of what happens on the disarmament front?

Mr. Fleischer. Regime change is the law of the land for the United States, as spoken by the Congress, signed by President Clinton and supported, of course, by President Bush.

Q. Ari, yesterday in the Rose Garden, Senator Warner harkened back to the '91 Gulf War resolution and he said, Mr. President, we delivered for your father and we'll deliver for you. I guess I had never thought of it in that way. Does the President think of this as a blood feud?

Mr. Fleischer. No, and I don't think that's at all what Senator Warner was saying, no. I think Senator Warner is pointing out that for 11 years, Saddam Hussein has been a constant menace to people who love freedom. And that's why the United States Congress in 1991 authorized the use of force, because Saddam Hussein invaded a sovereign country of Kuwait. That's what I think Senator Warner's reference was to. And the point is that, since that war ended, Saddam Hussein has engaged in even more of a militaristic approach by seeking to build up his weapons of mass destruction in absolute and total violation of the United Nations resolutions he swore to agree by, and the armistice that he signed as a result—as an agreement to end the war.

* * * *

Q. Ari, in an op-ed piece in the Washington Post today, Sandy Berger suggests dropping the threat of military action from the resolution the United States is presenting to the U.N. Security Council. Berger believes this would help its passage. Would the President accept such a compromise?

Mr. Fleischer. The President has made it clear that the resolution before the United Nations must include three things, and again those three things are to state that Iraq is not in compliance with its existing obligations to the world; what Iraq must do to come into compliance; and what the consequences will be to Iraq for failure to comply. The problem, in the President's judgment, is that if you remove that third provision, Iraq will have no incentive, none, none whatsoever, to change its behavior and disarm. They will continue in the same cat and mouse games they played throughout the '90s.

Remarks by United Nations Secretary-General Annan, October 3, 2002

Q. Mr. Secretary, the U.S. thinks that there should not be really inspections before a resolution. Officials have talked about thwarting inspections—using that type of language. What is your sense?

Secretary-General Annan. Well, I think the [Security] Council will be hearing from Mr. [Hans] Blix [Executive Chairman, U.N. Monitoring, Verification and Inspection Commission] this morning and I'm just going up to meet with Mr. Blix and [Mr. Mohamed] El Baradei [Director-General, International Atomic Energy Agency] who have just come from Vienna. Blix, until now, has been guided by approved Security Council resolutions. If the Council were to pass a new resolution giving him fresh guidelines, he will have to factor that in before he continues with his work. It would be up to the Council today or the coming week to determine what the next stage would be. Of course, they are discussing a new resolution which may be passed. But Blix, in the meantime, continues his preparations.

Q. Normally, it would be a Council matter, but you are involved, you're named, you're the MOU. So do you think there's enough to allow the inspections to continue and let other things take care of themselves on the side?

Secretary-General Annan. I think from the discussions Blix had in Vienna, there is a basis to go forward. But the Council is discussing whether or not the regime should not be tightened and strengthened to ensure that we don't repeat some of the weaknesses of the past. And I'm waiting to see how the discussions come out. And I think it is legitimate that the Council should be discussing these issues. But the focus is on disarmament.

White House Press Briefing, October 4, 2002

As Congress begins an important week in which it is expected to vote on the President's proposed resolution to authorize the use of force in Iraq, the President will speak to the nation Monday night in Cincinnati about the threat of Saddam Hussein and Iraq present to world peace.

The President thinks the nation and the Congress will benefit from a discussion of the issues involved and the important moment our nation faces. The speech will be at 8:00 p.m., at the Cincinnati Museum Center. And that will be Monday, Cincinnati.

Q. Does he plan to have any new information about Iraq, any new argument?

Mr. Fleischer. Well, let me put it this way, I think it's going to be a newsworthy speech. Obviously, you all will be there and you can make your own judgements about what is new, etc. But I think it will be a notable and newsworthy speech.

Q. Is it a forum where he'll be taking questions? I mean, why Cincinnati? Why not do it from the Oval?

Mr. Fleischer. It's a speech to a seated audience, it's going to be some 400 to 500 people. It's hosted by the Chamber of Congress, in conjunction with the United Way and the World Affairs Council of Cincinnati.

And the President looks at the debate that is about to begin in the Congress and the vote that is about to take place in the Congress as a part of the great tradition of America's democracy, in which the people's elected representatives speak from their heart, speak on the basis of principle. And whether they agree or disagree with the President, they inform the public about their views and why they hold those views.

And the President sees this as his role as President to similarly speak to the country through this audience in a way that is thoughtful, that is deliberative, so that the issues that the country is asking itself can be addressed by its elected leaders, including the President.

We are not asking the networks for time. We are doing this at 8:00 p.m. at night because the President wants people to know what he is saying. But, again, I think it will be a newsworthy speech. But just so you understand the levels in which Presidents give speeches, it is not a speech in which he is asking the networks for time.

Remarks by Secretary of State Powell, UNMOVIC Chairman Blix, and International Atomic Energy Agency Director El Baradei, October 4, 2002

Secretary Colin Powell, Dr. Hans Blix, and Dr. Mohamed El Baradei delivered their remarks following a meeting in Washington, DC.

Secretary Powell. Well, good afternoon, ladies and gentlemen. We've just completed an excellent set of discussions with Dr. Blix and Dr. El Baradei of the IAEA and of UNMOVIC. As you know, they briefed the Security Council yesterday on their discussions in Vienna with the Iraqi Government on how to move forward with inspections, and we were anxious to hear from both of them as to how those discussions went.

I reaffirmed to them that it was our intention to support them to the fullest, and we think the best way to support their efforts is with a new U.N. Security Council resolution setting out very tough standards and conditions for the conduct of new inspections. I think we have an agreement that such a resolution would be useful, and I think increasingly the members of the Council are coming to the conclusion that such a resolution would be useful.

There are a number of other issues outstanding with respect to the nature of that resolution and those discussions will continue between myself and my colleagues on the Security Council.

I want to express my appreciation to my two gentlemen here for their being with us today and for their dedication to this work, and it is our intention to support them fully. And so I would ask each of them to say a word and then we'll be able to take one or two questions.

Dr. Blix. All right. We have recently been in Vienna and discussed with the Iraqi representatives on practical arrangements concerning inspection. We know from long experience that the devil sits in the details and we have been able to clarify quite a number of them. There are still some loose ends which will need to be settled and the Security Council resolution that is now being discussed is one that I think we would welcome. It could clarify further matters and it will also put—place the Iraqis clearly before the need to give a clear declaration of what they have. So we welcome that effort. I had the impression also that in the Council there was very broad support for having a new resolution.

Dr. El Baradei. We, I think, made it clear in our consultation in the Security Council that we need full backing of the Security Council. We have made some good progress on the practical arrangements to go back to Iraq in Vienna, but we need the full backing and support of the Security Council.

I think we had very good, constructive discussion with the Council yesterday and we had excellent meeting with Secretary Powell and his colleagues here today. We all agree that the endgame should be a complete disarmament of Iraq and that's the common objective we all working for.

Q. Dr. Blix was ready to move advance people in, at least, by, you know, mid—a little past mid-October. Do you think there will be a new resolution in time to go ahead with those arrangements?

Secretary Powell. I don't know when we will have a new resolution. As I have said since we began this process on the 12th of September, I think it was a matter of weeks, not months. And so I don't want to put a timeline on it.

And I will let Dr. Blix speak to the other half of that question. But I think it would be more appropriate for the team to wait for the new resolution, and I cannot tell you how long it would take. And Dr. Blix may want to add a word to that.

Dr. Blix. Well, we hope that the path will not be very long to a new resolution, and the convergence that we began to see yesterday I think is a hopeful one. But I also explain to everybody that it would be somewhat awkward for us to go in and then find that a new resolution was coming there which would call for us—ask us to do something more or different which would require other practical arrangements.

So we look forward to a speedy negotiation of a resolution and for us to come in very shortly thereafter.

Q. Mr. Secretary, we've heard you stress, put emphasis, on the need for a one resolution solution and we know very well that the French, for instance, oppose that. Is there any likelihood that at the end of the day, to get to a compromise, we would see the United States accept a two resolution solution?

Secretary Powell. Well, we still believe a one resolution solution is the better way to go. The reason we have seen any movement on the Iraqi side in the last three weeks is because of the pressure that's been put upon them. They're not doing this out of the goodness of their hearts or because suddenly they realize they had to come clean; it's pressure, and one resolution keeps that pressure on.

I do understand the position of the French Government and some of the other members of the Security Council with respect to the concept of two resolutions, and we're in consultations with them. We're in a consultative process. They have their point of view, we have our point of view, and we'll try to find a way to resolve these different points of view.

Q. Mr. Secretary, this is for Mr. Secretary and Dr. Blix. Could you talk a little bit more about what this—what more authority this resolution would give Dr. Blix to conduct the kind of inspections he needs to conduct and whether it centers around the consequences?

Dr. Blix, do you think you need a resolution that has tough consequences in order to conduct your work?

Dr. Blix. I think it is clear that there has to be constant pressure to keep the Iraqis to comply with the resolution. There was an erosion over the years in the past. So that has to be there, but exactly the formulation of that, whether it is one resolution or two, this I think that we leave to them. We have not much influence on that.

Secretary Powell. We want to make sure that the new resolution demands access to all sites without any conditions that would hamper the work of the inspectors. There has been an erosion of the inspection regime in recent years, as Dr. Blix just said, and we have got to fix that, correct it, and make sure that Iraq is not given any opportunity to frustrate the work of the inspections teams if they go in.

Q. Mr. Secretary, what do you make of the position of Russia, which seems to be fluctuating between saying they're looking—they're sympathetic to the U.S. draft and saying they don't even believe there should be a new resolution? With your relationship with Igor, you must have a pretty good inside line on this.

Secretary Powell. Foreign Minister Igor Ivanov and I are in constant communication. I spoke to him again yesterday. And they understand our point of view and I understand their point of view, and we'll find a way to resolve—I'm confident we'll find a way to resolve—any differences that exist.

This is a negotiation. It's a very complex one. It's a very intricate one. There are 15 Security Council members who have an equity in this. They are all sovereign nations with a point of view, and we have to listen to all those points of view and find a way to go forward. But I am optimistic as this week has gone by because of the kind of presentations that were made by these two gentlemen to the Security Council and an understanding on the part of the Security Council that if inspectors are going to go back in, they have to go back in without any restrictions on what they are able to do and there has to be pressure maintained on the Iraqi regime through the likelihood of action taken if they try to frustrate this inspection regime the way they have other inspection regimes in the past.

Remarks by Deputy Secretary of Defense Wolfowitz, October 4, 2002

Deputy Secretary Paul Wolfowitz was interviewed by Mark Mazzetti of the U.S. News and World Report.

Q. The first question I wanted to ask was on the idea of the Saddam threat, and this is something that you've obviously thought about a great deal. And I would like to ask what is it that makes regime change now so important? Is the most pressing threat the idea that Saddam could have a nuclear weapon in a small period of time? Or is it the idea that terrorists could get weapons of mass destruction and strike at the United States? What, in your mind, is the greatest threat?

Deputy Secretary Wolfowitz. Well, let me say first in general terms, the problem here is that time is not on our side. When people say, "Why now," they imply that somehow it'll be better later. As I think Senator Lieberman said, "Every additional day that"—this is a direct quote—"Every additional day that Saddam Hussein is in power in Iraq is an additional day of danger." And that's absolutely correct. The focus on nuclear weapons is actually a bit distracting from the fact that he has large quantities of anthrax and botulin toxin and aflatoxin. When he declared to the inspectors some time ago that he had, for example, 2,000 plus gallons of concentrated anthrax, UNSCOM inspectors estimated he had three to four times the amount that were declared, and no evidence that he destroyed what he claimed to destroy. So that's a perfect weapon to hand over to a terrorist, and you don't know when a threat like this will be imminent.

I mean, think about it this way. The pilots who did the World Trade Center attack and the Pentagon attack were here in the United States in early 2000, and the entire crew was here by spring of last year. So if we had gone to war with Afghanistan in June or July of last year, it would have already been too late to prevent September 11th. We don't know when it will be too late to have dealt with Saddam, and he's dangerous already.

Q. Do you think that if we don't act, then he will inevitably not only get a nuclear weapon, but his weapons will inevitably get in the hands of terrorists, and who will strike at the United States? I mean, do you think all of this is inevitable?

Deputy Secretary Wolfowitz. Does it have to be inevitable to do something about it? I think it is highly probable and extremely dangerous. And the question comes, why would we continue to tolerate it, when we've had eleven years of flouting the United Nations, sixteen different resolutions that he has defied. And frankly, part of the point here is that we have an opportunity to deal with this threat like no other because, in fact, there has been a very clear declaration by the international community of the requirement that he disarm. All this talk about the, you know, that we're inventing some new doctrine is total speculation. With respect to Iraq, there's no new doctrine whatsoever. This is eleven years of old, and unfortunately, failed policy.

Q. You and Secretary Rumsfeld talked a great deal about weighing the risks of war, and the risk of action versus the risk of non-action—or inaction, sorry. And you talk a lot about what the risks of inaction are, and I was wondering if I could just get you to talk a little bit about what, in your mind, are some of the risks of action? What keeps you up at night in terms of things that could go wrong, or risks that could be borne out if, in fact, regime change by military force does go into place?

Deputy Secretary Wolfowitz. Well, first of all, just to frame this clearly, the risks of inaction are the continuing and growing danger that tens of thousands, or even hundreds of thousands, of Americans will die in some catastrophic attack with a biological weapon, or if we wait long enough, a nuclear weapon. So the risks of inaction are severe. Anytime you send American troops into combat, you're running a serious risk of people dying for their country. And I don't believe you should send American troops to die, except in defense of the country, but that's one of the major risks. And the other major risk is that we know he has these weapons, and there is a danger at any point that he may use them in some terrible way. But our ability to prevent that now, if there's a military confrontation, is greater than it will be a year from now, or two years from now, or three years from now. So—

Q. Sorry. And that is because?

Deputy Secretary Wolfowitz. Because our capabilities are great now, and his are more limited. So it's—if you're going to act, and I believe we have to act, the sooner you act, the lower the risks, but one shouldn't minimize the risk that he will do something terrible with what he's got. One place where I believe that people seriously exaggerate the risks, either out of ignorance, or just repeating some of the same errors that we heard eleven years ago about how the Middle East would go up in flames if there was a war with Iraq, I believe, frankly, that the risks of dealing with a post-Saddam Iraq are not only exaggerated, but are largely misstated.

I think there's an opportunity here, actually, to help liberate what most people say is perhaps the most talented population in the Arab world, including 4 million very successful exiles, who, many of whom would want to go back to Iraq from what is one of the worst tyrannies in the modern world. And that is a huge strategic advantage on our side. This, like every other regime that supports terrorism, rules its people by terror. We saw with the Taliban what a huge weakness that created for the regime. I think it's an even bigger weakness for the Iraqi regime. I think there are very few people in Iraq who want to be the last person to die for Saddam.

Q. And even getting before the post-Saddam—idea of a post-Saddam Iraq, I mean, there seems to be concern in the Middle East and elsewhere that the actual attack itself would create instability, and the idea that he could use these weapons of mass destruction certainly against Israel. I mean, is this something that—as someone who went to Israel during the Gulf War to urge restraint, how concerned are you about Israel being brought into this?

Deputy Secretary Wolfowitz. I'm very concerned that, at any point, that clique in Baghdad, and it is a very small clique, will do what they can to make the situation worse. That is one of the real concerns. But I really believe on this issue about broader instability in the Middle East, I think when people see huge crowds in Basrah and Kirkuk and Mosul and Baghdad eventually cheering the arrival of American troops, and saying, "Why didn't you come sooner," I think the air will go out of a lot of whatever excitement there may be temporarily.

Q. So the notion of mass unrest in the Arab street you think, once again, is something that is being overstated right now?

Deputy Secretary Wolfowitz. It was definitely overstated eleven years ago. As Yogi Berra says, "It's dangerous to make predictions, especially about the future."

Q. Right.

Deputy Secretary Wolfowitz. But I think to the extent we have insight into what the conditions are like in that country, there's every reason to believe that this is going to be a liberation of the Iraqi people, not a war against the Iraqi people.

Q. Could the—do you think the Pentagon can do a better job than was done during the Gulf War of trying to either take out Scuds being launched, or prohibit Saddam from actually using these WMD—or the WMDs that he has? You said this is a concern of yours, but do you think the capabilities are better?

Deputy Secretary Wolfowitz. No question the capabilities are better. Our capabilities to detect are better. Our capabilities to attack targets on the ground quickly are better, and our capability to intercept missiles, and the Israeli capability to intercept missiles, are vastly better, but that may not be good enough to prevent something. I should emphasize—by the way, I hope you'll put this primarily in whatever we say— that the President has not made a decision to use force—

Q. Right.

Deputy Secretary Wolfowitz.—and in fact, though it may be improbable, Saddam Hussein has shown himself over many years to be a survivor. And it may be improbable that he will finally give up his ambitions to have weapons of mass destruction, but he may be finally confronted with the fact that this is the only way he can survive. And if he faces that choice clearly, it's just possible he will have an extraordinary change of heart, and we'll be able to do this without a war.

Q. And based on your studying of Saddam and your studying of the Iraqi regime, how would you gauge the probability of that?

Deputy Secretary Wolfowitz. Based on the fair amount of trying to figure them out, I wouldn't attempt to predict how they'll behave. That's what makes them so dangerous.

Q. And just going back to this threat issue, obviously, there's been a lot of concern raised among U.S. allies about a possible attack. And I'm wondering why you think that allies, our allies, seem to gauge the threat differently than certainly the U.S. and Britain seem to be, who are obviously most prominent in talking about the Saddam threat. Is it just a question that they gauge it differently, or that they just don't have certainly the September 11th experience? What is your thinking on that?

Deputy Secretary Wolfowitz. Well, if you go and look at the magazines that were published in Baghdad on the anniversary of September 11th, including one that shows the World Trade Center burning and in Arabic says, "God's Judgment," maybe they don't feel quite as targeted as we do. I think in the case of some countries, they have been in the business of courting Baghdad for economic benefits for a long time, and it's a hard habit to break. And there are some countries that are just terribly afraid, for good reason, of antagonizing this man. It's—you don't ask the small shopkeeper to take on the Mafia. You expect the law enforcement people to do it, and that's—in this case, it's the United States.

I do think that you are seeing increasingly, thanks to the President's speech to the United Nations, a clear demonstration that we intend to go the U.N. route if it all possible, that even countries like Saudi Arabia are—have shifted their position quite significantly in just the last few weeks.

Remarks by President Bush, October 5, 2002

President Bush delivered the following radio address to the nation.

Good morning. This week leaders of the Congress agreed on a strong bipartisan resolution authorizing the use of force if necessary to disarm Saddam Hussein and to defend the peace. Now both the House and the Senate will have an important debate and an historic vote. Speaker Hastert and Leader Gephardt and Leader Lott did tremendous work in building bipartisan support on this vital issue.

The danger to America from the Iraqi regime is grave and growing. The regime is guilty of beginning two wars. It has a horrible history of striking without warning. In defiance of pledges to the United Nations, Iraq has stockpiled biological and chemical weapons, and is rebuilding the facilities used to make more of those weapons. Saddam Hussein has used these weapons of death against innocent Iraqi people, and we have every reason to believe he will use them again.

Iraq has longstanding ties to terrorist groups, which are capable of and willing to deliver weapons of mass death. And Iraq is ruled by perhaps the world's most brutal dictator who has already committed genocide with chemical weapons, ordered the torture of children, and instituted the systematic rape of the wives and daughters of his political opponents.

We cannot leave the future of peace and the security of America in the hands of this cruel and dangerous man. This dictator must be disarmed. And all the United Nations resolutions against his brutality and support for terrorism must be enforced.

The United States does not desire military conflict, because we know the awful nature of war. Our country values life, and we will never seek war unless it is essential to security and justice. We hope that Iraq complies with the world's demands. If, however, the Iraqi regime persists in its defiance, the use of force may become unavoidable. Delay, indecision, and inaction are not options for America, because they could lead to massive and sudden horror.

Should force be required to bring Saddam to account, the United States will work with other nations to help the Iraqi people rebuild and form a just government. We have no quarrel with the Iraqi people. They are the daily victims of Saddam Hussein's oppression, and they will be the first to benefit when the world's demands are met.

American security, the safety of our friends, and the value

Remarks by President Bush, October 7, 2002

President Bush delivered the following address to the nation from Cincinnati, OH.

Tonight I want to take a few minutes to discuss a grave threat to peace, and America's determination to lead the world in confronting that threat.

The threat comes from Iraq. It arises directly from the Iraqi regime's own actions—its history of aggression, and its drive toward an arsenal of terror. Eleven years ago, as a condition for ending the Persian Gulf War, the Iraqi regime was required to destroy its weapons of mass destruction, to cease all development of such weapons, and to stop all support for terrorist groups. The Iraqi regime has violated all of those obligations. It possesses and produces chemical and biological weapons. It is seeking nuclear weapons. It has given shelter and support to terrorism, and practices terror against its own people. The entire world has witnessed Iraq's eleven-year history of defiance, deception and bad faith.

We also must never forget the most vivid events of recent history. On September the 11th, 2001, America felt its vulnerability—even to threats that gather on the other side of the earth. We resolved then, and we are resolved today, to confront every threat, from any source, that could bring sudden terror and suffering to America.

Members of the Congress of both political parties, and members of the United Nations Security Council, agree that Saddam Hussein is a threat to peace and must disarm. We agree that the Iraqi dictator must not be permitted to threaten America and the world with horrible poisons and diseases and gases and atomic weapons. Since we all agree on this goal, the issues is : how can we best achieve it?

Many Americans have raised legitimate questions: about the nature of the threat; about the urgency of action—why be concerned now; about the link between Iraq developing weapons of terror, and the wider war on terror. These are all issues we've discussed broadly and fully within my administration. And tonight, I want to share those discussions with you.

First, some ask why Iraq is different from other countries or regimes that also have terrible weapons. While there are many dangers in the world, the threat from Iraq stands alone—because it gathers the most serious dangers of our age in one place. Iraq's weapons of mass destruction are controlled by a murderous tyrant who has already used chemical weapons to kill thousands of people. This same tyrant has tried to dominate the Middle East, has invaded and brutally occupied a small neighbor, has struck other nations without warning, and holds an unrelenting hostility toward the United States.

By its past and present actions, by its technological capabilities, by the merciless nature of its regime, Iraq is unique. As a former chief weapons inspector of the U.N. has said, "The fundamental problem with Iraq remains the nature of the regime, itself. Saddam Hussein is a homicidal dictator who is addicted to weapons of mass destruction."

Some ask how urgent this danger is to America and the world. The danger is already significant, and it only grows worse with time. If we know Saddam Hussein has dangerous weapons today—and we do—does it make any sense for the world to wait to confront him as he grows even stronger and develops even more dangerous weapons?

In 1995, after several years of deceit by the Iraqi regime, the head of Iraq's military industries defected. It was then that the regime was forced to admit that it had produced more than 30,000 liters of anthrax and other deadly biological agents. The inspectors, however, concluded that Iraq had likely produced two to four times that amount. This is a massive stockpile of biological weapons that has never been accounted for, and capable of killing millions.

We know that the regime has produced thousands of tons of chemical agents, including mustard gas, sarin nerve gas, VX nerve gas. Saddam Hussein also has experience in using chemical weapons. He has ordered chemical attacks on Iran, and on more than forty villages in his own country. These actions killed or injured at least 20,000 people, more than six times the number of people who died in the attacks of September the 11th.

And surveillance photos reveal that the regime is rebuilding facilities that it had used to produce chemical and biological weapons. Every chemical and biological weapon that Iraq has or makes is a direct violation of the truce that ended the Persian Gulf War in 1991. Yet, Saddam Hussein has chosen to build and keep these weapons despite international sanctions, U.N. demands, and isolation from the civilized world.

Iraq possesses ballistic missiles with a likely range of hundreds of miles—far enough to strike Saudi Arabia, Israel, Turkey, and other nations—in a region where more than 135,000 American civilians and service members live and work. We've also discovered through intelligence that Iraq has a growing fleet of manned and unmanned aerial vehicles that could be used to disperse chemical or biological weapons across broad areas. We're concerned that Iraq is exploring ways of using these UAVS for missions targeting the United States. And, of course, sophisticated delivery systems aren't required for a chemical or biological attack; all that might be required are a small container and one terrorist or Iraqi intelligence operative to deliver it.

And that is the source of our urgent concern about Saddam Hussein's links to international terrorist groups. Over the years, Iraq has provided safe haven to terrorists such as Abu Nidal, whose terror organization carried out more than 90 terrorist attacks in 20 countries that killed or injured nearly 900 people, including 12 Americans. Iraq has also provided safe haven to Abu Abbas, who was responsible for seizing the Achille Lauro and killing an American passenger. And we know that Iraq is continuing to finance terror and gives assistance to groups that use terrorism to undermine Middle East peace.

We know that Iraq and the al Qaeda terrorist network share a common enemy—the United States of America. We know that Iraq and al Qaeda have had high-level contacts that go back a decade. Some al Qaeda leaders who fled Afghanistan went to Iraq. These include one very senior al Qaeda leader who received medical treatment in Baghdad this year, and who has been associated with planning for chemical and biological attacks. We've learned that Iraq has trained al Qaeda members in bomb-making and poisons and deadly gases. And we know that after September the 11th, Saddam Hussein's regime gleefully celebrated the terrorist attacks on America.

Iraq could decide on any given day to provide a biological or chemical weapon to a terrorist group or individual terrorists. Alliance with terrorists could allow the Iraqi regime to attack America without leaving any fingerprints.

Some have argued that confronting the threat from Iraq could detract from the war against terror. To the contrary; confronting the threat posed by Iraq is crucial to winning the war on terror. When I spoke to Congress more than a year ago, I said that those who harbor terrorists are as guilty as the terrorists themselves. Saddam Hussein is harboring terrorists and the instruments of terror, the instruments of mass death and destruction. And he cannot be trusted. The risk is simply too great that he will use them, or provide them to a terror network.

Terror cells and outlaw regimes building weapons of mass destruction are different faces of the same evil. Our security requires that we confront both. And the United States military is capable of confronting both.

Many people have asked how close Saddam Hussein is to developing a nuclear weapon. Well, we don't know exactly, and that's the problem. Before the Gulf War, the best intelligence indicated that Iraq was eight to ten years away from developing a nuclear weapon. After the war, international inspectors learned that the regime has been much closer—the regime in Iraq would likely have possessed a nuclear weapon no later than 1993. The inspectors discovered that Iraq had an advanced nuclear weapons development program, had a design for a workable nuclear weapon, and was pursuing several different methods of enriching uranium for a bomb.

Before being barred from Iraq in 1998, the International Atomic Energy Agency dismantled extensive nuclear weapons-related facilities, including three uranium enrichment sites. That same year, information from a high-ranking Iraqi nuclear engineer who had defected revealed that despite his public promises, Saddam Hussein had ordered his nuclear program to continue.

The evidence indicates that Iraq is reconstituting its nuclear weapons program. Saddam Hussein has held numerous meetings with Iraqi nuclear scientists, a group he calls his "nuclear mujahideen"—his nuclear holy warriors. Satellite photographs reveal that Iraq is rebuilding facilities at sites that have been part of its nuclear program in the past. Iraq has attempted to purchase high-strength aluminum tubes and other equipment needed for gas centrifuges, which are used to enrich uranium for nuclear weapons.

If the Iraqi regime is able to produce, buy, or steal an amount of highly enriched uranium a little larger than a single softball, it could have a nuclear weapon in less than a year. And if we allow that to happen, a terrible line would be crossed. Saddam Hussein would be in a position to blackmail anyone who opposes his aggression. He would be in a position to dominate the Middle East. He would be in a position to threaten America. And Saddam Hussein would be in a position to pass nuclear technology to terrorists.

Some citizens wonder, after 11 years of living with this problem, why do we need to confront it now? And there's a reason. We've experienced the horror of September the 11th. We have seen that those who hate America are willing to crash airplanes into buildings full of innocent people. Our enemies would be no less willing, in fact, they would be eager, to use biological or chemical, or a nuclear weapon.

Knowing these realities, America must not ignore the threat gathering against us. Facing clear evidence of peril, we cannot wait for the final proof—the smoking gun—that could come in the form of a mushroom cloud. As President Kennedy said in October of 1962, "Neither the United States of America, nor the world community of nations can tolerate deliberate deception and offensive threats on the part of any nation, large or small. We no longer live in a world," he said, "where only the actual firing of weapons represents a sufficient challenge to a nations security to constitute maximum peril."

Understanding the threats of our time, knowing the designs and deceptions of the Iraqi regime, we have every reason to assume the worst, and we have an urgent duty to prevent the worst from occurring.

Some believe we can address this danger by simply resuming the old approach to inspections, and applying diplomatic and economic pressure. Yet this is precisely what the world has tried to do since 1991. The U.N. inspections program was met with systematic deception. The Iraqi regime bugged hotel rooms and offices of inspectors to find where they were going next; they forged documents, destroyed evidence, and developed mobile weapons facilities to keep a step ahead of inspectors. Eight so-called presidential palaces were declared off-limits to unfettered inspections. These sites actually encompass twelve square miles, with hundreds of structures, both above and below the ground, where sensitive materials could be hidden.

The world has also tried economic sanctions—and watched Iraq use billions of dollars in illegal oil revenues to fund more weapons purchases, rather than providing for the needs of the Iraqi people.

The world has tried limited military strikes to destroy Iraq's weapons of mass destruction capabilities—only to see them openly rebuilt, while the regime again denies they even exist.

The world has tried no-fly zones to keep Saddam from terrorizing his own people—and in the last year alone, the Iraqi military has fired upon American and British pilots more than 750 times.

After eleven years during which we have tried containment, sanctions, inspections, even selected military action, the end result is that Saddam Hussein still has chemical and biological weapons and is increasing his capabilities to make more. And he is moving ever closer to developing a nuclear weapon.

Clearly, to actually work, any new inspections, sanctions or enforcement mechanisms will have to be very different. America wants the U.N. to be an effective organization that helps keep the peace. And that is why we are urging the Security Council to adopt a new resolution setting out tough, immediate requirements. Among those requirements: the Iraqi regime must reveal and destroy, under U.N. supervision, all existing weapons of mass destruction. To ensure that we learn the truth, the regime must allow witnesses to its illegal activities to be interviewed outside the country—and these witnesses must be free to bring their families with them so they all beyond the reach of Saddam Hussein's terror and murder. And inspectors must have access to any site, at any time, without pre-clearance, without delay, without exceptions.

The time for denying, deceiving, and delaying has come to an end. Saddam Hussein must disarm himself—or, for the sake of peace, we will lead a coalition to disarm him.

Many nations are joining us in insisting that Saddam Hussein's regime be held accountable. They are committed to defending the international security that protects the lives of both our citizens and theirs. And that's why America is challenging all nations to take the resolutions of the U.N. Security Council seriously.

And these resolutions are clear. In addition to declaring and destroying all of its weapons of mass destruction, Iraq must end its support for terrorism. It must cease the persecution of its civilian population. It must stop all illicit trade outside the Oil For Food program. It must release or account for all Gulf War personnel, including an American pilot, whose fate is still unknown.

By taking these steps, and by only taking these steps, the Iraqi regime has an opportunity to avoid conflict. Taking these steps would also change the nature of the Iraqi regime itself. America hopes the regime will make that choice. Unfortunately, at least so far, we have little reason to expect it. And that's why two administrations—mine and President Clinton's—have stated that regime change in Iraq is the only certain means of removing a great danger to our nation.

I hope this will not require military action, but it may. And military conflict could be difficult. An Iraqi regime faced with its own demise may attempt cruel and desperate measures. If Saddam Hussein orders such measures, his generals would be well advised to refuse those orders. If they do not refuse, they must understand that all war criminals will be pursued and punished. If we have to act, we will take every precaution that is possible. We will plan carefully; we will act with the full power of the United States military; we will act with allies at our side, and we will prevail.

There is no easy or risk-free course of action. Some have argued we should wait—and that's an option. In my view, it's the riskiest of all options, because the longer we wait, the stronger and bolder Saddam Hussein will become. We could wait and hope that Saddam does not give weapons to terrorists, or develop a nuclear weapon to blackmail the world. But I'm convinced that is a hope against all evidence. As Americans, we want peace—we work and sacrifice for peace. But there can be no peace if our security depends on the will and whims of a ruthless and aggressive dictator. I'm not willing to stake one American life on trusting Saddam Hussein.

Failure to act would embolden other tyrants, allow terrorists access to new weapons and new resources, and make blackmail a permanent feature of world events. The United Nations would betray the purpose of its founding, and prove irrelevant to the problems of our time. And through its inaction, the United States would resign itself to a future of fear.

That is not the America I know. That is not the America I serve. We refuse to live in fear. (Applause.) This nation, in world war and in Cold War, has never permitted the brutal and lawless to set history's course. Now, as before, we will secure our nation, protect our freedom, and help others to find freedom of their own.

Some worry that a change of leadership in Iraq could create instability and make the situation worse. The situation could hardly get worse, for world security and for the people of Iraq. The lives of Iraqi citizens would improve dramatically if Saddam Hussein were no longer in power, just as the lives of Afghanistan's citizens improved after the Taliban. The dictator of Iraq is a student of Stalin, using murder as a tool of terror and control, within his own cabinet, within his own army, and even within his own family.

On Saddam Hussein's orders, opponents have been decapitated, wives and mothers of political opponents have been systematically raped as a method of intimidation, and political prisoners have been forced to watch their own children being tortured.

America believes that all people are entitled to hope and human rights, to the non-negotiable demands of human dignity. People everywhere prefer freedom to slavery; prosperity to squalor; self-government to the rule of terror and torture. America is a friend to the people of Iraq. Our demands are directed only at the regime that enslaves them and threatens us. When these demands are met, the first and greatest benefit will come to Iraqi men, women and children. The oppression of Kurds, Assyrians, Turkomans, Shi'a, Sunnis and others will be lifted. The long captivity of Iraq will end, and an era of new hope will begin.

Iraq is a land rich in culture, resources, and talent. Freed from the weight of oppression, Iraq's people will be able to share in the progress and prosperity of our time. If military action is necessary, the United States and our allies will help the Iraqi people rebuild their economy, and create the institutions of liberty in a unified Iraq at peace with its neighbors.

Later this week, the United States Congress will vote on this matter. I have asked Congress to authorize the use of America's military, if it proves necessary, to enforce U.N. Security Council demands. Approving this resolution does not mean that military action is imminent or unavoidable. The resolution will tell the United Nations, and all nations, that America speaks with one voice and is determined to make the demands of the civilized world mean something. Congress will also be sending a message to the dictator in Iraq: that his only chance—his only choice is full compliance, and the time remaining for that choice is limited.

Members of Congress are nearing an historic vote. I'm confident they will fully consider the facts, and their duties.

The attacks of September the 11th showed our country that vast oceans no longer protect us from danger. Before that tragic date, we had only hints of al Qaeda's plans and designs. Today in Iraq, we see a threat whose outlines are far more clearly defined, and whose consequences could be far more deadly. Saddam Hussein's actions have put us on notice, and there is no refuge from our responsibilities.

We did not ask for this present challenge, but we accept it. Like other generations of Americans, we will meet the responsibility of defending human liberty against violence and aggression. By our resolve, we will give strength to others. By our courage, we will give hope to others. And by our actions, we will secure the peace, and lead the world to a better day. s of our country lead us to confront this gathering threat. By supporting the resolution now before them, members of Congress will send a clear message to Saddam: His only choice is to fully comply with the demands of the world. And the time for that choice is limited. Supporting this resolution will also show the resolve of the United States, and will help spur the United Nations to act.

I urge Americans to call their members of Congress to make sure your voice is heard. The decision before Congress cannot be more consequential. I'm confident that members of both political parties will choose wisely.

Remarks by Senator Kennedy (D-MA) and Senator Specter (R-PA), October 7, 2002

Senator Edward Kennedy and Senator Arlen Specter delivered their remarks on the Senate floor.

Senator Kennedy. Mr. President, we face no more serious decision in our democracy than whether or not to go to war. The American people deserve to fully understand all of the implications of such a decision.

The question of whether our Nation should attack Iraq is playing out in the context of a more fundamental debate that is only just beginning—an all-important debate about how, when and where in the years ahead our country will use its unsurpassed military might.

On September 20, the administration unveiled its new National Security Strategy.

This document addresses the new realities of our age, particularly the proliferation of weapons of mass destruction and terrorist networks armed with the agendas of fanatics. The Strategy claims that these new threats are so novel and so dangerous that we should "not hesitate to act alone, if necessary, to exercise our right of self-defense by acting pre-emptively." In the discussion over the past few months about Iraq, the administration, often uses the terms "pre-emptive" and "preventive" interchangeably. In the realm of international relations, these two terms have long had very different meanings.

Traditionally, "pre-emptive" action refers to times when states react to an imminent threat of attack. For example, when Egyptian and Syrian forces mobilized on Israel's borders in 1967, the threat was obvious and immediate, and Israel felt justified in pre-emptively attacking those forces. The global community is generally tolerant of such actions, since no nation should have to suffer a certain first strike before it has the legitimacy to respond.

By contrast, "preventive" military action refers to strikes that target a country before it has developed a capability that could someday become threatening. Preventive attacks have generally been condemned. For example, the 1941 sneak attack on Pearl Harbor was regarded as a preventive strike by Japan, because the Japanese were seeking to block a planned military buildup by the United States in the Pacific.

The coldly premeditated nature of preventive attacks and preventive wars makes them anathema to well-established international principles against aggression. Pearl Harbor has been rightfully recorded in history as an act of dishonorable treachery.

Historically, the United States has condemned the idea of preventive war, because it violates basic international rules against aggression. But at times in our history, preventive war has been seriously advocated as a policy option.

In the early days of the cold war, some U.S. military and civilian experts advocated a preventive war against the Soviet Union. They proposed a devastating first strike to prevent the Soviet Union from developing a threatening nuclear capability. At the time, they said the uniquely destructive power of nuclear weapons required us to rethink traditional international rules.

The first round of that debate ended in 1950, when President Truman ruled out a preventive strike, stating that such actions were not consistent with our American tradition. He said, "You don't 'prevent' anything by war .... except peace." Instead of a surprise first strike, the nation dedicated itself to the strategy of deterrence and containment, which successfully kept the peace during the long and frequently difficult years of the Cold War.

Arguments for preventive war resurfaced again when the Eisenhower administration took power in 1953, but President Eisenhower and Secretary of State John Foster Dulles soon decided firmly against it. President Eisenhower emphasized that even if we were to win such a war, we would face the vast burdens of occupation and reconstruction that would come with it.

The argument that the United States should take preventive military action, in the absence of an imminent attack, resurfaced in 1962, when we learned that the Soviet Union would soon have the ability to launch missiles from Cuba against our country. Many military officers urged President Kennedy to approve a preventive attack to destroy this capability before it became operational. Robert Kennedy, like Harry Truman, felt that this kind of first strike was not consistent with American values. He said that a proposed surprise first strike against Cuba would be a "Pearl Harbor in reverse."

For 175 years, [he said] we have not been that kind of country.

That view prevailed. A middle ground was found and peace was preserved.

Yet another round of debate followed the Cuban Missile Crisis when American strategists and voices in and out of the administration advocated preventive war against China to forestall its acquisition of nuclear weapons. Many arguments heard today about Iraq were made then about the Chinese communist government: that its leadership was irrational and that it was therefore undeterrable. And once again, those arguments were rejected.

As these earlier cases show, American strategic thinkers have long debated the relative merits of preventive and pre-emptive war. Although nobody would deny our right to pre-emptively block an imminent attack on our territory, there is disagreement about our right to preventively engage in war.

In each of these cases a way was found to deter other nations, without waging war.

Now, the Bush Administration says we must take pre-emptive action against Iraq. But what the Administration is really calling for is preventive war, which flies in the face of international rules of acceptable behavior.

There is no doubt that Saddam Hussein is a despicable dictator and that he must be disarmed. But the Administration has not made a persuasive case that the threat is so imminent that we should risk going it alone. We should resort to war only as a last resort. If we work through the United Nations for free, unfettered inspections, we strengthen our hand with our allies, our hand against Saddam Hussein and our ability to disarm him.

The Administration's new National Security Strategy states "As a matter of common sense and self-defense, America will act against such emerging threats before they are fully formed."

The circumstances of today's world require us to rethink this concept. The world changed on September 11, and all of us have learned that it can be a drastically more dangerous place. The Bush administration's new National Security Strategy asserts that global realities now legitimize preventive war and make it a strategic necessity.

The document openly contemplates preventive attacks against groups or states, even absent the threat of imminent attack. It legitimizes this kind of first strike option, and it elevates it to the status of a core security doctrine. Disregarding norms of international behavior, the Bush strategy asserts that the United States should be exempt from the rules we expect other nations to obey.

I strongly oppose any such extreme doctrine and I'm sure that many others do as well. Earlier generations of Americans rejected preventive war on the grounds of both morality and practicality, and our generation must do so as well. We can deal with Iraq without resorting to this extreme.

It is impossible to justify any such double standard under international law. Might does not make right. America cannot write its own rules for the modern world. To attempt to do so would be unilateralism run amok. It would antagonize our closest allies, whose support we need to fight terrorism, prevent global warming, and deal with many other dangers that affect all nations and require international cooperation. It would deprive America of the moral legitimacy necessary to promote our values abroad. And it would give other nations—from Russia to India to Pakistan—an excuse to violate fundamental principles of civilized international behavior.

The administration's doctrine is a call for 21st century American imperialism that no other nation can or should accept. It is the antithesis of all that America has worked so hard to achieve in international relations since the end of World War II.

This is not just an academic debate. There are important real world consequences. A shift in our policy toward preventive war would reinforce the perception of America as a "bully" in the Middle East and would fuel anti-American sentiment throughout the Islamic world and beyond.

It would also send a signal to governments the world over that the rules of aggression have changed for them too, which could increase the risk of conflict between countries such as Russia and Georgia, India and Pakistan, and China and Taiwan.

Obviously, this debate is only just beginning on the administration's new strategy for national security. But the debate is solidly grounded in American values and history.

It will also be a debate among vast numbers of well-meaning Americans who have honest differences of opinion about the best way to use United States military might. The debate will be contentious, but the stakes, in terms of both our national security and our allegiance to our core beliefs, are too high to ignore.

I look forward to working closely with my colleagues in Congress to develop an effective, principled policy that will enable us to protect our national security, and respect the basic principles that are essential for the world to be at peace. I yield the floor.

Senator Specter. Mr. President, I have sought recognition, as noted, to discuss the pending resolution. At the outset, I commend the President for coming to Congress. Originally the position had been articulated by the White House that congressional authority was not necessary. The President, as Commander in Chief, has the authority under the Constitution to act in cases of emergency. But if there is time for discussion, deliberation, and debate, then in my view it is a matter for the Congress.

Senator Harkin and I introduced a resolution on July 18 of this year calling for the President to come to Congress before using military force.

When the President made his State of the Union speech and identified the axis of evil as Iran, Iraq, and North Korea, followed by the testimony of Secretary of State Powell that there was no intention to go to war against either North Korea or Iran, it left the obvious inference that war might be in the offing as to Iraq.

I spoke extensively on the subject back on February 13, 2002, raising a number of issues: What was the extent of Saddam Hussein's control over weapons of mass destruction? What would it cost by way of casualties to topple Saddam Hussein? What would be the consequence in Iraq? Who would govern after Saddam was toppled?

What would happen in the region, the impact on the Arab world, and the impact on Israel? I believe it is vastly preferable on our resolution to focus on the question of weapons of mass destruction as opposed to the issue of regime change. When we talk about regime change, there is a sense in many other nations that the United States is seeking to exert its will on another sovereign nation. Much as Saddam Hussein deserves to be toppled, when we move away from the focus of containing weapons of mass destruction, it is my view we lose a great deal of our moral authority.

There is no doubt Saddam Hussein has been ruthless in the use of weapons of mass destruction with the use of chemicals on his own people, the Kurds, and in the Iran-Iraq war. There is very substantial evidence Saddam Hussein has storehouses of biological weapons, and there is significant evidence he is moving as fast as he can toward nuclear weapons. So when we talk about self-defense, when we talk about ridding the world of the scourge, that is a very high moral ground. When we talk about regime change, it raises the concern of many leaders of many nations as to who is next—maybe they are next.

I suggest it is possible to achieve regime change in a way superior to articulating or planning an attack with the view to toppling Saddam Hussein. I believe the way to achieve regime change, consistent with international principles, is to try Saddam Hussein as a war criminal. I introduced a resolution on March 2, 1998, which was passed by the U.S. Senate on March 13, 1998, calling for the creation of a military tribunal, similar to the war crimes tribunal at The Hague, similar to the war crimes tribunal in Rwanda, so that Saddam Hussein could be tried as a war criminal. There is no doubt on the evidence available that Saddam Hussein has committed war crimes. Without going into all of the details set forth in the resolution, I ask unanimous consent that it be printed at the conclusion of my remarks.

Herein, there is a very ample statement for the basis for trying Saddam Hussein and trying him successfully as a war criminal. In doing that, we would be following the precedent of trying former Yugoslavian President Milosevic as a war criminal. I have made some seven visits to The Hague and have participated in marshaling U.S. resources from the Department of Justice, also specifically from the FBI, also from the CIA during the 104th Congress back in 1995 and 1996, when I was chairman of the Intelligence Committee; and we now see the head of state, Slobodan Milosevic, on trial.

We had the experience of the war crimes tribunal in Rwanda, which achieved an international precedent in convicting former Prime Minister Jean Kambanda of Rwanda, the first head of state to be convicted. He is now serving a life sentence.

So it is my suggestion that the objective of regime change can be accomplished in accordance with existing international standards, on a multilateral basis, without having other nations in the world saying the superpower United States is trying to throw its weight around. It might take a little longer, but as is evidenced from the proceedings in Rwanda as to the former Prime Minister of Rwanda, and as evidenced from the proceedings of Milosevic, that is an ordinary successful progress of the law. The most difficult issue pending on the resolutions as to the use of force on Iraq, the most difficult issue, in my opinion, is the question of whether the United Nations authorizes the use of force.

I commend the President for his efforts to organize an international coalition. President George Herbert Walker Bush did organize an international coalition in 1991, and prosecuted the war against Iraq with great success, enlisting the aid of the Arab nations, including Egypt, Syria, and other countries. That is the preferable way to proceed, if it can be accomplished.

The obvious difficulty in conditioning the President's authority to use force on a United Nations resolution is the United States would be subjecting itself to the veto by either China, or Russia, or even France, and we prize our sovereignty very highly—justifiably so. The conundrum, then, is whether we will get that kind of an international coalition that would have the weight of world public opinion, would have the weight of the U.N. behind them.

The difficulties of having the United States act alone would be the precedent that would be set. It could be a reference point for China, for example, looking at Taiwan, where China has made many bellicose warlike statements as to its disagreements with Taiwan. If the United States can act unilaterally, or without United Nations sanction, there would be a potential argument for a country like China proceeding as to Taiwan. There would be a potential argument for a nation like India proceeding as to Pakistan, or vice versa, Pakistan proceeding as to India, which could be a nuclear incident. Both of those countries have nuclear power.

This is a question I believe has to be debated on the floor of the U.S. Senate. I have not made up my mind as to whether it is preferable to condition the use of force on a United Nations resolution, and I am cognizant of the difficulties of giving up sovereignty and being subject to the veto of China, which I don't like at all, or being subject to the veto of Russia, which I don't like at all, or being subject to the veto of France, again something I do not like. But I think we have to recognize when we are authorizing the use of force, and if the President takes the authorization and is not successful going to the U.N. to get a coalition, we will be establishing a precedent that may have ramifications far into the future, at some point in time when the United States may not be the superpower significantly in control of the destiny of the world with our great military power.

I am glad to see the President is moving ahead with an effort to get inspections in the United Nations, and Secretary of State Powell met last Friday with the U.N. inspection chief, who agreed there ought to be broader authority for the U.N. inspection than that which was in place in 1998 when Iraq ousted the U.N. inspectors. Hans Blix supported the position the United States has taken. Yesterday, on a Sunday talk show, the Iraqi Ambassador to the U.N. made a comment to the effect there was no huge problem on having U.N. inspectors come, even to the Presidential compounds.

That is probably a typical Iraqi statement: holding out an offer one day and revoking it the next. I do believe it is important that we exhaust every possible alternative before resorting to the use of our armed forces, and to have the inspectors go back into Iraq is obviously desirable. We must have the inspectors, though, go into Iraq in a context where there are no holds barred. In August, Senator Shelby and I visited the Sudan. The Sudan is now interested in becoming friendly with the United States. Our former colleague, Senator Jack Danforth, has brokered the basic peace treaty which still has to be implemented in many respects. But as a part of the new Sudanese approach, the Government of Sudan has allowed U.S. intelligence personnel to go to Sudanese factories, munitions plants, and laboratories with no announcement or minimal announcement of just an hour, break locks, go in, and conduct inspections. That would be a good model for the inspection of Iraq. If, in fact, the Iraqis will allow unfettered, unlimited inspections, it is conceivable that would solve the problem with respect to the issue of weapons of mass destruction.

Certainly that ought to be pursued to the maximum extent possible. If, and/or when the Iraqis oust the U.N. inspectors or limit the U.N. inspectors, raising again the unmistakable inference that Saddam Hussein has something to hide, then I think there is more reason to resort to force as a last alternative and, in that context, a better chance to get other countries, perhaps countries even in the Arab world, to be supportive of the use of force against Iraq at the present time as they were in the gulf war in 1991.

Extensive consideration has to be given, in my judgment, to the impact on the Arab world. Egyptian President Mubarak has been emphatic in his concern as to what the impact will be there. So we ought to make every effort we can to enlist the aid of as many of the nations in the Arab world as possible.

If Saddam Hussein rebuffs the United Nations, again raising the unmistakable inference that he has something to hide, then I think the chances of getting additional allies there would be improved.

With respect to the situation with Israel, there is, again, grave concern that a war with Iraq will result in Scud missiles being directed toward Israel. Some 39 of those Scud missiles were directed toward Israel during the gulf war. Their missile defense system was not very good. Now we know that Israel has the Arrow system, but still all of Israel is not protected. The Arrow system has not been adequately tested.

In the gulf war in 1991, the Israeli Prime Minister Yitzhak Shamir honored the request of President Bush not to retaliate. It is a different situation at the present time with Israeli Prime Minister Sharon having announced if Israel is attacked, Israel will not sit back again.

When former National Security Adviser Brent Scowcroft published a very erudite op-ed piece in the Wall Street Journal in August, he raised the grave concern that with Israeli nuclear power, there could be an Armageddon in the Mideast. Former National Security Adviser Brent Scowcroft was advising caution; that we ought not proceed without exhausting every other alternative.

A similar position was taken by former Secretary of State James Baker in an op-ed piece, again in August, in the New York Times urging that inspections be pursued as a way of possibly avoiding a war.

Remarks by Secretary of State Powell, Senator Lieberman (D-CT), Senator Bayh (D-IN), and Senator McCain (R-AZ), October 8, 2002

Secretary Powell. Ladies and gentlemen it is my pleasure to be here this afternoon to meet with Senator Lieberman, Senator Warner, Senator Buchanan, Senator Bayh, and also joined by Senator Allard to express my appreciation for the fine work they have done in moving this resolution forward.

It is a resolution that I think will grow very, very solid and strong, overwhelming bipartisan and bicameral support. It is a resolution that will definitely strengthen my hand as I try to do the diplomatic work up in New York to get a U.N. Security Council resolution. I think the resolution is timely, and we need it now. We need it now because the President has laid the challenge squarely before the world and then again last night squarely before the American people.

We are faced with a dangerous situation. We are faced with a regime, which has ignored U.N. resolutions for many years and will continue to ignore them unless they are dealt with now.

The President has said he is not looking for war. He has given the United Nations an opportunity to find a peaceful solution. He has given Iraq an opportunity to find a peaceful solution. But the one thing that cannot be tolerated is that Iraq continues to have weapons of mass destruction. Iraq will be disarmed one way or the other.

All of my colleagues at the United Nations and others I have spoken to around the world clearly see the threat. I think there is increasing support for a U.N. resolution, which puts in place a much stronger inspection mandate, and I think there is mutual understanding of the fact that the only reason Iraq is trying to respond now is because the threat of force is there. We have to keep that in place. We have to make sure they understand there are consequences if the fail to act this time.

So our strategy is straightforward and our strategy, frankly, requires the kind of strong resolution that is now being debated on both the House floor and the Senate floor. I want to express once again my thanks to the gentleman who are here with me this afternoon and all the others in the Congress who are supporting the resolution, a resolution that was discussed with the leadership.

The President put forward some ideas. Some ideas came back, and now we are all unified behind this resolution, and I am sure it will win overwhelming support in both the House and Senate.

Senator Lieberman. Very briefly, thanks to Secretary Powell for the opportunity to meet with him, for the strong leadership he has given America's cause and the world's cause in the diplomacy at the United Nations and the capitals around the world. I think Secretary Powell's diplomatic leadership punctuates the point that all four of us co-sponsors of this urgent issue have made repeatedly, including this morning on the floor and that the President made last night in his remarks in Cincinnati: War is the last resort.

But over the last 11 years, the world community has tried just about everything else to get Saddam Hussein to keep the promise to disarm that he made to achieve the end of the Gulf War. We've tried inspections; we've tried sanctions; we've tried oil-for-food; we've tried limited military action, and they haven't worked.

That is why in this resolution we are essentially authorizing the President, and hopefully the United Nations, to say to Saddam Hussein, "Disarm or we will be forced to make war against you to achieve the disarmament that you promised at the end of the Gulf war."

Mr. Secretary, I want to say to you that we have offered the bipartisan resolution that we negotiated with the Administration this morning in the Senate. We're having a very good, thoughtful debate as befits a matter of life and death, literally.

But I want to express to you what I believe is the opinion of my colleagues here: our confidence that, when the roll is called on this bipartisan resolution, there will be overwhelming bipartisan support to give the President as Commander-in-Chief the authority that we believe he needs to protect America's interests.

Thank you very much.

Senator Bayh. I'd make three brief points. First, we support this resolution, not because we favor war, but because we believe this offers our best hope of maintaining the peace.

Secondly, we support this resolution not because we prefer that America act alone, but because this resolution gives us the best opportunity to rally our allies together with the support of the United Nations in a course of action we believe to be justifiable.

Finally, I would say that we support this resolution because of the lessons learned on September the 11, the principal one being that we waited too long to deal with the gathering threat in Afghanistan. And because of that delay, 3,000 innocent Americans lost their lives. We must not make that mistake again.

All the arguments being offered against this resolution would have been made if we had recommended taking action against Afghanistan 2 years ago. Those arguments would have wrong then; they are wrong today. So I'm pleased to join with my colleagues on a bipartisan basis and the leadership of the Administration in supporting this resolution because it's in the best interest of the American people.

Senator McCain. It's very important to the American people that we go through this process—the process of debate, and a resolution of approval on the part of both Houses of Congress, which as my colleagues said, will be overwhelming.

They also expect the Secretary of State to do his job, which he is doing in an outstanding fashion with the United Nations to get a resolution from the Security Council. Then the American people will be confident that we have taken every step necessary to build a consensus and have done everything we can to avoid conflict if that occasion should arise. They will be confident that we've done everything we can to avoid a war, but at the same time, if the president has to take military action, he will have the support of the American people and the United Nations.

Q. Mr. Secretary, respectfully, what message are you bringing to the Senators? Are you trying to reassure people or—

Secretary Powell. The importance of this resolution—and I want to reassure the American people that the American Government, neither the President nor the Congress, is leaping into something without thinking. That is why we need this kind of debate. That is why it was very useful to have a discussion about what the resolution should look like. And we have come up, I think now, with a resolution that serves our intended purpose.

So the message to the American people is war is a last resort, but we have seen what happens if you are not prepared to go to war: you will get this kind of violation of international law. We cannot let Saddam Hussein walk away this time without there being consequences for continued violation of international obligations.

As the President has said, we will not turn away from this challenge, we will not ignore this problem; it has to be dealt with and it's going to be dealt with now, one way or the other.

Letter from UNMOVIC Chairman Blix and IAEA Director General El Baradei to General Al-Saadi, October 8, 2002

Dear General Al-Saadi, Advisor, Presidential Office, Baghdad, Iraq,

During our recent meeting in Vienna, we discussed practical arrangements that are prerequisites for the resumption of inspections in Iraq by UNMOVIC and the IAEA. As you recall, at the end of our meeting in Vienna we agreed on a statement which listed some of the principal results achieved, particularly Iraq's acceptance of all the rights of inspection provided for in all of the relevant Security Council resolutions. This acceptance was stated to be without any conditions attached.

During our 3 October 2002 briefing to the Security Council, members of the Council suggested that we prepare a written document on all of the conclusions we reached in Vienna. This letter lists those conclusions and seeks your confirmation thereof. We shall report accordingly to the Security Council.

In the statement at the end of the meeting, it was clarified that UNMOVIC and the IAEA will be granted immediate, unconditional and unrestricted access to sites, including what was termed "sensitive sites" in the past.

As we noted, however, eight presidential sites have been the subject of special procedures under a Memorandum of Understanding of 1998. Should these sites be subject, as all other sites, to immediate, unconditional and unrestricted access, UNMOVIC and the IAEA would conduct inspections there with the same professionalism.

We confirm our understanding that UNMOVIC and the IAEA have the right to determine the number of inspectors required for access to any particular site. This determination will be made on the basis of the size and complexity of the site being inspected. We also confirm that Iraq will be informed of the designation of additional sites, i.e. sites not declared by Iraq or previously inspected by either UNSCOM or the IAEA, through a Notification of Inspection (NIS) provided upon arrival of the inspectors at such sites.

Iraq will ensure that no proscribed material, equipment, records or other relevant items will be destroyed except in the presence of UNMOVIC and/or IAEA inspectors, as appropriate, and at their request. UNMOVIC and the IAEA may conduct interviews with any person in Iraq whom they believe may have information relevant to their mandate. Iraq will facilitate such interviews. It is for UNMOVIC and the IAEA to choose the mode and location for interviews.

The National Monitoring Directorate (NMD) will, as in the past, serve as the Iraqi counterpart for the inspectors. The Baghdad Ongoing Monitoring and Verification Centre (BOMVIC) will be maintained on the same premises and under the same conditions as was the former Baghdad Monitoring and Verification Centre. The NMD will make available services as before, cost free, for the refurbishment of the premises.

The NMD will provide free of cost: (a) escorts to facilitate access to sites to be inspected and communication with personnel to be interviewed; (b) a hotline for BOMVIC which will be staffed by an English speaking person on a 24 hour a day/seven days a week basis; (c) support in terms of personnel and ground transportation within the country, as requested; and (d) assistance in the movement of materials and equipment at inspectors' request (construction, excavation equipment, etc.). NMD will also ensure that escorts are available in the event of inspections outside normal working hours, including at night and on holidays.

Regional UNMOVIC/IAEA offices may be established, for example, in Basra and Mosul, for the use of their inspectors. For this purpose, Iraq will provide, without cost, adequate office buildings, staff accommodation, and appropriate escort personnel.

UNMOVIC and the IAEA may use any type of voice or data transmission, including satellite and/or inland networks, with or without encryption capability. UNMOVIC and the IAEA may also install equipment in the field with the capability for transmission of data directly to the BOMVIC, New York and Vienna (e.g. sensors, surveillance cameras). This will be facilitated by Iraq and there will be no interference by Iraq with UNMOVIC or IAEA communications.

Iraq will provide, without cost, physical protection of all surveillance equipment, and construct antennae for remote transmission of data, at the request of UNMOVIC and the IAEA. Upon request by UNMOVIC through the NMD, Iraq will allocate frequencies for communications equipment.

Iraq will provide security for all UNMOVIC and IAEA personnel. Secure and suitable accommodations will be designated at normal rates by Iraq for these personnel. For their part, UNMOVIC and the IAEA will require that their staff not stay at any accommodation other than those identified in consultation with Iraq. On the use of fixed-wing aircraft for transport of personnel and equipment and for inspection purposes, it was clarified that aircraft used by UNMOVIC and IAEA staff arriving in Baghdad may land at Saddam International Airport. The points of departure of incoming aircraft will be decided by UNMOVIC. The Rasheed airbase will continue to be used for UNMOVIC and IAEA helicopter operations. UNMOVIC and Iraq will establish air liaison offices at the airbase. At both Saddam International Airport and Rasheed airbase, Iraq will provide the necessary support premises and facilities. Aircraft fuel will be provided by Iraq, as before, free of charge.

On the wider issue of air operations in Iraq, both fixed-wing and rotary, Iraq will guarantee the safety of air operations in its air space outside the no-fly zones. With regard to air operations in the no-fly zones, Iraq will take all steps within its control to ensure the safety of such operations.

Helicopter flights may be used, as needed, during inspections and for technical activities, such as gamma detection, without limitation in all parts of Iraq and without any area excluded. Helicopters may also be used for medical evacuation.

On the question of aerial imagery, UNMOVIC may wish to resume the use of U-2 or Mirage overflights. The relevant practical arrangements would be similar to those implemented in the past.

As before, visas for all arriving staff will be issued at the point of entry on the basis of the U.N. Laissez-Passer or U.N. Certificate; no other entry or exit formalities will be required. The aircraft passenger manifest will be provided one hour in advance of the arrival of the aircraft in Baghdad. There will be no searching of UNMOVIC or IAEA personnel or of official or personal baggage. UNMOVIC and the IAEA will ensure that their personnel respect the laws of Iraq restricting the export of certain items, for example, those related to Iraq's national cultural heritage. UNMOVIC and the IAEA may bring into, and remove from, Iraq all of the items and materials they require, including satellite phones and other equipment. With respect to samples, UNMOVIC and IAEA will, where feasible, split samples so that Iraq may receive a portion while another portion is kept for reference purposes. Where appropriate, the organizations will send the samples to more than one laboratory for analysis.

We would appreciate your confirmation of the above as a correct reflection of our talks in Vienna. Naturally, we may need other practical arrangements when proceeding with inspections. We would expect in such matters, as with the above, Iraq's cooperation in all respect.

Yours sincerely,

Hans Blix

Mohamed El Baradei

Remarks by Secretary Powell, October 9, 2002

Secretary Colin Powell was interviewed on CNN's Larry King Live.

Q. It's always a great pleasure to welcome him to this program, the Secretary of State of the United States, Colin Powell. Now, Secretary Powell, we'll begin with your response to the assessment raised in the letter by the Deputy CIA Director stating that Baghdad now appears to be drawing a line short of conducting terrorist attacks. Is this now in opposition to what the President said the other night?

Secretary Powell. Well, I don't know, Larry. I always take with a grain of salt anything that comes out of Baghdad, and we are always trying to make an assessment. But, you know, what you have to do in this case is measure Saddam Hussein's intentions, and his intentions for many years have included developing weapons of mass destruction to threaten his neighbors and threaten the United States if he thought that would serve his purposes, and we know that over the years he has supported terrorist organizations.

So it is not just what he might be doing at any moment in time; it's what his overall intentions have been for that long period of time. We are going to give him a challenge now, hopefully with a strong Congressional resolution, with a strong U.N. resolution, to change his ways, change the behavior of that regime, or the regime will have to be changed. And we're hard at work on that, and I think the President has been doing a terrific job in making the case.

Q. Mr. Secretary, therefore, is the CIA's assessment wrong or is the CIA just relating what they hear?

Secretary Powell. It's an assessment, Larry, and it's always a function of the information they have available to them at any particular point in time. Assessments rise in likelihood of occurrence or not a likelihood of occurrence depending on information that comes in. So we always have to see an assessment like that as a snapshot at a point in time.

Q. A great general once told me, Chappie James—I know you knew him well.

Secretary Powell. Very well.

Q.—that no one hates war more than a warrior. You've been a warrior. Do you fear the possibility that if a military action does occur, it becomes a self-fulfilling prophecy and Iraq then uses its chemical weapons on a state like Israel?

Secretary Powell. War should never be a self-fulfilling prophecy; it should always be a deliberate act by people acting rationally, hopefully. And in this case, as the President said the other night, we are trying to see war as a last resort. There is a way to avoid war, but it must include the disarmament of Saddam Hussein, taking away his weapons of mass destruction and the capability to produce them.

If that can be done through the international community rallying around the President's agenda, the international community coming together and supporting the resolutions that the U.N. has passed for many years, and the new resolution that I think will be put before the U.N., then we can solve this problem, hopefully, without war.

But if it takes military action to solve this problem, then that's what we will do, either in concert with other nations under a U.N. mandate or, if necessary, the President is prepared to act with just like-minded nations without a U.N. mandate. But it's much better to do it with the international community coming together.

Q. Just to make this clear: Saddam Hussein—and he might be watching for all we know, we are seen in Baghdad—he has to do what that would prevent him facing military action? What does he have to do?

Secretary Powell. He has to eliminate all of his weapons of mass destruction, and the only way we can be sure of that is to send inspectors in who have total access to any place in Iraq to see whoever they have to see anytime they decide they have to go see that place or person without any interference. We will see whether or not the Iraqi regime is prepared to cooperate on that basis. And if they cooperate on that basis and they can assure the international community that they have been disarmed, that will take care of at least one of the many U.N. resolutions, and I think we will have a different situation that we will have to examine at that time.

Q. What's the timetable? When does he have to start doing this?

Secretary Powell. Well, he should have been doing it over the years. He should have done it in 1991. I think it is important for us to act promptly now. That's why I hope the United States Congress will act promptly on its resolution, the resolution that President Bush helped draft with the Congress, because that will show that America is united behind this effort; and with that Congressional resolution, then I think our efforts to get a U.N. resolution are strengthened. And I hope that this will all come about in the not too distant future, within a matter of days, or perhaps a week or two.

Q. It has always been said that you were one opposed to us acting unilaterally. Do you still favor that position that we don't do it without the U.N. and Congressional approval?

Secretary Powell. I think it is always best to rally friends to a cause that they should be rallied to, a cause that we all should believe in. And in this instance, we can rally the international community. The President did exactly just that on the 12th of September when he went before the United Nations and reminded them of their responsibilities, laid out the indictment against the Iraqi regime, and then said clearly what the Iraqi regime had to do, and then he made it also clear that there had to be consequences if Iraq did not comply this time.

It is always best to see if you can do it with like-minded nations and with the support of the international community; but at the same time, if the United States is in danger, at risk, the President has the inherent right as President of the United States to do whatever is required to protect us. That might sometimes require unilateral action. It is not because we don't like multilateral action, but because it is necessary to act unilaterally. And that is not a new position; it has happened very often in the course of our history.

Q. Are you frankly, Mr. Secretary, optimistic or pessimistic about the response of Iraq?

Secretary Powell. I have stopped trying to handicap the Iraqi regime a long time ago. All I know is that I think the international community is coming together this time to put down a strong demand.

There is no debate in New York among the Security Council members about the fact that Saddam Hussein has violated these resolutions. There is also no debate among my colleagues in the Security Council that we need to have a tough inspection regime that is any time, any place, anybody.

The discussion is: How do you link consequences to their failure to act this time? So it is not a matter of being optimistic or pessimistic. We will just see what they do. I do know that there is a new determination, a new understanding within the international community that we cannot turn away from it this time, we cannot look away and trust Saddam Hussein to do the right thing; he has to know that there will be consequences for violating whatever new resolution is put down.

This is not a matter of negotiation with him or measuring optimism or pessimism from day to day; this is a realistic approach, it's a real approach, it's a way to solve a problem and see if we can do it without going to war. But there must be consequences for failure to comply, and if those consequences include going to war, then I hope the international community will understand the importance of us doing this as an international community.

Q. Mr. Secretary, no state likes to start a war, so the obvious is: What is the threat to this state, the United States, in starting it? What can he do to us?

Secretary Powell. His conventional military capability—tanks, planes, divisions—nowhere near the capability they had 12 years ago at the time of the Gulf war. The Gulf war succeeded in bringing that conventional capability down to size.

What would concern us are the weapons of mass destruction, the very reason that such a conflict may be necessary. We do know that he has stocks of biological weapons, chemical weapons. We don't believe he has a nuclear weapon, but there's no doubt he has been working toward that end. And that's what we want to make sure does not happen: him to be in possession of a nuclear weapon. So he could use these chemical and biological weapons against our forces going in; but more seriously, he could use them against neighbors or against his own people, as he has done in the past.

At the time of the Gulf war 12 years ago, we also attributed him with the capability to use chemical and biological weapons and we took the risk at that time, protecting our troops as they went into battle, and he demonstrated that he would strike at his neighbors. He fired scud missiles at Israel and at Saudi Arabia. He caused casualties, but those missiles did not contain chemical or biological agents. I don't know whether they would or would not this time.

But we have to make sure that if it comes to conflict we do everything we can to protect our friends in the region and we also send out a clear deterrent message to the Iraqi regime about the inadvisability of using such weapons, and especially get that message down to the commanders and units that might be the ones ordered to use those weapons and let them know they would be held to account for the consequences of such use.

Q. You were a commander. Would a commander listen to the statements made, threatening statements made, by another nation?

Secretary Powell. If that commander thought that he might face the consequences of not listening, if that individual thought he could be brought to justice for this kind of crime against humanity, and if that individual started to lose confidence in his leadership, recognizing that his leadership was about to be removed, then there may be a different calculation going through his mind and he might well be paying close attention to what we're saying.

Q. A few other things, Mr. Secretary. Israel supports the United States completely in this, yet they face the most immediate danger. Is this a dichotomy?

Secretary Powell. Well, they do face a danger. I think Saddam Hussein and the weapons he's been developing are a danger to all the nations in the region, to include Israel. And so that's why Israel has been a strong supporter of the need for the international community or for nations who are inclined to act together, if not under the umbrella of the international community, to deal with this threat.

Q. So much has been written about rifts, and we've dealt and discussed this before. Under what circumstances, Mr. Secretary, would a cabinet member, yourself, resign? In other words, you're a good soldier and good soldiers have to support. Is there a circumstance under which you would say, "I can't live with what we're doing"?

Secretary Powell. Larry, there's no point in getting into this kind of a discussion. We are knitted together as a cabinet team, as a national security team, on this issue, under the leadership of the President. He has given us clear guidance. He has given us clear instructions and he's given us a vision of what we have to accomplish. And we know what we have to do. We have to be firm at this moment in history. We have to be united as a cabinet, as a nation, and I think we are. And we also should be united as an international community, the United Nations coming together.

And it is all for the purpose of removing a threat to the region, a threat to the people of Iraq, and a threat potentially to the United States if we do not now disarm Iraq one way or the other.

And so the question you posed—that nice, hypothetical, rhetorical one—has no relevance at the moment.

White House Press Briefing, October 9, 2002

Q. One question, Ari, about—I know you were asked at the gaggle this morning about the CIA report related to Saddam Hussein and terrorism. Related to that, do you think it's—do you think you can share a little more with the American people what's on the President's mind with regard to what is a pretty big question, the unknown related to Saddam Hussein and his biological and chemical weapons status, whether he might use that against American troops should a decision be made to go into combat? What's the policy or the plan to deal with that? It's a pretty scary prospect, I think, for a lot of people.

Mr. Fleischer. Well, one, the very fact that you raise a valid issue is another reason why Saddam Hussein presents such a threat to the world, because the very fact that people say he has these weapons, he may use these weapons—despite the fact that he denies he has them—suggests that blackmail is something the United States has to consider. The fact that he might do this means the United States has to limit what it does to prevent him from harming people is a fact that Saddam Hussein counts on to hold the world at abeyance. And that's why the President feels so strongly it is important to—for the world to continue to pressure Saddam Hussein to disarm.

As for the specifics, David, as you know the President said in his speech that he is basically giving advice to Saddam Hussein's military not to listen to Saddam Hussein if they are told by Saddam Hussein to use these weapons. But, of course, the military is trained, the military is ready, the military is able to deal with such threats. The President hopes it won't come to that point.

Q. But if I can just follow on that—but should the American people—don't they deserve a little bit more information to deal with what is the biggest unknown and the most menacing unknown of combat?

Mr. Fleischer. What type of information are you suggesting?

Q. Well, how specifically we plan to deal with the potential that the CIA is talking about of a terrorist strike launched away from troops, or using his weapons of mass destruction against troops and how we would try to counteract it, and what might follow.

Mr. Fleischer. Well, of course, on the question of what we would do specifically from a military point of view, I think the military would be somewhat reluctant to describe every tactic they would take, because that would be information that an enemy would want to know. In order to hone an attack or have a more effective attack, they would, of course, want to know what defenses are available to those who might be attacked. So there are some limits on what can be said about that publicly, and I think people understand that.

But this is why in the President's speech he cited—and the President raised this himself when he said there is no easy or risk-free course of action. Some argue we should wait, and the President said, that's the riskiest of all options. The longer we wait, the stronger and bolder Saddam Hussein will become. And the President has said that an Iraqi regime faced with its own demise may attempt cruel and desperate measures. This is a reflection on how serious we take the threat from Saddam Hussein.

Q. Ari, one thing the President did not say was what Secretary Tenet said—Director Tenet said in that letter, and that is that Saddam has drawn a line against weapons of mass destruction, and there's a low probability that he will use them unless he sees a threat coming from the U.S., unless he is cornered. Does the President agree with that assessment, or not?

Mr. Fleischer. Well, the President, of course, has this information from the CIA and uses this in all his analysis, and he has no quarrels with what he has received from the CIA. It goes into the full context of all the information he receives about the threat that Saddam Hussein poses, and the threat that he presents. And the point that I make to you on that is that, when you talk about the probabilities, as the President said in his own speech last night, or two nights ago, he said, "We can wait and hope that Saddam does not give weapons to terrorists or develop a nuclear weapon to blackmail the world, but I am convinced that that is a hope against all evidence. As Americans, we want peace, we work and sacrifice for peace. But there can be no peace if our security depends on the will and whims of a ruthless and aggressive dictator."

And that's the problem, Ron, that this issue presents—that the only person who has sure knowledge of whether Saddam Hussein will use those weapons is Saddam Hussein. And you have to be aware of the fact that to suggest that as a result of unknowns, the President cannot defend the American people—that relies on us trusting Saddam Hussein, and being willing to say that since Saddam Hussein is the only one who knows whether he'll use those weapons, we can't act or should not act, because we'll rely on his will and whim.

Q. So even though in one part of the CIA Director's memo, where he clearly says there's a low probability that Saddam will strike unless he's cornered, the President, as he says in the speech, believes he's not going to risk one life on Saddam Hussein's word?

Mr. Fleischer. Well, I think—you also have to report what the rest of the statement was from the Director, because it wasn't just that truncated part of it. It was, in full fashion, the Director of the CIA had more to say than that. He went on to say that "there is no question that the likelihood of Saddam using WMD"—weapons of mass destruction—"against the United States and its allies in the region for blackmail, deterrence, or otherwise, rose as he continues to build his arsenal. His past use of WMD against civilian and military targets shows that he produces those weapons to use, and not just deter."

So that's the full context of what the Director said. And let me put it to you this way: Another way to look at this is if Saddam Hussein holds a gun to your head even while he denies that he actually owns a gun, how safe should you feel?

Q. I was going down the same road as Ron. I'm just wondering how you get this difference of opinion out there. Obviously, it's a national intelligence estimate. They're both working off of the same intelligence. How is it the President says, on the one hand, during his speech on Monday that at any given moment, this could happen, where the Deputy Director of the CIA reports the probability of that is low?

Mr. Fleischer. Well, keep in mind, too, and to be precise and to be accurate for both, when the President said at any given moment it could happen, he is referring to the transfer of weapons to terrorist organizations.

Q.—what the Deputy Director was saying.

Mr. Fleischer. No, I think his quote actually is, as you see, about Saddam Hussein, Iraq using them himself.

Q. I read that as engaging in terrorist activities.

Mr. Fleischer. The quote in the letter that's been public now since last night is, "My judgment would be that the probability of him initiating an attack," and then he goes on to describe it, initiating—

Q.—saying anything about the transfer—

Mr. Fleischer. The difference is him initiating versus the transfer. But the point the President is making on all of this, it depends on Saddam Hussein's decisions. And the trust, therefore, has to fall to Saddam Hussein not to use what he has.

And another way to look at this, I think, to keep this in the context of what is known, is what was the probability that Saddam Hussein would invade Iran? He did. What was the probability of Saddam Hussein invading Kuwait? He did. What was the probability of Saddam Hussein using chemical weapons against his own people? He did. There are some things that are clearly known from history that we have to learn from, lest we make mistakes, to protect the American people into the future.

The other thing, and let me just draw this to the general nature of intelligence information, sometimes it is the very fact of intelligence information that the only way of surely knowing anything is to know it in the past because it's too late and the damage has been done. You always have to remember, particularly with a country like Iraq, that they engage in deception and they engage in a great bit of planning to deploy in a way that we will never know. And so intelligence is limited in what it can tell you with certainty. The risks, however, as the President said, when dealing with Saddam Hussein and his history and his abilities, are such that the American people face a growing threat.

* * * *

Q. Helen's right. And I have a question—how much does oil have to do with the assessment of the threat from Saddam Hussein? President Bush didn't mention it.

Mr. Fleischer. I'm not sure I follow your question.

Q. Well, you keep talking about blackmail. You're talking about blackmailing the region to get control of the oil supplies. How significant is that in the President's thinking?

Mr. Fleischer. I see. Well, if you take a look at what the President said when he went to the United Nations, and what Congress said when it passed the Iraq Liberation Act for regime change in 1998, that issue is not in play.

The issue is the enforcement of the United Nations resolutions urging—calling on Iraq to make certain that they disarm, that they cease the development of weapons of mass destruction, they cease the hostility towards its neighbors, the repression of minorities. And Congress stated similar positions in 1998. Those are the factors, Terry, that threaten the peace.

Q. But when you talk about the potential—the very real potential that if he gets a nuclear weapon he'll be able to blackmail the world, what would we be concerned that he wants, that he would demand?

Mr. Fleischer. Think if Saddam Hussein had nuclear weapons at the time he invaded Iran, or the time he invaded Kuwait. If he had invaded Kuwait in possession of nuclear weapons, think how much harder it would have been to put the coalition together to forcibly remove Saddam Hussein from Kuwait. If he has them, he knows that that calculation changes and changes dramatically.

And the risk with Saddam Hussein is, while others may have nuclear weapons, Saddam Hussein has a military history of invading his neighbors, using the military tools he has to accomplish through force what cannot and should not be accomplished, that is the takeover of others. And that's why the U.N., as part of its resolution cited the need for him to cease his hostility toward his neighbors.

Q. But if his neighbors didn't have so much oil—there are countries in Africa which invade each other and we don't get involved—most security analysts take a look at it and say oil is a central aspect to the nation's security. And Saddam Hussein getting control of the world's oil supplies—are you saying oil is not at all a factor in the President's thinking?

Mr. Fleischer. I think when you take a look at what the United Nations voted for, what the Congress voted for, what President Clinton signed, and what President Bush supports, that is not a factor.

Q. So oil is not a factor?

Mr. Fleischer. That is not a factor. This is about preserving the peace and saving the lives of Americans. And it's also—a factor that is new is what took place on September 11th, and the awakening here that we are vulnerable to attacks on our own soil, now, and that Saddam Hussein, if he links up with terrorists, has an interest in harming us.

Q. So the stability of oil prices is not a national security or an economic matter—how can you say that it's not a factor? I just don't understand that.

Mr. Fleischer. The question is about any potential use of military force. And this is about saving the lives of American people.

Q. Saddam Hussein's oil reserves are not at all a factor in any of the geopolitical calculations?

Mr. Fleischer. No, the question as I took it was about whether or not this is a factor in what makes us—

Q.—on a broader question.

Mr. Fleischer. I think the reasons are exactly as the President stated. Now, there are implications as a result of any action that will have effects on the economy. And no one can predict what those will or will not be. The past history, at least in 1991, shows that the projections and the predictions were dire and were wrong, but I think it's impossible to state what the impact will be if this comes to pass.

Q. But the White House doesn't have anybody looking at what those implications would be?

Mr. Fleischer. Again, I think it's impossible to state with any precision what that effect might be. But the question as I took it—get back to cause and motive for why we are considering military action.

Remarks by Representatives Stark (D-CA), Castle (R-DE), Reyes (D-TX), Pomeroy (D-ND), Kleckza (D-WI), Sununu (R-NH), and Goodlatte (R-VA), October 9, 2002

The following remarks were made during the House debate on the resolution authorizing the use of force in Iraq.

Representative Stark (D-CA). Mr. Speaker, I rise in opposition to this resolution. I am deeply troubled that lives may be lost without a meaningful attempt to bring Iraq into compliance with U.N. resolutions through careful and cautious diplomacy.

The bottom line is that I do not trust the President and his advisors.

Make no mistake. We are voting on a resolution that grants total authority to a President who wants to invade a sovereign nation without any specific act of provocation. This would authorize the United States to act as the aggressor for the first time in our history. And it sets a precedent for our Nation or any nation to exercise brute force anywhere in the world without regard to international law or international consensus. Congress must not walk in lockstep behind a President who has been so callous as to proceed without reservation as if the war is of no real consequence.

Mr. Speaker, 3 years ago, in December, Molly Ivins, an observer of Texas politics wrote, "For an upper-class white boy, Bush comes on way too hard, at a guess, to make up for being an upper-class white boy. Somebody," she wrote, "should be worrying about how all this could affect his handling of future encounters with some Saddam Hussein." Pretty prophetic, Ms. Ivins.

Let us not forget that our President, our Commander in Chief, has no experience or knowledge of war. In fact, he admits that he was at best ambivalent about the Vietnam War. He skirted his own military service and then failed to serve out his time in the National Guard; and he reported years later that, at the height of the conflict in 1968, he did not notice any "heavy stuff" going on.

So we have a President who thinks foreign territory is the opponent's dug-out and Kashmir is a sweater. What is most unconscionable is that there is not a shred of evidence to justify the certain loss of life. Do the generalized threats and half-truths of this administration give any one of us in Congress the confidence to tell a mother or father or family that the loss of their child or loved one was in the name of a just cause? Is the President's need for revenge for the threat once posed to his father enough to justify the death of any American? I submit the answer to these questions is no.

Aside from the wisdom of going to war as Bush wants, I am troubled by who pays for his capricious adventure into world domination. The Administration admits to a cost of around $200 billion. Now, wealthy individuals will not pay; they have big tax cuts already. Corporations will not pay; they will just continue to cook the books and move overseas and send their contributions to the Republicans. Rich kids will not pay; their daddies will get them deferments as Big George did for George W.

Well, then, who will pay? School kids will pay. There will be no money to keep them from being left behind, way behind. Seniors will pay. They will pay big time as the Republicans privatize Social Security and continue to rob the trust fund to pay for this capricious war. Medicare will be curtailed and drugs will be more unaffordable, and there will not be any money for a drug benefit because Bush will spend it on a war.

Working folks will pay through loss of jobs, job security, and bargaining rights. And our grandchildren will pay, through the degradation of our air and water quality, and the entire Nation will pay as Bush continues to destroy civil rights, women's rights, and religious freedom in a rush to phoney patriotism and to courting the messianic Pharisees of the religious right.

The questions before the Members of this House and to all Americans are immense, but there are clear answers. America is not currently confronted by a genuine, proven, imminent threat from Iraq. The call for war is wrong.

What greatly saddens me at this point in our history is my fear that this entire spectacle has not been planned for the well-being of the world, but for the short-term political interests of our President.

Now, I am also greatly disturbed that many Democratic leaders have also put political calculation above the President's accountability to truth and reason by supporting this resolution.

But I conclude that the only answer is to vote "no" on the resolution before us.

* * * *

Representative Castle (R-DE). Mr. Speaker, I thank the distinguished chairman of the Permanent Select Committee on Intelligence not only for yielding to me but for the extraordinary work he does for this country on a day-in-and-day-out basis in a very difficult circumstance right now.

The vote on the resolution to authorize the use of force to disarm Saddam Hussein is one of the most important decisions we will ever have to make as Members of the House of Representatives. Every Member of Congress wants to do what is right, not only for America but for the entire world.

Today I speak both as the Representative of the people of Delaware and as a member of the Permanent Select Committee on Intelligence. Like many, I have been traveling throughout my State over the past few weeks, and Iraq is on everyone's minds. Individuals have crossed the street to give me their opinions, and seniors have approached me at our annual beach day event.

I have received many personal letters, e-mails, and phone calls from people who have taken the time to sit down and really think about this very difficult issue. They know Saddam Hussein is a tyrannical dictator and would like to see him go. They hope war can be avoided but also want to support the President.

They want to know if immediate military action is necessary and if the risks to our young men and women in uniform are necessary; how will other nations respond if the United States decides to enter the conflict without United Nations' support; what could be the effect on the stability of the Middle East and the fate of the Iraqi people.

I share many of their concerns. That is why I have tried to gather as much information as possible by reading reports, attending briefings, and talking with other Members of Congress. Here is what I have learned: the security of our Nation is at risk.

For the past several months, I have participated in intelligence hearings on the September 11 terrorist attacks and have studied the hatred some nations and groups have toward America. Saddam Hussein is encouraging and promoting this hatred by openly praising the attacks on the United States. The Director of Central Intelligence recently published an unclassified summary of the evidence against Saddam Hussein, and it is substantial.

We know that Iraq has continued building weapons of mass destruction, energized its missile program, and is investing in biological weapons. Saddam Hussein is determined to get weapons-grade material to develop nuclear weapons. Its biological weapons program is larger and more advanced than before the Gulf War. Iraq also is attempting to build unmanned vehicles, UAVs, to possibly deliver biological warfare agents. All of this has been done in flagrant violation of the U.N. Security Council resolutions.

Some may react to this evidence by saying that, in the past, other countries have had similar arsenals and the United States did not get involved. But as President Bush has told us and as Secretary of Defense Rumsfeld reiterated yesterday in a meeting, Saddam Hussein's Iraq is different. This is a ruthless dictator whose record is despicable. He has waged war against his neighbors and on his own people. He has brutalized and tortured his own citizens, harbored terrorist networks, engaged in terrorist acts, lied, cheated, and defied the will of the international community.

Mr. Speaker, I have examined this information and some of the more specific classified reports. The bottom line is, we do not want to get caught off guard. We must take all precautions to avoid a catastrophic event similar to September 11.

In recent meetings, the National Security Adviser, Dr. Condoleezza Rice, rightly called this coercive diplomacy. It is my hope that through forceful diplomacy, backed by clear resolve, we can avoid war. Unfortunately, Saddam Hussein's history of deception makes a new attempt to disarm him difficult. Additionally, our goal to disarm him must also be connected to a plan to end his regime, should he refuse to disarm.

For all these reasons, I would encourage all of us to support this resolution as the best resolution to make this happen.

* * * *

Representative Pomeroy (D-TX). Mr. Speaker, I thank the gentleman for yielding time to me.

Mr. Speaker, when it comes to Iraq, it is time for the United States of America to state forcefully and without equivocation: Enough is enough. Either Saddam Hussein yields to the resolutions of the United Nations, providing for completely unrestricted inspection and disarmament, or the United States and other nations will use military force against his government to enforce his compliance.

This is terribly, terribly serious business, Mr. Speaker, potentially one of life and death for those that will be involved in prosecuting this action. Therefore, I, like so many others, have expressed the view that this vote is one of the most important votes that I will ever cast in this Chamber on behalf of the people of North Dakota.

I reached the conclusion that the resolution authorizing the President to use force should pass, and I do that based upon the following undeniable and uncontroverted facts:

First, Saddam Hussein is a uniquely evil and threatening leader. His past is absolutely replete with nonstop belligerence and aggression, as well as atrocities.

Two, he has been determined to have developed weapons of mass destruction, biological and chemical. He continues to seek nuclear capacity and is believed to be within mere months of having that capacity, in the event he could get his hands on the requisite materials.

Three, he now continues to produce weapons of mass destruction, having effectively completely thwarted the inspection and disarmament requirements of the United Nations; and he has made it increasingly difficult to detect his production facilities, even as he continues to add to his arsenals.

Four, he is harboring and has well-developed relationships with terrorists, including senior al Qaeda operatives.

Five, he certainly has demonstrated that he is not above using weapons of mass destruction. Indeed, he has used them on his own people.

Now, under these terrible circumstances, I have concluded that doing nothing is simply not acceptable for the United States of America. We need to act, and determining exactly how to act is the question before this Chamber.

I believe that we should support the President as he builds an international consensus to reinstitute completely unfettered inspections, or to use force in the event it is not forthcoming. In dealing with Saddam Hussein, I believe our only hope of enlisting the cooperation of his government is if he knows for an absolute certainty there will be terrible consequences if he does not comply.

Therefore, in looking at the resolutions before this body, I think we can only conclude that the President needs the authorization to act if he is to have any hope of enlisting the cooperation from Saddam Hussein. A two-vote alternative in my view sends a mixed signal: Go try and enlist his cooperation, and we will evaluate what to do if you do not succeed.

The administration has made it very, very clear, and I have heard the President express this personally, that the use of force would be his absolute last wish. I believe, therefore, we need to give him the resolution and the authority from this body that, first, seek disarmament and under terms that are unlike any other imposed upon Iraq any time, anywhere, by any person; and in the event that is not forthcoming, there shall be force to insist on his cooperation, or to replace the regime and obtain cooperation from a new government.

I understand, Mr. Speaker, the difficulty of this decision. But, again, the facts are clear, and doing nothing is not acceptable. I urge adoption of the resolution.

* * * *

Representative Reyes (D-WI). Mr. Speaker, I thank the gentleman for yielding me time on this very important issue that we debate.

There are many things that make me proud to be an American. One of them is to be here today to be able to debate this issue. As my previous colleague stated when he quoted a general that said that war is hell, take it from somebody that has been there. Thirty-five years ago, I found myself half a world away in a place called Vietnam. I can tell my colleagues that war is hell. There are a lot of us here today that have had that same experience, but are taking different positions on this resolution. Some of my colleagues have asked why, when they hear my friend and colleague, the gentleman from California (Mr. Cunningham), talk about his experience and his favoring in support of the resolution.

I will tell my colleagues that I intend to vote against this resolution. I intend to do so because in meetings I have held in my district, mothers and fathers and veterans come to me and tell me, please, do not let us get back into a war without exhausting all other avenues. I think every one of us in this House brings our own experiences as we represent our constituents. Every one of us here wrestles with a very tough decision as to whether or not to go forward with a resolution on war. Every one of us understands that we are a nation of laws, that we lead the world by example, that we have a great respect for process and to protect the rights of everyone.

That is why, Mr. Speaker, I reluctantly today rise in opposition against this resolution, because I think that the President has not made a case as to why Iraq and why attack Saddam Hussein. As a member of the Committee on Intelligence, I have asked consistently the questions to those that have come before us with information, I have asked the question of what is the connection between 9-11 and Iraq and Saddam Hussein. None.

What is the connection between Iraq and Saddam Hussein and al Qaeda? Very little, if any.

As to the weapons of mass destruction, the delivery systems and all of these things, we have clearly heard that there is a lot of speculation about those capabilities.

Last week, I was part of a group of colleagues that met with a retired general that was in charge of this conflicted area of our world. He was asking the same question that we were: Why Iraq, and why Saddam Hussein?

In fact, when we asked him to list in priority order a war against Iraq and Saddam Hussein, he listed it as his seventh priority. When we asked him, what would you do in our situation, he was as perplexed as we are being in this situation.

September 11 changed things. I concede that. More than that, for me personally being first-time grandfather changed things as well. I bring to this position and to this decision the experience that I brought as a Member of Congress.

My staff asked me, Congressman, what are you going to say to the troops? Because I have taken the opportunity to go out and visit our troops in Afghanistan three times since Easter. I know the conditions they are living in, and I know the conditions they are fighting in. Those are similar to the same conditions of some 35 years ago. War is hell, and we ought to exhaust every single possible remedy before going to war, before subjecting our troops, our men and women in uniform, to those kinds of consequences.

So I tell my staff, I will tell the troops the same thing that I will tell the American people on the floor of Congress, that I oppose this resolution because I think that the case has not been made. I do not take giving my support for war lightly, as neither do my colleagues on both sides of the aisle. But each one of us has to wrestle with his or her own conscience.

I want to make sure that my granddaughter, Amelia, maybe 35 years from now, can look and say, my grandfather made his decision on the information that he had. He opposed the resolution because he did not think it was the right thing to do.

But I will tell the Members this: When and if the President makes a decision to commit troops, when and if the President commits us to a war, I intend to be there. Because my experience in coming to this Congress, my experience of some 35 years ago, returning from Vietnam and seeing all the protests and seeing all the signs and seeing all the things that they were calling us, was very divisive.

So it is inherent upon us to do what our conscience dictates on this issue today. I oppose it reluctantly under those circumstances, but I will support whatever decision our President and our country makes.

* * * *

Representative Kleczka (D-WI). Mr. Speaker, although we all know this war resolution will pass, I nevertheless must question the wisdom and morality of an unprovoked attack on another foreign nation. The guiding principle of our foreign policy for over 50 years has been one of containment and deterrence. This is the same strategy that kept the former Soviet Union in check, a power whose possession of weapons of mass destruction had been proven and not speculated, and in fact led to its downfall.

The administration asserts that this time-tested policy is not sufficient to deal with this, yes, dangerous but small, economically weakened Middle Eastern nation. Instead, they support a new policy of a unilateral preemptive attack against Iraq, citing the unproven possibility that Saddam Hussein might be a risk to the security of the United States.

The long-term effects of this go-it-alone, shoot-first policy will be to lose the high moral ground we have exercised in the past to deter other nations from attacking militarily when they felt their security was at stake. The next time Pakistani and Indian troops mass at their borders with both nations' fingers on nuclear triggers, what moral authority will we have to prevent a potential catastrophe? They would justifiably ignore our pleas for diplomatic or negotiated approaches and instead simply follow our lead.

The administration continues to assert that Iraq is an urgent threat to our national security and that we are at risk of an Iraqi surprise attack. But the resolution before us offers no substantiation of these allegations, speaking only of hunches, probabilities, and suspicions. That is not sufficient justification to start a war.

Further, there is reference to the 9/11 terrorism we suffered and the assertion that members of al Qaeda are in Iraq. After extensive investigation, our intelligence community could find no link between the Iraqi regime and the plot that led to last year's deadly terrorist attacks.

Also it has become reported that al Qaeda members are in Iran, Pakistan and Saudi Arabia. Do we attack them next?

The resolution further asserts also without any evidence that there is a great risk that Iraq could launch a surprise attack on the United States with weapons of mass destruction. It is fact that Saddam does not possess a delivery system that has the throw power of 8,000 miles or anything even close. And if there is such a great risk that he has and will use biological and chemical weapons against us, why did he not do so in the Gulf War? The answer is because he knew that our response would be strong, swift, and fatal. Hussein is not a martyr; he is a survivalist.

Similarly, the evidence does not show that Iraq has any nuclear capabilities. General Wesley Clark, former commander of NATO forces in Europe, contends that "despite all the talk of 'loose nukes,' Saddam does not have any," or the highly enriched uranium or plutonium to enable him to construct them.

Air Force General Richard B. Myers, chairman of the Joint Chiefs of Staff, recently concurred, admitting that the consensus is that Saddam Hussein "does not have a nuclear weapon, but he wants one."

One of the goals of the President is to force a regime change in Iraq. Who are we to dictate to another country that their leadership must be changed? What would be our reaction if another country demanded or threatened to remove President Bush? All of us, Republicans and Democrats alike and each and every American, would be infuriated by such an inference and rise up against them. Changes in regimes must come from within.

The result of voting for this resolution will be to give the President a blank check with broad authority to use our Armed Forces to unilaterally attack Iraq. He merely has to tell us why he believes that continued diplomatic efforts will fail and does not have to give that information to Congress until 48 hours after he has begun the war.

The more meaningful provision would be to provide for a two-step process where after all diplomatic efforts have failed, the President would come back to Congress and make the case that military force is now necessary.

Our colleague, the gentleman from South Carolina (Mr. Spratt), has that provision in his alternative and it deserves our careful consideration. Let us make no mistake about it, Hussein is a brutal dictator who has flagrantly defied the will of the world community. But the case has simply not been made either by this resolution or by the administration that there is a clear and present danger to the security of the United States which would warrant this Nation embarking on its first unprovoked preemptive attack in our 226-year history.

The President must continue to work together with our allies in the U.N. Security Council to ensure that the Iraqi regime is disarmed. Mr. Speaker, war should always be the last resort and not the first. For all these reasons, I cannot support this resolution and must vote "no."

* * * *

Representative Sununu (R-NH). Mr. Speaker, I rise today in support of the resolution, a resolution which I believe will send a clear and an unmistakable message to our own citizens, our allies, and our enemies, as well, that Congress stands behind our President in defense of America's national security interests.

Mr. Speaker, there is no more serious an issue for Congress to debate than the question of authorizing the use of America's Armed Forces. We are a peaceful Nation, preferring instead to rely on diplomacy in our relations with other countries.

On the question of Iraq in particular, the United States and the United Nations have been exceedingly patient, working steadily to integrate Iraq into the community of law-abiding nations, but to date we have failed. In the decades since Desert Storm, Iraq has chosen a very different path. Iraq has worked to develop weapons of mass destruction, including chemical and biological agents; and Saddam Hussein has repeatedly ignored U.N. resolutions demanding that he disarm. He has refused to allow weapons inspectors access to potential sites. Thus, the threat of obtaining stocks of these terrible weapons continues to grow.

Most troubling of all, Saddam Hussein has shown, has demonstrated, his willingness to use such horrible weapons against other nations and against his own people. Only when military action is imminent does the Iraqi regime begin to discuss allowing inspectors to return, but the restrictions they wish to place on these inspectors would effectively render their mission useless and, instead, simply delay action and allow a covert weapons program to begin to bear terrifying results.

If we wait until Iraq succeeds in achieving these goals, we will have waited too long.

The resolution we are debating today encourages a diplomatic solution to the threat that Iraq poses to our national security. The President has called on the U.N. to act effectively to enforce Iraq's disarmament and ensure full compliance with Security Council resolutions. But if the U.N. cannot act effectively, this resolution will provide the President with full support to use all appropriate means.

Mr. Speaker, neither I nor any Member of this body want to see a renewed conflict in Iraq. We must be prepared to act give the President flexibility that he needs to respond to this gathering threat to protect American lives and address the threat to global peace.

I urge my colleagues to support the resolution.

* * * *

Representative Goodlatte (R-VA). Mr. Speaker, I thank the gentleman for yielding me this time.

On the eve of potential military action abroad, I am reminded of President Reagan's speech before the British House of Commons when he said, "If history teaches anything, it teaches self-delusion in the face of unpleasant facts is folly." Reagan was speaking to a people who knew well the ravages of war and the terrible price of appeasement.

Churchill called World War II the unnecessary war. He did not mean that it was unnecessary to rise to the occasion and defeat Nazism, he meant that had we taken early notice of Hitler's clearly stated intentions rather than naively drifting through the 1930s, a world war may not have been necessary. Weary of conflict, some of the allies adopted a policy of peace at any price, but no peace that a freedom-loving people could tolerate.

While the circumstances are different, there are lessons to be drawn from the annals of history. Just because we ignore evil does not mean that it ceases to exist. Appeasement invites aggression. Dictators, tyrants and megalomaniacs should not be trusted.

Saddam Hussein has used weapons of bioterror against his own countrymen. He has committed genocide, killing between 50,000 and 100,000 people in northern Iraq. His regime is responsible for widespread human rights abuses, including imprisonment, executions, torture and rape. Just in the past 12 years, he has invaded Kuwait, he has launched ballistic missiles at Israel, Saudi Arabia, Bahrain, and previously at Iran.

Following the Gulf War, he arrogantly defied the international community, violating sanctions and continued in the development of weapons of mass destruction while evading international inspectors. His regime has violated 16 U.N. resolutions devoid of consequences.

Most ominously, in the wake of the September 11 terrorists' attacks, Saddam has quantifiable links to known terrorists. Iraq and al Qaeda have had high-level contacts stretching back a decade.

We know based on intelligence reports and satellite photos that Saddam is acquiring weapons of mass destruction. He possesses stockpiles of biological and chemical weapons, and he is aggressively seeking nuclear weapons. Every weapon he possesses is a violation of the Gulf War truce. A crazed man in possession of these instruments of death is a frightening prospect, indeed.

Had Saddam possessed nuclear capabilities at the time of the Gulf War, we may not have gone into Kuwait. Should he acquire nuclear capabilities, his aggressions would be virtually unchecked. Deterrence can no longer be relied upon.

President Bush was accurate to characterize Saddam as a grave and gathering danger. The President challenged the U.N., calling into question their relevance should they leave unchecked Saddam's blatant disregard for their authority. He consulted Congress and made a case to the American people. The President should continue to push for a U.N. resolution with uncompromising and immediate requirements for the Iraqi regime, thereby rejecting the tried course of empty diplomacy, fruitless inspections, and failed containment.

Americans looked on in horror as the events of September 11 unfolded. At the end of the day, the skyline of one of our greatest cities was forever changed; the Pentagon, a symbol of America's military might, was still smoldering; and a previously indistinguishable field in western Pennsylvania had suddenly and terribly become an unmarked grave for America's newest heroes.

In the aftermath, Americans have been asking questions, some of which we may never have satisfying answers to. But today we know that a sworn enemy is pursuing weapons of mass destruction. It is incumbent upon the free world, led by the United States, to dismantle these destructive capabilities. We have before us a resolution which will authorize, if necessary, the use of America's military to enforce the demands of the U.N. Security Council.

There is no greater responsibility for us as elected officials than to provide for the common defense of our fellow countrymen. In voting for this resolution, we send a message to a tyrant that he should not rest easy; that those who would venture to strike at our Nation will encounter consequences. We send a message to the Iraqi people that the world has not forgotten them and their suffering at the hands of a madman. We send a message to the world community that we are unified as a Nation; that the President possesses the full faith and backing of this distinguished body; that we are committed to defending the liberties which are the very foundation of our Republic; and that we are steadfast in our resolve in the war on terror.

Remarks by Senators Leahy (D-VT), Kerry (D-MA) and Hagel (R-NE), October 9, 2002

The following remarks were made during the Senate debate on the resolution authorizing the use of force in Iraq.

Senator Leahy (D-VT). Mr. President, I have enjoyed this colloquy and would yield further, but I know there are other Senators awaiting their turn to speak.

On September 26, I spoke at length in this Chamber about the important issue before us. I voiced my concerns and the concerns of a great many Vermonters—in fact, a great many Americans from whom I have heard. I spoke about the President's plan to send Americans into battle to overthrow Saddam Hussein.

Many Senators have also expressed their views on this difficult decision. As I prepared to speak 2 weeks ago, I listened to Senator Bingaman urge the administration to seriously consider a proposal for "coerced inspections." After I finished speaking, Senator Johnson voiced his support for providing the President with the broad authority he seeks to use military force against Iraq.

The opportunity and responsibility to have this debate is one of the cornerstones on which this institution, and indeed this country is built. Some have suggested that expressing misgivings or asking questions about the President's plan to attack Iraq is somehow unpatriotic. Others have tried to make it an election year issue on bumper stickers or in TV advertisements.

These attempts are misguided. They are beneath the people who make these attempts and they are beneath the issue. This is an issue of war. An issue of war should be openly debated. That is a great freedom of this Nation. We fought a revolution to have such debates.

As I and others have said over and over, declaring war is the single most important responsibility given to Congress. Unfortunately, at times like this, it is a responsibility Congress has often shirked. Too often, Congress has abdicated its responsibility and deferred to the executive branch on such matters. It should not. It should pause and read the Constitution.

In the Senate, we have a duty to the Constitution, to our consciences, and to the American people, especially our men and women in uniform, to ask questions, to discuss the benefits, the risks, the costs, to have a thorough debate and then vote to declare war or not. This body, the Senate, is supposed to be the conscience of the Nation. We should fulfill this great responsibility.

In my 28 years in the Senate, I can think of many instances when we asked questions and took the time to study the facts. It led to significant improvements in what we have done here.

I can also remember times when Senators in both parties wished they had taken more time to carefully consider the issues before them, to ask the hard questions, or make changes to the legislation, despite the sometimes overwhelming public pressure to pass the first bill that came along.

I know following the Constitution is not always politically expedient or popular. The Constitution was not designed to be politically expedient, but following the Constitution is the right course to take. It is what we are sworn to do, and there is no question that having this debate, which really began some months ago, has helped move the administration in the right direction.

Today, we are considering a resolution offered by Senator Lieberman to authorize the use of force. Article I of the Constitution gives the Congress the sole power to declare war. But instead of exercising this responsibility and voting up or down on a declaration of war, what have we done? We have chosen to delegate this authority and this burden to the executive branch.

This resolution, like others before it, does not declare anything. It tells the President: Why don't you decide; we are not going to.

This resolution, when you get through the pages of whereas clauses, is nothing more than a blank check. The President can decide when to use military force, how to use it, and for how long. This Vermonter does not sign blank checks.

Mr. President, I suppose this resolution is something of an improvement. Back in August the President's advisors insisted that there was not even any need for authorization from Congress to go to war. They said past resolutions sufficed.

Others in the administration argued that the United States should attack Iraq preemptively and unilaterally, without bothering to seek the support of the United Nations, even though it is Iraq's violations of U.N. resolutions which is used to justify military action.

Eventually, the President listened to those who urged him to change course and he went to the United Nations. He has since come to the Congress. I commended President Bush for doing that.

I fully support the efforts of Secretary Powell to negotiate a strong, new Security Council resolution for the return of weapons inspectors to Iraq, backed up with force, if necessary, to overcome Iraqi resistance.

Two weeks ago, when the President sent Congress his proposed resolution authorizing the use of force, I said that I hoped his proposal was the beginning of a consultative, bipartisan process to produce a sensible resolution to be acted on at the appropriate time.

I also said that I could envision circumstances which would cause me to support sending U.S. Armed Forces to Iraq. But I also made it clear that I could never support the kind of blank check resolution that the President proposed. I was not elected to do that.

I commend Senator Daschle, Senator Hagel, and others who tried hard to work with the administration to craft a bipartisan resolution that we could all support.

But while the resolution that we are considering today is an improvement from the version that the President first sent to Congress, it is fundamentally the same. It is still a blank check. I will vote against this resolution for all the reasons I have stated before and the reasons I will explain in detail now.

Mr. President, there is no dispute that Saddam Hussein is a menace to his people and to Iraq's neighbors. He is a tyrant and the world would be far better without him.

Saddam Hussein has also made no secret of his hatred of the United States, and should he acquire a nuclear weapon and the means to deliver it, he would pose a grave threat to the lives of all Americans, as well as to our closest allies.

The question is not whether Saddam Hussein should be disarmed; it is how imminent is this threat and how should we deal with it?

Do we go it alone, as some in the administration are eager to do because they see Iraq as their first opportunity to apply the President's strategy of preemptive military force?

Do we do that, potentially jeopardizing the support of those nations we need to combat terrorism and further antagonizing Muslim populations who already deeply resent our policies in the Middle East?

Or, do we work with other nations to disarm Saddam, using force if other options fail?

The resolution now before the Senate leaves the door open to act alone, even absent an imminent threat. It surrenders to the President authority which the Constitution explicitly reserves for the Congress.

And As I said 2 weeks ago, it is premature.

I have never believed, nor do I think that any Senator believes, that U.S. foreign policy should be hostage to any nation, nor to the United Nations. Ultimately, we must do what we believe is right and necessary to protect our security, whenever it is called for. But going to war alone is rarely the answer.

On Monday night, the President spoke about working with the United Nations. He said: "To actually work, any new inspections, sanctions, or enforcement mechanisms will have to be very different. America wants the U.N. to be an effective organization that helps keep the peace. That is why we are urging the Security Council to adopt a new resolution setting out tough, immediate requirements."

I could not agree more. The President is right. The status quo is unacceptable. Past U.N. resolutions have not worked. Saddam Hussein and other Iraqi officials have lied to the world over and over and over. As the President points out, an effort is underway in the U.N. Security Council—led by the United States—to adopt a strong resolution requiring unconditional, unimpeded access for U.N. weapons inspectors, backed up with force if necessary.

That effort is making steady progress. There is wide acceptance that a new resolution is necessary before the inspectors can return to Iraq, and this has put pressure on the other nations, especially Russia and France, to support our position.

If successful, it could achieve the goal of disarming Saddam without putting thousands of American and innocent Iraqi lives at risk or spending tens of billions, or hundreds of billions, of dollars at a time when the U.S. economy is weakening, the Federal deficit is growing, and the retirement savings of America's senior citizens have been decimated.

Diplomacy is often tedious. It does not usually make the headlines or the evening news. We certainly know about past diplomatic failures. But history has shown over and over that diplomatic pressure cannot only protect our national interests, it can also enhance the effectiveness of military force when force becomes necessary.

The negotiations are at a sensitive stage. By authorizing the use of force today, the Congress will be saying that irrespective of what the Security Council does, we have already decided to go our own way.

As Chairman and sometime Ranking Member of the Foreign Operations Subcommittee for over a decade, I have received countless letters from Secretaries of State—from both Democratic and Republican Administrations—urging Congress not to adopt legislation because it would upset ongoing negotiations. Why is this different?

Some say the President's hand will be strengthened by Congress passing this resolution. In 1990, when the United States successfully assembled a broad coalition to fight the gulf war, the Congress passed a resolution only after the—had acted. The world already knows that President Bush is serious about using force against Iraq, and the votes are there in Congress to declare war if diplomatic efforts fail and war becomes unavoidable.

More importantly, the resolution now before the Senate goes well beyond what the President said on Monday about working through the United Nations. It would permit the administration to take precipitous, unilateral action without following through at the U.N.

Many respected and knowledgeable people—former senior military officers and diplomats among them—have expressed strong reservations about this resolution. They agree that if there is credible evidence that Saddam Hussein is planning to use weapons of mass destruction against the United States or one of our allies, the American people and the Congress would overwhelmingly support the use of American military power to stop him. But they have not seen that evidence, and neither have I.

We have heard a lot of bellicose rhetoric, but what are the facts? I am not asking for 100 percent proof, but the administration is asking Congress to make a decision to go to war based on conflicting statements, angry assertions, and assumption based on speculation. This is not the way a great nation goes to war.

The administration has also been vague, evasive and contradictory about its plans. Speaking here in Washington, the President and his advisors continue to say this issue is about disarming Saddam Hussein; that he has made no decision to use force.

But the President paints a different picture when he is on the campaign trail, where he often talks about regime change. The Vice President said on national television that "The President's made it clear that the goal of the United States is regime change. He said that on many occasions."

Proponents of this resolution argue that it does put diplomacy first. They point to section 4, which require the President to determine that further diplomatic or other peaceful means alone will not adequately protect the national security, before he resorts to military force. They say that this ensures that we will act only in a deliberative way, in concert with our allies.

But they fail to point out that the resolution permits the President to use unilateral military force if he determines that reliance on diplomacy along.

".... is not likely to lead to enforcement of all relevant United Nations Security Council resolutions regarding Iraq ....."

Unfortunately, we have learned that "not likely" is a wide open phrase that can be used to justify just about anything. So let us not pretend we are doing something we are not. This resolution permits the President to take whatever military action he wants, whenever he wants, for as long as he wants. It is a blank check.

We have the best trained, best equipped Armed Forces in the world, and I know they can defeat Iraq. I hope, as we all do, that if force is used the Iraqi military surrenders quickly.

But if we have learned anything from history, it is that wars are unpredictable. They can trigger consequences that none of us would intend or expect. Is it fair to the American people, who have become accustomed to wars waged from 30,000 feet lasting a few weeks with few casualties, that we not discuss what else could happen? We could be involved in urban warfare where large numbers of our troops are killed.

And what of the critical issue of rebuilding a post-Saddam Iraq, about which the Administration has said virtually nothing? It is one thing to topple a regime, but it is equally important, and sometimes far more difficult, to rebuild a country to prevent it from becoming engulfed by factional fighting.

If these nations cannot successfully rebuild, then they will once again become havens for terrorists. To ensure that does not happen, do we foresee basing thousands of U.S. troops in Iraq after the war, and if so, for how many years? How many billions of dollars will we spend?

Are the American people prepared to spend what it will take to rebuild Iraq even when the administration is not budgeting the money that is needed to rebuild Afghanistan, having promised to do so? Do we spend hundreds of billions in Iraq, as the President's Economic Adviser suggested, while not providing at home for homeland defense, drought aid for farmers, education for our young people, and other domestic priorities?

Who is going to replace Saddam Hussein? The leading coalition of opposition groups, the Iraqi National Congress, is divided, has questionable support among the Iraqi people, and has made little headway in overthrowing Saddam. While Iraq has a strong civil society, in the chaos of a post-Saddam Iraq another dictator could rise to the top or the country could splinter along ethnic or religious lines.

These are the questions the American people are asking and these are the issues we should be debating. They are difficult issues of war and peace, but the administration, and the proponents of this resolution, would rather leave them for another day. They say: vote now! and let the President decide. Don't give the U.N. time to do its job. Don't worry that the resolution is a blank check.

I can count the votes. The Senate will pass this resolution. They will give the President the authority he needs to send United States troops to Iraq. But before the President takes that step, I hope he will consider the questions that have been asked. I hope he considers the concerns raised by former generals, senior diplomats, and intelligence officials in testimony before Congress. I hope he listens to concerns raised privately by some of our military officers. Above all, I hope he will listen to the American people who are urging him to proceed cautiously and not to act alone.

Notwithstanding whatever disagreements there may be on our policy toward Iraq, if a decision is made to send troops into battle, there is no question that every Member of Congress will unite behind our President and our Armed Forces.

But that time has not yet come. Based on what I know today, I believe in order to solve this problem without potentially creating more terrorists and more enemies, we have to act deliberately and not precipitously. The way the United States responds to the threat posed by Iraq is going to have consequences for our country and for the world for years to come.

Authorizing a U.S. attack to overthrow another government while negotiations at the United Nations are ongoing, and before we exhaust other options, could damage our standing in the world as a country that recognizes the importance of international solutions. I am afraid that it would be what the world expects of a superpower that seems increasing disdainful of international opinion or cooperation and collective diplomacy, a superpower that seems more and more inclined to "go it alone."

What a dramatic shift from a year ago, when the world was united in its expressions of sympathy toward the United States. A year ago, the world would have welcomed the opportunity to work with us on a wide agenda of common problems.

I remember the emotion I felt when I saw "The Star Spangled Banner" sung by crowds of people outside Buckingham Palace in London. The leading French newspaper, Le Monde, declared, "We are all Americans." China's Jiang Zemin was one of the first world leaders to call Washington and express sympathy after September 11.

Why squander the goodwill we had in the world? Why squander this unity? If September 11 taught us anything, it is that protecting our security involves much more than military might. It involves cooperation with other nations to break up terrorist rings, dry up the sources of funding, and address the conditions of ignorance and despair that create breeding grounds for terrorists. We are far more likely to achieve these goals by working with other nations than by going it alone.

I am optimistic that the Administration's efforts at the U.N. will succeed and that the Security Council will adopt a strong resolution. If Saddam Hussein refuses to comply, then force may be justified, and it may be required.

But we are a great nation, with a wide range of resources available to us and with the goodwill of most of the world. Let us proceed deliberately, moving as close to our goal as we can by working with our allies and the United Nations, rather than writing a blank check that is premature, and which would continue the trend of abdicating our constitutional authority and our responsibility.

Mr. President, that trend started many years ago, and I have gone back and read some of the speeches the Senators have made. For example, and I quote:

The resolution now pending is an expression of American unity in this time of crisis.

It is a vote of confidence ..... but is not a blank check for policies that might in the future be carried on by the executive branch of the Government without full consultation by the Congress.

Do these speeches sound familiar? They were not about Iraq. They were spoken 38 years ago when I was still a prosecutor in Vermont. At the end of that debate, after statements were made that this resolution is not a blank check, and that Congress will always watch what the Executive Branch is doing, the Senate voted on that resolution. Do you know what the vote was? 88 to 2. It passed overwhelmingly.

In case everyone does not know what resolution I am talking about, I am talking about the Tonkin Gulf resolution. As we know all too well, the Tonkin Gulf resolution was used by both the Johnson and Nixon administrations as carte blanche to wage war on Vietnam, ultimately involving more than half a million American troops, resulting in the deaths of more than 58,000 Americans. Yet, even the Tonkin Gulf resolution, unlike the one that we are debating today, had a sunset provision.

When I came to the Senate, there were a lot of Senators, both Republicans and Democrats, who had voted for the Tonkin Gulf resolution. Every single Senator who ever discussed it with me said what a mistake it was to write that kind of blank check on the assurance that we would continue to watch what went on.

I am not suggesting the administration is trying to mislead the Congress about the situation in Iraq, as Congress was misled on the Tonkin Gulf resolution. I am not comparing a possible war in Iraq to the Vietnam war. They are very different countries, with different histories, and with different military capabilities. But the key words in the resolution we are considering today are remarkably similar to the infamous resolution of 38 years ago which so many Senators and so many millions of Americans came to regret.

Let us not make that mistake again. Let us not pass a Tonkin Gulf resolution. Let us not set the history of our great country this way. Let us not make the mistake we made once before.

＊ ＊ ＊ ＊

Senator Kerry (D-MA). Mr. President, I thank my good friend from Arizona for his introduction and for his generous comments about the role that Senator Hagel and I have played.

My colleague, Senator Hagel, and I share seats on the Foreign Relations Committee. We have both followed this issue for a long period of time.

Obviously, with respect to an issue that might take Americans to war, we deserve time, and there is no more important debate to be had on the floor of the Senate. It is in the greatest traditions of this institution, and I am proud to take part in that debate now.

This is a debate that should be conducted without regard to parties, to politics, to labels. It is a debate that has to come from the gut of each and every Member, and I am confident that it does. I know for Senator Hagel, Senator McCain, and myself, when we pick up the newspapers and read about the residuals of the Vietnam war, there is a particular sensitivity because I do not think any of us feel a residual with respect to the choices we are making now.

I know for myself back in that period of time, even as I protested the war, I wrote that if my Nation was again threatened and Americans made the decision we needed to defend ourselves, I would be among the first to put on a uniform again and go and do that.

We are facing a very different world today than we have ever faced before. September 11 changed a lot, but other things have changed: Globalization, technology, a smaller planet, the difficulties of radical fundamentalism, the crosscurrents of religion and politics. We are living in an age where the dangers are different and they require a different response, different thinking, and different approaches than we have applied in the past.

Most importantly, it is a time when international institutions must rise to the occasion and seek new authority and a new measure of respect.

In approaching the question of this resolution, I wish the timing were different. I wish for the sake of the country we were not here now at this moment. There are legitimate questions about that timing. But none of the underlying realities of the threat, none of the underlying realities of the choices we face are altered because they are, in fact, the same as they were in 1991 when we discovered those weapons when the teams went in, and in 1998 when the teams were kicked out.

With respect to Saddam Hussein and the threat he presents, we must ask ourselves a simple question: Why? Why is Saddam Hussein pursuing weapons that most nations have agreed to limit or give up? Why is Saddam Hussein guilty of breaking his own cease-fire agreement with the international community? Why is Saddam Hussein attempting to develop nuclear weapons when most nations don't even try, and responsible nations that have them attempt to limit their potential for disaster? Why did Saddam Hussein threaten and provoke? Why does he develop missiles that exceed allowable limits? Why did Saddam Hussein lie and deceive the inspection teams previously? Why did Saddam Hussein not account for all of the weapons of mass destruction which UNSCOM identified? Why is he seeking to develop unmanned airborne vehicles for delivery of biological agents?

Does he do all of these things because he wants to live by international standards of behavior? Because he respects international law? Because he is a nice guy underneath it all and the world should trust him?

It would be naive to the point of grave danger not to believe that, left to his own devices, Saddam Hussein will provoke, misjudge, or stumble into a future, more dangerous confrontation with the civilized world. He has as much as promised it. He has already created a stunning track record of miscalculation. He miscalculated an 8-year war with Iran. He miscalculated the invasion of Kuwait. He miscalculated America's responses to it. He miscalculated the result of setting oil rigs on fire. He miscalculated the impact of sending Scuds into Israel. He miscalculated his own military might. He miscalculated the Arab world's response to his plight. He miscalculated in attempting an assassination of a former President of the United States. And he is miscalculating now America's judgments about his miscalculations.

All those miscalculations are compounded by the rest of history. A brutal, oppressive dictator, guilty of personally murdering and condoning murder and torture, grotesque violence against women, execution of political opponents, a war criminal who used chemical weapons against another nation and, of course, as we know, against his own people, the Kurds. He has diverted funds from the Oil-for-Food program, intended by the international community to go to his own people. He has supported and harbored terrorist groups, particularly radical Palestinian groups such as Abu Nidal, and he has given money to families of suicide murderers in Israel.

I mention these not because they are a cause to go to war in and of themselves, as the President previously suggested, but because they tell a lot about the threat of the weapons of mass destruction and the nature of this man. We should not go to war because these things are in his past, but we should be prepared to go to war because of what they tell us about the future. It is the total of all of these acts that provided the foundation for the world's determination in 1991 at the end of the gulf war that Saddam Hussein must:

".... unconditionally accept the destruction, removal, or rendering harmless under international supervision of his chemical and biological weapons and ballistic missile delivery systems ..... [and] unconditionally agree not to acquire or develop nuclear weapons or nuclear weapon-usable material."

Saddam Hussein signed that agreement. Saddam Hussein is in office today because of that agreement. It is the only reason he survived in 1991. In 1991, the world collectively made a judgment that this man should not have weapons of mass destruction. And we are here today in the year 2002 with an uninspected 4-year interval during which time we know through intelligence he not only has kept them, but he continues to grow them.

I believe the record of Saddam Hussein's ruthless, reckless breach of international values and standards of behavior which is at the core of the cease-fire agreement, with no reach, no stretch, is cause enough for the world community to hold him accountable by use of force, if necessary. The threat of Saddam Hussein with weapons of mass destruction is real, but as I said, it is not new. It has been with us since the end of that war, and particularly in the last 4 years we know after Operation Desert Fox failed to force him to reaccept them, that he has continued to build those weapons.

He has had a free hand for 4 years to reconstitute these weapons, allowing the world, during the interval, to lose the focus we had on weapons of mass destruction and the issue of proliferation.

The Senate worked to urge action in early 1998. I joined with Senator McCain, Senator Hagel, and other Senators, in a resolution urging the President to "take all necessary and appropriate actions to respond to the threat posed by Iraq's refusal to end his weapons of mass destruction program." That was 1998 that we thought we needed a more serious response.

Later in the year, Congress enacted legislation declaring Iraq in material, unacceptable breach of its disarmament obligations and urging the President to take appropriate action to bring Iraq into compliance. In fact, had we done so, President Bush could well have taken his office, backed by our sense of urgency about holding Saddam Hussein accountable and, with an international United Nations, backed a multilateral stamp of approval record on a clear demand for the disarmament of Saddam Hussein's Iraq. We could have had that and we would not be here debating this today. But the administration missed an opportunity 2 years ago and particularly a year ago after September 11. They regrettably, and even clumsily, complicated their own case. The events of September 11 created new understanding of the terrorist threat and the degree to which every nation is vulnerable.

That understanding enabled the administration to form a broad and impressive coalition against terrorism. Had the administration tried then to capitalize on this unity of spirit to build a coalition to disarm Iraq, we would not be here in the pressing days before an election, late in this year, debating this now. The administration's decision to engage on this issue now, rather than a year ago or earlier, and the manner in which it has engaged, has politicized and complicated the national debate and raised questions about the credibility of their case.

By beginning its public discourse with talk of invasion and regime change, the administration raised doubts about their bona fides on the most legitimate justification for war—that in the post-September 11 world the unrestrained threat of weapons of mass destruction in the hands of Saddam Hussein is unacceptable, and his refusal to allow U.N. inspectors to return was in blatant violation of the 1991 cease-fire agreement that left him in power. By casting about in an unfocused, undisciplined, overly public, internal debate for a rationale for war, the administration complicated their case, confused the American public, and compromised America's credibility in the eyes of the world community. By engaging in hasty war talk rather than focusing on the central issue of Iraq's weapons of mass destruction, the administration placed doubts in the minds of potential allies, particularly in the Middle East, where managing the Arab street is difficult at best.

Against this disarray, it is not surprising that tough questions began to be asked and critics began to emerge.

Indeed over the course of the last 6 weeks some of the strongest and most thoughtful questioning of our Nation's Iraq policy has come from what some observers would say are unlikely sources: Senators like Chuck Hagel and Dick Lugar, former Bush Administration national security experts including Brent Scowcroft and James Baker, and distinguished military voices including General Shalikashvili. They are asking the tough questions which must be answered before—and not after—you commit a nation to a course that may well lead to war. They know from their years of experience, whether on the battlefield as soldiers, in the Senate, or at the highest levels of public diplomacy, that you build the consent of the American people to sustain military confrontation by asking questions, not avoiding them. Criticism and questions do not reflect a lack of patriotism—they demonstrate the strength and core values of our American democracy.

It is love of country, and it is defined by defense of those policies that protect and defend our country.

Writing in the *New York Times* in early September, I argued that the American people would never accept the legitimacy of this war or give their consent to it unless the administration first presented detailed evidence of the threat of Iraq's weapons of mass destruction and proved that it had exhausted all other options to protect our national security. I laid out a series of steps that the administration must take for the legitimacy of our cause and our ultimate success in Iraq—seek the advice and approval of Congress after laying out the evidence and making the case, and work with our allies to seek full enforcement of the existing cease-fire agreement while simultaneously offering Iraq a clear ultimatum: accept rigorous inspections without negotiation or compromise and without condition.

Those of us who have offered questions and criticisms—and there are many in this body and beyond—can take heart in the fact that those questions and those criticisms have had an impact on the debate. They have changed how we may or may not deal with Iraq. The Bush administration began talking about Iraq by suggesting that congressional consultation and authorization for the use of force were not needed. Now they are consulting with Congress and seeking our authorization. The administration began this process walking down a path of unilateralism. Today they acknowledge that while we reserve the right to act alone, it is better to act with allies. The administration which once seemed entirely disengaged from the United Nations ultimately went to the United Nations and began building international consensus to hold Saddam Hussein accountable. The administration began this process suggesting that the United States might well go to war over Saddam Hussein's failure to return Kuwaiti property. Last week the Secretary of State and on Monday night the President made clear we would go to war only to disarm Iraq.

The administration began discussion of Iraq by almost belittling the importance of arms inspections. Today the administration has refocused their aim and made clear we are not in an arbitrary conflict with one of the world's many dictators, but a conflict with a dictator whom the international community left in power only because he agreed not to pursue weapons of mass destruction. That is why arms inspections—and I believe ultimately Saddam's unwillingness to submit to fail-safe inspections—is absolutely critical in building international support for our case to the world.

That is the way in which you make it clear to the world that we are contemplating war not for war's sake, and not to accomplish goals that don't meet international standards or muster with respect to national security, but because weapons inspections may be the ultimate enforcement mechanism, and that may be the way in which we ultimately protect ourselves.

I am pleased that the Bush administration has recognized the wisdom of shifting its approach on Iraq. That shift has made it possible, in my judgment, for the Senate to move forward with greater unity, having asked and begun to answer the questions that best defend our troops and protect our national security. The Senate can now make a determination about this resolution and, in this historic vote, help put our country and the world on a course to begin to answer one fundamental question—not whether to hold Saddam Hussein accountable, but how.

I have said publicly for years that weapons of mass destruction in the hands of Saddam Hussein pose a real and grave threat to our security and that of our allies in the Persian Gulf region. Saddam Hussein's record bears this out.

I have talked about that record. Iraq never fully accounted for the major gaps and inconsistencies in declarations provided to the inspectors of the pre-Gulf war weapons of mass destruction program, nor did the Iraq regime provide credible proof that it had completely destroyed its weapons and production infrastructure.

He has continually failed to meet the obligations imposed by the international community on Iraq at the end of the Persian Gulf the Iraqi regime provide credible proof war to declare and destroy its weapons of mass destruction and delivery systems and to forego the development of nuclear weapons. during the 7 years of weapons inspections, the Iraqi regime repeatedly frustrated the work of the UNSCOM—Special Commission—inspectors, culminating in 1998 in their ouster. Even during the period of inspections, Iraq never fully accounted for major gaps and inconsistencies in declarations provided to the inspectors of its pre-gulf war WMD programs, nor did the Iraqi regime provide credible proof that it had completely destroyed its weapons stockpiles and production infrastructure.

It is clear that in the 4 years since the UNSCOM inspectors were forced out, Saddam Hussein has continued his quest for weapons of mass destruction. According to intelligence, Iraq has chemical and biological weapons as well as missiles with ranges in excess of the 150 kilometer restriction imposed by the United Nations in the cease-fire resolution. Although Iraq's chemical weapons capability was reduced during the UNSCOM inspections, Iraq has maintained its chemical weapons effort over the last 4 years. Evidence suggests that it has begun renewed production of chemical warfare agents, probably including mustard gas, sarin, cyclosarin, and VX. Intelligence reports show that Iraq has invested more heavily in its biological weapons programs over the 4 years, with the result that all key aspects of this program—R&D, production and weaponization—are active. Most elements of the program are larger and more advanced than they were before the gulf war. Iraq has some lethal and incapacitating agents and is capable of quickly producing and weaponizing a variety of such agents, including anthrax, for delivery on a range of vehicles such as bombs, missiles, aerial sprayers, and covert operatives which could bring them to the United States homeland. Since inspectors left, the Iraqi regime has energized its missile program, probably now consisting of a few dozen Scud-type missiles with ranges of 650 to 900 kilometers that could hit Israel, Saudi Arabia and other U.S. allies in the region. In addition, Iraq is developing unmanned aerial vehicles UAVs, capable of delivering chemical and biological warfare agents, which could threaten Iraq's neighbors as well as American forces in the Persian Gulf.

Prior to the gulf war, Iraq had an advance nuclear weapons development program. Although UNSCOM and IAEA International Atomic Energy Agency inspectors learned much about Iraq's efforts in this area, Iraq has failed to provide complete information on all aspects of its program. Iraq has maintained its nuclear scientists and technicians as well as sufficient dual-use manufacturing capability to support a reconstituted nuclear weapons program. Iraqi defectors who once worked for Iraq's nuclear weapons establishment have reportedly told American officials that acquiring nuclear weapons is a top priority for Saddam Hussein's regime.

According to the CIA's report, all U.S. intelligence experts agree that Iraq is seeking nuclear weapons. There is little question that Saddam Hussein wants to develop nuclear weapons. The more difficult question to answer is when Iraq could actually achieve this goal. That depends on is its ability to acquire weapons-grade fissile material. If Iraq could acquire this material from abroad, the CIA estimates that it could have a nuclear weapon within 1 year.

Absent a foreign supplier, it might be longer. There is no question that Saddam Hussein represents a threat. I have heard even my colleagues who oppose the President's resolution say we have to hold Saddam Hussein accountable. They also say we have to force the inspections. And to force the inspections, you have to be prepared to use force.

So the issue is not over the question of whether or not the threat is real, or whether or not people agree there is a threat. It is over what means we will take, and when, in order to try to eliminate it.

The reason for going to war, if we must fight, is not because Saddam Hussein has failed to deliver gulf war prisoners or Kuwaiti property. As much as we decry the way he has treated his people, regime change alone is not a sufficient reason for going to war, as desirable as it is to change the regime.

Regime change has been an American policy under the Clinton administration, and it is the current policy. I support the policy. But regime change in and of itself is not sufficient justification for going to war—particularly unilaterally—unless regime change is the only way to disarm Iraq of the weapons of mass destruction pursuant to the United Nations resolution.

As bad as he is, Saddam Hussein, the dictator, is not the cause of war. Saddam Hussein sitting in Baghdad with an arsenal of weapons of mass destruction is a different matter.

In the wake of September 11, who among us can say, with any certainty, to anybody, that those weapons might not be used against our troops or against allies in the region? Who can say that this master of miscalculation will not develop a weapon of mass destruction even greater—a nuclear weapon—then reinvade Kuwait, push the

Kurds out, attack Israel, any number of scenarios to try to further his ambitions to be the pan-Arab leader or simply to confront in the region, and once again miscalculate the response, to believe he is stronger because he has those weapons?

And while the administration has failed to provide any direct link between Iraq and the events of September 11, can we afford to ignore the possibility that Saddam Hussein might accidentally, as well as purposely, allow those weapons to slide off to one group or other in a region where weapons are the currency of trade? How do we leave that to chance?

That is why the enforcement mechanism through the United Nations and the reality of the potential of the use of force is so critical to achieve the protection of long-term interests, not just of the United States but of the world, to understand that the dynamic has changed, that we are living in a different status today, that we cannot sit by and be as complacent or even negligent about weapons of mass destruction and proliferation as we have been in the past.

The Iraqi regime's record over the decade leaves little doubt that Saddam Hussein wants to retain his arsenal of weapons of mass destruction and, obviously, as we have said, grow it. These weapons represent an unacceptable threat.

I want to underscore that this administration began this debate with a resolution that granted exceedingly broad authority to the President to use force. I regret that some in the Congress rushed so quickly to support it. I would have opposed it. It gave the President the authority to use force not only to enforce all of the U.N. resolutions as a cause of war, but also to produce regime change in Iraq, and to restore international peace and security in the Persian Gulf region. It made no mention of the President's efforts at the United Nations or the need to build multilateral support for whatever course of action we ultimately would take.

I am pleased that our pressure, and the questions we have asked, and the criticisms that have been raised publicly, the debate in our democracy has pushed this administration to adopt important changes, both in language as well as in the promises that they make.

The revised White House text, which we will vote on, limits the grant of authority to the President to the use of force only with respect to Iraq. It does not empower him to use force throughout the Persian Gulf region. It authorizes the President to use Armed Forces to defend the "national security" of the United States—a power most of us believe he already has under the Constitution as Commander in Chief. And it empowers him to enforce all "relevant" Security Council resolutions related to Iraq. None of those resolutions or, for that matter, any of the other Security Council resolutions demanding Iraqi compliance with its international obligations, calls for a regime change.

In recent days, the administration has gone further. They are defining what "relevant" U.N. Security Council resolutions mean. When Secretary Powell testified before our committee, the Foreign Relations Committee, on September 26, he was asked what specific U.N. Security Council resolutions the United States would go to war to enforce. His response was clear: the resolutions dealing with weapons of mass destruction and the disarmament of Iraq. In fact, when asked about compliance with other U.N. resolutions which do not deal with weapons of mass destruction, the Secretary said:

The President has not linked authority to go to war to any of those elements.

When asked why the resolution sent by the President to Congress requested authority to enforce all the resolutions with which Iraq had not complied, the Secretary told the committee:

That's the way the resolution is currently worded, but we all know, I think, that the major problem, the offense, what the President is focused on and the danger to us and to the world are the weapons of mass destruction.

In his speech on Monday night, President Bush confirmed what Secretary Powell told the committee. In the clearest presentation to date, the President laid out a strong, comprehensive, and compelling argument why Iraq's weapons of mass destruction programs are a threat to the United States and the international community. The President said:

Saddam Hussein must disarm himself, or, for the sake of peace, we will lead a coalition to disarm him.

This statement left no doubt that the casus belli for the United States will be Iraq's failure to rid itself of weapons of mass destruction.

I would have preferred that the President agree to the approach drafted by Senators Biden and Lugar because that resolution would authorize the use of force for the explicit purpose of disarming Iraq and countering the threat posed by Iraq's weapons of mass destruction.

The Biden-Lugar resolution also acknowledges the importance of the President's efforts at the United Nations. It would require the President, before exercising the authority granted in the resolution, to send a determination to Congress that the United States tried to seek a new Security Council resolution or that the threat posed by Iraq's WMD is so great he must act absent a new resolution—a power, incidentally, that the President of the United States always has.

I believe this approach would have provided greater clarity to the American people about the reason for going to war and the specific grant of authority. I think it would have been a better way to do this. But it does not change the bottom line of what we are voting for.

The administration, unwisely, in my view, rejected the Biden-Lugar approach. But, perhaps as a nod to the sponsors, it did agree to a determination requirement on the status of its efforts at the United Nations. That is now embodied in the White House text.

The President has challenged the United Nations, as he should, and as all of us in the Senate should, to enforce its own resolutions vis-a-vis Iraq. And his administration is now working aggressively with the Perm 5 members on the Security Council to reach a consensus. As he told the American people Monday night:

America wants the U.N. to be an effective organization that helps keep the peace. And that is why we are urging the Security Council to adopt a new resolution setting out tough, immediate requirements.

Because of my concerns, and because of the need to understand, with clarity, what this resolution meant, I traveled to New York a week ago. I met with members of the Security Council and came away with a conviction that they will indeed move to enforce, that they understand the need to enforce, if Saddam Hussein does not fulfill his obligation to disarm.

And I believe they made it clear that if the United States operates through the U.N., and through the Security Council, they—all of them—will also bear responsibility for the aftermath of rebuilding Iraq and for the joint efforts to do what we need to do as a consequence of that enforcement.

I talked to Secretary General Kofi Annan at the end of last week and again felt a reiteration of the seriousness with which the United Nations takes this and that they will respond.

If the President arbitrarily walks away from this course of action—without good cause or reason—the legitimacy of any subsequent action by the United States against Iraq will be challenged by the American people and the international community. And I would vigorously oppose the President doing so.

When I vote to give the President of the United States the authority to use force, if necessary, to disarm Saddam Hussein, it is because I believe that a deadly arsenal of weapons of mass destruction in his hands is a threat, and a grave threat, to our security and that of our allies in the Persian Gulf region. I will vote yes because I believe it is the best way to hold Saddam Hussein accountable. And the administration, I believe, is now committed to a recognition that war must be the last option to address this threat, not the first, and that we must act in concert with allies around the globe to make the world's case against Saddam Hussein.

As the President made clear earlier this week, "Approving this resolution does not mean that military action is imminent or unavoidable." It means "America speaks with one voice."

Let me be clear, the vote I will give to the President is for one reason and one reason only: To disarm Iraq of weapons of mass destruction, if we cannot accomplish that objective through new, tough weapons inspections in joint concert with our allies.

In giving the President this authority, I expect him to fulfill the commitments he has made to the American people in recent days—to work with the United Nations Security Council to adopt a new resolution setting out tough and immediate inspection requirements, and to act with our allies at our side if we have to disarm Saddam Hussein by force. If he fails to do so, I will be among the first to speak out.

If we do wind up going to war with Iraq, it is imperative that we do so with others in the international community, unless there is a showing of a grave, imminent—and I emphasize "imminent"—threat to this country which requires the President to respond in a way that protects our immediate national security needs.

Prime Minister Tony Blair has recognized a similar need to distinguish how we approach this. He has said that he believes we should move in concert with allies, and he has promised his own party that he will not do so otherwise. The administration may not be in the habit of building coalitions, but that is what they need to do. And it is what can be done. If we go it alone without reason, we risk inflaming an entire region, breeding a new generation of terrorists, a new cadre of anti-American zealots, and we will be less secure, not more secure, at the end of the day, even with Saddam Hussein disarmed.

Let there be no doubt or confusion about where we stand on this. I will support a multilateral effort to disarm him by force, if we ever exhaust those other options, as the President has promised, but I will not support a unilateral U.S. war against Iraq unless that threat is imminent and the multilateral effort has not proven possible under any circumstances.

In voting to grant the President the authority, I am not giving him carte blanche to run roughshod over every country that poses or may pose some kind of potential threat to the United States. Every nation has the right to act preemptively, if it faces an imminent and grave threat, for its self-defense under the standards of law. The threat we face today with Iraq does not meet that test yet. I emphasize "yet." Yes, it is grave because of the deadliness of Saddam Hussein's arsenal and the very high probability that he might use these weapons one day if not disarmed. But it is not imminent, and no one in the CIA, no intelligence briefing we have had suggests it is imminent. None of our intelligence reports suggest that he is about to launch an attack.

The argument for going to war against Iraq is rooted in enforcement of the international community's demand that he disarm. It is not rooted in the doctrine of preemption. Nor is the grant of authority in this resolution an acknowledgment that Congress accepts or agrees with the President's new strategic doctrine of preemption. Just the opposite. This resolution clearly limits the authority given to the President to use force in Iraq, and Iraq only, and for the specific purpose of defending the United States against the threat posed by Iraq and enforcing relevant Security Council resolutions.

The definition of purpose circumscribes the authority given to the President to the use of force to disarm Iraq because only Iraq's weapons of mass destruction meet the two criteria laid out in this resolution.

Congressional action on this resolution is not the end of our national debate on how best to disarm Iraq. Nor does it mean we have exhausted all of our peaceful options to achieve this goal. There is much more to be done. The administration must continue its efforts to build support at the United Nations for a new, unfettered, unconditional weapons inspection regime. If we can eliminate the threat posed by Iraq's weapons of mass destruction through inspections, whenever, wherever, and however we want them, including in palaces—and I am highly skeptical, given the full record, given their past practices, that we can necessarily achieve that—then we have an obligation to try that as the first course of action before we expend American lives in any further effort.

American success in the Persian Gulf war was enhanced by the creation of an international coalition. Our coalition partners picked up the overwhelming burden of the cost of that war. It is imperative that the administration continue to work to multilateralize the current effort against Iraq. If the administration's initiatives at the United Nations are real and sincere, other nations are more likely to invest, to stand behind our efforts to force Iraq to disarm, be it through a new, rigorous, no-nonsense program of inspection, or if necessary, through the use of force. That is the best way to proceed.

The United States, without question, has the military power to enter this conflict unilaterally. But we do need friends. We need logistical support such as bases, command and control centers, overflight rights from allies in the region. And most importantly, we need to be able to successfully wage the war on terror simultaneously. That war on terror depends more than anything else on the sharing of intelligence. That sharing of intelligence depends more than anything else on the cooperation of countries in the region. If we disrupt that, we could disrupt the possibilities of the capacity of that war to be most effectively waged.

I believe the support from the region will come only if they are convinced of the credibility of our arguments and the legitimacy of our mission. The United Nations never has veto power over any measure the United States needs to take to protect our national security. But it is in our interest to try to act with our allies, if at all possible. And that should be because the burden of eliminating the threat posed by weapons of mass destruction should not be ours alone. It should not be the American people's alone.

If in the end these efforts fail, and if in the end we are at war, we will have an obligation, ultimately, to the Iraqi people with whom we are not at war. This is a war against a regime, mostly one man. So other nations in the region and all of us will need to help create an Iraq that is a place and a force for stability and openness in the region. That effort is going to be long term, costly, and not without difficulty, given Iraq's ethnic and religious divisions and history of domestic turbulence. In Afghanistan, the administration has given more lipservice than resources to the rebuilding effort. We cannot allow that to happen in Iraq, and we must be prepared to stay the course over however many years it takes to do it right.

The challenge is great: An administration which made nation building a dirty word needs to develop a comprehensive, Marshall-type plan, if it will meet the challenge. The President needs to give the American people a fairer and fuller, clearer understanding of the magnitude and long-term financial cost of that effort.

The international community's support will be critical because we will not be able to rebuild Iraq singlehandedly. We will lack the credibility and the expertise and the capacity.

It is clear the Senate is about to give the President the authority he has requested sometime in the next days. Whether the President will have to use that authority depends ultimately on Saddam Hussein. Saddam Hussein has a choice: He can continue to defy the international community, or he can fulfill his longstanding obligations to disarm. He is the person who has brought the world to this brink of confrontation.

He is the dictator who can end the stalemate simply by following the terms of the agreement which left him in power.

By standing with the President, Congress would demonstrate our Nation is united in its determination to take away that arsenal, and we are affirming the President's right and responsibility to keep the American people safe. One of the lessons I learned from fighting in a very different war, at a different time, is we need the consent of the American people for our mission to be legitimate and sustainable. I do know what it means, as does Senator Hagel, to fight in a war where that consent is lost, where allies are in short supply, where conditions are hostile, and the mission is ill-defined.

That is why I believe so strongly before one American soldier steps foot on Iraqi soil, the American people must understand completely its urgency. They need to know we put our country in the position of ultimate strength and that we have no options, short of war, to eliminate a threat we could not tolerate.

I believe the work we have begun in this Senate, by offering questions, and not blind acquiescence, has helped put our Nation on a responsible course. It has succeeded, certainly, in putting Saddam Hussein on notice that he will be held accountable; but it also has put the administration on notice we will hold them accountable for the means by which we do this.

It is through constant questioning we will stay the course, and that is a course that will ultimately defend our troops and protect our national security.

President Kennedy faced a similar difficult challenge in the days of the Cuban missile crisis. He decided not to proceed, I might add, preemptively. He decided to show the evidence and proceeded through the international institutions. He said at the time:

The path we have chosen is full of hazards, as all paths are ..... The cost of freedom is always high, but Americans have always paid it. And one path we shall never choose, and that is the path of surrender, or submission.

So I believe the Senate will make it clear, and the country will make it clear, that we will not be blackmailed or extorted by these weapons, and we will not permit the United Nations—an institution we have worked hard to nurture and create—to simply be ignored by this dictator.

* * * *

Senator Hagel (R-NE). Madam President, the Senate is, by design, a deliberative institution. Over this past week, we have witnessed thoughtful debate and commentary on how to meet the challenge of Saddam Hussein's Iraq. Ours is not an academic exercise; debate informs our decision whether to authorize the President to use force if necessary to enforce U.N. Security Council resolutions dealing with Iraqi disarmament.

There are no easy answers in Iraq. The decision to commit our troops to war is the most difficult decision Members of Congress make. Each course of action we consider in Iraq leads us into imperfect, dangerous, and unknown situations. But we cannot avoid decision on Iraq. The President cannot avoid decision on Iraq. The risks of inaction are too high. We are elected to solve problems, not just debate them. The time has come to chart a new course in Iraq and in the Middle East.

History informs our debate and our decisions. We know tyranny cannot be appeased. We also know our power and influence are enhanced by both a nobility of purpose and the support of allies and institutions that reinforce an international commitment to peace and prosperity. We know war has its own dynamic, that it favors neither ideology, nor democracy, nor tyranny, that men and women die, and that nations and individuals who know war are never again the same.

President Bush has rightly brought the case against Iraq back before the United Nations. Our problems with Iraq, as well as terrorism and the worldwide proliferation of weapons of mass destruction, are not America's alone. Israel, Iran, Turkey, Saudi Arabia, Kuwait, Iraq's own Kurdish population, and other nations and peoples are on the front lines of Saddam Hussein's ambitions for weapons of mass death.

The United Nations, with American leadership, must act decisively to end Saddam Hussein's decade-long violations of U.N. Security Council resolutions.

America's best case for the possible use of force against Iraq rests with the American and international commitment to enforcing Iraq's disarmament. The diplomatic process is not easy, and we face the competing interests and demands of Russia, France, China, and others, whose interests in Iraq may not always be the same as ours. A regional and international coalition is essential for creating the political environment that will be required for any action we take in Iraq, and especially for how we sustain a democratic transition in a post-Saddam Iraq. We cannot do it alone.

America—including the Congress—and the world, must speak with one voice about Iraqi disarmament, as it must continue to do so in the war on terrorism.

Because the stakes are so high, America must be careful with her rhetoric and mindful of how others perceive her intentions. Actions in Iraq must come in the context of an American-led, multilateral approach to disarmament, not as the first case for a new American doctrine involving the preemptive use of force. America's challenge in this new century will be to strengthen its relationships around the world while leading the world in our war on terrorism, for it is the success of the first challenge that will determine the success of the second. We should not mistake our foreign policy priorities for ideology in a rush to proclaim a new doctrine in world affairs. America must understand it cannot alone win a war against terrorism. It will require allies, friends, and partners.

American leadership in the world will be further defined by our actions in Iraq and the Middle East. What begins in Iraq will not end in Iraq. There will be other "Iraqs." There will be continued acts of terrorism, proliferating powers, and regional conflicts. If we do it right and lead through the U.N., in concert with our allies, we can set a new standard for American leadership and international cooperation. The perception of American power is power, and how our power is perceived can either magnify or diminish our influence in the world. The Senate has a constitutional responsibility and an institutional obligation in this effort.

Federalist Paper No. 63 specifically notes the responsibilities of the Senate in foreign affairs as follows:

An attention to the judgment of other nations is important to every government for two reasons: The one is that independently of the merits of any particular plan or measure, it is desirable, on various accounts, that it should appear to other nations as the offspring of a wise and honorable policy; the second is that, in doubtful cases, particularly where the national councils may be warped by some strong passion or momentary interest, the presumed or known opinion of the impartial world may be the best guide that can always be followed. What has not America lost by her want of character with foreign nations and how many errors and follies would she not have avoided, if the justice and propriety of her measures had, in every instance, been previously tried by the light in which they would probably appear to the unbiased part of mankind?

Remarkable words. The resolution before us today should be tried in that same light as the Federalist Papers points out. The original resolution proposed by the Bush administration, S.J. Res. 45, would have been a setback for this institution. It did not reflect the best democratic traditions of either Congressional-Executive relations, or the conduct of American foreign policy.

S.J. Res. 46, sponsored by Senators Lieberman, Warner, McCain, and Bayh, is a far more responsible and accountable document than the one we started with 3 weeks ago. I congratulate my colleagues, especially Senators Lugar, Biden, and Daschle, and the four sponsors of this resolution, for their efforts and leadership in getting it to this point.

S.J. Res. 46 narrows the authorization for the use of force to all relevant U.N. resolutions regarding Iraq, and to defending our national interests against the threats posed by Iraq. It includes support for U.S. diplomatic efforts at the U.N.; a requirement that, before taking action, the President formally determines that diplomatic or other peaceful means will not be adequate in meeting our objectives; reference to the war powers resolution requirements; and periodic reports to Congress that include those actions described in the section of the Iraq Liberation Act of 1998 regarding assistance and support for Iraq upon replacement of Saddam Hussein. This resolution recognizes Congress as a coequal partner in dealing with the threat from Saddam Hussein's Iraq.

If disarmament in Iraq requires the use of force, we need to consider carefully the implications and consequences of our actions. The future of Iraq after Saddam Hussein is also an open question. Some of my colleagues and some American analysts now speak authoritatively of Sunnis, Shiites, and Kurds in Iraq, and how Iraq can be a test case for democracy in the Arab world.

How many of us really know and understand much about Iraq, the country, the history, the people, the role in the Arab world? I approach the issue of post-Saddam Iraq and the future of democracy and stability in the Middle East with more caution, realism, and a bit more humility. While the people of the Arab world need no education from America about Saddam's record of deceit, aggression, and brutality, and while many of them may respect and desire the freedoms the American model offers, imposing democracy through force in Iraq is a roll of the dice. A democratic effort cannot be maintained without building durable Iraqi political institutions and developing a regional and international commitment to Iraq's reconstruction. No small task.

To succeed, our commitment must extend beyond the day after to the months and years after Saddam is gone. The American people must be told of this long-term commitment, risk, and costs of this undertaking.

We should not be seduced by the expectations of "dancing in the streets" after Saddam's regime has fallen, the kites, the candy, and cheering crowds we expect to greet our troops, but instead, focus on the great challenges ahead, the commitment and resources that will be needed to ensure a democratic transition in Iraq and a more stable and peaceful Middle East.

We should spend more time debating the cost and extent of this commitment, the risks we may face in military engagement with Iraq, the implications of the precedent of United States military action for regime change, and the likely character and challenges of a post-Saddam Iraq. We have heard precious little from the President, his team, as well as from this Congress, with a few notable exceptions, about these most difficult and critical questions.

We need only look to Afghanistan where the Afghan people joyously welcomed our liberation force but, months later, a fragile transition government grapples with rebuilding a fractured political culture, economy, and country.

However, Iraq, because of its resources, geography, capabilities, history, and people, offers even more complications and greater peril and, yes, greater opportunities and greater promise. This is the vast unknown, the heavy burden that lies ahead.

The Senate should not cast a vote in the hopes of putting Iraq behind us so we can get back to our campaigns or move on to other issues next year. The decision to possibly commit a nation to war cannot and should not ever be considered in the context of either party loyalty or campaign politics. I regret that this vote will take place under the cloud and pressure of elections next month. Some are already using the Iraq issue to gain advantage in political campaigns. It might have been better for our vote to have been delayed until after the elections, as it was in 1990. Authorizing the use of force against Iraq or any country for any purpose should always be weighed on its own merits, not with an eye on the politics of the vote or campaign TV spots. War is too serious, the human price too high, and the implications unforeseen.

While I cannot predict the future, I believe that what we decide in this Chamber this week will influence America's security and role in the world for the coming decades. It will serve as the framework, both intentionally and unintentionally, for the future. It will set in motion a series of actions and events that we cannot now understand or control.

In authorizing the use of force against Iraq, we are at the beginning of a road that has no clear end. The votes in Congress this week are votes for an intensification of engagement with Iraq and the Middle East, a world of which we know very little and whose destiny will now be directly tied to ours.

America cannot trade a new focus on Iraq for a lesser effort in the Israeli-Palestinian conflict. The bloodshed between Israel and the Palestinians continues, and the danger mounts. Stability in Afghanistan is not assured. We must carry through with our commitment. Stability in this region depends on it. America's credibility is at stake, and long-term stability in central and South Asia hangs in the balance.

We must also continue to pay close attention to North Korea where there is no guesswork about nuclear weapons. There on the Korean peninsula reside nuclear weapons, ballistic missiles, and 37,000 American troops. Despite setting the right course for disarmament in Iraq, the administration has yet to define an end game in Iraq or explain the extent of the American commitment if regime change is required, or describe how our actions in Iraq might affect our other many interests and commitments around the world.

I share the hope of a better world without Saddam Hussein, but we do not really know if our intervention in Iraq will lead to democracy in either Iraq or elsewhere in the Arab world. America has continued to take on large, complicated, and expensive responsibilities that will place heavy burdens on all of us over the next generation. It may well be necessary, but Americans should understand the extent of this burden and what may be required to pay for it and support it in both American blood and trade.

As the Congress votes on this resolution, we must understand that we have not put Iraqi issues behind us. This is just the beginning. The risks should not be understated, miscast, or misunderstood. Ours is a path of both peril and opportunity with many detours and no shortcuts.

We in the Congress are men and women of many parts. For me, it is the present-day Senator, the former soldier, or concerned father who guides my judgment and ultimate vote? It is pieces of all, for I am pieces of all. The responsibilities of each lead me to support the Lieberman-McCain-Warner-Bayh resolution, for which I will vote.

In the end, each of us who has the high honor of holding public office has the burden and privilege of decision and responsibilities. It is a sacred trust we share with the public. We will be held accountable for our actions, as it must be.

Remarks by Representative Gephardt (D-MO), Representative Armey (R-TX), Representative Pelosi (D-CA) and Representative DeLay (R-TX), October 10, 2002

The following remarks were made during the House debate on the resolution authorizing the use of force in Iraq.

Representative Gephardt (D-MO). Mr. Speaker, 26 years ago, I was fortunate to be elected by my constituents to serve in this House, and I represent today the district in which I was born. I am proud that the people of my district trust me to try to represent them every day. It is an honor that I feel every day that I walk into this building, that I am carrying the hopes and wishes of over a half a million people in Missouri, and I know today is a moment of sacred responsibility.

We come into this building hundreds of times during the year to cast very important votes, but on days like today, when we consider how we will protect our Nation, our people, the districts we come from and represent, these are the days when we must look deep inside and make sure that what we are doing is right.

Our gravest responsibility as legislators is authorizing the President to use military force. Part of the majesty of our democracy is that we do not entrust this power to one human being, the President, but we share it with a co-equal branch of this government; and in a democracy, the decision to put American lives on the line or perhaps go to war is ultimately a decision of the American people through their elected representatives.

No one wants to go to war. No one wants to put our young men and women in harm's way, and I know we hope that our actions today will avert war. But our decision is not so simple, because we must weigh the dangers of sending our young people into hostilities against the threat presented by Iraq to our citizens' safety.

Every Member of Congress must make their own decision on the level of the threat posed by Iraq and what to do to respond to that threat. I have said many times to my colleagues that each Member should be guided by his or her conscience, free from others trying to politicize the issue or questioning others' motives.

This is an issue of life and death, and the preoccupation by some to ascribe political motives to the conclusion of each of us demeans all of us and what we are here to do.

Let me say to my colleagues and my constituents in Missouri why I have decided to vote for this resolution.

First, September 11 has made all the difference. The events of that tragic day jolted us to the enduring reality that terrorists not only seek to attack our interests abroad but also to strike us here at home. We have clear evidence now that they even desire to use weapons of mass destruction against us.

Before 9/11, we experienced the terrorist attacks on Khobar Towers, the USS Cole, on two embassies in Africa, but we did not believe it would happen here. On 9/11, it did happen here; and it can happen again.

September 11 was the ultimate wake-up call. We must now do everything in our power to prevent further terrorist attacks and ensure that an attack with a weapon of mass destruction cannot happen. The consequences of such an attack are unimaginable. We spent 50 years in a Cold War and trillions of dollars deterring a weapon of mass destruction attack on the United States by another country. Now we must prevent such an attack by terrorists who, unlike our previous adversaries, are willing to die.

In these new circumstances, deterrence well may not work. With these new dangers, prevention must work.

If my colleagues worry about terrorists getting weapons of mass destruction or their components from countries, the first candidate we must worry about is Iraq. The 12-year history of the U.N. effort to disarm Iraq convinces me that Iraq is a problem that must be dealt with diplomatically if we can, militarily if we must.

I did not come to this view overnight. It has, instead, evolved over time, as we have learned the facts about the Iraqi regime with clarity. As you know, I opposed the use of force against Iran in 1991 in favor of giving sanctions more time to work. Others supported force, but thought that by dislodging Iraq from Kuwait we would neutralize the threat. In hindsight, both of these assessments were wrong.

In 1991, no one knew the extent to which Saddam Hussein would sacrifice the needs of his people in order to sustain his hold on power, deceive the international community in order to preserve his weapons of mass destruction programs, or take hostile actions against U.S. interests in the region.

Saddam Hussein's track record is too compelling to ignore, and we know that he continues to develop weapons of mass destruction, including nuclear devices; and he may soon have the ability to use nuclear weapons against other nations. I believe we have an obligation to protect the United States by preventing him from getting these weapons and either using them himself or passing them or their components on to terrorists who share his destructive intent.

As I stated in a speech in June, I believe we must confront the threat posed by the current Iraqi regime directly. But given the stakes involved, and the potential risks to our security and the region, we must proceed carefully and deliberately. That is why I felt it was essential to engage in negotiations in order to craft an effective and responsible authorization for the use of force, if necessary, so we can defend our Nation and enforce U.N. resolutions pertaining to Iraq.

At the insistence of many of us, the resolution includes a provision urging President Bush to continue his efforts to get the U.N. to effectively enforce its own resolutions against Iraq. I have told the President directly, on numerous occasions, that in my view, and in the view of a lot of us, he must do everything he possibly can to achieve our objectives with the support of the United Nations. His speech to the U.N. on September 12 was an excellent beginning to this effort.

Exhausting all efforts at the U.N. is essential. But let us remember why. We started the U.N. over 50 years ago. We remain the greatest advocate of the rule of law, both domestically and internationally. We must do everything we can to get the U.N. to succeed. It is in our own self-interest to do that. In 1945, Harry Truman told the Senate that the creation of the U.N. constituted, in his words, an expression of national necessity. He said the U.N. points down the only road to enduring peace. He said let us not hesitate to start down that road, with God's help, and with firm resolve that we can and will reach our goal: peace and security for all Americans.

Completely bypassing the U.N. would set a dangerous precedent that would undoubtedly be used by other countries in the future to our and the world's detriment. It is too high a price to pay. I am glad the President said in his speech Monday that diplomacy is the first choice for resolving this matter.

This resolution also limits the scope and duration of the President's authority to use force. It requires Presidential determinations before our Armed Forces may be used against Iraq, including assurances to Congress that he has pursued all diplomatic means to address this threat and that any military action will not undermine our ongoing efforts against terrorism.

Finally, the bill provides for regular consultation with and reporting to Congress on the administration's diplomatic and military efforts and, of great importance to all Americans, the planning for assistance, reconstruction, and regional stabilization efforts in a postconflict Iraq.

The efforts we must undertake in a postconflict Iraq could be the most enduring challenge we face in this entire endeavor, which is another reason for doing everything humanly possible to work through the U.N. to reach our goals.

Now a word on what this resolution, in my view, is not. In my view, it is not an endorsement or an acceptance of the President's new policy of preemption. Iraq is unique, and this resolution is a unique response. A full discussion of the President's new preemption policy must come at another time. But the acceptance of such a momentous change in policy must not be inferred from the language of this resolution.

It is also important to say that, thus far, the President's predominant response to 9-11 has been the use of military power. Obviously, self-defense requires the use of effective military force. But the exercise of military power is not a foreign policy. It is one means of implementing foreign policy. In the post-9-11 world, we must motivate and inform our citizens about how we construct a foreign policy that promotes universal values, improves living standards, increases freedom in all countries and, ultimately, prevents thousands and thousands of young people across this world from deciding to become terrorists. We will never defeat terrorism by dealing with its symptoms. We must get to its root causes.

In anticipation of the serious debate and vote that we have finally reached today, I have had many conversations with my colleagues and friends in this body, friends and colleagues that I respect deeply. I know for many of you this resolution is not what you want, and it is true for Democrats and some Republicans. And in some ways it is true for me. Many of my colleagues have had compelling arguments and important differences with this language. These differences do not diminish my respect or my trust for my colleagues as the true representatives of the people in this great Nation.

I believe, as a whole, the resolution incorporates the key notion that we want to give diplomacy the best possible opportunity to resolve this conflict, but we are prepared to take further steps, if necessary, to protect our Nation. I have heard in this debate some Members say they love America. I love America. I think every Member of this body loves America. That is not the issue. The issue is how to best protect America, and I believe this resolution does that.

I want to say a final word to those watching beyond our borders. To our friends around the world, I say thank you for standing with us in our time of trial. Your support strengthens the bonds of friendship between our people and the people of the world.

To our enemies, who watch this democratic debate and wonder if America speaks with one voice, I say have no doubt. We are united as a people in defending ourselves and we debate the best means for doing that. Do not mistake our resolve. Do not underestimate our determination. Do not misunderstand that we stand here today not as arguing Republicans and Democrats but as Americans, using the sacred right of free speech and thought and freedom to determine our collective course.

Finally, I thank God for those who have gone before us and used their freedom wisely, for those who have died to protect it and have created a stronger Nation and a better world because of their bravery. I pray that we may act today as wisely and courageously as those who have gone before. God bless this House. God bless America.

Mr. Speaker, as a co-author of H.J. Res. 114, I would like to take this opportunity to address certain elements of the joint resolution in order to clarify their intent.

As I stated in a speech I delivered in June, I believe we must confront the threat posed by the current Iraqi regime directly. But given the stakes involved and the potential risks to our security and the region, we must proceed carefully and deliberately.

That's why I felt it was essential to engage in negotiations in order to craft an effective and responsible authorization for the use of force if necessary—so we can defend our nation and enforce U.N. resolutions pertaining to Iraq.

At the insistence of many of us, the resolution includes provisions urging President Bush to continue his efforts to get the U.N. to effectively enforce its resolution against Iraq. I have told the President directly, on numerous occasions, that in my view of a lot of us, he must do everything he possibly can to achieve our objectives with the support of the United Nations. His speech to the U.N. on September 12 was an excellent beginning to this effort. Exhausting all efforts at the U.N. is essential.

Completely bypassing the U.N. would set a dangerous precedent that would undoubtedly be used by other countries in the future to our and the world's detriment. That is too high a price to pay. I am glad the President said in his speech Monday that diplomacy is the first choice for resolving this critical matter.

This resolution also limits the scope and duration of the President's authority to use force, unlike the Administrations original proposal. The resolution and its accompanying report define the threat posed by Iraq as consisting primarily of its weapons of mass destruction programs and its support for international terrorism. They also note that we should continue to press for Iraqi compliance with all outstanding U.N. resolutions, but suggest that we only contemplate using force to implement those that are relevant to our nation's security.

As for the duration of this authorization, this resolution confines it to the continuing threat posed by Iraq; that is, its current and ongoing weapons programs and support for terrorists. We do not want Congress to provide this or subsequent Presidents with open-ended authority to use force against any future threats that Iraq might pose to the United States that are not related to its current weapons of mass destruction programs and support for international terrorism. The President would need to seek a new authorization from Congress to respond to any such future threats.

Third, this resolution requires important presidential determinations to Congress before our Armed Forces are used against Iraq. These include assurances by the President that he has pursued all diplomatic and other peaceful means to address the continuing threat posed by Iraq, and that any military action against Iraq will not undermine our ongoing efforts against terrorism. These determinations ensure that the Executive Branch remains accountable to Congress if it resorts to military force, and stays focused on the broader war on terrorism that must remain of highest priority.

Finally, the bill provides for regular consultation with and reporting to Congress on the Administration's diplomatic and military efforts and, of great importance to all Americans, on the planning for assistance, reconstruction and regional stabilization efforts in a post-conflict Iraq. The efforts we must undertake in a post-conflict Iraq could be the most enduring challenge we face in this entire endeavor, which is another reason for doing everything humanly possible to work through the U.N. to reach our goals.

* * * *

Representative Armey (R-TX). Mr. Speaker, let me just take a moment to appreciate this body. I had resolved to cherish my last days in this body by being as attentive as I could to everything that I had the privilege of experiencing.

For the past 2 days, I have watched my friends in this body, from both sides of the aisle, from both sides of the issue, conduct what has to be regarded as one of the greatest debates we have seen in this body during my tenure here. I have been struck in the last 2 days with the sobriety, the thoughtfulness, the eloquence, and the respect with which the countervailing positions have been presented. And I would like to say thank you to my colleagues for letting me be part of this debate.

The distinguished minority leader, the gentleman from Missouri (Mr. Gephardt), had a sentence in his speech we heard just a minute ago where he said we had to see the facts with clarity. To see the facts with clarity. This is not an ideological debate. This is not a debate about philosophy. This is a debate about the sober business of safety in the face of danger, honor in the face of fear, responsibility in the face of timidity. We must turn to the facts when we face issues of this gravity, and we have done that.

Intensely, for the last month or so, most of us have been looking at the facts that we hoped we would never have to pay attention to. Let me just relate some of my travels in this past month through the facts.

Is Saddam evil? Who could doubt it? The evils that this man perpetrates, as described on this floor by our young colleague, the gentleman from Wisconsin (Mr. Ryan), from a book he read from, strike terror in the heart of the worst that we have ever seen before.

This man is evil. It is an evil that this world should never have to observe and that the poor victims, particularly those in Iraq, should not have to live with on a daily basis. The atrocities are beyond belief, beyond tolerance. And those poor people in Iraq live with it each day, afraid to leave their home, afraid to speak at their own dinner table, frightened for their children who might be tortured in order to punish the parents' careless moment.

Saddam is evil. That is a fact.

Does he have dangerous assets? More so than we thought, more so than we ever wanted to believe. And does he have an ongoing, consistent program and plan to acquire, to enhance those evil assets that are described by the term weapons of mass destruction, beyond what any of us imagined?

The acquisition of the weaponry, the resources, the resourcefulness, the ability to put together the device that would destroy hundreds of thousands in a fell swoop has never been even mitigated against by the commitments he made to the U.N. 11 years ago.

Can he strike our interests, our citizens, our land, and our responsibilities with them? Irrefutably, yes. Through the conventional means that we recognize and fear, things like SCUD missiles, yes. American people, American citizens, American resources in his immediate area, through the insidious means that would be deployed by his ongoing working relationship with a myriad of evil terrorist organizations, yes. Through simple-looking, innocent-looking little suitcases left in a train depot, a service station, an airport in Chicago, Illinois. Yes, he can strike us, our interests and our responsibilities. I know no other way to put that.

America is the most unique Nation ever in the history of the world. We have accepted responsibility for freedom, safety, and dignity of people other than ourselves. Those proud nations with those brave people that live as islands of freedom and hope within seas of threat and terror look for and understand they can depend upon the protection of the United States. That is who we are, that is who we have been, our heroes, our parents.

They spent their heroism, they spent their life all too often on foreign, distant lands fighting for the freedom of people other than themselves. No other nation has ever done that like we have done.

A nation such as Israel, not exclusively Israel, but right now in the world today, at a level of danger that is unparalleled by any other nation of the world, Israel struggles for its freedom, safety and dignity; and it is in imminent, immediate danger by a strike from Saddam Hussein. And that represents a responsibility we have, not only to what role we have played in the world, not only to our heroes who have acted it out and sacrificed, but to the character of this Nation that we cherish and protect.

I have said it as clearly as I can. To me, an attack on Israel is an attack on America; and it is imminently in danger.

Will he do so? Who can doubt that? He has a record of having done so that is deplorable in the most evil and insidious ways. The question is when will he do so; not will he do so.

Why does one violate one's own commitments to the world, to the United Nations accord with resolve, and consistently acquire these resources if you have no intent to use them? Why do you deny your own citizens the resources for food and shelter and clothing and health care in order to divert that to the expenditure on weapons of mass destruction and instruments of horror if you do not intend to use them? Why would he deny his own clear volitions in actions past if he had the resources to strike? Saddam will strike.

Is action against Saddam compliant with the character of our great Nation? I struggled with this. It was a hurdle for me for a long time. It all gets involved with this question of preemptive strike.

First of all, it is not a preemptive strike. This is a man who has consistently been in violation of his own commitments to the world for 11 years. As I put it, this snake is out of his hole. We are not striking an innocent here, we are correcting an error of complacency. So it is not a question of a new doctrine.

But even if we were to examine the doctrine of preemptive strike, let us not forget the Cuban missile crisis. An embargo on the high seas is an act of war, and the threat to us I would submit was not as dangerous as it was at that time, and it was certainly not so insidious as it is today.

There have been other instances in our history. When necessary, America does what it needs to do to keep America safe. America does have a pride which is exhibited in movies like "13 Days" for the courage that was displayed when the action was necessary.

There is an argument that this is a diversion from the war on terrorism. If we are going to conduct a war on terrorism, then we must stop that person who is most likely and most able to arm the terrorists with those things which will frighten us the most. A strike on Saddam is an integral part, a necessary part, of the war on terrorism.

Now we turn to questions about our ability. Can we be swift and decisive and conduct this operation with minimal risk to the brave men and women that we ask to carry it out?

It is possible. We saw that in Desert Storm. It is even more possible now. It will be a difficult operation, and our people will be at risk. But we have the resources and the resourcefulness, and we have the ability to plan and execute an operation that rids the world of this scourge conducted by our young men and women and their allies in such a manner to keep them at minimal risk.

That is all we can do, the moral imperative that we have, when we ask our brave young men and women who have volunteered to serve this Nation and the world in the cause of freedom, to take the field of danger, we have an obligation, and we can say we can construct the plan, outfit you in such a way, support you in such a manner that you can carry out this deed with minimal risk. We can do that. We will do that. We have an administration. We have a Secretary of Defense that respects our people.

Should we vote this resolution that says in effect that we, the Congress of the United States, the representation of the people of the United States, say, Mr. President, we trust you and we rely on you in a dangerous time to be our Commander-in-Chief and to use the resources we place at your disposal? Yes, even by two bills we will vote on later today, to protect freedom? The answer is, yes.

Mr. President, we are about to give you a great trust. Those brave young men and women who have volunteered in our Nation's military services of their own free will to take their place in history alongside the American heroes of the past deserve our respect and our support, Mr. President. We trust that you will plan for them, use them, care for them, and be guided by your own notion of tender mercies.

But we also have an obligation to the parents, the children, the siblings, the grandparents of those brave young men and women. We lend our children to the cause of liberty. I have said so many times. I do not care if he is 240 pounds of solid muscle, the brightest kid in the class, when he puts on that uniform, he is my baby and I have fear, and I demand that you treat him properly as his Commander-in-Chief.

We all have that right to expect. Can we expect that from this President? I would say so.

Mr. Speaker, I was speaking yesterday with the gentleman from Indiana (Mr. Buyer), who remembered embarking for Desert Storm, saying good-bye to his family.

At the last moment, he approached his father, proud veteran of the Korean War with his veteran's hat. His proud father put his hands on Steve's shoulder and looked at him and said, "You are the best I have to give."

Mr. President, we trust to you the best we have to give. Use them well so they can come home and say to our grandchildren, Sleep safely, my baby.

* * * *

Representative Pelosi (D-CA). Mr. Speaker, I thank the gentleman for yielding me this time and for his extraordinary leadership in presenting this option to the House of Representatives. I also want to commend him for his leadership as a person who speaks for our Armed Services in this Congress, his commitment to provide for the common defense, as provided for in the Preamble of our Constitution. Today, we are all benefiting from his wisdom.

The Spratt substitute, Mr. Speaker, captures many of the concerns of the American people who overwhelmingly support a multilateral approach to dealing with Saddam Hussein. The Spratt substitute also honors the Constitution when it says that Congress shall declare war.

Some who have opposed the Spratt substitute have done so on the basis that we do not have time to come back to the Congress. This is simply not true. As called for in the Spratt substitute, should the Security Council fail to act in a satisfactory way, we come back to the Congress.

I want to speak to the issue of time by quoting what is now declassified but is contained in a letter from the Director of the Central Intelligence Agency to the chairman of the Senate Permanent Select Committee on Intelligence, this letter, signed by George Tenet. When asked if Saddam did not feel threatened, is it likely he would initiate an attack using a weapon of mass destruction, the Director of Central Intelligence responds in this letter and says, "My judgment would be that the probability of him," Saddam, "initiating an attack, let me put a time frame on it, in the foreseeable future, given the conditions we understand now, the likelihood I think would be low."

This is the Director of Central Intelligence saying the likelihood of Saddam initiating an attack using weapons of mass destruction, the likelihood, would be low. So it is not about time. It is about the Constitution. It is about this Congress asserting its right to declare war when we are fully aware of what the challenges are to us, and it is about respecting the United Nations and a multilateral approach, which is safer for our troops.

Force protection. I have been on the Permanent Select Committee on Intelligence for 10 years, longer than anyone. My service there is coming to an end. But in the time that I have been there, force protection is one of our top priorities, to protect the men and women in uniform.

This letter goes on to say, "If we initiate an attack," if he felt he was threatened, "if we initiate an attack and he thought he was in extremis or otherwise, what is the likelihood in response to our attack that he would use chemical and biological weapons?" The response, "Pretty high."

We are placing our young people in harm's way in a way that can be avoided by taking a multilateral approach first. I commend the gentleman from South Carolina for his leadership. I will support this with great pride, and I thank him for giving us that opportunity.

* * * *

Representative Delay (R-TX). Mr. Speaker, I thank the chairman for yielding me the time, and I commend the chairman and the ranking member for the work that they have done, not just on this but the whole issue of the war on terror.

Mr. Speaker, Americans have always had to summon courage to disregard the timid counsel of those who would mortgage our security to the false promises of wishful thinking and appeasement. The perils of complacency were driven home to us in September of last year. We saw in tragic detail that evil is far more than some abstract concept. No longer should America allow dangers to gather and multiply. No longer should we stand idle as terrorists and terrorist states plot to murder our citizens.

As a free society, we have to defeat dangers before they ripen. The war on terrorism will be fought here at home, unless we summon the will to confront evil before it attacks.

President Bush certainly understands this imperative for action. The President is demonstrating the strong, moral leadership to find and defeat threats to the United States before they strike. Because once a madman like Saddam Hussein is able to deliver his arsenal, whether it is chemical, biological or nuclear weapons, there is no telling when an American city will be attacked at his direction or with his support.

A nuclear armed Iraq would soon become the world's largest safe haven and refuge for the world's terrorist organizations. Waiting to act until after Saddam has nuclear weapons will leave free nations with an awful dilemma. Will they, on the one hand, risk nuclear annihilation by confronting terrorists in Iraq or will they give in to fear by failing to confront these terrorist groups?

For that reason, regime change in Iraq is a central goal of the war on terror. It is vital because a war on terrorism that leaves the world's leading purveyor and practitioner of terror in power would be a bald failure.

Some call Hussein a diversion, but far from being a diversion, confronting Saddam Hussein is a defining measure of whether we still wage the war on terror fully and effectively. It is the difference between aggressive action and misguided passivity.

The question we face today is not whether to go to war, for war was thrust upon us. Our only choice is between victory or defeat.

And let us just be clear about it. In the war on terror, victory cannot be secured at a bargaining table.

Iraq's vile dictator is a central power of the axis of evil. President Bush and this Congress are committed to removing the threat from Saddam Hussein's terrorist state. Only regime change in Iraq can accomplish that objective. Only regime change can remove the danger from Saddam's weapons of mass destruction. Only by taking them out of his hands and destroying them can we be certain that terror weapons will not wind up in the hands of the terrorists.

Saddam Hussein is seeking the means to murder millions in just a single moment. He is trying to spread that grip of fear beyond his own borders, and he is consumed with hatred for America.

But I am not here today to offer that definitive indictment of Iraq's tyrant. That has already been very clearly documented and well-established in this debate.

In the wicked litany of crimes against humanity, Saddam Hussein has composed a scarlet chapter of terror. Our only responsible option is to confront this threat before Americans die. Time works to the advantage of our enemies, not ours.

Under our Constitution, America speaks through the United States Constitution; and our resolution is very, very clear. The enemies of a free and a moral people will find no safe harbor in this world.

Today, the free world chooses strength over temporizing and timidity. Terrorists and tyrants will see that the fruits of their evil will be certain destruction by the forces of democracy.

Now we seek broad support, but I am telling my colleagues that fighting this war on terrorism by committee or consensus is a certain prescription for defeat. We will defend our country by defeating terrorists wherever they may flee around the world.

None of us take the gravity of this vote and its ramifications lightly, but history informs us that the dangers of complacency and inaction far outweigh the calculated risks of confronting evil.

In the fullness of time, America will be proud that in our hour of testing we chose the bold path of action, not the hollow comfort of appeasement.

So let us just take this stand today against tyranny. Let us take this stand against terror. Let us take this stand against fear. Let us stand with the President of the United States.

I say to my colleagues, just trust the cherished principles on which we were founded. Put faith in freedom and raise our voices and send this message to the world: The forces of freedom are on the march and terrorists will find no safe harbor in this world.

Chapter 4 ━━━━━━━━━━━━━

October 10–November 7, 2002
Congress Authorizes Use of Force; U.S. Intensifies Diplomatic Efforts at the United Nations

CHRONOLOGY

2002

October 10. The United States Congress passes a joint resolution which explicitly authorizes the President to use the Armed Forces of the United States as he determines to be necessary and appropriate. Canada announces that it will be part of any military coalition sanctioned by the United Nations to invade Iraq.

Sources: Chronology entries are drawn from www.abc.com, www.bbc.com, www.nytimes.com, www.reuters.com, www.washingtonpost.com, www.wikipedia.com, and staff research.

DOCUMENTS

Remarks by President Bush, October 10, 2002

I would like to thank the members of the House of Representatives, just as I thanked Speaker Hastert and Leader Gephardt a few minutes ago, for the very strong bipartisan vote authorizing the use of force in Iraq if it becomes necessary.

The House debate was conducted in the best traditions of the United States Congress. It was spirited, it was civil, and it was informed. This is a debate and a decision that all Americans can be proud of.

I'm also pleased with the progress being made in the Senate, and I look forward to a final vote soon.

The House of Representatives has spoken clearly to the world and to the United Nations Security Council: the gathering threat of Iraq must be confronted fully and finally. Today's vote also sends a clear message to the Iraqi regime: it must disarm and comply with all existing U.N. resolutions, or it will be forced to comply. There are no other options for the Iraqi regime. There can be no negotiations. The days of Iraq acting as an outlaw state are coming to an end.

The United States is committed to helping make the world more peaceful and more just. We are committed to freedom for all. We're also committed to protecting human dignity, and today's vote is an important step toward fulfilling those great American commitments.

White House Press Briefing, October 10, 2002

Q. If the President gets the same kind of a vote from the Senate, does he feel that he can immediately or at any point have a free hand to go to war?

Mr. Fleischer. Well, under the Constitution, Helen, the President, of course, does have the authority—

Q.—or even with or without allies.

Mr. Fleischer. Under the Constitution, the President does have the authority as Commander-in-Chief to make those determinations. The President has asked—said he would ask the Congress to weigh in on this matter, and the Congress is doing so and doing it today. And the President thinks that will be very helpful in keeping the peace. The President has made no decisions about what the next step will be. Clearly, we will continue to talk to the United Nations about the inspection process, and that's where the matter currently stands.

Q. But he would never go back to Congress again for another go-ahead? I mean, he considers this the green light?

Mr. Fleischer. The Congress is speaking today about authorization of the use of force. Today's vote by the Congress is an important vote.

* * * *

Q. On Iraq, the Iraqi government is taking reporters around to al Furat manufacturing facility and the Nassr engineering facility. These were mentioned obliquely by the President Monday night, the White House released satellite photographs of them, and the Iraqis I guess are taking reporters around to show that everything is hunky-dory there. You got any reaction to that?

Mr. Fleischer. I think that reporters are seeing the same cat and mouse games get played with themselves, and they walk away scratching their heads, wondering what it is they just saw and what was concealed. I think Iraq has shown a 10-year-long history of being able to take guests into Iraq, having moved facilities around, having mobile facilities available, hiding information, allowing things to be seen that only they want to be seen. And so it's very hard, I think, for anybody, unless they are a real independent expert with the proper equipment, to walk into a facility and have a clear understanding of what it is that is either taking place there, used to take there, or may be taking place on another side of a wall through which they cannot see.

Q. Ari, it's clear from the satellite photos that the White House provided to us on Monday that there has been new construction at those two facilities. But do you have any way of legitimately knowing what's inside those buildings?

Mr. Fleischer. Well, the best way to know what is inside those buildings is either through intelligence, which I will not discuss, or through the return of inspectors, who have the authority to go into those buildings any time, anyplace, anywhere, with any equipment and get their job done.

But your assessment is accurate. The photos that were released showed the rebuilding of a building. People can make their own interpretations about what's going on inside those buildings, but the point is that facilities that were associated with these weapons of mass destruction that we knew were used for the purpose of creation of weapons of mass destruction have been destroyed and then these same facilities rebuilt. The best way to know what's going on is through the other two means I said.

Q. But to your point that Iraq is paying a cat and mouse game with reporters, you really don't have any legitimate idea what's in that building, so you can't really say that they're playing a cat and mouse game, can you?

Mr. Fleischer. I think if you want to take Saddam Hussein's word for it, people are free to do that. And his word hasn't proven very good.

Q. Ari, the President in Cincinnati said that if he makes a decision to go to war, that he would, in the aftermath, support a unified Iraq, which is a significant statement. So what evidence can the administration point to now that there is a viable alternative to Saddam Hussein, an opposition that is capable of leading in his absence? Especially given the fact that Americans have a lot of information to chew on about the Northern Alliance as a viable alternative to the Taliban prior to that—

Mr. Fleischer. It's a very interesting question, and I think the easiest way to express it, David, is the President has a universal faith in mankind that mankind does not want to be governed by despots, that people are capable of self-government around the world. That's particularly true in an educated, relatively advanced nation like Iraq. No people choose to have a leader who engages in the type of dictatorial, despotic, tyrannical types of actions that Saddam Hussein has taken.

Another way to say it is when Saddam Hussein has been such a brutal dictator, he has no shortage of people who would like to see him gone, and who could do a much better job governing once he is gone. More specifically then, we will continue, the United States government will continue to work with people both inside and outside Iraq who have an interest in advancing the cause of government that is representative of the people. I don't think anybody thinks that Saddam Hussein is representative of the Iraqi people.

Q. But—okay, well, tell us about that. What are we doing? Don't the American people have the right to chew over what the alternatives are here, and know what the government is doing to pave the way toward dealing with the aftermath of invasion, should it come to that?

Mr. Fleischer. I don't think—it's impossible to predict with certainty what type of government would replace Saddam Hussein. It's fair to say that whatever it is, it will be an improvement. Whatever it is, it will also represent what the President has said about a government that represents the people. And that's why there are various groups, both inside and outside Iraq, who are dedicated to that.

Q. What are we doing? What are we doing to work with these groups to support them?

Mr. Fleischer. Through the—okay, through the 1998 Iraq Liberation Act funds were made available to work with Iraqi opposition groups. They've been having gatherings to discuss types of government that could possibly replace Saddam Hussein. There's not unanimity within those groups about how to proceed, but—

Q. But you still don't have any evidence to present to the public that there is a viable alternative as we stand here today?

Mr. Fleischer. If you're suggesting that because there is no known immediate successor to Saddam Hussein, that until one can be known, Saddam Hussein is a risk that should be left in place, the President does not agree with that approach.

Q. Obviously, I didn't say that. But what I'm asking you is, do you have anything beyond faith in mankind to tell people that the government is preparing to pave the way toward an alternative leadership?

Mr. Fleischer. It's the issues I mentioned. And also, I think that it's fair to say if you look at Afghanistan as a model—and this is where the—faith in mankind, don't misinterpret what I'm saying here, this is something that we hold dearly as Americans, the universal value that be believe is God-given for people to be free, for people to have a government that represents themselves, not a government that controls, not a government that is dominant over them. That is a powerful force throughout the world. That is a force for freedom and that is a force for good government.

Saddam Hussein has used his powers in a ruthless manner to oppress the people of Iraq. And as I said, the President will continue to work through, and the United States will continue to work through these groups. And Afghanistan has shown that when despots are thrown out, there are a great many good people who would like to take their place and who can make for a better day for the people of that country. That is the case with President Karzai of Afghanistan and many other people who participate in the loya jirga there.

Q.—on the record here, are you then putting the administration behind a commitment that should regime change happen in Iraq, the United States will commit to a democracy in Iraq? Not support a strong man, not support some kind of interim general, but that the United States will commit to trying to establish a democracy in Iraq.

Mr. Fleischer. I think if you look at the history of the United States, and President Bush is dedicated to this, the fact of the matter is that after a military operation, the

United States has been a marvelous, wonderful force for democracy around the world. That is the case with Japan, that is the case with Germany, that was the case with Afghanistan. And while not everything can immediately and fully move to democracies around the world, and we understand that, the United States has been a wonderful, powerful force pushing toward democracy around the world. Central and Latin America are the most recent, now 10-year-long examples of that trend around the world, with the help of the United States.

Q. After a many-decade history where we were not supporting democracy in that part—

Mr. Fleischer. You can take that up with many decades ago. But the point remains the same, and what I said is a government that represents the people, and the President will continue to push for the direction of a government that represents the people.

Q. Ari, would you expect the votes today in the House will serve to provide some momentum in any way to the developments within the U.N. and the efforts to get a resolution there?

Mr. Fleischer. Well, the President hopes so. The President thinks that there is a good possibility that Congress, having spoken and spoken strongly, the American people coming together, and our nation speaking in one voice, will send a signal to the United Nations and United Nations Security Council that President Bush and our people are united in the belief that a strong resolution is the most effective way to keep the peace, and that the United States and her allies are prepared to take action if the United Nations will not.

Q. And today, what is he doing today, specifically on Iraq? He spoke with Chirac yesterday. Is he going to reach out to any other—

Mr. Fleischer. Well, he's been watching—he's monitoring the vote and keeping informed about the vote, and we look forward to the conclusions of the vote. And I'll keep you filled in if there will be any additions to the President's schedule later on. We're looking at the timing of what's happening in both the House and the Senate. It remains unclear I think even to the people who will do the voting, particularly in the Senate, about what time their vote may take place.

Q. Ari, now that the President is sure to get what could be called a mandate from both Houses on the Iraq situation, does he have a timetable for the U.N. to issue a new resolution? Or is he just willing to wait until they come around? Or does he have a time frame?

Mr. Fleischer. The timetable is exactly as the President said on September 12th in his speech to the United Nations. The President said—he urged the United Nations to act in a matter of days and weeks, not months. Clearly, now, it's been a matter of some weeks. It is not yet a matter of months. So it still was in the timetable that the President originally established.

Q. And a second question, Ari. You keep referring to the United States and its allies—

Mr. Fleischer. Correct.

Q.—will use force. Well, as far as we hear, allies—I guess the United Kingdom is one ally, but do you mean, by "allies" and "force", do you mean permission for over-flights, refueling, use of bases, or storing weapons? What do you mean—military help?

Mr. Fleischer. I think it can be all of the above. The President has said in many of his public events that the United States and a coalition of allies will act if the United Nations does not act.

And this is why I've made the point before that this notion of somehow the United States would do something unilateral is just as wrong as wrong can be. The only question is will the multilateral action come thanks to the United Nations, or will the multilateral action come as a result of a large coalition that the United States will assemble because the United Nations failed to act? The President hopes that will not be the case, but he is prepared if that is the case.

* * * *

Q. Ari, if I can just go back to your statement just a moment ago that the President would act not unilaterally, but with a coalition; the only question is, does the coalition have U.N. endorsement or not. If that's the President's position, does the exact wording of that U.N. endorsement become less important? In other words, do you necessarily need "all necessary means" or something, if he's committed that he can—he's going to act to enforce it, basically no matter what the U.N.—final U.N. resolution says?

Mr. Fleischer. Well, the President went to the United Nations because the President thinks it's important for the United Nations to have a role in keeping peace around the world. That's why he went. He didn't have to go. He made the judgment and the decision that it was important for the U.N. that an American President go there and remind the U.N. about the resolutions that it passed, and the fact that Saddam Hussein has violated them with impunity, and raised the question to the U.N., what do you intend to do about it. And he hopes that the U.N. will not leave that question unanswered.

That's why he chose to go. But the President is also saying that if he decides to take any further action, it's clear now that it would not be unilateral, it will be with a coalition. And the only question is, does the U.N. play a role on that coalition.

Now, on the language that is currently being discussed at the United Nations, what's important, David—and the President has stressed this in his conversations with world leaders, and this is what our diplomats are focusing on in their negotiations—the resolution must describe that there will be consequences if Iraq fails to act. It must be, the resolution must include that. And the reason for the President saying that and thinking it's so important is because if it's not in there, then Saddam Hussein is free to play his games once again. And the President thinks the best way to keep the peace is for Saddam Hussein to understand that the world this time is serious.

Within that, there is room for diplomacy about how to exactly phrase what those consequences are, and that's what the diplomats are currently working on, the exact phraseology of it. I'm not—to get specifically now to your very question, I'm not going to negotiate that in public, what the exact words could or could not be. Don't take that as a reading that something may be in or out; obviously, that's something the diplomats will do and do in private.

Q. I'm sorry, if you say that it must describe there will be consequences, is it sufficient to say there will be consequences? Or in the President's mind, does the resolution have to describe exactly what those consequences would be?

Mr. Fleischer. The President thinks the more clearly the consequences are stated, and the more—and the stronger they are, the better the chance of keeping the peace, because Saddam Hussein will know that this time the world is serious.

Q. Ari, can you talk to us about the President's plans over the next few weeks to campaign for Republicans, and how this reflects his priorities over that period?

Mr. Fleischer. Sure. Between now and the election, the President will have several items on his travel agenda. This will include traveling around the country to support candidates who support his agenda. Obviously, with the Congress as closely divided as it is—a Congress that has failed to act on a great many priorities for the American people, including helping the economy to recover and grow by creating jobs, passage of homeland security—every vote in the Congress counts. And so he will spend some time on the road working to build support for candidates who share his vision.

He also has, of course, a summit with the President of China coming up at his ranch in Crawford. He will travel to Mexico, where he'll take part in the APEC Summit of leaders from the Pacific Ocean countries, including leaders from Japan and China, again, and Russia, as well as Mexico and Canada and other nations. So the President will have quite a bit of business to conduct between now and the election. He'll conduct much of it on the road.

Q. But you're not minimizing the fact that he's going to be pretty much solidly campaigning for his party's candidates for the last couple weeks running up to the election?

Mr. Fleischer. I think I just described to you what the President's agenda is. It consists of travel on behalf of candidates across the country, a summit meeting with the President of China, an international meeting outside the country in Mexico and, of course, other business.

Q. Is that the proper thing for him to be doing when he's trying to prepare the nation for war?

Mr. Fleischer. I think, particularly—let me put it to you this way. In all times, whether our nation is at war or our nation is at peace, what makes us strong is our democratic process. And everybody, in both parties, should proudly stand up and participate in our democratic process.

Remarks by Senator Kennedy (D-MA) and Senator Byrd (D-WV), October 10, 2002

Senator Kennedy. Mr. President, I welcome this opportunity to commend our outstanding colleague, Senator Robert Byrd, for his thoughtful and eloquent op-ed article in The New York Times this morning. In his article, Senator Byrd rightfully condemns the failure of Congress to take adequate time to exercise our all-important constitutional responsibility in deciding whether or not America should go to war with Iraq.

Instead of fairly assessing the full consequences of the administration's proposal, Congress is allowing itself to be rushed into a premature decision to go to war. Many of us agree with Senator Byrd, and so do large numbers of Americans across the country.

We owe the Senate and the Nation a more thoughtful deliberation about war. Senator Byrd's article is a powerful statement urging Congress not delegate our constitutional power to the President, and I ask unanimous consent that it be printed in the record.

Senator Byrd. (From the New York Times, October 10, 2002). A sudden appetite for war with Iraq seems to have consumed the Bush administration and Congress. The debate that began in the Senate last week is centered not on the fundamental and monumental questions of whether and why the United States should go to war with Iraq, but rather on the mechanics of how best to wordsmith the president's use-of-force resolution in order give him virtually unchecked authority to commit the nation's military to an unprovoked attack on a sovereign nation.

How have we gotten to this low point in the history of Congress? Are we too feeble to resist the demands of a president who is determined to bend the collective will of Congress to his will—a president who is changing the conventional understanding of the term "self-defense"? And why are we allowing the executive to rush our decision-making right before an election? Congress, under pressure from the executive branch, should not hand away its Constitutional powers. We should not hamstring future Congresses by casting such a shortsighted vote. We owe our country a due deliberation.

I have listened closely to the president, I have questioned the members of his war cabinet. I have searched for that single piece of evidence that would convince me that the president must have in his hands, before the month is out, open-ended Congressional authorization to deliver an unprovoked attack on Iraq. I remain unconvinced. The president's case for an unprovoked attack is circumstantial at best. Saddam Hussein is a threat, but the threat is not so great that we must be stampeded to provide such authority to this president just weeks before an election.

Why are we being hounded into action on a resolution that turns over to President Bush the Congress's Constitutional power to declare war? This resolution would authorize the president to use the military forces of this nation wherever, whenever and however he determines, and for as long as he determines, if he can somehow make a connection to Iraq. It is a blank check for the president to take whatever action he feels "is necessary and appropriate in order to defend the national security of the United States against the continuing threat posted by Iraq." This broad resolution underwrites, promotes and endorses the unprecedented Bush doctrine of preventive war and pre-emptive strikes—detailed in a recent publication, "National Security Strategy of the United States"—against any nation that the president, and the president alone, determines to be a threat.

We are at the gravest of moments. Members of Congress must not simply walk away from their Constitutional responsibilities. We are the directly elected representatives of the American people, and the American people expect us to carry out our duty, not simply hand it off to this or any other president. To do so would be to fail the people we represent and to fall woefully short of our sworn oath to support and defend the Constitution.

We may not always be able to avoid war, particularly if it is thrust upon us, but Congress must not attempt to give away the authority to determine when war is to be declared. We must not allow any president to unleash the dogs of war at his own discretion and for an unlimited period of time.

Yet that is what we are being asked to do. The judgment of history will not be kind to us if we take this step.

Members of Congress should take time out and go home to listen to their constituents. We must not yield to this absurd pressure to act now, 27 days before an election that will determine the entire membership of the House of Representatives and that of a third of the Senate. Congress should take the time to hear form the American people, to answer their remaining questions and to put the frenzy of ballot-box politics behind us before we vote. We should hear them well, because while it is Congress that casts the vote, it is the American people who will pay for a war with the lives of their sons and daughters.

House Joint Resolution 114, October 10, 2002

House Joint Resolution 114, "To authorize the use of United States Armed Forces against Iraq," was approved in the House of Representative by a vote of 296 to 133.

Whereas in 1990 in response to Iraq's war of aggression against and illegal occupation of Kuwait, the United States forged a coalition of nations to liberate Kuwait and its people in order to defend the national security of the United States and enforce United Nations Security Council resolutions relating to Iraq ;

Whereas after the liberation of Kuwait in 1991, Iraq entered into a United Nations sponsored cease-fire agreement pursuant to which Iraq unequivocally agreed, among other things, to eliminate its nuclear, biological, and chemical weapons programs and the means to deliver and develop them, and to end its support for international terrorism;

Whereas the efforts of international weapons inspectors, United States intelligence agencies, and Iraqi defectors led to the discovery that Iraq had large stockpiles of chemical weapons and a large scale biological weapons program, and that Iraq had an advanced nuclear weapons development program that was much closer to producing a nuclear weapon than intelligence reporting had previously indicated;

Whereas Iraq, in direct and flagrant violation of the cease-fire, attempted to thwart the efforts of weapons inspectors to identify and destroy Iraq's weapons of mass destruction stockpiles and development capabilities, which finally resulted in the withdrawal of inspectors from Iraq on October 31, 1998;

Whereas in Public Law 105-235 (August 14, 1998), Congress concluded that Iraq's continuing weapons of mass destruction programs threatened vital United States interests and international peace and security, declared Iraq to be in 'material and unacceptable breach of its international obligations' and urged the President 'to take appropriate action, in accordance with the Constitution and relevant laws of the United States, to bring Iraq into compliance with its international obligations';

Whereas Iraq both poses a continuing threat to the national security of the United States and international peace and security in the Persian Gulf region and remains in material and unacceptable breach of its international obligations by, among other things, continuing to possess and develop a significant chemical and biological weapons capability, actively seeking a nuclear weapons capability, and supporting and harboring terrorist organizations;

Whereas Iraq persists in violating resolution of the United Nations Security Council by continuing to engage in brutal repression of its civilian population thereby threatening international peace and security in the region, by refusing to release, repatriate, or account for non-Iraqi citizens wrongfully detained by Iraq , including an American serviceman, and by failing to return property wrongfully seized by Iraq from Kuwait;

Whereas the current Iraqi regime has demonstrated its capability and willingness to use weapons of mass destruction against other nations and its own people;

Whereas the current Iraqi regime has demonstrated its continuing hostility toward, and willingness to attack, the United States, including by attempting in 1993 to assassinate former President Bush and by firing on many thousands of occasions on United States and Coalition Armed Forces engaged in enforcing the resolutions of the United Nations Security Council;

Whereas members of al Qaida, an organization bearing responsibility for attacks on the United States, its citizens, and interests, including the attacks that occurred on September 11, 2001, are known to be in Iraq ;

Whereas Iraq continues to aid and harbor other international terrorist organizations, including organizations that threaten the lives and safety of United States citizens;

Whereas the attacks on the United States of September 11, 2001, underscored the gravity of the threat posed by the acquisition of weapons of mass destruction by international terrorist organizations;

Whereas Iraq's demonstrated capability and willingness to use weapons of mass destruction, the risk that the current Iraqi regime will either employ those weapons to launch a surprise attack against the United States or its Armed Forces or provide them to international terrorists who would do so, and the extreme magnitude of harm that would result to the United States and its citizens from such an attack, combine to justify action by the United States to defend itself;

Whereas United Nations Security Council Resolution 678 (1990) authorizes the use of all necessary means to enforce United Nations Security Council Resolution 660 (1990) and subsequent relevant resolutions and to compel Iraq to cease certain activities that threaten international peace and security, including the development of weapons of mass destruction and refusal or obstruction of United Nations weapons inspections in violation of United Nations Security Council Resolution 687 (1991), repression of its civilian population in violation of United Nations Security Council Resolution 688 (1991), and threatening its neighbors or United Nations operations in Iraq in violation of United Nations Security Council Resolution 949 (1994);

Whereas in the Authorization for Use of Military Force Against Iraq Resolution (Public Law 102-1), Congress has authorized the President 'to use United States Armed Forces pursuant to United Nations Security Council Resolution 678 (1990) in order to achieve implementation of Security Council Resolution 660, 661, 662, 664, 665, 666, 667, 669, 670, 674, and 677';

Whereas in December 1991, Congress expressed its sense that it 'supports the use of all necessary means to achieve the goals of United Nations Security Council Resolution 687 as being consistent with the Authorization of Use of Military Force Against Iraq Resolution (Public Law 102-1),' that Iraq's repression of its civilian population violates United Nations Security Council Resolution 688 and 'constitutes a continuing threat to the peace, security, and stability of the Persian Gulf region,' and that Congress, 'supports the use of all necessary means to achieve the goals of United Nations Security Council Resolution 688';

Whereas the Iraq Liberation Act of 1998 (Public Law 105-338) expressed the sense of Congress that it should be the policy of the United States to support efforts to remove from power the current Iraqi regime and promote the emergence of a democratic government to replace that regime;

Whereas on September 12, 2002, President Bush committed the United States to 'work with the United Nations Security Council to meet our common challenge' posed by Iraq and to 'work for the necessary resolutions,' while also making clear that 'the Security Council resolutions will be enforced, and the just demands of peace and security will be met, or action will be unavoidable';

Whereas the United States is determined to prosecute the war on terrorism and Iraq's ongoing support for international terrorist groups combined with its development of weapons of mass destruction in direct violation of its obligations under the 1991 cease-fire and other United Nations Security Council resolutions make clear that it is in the national security interests of the United States and in furtherance of the war on terrorism that all relevant United Nations Security Council resolutions be enforced, including through the use of force if necessary;

Whereas Congress has taken steps to pursue vigorously the war on terrorism through the provision of authorities and funding requested by the President to take the necessary actions against international terrorists and terrorist organizations, including those nations, organizations, or persons who planned, authorized, committed, or aided the terrorist attacks that occurred on September 11, 2001, or harbored such persons or organizations;

Whereas the President and Congress are determined to continue to take all appropriate actions against international terrorists and terrorist organizations, including those nations, organizations, or persons who planned, authorized, committed, or aided the terrorist attacks that occurred on September 11, 2001, or harbored such persons or organizations;

Whereas the President has authority under the Constitution to take action in order to deter and prevent acts of international terrorism against the United States, as Congress recognized in the joint resolution on Authorization for Use of Military Force (Public Law 107-40); and

Whereas it is in the national security interests of the United States to restore international peace and security to the Persian Gulf region:

Now, therefore, be it resolved by the Senate and House of Representatives of the United States of America in Congress assembled,

SECTION 1. SHORT TITLE.

This joint resolution may be cited as the 'Authorization for Use of Military Force Against Iraq Resolution of 2002'.

SEC. 2. SUPPORT FOR UNITED STATES DIPLOMATIC EFFORTS.

The Congress of the United States supports the efforts by the President to—

1. strictly enforce through the United Nations Security Council all relevant Security Council resolutions regarding Iraq and encourages him in those efforts; and

2. obtain prompt and decisive action by the Security Council to ensure that Iraq abandons its strategy of delay, evasion and noncompliance and promptly and strictly complies with all relevant Security Council resolutions regarding Iraq .

SEC. 3. AUTHORIZATION FOR USE OF UNITED STATES ARMED FORCES.

(a) AUTHORIZATION—The President is authorized to use the Armed Forces of the United States as he determines to be necessary and appropriate in order to—

1. defend the national security of the United States against the continuing threat posed by Iraq; and

2. enforce all relevant United Nations Security Council resolutions regarding Iraq .

(b) PRESIDENTIAL DETERMINATION—In connection with the exercise of the authority granted in subsection (a) to use force the President shall, prior to such exercise or as soon thereafter as may be feasible, but no later than 48 hours after exercising such authority, make available to the Speaker of the House of Representatives and the President pro tempore of the Senate his determination that—

1. reliance by the United States on further diplomatic or other peaceful means alone either (A) will not adequately protect the national security of the United States against the continuing threat posed by Iraq or (B) is not likely to lead to enforcement of all relevant United Nations Security Council resolutions regarding Iraq; and

2. acting pursuant to this joint resolution is consistent with the United States and other countries continuing to take the necessary actions against international terrorist and terrorist organizations, including those nations, organizations, or persons who planned, authorized, committed or aided the terrorist attacks that occurred on September 11, 2001.

(c) War Powers Resolution Requirements—

1. SPECIFIC STATUTORY AUTHORIZATION—Consistent with section 8(a)(1) of the War Powers Resolution, the Congress declares that this section is intended to constitute specific statutory authorization within the meaning of section 5(b) of the War Powers Resolution.

2. APPLICABILITY OF OTHER REQUIREMENTS—Nothing in this joint resolution supersedes any requirement of the War Powers Resolution.

SEC. 4. REPORTS TO CONGRESS.

(a) REPORTS—The President shall, at least once every 60 days, submit to the Congress a report on matters relevant to this joint resolution, including actions taken pursuant to the exercise of authority granted in section 3 and the status of planning for efforts that are expected to be required after such actions are completed, including those actions described in section 7 of the Iraq Liberation Act of 1998 (Public Law 105-338).

(b) SINGLE CONSOLIDATED REPORT—To the extent that the submission of any report described in subsection (a) coincides with the submission of any other report on matters relevant to this joint resolution otherwise required to be submitted to Congress pursuant to the reporting requirements of the War Powers Resolution (Public Law 93-148), all such reports may be submitted as a single consolidated report to the Congress.

(c) RULE OF CONSTRUCTION—To the extent that the information required by section 3 of the Authorization for Use of Military Force Against Iraq Resolution (Public Law 102-1) is included in the report required by this section, such report shall be considered as meeting the requirements of section 3 of such resolution.

Statement by President Bush, October 11, 2002

With tonight's vote in the United States Senate, America speaks with one voice. The Congress has spoken clearly to the international community and the United Nations Security Council. Saddam Hussein and his outlaw regime pose a grave threat to the region, the world, and the United States. Inaction is not an option, disarmament is a must.

I commend members of the Senate for the strong bipartisan vote authorizing the use of force, if necessary. The Senate, like the House, conducted this important debate and vote in the finest traditions of our democracy.

Our nation seeks a more just and more peaceful world. Our nation seeks a safer and better world. America will never waver in its commitment to these ideals.

Remarks by Secretary of State Powell, October 11, 2002

Secretary Colin Powell was interviewed on NPR's "All Things Considered."

Q. I would like to ask you first, Senator John Warner of Virginia, among many others, said last night of the Iraq resolution that passed, "It is an act to declare war, to put in place the tools for our President, our Secretary of State, to get the strongest possible resolution in the United Nations." Could you tell us, if there is not a strong resolution agreed to by all the permanent members of the U.N., all those with veto power, would that alter U.S. plans to proceed with military action against Iraq?

Secretary Powell. Well, our plans right now are to work with the United Nations to get a strong resolution with as many votes for it as possible in order to put pressure on Saddam Hussein to disarm. And we're not going to the U.N. to look for a reason to go to war. We're going to the U.N. to look for a way of disarming this very dangerous regime. But the only way that will work is if there are consequences for his failure to disarm, his failure to act. And the Congressional resolution that passed last night shows unity of purpose and unity of effort within the American Government, and that will help me convey to my colleagues at the Security Council that this is time for them to show the same kind of unity.

Q. Secretary General Kofi Annan said today he thinks it's unlikely that the Security Council would back a single resolution calling for both tighter arms inspections and also authorizing a military strike. If the U.S. had to settle for a two-stage resolution, would it be worth deferring plans, military plans, in order to increase the chance of international support for an attack later on?

Secretary Powell. Well, we still think one resolution is better and I have the greatest respect for Kofi Annan and his views, but in this case I still think one resolution is better for the simple reason is that it doesn't give Iraq an opportunity to look at what's happening in the Security Council and say, "well, you know, I can still frustrate them because it will force them to take another vote on this issue," and so I still believe, and the American position is that we should try to get it all in one resolution.

Q. But if you can't get it—

Secretary Powell.—but you know, it is a Security Council of 15 nations, so I am in consultation with other members of the Security Council trying to take their views into account and see if there's not a way to bridge this.

Q. And it is, in fact, compromising U.S. plans one element of a possible bridge?

Secretary Powell. Our plans are that we have to continue with our military plan-ning and examining military options in the case that Saddam Hussein once again refuses to comply with the new resolution. There should be little optimism that he is going to comply. His record is very bad. And we hope he will comply, but I am also sure he will not comply if he doesn't believe that there is a likelihood he will be made to comply. And that is why it is so important that we not show weakness at this time and the international community comes together. The best way to avoid war is for us to be strong now, both here in the United States and within the United Nations, in order to show that the will of the international community must be obeyed.

Q. The *New York Times* reports today on administration plans for a post-Saddam Iraq, a post-war Iraq, and it sounds a lot like post-war Japan or Germany half a cen-tury ago. Should Americans assume that if we go to war against Iraq there will be U.S. forces based there for several years and that an American general will govern there the way McArthur did in Japan?

Secretary Powell. Well, I think what the American people should realize is that should it come to that and the President hope is does not come to that, but should it come to that, we would have an obligation, really, to put in place a better regime. And we are obviously doing contingency planning, and there are lots of different models from history that one could look at: Japan, Germany, but I wouldn't say that anything has been settled upon even though *The New York Times'* story reflected one particular model.

Q. But would going to war assume that we would be going to base troops there for some time into the future?

Secretary Powell. Well, if you're going to war, obviously troops are going to a the-ater and to a country and in the immediate aftermath of such a conflict, there would have to be a need for some presence until such time as you can put in place a better system. I mean, the United States has done this many times in the course of the last 50 or 60 years and we always try to get out as quickly as we can once we have reestablished peace, put in place a stable system, it is never our intention to go and stay in a place and to impose our will by the presence of our military forces.

Remarks by President Bush, October 14, 2002

Q. Are you prepared to meet the French halfway on their concerns on the trigger of the use of force? Specifically, are you willing to drop the language that specifies the use of any and all means to—

President Bush. John, I think what's important is that, first of all, we are working with all parties to get a resolution done. I talked about it again, I talked to Tony Blair about that subject. What I'm interested in is making sure that Saddam Hussein is disarmed. He said he wouldn't have weapons of mass destruction; it is in our national interest that he not have weapons of mass destruction. And anything we do must make it very clear that Saddam must disarm, or there will be consequences. And how that language is worked out is up to the diplomats.

But I am very firm in my desire to make sure that Saddam is disarmed. Hopefully, we can do this peacefully. The use of the military is my last choice, is my last desire. But doing nothing, allowing the status quo to go on, is unacceptable, particularly since we've got a new war on terror that we've—that was launched on September the 11th, 2001; particularly since oceans no longer protect America from people who hate us.

And so we'll see how it plays out. But I'm anxious to work with the international community. If I wasn't I wouldn't have gone to the United Nations.

Q. Are you willing to be a little more oblique about that particular part of the language?

President Bush. Well, we'll just see how it comes. What I'm not—what I want is a firm resolution that says, you disarm, and an inspection regime that is there not for the sake of inspectors, but is there to achieve the objective of disarming Mr. Saddam Hussein. It's his choice to make. And in order to make sure the resolution has got any kind of credence with Mr. Hussein, there has to be a consequence.

* * * *

Q. Sir, could we ask you one more question, sir? Senator Graham last week said that the number one threat to this nation still remains al Qaeda and questioned the wisdom about going after Saddam Hussein while al Qaeda remains the number one threat. Based on what's happened for the last week in terms of Yemen, Kuwait, and Bali, does it suggest that that argument does hold some water?

President Bush. I think they're both equally important, and they're both dangerous. And as I said in my speech in Cincinnati, we will fight if need be the war on terror on two fronts. We've got plenty of capacity to do so. And I also mentioned the fact that there is a connection between al Qaeda and Saddam Hussein. The war on terror, Iraq is a part on the war on terror. And he must disarm.

And so I—I respect the opinion of a lot of people, and I respect his opinion. But if we don't deal with Saddam Hussein and disarm him—hopefully, it will be done peacefully—he becomes more and more dangerous. And someday we don't want to step back and say, where was the United States government? How come we didn't act? And we've got plenty of capacity to fight the war against al Qaeda, which is going to take a while. We just learned a lesson this weekend: it's going to take a while to succeed. And at the same time, the United Nations hopefully will pass—will show their strong desire to disarm Saddam and we can get after it, get him disarmed before he hurts America. And I'm absolutely confident we can achieve both objectives, John.

Memorandum from Secretary of Defense Rumsfeld, Released October 14, 2002

This memorandum was written by Defense Secretary Donald H. Rumsfeld in March 2001 and revised as late as the first week of October, 2002. It is titled "Guidelines to be Considered When Committing U.S. Forces," This version was printed by the New York Times on October 14, 2002. The original was provided to the New York Times by the Department of Defense.

Is the proposed action truly necessary?

A Good Reason: If U.S. lives are going to be put at risk, whatever is proposed to be done must be in the U.S. national interest. If people could be killed, ours or others, the U.S. must have a darn good reason.

Diplomacy: All instruments of national power should be engaged before resorting to force, and they should stay involved once force is employed.

Basis for the Action: In fashioning a clear statement of the underpinning for the action, avoid arguments of convenience. They can be useful at the outset to gain support, but they will be deadly later. Just as the risks of taking action must be carefully considered, so, too, the risk of inaction needs to be weighed.

Is the proposed action achievable?

Achievable: When the U.S. commits force, the task should be achievable—at acceptable risk. It must be something the U.S. is capable of accomplishing. We need to understand our limitations. The record is clear; there are some things the U.S. simply cannot accomplish.

Clear Goals: To the extent possible, there should be clear, well-considered and well-understood goals as to the purpose of the engagement and what would constitute success, so we can know when we have achieved our goals. To those who would change what is falls the responsibility of helping provide something better. It is important to understand that responsibility and accept it.

Command Structure: The command structure should be clear, not complex—not a collective command structure where a committee makes decisions. If the U.S. needs or prefers a coalition to achieve its goals, which it most often will, we should have a clear understanding with coalition partners that they will do whatever might be needed to achieve the agreed goals. Avoid trying so hard to persuade others to join a coalition that we compromise on our goals or jeopardize the command structure. Generally, the mission will determine the coalition; the coalition should not determine the mission.

Is it worth it?

Lives at Risk: If an engagement is worth doing, the U.S. and coalition partners should be willing to put lives at risk. Resources: The military capabilities needed to achieve the agreed goals must be available and not committed or subject to call elsewhere halfway through the engagement. Even with a broad coalition, the U.S. cannot do everything everywhere at once.

Public Support: If public support is weak at the outset, U.S. leadership must be willing to invest the political capital to marshal support to sustain the effort for whatever period of time may be required. If there is a risk of casualties, that fact should be acknowledged at the outset, rather than allowing the public to believe an engagement can be executed antiseptically, on the cheap, with few casualties.

Impact Elsewhere: Before committing to an engagement, consider the implications of the decision for the U.S. in other parts of the world—if we prevail, if we fail, or if we decide not to act. U.S. actions or inactions in one region are read around the world and contribute favorably or unfavorably to the U.S. deterrent and influence. Think through the precedent that a proposed action, or inaction, would establish.

If there is to be action

Act Early: If it is worth doing, U.S. leadership should make a judgment as to when diplomacy has failed and act forcefully, early, during the pre-crisis period, to try to alter the behavior of others and to prevent the conflict. If that fails, be willing and prepared to act decisively to use the force necessary to prevail, plus some. Unrestricted Options: In working to fashion a coalition or trying to persuade Congress, the public, the U.N., or other countries to support an action, the National Command Authorities must not dumb down what is needed by promising not to do things (i.e., not to use ground forces, not to bomb below 20,000 feet, not to risk U.S. lives, not to permit collateral damage, not to bomb during Ramadan, etc.). That may simplify the task for the enemy and make our task more difficult. Leadership should not set arbitrary deadlines as to when the U.S. will disengage, or the enemy can simply wait us out.

Finally

Honesty: U.S. leadership must be brutally honest with itself, the Congress, the public and coalition partners. We must not make the effort sound even marginally easier or less costly than it could become. Preserving U.S. credibility requires that we promise less, or no more, than we are sure we can deliver. It is a great deal easier to get into something than it is to get out of it!

Note

Guidelines, Not Rules: I believe these guidelines are worth considering. However, they should not be considered rules to inhibit the U.S. from acting in our national interest. Rather, they are offered simply as a checklist to assure that when the U.S. does engage, it does so with a full appreciation of our responsibilities, the risks, and the opportunities. Our future promises to offer a variety of possible engagements. The value of this checklist will depend on the wisdom with which it is applied. Decisions on military engagement always will be based on less than perfect information, often under extreme pressure of time. These guidelines likely will be most helpful not in providing specific answers, but rather in helping to frame and organize available information.

White House Press Briefing, October 15, 2002

Q. Negotiations with the French over a U.N. resolution seem to be deadlocked. How much longer is the President going to put up with this? Is he going to pull the plug?

Mr. Fleischer. Number one, I would not characterize it as deadlocked. I think the fair way to describe it is the discussions are ongoing, they do continue. No breakthroughs have taken place to date, but the conversations continue.

Q. How long is the President willing to let them continue? It's been going on now for weeks.

Mr. Fleischer. Just as the President said at the United Nations when he announced that he wanted to go through the United Nations and propose a resolution, the President said then that he was content to wait for days and weeks, not months. It still is within that days and weeks time frame. It has not reached months. And we'll see, if it goes on for the period of time beyond what the President has said. It has not yet, Bill.

* * * *

Q. Why is [President Bush] sending thousands of soldiers and people to the Persian Gulf, including planes and tanks and carriers and so forth if he's not planning a war?

Mr. Fleischer. Well, I think if you take a look at the actions of Saddam Hussein— he threw out the weapons inspectors in 1998. I think there would be absolutely no discussion by Saddam Hussein—

Q. For 11 years he's been contained and everybody knows that. So why do you want to go to war?

Mr. Fleischer. Are you opposed to having the weapons inspectors return?

Q. No, no, I think it would be good to have them go back. But I don't keep you should keep threatening war every day.

Mr. Fleischer. I think one of the reasons that there is even now talk of the weapons inspectors going back is because the President has been firm and tough. If the President had not been firm, there would be no discussion in the United Nations about the return of the inspectors. So one of the things the President believes is that the best way to preserve peace and to make certain that Iraq does what it promised to do, and that's to disarm, is for the United States to show—and to mean it—that we are resolute, we are determined to enforce the peace and make certain Saddam Hussein disarms.

Remarks by President Bush, October 16, 2002

Thank you all. Please be seated. Good morning. Welcome to the White House. I want to thank the members of my Cabinet who have joined us. I want to thank the members of Congress who are here on the stage. I want to thank the members of Congress who are here in the audience. I'm honored to have you here.

The resolution I'm about to sign symbolizes the united purpose of our nation, expresses the considered judgment of the Congress, and marks an important event in the life of America. The 107th Congress is one of the few called by history to authorize military action to defend our country and the cause of peace.

This is among the most serious and difficult decisions a legislator can face. Members of both Houses, both political parties, have deliberated with care, and they have spoken with clarity on behalf of the American people. We will face our dangers squarely, and we will face them unafraid.

With this resolution, Congress has now authorized the use of force. I have not ordered the use of force. I hope the use of force will not become necessary. Yet, confronting the threat posed by Iraq is necessary, by whatever means that requires. Either the Iraqi regime will give up its weapons of mass destruction, or, for the sake of peace, the United States will lead a global coalition to disarm that regime. If any doubt our nation's resolve, our determination, they would be unwise to test it.

The Iraqi regime is a serious and growing threat to peace. On the commands of a dictator, the regime is armed with biological and chemical weapons, possesses ballistic missiles, promotes international terror and seeks nuclear weapons. The same dictator has a history of mass murder, striking other nations without warning; of intense hatred for America; and of contempt for the demands of the civilized world.

If Iraq gains even greater destructive power, nations in the Middle East would face blackmail, intimidation or attack. Chaos in that region would be felt in Europe and beyond. And Iraq's combination of weapons of mass destruction and ties to terrorist groups and ballistic missiles would threaten the peace and security of many nations. Those who choose to live in denial may eventually be forced to live in fear.

Every nation that shares in the benefits of peace also shares in the duty of defending the peace. The time has arrived once again for the United Nations to live up to the purposes of its founding to protect our common security. The time has arrived once again for free nations to face up to our global responsibilities and confront a gathering danger.

In 1991, Iraq was given 15 days to fully disclose all weapons of mass destruction. The dictator has successfully defied that obligation for 4,199 days. The dictator has—and during this 11-year period of his dictatorship the regime has become highly skilled in the techniques of deception. It has blocked effective inspections of so-called presidential sites—actually 12 square miles with hundreds of structures where sensitive materials could be hidden. The regime has forged documents, disabled surveillance cameras, and developed mobile weapons facilities to keep ahead of any inspector.

The Iraqi regime has frustrated the work of international inspectors by firing warning shots, by tapping the telephones, confiscating their documents, blocking aerial inspection flights and barring access to sites for hours while evidence is carried away. At one location, inspectors actually witnessed Iraqi guards moving files, burning documents, and then dumping the ashes in a river. Aboard U.N. helicopters, Iraqi escorts have physically struggled with inspectors to keep them from approaching certain areas.

For Iraq, the old weapons inspection process was little more than a game, in which cheating was never punished. And that game is over. The ploys and promises of the Iraqi regime no longer matter. The regime is free to continue saying whatever it chooses; its fate depends entirely on what it actually does.

Our goal is not merely to limit Iraq's violations of Security Council resolutions, or to slow down its weapons program. Our goal is to fully and finally remove a real threat to world peace and to America. Hopefully this can be done peacefully. Hopefully we can do this without any military action. Yet, if Iraq is to avoid military action by the international community, it has the obligation to prove compliance with all the world's demands. It's the obligation of Iraq.

Compliance will begin with a accurate and full and complete accounting for all chemical, biological and nuclear weapons materials, as well as missiles and other means of delivery anywhere in Iraq. Failure to make such an accounting would be further indication of the regime's bad faith and aggressive intent. Inspectors must have access to any site in Iraq, at any time, without pre-clearance, without delay, without exceptions. Inspectors must be permitted to operate under new, effective rules. And the Iraqi regime must accept those rules without qualification or negotiation.

To ensure that we learn the truth, the regime must allow witnesses to its illegal activities to be interviewed outside of the country. These witnesses must be free to bring their entire families with them, so they're beyond the reach of Saddam Hussein's terror, Saddam Hussein's torture, Saddam Hussein's murder.

In addition to declaring and destroying all of its weapons of mass destruction, Iraq, in accordance with U.N. Security Council demands, must end its support for terrorism. As the U.N. demands, Iraq must cease the persecution of its civilian population. As the U.N. demands, Iraq must stop all illicit trade outside the oil-for-food program. Iraq must also release or account for all Gulf War personnel, including an American pilot whose fate is still unknown.

The United States takes the resolutions of the Security Council seriously. We urge other nations to do the same. We're working to build the broadest possible coalition to enforce the demands of the world on the Iraqi regime. I've told all the members of the United Nations, America will play its historic role in defeating aggressive tyranny.

I hope the good people of Iraq will remember our history, and not pay attention to the hateful propaganda of their government. America has never sought to dominate, has never sought to conquer. We've always sought to liberate and to free. Our desire is to help Iraqi citizens find the blessings of liberty within their own culture and their own traditions. The Iraqi people cannot flourish under a dictator that oppresses them and threatens them. Gifted people of Iraq will flourish if and when oppression is lifted.

When Iraq has a government committed to the freedom and well-being of its people, America, along with many other nations, will share a responsibility to help Iraq reform and prosper. And we will meet our responsibilities. That's our pledge to the Iraqi people.

Like the members of Congress here today, I've carefully weighed the human cost of every option before us. If we go into battle, as a last resort, we will confront an enemy capable of irrational miscalculations, capable of terrible deeds. As the Commander-in-Chief, I know the risks to our country. I'm fully responsible to the young men and women in uniform who may face these risks. Yet those risks only increase with time. And the costs could be immeasurably higher in years to come.

To shrink from this threat would bring a false sense of temporary peace, leading to a future in which millions live or die at the discretion of a brutal dictator. That's not true peace, and we won't accept it.

The terrorist attacks of last year put our country on notice. We're not immune from the dangers and hatreds of the world. In the events of September the 11th, we resolved as a nation to oppose every threat from any source that could bring sudden tragedy to the American people. This nation will not live at the mercy of any foreign power or plot. Confronting grave dangers is the surest path to peace and security. This is the expectation of the American people, and the decision of their elected representatives.

I thank the Congress for a thorough debate and an overwhelming statement of support. The broad resolve of our government is now clear to all, clear to everyone to see: We will defend our nation, and lead others in defending the peace.

May God bless your work.

Statement by President Bush, October 16, 2002

Today I have signed into law H.J. Res. 114, a resolution "To authorize the use of United States Armed Forces against Iraq." By passing H.J. Res. 114, the Congress has demonstrated that the United States speaks with one voice on the threat to international peace and security posed by Iraq. It has also clearly communicated to the international community, to the United Nations Security Council, and, above all, to Iraq's tyrannical regime a powerful and important message: the days of Iraq flouting the will of the world, brutalizing its own people, and terrorizing its neighbors must—and will—end. Iraq will either comply with all U.N. resolutions, rid itself of weapons of mass destruction, and in its support for terrorists, or it will be compelled to do so. I hope that Iraq will choose compliance and peace, and I believe passage of this resolution makes that choice more likely.

The debate over this resolution in the Congress was in the finest traditions of American democracy. There is no social or political force greater than a free people united in a common and compelling objective. It is for that reason that I sought an additional resolution of support from the Congress to use force against Iraq, should force become necessary. While I appreciate receiving that support, my request for it did not, and my signing this resolution does not, constitute any change in the long-standing positions of the executive branch on either the President's constitutional authority to use force to deter, prevent, or respond to aggression or other threats to U.S. interests or on the constitutionality of the War Powers Resolution. On the important question of the threat posed by Iraq, however, the views and goals of the Congress, as expressed in H.J. Res. 114 and previous congressional resolutions and enactments, and those of the President are the same.

Throughout the past months, I have had extensive consultations with the Congress, and I look forward to continuing close consultation in the months ahead. In addition, in accordance with section 4 of H.J. Res. 114, I intend to submit written reports to the Congress on matters relevant to this resolution every 60 days. To the extent possible, I intend to consolidate information in these reports with the information concerning Iraq submitted to the Congress pursuant to previous, related resolutions.

The United States is committed to a world in which the people of all nations can live in freedom, peace, and security. Enactment of H.J. Res. 114 is an important step on the road toward such a world.

White House Press Briefing, October 16, 2002

Q. Ari, the President said he was, quote, fully—he wanted—his goal was to fully and finally remove a real threat. Was he talking about weapons of mass destruction or Saddam Hussein? Or both?

Mr. Fleischer. He's talking about both. The policy of the United States is both. We talk in the United Nations about the enforcement of the resolutions which focus on disarmament; end of hostility towards the neighbors; end of repression of minorities, which the President also spoke about. And of course, the policy of the United States is regime change. And today, given the signature by the President on the bipartisan authorization to use force it is the position of the United States now in 2002 that force is authorized in the event that Saddam Hussein does not comply.

* * * *

Q. The President said at the U.N. on September 12th that it would be days not—weeks not months for a new U.N. resolution. It's been now more than a month. What kind of time line does this administration have for—

Mr. Fleischer. Well, you described it exactly right. It's just as the President announced. It will be, as he said, days and weeks, not months. And we are not yet at month-plurals.

Q. We're at more than a month, though.

Mr. Fleischer. We are at more than a month, but we're not at months. Not to put too fine a line on it, but the President's words speak for themselves. We are still at the time where it's weeks. I think that the President would get concerned, indeed, if it became a matter of months. And it has not reached a matter of months yet, it is still less than two—it's more than one. It's taking its time. And the President understood when he went up to the United Nations that they're—the United Nations is a deliberative body. They meet, they talk, the drafting of resolutions is a fine art that is practiced at the United Nations. And the President has said that that is the course he wanted to pursue, and he's pursuing it. So we'll see exactly how long it takes them. They don't have forever. And the President is mindful of that.

Q. Is the President going to ask Prime Minister Sharon not to speak at all about any possible retaliation against Iraq? And what's the administration's position of

Israel saying that it would retaliate this time around if Iraq did launch any attack on Israel?

Mr. Fleischer. Well, one, I think the very premise of your questions underscores how dangerous Iraq is. The very fact that people ask a question, a serious one about Iraq attacking its neighbors once again shows how threatening the Iraqi regime is.

But we are worried and concerned about the risk of Iraq attacking its neighbors. We share the concern of all the countries in the region about the aggressive, invading Iraqi regime. I want to remind you that over the last 20 years, Iraq has invaded its Muslim neighbors—it's invaded Iran, it's invaded Kuwait; it's launched missiles at Saudi Arabia, at Iran. It's also launched missiles at Israel, of course.

We're going to closely consult with our friends and allies in the region about this threat and ways to reduce the risk from this threat. And again, the President has not made any determination about whether he would or would not engage in military action. But no matter what decisions are made, we will consult closely with all our friends in the region, including Israel.

Q. Regarding the resolution signing ceremony today, were Congressman Gephardt and Senator Daschle invited and, if so, did they express any reasons for why they chose not to show up today?

Mr. Fleischer. All members of Congress who voted for the resolution were invited. So they were invited and they apparently had scheduling issues or some other issue that—

Q. Did they indicate to you there were—

Mr. Fleischer. I'll have to find out what the exact reason was. I don't know if they were traveling or out of town, had a scheduling conflict. But the President was very pleased to welcome many Democrats and Republicans alike who came down for the ceremony.

* * * *

Q. Ari, when the President said that those countries were living in denial now may live in fear later on, he had spoken just a few phrases before about Europe. Did he have France in mind? And did he have Russia in mind?

Mr. Fleischer. You know, the President didn't name those countries, but it's a valid statement. And this is why the President has said that, talking about the United Nations, the importance of putting calcium in the United Nations' spine.

The point is, until President Bush went to New York on September 12th, the United Nations and many nations of the world were happy to look the other way at Saddam Hussein's flagrant violations of the U.N. resolutions. What, after all, were they doing about it until President Bush went to New York?

There is a tendency in the world to allow the current path to continue even with the risks that that can take for war and peace, rather than confront the evil that is menacing and growing. And that is why the President went to New York, to remind the world about the importance of standing strong and standing up to those nations, because sometimes nations can allow the current path to continue and, therefore, live in fear as a result.

You know, one of the examples, David, that the President is constantly talking about when he has visitors coming to see him that are in the Oval Office or in foreign countries or when members of Congress come to town, is—if you remember the President came back from the ranch on September 3rd and immediately had a meeting with members of Congress. He came back, I think, September 2nd. On September 3rd, he had a meeting with members of Congress where, for the first time, the President spoke on Iraq and Congress came back and he said that if he was going to take action, he would ask for the Congress to vote, which they just did.

That same afternoon, the President met with the President of Estonia in the Oval Office, and the President started to talk to the President of Estonia about his views of the situation in Iraq. And the President of Estonia interrupted the President and he said, you don't need to talk to me about Iraq. And the President was a little bit surprised. People kind of like to hear what his thinking is on Iraq. And he said, you don't have to explain to us the great democracies in mid-to late 1930s did nothing as a storm gathered and, as a result, we lived in tyranny and oppression for 50 years. And we understand what it's like to yearn to be free and how it's important to take action in the face of a growing storm so that people can be free.

And that's a lesson that the President has kept with him. And that's why the President speaks in the language he does, because he sees a gathering and growing menace to the world and he is trying to bring the world to action against it.

Q. One of those great democracies was, in fact, France, and saw the results of that. What I'm trying to correlate is—

Mr. Fleischer. It's not a country-specific message, David.

Q. I understand that. But, obviously, now your diplomacy at the U.N. is focused on France, Russia—to some degree, China. Is—was the President's wording today an indication of any kind of a toughening line that he is taking with those three countries—the leaders of whom he'll be seeing, with the exception of the French—

Mr. Fleischer. No, I really think what's happening now at the United Nations is going to be resolved one way or another through diplomatic means. I'm not certain that we're at the point at this stage where any one speech given by any one President is going to change the votes in the United Nations, or the approach—the language in the United Nations. I really think it is at the diplomatic level. So what the President was saying was not country-specific. But it is a very valid point about what can happen to nations that do not act.

Remarks by United Nations Secretary-General Annan, October 16, 2002

Q. [What is the role of the United Nations in the war against terror and the U.S. plan with regard to Iraq?]

Secretary-General Annan. Let me say that the U.N. was very quick to react to the war on terrorism after 11th September. It was the Security Council and the General Assembly [that] acted very promptly. The Security Council approved the Resolution 1373, which demanded governments to work together in the fight against terrorism, demanding that they should not give them financial support, logistical support: they should not give them save harbor. And if we all did it and cooperated, I think we can deny the terrorists their opportunities.

And of course given what happened in Indonesia, the Council has condemned it but it underscores the importance for international action. That is the only we can defeat terrorism. And we are going to intensify our efforts, but of course each Government has to play its role.

On the question of Iraq, the Security Council is seized of the matter and they are discussing what steps they should take. They are reviewing the possibility of approving a new resolution, a resolution that will strengthen the disarmament program, strengthen the hands of the inspectors and send them back to Iraq with the demand that the Iraqi Government cooperates and complies with Security Council resolutions. And of course if Iraq were to continue to defy, the chief inspector will report back to the Council and the Council would decide what to do. But I think that Iraq must understand that it has to perform. There is a universal message to the Government and the leaders of Iraq—do comply with the U.N. resolutions. And I hope they heed this appeal that is coming from every corner of the world, including from their friends and neighbors in the region.

Q. Today the debate starts in the Security Council on the resolution and there is obviously the U.S. and Britain call for one resolution and while other permanent members are for two. Now how will you—how do you think that this deadlock can be opened, solved, and would this two step resolution work better or would it show less of a threat on Iraq. Would that be less forceful threat. And then yesterday Iraqis voted Saddam Hussein for another seven-year term. What do you think? Is it valid confirmation that people of Iraq support Saddam and would this election result have some impact on the resolution issue?

Secretary-General Annan. I think the question whether there would be one or two resolutions is something that is being hotly debated and discussed by the Member States in New York. What I firmly believe is that at the end of the day, when those discussion are over, the Council will come up with an optimal decision, an optimal decision that will allow the inspectors to go back with a strengthened hand and continue their work. And it's a decision that would also underscore the determination and the desire of the international community to ensure that the disarmament tasks are carried out.

I think as soon as the Council itself is so seized, and you yourself indicated there is going to be a debate in the Council, and there may well be about 70 speakers, countries who will speak, we should wait and see what happens at the end of debate. But whatever it is, I think the Council will come up with an optimal decision and hopefully a united decision which will send a strong message of the will of international community.

As to the question of the vote in Iraq, think the Iraqi people did vote, but of course there was only one candidate on the list. I don't think the voting in Iraq will have any impact on the discussions that are going on the Security Council. The Council has work to do and I'm sure they will proceed with it and I think that's it. Bayarlalaa. [Thank you.]

Excerpts from the United Nations Security Council Debate on the Situation in Iraq, October 16-17, 2002

United Nations Deputy Secretary-General Louise Fréchette. As you know, the Secretary-General very much wished to attend this debate in person, but is unable to do so because of his commitment to visit a number of Member States in Asia this week. He is, however, very anxious to give the Council the benefit of his views on an issue of such great importance. Exceptionally, therefore, he has asked me to read you the following statement on his behalf:

"I applaud you for holding this open debate on Iraq, and much regret that I cannot be with you in person.

"The situation created by Iraq's failure to comply fully with the resolutions of this Council since 1991 is indeed one of the gravest and most serious facing the international community today.

"It poses a great challenge to this Organization, and in particular to the Security Council. In Article 24 of the Charter, the Member States have conferred primary responsibility on this Council for the maintenance of international peace and security.

"That is a grave responsibility indeed, and it is essential that the Council face up to it.

"But let me add that the situation also presents the United Nations with an opportunity. If we handle this properly, we may actually strengthen international cooperation, the rule of law and the United Nations—enabling it to move forward in an purposeful way, not only in this immediate crisis but in the future as well.

"It is therefore entirely proper that the Council should debate its course of action, not only in private consultations but also only in public, so that Member States not currently serving on the Council may have an opportunity to give their views. For myself, I stated my views on this matter very clearly on 12 September, when I had the honor to address the General Assembly. The Council may recall that on that occasion I said that efforts to obtain Iraq's compliance with the Council's resolutions must continue. I appeal to all who might have influence with Iraq's leaders to impress on them the vital importance of accepting the weapons inspections. I myself urged Iraq to comply with its obligations, for the sake of its own people and for the sake of world order.

In his speech in the general debate on the same day, the President of the United States also insisted that Iraq must comply with its obligations under the Council's resolutions, and a large number of other States joined in that appeal.

"Four days later, I received a letter from the Iraqi Foreign Minister informing me of his Government's decision 'to allow the return of the United Nations weapons inspectors to Iraq without conditions'. Since then, Mr. Hans Blix, Executive Chairman of the United Nations Monitoring, Verification and Inspection Commission (UNMOVIC) and the Director General of the International Atomic Energy Agency (IAEA), Mr. Mohammed ElBaradei, met with an Iraqi delegation on 30 September and 1 October to discuss the practical arrangements for the resumption of inspections. Iraq's decision to readmit the inspectors without condition is an important first step, but only a first step.

"Full compliance remains indispensable, and it has not yet happened. Iraq has to comply. It must implement the disarmament program required by the resolutions of the Council. Weapons inspectors will be returning to Iraq after a four-year absence, under a new structure and new leadership, to verify the implementation of that program. The inspectors must have unfettered access, and the Council will expect nothing less. It may well choose to pass a new resolution strengthening the inspectors' hands so that there are no weaknesses or ambiguities. I consider that such a step would be appropriate. The new measures must be firm, effective, credible and reasonable. If Iraq fails to make use of this last chance, and if defiance continues, the Council will have to face its responsibilities. It my experience it always does so best and most effectively when its members work in unison.

"Let me therefore conclude by urging the President and his colleagues to make every effort to retain their unity of purpose. If you allow yourselves to be divided, the authority and credibility of the Organization will undoubtedly suffer; but if you act in unison, you will have greater impact and a better chance of achieving your objective, which must be a comprehensive solution that includes the suspension and eventual ending of the sanctions that are causing such hardship for the Iraqi people, as well as the timely implementation of other provisions of your resolutions. If the Council succeeds in this, it will strengthen the United Nations in a way that will place future generations in its debt."

South African Representative Kumalo. We come before the Council because we believe that the Council is being asked to consider a matter that has important repercussions for the entire United Nations. According to the Preamble to the Charter, the United Nations was founded with the explicit determination "to save succeeding generations from the scourge of war". We are here to voice our concerns regarding the possibility that the United Nations is now being asked to consider proposals that open up the possibility of a war against a Member State.

The situation between Iraq and Kuwait must be addressed comprehensively by the United Nations so as to allow the Security Council to lift sanctions against Iraq, which continue to have dire humanitarian consequences. Iraq should comply with the relevant Security Council resolutions, including the provisions relating to the repatriation of all Kuwaiti and third country nationals and the return of all Kuwaiti property. All

Member States are bound by Security Council resolutions, and no Member should be exempted from carrying out obligations as determined by the Council.

We therefore welcome the announcement by the Government of Iraq to allow United Nations weapons inspectors to return without any conditions. We believe this offers the prospect for a peaceful resolution of this matter. We would urge the Security Council to allow the inspectors to return to Iraq as soon as possible.

We called for this meeting to offer our encouragement to the Security Council to seize this opportunity, which could possibly lead to a lasting peaceful solution to the long-standing matter between Iraq and Kuwait.

During the general debate of the fifty-seventh session of the General Assembly, the Foreign Ministers of the Non-Aligned Movement were seized with the debate on Iraq. They welcomed the decision by the Government of Iraq to allow the unconditional return of weapons inspectors in accordance with the relevant Security Council resolutions. They further stated that "in this regard, we wish to encourage Iraq and the United Nations to intensify their efforts in search of a lasting, just and comprehensive solution to all outstanding issues between them in accordance with the relevant United Nations Security Council resolutions." The Ministers reaffirmed respect for the sovereignty, territorial integrity and political independence of Iraq and Kuwait, in accordance with the relevant Security Council resolutions. They emphasized the need for a peaceful solution of the issue of Iraq in a way that preserves the authority and credibility of the Charter of the United Nations and international law, as well as peace and stability in the region. The Ministers also reiterated the Non-Aligned Movement's firm rejection of any type of unilateral action against any Member State of the United Nations.

We welcome the agreement of 1 October 2002 between the Government of Iraq, the United Nations Monitoring, Verification and Inspection Commission (UNMOVIC) and the International Atomic Energy Agency (IAEA) on the practical arrangements necessary for the immediate resumption of inspections, in accordance with the provisions of the relevant Security Council resolutions. The timetable for the return of the inspectors that has been presented to the Security Council by Mr. Hans Blix, Executive Chairman of UNMOVIC, and Mr. ElBaradei, Director General of the IAEA, is also welcomed. It would therefore be inconsistent with the spirit and letter of the United Nations Charter if the Security Council were to authorize the use of military force against Iraq at a time when Iraq has indicated its willingness to abide by the Security Council's resolutions.

In our view, the way has now been cleared for the immediate return of the United Nations weapons inspectors to Iraq. We have full confidence that Mr. Blix and the United Nations inspectors will undertake their duties with utmost professionalism. We hope that the Security Council shares our confidence in the abilities and credibility of UNMOVIC and the IAEA in carrying out this task. We urge the Council to allow the United Nations inspectors to return to Iraq to resume their important work without delay. It would be tragic if the Council were to prejudge the work of the inspectors before they set foot in Iraq. There will be enough time for the Council to review the work of the inspectors since Mr. Blix and his team are required to report progress to the Council.

We have followed with interest the public discussion on the elements for a possible resolution on Iraq. It has been brought to our attention that the significant consultations are limited to the permanent members of the Security Council and their capitals. There have even been suggestions that permanent members should be given new and exclusive roles in dealing with the resolution of the Iraqi issue.

It has always been a source of comfort and satisfaction for those of us who are not in the Security Council that there are ten elected members who we chose to represent our views. We believe that these elected members have their own special role to play in the Council's deliberations, because they bring credibility and balance to decision-making within the Council. We are therefore concerned if elected members are excluded from consultations on the most pressing issues before the Council. This is can only lead to the erosion of the authority and legitimacy of the Security Council as a whole.

The Security Council represents our collective security concerns and should ultimately be accountable to the entire United Nations. The maintenance of international peace and security is a core function of the United Nations. Therefore, the Security Council cannot be party to increasing the humanitarian suffering of civilians who are caught up in conflict situations. Nor can the Council allow itself to agree to decisions that will subject and condemn large numbers of innocent civilians to conditions of war in efforts to enforce its resolutions. Through the United Nations Charter, we adopted a system of collective security, and we now have to act with resolve to protect our rules-based system of international relations. The norms and fundamental principles of international law must be our basis to establish the conditions for peace, justice and human dignity.

The Security Council should ensure that there is consistency in the way it acts to enforce its own decisions and avoid subjectivity and vagueness in its resolutions. The Council should be explicit and clearly define the objectives of its resolutions and set clear, implementable benchmarks for compliance. This would facilitate the efforts by Member States to fully comply with their obligations.

Open-ended sanctions regimes imposed by the Security Council are counterproductive insofar as they exacerbate the humanitarian situation. In Iraq, 11 years of sanctions have brought endless suffering to the ordinary people. We hope that the Security Council will dispatch the inspectors to Iraq as soon as possible and allow the people of Iraq to focus their attention on rebuilding their country.

Iraqi Representative Aldouri. We would also like to express our thanks and gratitude to the friendly State of South Africa for its initiative on behalf of the Non-Aligned Movement on requesting the convening of this meeting to give a chance to the Members States of the United Nations to express their views on this matter, which is not only about relations between Iraq and the Security Council, but also about international relations in general. It is also a matter that relates to the capacity of the international community to face up to the American tendency to practice hegemony and aggression, and to stand steadfastly by the principles of the United Nations Charter. We hope that the Security Council will take the views that we will hear today and tomorrow into account.

The deterioration in international relations has reached a point where the American Administration unabashedly declares its plans to invade and occupy Iraq, using military force and even appointing an American governor, therein changing the map of the region by force and putting their hands on the sources of energy there. The United States also wants the Security Council to give it a blank cheque to colonize Iraq, not just Iraq but the entire Arab Mashrq, which it plans to violate as part of its plan to subject the entire world to American hegemony. The United States of America has taken advantage of illegal means of pressure and a tremendous propaganda mechanism to disseminate lies concerning Iraq, one lie after the other, the latest being the pretence that Iraq owns weapons of mass destruction and the alleged threat of such weapons to world security.

I believe that everyone knows that there are no nuclear, chemical or biological weapons of mass destruction in Iraq and that Iraq implemented many years ago the disarmament requirements set out in paragraphs 8 to 13 of resolution 687 (1991). This has been recognized by the International Atomic Energy Agency (IAEA), which has declared that there are no pending issues concerning disarmament in Iraq. The United Nations Special Commission (UNSCOM) also recognized that fact. Ambassador Rolf Ekeus, the former Executive Chairman of UNSCOM, declared on 13 January 1993 that Iraq had implemented 95 per cent of its obligations, an assertion that he repeated in an interview for the Swedish Broadcasting Corporation on 7 September 2002.

I should like to beg the Security Council's indulgence in describing in depth Iraq's implementation of resolution 687 (1991) over the past seven years and seven months. Suffice it to say that 276 inspection teams, made up of a total of 3,845 inspectors, in addition to 80 delegations in the form of special missions, undertook 3,392 visits to Iraqi sites. Among these teams were 94 teams specializing in meetings and interviews, which met for a total of 2,359 hours with 1,378 people connected directly or indirectly with Iraq's previous programmes. There were 192 monitoring teams involving 1,332 inspectors who undertook 10,256 inspection visits to sites subject to the monitoring system, as well as other sites. Although 595 sites were subject to monitoring pursuant to the mechanism for monitoring Iraqi exports and imports under resolution 1051 (1996), 74 sites were added, including in border and customs areas, harbors, hospitals and health centers.

UNSCOM and IAEA used 140 surveillance cameras at 29 sites and 30 sensors at 23 sites, as well as 1,929 labels on 1,832 facilities and pieces of equipment in monitoring 161 sites. UNSCOM placed 9,026 labels on 99 types of missile with a range of less than seven kilometers. UNSCOM and IAEA also undertook 2,967 helicopter sorties in their work, for a total of 4,480 flight hours. The United States undertook 434 U-2 surveillance sorties for a total of 1,800 flight hours. Iraq submitted 1,744,000 pages of documents to UNSCOM and IAEA, along with a number of videotapes and nine kilometers of microfilm, containing 600,000 pictures and 50,000 microfilm slides.

All of this demonstrates to the Security Council that Iraq has honored all its requirements, despite the many harmful and insulting practices of the inspection units, including the espionage carried out by the American and British inspectors, in particular, in implementation of the well-known plots and plans devised by the United States to maintain the embargo and to jeopardize Iraqi national security. This was recognized by many inspectors, UNSCOM Executive Chairman Ekeus and the chief United States inspector Scott Ritter among them.

Iraq has consented to all these sacrifices in the hope that its cooperation would lead the Security Council to honor its obligations under resolution 687 (1991). Foremost among those obligations are lifting the comprehensive embargo imposed on Iraq, ensuring respect for Iraq's national security, and addressing the regional security imbalance embodied in Israel's possession of a vast arsenal of nuclear, chemical and biological weapons, long-range missiles and their delivery systems. However, when the United States sensed that the pretext of inspections had become an inadequate excuse for maintaining the comprehensive embargo and for repeated American and British aggressions, it asked the inspection team led by Mr. Butler to leave Iraq on 15 December 1998. In other words, the inspectors did not leave because Iraq asked them to, but because Mr. Butler asked them to do so, as instructed by the United States.

One day after the inspectors left Iraq, there was a vast military attack against Iraq, which claimed the lives of hundreds of Iraqi citizens and destroyed several economic and service institutions, including sites that had been under the surveillance and monitoring of UNSCOM and the IAEA.

Following that, the United States dragged the Security Council along a very long and complex path of discussions in order to redraft Council resolutions, impose new conditions on Iraq and set up new inspection committees, believing that the continued absence of inspectors justified continuing the embargo, which would mean that one day the Iraqi people would kneel to the will of the United States.

Thus, the inspectors left Iraq and the overall embargo continued from 6 August 1990, claiming the lives of Iraqi citizens, so much so that the number of embargo victims has reached 1,750,000 Iraqi citizens, as of the end of September of this year.

The embargo continues to represent a moral problem for the United Nations, as described by the Secretary-General. It also is a blatant violation of several provisions of the Charter of the United Nations, such as Article 24, which calls for the Security Council to work in keeping with the purposes and principles of the Charter. It is also a violation of Article 1, paragraph 1, which states that sanctions and other measures adopted for the maintenance of international peace and security should be in keeping with the principles of international law and justice.

The sanctions are a violation of Article 1, paragraph 2 of the Charter, which deals with respect for the principle of equality among peoples—their equal rights and their right to self-determination—since no sanctions should be imposed that will cause international disagreements that are incompatible with the legal rights of the State or that prejudice the people's right to self-determination.

The sanctions are also a violation of Article 1, paragraph 3 of the Charter, which concerns the promotion of and respect for human rights. The system of sanctions also violates Article 2, paragraph 7 of the Charter, which does not allow the United Nations to intervene in matters that are essentially within the domestic jurisdiction of any State.

Sanctions also go against Article 55 of the Charter, which calls upon the United Nations to guarantee higher standards of living for all people and to work towards economic and social progress and development. We do not want to dwell at length on the fact that they are also a violation of many other international conventions and instruments on human rights.

All this has been documented by United Nations agencies, humanitarian organizations, human rights organizations and many researchers and writers in this area. The sanctions imposed on Iraq have caused a humanitarian catastrophe comparable to the worst catastrophes that have befallen the world throughout history. The sanctions have claimed the lives of thousands of children, women and elderly people. They constitute genocide by any standard; the number of victims goes far beyond the victims of the use of weapons of mass destruction throughout history. Parallel to the imposition of the comprehensive embargo, since April of 1991 the United States and Britain have declared two no-fly zones in the south and north of Iraq, in blatant violation of the Charter and the established rules of international law, as well as the relevant resolutions of the Security Council, which have underlined the importance of respecting Iraq's sovereignty, territorial integrity and political independence.

By imposing those no-fly zones, the United States and Britain have carried out military aggression continuously, killing thousands of Iraqi citizens and destroying property. Those two States are violating daily the resolutions of the Security Council and carrying out continuous aggression against Iraq. The Council has been unable to put an end to such aggression or even to condemn it.

In order to end the impasse in the situation with the Security Council, Iraq took the initiative of opening a dialogue with the Secretary-General, with the aim of achieving full implementation of the obligations contained in resolutions of the Council in a balanced and equitable manner and in accordance with international law and the Charter of the United Nations.

The Iraqi side held four meetings with the Secretary-General which led to some progress but which did not achieve their objective. This was due to pressure by the United States, which prevented the Council from participating in the efforts to seek a comprehensive solution that would deal with all aspects of the relationship between Iraq and the Council while guaranteeing the implementation of all the requirements of the Council's resolutions—I repeat, guaranteeing the implementation of all requirements of the Security Council.

This American position actually means that a comprehensive solution would not serve the aggressive intentions of the United States against Iraq and the region as a whole. That is the very reason which has led the United States to prevent the Security Council from examining the possibility of implementing operative paragraph 6 of the Council's resolution 1382 (2001). This paragraph calls on the Security Council to reach a comprehensive settlement concerning the relationship between Iraq and the Council, including clarification concerning the implementation of resolution 1284 (1999).

In response to the calls and appeals of the Secretary-General of the United Nations, the Secretary-General of the League of Arab States, the Arab States and many friendly countries, the Iraqi Government on 16 September 2002 agreed, unconditionally, to the return of United Nations weapons inspectors, in order to dissipate any doubts concerning Iraq's continued possession of weapons of mass destruction, and as a first step towards a solution that would include lifting the overall embargo imposed on Iraq and implementing the other provisions of relevant Security Council resolutions.

In his letter dated 16 September 2002, the Secretary-General conveyed to the President of the Security Council Iraq's agreement and mentioned the following:

"As I had the honor to mention to the General Assembly a few days ago, this decision by the Government of the Republic of Iraq is the indispensable first step towards an assurance that Iraq no longer possesses weapons of mass destruction and, equally important, towards a comprehensive solution that includes the suspension and eventual ending of the sanctions that are causing such hardship for the Iraqi people and the timely implementation of other provisions of the relevant Security Council resolutions." (S/2002/1034, p. 1)

The Iraqi technical delegation held talks in Vienna on 30 September and 1 October 2002 with delegations from the United Nations Monitoring, Verification and Inspection Commission (UNMOVIC) and the International Atomic Energy Agency (IAEA) under the chairmanship of Mr. Hans Blix and Mr. Mohamed ElBaradei. Both delegations agreed on arrangements for the return of the weapons inspectors and chose 19 October 2002 as the date when the first UNMOVIC team would reach Baghdad.

The Iraqi delegation, in the course of that meeting submitted the semi-annual reports concerning the sites that are subject to monitoring, and that had not been monitored since the inspectors left Iraq four years ago. These reports show Iraq fully respects its obligations pursuant to Security Council resolution 687 (1991), despite the absence of the monitoring and inspection teams. Bear in mind that these developments clearly reflect the wishes of Iraq and the United Nations and their readiness to begin confidence-building measures and pave the way for the Security Council to implement its own obligations.

In spite of these developments the United States of America has tried to hamper such agreements by increasing its threats against Iraq, appearing before the Security Council in order to obtain the blank check needed to carry out its aggression and by calling for the imposition of unfair, impossible and arbitrary conditions on Iraq. These conditions are, at the least, an insult to the international community, the United Nations and international law and constitute a return to the law of the jungle.

The war hysteria that seems to have hit the current American Government is fed by hatred and by a desire to settle old accounts and impose its hegemony on the world politically, militarily, and economically. The United States is not interested in the implementation of the Security Council resolutions, for the United States of America is the main ally of Israel, which has refused to implement more than twenty-eight Security Council resolutions and scores of General Assembly resolutions that have called on Israel to withdraw from occupied Arab territories and to allow Palestinian refugees to return to their homes. The United States of America has been providing Israel with state-of-the-art weapons to kill the heroic Palestinian people and destroy their property.

This aggressive American hysteria has nothing to do with ending the proliferation of weapons of mass destruction in the world, for the United States of America possesses the largest arsenal of weapons of mass destruction and has a longer history of using these weapons against people, starting with Hiroshima and Nagasaki, then Viet Nam and most recently by using depleted uranium against Iraq and Yugoslavia. The United States is the country that revoked the Antiballistic Missile Treaty. It unilaterally hampered the implementation of paragraph 14 of Security Council resolution 687 (1991) which calls for making the Middle East a zone free of weapons of mass destruction.

Allow me to mention, as an example, a statement of the former Director-General of the Organization for the Prohibition of Chemical Weapons, Mr. Jos Bustani, published in Le Monde Diplomatique in July of this year, where he stated

"From the very beginning we were faced with difficulty when the Americans refused to allow the members of the organization to carry out their inspections. Very often the inspectors could not enter the laboratories so we remained unable to ascertain that they were actually producing chemical material for peaceful purposes only. It was very difficult for us to examine the samples, for it was not possible to carry out such an inspection, except in the American laboratories. In the final analysis, we had no guarantee as to the validity of the results. At every inspection operation the Americans were trying to change the rules of the game."

We call on the international community loudly to voice their objections to the aggressive designs of the United States of America against Iraq, in order to prevent it from using the Security Council as a tool to carry out its policy of aggression. Not to speak out in the face of these attempts would have serious repercussions on international peace and security, for this would be the beginning of the end of the collective security system as set out in the Charter of the United Nations and of all other instruments, agreements and conventions governing international relations. The key principles underpinning all of these include resorting first to peaceful means in the settlement of conflicts; refraining from the use of force, or the threat thereof, and from violating the territorial integrity or political independence of any State; respecting equal sovereignty among States Members of the United Nations; and following a policy of non-intervention in matters that fall under the jurisdiction of a given State. This hegemonistic attitude will claim many victims if we do not bridle it.

Today we must urgently reject Washington's attempts to hinder the return of the inspectors. It is doing so even though Iraq has taken all the necessary practical measures and arrangements and paved the way for the return of the inspectors and made the necessary preparations for them to carry out their work easily.

Iraq has pledged to cooperate with the inspectors in every possible way so as to facilitate their task of ascertaining that there are no weapons of mass destruction in Iraq.

There is therefore absolutely no need for the adoption a new Security Council resolution. The attempts being made by the United States of America to hamper and delay the return of the inspectors and to make the Security Council adopt a new resolution laying down conditions that are impossible to respect are but a pretext for aggression against Iraq. The goal of that aggression is the colonization of our country and the imposition of American domination over our oil, as a first step towards the imposition of American colonialism in the region as a whole and the control of its oil and towards allowing Israel to continue its genocidal war against the Palestinian people and its aggression against the Arab countries.

The United States of America does not want the inspectors to return, because if they do there will be proof that the Americans have consistently lied and made false allegations. At that point the Security Council would have to lift the unjust embargo against Iraq, ensure respect for its national and regional security concerns, and implement of the other requirements set out in Council resolutions; and that is exactly what the United States of America does not want.

Finally, we are confident that, now that Iraq has expressed its readiness before the Security Council unconditionally to receive the inspectors, the States Members of the United Nations will defend its decisions, just as all peoples have done in rejecting the American war of aggression.

Kuwaiti Representative Abulhasan. The Security Council is debating today the current situation between Iraq and the United Nations against the somber backdrop of ominous precursors of an imminent war in one of the most sensitive and strategic regions of the world, which would have a direct impact on the crucial lifelines of the world economy and subsequently on global stability.

The debate has taken on even greater significance in view of the complex and difficult situation of the international community as it endeavors to channel substantial energies and resources to the combat against terrorism and to identify its underlying causes, uproot it and resolve any problems that might be perceived as justifications or pretexts for the commission of such heinous crimes.

In the face of this common threat, the world must be united in its goals, in shouldering its responsibilities and in taking action. This should be done only within the framework of the United Nations system, because unilateral actions taken as a result of being in a position of power could prove, down the road, as ineffective as a reluctance to pitch in due to weakness. Truly effective and meaningful action should therefore be driven by a sense of our common destiny in the face of a threat that is blind to nationality, religion, race and culture.

This, perhaps, explains the overwhelming international support for the statement made by the Secretary-General when on 12 September last he introduced his annual report on the work of the Organization at the beginning of the General Assembly's general debate. In that introduction, he stressed the need to strengthen collective action to ensure respect for international law and to abide by the legality of the United Nations in confronting any threat to international peace and security.

The President of the United States of America, speaking on the same day and from the same rostrum, stated that the United Nations should take on that obligation. That position can be considered as an endorsement of joint international action within the framework of the United Nations, which must characterize any approach to issues relating to international peace and security.

Kuwait feels very strongly that any action taken must be taken within the United Nations legal framework. Without such a framework, Kuwait would probably not have been liberated from Iraqi occupation early in 1991. Furthermore, the issues that emerged as a result of that occupation, and which are still unresolved with regard to Iraq, would not have assumed such great international significance.

In this respect, my delegation supports the convening of this open debate in the Security Council. Indeed, we consider it as further evidence that the current situation with regard to Iraq must be resolved between Iraq and the United Nations, not between Iraq and any particular country or group of countries.

Over the past few months the Security Council has been involved in intensive efforts to find a peaceful solution to the current crisis, which arose as a result of the rejection by Iraq of resolution 1284 (1999) by blocking the return of United Nations weapons inspectors to Iraq. That position prompted the international community to insist that the United Nations continue to play its essential role and that the Security Council's credibility be reaffirmed through the implementation of its relevant resolutions, as required by the Charter.

Kuwait hopes that the current international momentum can be maintained so as to ensure that Iraq fully implements all relevant resolutions. The unity of the Security Council is essential; without it, the message from the Council will not reach Iraq with full force and the Council will not achieve its true objective—full compliance with the relevant resolutions. Only such compliance will ensure peace and security throughout the region and allow the dark clouds of war that are looming on the horizon to dissipate.

I would like to sum up the position of the State of Kuwait regarding the current situation. First, we welcome the steps taken by the Iraqi Government to readmit United Nations weapons inspectors without restrictions or conditions. My Government considers that to be a move in the right direction.

Second, we consider that full compliance by the Government of Iraq with all the operational procedures, rules, controls and requirements set out by the United Nations Monitoring, Verification and Inspection Commission to ensure an effective and fruitful inspection process within the time frame that has been set out to be the only yardstick for evaluating Iraq's seriousness and credibility with regard to the unconditional and unfettered readmission of the inspectors.

Third, ever since the early clouds of war began to gather as a result of Iraq's persistent rejection of the return of inspectors, Kuwait has declared that it was not in favor of the use of military force against Iraq because we feared serious negative consequences that would exacerbate the suffering and hardship of the brotherly people of Iraq, who have already endured so much.

We in Kuwait are very sensitive to the suffering of the Iraqi people. That is why we have called on the Government of Iraq time and again to save the people of Iraq from their grave situation by fully implementing all relevant Security Council resolutions without selectivity or procrastination, and by putting the welfare of the people ahead of all other narrow interests.

Fourth, force must be used only as a last resort after all other available means have been exhausted, and must be within the United Nations legal framework. The Kuwaiti position is completely in line with those of the Gulf Cooperation Council, the Arab Summit that took place at Beirut last March and the ministerial meeting of the League of Arab States, held at Cairo last September. All of those forums rejected the use of military force outside the United Nations framework against any Arab State, especially Iraq, as well as any measures that might jeopardize Iraq's sovereignty and territorial integrity.

Fifth, Kuwait maintains that the Secretary-General's 1998 concept of diplomacy backed by force aimed at ensuring the necessary compliance with Security Council resolutions has been shown to be valid once again in the context of seeking a peaceful solution to the Iraqi question.

Ongoing efforts to ensure compliance by Iraq with the provisions of relevant Security Council resolutions relating to Iraq should not be confined to the question of the return of inspectors to Iraq and the elimination of weapons of mass destruction. Despite the paramount importance of that matter, it is still only one of the major obligations that Iraq must fulfill. Iraq has other key obligations, including some that relate directly to my country, Kuwait, most importantly the question of Kuwaiti prisoners of war and third country nationals held in Iraq. Those obligations are set forth in Security Council resolutions 686 (1991), 687 (1991) and 1284 (1999), all of which require Iraq to cooperate fully with the International Committee of the Red Cross (ICRC) in order to ensure a speedy resolution of the matter.

Regrettably, since 1998 the Iraqi Government has been boycotting the meetings of the Tripartite Commission, chaired by the ICRC and charged with accounting for those innocent victims. All of the worthy efforts of the Secretary-General and his High-Level Coordinator on this issue, Ambassador Yuli Vorontsov, as well as the repeated calls made by the Council after every four-month periodic review of the Coordinator's reports, have thus far been in vain. Here, I would like to emphasize that no one else can comprehend the intransigence of the Iraqi position regarding this purely humanitarian issue, which should not have been allowed to drag on for the past 12 years. The Government of Iraq has been attempting to justify its non-participation in the Tripartite Commission, despite the fact that Iraq was one of the States signatories to the Riyadh Agreement of 1991, and despite the fact that such participation was set forth as a specific obligation in section B of resolution 1284 (1999). Iraq's argument for refusing to sit down with the representatives of the United States and the United Kingdom is that those two countries launched military attacks against it in 1998 and that there are no dossiers on any nationals from those two States.

Following Iraq's acceptance of the unconditional and unrestricted return of inspectors, my delegation wonders how Iraq can seek to bar individuals of any nationality from participating in the inspection teams. Would the Council permit such exclusions? I am confident that the Council will not condone such a position. Also, I am sure that the Government of Iraq will not make such a request. Following that line of reasoning, how could the Government of Iraq refuse to cooperate with the Tripartite Commission because of the involvement of nationals from certain States, while allowing those same States to participate in the inspection operations?

Regarding the argument that there are no dossiers on nationals from either the United Kingdom or the United States, I wonder how Iraq can accept inspectors of all nationalities, individuals who have the required technical qualifications and experience in the area of weapons of mass destruction, while the same criteria of technical qualifications and knowledge of the military operations to liberate Kuwait are not applied in the case of the missing persons issue. Both United States and United Kingdom forces were major parties in the war to liberate Kuwait. Therefore, those two countries are quite familiar with all the events during that difficult period. In fact, that is all the more reason why those two countries should participate in the meetings of the Tripartite Commission.

We demand that Iraq respond with regard to this issue in order to resolve it once and for all. We expect Iraq to give concrete demonstration of the good intentions it expressed at the Beirut Arab Summit when it pledged to find a quick and definitive solution to the question of Kuwaiti and third country prisoners and hostages. To that end, we are awaiting Iraq's participation in the coming meetings of the Tripartite Commission on 24 October in Geneva under the chairmanship of the International Committee of the Red Cross. Iraq must abandon its worn-out pretexts and justifications, which are totally unacceptable in form and content.

The question of Kuwaiti and third country detainees in Iraq is not a bilateral issue between Kuwait and Iraq. Nor is the issue suited to be considered by a regional organization, as the Government of Iraq currently seeks to have done. Rather it is an issue of international commitment, as stressed in a number of Security Council resolutions. The Council has been seized of this matter from the very beginning and has been holding consultations on the issue once every four months. Kuwait takes this opportunity to call on the international community and the Council to maintain pressure on Iraq to persuade it that its cooperation in resolving this issue should arise from explicit political will and not from a sense of fear that will dissipate as soon as threats of the use of force are dropped.

I request that the Council ensure that the question of Kuwaiti and third country prisoners held in Iraq be a key element in any Council resolution adopted on the current situation between Iraq and the United Nations. Indeed, this is the most propitious time to break the deadlock on this humanitarian question. The Security Council and the United Nations system cannot be true to themselves unless they honor their commitments, demonstrate respect for human rights and address human suffering effectively. In that context, we expect the Council to give as much attention to the suffering endured by the people of Kuwait since 1990 as it devotes to saving the region from the evils and horrors of weapons of mass destruction. For, in the end, all efforts of the United Nations system, and the Council in particular, aim at protecting human life, human dignity, families and communities. That function constitutes the first step towards global security and stability.

In closing, let me reiterate Kuwait's clear position. We invite the Government of Iraq to heed the appeals of the international community and all nations in our area, especially those in the Gulf region, and to make every possible effort in a spirit of sincerity to comply with all relevant Security Council resolutions. Furthermore, Iraq should strictly abide by the will of the international community, represented by the Council, in order to avoid a war and its consequences and the additional suffering that it will cause the brotherly people of Iraq. Such a war will certainly affect all citizens of the region, who aspire to live in peace and tranquillity and to devote all their energy towards meeting economic, social and cultural challenges.

All of us should live up to our responsibilities and acquire wisdom and far-sightedness. God entrusted us with the present and all its potential in order to build the future with all its requirements. Without peace, we shall not be able to use the present for our own sake, nor can we ensure the future for our children.

Arab League Observer Mahmassani. On 16 September 2002, following the tireless efforts by the Secretary-General Mr. Kofi Annan, and the Secretary-General of the League of Arab States, Mr. Amr Moussa, Iraq accepted the return of inspectors of the United Nations Monitoring, Verification and Inspection Commission (UNMOVIC) without restrictions or conditions, a step that was welcomed by the international community.

Following that, an agreement between Iraq and the Executive Chairman of UNMOVIC was reached in Vienna on the arrangements for the return of the weapons inspectors. World markets have been relieved, and the Dow Jones index gained $1 billion in one minute. That relaxation did not last for long, since some have requested that inspectors not return until a new draft resolution is prepared.

Iraq has declared that it is free of all weapons of mass destruction and that it is committed to all relevant Security Council resolutions. Therefore, we believe that the present situation requires the return of the inspectors to Iraq as soon as possible, in accordance with relevant Security Council resolutions, in order to fulfill their tasks and to present a report to the Security Council so it can lift the sanctions imposed on Iraq. There is no reason for the delay in the Council's work, and there is no reason to prejudge the results of the inspectors and to prepare for war.

We would like to recall that Article 2 of the United Nations Charter states that all Member States shall refrain in their international relations from the threat or use of force against the territorial integrity or political independence of any State.

The League of Arab States, at the Beirut Summit on 27 and 28 March 2002, completely rejected any strike against Iraq or any threat against the safety and security of any Arab country. We requested that sanctions against Iraq be lifted and called for respect for its territorial integrity and security. We also welcomed Iraq's reaffirmation of the Council's call for respect for the independence and sovereignty of Kuwait, and we have called for implementation of resolutions of international legitimacy and for adoption of policies of good intentions.

Security Council resolution 687 (1991) also called for the entire region of the Middle East to be free of all weapons of mass destruction, including nuclear weapons. Israel has rejected that and is the only nuclear State in the region. It has large stocks of nuclear weapons and biological and chemical weapons of mass destruction and the ability to strike any region in the Arab world.

Why does the Security Council not adopt a resolution to force Israel to dismantle its weapons of mass destruction? Why is there this double standard? Article 25 of the United Nations Charter states that Member States of the United Nations undertake to accept Security Council resolutions and implement them in accordance with the Charter. All Council resolutions should be implemented. Israel has violated scores of them in its conflict with the Arab side. Why does the Security Council not adopt a resolution forcing Israel to implement its resolutions?

The Secretary-General of the United Nations stated lately that every time he is in a press conference he is asked about double standards. In its last issue, on 12 October 2002, the Economist magazine addressed this particular matter.

"This question is no longer being asked by Arabs alone. 'No war against Iraq, Free Palestine' has become the slogan of anti-war demonstrations in Europe and America. The two conflicts have become entwined in the public mind in a way that the West's politicians cannot ignore. When he sought last week to talk his skeptical Labor Party into supporting action against Iraq, Tony Blair, Britain's Prime Minister, got his biggest cheer for the bit of his speech that said U.N. resolutions should apply in Palestine as much as Iraq."

We are extremely concerned about the increasing possibility of war breaking out against an Arab country. A dark, ominous cloud is gathering on the horizon, threatening the peace and safety of the entire region. We call for the expeditious return of UNMOVIC inspectors to Iraq to fulfill their tasks in order to allow the region and the entire world to breathe easily again. We completely reject the waging of war against an Arab country. The imposition of a new military conflict on the Middle East will be a grave mistake that will be very difficult to contain or control. War against Iraq will open a Pandora's box. Violence and civil war will sweep the entire country, fragmenting it. This in turn will undermine the entire Arab region, which has already been plagued with extreme anger due to the Israeli occupation and preparations for another military attack against another brotherly State.

War against Iraq will annul the current world order, the United Nations Charter and international law. It would expose States, particularly those of the South, to the danger of attacks on the pretext of preventive measures, leading the entire world back to the era of the League of Nations.

Upholding the United Nations Charter, international legitimacy and the solidarity and unity of the international community is the only means to face up to the crises of the twenty-first century, to maintain international peace and security and to "save succeeding generations the scourge of war, which twice in our lifetime has brought untold sorrow to mankind".

Danish Representative Lj. I have the honor of speaking on behalf of the European Union. The countries of Central and Eastern Europe associated with the European Union—Bulgaria, the Czech Republic, Estonia, Hungary, Latvia, Lithuania, Poland, Romania, Slovakia and Slovenia—and the associated countries of Cyprus, Malta and Turkey, as well as the European Free Trade Association (EFTA) country of the European Economic Area, Iceland, align themselves with this statement.

Let me begin by stating that the European Union and the peoples of its member States bear no grudge against the people of Iraq. The European Union respects the sovereignty, territorial integrity and political independence of Iraq. In 1990, the Iraqi regime chose to invade its small and defenseless neighbor Kuwait. A broad coalition of countries from all over the world stood up against this aggression. After the international community had liberated Kuwait, Iraq accepted, inter alia, to give up all its weapons of mass destruction and its long-range ballistic missiles as a condition for lifting the sanctions imposed on Iraq by the Security Council.

For nearly 12 years, the Government of Iraq has failed to cooperate fully on the elimination of its weapons of mass destruction and on the dismantling of its capability for producing such weapons. In 1991, the Security Council established the United Nations Special Commission (UNSCOM) to implement the disarmament process. The Commission was, however, several times faced with unacceptable conditions imposed by the Iraqi regime, which came to a head in 1998, when further access on the part of the weapons inspectors to Iraqi territory was denied. In 1999, the Security Council, in its resolution 1284 (1999), established the United Nations Monitoring, Verification and Inspection Commission (UNMOVIC) to pick up where UNSCOM had left off. As we all know, UNMOVIC has never been allowed to carry out its mandate in Iraq. As a result, no inspections have taken place in Iraq for more than four years, giving rise to serious concerns on the part of the international community as to the intentions of the Government of Iraq to respect binding obligations under international law.

The Secretary-General of the United Nations has worked incessantly to persuade the Iraqi regime to honor its obligations and to let the weapon inspectors from UNMOVIC and the International Atomic Energy Agency (IAEA) return to Iraq. Only under strong pressure from the international community has Iraq recently indicated its preparedness to receive the weapons inspectors without any conditions. This newly found position by the Iraqi regime should now be put to the test, and complete disarmament in respect of weapons of mass destruction achieved. UNMOVIC and IAEA should resume inspections as soon as possible on the basis of a reinforced mandate incorporating the practical arrangements set out in the joint letter of UNMOVIC and IAEA to Iraq dated 8 October.

The existing Security Council resolutions, the results of the Vienna talks as contained in the joint letter of the heads of UNMOVIC and IAEA, as well as any new rules the Security Council may deem necessary, should constitute the new governing standard for compliance by the Government of Iraq. This governing standard for inspections should be put to a real test as soon as possible. The Government of Iraq should make no mistake about the fact that noncompliance with this inspection regime would have serious consequences.

The European Union reiterates its demand that Iraq must adhere fully to all the relevant resolutions of the Security Council, in particular it must let the United Nations weapons inspectors return to Iraq without any preconditions and fully cooperate with the inspection teams in all aspects, including the granting of immediate and unhindered access to all sites and facilities in Iraq that the inspectors might wish to investigate. The European Union supports a new Security Council resolution strengthening the rights of inspectors so as to ensure that they can, as effectively as possible, carry out the disarmament required by the relevant resolutions. An effective inspection process in Iraq is a necessary tool for securing the dismantling of all weapons of mass destruction and long-range ballistic missiles, which is our common goal. Iraq must let the inspectors in and fully cooperate in allowing them to carry out their mandate, or be held accountable for its failure to do so. The European Union reiterates its full support for the efforts of the Security Council and of the Secretary-General in finding a solution to the Iraq question. The European Union emphasizes the vital importance of safeguarding and respecting the crucial role of the Security Council—present and future—in maintaining international peace and security in accordance with the United Nations Charter and in the solution of international conflicts.

We encourage all members of the Security Council to take a speedy decision that maintains strong pressure on Iraq and gathers the widest possible support within the Council. with its resolutions, and the exchanges among the permanent members in particular, will be enriched and duly inspired by what they hear in this session from so many speakers.

Turkish Representative Pamir. At the outset, Sir, I would like to congratulate you on your assumption of the presidency of the Security Council for the month of October. I wish you every success as you carry out this important responsibility. I would also like to heartily thank your predecessor, the Permanent Representative of our good neighbor Bulgaria, for the way he conducted the challenging work of the Council over the past month. Last, but not least, I also wish to thank the Permanent Representative of South Africa, who, on behalf of the Non-Aligned Movement (NAM), invited the Security Council to discuss this issue during an open debate. As such, this meeting allows all of us, members of the Council and non-members alike, to really see where the feelings and views of the international community really stand today on an issue that is of primary importance to world peace and stability. We do not doubt that the deliberations of the Security Council on the matter of Iraqi compliance with its resolutions, and the exchanges among the permanent members in particular, will be enriched and duly inspired by what they hear in this session from so many speakers.

I also wish to commend the untiring efforts of the Secretary-General to persuade the Iraqi Government of the necessity of full compliance with the Security Council resolutions.

Turkey has aligned itself with the statement just made on behalf of the European Union by my colleague, the Permanent Representative of Denmark. The statement of the European Union is to be seen and understood for what it is: a dispassionate description of a longstanding issue, on the one hand, and on the other, a judicious assessment of the road ahead. I wish to expound on a number of points that are already included in that statement.

First, the Iraqi issue is indeed a long-standing one. Before we lament this critical moment and abhor the dangers it poses, we must remember how we arrived at this unenviable juncture. The Iraqi issue has continued to exist in its various aspects—such as sanctions, disarmament, humanitarian matters like the repatriation of all Kuwaiti and third-country nationals and the return of Kuwaiti property—for no less than 12 years. Throughout those years, the Iraqi people have suffered the debilitating, and at times gruesome, effects of the unintended consequences of measures taken under Chapter VII of the United Nations Charter.

As we longed for stability in the southern part of our country during that time, Turkey received a raw deal. Northern Iraq was turned into a no-man's land, and quickly thereafter into a safe haven for terrorists from where they could conduct their operations into Turkey, gather strength and find rest in order to regroup and start again. We had to bury thousands of souls in our hearts as we determinedly fought this organized evil. At that time world public opinion was still in its infancy and was therefore selfishly equivocal with regard to the ways of combating terrorism.

Turkey's trading routes were also disrupted during those years, which caused widespread unemployment and an awesome loss of revenue. At a time when people everywhere were talking about the so-called benefits of globalization and about a shrinking world, Turkey found itself unable to trade with the southern part of its country.

Obviously, this issue is neither a lurking danger nor a distant event for Turkey. We have been living with the manifold consequences of the deterioration in stability in neighboring Iraq. Therefore, in our sincere desire for a restoration of normalcy, we have tried for years to explain to our neighbor the dangers inherent in non-compliance with Security Council resolutions. We tried to impress upon the Iraqi leadership that its continued failure to cooperate with the international community in the elimination of its weapons of mass destruction and of its capabilities to produce those weapons would unleash dangers of all sorts. At long last, after four years, the Iraqi Government last month decided to allow the unconditional return of United Nations weapons inspectors. We very much hope that this signals more than preparedness, and that the international community will choose to test the veracity of the Iraqi position.

It was in that hope that we welcomed the results of the Vienna talks between Iraqi officials and officials of the United Nations Monitoring, Verification and Inspection Commission (UNMOVIC) and the International Atomic Energy Agency (IAEA) concerning practical arrangements regarding inspections. We note that a number of ranking Iraqi officials now assure the international community of Iraq's full cooperation, including the provision of unhindered access to wherever the inspectors deem appropriate to inspect and investigate. However, we also note that the letters sent to the Executive Chairman of UNMOVIC and the Director General of IAEA fell short of total clarity, as they lacked a vocal and unambiguous "yes" to unconditional and unrestricted inspections.

We are passing through the final hours before the Iraqi Government fully understands the gravity of the situation. They should adhere fully to all the relevant resolutions without vainly trying to set forth any preconditions. A new draft resolution should help the Iraqi Government to do precisely that. Not that the previous resolutions are incomplete or legally deficient in any way. Rather, the ongoing quest for a new resolution stems from the actual need to show the world, and large segments of public opinion practically everywhere, that the means available to the Security Council to peacefully dispose of this matter are well and truly exhausted.

In other words, a new draft resolution should help the Iraqi Government to fully understand that the international community is not divided on the straightforward and urgent need for speedy and unhindered inspections to take place in that country, and that it is equally united on the need to hold the Iraqi Government accountable in the event of its failure to keep its word. We hope that the text of such a resolution will display the unanimity of the Security Council, empower the inspectors with an effective mandate and, at the same time, incorporate clear provisions in case of both compliance and noncompliance.

The time for hardening rhetoric has indeed came to an end. It is time to match words with deeds. No one in the Chamber doubts the seriousness of the stage we are passing through. This is not one more critical stage in this long episode; it is a seriously critical stage. As part of that already problematic geography, as a traditional Power in that part of the world and, more importantly, as people who have special historic and cultural relations and links to the people of Iraq and the region, we have serious concerns regarding any miscalculations that might destabilize the region. After all, no military action has brought a lasting and viable solution in the Middle East. On the contrary, military action has further complicated already difficult problems, perpetuating them for future generations of innocent victims who have, sadly, borne witness to the futility of prolonging conflicts.

We also fear that further destabilization in the Middle East may well trigger the inherent propensity to disrupt the fight against new forms of terrorism. Today the single most important task is to harness the full support of the Security Council and the international community. To repeat, we need a Security Council that speaks the same language and that employs the same pitch inside and outside this Chamber.

Turkey spares no effort to ensure that peace and security prevail in the region, and will continue to do so. We know full well that we have historic responsibilities in securing the reign of hope and dignity in our region. We work towards enlightened ends, and we will never waver when the defense of those goals is called for. Respect for the sovereignty, independence and territorial integrity of our neighbors, as well as other principles of good-neighbourliness, will continue to guide us.

Palestinian Observer Al-Kidwa. Like other Arab and Islamic countries and the overwhelming majority of the world's peoples and States, Palestine is deeply concerned and harbors serious apprehensions about what we are witnessing with regard to the increasing possibilities of a new outbreak of war in the Middle East region. We are also worried about the growing possibility of the use of military force against Iraq—a sisterly Arab member country of the United Nations—as well as about the possibility of invading and occupying it. Were such things to occur, they would of course lead to further destruction in Iraq and to further suffering for its people. Moreover, such events would also have profound negative consequences on the region as a whole, encourage extremism and heighten hatred towards those who actually undertook such actions. It is very difficult to imagine stability in either Iraq or the region if such events take place. Using military force or going to war is definitely no solution. It must be avoided.

Despite the beating of war drums we have been hearing recently, there have been some positive developments. On the one hand, this question has been referred to the United Nations instead of taking unilateral action; and, on the other hand, Iraq has accepted the unconditional return of inspectors. We believe we should build on these two elements and that the current crisis should be resolved through a rapid return of inspectors to ensure that there are no weapons of mass destruction, thereby reassuring the international community with regard to this important issue.

The Security Council has adopted enough resolutions on this subject. The recent negotiations in Vienna and Iraq's subsequent position seem to point to the possibility of reaching acceptable arrangements between the United Nations and Iraq with a view to ensuring full compliance with the resolution calling for the destruction of all weapons of mass destruction and verifying that there are no such weapons in Iraq. Nevertheless, if the members of the Council find it necessary to adopt a new resolution, it will be important that such a resolution not contain impossible demands or mandate the use of force in advance. A new Council resolution should serve as a bridge leading to the implementation of its previous resolutions and not as a bridge to war.

Just prior to the last crisis, Arab States had indeed made great headway towards Arab reconciliation with regard to the situation between Iraq and Kuwait. The Beirut Summit was a very important step in that direction. We would like to reiterate our commitment to the spirit of the Summit and to its decisions and resolutions, including with regard to cooperating with the Tripartite Commission to resolve the issues of the return of Kuwaiti property and of Kuwaiti prisoners and third-party citizens being held in Iraq.

It is very difficult for the Arab street to believe that the use of force against Iraq would serve to uphold international law and legitimacy or to ensure respect for the resolutions of the Security Council. It is doubly difficult to believe when all Arabs— and indeed the entire world—have witnessed how Security Council resolutions are violated and rejected and how the provisions of international law are flouted by a single State. That State is, of course, Israel, which is considered by the Council to be the only occupying Power in the world today and which, incidentally, has illegally acquired several weapons of mass destruction. Just a few hours ago, Israeli tanks once again destroyed the homes of civilians in Rafah, killing at least five people and injuring forty. What we need here is for Members to try to regain, even partially, credibility for the Council and for this international Organization.

Israeli Representative Lancry. Israel feels compelled to take the floor in the light of the numerous charges, made in the course of this debate, that the Security Council has adopted a double standard with regard to Israel's compliance with Council resolutions.

In fact, those statements are the strongest proof that there is indeed a double standard: one directed against Israel. What else could explain such a deliberate blindness to the fundamental differences between Iraq's defiance of the Council and Israel's commitment to a peaceful settlement of conflict with its neighbors? What else could explain the failure to see any distinction between binding resolutions, adopted under Chapter VII of the Charter—resolutions that set out specific actions to be taken by Iraq, independent of the actions of any other party—and interdependent recommendations or statements of principle, adopted under Chapter VI, that are designed to move all the parties forward in the Middle East? The Charter of the United Nations is itself founded on the understanding that different situations and disputes require different responses and that not every conflict requires identical action. The distinction between resolutions adopted under Chapter VI and those adopted under Chapter VII recognizes that in certain cases the Council might wish to express itself in the form of a recommendation or in a broadly outlined statement of principles, rather than an explicit demand of one particular Member State.

What else but a double standard could possibly blur the gaping distinctions between Iraq, which has repeatedly violated and flouted the resolutions of the Council, and Israel, which has repeatedly taken significant steps, at considerable risk to its own security, to implement the Council's will? Indeed, the principles set out by the Council in resolutions 242 (1967) and 338 (1973) provided the basis for Israel's peace treaties with Egypt and Jordan, and will hopefully enable us to reach peace with our other neighbors as well. All parties accepted those resolutions as the basis of the Madrid Peace Conference. They also provided the basis for our peacemaking with the Palestinians, for our mutual recognition, for the Oslo accords and for nearly a decade of peace negotiations. Those negotiations broke off as a result of the decision by the Palestinian side to revert to a strategy of violence and terrorism and as a result of its rejection, both in word and deed, of the right of States in the region to live in peace within secure and recognized boundaries, as required by resolutions 242 (1967) and 338 (1973).

In May 2000, Israel fully implemented its obligations under Security Council resolution 425 (1978), a fact that has been confirmed by the Secretary-General and endorsed by the Council. Despite that, Hizbullah terrorists have continued to launch cross-border attacks against Israel. The group has abducted three Israeli soldiers and one civilian, jeopardized security and stability in the area and threatens to provoke a broader regional confrontation. These illegal and dangerous activities are carried out in blatant violation of resolution 425 (1978) and with the ongoing support of the Government of Syria, which is itself a member of the Council, and the acquiescence of the Government of Lebanon.

Israel has also taken significant steps to implement the resolutions adopted by the Council since September 2000. Following the adoption of resolution 1402 (2002), Israel has gradually withdrawn its troops from Palestinian cities, including Ramallah, successfully negotiated a peaceful end to the stand-off at the Church of the Nativity and redeployed our forces to the perimeter of population centers, in the hope that reciprocal Palestinian measures called for in the resolution would follow. But despite the call on the Palestinian Authority to adhere to a meaningful cease-fire and to end all acts of violence, terror and incitement, it did none of those things. Similarly, the recently adopted resolution 1435 (2002) placed obligations on both parties, including a call upon the Palestinian Authority to end all acts of violence, terror and incitement, and to bring to justice those responsible for terrorist acts. The Palestinian Authority has thus far refused to live up to its obligation to arrest and prosecute terrorists and has thereby forced Israel to take actions to protect its citizens. In short, these obligations were totally ignored by the Palestinian Authority.

Unlike resolutions concerning Iraq, the Council's resolutions on the Israeli-Palestinian conflict do not envision Israeli actions without reciprocal commitment and implementation by other parties to the dispute. They are part and parcel of a number of interdependent actions aimed at ending violence and terrorism and returning the parties to a political process. They cannot be compared to resolutions adopted under Chapter VII, which address the threat posed by the aggressive intentions of one regime to both the region and the world.

But beyond all that lies a more significant, and indeed more fundamental, distinction between Iraq and Israel. Israel is a country confronting the daily threat of terrorist attacks against its civilians, as well as repeated threats to destroy it, including threats from remote neighbors like Iran and Iraq. Are we to forget that just months before the Gulf War, Saddam Hussein threatened to "completely burn half of Israel", and that in the course of that war 39 Iraqi Scud missiles fell on Israeli cities without any provocation?

Is there a double standard, as certain Member States have alleged? There is a simple test. Take two States, one a dictatorship and serial violator of Council resolutions and human rights that is dedicated to the acquisition of chemical, biological and nuclear weapons and fighting for regional domination; the other is a democracy upholding the principles of the rule of law and freedom of speech, a people whose survival has been tested for decades but who are still committed to peace, both for themselves and for future generations in the Middle East.

The Israeli-Palestinian conflict is a serious one, and deservedly a source of international concern. But the cause of peace in the Middle East is not served by the charges we have heard in the course of this debate, nor is it served by false comparisons and deliberate obfuscation intended not to foster constructive action, but rather to prevent it. We cannot lose sight of the fact that the resolution of the conflict in the Middle East is only possible through both sides fulfilling their obligations and negotiating the terms of a final settlement in an atmosphere of partnership and cooperation. We hope that other Member States will do their utmost to help create such an atmosphere.

British Representative Sir Jeremy Greenstock. You were right, Sir, to schedule this debate. The United Kingdom was one of the first to call for it. The Council needs to hear the voice of the wider membership, particularly when we are on the edge of decisions that could make the difference between war and peace.

It is a debate, clearly, that is about more than Iraq. The delegation and I have been listening carefully to it. The issues in our minds, whether we all refer to them or not, go much wider: the security of the whole neighborhood of Iraq; the reinforcement of our collective effort to eliminate terrorism; justice for Palestine and security for Israel within the law; the role of the Security Council when serious matters of national security are before its members and the overall effectiveness of the United Nations itself.

I wish to be very clear. The United Kingdom's firm objective is the complete disarmament of Iraq in the area of weapons of mass destruction, by peaceful means. I repeat, our first preference is a peaceful solution to the current crisis surrounding Iraq. Ensuring that there is such a solution lies in the hands of Iraq. In 1991, following the Gulf War, the Security Council set out the conditions governing the cease-fire between Iraq and the international coalition. Sadly, over eleven years later, Iraq remains in material breach of these obligations. We all know of the myriad ways in which Iraq sought, almost immediately after inspections began, to frustrate inspections and intimidate inspectors.

We all know of the succession of allegedly final declarations submitted by Iraq after inspectors discovered some new incriminating fact or evidence. We all know how Iraq tried to limit and hinder inspections to the extent that in August 1998 the then head of the United Nations Special Commission (UNSCOM) said it was impossible for him to do his job. We all know of the outstanding weapons of mass destruction for which UNSCOM was unable to account. We all know of the multiple warnings sent to Iraq in resolution after resolution and presidential statement after presidential statement.

No shadow of a doubt remains that Iraq has defied the United Nations—not any particular Member State, the United Nations—over the whole of this period. As Prime Minister Blair has said

"it is not that for 10 years Saddam Hussein has not been a problem, he has been a problem throughout the last 10 years. What has changed is first, that the policy of containment isn't any longer working, certainly without a massive change in the way that the regime is monitored and inspected; and secondly, we know from 11 September that it is sensible to deal with these problems before, not after."

Iraq could have invited the inspectors back without conditions at any time in the last few years. Sanctions could have been lifted and Iraqis restored to a normal life.

They are a talented and spirited people; but they have been betrayed and stunted by a Government unworthy of them. Only Baghdad's insistence on retaining weapons of mass destruction capability has blocked that path of good sense and humanity. Only under the recent intense diplomatic pressure, and particularly the threat of military action, has the Iraqi Government's letter of 16 September 2002 emerged.

These Iraqi words, while necessary, are of themselves not enough. We remain deeply perturbed by evidence that Iraq believes it can hide its weapons of mass destruction rather than declare them, that it can again fool the inspectors and play games with them. The United Kingdom analysis, backed up by reliable intelligence, indicates that Iraq still possesses chemical and biological materials, has continued to produce them, has sought to weaponize them, and has active military plans for the deployment of such weapons. The United Kingdom analysis, backed up by reliable intelligence, shows that Iraq has in recent years tried to buy multiple components relevant to the production of a nuclear bomb. The United Kingdom analysis, backed up by reliable intelligence, points to the retention of extended-range missiles and to the employment of hundreds of people in projects to develop weapons with a range of over 1,000 kilometers that could carry both weapons of mass destruction and conventional warheads.

It would be an abdication of responsibility to ignore this challenge to the international community. We cannot afford to bury our heads in the sand and pretend the problem does not exist. We cannot accept the Iraqi Government's word at face value, knowing what we know.

We wish to see the Security Council, which Iraq has been defying for so long, express its will and its unity in a clear, strong resolution. That resolution must give the regime in Baghdad an unequivocal choice: complete weapons of mass destruction disarmament and normal membership of the international community, or refusal and the inevitable consequences.

The United Kingdom has made it clear to Iraq, privately at a senior official level, that this choice is being offered genuinely. It represents a single, final chance for Iraq. If this is understood, and if the Council keeps its nerve, then maybe there is a prospect that Iraq will finally comply with its obligations and that military action can be averted. If we fail to send that tough signal, we shall be ignoring the realities. The weaker we collectively appear, the more probable it is that military action will be the outcome.

An essential component of this message is to ensure that inspections — United Nations inspections — are effective. That means giving the inspectors the penetrating strength to ensure the successful weapons-of-mass-destruction disarmament of Iraq. We cannot afford a return to the ambiguous modalities and memorandums of understanding (MOUs) of the past; we cannot afford exceptions to unconditional, unrestricted and immediate access; we cannot afford to have inspectors again standing by helplessly while crucial documents are burned or while convoys leave from the back door as inspectors arrive at the front; we cannot afford interviews compromised by intimidating minders. The recent Iraqi letters on practical arrangements, the language of which brings back the obfuscations of the past, reinforce the need for strengthened inspections and for practical arrangements to be made legally binding. Stronger inspections will be crucial to ensuring that all countries have confidence in them and that Iraq makes the decision to comply rather than to continue hiding its weapons of mass destruction—crucial, if we are to succeed in achieving a peaceful resolution of this issue.

I have heard loud and clear the concerns of many speakers that, on a decision so crucial, we should not rush into a war; that on a decision so crucial, any Iraqi violations must be discussed by the Security Council. Let me make totally clear that the United Kingdom Government would expect there to be a detailed Security Council discussion if either Mr. Blix or Mr. ElBaradei, whose professionalism and independence are not in question, reports that Iraq is not fully cooperating with the inspections process. We would want at that point to hear the views of all our Security Council colleagues.

I have heard in a number of interventions a concern that the non-permanent members of the Council have been kept in the dark. Some have even spoken of humiliation. I believe the facts have been misrepresented. None of the permanent members has been in a position so far to bring a draft resolution to each other here or to the Council as a whole. The permanent five have done no negotiating on a text in New York. Discussion in capitals has taken place on bilateral channels. Of course our Governments have been working to make a negotiation worthwhile; proper preparation is a responsible approach. We, the United Kingdom and the United States, have met with the non-permanent 10 twice as often since 12 September as we have with the other permanent members. Once there is a draft with a prospect of broad acceptance in the Council, no Council member will be excluded from discussion. Let us remain connected with reality in this respect.

I could not close these remarks without referring to the fact that Iraq is in breach of other Security Council obligations, including on the repatriation of all Kuwaiti and third-country nationals and the return of all Kuwaiti property. These other violations may not threaten international peace and security in the same way as the issue of Iraqi weapons of mass destruction, but they are perhaps more important issues in human and emotional terms, particularly for the families concerned. There can be no humane reason why Iraq has failed to comply for so long. We call on Iraq now to rectify that non-compliance, including by resuming its participation in the Tripartite Commission under the auspices of the International Committee of the Red Cross.

Chinese Representative Zhang Yishan. I should like at the outset to express our appreciation to South Africa for having requested, on behalf of the countries of the Non-Aligned Movement, that the Council hold this emergency open debate. I should like also to thank you, Mr. President, for having made prompt arrangements in this respect.

The absence for so long of a solution to the question of Iraq has not served peace and stability in the Gulf region or the authority and credibility of the Security Council, nor has it been conducive to improving the humanitarian situation in Iraq. An early and appropriate settlement of the Iraqi question is the important and urgent task facing the international community and the United Nations in particular.

To hold an open debate and earnestly heed the views of a large number of Member States under such circumstances will undoubtedly enable the Council better to handle the Iraqi question. The Chinese Government has consistently maintained that Iraq should unconditionally and strictly implement the relevant Security Council at an early date and fully cooperate with the United Nations on questions of weapons inspections and other questions.

We believe also that the international community should work tirelessly to seek a comprehensive settlement of the Iraqi question through political and diplomatic means on the basis of the relevant Council resolutions. Over the past few days, dozens of countries have participated in this open debate, which clearly attests to the importance that a large number of Member States attach to the question of Iraq, and to their concerns about the possible implications of this question for international relations.

The overwhelming majority of States have emphasized during the debate that the question of Iraq should be settled within the framework of the United Nations, that the Security Council should play a central role in the process and that the unity of the Security Council is of paramount importance.

A number of countries, especially the Arab States, have also expressed their strong for wish for peace, not war. They have pointed out that war can only further exacerbate the already tense situation in the Middle East. The independence, sovereignty and territorial integrity of Iraq, Kuwait and other countries of the region should be respected. These views and positions are very important, and we agree with them. We hope that the Security Council will give them serious consideration.

The question of disarmament is at the core of the Iraqi question. On the basis of resolution 687 (1991), Iraq must destroy all weapons of mass destruction in its possession and refrain from developing or using such weapons. But since the end of 1998, the United Nations disarmament process in Iraq has been suspended. Only when the United Nations weapons inspectors return to Iraq and conduct effective inspections can the truth ultimately emerge.

We are pleased to note that, thanks to the positive endeavors of Secretary-General Kofi Annan, Secretary-General Moussa of the Arab League and other concerned parties, the Iraqi side announced last September that it would unconditionally accept the return of weapons inspectors. The United Nations Monitoring, Verification and Inspection Commission (UNMOVIC) and the International Atomic Energy Agency (IAEA) then engaged in a dialogue with the Iraqi side on practical arrangements for the inspection and achieved positive results. We hope that Iraq will honor its commitments and translate them into actual deeds.

We believe that the United Nations weapons inspectors should return to Iraq as soon as possible to conduct independent, fair and professional inspections and report truthfully and in a timely manner to the Council the results of such inspections, so that the Council can draw objective, fair and realistic conclusions on that basis.

Under such circumstances, it is not that we cannot consider the adoption by the Council of a new resolution on the question of the inspection. Such a draft resolution, however, should call for support for UNMOVIC and the IAEA. Its contents should be practical and feasible, in the interests of an appropriate settlement of the Iraqi question.

The Iraqi question involves many elements in addition to disarmament, including the humanitarian situation in Iraq and the missing Kuwaiti nationals and property. We call on all the parties concerned to continue to earnestly implement the oil-for-food program and make further efforts to improve the humanitarian situation in Iraq. We would also like to urge the Iraqi side to implement, as soon as possible, its obligations in accordance with relevant Security Council resolutions and to take concrete steps for an early settlement of the question of the missing Kuwaitis and third country nationals.

The Iraqi question has reached a crucial juncture. The international community in general has high hopes of the Security Council. It hopes that the Council will be able to effectively undertake its responsibility to maintain international peace and security and take action to safeguard the purposes and principles of the Charter. The Chinese Government is ready to join other countries in promoting an appropriate settlement of the Iraqi question within the Security Council.

United States Representative Negroponte. On 12 September, President George Bush outlined to the General Assembly the history of Iraq's defiance of Security Council resolutions, listed the steps that Iraq must take if it wants peace and stated that the United States would work with the Security Council to hold Iraq to account.

President Bush's speech was a declaration of purpose, not a declaration of war. It put the United Nations in the spotlight and challenged the international community to restore the Security Council's relevance on this issue by confronting this threat to international peace and security and 11 years of failure by Iraq to accept the demands made of it after its invasion and destruction of Kuwait.

The threat today is serious and unique, and it arises directly from the Iraqi regime's own actions: its history of aggression and brutality, its defiance of the international community and its drive towards an arsenal of terror and destruction. This is a regime that has invaded two of its neighbors and tried to annihilate one of them; a regime that has used chemical weapons on its neighbors and its very own citizens; a regime that has lied about its development of weapons of mass destruction; a regime that signed the Nuclear Non-Proliferation Treaty and then proceeded to develop a major nuclear weapons program.

Eleven years ago, as one of the conditions for ending the Persian Gulf war, the Security Council required the Iraqi regime to destroy its weapons of mass destruction and cease all development of such weapons. As President Bush noted yesterday when signing the Congressional resolution on Iraq, at that time Iraq was given 15 days to fully disclose its weapons of mass destruction. The Baghdad regime has defied this obligation for 4,199 days.

The Security Council also demanded, 11 years ago, that Iraq return all prisoners from Kuwait and other lands and renounce all involvement with terrorism. Iraq agreed to these demands and more at the time, and these are commitments with which Iraq must comply. The Council has tried in every way to bring Iraq to peaceful fulfillment of the Gulf war cease-fire, yet the Iraqi regime has violated all of its obligations. As President Bush said earlier this month in Cincinnati, "the entire world has witnessed Iraq's 11-year history of defiance, deception and bad faith".

The Security Council is not the only international body that has focused on the behavior of the Iraqi regime. Last year, a year when the United States was not a member, the Commission on Human Rights, based in Geneva, adopted resolution 2001/14, which strongly condemns the "systematic, widespread and extremely grave violations of human rights and international humanitarian law by the Government of Iraq, resulting in an all-pervasive repression and oppression sustained by broad-based discrimination and widespread terror".

Today, exactly five weeks after the President spoke, we meet for the first time to publicly discuss the message that the Security Council will send to Iraq and to its leader, Saddam Hussein. Our view of that message has been clear from 12 September. There can be no more business as usual or toothless resolutions that Iraq will continue to ignore. Our intent is that the Council should meet the challenge and stand firm, resolute and united in adopting a draft resolution that holds Iraq to its commitments, lays out clearly what Iraq must do to comply and states that there will be consequences if Iraq refuses to do so.

We expect the Council to act, and when the Council adopts a draft resolution that sends a clear and united message to Iraq that it must fulfill its obligations, Iraq will have a choice. It will have to decide whether to take this last chance to comply. We hope that it will choose to comply. If it does not, we will seek compliance and disarmament by other means.

This is not an easy issue for any of us on the Council. The world's united response to aggression by Iraq in 1990 and 1991, expressed through a series of unique, groundbreaking Security Council resolutions, brought the world body closest to the visions of its founders. The Council's requirements were far reaching, commensurate with both the threat and the Council's determination that Iraq never again possess the means to threaten and even destroy its neighbors.

In the ensuing decade, however, Iraq's failure to implement this body's peace terms became for the United Nations a question of enormous significance. The challenge now is whether the United Nations can perform the function its founders envisaged. We very much hope the answer will be, "Yes".

The five weeks since the President came to the United Nations to discuss the threat posed by Iraq have passed quickly. We have seen signs of emerging Council unity during intensive discussions here and in capitals, involving the highest levels of our respective Governments. We have also seen clear signs that Iraq is reverting to form. We have seen Iraq invite inspectors to return without conditions, and then immediately place conditions. We have seen requests for clarity from the United Nations Monitoring, Verification and Inspection Commission (UNMOVIC) and the International Atomic Energy Agency (IAEA) on practical arrangements met by Iraqi obfuscation and multiple answers, which in fact avoid answering at all.

Not surprisingly, in the first test of the so-called new Iraqi cooperation, Iraq has shown that it hopes to return to the word games, ephemeral commitments and misdirection of the past, while continuing to develop the world's deadliest weapons.

That is why a clear, firm message from the Council is so important. Miscalculation by Iraq will be dangerous. This body and, indeed, the entire membership of the United Nations do no favor to the people of Iraq, do no favor to those who seek a better future for Iraq, do no favor to the countries of the region and do no favor to the credibility of the United Nations if they create the impression that an outcome in which Iraq retains its chemical, biological and nuclear weapons programmes is an acceptable or possible outcome.

Over the past five weeks, a consensus has been forming in the Council that the time for denial, deception and delay has come to an end and that Iraq must be verifiably disarmed. There is growing agreement that there must be immediate, unconditional and unrestricted inspections of all Iraqi facilities that may have a role in the development of weapons of mass destruction.

The United States, together with the United Kingdom, has shared with the other members of the Council the elements of our vision of a resolution that will address Iraq's material breach of its obligations under relevant Security Council resolutions, specify the types of access and authorities that UNMOVIC and IAEA must have to be able to effectively verify Iraqi disarmament, make clear Iraq's obligations and articulate to Iraq that there will be consequences to non-compliance.

The United States believes that the best way to ensure Iraqi compliance is through one resolution that is firm and unambiguous in its message.

We are considering the reactions we have received and will be placing before the Council, in the near future, a resolution with clear and immediate requirements—requirements that Iraq would voluntarily meet if it chooses to cooperate. We have also shared these elements with the Executive Chairman of UNMOVIC and the Director General of the International Atomic Energy Agency. While they can and should speak for themselves, both Mr. Blix and Mr. ElBaradei have made it clear that they would welcome a new Security Council resolution that strengthens their hands and allows for more effective inspections.

While all this diplomatic activity has been taking place, in the United States we have been having our own great national debate. Last week, the House of Representatives and the Senate passed a joint resolution that expressed support for the administration's diplomatic efforts in the Security Council to ensure that "Iraq abandons its strategy of delay, evasion and non-compliance" and authorized the use of United States armed forces should diplomatic efforts fail. This resolution tells the world that the United States speaks with one determined voice.

Yesterday, when President Bush signed this resolution, he said that he had not ordered the use of force. The United States hopes that the use of force will not become necessary. But the President also said that the choice for Iraq is straightforward: "Either the Iraqi regime will give up its weapons of mass destruction, or, for the sake of peace, the United States will lead a global coalition to disarm that regime."

Now, the spotlight is back on the Security Council. We hope and expect that the Council will act and play its proper role as a safeguard of our common security. If it fails to do so, then we and other States will be forced to act.

The approach of the United States and the United Kingdom aims at clarity — clarity with respect to what Iraq must now do to fulfill its 1991 obligations to restore peace and security in the region; clarity with respect to what inspectors must be allowed to do; and clarity with respect to our seriousness. Without such clarity, there is too high a danger that Iraq will miscalculate. And miscalculation by Iraq will lead to precisely the military action we all hope to avoid.

The Security Council faces a defining moment. The Council works best on Iraq when it works together. As we witnessed last spring with the successful passage of resolution 1409 (2002) and the establishment of the Goods Review List, when the Security Council is resolute and united, its actions produce results. We must stand together and show Iraq that its failure to comply will no longer be tolerated.

French Representative Levitte. Since December 1998, United Nations disarmament inspectors have no longer been present in Iraq. For nearly four years now, the international community has not been able to verify whether Iraq possesses weapons of mass destruction and whether it is pursuing programmes to that end.

By refusing to allow the return of United Nations inspectors, Iraq has defied the international community and the authority of the Security Council. Even though France does not possess irrefutable proof, there are several indications that Iraq has used this situation to pursue or resume its prohibited programmes, notably in the chemical and biological areas. The behavior of the Baghdad authorities has given rise to strong suspicions in this regard.

This situation cannot be tolerated. The proliferation of weapons of mass destruction and their delivery systems, in Iraq or elsewhere, constitutes a serious threat to international security. In the face of this challenge, it is the Security Council's duty to place firmness and lucidity in the service of a common objective. For France, that objective is the disarmament of Iraq. This implies the return of the inspectors and the resumption of monitoring on the ground.

On 16 September, Iraq, under unanimous pressure from the international community and thanks to the efforts of the United Nations Secretary-General and the Secretary General of the League of Arab States, agreed to the unconditional return of the inspectors. During discussions conducted in Vienna by the Executive Chairman of the United Nations Monitoring, Verification and Inspection Commission (UNMOVIC) and the Director General of the International Atomic Energy Agency (IAEA), Baghdad confirmed this decision. Practical arrangements were made for carrying out inspections. UNMOVIC and the IAEA must now return to Iraq as soon as possible. The United Nations must verify the sincerity of its commitments. In the light of past experience, the international community cannot be satisfied with words alone. Iraq must translate its promises into concrete, verifiable and lasting acts.

Here and there, doubts and reservations have been expressed about the inspectors' ability to fulfill their mission. France has the greatest confidence in the ability of Mr. Blix and Mr. ElBaradei to achieve the mandate entrusted to them by the Security Council with the utmost rigor and professionalism. In any case, there is no reason to question the effectiveness of their teams a priori, as the inspection regime established under resolution 1284 (1999) has not yet been tested on the ground.

Furthermore, the outcome of United Nations inspections has been very positive. It is a fact that United Nations Special Commission (UNSCOM) inspectors destroyed more weapons of mass destruction between 1991 and 1998 than did the military operations during the Gulf War. In 1998, the IAEA believed it had succeeded in dismantling the Iraqi nuclear program. It was not the inspections that failed, but the international community's ability to enforce its decisions in a sufficiently firm and united manner. France, however, is fully disposed to support measures strengthening the inspection regime, insofar as that proves necessary to facilitate the inspectors' work. The question of immediate access to the presidential sites, for example, must be examined by the Security Council.

On the other hand, we reject measures that would in fact multiply the risk of incidents without improving the effectiveness of the work carried out by UNMOVIC and the IAEA. We also set store by the multinational, independent nature of the inspectors;

any measure countering this fundamental element would be tantamount to repeating past mistakes and would not have our support.

Finally, it is the opinion of Mr. Blix and Mr ElBaradei—that is, those who will have to lead the inspections on the ground—that should guide the Security Council in its choices. It is up to them to determine what would help them achieve their mission. Our duty is to assist them, not to complicate their task.

France attaches importance to the principle of collective security, which lies at the heart of the functioning of our Organization and the international order. The Iraqi question cannot be an exception. That is why we are proposing a two-stage approach. During the first stage, the Security Council should adopt a resolution clearly specifying the "rules of the game." It would define the inspection regime with a view to ensuring that the inspectors can accomplish their mission fully and without any hindrance. This resolution should also send a clear warning to Iraq that the Council will not tolerate new violations.

During the second stage, if UNMOVIC or the IAEA observe that Iraq is refusing to cooperate fully with inspectors, the Security Council would meet immediately to decide on the appropriate measures to take, without ruling out anything a priori.

France believes that this approach, which is also the one proposed by the Secretary-General in his message to the Council, is the only one that can offer us the unity, cohesion, fairness and legitimacy so crucial to the effectiveness of our action.

The unity of the Security Council is absolutely vital. In the past, Iraq has taken advantage of divisions within the international community to renege on its obligations and defy the Council's authority. Only a united front will convince it not to repeat this error. Only a two-stage approach will allow us to preserve our Council's unity; any kind of "automaticity" in the use of force will profoundly divide us.

The two-stage approach is, rather, the choice of cohesion. United in sending Iraq a message of firmness in an initial resolution, the Security Council will, we have no doubt, remain united to assume all of its responsibilities during the second stage, should Iraq violate its commitments.

The Security Council must also demonstrate fairness by showing Iraq that war is not inevitable if it fully and scrupulously fulfills its obligations. This new behavior would open the way to the suspension and then the lifting of sanctions, in accordance with Security Council resolutions.

Finally, given the gravity of the situation, in which nothing less than peace or war is at stake, it is essential for the Security Council to remain in charge of the process every step of the way. This is fundamental for the legitimacy of our action and essential for maintaining unanimous support for our common objectives.

This debate constitutes an important, perhaps even cardinal, moment for our Council and, beyond that, for our Organization. What is at stake in the ongoing negotiations is fundamental: even beyond Iraq, we are talking about the future of the international order, relations between North and South, and notably, our relationship with the Arab world. An action of uncertain legitimacy, one that does not enjoy the support of the international community, would not be understood and could gravely affect these relations.

By placing this action within the framework of collective security, the French approach aims to ensure its legitimacy and effectiveness, while respecting the principles defined by the United Nations Charter.

Russian Representative Lavrov. The Russian Federation actively supported the request of the Non-Aligned Movement to convene this open debate on Iraq. It gives the Security Council an opportunity to hear and consider the opinions of all States Members of the United Nations before determining how to proceed on the question of Iraq. This approach is in full consonance with the United Nations Charter.

For almost 12 years now, the international community has sought a way to settle the Iraqi situation. Throughout that time, the Security Council has adopted more than 50 resolutions and endured several severe crises. The current ongoing impasse is rooted not only in the position of the Iraqi side, although we are far from condoning Baghdad's behavior, while the need for Iraq to meet all its obligations under Security Council resolutions has been frequently alluded to yesterday and today. We fully support such assessments. At the same time, in a number of instances the Security Council has been unable to hold up its own end with respect to an objective assessment of the situation and to meeting its own obligations to work for a comprehensive settlement in the Persian Gulf.

Throughout their many years of work in Iraq, the United Nations Special Commission (UNSCOM) and the International Atomic Energy Agency (IAEA) conducted some 7,000 inspections. As a result, they achieved significant progress in shutting down Iraq's weapons of mass destruction programmes. The inspections allowed us to destroy more components of weapons of mass destruction than were destroyed by the military strikes against Iraq during the Gulf War. We have managed to structure a material balance in the nuclear sphere which, in 1998, in the opinion of IAEA, allowed us to convert this file into a long-term monitoring regime.

Unfortunately, the Security Council was not able to recognize this fact four years ago. It is an important thing that this conclusion was supported by the Director General of IAEA, Mr. ElBaradei, in his letter to the President of the Security Council of 14 October, in which he clearly indicated that there are no outstanding unresolved nuclear disarmament issues. This has been circulated to Security Council Members and everyone can become acquainted with it.

There is a virtually complete picture of the missile situation as well. A significant portion of the stocks of chemical weapons have been destroyed, although there were some outstanding issues requiring further clarification. The largest problems persisted in the biological sphere. But on these issues and all the outstanding issues, solutions were possible. At any rate, documents of the former UNSCOM testify that such was the case.

However, this did not in fact happen. In December 1998 the head of the former UNSCOM provoked a crisis, arbitrarily withdrawing inspectors from Iraq without the approval of the Security Council. His report came to the Council only after United States and United Kingdom aviation had launched military strikes against Iraq. In fact, the United States Government, after these strikes, stated that the strikes had dealt with the issue of eliminating the vestiges of Iraqi weapons of mass destruction programmes, although the relevant information was not given to the Security Council.

The former UNSCOM, in this way, through its acts of provocation, fully discredited itself and simultaneously undermined the pre-December 1998 prospects for reaching a comprehensive settlement. The Security Council then found itself in a profound crisis not of its own making on the question of Iraq and for a long time was unable to get out of this impasse. And then, a year later, we drafted Security Council resolution 1284 (1999), which allowed us to renew the inspections on a new genuinely international basis. However, this resolution contained extremely ambiguous criteria for suspension of the sanctions, which gave an opportunity to individual Security Council members at their discretion to maintain the embargo indefinitely.

For this reason Russia, together with France, China and Malaysia, abstained in the vote on resolution 1284 (1999). We made proposals to give concrete substance to the criteria of sanctions suspension in the context of a comprehensive settlement. These proposals are well known and they remain in force. We will not forget the fact that in resolution 1382 (2001), the members unanimously stated their commitment to a comprehensive settlement on the basis of existing Council decisions, including a fine-tuned Security Council resolution 1284 (1999). The Security Council must carry out these commitments, as the other part of Council resolution 1382 (2001) was carried out, and create a goods review list. So there were two parts to the resolution. One part of it has been complied with, the other has not.

Russia, being a responsible member of the international community, has done and will do its utmost to prevent a renewal of Iraqi weapons of mass destruction programmes. We are prepared to cooperate on this matter with all States. Up to now, we, like all unbiased observers, have not seen any kind of persuasive evidence that there are weapons of mass destruction in Iraq or programmes to develop them. Nor have we seen any other facts that would situate Iraq in the context of combating terrorism. The only way to remove any doubts is the immediate redeployment of the international inspectors to Iraq.

And today, there are no legal or technical impediments to doing this. Moreover, as a result of the intensive efforts of a whole host of countries, including Russia, as well as the United Nations Secretary-General, the leadership of UNMOVIC and IAEA, Baghdad has consented, not only to an unconditional return of the United Nations inspectors, but also to UNMOVIC's and IAEA's new, enhanced and very effective parameters for conducting the inspections.

In this way we have everything we need to ensure that there is no renewal of the proscribed military programmes in Iraq and that there is a political and diplomatic settlement of the crisis. We see no reason to delay deployment of the UNMOVIC and IAEA structures in Iraq. Neither formally nor legally, in order to begin the inspections, do we need any new decisions to be taken by the Security Council. This has been confirmed by Messrs. Blix and ElBaradei. They do not need new decisions. They need clarity.

Do all Security Council members support the swift redeployment of the inspectors in Iraq? If the Council has a prevailing desire to give further support to UNMOVIC and the IAEA in the interest of an effective implementation of existing resolutions, then we will be prepared to look at the relevant proposals, including and based on the great importance of maintaining Council unity.

We are calling for collective steps by the international community. Unilateral actions do not facilitate the efforts for a settlement, as we see over and over again, according to the example of the unilaterally announced so-called no-fly zones. At the same time, with the efforts of non-renewal of Weapons of Mass Destruction programmes in Iraq, we must continue to press for Iraq's compliance with all other Security Council requirements, particularly the need to shed light on the fate of the missing detainees, a swift conclusion of the process underway to return the Kuwaiti archives and a return of Kuwaiti property. When we listen to the media, we might get the impression that the most important thing is to reach an agreement on whether or nor we are adopting one resolution or two. In fact, the issue is not how many resolutions, or do we need any resolutions. That diverts attention from the crux of the matter. But in fact we believe that the crux of the matter is the following.

If we are all sincerely interested in the nonrenewal of weapons of mass destruction programmes in Iraq, then what is the remaining issue? What are we waiting for? The inspectors can travel as early as tomorrow and Iraq knows that it must fully and scrupulously cooperate with the inspectors. If we are talking not about the deployment of the inspections but about an attempt to use the Security Council to create a legal basis for the use of force, or even for a regime change of a United Nations Member State—and this goal has been constantly and publicly alluded to by several officials—then we see no way how the Security Council could give its consent to that. I reiterate that the crux of the matter is not in the number of resolutions.

The Charter powers of the Security Council allow it at any time to make decisions about any measures which could be required to eliminate real threats. The important thing now is to achieve a comprehensive settlement, based on political and diplomatic methods, with the central role of the Security Council and in strict compliance with Council resolutions on the norms of international law.

In this we see the common platform for the United Nations work on Iraq and we are prepared to interact on this platform with other members of the Security Council. This is what we have been called to by the vast majority of the international community during the discussions yesterday and today. That is the opinion of the world community. And that is geopolitical reality as well. We are convinced that Security Council members will not be able to ignore this call.

Iraqi Representative Aldouri. I should like to thank everyone who has participated in this debate. It has certainly further developed discussion on the issue of Iraq, and I believe that it has been very useful to the Council, to the rest of the United Nations and to the world.

This important and serious debate has been held to offset significant efforts that have sought to mislead public opinion. I should like to thank all those who have made statements that have faithfully described reality, because before now reality had been revealed only in part. The time called for the debate was fairly short, and it was quite difficult to acquire all the necessary data from the period since 1999 so that everyone could participate fully in this debate.

I should like to begin my statement where the President left off in his statement, when he spoke about the Sumerian, Babylonian and Akkadian civilizations in Iraq—Iraq, the land of water, oil and minds, the Iraq of the Abbassid civilization. Even without oil or water, would we have experienced the situation that we are now experiencing? I shall not dwell on a political analysis of this issue. The Council is fully aware that the only objectives of the approaching war are oil, wealth and hegemony—control over the wealth in the region and the world. I shall not go into detail. I shall say only that the world is now split into two and that the larger part favors peace, negotiations and diplomacy under the Charter of the United Nations, unity in the United Nations and the very future of the Organization.

I am definitely in that camp. I fervently desire peace, understanding and conciliation, and I care about the future of this international Organization. It was recently jeopardized by the statement of one major Power that, if the United Nations failed to take into account the interests of that State, it would go its own way. It was not Iraq that made that statement, it was another major Power that feels it has immense power in the world. It was the National Security Adviser who made that statement. It seemed that we had nearly written the Organization's epitaph.

We ourselves support those who believe in peace, diplomacy, understanding, the implementation of resolutions adopted by the United Nations and the provisions of the Charter. I should like to thank and pay tribute to all those who have spoken to that effect. But while we were engaged in this debate, we witnessed a major event that nearly amounted to a declaration of war, aimed at striking Iraq, although a debate was being held here. It was a virtual declaration of war. War legislation was adopted and celebrated with great pomp and ceremony by the President and the leaders of a certain country, and it was against Iraq, a small country thousands of kilometers away from that superpower, which is the primary Power in the world today. It is my hope that that country's President and his colleagues, who celebrated that declaration of war in the form of legislation, have all heard what has been said in this debate by those who favor peace and security.

I said earlier that the world has been split into two, one part favoring peace and the other part—which is actually a very small minority, but an extremely active minority, made up of virtually two States—favoring war. But I wonder: how can a State go along with the warlike approach of another State? The representative of one State said here that if the Council does not take a decision, then his State will act as it sees fit. The text of his statement has been photocopied and is available to Council members. Its message is clear: if the Council refuses to declare war on Iraq, then that State will do it for the Council. That was one voice in this debate.

I am, however, happy to see that the majority of the members of the United Nations are still anxious to preserve peace, the rights of peoples and the Charter of the United Nations, as well as principles that I myself have advocated, and have in fact taught for 30 years in this very country. Those principles are nevertheless being trampled underfoot on a daily basis in our world. Like others who have spoken in the Security Council today, and indeed like the overwhelming majority of the Members of the United Nations, I believe that it is necessary to preserve the credibility of the United Nations in order to guarantee its future. I can assure the Council that it will certainly not be Iraq that will undermine or weaken the Organization. Rather, we will work tirelessly to restore the credibility of the United Nations, which has been called into question, not by small countries like my own but by some major Powers.

Many speakers, members and non-members of the Council alike, have expressed their trust in Mr. Blix and Mr. ElBaradei. Indeed, the Government of Iraq also has full confidence in those two gentlemen. Our doors are wide open to them and to their inspectors. Let them come as soon as possible; they will be quite welcome in Iraq. Our doors are widen open, as are our palaces, houses, hospitals and schools. Let them come and go where they wish. As I say, our doors are wide open to them. We are not afraid. We are open to Mr. Blix, Mr. ElBaradei and their inspectors. They are welcome to send the inspectors on 19 October, which is just a couple of days away. Let them come to Iraq, where they will be welcomed and where they and their teams will be able to go where they wish. That is our position regarding Mr. Blix. We have trust in him.

Actually, though, why do we have to reconfirm our trust in Mr. Blix? When has there ever been any question about our confidence in him? Who raised the issue of their being any doubt about him? I do not think anyone has questioned him. In order to be able to explain the evolution of events we therefore have to look back to the United Nations Special Commission (UNSCOM) and Mr. Butler, who was entrusted with the task of leading UNSCOM. There had been some rumors here and there about Mr. Butler in the past, but we are now talking about Mr. Blix and the need to have confidence in him. However, let me reassure the Council that Iraq has full trust in Mr. Blix and that he and his team will be welcomed in Iraq.

Some speakers have said that Iraq has violated all of the Security Council's resolutions. That assertion is perhaps due to the rather frightening lack of familiarity with UNSCOM documents. It has also been said that Iraq expelled UNSCOM and the inspectors in 1998. However, as everyone in fact knows, Mr. Butler was receiving his orders directly from the United States and the United Kingdom, which were constantly urging him to leave Iraq. Those calls were in fact sufficient to get him to leave Iraq. As the representative of the Russian Federation pointed out, Iraq was bombed 24 hours after Mr. Butler's departure. I would invite everyone who is not familiar with those events to look into the dossier on this case and to familiarize themselves with its contents.

I have spoken about the number of meetings held and about the amount of time spent on inspections and in Iraqi airspace, so I need not repeat that now. Neither Mr. Ikeus nor Mr. Butler nor the inspection teams were able to point to a single element that could indicate the presence of weapons of mass destruction in Iraq — apart, of course, from the information provided by Iraq.

Iraq destroyed the weapons it had, opened up its doors and provided copious documentation. Iraq was therefore acting in good faith and with good will. Iraq itself took the decision to reject weapons of mass destruction. I think that the fact that we have welcomed the return of inspectors is further evidence of that rejection. We fully and forever turned our back on weapons of mass destruction and we destroyed them. The representative of Norway has expressed some apprehension about Iraqi weapons reaching his country. I do not know the distance between Iraq and Norway, but I would like to reassure him that our hands are now clean and that there are no weapons of mass destruction in Iraq.

Everything that has been said about the issue of weapons of mass destruction has been part of a disinformation campaign. We hope that inspectors will return soon so that they themselves can tell the international community that Iraq's hands are now clean and that it has no weapons of mass destruction. Iraq has no such materials. I just wanted to reassure anyone who still has any doubts about this as a result of that dis-information campaign.

I would like to thank some of my colleagues, including members of the Council, and especially the representative of Singapore, who have said that sanctions will be lift-ed once the inspectors return to Iraq and they report to the Security Council that there are no weapons of mass destruction in my country. The Iraqi people would then get some relief. I fear that they are being too optimistic, however. American and British individuals have made clear statements to the effect that sanctions and the embargo will never be lifted until there has been "regime change" in Iraq. In fact, those state-ments are documented and are available to the Council and the Secretary-General. Everyone knows about documents containing such statements. This is a domestic political issue pertaining to the interests of the United States and the United Kingdom. We have said that we are willing to welcome inspectors. But there is also the question of lifting the embargo, which, as I have also said, is a political matter for those two countries.

Several speakers have also referred to the memorandum of understanding to say that Iraq had not facilitated its implementation. However, although we had billions or tens of billions of dollars in a trust fund, about 2,000 contracts for medicines and medical supplies were pending due to a hold by the United States. Those contracts also included equipment necessary to provide drinking water and to produce food for the people of Iraq. We have lost untold thousands of people as a result of the lack of drink-ing water and foodstuffs. In fact, the United States even banned the export of chlorine to Iraq, which is essential to treating drinking water. There are many other examples, but I shall not go into them.

The representative of the United Kingdom said that he was really distressed about the situation of the Iraqi people. They can well say that they have nothing against our people, only against the Iraqi Government. There were four billion dollars available in the fund that could have been used had it not been for the veto by the United States and the United Kingdom.

In respect to contractors, 2,000 contracts were stopped. I heard a colleague men-tion the lack of money in the fund. There are really four reasons for that, but the cen-tral one is that the United States and the United Kingdom imposed a retroactive pric-ing mechanism for our oil. In other words, if I want to buy Iraqi oil today, I sign a con-tract, then the United States and the United Kingdom say that I have to wait for a month before a price can be quoted. Naturally, one does not want to conclude such a contract, because oil prices are so volatile. That was a deliberate policy of these two countries to thwart the memorandum of understanding and make sure that it could not work. In the past, the mechanism worked. Hopefully things will soon improve again, and so will the situation of the fund. Those who are shedding crocodile tears for the Iraqi people have also made statements relating to war and destruction, as has been reported widely in the Western and United States media.

There was another point made by several speakers. I am not sure whether I should mention it, but I would like to make one point in connection with it. That is the ques-tion of some Kuwaiti property—some, I stress—that is about to be returned to the owners as per Iraqi-Kuwaiti arrangements. I recognize what was said about the Kuwaitis and their wish to get their property back without any problems whatsoever, a matter that I appreciate. Another representative spoke of the matter and tried to politicize the issue. Before concluding, I would like to mention the agreement between Mr. Blix and Mr. ElBaradei on the one hand, and Iraqi authorities on the other. We have heard a lot in the media about this. Both yesterday and today, here at this meeting, some supporters of the American position said that the agreement between Iraq and Mr. Blix had only just been signed and Iraq was already looking for another margin or space as delaying tactics, seeking other interpretations in order to deprive the agreement of any significant meaning or content whatsoever.

Iraq approved and signed the agreement in Vienna and is bound by all its provisions. We even issued an official communique inviting the inspectors to return to Iraq and undertook to fully cooperate with them. We are willing to work and resolve any problems that occur. We are confident that the inspectors will face no impediments in carrying out their work. I would like to give assurances that any doubt cast on this agreement is inaccurate. In an exchange of letters it is quite natural that there be some misunderstanding about the actual meaning of words, but that is all there is.

On the substance of what was agreed on in Vienna, I affirm that there is no misunderstanding as to what was agreed there, and we will not in any way hinder the work of the weapons inspectors. I believe that we are all civilized persons, as you all said. We have a history that covers several civilizations and millennia.

Many who participated in this debate noted that goodwill is present and that we will cooperate with UNMOVIC. So I would like to say that the new resolution being spoken of in the media and in negotiations about its text—the contents of which we do not know—will not be about ensuring that UNMOVIC and the inspectors do their work, but rather will prevent the inspectors from doing their work. We urge the inspectors to come tomorrow or the day after to do their work. We will create no problems.

Of course some say that this is just rhetoric, but I say that I am not an experienced diplomat familiar with all these rhetorical flourishes. I speak as an Iraqi who is sincere in my intention. The United Nations does not need another resolution. That is my view, though I know that it will not change the views of the superpower. But I want to ensure all the peace-loving countries that reject war that the new text is geared towards preventing the inspectors from returning to Iraq. We want them to come and do their work, and we are resolved to implement the resolution in spirit and in letter.

I thank you very much, Mr. President, for giving me this right of reply to comment on what has been said by other speakers in this debate.

Remarks by Secretary of State Powell, October 17, 2002

Secretary Colin Powell delivered his remarks following meetings with members of the United Nations Security Council at U.N. Headquarters, New York, New York.

Q. Mr. Secretary, have you reached an agreement with France for a new U.N. resolution on Iraq?

Secretary Powell. We are in consultations with our French colleagues as well as our Russian and Chinese and British colleagues and other members of the Security Council on a resolution. Those conversations are going well and they're continuing and let me just reinforce our belief that one resolution is what is appropriate. A resolution that makes it clear that Iraq has been in violation, material breach of U.N. resolutions for a long period of time (inaudible) continued violation. Next we have to have a strong inspection regime if inspectors are to go back in. I've had conversations with Dr. Hans Blix this afternoon (inaudible) or if Iraq once again fails to abide by U.N. resolution, there have to be consequences and action has to be taken and that remains our position as we work with our Security Council colleagues. We are trying to break some of the differences that exist between our views and their views. But I just think that our views are rather directly clear.

Q. [*Inaudible*] American proposal of the latest resolution. Will that prepare the authority for the United States to use military action or will they have to come back to get authority in a second resolution?

Secretary Powell. The United States does not [*inaudible*] original authority even now until necessary to take action to defend ourselves. The President brought the problem to the United Nations in a very powerful speech on the 12th of September, I think laid out the case clearly and asked the U.N. to act to make sure that everybody knew that this was a real [*inaudible*] have done. Secondly, if inspectors go back in, they have to go back in under much more powerful instructions and with much more support and there is no opportunity for the Iraqis to deter the inspectors from their work [*inaudible*]. Thirdly, there must be a threat, there must be consequences for their continued failure. Now, we hope that the U.N. Security Council, as it considers this, and as they come to a conclusion of this discussion, will make sure all of those elements are in whatever resolution is passed. We have not tabled a resolution, we have not tabled a resolution at all. We are having conversations with our Security Council colleagues and in due course, when those consultations are completed, the whole world will know what the position of the Council is.

Q. Are you confident it can still be reached that a trigger mechanism that will be supported by Washington and the other members of the Council?

Secretary Powell. I don't think that a trigger mechanism is the right impression. The United States in now operating behind the authority given to the President by the joint resolution of the Congress last week. That joint resolution is clear. The United States should work with the United Nations to see if they can collectively deal with this problem and if it becomes necessary as a result of continued Iraqi violation of international law, it becomes necessary to apply force, the joint resolution says that the President should work with the United Nations to see if everybody will come to an agreement to do that. But at the same time, the resolution says that the President has the authority to act as President of the United States in the best interest of the United States in concert with well-minded nations, whether the United Nation is active or not. What we are trying to do is make this case to the United Nations that collective action is better, but there has to be an action. That is a clear action that the Iraqis understand that they are in violation. What the language will ultimately look like, where we will get agreement, whether nations will choose to preserve their prerogative remains to be seen. But our position is firm. We believe one resolution is appropriate and obviously the Council can always go out and have other discussion at any time it chooses. But any resolution that emerges from this will be a resolution that preserves the authority and right of the President of the United States to act in self defense of the American people, of our neighbors, in working in concert with the international community or with like-minded nations, if the international community through the U.N. does wish to act.

Q. If Iraq is shown to be in violation, is the United States prepared to consult with the Council for launching its [*inaudible*]?

Secretary Powell. We are in constant consultation with leaders around the world, and the resolution, I think will be clear when we finally finish the wording that other nations have the right to do what they wish to do with respect to consultations or further discussions. But the United States in the presence of continued violations, does [*inaudible*] will have the authority to do what we believe is necessary to protect our people and protect our friends. It is inherent in the laws of the United States and in constitutional position that the President [*inaudible*].

Remarks by Secretary of State Powell, October 17, 2002

Secretary Colin Powell made the following remarks at the annual Alfred E. Smith Memorial Foundation Dinner in New York, New York.

We are now engaged in a great debate about Iraq—Iraq, a country that is a state sponsor of terrorism and in possession of weapons of mass destruction. It is an unholy combination.

The President came to New York and went before the United Nations on September 12th, the day after the anniversary of 9/11, and he laid out the case. He reminded the world that Saddam Hussein already has used weapons of mass destruction against his own citizens and against his neighbors. He has not abandoned such weapons or his intention to acquire more, including nuclear weapons.

The President presented on the 12th of September here an unassailable indictment of Saddam Hussein's flagrant violation of all 16 United Nations resolutions. The President also described Saddam Hussein's history of threatening his neighbors and repressing his own citizens.

He has gotten away with it for eleven years. We are determined, once and for all, that he will not get away with it any longer.

The President came to the United Nations not to make a declaration of war, but to make a declaration of purpose. He came to rally the United Nations to deal with Saddam Hussein's blatant disregard of the United Nations' solemn authority. He also described what can be done to disarm Iraq without resorting to war.

We need a tough new resolution that will send the inspectors back in with the authority to do their job and disarm Iraq. And it is not for Iraq to dictate the conditions to the United Nations, but for the United Nations to dictate the conditions to Iraq.

The plain truth, however, is that the inspectors won't be able to do their jobs unless Iraq cooperates. This time, Iraq must face consequences for continued failure to disarm.

The United States Congress last week passed a strong resolution authorizing the President to impose those consequences. The resolution supports and encourages action within the U.N.. It recognizes, however, that the world faces a real and present danger and if the United Nations does not act, the United States, joined by other nations, willing nations, must act, and we will act.

I also know that Iraq will not have a single defender among the circle of civilized nations. Not one. Nor are Saddam and his regime likely to have very many defenders among their own people.

As President Bush has said, our objective in the war against terrorism and in confronting Iraq is not just a safer, but a better, world. Our goal is not just to free the people from fear, but to create fresh hope in the process.

In the challenging months ahead, the men and women that I lead in the Department of State will be proud to do their part.

Remarks by Secretary of Defense Rumsfeld, October 17, 2002

Last week there was a strong vote in Congress to authorize the president to use force. It sent a strong signal to the Iraqi regime and to the world that our country is united in its goal of working with the United Nations to seek disarmament in Iraq.

As the president made clear in his address last week, none of us desire to see military conflict, because we know the awful nature of war. A decision to use force is never easy. No one with any sense considers war a first choice. In the recent congressional debate, many important questions were raised about the risks of military action.

When I came to the Pentagon last year, I prepared a list of issues that I have found useful in considering before making a recommendation with respect to the use of force. I update those guidelines from time to time, and I thought I would mention a few of them today. A copy of the guidelines is available in the press office, if anyone wants one.

First, is the proposed action truly necessary? Certainly if lives are going to be put at risk, whether they're U.S. lives or the lives of other foreign nationals, there must be a darn good reason.

I suggest that all instruments of national power should be engaged before, during and after any possible use of force. There is clearly an interaction between diplomacy and the potential of the use of force.

And I would submit that—a good example of it exists today. The Iraqis have refused inspections for years now, and because of the threat of the use of force and because the United Nations is considering that, the Iraqis have now volunteered that they might consider one type of inspection or another. Whether they'll stick with that or not is another question. But I think it's an example of that interaction.

When the U.S. commits force, the task should be achievable and at an acceptable risk. It has to be something that the United States is truly capable of doing. We need to understand that we have limitations. There are some things that this country and other countries simply can't do. There should be clear goals both as to the purpose of the engagement and what would constitute success so we can know when our goals have been achieved. Decisions, in my view, ought not to be made by committees. If the U.S. needs or prefers a coalition, which in my view it almost always will, it's important to avoid trying so hard to persuade others to join a coalition that it could compromise the goals or jeopardize the command structure. The mission needs to determine the coalition.

Third, if a proposed action is necessary and doable, is it worth it? If an engagement is worth doing, then we need to recognize that ultimately lives could be put at risk, and leaders have to be willing to invest the political capital necessary to marshal support necessary to sustain the effort for whatever period of time conceivably could be required. When there's a risk of casualties, that risk should be acknowledged at the outset, rather than allowing the American people or others to think that an engagement can be executed antiseptically.

Next, before acting, one needs to consider the implications of the decision in other parts of the world. When the United States does something in one location, that action is read all across the globe. So too with an inaction—it can be read all across the globe. And those actions and/or inactions can contribute either favorably or unfavorably to the U.S. deterrent and to our influence in other parts of the globe.

Finally, if there's to be an action, it seems to me that it's important to make a judgment as to when diplomacy has failed and to act forcefully during the pre-crisis period to try to alter behavior and prevent a conflict; if that fails, to be prepared to use whatever force is necessary to prevail, plus some.

It's important not to dumb-down what's needed by promising not to do things, it seems to me. We've seen instances where people have said, "We won't use ground forces," or "We won't risk lives," or "We won't permit collateral damage," or "We won't bomb below 15,000 feet," or "We'll set an arbitrary deadline that it will end as of this date." Those promises, those declarations, it seems to me, have the net effect of simplifying the task for an enemy, and it makes the task for the coalition much more difficult.

I think it's also important to be brutally honest. We need to avoid making any effort sound even marginally easier or less costly than it in fact could become. Preserving U.S. credibility requires that we promise less, or at least know more, than we believe we can deliver. And remember that it's a great deal easier to get into something than it is to get out of it. There may be times when national security requires that the U.S. act without clear answers to some of these questions. These questions, really, that I've posed to myself I think of as guidelines: not a perfect checklist, but simply—and certainly not hard and fast rules. But they're prepared as a checklist so that as people are considering the possible use of force, it is done with the fullest appreciation of our responsibilities and all the risks.

Remarks by United Nations Secretary-General Annan, October 18, 2002

Q. Mr. Secretary-General, President Chirac speaking today in Beirut about the Iraq crisis said the world had to resist what he called "temptations of adventure." Is the world at a risk of succumbing to temptations of adventure and what is your latest assessment of deliberations between the U.N. members over the Iraq crisis?

Secretary General Annan. I think this is an issue that we all take seriously. The Security Council and the entire membership of the United Nations, as evidenced by the debate going on in the Council right now where the vast majority of the membership spoke and expressed their views. I think, at the end of the day, the Council will act, will take an optimal decision, the decision I that suspect will strengthen the hands of the inspectors and the disarmament effort, sending the inspectors in and demand that Iraq cooperates. And I think it is important that Iraq cooperates and does not continue to defy the international community. Were it to do that, the Council will meet again or the Council will have to decide what further measures to take. But I think it is an issue that the entire international community is seized [with] and I hope the Council will act in unity, in unison and come up with an optimal decision.

* * * *

Q. Can you tell us your opinion on the position of Russia with regard to the Iraq problem?

Secretary-General Annan. I don't speak for Russia. But let me say that Russia is fully engaged with other members of the Security Council, particularly with the permanent members in intensive discussions to find a way out of the current crisis surrounding the Iraqi issue. And I spoke to Foreign Minister [Igor] Ivanov recently about the resolutions under discussion and they are playing an active and their full role. And as I said I expect the Council to approve the resolution within the next week or so.

Remarks by Secretary of State Powell, October 20, 2002

Secretary Colin Powell was interviewed on Fox News Sunday by Tony Snow and Brit Hume.

Q. We appear to be near, at the U.N., an agreement on passage of a resolution on Iraq. But the confident signals that have been coming from Washington and some of diplomats at the U.N. seem, at least on the surface, to be contradicted by comments from other diplomats, France and others. What is going on here?

Secretary Powell. Well, it's the U.N. at work: 15 sovereign nations in the Security Council who are trying to move forward on a particular issue. We have had very productive conversations over the last several days with some of our Security Council colleagues, and early this week we will be presenting a resolution that contains all the elements we believe should be in such a resolution, and as a result of discussions with the French and the British and the Russians and the Chinese and others, I think it's a resolution that will draw good support from the Security Council.

But there's still a ways to go. Once you put a resolution down, then everybody gets to comment on it, and there will be some tough debates ahead. But it will be a resolution, I believe, that will clearly lay out the violations of Saddam Hussein, the fact that we need a very new and tough inspection regime, and the fact that there will have to be consequences that flow from any continued violation on the part of Saddam Hussein of the inspection regime.

Q. Do you have the agreement already that you need from the Permanent 5 members of the U.N. Security Council on those provisions you just spoke of?

Secretary Powell. They haven't all seen every element of it, and that's what we will do early this week, and then the discussion will begin.

Q. Well, let's talk about just for a moment on the—the issue of inspections seems to be basically non-controversial in terms of everybody wants that.

Secretary Powell. Everybody wants that.

Q. What about the issue of consequences now?

Secretary Powell. The issue of consequences, there are different points of view. The point of view we hold is that there have to be consequences, and we believe that the President of the United States has all the authority he needs now and this new resolution will in no way diminish his authority if he feels he has to act with like-minded nations to deal with continued Iraqi violations.

Q. What about the issue of one resolution versus two?

Secretary Powell. Initially, there will be one resolution. That is what we are supporting. And we believe that that one resolution will give the President what he needs and in no way diminishes his authority.

Now, will that one resolution be sufficient to get all other members to join in an effort, if an effort is needed at this time? That remains to be seen. There is no way to keep other members of the Security Council from going before the Council and asking for a discussion, asking for a debate and asking for other resolutions. But right now, we are focusing on this one resolution.

Q. I'm sorry, just one question. It comes down to this: We believe that the one resolution you now feel confident you will get, specifying inspections and consequences, would be sufficient for the President to act, and you have no objection if there are further resolutions?

Secretary Powell. I can't object because I don't know what further resolutions might be. But the resolution I hope will come out of the Security Council will lay out the indictment, will put in place a new, tough, take-it-or-leave-it inspection regime for Saddam Hussein, and will make it clear that consequences will flow from continued violation. How those consequences will flow remains to be seen with respect to the United States and other like-minded nations who, in the presence of continued violations on the part of the Iraqis, believe they will have all the authority necessary if they decide to act, whether other members of the body choose to act with us at that time remains to be seen.

Q. All right, let's run through this quickly, then. Completely open inspections, no conditions. That's an absolute must.

Secretary Powell. Yes.

Q. Secondly, there are going to be timetables.

Secretary Powell. Yes.

Q. And how soon must Iraq (a) provide a full accounting of what it has and (b) permit unconditional searches?

Secretary Powell. Tony, I would rather that come out of the negotiation process with the Security Council members this week, rather than me prejudge what they might decide.

Q. Also, is it your view that the U.N. Charter, if Iraq is found in "material breach" of previous resolutions, already grants you the authority to use force, and that is the reason why you don't need a second resolution?

Secretary Powell. I think that argument can be made, and we'll be making that argument with our friends. In fact, Iraq has been in violation of these many resolutions for a period of 11 years. And the President, acting in his authority as Commander-in-Chief, and consistent with the United Nations Charter, and especially empowered by the congressional resolution last week that says work with the United Nations, try to get a tough resolution, and you can operate within the United Nations framework if military action is required and it is approved by the United Nations; but, if the United Nations, the Security Council, in the presence of violations, is not willing to then authorize military force, you, Mr. President, have the authority you need under our Constitutional and in accordance with our laws, and under self-defense aspects of the U.N. Charter, to take military action with like-minded nations.

So if it comes to military action, it could be done one of two ways: the United States, with like-minded nations, taking it—and we believe all the authority that is necessary for us to do so—or with all other nations as part of a U.N. resolution.

* * * *

Q. Sir, very quickly, I'd like to get your reaction to two quotes. One is from our next guest, Senate Majority Leader Tom Daschle. He is talking about the Bush Administration foreign policy. He says, "I don't know if we've ever seen a more precipitous drop in international stature and public opinion with regard to this country as we have in the last two years."

Your reaction?

Secretary Powell. Well, I would disagree with Senator Daschle. I think the United States is seen as a nation that believes in principles, that we will act on our principles, we will work in concern with our friends and allies around the world, and where there is a particular issue where we can't get consensus but it is in our interest to act, we will act. And I think that we are showing leadership in this world, we are showing the principled use of our economic strength, our moral strength, as well as our military strength.

White House Press Briefing, October 21, 2002

Q. Zbigniew Brzezinski said that the chances of war are now greatly diminished. Does the President agree with that? And can you give us a—on what's happening at the Security Council?

Mr. Fleischer. The Security Council came in at 11:00 a.m. this morning for discussions among the Permanent Five on the resolution. And I think it's fair to say that the discussions will continue and we feel that progress is being made on getting an agreement around the language that's been under discussion for several weeks now. We'll see exactly what course the United Nations Security Council takes. I can't predict the exact dates that they will take concrete action, but I think it's moving forward nicely.

Q. What about Brzezinski saying that war is now reduced, the chances of war?

Mr. Fleischer. I haven't seen what he said, so I'd hesitate to comment.

Q. Ari, does the United States government see any merit whatsoever in the fact that Saddam Hussein has decreed practically a general amnesty?

Mr. Fleischer. Well, as Secretary Powell said yesterday that can also be read as a political ploy. Nobody knows how many prisoners there are in Iraq. Nobody knows if Saddam Hussein has released a tenth of them, a quarter of them, half of them. So it's very hard to make sense of what Saddam Hussein has done.

The other issue that would be important here, too, is the President, when he went to the United Nations in September, talked about the need for Saddam Hussein to account for the 600 people that remain unaccounted for since the Persian Gulf War. We have no indication that his actions yesterday have touched on the fate of any of those 600.

Q. As far as the negotiations at the U.N., do you feel that Washington and Paris are closer now to an agreement, and do you expect a resolution this week?

Mr. Fleischer. Well, I'm not going to predict the ultimate course. I think that's very risky for anybody to predict what the United Nations will do in final form. But as I indicated, progress is being made. The talks are continuing, but it's moving forward and moving forward nicely.

Q. Ari, yesterday Secretary of State Powell indicated that there may very well be a second resolution that will ultimately be voted on. However, it's his position, or the United States' position that once the initial resolution is accepted, if it is in the U.N., that the U.S. will have all the authorization it needs to take action should it come to those steps. Can you explain exactly what kind of language there would be in such a resolution in which the United States could very well still act on its own, however, there may be nations—other member nations who say, no, we have to have another vote?

Mr. Fleischer. Well, the resolution that's being discussed is a very strong resolution. It makes clear that the inspection regime of the '90s will be replaced with a new and much tougher, more effective inspection regime in this century. And it also makes clear that there will be serious consequences if Saddam Hussein fails to honor his obligations. And it's a very important action for the United Nations Security Council to adopt this resolution. We hope that they will.

It is always the right of any nation that is a member of the United Nations Security Council to come forward at any time, and all times, with any resolution that they see fit. But it will—clear, based on this resolution that the United States will have all the authority that it needs, along with our allies.

Q. Do you expect at this point that there will be a second resolutions? Are you anticipating—

Mr. Fleischer. As I indicated, it's always the right of a sovereign nation of the 15 nations of the United Nations Security Council to step forward with a resolution at any time of their choosing, on any issue, at all times. I'm not in a position to predict in this case, vis a vis Iraq, whether that will or will not take place.

* * * *

Q. I'm still not clear about the status of the United Nations. Is there actually a U.S. draft on the floor that's being discussed? You made reference to something that's being discussed.

Mr. Fleischer. Yes. The technical word at the United Nations is to "table" a resolution—which, unlike in the Congress, when you table something you put it off. At the United Nations, when you table something, you put it on. And I would have to refer you up to the U.N. to see what the exact timing of it is going to be. That's going to be a U.N. matter and they can discuss with you the exact timing of it.

Q. You referred earlier to something that is being discussed there now that you liked, that you thought was strong. You're talking about our version of events, what we and the British have come up with; are you not?

Mr. Fleischer. Sure, that's the way everything has been talked about. The United States-British draft language that has been shopped around and is making progress.

* * * *

Q. After all these years, the Iraqis not only released all their political prisoners but also shipped back several truckloads of documents that had been stolen from Kuwait. After all this time, to do two of those things in the course of two or three days, what do you make of this?

Mr. Fleischer. Well, as Secretary Powell said, the release of the prisoners appears to be a political ploy. But it's hard to know what to make of all of this. Saddam Hussein does not often act in a way that is clear or that is rational or even that is open and conclusive. That's why I indicated earlier that nobody knows how many prisoners have really been released. Nobody knows how many he had.

And, so, it's very hard to make any real meaningful interpretations of what he has done. He remains a threat and a menace.

* * * *

Q. On other thing on the U.N. resolution, if I may. the position is clear on tough rules for new inspections, single resolution and so forth. What is the current U.S. position on whether or not there should be armed escorts for inspectors, and whether or not members of the P-5 should be able to have the right to insist on their own representatives?

Mr. Fleischer. Okay, let me do this. Much of that will be found in the exact language of the resolution that's being discussed at the United Nations. And so as soon as that is ready to be released publicly, I think you'll find your answers to that. And I will try to keep you advised at what the timing of that may be.

Remarks by Secretary of State Powell, October 22, 2002

Secretary Colin Powell was interviewed by Oprah Winfrey on the "Oprah Winfrey Show."

Q. We also went to Secretary of State Colin Powell to answer some of those questions. As a four-star general, Colin Powell oversaw the Persian Gulf war. As Secretary of State, he's trying to convince our allies that now is the time to stop Saddam Hussein.

Secretary Powell. Right now we're not talking about war. Right now we're talking about finding a peaceful solution to this. Nobody wants war. President Bush does not war. I do not want war. But do we want Saddam Hussein to have nuclear, chemical and biological weapons that he can use, as he has used these kinds of weapons in the past against his neighbors, against his own people, or perhaps against us someday? This is the time to stop him. He has been told to stop by the international community.

It's not the United States who is at fault here; it is Saddam Hussein and Iraq that is at fault. And it is a problem he is wholly responsible for, and he cannot be allowed to get away with it.

There has been a containment policy in effect, but we have seen that during the period of this containment policy Iraq has continued to try to develop weapons of mass destruction. They have chemical weapons; they have biological weapons; they're trying to acquire nuclear weapons. They've been in violation of all of these containment resolutions for the last 11 years.

He has shown previously that he is not that inhibited. What we don't want him to be able to do is to achieve greater capability because then he would be even less inhibited.

One thing you can be sure of: He isn't going to disarm, he is not going to let the inspectors in, unless he is fearful of a conflict that would remove him from power. He has demonstrated for 11 years that he will ignore, stiff and laugh at the world's opinion. That laughter has to stop.

If peace can be maintained while disarming Saddam Hussein and disarming the Iraqi regime, fine. But if it takes conflict, we must keep the prospect of conflict there or else he will not cooperate.

The concern we should have is that Saddam Hussein might blow up his infrastructure, his own oil wells, as he goes down to defeat. If we are going in if we have to go in, and we hope we don't have to go in, we will go in to remove a dictatorial regime and take away his weapons of mass destruction.

And as we have demonstrated repeatedly in recent years, we will fight a conflict, if it comes to a conflict, with sophisticated weapons, with precision weapons, in a way that minimizes loss of civilian life. Will there be some loss? Of course, there always is. That's why war should be avoided.

But forestalling action is forestalling the inevitability, rather. I mean, it just leads to the inevitability of Saddam becoming more dangerous, the Iraqi regime becoming more dangerous, in the months and years ahead.

Remarks by Chairman of the Joint Chiefs of Staff Myers and Secretary of Defense Rumsfeld, October 22, 2002

Q. General Myers, and I know it's an "if," based on this discussion and the question, but isn't Saddam getting almost an inordinate amount of time to plan and prepare for any possible invasion? And if so, doesn't that put U.S. troops in greater harm's way? For instance, there was a published report today that the U.S. has decided in a sense not to fight in the cities and play Saddam's game. Are you at all concerned about this extra time that it's taking?

General Myers. The short answer is that the U.S. military remains capable of responding to the president whenever he asks that it respond for crisis prevention, for conflict, across the entire spectrum, whenever. And the last thing that we want to do is limit the president or the rest of the national command authority's flexibility in responding to crisis. And we're postured—I can tell you we're postured in that way that that will not be a problem.

Q. But capable is one thing, sir, but, I mean, do you see the possibility now, because of the time, you know, elapsing here, for a greater threat to our forces? I mean, there's no question, from what you say, that the U.S. is capable, but what about losses?

General Myers. In a hypothetical situation, the longer you wait, obviously, an adversary has time to prepare, but so do you, to prepare for the consequences. So I would say no. I think—we have a very strong military force. We have potentially great coalition partners and, as we said before, that will contribute in many different ways, and we'll be ready for whatever whenever.

Q. Mr. Secretary, do you believe that it's possible to disarm Iraq with Saddam Hussein remaining in power?

Secretary Rumsfeld. The—if one thinks about it, inspections are designed for a situation where a country decides it wants to be cooperative, and it wants to prove to the world that it has done something that the world wants them to do. Therefore, they invite in inspectors, and they then behave in a totally cooperative way, so that those inspectors can in fact do their task of informing the world that the host country has been behaving in a hospitable and open manner.

Inspections don't work, really, in a situation that's hostile. They can do some things. They can, on occasion, talk to inspectors—correction: to defectors. The inspectors can talk to defectors and learn things that can be helpful, and they can discover some things. But in terms of being able to disarm a country, unless that country is cooperative, it is—it strikes me as a very, very difficult thing to accomplish. I can't quite imagine how that could happen, except through the cooperation of the country.

Therefore, the answer to the question is for everybody, in the United Nations or in this room or in the country, to answer for themselves: How do we feel about Saddam Hussein's behavior over the past 11 years and in the past 11 months and in the past 11 weeks or days? Does it lead one to believe that he's likely to behave in that manner or not?

Q. If I could follow up, the administration seems to be sending a signal that regime change could come by simply a change in the way the regime operates and not a physical removal of Saddam Hussein. Is military—the threat of military action possibly enough to get Saddam Hussein to change the way that he's operated in the past—more than a decade?

Secretary Rumsfeld. Oh, I think, again, each person can answer that for themselves. They can look at the record, they can look at Saddam Hussein, they can look at the country.

Q. How do you answer it?

Secretary Rumsfeld. Very carefully.

* * * *

Q. I'm sort of having a hard time reconciling all of this and not coming up with the flip answer that the reason that the United States is considering and possibly preparing to use force in Iraq is because of a massive intelligence failure. And we don't know what we don't know, so let's go do this.

Secretary Rumsfeld. I don't like the phrase "intelligence failure." And I purposely didn't use it with respect to the—I don't think I used it—with respect to the Cuban missile crisis. I wouldn't use it with respect to September 11th.

I think the point I like to make is that we're living in a big world, where these technologies and capabilities are spreading across the globe. And many more countries and many more terrorist networks are going to be able to get their hands on them, and are getting their hands on them. And that it's not possible to know everything that's going on in this globe—no matter how good you are, no matter how effective your intelligence gathering is. You can know a lot, and you can make good estimates and guesses, but there are—we have to accept that we're going to live in a world of little or no warning, a world of surprises if you're still surprised.

But if you know that those capabilities are out there, and you know you can't know exactly where they are, or exactly who has them, or exactly what method they may or may not use to attack you, then you ought not to be surprised. The only thing surprising to me is that people are surprised, because that's the nature of our world.

And the Cuban missile crisis, one can say, was an intelligence failure. Anyone with 20/20 hindsight can go back and say they failed to know that. And that's not inaccurate from a grammatical standpoint, or from a semantic standpoint. It is, however, I think, an unrealistic expectation to think that it's possible to know exactly what's going in the—on the minds of people, or whether they have intent, whether they necessarily have capability because they have very effective means of denial and deception. And it's constantly a moving target.

And I think what we have to do is to just—I don't know if I'm leading you out of your cul-de-sac, but—but it seems to me, that what I was trying to say is, there was an instance where we did not know, months after a decision has been made to put those missiles in Cuba. We did not know that. At some moment, they were seen physically.

Now, that is not often the case, when you can see something physically. If it's underground, you're not going to see it. If it's something other than a large mass, like a ballistic missile, you may not see it. If it's chemical or biological you might not see it. We saw it, and then the president made a decision, President Kennedy, and he said: That's unacceptable; no one's fired a missile at us, no one's announced they intended to do that, but that's not acceptable. And he imposed a quarantine, a blockade which he called a quarantine, euphemistically, because he was acting to prevent or preempt their ability to use those missiles against us from the island of Cuba. And he did it at the last moment and was fortunate in succeeding.

* * * *

Q. Your view on [the possible use of containment in Iraq] sir?

Secretary Rumsfeld. There's no question but that there have been times in history, in my lifetime, when containment has worked. There have also been times when containment or deterrence have not worked. And one has to look across a spectrum of activities and recognize the reality that some set of capabilities deter certain kinds of behavior but not others.

With respect to containment, if you wanted to use that word and say that a containment of Iraq might be an appropriate approach, the reality is that for 11 years, the United States has attempted to do that. They have worked with other countries, through the United Nations, some 16 resolutions. They have attempted to diplomatically restrict Iraq, with the hope of creating incentives for them to give up weapons of mass destruction. It's failed. They've used economic sanctions. And for a while, the economic sanctions pinched. But today they not only don't pinch, but they may very well even result in higher revenues for Iraq than were those sanctions not there. And so that has not worked, because he's made a conscious judgment that he'd rather have weapons of mass destruction than the food or the revenues from the oil liftings.

And the third approach of military activity has also been used, and it's been used first in Desert—in the Gulf War and then, second, in—Desert Shield I guess it was called, and—pardon me?

Q. Desert Fox in December '98.

Secretary Rumsfeld. Desert Fox. And then, third, it's been used in the northern and southern no-fly zones—military weaponry and capability. And all three have failed. And they failed over a sustained period, which is not a month or a week or a year; it's 11 years of—

Q. To do what?

Secretary Rumsfeld. They have failed to bring about a situation where Saddam Hussein would do what he promised to do at the end of the Gulf War, namely, give up his weapons of mass destruction and adhere to those resolutions.

Now, anyone who wants can rewrite history, anyone who wants can give speeches and say things they'd like to say. But the fact is that at some point, I think most reasonable people would have to agree that 11 years is a long time; that the economic sanctions are not working; the borders are porous, the weapons are flowing in; and third, that the diplomatic efforts have not failed. So, if one is enamored of the word containment, it's pretty clear that they have not been, are not currently, and I would submit, are unlikely, prospectively, to feel contained.

Deterrent, one can also raise, and say, are they deterred? We know that the fact that the United States has nuclear weapons did not deter the Korean War. It did not deter the Vietnam War. It did not deter Saddam Hussein from invading Kuwait, and it did not deter a bucket of other things. It happened that those deterrents did work with the Soviet Union, one would think, and created a relatively stable situation between two powers.

But it never worked with respect to terrorist states. It never worked with respect to lesser contingencies. And I think that that's an accurate reading of history. And I hope you do, too.

White House Press Briefing, October 22, 2002

Q.—is reporting the Russian reaction to the latest resolution is that they find it "unacceptable." What is your reaction to that?

Mr. Fleischer. One, that's the first I've heard such reaction. I think you can anticipate, as we've seen throughout this multi-week process, a series of statements, sometimes which are not supported by what is said in private. We'll continue the work in the United Nations. It is ongoing. It is coming down to the end. The United Nations does not have forever, and we'll continue to work it and see when we get an agreement, if we get an agreement, how to proceed.

Q.—you say that the United Nations can't do this forever. I mean, is that signaling an impatience on your part?

Mr. Fleischer. Well, it's a fact that they don't have forever. The United Nations is entering the final stages on this, and we would like to see an agreement reached.

Q. Ari, just for the record, are you still opposed to a two-resolution process?

Mr. Fleischer. Correct, that position remains the same; one resolution is appropriate.

* * * *

Q. Does regime change mean that you want to change the leader of Iraq, or you want to change the nature of the regime?

Mr. Fleischer. The objective is for Saddam Hussein's Iraq to disarm, to stop threatening its neighbors, to stop repressing minorities within its own country. And that's why Congress passed the policy of regime change.

Q. Well, which of those definitions is correct?

Mr. Fleischer. Well, let's do it—let me cut to the bottom line on it. What I would propose is that in the event Saddam Hussein gives the order, and under his leadership and direction disarms Iraq, gives up its weapons of mass destruction, has no more chemical weapons, no more biological weapons, stops using hostility as a way to deal with its neighbors, stops repression of minorities with his own country, give me a call. After you cover Saddam Hussein doing these things, let's talk about it. Until then, the President is focused on making sure that these developments take place as a result either of the U.N. resolutions being enforced, or by whoever in Iraq taking these actions to make it happen. But this is probably the mother of all hypotheticals. Give me a phone call when it happens.

White House Press Briefing, October 23, 2002

Q. Ari, what happens if the Security Council fails to reach an agreement on a new resolution against Iraq?

Mr. Fleischer. Well, let's see what happens at the United Nations. No one is going to know what the outcome of any vote at the United Nations Security Council will be until members of the Security Council raise their hand and vote. And there is movement in New York. We'll see ultimately where it takes us, but the diplomats are earning their salaries and are working very hard on the actual language now.

Q. Do you all have any deadline? Are you looking at this week for the U.N. to either reach some consensus, or are you planning to take this resolution to the full council?

Mr. Fleischer. They are hard at work in New York, and I think the best way to describe where they are is the end is coming into sight, but it's not here yet. They have some amount of time left, but not a lot. And the President knows that, and I think the U.N. knows that, too.

Q.—some amount of time left, what that means?

Mr. Fleischer. I would not hazard a guess on it. The U.N. is a very deliberative body—and this has probably been the most deliberative debate of the United Nations Security Council in the history of the United Nations. It's been a thoughtful debate, a deliberative debate and a lengthy debate. It's coming to an end, but it's not here yet.

Q. And I have one more. Not to go over the language, what you're willing to accept or not, but are you all at the point where you feel like you've negotiated enough, that you've made enough compromises that your position is pretty set on what United States will support in a resolution?

Mr. Fleischer. I think that everybody clearly understands that the American position is a position that's shared by many—and we'll see if it's shared by all—is that there must be a tough inspection regime, that there must be consequences if Saddam Hussein fails to honor the previous United Nations resolutions, and that there must be a finding that Saddam Hussein is in material breech, as the United Nations has previously found.

Q. Is the U.S. calling a full Security Council meeting for this afternoon?

Mr. Fleischer. There is movement and that is not ruled out. There very well may be additional action broadened to the E-10 beyond the P-5—in other words, to all 15 members of the Security Council. Any such announcement will come out of New York.

Q. Does that mean that there has been or has not been agreement reached between the U.S. and France?

Mr. Fleischer. Well, while there is movement which is, in and of itself, a good thing, it is impossible to say whether or not movement will yield to agreement. The process is moving forward and we'll see ultimately if that process leads to agreement. It does not necessarily mean that everybody yet agrees. That's why I said that there is only one way to know if everybody agrees, and that's when they raise their hand.

Q. And on that issue, when it goes to the full Security Council, the United States will need the votes of others outside of the Permanent Five. Mexico is one of those countries. Does the President expect Mexico to vote in favor of this? Has he talked to President Fox about this?

Mr. Fleischer. I don't think it would be my role to describe how a sovereign nation will vote. Of course, the President hopes Mexico will support the American position. We'll find out.

Q. Ari, if there's not an agreement among the P-5 on the language of a U.N. resolution, might the United States take it to the Elected 10 as a form of putting a leaver on some of the intransigent members of the P-5?

Mr. Fleischer. As I indicated there, there is movement and that's a very good possibility. That could clearly be one of the ways the movement is expressed. I think if that were to be the case you would hear from people in New York. And it's something you should keep your eye on.

Q. Are we hearing from some of our allies on the E-10 that, let's get going on this, bring it to us, and we'll put the arm on France?

Mr. Fleischer. I think people understand that after 11 years of Saddam Hussein defying the United Nations, the United Nations has to face up to its mission. And one way or another the United Nations is going to have to make a decision. They've been engaged in a very thoughtful and deliberative debate, and the debate is coming to a close. And the members of the Security Council feel the debate coming to a close, and I think they want to do their part to constructively engage on what type of closing this will be. The events are coming together.

Q. Would the French not see this as ganging up and dig their heels in even further?

Mr. Fleischer. Again, it's not my place to characterize what other nations would think or not think. I have no reason to believe that would be accurate. Everybody understands that at a certain point, and the point is arriving, the United Nations Security Council has to make a decision.

* * * *

Q. The President has always prided himself in having a lot of patience. And you have told us from this podium that we're still within the time frame for a resolution at the U.N. But were the President's patience wearing a little thin yesterday when he said he doesn't want the U.N. to be like the League of Nations, or when he doesn't want it to be just a debating body?

Mr. Fleischer. When the President says he doesn't want the U.N. to be like the League of Nations, it's not a sign of patience or impatience. It's a fact. And the United Nations has an important decision before it, and it's the decision that the President laid out on September 12th. And I think that this is why the United Nations Security Council has approached this issue with the care and the deliberation that it has.

The fact of the matter is, until the President went to New York and made the speech on September 12th, the United Nations was slumbering in terms of whether it would hold Iraq accountable for the resolutions that it previously passed. And that wasn't acceptable. And now the world is facing up to what is, or is not, acceptable, and we'll see.

* * * *

Q. Ari, the full text of the U.N. resolution, as proposed by the U.S., was introduced yesterday morning to the P-5. Has the U.S. accepted any changes in that text since then?

Mr. Fleischer. There are going to be continuing conversations, and they are really working now on the every word, every sentence, every paragraph level. The diplomats are earning their keep. They are doing what they should be doing for a living. Nobody has ruled out that there could be any changes. But the core of the resolution must be as I described it earlier in order for the U.N. to keep the peace, and that is that there must be material breach, there must be consequences, and there must be a tough inspection regime.

Q. Consequences—a mention of serious consequences, or consequences must be part of the language of resolution?

Mr. Fleischer. That's been made very plain.

Q. So you're saying the U.S. is willing to accept changes, but not to change those items you just mentioned?

Mr. Fleischer. Well, let me turn it around. Can you imagine after a decade of Saddam Hussein defying the United Nations and after having successfully thrown out the inspectors for four years, the United Nations message to Saddam Hussein is, you can continue to do it because there won't be consequences? That's rather hard to imagine now that the United Nations Security Council is hard at work at bringing this to a successful resolution.

Remarks by Secretary of State Powell, October 23, 2002

Secretary Colin Powell delivered his remarks while in Los Cabos, Mexico for a meeting of APEC foreign ministers.

Q. Can you tell us anything on the latest developments in the Security Council? Do you feel that you're making progress towards a resolution?

Secretary Powell. Well, we've had intense but useful conversations with the Perm Five Members over the last couple of days and we felt that sufficient progress had been made that it was appropriate at this time to circulate the resolution in its current form to all 15 members and that's what Ambassador Negroponte did earlier today. Now all fifteen members will have an opportunity to examine our proposed resolution in detail, and then I believe they'll be meeting again on Friday to go over it, as is the case in such matters, line by line, paragraph by paragraph.

We have listened carefully to our friends in the Perm Five and also consulted with the 10 elected members, and we have tried to be accommodating where it was appropriate, but we are not going to move off basic principles, and the basic principles are those you've heard us discuss on a number of occasions of recent weeks. One, there has to be a clear indictment that Iraq has been in material breach of its obligations. Two, there have to be consequences for this kind of behavior if it continues. Three, let's put in place a tough inspection regime, an inspection regime that cannot be defeated or deterred or disrupted by Iraqi misbehavior.

We've been working very close with Dr. Hans Blix and Dr. ElBaradei of IAEA, to hear their ideas of the kind of regime they'd like to see and have them listen to our ideas as well. And what we want to do is give them what they need to do the job, and that job has to be the disarmament of Iraq, of weapons of mass destruction. And it's also absolutely clear that this issue of consequences has to remain in any resolution so that Iraq knows that if it continues this pattern of violation, it will suffer consequences. This is not a new concept or new language, it is language that has been in previous U.N. resolutions with respect to consequences of continued failure to comply.

So we will continue our discussions and consultations, and we'll see where we go. I don't think this will go on for a much, much longer period of time, there is now a resolution before the Security Council for circulation, we'll see what comments come back.

President Bush will have an opportunity to engage a number of leaders over the next several days, President Jiang Zemin of China on Thursday, and President Putin on Saturday, and also President Fox on Saturday, President Fox of course, as you all know, Mexico is one of the members of the Security Council, one of the elected members of the Security Council, and there are other meetings that are taking place that will move the process along.

Q. Do you still consider this a negotiation? Is there anything to negotiate as far as the United States is concerned, will we accept amendments to the resolution? Do you expect there to be any changes at all?

Secretary Powell. It is a consultation, we put it out for circulation, meaning that a number of countries are reading it complete for the first time in its current version, and when they get back together on Friday, no doubt that members will have had 24 hours to consult with their capitals, and will come forward with ideas, and we will listen to those ideas, but we have done a great deal in recent weeks to try to accommodate some of the issues that were raised, but we cannot walk away from the basic principles that I described earlier, or else there's no point in it.

It cannot just be another pointless resolution that Iraq can sit back and smile at, and not comply with in the knowledge that there will be no consequences as a result of their non-compliance. That is not acceptable. The United States will not accept that, President Bush has made it clear that this would be an unacceptable outcome.

Q. Listening to their views, would you, is the United States open to any changes in this second revision?

Secretary Powell. We have been, because we are listening to their views and consulting, obviously, if they come up with points that seem to make sense and don't violate the principles that I've laid out, we would certainly look at it. I can't say whether any changes would be accepted or not, but it's not a fiat that we have put down. It is a circulating draft, and we will see what reaction it draws. I have to give all of the members time to reflect on it, and consult with their capitals.

Q. Does the fact that you are opening it now to the E-10 as well mean that you are pretty confident, you have to be very confident, since you can't have a rejection from the P-5, I mean, are you confident that there's not going to be a rejection?

Secretary Powell. I'm not going to predict what any member of the body would do, the Security Council would do, especially members of the P-5, they can speak for themselves, but I think that a lot of the work that has taken place over the last couple of weeks have dealt with some of the concerns, some of the issues that were raised by members of the Security Council. We felt that the resolution reached the point where it was appropriate to expand it out beyond the Permanent Five to all 15 members, so I wouldn't have done that unless I had thought that we had put down a resolution that is deserving of support, but that will be for each member country to decide.

White House Press Briefing, October 24, 2002

Q. Ari, on another subject, President Fox today said he had sympathies for the French and Russian argument on the U.N. resolution, and he declined to back what the French and the Russians want to do. Will the President try to change his mind?

Mr. Fleischer. I haven't heard that, so I would hesitate to comment on it. But of course the President looks forward to talking to all members of the Security Council that he'll see at APEC. But he'll have other conversations with President Fox, too. So they'll—I'm sure the topic of Iraq is going to come up in the President's conversations with the President of Mexico.

Remarks by Secretary of State Powell, October 24, 2002

Secretary Colin Powell delivered his remarks while in Los Cabos, Mexico for a meeting of APEC foreign ministers.

Q. Regarding the Iraq attack, it is said you are preparing the military activity in Iraq. What do you think will be the impact of the APEC economy after you start attacking Iraq? Thank you.

Secretary Powell. The United States is working hard to find a diplomatic solution, which is why we have engaged the United Nations Security Council in the most intense set of discussions. Those discussions are continuing at the United Nations in New York and I have had a number of very helpful discussions here among my APEC colleagues.

We are very mindful of the concerns that you raised. Obviously, we always have to plan for whatever contingencies might exist in the future but no decision has been made with respect to military action. President Bush has said repeatedly that he hopes that this can be solved peacefully.

But it is absolutely clear—and I think there is agreement among my colleagues and agreement among all of the members of the international community—that Iraq must face its obligations, it must stop violating the U.N. resolutions that apply to it, Iraq must give up its weapons of mass destruction.

And I hope that the United Nations will come to closure in the near future on a new Security Council resolution that will make it clear that if inspectors go back in, they go back in with new authority and with all of the ability to disarm Iraq that they might need to complete that mission, and that finally, there must be consequences if Iraq does not comply with this resolution.

So let us all hope that this is a matter that can be resolved peacefully, but the outcome has to be Iraq disarmed of weapons of mass destruction.

When we see the kinds of terrorist attacks that afflict so many countries represented here today and we see what's happening around the world, it's clear that as part of the efforts against terrorism there also has to be an effort against those nations that develop weapons of mass destruction which, if they fell into the hands of terrorists, would be the worst sort of consequences for all of us to contemplate.

And so I believe that our efforts with respect to Iraq should be considered part of our overall campaign against terrorism. We have no ill will against the people of Iraq but we believe that they are led by a very despotic, dictatorial regime, and this regime has to respond to the demands of the international community.

Remarks by Secretary of Defense Rumsfeld, October 24, 2002

Secretary Rumsfeld was interviewed by Jim Clancy and Zain Verjee of CNN International.

Q. Mr. Secretary, it is not an exaggeration to say I think the people around the world probably know you better than they do George W. Bush, the President of the United States, because they see you so often in this room at the briefings talking about important issues, issues that affect everyone around the globe. But if I watch their response, if I listen to what they're saying, I hear from them constantly, even from those who would like to support the United States, that the evidence simply isn't there to support unilateral action against Baghdad.

Secretary Rumsfeld. Interesting. The President, of course, has not proposed unilateral action against Baghdad, and so I suppose it's not surprising that people don't feel that a decision has been made or that it's time to be supportive of that. What he has—is trying to do is very difficult. It is to connect the dots, what might happen before something happens. If you think in the United States, right now the Congress of the United States is holding hearings on what happened on September 11th last year, and they're trying to connect the dots. What did somebody know? And what might we have done to have prevented that attack? What could the intelligence community or the law enforcement community or the people who hand out visas—all of those things—how might that have been avoided? And that's a difficult thing to do. They're having a great deal of difficulty trying to do that. It's even more difficult to do before the fact.

Now, you used the word "unilateral," which I think is kind of a catchphrase to mean nothing should happen—

Q. I mean, you're pushing the envelope. You're leaning forward, in your own terminology.

Secretary Rumsfeld. Yeah, the fact of the matter is that the President has put together 90 nations in the global war on terrorism. It's the largest coalition in the history of humankind. It's breathtaking in its breadth and its depth. And they are cooperating all across the globe with intelligence sharing and closing bank accounts of terrorists. It's been a wonderfully successful effort. I can assure you that, if the President decides that something needs to be done, which he has not, with respect to Iraq and if Iraq resists the kinds of inspections that clearly the United Nations as a world body has been attempting to impose on Iraq since 1991, that it would not be alone. There are dozens of countries—

Q. But right now—

Secretary Rumsfeld.—who have supported the United States and are supporting the United States. And in the event anything is decided, I can assure you there would be a large number of countries participating.

Q. But right now we're not to that point. The point that we're at right now—

Secretary Rumsfeld. Because the President hasn't made a decision.

Q. That's right. Among other reasons. Another reason that people say is the evidence—now, you're talking about the war on terror.

Secretary Rumsfeld. Mmm-hmm [in agreement.]

Q. This link between al Qaeda and Baghdad, people say it doesn't even exist; there isn't a shred of evidence to show that such a link even exists.

Secretary Rumsfeld. You're correct. People are saying that. It happens not to be true.

Q. Well, what is the truth then? What is the evidence?

Secretary Rumsfeld. Well, the truth is that the Central Intelligence Agency, the director of Central Intelligence, has testified and made public some unclassified instances of the relationship between Saddam Hussein's Iraq and al Qaeda. It's there. It's a matter of record. And it's still evolving. It's still unfolding. There's no question but that Iraq is a terrorist state. They've been on the terrorist list for many years. There's no question but that they have used chemicals on their own people as well as their neighbors. There's no question but that they have biological weapons.

Q. That's proved. The al Qaeda link, though, is what I think people all around the world are looking and saying this isn't so much a case, in their view, that it's imminent danger to the United States of America. They see an imminent opportunity by Rumsfeld, Wolfowitz and others to push a very hard-line agenda for regime change, not only in Iraq but beyond Iraq.

Secretary Rumsfeld. Hmm. Well, I don't deny for a minute that some people in the press like to paint it that way.

Q. Well, it's not only in the press.

Secretary Rumsfeld. But the fact is that that's just simply not true. Our job in the Department of Defense is not to make recommendations with respect to these things. It's to be prepared to develop contingency plans for the kinds of things that might occur and, in the event that the President and the Congress and the country decide to do something, be capable of doing it effectively on behalf of the country.

* * * *

Q. Mr. Secretary, you talk a lot—and I want to give you an opportunity to bring the point home—about why development of weapons of mass destruction and the war against terror, the spread of terror around the globe, really have a lot to do with all of us in the world, that this isn't just a U.S. issue whether these two things meet, terrorism and weapons of mass destruction.

Secretary Rumsfeld. The—first, the issues you're raising and that you say people are raising, I think are important issues. And they're issues that need to be discussed. It's useful that they are elevated into the public debate and the public dialogue. I find that helpful. We spend a great deal of time analyzing the variety of risks that could occur in the event that force were used, as well as the risks that could occur in the event that nothing is done. And so I think it's a helpful thing to have that kind of a debate and dialogue in the world, and we welcome it.

The nexus between weapons of mass destruction and terrorist states is at the heart of the problem. In the last century we were dealing essentially with conventional capabilities. Nuclear weapons have existed since 1945. They've not been used in anger since that year. It's a wonderful compliment to human beings that those things have existed and not been used. The 21st century is a different situation. With the end of the Cold War and the end of the Soviet Union, the movement of these technologies all across the globe into the hands of lots of people—chemical weapons, biological weapons, and in increasing number of instances, nuclear weapons—mean that the nature of the threat is not that two or three hundred people or even two or three thousand people will die, but that potentially twenty, thirty, or forty thousand people can die—two hundred thousand people can die. And, therefore, one has to consider that in a different context, a different security environment.

Q. Let me follow that up and just ask you this: If Saddam Hussein admitted—says, "I've got weapons of mass destruction; bring the inspectors in; destroy them; we're not going to—set up a monitoring program," would the U.S. back down on the idea of a regime change?

Secretary Rumsfeld. Well, the regime change is something that the Congress of the United States passed, oh, gosh, I think in 1998. It's been a number of years. It's been the policy of the United States. The people who have watched Saddam Hussein over a period of time have seen him systematically lie and resist inspections. Inspections only work in a country that wants to cooperate with them and they've decided they want the international community to come in and then they can prove to the world that they're honest, open and exactly what they say. You know, you say what if he were to decide to do that. That's like saying what if I were to decide to jump over the moon. The likelihood of him doing that is so small. I just—it's—he has a record systematically of preventing inspections and of denying his people the billions of dollars from his oil revenues that he could have if the sanctions were lifted, which he refuses to do because he's unwilling to have inspections because he's determined to have weapons of mass destruction.

Q. Are you as determined to see that he's out of power?

Secretary Rumsfeld. It's not for me. I'm the Secretary of Defense of the United States.

Q. But you have your own personal views?

Secretary Rumsfeld. Well, my goodness, I give my personal views to the President of the United States, and it's for him to make those decisions—and the Congress and the world. And he's been very measured. He's been very balanced on it. He's decided to go to the Congress and received an overwhelming vote. It apparently is the vote of the Congress that regime change is the policy of the United States. He's gone to the United Nations and made his case. And the evidence of the distinctive nature of the Iraqi regime, it seems to me, is compelling and powerful. He made a very strong case. I think people ought to re-read that speech.

* * * *

Q. Welcome back to Q&A and our conversation with Donald Rumsfeld, the U.S. Secretary of Defense.

It was back in 1983 I think, and it was right when the State Department was announcing they had evidence that Iraq had used chemical weapons against the Iranians during that long and brutal war, you had to go to Baghdad on a U.S. diplomatic mission. You got to meet Saddam Hussein. I want to get a little bit of your impressions about the man personally. Are you sure it was him? Because he's supposed to have doubles.

Secretary Rumsfeld. He does have doubles. Well, he said he was him, but we had a—I went in at the request of President Reagan and Secretary of State George Schultz to serve as Middle East envoy for a period after we had 241 Marines killed in Beirut, Lebanon. And I—one of the pieces was to visit the various countries in the region and see if we couldn't put some pressure on Syria that was occupying Lebanon at the time, and still is to this day, and engaging in terrorist activities, which they still are today—cooperating with Iran and bringing terrorists down through the Bekaa Valley into Lebanon and Israel. But one of the pieces of it was to go to Iraq. They were engaged in a conflict with Iran, and our interest was in having them be more of a balance in the—

with respect to the Middle East situation and complicate the world for Syria. And so we went in and visited with him briefly and—or for a day or so—and had a good meeting. He's—he clearly is a survivor. He's tough. And he has—runs a very repressive, vicious regime.

Draft Resolution Submitted to the President of the United Nations Security Council by the United Kingdom and United States, October 25, 2002

This draft served as the formal basis for discussions among members of the Security Council concerning action with regard to Iraq.

The Security Council,

Recalling all its previous relevant resolutions, in particular its resolutions 661 (1990) of 6 August 1990, 686 (1991) of 2 March 1991, 678 (1990) of 29 November 1990, 687 (1991) of 3 April 1991, 688 (1991) of 5 April 1991, 986 (1995) of 14 April 1995, and 1284 (1999) of 17 December 1999, and all the relevant statements of its President,

Recognizing the threat Iraq's non-compliance with Security Council resolutions and proliferation of weapons of mass destruction and long-range missiles poses to international peace and security,

Recalling that its resolution 678 (1990) authorized member States to use all necessary means to uphold and implement its resolution 660 (1990) of 2 August 1990 and all relevant resolutions subsequent to resolution 660 (1990) and to restore international peace and security in the area,

Further recalling that its resolution 687 (1991) imposed obligations on Iraq as a necessary step for achievement of its stated objective of restoring international peace and security in the area,

Deploring the fact that Iraq has never provided an accurate, full, final, and complete disclosure, as required by resolution 687 (1991), of all aspects of its programmes to develop weapons of mass destruction and ballistic missiles with a range greater than one hundred and fifty kilometers, and of all holdings of such weapons, their components and production facilities and locations, as well as all other nuclear programmes, including any which it claims are for purposes not related to nuclear-weapons-usable material,

Deploring further that Iraq repeatedly refused to allow access to sites designated by the United Nations Special Commission (UNSCOM), refused to cooperate fully and unconditionally with UNSCOM and International Atomic Energy Agency (IAEA) weapons inspectors, as required by resolution 687 (1991), ultimately ceased all cooperation with UNSCOM and IAEA in 1998, and for the last three years has failed to provide immediate, unconditional, and unrestricted access to the United Nations Monitoring, Verification and Inspection Commission (UNMOVIC) established in resolution 1284 (1999) as the successor organization to UNSCOM, and the IAEA, as it was first obliged to do pursuant to resolution 687 (1991), and as the Council has repeatedly demanded that it do, and regretting the consequent prolonging of the crisis in the region and the suffering of the Iraqi people,

Deploring also that the Government of Iraq has failed to comply with its commitments pursuant to resolution 687 (1991) with regard to terrorism, pursuant to resolution 688 (1991) to end repression of its civilian population and to provide access by international humanitarian organizations to all those in need of assistance in Iraq, and pursuant to resolutions 686 (1991), 687 (1991), and 1284 (1999) to return or cooperate in accounting for Kuwaiti and third country nationals wrongfully detained by Iraq, or to return Kuwaiti property wrongfully seized by Iraq,

Recalling that in its resolution 687 (1991) the Council declared that a cease-fire would be based on acceptance by Iraq of the provisions of that resolution, including the obligations on Iraq contained therein,

Determined to ensure full and immediate compliance by Iraq without conditions or restrictions with its obligations under resolution 687 (1991) and other relevant resolutions and recalling that the resolutions of the Council constitute the governing standard of Iraqi compliance,

Recalling that the effective operation of UNMOVIC, as the successor organization to the Special Commission, and the IAEA, is essential for the implementation of resolution 687 (1991) and other relevant resolutions,

Noting the letter dated 16 September 2002 from the Minister for Foreign Affairs of Iraq addressed to the Secretary-General is a necessary first step toward rectifying Iraq's continued failure to comply with relevant Security Council resolutions,

Noting further the letter dated 8 October 2002 from the Executive Chairman of UNMOVIC and the Director-General of the IAEA to General Al-Saadi of the Government of Iraq laying out the practical arrangements, agreed in Vienna, that are prerequisites for the resumption of inspections in Iraq by UNMOVIC and the IAEA, and expressing the gravest concern at the continued failure by the Government of Iraq to provide confirmation of the arrangements as laid out in that letter,

Determined to secure full compliance with its decisions,

Acting under Chapter VII of the Charter of the United Nations,

1. Decides that Iraq is still, and has been for a number of years, in material breach of its obligations under relevant resolutions, including resolution 687 (1991),

    in particular through Iraq's failure to cooperate with United Nations inspectors and the IAEA, and to complete the actions required under paragraphs 8 to 13 of resolution 687 (1991);

2. Recalls that the Council has repeatedly warned Iraq that it will face serious consequences as a result of its continued violations of its obligations;

3. Decides that, in order to begin to comply with its disarmament obligations, in addition to submitting the required biannual declarations, the Government of Iraq shall provide to UNMOVIC, IAEA, and the Security Council, not later than 30 days from the date of this resolution, a currently accurate, full and complete declaration of all aspects of its programmes to develop chemical, biological and nuclear weapons, ballistic missiles, and other delivery systems such as unmanned aerial vehicles and dispersal systems designed for use on aircraft, including any holdings and precise locations of such weapons, components, subcomponents, stocks of agents, and related material and equipment, the locations and work of its research, development and production facilities, as well as all other chemical, biological and nuclear programmes,

including any which it claims are for purposes not related to weapon production or material;

4. Decides that false statements or omissions in the declarations submitted by Iraq pursuant to this resolution and failure by Iraq at any time to comply with, and cooperate fully in the implementation of, this resolution shall constitute a further material breach of Iraq's obligations;

5. Decides that Iraq shall provide UNMOVIC and IAEA immediate,

unimpeded, unconditional, and unrestricted access to any and all, including underground, areas, facilities, buildings, equipment, records, and means of transport which they wish to inspect, as well as immediate, unimpeded, unrestricted, and private access to all officials and other persons whom UNMOVIC or IAEA wish to interview in the mode or location of UNMOVIC's or IAEA's choice pursuant to any aspect of their mandates; further decides that UNMOVIC and IAEA may at their discretion conduct interviews inside or outside of Iraq, may facilitate the travel of those interviewed and family members outside of Iraq, and that, at the sole discretion of UNMOVIC and IAEA, such interviews may occur without the presence of observers from the Iraqi government; and instructs UNMOVIC and requests the IAEA to resume inspections no later than 45 days following adoption of this resolution and to update the Council 60 days thereafter;

6. Endorses the 8 October 2002 letter from the Executive Chairman of UNMOVIC and the Director General of the IAEA to General Al-Saadi of the Government of Iraq, which is annexed hereto, and decides that the contents of the letter shall be binding upon Iraq;

7. Decides further that, in view of the prolonged interruption by Iraq of the presence of UNMOVIC and IAEA and in order for them to accomplish the tasks set forth in paragraph 3 above and notwithstanding prior understandings, the Security Council hereby establishes the following revised or additional authorities, which shall be binding upon Iraq notwithstanding prior understandings, to facilitate their work in Iraq:

• UNMOVIC and IAEA shall determine the composition of their inspection teams in such a way as to ensure that these teams are composed of the most qualified and experienced experts available, and all UNMOVIC and IAEA personnel shall enjoy the privileges and immunities corresponding to those of experts on mission;

• UNMOVIC and IAEA shall have unrestricted rights of entry into and out of Iraq, the right to free, unrestricted, and immediate movement to and from inspection sites, and the right to inspect any sites and buildings, including immediate, unimpeded, unconditional, and unrestricted access to Presidential Sites equal to that at other sites, notwithstanding the provisions of resolution 1154 (1998);

• UNMOVIC and IAEA shall have the right to be provided by Iraq the names of all personnel associated with Iraq's chemical, biological, nuclear and ballistic missile programmes and the associated research, development and production facilities;

• Security of UNMOVIC and IAEA facilities shall be ensured by sufficient United Nations security guards;

• UNMOVIC and IAEA shall have the right to declare for the purposes of freezing a site to be inspected no-fly/no-drive zones, exclusion zones, and/or ground and air transit corridors;

• UNMOVIC and IAEA shall have the free and unrestricted use and landing of fixed and rotary winged aircraft, including unmanned reconnaissance vehicles;

• UNMOVIC and IAEA shall have the right at their sole discretion verifiably to remove, destroy, or render harmless all prohibited weapons, subsystems, components, records, materials, and other related items, and the right to impound or close any facilities or equipment for the production thereof;

• UNMOVIC and IAEA shall have the right to free import and use of equipment or materials for inspections and to seize and export any equipment, materials, or documents taken during inspections, without search of UNMOVIC or IAEA personnel or official or personal baggage; and

• UNMOVIC and IAEA shall have access to any information that any member State is willing to provide;

8. Decides further that Iraq shall not take or threaten hostile acts directed against any representative or personnel of the United Nations or of any Member State taking action to uphold any Security Council resolution;

9. Requests the Secretary-General immediately to notify Iraq of this resolution and decides that within seven days following such notification, Iraq shall state its acceptance;

10. Requests all Member States to give full support to UNMOVIC and the IAEA in the discharge of their mandates, including by providing any information on Iraqi attempts since 1998 to acquire prohibited items and by recommending sites to be inspected, persons to be interviewed, conditions of such interviews, and data to be collected, the results of which shall be reported to the Council by UNMOVIC and the IAEA;

11. Directs the Executive Chairman of UNMOVIC and the Director General of the IAEA to report immediately to the Council any interference by Iraq with inspection activities, as well as any failure by Iraq to comply with its disarmament obligations, including its obligations regarding inspections under this resolution;

12. Decides to convene immediately upon receipt of a report in accordance with paragraph 11 above, in order to consider the situation and the need for full compliance with all of the relevant Security Council resolutions in order to restore international peace and security;

13. Decides to remain seized of the matter.

Draft United Nations Security Council Resolution from the Russian Federation, October 25, 2002

This draft resolution concerning action with regard to Iraq was informally circulated by the Russian Federation to members of the Security Council. A similar draft resolution was circulated by the Government of France on October 2, 2002.

The Security Council,

Reaffirming its resolutions 687 (1991), 699 (1991),707 (1991), 715 (1991), 1060 (1996), 1154 (1998) and 1284 (1999) and all other relevant resolutions and statements of its President, which establish the criteria for Iraqi compliance,

Reaffirming also its resolution 1382 (2001) and its intention to implement it fully,

Noting with grave concern the absence in Iraq of any international monitoring, inspection and verification body with regard to weapons of mass destruction and ballistic missiles since December 1998,

Commending the Secretary General and the Secretary General of the League of Arab States for their unrelenting efforts,

Taking note of the letter dated 16 September 2002 of the minister of foreign affairs of the Republic of Iraq (S/2002/1034) in which Iraq accepts the return of the United Nations weapons inspectors to Iraq without conditions,

Welcoming the efforts of the Executive. Chairman of UNMOVIC and the Director General of IAEA, and taking note of the agreement reached in Vienna on the practical arrangements necessary for the immediate resumption of inspections in accordance with the provisions of the relevant resolutions, on the basis of the proposals made by UNMOVIC and lAEA,

Underlying that the resumption of inspections by UNMOVIC and IAEA would be a first step towards a comprehensive settlement based on full implementation of all relevant resolutions of the Council, full compliance by Iraq of its obligations in the field of disarmament, and opening the way to ending the prohibitions referred to in Council's resolution 687,

Determined to secure full compliance with its relevant resolutions, in particular its resolutions 687 (1991) and 1284 (1999). Recalling the objective of the establishment of a nuclear weapon-free zone in the region of the Middle East,

Reiterating the commitment of all Member States to the sovereignty, territorial integrity and political independence of Iraq, Kuwait and other neighboring States,

Acting under Chapter VII of the Charter of the United Nations,

1. Demands that Iraq cooperate immediately, unconditionally and actively with the United Nations Monitoring, Verification and Inspection Commission (UNMOVIC) and the International Atomic Energy Agency (IAEA);

2. Reaffirms all the obligations of Iraq contained in all relevant resolutions and, in particular resolutions 687 (1991), 699 (1991), 707 (1991) and 715 (1991), 1051 (1996), 1154 (1998) and 1284 (1999) with regard to immediate, unconditional and unrestricted access in Iraq to any and all areas, facilities, equipments, records, means of transport which UNMOVIC and the IAEA wish to inspect as well as to all officials and other persons under the authority of the Iraqi Government whom UNMOVIC and the IAEA wish to interview so that both organs may fully discharge their mandate, and underlines that Iraq will be fully accountable for the safety of the teams of UNMOVIC and IAEA;

3. Endorses the letter dated 8 October 2002 from the Executive Chairman of UNMOVIC and the Director General of IAEA to General Al-Saadi of the Government of Iraq, which is annexed hereto and the practical arrangements contained therein;

4. Directs the Executive Chairman of UNMOVIC to improve the modalities necessary to ensure the full implementation of the provisions of the memorandum of understanding (S/1998/166) endorsed by the Security Council in its resolution 1154 (1998) so as to allow UNMOVIC and lAEA teams immediate, unconditional and unrestricted access as referred to in paragraph 2 above;

5. Demands that Iraq, in order to facilitate the establishment by UNMOVIC and IAEA of their work program as referred to in Security Council's resolution 1284

(1999), provides without delay a complete, detailed and updated declaration on all its past programmes and remaining capacities to develop weapons of mass destruction and ballistic missiles with a range greater than 150 km;

6. Member States and in particular those with special capabilities in this field, to cooperate fully with UNMOVIC and lAEA by providing them any information related to prohibited programmes in accordance with the procedures developed by UNMOVIC in this area;

7. Supports the Secretary General in his ongoing efforts, in particular to ensure the implementation of this resolution, and expresses its full confidence in and support for IAEA and its Director General, and UNMOVIC and its Executive Chairman, in the discharge of their mandate with all necessary professionalism and strictness;

8. Confirms the full relevance of the goals of section D of resolution 1284 (1999) and its intention to act accordingly,

9. Directs the Executive Chairman of UNMOVIC and the Director General of lARA to report immediately to the Council any serious failure by Iraq to comply with its obligations referred to in paragraphs 2, 3 and 4 above;

10. Decides to convene immediately upon receipt of a report in accordance with paragraph 9 above, in order to consider the situation and the needed steps to ensure full compliance with relevant Security Council resolutions;

11. Decides to remain seized of the matter.

Remarks by United Nations Secretary-General Annan, October 25, 2002

Q. Sir, we understand that negotiations are starting in a hard way about Iraq in the Security Council and that now even Russia and France are submitting their own version of a working paper. Do you feel that this is going to slow things down? What do you think about the state of negotiations now?

Secretary-General Annan. First of all, we shouldn't forget that the resolution, the draft resolution, was given to the members only this week, on Monday. There's been lots of discussions in capitals between the P-5 but the Council as such just got the resolution. And I think there's going to be quite a lot of discussions amongst the members. And it's appropriate, because we're dealing with a very serious matter. It's democracy in practice; it takes a bit of time but with patience, we'll get an optimal decision.

* * * *

Q. Mr. Secretary-General, there is a possibility we might not reach a resolution. Ari Fleischer said there is a 50-50 chance. Now, we understand from Hans Blix and El-Baradei that the only reason they are not there is because they don't want a resolution to come and change their mandate halfway. If we don't reach a resolution, an agreement—and I'm sure you'd like to see a unified Council—do you see any reason why they shouldn't go to Iraq straight away?

Secretary-General Annan. In the first place, I do expect a Council resolution and I expect it to be unanimous. There's hard discussions going on, and I hope in the end they will be fruitful, and that the inspectors will go back to Iraq with the support of a united Council behind them.

Remarks by Secretary of State Powell, October 26, 2002

Secretary Colin Powell delivered his remarks while attending a meeting of APEC leaders in Los Cabos, Mexico.

Q. Mr. Secretary, you talked about the six weeks of diplomacy on the Iraq resolution and, yet, in the last 24 hours at least four countries that will have a vote on the Security Council—Mexico, Russia, China and France—have either opposed the resolution or resisted a public opportunity to embrace it. Can you tell us whether it's as bad as it looks publicly, or whether you can point to any sign of the progress that has been made in the last six weeks that would give any hope that this resolution might actually pass?

Secretary Powell. A lot of progress has been made in the last six weeks. And I don't want to say that we're near a solution because it may evade us. But I think we have successfully narrowed down the differences to a few key issues. And if we can resolve these few key issues in the days ahead, then I think we might get a resolution that will be strong.

Everybody is committed to getting a strong resolution. A weak resolution would not serve the interest of the United Nations, it would not disarm Iraq, and I think it would be an abject failure. So I think everybody is committed to a strong resolution and we have narrowed down the differences considerably. It remains to be seen whether we can resolve those remaining differences.

Q. What are the sticking points?

Secretary Powell. How you characterize future Iraqi violations in the presence of a new resolution, how you characterize it and what happens once it has been characterized.

Remarks by Secretary of State Powell, October 28, 2002

Secretary Colin Powell was interviewed by a group of European journalists.

Q. Mr. Secretary, do you have a deadline in mind for the negotiations in the U.N.?

Secretary Powell. I don't have a specific deadline. But obviously, we have to bring this to closure in the near future. We have narrowed our differences considerably, but there still are differences. We are working hard to see if those differences can be resolved. If they can be resolved, they'll be resolved shortly, I think. It's not a matter of needing to send it out for analysis.

If those differences can be resolved, I think we can get a resolution that will enjoy broad support. If those differences cannot be resolved, then we will have difficulty. But I've been working all day long on this issue. It is narrowing, but I'm not yet ready to declare success or failure. We're hard at work. This is a very important issue. The United States, as I've said all along, wants to hear from its partners in the Security Council, believes that it would be the in the best interest of resolving this issue to have a resolution that enjoys strong support from the Council. And it would be the best possible signal to Iraq that it is time for them to cooperate.

But the resolution must be clear with respect to Iraq's violations. The resolution must be clear with respect to the tough inspection regime. I think Dr. Blix and Dr. ElBaradei spoke to that earlier today. And it must be an inspection regime that will not give Saddam Hussein the opportunity to deceive it. I think there is a strong view throughout the Council on that point. It must be a resolution that one way or the other—and this is where the points of disagreement are—but one way or the other, it must lead to consequences if Iraq fails again.

And I don't think there is disagreement on that point either. The disagreement is how you determine and arrive at those consequences. It would be much better for all concerned if we could find a way that the Council is united and worked together as a council on these elements that I've just discussed. And that's what we're trying to achieve. But as the President has made clear all along, this is a problem that we cannot turn our head away from, that we believe strongly the United Nations—us, as part of the United Nations—should meet its obligation at this time and not let Iraq, once again, thwart the will of the international community.

And I hope we'll be able to achieve that outcome. If we are unable to achieve that outcome, as the President has said, the United States will not look away and walk away from this problem. We don't want to be in the position some time in the future of seeing Iraq in possession of these weapons and threatening the world with these weapons or even using these weapons or letting others use these weapons, and then look in the mirror and ask ourselves the question, "Why didn't we do something when we could?"

Q. You said Saturday in Los Cabos that there were maybe two issues remaining. One was the characterization of future violations and the consequences. Are we still there or do you think—

Secretary Powell. Yes, it's—it's pretty much the—you know, I'm a car—I love cars. But that's where the gears—that's where the gears still grind a little bit. So I'm working on the clutch.

Q. But is—

Secretary Powell. Yes, that's where the gears are not quite meshed. And even when we solve these two areas, there are other issues that people will want to discuss. It's a fairly extensive resolution. But these—the two that you just touched on, that I touched on in Los Cabos, are the key ones. And when those are resolved—if those are resolved—and I hope they will be—if those are resolved, there will be other areas people will wish to discuss.

But I think the major problem will be resolved—the major problems will be resolved. I mean, I take note of the fact that when we started out debating this, there was a lot of concern about this tough inspection regime. And everybody thought that would be the biggest problem. But we have listened to the comments from others. We have adjusted our position. Others have adjusted their position and accepted some of the ideas we have. Dr. Blix and Dr. ElBaradei appeared before the Council today for a long period.

My best information so far is that we're pretty okay with respect to the inspection regime instructions for the new resolution.

Q. On Wednesday your old friend Joschka Fischer will come, and in case war against Iraq is inevitable what do you expect which stance the German Government should take? And what—how would you characterize German-American relations about two months after these heavy turbulences? When are we back to normal?

Secretary Powell. On your second point, I would not presume to tell the German Government what its position should be. It's a democratic government, as we've learned from the latest election, and I'm sure Chancellor Schroeder can determine his position.

I will talk to my old friend—and good friend—Joschka Fischer in direct terms about what we think and what we believe is the right course of action, as I have in the past, and I will be as vigorous as I can be in presenting the U.S. position. I never believe that war is inevitable. The U.S. position is not designed to find a war. The U.S. position is designed to solve a danger that threatens the region, the Persian Gulf region, that threatens the world, from a dictator. The U.S. position is to try to solve this problem and not walk away from it, and to try to solve it peacefully.

If the United States was looking for a war and was not interested in any peaceful solution, the President of the United States would not have gone to the United Nations on the 12th of September and give the speech that he gave. And he would not have spent these last six weeks—and my hair would be less gray than it is now—if all we were looking for was an excuse for war.

The President of the United States has demonstrated repeatedly that he has strong views, he has strong principles. He is a leader who brings patience and deliberation to his decision-making process. He has done that in this instance. And so war is never inevitable. This President doesn't believe war is inevitable, and I will try to persuade Joschka of that.

With respect to U.S.-German relations, we have been in some turbulent times in recent weeks, if I can use that expression. I said we hit a pothole the last time we talked about this. But, you know, one of my old mentors when I was a young brigadier said to me when I was mad one day, he said—and I was upset and I was telling him how upset I was, and he did not have any particular sympathy for my being upset. He was much senior to me so he didn't have to have any such sympathy for me, but he said something I'll never forget. He said, "The best thing about being upset is you get over it."

So we have a problem and we'll get over the problem, for the simple reason that Germany and the United States are two nations that are bound together by a common purpose, by common values, by common beliefs and democracy and all the other things that have kept us together as strong partners for the last half-century. Differences will come along that will irritate the relationship from time to time, but the strength of the relationship will allow us to get over this.

When I reflect, as I will with Joschka on Wednesday, all that we have done together in the two years of this administration, the 22 months of this administration—Afghanistan, the Bonn conference, the Loya Jirga sponsored by Germany, Germany's work now in helping train police forces of Afghanistan, Germany's dealing with its constitutional issues in order to be able to use competent German forces in places like Bosnia and Task Force Fox, all the other things that we have done with Germany together. This is the measure of the relationship and we will get through this rough patch, of this I have no doubt, and I don't think Joschka has any doubt because we're just too close to one another.

Now, if I was a mischievous person, I could take note of the fact that there seemed to be some differences within the European Union this past weekend. So friends can argue with one another and have heated arguments, but that does not mean they are not friends. It means that friends have heated arguments. Within a family there are occasionally arguments; there are occasionally disagreements. And I enjoyed—never mind.

Q. Sir, to continue with Iraq, the French suggested that there might be an urgent meeting of foreign ministers. Would you support that idea?

Secretary Powell. It's an option. I've discussed this idea with Dominique de Villepin earlier today and with Minister Straw and Minister Ivanov and Minister Tang. But it's premature now to decide whether we should meet or not. I think we'll know better in another day or two.

Q. To go to Russia, though, how close are we to the next meeting between Presidents Bush and Putin? And also—

Secretary Powell. Between President Bush and Putin?

Q. Yes, I understand a new meeting is discussed.

Secretary Powell. Yes, I think there will be an opportunity later this fall. I don't know if anything's been announced yet.

* * * *

Q. Mr. Secretary, can we go back to Iraq for a second? You said that the United States is not looking for an excuse for war. But as you well know, the principal concern, particularly from countries such as France, is about language that appears to authorize the use of force or would be seen as a trigger for force.

Are you so opposed to a second resolution? What are your reasons for opposing a second resolution, and are you so opposed that you're prepared to walk away from what's obviously been intensive debate over the last six weeks?

Secretary Powell. We felt strongly that the violation of U.N. Security Council resolutions was flagrant, obvious and unquestionable. Nobody disagrees with that. We also believe that if you sent the inspectors back in, the only way Iraq was going to cooperate is if they knew consequences would follow. We believed it was the strongest possible signal to Iraq to include a statement of those consequences in one resolution, and that's why we put "all necessary means" in our first resolution proposal when we started discussing this.

A number of our friends said that is a little too far for us, we believe, and we believe strongly, that there ought to be a break in there where the Council can consider whether or not "all necessary means" or whatever the Council decides to do should be put into another resolution. So then you had the two-resolution debate. We listened carefully. We saw that it would be useful to find a way to bridge that difference, and we did. And we moved away from "all necessary means," and we moved to another formulation that had Dr. Blix or Dr. ElBaradei reporting to the Council if they couldn't do their job, a new violation, a new breach. Then the Council could consider this situation and the need for full implementation.

So that gives all of those who wanted the opportunity to debate this before the Council took action, that opportunity. Now, some people say that gives you a second resolution; it might just give you a second debate; it might give you a second, third and fourth resolution. By our willingness to show flexibility on that point, we essentially believe we have accommodated those who wanted an opportunity to decide this. They have now the opportunity to decide or not to decide it, to pass a second resolution or offer a second resolution or not, and we will be part of that debate. We're part of that Security Council.

We had to make sure that we did not do it in such a way that a set of handcuffs were being put upon the United States and other nations who, in the absence of the Security Council's second resolution if one were to come about, but in the presence of continued Iraqi violation, could not at some point in the future act.

I think the circle gets squared because when Dr. Blix or Dr. ElBaradei report to the Council that Iraq is not complying, and there are some people who suggest this is what Iraq will do, most of—I think everybody's hoping Iraq will stop this nonsense and cooperate fully. But if they don't cooperate and Dr. Blix or ElBaradei report these failures, this new violation, this new breach, this new problem, then we don't want to find ourselves handcuffed so that nothing can happen.

It's also clear that it will take some time for people to make a judgment, not only the Security Council under the terms of the resolution we proposed, but also the United States Government and our allies who might be willing to do, you know, like-minded nations like Kosovo, deciding to act in the absence of a new resolution.

There will be time for this to be considered, both courses of action, and we would certainly prefer to see the U.N. act in a multilateral way. That would be a preferred course of action.

I think the circle is squared by the simple fact that there will be time. The situation is not going to be so spring-loaded that from a violation reported by Dr. Blix or ElBaradei that something happens the next morning. The language that we proposed is that the Council will immediately convene to consider what the two doctors or one of the two doctors have reported.

Q. But why did you actually not take the French proposition? Because it would enhance the international support dramatically.

Secretary Powell. Because we didn't think the French—well, let me answer it this way. There were some French ideas and American ideas and there are Russian ideas and Chinese ideas, and we are working hard now to see if we can blend them into a proposal that all sides will find useful and that will no longer be the French or the American proposal. The French had difficulties with our proposal. They thought it was a little too far down the road of action. And we had trouble with the French original French proposal when they were shopping last week because we felt it wasn't strong enough with respect to the indictment and what happens, what the serious consequences could be.

So what we're trying to do is to find a blend that will satisfy as many members of the Council as possible. And it's not clear what the vote would be on either version today.

Q. But you'd still be leaving the definition of what the serious consequences would be to a later resolution would be insufficient or too weak to get Iraq to comply?

Secretary Powell. But that's where we—that's the position we have now. So obviously, we don't think it's too weak because Iraq knows that if they violate the will of the Council this time and do not comply, do not cooperate, frustrate the work of the inspectors, there are consequences ahead, either multilaterally under a U.N. authority, the U.N. authority, or, as the President has said, the Kosovo model of like-minded nations coming together might be the way to crack the problem.

Q. You said on Saturday that if an agreement was not possible, if an agreement was not possible, the Security Council should come to realize that it was not possible.

Secretary Powell. I mean, if we—

Q. So how do you do it? Is it through a vote?

Secretary Powell. Well, that—

Q. And second, is the vote is the same if there is no majority for your resolution or if one of the Permanent Members uses its veto power?

Secretary Powell. Say the first part of your question?

Q. Do you go to a vote to realize, as you said, that there's no agreement? And second, is the vote the same for the U.S. whether there is a majority against the U.S.-U.K. proposal or one of the Permanent 5 uses its veto power?

Secretary Powell. I wouldn't want to hypothesize on what we might or might not do or what we might or might not vote for or against in the absence of something specific. But the way you ultimately have to resolve this is, I am sure that somebody sooner or later will say, okay, look, we think this is as far as we can go with our position and therefore we present it to the Council for a vote. Then the Council will vote, and it either will succeed or it will fail. You can follow the logic trail from that as easily as I can. If it succeeds, fine. If it fails, then there is an option for an other resolution which might succeed or fail.

It is possible that you could end up at the end of this—and I'm just mathematically taking you down the road—you could end up with no resolution that could gain the support of the Council. But I don't—you know, I'm not predicting that. I'm just mathematically telling you what the procedure is.

I think that it's possible still to blend these positions into a resolution that will enjoy strong support and it will be a strong resolution that will meet the tests that I think all of the international community agree upon, even though the methodology we don't agree upon: a clear statement that they have been in violation of these resolutions, a tough inspection regime, and a clear statement that there have to be consequences for continued violations. I know of no member of the Council—I can maybe think of one, but I can for the most part think of no member of the Council—most members of the Council, almost all the members of the Council would agree with this.

When I speak to my colleagues—and pick any one you want—they don't disagree with this. There have to be consequences. And, you know, those who say, well, look at all Iraq is doing now. Oh, my, they're inviting inspectors in and they want you and they're mad that they didn't show up in the 19th last week like they were supposed to. Why are they doing this? Because of the goodness of their heart? Oh, why didn't you tell us we were in violation before? I must tell you, the letter must have been lost in the mail. You know, nonsense. It's because there's pressure being put on them. Pressure that says there will be consequences; you are not going to be allowed to get away with this again. No, cooperate.

And that's why they're doing all this. That's why they threw the first, you know, ball in the game on the day—the Monday after the Thursday, 12 September. On Monday they suddenly say they're letting everybody in. And then Thursday they were starting to change their mind and then the next Monday they had another proposal. And then presidential sites—sure, you can look at them—oh, no, we didn't mean it. Dr. Blix sent them a letter, which they haven't really answered yet.

It's a game we have seen for years and there have to be consequences for a nation that will play this kind of unilateral game against the whole international community. One nation against 190. And it's a game that has to come to an end. And nobody disagrees with this. Nobody disagrees with this. What we're having our debate about is different points of view of how best to achieve the same thing.

Remarks by United Nations Secretary-General Annan, October 28, 2002

As you know, the [Security] Council is discussing Iraq and what I can tell you is that they are in very serious deliberations on this topic. And Mr. El-Baradei and Mr. Blix are there with them, clarifying their needs and answering questions that the Council members have posed. And I think after that, of course, the Council members themselves will have to get into discussions on the issue. But it is a very, very serious discussion. It's a grave matter. It's a question of war and peace. And I think it is appropriate that the Council goes about it in a deliberate manner.

Q. After listening, Mr. Kofi Annan, to these two experts, are you more assured that the Council would be able to reach some sort of a compromise solution?

Secretary-General Annan. I'm still hopeful that the Council will come up with a resolution—a resolution that all of them can sign on to, or a vast majority. But it would require some compromises to get compromises. And I have not given up that hope, no.

White House Press Briefing, October 29, 2002

Q. Ari, the President's U.N. resolution spells out clear deadlines for Saddam Hussein, and a clear timetable for inspections that could lead to war. The President at every campaign stop across America talks in a hypothetical fashion about what should happen if that U.N. resolution would fail, that he'll lead a coalition to disarm Saddam. What are the deadlines and timetables for the backup plan?

Mr. Fleischer. The President has not indicated there are hard deadlines as such. I think that it's clear from listening to the President speak that the end is coming near. The United Nations is still hard at work on this matter. They have made some progress, and it's still unclear what the ultimate outcome will be in New York.

Q. Perhaps I wasn't clear. My question was, what are the deadlines and timetables for his backup plan? That is, acting with either congressional authorization or existing U.N. authorization.

Mr. Fleischer. Again, the President has not established any hard deadlines. And again, let's see what the United Nations does before I'm prepared to discuss anything that could be an alternative.

Q. Would they be similar to the U.N. deadlines which is seven days to comply, 30 days for a full list of weapons of mass destruction, 45 days for inspectors, and 60 days for—

Mr. Fleischer. The President is still working through the United Nations. Let's see if the United Nations is able to get the job done or not.

* * * *

Q. [The president] says if the United Nations won't act, if Saddam Hussein does not disarm, the U.S. will lead a coalition to disarm him. Who—what nation, aside from the United Kingdom, has publicly committed to join such a coalition?

Mr. Fleischer. Well, I was asked this question about two or three weeks ago when the President first started talking about this. And, one, make no mistake, that if the United Nations fails, international action will still follow. The only issue at that time will be the fact that the United Nations wrote itself out of any international action.

I think, Terry, what is appropriate now, in the President's judgment, is for the U.N. to proceed. Let us see if the U.N. is able to do the job or not. If they are not, then I think you will have no questions about who will proceed with the coalition the United States and others will form. I think at that time it will be appropriate for those nations to be named. But at this point, the President is still content to work through the United Nations. We'll see where ultimately that goes.

Q. Right now no public commitments aside from the—even the United Kingdom, I guess, has said that unless—

Mr. Fleischer. You can rest assured that what the President said is based on the information he has gotten as he talks to other nations. But again, because the President went to the United Nations September 12th and said that he wanted to work with the United Nations for days and weeks, not months—while time is running out in New York, they still have some time left to get the job done.

Q. Why is the time running out?

Mr. Fleischer. Because I think that everybody at the United Nations—the people who strongly support the President's position, people who are still trying to figure out where they are, and those who may oppose—for example, like Syria—they all recognize that it's getting time to bring this to a conclusion.

* * * *

Q. On the U.N., Hans Blix and Mohammed El-Baradei briefed the Security Council yesterday. What was the significance of their testimony? What is your view of what they told the Security Council about the regime for inspections?

Mr. Fleischer. Well, the briefing that was done by two of the leaders of the inspection regime was very notable. It was notable for what it said about the importance, in their judgments, about having—these are my words—but a tough and effective resolution so they can go about and do their jobs. They did both express a concern about going back into the country in the absence of a clear, strong resolution.

In addition, when they were asked about whether or not the resolution needed to have the words "material breech" in it, they did indicate—and I want to find the verbatim on this to be precise—but a reporter asked Dr. Blix, will it help you if "material breech" will be defined in the resolution? And his answer was, "I think it helps us if Iraq is conscience that non-cooperation will entail reactions by the Council."

They both were diplomatic in stating that it is up to the United Nations Security Council to settle the exact words and make any determinations from that point forward. But that's a very notable statement about the inspectors themselves believing they think it helps if Iraq is conscience that non-cooperation will entail reactions by the Council. I think the last thing the inspectors want to do is go in there and be led around again in more cat-and-mouse games. They want to do their job, they want to disarm Saddam Hussein.

Q.—Russians had objected to the inspections regime in the U.S. and British resolution, saying that they were unrealistic and unimplementable. Does the U.S. now believe that any of the Russian concerns have faded away, or at least been softened by the Blix and El-Baradei—

Mr. Fleischer. Well, again, what keeps striking me about this whole process at the United Nations is the swirl of words, some of which are repeated privately, some of which are not; some of which are said publicly for no other intention or purpose than to be said publicly. And that's the nature of diplomacy. That doesn't apply to only one nation, that simply is how these things sometimes go. So the real action will remain action behind closed doors and the Security Council, and we'll see where that leads. No one has a clear picture of it yet, but ultimately it will go.

Remarks by Secretary of State Powell, Secretary of Defense Rumsfeld, and Australian Defense Minister Hill, October 29, 2002

Secretary Colin Powell, Secretary Donald Rumsfeld, and Minister Robert Hill delivered their remarks after meeting in Washington, DC.

Q. Mr. Secretary, on Iraq. Some of us are reporting that the United States is now prepared to make changes on the margins of the resolution, not the key core issues, in order to get an agreement so the resolution can be approved by the Security Council. I wonder if you can tell us whether you think that's enhanced—if the reports are correct—enhanced chances of an agreement.

And if I can ask a specific, how long do you feel, how much time do you feel, if you would, Iraq should be given to list its chemical and biological weapons? The original idea was 23 or 30 days, however you look at it.

Secretary Powell. The U.S. draft resolution that's up there being considered by the Council says 30 days for the presentation of a declaration from Iraq, and we still think that's enough time. They know what they have, and they can respond in that amount of time.

With respect to the resolution, there are still a couple of outstanding issues that are rather basic. Our friends in the Security Council know our views on these issues and we know theirs. There may be a way to bridge these remaining differences, and that's what we are working on very intensively today. Either between my conversations with others or Ambassador Negroponte's conversations with others, we've been in touch with all of our colleagues, permanent colleagues on the Security Council today. I've had two conversations as well with Kofi Annan.

So we're hard at work and I think we're getting closer, but our basic principles remain the same. A clear indictment of Saddam Hussein's past behavior and current behavior has to be in the resolution. There has to be a very tough inspection regime, and I'm very pleased that Dr. Hans Blix of UNMOVIC and Dr. ElBaradei of IAEA in their presentation yesterday to the Security Council were supportive of the tough inspection regime that's in our draft resolution, with some little tweaks in the margins, but in principle they agree with it.

And there have to be consequences, otherwise Iraq will try to deceive and distract. They may try anyway even in the face of consequences. And there have to be consequences, and we cannot accept any language that suggests that in the presence of new Iraqi violations, those violations would be ignored and there would be no consequences.

How those consequences would ultimately be administered, dealt with, it can either be by an action of the Security Council or, as President Bush has repeatedly said, if the Council does not act, if the United Nations chooses not to act, the President has what he believes is the authority needed, and frankly, the obligation to act with like-minded nations to disarm Iraq.

But there is a way, I think, to preserve both of these positions—the Council acting or the United States acting—and we have worked to accommodate both of those positions within the draft resolution that is before the Security Council now.

Q. I have a question to Secretary Rumsfeld and also Senator Hill. Secretary Rumsfeld, does the U.S. want Australia to be part of any military force to disarm Iraq, if necessary, without a specific U.N. resolution? And were specific elements of that discussed today?

To Senator Hill, given the need for Australia to focus on the Southeast Asian region, is the Australian Government prepared to make such a commitment and would ground forces be involved?

Secretary Rumsfeld. Well, with respect to the first part of the question, the President of the United States has not made a decision as to whether or not force will be required with respect to Iraq so we've not gotten to that point. I would only say that whatever the United States ever does, we value having a close working relationship with Australia and, as always, those decisions are up to Australia.

Defense Minister Hill. Well, we share the goal and determination of the United States to see an end to the weapons of mass destruction program of Saddam Hussein and we are seeking to do that through the United Nations process and we trust that that will be successful. We are pleased that the United Nations Security Council has now accepted its responsibility and is addressing the issue.

So I wouldn't want to preempt that because I'm hopeful that that will work and it can be achieved without the use of armed force. But our bottom line is that we do want to see an end to this program. It's gone on for too long, and I think we're at the stage now where through the processes that were embarked upon it must now end and the threat must therefore be removed.

Q. Mr. Secretary, Secretary Powell, it's been six weeks, I believe, since the President addressed the United Nations on September 12th. How long are you prepared to wait before forcing a vote in the Security Council and perhaps making some of our friends and allies stand up and be counted?

And I'd like to ask Secretary Rumsfeld whether you believe that anything is being lost by this period and whether there will come a point where you think it is necessary for the U.S. to take some kind of unilateral decisions here.

Secretary Powell. It has been six weeks, but this has been a very complex issue and I think we have accomplished quite a lot in six weeks—getting a tough inspection regime, getting agreement, I believe, on most of the resolution, and listening to our friends and allies and trying to accommodate their views.

But I think your question is correct, Andrea, in the sense that we're getting close to a point where we'll have to see whether or not we can bridge these remaining differences in the very near future. I don't want to give you days or a week, but it certainly isn't much longer than that. I think sometime in the very near future we will have to see whether or not we can get, for the most part, consensus on our resolution, and if not, we'll have to make a judgment as to whether we start putting resolutions up, competing resolutions for votes.

So I think it's in the very near future, but we are closer. And what I'm impressed with right now is that all of the ministers that I'm in contact with are anxious to find a solution that would draw the greatest number of yea votes for such a resolution.

Q. Secretary Rumsfeld, are you concerned that if this stretches out very much longer, if this stretches out too much longer, that it will diminish the ability of a military force to launch a successful action, if it is necessary to disarm Saddam Hussein militarily?

Secretary Rumsfeld. Well, as anything in life, there are advantages and disadvantages to different courses of action, and clearly the President of the United States made a judgment that going to our Congress first and to the United Nations second had more advantages than disadvantages. And those were all considered and weighed at the outset, and I fully agree with his decision to do so.

* * * *

Q. A question for Secretary Powell and for Secretary Rumsfeld. Secretary Powell, how much time do you believe that the Security Council ought to have if the inspectors encounter obstacles in Iraq? How much time should the Security Council have to consider that and decide on a response?

And for Secretary Rumsfeld, do you have any confidence that the inspections can be thorough enough to uncover all that Saddam Hussein has in the way of weapons of mass destruction and is it basically a fruitless exercise?

Secretary Powell. On the first question, I can't give you an artificial answer. I do know that we've structured the resolution in a way that when it becomes obvious to Dr. Blix or to Dr. ElBaradei that they're being frustrated in their work and there is a violation, they are to report immediately to the Council, and the Council is to convene immediately to consider this report. I can't tell you now how long it might take them to consider such a report or what action they might take, but as their clock is ticking there is a clock that is also ticking on the U.S. side as to whether or not the violation is of such a nature that the President makes a judgment in due course that he should act if the U.N. chooses not to act.

Secretary Rumsfeld. With respect to inspections generally, they tend to be designed and fashioned to be used on a country that has made a conscious decision that it wanted to open its doors to the world community, allow inspectors to come in and validate something that they want the world to know, namely that, in this case, that they do not have weapons of mass destruction.

Needless to say, to the extent a country is not cooperative, it is relatively easy for them to frustrate and make difficult the inspection process. So it's generally used in a case where a country wants to open its doors and prove to the world that it is doing precisely that which the world is hoping it would do.

In terms of finding and disposing of or disarming all of Iraq's weapons of mass destruction, they have been on a conscious effort of dispersing them across their country in a variety of locations, and that is a process that even in the best of circumstances with full cooperation that they would—it would still take a good deal of time.

Remarks by Secretary of State Powell and German Foreign Minister Fischer, October 30, 2002

Secretary Colin Powell and Minister Joschka Fischer delivered their remarks after meeting in Washington, DC.

Secretary Powell. Well, good evening, ladies and gentlemen. It's been my pleasure to again host my colleague, Joschka Fischer. We've just completed a very full discussion of our bilateral relations as well as our alliance relations.

We also talked about the situation in Iraq and I updated the Minister on the work we are doing in the United Nations to obtain a resolution that is tough, puts the inspectors back in, and communicated to him our position with respect to the need for consequences in such a resolution. And the Minister, of course, expressed his opinion, and I'm sure he will in a moment here.

* * * *

From time to time, there are disturbances in the relationship, there are points where we have disagreements, and as befitting the kind of relationship we have, we are confident that in due course we will get over these disagreements and we'll find ways to resolve any differences that may exist.

Foreign Minister Fischer. I am very glad to be here. And we discussed a wide range of issues and international affairs. We discussed about the war against terror and the situation in the Middle East, the situation with the resolution about Iraq and the Security Council. And we think and we agree that there should be found now an agreement and that all relevant resolutions must be implemented immediately by the regime in Baghdad so that Hans Blix and his team can start their job immediately.

There is a disagreement about possible military action, but nevertheless we are full supportive for the implementation of the Security Council resolution and the beginning of the job of Blix and his team.

* * * *

Q. Mr. Secretary, I wonder if I could ask you to clarify what you said a few hours ago on a radio interview. You spoke of the inspectors needing months to do their job and you said the President will wait until they complete the job.

Are you foreclosing military action before the inspections are conducted and the reports come back?

Secretary Powell. No. I think the clear impression that I was—the impression I was trying to convey is that once the inspectors go in it will take some time for them to do their job. They won't be able to do their job unless Iraq cooperates. And if there is immediately non-cooperation on the part of Iraq, that, I think, is an absolute red line and that has to come back to the Council immediately. But it will take some time for the inspectors do to their job.

But we have to see whether or not Iraq will cooperate and permit the inspectors to do their job, and during that period, obviously, in execution of such a resolution, the United States and all member nations of the Security Council and of the United Nations will watch and see how the inspections are going and whether or not there is a level of cooperation with Iraq that suggests the inspections should continue.

Q. But that will not handcuff, to use your word, the U.S.?

Secretary Powell. No, there is nothing that we propose in this resolution or we would find acceptable in a resolution that would handcuff the President of the United States from doing what he feels he must do to defend the United States, defend our people, and defend our interests in the world.

But he is also anxious to pursue this matter through the United Nations. He has demonstrated that clearly with his speech on the 12th of September. I think we've demonstrated by the patience we have shown and by our willingness to listen to the views of others over the last six-plus weeks. But at no time will the United States foreclose its ability to act in its interests in accordance with its constitutional obligations to protect the nation and protect the people.

And I believe that with a little more hard work on the part of all concerned, we can find a way to accommodate the interests of our friends without in any way, as I've said before, handcuffing the United States.

Q. Mr. Fischer, is Germany in line with Russia, France and Mexico in the Security Council? Do you agree with their position?

And Mr. Powell, is it true that the United States, it is upset with Mexico because their position on Iraq in the Security Council?

Can I have both comments, too?

Foreign Minister Fischer. Well, we are—we will be a member of the Security Council beginning with January the 1st, but up to now we are not a member of the Security Council. We have an interest of an agreement between the members of the Security Council because we think that if there is an agreement this will be a strong message to the regime in Baghdad if there is an agreed, common, unified position. Therefore, we hope that the members of the Security Council will find such a position to give a strong message and that then we think that Blix must start immediately his job and go into Iraq and do what he really has to do. This is our position.

Secretary Powell. With respect to Mexico, President Bush and President Fox had good discussions about the Iraq situation at the summit, APEC summit meeting in Los Cabos. And no, we're not upset. We had good discussions and we're confident that Mexico will weigh this issue very carefully and will vote in a way that represents their interests.

And we hope that a case will be made that the resolution the United States put forward will be worthy of Mexican support. But that's a decision for the Mexican President to make. But no, we're not upset. We're talking to all of our friends in the Security Council and listening to different points of view.

Q. Mr. Secretary, is the atmosphere still poisoned between Germany and the United States?

Secretary Powell. I wouldn't say there is a poisoned atmosphere. I would say that we are two friends, two allies, that occasionally find ourselves with areas of disagreement and some rough spots. And as I think both Joschka and I have said, we don't hide from these disagreements, we don't pretend there are no rough spots. There are rough spots. But because we are friends and our two nations are allied, we will find ways to get these disagreements and rough spots behind us in due course.

Q. Mr. Secretary, you have indicated that there is some agreement or approaching an agreement with the French in the Security Council. Are you approaching agreement on a two-resolution approach?

Secretary Powell. We are working on one resolution and the approach that we're looking at would permit the Security Council to immediately convene in the presence of continued or new Iraqi violation of resolutions. And in that discussion that would take place when the Security Council convenes, the Security Council can choose to do what it chooses to do, whether that's another resolution or just a continued debate.

While that discussion and debate is taking place, the United States retains its full authority to do whatever the United States feels it might need to do to protect its interests. But there will be a period of time there while the situation is being examined for the Security Council to consider additional moves and for the United States to consider what is in its best interest.

* * * *

Q. Russia is dropping some of its objections to the text that we've seen clearly on the "material breach." What kind of reassurances is it asking from the U.S. in exchange for coming further to your side on this?

Secretary Powell. I think it's best that we let these diplomatic exchanges take place in a nice, quiet, diplomatic rooms.

Q. Mr. Fischer, can you tell us whether you support the current efforts by the United States administration to get this resolution coming to an end?

Foreign Minister Fischer. I cannot give any details about the present negotiation situation because we are not part of the negotiations in New York. We support a unified position of the Security Council and we hope that especially the P-5 members can agree on a common approach.

Remarks by Secretary of State Powell, October 30, 2002

Secretary Colin Powell was interviewed by Neil Conan on National Public Radio.

Q. Mr. Secretary, you spoke yesterday with a group of European journalists, and you said you were being flexible in offering the Security Council a second debate to authorize war should Iraq fail inspection, but you wanted to emphasize that the United States would not be handcuffed. What did you mean by that?

Secretary Powell. What I meant was that the President really believes this problem has to be dealt with now, before it gets any worse, and he would much prefer to see it dealt with by the international community.

Iraq's offense is against the United Nations for ignoring the many resolutions that Iraq has been bound by for these past 11 years, and so we would like to see it done through the multilateral organization of the U.N..

We want a tough resolution that puts in inspectors to go back in with the toughest set of standards to see if Iraq will cooperate. If Iraq cooperates, then we can find a peaceful solution to this if it results in their disarmament; but we also know that Iraq will not cooperate unless the element of pressure in the form of potential military force is there, and we want to make sure that that pressure is there.

Now, some of our friends in the Security Council say, well, therefore, that has to come back to the Security Council for its consideration, and we say, fine, it can come back to the Security Council for its consideration, but if the Security Council refuses to act, the United States must be free, with other likeminded nations, to act to deal with this danger.

But we will participate in whatever debate the Security Council chooses to have in whether a decision is made to provide a second resolution authorizing force or not, but the United States cannot find itself handcuffed to an extended debate in the presence of a new Iraqi violation and new Iraqi material breaches.

Q. In the Los Angeles Times today, a French diplomat is quoted as saying, "This is a matter of principle. This is about the rules of the game in the world today, about putting the Security Council in the center of international life, and not permitting a nation, whatever nation it may be, to do what it wants, when it wants, where it wants."

Secretary Powell. He might just as easily have been referring to Iraq than the United States. It's Iraq that has decided to do what it wants to do, when it wants to do it, notwithstanding the international rules of the road.

The United Nations passed 16 resolutions telling him to disarm. He frustrated, Saddam Hussein frustrated the inspectors for years, and violated the international community.

Now, is the international community supposed to simply say, well, oh, never mind, and look away?

And so the United States took this problem to the international community and is asking it to act. We hope it will act. And the one who is the violator of international standards and law is Saddam Hussein and the Iraqi regime, which has gassed its own people, gassed its neighbors, and invaded its neighbors. It's not the United States that's done all that, it's Iraq that's done all that.

Q. Let me put the same question another way and this time, I'll get a quote from Francis Fukuyama who wrote, on September the 11th, "Americans are largely innocent of the fact that much of the rest of the world believes that it is American power, and not terrorists with weapons of mass destruction, that is destabilizing the world, and nowhere are these views more firmly held than among America's European allies."

Secretary Powell. I don't agree with Francis, as much as I respect his opinion. The fact of the matter is, America isn't out terrorizing the world.

If you look at where American armed forces have gone over the last 10 years, they went into Kuwait to do what? To overthrow an invasion of a Muslim nation by another Muslim nation, Iraq invasion of Kuwait.

We sent our brave young men and women into Kosovo to do what? To rescue a Muslim population.

We sent our young men and women into Afghanistan after we were attacked by terrorists operating out of Afghanistan to do what? To free a Muslim people. And now, our young men and women are over there not terrorizing anybody, not threatening anybody, but building a new nation where people are free, where women can come out and participate in the society, where children can go to school and get an education that is useful, where reconstruction has begun.

1.9 million Afghan refugees have returned to Afghanistan since the United States invaded, as some might call it. What we did was free Afghanistan. And those 1.9 million Muslims are voting with their feet for the opportunity, to get to the opportunity created by America.

Our European allies know that. Most of our European allies participated with us in these efforts.

So although there may be disagreements from time to time—as there is now between some of our European allies and the United States, but not all of them—a number of our European allies are solidly supportive, the United Kingdom, Italy, Spain, a number of the Benelux countries, but it is not a monolithic alliance, transatlantic alliance, and there will be disagreements; and we work our way, through debate and dialogue, through these disagreements.

Q. President Bush has been speaking today with Chief U.N. Weapons Inspector Hans Blix to outline inspection processes that could validate Iraq's disarmament. How much time would this take?

Secretary Powell. That's a good question. A lot depends on the level of cooperation.

I was listening to an earlier segment of your show, and some of the callers said there must be cooperation, there has to be cooperation in order to have a good inspection regime, and that's certainly true. You're going to get a much better inspection regime with cooperation. If they don't cooperate, then it has to be far more intrusive as it was in the early '90s.

I can't tell you how long it'll take, but it's certainly a matter of months before Dr. Blix and the head of the IAEA, Mr. ElBaradei, would come back and say, we have made our determination whether or not they are continuing to pursue this kind of technology.

And we understand that it will take time, and the President understands that that means that we will have to wait for them to do their work and complete their report.

When the President met with them this morning—and I was present at the meeting—he made it clear to them that we have confidence in them and that we're going to give them all the support we can so that they can do the job, and their job is to find out the truth, and the Security Council will then make its determination of what should follow.

Q. I know you have to leave shortly, but can you give us a better appreciation of the timeline on a vote in the Security Council?

Secretary Powell. I would say that we are narrowing the differences. I've been on the phone most of the day with my colleagues in the Security Council, and I think we're getting much closer, and I would say that this will break in one way or another, either with agreement, or if we don't get agreement, different sides can put down different resolutions to see who has the votes.

I think this is all going to happen, certainly toward the—by the end of next week. I'd be surprised if it went into the following week.

White House Press Briefing, November 2, 2002

Q. How close are we to a resolution on Iraq?

Mr. Fleischer. The U.N. does not work over the weekends, and so there are going to be some phone calls made at various levels—

Q. By the President?

Mr. Fleischer. No, not by the President. But I do not anticipate any action by the United Nations over the weekend.

Q. Do you think early next week there could be a compromise?

Mr. Fleischer. Scott, I'd hazard a guess at the date. The talks are continuing to move along; a productive week at the United Nations, and in the discussions around the world. I would hazard to make a hard guess as to the timing.

Q. We've been given to understand there would be new U.S. draft that took account of some of the back-and-forth, the French-Russians, early next week. Is that the case?

Mr. Fleischer. We'll see what ultimately they decide to finalize. I think the talks are continuing and, obviously, whatever is the best summary of how these talks have moved will be represented in the final draft that is put to a vote.

Q. Is what Colin Powell said the other day still active, that we're looking to have a vote by the end of next week?

Mr. Fleischer. I think he indicated—I don't think he was that precise in his language. He indicated it could be this coming week, could be the week after, is I think how the Secretary put it.

Q. He said he doubted it would go to the following week.

Mr. Fleischer. Yes, I think he left the door open. Again, it's impossible to guess. And this will come together when it comes together. As I said, it was a productive week, and I think everybody has seen that. I just don't want to guess a date.

Q. Can the President live with the possibility that it would slide beyond November the 12th?

Mr. Fleischer. Again, I'm just not going to get into the hard date guessing business. The President would like to see this wrapped up though.

Remarks by President Bush, November 3, 2002

President Bush delivered his remarks during a campaign stop in Sioux Falls, South Dakota.

What's important for us as we work to secure the homeland is to remember the stakes have changed. After September the 11th, world changed. It changed for a lot of reasons. Perhaps the most profound reason on a foreign policy perspective, or from a homeland security perspective, is that we're no longer protected by two big oceans. Used to be if there was a threat overseas we could deal with it if we chose to do so, but we didn't have to worry about something happening here at home. It used to be oceans could protect us from conflict and from threats.

But that's changed, and it's important to have people in the Senate who are clear-eyed realists. It's important to have people who see the world the way it is, not the way we hope it is. And the world is a dangerous place, particularly with people like Saddam Hussein in power.

Saddam Hussein is a man who told the world he wouldn't have weapons of mass destruction, but he's got them. He's a man who a while ago who was close to having a nuclear weapon. Imagine if this madman had a nuclear weapon. It's a man who not only has chemical weapons, but he's used chemical weapons against some of his neighbors. He used chemical weapons, incredibly enough, against his own people. He can't stand America. He can't stand some of our closest friends.

And, not only that, he is—would like nothing better than to hook-up with one of these shadowy terrorist networks like al Qaeda, provide some weapons and training to them, let them come and do his dirty work, and we wouldn't be able to see his fingerprints on his action.

No, he's a threat. And that's why I went to the United Nations. I went to the United Nations because, I said to that august body, you need to hold this man to account. For 11 years, in resolution after resolution after resolution he's defied you. For the sake of keeping the peace, we want you to be effective. For the sake of keeping the world free, we want you to be an effective body. It's up to you, however. You can show the world whether you've got the backbone necessary to enforce your edicts or whether you're going to turn out to be just like the League of Nations, your choice to make.

And my message to Saddam Hussein is that, for the sake of peace, for the sake of freedom, you must disarm like you said you would do. But my message to you all and to the country is this: for the sake of our future freedoms, and for the sake of world peace, if the United Nations can't act, and if Saddam Hussein won't act, the United States will lead a coalition of nations to disarm Saddam Hussein.

I want you to know that out of the evil done to America is going to come some great good. I truly believe that. I believe by being firm and strong, we can keep the peace. I know that if we remember our values, remember that freedom is not America's gift to the world, freedom is a God-given gift to the world—if we remember that value—we remember our uniqueness and the values we hold dear, we can bring peace, and that's going to happen. And here at home, we'll have a better America, too. A better America.

Out of the evil done to this country is going to come a society which is more hopeful. See, you and I know that amongst our plenty, there are people who hurt, people who are hopeless, addicted, people who wonder if there is such a thing as love. People when you say, gosh, the American Dream applies to you, they don't have any idea what you're talking about.

White House Press Briefing, November 4, 2002

Q. Ari, there was a report on NBC this morning that the United States and France have reached a compromise on a meeting of the term "material breach" in the Security Council resolution. Is that accurate?

Mr. Fleischer. Nobody has brought anything like that to my attention. The talks continue at a productive level and we are hopeful that we will be able to move forward with one voice at the United Nations Security Council.

Q. Is there any reason to—is there any reason for this hopefulness? Anything different?

Mr. Fleischer. No, I think it's—what I'm reflecting is the tenor of the conversations that have been taking place for the last week. I did not see this NBC news report. As I indicated, nobody had brought anything that to my attention.

Q. Or anything else that makes you even more hopeful?

Mr. Fleischer. Well, this is the product of long diplomacy, and we still don't know where it will end up. I need to put that caution in here: we do not know. But the President made the determined course on September 12th to speak in very clear, black and white, moral terms to the United Nations. Then he launched a methodical, diligent, diplomatic campaign. We'll see ultimately if this campaign is successful. But, clearly, the differences have been narrowed to several issues, and we'll see if we can finalize those issues.

Q.—assurances from Fox of support?

Mr. Fleischer. I cannot characterize what a foreign leader says. It's continuing consultation.

Q.—the President took in his remarks to Fox?

Mr. Fleischer. Stressing the importance of the United Nations speaking with one voice and the threat Saddam Hussein poses and the need for the United Nations Security Council to act in a meaningful way this time.

Remarks by Secretary of State Powell, November 4, 2002

Q. Thank you, sir. I guess my first question is, what is the deadline for the U.S. for reaching a resolution in the Security Council? I mean, last week you said that it should be next week.

Secretary Powell. Today's Monday.

There is no deadline or no cutoff, but obviously we just can't keep discussing and negotiating and debating. I think we are getting very close to the point where we will put forward a U.S. resolution. I have been in intense conversations over the last several days with my colleagues in the Security Council and I think we are very close.

I think we are all united behind the need for a strong resolution, a resolution that makes clear Iraq's failure to comply with previous resolutions, that puts in place an exceptionally strong inspection regime so that Iraq cannot deceive it the way it did previously, and a clear understanding that if Iraq violates this resolution and fails to comply, then the Council has to take into immediate consideration what should be done about that, while the United States and other likeminded nations might make a judgment about what we might do about it if the Council chooses not to act.

Those elements have been there from the beginning and I think we have found a way to accommodate the concerns and items that have been presented to us by not only the Permanent Members of the Security Council, but we have been very sensitive to what the elected members also had to say to us, which is one reason we are having this session here today.

So it has taken a while. We are not into months yet, so I am okay with respect to my earlier statements of days and weeks but not months. But it will come to a head, I think, in the near future, but I don't have a deadline.

Q. Mr. Secretary, if a resolution is agreed on on inspection in Iraq, what is the ideal U.S. timeframe for Mr. Blix to report back to the Security Council?

Secretary Powell. The resolution will contain dates, a 30-day period—if it passes— we believe a 30-day period for the Iraqis to provide a declaration would be a useful way to get started to see whether they are serious. Then Dr. Blix has a timetable for how long it will take inspectors to get in. Dr. Blix and Mr. ElBaradei have their timetables. So time will pass while the inspections are taking place, and that is one of the built-in requirements of the inspection regime. If you are going to have an inspection regime, then you have to give time for the inspectors to do their work.

But we will know very early on whether Saddam Hussein and the Iraqi government plan to cooperate. We will know in short order, by the nature of the declaration they send in, if the Council passes such a requirement, and whether or not they are showing the level of cooperation that is appropriate or which would allow Dr. Blix and Mr. ElBaradei to do their job.

So, yes, some can argue it will take months and months and months and months and months for the inspectors to look at everything they will want to look at, but we will know early on whether or not Iraq is intending to cooperate or not to cooperate. That is the real test for Iraq. Now, Iraq has made many moves since the 12th of September when the President gave his speech. Each one of the moves they made has constituted an attempt to tie the U.N. up in knots and to force the U.N. to play the same game that Iraq always wins at. And this time it is a strong resolution with a strong inspection regime and the possibility of consequences afterwards if Iraq violates. It will not just be another situation where Iraq lets the inspectors in and they can't do their job because of Iraqi actions. Iraq has to know that that will not be acceptable, and the international community should not accept it and I hope will not accept it, if that is the way Iraq decides to behave.

Q. "Early on." Is that January?

Secretary Powell. I said January about what?

Q. "Early on." In your view, is that January?

Secretary Powell. No, I'm not going to give you—to do what?

Q. To assess the seriousness of Saddam Hussein.

Secretary Powell. No, it would be within a few weeks after the resolution is passed. If Iraq says no, we're not going to cooperate, we're not going to give you a declaration, we're not going to let the inspectors in and starts to place all kinds of conditions on the U.N. resolution, then we would know in a very short period of time that Iraq is not planning to cooperate, and that would say something to the Security Council.

Once the inspectors go in, if they are allowed to go in under the conditions the U.N. dictates, not Iraq dictates, then it will take some time for the inspectors to determine whether or not Iraq is continuing to cooperate. It is a function of what the inspectors find or don't find.

You are trying to get me to say when there is a deadline to go to war. This is not a resolution for war. This is a resolution to try to resolve a crisis in international relations that has been put before the United Nations, not by the United States, but by Iraq. Everybody keeps pointing fingers at the international community and at the United States, when the person who is the perpetrator of this crime is Saddam Hussein and Iraq. It cannot be allowed to continue, and that is the strong point of view of the United States and I think it is the strong point of view of the United Nations. This can't continue this way. The United Nations simply cannot be dictated to this way by someone who is not obeying U.N. resolutions.

But whether it will lead to conflict or war that remains to be seen. That judgment, really, is in the hands of the U.N., the United States, likeminded nations, and ultimately whether Iraq is going to come into compliance with international law or not.

Q. Mr. Secretary, could I ask you who determines if there is to be a new material breach, and can the United States do that unilaterally?

And secondly, could I say, you know, arithmetically when the resolution is put to the Security Council, you need a majority of nine. What would you say to countries like Ireland and Mexico—which would very much like a second resolution—to convince them that one resolution is enough?

Secretary Powell. The one resolution that we are working on now is not a resolution that forces the U.N. to take military action in the presence of an Iraqi violation. Ireland, Mexico, a number of other nations in the Security Council—France, China, Russia, others—wanted an opportunity for the Security Council to debate what the international community or what the Security Council should do in the presence of Iraqi violation.

The resolution that we have been working on does that. It says that if there is a continued show of intransigence on the part of Iraq and the inspectors are unable to do their job, this gets referred to the Council for the Council to discuss and debate. The Council may choose to pass another resolution. The United States, as part of the Council, would participate in that debate.

But we had to structure the resolution in a way that while this process is ongoing, the United States is not handcuffed so that if, at the end of whatever the Security Council decides to do, or in the process, if it looks like the Security Council will not choose to act, the United States is not handcuffed if the United States feels that, with other likeminded nations, action is required. This is not an unprecedented scenario. Kosovo happened this way when the United States and likeminded nations believed it was necessary to act in the presence of this emergency.

The question of what triggers that is one of the items that is being discussed now. We believe that Iraq now is in material breach, has been in material breach. So material breach is there. It exists now. We also believe that there is a precedent for determining a new material breach or a future material breach. If you look at U.N. Resolution 707 from 1991, it says in the presence at that time of Iraqi intransigence that if Iraq fails to provide information or if Iraq does not comply, that is a fact that constitutes a material breach. It's 11 years old.

We think that is not a bad precedent, but we will have to discuss with our colleagues how best to deal with this question. It is one of the remaining questions, as you all know, on what constitutes a new material breach, and is that an immediate trigger or is that just send it to the Council for discussion.

Q. Mr. Secretary, France, Germany and Russia appear to have put up far more resistance than the United States expected. Does the U.S. look worse after going through this experience?

Secretary Powell. No. Everybody was concerned about this issue over the summer and wondering what the United States was going to do. There are all sorts of speculations about the position of the United States. We heard lots of commentary about unilateralism, about going off on our own, about "cowboyism." What President Bush did was he strode to the lectern at the United Nations 57th General Assembly and he presented the case, and he asked the major multilateral organization of the world, whose resolutions have been steadfastly ignored by Iraq, a country that invades its own neighbors and gasses its own people, and he put the problem to them.

Now, there have been a number of nations who feel differently about the seriousness of the problem or what should be done about the problem, and we have been in discussion with those. You have touched on several. Germany has a view that says yes, this is all very bad but we don't think it warrants military action under any circumstances that we can see. Other nations have said it may warrant military options, but only if the Council convenes again to consider it and make a decision at that point.

We have tried to accommodate all those positions and I think we have in the resolution that we are working on now and hopefully coming to closure on now. But I don't think we look any worse off. I think we look better off, having taken this issue to the United Nations and reminding everybody of the nature of this regime, what this regime has done, what it is about, and that it is a call for unified action.

And, frankly, if the U.N. doesn't step up to its responsibilities in this regard, I think it is the U.N. that will look bad, not the United States.

But, you know, we understand that every nation, and every nation represented here by its correspondents, is a sovereign nation with its own parliament, its own legislature, its own elected head of the state and government, its own foreign minister. I have spent an enormous amount of time, up until to ten minutes before my daughter's wedding on Saturday—the phone was only shut down when I started down the aisle—I have spent an enormous amount of time working with all of my colleagues in the international community to listen, to understand, to build bridges between different positions.

So I think we have demonstrated that we do have a high regard for the opinion of other nations. Even when there is strong disagreement, we have high regard for the friends that we have around the world and their opinions. We try to accommodate those opinions, but, at the same time, we hope that our friends will listen to our views as well and try to accommodate our views. There will be occasions when, on matters of principle, we might have to move in two directions. This is a case where I think the international community is coming together.

Q. My question is what is the scenario for a post-Iraq and is the U.S. perceiving some kind of prolonged occupation, just like in Japan?

Secretary Powell. The United States has made no decision for war, which has to be the trigger for the your question. Should conflict come and the only way this can be resolved is through conflict, we have given considerable thought to what should come afterwards because if a conflict comes, it must involve, then, the removal of the regime because the regime simply will not respond to its obligations to the U.N..

And after regime removal, the United States or any group of nations that have gone in, or the U.N., if it has gone in under Chapter 7, has an obligation to help the people of Iraq liberate themselves and put in place a better government. There are many models that people are looking at. No model has been settled on because there is no war that has been decided upon.

But we have come to the clear decision within the United States that should it come to this, we would have an obligation to help the people of Iraq put in place a new government representative of the people and in a way that does not destabilize the region. We have considerable experience and considerable success in having done this a number of times over the past 50 or 60 years with considerable success.

Q. Sir, in the case of Mexico—and of course I have to ask you about Mexico—there is no immigration agreement. There is a problem with water and the Fox government defers with the Bush Administration on the possible solution.

I think, they are saying, of course, they want to get to an agreement, they don't want to vote against, but can you tell us what is the future you see for the bilateral relationship?

Secretary Powell. I think the bilateral relationship is strong now and will remain strong in the future. With respect to Iraq, I had two conversations with Foreign Secretary Castaneda—Richard [Boucher] will correct me if I have gotten them wrong, but I think I spoke to him both Friday and Saturday. President Fox and President Bush stay in close touch on this matter.

Mexico, a sovereign nation, will have to make its own choice and its own decision with respect to the Iraq resolution. I hope the resolution that we will be putting forward is one that Mexico will find that it can support.

* * * *

Q. Yes, I wanted to get back to this question of—on the important question of regional stability, Mr. Secretary, which you raised. We had elections yesterday in Turkey with the election of an Islamist party. You have the Saudi Foreign Minister's statement saying that there will be no U.S. troops on Saudi soil. And you've got developments in Israel with the emergence of an extremely—a narrow right-wing coalition, the loss of the Labor Party there.

So how do you maintain, you know, all these portents are not very good for regional stability in the event of a war.

Secretary Powell. I am pleased that the initial statements coming from the AKP—the party that did the best in the Turkish elections—are rather forthcoming and positive with respect to economic reform. To some extent, this election will clarify the political situation in Turkey. The fact that the party has an Islamic base to it in and of itself does not mean that it will be anti-American in any way. In fact, the initial indication we get is that the new party, which will form the new government, understands the importance of a good relationship with the United States.

The Saudi Foreign Minister's statement—we will wait to see whether he adds anything to that or clarifies it.

The question, really, at this point is moot because we have not asked them for the use of bases. There is not yet a U.N. resolution, nor is there anything that has triggered a military operation that would require us to ask for the use of their bases or for the use of their forces at this time.

We are using their bases now. We have Americans and bases throughout that part of the world and we have good relations with the Saudis. So we will wait to see whether there is or is not a need. We hope there is not a need because we are hoping to resolve this situation peacefully.

Q. And on Israel?

Secretary Powell. Oh, I'm sorry. Israel. We will also wait to see. It's not clear—

Q. But how do you put pressure on a government with Netanyahu and Sharon to move this process along?

Secretary Powell. Mr. Netanyahu—I don't think I have heard his answer yet so I don't think I will speculate on the nature of this government because it apparently is still being formed and it is not clear. I just think it is premature for me to comment because I don't believe Mr. Netanyahu has yet joined the government.

Q. Mr. Secretary of State, could I go back to—could you talk us through the timetable on Iraq? I understood that the 30 days was flexible and that you might give longer to Iraq to come up with a full list of their—

Secretary Powell. There is an idea that—30 days was the original idea there. There are some ideas that for some parts of their holdings they may need more time. That hasn't been decided. Right now, 30 days is the period that we have in our resolution for them to declare what it is they have.

Q. And then after 30 days, what happens?

Secretary Powell. After 30 days, the declaration comes in and in that 30-day period, Dr. Blix and Mr. Baradei have the opportunity to start preparing themselves. But if the declaration comes in and it seems to be a declaration that we should find forthcoming and in evidence of cooperation, then Dr. Blix is prepared to start inspections.

But I would rather not answer for Dr. Blix and how—the timelines and whatnot—because that really is his portfolio, not mine.

Q. So if there's going to be a war, it's not going to be this year?

Secretary Powell. Everybody keeps looking for a war. We keep looking for peace. I know that is the question on the minds of your readers, but the United States is trying to put forward a resolution that will find a peaceful solution. The President has said this on many occasions. We will see whether or not we will have war and peace based on what Iraq does or does not do.

* * * *

Q. Okay, I have one more question that just came up to me. You had the experience of building a coalition in the United Nations last time. What's the difference this time? Why isn't it so easy? Or was it easy?

Secretary Powell. Last time we had something that was a little clearer in the minds of the world. We had an invasion. We had a blatant, unmistakable invasion. There they were. The Iraqi army was sitting in Kuwait, poised to go into Saudi Arabia. It was something that the international community rallied to immediately.

Eleven years later, here we have a somewhat different situation. We have 11 years worth of violation of resolutions. But I think what we are now seeing is a coalition is forming, not necessarily a coalition for war, but a coalition for peace, a coalition that understands that peace will only come in this part of the world if Iraq is disarmed, and a coalition that is saying to Iraq you have violated your obligations and it cannot be tolerated.

So I hope this coalition forms again. It is a different coalition than the one that we created 12 years ago with respect to military action, and hopefully it will signal the same—it will give the same sort of clear political signal to Iraq that their actions will no longer be tolerated.

White House Press Briefing, November 5, 2002

Q. On the U.N. resolution, I understand that revised language from the State Department is going up to New York today. Are you planning to present today to the Security Council or tomorrow? And how did you fudge the language in material breach to get the French to agree to it?

Mr. Fleischer. Fudge, question mark, question mark, question mark?

Q. Yes, fudge.

Mr. Fleischer. Well, the President began this course on September 12th, and this course is almost at its final day. The President believed that it was important to go the United Nations and test the United Nations to see if the international community could act in a way that was strong, effective and in a way that results in inspectors having the tools they need to do their jobs, to disarm Saddam Hussein.

The President chose a multilateral path. And we will ultimately see now, shortly, whether or not the U.N. will be successful. It didn't have to be this way. The President could have chosen to act, probably with the support of the American people, in a different way, but he laid out this course.

We are very close. I cannot tell you at this moment whether or not something will be tabled today, tomorrow or the next day. But a productive two weeks are becoming even more productive. But there are no assurances about what will happen next, still.

Q. Okay, then on the fudge question, how did you work the question in, I guess—

Mr. Fleischer. John, I think what I'd like to do is, until a motion is tabled, I'm not going to describe any of the language. There still are conversations going on with the members of the Security Council about the exact language.

Q. But you know what the French wanted, they wanted the Security Council to decide what constituted a further material breach.

Mr. Fleischer. Let me just say that this has been a very dedicated effort by America's diplomats, and a very important one. The diplomats have worked very hard to work with our friends and allies to find agreement on language. It's a reflection of the path that the President committed to. It's a reflection of the efforts made by the U.N. officials, by the State Department officials, by others in our government, to bring this to a point where we could keep the United Nations Security Council together.

This has been a test of the Security Council. We still have a final stage to go through with the Security Council. But I'm not going to characterize any of the specific word changes at this moment. I think that will all come out shortly, I'm just not prepared to do so at 11:30 a.m. central time.

Q. But I take it, though, that this isn't a game of brinkmanship. You work the language and you work with friends and Russia to the point where everybody is comfortable with it. You're not about to lay down something that will draw a veto?

Mr. Fleischer. It's been a very healthy dose of good, solid diplomacy, backed up by a clear understanding that President Bush was determined to take action if the United Nations did not, and that he would do so in a multi-lateral way.

Q. How confident are you that there will be a vote this week?

Mr. Fleischer. Again, I'm not prepared to make any specific guesses about whether these will be tabled today, tomorrow or whatever day. That's something that the diplomats will make a final determination of.

Q. And if it doesn't happen this week, when will the clock that you've said all along is ticking, when will it run out?

Mr. Fleischer. I'm just not prepared to make any guesses on the final timetable. But it's abundantly clear that we are reaching the point of finality.

Q. Has he made any phone calls on this today?

Mr. Fleischer. I'll let you know if he does. I don't anticipate any.

Q. And so far, has he been heartened or disheartened by the process at the U.N.?

Mr. Fleischer. The President will make his final judgement after a vote is cast. This has been a slow process, but an important one. The President committed to this process. One of the ironies of this entire debate is the phony charge against President Bush that he would engage in unilateralism. What President Bush has done is demonstrated strength and determination, which has given multilaterialsm a chance. Unilateralism was the way of the '90s, because the multilateral organization known as the Security Council was slumbering, and the unilateralist was Saddam Hussein. Thanks to the President's strength and leadership by going up to New York and saying, this is your chance, the United Nations, to be relevant, the President changed the equation of what it means to be unilateral and what it means to be multilateral.

The fact of the matter is it was the President's black and white language, the President's moral standing and moral clarity that gave impetus to the multilateral United Nations to finally wake up and look at the Iraq situation seriously. We'll see ultimately what the outcome is. That still is a question mark. We'll see.

United States' Draft Security Council Resolution on Iraq, November 6, 2002

Recalling all its previous relevant resolutions, in particular its resolutions 661 (1990) of 6 August 1990, 678 (1990) of 29 November 1990, 686 (1991) of 2 March 1991, 687 (1991) of 3 April 1991, 688 (1991) of 5 April 1991, 707 (1991) of 15 August 1991, 715 (1991) of 11 October 1991, 986 (1995) of 14 April 1995, and 1284 (1999) of 17 December 1999, and all the relevant statements of its president,

Recalling also its resolution 1382 (2001) of 29 November 2001 and its intention to implement it fully, Recognizing the threat Iraq's noncompliance with council resolutions and proliferation of weapons of mass destruction and long-range missiles poses to international peace and security,

Recalling that its resolution 678 (1990) authorized member states to use all necessary means to uphold and implement its resolution 660 (1990) of 2 August 1990 and all relevant resolutions subsequent to resolution 660 (1990) and to restore international peace and security in the area,

Further recalling that its resolution 687 (1991) imposed obligations on Iraq as a necessary step for achievement of its stated objective of restoring international peace and security in the area,

Deploring the fact that Iraq has not provided an accurate, full, final, and complete disclosure, as required by resolution 687 (1991), of all aspects of its programs to develop weapons of mass destruction and ballistic missiles with a range greater than 150 kilometers, and of all holdings of such weapons, their components and production facilities and locations, as well as all other nuclear programs, including any which it claims are for purposes not related to nuclear-weapons-usable material,

Deploring further that Iraq repeatedly obstructed immediate, unconditional, and unrestricted access to sites designated by the United Nations Special Commission (UNSCOM) and the International Atomic Energy Agency (IAEA), failed to cooperate fully and unconditionally with UNSCOM and IAEA weapons inspectors, as required by resolution 687 (1991), and ultimately ceased all cooperation with UNSCOM and the IAEA in 1998,

Deploring the absence, since December 1998, in Iraq of international monitoring, inspection, and verification, as required by relevant resolutions, of weapons of mass destruction and ballistic missiles, in spite of the council's repeated demands that Iraq provide immediate, unconditional, and unrestricted access to the United Nations Monitoring, Verification and Inspection Commission (UNMOVIC), established in resolution 1284 (1999) as the successor organization to UNSCOM, and the IAEA, and regretting the consequent prolonging of the crisis in the region and the suffering of the Iraqi people,

Deploring also that the Government of Iraq has failed to comply with its commitments pursuant to resolution 687 (1991) with regard to terrorism, pursuant to resolution 688 (1991) to end repression of its civilian population and to provide access by international humanitarian organizations to all those in need of assistance in Iraq, and pursuant to resolutions 686 (1991), 687 (1991), and 1284 (1999) to return or cooperate in accounting for Kuwaiti and third country nationals wrongfully detained by Iraq, or to return Kuwaiti property wrongfully seized by Iraq,

Recalling that in its resolution 687 (1991) the council declared that a cease-fire would be based on acceptance by Iraq of the provisions of that resolution, including the obligations on Iraq contained therein,

Determined to ensure full and immediate compliance by Iraq without conditions or restrictions with its obligations under resolution 687 (1991) and other relevant resolutions and recalling that the resolutions of the council constitute the governing standard of Iraqi compliance,

Recalling that the effective operation of UNMOVIC, as the successor organization to the Special Commission, and the IAEA, is essential for the implementation of resolution 687 (1991) and other relevant resolutions,

Noting the letter dated 16 September 2002 from the minister for foreign affairs of Iraq addressed to the secretary-general is a necessary first step toward rectifying Iraq's continued failure to comply with relevant council resolutions,

Noting further the letter dated 8 October 2002 from the executive chairman of UNMOVIC and the director general of the IAEA to General Al-Saadi of the government of Iraq laying out the practical arrangements, as a follow-up to their meeting in Vienna, that are prerequisites for the resumption of inspections in Iraq by UNMOVIC and the IAEA, and expressing the gravest concern at the continued failure by the government of Iraq to provide confirmation of the arrangements as laid out in that letter,

Reaffirming the commitment of all member states to the sovereignty and territorial integrity of Iraq, Kuwait, and the neighboring states,

Commending the secretary-general and the members of the League of Arab States and its secretary-general for their efforts in this regard,

Determined to secure full compliance with its decisions, Acting under Chapter VII of the Charter of the United Nations,

1. Decides that Iraq has been and remains in material breach of its obligations under relevant resolutions, including resolution 687 (1991), in particular through Iraq's failure to cooperate with United Nations inspectors and the IAEA, and to complete the actions required under paragraphs 8 to 13 of resolution 687 (1991);

2. Decides, while acknowledging paragraph 1 above, to afford Iraq, by this resolution, a final opportunity to comply with its disarmament obligations under relevant

resolutions of the council; and accordingly decides to set up an enhanced inspection regime with the aim of bringing to full and verified completion the disarmament process established by resolution 687 (1991) and subsequent resolutions of the council;

3. Decides that, in order to begin to comply with its disarmament obligations, in addition to submitting the required biannual declarations, the government of Iraq shall provide to UNMOVIC, the IAEA, and the council, not later than 30 days from the date of this resolution, a currently accurate, full, and complete declaration of all aspects of its programs to develop chemical, biological, and nuclear weapons, ballistic missiles, and other delivery systems such as unmanned aerial vehicles and dispersal systems designed for use on aircraft, including any holdings and precise locations of such weapons, components, sub-components, stocks of agents, and related material and equipment, the locations and work of its research, development and production facilities, as well as all other chemical, biological, and nuclear programs, including any which it claims are for purposes not related to weapon production or material;

4. Decides that false statements or omissions in the declarations submitted by Iraq pursuant to this resolution and failure by Iraq at any time to comply with, and cooperate fully in the implementation of, this resolution shall constitute a further material breach of Iraq's obligations and will be reported to the council for assessment in accordance with paragraph 11 or 12 below;

5. Decides that Iraq shall provide UNMOVIC and the IAEA immediate, unimpeded, unconditional, and unrestricted access to any and all, including underground, areas, facilities, buildings, equipment, records, and means of transport which they wish to inspect, as well as immediate, unimpeded, unrestricted, and private access to all officials and other persons whom UNMOVIC or the IAEA wish to interview in the mode or location of UNMOVIC's or the IAEA's choice pursuant to any aspect of their mandates; further decides that UNMOVIC and the IAEA may at their discretion conduct interviews inside or outside of Iraq, may facilitate the travel of those interviewed and family members outside of Iraq, and that, at the sole discretion of UNMOVIC and the IAEA, such interviews may occur without the presence of observers from the Iraqi government; and instructs UNMOVIC and requests the IAEA to resume inspections no later than 45 days following adoption of this resolution and to update the council 60 days thereafter;

6. Endorses the 8 October 2002 letter from the executive chairman of UNMOVIC and the director general of the IAEA to General Al-Saadi of the government of Iraq, which is annexed hereto, and decides that the contents of the letter shall be binding upon Iraq;

7. Decides further that, in view of the prolonged interruption by Iraq of the presence of UNMOVIC and the IAEA and in order for them to accomplish the tasks set forth in this resolution and all previous relevant resolutions and notwithstanding prior understandings, the council hereby establishes the following revised or additional authorities, which shall be binding upon Iraq, to facilitate their work in Iraq:

• UNMOVIC and the IAEA shall determine the composition of their inspection teams and ensure that these teams are composed of the most qualified and experienced experts available;

• All UNMOVIC and IAEA personnel shall enjoy the privileges and immunities provided in the Convention on Privileges and Immunities of the United Nations and the Agreement on the Privileges and Immunities of the IAEA;

• UNMOVIC and the IAEA shall have unrestricted rights of entry into and out of Iraq, the right to free, unrestricted, and immediate movement to and from inspection sites, and the right to inspect any sites and buildings, including immediate, unimpeded, unconditional, and unrestricted access to presidential sites equal to that at other sites, notwithstanding the provisions of resolution 1154 (1998);

• UNMOVIC and the IAEA shall have the right to be provided by Iraq the names of all personnel currently and formerly associated with Iraq's chemical, biological, nuclear, and ballistic missile programs and the associated research, development, and production facilities;

• Security of UNMOVIC and IAEA facilities shall be ensured by sufficient U.N. security guards:

• UNMOVIC and the IAEA shall have the right to declare for the purposes of freezing a site to be inspected, exclusion zones, including surrounding areas and transit corridors, in which Iraq will suspend ground and aerial movement so that nothing is changed in or taken out of a site being inspected;

• UNMOVIC and the IAEA shall have the free and unrestricted use and landing of fixed and rotary winged aircraft, including manned and unmanned reconnaissance vehicles:

• UNMOVIC and the IAEA shall have the right at their sole discretion verifiably to remove, destroy, or render harmless all prohibited weapons, subsystems, components, records, materials, and other related items, and the right to impound or close any facilities or equipment for the production thereof; and

• UNMOVIC and the IAEA shall have the right to free import and use of equipment or materials for inspections and to seize and export any equipment, materials, or documents taken during inspections, without search of UNMOVIC or IAEA personnel or official or personal baggage;

8. Decides further that Iraq shall not take or threaten hostile acts directed against any representative or personnel of the United Nations or of any member state taking action to uphold any council resolution;

9. Requests the secretary-general immediately to notify Iraq of this resolution, which is binding on Iraq; demands that Iraq confirm within seven days of that notification its intention to comply fully with this resolution; and demands further that Iraq cooperate immediately, unconditionally, and actively with UNMOVIC and the IAEA;

10. Requests all member states to give full support to UNMOVIC and the IAEA in the discharge of their mandates, including by providing any information related to prohibited programs or other aspects of their mandates; including on Iraqi attempts since 1998 to acquire prohibited items, and by recommending sites to be inspected, persons to be interviewed, conditions of such interviews, and data to be collected, the results of which shall be reported to the council by UNMOVIC and the IAEA;

11. Directs the executive chairman of UNMOVIC and the director general of the IAEA to report immediately to the council any interference by Iraq with inspection activities, as well as any failure by Iraq to comply with its disarmament obligations, including its obligations regarding inspections under this resolution;

12. Decides to convene immediately upon receipt of a report in accordance with paragraphs 4 or 11 above, in order to consider the situation and the need for full compliance with all of the relevant council resolutions in order to restore international peace and security;

13. Recalls, in that context, that the council has repeatedly warned Iraq that it will face serious consequences as a result of its continued violations of its obligations;

14. Decides to remain seized of the matter.

White House Press Briefing, November 6, 2002

Q. I wanted to ask you about the Iraq resolution. The resolution that has now been circulated at the U.N. Security Council, A, is it going to pass; B, is this what the President wanted all along; C, hasn't he given up a lot? I guess, I'll ask D, as well—does he feel that he has the right under this resolution to see Iraqi defiance and say, we're going to combat it with military force?

Mr. Fleischer. Well, one, the President views this as has been a long, but a very constructive and important process by focusing on diplomacy and asking the United Nations to fulfill its important responsibilities to keep the peace.

The President made the decision to go to the United Nations. He set this course in motion, and the course he set in motion is now coming to a head. The United States is seeking a vote on this resolution on Friday this week. We, in New York, laid down the resolution today. This is a revised text of our resolution that makes crystal clear that Iraq must disarm.

For six weeks, efforts by the President, by Secretary Powell, by Ambassador Negroponte in New York, we have put together the key elements of a resolution that we hope will meet with support of all the members of the Security Council. The resolution we'll circulate takes into views—takes into account the views that we heard from our allies on the Security Council. And it meets the goals that the President identified from the start.

From the start the President made clear that any resolution to be voted on had to say that Iraq is in material breach. This resolution does. He made it clear that it had to provide for a very tough inspection regime. This resolution does that. And the President made it clear the there will be serious consequences if Iraq fails to disarm. This resolution accomplishes all of those core principles. And it does so in a way that we believe will also attract the support of our allies whose voices are important and whose voices the President wanted to listen to.

Q. Those voices, principally, were concerned about—they wanted this issue to go back to the Security Council if there was further Iraqi defiance. Under this draft, do we have to go back to the Security Council? Or is the President empowered to make a decision on his own?

Mr. Fleischer. Under this draft, and as always at the United Nations, it is the prerogative and the right of any member of the Security Council to convene, to hold a meeting as they judge wise and see fit. Nothing in this resolution handcuffs the President, and the President thinks it is very important and has committed to further consultations.

Q. This would have the international legal authority, this resolution alone, that the President would be able to take the country to war against Iraq?

Mr. Fleischer. It's exactly as I just stated.

Remarks by United Nations Secretary-General Annan, November 6, 2002

The discussions are going on in very good spirit and I think we are making progress.

* * * *

Q. Do you have any idea if the U.S. is going to have a resounding support of its resolution?

Secretary-General Annan. I have always maintained that it is important that the Council speaks with one voice and I hope everyone will be seeking a broad consensus. I would prefer to see a unanimous decision—15-0.

* * * *

Q. Are you being given that indication in the meeting today?

Secretary-General Annan. I have always given that indication all along. That has always been my position. That is when we are really effective. Thank you.

Remarks by President Bush, November 7, 2002

Q. Mr. President, how confident are you that the Security Council will approve the tough new resolution on Iraq? And if that happens, what happens next; what's the next step? Is war inevitable?

President Bush. Well, first of all, the resolution we put down is a tough new resolution. It talks about material breach and inspections and serious consequences if Saddam Hussein continues to defy the world and not disarm. So, one, I'm pleased with the resolution we put down. Otherwise, we wouldn't have put it down.

I just talked to Jacques Chirac, and earlier today I talked to Vladimir Putin. I characterize our conversation—I'm loathe to put words in somebody else's mouth. That's, evidently, not the case with a lot of people in Washington, but nevertheless, I am. And I'm optimistic we'll get the resolution vote tomorrow—let me put it to you that way.

And, Steve, the resolution is a disarmament resolution; that's what it is. It's a statement of intent to, once and for all, disarm Saddam Hussein. He's a threat. He's a threat to the country, he's a threat to people in his neighborhood. He's a real threat. And it's now time for the world to come together and disarm him. And when this resolution passes, I will—we'll be able to say that the United Nations has recognized the threat, and now we're going to work together to disarm him.

And he must be cooperative in the disarmament. So the job of inspectors is to determine his level of cooperation, see. He has got to be the agent of disarming; he's got to agree that what we're doing is what he said he we do. And just like the United Nations has agreed that it is important to disarm him, for the sake of peace, and so the next step will be to put an inspection regime in there to—after all the declarations and after all the preamble to inspections, that he's got to show the world he's disarming. And that's where we'll be next.

* * * *

Q. You are leaving the impression that you wouldn't mind if you go to war against Iraq, but you deal with another nation which may have weapons in a different way. But there are two other impressions around. One, that you have an obsession with going after Saddam Hussein at any cost. And also that you covet the oil fields.

President Bush. Yes. Well, I'm—some people have the right impressions and some people have the wrong impressions.

Q. Can you—

President Bush. Well, those are the wrong impressions.

Q. Okay.

President Bush. I have a deep desire for peace. That's what I have a desire for. And freedom for the Iraqi people. See, I don't like a system where people are repressed through torture and murder in order to keep a dictator in place. It troubles me deeply. And so the Iraqi people must hear this loud and clear, that this country never has any intention to conquer anybody. That's not the intention of the American people or our government. We believe in freedom and we believe in peace. And we believe the Iraqi dictator is a threat to peace. And so that's why I made the decisions I made, in terms of Iraq.

Q. Thank you, sir. On Iraq, you've said many times that if Saddam Hussein does not disarm, he will be disarmed militarily, if necessary, by the U.N. or the U.S. and others. There's a school of thought that says that going to war against Iraq would be a dangerous and misguided idea because it would generate a tremendous amount of anger and hatred at the United States, and out of that you'd essentially be creating many new terrorists who would want to kill Americans. What's wrong with that analysis?

President Bush. Well, that's like saying we should not go after al Qaeda because we might irritate somebody and that would create a danger to Americans. My attitude is you got to deal with terrorism in a firm way. And if they see threats you deal with them in all different kinds of ways. The only way, in my judgment, to deal with Saddam Hussein is to bring the international community together to convince him to disarm.

But if he's not going to disarm, we'll disarm him, in order to make the world a more peaceful place. And some people aren't going to like that—I understand. But some people won't like it if he ends with a nuclear weapon and uses it. We have an obligation to lead. And I intend to assume that obligation to make the world more peaceful.

Terry, listen, there's risk in all action we take. But the risk of inaction is not a choice, as far as I'm concerned. The inaction creates more risk than doing our duty to make the world more peaceful. And obviously, I weighed all the consequences about all the differences. Hopefully, we can do this peacefully—don't get me wrong. And if the world were to collectively come together to do so, and to put pressure on Saddam Hussein and convince him to disarm, there's a chance he may decide to do that.

And war is not my first choice, don't—it's my last choice. But nevertheless, it is a— it is an option in order to make the world a more peaceful place.

* * * *

Q. Mr. President, thank you very much. You have put a lot of effort toward getting the United Nations to rally the world to disarm Saddam Hussein. And yet you and your aides have expressed a great deal of skepticism about whether Saddam Hussein will actually comply. Can you give us an idea, sir, how long you think it might take for the world to know whether Saddam Hussein actually intends to go along with the call of the world to disarm? Will it be a matter of days or weeks, months, or perhaps a year, sir?

President Bush. Well, Wendell, this much we know—it's so far taken him 11 years and 16 resolutions to do nothing. And so we've got some kind of history as to the man's behavior. We know he likes to try to deceive and deny, and that's why this inspection regime has got to be new and tough and different. The status quo is unacceptable, you know, kind of send a few people in there and hope maybe he's nice to them and open up the baby milk factory—it's unacceptable.

And so that's why you'll see us with a different inspection regime, one that works to see to it that Saddam Hussein disarms. It's his responsibility to disarm. I don't put timetables on anything. But for the sake of peace—sooner, better.

And we'll see. But you must know that I am serious—so are a lot of other countries—serious about holding the man to account. I was serious about holding the U.N. to account. And when they pass this resolution, which I hope they do tomorrow, it shows that the U.N. is beginning to assume its responsibilities to make sure that 11 years of defiance does not go unanswered. It's very important that the U.N. be a successful international body because the threats that we face now require more cooperation than ever. And we're still cooperating with a lot of nations. We're still sharing intelligence and cutting off money the best we can. And there's still law enforcement efforts taking place all around the world.

And that's why the international—this international body called the U.N. is an important body for keeping the peace. And it's very important that they're effective. And we'll see tomorrow—starting tomorrow.

And then the key on the resolution, I want to remind you, is that there are serious consequences. And that's one of the key elements to make sure that everybody gets the picture that we are serious about a process of disarming him in the name of peace. Hopefully, he'll choose to do so himself.

* * * *

Q. Thank you, Mr. President. You said this afternoon that the U.N. Security Council vote tomorrow would bring the civilized world together against Iraq. But broad opposition remains all over the world to your policy. Will you continue to try to build support and, if so, how will you do that? Or do you think that a Security Council vote would be all the mandate you need?

President Bush. First of all, broad opposition around the world not in support of my policy on Iraq?

Q. Yes, sir.

President Bush. Well, I think most people around the world realize that Saddam Hussein is a threat. And they—no one likes war, but they also don't like the idea of Saddam Hussein having a nuclear weapon. Imagine what would happen. And by the way, we don't know how close he is to a nuclear weapon right now. We know he wants one. But we don't know. We know he was close to one at one point in time; we have no idea today. Imagine Saddam Hussein with a nuclear weapon. Imagine how the Israeli citizens would feel. Imagine how the citizens in Saudi Arabia would feel. Imagine how the world would change, how he could alter diplomacy by the very presence of a nuclear weapon.

And so a lot of people—serious people around the world are beginning to think about that consideration. I think about it a lot. I think about it particularly in the regard of making the world a more peaceful place.

And so it's very important for people to realize the consequences of us not taking the case to the U.N. Security Council. People need to think about what would happen if the United States had remained silent on this issue and just hoped for a change of his attitude, or maybe hoped that he would not invade somebody again, or just hoped that he wouldn't use gas on his own people when pressure at home began to mount.

I'm not willing to take those kind of risks. People understand that. I think a lot of people are saying, you know, gosh, we hope we don't have war. I feel the same way, I hope we don't have war. I hope this can be done peacefully. It's up to Saddam Hussein, however, to make that choice.

I also want to remind you that, should we have to use troops, should it become a necessity in order to disarm him, the United States, with friends, will move swiftly with force to do the job. You don't have to worry about that. We will do—we will do—we will do what it takes militarily to succeed.

I also want to say something else to people of Iraq, that the generals in Iraq must understand clearly there will be consequences for their behavior. Should they choose, if force is necessary, to behave in a way that endangers the lives of their own citizens, as well as citizens in the neighborhood, there will be a consequence. They will be held to account.

And as to the Iraq people, what I said before—the Iraqi people can have a better life than the one they have now. They can have a—there are other alternatives to somebody who is willing to rape and mutilate and murder in order to stay in power. There's just a better life than the one they have to live now.

I think the people of the world understand that too, Judy. I don't take—I don't take—I don't spend a lot of time taking polls around the world to tell me what I think is the right way to act; I've just got to know how I feel. I feel strongly about freedom. I feel strongly about liberty. And I feel strongly about the obligation to make the world a more peaceful place. And I take those responsibilities really seriously.

* * * *

Q. Your CIA Director told Congress just last month that it appears that Saddam Hussein "now appears to be drawing a line short of conducting terrorist attacks against the United States." But if we attacked him he would "probably become much less constrained." Is he wrong about that?

President Bush. No. I think that—I think that if you would read the full—I'm sure he said other sentences. Let me just put it to you, I know George Tenet well. I meet with him every single day. He sees Saddam Hussein as a threat. I don't know what the context of that quote is. I'm telling you, the guy knows what I know, that he is a problem and we must deal with him.

And, you know, it's like people say, oh, we must leave Saddam alone; otherwise, if we did something against him, he might attack us. Well, if we don't do something, he might attack us, and he might attack us with a more serious weapon. The man is a threat, Hutch, I'm telling you. He's a threat not only with what he has, he's a threat with what he's done. He's a threat because he is dealing with al Qaeda. In my Cincinnati speech, I reminded the American people, a true threat facing our country is that an al Qaeda-type network trained and armed by Saddam could attack America and leave not one fingerprint. That is a threat. And we're going to deal with it.

The debate about whether we're going to deal with Saddam Hussein is over. And now the question is how do we deal with him. I made the decision to go to the United Nations because I want to try to do this peacefully. I want Saddam to disarm. The best way to convince him to disarm is to get the nations to come together through the U.N. and try to convince him to disarm.

We're going to work on that. We've been spending a lot of time—I wouldn't exactly call it gnashing of teeth, but working hard on the U.N. resolution. It took a while, but we've been grinding it out, trying to bring a consensus, trying to get people together, so that we can say to the world the international community has spoken through the Security Council of the United Nations and now, once again, we expect Saddam to disarm.

This would be the 17th time that we expect Saddam to disarm. This time we mean it. See, that's the difference—I guess. This time it's for real. And I say it must not have been for real the last 16 times because nothing happened when he didn't. This time something happens. He knows—he's got to understand that. The members of the U.N. Security Council understand that. Saddam has got to understand it so he, so, in the name of peace, for a peaceful resolution of this, we hope he disarms.

Remarks by Secretary of State Powell, November 7, 2002

Secretary Colin Powell was interviewed by the Associated Press.

Q. Guess what. Iraq. It is in the bag do you think? Is it a done deal? Richard said the other day you're making a couple of modifications they've asked for.

Secretary Powell. We're still working on some suggestions. If you followed the discussions at the U.N. yesterday, you know that different delegations raised issues. Yesterday was the first time we formally tabled a resolution. Really it was the third draft that we had of it. And we have to give our other Security Council colleagues time to reflect on it. So some changes have come forward and we're looking at all of those.

But I am still hopeful that we will have a vote in the very near future, perhaps tomorrow, and we're still driving toward that goal. Maybe it will or will not occur, but we're still hopeful there will be a vote tomorrow. And we're working off the remaining differences, in touch with my various colleagues, as I have been in the past. I've spoken to Foreign Minister Straw this morning, and I expect to speak to Minister Ivanov and Minister de Villepin and perhaps others before the day is out.

Q. Is it still true that the bottom line is intact?

Secretary Powell. Yes.

Q. The tough provisions are still—

Secretary Powell. Yes. I think as you've heard me say many times before, Barry, I think it was essential that we have a resolution that acknowledges Iraq's material breaches of the past and of the present—they have not gone away—and that we made clear that further violations related to this resolution should be also considered material breaches, and that we have in place a tough inspection regime and that the Council has to be prepared to make sure that Iraq understands that there will be consequences for continued violation of resolutions. So our lines are crystal clear.

But I think it's clear to everyone that we took this time, this seven weeks now, almost—I think it's seven weeks today since the President gave his speech. We took this time to talk to our friends and allies to make the case. And there were tough discussions and negotiations and we tried to listen and to accommodate them. They had their principles and red lines and we had ours, and we found a way to converge. And I think the convergence is near complete.

Q. Are you going to go up there, do you think, to bring it home?

Secretary Powell. I haven't made a decision on that.

Q. What is a reasonable amount of time to give inspections a real chance to work?

Secretary Powell. Well, what we're looking for, really, in the first instance in the days and weeks following the passage of a resolution is whether or not the Iraqis are going to cooperate in a way in which they have not cooperated in the past. If they don't intend to cooperate, I think that will become obvious rather soon, and the U.N. will then have to make its judgment as to whether they want to participate in a charade with the Iraqi Government again or whether they want immediately to convene to see whether something else should be done.

If Iraq does indicate a clear willingness to cooperate—and I have no idea whether they will or they won't, but the history is not good on this, as my colleague Donald Rumsfeld repeatedly reminds the world—but if they decide to cooperate this time, then Dr. Blix and Mr. ElBaradei will go in and start to do their work.

It will take some time for them to bring their baselines up to 2002, to deploy their people, and to start doing inspections. I cannot speak for them as to how many months they think it would take, but certainly it will take time for these inspections to be conducted, and a lot will depend on what the inspections find and how extensive the inspections are. So I can't give you a precise timeline with respect to how many months it will take.

And then I could ask the question back, "Take to do what?" Take to exhaust everything one can look at? Take to come to a conclusion that these weapons do or do not exist, and if they do exist, we've found them and we've destroyed them? I'm reluctant to speculate on how long it could take because then that gets us into a discussion, "Well, when does the war begin?" And I am very reluctant to do that for obvious reasons, because I don't know.

Q. But months is, when you said—

Secretary Powell. The plan that Dr. Blix is executing on, the basic design of the UNMOVIC inspection regime, is something that takes months, not weeks.

Remarks by United Nations Secretary-General Annan, November 7, 2002

Q. I was wondering if you heard anything from Baghdad since the U.S. has presented this draft resolution.

Secretary-General Annan. No, not directly, not directly. But I think we'd probably have a reaction once there has been a final decision. And we are all hoping that it would be sometime tomorrow.

* * * *

Q. Do you have any reason for optimism, or do you have any indication of how Baghdad will react once the [Security] Council, if it does, pass the text of the resolution?

Secretary-General Annan. We've been getting different signals. I mean, they had indicated to cooperate and they have raised some questions. And again I think we will have to see the resolution passed and to have the inspectors return and see what happens on the ground.

* * * *

Q. And you hope that this could avoid a U.S.-led military strike?

Secretary-General Annan. I think for the Council the issue is disarmament. If Iraq cooperates and the inspectors can get that work done, I think the Council will be less inclined to think in terms of military action.

Chapter 5

November 8–December 18, 2002
United Nations Security Council Resolution 1441 Affords Iraq a "Final Opportunity" to Comply with Disarmament Obligations

CHRONOLOGY

2002

November 8. The United Nations Security Council unanimously adopts Resolution 1441, stating that United Nations inspectors must be given the unconditional right to search anywhere in Iraq for banned weapons, and that Iraq must within seven days acknowledge that right. The resolution further requires Iraq to make an "accurate full and complete" declaration of its nuclear, chemical, biological and ballistic weapons and related materials used in civilian industries within 30 days. The resolution requires violations to be reported back to the Security Council by inspectors before any actions are taken against Iraq for violating weapons bans.

November 13. Iraq states its acceptance of U.N. Security Council Resolution 1441 and informs the U.N. that it will abide by the resolution, "despite its bad contents." In the letter, Iraq also denies that it possesses any weapons of mass destruction. Weapons inspectors arrive in Baghdad again after a four-year absence.

November 25. The UNSC extends the "Oil-for-Food" program to give Security Council members time to reach agreement on which goods would be placed on a "goods review list" which are goods that require approval before Iraq can use its revenues to purchase them.

December 4. The U.N. Oil-for-Food program is unanimously renewed by the Security Council for another six months, and shortly thereafter accepted by the Iraqi government.

December 7. Iraq files a 12,000-page weapons declaration with the IAEA and U.N. in order to meet requirements of Resolution 1441. Turkey moves approximately 15,000 soldiers to the border with Iraq.

December 12. Iraq cancels a $3.8 billion contract with three Russian companies—Lukoil, Zarubezhnest, and Machinoimport—to develop the very large West Qurna oil field.

Sources: Chronology entries are drawn from www.abc.com, www.bbc.com, www.nytimes.com, www.reuters.com, www.washingtonpost.com, www.wikipedia.com, and staff research.

DOCUMENTS

United Nations Security Council Resolution 1441, November 8, 2002

The Security Council,

Recalling all its previous relevant resolutions, in particular its resolutions 661 (1990) of 6 August 1990, 678 (1990) of 29 November 1990, 686 (1991) of 2 March 1991, 687 (1991) of 3 April 1991, 688 (1991) of 5 April 1991, 707 (1991) of 15 August 1991, 715 (1991) of 11 October 1991, 986 (1995) of 14 April 1995, and 1284 (1999) of 17 December 1999, and all the relevant statements of its President,

Recalling also its resolution 1382 (2001) of 29 November 2001 and its intention to implement it fully,

Recognizing the threat Iraq's non-compliance with Council resolutions and proliferation of weapons of mass destruction and long-range missiles poses to international peace and security,

Recalling that its resolution 678 (1990) authorized Member States to use all necessary means to uphold and implement its resolution 660 (1990) of 2 August 1990 and all relevant resolutions subsequent to resolution 660 (1990) and to restore international peace and security in the area,

Further recalling that its resolution 687 (1991) imposed obligations on Iraq as a necessary step for achievement of its stated objective of restoring international peace and security in the area,

Deploring the fact that Iraq has not provided an accurate, full, final, and complete disclosure, as required by resolution 687 (1991), of all aspects of its programs to develop weapons of mass destruction and ballistic missiles with a range greater than one hundred and fifty kilometers, and of all holdings of such weapons, their components and production facilities and locations, as well as all other nuclear programs, including any which it claims are for purposes not related to nuclear-weapons-usable material,

Deploring further that Iraq repeatedly obstructed immediate, unconditional, and unrestricted access to sites designated by the United Nations Special Commission (UNSCOM) and the International Atomic Energy Agency (IAEA), failed to cooperate fully and unconditionally with UNSCOM and IAEA weapons inspectors, as required by resolution 687 (1991), and ultimately ceased all cooperation with UNSCOM and the IAEA in 1998,

Deploring the absence, since December 1998, in Iraq of international monitoring, inspection, and verification, as required by relevant resolutions, of weapons of mass destruction and ballistic missiles, in spite of the Council's repeated demands that Iraq provide immediate, unconditional, and unrestricted access to the United Nations Monitoring, Verification and Inspection Commission (UNMOVIC), established in resolution 1284 (1999) as the successor organization to UNSCOM, and the IAEA, and regretting the consequent prolonging of the crisis in the region and the suffering of the Iraqi people,

Deploring also that the Government of Iraq has failed to comply with its commitments pursuant to resolution 687 (1991) with regard to terrorism, pursuant to resolution 688 (1991) to end repression of its civilian population and to provide access by international humanitarian organizations to all those in need of assistance in Iraq, and pursuant to resolutions 686 (1991), 687 (1991), and 1284 (1999) to return or cooperate in accounting for Kuwaiti and third country nationals wrongfully detained by Iraq, or to return Kuwaiti property wrongfully seized by Iraq,

Recalling that in its resolution 687 (1991) the Council declared that a ceasefire would be based on acceptance by Iraq of the provisions of that resolution, including the obligations on Iraq contained therein,

Determined to ensure full and immediate compliance by Iraq without conditions or restrictions with its obligations under resolution 687 (1991) and other relevant resolutions and recalling that the resolutions of the Council constitute the governing standard of Iraqi compliance,

Recalling that the effective operation of UNMOVIC, as the successor organization to the Special Commission, and the IAEA is essential for the implementation of resolution 687 (1991) and other relevant resolutions,

Noting that the letter dated 16 September 2002 from the Minister for Foreign Affairs of Iraq addressed to the Secretary-General is a necessary first step toward rectifying Iraq's continued failure to comply with relevant Council resolutions,

Noting further the letter dated 8 October 2002 from the Executive Chairman of UNMOVIC and the Director-General of the IAEA to General Al-Saadi of the Government of Iraq laying out the practical arrangements, as a follow-up to their meeting in Vienna, that are prerequisites for the resumption of inspections in Iraq by UNMOVIC and the IAEA, and expressing the gravest concern at the continued failure by the Government of Iraq to provide confirmation of the arrangements as laid out in that letter,

Reaffirming the commitment of all Member States to the sovereignty and territorial integrity of Iraq, Kuwait, and the neighboring States, Commending the Secretary-General and members of the League of Arab States and its Secretary-General for their efforts in this regard,

Determined to secure full compliance with its decisions,

Acting under Chapter VII of the Charter of the United Nations,

1. *Decides* that Iraq has been and remains in material breach of its obligations under relevant resolutions, including resolution 687 (1991), in particular through Iraq's failure to cooperate with United Nations inspectors and the IAEA, and to complete the actions required under paragraphs 8 to 13 of resolution 687 (1991);

2. *Decides*, while acknowledging paragraph 1 above, to afford Iraq, by this resolution, a final opportunity to comply with its disarmament obligations under relevant resolutions of the Council; and accordingly decides to set up an enhanced inspection

regime with the aim of bringing to full and verified completion the disarmament process established by resolution 687 (1991) and subsequent resolutions of the Council;

3. *Decides* that, in order to begin to comply with its disarmament obligations, in addition to submitting the required biannual declarations, the Government of Iraq shall provide to UNMOVIC, the IAEA, and the Council, not later than 30 days from the date of this resolution, a currently accurate, full, and complete declaration of all aspects of its programs to develop chemical, biological, and nuclear weapons, ballistic missiles, and other delivery systems such as unmanned aerial vehicles and dispersal systems designed for use on aircraft, including any holdings and precise locations of such weapons, components, subcomponents, stocks of agents, and related material and equipment, the locations and work of its research, development and production facilities, as well as all other chemical, biological, and nuclear programs, including any which it claims are for purposes not related to weapon production or material;

4. *Decides* that false statements or omissions in the declarations submitted by Iraq pursuant to this resolution and failure by Iraq at any time to comply with, and cooperate fully in the implementation of, this resolution shall constitute a further material breach of Iraq's obligations and will be reported to the Council for assessment in accordance with paragraphs 11 and 12 below;

5. *Decides* that Iraq shall provide UNMOVIC and the IAEA immediate, unimpeded, unconditional, and unrestricted access to any and all, including underground, areas, facilities, buildings, equipment, records, and means of transport which they wish to inspect, as well as immediate, unimpeded, unrestricted, and private access to all officials and other persons whom UNMOVIC or the IAEA wish to interview in the mode or location of UNMOVIC's or the IAEA's choice pursuant to any aspect of their mandates; further decides that UNMOVIC and the IAEA may at their discretion conduct interviews inside or outside of Iraq, may facilitate the travel of those interviewed and family members outside of Iraq, and that, at the sole discretion of UNMOVIC and the IAEA, such interviews may occur without the presence of observers from the Iraqi Government; and instructs UNMOVIC and requests the IAEA to resume inspections no later than 45 days following adoption of this resolution and to update the Council 60 days thereafter;

6. *Endorses* the 8 October 2002 letter from the Executive Chairman of UNMOVIC and the Director-General of the IAEA to General Al-Saadi of the Government of Iraq, which is annexed hereto, and decides that the contents of the letter shall be binding upon Iraq;

7. *Decides* further that, in view of the prolonged interruption by Iraq of the presence of UNMOVIC and the IAEA and in order for them to accomplish the tasks set forth in this resolution and all previous relevant resolutions and notwithstanding prior understandings, the Council hereby establishes the following revised or additional authorities, which shall be binding upon Iraq, to facilitate their work in Iraq:

• UNMOVIC and the IAEA shall determine the composition of their inspection teams and ensure that these teams are composed of the most qualified and experienced experts available;

• All UNMOVIC and IAEA personnel shall enjoy the privileges and immunities, corresponding to those of experts on mission, provided in the Convention on Privileges and Immunities of the United Nations and the Agreement on the Privileges and Immunities of the IAEA;

• UNMOVIC and the IAEA shall have unrestricted rights of entry into and out of Iraq, the right to free, unrestricted, and immediate movement to and from inspection sites, and the right to inspect any sites and buildings, including immediate, unimpeded, unconditional, and unrestricted access to Presidential Sites equal to that at other sites, notwithstanding the provisions of resolution 1154 (1998) of 2 March 1998;

• UNMOVIC and the IAEA shall have the right to be provided by Iraq the names of all personnel currently and formerly associated with Iraq's chemical, biological, nuclear, and ballistic missile programs and the associated research, development, and production facilities;

• Security of UNMOVIC and IAEA facilities shall be ensured by sufficient United Nations security guards;

• UNMOVIC and the IAEA shall have the right to declare, for the purposes of freezing a site to be inspected, exclusion zones, including surrounding areas and transit corridors, in which Iraq will suspend ground and aerial movement so that nothing is changed in or taken out of a site being inspected;

• UNMOVIC and the IAEA shall have the free and unrestricted use and landing of fixed-and rotary-winged aircraft, including manned and unmanned reconnaissance vehicles;

• UNMOVIC and the IAEA shall have the right at their sole discretion verifiably to remove, destroy, or render harmless all prohibited weapons, subsystems, components, records, materials, and other related items, and the right to impound or close any facilities or equipment for the production thereof; and

• UNMOVIC and the IAEA shall have the right to free import and use of equipment or materials for inspections and to seize and export any equipment, materials, or documents taken during inspections, without search of UNMOVIC or IAEA personnel or official or personal baggage;

8. *Decides* further that Iraq shall not take or threaten hostile acts directed against any representative or personnel of the United Nations or the IAEA or of any Member State taking action to uphold any Council resolution;

9. *Requests* the Secretary-General immediately to notify Iraq of this resolution, which is binding on Iraq; demands that Iraq confirm within seven days of that notification its intention to comply fully with this resolution; and demands further that Iraq cooperate immediately, unconditionally, and actively with UNMOVIC and the IAEA;

10. *Requests* all Member States to give full support to UNMOVIC and the IAEA in the discharge of their mandates, including by providing any information related to prohibited programs or other aspects of their mandates, including on Iraqi attempts since 1998 to acquire prohibited items, and by recommending sites to be inspected, persons to be interviewed, conditions of such interviews, and data to be collected, the results of which shall be reported to the Council by UNMOVIC and the IAEA;

11. *Directs* the Executive Chairman of UNMOVIC and the Director-General of the IAEA to report immediately to the Council any interference by Iraq with inspection activities, as well as any failure by Iraq to comply with its disarmament obligations, including its obligations regarding inspections under this resolution;

12. *Decides* to convene immediately upon receipt of a report in accordance with

paragraphs 4 or 11 above, in order to consider the situation and the need for full compliance with all of the relevant Council resolutions in order to secure international peace and security;

13. *Recalls*, in that context, that the Council has repeatedly warned Iraq that it will face serious consequences as a result of its continued violations of its obligations;

14. *Decides* to remain seized of the matter.

Remarks by Representatives of Members of the United Nations Security Council upon the Passage of Resolution 1441, November 8, 2002

Security Council President. Members of the Council have before them document S/2002/1198, which contains the text of a draft resolution submitted by the United Kingdom of Great Britain and Northern Ireland and the United States of America.

It is my understanding that the Council is ready to proceed to the vote on the draft resolution. Unless I hear any objection, I shall put the draft resolution to the vote now.

There being no objection, it is so decided.

[A vote was taken by show of hands.

In favor: Bulgaria, Cameroon, China, Colombia, France, Guinea, Ireland, Mauritius, Mexico, Norway, Russian Federation, Singapore, Syrian Arab Republic, United Kingdom of Great Britain and Northern Ireland, United States of America.]

Security Council President. There were 15 votes in favor. The draft resolution has been adopted unanimously as resolution 1441 (2002).

I should now like to give the floor to the Secretary-General, Mr. Kofi Annan.

Secretary-General Annan. The Security Council resolution adopted today has strengthened the cause of peace and given renewed impetus to the search for security in an increasingly dangerous world. The resolution sets out in clear terms Iraq's obligation to cooperate with the United Nations in ensuring the full and final disarmament of its weapons of mass destruction. It leaves no doubt as to what these obligations are or as to how they must be fulfilled. Iraq now has a new opportunity to comply with all the relevant resolutions of the Security Council.

I urge the Iraqi leadership, for the sake of its own people and for the sake of world security and world order, to seize this opportunity and thereby begin to end the isolation and suffering of the Iraqi people. If Iraq's defiance continues, however, the Security Council must face its responsibilities.

This resolution is based on law, collective effort and the unique legitimacy of the United Nations. It represents an example of multilateral diplomacy serving the cause of peace and security. It reflects a renewed commitment to preventing the development and spread of weapons of mass destruction and the universal wish to see this goal obtained by peaceful means.

I commend the leaders and the Council members, who have worked so hard to negotiate this resolution. I know that it has not been easy to reach agreement. It has required both patience and persistence. But the effort has been well worthwhile. Whenever the Council is united, it sends a very powerful signal. And I hope that Iraq will heed that signal.

I also wish to recognize those countries, especially members of the League of Arab States, who persuaded Iraq to change its previous position. It is important that Governments with influence on Iraq remain engaged in the efforts to obtain Iraq's compliance with its international obligations. The road ahead will be difficult and dangerous. But empowered by this resolution, the United Nations Monitoring, Verification and Inspection Commission and the International Atomic Energy Agency stand equipped to carry out their vital task. To succeed, they will require full and unconditional cooperation on the part of Iraq and the continued determination of the international community to pursue its common aim in a united and effective manner.

This is a time of trial—for Iraq, for the United Nations and for the world. The goal is to ensure the peaceful disarmament of Iraq in compliance with Security Council resolutions and a better, more secure future for its people. How this crisis is resolved will affect greatly the course of peace and security in the coming years, in the region and in the world.

I commend the Council for acting today with purpose and resolve.

United States Representative Negroponte. This resolution constitutes the world community's demand that Iraq disclose and destroy its weapons of mass destruction. On 12 September, President Bush came to the General Assembly seeking to build an international consensus to counter Iraq's persistent defiance of the United Nations. Over a decade ago, after evicting Iraq from Kuwait, the Security Council determined that peace and security in the Persian Gulf region required that Iraq, verifiably, give up its weapons of mass destruction. The Council reached that decision because of Iraq's record of aggression against its neighbors and its use of chemical and biological weapons. For 11 years, without success, we have tried a variety of ways, including diplomacy, inspections and economic sanctions, to obtain Iraqi compliance. By this resolution, we are now united in trying a different course. That course is to send a clear message to Iraq insisting on its disarmament in the area of weapons of mass destruction and delivery systems, or face the consequences.

The resolution we have just adopted puts the conflict between Iraq and the United Nations in context and recalls the obligations on Iraq and the authorities of Member States to enforce them. It begins by reference to Iraq's invasion of Kuwait in August 1990 and the international community's response. It recalls that the ceasefire ending the 1991 Gulf war was conditioned on Iraq's disarmament with respect to nuclear, chemical and biological weapons, together with their support infrastructures; ending its involvement in, and support for, terrorism; and its accounting for, and restoration of, foreign nationals and foreign property wrongfully seized. In addition, the Council demanded that the Iraqi Government stop oppressing the Iraqi people. Iraq has ignored those obligations essential to peace and security.

The resolution confirms what has been clear for years: that Iraq has been and remains in violation of disarmament obligations—"material breach" in lawyers' language. The Council then decides to afford Iraq a final opportunity to comply. As a means to that end, the resolution then establishes an enhanced, strengthened inspection regime. The resolution gives the United Nations Monitoring, Verification and Inspection Commission (UNMOVIC) and the International Atomic Energy Agency (IAEA) a new, powerful mandate. Its core is immediate and unimpeded access to every site, including presidential and other sensitive sites, structure or vehicle they choose to inspect and equally immediate and unimpeded access to people they wish to interview. In other words, anyone, anywhere, any time. And the resolution gives UNMOVIC and the IAEA the power to do their work properly and to ensure the verifiable destruction of Iraq's weapons of mass destruction and associated infrastructure and support programs.

Let us be clear: the inspections will not work unless the Iraqi regime cooperates fully with UNMOVIC and the IAEA. We hope all Member States now will press Iraq to undertake that cooperation. This resolution is designed to test Iraq's intentions: will it abandon its weapons of mass destruction and its illicit missile programs or continue its delays and defiance of the entire world? Every act of Iraqi non-compliance will be a serious matter, because it would tell us that Iraq has no intention of disarming.

As we have said on numerous occasions to Council members, this resolution contains no "hidden triggers" and no "automaticity" with respect to the use of force. If there is a further Iraqi breach, reported to the Council by UNMOVIC, the IAEA or a Member State, the matter will return to the Council for discussions as required in paragraph 12. The resolution makes clear that any Iraqi failure to comply is unacceptable and that Iraq must be disarmed. And, one way or another, Iraq will be disarmed. If the Security Council fails to act decisively in the event of further Iraqi violations, this resolution does not constrain any Member State from acting to defend itself against the threat posed by Iraq or to enforce relevant United Nations resolutions and protect world peace and security.

To the Government of Iraq, our message is simple: non-compliance no longer is an option. To our colleagues on the Security Council, our message is one of partnership: over seven weeks, we have built international consensus on how to proceed towards Iraq, and we have come together, recognizing that our collective security is at stake and that we must meet this challenge, as proposed by President Bush on 12 September.

To the Secretary-General, Mr. Blix, and Mr. El-Baradei: We urge you to make full use of the tools given to you in this resolution, and we pledge our full support. And we urge every Member of the United Nations to offer you all assistance possible.

To the Governments and peoples of the Arab world, including the people of Iraq: the purpose of this resolution is to open the way to a peaceful solution of this issue. That is the intention and wish of my Government. When the Baghdad regime claims that the United States is seeking to wage war on the Arab world, nothing could be farther from the truth. What we seek, and what the Council seeks by this resolution, is the disarmament of Iraq's weapons of mass destruction. We urge you to join us in our common effort to secure that goal and assure peace and security in the region.

President Bush asked the Security Council to take on the challenge posed by Iraq. He asked that it find Iraq in material breach of its ongoing obligations, that it establish an enhanced inspection regime as a means for obtaining the disarmament of Iraq in the area of weapons of mass destruction, and that it make clear that the most serious consequences for Iraq would follow continued defiance. This resolution accomplishes each of these purposes. Moreover, it does so as a result of intense and open discussions with our Security Council partners. In this process, different views about the shape and language of a resolution were fused into the common approach we and our British partners wanted to create.

This resolution affords Iraq a final opportunity. The Secretary-General said on 12 September—and he repeated it again today—that "If Iraq's defiance continues, the Security Council must face its responsibilities" (A/57/PV.2, p.3). We concur with the wisdom of his remarks. Members can rely on the United States to live up to its responsibilities if the Iraq regime persists with its refusal to disarm.

British Representative Sir Jeremy Greenstock. I start by thanking the Secretary-General for his presence, for his powerful statement and for his wisdom in advising the Council over these past weeks. I said at the Council's open debate on Iraq, on 17 October, that no shadow of a doubt remained that Iraq has defied the United Nations—not any particular Member State: the United Nations—over the last 11 years. I itemized on that occasion the ways in which Iraq has sought to frustrate and hinder inspections since 1991.

With the adoption of this resolution, the Security Council has clearly stated that the United Nations will no longer tolerate this defiance. As paragraph 2 makes crystal clear, Iraq is being given a final opportunity to comply with its disarmament obligations; a final opportunity to remedy its material breach of resolution 687 (1991) set out in paragraph 1. The regime in Baghdad now faces an unequivocal choice: between complete disarmament and the serious consequences indicated in paragraph 13.

The fact that this resolution has the unanimous support of Council members sends, as the Secretary-General has just said, the most powerful signal to Iraq that this is the only choice, that it can no longer evade its obligations under United Nations resolutions. Because of the strength of this signal, there is at last a chance that Iraq will finally comply with its obligations and that military action can be averted.

A key part of the resolution we have adopted today is the provisions giving inspectors the penetrating strength needed to ensure the successful disarmament of Iraq. I am glad that the Council has recognized that we could not afford a return to the ambiguous modalities and memorandums of understanding of the past; that we could not afford exceptions to unconditional, unrestricted and immediate access; that we could not afford to have inspectors again standing by helplessly while crucial documents are burned or while convoys leave from the back doors as inspectors arrive in the front; and that we could not afford interviews compromised by intimidating minders.

The provisions we have agreed, including making legally binding the practical arrangements set out by the inspectors themselves, will significantly strengthen the hand of the United Nations Monitoring, Verification and Inspection Commission (UNMOVIC) and the International Atomic Energy Agency (IAEA). This will reinforce international confidence in the inspectors. It will also, I hope, lead Iraq away from a fatal decision to conceal weapons of mass destruction. If Iraq is genuinely committed to full weapons of mass destruction disarmament, it can ensure that inspections get off to a flying start by providing the complete and accurate declaration required under paragraph 3. The United Kingdom has full confidence in Mr. Blix and Mr. ElBaradei and their teams, and full respect for their integrity and independence, as they embark on a crucial and difficult task.

We heard loud and clear during the negotiations the concerns about "automaticity" and "hidden triggers" — the concern that on a decision so crucial we should not rush into military action; that on a decision so crucial any Iraqi violations should be discussed by the Council. Let me be equally clear in response, as a co-sponsor with the United States of the text we have just adopted. There is no "automaticity" in this resolution. If there is a further Iraqi breach of its disarmament obligations, the matter will return to the Council for discussion as required in paragraph 12. We would expect the Security Council then to meet its responsibilities.

Ultimately, the choice lies with Iraq as to whether to take the peaceful route to disarmament. The United Kingdom hopes that Iraq will fully cooperate with the United Nations, meet its obligations and take the path back to the lifting of sanctions laid out in resolutions 1284 (1999) and 687 (1991). The disarmament of Iraq in the area of weapons of mass destruction by peaceful means remains the United Kingdom's firm preference. But if Iraq chooses defiance and concealment, rejecting the final opportunity it has been given by the Council in paragraph 2, the United Kingdom — together, we trust, with other Members of the Security Council — will ensure that the task of disarmament required by the resolutions is completed.

French Representative Levitte. France considers that the resolution that has just been adopted unanimously is a good resolution for the following reasons. The resolution strengthens the role and authority of the Security Council. That was the main and constant objective of France throughout the negotiations which have just concluded. That objective was reflected in our request that a two-stage approach be established and complied with, ensuring that the Security Council would maintain control of the process at each stage.

That objective has been attained: in the event that the Executive Chairman of the United Nations Monitoring, Verification and Inspection Commission (UNMOVIC) or the Director General of the International Atomic Energy Agency (IAEA) reports to the Security Council that Iraq has not complied with its obligations, the Council would meet immediately to evaluate the seriousness of the violations and draw the appropriate conclusions. France welcomes the fact that all ambiguity on this point and all elements of automaticity have disappeared from the resolution.

As we wished, the resolution we have just adopted also gives the Executive Chairman of UNMOVIC and the Director General of IAEA a clear mandate and stronger authority to carry out their mission. Their teams will be able to have immediate and unrestricted access to all sites they wish to inspect. They will be able to hear, at their convenience, all Iraqi leaders involved in activities covered by the resolution. Multinational composition will guarantee impartiality. They will have all the technical and logistical arrangements necessary to carry out their tasks.

Naturally, the inspectors will have to count on the complete cooperation of the Iraqi authorities to verify that Iraq does not have weapons of mass destruction and to ensure its disarmament. To begin with, Iraq within seven days must unambiguously state its decision to apply in full this resolution and to cooperate actively with the inspectors. It must within 30 days provide a declaration which will facilitate their work.

France is fully confident that Mr. Blix and Mr. ElBaradei will make full use of the new powers they have been given and that they will rigorously and professionally discharge the essential responsibilities entrusted to them by the Security Council. With their mandate and greater authority, their teams must now proceed immediately to Iraq to resume inspections. In the course of the day, France, Russia and China will make public a joint statement stressing the scope of the text of the resolution just adopted.

This resolution represents a success for the Security Council and the United Nations. That success must now become a success for peace. As President Jacques Chirac of France said yesterday, all of France's diplomatic efforts in recent weeks were directed towards giving peace a chance. In other words, those efforts sought to achieve the peaceful disarmament of Iraq. France's goal is to work tirelessly to ensure stability in the region.

It is against that backdrop, and through collective responsibility, that the efforts of the international community to disarm Iraq should be carried out. War can only be the last recourse. The rules of the game spelled out by the Security Council are clear and demanding and require the unfailing cooperation of Iraqi leaders. If Iraq wants to avoid confrontation it must understand that this is its last opportunity.

Russian Representative Lavrov. At the very beginning of our work in the Council on this matter, we started with the need to ensure that international inspectors be sent to Iraq as soon as possible, responding to the clearly stated consent by Baghdad to the inspection and monitoring activities of UNMOVIC and the International Atomic Energy Agency (IAEA) in Iraq, without preconditions. Sharing the concern of all members of the Security Council and the heads of UNMOVIC and IAEA to ensure the most effective inspection activity possible, our delegation participated constructively in work on additional procedures for inspections that would ensure there would be no resumption of Iraqi programs for weapons of mass destruction and at the same time would create the conditions for a comprehensive settlement of the situation around Iraq, including the lifting of sanctions.

At all stages of this work, we were guided by the need to direct the process of a settlement onto a diplomatic and political path and not to allow a military scenario. As a result of intensive negotiations, the resolution just adopted contains no provisions for the automatic use of force. It is important that the resolution's sponsors today officially confirmed in the Security Council that that is their understanding and that they provided an assurance that the resolution's objective is the implementation of existing Security Council decisions concerning Iraq through inspections by the United Nations Monitoring, Verification and Inspection Commission (UNMOVIC) and by the International Atomic Energy Agency (IAEA). That is an objective shared by all members of the Council. In that connection, it is of fundamental importance that the resolution clearly confirms that all Members of the United Nations respect the sovereignty and territorial integrity of Iraq and of all other States in the region. It is also confirms the need for full implementation of resolution 1382 (2001), whereby members of the Security Council undertook to seek a comprehensive settlement of the Iraq problem, which assumes the lifting of sanctions.

In addition, we note that the new resolution contains strengthened inspection procedures, which are necessary only to hasten attainment of the goal of nonresumption of Iraqi programs relating to weapons of mass destruction. Those procedures will be implemented by the heads of UNMOVIC and of the IAEA, fully mindful of their responsibility, which requires professionalism, objectivity and impartiality.

The resolution's wording is not ideal — a fact that the sponsors themselves acknowledge — but that reflects the very complicated nature of the compromise that was reached. The Russian Federation made a choice based on principle to support the resolution, guided by its special responsibility, as a permanent member of the Security Council, for the maintenance of international peace and security. What is most important is that the resolution deflects the direct threat of war and that it opens the road towards further work in the interests of a political diplomatic settlement.

It is particularly important that—as many of my colleagues have said today—in the event of any kind of disagreement over disarmament matters, it is the heads of UNMOVIC and of the IAEA who will report that to the Security Council, and that it is the Council that will consider the situation that has developed. That is the sequence set forth clearly in paragraphs 4, 11 and 12 of the resolution.

We also note the following clarifying points, presented by the sponsors when they introduced the resolution and confirmed by the heads of UNMOVIC and of the IAEA.

First of all, with regard to paragraph 3, more than 30 days will probably be needed for Iraq to submit information on non-military programs in the chemical and biological areas. However, any delay there will not constitute a violation.

Concerning paragraph 7, nothing in the resolution affects the status of UNMOVIC, of the IAEA or of members of their staff, as independent international personnel. The cooperation of Member States with UNMOVIC and with the IAEA will be carried out fully in accordance with the status and mandates of those organizations.

Paragraph 8 refers to personnel of the United Nations, to those of the IAEA and to any other personnel whom Members of the United Nations may provide to UNMOVIC or to the IAEA on the request of those organizations.

Like all other members of the Security Council, we join in the appeal made today by the Secretary-General on the need for Iraq to comply with all of its disarmament commitments and to cooperate fully with the inspectors of UNMOVIC and of the IAEA, on the basis of the resolution adopted today and Baghdad's declared willingness to cooperate. We note the important role that has been played and continues to be played by the Secretary-General of the United Nations, by the Secretary-General of the League of Arab States and by members of the League in ensuring a comprehensive political settlement of the situation concerning Iraq.

Implementation of the resolution will require goodwill on the part of all those involved in the process of seeking a settlement of the Iraq question. They must have the willingness to concentrate on moving forward towards the declared common goals, not yielding to the temptation of unilateral interpretation of the resolution's provisions and preserving the consensus and unity of all members of the Security Council.

Security Council President. I shall now make a statement in my capacity as the representative of China.

First, I wish to thank the Secretary-General for attending today's meeting and for his important and wise statement.

The Chinese delegation voted in favor of the resolution that has just been adopted. Our decision was based on the Chinese Government's consistent and clear-cut position on the question of Iraq. China stands firmly for a peaceful solution to the question of Iraq, through political and diplomatic means and within the framework of the United Nations. China has always urged Iraq to fully and strictly implement relevant Security Council resolutions and to cooperate fully with the United Nations with a view to thoroughly accounting for and destroying its weapons of mass destruction.

China has consistently held that, in seeking a comprehensive settlement of the question of Iraq, the sovereignty and territorial integrity, as well as the legitimate concerns, of Iraq should be respected and that the Security Council should, depending on Iraq's implementation of relevant resolutions, consider suspending and eventually lifting the sanctions against Iraq, which have been in force for 12 years.

We support dialogue between the Secretary-General and the Iraqi side in order to break the stalemate and welcome efforts by the Arab League and other organizations aimed at a peaceful resolution of the question of Iraq. We also welcome the announcement by Iraq in September that it would unconditionally accept a return of United Nations inspectors, and its subsequent talks with the United Nations Monitoring, Verification and Inspection Commission (UNMOVIC) and the International Atomic Energy Agency (IAEA) on practical arrangements concerning inspections.

We are in favor of strengthening the effectiveness of inspections. At the same time, we believe that relevant provisions relating to the inspections should be practical and feasible. We appreciate the work done by UNMOVIC and the IAEA with regard to the inspections, and hope that they will be able to return to Iraq at an early date to conduct independent, fair, professional and effective inspections, reporting to the Security Council the result of their inspections in a truthful and timely manner. That would enable the Council to draw objective, fair and realistic conclusions and decide on the next steps in the light of the situation and the views of the various parties concerned.

China supports the two-stage approach. The Chinese delegation actively participated at all stages of the consultations on the draft resolution, and put forward its views and suggestions in a constructive manner. We are pleased to note that, after many rounds of consultations, the sponsors of the draft resolution accommodated our concerns, and the Council members have finally reached consensus.

As the sponsors pointed out in their statements earlier, the purpose of the resolution is to achieve the disarmament of Iraq through effective inspections. The text no longer includes automaticity for authorizing the use of force. According to the resolution that has just been adopted, only upon receipt of a report by UNMOVIC and the IAEA on Iraq's non-compliance and failure to cooperate fully in the implementation of the resolution, will the Security Council consider the situation and take a position.

We are also pleased to note that, at the request of many members, including China, the resolution now includes other important elements, for example, reaffirming the commitment of all Member States to the sovereignty and territorial integrity of Iraq, Kuwait and other neighboring States, commending the Secretary-General and members of the League of Arab States and its Secretary-General for their efforts and recalling its resolution 1382 (2001) and its intention to implement it fully.

The Security Council bears the primary responsibility for the maintenance of international peace and security—a responsibility that is entrusted to it by the Charter. Now that the Security Council has adopted this important resolution at this crucial moment, we hope that it will contribute to preserving the authority of the Council, facilitate a political settlement of the question of Iraq and enable an early return of United Nations inspectors to Iraq.

It is our hope that Iraq will implement the resolution in good faith, fully cooperate with United Nations weapons inspectors and fully comply with its disarmament obligations, so as to create conditions for an early and comprehensive resolution of the question of Iraq.

We would also like to point out that the United Nations inspectors should draw lessons from the United Nations Special Commission. We trust that UNMOVIC and the IAEA will strictly abide by the mandate provided by the Security Council in its resolutions and faithfully fulfill its duties. Finally, we once again strongly appeal to all parties to continue to strive for a political solution to the Iraqi issue. That is the common aspiration of the entire international community, particularly the Gulf States and the Arab States. We sincerely hope that the adoption and smooth implementation of the resolution will be conducive to the effective carrying out of weapons inspections in Iraq and facilitate a final and comprehensive resolution of the Iraqi issue within the framework of the United Nations.

Remarks by President Bush, November 8, 2002

Good morning. With the resolution just passed, the United Nations Security Council has met important responsibilities, upheld its principles and given clear and fair notice that Saddam Hussein must fully disclose and destroy his weapons of mass destruction. He must submit to any and all methods to verify his compliance. His cooperation must be prompt and unconditional, or he will face the severest consequences.

The world has now come together to say that the outlaw regime in Iraq will not be permitted to build or possess chemical, biological or nuclear weapons.

That is the judgment of the United States Congress, that is the judgment of the United Nations Security Council. Now the world must insist that that judgment be enforced. Iraq's obligation to disarm is not new, or even recent. To end the Persian Gulf War and ensure its own survival, Iraq's regime agreed to disarm in April of 1991. For over a decade the Iraqi regime has treated its own pledge with contempt.

As today's resolution states, Iraq is already in material breach of past U.N. demands. Iraq has aggressively pursued weapons of mass destruction, even while inspectors were inside the country. Iraq has undermined the effectiveness of weapons inspectors with ploys, delays, and threats—making their work impossible and leading to four years of no inspections at all.

The world has learned from this experience an essential lesson, inspections will not result in a disarmed Iraq unless the Iraqi regime fully cooperates. Inspectors do not have the power to disarm an unwilling regime. They can only confirm that a government has decided to disarm itself. History has shown that when Iraq's leaders stall inspections and impede the progress, it means they have something to hide.

The resolution approved today presents the Iraqi regime with a test—a final test. Iraq must now, without delay or negotiations, fully disarm; welcome full inspections, welcome full inspections, and fundamentally change the approach it has taken for more than a decade.

The regime must allow immediate and unrestricted access to every site, every document, and every person identified by inspectors. Iraq can be certain that the old game of cheat-and-retreat tolerated at other times will no longer be tolerated.

Any act of delay or defiance will be an additional breach of Iraq's international obligations, and a clear signal that the Iraqi regime has once again abandoned the path of voluntary compliance.

With the passage of this resolution, the world must not lapse into unproductive debates over whether specific instances of Iraqi noncompliance are serious. Any Iraqi noncompliance is serious, because such bad faith will show that Iraq has no intention of disarming. If we're to avert war, all nations must continue to pressure Saddam Hussein to accept this resolution and to comply with its obligations and his obligations.

America will be making only one determination: is Iraq meeting the terms of the Security Council resolution or not? The United States has agreed to discuss any material breach with the Security Council, but without jeopardizing our freedom of action to defend our country. If Iraq fails to fully comply, the United States and other nations will disarm Saddam Hussein.

I've already met with the head of the U.N. Inspections Program and the head of the International Atomic Energy Agency, which has responsibility for nuclear matters. I've assured them that the United States will fully support their efforts, including a request for information that can help identify illegal activities and materials in Iraq.

I encourage every member of the United Nations to strongly support the inspection teams. And now the inspectors have an important responsibility to make full use of the tools we have given them in this resolution.

All patriotic Iraqis should embrace this resolution as an opportunity for Iraq to avoid war and end its isolation. Saddam Hussein cannot hide his weapons of mass destruction from international inspectors without the cooperation of hundreds and thousands of Iraqis—those who work in the weapons program and those who are responsible for concealing the weapons. We call on those Iraqis to convey whatever information they have to inspectors, the United States, or other countries, in whatever manner they can. By helping the process of disarmament, they help their country.

Americans recognize what is at stake. In fighting a war on terror, we are determined to oppose every source of catastrophic harm that threatens our country, our friends, and our allies. We are actively pursuing dangerous terror networks across the world. And we oppose a uniquely dangerous regime—a regime that has harbored terrorists and can supply terrorists with weapons of mass destruction; a regime that has built such terrible weapons and has used them to kill thousands; a brutal regime with a history of both reckless ambition and reckless miscalculation.

The United States of America will not live at the mercy of any group or regime that has the motive and seeks the power to murder Americans on a massive scale. The threat to America also threatens peace and security in the Middle East and far beyond. If Iraq's dictator is permitted to acquire nuclear weapons, he could resume his pattern of intimidation and conquest and dictate the future of a vital region.

In confronting this threat, America seeks the support of the world. If action becomes necessary, we will act in the interests of the world. And America expects Iraqi compliance with all U.N. resolutions.

The time has come for the Iraqi people to escape oppression, find freedom and live in hope.

I want to thank the Secretary of State Colin Powell for his leadership, his good work and his determination over the past two months. He's worked tirelessly and successfully for a resolution that recognizes important concerns of our Security Council partners and makes Iraq's responsibilities clear.

I also thank our Ambassador to the United Nations, John Negroponte and his team at our U.N. mission in New York for their hard work and outstanding service to our country. Secretary of State Powell's team has done a fine job. The American people are grateful to the Security Council for passing this historic resolution.

Members of the Council acted with courage and took a principled stand. The United Nations has shown the kind of international leadership promised by its charter and required by our times. Now comes the hard part. The Security Council must maintain its unity and sense of purpose so that the Iraq regime cannot revert to the strategies of obstruction and deception it used so successfully in the past.

The outcome of the current crisis is already determined: the full disarmament of weapons of mass destruction by Iraq will occur. The only question for the Iraqi regime is to decide how. The United States prefers that Iraq meet its obligations voluntarily, yet we are prepared for the alternative. In either case, the just demands of the world will be met.

Remarks by United Nations Secretary-General Annan and UNMOVIC Chairman Blix, November 8, 2002

Secretary-General Annan. I think we are all very pleased that the Council has adopted this Resolution [1441] unanimously. As you heard most Council members indicate, and in my own statement, we believe Iraq now has a chance to press ahead with disarmament of the weapons of mass destruction. And I hope Iraq will seize this moment and this opportunity.

And I have also appealed to all governments with influence to remain engaged and encourage and urge Iraq to comply. I am particularly looking to the contribution of the Arab League states who were very instrumental in helping Iraq to change its position and I hope they will remain engaged to get the message across that it not enough to let the inspectors come in—it is a good beginning—but what is important is performance. And I hope Iraq will perform and offer the chief [weapons] inspectors the full cooperation that they deserve.

I think the Security Council took its time, acted patiently, and in the end we have an optimal decision and result and I am very, very pleased. I know I kept telling some of you that "we will have unanimity", "we will have fifteen votes' and you didn't believe me. But here we are.

Q. Mr. Secretary-General, what can you do to preserve the integrity of UNMOVIC? The Chinese, the President of the Security Council referred to lessons to be learned from UNSCOM. A major problem with UNSCOM was that its integrity was in question. What are you going to do to ensure that the same thing doesn't happen ?

Secretary-General Annan. I think that the establishment of UNMOVIC is an attempt by the Security Council to correct some of the past weaknesses and errors. And here we have two strong leaders, we have a team of inspectors who have been very carefully picked, from all over the world, who have been given training, including sensitivity training and who have strict instructions to stick to what they are in Iraq to do and nothing else. And I think under the leadership of Mr. Blix and Dr. ElBaradei we can look forward to that kind of performance.

Q. The stick has been mentioned in this Resolution in more than one place, about consequences. Yet there are no carrots for the Iraqis. Isn't there any reward for complying, and why wasn't it mentioned in this?

Secretary-General Annan. I think in the statements by the members this morning, there was quite a lot of encouragement for Iraq to honor its obligations and commitments to the Council so that we can see a situation where Iraq will join the international community, that the sanctions will be lifted, and the people of Iraq, who have suffered for so long, will live normal lives again. And I think most of the speakers referred to this need.

Q. What do you feel about the fact that the Security Council ? Sort of put aside the Memorandum of Understanding that you had signed already and taken up in the Resolution. Do you think it's possible that the Iraqis can cooperate by allowing inspectors into the palaces?

Secretary-General Annan. I think the Security Council Resolution of today is the governing document, and Iraq has to comply. What you are referring to [inaudible] of a different era—we have a new ballgame now and Iraq has to comply.

Q. Sir, the U.S. Ambassador talked about the Resolution not restraining any member state to act against Iraqi non-compliance. Does that concern you that a member state may take it upon itself to respond that way?

Secretary-General Annan. Well, I think the Ambassador also indicated that if there is no automatic trigger in the current Resolution as it stands, and that if the inspectors were to report back that Iraq is not cooperating and is not complying, the Council would meet again and take an appropriate decision. What the Ambassador was referring to, is when the Council comes back the second time around and engages in discussion, they all hope that the Council will face up to its decisions, in effect saying, we are not going to be tied down. But I think the Council will have the chance to look at this issue again based on the report of the inspectors. What is important is that there are no triggers in this resolution and the Council will be back to review what the inspectors bring back.

* * * *

Q. Dr. Blix, could you tell us, over the next week or two, what your next steps are?

Dr. Blix. Well, I should safely say first that we are very pleased that the Resolution was adopted by unanimity—that strengthens our mandate very much. Secondly, as to the timetable, we are planning to go to Baghdad on Monday the 18th of this month— so it will be within the seven to ten days that we had planned.

Remarks by Secretary of State Powell, November 8, 2002

Secretary Colin Powell was interviewed by the Middle East Broadcasting Corporation.

Q. We have with us from Washington, Mr. Colin Powell. Mr. Powell, good evening, sir. After eight weeks of deliberations in the Security Council about the resolution and the amendment the Security Council agreed on the resolution. Do you understand that this resolution will tie the hands of U.S. from taking any unilateral movement towards Iraq except through the Security Council?

Secretary Powell. I think this is an excellent resolution and I am very pleased that all 15 members of the Security Council agreed. This wasn't a resolution to go to war. This was a resolution of purpose: to find a peaceful solution to a very serious problem. That problem was Saddam Hussein's development of weapons of mass destruction, weapons of mass destruction that threaten his neighbors, threatens his own people, and wastes the treasure of the Iraqi people.

So the United States was not looking for a way to keep from going to war. We were looking for a solution that would be peaceful. If Saddam Hussein violates this resolution, then the Security Council will meet again to consider what should be done, and that might include the use of military force. The United States would participate in that conversation in the Security Council, but at the same time, the United States would always retain its option to use its forces in concert with other nations if the Security Council should choose not to act.

But we are not talking about war now. We are talking about a peaceful solution. And all it would take to get to that peaceful solution is for Saddam Hussein to cooperate with the inspectors, with the United Nations, and give up weapons of mass destruction. Saddam Hussein is the problem, not the United Nations, not the United States.

Q. Mr. Powell, do you understand that the U.S. will keep its options and it will not only move through the Security Council?

Secretary Powell. We have moved with the Security Council for the last seven and a half weeks to come up with this resolution, but we will always have an option of acting to defend ourselves or to defend our friends in the region with other nations who feel the same way working with us. It is always preferable to work through the Security Council, and that is why we have worked through the Security Council for this resolution. And if Saddam Hussein violates this resolution, we would also work with the Security Council while it deliberates what to do.

The focus shouldn't be what the United States might or might not do in the future. The focus should be what is Saddam Hussein going to do now to get out of the violations that he has been committing for the last 11 years that has put peace at risk in that part of the world. It is not the United States who has attacked the neighbors of Iraq. It is Iraq who has attacked its own neighbors. It is not the United States or any other nation that has gassed the people of Iraq. It is Saddam Hussein who has gassed his own people.

He has wasted the treasure of the Iraqi people—money that could have gone to education, healthcare, infrastructure repair, so many things—have gone to developing weapons of mass destruction. And what the international community is now saying is it is time for this to stop.

Q. Mr. Powell, we want to know who will decide that Iraq has violated the resolution of the Security Council. Is it the United Nations or the United States?

Secretary Powell. The inspectors will go in and do their job and we will know soon enough whether or not Iraq is cooperating or not cooperating, and then we will see what the inspectors find. Under the resolution passed today, Dr. Blix of the UNMOVIC group and Mr.

ElBaradei of the International Atomic Energy Agency will report their findings to the Security Council for the Security Council to consider.

But any member state can see what is going on and make a judgment as to whether or not Iraq is cooperating. But let's not look for a way to get to war. Let's look for a way to get to peace. What President Bush and the American Government is interested in now is how to get to peace, not how to get to war, how to disarm Saddam Hussein so that the region becomes more peaceful and more stable.

Q. Mr. Secretary, through this resolution it seems that you looked at the idea of toppling the Iraqi regime. Is the Iraqi regime less dangerous than before?

Secretary Powell. I believe the Iraqi regime is a dangerous regime. It does not respect its own people. It threatens its neighbors. It violates international agreements. But it is especially dangerous in the possession of weapons of mass destruction. The U.N. has spoken clearly about this since 1991. Saddam Hussein and this regime have ignored the United Nations. And the United Nations has spoken clearly today. Its will cannot be and must not be ignored.

Remarks by Secretary of State Powell, November 8, 2002

Secretary Colin Powell was interviewed by the Lebanese Broadcasting Corporation.

Q. What is the purpose, what is the aim from going back to the Security Council in case Iraq refuses to abide by this resolution or breaches it? Is it to issue a new resolution or for another purpose?

Secretary Powell. Well, good evening, first of all and Ramada Karim to all of your viewers.

The resolution that was passed today by the Security Council has several parts to it: one, to again remind everybody of Iraq's failure to abide by previous resolutions, secondly, to put in place a solid inspection regime so that the inspectors can go back into Iraq and see whether or not they still have weapons of mass destruction. If Iraq cooperates with the inspectors, then we have a peaceful way out of this problem.

If Iraq does not cooperate or if Iraq makes it clear that they intend to continue to develop weapons of a chemical nature, a biological nature, nuclear weapons that are so threatening to the people of the region, then the Security Council will come together again and make a judgment about what should happen at that time.

I can't predict what the Security Council will decide to do at that time, but I must say that the United States will be watching this carefully and will always keep open the option of working with other nations to force Iraq to give up these weapons of mass destruction.

Q. But in this resolution it was mentioned that this was the last chance for Iraq, but Iraq says, they said a new resolution is only a preparation for a military attack under an international cover. What is your comment?

Secretary Powell. Well, they are wrong. It is not an excuse for a military attack. If we wanted to conduct a military attack, we would not have needed an excuse. This was an effort for the international community to come together and say to the world that Iraq has violated its obligations to the international community.

The United States is not looking for an opportunity to hurt the Iraqi people. The United States is trying to get rid of these terrible weapons that Saddam Hussein is developing and which he has used—he has used against Iran in the past, he has used against his own people, and so what we are interested in is disarmament. We hope that through this resolution disarmament can be accomplished peacefully. We are not looking for an excuse for war.

Americans don't like war. We don't want war, and we do not go out looking for wars in an aggressive way. We fight wars when it is necessary to defend our interests and the interests of our friends. But in this case, we want to help the Iraqi people use the oil treasure that they have for peaceful purposes to improve their society and not to develop weapons and missiles that threaten their neighbors.

Q. Mr. Powell, about this resolution, how were you able to cancel the reservations, the French and Russian reservations on this resolution, especially?

Secretary Powell. We worked very closely with the Russians and the French and all the other members of the Security Council and we listened to the concerns they had about our original proposal. We were able to modify our position, they were able to change some of their positions so that slowly we were all able to come into agreement, to include Syria, come into agreement that Iraq has been responsible for these violations in the past, that we need a new, tough inspection regime and that we have to hold out the likelihood of consequences if Iraq fails to comply with this new resolution.

What we have seen over the years is that in the absence of some pressure on Iraq, it will not comply. It will merely frustrate the work of the inspectors. And this time we believe it is important that we keep the pressure on for Iraq to comply.

This is not just the United States speaking now. All 15 members of the Security Council and through them all members of the United Nations, the entire international community, are united in this effort.

Remarks by Secretary of State Powell, November 8, 2002

Secretary Colin Powell was interviewed by Al-Jazeera television.

Q. Good evening to you, Mr. Secretary. After weeks of deliberations, and you have managed to get to a resolution.

Secretary Powell. Yes. I am very pleased that we were able to achieve a unanimous vote on a resolution this afternoon.

Q. What are the kinds of negotiations that went on between you and the French and the Russians, in particular, to get to this resolution in the end?

Secretary Powell. We worked very closely with the French and the Russians and all of the other members of the Security Council in reconciling different points of view and different positions that were held. I think the Russians and the French were anxious to make sure that the United States didn't have what they called "triggers" in the resolution that would automatically lead to conflict.

We took their concerns very much to heart, and in a spirit of openness and trying to solve a problem—and the problem was Iraq's violation of previous resolutions—how to put together a solid resolution with a good inspection regime, a resolution that would have consequences if Iraq continued to violate this resolution, as well as others—and we were able to reach an agreement.

I think that it is an agreement that shows that the international community is unified in demanding that Iraq do what Iraq should have done long ago: stop trying to develop weapons of mass destruction that could be used against people in the region; use that money they have, that treasure they have, that comes from oil, use all of the intelligence capability of the Iraqi people, their skills, their experience, to make products for peace, not weapons for war.

And we hope now the Iraqis will understand that a better future awaits them if they will comply with the terms of this resolution.

Q. Before talking about consequences, and severe ones, for that matter, that we hear some officials are talking about, threatening to use force by one side and automatically—this is the United States—this has pushed Russia and France to stop their objection to the proposed resolution.

Is this true, in your opinion, Mr. Secretary?

Secretary Powell. No, not at all. What we succeeded in doing is getting all 15 members of the Security Council together behind a single resolution which says Iraq has violated previous resolutions let us put in place a strong inspection team with a strong mandate, and let us go in and see if Iraq now is finally willing to cooperate, willing to destroy these weapons of mass destruction; and if it is not willing to destroy these weapons of mass destruction, then the Security Council has the responsibility to assemble again and decide what consequences are appropriate; and the United States retains its option to act if the Security Council doesn't act.

But this resolution should be seen not as a resolution for war, but as a resolution for purpose: to remove dangerous weapons from the region; to stop Saddam Hussein and the Iraqi regime from developing the kinds of weapons that they have used against their own people and they have used against neighbors, in fact, against Iran, missiles that have been fired against Saudi Arabia. It is to bring an end to this development of weapons of mass destruction and to show the way to a better life for the Iraqi people.

Q. The question which we find very pressing, Mr. Secretary, if Iraq really agreed and cooperated with the inspectors and got rid of its weapons, will, in the United States, you stop talking about changing regime in Iraq, then?

Secretary Powell. If the Iraqi regime got rid of these weapons of mass destruction and were fully cooperating with the inspectors, then, in effect, it has changed its policies; it is a changed regime.

The reason for regime change in the beginning, in 1998, under the previous American Presidential administration, was because Iraq would not disarm, it would not comply with the resolutions. If it complies with those disarmament resolutions, in effect, it has adopted new policies, which suggest a change in the thinking in Baghdad and a changed regime.

Remarks by Secretary of State Powell, November 8, 2002

Secretary Colin Powell was interviewed on Abu Dhabi TV.

Q. Mr. Secretary, there are only two options for Saddam today after the resolution: either he complies or he doesn't. If he does, do you foresee any scenario under which Saddam would stay in power, with an Iraq free of sanctions?

Secretary Powell. Well, it remains to be seen. I mean, there is a logical path that could lead to that, but right now we have to wait and see whether or not he is willing to cooperate. He has not demonstrated previously his willingness to cooperate, and that is why now we have to keep maximum pressure—and, frankly, we have to keep the possibility of military action present—in order to force his cooperation. Without that pressure, he won't cooperate.

If he cooperates and gets rid of his weapons of mass destruction, and those weapons have been verified to be gone, then we have a new situation, and we will have to examine the situation at that time.

Q. Would you be willing to lift sanctions then?

Secretary Powell. As you well know, at the end of the resolutions, sanctions ultimately are linked to his performance under these resolutions. So, at some point, the resolutions provide for the lifting of sanctions. But I don't see that any time in the near future.

Q. And what if that happens? Will that leave U.S. policy—stated policy several times—that we need a regime change in Baghdad to free Iraqi people? If he complies, how would that leave the people?

Secretary Powell. I think the Iraqi people would be a lot better off with a different leader. Right now, we are focusing on weapons of mass destruction. And the U.S. policy of regime change was put in in 1998 because we didn't see any other way for him to comply with the resolutions. He wasn't complying, and so we thought regime change must be the only way.

Well, we are giving him another chance to see whether he will change the nature of his regime, change his policies, by giving up weapons of mass destruction in the presence of this unified international pressure. And if he were to do that, then we will see. I still think it would be better off if the Iraqi people had different leadership, leadership that was democratically based, leadership that was willing to provide for the people of Iraq.

There are many other resolutions he has violated, with respect to human rights, terrorist activity. But right now, we are focusing on weapons of mass destruction, and if we could get that dealt with, then we'd see where we are and whether the Iraqi people want to continue to have Saddam Hussein as their leader.

Q. And then why not give him an incentive to cooperate with this new resolution?

Secretary Powell. He has incentive. His incentive is that, right now, his incentive is he will avoid regime change in a more forceful way. But why should we give him incentive? He is the one who is in violation. His incentive should be to get out of violation. This isn't a problem that the United States has created or the United Nations has created. It is a problem he has created. So he should take the action to remove these violations and to get on the good side of the international community. We don't owe him any incentives. We owe him nothing more than an opportunity to do what he is supposed to do and to be accountable to the international community.

Q. In the worst case scenario, Mr. Secretary, if the United States decides to go to war against Iraq, is there any concern in this building or somewhere else in this town

about so-called "Arab street?" While the Israeli-Palestinian is not resolved, you're going towards another Arab country? Is there any concern about reaction of the Arab street?

Secretary Powell. We, of course, are doing everything we can to try to find a way forward with respect to achieving a Middle East peace, which would result in the creation of a Palestinian state that President Bush is committed to try to create within a three-year period.

But, at the same time, you cannot ignore other dangers, other problems, such as that presented by Saddam Hussein. So we are sensitive to the feelings in the Arab street and we will always remain sensitive to the feelings in the Arab street, but we still have to do what we think is necessary to do to protect our friends in the region and to protect our own interests.

And we are hopeful that it will not be necessary to go to war. President Bush did not go to the United Nations to declare war. He went to the United Nations to say we have a problem and let's give Saddam Hussein one more chance to solve this problem, and let's see if we can do it peacefully.

Q. And, sir, what's your evaluation so far to the so-called roadmap? It seems like it's leading nowhere when it comes to the Israeli-Palestinian issue.

Secretary Powell. We have had a number of discussions on the roadmap and we have shared it with our friends in the region, our Arab friends, our Palestinian friends and our Israeli friends. And there is a lot of comment on the roadmap, but we will continue to refine the roadmap and then present it to all of the parties.

What we really do have to have now, though, is security in the area—the end of violence, the end of suicide bombing, responsible leadership emerging out of the Palestinian Authority. We are starting to see some signs of responsible leadership coming forward. Chairman Arafat has not used his leadership role well, and we have said so openly. And we hope that more responsible leadership will come forward.

We are pressing the Israeli side to return the tax revenues that belong to the Palestinian people so that a budget can be formed and a budget can be executed.

But the United States is deeply engaged in trying to find a way forward through this crisis, and we will remain deeply engaged. And our goal is to secure a peace where two states can live side by side in peace, a Palestinian state called Palestine and a Jewish state, the state of Israel.

Q. One last question, Mr. Secretary. Some observers are expressing some concern that some Arab regimes, some of your friends in the area, will not be able to survive violence between the Palestinians and Israelis and violence in Baghdad at the same time. Do you share that concern?

Secretary Powell. No, I think that the friends that we have in the region understand that we are committed to finding a solution that will lead to peace and they also understand the dangers presented by Saddam Hussein. So I think while there would be turmoil in the event of a conflict in the region, I think it is our responsibility to explain our case and make sure people knew why this was necessary.

But right now, I am not thinking about that. Right now, I am thinking about how can we put maximum pressure on Saddam Hussein so that he will cooperate and get out of this problem he has created for himself and provide a better life for the Iraqi people. That is what we are interested in. That is what President Bush is interested in.

When you think of all the money that he has wasted on wars, wasted on weapons, wasted on nuclear development, that could have gone to education, to healthcare, to helping other countries—because this is a wealthy country, Iraq—it could be helping its neighbors, it could be helping the Palestinians in a more positive way than it has ever done. And all that money is being wasted on these weapons. It's a shame and it's a time to bring this shame to an end.

Remarks by Secretary of Defense Rumsfeld and German Minister of Defense Struck, November 8, 2002

Secretary Rumsfeld. The passage this morning of the U.N. resolution. It is the result of a good deal of hard work over the past several weeks. President Bush has rallied our country and the world to address the dangers that are posed by the Saddam Hussein regime in Iraq. Until President Bush spoke out on this subject, the world was drifting along and Iraq was hard at work on developing weapons of mass destruction, having thrown out the U.N. inspectors.

The president took his case to the Congress first, and the American people, and the Congress responded.

He then took his case to the United Nations, and the Security Council has now responded.

The world's attention is now turning to Baghdad. The Iraqi regime has a choice to make. He can give up his weapons of mass destruction or, as the president has said, he will lose power. The burden of proof is not on the United States or the United Nations to find weapons of mass destruction in Iraq and destroy them. The burden of proof is on Saddam Hussein to prove to the world that he is in fact disarming, as he agreed to do a decade ago and as is now required by some 17 U.N. resolutions.

As the president made clear this morning, inspections can be effective only if the target nation has made a choice to disarm and the country wants to prove to the world that it's in fact doing so. Inspections cannot be effective in uncovering deceptions and violations if the target country is determined not to cooperate. The task the international community now faces is to determine what choice Saddam Hussein will make. Has he accepted, finally, that he has no choice left but to disarm, or as before, has he simply made a tactical retreat in the hope of keeping his weapons of mass destruction aspirations alive?

We know this much: the only thing that has brought us to this point is the growing threat of pressure on the Iraqi regime, and the only way to finish the job facing the U.N. today is that Iraq be disarmed. And to do that, it's necessary to keep the pressure up.

Since 1998, the Iraqi regime has refused to allow any inspectors into the country. They're reversing course in this period only when they began to realize they had little choice. And the minute that Saddam Hussein and his small ruling clique sense that they're out of danger, I suspect that they'll have no further incentive to cooperate, and any U.N. inspection and disarmament efforts could then fail.

There will be a number of opportunities in the coming weeks to discover their intentions. Needless to say, Iraq ought not to take or threaten hostile action against inspectors or coalition aircraft upholding U.N. inspections.

Within seven days, the—Iraq is required to confirm an intention to comply. Within 30 days Iraq is—must fully and truthfully declare all of its weapons of mass destruction capabilities, its programs and stockpiles. They need to comply with demands to inspect any site and interview any individual that inspectors see fit, including interviews outside of Iraq.

As the president said this morning, any act of delay or defiance will be considered an additional breach of Iraq's international obligations, and "if Iraq fails to comply fully, the U.S. and other nations will disarm Saddam Hussein," unquote.

During this period, the United States will continue to patrol the skies over Iraq. We'll continue working with our friends and allies to keep the pressure on them to respond favorably to the U.N. resolution, and we'll continue working with the Iraqi opposition to prepare in the event that they fail to cooperate. Continuing—we will also continue developing humanitarian relief and reconstruction plans for a post-Saddam Hussein Iraq.

Saddam Hussein needs to understand that this is his regime's chance to come into compliance with all U.N. Security Council resolutions. The choice does not rest in Washington. It does not rest in New York. It rests in Baghdad. For the sake of peace, let's hope that the Iraqi regime chooses wisely.

Minister Struck. And I would now like to read a short statement on the decision taken by the U.N. Security Council today. I welcome the unanimous decision taken by the Security Council of the United Nations. In doing so, the Security Council has lived up to its responsibility for international peace and security. And I'd like to add explicitly, with today's decision in New York, the line and the approach of President Bush to cooperate with—to go through the United Nations, to choose the way of multilateral approach, has proven to be correct.

Today, the international community has given Saddam Hussein a very last chance to fulfill his international obligations. The inspectors must return to Iraq as quickly as possible. It must be made possible for them to return as quickly as they can.

And the Federal Republic of Germany will support the work of the inspectors by offering personnel and equipment.

Moreover, the unanimous decision of the Security Council is a strong and clear signal towards Iraq. Now we do have a real chance that we can urge Iraq to really disarm in accordance with international law and the U.N. Charter.

* * * *

Q. I think you said that needless to say, coalition aircraft must not—that the Iraqis must not challenge coalition aircraft, as you said, upholding inspections. Do you mean by that the aircraft that are policing the northern and southern no-fly zones?

Or is the United States going to provide additional aircraft, such as attack helicopters, in order to protect the inspectors?

Secretary Rumsfeld. The issue—those issues are being worked out. And I'm not quite sure who is doing it, but someone in this building and someone in the State Department are beginning the process of working with the—Mr. Blix and the U.N. to determine exactly how all of that is going to work and be deconflicted.

Q. Well, but, if we can talk about the—

Secretary Rumsfeld. Oh!

Q.—the no-fly zones. Would those planes policing the no-fly zones be considered part of the inspections?

Secretary Rumsfeld. I can't speak for the United Nations on something like that. I mean, clearly, they are there to enforce U.N. resolutions, and that's why the coalition forces fly them. And we have various types of activities that go on. It's not for me to give you a legal definition of what somebody else would say.

Q. Has Germany decided to back the U.S. in a use of force if the inspections do fall apart?

Defense Minister Struck. You know Germany's position on that question you raised. I can only say that we support the U.N. resolution. And today Chancellor Schroeder and President Bush had a conversation and they also talked about the relations between Germany and the U.S. And let me add that Germany makes a contribution to the Operation Enduring Freedom.

Q. Mr. Secretary, could you imagine that Germany, given the position of the German government they wouldn't take an active role in a possible war in Iraq, could support the United States somehow else, in a different way, in a more—in a passive role—let's put it like this—by giving some different support for a possible war in Iraq?
And the same question to the German minister.

Secretary Rumsfeld. All right, we'll let both of us answer that.
I've always believed that the United States is best off getting the maximum amount of help we can. And the way to do that is to let other countries decide what they want to do and characterize what it is they may want to do.
I have no idea what the circumstance will be as to how the inspections will play out. I have no idea how the—in the event that he does not cooperate, in what way the U.N. would then make a judgment. Therefore, it's next to impossible for me to know how any given country is going to react, since you don't know how things play out. And each country will do that in their own way, in a way that's consistent with their constitutions, that's consistent with their political circumstance. And as far as I'm con-

cerned, that's just fine. I think each country ought to do whatever it is they believe is right and best for them.

Defense Minister Struck. Yes, that's a very decisive point. And Saddam Hussein, he has to realize what a great responsibility he bears on his shoulders. It is up to him to prevent any further action, and it's up to him to accept the U.N. decision that's been taken today. And this question you raise on a more theoretical level will be answered if he does not accept and live up to this U.N. vote.

Washington Post Op-Ed by Secretary of State Powell, November 10, 2002

On Sept. 12, President Bush went before the United Nations and challenged the Security Council to meet its responsibility to act against the threat to international peace and security posed by Iraq. The council's unanimous passage of Resolution 1441 was a historic step for the United Nations toward ridding Iraq of its weapons of mass destruction by peaceful means.

The international community has given Saddam Hussein and his regime one last chance. It is now for Baghdad to seize it.

Seven weeks of consultation, debate and negotiation in the Security Council only forged a deeper agreement and a stronger resolve among the world that Iraq must fully and finally disarm. It should now be clear to Saddam Hussein that this is not just a matter between Iraq and the United States, but between Iraq and a united world.

After 11 years of flouting dozens of U.N. resolutions and statements, Hussein's contempt for the international community is obvious. We are all well acquainted with the tactics of denial, deceit and delay that he has used time and again to avoid compliance. We are also well aware of the brutal and aggressive nature of his regime. He has twice invaded his neighbors and he has used chemical weapons not just against other countries but against his own citizens: men, women and children.

During the four years since inspectors have been barred from Iraq, Hussein has done everything he can to acquire and develop more weapons of mass destruction—whether biological, chemical or nuclear. He has no scruples about using the weapons that he possesses or about providing them to terrorists should that suit his interests.

Long experience with Saddam Hussein and his regime tells us that he will respond only when confronted with steadfast resolve and the threat of force. Every member of the Security Council understands that if Hussein fails to comply with Resolution 1441, there must be serious consequences.

The words of the resolution are unambiguous:

• The Security Council has found Iraq in material breach of its solemn obligations.

• Iraq has been given one week to state whether it intends to comply with Resolution 1441.

• Iraq must produce a comprehensive declaration of its weapons programs.

• Iraq must submit to an inspection regime that is far tougher and far more thorough than ever before.

Saddam Hussein must give the inspectors immediate, unimpeded, unconditional and unrestricted access to uncover the weapons of mass destruction that he has had so many years to hide. Access not just to places such as presidential palaces but to people and other sources of information will be critical, because you have to know where and when to look in order to find biological and chemical weapons that are easy to conceal and move. Without access to key people and information, the inspectors would have to search under every roof and in the back of every truck.

The chief U.N. inspector, Hans Blix, and the director general of the International Atomic Energy Agency, Mohamed ElBaradei, have been given the robust regime they need. The United States will support the inspectors in every way. Other U.N. members will do the same.

The disarmament process must now begin. The first inspectors plan to arrive in Iraq one week from tomorrow. The world will be watching. The inspectors are required to update the Security Council 60 days after inspections start. Inspectors also are required to inform the council whenever they encounter interference or obstacles. As President Bush said on Friday, U.S. policy will be one of zero tolerance.

In the days and weeks of inspections that lie ahead, the international community can expect Iraq to test its will. Backing Resolution 1441 with the threat of force will be the best way to not only eliminate Iraq's weapons of mass destruction but also to achieve compliance with all U.N. resolutions and reach our ultimate goal: an Iraq that does not threaten its own people, its neighbors and the world.

President Bush and both houses of Congress have emphasized that the United States prefers to see Iraq disarm under U.N. auspices without a resort to force. We do not seek a war with Iraq, we seek its peaceful disarmament. But we will not shrink from war if that is the only way to rid Iraq of its weapons of mass destruction. The Security Council has confronted Saddam Hussein and his regime with a moment of truth. If they meet it with more lies, they will not escape the consequences.

Remarks by Secretary of State Powell, November 10, 2002

Secretary Colin Powell was interviewed on CNN's "Late Edition" by Wolf Blitzer.

Q. Congratulations on the big win at the U.N. Security Council. But the key question is this: Will Saddam Hussein comply?

Secretary Powell. We don't know. He has not complied in the past, and that is why we put in this resolution that this is a last chance. If he does not comply this time, that lack of compliance goes right to the Security Council for it to convene immediately and consider what should be done, and serious consequences are held out within this current resolution.

I can assure you that if he doesn't comply this time we are going to ask the U.N. to give authorization for all necessary means. If the U.N. is not willing to do that, the United States with likeminded nations will go and disarm him forcefully. The President has made this clear.

Q. So you will go to war against Iraq, Saddam Hussein's regime, if he doesn't comply?

Secretary Powell. The President has made it clear that he believes it is the obligation of the international community, in the face of new noncompliance, to take whatever action is necessary to remove those weapons of mass destruction. If the U.N. does not act, then the President is prepared to act. He has made it clear for months.

Q. You wouldn't be surprised if Saddam Hussein were skeptical, because these threats have been made before. Even the President, the other day, in his news conference acknowledged it. Listen to what the President said:
"This would be the 17th time that we expect Saddam to disarm. This time we mean it. See, that's the difference, I guess. This time it's for real."
Seventeen times these threats have been made. Why should he believe you this time?

Secretary Powell. Because the 17th resolution is a lot different from all the previous ones. This time a mechanism has been put into this resolution so that if he does not cooperate with the inspectors—they can't get their job done—they are told to report back to the Security Council, not play rope-a-dope in the desert with them. They are to report back to the Security Council and tell the Council 'we are not getting the job done,' 'they're not cooperating with us,' or 'we've found these violations and it is a problem for us.' The resolution says the Security Council will convene immediately at that moment to consider what should be done about this.

So there can be no mistake about it this time and I don't think he is making any mistakes about it. He is facing a 15-0 vote in the Security Council. He did not have that the last couple of times around.

The Arab League is meeting today with Iraq in Cairo and I hope that they will see the wisdom of encouraging the Iraqis not to misjudge the intent and determination of the international community and especially of the United States.

Q. Let's be precise on what the resolution says, and I'll put it up on the screen:
"Failure by Iraq at any time to comply with and cooperate fully in the implementation of this resolution shall constitute a further material breach of Iraq's obligations and will be reported to the Council for assessment."
But there is ambiguity between the U.S. stance, the French, the Russians, the Chinese; what happens next.

Secretary Powell. No, there is no ambiguity. It says clearly that if there is this violation, that very fact of a violation is a material breach. It is not a judgment to be made by somebody else—either by Dr. Blix or the head of UNMOVIC or by the Security Council. It is a material breach.

And at that point, it is referred to the Security Council under Paragraph 12 for the Security Council to make a judgment as to what should be done. While the Security Council is doing that, the United States will also be reviewing the nature of this breach and making a judgment as to whether it should prepare, or begin to prepare, to take military action either as part of the U.N. effort, if the U.N. decides to do that, or separately with likeminded nations if that turns out to be the direction in which we are heading.

Q. When I interviewed the Russian Ambassador to the U.N., Sergey Lavrov, on Friday, he said if they come back, the U.N. weapons inspectors Dr. Blix and Dr. ElBaradei, and they say there have been some problems, they will look closely to see how serious the noncompliance is before they decide what to do.

Will the U.S. say there are serious problems and there are some not-so-serious problems?

Secretary Powell. We will have to wait and see. We believe we ought to approach this with a zero tolerance attitude because we have been down this road with Saddam Hussein before. And so we will have to wait and see what Dr. Blix or Dr. ElBaradei would say and then the assessment is made within the Security Council.

We are part of the Security Council. We will be part of that assessment. You can be sure we will be pressing the Security Council at that point to show very little tolerance or understanding for any of the kinds of excuses that Saddam Hussein might put forward.

Q. But just to be precise, the U.S. position is a second resolution, a formal resolution, authorizing the use of force is not necessary?

Secretary Powell. We understand that a second resolution would bring the whole Council to all necessary means. But if the Council is unable to agree on a second resolution, the United States believes, because of past material breaches, current material breaches and new material breaches, there is more than enough authority for it to act with likeminded nations, if not with the entire Council supporting an all necessary means new resolution.

Q. I want to put up on the screen the timetable that this resolution spells out. Iraq must agree to comply by November 15. You anticipate that will happen?

Secretary Powell. We will see.

Q. You have some doubt that that might not happen?

Secretary Powell. I do not have any doubts and I do not have any forecasts, and I do not know whether they will or they will not. We will see what they do next Friday. I do not want to start handicapping the Iraqi regime.

Q. By December 8, they must declare all their programs of weapons of mass destruction—chemical, biological, nuclear. Full inspections have to begin no later than December 23, although Dr. Blix seems to think they could begin even earlier than that. But by February 21 of next year, the inspectors have to report back to the Security Council, at the latest.

Now, you're a General. That timetable seems to coincide with the weather factors as far as a military invasion is concerned—February, March, April, it starts getting very hot in that part of the world. Is there a link there between the weather and this timetable?

Secretary Powell. No, we did not create this timetable. It is a timetable that was provided by Dr. Blix. But you know battles have been fought in the heat of the day before, and it gets cool at night when the American army is particularly effective. So I would not believe that there are some red lines out there that give us a timeline beyond which Iraq will not be suffering any consequences.

But the more important point here is not when the inspectors report back, but what level of cooperation are they receiving from Iraq. We are not going to wait until February to see whether Iraq is cooperating or not. If Iraq is not cooperating, Dr. Blix and Mr. ElBaradei will discover that rather quickly. The United States and the United Nations will be able to make a judgment as to cooperation very quickly, not sometime in February.

Q. And the Iraqis should be under no illusions the U.S. military, the Pentagon, a place you once worked at, they're moving forward with war plans?

Secretary Powell. It would be imprudent of the Pentagon not to be developing contingency plans. They are always developing contingency plans. I am sure they will put a plan together that will accomplish any military objective that the President has assigned to them.

Q. Now, you know that for months now there have been all sorts of reports in the news media, splits within the Bush Administration, about the usefulness of going back to the U.N., the usefulness of resuming inspections. I want you to listen to what the Vice President, Dick Cheney, your boss, your former boss and your current boss, said on August 26 regarding a return of inspectors:

"A person would be right to question any suggestion that we should just get inspectors back into Iraq and then our worries will be over. Saddam has perfected the game of cheat-and-retreat and is very skilled in the art of denial and deception. A return of inspectors would provide no assurance whatsoever of his compliance with U.N. resolutions."

Does that reflect what you believe?

Secretary Powell. He is absolutely right. I agree with him. The return of the inspectors, in and of themselves, will not lead to disarmament in the face of an uncooperative attitude on the part of the Iraqis.

What makes it different this time is that if they display that uncooperative attitude, if they are cheating and deceiving and doing all those things to prevent the inspectors from doing their job, and then they are going to face the most serious consequences. The President has made clear what those consequences are.

What Vice President Cheney was saying was you just cannot think: 'inspectors are there, the problem is over, everything is dealt with'—not at all. We have to see cooperation from the Iraqi regime. There has to be an inspection regime that can get the job done. They can only get their job done if there is openness and a cooperative attitude on the part of the Iraqi regime that we have not seen before. If we do not see it this time, then we go right back to the U.N. for consideration of the application of serious consequences.

Q. And so you're saying flatly this is Saddam Hussein's last change—no ifs, ands or buts?

Secretary Powell. Read the resolution. It says that.

Q. I want to give you a chance to respond to those who have suggested that you may be the odd man in the administration, that you have some critics within the administration. The New York Times wrote in an editorial at the end of July, "The sharks circling around Mr. Powell include Vice President Dick Cheney, Defense Secretary Donald Rumsfeld and his Deputy Paul Wolfowitz, and the White House Political Director Karl Rove. Mr. Rove is especially eager to bend policy to placate the Republican right."
Go ahead and respond to that.

Secretary Powell. I do not have to respond to that. This goes on all the time. I have seen it in every administration I have ever been a part of.
We have our discussions; we debate issues—all for the purpose of serving the President. The only one in the pool that I worry about is the President and I know that I am doing what he wanted done.

Q. Were there any concessions, quid pro quos, offered to Russia, France, China, Syria, in exchange for their affirmative vote?

Secretary Powell. No. What we did was go in with a very hard position initially, a tough negotiating position, with a negotiating position that, if we had asked everyone to vote for we would not have gotten any votes for it other than our own. Then we listened to other nations. There are 15 nations on the Security Council. They are all sovereign, they all have principles, and they all have their own red lines. We listened to them and we tried to accommodate them in every way that we could in order to get consensus. But we did it in a way that did not violate any of our principles or any of our red lines, and we succeeded.
We got a resolution that got exactly what the President said he wanted on the 12th of September when he spoke before the U.N.—an indictment of Saddam Hussein, a tough inspection regime, and consequences if he violated this inspection regime. We got that in this resolution but we did it in a way that brought our friends back on board—brought the Syrians on board. We gave nothing away with respect to principles or under-the-table deals. It was good, tough negotiating among nations that have respect for one another.
The other thing it did, it pulled the United Nations back together. The Security Council has been in disarray, the U.N. has been in disarray, over this issue for years. Now the Security Council and the U.N. are back together with a single, strong, pow-

erful message to Iraq: You cannot violate the will of the international community by keeping these kinds of weapons in your inventory. They must be removed; you must be disarmed.

Q. So you can flatly say that as far as the Russians, for example, are concerned, no promises as far as a U.S. stance on the issue of Chechnya, for example?

Secretary Powell. No, we made no such deals. We talk about all of these other issues—Chechnya or anything else—on their own merits and there were no deals cut for this resolution.

Q. And no deals with the French as far as future oil sales involving Iraq are concerned?

Secretary Powell. No. Wolf, I was the chief negotiator on this along with my colleagues in New York, Ambassadors Negroponte and Cunningham, both of whom and their teams, did an outstanding job. The whole team within Washington: Secretary Rumsfeld, Vice President Cheney, Dr. Rice especially—our whole team worked together and no deals like that were cut.

Q. The President was very precise in his language used in the Rose Garden on Friday. You were standing right next to him. At one point, he referred to Iraq as an 'outlaw regime.' Outlaw regime. There is nothing in this U.N. Security Council resolution that speaks about regime change, as you know.
What exactly is the Bush Administration policy as far as the need to get rid of Saddam Hussein's regime?

Secretary Powell. We think that the people of Iraq would be better off, the region would be better off and the world would be better off, if Saddam Hussein was no longer in power. That has never been the position of the United Nations through all of these previous resolutions. So working within the United Nations we did not expect to come up with a policy of regime change.

Regime change is a United States policy that was put in place back in the Clinton Administration in 1998 because Iraq was violating all of these resolutions with respect to disarmament—and other resolutions. It was thought the only way you could get disarmament was through regime change.

We inherited that policy. We thought it was a good policy and it remains our policy to this day. We will see whether, in the area of disarmament with this resolution we find a regime that is changing itself, that has decided to cooperate with the international community.

But beyond that do we still think the world would be better off and the Iraqi people would be better off—would live a better life—if they had a different leadership? Yes we still do and will continue to feel so.

Q. So what incentive does Saddam Hussein personally have to cooperate if the United States says, you know what, we're going to get rid of you if you cooperate or if you don't cooperate?

Secretary Powell. Right now he knows that if he does not cooperate with respect to this U.N. resolution which deals fundamentally with disarmament—although it does in its perambulatory paragraphs talk about his other violations of resolutions-he knows if he violates this resolution military force is coming in to take him and his regime out.

Q. Has Saddam Hussein committed war crimes?

Secretary Powell. I think he has, yes. I mean, when you gas your own people, when you use these kinds of weapons of mass destruction, I think a case can be made. We are always assembling information that might be suitable and useful for such a case.

Q. So if you do capture him alive, do you think he would go before a war crimes tribunal?

Secretary Powell. I don't know the answer to that right now. We are assembling information but I think he certainly has demonstrated criminal activities. He has invaded neighbors that were doing nothing to him—his invasion of Kuwait. He has done a lot of things that I think he should be held accountable to, and for.

Q. And the President spoke a little bit about this as far as his generals are concerned the other day, issuing a warning to them specifically not to use weapons of mass destruction if Saddam Hussein were to order them to do so. Listen to what the President said:
"The generals in Iraq must understand clearly there will be consequences for their behavior. Should they choose, if force is necessary, to behave in a way that endangers the lives of their own citizens, as well as citizens in the neighborhood, there will be a consequence. They will be held to account."
As you know—

Secretary Powell. He did not say weapons of mass destruction.

Q. Well, what exactly—because, as you know, this program is seen around the world, including in Iraq, so go ahead and explain precisely what the President said.

Secretary Powell. What he was saying directly to the generals in Saddam Hussein's army is that should it come to conflict, and we hope it can be solved peacefully—he also says that all the time, but if it comes to conflict you can be sure that one: you will lose, and two: you will be held to account for your actions.

Q. All right. So go ahead. What does that mean?

Secretary Powell. It means you will be held to account for your actions. You can either have the option of deciding that you are serving somebody who is not going to be in power in a few days and perhaps lay down your arms quickly—and we saw some of this during the course of the Gulf war 12 years ago.To resist what I am convinced will be inevitable would be foolish on their parts.

* * * *

Q. If you could explain this, I would be happy. What exactly does the U.S. want Israel to do in the event that scuds once again were launched against Israeli targets?

Secretary Powell. Israel has to be concerned about its own self-defense and no American President would say to an Israeli Prime Minister that you do not have the option of deciding how to defend yourself.

But in the instance of such an attack we would hope that the Israeli Prime Minister would consider all the consequences of such an action. There are different kinds of attacks that might come—might be directed toward Israel in such a set of circumstances. I am sure there would be consultations between us and the Prime Minister of Israel at that time.

Remarks by Secretary of State Powell, November 10, 2002

Secretary Colin Powell was interviewed on CBS's "Face the Nation" by Bob Schieffer and Gloria Borger.

Q. Mr. Secretary, a big week for you. The U.N. passed a very strong resolution. I guess the first question: Have you had any reaction from Iraq at this point?

Secretary Powell. Not yet. I understand that Saddam Hussein has called the national assembly in to conference to begin to meet and consider this. And the only quasi-official statement we've received is that they would look at this resolution calmly. They should look it calmly, they should look at it seriously, and they should comply.

Q. What do you now feel that the United States has a right to do? Do we need to go back to the United Nations at some point now if they don't comply with these various deadlines that you've set up?

Secretary Powell. If they don't comply, the resolution provides for the Security Council to convene immediately and consider what should be done. And the resolution also says Iraq can expect to face serious consequences.

Now, while the Security Council is meeting once again in the presence of this noncompliance, the United States will be participating in that debate in the Security Council. But at no time have we given up our authority. If we find that debate is going nowhere, if the U.N. chooses not to act, we have not given up our authority to act with likeminded nations who might wish to join us in such an action.

So we found a compromise where the United Nations gets the opportunity to consider this violation again, this new material breach, and to decide what the Security Council should do. But, at the same time, the United States has not given up its ability to act if it believes it's necessary to do so.

Q. So let me just make sure I understand what you're saying. And as I understand it, the last deadline they have to meet is sometime in late February, around the 21st or so. If, sometime between now and then, the United States feels that Iraq has violated this in some way, made what you've called a material breach, we could, and believe we have the right, to take military action at that point?

Secretary Powell. We believe the first thing that would happen would be it would go to the Security Council. We would bring it to the Security Council if we saw that Iraq simply wasn't cooperating with the inspectors.

Say they let the inspectors in; they provided us a declaration that seems to be something we can accept. It remains to be seen whether they will do that or not in 30 days. The inspectors go back in, but Iraq is not cooperating with them. They are playing the same game they played before.

Then we can say to the Security Council we need to get together and talk about this. Or, Dr. Blix or Dr. ElBaradei of the IAEA—International Atomic Energy Commission—Dr. Blix of UNMOVIC—the inspectors—can report to the Security Council under the terms of the resolution that they are not doing what they are supposed to do, in which case the U.N. Security Council can decide whether or not action is required. At the same time we will participate in that debate but also reserve our option of acting.

Q. And not necessarily be bound by what the Security Council might decide at that point?

Secretary Powell. We are not bound. But, clearly, if the Security Council acts, it acts with the force of international law. We will see whether it chooses to do so or not.

Q. Mr. Secretary, there are reports today that there's going to be a first early test, and that is that the weapons inspectors are going to say to Saddam Hussein, give us a comprehensive list of where these weapons are, and then they are going to compare that list with their own list. How long would that take?

Secretary Powell. The resolution requires Iraq to come forward with that declaration in 30 days. So 30 days from this past Friday, Iraq has to come forward with a declaration listing everything called for by the resolution.

Q. So, if Saddam gives what you consider to be a false declaration, would you consider that to be a material breach?

Secretary Powell. The resolution says that if the declaration is false, and if they're not complying—and if the declaration is false, they're not complying—then that constitutes, in and of itself, the very fact of that noncompliance is a material breach under the terms of the resolution, at which point this material breach is reported to the Council for the Council to decide what to do.

At that point, the United States will participate in the Council discussions, but also retains the ultimate right, if it chooses to do so at some point, to take action separately from the Council if the Council does not act.

Q. When you get down to these inspections, can you tell our viewers and us exactly how these inspections are going to work—unannounced, no notice, everywhere at the same time?

Secretary Powell. We have gotten in this resolution a tough inspection regime where Dr. Blix and Dr. ElBaradei can go wherever they have to go, whenever they want to go, with little announcement. There has to be some announcement, but it will be very short, that they are coming so that there isn't—

Q. How short?

Secretary Powell. Well, we're talking just a matter of hours. We're not going to give him days to cook the books once again. But at the same time, you have to let someone know you are coming so that they are ready to receive you.

But it is not so much whether they catch somebody doing something as it is are the Iraqis finally cooperating. If they are cooperating, the inspectors can do their job. If they are not cooperating, they can inspect for 12 years and not get anywhere. And that is the big difference in this resolution. The resolution says we are expecting cooperation, and if there is no cooperation, that lack of cooperation will be reported to the Council because the inspectors cannot get their jobs done.

We are going to give Dr. Blix and Dr. ElBaradei all the support we can, all the information we can, with respect to the things that they should be looking at. I am confident, after a number of meetings with both of these gentlemen, that they are thorough professionals; they know what they have to do; they have to call it the way they see it. Then the judgment is up to somebody else, the Security Council or the United States and likeminded nations, as to whether or not because the Iraqis are not complying, not cooperating, it is time to take military action to remove this regime.

Remarks by United Nations Secretary-General Annan, November 12, 2002

Q. Your reaction to the Iraqi Parliament rejection so far of this resolution.

Secretary-General Annan. I've written to the Iraqi government and I'm expecting to hear formally from them. So I don't want to put too much on what the Parliament has said until I hear from the Government.

Q. Is this a new letter or are you talking about the fax from Friday?

Secretary-General Annan. The Friday fax. So I expect to hear from them by the 15th.

Q. Is it a bad sign?

Secretary-General Annan. Governments have a way of managing their own environment and I think most of it was for their own people.

Q. How do you think the inspectors will do when they go in there? What kind of level of trust do you have on Hans Blix, previous inspectors, chief inspectors you have sometimes had difficulties with?

Secretary-General Annan. I think Mr. Blix is a very experienced man, with keen judgement. He has work in Iraq before and he is familiar with the Iraqis. And I expect him to do very well. And they are going with their hands strengthened with a new resolution. And I expect Dr. Blix and Dr. ElBaradei will use those new tools very effectively.

Q. How do you explain the differences between the U.S. saying they can do what they want to do and the [Security] Council saying there will be a meeting if there's a problem with Iraq?

Secretary-General Annan. I think the resolution is very clear. If the inspectors do report back that Iraq is defiant, there will be a Council meeting to discuss the situation and to determine what to do.

Q. What about the President of the United States? You're seeing him. Would it be to congratulate him on the election results or do you need anything on Iraq?

Secretary-General Annan. No, we have quite a few other issues to discuss. The world is a big place.

Letter from Iraqi Foreign Affairs Minister Sabri to United Nations Secretary-General Annan, November 13, 2002

In the Name of God, the Merciful, the Compassionate
"Go to Pharaoh; he has overstepped the bounds. But speak to him with gentle words so that hopefully he will pay heed or show some fear" Almighty God has spoken the truth.
    Sir,
    You may recall the enormous uproar created by the President of the United States of America in the greatest and most wicked slander against Iraq, in which he was followed in his malicious intent and preceded in word and infliction of harm by his lackey Tony Blair, when they spread the rumor that Iraq might have produced or might

have been on the way to producing nuclear weapons during the period since 1998 in which the international inspectors were absent. They later asserted that Iraq had indeed produced chemical and biological weapons, though they know as well as we do, and other States are in a position to know, that this is a an utterly unfounded fabrication. But does knowledge of the truth even enter into the vocabulary of political interaction in our time, after evil has been unleashed to the fullest within the American administration and any hope of good has been dashed? Indeed, is there any good to be expected or hoped for from American administrations now that they have been transformed by their greed, by Zionism and by other well-known factors into the false god of our time?

After some States and the public were taken in by this lie, while others remained silent, Iraq confronted them with its consent to the return of the international inspectors after agreeing with you, as representative of the United Nations in New York, on 16 September 2002, and in a press statement issued jointly in Vienna on 30 September/1 October 2002 by an Iraqi technical delegation headed by Amer Al-Saadi, Chief Inspector Hans Blix and Mohamed ElBaradei, Director General of the International Atomic Energy Agency (IAEA). Yet a few hours after Iraq's consent to the return of the inspectors became an established fact, including agreement on 19 October 2002 as the date of their arrival, Colin Powell, the American Secretary of State, declared that he would refuse to have the inspectors go to Iraq. The gang of evil began once again to talk of the need to adopt a new resolution in order to entertain the people of the world with something new, rather than following the teams of inspectors and witnessing the facts stated by Iraq, namely that it neither had produced nor possessed any nuclear, chemical or biological weapons of mass destruction during the absence of the inspectors. The officials in the international Organization and its agencies, however, and especially those from the permanent members of the Security Council, rather than engaging in such monitoring so as to expose those responsible for their lies and false accusations, busied themselves with discussions of the nature and wording of the new resolution. They would strike or add a letter here and letter there, a word here and a word there, until they reached agreement, on the argument that it was better to take the kicks of a raging bull in a small ring than to face its horns in an open space.

This took place under the pressure of the American administration and its threats to withdraw from the international Organization unless it agreed to what America wanted, which was at best evil in the extreme and a reason for embarrassment for every honest and free member of the international Organization who recalls the provisions of the Charter and sees that there are some who feel shame on behalf of those members who are shameless.

We have told members of the Security Council whom we have contacted or who have contacted us, when they spoke to us of the pretexts of the Americans and their threats of aggression against our country, either by themselves or with whomever might stand with them if the Security Council did not agree to what they wanted, that we preferred, if it was inevitable, to have America alone attack us and to confront it, placing our trust in God, rather than having it obtain international cover with which to camouflage its lies in whole or in part, bringing falsehood closer to the truth so that it might stab the truth with the dagger of evil and perfidy. Indeed, we have confronted it before, at a time when it could be characterized the same way, and that was one of the reasons for its isolation in the human environment all over the globe.

America's aggressiveness and single-handed infliction of injustice and destruction on its victims, chief among them Muslim and Arab believers, constitute the main reason for its withdrawing its ambassadors and other staff, closing its embassies and limiting its interests in many parts of the world, in addition to the hatred of the peoples of the world for its aggressive policies and objectives. This is a situation which no other country in the world has experienced before, not even the fathers of colonialism in earlier times. Yet the Security Council, or more exactly those who basically run it, instead of leaving the American administration and its lackey, behind whom stands hateful Zionism, to reap the consequences of the evil they have sown, have saved iniquity rather than curbing it. We shall see, and then remorse will not be of any avail as they bite their fingers.

The influence of any international organization is based on the conviction and trust of the community in which it exists, once the organization declares that it has been established to serve goals important to that community. We fear that the United Nations will lose the trust and interest of peoples, if that has not already taken place, once it has been exhausted by powerful interests, wherever those interests converge at the expense of other peoples or flatter each other and haggle over what is false at the expense of what is true. Thus the United Nations and its agencies will collapse just as the League of Nations did before it. The responsibility for this will not rest on the American administration alone, but on all those who, in their weakness, work for its interests, yielding to its threats, enticements or promises.

He who fails to speak out the truth is a voiceless demon. Nothing is more distressing than the silence of the representatives of States in the Security Council during their discussion of the American draft in the face of the question raised by the representative of Mexico regarding the possibility of lifting the sanctions imposed on Iraq. During the consultations in the Security Council concerning resolution 1441 on 7 November 2002, the Mexican representative said that he was not satisfied with the explanations provided by the American ambassador concerning the absence of any reference to the lifting of the sanctions and the establishment in the Middle East of a zone free from weapons of mass destruction, adding that he would convey this to his Government in order to receive instructions. The British representative replied that he had listened to the statements of the delegations of Syria and Mexico regarding the inclusion in the resolution of a paragraph on the lifting of the sanctions. He said that Iraq had previously been afforded an opportunity to rid itself of weapons of mass destruction, but had ignored it and made a decision to keep them. Consequently, any reference to the lifting of the sanctions while Iraq still had such weapons was improper. Nevertheless, an indirect reference to that effect was being included. We should add that none of the representatives asked him when, how or where such an alleged decision had been taken by Iraq to keep weapons of mass destruction. The delegates treated the statement of the British representative as though it related to a matter that did not concern them, or rather, as though telling the truth was of no concern to them. Do not this and other things, together with the decline in the prestige of international organizations of this nature, point to the possibility of the collapse of this international Organization, which was founded to maintain international peace and security, but has turned into a kitchen for haggling over the interests of the big powers and for providing cover for war, destruction, blockades and the starvation of peoples?

The future will be determined in the light of the potential for reform, or the inability to achieve reform, as will the future of the United Nations. All those who show their concern in deed and not merely in word to foster this international Organization and its work on the basis of its Charter so that stability, justice and fairness prevail throughout the world as a route to peace, freedom and cooperation among peoples are called upon to exercise caution and act in accordance with international law and the Charter of the United Nations and not at whim in accordance with the unrestrained tendencies of those who threaten the world with their weapons and evil endeavors and those who narrow-mindedly look to their own interests, which they seek to achieve by bargaining at the expense of truth, justice and fairness.

We know that those who pressed the case in the Security Council for the adoption of Security Council resolution 1441 (2002) have objectives other than to ascertain that Iraq has developed no weapons of mass destruction in the absence of the inspectors from Iraq since 1998. You are aware of how they left Iraq and who was the cause of their departure. Although we are aware that, following the widely known understanding between the representatives of Iraq and the Secretary-General and the press statement issued by Blix, ElBaradei and the representatives of Iraq, there are no facts or principles of justice and fairness to necessitate the adoption of that resolution in the name of the Security Council, we hereby inform you that we will deal with resolution 1441 (2002), despite its iniquitous contents, even though it is to be implemented against the background of the intentions harbored by those of bad faith. Based as this is in an attempt to spare our people harm, we shall not forget, just as others should not forget, that the preservation of our people's dignity and of their security and independence within their homeland is a sacred and honorable national duty on the agenda of our leadership and our Government. The same is true of the protection of the homeland and its sovereignty, together with that of the people and their security, interests and high values, from antagonists and oppressors. Hence, as we said in the aforementioned agreement and press statement, we are ready to receive the inspectors so that they can perform their duties and ascertain that Iraq has produced no weapons of mass destruction in their absence from Iraq since 1998 under the circumstances known both to you and to the Security Council. We request you to inform the Security Council that we are ready to receive the inspectors in accordance with the established dates. All concerned parties should remember that we are in our holy month of Ramadan and that the people are fasting, and that after this month is a feast. The concerned bodies and officials, however, will cooperate with the inspectors against this entire background and that of the tripartite statement of France, the Russian Federation and China. The Government of Iraq will also take all of this into consideration when dealing with the inspectors and with all matters relating to their demeanor and the intentions of any one of them who demonstrates bad faith or an inappropriate approach to preserving the national dignity, independence and security of the people and the security, independence and sovereignty of the homeland. We are eager for them to accomplish their task in accordance with international law as soon as possible. If they do so in a professional and lawful manner, and without previously planned goals, the fabrications of the liars will be revealed to the public and the declared aim of the Security Council will be achieved. At that point, the Security Council will become legally obligated to lift the embargo from Iraq, failing which all persons of goodwill throughout the world, in addition to Iraq, will tell it to lift the embargo and all the other unjust sanctions from Iraq. Before the public and the law, the Council will be under obligation to apply paragraph 14 of its resolution 687 (1991) to the Zionist entity (Israel) and thereafter to the entire region of the Middle East so that it is free of weapons of mass destruction. The worldwide number of fair-minded persons will increase, together with Iraq's potential to drive from its environment the cawing of the crows of evil, who daily raid its lands, demolish its property and take the lives of those hit by their bombs, if not already claimed by the evil-doers themselves. When this happens, it will help to stabilize the region and the world, if accompanied by a solution not based on double standards to end the Zionist occupation of Palestine and if the aggressors desist from their attacks against Muslims and the world.

We therefore reiterate, through you, the same statement to the Security Council: send the inspectors to Iraq to ascertain as much and, if their conduct is thoroughly supervised to ensure that it is lawful and professional, everyone will be assured that Iraq has produced no nuclear, chemical or biological weapons of mass destruction, whatever allegations to the contrary are made by the evil pretenders. The fabrications of the liars and the deceit of the charlatans in the American and British administrations will be revealed before the world in contrast to the truthfulness of the proud Iraqis and the correctness of what they say and do. If, however, the opportunity is left for the whim of the American administration and the desires of Zionism, coupled with the followers, intelligence services, threats and foul inducements of each, to manipulate and play with the inspection teams and among their ranks, the picture will be muddled and the ensuing confusion will distort the facts and push matters in a dangerous direction, to the edge of the precipice, a situation wanted neither by the fair-minded nor by those, including my Government, who seek to uncover the facts as they stand. The fieldwork and the implementation will be the deciding factors as to whether the true intent was for the Security Council to ascertain that Iraq is free of those alleged weapons or whether the entire matter is nothing more than an evil cover for the authors of the resolution, with their vile slander and their shamelessness in lying to the public, including their own peoples.

So let the inspectors come to Baghdad to perform their duty in accordance with the law, whereupon we shall hear and see, together with those who hear, see and act, each in accordance with his obligations and rights as established in the Charter of the United Nations and international law. The final frame of reference continues to be resolution 687 (1991), which imposes obligations on the Security Council and Iraq, as well as the code of conduct contained in the agreement signed with the Secretary-General in New York on 16 September 2002 and the press statement issued jointly with Hans Blix and ElBaradei in Vienna on 30 September-1 October 2002.

We hope that you will exercise your responsibilities by speaking to the oppressors and advising them that their unjust treatment of Muslims, faithful Arabs and all people has disastrous consequences and that God is omnipotent and capable of all things. Tell them that the people of Iraq are proud, faithful and militant, having fought and waged war against the former colonialism, imperialism and aggression, including that of the false god, for years and years. The price paid for the preservation of their independence, dignity and the high principles in which they believed was rivers of blood, together with a great deal of deprivation and damage to their wealth, alongside the immortal achievements and record in which they take pride. We hope that you will advise those who are ignorant not to push the situation to the edge of the precipice at the time of implementation, because the people of Iraq will not choose to live if the price is their dignity, their homeland, their freedom or the things sacrosanct to them. On the contrary, the price will be their lives if that is the only way forward to preserve what must be preserved.

Before concluding this letter of mine, I should like to inform you that I shall address a further detailed letter to you in due course, stating our comments on the procedures and measures contained in resolution 1441 (2002) that are inconsistent with international law, the Charter of the United Nations, the established facts and the requirements of previous relevant Security Council resolutions.

"Have you guaranteed that the One in heaven will not strike earth and cause it to tumble?"

Almighty God has spoken the truth.

God is great.

Remarks by President Bush and United Nations Secretary-General Annan, November 13, 2002

President Bush and Secretary-General Kofi Annan delivered their remarks after meeting in Washington, DC.

President Bush. First, I do want to welcome the Secretary General here. I'm grateful for your leadership at the United Nations. A while ago the United Nations Security Council made a very strong statement that we, the world, expects Saddam Hussein to disarm for the sake of peace. And the U.N. stepped up to its responsibilities, and I want to thank you for that, Mr. Secretary General. I appreciate your leadership.

I'm looking forward to our discussion. Of course I'll remind the Secretary General that our war against terror is a war against individuals whose hearts are full of hate. We do not fight a religion. As a matter of fact, by far, the vast majority of American citizens respect the Islamic people and the Muslim faith. After all, there are millions of peaceful-loving Muslim Americans.

Some of the comments that have been uttered about Islam do not reflect the sentiments of my government or the sentiments of most Americans. Islam, as practiced by the vast majority of people, is a peaceful religion, a religion that respects others. Ours is a country based upon tolerance, Mr. Secretary General, and we respect the faith and we welcome people of all faiths in America. And we're not going to let the war on terror or terrorists cause us to change our values.

And so, Mr. Secretary General, I'm honored that you're here at the Oval Office. I'm proud to call you friend, and welcome.

Secretary-General Annan. Thank you very much, Mr. President. If I may comment on the last point you raised. I share your view entirely that every region and people of every faith have also been victims of terrorists. This is a scourge that affects all of us, regardless of region or religion. And we need to stand together to defeat terrorism.

And this is where the work of the United Nations and effective implementation of this Resolution 1373 is absolutely crucial. We need to work to deprive terrorists of the opportunities by not giving them haven, by not giving them financial and logistical support. And I think the counterterrorism committee of the Security Council is doing a good job in trying to make sure we all work together on it.

With regards to the Iraq decision, I want to thank you, Mr. President, for working with the United Nations and the Council and working through the Council. And I remember when you came to the U.N. on the 12th of September, nobody knew which way you were going to go. And in my own speech before yours, I was pleading that we go the multilateral route. And I think we were all relieved that we did—you did.

And I would want to say that the Council decision, which was unanimous, sent a powerful message that the entire international community would like to see the Security Council resolutions implemented.

Today I received a letter from the Iraqi government accepting the resolution, saying that they would work with the resolution. And Mr. Blix and his team will go back. We expect them to get there on the 18th and actively begin their work. This is a Chapter 7 resolution, and it must be implemented.

White House Press Briefing, November 13, 2002

Q. In it's 9-page letter to the U.N. Security Council accepting the conditions of Resolution 1441, Iraq makes the assertion that it has no weapons of mass destruction, that it is "clean." What's the White House's opinion on that declaration?

Mr. McClellan. Well, John, I haven't seen what's in the letter yet. I've heard the reports and I would remind you that this was never a question of accepting or rejecting the resolution. The U.N. resolution is binding on Iraq and the Iraqi regime. Saddam Hussein had no choice but to accept the resolution.

I would also remind you that we have heard this before from Saddam Hussein and the Iraqi regime. Now we need to see it by Saddam Hussein's actions. We need to—the onus continues to be on Saddam Hussein. This is his choice.

And I would go back through what the regime in Iraq needs to do: Iraq must provide a full accounting of all weapons of mass destruction—the programs, materials and delivery systems—within 30 days, that's what the resolution spells out; Iraq also must allow free, unimpeded, unconditional immediate access for weapons inspectors anywhere, any time, to anyone; and Iraq must also allow witnesses to weapons of mass destruction programs to be interviewed outside of the country and to bring their families with them; and Iraq must also stop firing on the U.S. and British aircraft patrolling the no-fly zones.

Q. But this assertion that Iraq possess no weapons of mass destruction, does that seem plausible to you?

Mr. McClellan. Well, John, again, I haven't seen the specifics of the letter, but the resolution clearly spells out for the regime in Iraq that any false information or omissions are considered a violation of the resolution and would be considered a further material breach. That's all spelled out in the resolution.

But, again, I would reiterate that—the latest reports that the regime in Iraq has agreed to cooperate and comply, that we have heard this before and now it's time to see it by their actions.

Q. If they don't stop firing on coalition planes in the no-fly zone, is that a material breach?

Mr. McClellan. I just indicated to you that part of the resolution calls for the regime in Iraq to stop firing on aircraft patrolling the no-fly zones. You're trying to get into "ifs" and hypotheticals and, as I said yesterday, I'm not going to get into every if and hypothetical. It makes clear in the resolution that if there are violations, that the countries, or the inspectors, are to report that to the Security Council where there will be further discussion about what consequences may follow. But just because there are discussions at the Security Council, I would remind you that that does not prohibit the President from using his authority to act with like-minded nations if need be.

Q. Scott, you noted that Iraq has 30 days, or until December 8th, to provide a complete accounting of its weapons of mass destruction. It has; they don't have any.

Mr. McClellan. Well, again, this letter apparently, I understand, has been delivered to the United Nations. We have not seen—or maybe we are reviewing this letter as I speak, but I have not seen the contents of the letter. We'll look at the letter and we'll go from there.

Q. Is the United States prepared to provide evidence to counter Iraq's assertion that it has weapons of mass destruction?

Mr. McClellan. Well, again, they have a 30-day deadline to list and disclose all that information. I haven't seen the contents of the letter, so I don't want to jump into what I haven't seen at this point. But it's been made clear, if there is false information or omissions, then that would be considered a violation.

Q. And saying that they had no weapons of mass destruction would be false information, according to the United States?

Mr. McClellan. Well, again, I haven't seen the contents of the letter. So let's—they have a 30-day time line to report all that information.

Remarks by Secretary of State Powell, November 13, 2002

Secretary Colin Powell was interviewed on BBC-TV by Jon Leyne.

Q. Well, on Resolution 1441, Iraq has requested, has demanded, has said it will now comply with the resolution. What's your response to that?

Secretary Powell. Well, they had no choice. The international community spoke last Friday on Resolution 1441 and one of the first requirements they put before Iraq was to acknowledge, accept this resolution. And notwithstanding all of the usual boilerplate language that was in the long Iraq letter, Iraq did what it was required to do under the resolution.

Q. Okay, the next thing it is required to do under the resolution is to provide a declaration, a 30-day declaration. Who decides whether there are omissions or false statements in that declaration?

Secretary Powell. We'll have to see what the declaration looks like when it comes in. And I think we know enough, and I think the inspection teams, UNMOVIC and IAEA, and frankly, other members of the Security Council, know enough with respect to what Iraq has done in the past and the baselines that existed in 1998 as to their holdings, and the work that has been done over the last 12 years to make a judgment as to whether the declaration they submit bears some relationship to the truth and the facts as I think we understand them.

Q. But can you, the United States, jump in, yourselves, and just say, we believe there are omissions, it is a material breach, the whole consequences therefore follow?

Secretary Powell. Well, as you know, the way the resolution is structured, if the declaration is false and if there are efforts to deny the inspectors the access that they need, then that constitutes, in and of itself, as a matter of fact, a material breach. It is not the United States that declares it, it stands on its own. Somebody will have to make a judgment as to whether it's accurate or not.

Q. Well, exactly. Who makes that judgment?

Secretary Powell. There are lots of ways to do that. Dr. Blix could make a judgment. We could make a judgment. Any member of the Council can look at this and say this just can't be, and then refer it to the Security Council for its assessment, which is what's called for in that part of the resolution.

Q. By calling for the resolution, as soon as there is—somebody decides—and it's not clear who—decides there's an omission, it is therefore automatically in material breach?

Secretary Powell. Joining many other material breaches, past and current.

Q. But it is a new one following the resolution?

Secretary Powell. It is a new one following the resolution, joining past ones and present ones. It is not as if there is no material breach now. There is material breach now.

Q. Which then leads the Security Council to meet with the possibility, of course, of all those consequences that would follow. That sounds an awful lot like the automaticity you said isn't in the resolution.

Secretary Powell. Not at all. I don't think it is. It says that if there is this failure in providing an accurate declaration and if they continue to frustrate the inspectors, then it gets referred to the Council for its assessment as to whether or not serious consequences could follow, or for whatever the Council might choose to do.

And at the same time, the United States is free, as is any other member of the Security Council, to make its own independent judgment as to whether or not it may wish to act in concert with likeminded nations. But there is no automaticity. It isn't as if one flips a switch and a light goes on. Judgments will be made, considerations will be taken, and there will be a great deal of discussion between the members of the Security Council as we review that particular material breach.

But the United States wants to work with members of the Security Council. It's better if we act collectively. But if there's not the collective will to act, then the United States certainly, as does any other member of the Security Council, retains its ability to act in self-defense.

Q. Going on beyond this declaration—say we get past that stage and the inspections are in progress—the sort of problems you're going to encounter probably won't be black and white. It will be a very gray area. And Iraq might say, "We'd like to let you in this building but we've lost the key." You know, "Somebody's car broke down on their way."

Secretary Powell. That kind of—that isn't a gray area. That's black and white. They're not letting us in the building.

Q. But they'll find gray areas.

Secretary Powell. Well, they can try to find gray areas. But if we see that the inspectors are just running into one gray area after another, or even the first gray area, that's a clear indication that Iraq does not intend to cooperate. And the instructions from the Council, I think, are rather clear. We expect cooperation. And we have had many conversations with Dr. Blix and with Dr. ElBaradei, and they have made the same point. They don't want to be part of a sham. They don't want to be part of a shell game where we're finding, you know, where is the quarter under the walnut, or however you play the game.

What they want to know is: Will they be put in a position where they can do their job? Will there be cooperation? And if Iraq keeps painting everything in gray, it won't work, and we expect that UNMOVIC and IAEA will report that to the Council for the action called for in the resolution.

Q. The point is that Iraq is going to try and do something that is not clear in that way, and you're going to have other members of the Council, quite possibly, saying it was an honest mistake, they forget about an appointment, somebody was sick. So who decides that?

Secretary Powell. Well, maybe we will, Jon, and maybe we won't. Maybe Iraq has to understand that this is not like 1999 when the Council did not speak with a single, clear voice and you had three abstentions among the Permanent Members of the Security Council the last effort at an inspection regime.

This time, all 15 have spoken clearly, with a much tougher resolution, and have made clear that we are expecting Iraqi cooperation; and if there's not Iraqi cooperation, the inspectors cannot do their job and the inspectors are expected to report that to the Security Council; the Security Council will assess the seriousness of this, and serious consequences, as the United Nations has said in the past, is a possibility.

It's clear. It's unambiguous. Yes, judgments will be made. Yes, there will be debate. But I think Iraq would be making a very great mistake if they think there are fissures within the Security Council of the kind they have exploited in the past. This time, there are none. We are all together on this. Every nation is saying the same thing to Iraq: cooperate, comply, disarm; you will be disarmed one way or the other.

Q. If you get to that point where the Council has agreed there's a material breach, or there is some argument, at least, within the Council, would you press forward, then, for a second resolution, as I think you seemed to intimate over the weekend?

Secretary Powell. What I've intimated is that the Council has the ability to do whatever it wishes once a situation has been reported to it that would constitute a new material breach. I don't know whether the Council will just want to debate it for a long period of time or whether they want to move immediately to another resolution, a new resolution. That's for the Council to decide.

Q. But would you press for one?

Secretary Powell. Well, I can't tell you what we would press for in the absence of what it is, why we're pressing for something.

But clearly, if it was the reality that Iraq was not cooperating, that they did not intend to disarm, that they were once again thwarting the will of the international community, that they wanted to treat this 17th resolution like they have treated all previous 16 resolutions, then you can bet we will be pressing for the United Nations, through the Security Council, to take appropriate action in accordance with this resolution. The whole purpose of this resolution, the guts of this resolution, was that there would be consequences for further misbehavior. That's what makes this resolution different.

So to have this misbehavior and to see it, and see this violation, and knowing that this individual has said I don't care what the international community thinks, I don't care what the Arab League thinks, I don't care what the Security Council thinks, I'm going to continue to violate international law, then of course we'll be pressing for action on the part of the Security Council.

Q. What happens in the other scenario, the other half of the scenario, where Saddam Hussein decides completely to comply with the U.N.'s demands, with Resolution 1441? Can you say for sure there would not be a war?

Secretary Powell. We will have to wait and see whether any such level of compliance is reached. But the President has made it clear from the very beginning that he wants to solve this peacefully. But solving it means disarmament. And if you have had disarmament to the satisfaction of the Security Council, then we have had disarmament to the satisfaction of the Security Council; and if that is also to the satisfaction of the United States, our security council, then we have found the peaceful solution the President said he is looking for.

Q. So Saddam Hussein stays in power?

Secretary Powell. We are looking for disarmament. We still think that the Iraqi people would be better off with a new leader, and I hope they will come to their senses in due course that a better life awaits all the people of Iraq without Saddam Hussein.

Regime change was and still is our policy because we have had the greatest doubts as to whether or not he'll ever comply. He didn't comply previously. He caused circumstances to exist which caused the withdrawal of the inspectors in 1998. That's why regime change became our policy, because it did not seem he would obey the international community, and the only way you could get disarmament was through regime change. And that remains our policy.

It's up to him to demonstrate that the regime has changed and perhaps we should look at it in a different light. But right now the burden is on him, not on the United States, not on the Security Council. The burden is on him to obey international law, get rid of weapons of mass destruction.

And let us not lose sight of the other U.N. resolutions that he has violated with respect to human rights, with respect to the return of prisoners, with respect to a lot of other things that he is responsible for. And we just can't walk away from those when disarmament occurs, if it occurs. So the burden is on him. If anybody is guilty in this matter, it is Saddam Hussein, not the United States, not the international community.

Q. Just briefly, after all that's been said about you and your position with the administration over the summer, did you realize the smallest of wry smiles after that resolution was passed unanimously?

Secretary Powell. Obviously, I was very pleased. Lots of things have been said about me in the course of the summer and in the course of the past 22 months. But that's part of the price of being in public life in my position.

The only thing I'm interested in is doing the best job I can as Secretary of State in representing the American people, serving the President of the United States in the conduct of foreign policy. And commentary plus or minus, good or bad, just comes with the job, and I've been around this town a long time and I know how to work my way through controversy and comment.

Remarks by United Nations Secretary-General Annan, November 13, 2002

Q. Mr. Secretary-General, is it your opinion, Sir, that with this letter, Iraq is in compliance with paragraph 9 of [Resolution] 1441, that they have stated their intention to comply with the Resolution?

Secretary-General Annan. Yes, Iraq has accepted. I think that the word, the acceptance and inviting the inspectors to come in is there, so we take it that they have accepted it, and Mr. [Hans] Blix and his team will go in on the 18th and begin their work actively.

Q. So, they have met the first deadline of Resolution 1441?

Secretary-General Annan. Yes.

Q. Mr. Secretary-General, is it your impression, some in the Administration say, "Look, we've heard this before." What is your level of confidence that things are different now? Or are they?

Secretary-General Annan. I think we—we all have to be a bit patient. The inspectors will be there in a few days, within a week, they will be there by the 18th and we are going to test it.

Q. Mr. Secretary-General, you discussed Cyprus with the President? Can you give us more details about your discussions on Cyprus?

Secretary-General Annan. I think the President, like other leaders, is encouraged that the Plan is out, and we are all hoping that the leaders will seize this opportunity and resolve the Cyprus issue once and for all. I have asked the leaders to react within a week, and I would hope to hear from them by the 18th and we will decide how we will take the issue forward.

Q. I am confused about what constitutes a "material breach" for the U.N. resolution. Did you get from the President Bush the feeling that he will be patient, or "zero tolerance" policy?

Secretary-General Annan. I think the resolution is clear as to what the inspectors have to do and the reporting procedures to the Council. Of course the President is determined that the disarmament will take place and that we should press ahead with our plans.

Q. To what extent do you feel that the Iraqi acceptance of the U.N. resolution has delayed military action?

Secretary-General Annan. I think the issue is not the acceptance, but performance on the ground. It's the performance on the ground and so, let the inspectors go in, and I urge the Iraqis to cooperate with them and to perform and I think that is the real test we are all waiting for.

Q. Mr. Secretary-General, the language in the letter, as you know, is quite bombastic. It includes a paragraph at the end in which Naji Sabri says that he will outline to you in a further letter what he believes are illegalities in resolution1441. Does that give you some sort of indication that they are going to start playing games?

Secretary-General Annan. I will wait to see whether it is an indication that they are going to play games, or is a message they are sending to their own people. I really don't know. What is important is that the resolution is mandatory. The resolution went into force the moment it was adopted and the inspectors are going to go there and do their work and they have to comply and we will see what happens when they are on the ground.

Q. The Iraqi Ambassador said today that Iraq has nothing to fear because it has no weapons of mass destruction. Based on everything you have seen, intelligence that has been shared with you, do you believe that to be a truthful statement, that Iraq has no weapons of mass destruction?

Secretary-General Annan. I really can't answer that question, until the inspectors come back. This is precisely why the inspectors are going back in, and with a new strengthened mandate, I hope they will be able to search and go wherever they want to do their work and come back and report to the Council, and that is why they are going. That is their mandate, to come back and certify whether Iraq has, or has no weapons of mass destruction.

Remarks by Secretary of Defense Rumsfeld, November 14, 2002

Secretary Donald Rumsfeld delivered his remarks on a CBS Radio program hosted by Steve Kroft.

Q. Well, thank you. There are many questions, and I would like to ask the first one, if it's all right. U.N. weapons inspectors are preparing to go to Iraq very shortly and begin searching for evidence of Saddam Hussein's weapons of mass destruction. What do you expect them to find, and what happens if they don't find anything? Is Saddam Hussein off the hook?

Secretary Rumsfeld. Well, we know that Saddam Hussein has chemical and biological weapons. And we know he has an active program for the development of nuclear weapons. I suppose what it would prove would be that the inspections process had been successfully defeated by the Iraqis if they find nothing. That's what one would know if that turned out to be the case. There's no question but that the Iraqi regime is clever. They have spent a lot of time hiding things, dispersing things, tunneling underground, taking documentation and moving it to different locations in the past, preventing inspectors from getting access, listening in on what inspectors intend to do. And before the inspectors arrive to do it, seeing that what was there is moved or the effort is frustrated in some way.

Q. Does Saddam Hussein win if that's the case?

Secretary Rumsfeld. I think the quotation you heard from the president kind of answered that question. The president believes it's important that the Iraqi regime be disarmed. He has indicated that his first choice would be that it would be done peacefully with the Iraqi regime acquiescing in the unanimous Security Council vote for the new resolution, and that they disarm themselves. The president has said that if not, he intends to lead a coalition of the willing to see that that happens.

Q. In the event that we ultimately go to war with Iraq, what do you think the Iraqi response will be in Iraq, and then what do you think the Iraqi response would be on U.S. soil?

Secretary Rumsfeld. Of course, those questions are awfully tough to answer. We're looking at all conceivable contingencies because, in any event, war is your last choice, not your first choice. There is a danger that Saddam Hussein would do things that he's done previously. He has, in the past, used chemical weapons, for example, on his own people. And he's used chemical weapons on his neighbors. And one has to be prepared and concerned that that could occur.

Terrorists have attacked the United States on September 11th, and U.S. interests around the world on other occasions. And I don't doubt for a minute that if he's able, he would like to try to see that terrorist attacks would occur in the event that force were to be used by the United Nations, or by a coalition of the willing.

However, I would have to say that I think that one ought not to think of that as a direct response to the use of force, because he's already done these things in the past, and his inclination and his words today suggest that he would like to do them today. So, I don't think that the use of force would necessarily precipitate it.

Q. Mr. Secretary, how likely do you consider it that he might, again, try to sabotage oil wells, possibly contaminate them with biological weapons, and things like that?

Secretary Rumsfeld. Well, of course, you're right. He did it in Kuwait when that invasion took place 10 or 12 years ago. It's a possibility. It was a terrible environmental disaster what he did. We were able to get the fires put out, and to restore the oil wells, and we certainly would be prepared to see that the fires are put out and that they're restored again if he were to do that. He would be harming his own people if he were to do that, but that wouldn't be the first time he'd done that.

Q. Thank you, Mr. Secretary. Thank you for taking my question. Very briefly, my question is as follows: Apart from the difficult task of ascertaining whether or not Saddam has hidden weapons of mass destruction within his geographic boundaries, there is certainly the possibility that he has hoarded them in third countries, or with organizations that have interests inimical to the United States. What, if anything, can we do to address that distinct possibility?

Secretary Rumsfeld. You're right. It is possible that Iraq, or any country could make arrangements with a terrorist network, and have them assist them in conducting terrorist attacks. It is also true that from time to time over my lifetime we've seen countries put their weapons in other locations to make—to complexify the problem for the other side. In fact, during the Gulf War, Iraq flew their air force into Iran so that they wouldn't be shot down by the United States of America. And there had been countries that had moved other types of weapons around. It's something we have to be sensitive to, and alert to, but I think it's a manageable problem.

Q. I'm the parent of an Army Reserve soldier who has already gone through his training and is on the next call up list to be deployed to the Persian Gulf area within the next few weeks, for a period of six months to two years. I'm not yet convinced that Iraq is such an imminent threat to the United States that it justifies having my son placed in harms way. If I were there in person, speaking to you, what would you say to convince me?

Secretary Rumsfeld. Well, first, we're grateful that your son is serving, and wants to serve. And I can't help but recognize the feelings that a parent has. What would I say to you? Well, I would look you in the eye and I would say, go back before September 11th and ask yourself this question, was the attack that took place on September 11th an imminent threat the month before, or two months before, or three months before, or six months before? When did the attack on September 11th become an imminent threat? When was it sufficiently dangerous to our country that had we known about it that we could have stepped up and stopped it and saved 3,000 lives? Now, transport yourself forward a year, two years, or a week, or a month, and if Saddam Hussein were to take his weapons of mass destruction and transfer them, either use them himself, or transfer them to the al Qaeda, and somehow the al Qaeda were to engage in an attack on the United States, or an attack on U.S. forces overseas, with a weapon of mass destruction you're not talking about 300, or 3,000 people potentially being killed, but 30,000, or 100,000 of human beings. So the question is, when is it such an immediate threat that you must do something, is a tough question. But if you think about it, it's the nexus, the connection, the relationship between terrorist states and weapons of mass destruction with terrorist networks that has changed our lives, and changed the security environment in the world. And right now in the Congress the intelligence committees in the House and the Senate are working very hard, trying to connect the dots as to who knew what before September 11th, how might it have been stopped. Our task, your task as a mother, and as a citizen, as a voter, and my task, is to try to connect the dots before something happens, not afterwards. People say, well where's the smoking gun? Well, we don't want to see a smoking gun from a weapon of mass destruction. We have an obligation to try to defend the people of our country and the interests we have, and that is why the president went to the United Nations and sought a resolution, and received unanimous support to try to see if we can't get a peaceful solution to the Iraqi problem.

* * * *

Q. Okay. I remember shortly after September 11th there was talk and rumor of there being a draft again, because we were low in reserves, and troops. I was wondering, since there's troops being deployed to different areas if that's even more of a possibility now, or if that's something that's being thought of right now?

Secretary Rumsfeld. Yes, we're not considering having a draft. We've been very fortunate in being able to attract and retain the number of men and women that are needed in the armed forces. Indeed, the Army, the Navy, the Air Force and the Marines all are meeting their recruiting quotas, and their retention quotas well in advance of their targets. Morale is high in the military, and there's absolutely no need, for the present, for us to even think about returning to a draft.

Q. Mr. Secretary, how dependent is the United States right now on the National Guard, and Reserve units?

Secretary Rumsfeld. Well, it is very dependent, because we have what's called a total force concept. We're arranged in a way that we keep on active duty the number of people we feel is necessary to maintain a ready force, and then we keep in the ready reserves the number of people that we feel are appropriate to augment that force. There's no way we can function in this somewhat dangerous and untidy world of ours without using Guard and Reserve from time to time. And they do an absolutely terrific job, they really do.

Q. My question is basically, in the event of what seems to be an almost inevitable war with Iraq, would the State of Israel be allowed to defend herself, and to what extent?

Secretary Rumsfeld. Any sovereign country certainly has the right, indeed the obligation, to defend themselves if they believe that their circumstance requires it. Our hope, and intention would be that in the event force were to be used in Iraq that the coalition of willing countries would be able to do the task, and it would not require Israel having to defend itself. But, needless to say, Israel would have to make that judgment themselves. You may recall that during the Gulf War, early in the 1990s, they did not become engaged in the conflict, which in my personal view was the correct decision, even though they were subject to having some SCUD missiles fired at them.

* * * *

Q. On the eventuality, or hypothetically if we do go in and overthrow the Iraqi regime currently in place, what is our position on the occupation of Iraq in the future? Thank you.

Secretary Rumsfeld. Yes, indeed, in the event that force had to be used, and the Saddam Hussein regime were to be gone, there would need to be a period of time when the coalition countries that were involved in removing the Saddam Hussein regime were in the country, and working to do several things. Number one, to find the weapons of mass destruction and destroy them. Number two, to see that the humanitarian assistance was provided. Number three, to see that the oil wells, to the extent that they'd been damaged, were back in working condition, and providing the kind of revenue that's going to be necessary for the health and welfare of the people in that country. And then at some point, some sort of a provisional government of Iraqis would find its way in the world. And other than saying it ought to be representative and protective of the minority groups in the country, I don't think it's for outsiders to necessarily prescribe precisely what that ought to look like. Just as Afghanistan found its way through this loya jirga process to a government form, I suspect that would be the case in Iraq, too. There's no question but that the institutions in Iraq that manage things like water and sewage, and those types of things would have to exist, and they'd have to be operating and functioning, so that the health and welfare of the people was looked out for. And at some moment, then there would be no coalition forces in the country, at that point where there was a stable situation. How long that would take is not knowable at the present time.

Q. Is it possible that there could be a U.S. military figure running the country for a period of time?

Secretary Rumsfeld. There's no question but that, in the event force were used, there would be a military command in the country. During that period you're trying to find and destroy the weapons of mass destruction, that simply is going to be a very difficult task. They have dispersed these things throughout the country, they've got so many underground facilities, they have things that are mobile, and the only way it will ever be found, in my view, effectively is if you find people who have been involved in it who are willing to come and talk to you about it, and tell you where they are. The last time the inspectors were in, that's how it happened. Two sons in laws of Saddam Hussein defected, went into Jordan, and the word came out and they told where these inspectors could go look, they went and looked, and they found weapons of mass destruction. And eventually Saddam Hussein talked his two sons in laws, I can't imagine it, but he did, talked them into coming back to Iraq, and then he killed them.

Q.Mr. Secretary, back in the '80s, when you were a Middle East envoy for the Reagan administration you actually met Saddam Hussein on one or two occasions. You're probably one of the few Americans who have met him. What do you remember about that meeting, and has it influenced your response in dealing with him in this crisis?

Secretary Rumsfeld. I remember the meeting well, but it hasn't influenced my response in this crisis at all. If you think back to that time, Iran and Iraq were in a war. Our friends in the Gulf region were concerned about the possibility that Iran could win. And were deeply concerned that it could upset, and create an instability in the entire region. So I was asked to go over there, and I met with Tariq Aziz and with Saddam Hussein and talked to him about our interests. And the fact that—it was one of the few countries from the Middle East war that we had not reestablished relationships with. So I was, I guess, the first senior American to go in there in some time. And we had a good discussion. He recognized his situation, and was interested in getting some assistance, so that he had better information. And I was Middle East envoy for about six months, right after 241 Marines had been killed by terrorists in Beirut, Lebanon, at the airport there. And it's my understanding that subsequent to my visit, the United States government did, in fact, provide some intelligence assistance to him, so that he—the war ended up kind of at a standstill, or a stalemate, rather than either country being defeated.

Q. Do you remember anything about it, did he impress you one way or the other?

Secretary Rumsfeld. Well, he's—I suppose anyone who lives in a country that he's the head of, like Saddam Hussein is, and sees his picture in every room in every building, in every city of the country, begins to inhale and believe that he's different. I suppose that could happen to most anybody. But, he is clearly a survivor, he is a brutal, repressive dictator; he has imposed enormous harm to his people. His determination to have weapons of mass destruction is so great that he's denied his people billions and billions, and billions of dollars of revenue they would have if he wanted to give up his weapons and have the sanctions lifted. But, he won't do it. He has an attitude about himself that suggests that he wants to try to destabilize the neighboring countries, and periodically describes them as illegitimate, and attempts to take them over. I guess he is a long-term dictator who has killed an awful lot of people. He's even used chemical weapons on his own people.

* * * *

Q. My question, how does our national security have anything to do with Iraq, and has the United States illegally armed Iraq?

Secretary Rumsfeld. Has the United States illegally armed Iraq? I don't know quite what you mean, but no, I don't know of anything the United States has done that's illegal at all. If you're asking, has the United States ever provided arms to Iraqis, as opposed to the Iraqi government, the answer is yes, there are various Iraqis that are in opposition to the Saddam Hussein regime and it is correct that some time, in past years, they have provided some military capabilities to some Iraqi opposition forces. And then there's the Kurdish forces in the north, and I believe that the United States, again, going back some years, provided some military equipment to the Kurdish forces in the north.

Q. I think he may be talking about when the United States was backing Iraq in the Iran-Iraq war.

Secretary Rumsfeld. Well, I am told that we did not, but I don't know, I was not in the government during that period. I saw an article in Newsweek that reported on some—I think it was various types of biologicals. And I'm told that they went through a medical relationship that we had with many countries in the world, and they were for medical purposes. But, I don't know of any weapons that went to Iraq. I do know that the United States government in the 1980s, I'm told, as I said, provided intelligence to Iraq.

Q. If the Iraqis use chemical weapons on our troops, would we consider responding with nuclear weapons? And I ask that, because my dad was a Marine at Iwo-Jima at the end of World War II, and I believe, and he believed that his life was saved by Hiroshima and Nagasaki.

Secretary Rumsfeld. It is always possible that Iraq, in the event of conflict, could use chemical or biological weapons. The United States government, the president and others, are communicating with people in Iraq, in the military, very forcefully that they ought not to use those weapons. If you think about it, Saddam Hussein can't use those weapons himself. He has to use intermediaries. He simply has to go through a general to a colonel, to some person who physically can do what it is required to actually employ a chemical or biological weapon. We are communicating with people in that regime, the truth. And the truth is that anyone who is any way connected with weapons of mass destruction and their use, in the event of a conflict, would be held accountable. And people who help to avoid that would be advantaged.

Q. How many Americans would you estimate might be killed in an invasion of Iraq? What number do you consider acceptable, and what about Iraqi civilian casualties?

Secretary Rumsfeld. There is no way to know the answers to those questions and, of course, they're terribly important questions. You don't ever want to use force and put men and women in uniform, or civilians, into the dangerous position where they could be injured or killed. The United States government in the Desert Storm conflict was actually on the ground fighting for four days. They Iraqi Army surrendered tens of thousands, a total of something like 70,000 troops started surrendering in the first three or four days of the war. They know what kind of a regime Saddam Hussein is running. They know what the damage that's done to the people of Iraq. They know the truth that the United States of America doesn't covet the land of any other country. They know this is not an issue between the United States, or England, or the coalition countries, or the United Nations and the Iraqi people, or the Iraqi Army. It has to do with a small clique in the Ba'ath Party leadership in Baghdad that Saddam Hussein uses to work his will. I think that there would be—in fact, there was one instance where hundreds and hundreds of Iraqi soldiers surrendered to a journalist who didn't even have a gun. So, the idea that it's going to be a long, long, long battle of some kind, I think, is belied by what happened in 1990. Now, can you be certain of that, no. Do you have to be prepared for the worst, yes. In the event that it becomes necessary the United States would do it in a manner that would be respectful of human life on all sides, but would be determined to do the job, and to finish it fast.

* * * *

Q. One of the questions I have for you is, can you elaborate a little bit about the connection between al Qaeda and Iraq as I think a lot of Americans are sort of perplexed by the lack of information we have about that, and could you just make that connection a little clearer for us?

    Secretary Rumsfeld. The reason people are perplexed is because it is perplexing. The terrorist states, one of which is Iraq. Another is Iran, and Libya, and Syria, and Korea, and Cuba, and they're all on the terrorist state list, have varying relationships with these so-called terrorist networks, Hezbollah, Hamas and al Qaeda, and six or eight others. In some cases, the relationships are quite well known, and well defined. For example, Iran works with Hezbollah, and against Israel, and sends weapons, and terrorists down into Damascus, and down into Beirut, Lebanon, and down into Israel to engage in terrorist acts.

    In other cases, it's rather mysterious, the relationship is, and they don't advertise it or publicize it. In some cases, it's because they're ideologically oriented, and agree with each other. In some cases, they have marriages of convenience, where they have a common enemy, so that even though they may be different philosophically, or religiously, their common enemy brings them together and they work together on things.

    I think that what I've done is, I see, of course, a lot of classified information, and what I've done is to go to the Central Intelligence Agency, and ask them, what is it that we can say about a relationship or a situation that is not going to damage our sources and methods, and expose anyone to harm, or reduce our ability to gather additional intelligence? And when that information comes back, I tended to almost repeat it word-for-word. And in the case of the relationship between Iraq and al Qaeda, the words that have come back as being appropriate for release publicly are something like this: That the relationship—that our understanding of the relationship between Iraq and al Qaeda is still developing. That there is no question but that there have been interactions between the Iraqi government, Iraqi officials, and al Qaeda operatives. They have occurred over a span of some eight or ten years to our knowledge. There are currently al Qaeda in Iraq. It is less hard—

    It is not possible for me to elaborate as to exactly what the linkage between the people in Iraq who are known Al Qaeda operatives, and the Iraqi Intelligence Service is. While I can't comment on that, I can say that if you're living in a dictatorship that's repressive, that is as controlling as the Saddam Hussein regime is, it's hard for one to believe that there would be senior people from the al Qaeda in that country and have the regime not be aware of them.

Q. What can effectively be done to limit the conflict, and what is your opinion about the possibility of a wider war breaking out?

Secretary Rumsfeld. In the event that force has to be used with Iraq, there will be no World War III. The Gulf War in the 1990s lasted five days on the ground. I can't tell you if the use of force in Iraq today would last five days, or five weeks, or five months, but it certainly isn't going to last any longer than that. And, it won't be a World War III. And if I were to characterize the difference between 1990 and today, the United States military is vastly more powerful. And the Iraqi Army and military capability has declined substantially. The difference is, the reason for needing to disarm Iraq, and that is chemical and biological weapons today, and a very robust effort to develop nuclear weapons tomorrow. And, that is the difference between today and then.

Q. Mr. Secretary, what do you say to people who think this is about oil?

Secretary Rumsfeld. Nonsense. It just isn't. There are certain things like that, myths, that are floating around. I'm glad you asked. It has nothing to do with oil, literally nothing to do with oil. It has nothing to do with the religion. People who have a viewpoint frequently throw up those two issues, and say, well, this is really against Muslims, which it certainly isn't. The United States is the country that went in and helped Kuwait, a Muslim country. We worked in Bosnia to stop ethnic cleansing. We've done Afghanistan. And it's certainly not about oil. Oil is fungible, and people who own it want to sell it, and it will be available.

Remarks by National Security Advisor Rice, November 15, 2002

Q. Dr. Rice, are you looking for a statement of support from the NATO meeting on Iraq? And are you looking for a military commitment? If not, why not?

Dr. Rice. This is a summit that is going to celebrate an historic moment for NATO, which is the expansion of NATO into territories that I think nobody ever thought NATO would expand into. And that is really the central purpose of this summit. It is also the central purpose of this summit to talk about how to improve NATO's capabilities to deal with the threats that we face today.

Now, of course, we expect that Iraq will be discussed and, of course, the President will discuss Iraq in bilaterals and probably in the NATO Council, as well. But there is a lot of work that has already gone on and is already going on in terms of coalition building for Iraq. We now have a U.N. Security Council resolution that is 15 to 0, so it's not just NATO that is united about what to do about Saddam Hussein, it's the entire world that is united.

I suspect that we will hear from NATO partners what they are prepared to do and what they can do, but that's not the purpose of this summit. The purpose of this summit is to invite new members in, to celebrate NATO's future, and to talk about how far NATO has come and how it remains a vital and viable alliance some 11 years after the end of the Cold War.

Q. So you're not expecting some sort of statement of support?

Dr. Rice. Well, there will undoubtedly be discussion of this and there probably will be statements about it. But that's not the central purpose of this meeting. But I assume that there will be some kind of statement from NATO about this.

Remarks by President Bush, November 18, 2002

Q. Mr. President, this week NATO will be celebrating an historic expansion, as well as focusing on transforming the Alliance to meet new threats, such as Iraq. You have spoken about the possibility of leading a coalition of the willing against Iraq. Why not speak about using NATO forces against Iraq, since, under NATO's charter, all members are supposed to come to the aid of any member under direct threat?

President Bush. Well, first of all, I hope we can do this peacefully. And by doing it peacefully, that means I hope Saddam Hussein disarms. Of course, we've hoped that for 11 years. We've hoped that for 16 resolutions. We now have a 17th resolution and this time, I intend to work with nations that love freedom and peace, make sure the resolution stands. And if he doesn't disarm, you're right, I'll lead a coalition of the willing to disarm him.

And there's all kinds of ways for that coalition to be formed. It could be formed with NATO if they choose. I have said to the U.N. Security Council we'll go back and discuss the matter with you. But Mr. Saddam Hussein must understand he'll be disarmed one way or the other. I hope it's done peacefully.

Q. The new members of NATO are quite small. Do you see them as contributing something significant militarily to the Alliance?

President Bush. I was hoping you'd ask, do I see them contributing something to the Alliance. I'll answer it that way. First, I'll answer it militarily—because I do believe they can contribute something really important, and that is they can contribute their love for freedom. These are countries which have lived in totalitarian states. They haven't been free. And now they've seen freedom and they love freedom. Just like America loves freedom. And that's going to be a really important—it will add some vigor to the relationship in NATO that's healthy and wholesome.

And I think they will. The key is to—I think they will help militarily—but the key is to change the military strategy of NATO. Lord Robertson understands this. It starts with the understanding that Russia is not our enemy. NATO doesn't need to be constructed to prevent the Warsaw Pact from invading Europe. After all, the Warsaw Pact doesn't exist. As a matter of fact, the Warsaw Pact is becoming NATO, slowly but surely. We don't need that type of mentality, and we've got to have a military strategy that addresses the true threats.

The threats we face are global terrorist attacks. That's the threat. And the more you love freedom, the more likely it is you'll be attacked. And therefore, the Article 5 that you referred to for NATO becomes very relevant in this war against terror.

The war against terror will not only be defeated—the terrorists will not only be defeated militarily, but the terrorists will be defeated as we share intelligence, and as we cut off money, and as we deny access, and as we stiffen up border requirements in order to make sure that people can't go from one spot to another with plots and/or messages to attack.

And so it's a different kind of war. And it's going to be an interesting meeting, because not only is the meeting going to expand, but the meeting is going to address how best to achieve this common objective. I'm absolutely convinced that the so-called military gap between America and all countries can be addressed with a good strategy. And that will be interesting for observers to watch. I think it's going to happen. I know that Lord Robertson, who runs NATO, is committed to developing a relevant strategy and one that will work.

White House Press Briefing, November 18, 2002

Q. These continued missile firings in the no-fly zones, taken in toto, could they constitute a material breach that was serious enough for us to take it to the U.N.? Or do we want to see material breach in the area of weapons?

Mr. McClellan. Well, again, John, the goal here with the new strong resolution out of the United Nations is disarmament. However, within that resolution, it makes very clear that Iraq needs to stop hostile acts against members who are carrying out previous U.N. resolutions and the—

Q. Sure, which is why I asked the question.

Mr. McClellan. Right. And the United States—the United States believes that firing upon our aircraft in the no-fly zone or British aircraft is a violation, it is a material breach. And what that—what the U.N. resolution allows us to do is it gives us the option, if we choose, to take that to the Security Council.

But make no mistake about it, our aircraft will continue to respond accordingly when fired upon in the no-fly zone.

Q. Understood. But if they continue to fire on us in the no-fly zones, will we take that, in toto, to be a pattern of obstruction or misbehavior that we'll consider taking to the U.N.? Or do we want to see a material breach on the weapons inspection front before we go to the U.N.? Are we willing to tolerate these firings?

Mr. McClellan. That's why I emphasized—no, we're not. I mean, we will respond accordingly. But we reserve that option of taking that to the Security Council when it comes to our aircraft in no-fly zones. But the issue here is disarmament, and this goes to the heart of the intentions of Saddam Hussein and his regime. Is he going to comply and cooperate with all the United Nations Security Council resolutions as called for under the resolution.

Q. But, Scott, it seems that, if we're taking the President at his word, zero tolerance means zero tolerance, and this is a material breach. Why isn't the administration exercising the option to return to the U.N. and say, this thing is over before it starts? Or is there a point of view that, okay, we have to make some kind of threshold judgments about when we're going to throw in the towel?

Mr. McClellan. Again, I think that's something that we will assess and review and use that option as available to us if we so choose to pursue it with the Security Council. But—

Q. Why not pursue that if there's already a material breach?

Mr. McClellan. It goes back to what I emphasized. The ultimate issue here is the disarmament of weapons of mass destruction by Saddam Hussein. I continue to emphasize our policy is one of zero tolerance when it comes to disarmament, and that's what we will continue to pursue.

Remarks by Secretary of Defense Rumsfeld, November 19, 2002

Q. Mr. Secretary, Reuters has a story, they quote Kofi Annan as saying in Pristina, something and I think I quote it fairly closely that he didn't think that the counsel would agree that the firings were in contravention of the most recent resolution?

Secretary Rumsfeld. I haven't seen it. My recollection is the current resolution incorporates prior resolutions.

Q. Prior resolutions actually justify the no fly zone.

Secretary Rumsfeld. Oh, is that a question?

Q. In that story, some countries didn't agree with the legitimacy of the no fly zone.

Secretary Rumsfeld. Whenever resolutions are fashioned, there tend to be compromises and there tend to be calculated ambiguities written into them to gain votes. So it's not surprising any time a resolution passes or even a piece of legislation in the congress that people have differing views about it, so it does not come as a surprise to me.

Q. Because he said that does it carry a lot of weight?

Secretary Rumsfeld. I have no idea what the reaction of the members of the council will be, I have been careful to say that it's not for me to make those judgments, it's up to the security council and individual members to come to conclusions.

I think that two things that are open and unknown and not knowable at the present time. One is how Saddam Hussein will react to the U.N resolution and whether or not he will come to a conclusion that it's all over I'll just go ahead and disarm or whether he'll come to the conclusion it's all over I'll leave the country and just go somewhere else. Or I'm not going to disarm, I'm going to stay here and I'm going to fight it.

So that's one category of questions that are open, the other is how the United Nations will behave. The United Nations sat there for years with 16 resolutions being violated. Just as we've seen a pattern of behavior on the part of Saddam Hussein we've also seen a pattern of behavior on the part of the United Nations and only time will tell what it, that is to say, the membership will conclude and I have no idea what they will conclude.

I don't know if that necessarily reflects the U.N. the center of gravity of the Security Council on any particular issue at any particular time. He certainly is the Secretary General and he certainly has a voice and a role on the other hand until President Bush went to the U.N. the U.N. was quite happy the way things were.

It seems and once he went and they voted unanimously that marked a considerable point of departure for the United Nations that had not been there prior to President Bush's presentation.

Expecting a continuum; a straight-line projection out of the United Nations given the sharp turn they've recently done may not be the wisest thing to do.

Q. No matter what the U.N. does on the no fly zones will the U.S. and Britain continue to take a measured response against being fired upon, do you plan to increase the response?

Secretary Rumsfeld. Oh, I'm not going to talk about what we might or might not do. You can be absolutely certain we'll not allow our aircraft to continue to be shot at with impunity we intend to respond.

* * * *

Q. Iraq has called U.N. inspectors of being basically spies and stooges for the U.S., this time around U.S. and British will there be a two way intelligence flow? This time will the U.S. be getting information back directly from the inspectors?

Secretary Rumsfeld. Not to my knowledge. With respect to the first part of your comment, I saw Mr. Butler on television, the former head of the inspections stating that there was in fact spying and throughout the entire time the Iraqis were spying on the inspectors and determining what they were going to do next so they could take steps to avoid having anything found. It seems to me that that's an interesting footnote in history.

* * * *

Q. Mr. Secretary you said you'd been getting offers every day from other countries to help disarm Iraq by force could you talk at all about the details of those offers? Do you expect further such offers at the NATO summit?

Secretary Rumsfeld. I don't know that I've said we're getting offers everyday. I may have, if I did, I think we're getting more accurately to say we're getting responses every day. And they fit into a variety of categories, one category is That we would like to be helpful and start planning now in the event that force is used with or without the U.N. resolution. Another category is we would like to be helpful and begin planning now but only if there is a U.N. resolution indicating that it's appropriate for member states to use appropriate force. Still others are saying we are not in a position to cooperate with Iraq but on the other hand we would be willing to provide assistance in other ways. That might be force protection in a host country. It might be back-fill and support for some of the things we're doing elsewhere in the world where as they don't feel they'd like to be involved in the event force is used in Iraq but they could be helpful to us and free up some of our capabilities.

A forth category would be we don't want to help. A fifth category would be in the event force is used and the regime is changed we would like to cooperate with a coalition of the willing after the fact to assist Iraq from a humanitarian standpoint, and that type of thing, like so many countries are doing in Afghanistan. So they're these various baskets and a large number of countries have responded to those and a recently some additional inquiries have gone out and there are a number of countries that are in the planning process.

I think one of the reason so many countries are currently involved with planning that they recognize that there would not have been a U.N. resolution absent the potential of the use of force. That the build up that's taken place and the cooperative arrangements that are being fashioned among a coalition or the willing reinforces the diplomacy and creates a much better environment for the united nations because it ought to persuade the Iraqi's that the united nations and the coalition countries are serious.

Q. Would it be a tragedy that this whole thing played out and Saddam Hussein was still in power?

Secretary Rumsfeld. These are issues for people other than me. I think the focus clearly has been that Saddam Hussein is determined to have weapons of mass destruction, and he's been unwilling to have inspectors in and he's been unwilling to disarm.

Now if the goal is to disarm him, the Saddam Hussein regime, and you have a long record of people believing that he is willing to forego billions and billions and billions of dollars because of his unwillingness to forego weapons of mass destruction, then it's not surprising that a lot of people take that next step and they say the only way to disarm is to have the regime change.

And second the congress' policy has been regime change; the prior administration's policy was regime change. This administrations policy has been regime change.

So the fact that it has not been competing—it has not been a part of the U.N. resolution therefore it ought not be surprising that it's more discussed by the United States than by the United Nations as a resolution.

Remarks by President Bush, November 20, 2002

President Bush delivered his remarks while visiting the Czech Republic on his trip to Europe.

Q. You said that you hope NATO comes along with you and Saddam Hussein will disarm one way or another. And yet, I don't hear any discussion about NATO collectively taking up arms against Iraq should war be necessary. Why is that? Why settle for just niche contributions from individual allies? And also, what role do you see Germany—

President Bush. What will I see—

Q. What role do you see Germany taking in a war against Iraq?

President Bush. Well, first, thank you for the "if we should go to war against Iraq." War is my last choice, my last option. I hope we can do this peacefully.

It is possible that Saddam Hussein gets the message that we're serious about disarmament and he should fully disarm—that's possible. The possibility becomes more real if he understands that there is a true consequence for his failure to disarm. And there is a true consequence. There's a serious consequence as the U.N. resolution addresses.

Now, you asked about two different parts of NATO—first, by niche I mean that in order for there to be an effective NATO, some countries can specialize and provide excellence. And the classic example is the Czech Republic's ability to deal with biological weapons, the aftermath of a biological weapon attack.

The Czech Republic is one of the very best in the world at a chemical and biological response capability. And that's what I was referring to when I talk about the capacity of each country to contribute a part of an effective strategy, a military strategy, as we head into the 21st century, as a vision which is yet to be implemented, which is a vision which will be discussed here in Prague.

Of course, the key reason we're here is to talk about NATO expansion and the benefits of NATO expansion, not only to encourage the spread of freedom in Europe, but also to be able to deal with the true threats we face in order to defend our freedoms. And my answer, as far as Iraq goes, is exactly what I've said previously: If the decision is made to use military force, we will consult with our friends, and we hope that our friends will join us.

And as to Germany's role, it's a decision Germany will make; just like it's a decision the Czech Republic will make; just like it's a decision Great Britain will make. It's a decision that each country must decide as to how, if, and when they want to participate, and how they choose to participate. The point is, is that we will have plenty of consultations with our friends.

Q. Mr. President, you've said that you have a zero tolerance attitude toward Iraqi violations. Secretary Rumsfeld and Kofi Annan say they're looking for a pattern of behavior over time. Which is right? How do you reconcile these two?

President Bush. Well, I think there is—we were talking about whether or not Saddam Hussein shooting at our airplanes, what that means—we'll deal with that. The United States will take appropriate action.

The thing that's important for people to understand is what we want to see is whether or not he's going to cooperate, whether or not he's heard what the world has said, whether or not he's heard what the world has said through the U.N. Security Council resolution.

See, what happens is people tend to focus on the inspectors as if the inspectors are the end. The final—the thing that's important, the final point of determination is whether or not he is disarmed.

So, what we're going to be looking for, and I hope the world joins us, is whether or not this man is cooperating with the will of the world. See, the world has recognized—many members of NATO have recognized that a Saddam Hussein and Iraq which possesses weapons of mass destruction is dangerous. Imagine a Saddam Hussein with a nuclear weapon. It's important for the Czech people to understand this is guy who has poisoned his own people. He's got such hate in his heart he's willing to use a weapon of mass destruction not only on his neighborhood, but on the people of his country.

He is a danger. And so, therefore, what we're looking for is to determine whether or not he is willing to cooperate, whether or not he has got the message that he must disarm.

The United Nations has said 16 different times, "You must disarm." And 16 times, he's said, oh, of course, I will—but never did. And so, the game's over with; we're through with that. And now he's going to disarm, one way or the other. In the name of peace, he will be disarmed.

Remarks by Deputy Secretary of Defense Wolfowitz, November 21, 2002

Deputy Secretary Paul Wolfowitz was interviewed by Indonesian and Australian Journalists.

Q. There was a report yesterday I think the State Department had sent out from cables to about 50 of its embassies [inaudible], alerting their embassies to talk to the countries about possible involvement in some future action in Iraq.

I was reading this book of Bob Woodward's, I don't know how accurate all of it is but I'm interested in one section which relates to Australia which was a question about what are you doing about the Australians who had Special Forces in Tampa?

The question was put to Mr. Rumsfeld who said, "We'll prepare a paper on this." Colin Powell is said to have smiled as though Mr. Rumsfeld was stalling. Then Mr. Rumsfeld said to him, "We want to include them if we can."

I guess my question is, how much do you really want the countries like Australia involved in your military actions? Is it just political cover? Or is in fact what Australia brings in the way of Special Forces or other force is that actually useful and would that be useful in Iraq?

Deputy Secretary Wolfowitz. Not to suck up to you but there aren't many countries like Australia. The Australian question is very easy to answer. Australians bring incredible military capability and professionalism and we have—It's small, from the point of view we have ten times as much, but what Australia has offered us is top of the line military personnel, military competence. Your Special Forces are as good as any in the world. And when you're in a difficult war, and this is a difficult war, the more high quality help you can get the better.

Your question sort of alludes to the possibility sometimes even lower quality help is helpful because it contributes in a more general way to your capability.

We had some 90 countries participating in one way or another in this war on terrorism. The numbers vary. I think that's partly because some of them obviously don't want to admit that they're cooperating. That's fine. We'll take it whatever form it comes in. But there is no question that both militarily and politically, that from our point of view coalitions are better than going it alone, even though there are some imperfections in that. But the price—It's more than worth the price from both a military and political point of view.

Q. Just to follow up, the Australians have announced in the last few days that they're withdrawing their SS forces from Afghanistan. Would they be useful to you if—Is that the sort of capability you would find useful in any action in Iraq?

Deputy Secretary Wolfowitz. Almost anywhere including Iraq. Those sort of elite military units are called elite for a reason. They're very very good. They're generally scarce. When we look at increasing our own Special Forces capabilities we recognize that you can't just take any average person and turn them into a capable Special Forces person. So it's a capability we have benefited from enormously in Afghanistan. We're quite comfortable with the idea of letting them go home for a rest because they might be needed again in the future.

Q. According to Woodward the Secretary of State pointed out a number of possible risks of any military action against Iraq including destabilization of Saudi Arabia, Egypt, Jordan, plus, to use a phrase from the book, it would suck all the oxygen out of everything else the U.S. was doing militarily and diplomatically across the board.

Are these the real risks of a military confrontation with Iraq? And if so, are they risks that we're prepared to take?

Deputy Secretary Wolfowitz. The Secretary of Defense put together a list of, I don't know if it's 19 or 20 awful things that could happen in the context of, if there is a war with Iraq. He's been pushing us to think very hard of all the things that can go wrong and unfortunately there are quite a few. The problem is there are also a lot of things that can go wrong if you continue having, as the President put it, one of the world's worst dictators in possession of the world's worst weapons so that's the thing you have to balance.

I think the only thing in the long list of risks that people like to assemble the one that I think is usually generally overstated is the supposed risk of instability if we lose Saddam Hussein as the controlling force over Iraq.

You know, I'm accused of being excessively optimistic here. I don't see how it could be any worse than it is with that man there. He's a destabilizing force in his country. He's a destabilizing force in his region. He mistreats his own people as horribly as any leader in the world except possibly the North Koreans. And I think rather than being a risk, I think there's a potential opportunity there. That's not a reason to go to war, but of all the risks I worry about, and I worry about a great many, I'd love to have the opportunity to deal with the risks of an Iraq without Saddam Hussein.

Q. Did you ever think that the President would get this far in the inspection process that we would have seen Blix and [*inaudible*] in Iraq?

Deputy Secretary Wolfowitz. Look, I think with real resolve and real determination we can change the way Saddam Hussein thinks. It didn't happen just by another resolution. It happened because of the resolution and determination of Congress.

Remarks by President Bush and British Prime Minister Blair, November 21, 2002

President Bush and Prime Minister Tony Blair delivered their remarks during the NATO Summit in Prague, Czech Republic.

Q. Mr. President, you put a formal request to Britain and other countries to supply troops for a possible conflict in Iraq.

President Bush. Is that a question, have we, or an asserted statement?

Q. I understood you had—

President Bush. Oh, I see.

Q.—and I wonder what your expectation was for what Britain might do.

President Bush. Well, my expectation is, is that we can do this peacefully, if Saddam Hussein disarms. That's my expectation. This is—Saddam Hussein has got a decision to make: Will he uphold the agreement that he has made. And if he chooses to do so by disarming peacefully, the world will be better off for it. If he chooses not to disarm, we will work with our close friends, the closest of which is Great Britain, and we will disarm him. But our first choice is not to use the military option. Our first choice is for Mr. Saddam Hussein to disarm. And that's where we'll be devoting a lot of our energies.

Q. And, Prime Minister, you have this request now. You also seem to have a prospect of another fire strike, as well. Do you believe that many British troops and reserves are going to have to prepare for a Christmas away from their family celebrations in either fighting fires, or fighting Saddam Hussein?

Prime Minister Blair. We will do what's necessary, both to secure ourselves at home, and to make sure that the will of the United Nations is enforced abroad. And I think what you will find here at this NATO summit is a totally united determination on behalf of the international community, reflected in the unanimous United Nations resolution, that Saddam Hussein has to disarm himself of all weapons of mass destruction. And how that happens is a choice for him.

We hope, and want it to happen, through the United Nations inspectors, mandated by the whole of the international community. But if he fails to cooperate with them, if he fails to do all he can—and it is within his power—to help that process of disarmament through the United Nations, then he will be disarmed by force. And that is the clear will of the international community.

And I think you will find now that there is a consensus for that position virtually right across the civilized world.

Remarks by Russian President Putin, November 22, 2002

President Vladmir Putin delivered his remarks after meeting with President Bush at the NATO Summit in the Czech Republic.

Q. And since we see President Putin so rarely, Mr. President, I hope you won't object if I ask President Putin a question, as well. And that is, sir, has the U.S. asked you to participate or contribute to any military action in Iraq if it becomes necessary, and what is your view on that?

President Putin. [W]e agree with the President of the United States and his colleagues who say that we have to make sure that Iraq has no weapons of mass destruction in its possession.

Diplomats have carried out a very difficult, a very complex work. And we do believe that we have to stay within the framework of the work being carried out by the Security Council of the United Nations. And we do believe that together with the United States we can achieve a positive result. As you know, our recent past gives us— we have a example of that kind; and the level achieved in our bilateral relations between Russia and the United States gives us hope that we can achieve such results.

Joint Statement by the United States and Russia, November 22, 2002

We have expressed our serious concern about the proliferation of weapons of mass destruction. In this context, we pledge our full support for the implementation of U.N. Security Council resolution 1441. We call on Iraq to comply fully and immediately with this and all relevant U.N. Security Council Resolutions, which were adopted as a necessary step to secure international peace and security.

We firmly support the efforts of the United Nations Monitoring, Verification and Inspection Commission Chairman and the International Atomic Energy Agency Director General to fulfill their responsibilities under U.N. Security Council resolutions.

We call on Iraq, in strict compliance with UNSC resolution 1441, to cooperate fully and unconditionally in its disarmament obligations or face serious consequences.

Remarks by French President Chirac and United Nations Secretary-General Annan, November 25, 2002

President Jacques Chirac and United Nations Secretary-General Kofi Annan delivered their remarks while meeting in Paris, France.

President Chirac. We welcomed the Secretary-General with great pleasure. You know that in France and for that matter in Europe, we have a great deal of respect and gratitude for Mr. Kofi Annan and the eminent role he plays in promoting peace and stability in a difficult world.

My first words for him were simply: Thank you Mr. Secretary-General. We discussed the situation in Iraq and all the crises that we face in the world, including in Africa, Asia, the Middle East and Latin America. I won't get into the details, but we touched on all these problems in which the Secretary-General and the United Nations have a positive and difficult role to play. We naturally talked about relations between France and the U.N. and our wish to see the U.N. and its Security Council be that special place where the norms and the governance of tomorrow are being elaborated. Regarding Iraq, the inspectors are arriving today. Our position is to support unconditionally U.N. resolution 1441. We need total transparency from the Iraqi authorities and all the facilities so that the inspectors can do their work. If there were any difficulty or problem, it should be exposed to the Security Council that would be authorized to take the decisions it would deem necessary.

Secretary-General Annan. Thank you Mr. President for your support. I believe that the U.N. cannot do anything without the support of your country and other governments and especially the world population. Regarding Iraq, we ask the Iraqi Government to cooperate fully with the inspectors and respect its commitments without reservations. It is the only way to avoid a military conflict in the region. I think that in its own interest, in the interest of its people and the interest of the entire world, the Iraqi Government must cooperate with Mr. Blix and Mr. ElBaradei. They will start their work on Wednesday. We are waiting for the full cooperation of the Iraqi Government.

Q. Mr. Secretary-General and Mr. President, do you trust the Iraqi authorities or don't you like the U.S.?

President Chirac. It is not a question of trust. It is a problem of fact. Iraq committed to recognize the validity of the inspections decided by the U.N. a long time ago. Today, it must comply. I cannot imagine that Iraq would not apply the resolution. If for any reason it was not, then the Security Council would deliberate on the report of the inspectors, that is to say on the report of Mr. Blix and Mr. ElBaradei, to see which conclusions the international community could draw and all conclusions are possible.

Secretary-General Annan. The President said it all, I have nothing to add.

Q. Mr. President, according to the U.S. scenarios, the war should take place shortly in Iraq and the Americans, according to the last information, wanted to occupy Iraq in 3 to 4 stages. What do you think and what will you do to stop such a scenario? Will the U.N. do something for the Iraqi people?

President Chirac. I have already had the opportunity to say that war is always the worst of solutions. I hope everyone is aware of that.

* * * *

Q. Mr. Secretary-General, Mr. Bush said that if Iraq did not provide a comprehensive list by 8 December, it would be a casus belli. Do you think that the war would be inevitable in such a case?

Secretary-General Annan. We have to wait until 8 December to see what Iraq will do. The Iraqis have promised to Mr. ElBaradei that they will provide the list by then. The list will have to be analyzed and the decision will be up to the Security Council.

Remarks by Secretary of State Powell, November 27, 2002

Secretary Colin Powell was interviewed on NPR's "Morning Edition" by Michele Keleman.

Q. So I wanted to start out talking a little bit about the weapons inspectors because they began their work today. The inspectors came back saying they had good signs of cooperation. But I wonder, from where you sit now, do you have faith in these U.N. teams that they're going to be as aggressive as the Bush administration wants them to be and that they'll quickly test Iraq's willingness to comply?

Secretary Powell. Well, we've had a number of conversations with the leaders of the inspection teams, Dr. Blix of UNMOVIC and Dr. ElBaradei of the International Atomic Energy Agency, and I am confident they're going to do their job. We're going to try to help them do their job with information and intelligence and additional resources. They are experts in this field and they know what the Iraqis have done in the past. They know how the Iraqis have deceived previous inspection regimes. And I think that both of these gentlemen want to do the best job they can because the whole world is watching this and so I think they'll be aggressive. I think they will try to get to the truth of the matter.

Q. You've also said that it's going to become pretty clear quickly whether the Iraqis are cooperating, and I wonder at what point the U.S. can say we think Iraq is in material breach of these violations. I mean, is there a debate going on within the administration right now, within the Bush Administration, about the threshold that Iraq has to meet?

Secretary Powell. No, there isn't a debate going on. We'll wait and see what happens rather than prejudge where that threshold might be.

As you noted, Michele, I have said in the past that what we're looking for is a new spirit of cooperation from Iraq and that spirit of cooperation will manifest itself quite early, I think, by giving access to the places that the inspectors wish to go on short notice, cooperating fully with the demands of the inspectors, putting forward a declaration that is due next week that is accurate and something that we can look at as a serious effort on their part.

And if they cooperate, then the inspectors should be able to do their job. And if they don't cooperate, then the U.S. resolution is clear. I am sure that Dr. Blix and Dr. ElBaradei will report that to the Council or we may report it to the Council if it's obvious, and the resolution permits us to do that, and then the Council will have to decide what it wishes to do while we decide what we might want to do.

Q. But is the U.S. already sort of looking at the pattern? For instance, there have been Iraqi air defenses shooting at U.S. and British planes in the no-fly zones.

Secretary Powell. They've been shooting at U.S. and British planes for, oh, eight or nine years now so this is a pattern of behavior that is inconsistent with what we believe their obligations are, and we are responding to them every time they do fire at our aircraft. But we don't see that series of incidents, firing at our aircraft and us firing back, as something that triggers the demands and the consequences of the new resolution. But we think the Security Council should take note of the fact that since we've passed this resolution Iraq continues to operate in this way.

Q. There's one other issue at the Security Council now. U.N. diplomats have been complaining that the U.S., and pointing particularly to the Defense Department more than to your Department, but saying that they're holding up this agreement to extend the Oil-for-Food program because the U.S. military wants more items on this list to be banned.

Why this last-minute maneuvering?

Secretary Powell. Well, we have been examining the list on a continuing basis ever since it came into effect this past May and we have come across items that we know the Iraqis are buying that would add to their military capability and—

Q. Such as?

Secretary Powell. For example, we know they're trying to find jammers for GPS or, you know, ground precision locating system devices that are used by our troops. And this is the kind of capability we think should be added to the goods review list.

And so rather than just roll it over this past Monday, we decided to just do a short technical rollover for nine days, rather than a six-month rollover, so we can consult with our colleagues in the U.N. about putting some more items on this very long list. It's over 400 pages long now. And that's what we're doing and we'll see how that turns out next week.

Q. You're also looking at three months versus the usual six months, and some have interpreted this to mean maybe the U.S. is getting ready for a war in the wintertime.

Secretary Powell. No. Frankly, the difference between three months and six months was a way of seeing whether or not a shorter time period would put more pressure on the process to add items to the list, but it isn't a reflection of when we think war might come or not come. We're hoping this can be solved peacefully. The President has said that repeatedly.

Q. But do you think that war can be averted and do President Bush's advisors, yourself included, really agree that that's going to be the best outcome?

Secretary Powell. The President has said repeatedly and publicly to us and he has said it to the international community, to the world, that he hopes Saddam Hussein will comply and get rid of these weapons of mass destruction and the capability to develop such weapons. It would be in the interest of the Iraqi people, the interest of the people of the region and the world and remove a danger to the world. And he hopes that Saddam Hussein will do this peacefully.

He sees war, President Bush sees war, as a last resort, and there is no dispute within the administration. The President has spoken clearly on this. But if war does come, you can be sure that the Armed Forces of the United States and the armed forces of other nations that I think would be with us in such a conflict will be ready to accomplish the mission of disarmament.

Q. I do want to ask you about the other nations, but first, there's been so much written lately in the media, Americans have been reading about this divide within the Bush Administration. When we got the weapons inspectors back in to Iraq, when the U.S. got this unanimous resolution at the Security Council, most commentators called this your shining moment, your moment of your diplomatic skills at work. And I wonder if this is a sign that you have the President's ear more now.

Secretary Powell. I've had the President's ear since we started together in January of 2001. I've never lacked for access. I've never lacked for the ability to present diplomatic options to the President.

I think the President is fortunate in having people within his Cabinet who have strong points of view, who are strong-willed. We have all known each other for many, many years and we know how to debate without ever being disagreeable. And we think the President is served and the nation is served when strong points of view are allowed to, shall we say, coexist for a while, and then they stop coexisting because the President decides. And we are blessed to have a President who can handle strong personalities in his national security team and then make the decision which we then all execute.

Q. Where is the balance now? I mean, do we have put to—does the U.S. have to put regime change off the table for the time being to allow the inspectors to—

Secretary Powell. Well, remember why regime change came into the equation. And that was back in 1998 and President Clinton announced it as U.S. policy and the Congress passed a law making it U.S. policy because Iraq had made it impossible for the inspectors to do their work and they left, and the only way it seemed we could get those weapons of mass destruction out was to change the regime. But if the inspectors can do it with a cooperative Iraqi regime, if they are cooperating this time, in effect, that would be something of a changed regime. The objective is to get the weapons of mass destruction out, one way or the other.

Q. But you disagree with Secretary Rumsfeld and Vice President Cheney on this issue?

Secretary Powell. No, the only one I agree with is the President. He has told us what our policy is and we all agree with the President and we are supporting the President. Do we have debates and discussions and different points of view and perspective? Yes, of course. We are people who do have opinions and those opinions come together to try to give the President the best information to make decisions for the American people. And this is the stuff of cocktail talk all over Washington and certain other quarters, but occasionally it gives us a good giggle within the team.

Q. I imagine so. Well, I think it raises the question for many Americans, though, when they look at this and they wonder where the balance is, are you in this administration for the long haul?

Secretary Powell. I have been Secretary of State going on two years, and if—that certainly is a long haul. It seems like it already. It'll be two years in January. And I have no idea what the basis of your question is or what you're trying to feel me out on because I serve at the pleasure of the President and we all serve at the pleasure of the President, and I'm pleased to have this opportunity to serve the American people again, but especially this President.

Q. I want to ask you about a side issue to Iraq, and that is the Bush Administration is now considering aid to Israel, an extra $4 billion military assistance, $10 billion in loan guarantees. Some reports have painted this as part of the efforts to prepare for war in Iraq. There's not only that aid package, but also an aid package for Turkey.

Where are we on this?

Secretary Powell. Well, Israel has real needs. Its economy has been seriously affected by the events of the last couple of years since the second Intifada began and it's costing them a great deal for the military operations they are conducting. And so they have let us know that they have these additional financial needs and we will certainly consider them, as we should for a good friend like Israel, and I'm sure the Congress will also consider it when they come back in session early next year.

Turkey also has needs and we are in touch with Turkey as to what their needs might be both in the absence of a conflict, we support Turkey, and if there were to be a conflict, how might that affect Turkey. They were seriously affected in a very negative way during the Gulf War and they are sensitive to such a potential problem in the event of a new conflict, as are we. So we stay in close touch with our Turkish friends.

Q. There will likely be concern in the Arab world if we do, if the U.S. Government does give another big aid package to Israel, that we've often heard in the past the U.S. is trying to underwrite settlement activity in the West Bank, for instance. How do you answer questions like that to the Arab world?

Secretary Powell. No, none of this aid will be underwriting settlement activity. We believe that settlement activity is something that should be stopped and it is part of the comprehensive solution to the problems in the Middle East and that has been our position for some time. So this money is not to underwrite settlement activity.

Q. Could it be used more as leverage to persuade Israel to stop?

Secretary Powell. We will judge it on its merits and we will see what case is made for the funds requested and we'll see how Congress chooses to dispose of that request.

Q. Do I have time for one more question on the Iraqi exiles meeting? Okay, one more question. The State Department has been doing a lot to get Iraqi exiles thinking about a post-Saddam Hussein regime, but your colleague in Belgium did not want this meeting to take place of Iraqi opposition figures in Belgium because he said it puts us into—it puts Belgium in an awkward position of looking at regime change when, in fact, inspections is what were really on the table, disarmament. Are you meeting resistance from—

Secretary Powell. No, the conference has been moved to London and the British authorities were very pleased to host it. So the meeting will go forward and I'll let the Belgian authorities speak for themselves. They thought there was some inconsistency between such a conference and their obligations under 1441. I didn't see it that way and the British don't see it that way.

White House Press Briefing, December 2, 2002

Q. Weapons inspectors in Iraq have now visited a couple of sites that both the President and Prime Minister Blair pointed to specifically as possible sources of new construction and new development of Iraqi weapons programs. It doesn't seem they found anything. What's the President's assessment of Iraqi cooperation—

Mr. Fleischer. The President's assessment of Iraqi cooperation is that it is far, far too soon to say. The regime is just beginning—the inspection regime is just beginning. They will continue to increase their numbers and their efforts. And the President has not reached any conclusions; it's too early to reach any conclusions.

Q. Does it undermine the President's credibility at all that these sites were pointed to by him and by Prime Minister Blair as very suspicious, and inspectors and reporters went there and didn't seem to find anything?

Mr. Fleischer. No, I think there's widespread agreement that those sites were the sites in which Iraq previously violated United Nations accords, and it underscores the President's concern about Iraq moving things around and the fact that in the '90s they did say they weren't in violation of the United Nations charters, they were living up to the United Nations charters. And everyone recognizes that they violated the U.N. resolutions at those sites. Just because they're not violating it at the same site today doesn't mean that Iraq can be taken at its word.

Q. That's not what the President said. But let me raise a broader question here. Back in August, the Vice President said that there was a danger in weapons inspectors going back into Iraq because it would perhaps convince the world that Saddam was back in the box, as he put it. Is that possibly what we're seeing here, as the inspectors show up at sites and don't find anything?

Mr. Fleischer. Well, I would encourage you, one, to listen to the President's speech this afternoon. The President is going to talk about the inspections in Iraq and what they mean and the importance of the December 8th deadline for Iraq to provide the United Nations, and therefore, the world, with a list of its weapons programs in violation of the United Nations resolutions.

Two, I don't think that it's fair to compare one week's worth of preliminary work to four years worth of the absence of inspectors. That's why the President's conclusion is it's much too soon to make any judgments.

Q. Does the President hope that there will be no weapons there?

Mr. Fleischer. The President wants—

Q. I mean, everything you say is so negative. It doesn't sound you people really want to not find anything there.

Mr. Fleischer. I think everything Saddam Hussein has done has been so negative that this President is accurately and realistically describing facts to the world. And as a result of the President accurately describing facts to the world—

Q. But you're going in with such a negative attitude.

Mr. Fleischer. Well, I think it's fair to say the President has gone into this with a can-do attitude to preserve the peace, and if it hadn't been for the President's efforts and leadership and willing to state facts realistically, there would be no inspectors inside Iraq, would there be? There wouldn't have. It was the President who caused this to happen.

Q. Have they ever threatened the United States? Has Iraq ever threatened the United States?

Mr. Fleischer. Only when they shoot at our pilots. Only when they attack their neighbors and America's interests abroad.

Q. During the Gulf War when we were shooting at them.

Mr. Fleischer. They were shooting at our pilots just recently.

Q. You continue to tell us that the President is very skeptical that the Iraqis will cooperate. So in the event that they do, as they have so far, do you have a plan B? What happens if this actually doesn't turn up anything? Then what do you do?

Mr. Fleischer. I urge you to wait until the President's speech this afternoon, and we will see precisely what the President says. And then there is also this interesting question about what will Iraq do when they have to honor the United Nations resolution and provide a list of their weapons that they hold in violation of United Nations resolutions. It's up to Saddam Hussein to produce that list.

Q. You're assuming in your answer that they have weapons of mass destruction which they are hiding. They say they do not; you say that they do.

Mr. Fleischer. I think the history of people who accept Saddam Hussein at face value and take his word for accurate is one of disappointment because they have been deceived. Saddam Hussein does not exactly have a track record of telling the world the truth. So he, on December 8th, has to indicate whether or not he has weapons. Let's see what he says. If he declares he has none, then we will know that Saddam Hussein is once again misleading the world.

Q. How will you know?

Mr. Fleischer. We have intelligence information about what Saddam Hussein possesses.

Q. So you say that you do have information that he has these weapons.

Mr. Fleischer. It's no secret. We've said many times—you've heard the President say repeatedly that he has chemical and biological weapons, and he has missiles that can reach an access of 150 kilometers, all three of which are violations of his sworn commitments to the United Nations.

Q. One quick follow. What happens on December 8th?

Mr. Fleischer. December 8th will mark the beginning of a process, a process of verification to find out whether or not Saddam Hussein is indeed telling the truth, and whether or not he has indeed disarmed. That will mark the beginning of that process. If Saddam Hussein indicates that he has weapons of mass destruction and that he is violating United Nations resolutions, then we will know that Saddam Hussein again deceived the world. If he said he doesn't have any, then I think that we will find out whether or not Saddam Hussein is saying something that we believe will be verifiably false.

Q. It's a process—what do you mean?

Mr. Fleischer. Well, it's a process of verification. That's the purpose of the President going to the United Nations and asking the world to support the effort to put the inspectors back into Iraq. And that process is now, as you know, underway and just beginning. So the inspectors will then begin, and increase their efforts to find weapons of mass destruction and obtain information.

But I want to remind you that much of this depends on Saddam Hussein's cooperation. The inspection regime cannot work on its own, without the cooperation of the Iraqi government. Iraq is a country the size of France. If they desire to hide things or move things, they have the means and the ability and the history of doing so. The inspection regime substantially depends on the cooperation of Iraqi officials.

Q. I'm curious about why you're saying it's just the beginning of the process on Sunday. If Iraq, as you say, using your hypothetical, if Iraq declares Sunday it has no weapons of mass destruction, why should that begin a process? Why should that not end it? Why don't you stand up and verify that they're lying and have them suffer the consequences?

Mr. Fleischer. Well, I think the timing, if there's anything that goes beyond that, will be determined by the President, and Saddam Hussein will have to figure out what the timing is. But I share with you the President's approach that this is the beginning of the process, and I make no statements to you about how long that process will be.

Q. In terms of moving the process forward after the 8th, is there a mechanism that's in place for the President to share the broader intelligence that he's—with specifics that he knows about—to compare that against the Iraqi statements?

Mr. Fleischer. Well, the President has shared much information with the American people in many of his speeches, including his speech in Cincinnati, for example, where he is trying to find the appropriate level of information that can be shared without endangering sources or methods. But suffice it to say the inspectors, of course, as is well-known, will have access to intelligence information from not only our government, from other governments, and that means they will be in the strongest position to do their job so that we can know if the Iraqis are telling the truth, or not; we can know whether or not he has disarmed.

Q. The theory would then be that you have the statement from Iraq on the 8th of what they have and what they don't have. Then information, if it hasn't already been, would be transmitted to the inspectors on the ground so that they could then go to cross-check, basically, against the Iraqi declarations, and at that point, presumably there would be some sort of unveiling of further information? Or would it all be kept at the classified or background level with the inspectors?

Mr. Fleischer. Under the U.N. resolution, the report that Saddam Hussein must file on December 8th is to be filed with the United Nations Security Council. They will be the recipient of Saddam Hussein's cataloging of what weapons of mass destruction he has, or perhaps he will say he has none. This is up to Saddam Hussein. That will get filed with United Nations Security Council, and of course, that will provide some level of information—or maybe no information for the inspectors to proceed and to do their jobs. And beyond that, I'm not prepared to say what type of information may or may not be declassified. I can't guess.

Q.—reports are circulated and then member countries comment on them, is that right?

Mr. Fleischer. I'd have to take a look at the exact resolution. As a practical matter, this would become—depending on what Saddam Hussein says or lists, this will become information then for the inspectors to use to fulfill their mission to make certain that he disarms.

Q. Ari, if the Iraqis were to declare they have no weapons of mass destruction, would the President require proof from the inspectors to the negative, or does he already have indications that would disprove that claim?

Mr. Fleischer. Well, I don't want to say with specificity what every potential hypothetical could or could not be.

Q. But does he have enough information now to act if Iraq claims they don't?

Mr. Fleischer. It was President Bush who made the determination to go to the United Nations and ask for the inspectors to be put back into Iraq. And the President successfully urged the world to take this action after four years of the inspectors being

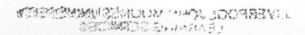

absent. And I think the world is pleased now that the inspectors are going in. The President wants to allow the inspectors to do their jobs, and that's what the President's approach will begin with.

Q. Is he confident they can, they could find—

Mr. Fleischer. Well, we'll find out. We'll find out.

Q. Ari, the British government is putting out a list of human rights violations by the government of Saddam Hussein. Amnesty International is saying that this has been known for a long time and Britain has looked the other way, probably the U.S. also. Now they're coming up with this argument and, according to Amnesty this is a way of preparing for war.

Mr. Fleischer. Well, I would hope that Amnesty International would welcome a dialogue around the world about human rights abuses, and that when a nation puts out a report, even if it's a report that characterizes or catalogues information that was previously discussed, Amnesty International would treat this as a serious document that describes accurately—and there's no dispute by Amnesty International about the accuracy of the document—the facts on the ground in Iraq.

Q. How long is the White House willing to go along with this whole inspection regime and diplomatic efforts at the U.N.? Is there a weeks or months or time limit to—

Mr. Fleischer. Well, again, President Bush is the one who sought the inspections. President Bush is the one, I think, more than anybody else around the world, who made them happen again after the absence of inspectors.

Saddam Hussein will have to figure out how long the United States intends to go along until we find out what Saddam Hussein is really doing. And the President has made certain—wants to make certain that the inspections are effective and that the inspectors have every resource they need to do their job. And that's what the President wants to see happen. The President wants the inspectors to be successful.

And the key to the success of the inspectors really rests with Iraq. As much help as the world can give to the inspectors, as many resources as inspectors can have, it remains a daunting challenge to find everything in a country the size of Iraq. And without cooperation from the Iraqis, the

chances for the inspectors to be successful is very, very limited. And so the President will continue to very closely monitor Iraq's behavior because what is at stake here is the disarmament of Iraq, so that peace can be preserved.

Q. Is there any time limit he's willing to wait out for this thing?

Mr. Fleischer. That's something Saddam Hussein will have to figure out.

Excerpts from Remarks by President Bush, December 3, 2002

President Bush delivered his remarks in New Orleans, Louisiana.

And that's why I started talking about Iraq and Saddam Hussein. Not only starting a debate in the halls of the United States Congress, which overwhelmingly supported any means necessary to deal with the threat to the United States, but also took the debate to the United Nations, and a couple of weeks ago to NATO.

It's important for our fellow Americans to understand that, when we're talking about Saddam Hussein, we're talking about a man who said he has had no weapons of mass destruction, yet we believe has weapons of mass destruction—a man who has not only had weapons of mass destruction, but he's used weapons of mass destruction. He used weapons of mass destruction on his neighbors and he used weapons of mass destruction on his own citizens. He's a man who has professed hate to America, as well as our friends and allies. He's a man who has got terrorist ties, a man who helps train terrorists. He's a threat and he's a danger.

I went to the United Nations because I felt like, in a world that required cooperation in this new war of the 21st century, that it was important the United Nations show some backbone, that the United Nations be something other than an empty debating society, that when they issue a resolution, they mean it. And on a 15-0 vote, the United Nations recognized the threat of Saddam Hussein and demanded that he disarm.

I then went to our close allies in NATO and said the same thing. I said, this man's a threat; he's a threat to us, he's a threat to you. He, too, must disarm. And now, as you've seen in your newspapers, inspectors are inside of Iraq. Inspectors are there not to play hide-and-seek with Mr. Saddam Hussein. Inspectors are there to verify the will of the world. And the will of the world says clearly, disarm. Saddam Hussein, for the sake of peace, must disarm. And if he refuses to disarm, if he tries to deceive his way out of disarmament, this nation—along with other willing nations—will disarm Saddam Hussein.

I say that—I say that because I believe in peace. I believe this is how you achieve peace, by being strong and resolute, by fighting terror and all forms of terror, by not allowing those who hate to try to dictate to those of us who love freedom. See, I believe out of the evil done to America is going to come some incredible good. Part of the good done to this—part of the evil done to this country is going to help lead the world to peace.

Oh, I know some don't believe that, but I do. I believe that if we remain steadfast and strong, if we remain true to our values, we'll achieve peace—not only peace for ourselves, but because we believe every life is precious, everybody matters, everybody has worth. We can achieve peace in parts of the world where they've quit on peace, where people have given up hope.

Remarks by Secretary of Defense Rumsfeld, December 3, 2002

As the United Nations weapons inspectors start their work in Iraq, it's I suppose worth remembering that what brought us to this point with inspectors in Iraq has been the increasing pressure on the Iraqi regime that's been backed by the coalition's credible threat of force, if necessary. For more than a decade Iraq has been pursuing weapons of mass destruction, in defiance now of—then of some 16 resolutions of the Security Council. Only when President Bush took the case to Congress first, and then to the United Nations, and made clear that he, and this country, and a coalition of the willing, were prepared to take military action if Iraq refused to disarm its weapons of mass destruction program, did the Iraqi regime allow the inspectors to return. I think it's useful to keep that sequence in mind. They didn't just suddenly one day decide to invite back the inspectors. With the passage of the new U.N. resolution and the strong statement by our NATO allies in Prague, Saddam Hussein now faces a choice: to disarm or face the possibility of being disarmed. I should add that the members of the U.N. also face a choice. When the Iraqis send in their declaration, if it's false, will the United Nations continue the pattern of the past of allowing Iraq to ignore U.N. resolutions, or will the member countries hold Iraq to its obligations? As inspections begin, it's worth underscoring another important fact: the burden of proof is not on the United Nations or on the inspectors to prove that Iraq has weapons of mass destruction. The burden of proof is on the Iraqi regime to prove that it is disarming, as required by the successive U.N. resolutions. As President Bush said here at the Pentagon yesterday, inspectors do not have a duty, or even an ability, to uncover weapons of mass destruction hidden in a country that is uncooperative. The responsibility of the inspectors is simply to confirm evidence of voluntary and total disarmament. Let me also make clear that disarmament is only one of the steps required of Iraq in Resolution 1441, and the 16 Security Council resolutions that preceded it. Resolution 1441 also calls for Iraq to end repression of its civilian population. That repression is well documented in the British government's new human rights dossier, which details the systematic terror that the Iraqi regime has and is currently inflicting on its own people. According to the U.K. report, some 100,000 Kurds in northern Iraq—innocent men, women and children—have been killed. Shi'ite Muslims, who make up more than half of the population of that country, have also been systematically attacked, and millions of Iraqis have been forced to flee their homeland. Torture is systematic in Iraq, and the most senior officials in the regime are involved. Electric shock, eye-gouging, acid baths, lengthy confinement in small metal boxes are only some of the crimes committed by this regime. That this pattern of human rights violations seems not of concern to some nations is disturbing. The British human rights dossier ought to remind us why Iraq's pursuit of weapons of mass destruction should be of the utmost concern to free people everywhere. A regime with weapons of mass destruction and such contempt for human life, even the lives of its own people, ought to be considered what it is: namely, a particular kind of danger.

Q. Mr. Secretary, you said that pressure on Iraq, the threat of military action, is the only thing that has brought it this far, and the fact that U.N. inspectors are now in Iraq. If Iraq on December 8th says that it has no weapons of mass destruction, is the United States prepared to further ratchet up that pressure by again moving large numbers of ground troops to the Gulf for a possible invasion?

Secretary Rumsfeld. There are a series of things that could occur in the days ahead, including what you indicated. I think it's due by December 8th, their declaration, but very likely could be on the 7th or something. There are a number of things like that that can occur as we go along. And of course at that point the president and other countries that participate in the Security Council will be making judgments about how they feel about whatever has been done. And then I am sure they will be consulting and making judgments about what they think about that.

Q. Well, might the U.S. unilaterally begin—openly begin moving large numbers of troops to ratchet up the pressure? And wouldn't you also have to notify the National Guard and Reserves of a possible large call-up in such a case?

Secretary Rumsfeld. I don't think I want to speculate on that. We don't really talk about deployments particularly, or operations. We had been moving forces around the world, as you know. We've got a somewhat higher level of presence in the Central Command area today than we did last week or the week before or the week before that. But I don't think I want to speculate about what the president might decide to do.

*   *   *   *

Q. Mr. Secretary, yesterday the president expressed a lack of optimism about the situation in Iraq. And yet the weapons inspectors seem to be getting cooperation, even to the point of going into one of the presidential palaces. We go back to early on in the verbal conflict against Iraq, the goal was regime change. And then by the time it got to the U.N. it became disarmament. And now listening to the president again it seems to be back on regime change. Can you straighten us out, what is the actual goal?

Secretary Rumsfeld. Well, I don't think anything's ever changed. Years ago—four, or five years ago, '98, '97—somewhere in that timeframe, '99—the Congress passed legislation calling for regime change in Iraq. That has been the position of the government. And the reason it's been the position of the United States government is quite simple: It is that the conclusion was made that he had refused to cooperate with some 16 U.N. resolutions, and that seemed to be a behavior pattern which suggested that he would be unlikely to do so in the future, and therefore the way to change—to achieve disarmament would be to change the regime, and have disarmament occur that way. When the president went to the United Nations, the U.N. Security Council addressed it in a slightly different way, and focused on disarmament, which had been the U.N. practice over a period of time. And I don't see any change in our—in the administration's position. I do recognize that the U.N. has emphasized disarmament.

Q. Mr. Secretary, so—Just to follow up. So the goal is actually twofold: disarmament and regime change?

Secretary Rumsfeld. I think, you know, beauty is in the eye of the beholder. It depends on who you talk to and when you talk to them. If you talk to somebody who concludes—frequently, if you talk to the Congress, that's our national position. If you talk to the U.N., you'll get different views from different people, because they—some have a higher degree of confidence that Saddam Hussein and his regime are going to decide that they want to cooperate, in which case they then could disarm, and that problem, that aspect of the problem—certainly not as his repression of his people, which is another part of the U.N. resolution, which I mentioned in my opening remarks. But that portion of it, disarmament, would have occurred voluntarily. So it depends on who you talk to and when you talk to them, and what their confidence level is as to whether or not Saddam Hussein's regime will change a decade-long pattern. Yes?

Q. Coming back to—[*inaudible*]—the inspections. There are some within the Iraqi opposition movement who say that rather than running around a country to these suspected weapons of mass destruction sites, that the inspectors should instead focus on the concealment mechanisms of the regime, such as the special security organization which supposedly has records about movements of equipment and so forth. I wondered what you thought about that. Should the inspectors try to go to the heart of the matter after these concealment mechanisms, or continuing a path of suspected sites?

Secretary Rumsfeld. Gosh, I don't know that I'm inclined to give advice to the inspectors. I—if one looks back historically, there are two or three things that stand out. One is inspections don't work unless it is a country that has decided to cooperate. In other words, you can't expect people to go into a country that is just enormous, with all that real estate and all that underground facilities and all of these people monitoring everything—everything anyone is doing—and expect them to engage in a discovery process and turn up something somebody is determined for them not to turn up. Inspections work when the country cooperates. They tend not to work if the country doesn't. So that's fact number one. Fact number two: If you go back and look at the history of inspections in Iraq, the reality is that things have been found—not by discovery, but through defectors. That is to say, someone in the country with certain knowledge figures out a way to get that information into the hands of the inspectors, or somebody else, who then gets it into the hands of the people. And they may be in the country or out of the country. And it is that certain knowledge of an individual who has been a participant in the program, and decided that they think it is not a good thing. And therefore they go to the inspectors, or they go to somebody else and say, Look, here's where it is, here's how they are hiding it, here's where they are going to move it—and you get the kind of information that means the game is up. You've got hard information, and only then, really only then, do you discover anything that somebody didn't tell you. Historically, that's been roughly the pattern.

Q. Mr. Secretary, what's the state of play of the vaccinations, smallpox vaccinations for the troops? And is there any evidence that Iraq has smallpox in their bioweapons program?

Secretary Rumsfeld. I'm not going to discuss intelligence about Iraq on that subject. I must say, I see so many leaks in the newspaper that pre-announce things that haven't been announced or finally decided that I have lost track. I have a meeting on a subject like smallpox. And then I have a second meeting on smallpox. And then a month later, I have a third meeting. And we're getting ready to do something. And then I read in the press that we're doing it—Hasn't been announced. Well, I didn't think it had been announced.

Q. Okay. Thank you. Mr. Secretary, the United States has categorically said that Iraq has an active bio, chemical and nuclear weapons program.

Secretary Rumsfeld. Because they do.

Q. Britain has said categorically that they have active bio, chemical and nuclear weapons programs. What happens on Saturday, or Sunday, when Iraq comes in and says, "No, we don't have any active programs. We have no weapons. We have some dual technology that is used for civilian purposes." How does that get resolved? Is it for the United States and Britain to prove they're right, for the Iraqis to prove they're right, or for UNMOVIC to say who's right?

Secretary Rumsfeld. The resolution I think is really quite clear on that. And, it does not leave it in the hands of UNMOVIC. It—as I recall, it has a provision that there are certain things UNMOVIC must do and assert or not assert as to their circumstance, and they have the ability to do that. They can say anything they wish, as I understand it, and it's up to the Security Council, also individual members, to make a decision at any moment as to what their particular view might be about that. And any member can take that issue to the Security Council under the resolution at any time that they believe that it's something that the Security Council ought to be seized on.

Q. What would the United States expect of the Security Council if this was to happen?

Secretary Rumsfeld. I can't speak for the United States. That's something that the president would have to decide. And I'm sure it would be the kind of thing he would decide after looking at all the things that had taken place during the preceding period, and then have discussions with various members of the Security Council, I suspect. But that really is more a presidential thing than a Department of Defense thing.

Remarks by Deputy Secretary of Defense Wolfowitz, December 3, 2002

Deputy Secretary Paul Wolfowitz delivered his remarks en route to Turkey.

The President asked me to visit two of our most important allies, U.K. and Turkey, as well as NATO. And the basic message that we are carrying is that the peaceful outcome, the peaceful resolution of the problem of Iraqi weapons of mass destruction requires a credible threat of force. And that is the message that I think is very well understood by our British allies. I think even Parliamentarians I've met with yesterday understand that point. We had, as always, very good discussions with British Defense Officials and the British Military. They have a very professional military [*inaudible*] excellent cooperation. Very helpful to have that kind of [*inaudible*]. I met with Defense Minister [*inaudible*], with parliamentary, undersecretary for foreign affairs Michael Brian. With Jonathan Powell, who I guess is the Prime Minister's chief of staff. Prime Minister Blair actually dropped in at the beginning of our meeting which was a gesture we appreciated. I think it was precisely also intended to show that how important he regards our cooperation. He had just finished meeting with a group of Iraqi women who were there to talk about human rights violations in Iraq. And it was the same day that Jack Straw issued that dossier on human rights conditions in Iraq. And it was quite clear that Blair had been personally quite moved by the exchanges with those women and it put a human face on the problem that we are dealing with. And I think it's, as I've said in another occasion, it's not an accident that people who build terror weapons and support terrorism also terrorize their own people. That's certainly true of Saddam Hussein.

Basically in Turkey we have the same message, which is that our goal remains to get a peaceful outcome and a peaceful implementation of Resolution 1441. But the only possible hope of doing that given the resistance that Saddam's put up over the last for eleven years is to convince him that that is his only alternative. And that means having a credible threat of force. It's important that he see that he is surrounded by the international community, not only in the political sense, but in a real, practical military sense. And Turkey has a very important role to play in that regard. The more support we get from Turkey, the more chance, the better our chances are of avoiding war. Our planning has got to proceed. To have a military option, you've got to do the serious planning and serious preparation. And that is an essential part of convincing Saddam that we are serious. As we have said over and over again, the president has not made the decision on using force. In fact, as he said, our hope is to avoid it, but that our goal is to disarm Iraq voluntarily, if possible, and by force, if necessary. Turkish participation, if it does come to the use of force, is very important in managing the consequences, in producing the result as decisively as possible, and also in helping to make sure that post-war Iraq is a positive force in the region, not a destabilizing one. So it's very crucial to have Turkey intimately involved in the planning process. It can make a big difference for every one, especially for Turkey. It's not simply some favor that we're asking the Turks to do for us. It's something that can make a much better situation for Turkey, should it become necessary to use force.

We are very well aware that the Turks are worried about the economic consequences of the crisis in the region. They've already paid a pretty high price for the sanctions and the isolation of Iraq over the last 11 years. In fact, if one takes a medium-and long-term view, a free and prosperous Iraq is going to be, I think, a huge gain for Turkey, economically and in other ways as well. But, if there is a crisis in the region, there are very likely to do some short-term economic consequences and that's obviously concerning Turkey and that's a subject we will be talking about.

Finally, as you've said, this trip happens to come within what may be the most important two or three weeks. Many, many years in the Turkish-European relations were both the possibility of a date for starting accession talks for Turkey to the EU on the table. The upcoming Copenhagen Summit and also the promising peace plan of the Secretary General of the United Nations has put forward on Cyprus at the same time. And all of that coming together with a brand new Government in Turkey, which came [*inaudible*] what people call the political earthquake in Turkey. So it's a pretty amazing time for a visit in Turkey. There would be every reason to make this visit even if we didn't have so much to talk about on the subject of Iraq. And we will be talking about Cyprus and the EU and the whole range of Turkish-EU relations. This is, as I think [*inaudible*] yesterday, it's been American policy for ten years officially, and I think longer, informally, to support Turkey's accession in the EU. We understand that that's a European decision; we understand that Turkey has a very long way to go to meet the standards of the European Union. But it is very important in our view to have that door open to Turkey. That's a real encouragement to meeting the standards. It's something that really can help to pull Turkey forward and become the kind of country that we will all benefit from having as a model for the Muslim world of what a free and democratic and secular Muslim society can achieve. So, the stakes in that regard are large and they are not unrelated also to the [*inaudible*].

Remarks by Deputy Secretary of Defense Wolfowitz, December 3, 2002

Deputy Secretary Paul Wolfowitz delivered his remarks during his visit to Turkey.

I'm delighted to be back in Turkey and so is my colleague Marc Grossman, who feels like Turkey is a second home. We had a very constructive meeting just now with Prime Minister Gul. I'd known him before, but this is my first chance to meet him as Prime Minister. It was a pleasure to learn that our president, President Bush, was the first foreign leader to call and congratulate him as prime minister. I think that is a nice symbol of the close relationship between our two countries. We discussed there's a lot on the Turkish agenda right now and we discussed a wide range of subjects. Very importantly, we talked about Iraq and our focus with Iraq is to try to bring about a peaceful resolution of the problem that's posed by Iraq's weapons of mass destruction and that requires persuading Saddam Hussein that there has to be a fundamental change. Turkish-American cooperation can be key to achieving that peaceful outcome which is what both our countries greatly desire. Of course it's not the only issue on Turkey's foreign agenda now.

* * * *

Q. There are reports about U.S. has formally presented its demands about Iraq?

Deputy Secretary Wolfowitz. Even before this government came into office we've had some extensive discussions with the Turkish Foreign Ministry and the Turkish Military about the various kinds of planning that can be done. But, let me emphasize: our focus now, including in that planning, is to do the things that we can to persuade Saddam Hussein that Resolution 1441 represents a new era. That we are not playing games any longer, that we have to have disarmament of Iraqi weapons of mass destruction. President Bush has said voluntarily if possible, by force if necessary. I believe that close U.N./American cooperation is going to be a key to achieving that desired goal of having Iraq disarm voluntarily.

Q. What about the military aspect of the planning?

Deputy Secretary Wolfowitz. Military planning is in that same context. Our focus now is on convincing Saddam Hussein that we are serious, the world is serious, U.S.-Turkish cooperation is serious. And the purpose I believe is to finally convince him that he has to change his ways. That's our real hope of gaining a peaceful resolution of this crisis. One more question.

Q. Did you talk about economic situation and aid to Turkey?

Deputy Secretary Wolfowitz. One thing that we did talk about is the deep concern in Turkey about the condition of the Turkish economy. We've been working closely with the Turkish Government in the IMF and bilaterally ever since the economic crisis broke. We've tried to help Turkey manage its way through it. We understand those anxieties. We are determined to support Turkey whatever comes to make sure that the Turkish economy continues to recover. If there is a crisis in this region, we know that Turkey is going to be one of the countries the most affected. We want to make sure we deal with that.

Remarks by Deputy Secretary of Defense Wolfowitz, December 3, 2002

Deputy Secretary Paul Wolfowitz was interviewed by Wolf Blitzer on CNN while visiting Turkey.

Q. Joining me now live from Ankara, Turkey, the Deputy Secretary of Defense. Paul Wolfowitz is on a mission to try to encourage support for the U.S. in the case of—in case of war with Iraq.

Mr. Secretary, thanks for joining us.

Are the Turks on board in case the President gives that order to go to war against Iraq?

Deputy Secretary Wolfowitz. Wolf, we have a brand new government here in Turkey, but it's an old ally, a country that's been with us in many crises in the past. And our chances of achieving a peaceful outcome here, of achieving the peaceful disarmament of Iraq's weapons of mass destruction is greatly increased by U.S.-Turkish cooperation. It's important for Saddam Hussein to understand that he's surrounded by an international coalition. And that, I think, is our best chance of getting through to him and understanding that he's got to have a fundamental change—own problems that this country will face.

Q. The Turkish military has always been a closed ally, a NATO ally of the United States. But this new government, which has a strong Islamic influence, obviously, are they going to be on board as well?

Deputy Secretary Wolfowitz. Well, you know, Wolf, they actually reject that label. They have a lot of religious roots, as do parties in other countries. One of the very striking things about this new party and this new government is how strongly they've made it clear that Turkey wants to be part of Europe, which means to be a part of the West, that they're committed to the values of separation of religion and government that underlie this modern, secular democracy.

Frankly, all the signs for this government continuing Turkey's strong traditions, democratic traditions, and even advancing them are very good.

Q. And what about the U.S. and the Turks as far as the Kurds in northern Iraq are concerned, the opposition forces closely aligned with the U.S. But, of course, there's been some tensions with Turkey longstanding, tensions. Are you working that problem out with the Turkish government?

Deputy Secretary Wolfowitz. We've been working it with both the Turkish government and with opposition forces and Kurdish groups. I believe the Kurds of northern Iraq really do understand that their destiny is in Iraq and as Iraqis, not to have a separate state. And we've made it clear over and over again, publicly and privately, that we are opposed to a separate state in northern Iraq. It's important if it comes to removal of the Saddam Hussein regime that the territorial integrity of Iraq be maintained. In fact, it will be a lot better when there's a democratic government in Baghdad.

Q. We heard earlier today from Kofi Annan, the U.N. Secretary-General, that things are moving along just fine as far as the U.N. inspections are concerned. It's been a week now. We heard the same line come from Mohamed al Baradei, the nuclear inspector, Hans Blix, the chief weapons inspector. But the President says he's not encouraged by what's happened so far.

Have you come up with any reason to be concerned about the inspections, at least of this first week?

Deputy Secretary Wolfowitz. Wolf, it's very early to make that kind of optimistic judgment. We certainly have to wait and see what the Iraqis come up with with this declaration that they're supposed to make on December 8th. But it's clear that if we want to have what has got to be a fundamental change of attitude on the part of the Iraqi regime, that they really do have to see themselves surrounded by a unified international coalition.

I think the people I've talked to in Turkey, from the Prime Minister on down, understand very clear that our real hope for a peaceful outcome to this crisis is to maintain the pressure on Saddam Hussein.

Q. Yesterday, the President said he's not encouraged by what he's seen so far, and he specifically cited the Iraqis continuing to fire on those U.S. and British planes patrolling the no-fly zones in the north and the southern parts of Iraq. If there's a zero tolerance policy, why isn't that, in and of itself, a casus belli for the U.S. to go to war against Iraq?

Deputy Secretary Wolfowitz. There's no question that that pattern of behavior hardly counts as cooperation, and I believe one of the things that is very clear here in Turkey is a great deal of realism about what it's going to take to produce a real change in attitude on the part of the Iraqi regime. It's not going to happen simply because we passed a new resolution. But that is a much tougher resolution than any they've confronted before. It's essential that they face a unified coalition that is prepared and able to use force if necessary.

Q. But does the Bush administration consider those fires—the firing at the U.S. and British planes in the no-fly zones a material breach of U.N. Security Council Resolution 1441, which was unanimously passed by the Security Council?

Deputy Secretary Wolfowitz. Wolf, you're getting into legal terms. I would just say it's certainly not a good sign of cooperation, and it's something that clearly we've got to take into account. We are looking for a fundamental change in attitude on the part of Iraq. Without that, there's no hope for peaceful disarmament. It's not something the inspectors can do on their own in the face of an Iraqi government that denies that it has these programs. So we're going to have to see. It's very important to see what they come forward with on December 8th, whether they admit what they have and open up and give us a chance to get rid of it. That will be a crucial test.

Q. But if you don't like what you see in that document that's released this coming weekend, if the Iraqis, according to the U.S. interpretation, Mr. Secretary, are lying, not telling the whole truth about what their capabilities are in weapons of mass destruction, what happens next? Do you then go back for this meeting at the U.N. Security Council? And then what?

Deputy Secretary Wolfowitz. Wolf, we're talking about obviously very big decisions that in our system the President of the United States is the one who has to make. What the President has made absolutely clear is his determination that we will disarm Iraq of those weapons one way or another; as he put it, voluntarily if possible, by force if necessary.

Q. And is regime change still the ultimate U.S. objective?

Deputy Secretary Wolfowitz. We've been—it's been a policy of the United States going back to the last administration, and it established in actually a bipartisan act of Congress called the Iraq Liberation Act, that makes very clear what ought to be pretty obvious, which is that we would be better off, the Iraqi people would be better off, and the whole world would be better off with a different government in Baghdad. But what we're focused on right now and what we are doing military planning for and mobilizing forces for is to enforce U.N. Security Council resolution that requires Iraqi disarmament, if it's necessary, and also to put the pressure on Saddam Hussein to make those fundamental changes.

Our goal right now is disarmament. But that isn't our only concern in Iraq.

Q. So, just to let—I'm going to let you go in a second. But just to pinpoint this fine point, even if the Iraqis did fully—

Deputy Secretary Wolfowitz. This is going to have to be the last one, I'm sorry, because I am late.

Q. Well, let me just ask you this. Even if the Iraqis fully comply with all of the U.N. resolutions, regime change still is the ultimate objective?

Deputy Secretary Wolfowitz. As I said, everyone would be better off with a representative government in Baghdad that treats its people decently, treats its neighbors properly and isn't hostile to the rest of the world. That would be a huge improvement. But our focus right now, the reason we're engaged in this kind of military planning, the reason we went to the United Nations for a strong resolution was to eliminate the single greatest danger, which is Saddam's weapons of mass destruction.

White House Press Briefing, December 4, 2002

Q. Ari, the chief Iraqi liaison officer, in a news conference this morning, said that the declaration they will make to the U.N. will not include any admission of Iraq having weapons of mass destruction. Since you have said repeatedly that the administration believes they have weapons of mass destruction, what's the next step?

Mr. Fleischer. Well, one of the reasons that the President is skeptical about Iraqi compliance is because of their past statements that were then contradicted by actual facts. And in this case, I remind you that in the '90s Iraq also denied that they had weapons of mass destruction, only for weapons inspectors to find those weapons of mass destruction. And then the weapons inspectors proceeded to destroy as much of it as they possibly could. It remains an issue we believe and we have said publicly they continue to have weapons of mass destruction, biological weapons and chemical weapons.

So this is not a new statement by Iraq. The last time they made it, events proved them false.

Q. Okay, but that said, they're going to say it in the declaration before the U.N. So does this mean that that is a breach and a reason that the U.S. could then go to the U.N. to take military action? Or are we going to let this play out? The inspectors say they're going to go back in January—

Mr. Fleischer. Let me try to review with you the steps that will be upcoming. And the President is less interested in any of these statements that Iraqis happen to make; he is more interested in what they put in writing and present, per their obligations to the United Nations Security Council.

On December 8th, the Iraqis have said that they will turn over, per their obligations to the U.N., a declaration of their weapons programs. That is up to the Iraqis to determine the length of it, what it says, the language it will be in. We have various reports that it may be hundreds, if not thousands of pages long. It may be in more than one language. We'll have to see what the Iraqis turn over.

It will then go to the United Nations, and then the United Nations will review it through the Security Council. It will be shared with member states of the United Nations Security Council and the General Assembly. And then the United States will carefully review it. We will take the appropriate amount of time to review it, to assess it, to study it. And then only at that point will I be able to indicate what the United States thinks of it. And I don't know because it depends much on what the Iraqis say and how much they provide how long that process will take. But it begins on the 8th.

Q. If I can try one more time. I mean, we know what they're going to say, if the officer is speaking on behalf of the country, which is, we have no weapons of mass destruction. There will be new stuff in the declaration, but nothing that is prohibited. So, given that, are they not already in defiance?

Mr. Fleischer. Well, the President will wait until they make the formal declaration, as required by the United Nations Security Council. However, the last time the Iraqis said they had no weapons of mass destruction, they turned out to be liars.

Q. So the inspectors will disprove any lie by the Iraqis?

Mr. Fleischer. That's the purpose of having the inspectors there. Whether the inspectors ultimately will be able to disprove any lie by the Iraqis remains to be determined. That depends on the resources of the inspectors. It also depends substantially on the compliance of Iraq with the inspection regime.

Q. Ari, the U.N. resolution clearly states that any false statements or omissions in the declaration due on the 8th will constitute further material breach. Will a false statement or an omission on that document be a trigger for war?

Mr. Fleischer. The President, again, will look forward to seeing the assessments and the studies of the document that Iraq presents on December 8th. This will be the beginning of a process. We will, the administration will review the information that we receive from the Iraqis. We have our own ways of determining whether something seems to be accurate or not—

Q. I understand that, but will a false statement on that declaration be a trigger for war?

Mr. Fleischer. As I indicated, this December 8th will be the beginning of a process. The trigger for war will be decided by Saddam Hussein, and only Saddam Hussein. Saddam Hussein has within his ability the means to avoid war. The President has said war is his last resort. Now, Saddam Hussein has to disarm. And Saddam Hussein has to figure out what the President means when the President says zero tolerance. The President hopes that Saddam Hussein interprets that to mean that he must do what he promised the world, and that is disarm. The burden is on Saddam Hussein.

Q. Well, if an omission or a false statement in the declaration does not automatically constitute a trigger for war, then what teeth are in that resolution?

Mr. Fleischer. Let me just say, when it comes to anything that you, as you put, is a trigger for war, if there were such a trigger for war, you would hear about that from the President and not from the staff. But the process begins on December 8th, and that is the path that the President sought to put into motion. And this process is now beginning.

Q. Talk about the acceleration of inspections after the 8th to verify the Iraqi declaration. Can you talk a little bit about sort of how—what acceleration means, and does it involve a widening of the number of people on the ground, sort of troop support, U.N.—what does it mean to accelerate and—

Mr. Fleischer. Under the plan that the United Nations has put in place to verify Iraqi compliance with U.N. resolutions, the United Nations is sending a growing number of inspectors into Iraq, and these inspectors will have a additional equipment that allows them to do their job. And the amount of equipment and the amount of inspectors grows over time, per the United Nations' plans.

What you have seen in the last five or six days or so has been the very, very beginning of a process where they have a small crew of people inside Iraq with a limited amount of equipment. You can anticipate that more people and more equipment will be arriving.

Q. Do you know how much that grows from the small—to what levels and—

Mr. Fleischer. I don't have the precise numbers of people, whether it's going to go from 17 to 111—I'd the have that. I don't keep that. That's the United Nations.

Q. Prior to the action on—earlier this fall we were talking about a robust inspection process, and that was described as involving troop support in some way to protect the inspections on the ground. Is that anticipated as an accelerated—as the inspection process accelerates?

Mr. Fleischer. No, the terms of the inspectors going to it was determined by the 15 to nothing United Nations Security Council vote, which, of course, the United States pushed for, and troops was not a part of that.

Q. First, on the first few days of the inspections, it's been a little confusing what the President's remarks were really aimed at. Does the White House regard these first few days of inspections as a meaningful indication of anything?

Mr. Fleischer. The White House, President Bush regards these first several days of inspections in the precise words that the President used—the beginning of a process. I've said that it was too soon to say what any of these preliminary inspections with the limited number of inspectors on the ground means to whether or not Saddam Hussein will indeed disarm. And I think it's pretty logical that the process is beginning. They have a small number of inspectors on the ground now, with not as many resources as they will have. After 11 years of defiance, after four years of the absence of inspectors, six days is not even close to enough time to determine whether Saddam Hussein is cooperating or complying with his mandate to disarm.

But it is the beginning of a process that the President thinks is an important process, that he called for, and he's pleased to see that the process of inspections is again resuming.

Q. How much concern is there that this could be a quagmire, that you could have months of no clear evidence one way or the other that the Iraqis do or do not have weapons of mass destruction?

Mr. Fleischer. Well, that's up to Saddam Hussein. Saddam Hussein can create a quagmire if he wants to. He certainly did in the 1990s. The President hopes that the inspection regime will be tough enough and vigorous enough to get at the bottom line, which the world wants to see, and that is that Saddam Hussein disarms. If it is a quagmire, it's because Saddam Hussein turned it into one.

Q. To follow up on Jim's question, I guess the first five days of inspections, there's no assessment by administration—I mean, do you feel like it's a meaningless process, that there's no sense of encouragement that there has been access granted to these presidential palaces, that this has gone without incident?

Mr. Fleischer. No, I think this is—don't interpret this to mean literally 365 days, but you're asking how did the year go based on the first morning of the first day. And it's an impossible assessment to make this quickly. That's why I've said it's too soon to say. You heard it directly from the President. I don't think this is complicated—the President said that these last several days with the inspectors there is the beginning of a process. His statement that he is not encouraged and his skepticism is based on 11 years of empirical evidence and behavior from Saddam Hussein which he violated United Nations resolutions and did everything he could to thwart the inspectors.

So I don't think anybody can draw conclusions based on five days, and that separate and apart from the bigger picture about, do you trust Saddam Hussein.

Q. Do you think Blix is characterizing his assessment when he says he's encouraged by what has taken place in the last five days?

Mr. Fleischer. Well, I think that he is a good man with a very difficult job, and he is doing his level best. And he will have additional resources as time goes along here, with more inspectors on the ground. And it's very important that they have the means and the ability, and that Saddam Hussein provides them with the cooperation so that they can do their job in a full, vigorous manner. That way, the world knows that the inspectors can check to see if Saddam Hussein has weapons or if he's moving around and hiding them and burying them and dividing them and diversifying them and putting them in small places that are hard to find in a country the size of France.

Remarks by Deputy Secretary of Defense Wolfowitz, December 4, 2002

Deputy Secretary Paul Wolfowitz delivered his remarks at a press conference during his visit to Turkey.

I will just make a few comments at the start.

We had a very busy day yesterday and a packed schedule from the moment we landed here until about eleven o'clock at night. It's, I think, representative of the very busy days that this new Turkish Government is having with a very very full agenda of international foreign policy issues. Even if there were no need to discuss the subject of Iraq, the agenda of Copenhagen, of Turkey's hopes to get a date for EU accession, the issue of Cyprus would be totally preoccupying and in some ways it was preoccupying. I think it is the reason why when our meeting went late with the Prime Minister, the Foreign Minister had already had to move on to see Jack Straw. So it's symbolic of just how busy things have been.

But I am very encouraged by the discussions we've had with this new Government. I saw the Defense Minister, had a long discussion with the Prime Minister, and an even longer dinner last night with Mr. Erdogan, the head of the party. In general what we found was a very strong affirmation of what we've been observing the last couple of weeks already, which is this government's commitment to Turkey's role in Europe, to Turkey's aspirations to join the European Union, to the values that have been at the heart of Turkish aspirations since the founding of Turkish democracy early in the last century, of freedom and democracy and a commitment to secularism. All of those things have been strongly expressed by this new government and, as I say, including by the Prime Minister and Mr. Erdogan.

It was also encouraging though not surprising to hear this new government express its strong support for what President Bush is trying to achieve and what the United Nations is trying to achieve with Iraq, to try, by presenting the Iraqi regime with a strongly unified international community, to achieve the disarmament of Iraqi weapons of mass destruction, hopefully and preferably peacefully, or voluntarily, but if necessary by the use of force. And I think if anything this new government has a better common understanding with us about the need to resolve that problem and about the need to have a credible threat of force behind the United Nations if we hope to resolve that problem peacefully.

At the same time very strongly hoping that in fact a peaceful outcome will be possible. But our chances of that peaceful outcome are definitely dependent on the Iraqi regime recognizing that they have no alternative to disarming themselves peacefully if they want to survive as a regime. And I think this new government understands that, and we heard very strong expressions of Turkish solidarity with the United States and of Turkish commitment to be with us as they have been with us in virtually every crisis of the past 50 years or 60 years. So I think all of that on the broad level is very encouraging.

On the sort of very concrete specific level, we have agreement to proceed with the next immediate steps of military planning and preparations. We need to take those steps before we will be in a position to make specific decisions about whether and where and which forces might be based in Turkey. There are some big issues that we need to discuss further and have more clarity about in the process, particularly I would say issues about how to manage the economic consequences of any military crisis with Iraq. I think we have a better understanding after this visit than we did before that there may be steps that can be taken to construct a kind of safety net—if I can use that term, I think that is what we talked about in Turkey's earlier economic crisis last year—a safety net that could actually minimize losses, as opposed to simply incurring them and dealing with them afterwards.

Secondly, we've got important issues to discuss about exactly what military measures would need to be taken in northern Iraq if there is a use of force to make sure that we achieve the goals that both our governments have agreed on: maintaining the territorial integrity of Iraq, ensuring that there is not an independent state established in northern Iraq, and that the rights of Iraqi Turkomen are respected. So we have some concrete military planning work to do, we have some sort of more political/military, political/economic/military planning to do, and we hope to have some more discussions at the highest levels of both our governments.

In fact, last night I was able to extend an invitation to Mr. Erdogan from President Bush to come to Washington. We are hopeful that he might be able to come as early next week, in which case we might be able to get one more round of discussions with him before Copenhagen. Obviously the Copenhagen issues are probably at the top of the Turkish agenda, but the subject of Iraq is right up there as well.

Q. Sir, yesterday you said that Turkey has a role to play towards Iraq policy. What kind of role do you foresee for Turkey. Can you give some details? For example, do you request from the Turkish Government the use of Turkish forces on the northern side? Can you give some details?

Deputy Secretary Wolfowitz. We're working on the details. The important role is the one that I think is very clear and should be very clear to the regime in Baghdad that Turkey is with us, that Turkey has been with us in the past, and that they're with us now and will be in the future. The Iraqi regime is literally surrounded by the international community, and has got to choose between disarming itself voluntarily or being disarmed by the use of force. If it comes to the use of force, the level of Turkish participation, or the level of U.S. forces that would operate out of Turkey is something that we still need to determine with precision. You can count on the fact—I think we can count on the fact—that Turkey will be with us. That's the important point.

It is also worth emphasizing that the range of possible Turkish participation is broader than probably any other coalition partner. It involves not only the use of bases, but possibly the use of land routes, the airspace, and questions too possibly about a role of Turkish forces. But the more extensive our role from here, the more extensive Turkish participation, I think depends also on getting more clarity between us—and in fact with the people of northern Iraq—about what we hope to see in northern Iraq after the Saddam Hussein regime. We've been very clear on the broad principles. I think we're now at the point of needing to have some more clarity about the details.

Q. **You've used a sentence something like we need to specifically decide which forces might be based and we need some further clarity. Now do we understand that now we have a commitment from the Turkish side to, for instance, base some American forces on Turkish land, that we would go on planning on that?**

Deputy Secretary Wolfowitz. To continue on planning, the commitment from the Turkish side is that Turkey will be with us. In exactly what ways they will be with us is something that we need to work out. We need to understand ourselves what the potential is of different Turkish facilities. We need to understand with real precision now how much money will have to be invested in different facilities to make them useful for American forces. We are not talking about small expenditures. We are talking about probably several hundred million dollars of potential, possible improvements to the range of facilities that we're looking at. So until we've done that work, we aren't in a position to make specific requests, and obviously the Turkish Government is not in a position to give us specific answers.

But, we do have agreement to proceed with the kind of planning work that will give both our governments those options. I think developing concretely the military options is a key part of trying to convince the Iraqi regime that this has to be resolved peacefully. I've noticed many comments in the Turkish press about the importance of exhausting every effort to resolve this problem peacefully if possible. [*Inaudible*] that is the view of the United States as well the view of our President. But it is also important for people to understand that—it may seem like a paradox—but you are not going to get to a peaceful resolution if you create any doubt in Saddam's mind ultimately there is the possibility of force behind it. It is always a prime balance to draw between affirming your interest in a peaceful resolution and making clear your resolve to settle the problem in one way or another. I think our President has been very clear on those points.

Q. **Would you say that all these efforts—millions and millions of dollars spent on rehabilitation of some facilities and everything—would you call it a step for deterrence or would you call it a step for an attack?**

Deputy Secretary Wolfowitz. I would call it an investment in peace, to be honest. But let's be clear. It is very important to be clear. If anyone thought I said we have decided to spend this kind of money, then you're several weeks at least ahead of me. What I said is we have to make decisions about whether to make that investment. And the Turkish Government has to make decisions about whether to have us make that kind of investment. Until we know with precision which facilities we are talking about and how much money we would be spending, neither government is quite yet at the point of a decision. So, don't make it sound as though we are rushing out to spend that money. But I think it is an investment in peace. It is part of deterrence, and our hope would be that we never have to use it. That would be the best possible outcome that would save a lot of money in the long run.

Q. How about the involvement of the Turkish military in the case of a crisis? Do you have a separate view on the possible role of the Turkish side—that the Turkish military could play? Because there are press reports that your side would like the role of the Turkish army, especially in northern Iraq, to be restricted to certain missions, whereas the Turkish side would have a bigger...

Deputy Secretary Wolfowitz. I have a lot of sympathy for the press reports, because people are grappling to try to understand what takes place, and understandably our military planning has to be a secret. So, there is a lot of speculation, and I can't give you precision. I can say that the range of issues that we still have to clarify is broad. There are a broad range of possibilities for Turkish participation. Stop me if I've said this already to this group—I've said it once or twice this morning—Turkey has more potentially to contribute to this effort than any other coalition partner. Both in facilities and over flight rights and bases of various kinds, and even possibly in forces. But the more one gets into discussion of Turkish Forces, the more clarity we have to have, the more clarity Turkey has to have, and the more clarity the people in northern Iraq have to have about exactly what final outcome we are looking at. I think that's clearly an important issue.

Q. Will there be a northern front?

Deputy Secretary Wolfowitz. I think it's clear from the statements of the senior officials of this government, the senior leaders of this government, that Turkey will be with us. Turkey being with us means that the Iraqi regime is literally surrounded by the international community. And they better take it seriously. This is really their last chance to decide to either have a peaceful resolution, which requires giving up those weapons, or have us do it by force. We much prefer a peaceful outcome.

Q. You know that Mr. Yasar Yakis made a statement and in the case of use of force, we will give the air bases, air space permission to United States. And during the dinner Mr. Erdogan gave the same statement, said the same thing or how can you evaluate this statement?

Deputy Secretary Wolfowitz. As I said, partly because there was so much other foreign affairs activity going on yesterday and our meeting with Prime Minister Gul went long, we did not get to meet with the Foreign Minister. So I don't have the benefit of having directly exchanged views with him. I think the public appetite for details, which is understandable, is ahead of the level of details that we have in our planning. What we have is a clear agreement to work out those details. The planning efforts and the preparatory efforts, which were in a bit of a holding pattern within the new Turkish Government, will now move forward and we will be able to make those kinds of concrete decisions.

The last two questions.

Q. [*nearly inaudible question regarding aid*] **can you just lighten up that issue? There are some amounts like 20 billion dollars worth of either investment or cash aid that can be given to Turkey. These of course are in all the headlines. Can you confirm these numbers on background?**

Deputy Secretary Wolfowitz. No I can't confirm any numbers. Because first of all I couldn't, but secondly I think what we understand—I now understand—after yesterday that I did not understand so much before is that if we do things in the right way, if we can find a way to construct the right kind of safety net beforehand, we can actually bring those potential losses way down. It's much better to take preventive steps than to have to deal with problems afterwards. Also, I want to repeat—if I didn't say it yet to this group—that it's important not only to think about the immediate short-term economic impact, which will be a negative one if there is military action, but also to think about the medium-term and long-term impact of a free and prosperous Iraq that is no longer under economic sanctions, that is trading freely with its neighbors, including particularly its immediate democratic neighbor here in Turkey. The upside for the Turkish economy, I think, is enormous. And the more—if it comes to the use of force—the more quickly we can resolve the issue the better it is from the economic point of view. So there is definitely a relationship between the level of Turkish participation in a military action, if it comes to it, and our ability to get past that quickly and minimize economic consequences.

Q. **What's the schedule in your mind for the next coming days? When do you think the first American troops can be based in Turkey? And did you request some sort of .. Is there a deadline for the Turkish Government in mind? And another different question as it is the last one: What is the American Government's thoughts about Mr. Erdogan being in his past an Islamic leader and now he is the leading figure in the country. You said that President Bush has invited him. Does he have any special thoughts about him being an important figure for the Islamic region?**

Deputy Secretary Wolfowitz. We aren't yet at the point of talking about stationing specific American forces in Turkey. And I think that is a significant political step for the Turkish Government, and probably one that engages the Parliament. That is something that's not for us decide, but for Turkey to decide. We would like to get to that point of decision sooner rather than later, because the more quickly we can actually be doing concrete things on the ground, I think, the stronger signal we will be sending to Saddam Hussein and the Iraqi regime that they really have to change their ways. But I think it's already very clear that in whatever form it comes we will be confronting—if it comes to it, if it comes to the use of force—Saddam, will be facing a military coalition from all directions, including here. But the exact time lines—we'd like to make them short as possible, but obviously that depends in the first instance on how long it takes to work out the military planning details, and then in the second instance it's a question of the Turkish Government, Turkish politics. And that's obviously something the Turks have to decide. On the broader question you raised, it's obviously up to Turks to choose their own government. They spoke very clearly in this last election. I've believed for a long time, and even more strongly since September 11, that Turkey, as a modern secular democracy and as a Muslim majority country, it represents a very important alternative to the Muslim world from the very backward-looking, constrained view that the terrorists and their spiritual colleagues would like to impose on the world's Muslims. And for that reason, I believe Turkey's success is very important to the world, and the United States in its larger battle for the hearts and minds of people in the Muslim world. I find it very encouraging that this new government, and the head of this party, who you say, I guess, has Islamist roots, but in fact specifically rejects the Islamic label, has made such an effort in its first days in office to try to persuade the European Union that Turkey wants to be and should be a member of the European Union. And they clearly do so recognizing that that means more moves in the direction of the free democratic institutions that sometimes are mistakenly called western institutions, but in fact are universal aspirations. I think Turkey is at a kind of strategic crossroads not only geographically, but in a kind of spiritual sense as well. So Turkey's success is based on those principles, and incredibly important to the whole world. And I'm very encouraged by the first couple weeks of this new government.

Remarks by Deputy Secretary of Defense Wolfowitz, December 4, 2002

Deputy Secretary Paul Wolfowitz delivered his remarks prior to his departure from Turkey.

Good morning. Let me just make a few points, and then I guess I'll have time for maybe a question or two. First of all it was a pleasure to be here in Turkey again, and an honor to see so many old friends and new friends. Second, we had a series of very positive and constructive discussions about Turkey's future, which is clearly a future of further integration with Europe, a future of economic strength, and a future of continued alliance and close cooperation with the United States. Third, I was honored last night to be able to extend formally an invitation from President Bush to Mr. Erdogan for an official visit to Washington. And fourth, I also discussed with the Prime Minister, the Defense Minister and others a range of very important matters regarding the threat posed by Iraq. Fifth, we reached agreement on the next steps in military planning and preparations, and I believe we've charted a course for the way forward, working together, so now it should be clearer than ever that Saddam Hussein is surrounded by the international community. And finally, this is vitally important, because the most likely route to achieving a peaceful resolution, a peaceful disarmament of Iraqi weapons of mass terror is through confronting Saddam Hussein with a unified international community. I have time for a question or two.

* * * *

Q. Sir, you've talked about possible investments in bases here, and we've read about letters asking for certain bases, positioning of troops. Do you foresee a big build-up of U.S. troops here in Turkey?

Deputy Secretary Wolfowitz. What I've referred to is that the next immediate step of our military planning preparations is to identify, with the kind of precision that military planners have to have, which facilities might actually be used, which forces might actually be based on those facilities, which investments are required to bring those facilities up to the standards necessary for forces to operate out of them. That would then bring us to an important decision point for both our governments. But until we've done that work—and we want to do it as quickly as possible—neither our government nor the Turkish Government can actually say with precision what we would do.

* * * *

Q. Yesterday you said that we are trying to convince Iraq, but if we can't manage it, we will have to use force. I want to learn that. First you in United States are trying to convince Iraq to accept the arms inspectors, and now and later you tried to convince them to be cooperative. And according to the inspectors, they are. So I want to learn what is the specific issue now that you are trying to convince Iraq?

Deputy Secretary Wolfowitz. It's a good question and I think the answer is very simple and clear. The Iraqi regime is required under the terms of some sixteen U.N. resolutions—and now the seventeenth one that was passed last month—to give up all of its biological and chemical and nuclear weapons, and ban programs to develop those weapons. And for eleven years they have resisted doing so. It is time for a new era. It's time for Iraq to give up those weapons. They have got to do so one way or another. It is up to Iraq to disarm. It's not up to the inspectors to disarm Iraq. What the inspectors can do, if there is a fundamental change in the attitude of Iraq, is to verify that that has happened. But we have to have a fundamental change in attitude. That's why it is so important that Saddam Hussein understand that he is indeed surrounded by the international community, and has no choice but to give up those weapons. Let me also say that because of all of this rather grim and serious talk, which is necessary, it's also, I think, important to point out that one way or another if we can achieve this objective of disarming Iraqi weapons of terror, we can look forward to a much better future for this whole region, including for Turkey. When I met with Mr. Erdogan last night, he spoke quite eloquently of some of the economic problems and suffering of people in the southeastern part of Turkey, the poorest part of this country. That is something that we believe can change with a new era, especially if there is a new regime in Baghdad that takes care of its own people, lives at peace with its neighbors, and focuses on peaceful economic development. That will be very positive not only for the United States and for the people of Iraq, but for the people of Turkey as well. Thanks very much.

Remarks by President Bush, December 5, 2002

Q. Mr. President, I've been out in the country on vacation and a lot of people have asked me, what are the chances that we're actually going to war with Iraq? I mean, how likely is war and what would trigger it?

President Bush. Right. That's the question that you should ask to Saddam Hussein. It's his choice to make. And Saddam Hussein must disarm. The international community has come together through the United Nations Security Council and voted 15 to nothing for Saddam Hussein to disarm. We recently got back from NATO where our NATO allies voted overwhelmingly to send this same message.

So, David, to answer your question, the question is whether or not he chooses to disarm. And we hope he does. For the sake of peace, he must disarm.

There are inspectors inside the country now, and the inspectors are there not to play a game of hide-and-seek; but they're there to verify whether or not Mr. Saddam Hussein is going to disarm. And we hope he does.

Q. But at what point would you make that decision?

President Bush. We hope he does. You'll see.

White House Press Briefing, December 5, 2002

Q. Ari, when Tariq Aziz of Iraq says that his country possesses no weapons of mass destruction, how do we know that he's not telling the truth?

Mr. Fleischer. Well, Iraq has lied before and they're lying now about whether they possess weapons of mass destruction. Tariq Aziz's statement is very much like statements that Iraq made throughout the '90s, denying that they had weapons of mass destruction when, of course, it was found that they indeed had weapons of mass destruction. And so I see little reason to believe Iraq now when they have such a history of lying in the past about this very topic.

Q. Well, I mean, you're saying, I don't see why, if they were lying in the past they wouldn't be lying now, but do you have anything that constitutes proof?

Mr. Fleischer. Let me cite for you something I think you will find constructive. This is July 31, 2002, Senator Biden's committee up on Capitol Hill, and this is a statement by Richard Butler, formerly of the United Nations. Quote—this is Richard Butler speaking—"It is essential to recognize that the claim made by Saddam's representative that Iraq has no weapons of mass destruction is false. Everyone concerned, from Iraq's neighbors to the U.N. Security Council to the Secretary of the U.N., with whom Iraq is currently negotiating on this issue—everyone simply, Mr. Chairman, is being lied to."

And Mr. Butler, formerly of the U.N., continued, "From the beginning, Iraq refused to obey the law. Instead it actively sought to defeat the application of the law in order to preserve its weapons of mass destruction capabilities."

Two more paragraphs—"The work of UNSCOM, the body created by the United Nations Security Council to take away Iraq's weapons of mass destruction, had various degrees of success—varying degrees," said Mr. Butler. "But above all, it was not permitted to finish the job. Almost four years have now passed since Iraq terminated UNSCOM's work, and in that period, Iraq has been free of any inspection and monitoring of its WMD programs."

And then Mr. Butler concluded, "This shows two key things. One, Iraq remains in breach of international law, and two, it has been determined to maintain a weapons of mass destruction capability at all costs."

President Bush has said Iraq has weapons of mass destruction; Tony Blair has said Iraq has weapons of mass destruction; Donald Rumsfeld has said Iraq has weapons of mass destruction; Richard Butler has said they do; the United Nations has said they do; the experts have said they do. Iraq says they don't. You can choose who you want to believe.

Q. So—but if you had this evidence other than what Richard Butler is talking about, why don't you lay it out on the table? Why don't you share it with the American public?

Mr. Fleischer. I think the burden now falls on Saddam Hussein and his opportunity to shed that burden comes this weekend when he will send to the United Nations a declaration of the weapons that he possesses. And I think it will be a very interesting day to see what he says in that document, and we shall see what he says he has. Also we'll see what he says he doesn't have.

Q. Why can't you present your own evidence, for god sake? Nobody is stopping you. And Butler knows damn well that we pulled the inspectors out.

Mr. Fleischer. I think, Helen, the burden is on Saddam Hussein to comply with the will of the United Nations and demonstrate—

Q. Did we pull the inspectors out of Iraq?

Mr. Fleischer.—and Saddam Hussein by shooting at the inspectors, by bugging their rooms, by stopping them from being able to do their work, by holding them in parking lots for days, by slamming the gates to facilities they had every right under international law to inspect created an environment which they were withdrawn.

Q. To what extent are you worried that you could lose international support if no—if the inspectors can't find any weapons?

Mr. Fleischer. Well, again, let's let events take their course. I think that it will be important to note what Saddam Hussein says when he submits this declaration over the course of the weekend. We'll see what he says, and we'll also see what he doesn't say when he submits this.

Q. Can you just step us through a little bit how the United States government is going to deal with this report? In other words, how information is going to get to various departments and agencies and experts, and what the administration is going to do with it?

Mr. Fleischer. Here's the procedure I think we can anticipate—and again, much of this depends on Iraq and what they will do in fact. We've heard much speculation about what Iraq will release in this report over the weekend. The word that we hear is that this report will be relatively voluminous, many, many pages, and it's unclear yet what language it will be in. It's possible it will be in Arabic and portions in English—we just don't know. So we'll see what Saddam Hussein produces.

And then we will be very thoughtful. We will be deliberative. We will study it, we will assess what it says, we will assess what it doesn't say. And the process will be that the report must be received by the United Nations in New York. It's unclear in what manner it will be transmitted to New York, whether Saddam Hussein will release it on the ground in Iraq, whether they will have to move them from Iraq physically to New York, how it will be physically transmitted, the amount of time for that, whether it's courier, electronic, we don't know. That's up to Saddam Hussein and the United Nations.

It will be received by the United Nations in New York. The Security Council will receive it. It will be shared with member states of the Security Council. And then you can anticipate that at the point that the United States government receives it, we will begin to study it carefully. We will assess what it says. Depending on how big it is will determine the amount of time it takes for us to study it.

Q. Who is going to study it in the United States government? Do you have teams of experts at the CIA, State, Department of Defense people here? Can you spell that out a little bit?

Mr. Fleischer. Sure. I think there will be many people in various government agencies who will take a very careful look at it from an expert point of view to determine what it is that this document shows, and it will be a large number of people who take a look at it.

Q. Now, Hans Blix and his team have said that they could be overwhelmed by this much information and documentation. It could take them a very long time, indeed, just to make their way through it. Is the United States prepared to provide translation assistance, analysis, sort of point the inspectors to special pages?

Mr. Fleischer. Our whole intention of having the inspectors return to Iraq was so we could work together to make certain that Saddam Hussein disarms. So as the report is received I think you're going to see the members of the Security Council, the

United States included, cooperate to discern what is in the document, to study it carefully, and also to see what is not in the document.

Q. Ari, three times you've mentioned what the report does not contain, which may in the end be more significant, of course, than what it does contain. While you're reluctant right now to provide us with sort of a footnotes and backup evidence for the kind of statements like the one you read from Mr. Butler, after the report is out, is it the administration's intent to make public or to provide to the inspectors evidence of areas that you believe are not covered in the Iraqi declaration?

Mr. Fleischer. Well, we will, of course, work closely with the inspectors, as we always have and always will, to make certain that they have the best information available so they can do their job. We—President Bush is the one who wanted them to go into Iraq, and now that they're in Iraq, we want them to be successful. So we will, of course, work with them to provide them information, as we have and as we will continue to do.

But you may want to look back at what the President said in signing the Defense Authorization bill at the Pentagon this week, when the President talked about the importance of this declaration being full, accurate, and complete.

Q. There have been moments in American history when Presidents have decided that it was worthwhile to make some intelligence data public to prove the case and not simply make the statement. Adlai Stevenson at the U.N. is a famous one, but there have been others. Is it the administration's intention at this point to attempt that, to provide backup evidence, whether it's in the form of satellite photographs or other intelligence, to indicate areas that you believe that Saddam Hussein is—

Mr. Fleischer. The burden of proof lies with Saddam Hussein. The world has seen Iraq lie for 10 years, and Iraq continues its ways of lying and deceiving to the world when it says it does not have weapons of mass destruction. When the authorities that I cited earlier, including—let me read you one additional report because I think this, too, is constructive, and it comes from, frankly, The New York Times.

This is April 10, 1998. "A team of independent experts who reviewed Iraq's progress in eliminating biological weapons at Baghdad's request has rejected Saddam Hussein's contention that he no longer has a germ warfare program." And this report was compiled by military and scientific experts from 13 countries, including the United States, Russia, China and France.

So given the overwhelming amount of history that the world has had dealing with Saddam Hussein, and his deceptions and lies about whether he does or doesn't have weapons of mass destruction, the burden this time lies with Saddam Hussein. And he can begin to shed that burden with what he reveals when he produces the declaration this weekend.

Q. The burden of proof may lie on him, but the burden of putting together a coalition, if you believed he has withheld information, obviously lies on the United

States. And the way you put together that coalition is providing evidence to back up your claims and the claims of others. The question is—

Mr. Fleischer. I think the President is—

Q.—are you prepared to do that in public?

Mr. Fleischer. I think in terms of assembling a coalition, the President is very well satisfied that the coalition is already assembling. The President has said that he will assemble a coalition of the willing, and the coalition has access to information and they know what I have just been saying to you, in citing these very public cases, including news reports.

Q. Why can't the public know?

Mr. Fleischer. We'll know this weekend, won't we, when Saddam Hussein makes his report.

Q. It's not your intention to make it public, is that where we're—

Mr. Fleischer. Not make public—

Q. It's not your intention to make public intelligence that would contradict whatever is in Saddam's—

Mr. Fleischer. All events in due course. Let Saddam Hussein make his report this weekend, which is what the United Nations asked to happen, and that is what the President called for.

Q. Is there any plan this weekend for the administration to respond to the declaration at all, any type of statement or is that something—

Mr. Fleischer. Again, let him send his report. We'll take a look at what he does and what he says, and we'll keep you apprised as we receive the information. I can't guess. If he sends in one piece of paper with one paragraph on it, then it's rather easy to study it and it won't take much time. If he sends in tens of thousands of pages worth of documents, it will require some time to take a look at.

Q. Is Bush meeting with the principals tomorrow to discuss how to respond to the declaration?

Mr. Fleischer. I haven't looked ahead at tomorrow's schedule in any case. He has a National Security Council meeting every day, so—you know I read that out every morning, I tell you he has the meeting. I'm not at liberty to go into any of what is discussed at National Security Council meetings, but the President meets with the NSC every day.

Q. Are you essentially confirming the statement of one member of the inspection team that if the U.S. has intelligence that points to Saddam's weapons of mass destruction program, it has not been shared with the inspectors? And if that's the case, why has it not been shared with the inspectors? And is it your plan to do so after the declaration—

Mr. Fleischer. Wendell, it is never the practice of the White House to discuss how we—what in any detail level we do with intelligence information. I've made it abundantly clear that we will continue to cooperate with the inspectors to provide them with information and tools they need so they can get the job done that the President has asked them to go into Iraq to do. We have an interest in working closely with them. But I never discuss publicly in any way—

Q. Well, having said that, you can then say whether or not the inspector is accurate in saying that if you have the intelligence it has not been shared with the team.

Mr. Fleischer. We will continue to work closely with the inspectors as the events go along, as we always have.

Q. Ari, you talk about the coalition is already assembling, in sort of response to David's question, you don't have to provide any additional information politically to bring this coalition together. How do you gauge the support in that light of Turkey for the operation, what's envisioned there? And can you expect to secure—can the U.S. expect to secure use of Turkey as a staging ground for U.S. troops?

Mr. Fleischer. Some two to three weeks ago, I think it was rather extensively reported that the State Department contacted some 50 nations around the world to discuss cooperation in the eventuality of a potential conflict with Iraq. And those conversations began at that point; they've been developing since then. And it is always my practice to allow nations to speak for themselves about what level of cooperation they are providing. So I am not going to get into any one nation specific.

I'll just repeat that the President is very satisfied that the international community agrees with him about the threat that Saddam Hussein presents. The international community and many of these nations that we are working most closely with see it the same way the President does. They, too, don't want war. They believe war should be a last resort, and they hope that Saddam Hussein will disarm so it can be averted. But make no mistake that the work of assembling a coalition continues.

Q. You just had a Defense official, Mr. Wolfowitz, come back from Turkey, where they talked about these sorts of issues. What's your sense of the success of his mission there?

Mr. Fleischer. I think as he described it, it was a very successful visit and he was pleased with his consultations with officials in Turkey. The President will be—the President, as you know, met with Turkish officials during his visit to the Czech Republic, and important members of the Turkish government or governing structure will be coming to visit the President next week.

Q. Ari, there was a poll released—I believe it was by the Pew Foundation—yesterday showing that overseas, that the United States is not held in as high esteem as it once was. Is this something that troubles the President? And what does he think might be contributing to that?

Mr. Fleischer. You know, I would encourage everybody to go back and take a look at the raw data in that poll and pay less attention to some of the interpretations that instantly came out that accompanied it. Because I think, if you look at it, what you'll see is, with the exception of some areas in the Muslim world where the President has already acknowledged the United States has a job to do and we have to bring people together between the United States and the Muslim world, but around the rest of the world, the poll showed overwhelming favorable notions of the United States of America, particularly among those who recently struggled against tyranny and oppression.

The numbers are astounding in terms of people in all parts of the world who look to the United States with a favorable image. And I think that's one of the reasons why you see so many people from around the world want to come to the United States to go to college and get good educations, because they see so much hope and opportunity in America, and opportunity for learning. And we welcome them. We want them to take advantage of it in a way that is consistent with our immigration laws, and then go back to their countries. And they are good emissaries for the wonderful spirit of the American people.

So I think this is one of the most stark example of a poll whose data showed one thing and whose instant analysis showed another.

Q. In that case, let's look at the Muslim world quickly at least. Obviously, if you go to war with Iraq, it might not sit too well with some other—some folks in the Muslim world. What exactly is it that the administration is tending to do to try to bring those folks closer?

Mr. Fleischer. Well, let me remind you that Syria voted with the United States on the Security Council resolution and so Iraq operates alone in terms of whether or not it should disarm. Syria has called on Iraq to disarm. I don't make any predictions about whether Syria will or will not take any part in anything beyond the vote in the United Nations, but I think the point is instructive. And I remind you about all the efforts the United States has made to help bring freedom to Muslims around the world, including Bosnia, including Afghanistan.

Q. This is the populace that was being polled. Is there any reason to think that the populace of these Arab nations will look more fondly on the United States if it invades Iraq?

Mr. Fleischer. Well, I think, given the fact that Iran was attacked by Iraq, given the fact that Kuwait was attacked by Iraq, and given the fact that Saudi Arabia was attacked by Iraq, I don't think you're going to find many citizens that believe that Saddam Hussein is an exact role model for the way Arab community wants to be seen.

Q. Ari, when you said the coalition is assembling over the past two weeks, what exactly does that mean? What's been going on?

Mr. Fleischer. It means just as I did in the follow-up, that the State Department contacted some 50 nations around the world in terms of possible cooperation, in the event that war becomes necessary, and that we are receiving good responses from many nations. And that the President believes that one of the best ways to avert war is to make absolutely certain that Saddam Hussein understands that, if he does not comply and disarm, we are ready to wage it and it will be waged successfully.

Q. What do you mean, good responses? Do you mean nations have stepped up and committed specific forces to a coalition force?

Mr. Fleischer. Nations have stepped up and committed specific levels of support. I won't get into what those may be, whether it is troops, whether it is equipment, whether it is overflight, whether it is landing bases. As I indicated, that is for each nation to do on its own. But you can assume all of the above in various regions of the world.

Q. So people have made specific commitments sort of along the lines that the President outlined at the NATO summit?

Mr. Fleischer. That's correct. That's correct.

Q. Ari, one of the Joint Chiefs yesterday shared a view in response to a question that the trigger for military disarmament in Iraq would most likely have to come after the inspectors were able to come up with the tangible goods to make the case that Iraq is lying. Does the President believe that that is the case? Because that would suggest that the burden of proof is more with the inspectors than with Iraq.

Mr. Fleischer. No, the burden of proof is clearly on Iraq. And one of the issues, again—I've said this before, and I hope you can just think about this in the most logical way of 100 inspectors working in a nation the size of France where, often, the ability to hide something is not so complicated, because what you're hiding is relatively small. And the amount of facilities that can be available underground or mobile makes your task of hiding or deceiving or moving relatively easy.

The burden falls on Saddam Hussein to comply. And this is why the President keeps saying this is not a game of hide and seek. If an adversary wants to hide, it's not hard to hide weapons of mass destruction from even the best inspectors, particularly in a country the size of Iraq. So Iraq is under an obligation under international law not to just not hide, but to cooperate. Iraq must cooperate, and this is what the inspectors and the world community will soon see if Iraq is indeed doing it or not.

Q. Can I follow up on that? If the inspection process is this difficult in the size of the country and with the number of inspectors, then how long is the President willing to let this process—which so far has looked on the outside like cooperation—continue?

Mr. Fleischer. Again, I want to remind you that, when you say it looks on the outside like cooperation, how do you square that with what Tariq Aziz just said when he said he has no weapons of mass destruction, unless Tariq Aziz's word is taken at face value. And I submit to you—and this is why I cited a public account—pull your own reporting for the last 10 years. Those reports I cited, particularly the first one, was not in the name of any government official, it was independent reporting—refuted Iraqi claims. So I know that when you also independently take a look at Iraqi claims, you do render a judgment about whether it's accurate or not.

Q. So the President does believe that Baghdad's word is enough of a trigger?

Mr. Fleischer. The President will wait for Iraq to submit its declaration, and then we will take a look at it, as I said, in a thoughtful, deliberative manner, take all appropriate time to review it, and then you will hear from the United States in various forms as time goes along.

Remarks by Secretary of State Powell, December 5, 2002

Secretary Colin Powell was interviewed by Thierry Thuillier of France 2 television.

Q. First, of course, I want to ask some questions about the Iraqi situation, as usual. In spite of U.N. inspectors, in Europe we feel that your rights or you know end of the story. War is coming soon?

Secretary Powell. No, I don't think war is necessarily coming soon. But whether war comes or not, it's up to Saddam Hussein. President Bush has made it clear that the international community expects Saddam Hussein to disarm. He took the case to the international community, the United Nations, on the 12th of September. The inspectors are now doing their work. The declaration has just come in, about to come in, about to be examined.

And if Saddam Hussein is cooperating with the United Nations, cooperating with the will of the international community, and is divulging everything that he has done and what he is doing now, then war can be avoided. President Bush has always said that he would prefer to solve this peacefully.

But we also know that the threat of war, the threat of force, is the only thing that has forced Saddam Hussein to come this far. Now we will see whether he is cooperating or not.

Q. But if Saddam Hussein denies to have possession of mass destruction weapons, why don't you believe Saddam Hussein?

Secretary Powell. Why should we believe him? He's been lying for 12 years. Would you believe him?

Q. He's a liar?

Secretary Powell. He's a liar. We'll see now whether he decides that the cost of lying is too great. The cost of lying now might result in his regime being destroyed by the armed forces of the international community. We will see whether he continues to lie or whether he cooperates with the United Nations and the international community.

This is not the United Nations or the United States on trial or being accused of anything. It is Saddam Hussein who is being accused by the international community of having weapons of mass destruction. And anybody who thinks that he does not have weapons of mass destruction simply is denying the obvious, denying reality. He has gassed his own people. He has invaded his neighbors.

We know from previous inspection regimes that he has developed these kinds of weapons. He had them in his possession. He denied it, but he was found out. And then he created circumstances which caused the inspectors to be pulled out four years ago. And now the inspectors are back, and let's see if he's willing to cooperate and tell the truth.

Q. Yes, but if U.N. inspectors don't find anything, what will happen?

Secretary Powell. We'll find out. We'll have to wait—

Q. You'll—

Secretary Powell. No, we'll have to wait and see. The U.N. inspectors may not find anything because Saddam Hussein is not cooperating and he is denying them access to places or he is practicing deception to keep them from finding.

Wouldn't that say to the international community that they must act if it is clear that Saddam Hussein is not being truthful, once again, in his declarations or that he is frustrating the ability of the inspectors to find out the truth? Then, I think the international community should say, "Enough, enough. This man can't be trusted."

Q. Yes, but, again, if U.N. inspectors don't find anything, what will happen? Because it's a possibility.

Secretary Powell. We will find out. If the U.N. inspectors do not find anything after an extensive search and after doing their work as well as they can, they will report those facts to the Security Council, as they are required to, and the Security Council will have to make an assessment and come to a judgment, as will the United States.

Q. How do you estimate the cooperation of the Iraqi regime as far as today?

Secretary Powell. So far, I think we should remain skeptical. Since the U.N. resolution was passed on the 8th of November, the Iraqis came back with two letters, which are very unsatisfactory, very accusatory, not a spirit of cooperation associated with these two letters. And so I think we should be skeptical.

Now, we are in the process of analyzing the declaration that will be arriving and we'll see whether or not Iraqi authorities are cooperating when they put forward this declaration. We have an idea, a pretty good idea, of what should be in such a declaration and we will see whether or not they are cooperating and being truthful.

With respect to what the inspectors have been able to do for their first week of moving around Iraq, Iraq has responded, let them into places and not delayed the inspectors. But this is just the beginning. This is just the first five days. We will see whether or not they are cooperative over time.

Q. Since several months, we are expecting the evidence that Iraqi develop weapons of mass destruction, but we see nothing from America, for example. Why?

Secretary Powell. That's simply not true. You are trying to make the case for Iraq instead of making the case against Iraq. We have put forward information. We have put forward papers. We have presented information to the international community. We have nine—eight years worth of inspection reports from UNSCOM, from the IAEA. We have evidence. We have seen it. We have reports that show Iraq developed weapons of mass destruction. The United Kingdom has put out a number of papers that deal with it.

And so the burden is not upon the international community to prove Iraq has it; let Iraq come forward and prove they don't have it. If they don't have it, you tell me, then, why they caused the inspectors to leave in 1998 and why they would not let them back in, if they don't have them.

Why aren't they forthcoming? Why aren't they saying, "Go anywhere, anytime." Why did it take the threat of war to get the Iraqi regime to say "Okay, we'll let the inspectors come back in"? Because suddenly they had a change of heart? No. Because suddenly they were facing military force and they realized they had to do something. They have been denying. They have been deceiving. They have been lying. And nobody should stand up and justify Iraq's actions. Iraq stands condemned by its own actions.

Q. So we can't deal with Saddam Hussein? It's not possible because he's a liar? The only solution is a war?

Secretary Powell. No, the solution is to see whether or not the threat of war and the threat of the regime being overthrown is enough to cause him to cooperate with the international community. We are skeptical. The President has been skeptical. I am skeptical. My other colleagues in the American Government are skeptical. I am sure most of my friends in the international community are skeptical.

So we will see whether or not he cooperates with the demands of the United Nations. If he cooperates, then war can be avoided. If he doesn't cooperate, then I believe it is an obligation of the international community to see that its will is imposed on Saddam Hussein by removing the regime and removing the weapons of mass destruction.

And if removing the regime is the only way to do it, then that will be necessary. We cannot allow a regime such as Saddam Hussein's to essentially look the United Nations in its face, this one nation, look in the face of the United Nations and say, "I ignore you. I don't care what you think. I don't care what the international community thinks. I want to keep developing nuclear weapons. I want to retain chemical weapons. I want to have biological weapons. I want to continue to be able to threaten the nations in my neighborhood. I may wish to invade again, like I have done before."

I don't think the international community can simply look away and say, "Oh, gosh, isn't that too bad? Saddam Hussein will not cooperate, therefore we can ignore the demands we have placed upon him."

Q. Is there an evidence of a link between al-Qaida and Iraq? Because we don't see any evidence for the moment. We have just pieces, but not real evidence.

Secretary Powell. We have no evidence, conclusive evidence, that Iraq and al-Qaida worked together with respect to 9/11, what happened on that tragic day here in the United States. We do know, however, that over the years there have been contacts between the Iraqi regime and al-Qaida elements. We also know that there are members of al-Qaida who are in Iraq, in different places in Iraq.

So there are some connections and we will continue to examine those connections. And as time goes by and more information comes out, more evidence presents itself, we'll continue to make our assessment. And as we find out information, we'll make it known to the world. But there have been contacts between Iraq and al-Qaida over the years.

Q. If you launch a war against Iraq, is America can go alone, if it's necessary?

Secretary Powell. The President has made it clear that he believes this matter has to be resolved; Iraq has to be disarmed. The international community can do it under the auspices of the Security Council. But if the United Nations chooses not to act in the face of continued Iraqi noncooperation, then the President is prepared to go with likeminded nations. We won't be alone. There are many nations who have already spoken up and said we understand the seriousness of this matter, and if it is necessary to undertake military action, we would prefer to do it within the context of a Security Council resolution, but if that is not the case, we are prepared to go with you.

Q. I want to be sure to understand. What is main goal if there is a war? What is the main goal? To disarm Saddam Hussein? To rebirth the regime? To build a democracy?

Secretary Powell. Should there be a conflict—and, once again, the President hopes there will not be a conflict—but should there be a conflict, it will be to remove this regime because the regime can't be dealt with. And we would be removing the regime for the purpose of getting rid of the weapons of mass destruction.

But having removed the regime, the United States and other likeminded nations, or the United Nations, the international community, would pick up an obligation to help the Iraqi people put in place a government that is representative of all the Iraqi people, that is not a dictatorship, that is not developing weapons of mass destruction, that will use the wealth of this nation, the tremendous wealth of this nation in the form of oil, for the purpose of helping the people, educating the people, providing health care for the people, building the infrastructure of the country, and not developing weapons. That would be an obligation that we would pick up. We would try to help Iraq get onto a path that would lead to a peaceful Iraq, living in peace with its neighbors, a representative form of government, and is no longer a threat to anybody in the world.

Q. And rebuild the regime, if it's necessary?

Secretary Powell. What?

Q. To change the regime if it's necessary?

Secretary Powell. Yes, yes. It has always been our policy. It's still our policy to change the regime. But it's important to remember why that is our policy. Regime change as a U.S. policy was decided upon in 1998 by President Clinton. And the reason President Clinton, supported by the American Congress, did it, was because Iraq would not get rid of its weapons of mass destruction.

So, as a result, it seemed to us the only way to get Iraq to do that, was to change the regime. But if Iraq now, in light of the pressure being brought to bear on it, decides to cooperate and get rid of its weapons of mass destruction, they are, in effect, changing their approach; it is a changed regime, and therefore we do not require a military change of regime.

Q. Are you ready to change the Middle East map? Don't you think it's very dangerous with the war in Iraq?

Secretary Powell. Certainly, it comes with certain risks and dangers. But we believe the danger of a Saddam Hussein developing weapons that can kill thousands upon thousands of people and who has a record of using weapons such as this nature, is also a very dangerous thing to leave in place. And we understand the risks in other parts of the region if a conflict takes place—

Q. At embassies, in countries, for instance?

Secretary Powell. Yes, yes, there will be problems. But there is also the prospect that with a changed regime in Baghdad, maybe things will change for the better in the Middle East. Maybe Israel will not feel as threatened. Maybe other nations in the region will not feel threatened any longer. And so there is a possibility that there are opportunities in such a conflict, as well as risks in such a conflict.

But at the end of the day, if a conflict does become necessary, war does become necessary, and a coalition goes in, I think the strategy we would do it quickly and create inside of Iraq, as quickly as possible, a government that is responsive to the needs of its people, and representative of its people, and that will live in peace with its neighbors. It seems to me this would be a stabilizing element in the region, not a destabilizing element.

Q. Do you know that in France modern people say that maybe we have to be frightened by America, by the superpower? Do you understand that, this feeling?

Secretary Powell. I hear it, but, you know, I believe it is mostly just commentary. How could, how could France every feel itself threatened in some way by American power? American power has served what purpose in Europe in the last 50 years? The last 100 years? What was American power used for? We were a power in 1918 when we did what? We came and fought alongside the French, and we brought an end to World War I. We were a power at the beginning of World War II, when we entered World War II two years after the war had broken out in Europe and France had been overrun.

What did we use that power for? Did we use it to subject a single nation, a single person, in all of Europe? What did we use that power for? We used it to free Europe. We used it to free our French friends, our French friends who have been our friends since our own revolution.

So France has no—should have no concern, nor any Frenchman should have any concern about American power. We have been friends for so many years.

The outgoing French Ambassador, my very good friend Francois Bujon, said, you know, France will always be a bad weather friend of the United States. It's a wonderful line. What it means is, we argue. Sometimes the relationship is prickly. France is a proud nation with its own interests. The purpose of French diplomacy is to represent French interests. My responsibility as Secretary of State is to represent American interests.

But more often than not, our interests coincide. So even when we are having our little debates, and sometimes we have a little fight, it's within a family. It's within a family that has been these two strong partners, France and the United States, and many other members of this Euro-Atlantic family. We have been through a lot together, and we will go through a lot more in the future. But we will always go through it as friends.

The United States does not wish to use its power to impose its will on anybody. We look for partners. We look for friends. We will represent our interests. We will stick by our principles. We want to be part of a multilateral community when it is appropriate to do so.

When we have things we feel strongly about, then we represent our own interests even if we can't join a consensus. France demonstrated this some years ago when it left the NATO Alliance, if you'll recall, and asked everybody to leave Paris. That was an expression of French interests at that time.

But these problems come, these problems go. The relationship between France and the United States is strong, will remain strong. I think it was particularly well demonstrated in the discussions on U.N. Resolution 1441. Dominique de Villepin and I, we talked every day, many times—always serious, sometimes funny, always in the spirit of friendship, accommodating each other's concerns and positions—and we came up with an outstanding result.

White House Press Briefing, December 6, 2002

Q. Let me ask about Iraq, if I can, and the declaration we're going to be getting supposedly tomorrow. U.N. officials have been telling us that they're expecting something that could run to thousands of pages, likely is going to be in Arabic, and it may well take weeks to digest, to translate. Is that acceptable to the administration, taking weeks to deal with something like that?

Mr. Fleischer. Well, it'll take as much time as is necessary to do the job right. We have asked Iraq, through the international community, to develop a list of what weapons it possesses and to come out with a certification of what they possess. That is Iraq's right and burden to do so. We look forward to reviewing it. Just as important as what's in there, we'll also be curious to see what is not in there. And Iraq will prepare it to turn it over per their obligations to the world, and the President will direct his administration to receive it, to look through it carefully—this will be done through the intelligence communities—and render a judgment.

Q. Is there no fear that, perhaps by loading it up with lots of detail and leaving it in Arabic that they're playing for time?

Mr. Fleischer. Well, I don't think the language is going to be a particular impediment. It has to be translated; there are translators who do these types of things. I think that one of—sometimes, one of the best ways to hide or to deceive is to come out with such a voluminous document that it makes people miss the things that aren't in there. You know, another way I put that is, just because Iraq turns over a phone book to the United Nations doesn't mean that nobody inside Iraq has an unlisted phone number.

And so there would be a variety of things that we want to find out about and whether or not Iraq has left information out of here. So we won't be fooled by the size of this document into thinking that the size alone dictates that Iraq has complied. We want to make certain that Iraq is listing everything they have obligation to list, full, accurate and complete, so the world knows that Saddam Hussein is serious about disarmament.

Q. Ari, can you discuss a little bit the reasoning behind the goal of enlisting inspectors' help in getting weapons scientists out of Iraq to help us locate other weapons? And what sort of commitment the administration may be prepared to make along the lines of asylum, witness protection programs, what are we talking about here?

Mr. Fleischer. History, in dealing with Iraq, has shown that one of the most valuable ways to get information about what is really going on with Iraq's weapons programs is to talk to the scientists and the weapons people inside Iraq who really know the facts about what's going on.

The inspectors, for all their abilities, don't have the ability to know and see everything. But there are many people inside Iraq who do know a lot more. And history has shown that some of those people who want to preserve peace, want to provide that information to the western world. And because of the brutal regime that Saddam Hussein has, many of these experts who have information they want to share, fear doing so because they know that, if they do, they risk imprisonment, torture, murder, their families will be at risk and they're vulnerable to the brutality of Saddam Hussein's regime.

So in the United Nations Security Council Resolution 1441, it makes explicit mention of the obligation on Iraq for the inspectors to have the right at a time and place of their choosing, including outside of Iraq, to interview any of these people inside Iraq. That often is one of the best ways that we can obtain information about whether Iraq is telling the truth. And so this is a very important part of the U.N. resolution.

Q. Can you amplify at all on what might be done to secure their asylum and their protection in this country? I mean, is it—there may not be a final decision. As you said this morning, modalities might have to be worked out. But is it at least in the discussion phase, this notion of protecting them along the lines the way you protect informers in mob cases in this country?

Mr. Fleischer. Well, let me put it to you this way. We attach great importance to the safety and the welfare and the nonintimidation of these experts in Iraq who have information that some of them may want to share with the West and with the United Nations, with the world and the United Nations. We take it very seriously and attach great importance to it. We hope the international community will do the same and attach the same amount of importance to it.

The exact way in which it could be done will be really a matter for the United Nations and the inspectors on the ground to work through. But, of course, much of the world stands ready to help because we saw in the '90s that is the way that much of the world got information about what was really going on inside Iraq.

Q. Just one more on this. You don't want to utter the words "witness protection program," but there is a commitment by this government to protect those Iraqis who are willing to give the international community information that would lead to the ultimate disarmament of Saddam?

Mr. Fleischer. We have a real and genuine concern to help protect the safety and the welfare of those inside Iraq who have information that can help preserve the peace. Because the information they have is very important information. And history has shown that there people inside Iraq who want to share it, but are fearful of doing so because of the brutal tactics of the Iraqi regime.

And under the Security Council resolution, Iraq is obligated not only to allow the inspectors to interview those scientists or weapons developers and designers, but also their families, and to remove them from Iraq. Those are the conditions Iraq has accepted.

* * * *

Q. The President and the Secretary of Defense say there's hard evidence that Saddam Hussein has weapons of mass destruction. When will that evidence be released? Once this white paper from Saddam is gone over, or when?

Mr. Fleischer. Well, again, per the United Nations Security Council resolution, the obligation is on Saddam Hussein to disarm. I think there's been no secret and everybody has recognized this—including Democrats, Republicans, previous administrations, arms experts, United Nations officials—that Saddam Hussein has claimed that he didn't have weapons of mass destruction when it was obviously the conclusion of all that he did.

Those conclusions are based, Ivan, on a variety of information that is available to administrations, and there is always the issue about protecting the sources and methods of how we receive that information. But I don't know anybody who takes what the administration and administrations and people in both parties have said, and the United Nations experts have said that Iraq does, indeed, have weapons of mass destruction, and thinks it's inaccurate or discounts it. And the President has made it perfectly plain, and I refer you to his Cincinnati speech where he walked people through why we believe and have concluded that they have weapons of mass destruction.

White House Press Release, December 7, 2002

The Iraqi regime today submitted to the United Nations Monitoring, Verification, and Inspection Commission (UNMOVIC) what it claims is a declaration of its programs to develop chemical, biological, and nuclear weapons, ballistic missiles, and other delivery systems. A "currently accurate, full and complete declaration" is required by United Nations Security Council resolution 1441. The U.S. Government will analyze this declaration with respect to its credibility and compliance with UNSCR 1441. We will continue to work with other countries to achieve the ultimate goal of protecting the peace by ending Saddam Hussein's pursuit and accumulation of weapons of mass destruction.

Remarks by President Bush, December 7, 2002

President Bush delivered the following radio address to the nation.

Good morning. This weekend is the deadline for the Iraqi regime to fully disclose to the U.N. Security Council all of its weapons of mass destruction. Disarming that regime is a central commitment of the war on terror. We must, and we will, prevent terrorist groups and outlaw regimes from threatening the American people with catastrophic harm.

Saddam Hussein has been under a duty to disarm for more than a decade. Yet he has consistently and systematically violated that obligation and undermined U.N. inspections. And he only admitted to a massive biological weapons program after being confronted with the evidence.

Now the U.N. Security Council and the United States have told Saddam Hussein, the game is over. Saddam Hussein will fully disarm himself of weapons of mass destruction, and if he does not, America will lead a coalition to disarm him.

As the new inspections process proceeds, the United States will be making only one judgment: Has Saddam Hussein changed his behavior of the last 11 years and decided to cooperate willingly and comply completely, or has he not?

Inspections will work only if Iraq complies fully and in good faith. Inspectors do not have the duty or the ability to uncover terrible weapons hidden in a vast country. The responsibility of inspectors is simply to confirm evidence of voluntary and total disarmament. Saddam Hussein has the responsibility to provide that evidence, as directed, and in full.

The world expects more than Iraq's cooperation with inspectors. The world expects and requires Iraq's complete, willing and prompt disarmament. It is not enough for Iraq to merely open doors for inspectors. Compliance means bringing all requested information and evidence out into full view, to show that Iraq has abandoned the deceptions of the last decade. Any act of delay or defiance will prove that Saddam Hussein has not adopted the path of compliance, and has rejected the path of peace.

Thus far we are not seeing the fundamental shift in practice and attitude that the world is demanding. Iraq's letters to the U.N. regarding inspections show that their attitude is grudging and conditional. And in recent days, Iraq has fired on American and British pilots enforcing the U.N.'s no-fly zone.

Iraq is now required by the United Nations to provide a full and accurate declaration of its weapons of mass destruction and ballistic missile programs. We will judge the declaration's honesty and completeness only after we have thoroughly examined it, and that will take some time. The declaration must be credible and accurate and complete, or the Iraqi dictator will have demonstrated to the world once again that he has chosen not to change his behavior.

Americans seek peace in the world. War is the last option for confronting threats. Yet the temporary peace of denial and looking away from danger would only be a prelude to a broader war and greater horror. America will confront gathering dangers early. By showing our resolve today, we are building a future of peace.

Presidential Determination No. 2003-06, December 9, 2002

Subject: Presidential Determination on Authorization to Furnish Drawdown Assistance to the Iraqi Opposition under the Iraq Liberation Act of 1998

Pursuant to the authority vested in me as President of the United States, including under sections 4(a)(2) and 5(a) of the Iraq Liberation Act of 1998 (Public Law 105-338) (the "Act"), and consistent with Presidential Determination 99-13, I hereby direct the furnishing of up to $92 million in defense articles from the Department of Defense, defense services from the Department of Defense, and military education

and training in order to provide assistance to the following organizations:
- Iraqi National Accord;
- Iraqi National Congress;
- Kurdistan Democratic Party;
- Movement for Constitutional Monarchy;
- Patriotic Union of Kurdistan;
- Supreme Council of the Islamic Revolution in Iraq;

and to such other Iraqi opposition groups designated by me under the Act before or after this determination. The assistance will be allocated in accordance with plans being developed by the Department of Defense and the Department of State.

The Secretary of State is authorized and directed to report this determination to the Congress and to arrange for its publication in the Federal Register.

White House Press Briefing, December 9, 2002

Q. There's a growing anti-war movement in this country against potential war with Iraq. There's a series of protests scheduled across the country tomorrow. What's the administration's position on that? Do you think that this is going to be a problem that you'll have to face as you go forward putting pressure on Saddam Hussein? Are these people misinformed about the issues?

Mr. Fleischer. No, I think peaceful protest is one of America's most time-honored traditions, and properly so. We're a stronger nation thanks to people from both sides of any debate who feel the right to demonstrate their beliefs in the peaceful manner of their choice.

Q. Is this going to complicate your efforts to squeeze Saddam Hussein?

Mr. Fleischer. No, I think that—again, this is part of the America tradition. And the President believes that the overwhelming majority of the American people agree with him that Saddam Hussein is a threat, and that he needs to be dealt with. And we hope that the provisions that have been put in place, through the inspections and through the collective will of the international community, will help Saddam Hussein come to the realization that he must disarm.

Q. And given that now Iraq has handed in a declaration and said, announced, it has no weapons of mass destruction, what's the inspectors' role now?

Mr. Fleischer. Well, the inspectors' role will be exactly prescribed in the Security Council resolution covering the inspections, which is to receive unlimited, unconditional access to all sites in Iraq so they can inspect to determine whether or not Saddam Hussein has, indeed, disarmed. It's a very difficult task. And we want to help them to do it.

Q. How is the administration going to help them do that?

Mr. Fleischer. Well, number one we're helping them to do it by getting them into the country. They couldn't do it having been thrown out of the country. Now that the President has gone to the United Nations and asked for the return of the inspectors, they're now able to do their job. And they are growing in numbers, growing in material. They still have an extraordinarily difficult task given the size of the country and the ease of which material can be hidden or moved. So that is the challenge that they face, and that is the purpose of their mission.

Q. Back in August, Vice President Cheney warned against this scenario, explicitly, saying it was dangerous. What changed?

Mr. Fleischer. Well, I think that the Vice President said what the President thinks, what all people in the administration think, and the Vice President also recognizes the value of having the inspectors there while we all say it's not a guarantee. I think when you take a look at the realm of what is possible inside Iraq with the inspectors, there's a clear recognition said by the President and the Vice President that we want the inspectors to be there so they can do their level best to determine whether Saddam Hussein disarmed. But the presence of inspectors in and of itself is not a guarantee of disarmament.

Q. Ari, do you have—does the United States now have in its possession the declaration made by the Iraqis, and do you have an estimate now how long it will take to analyze that?

Mr. Fleischer. I have not seen any reliable estimate of how long it will take to analyze, other than it's going to take whatever time is right and appropriate. The analysis of this document is going to be done in a very thoughtful, thorough and complete way. We want to be very deliberative as we move through and look at this document to determine with the international community what this indicates about Saddam Hussein and his disarmament.

In terms of the document, we are in the process. The United States is assisting the President of the Security Council with copying and distribution of the declaration.

Q. And I think the IAEA official there was saying it could take the inspectors as long as a year to verify compliance on that front. Is that a realistic estimate?

Mr. Fleischer. I'm not in a position to judge how long it will take the inspectors to do their job. That really depends on Iraqi cooperation. If the Iraqis cooperate, their job is made much easier. If the Iraqis don't, their job is made much harder.

Q. Will you be sharing more information now, more intelligence information with the inspectors now that the document has been handed over?

Mr. Fleischer. We're going to continue to cooperate with the inspectors, of course.

Q. There are those who believe that the only way inspections will be successful is

to have defectors inside of Iraq tell where things are. And there are published reports that Dr. Rice spent some time with Hans Blix and tried to forcefully stress point five of the resolution. Does the President believe that, too, is really the only way to get this done to make the inspections effective?

Mr. Fleischer. Well, I don't know that it's the only way for the inspectors to be effective. The inspectors are going to work very hard to be effective with whatever means they have. But it's certainly an enhanced way for the inspectors to be effective.

History has shown that very often the best quality information the inspectors were able to discover in the '90s was a result of information they received from people inside Iraq—scientists and weapons experts—who had information that they wanted to share.

Q. Ari, you said that this declaration from Iraq would be the beginning of a process.

Mr. Fleischer. Correct.

Q. To Terry's point of what the Vice President has said, he fears that if this goes on forever, inspecting one site a day or two sites a day, that it loses its urgency, that the world consensus you now have to deal with this would dissipate over time. Is there a time frame within the administration that says, okay, if you say you have no weapons of mass destruction prove to us within X that you have destroyed this, destroyed that, show us this site?

Mr. Fleischer. I think the time frame begins with the submission of this declaration by Iraq. And it will continue with the United States engaging in the analysis of the declaration to see what it says. I think those events may help determine the time frame. I have not heard the President engaged in any speculation about what the time frame may be beyond that. But the President is taking it in turn. And the turn now is to review the declaration Iraq has presented.

Q. He urged the U.N. to act on this in days and weeks, you'll remember, not months and years. Does he believe there has to be—Iraq says it's now—now the burden is on the United States to prove they're lying. Obviously, you view it differently. Does the administration have a sense that this needs to be resolved within a period of days and weeks, months?

Mr. Fleischer. Yes, that's what I indicated. I have not heard the President engage in any speculation on that. The President's statement about days and weeks applied to the vote that the United Nations cast. And the vote felt just shy of two months. The President went to the United Nations on September 10th. The United Nations voted in early November, if I recall, for their 15 to nothing resolution that gave Iraq the 30 days. The 30 days expired last week—just this past weekend, so it actually is moving very much along the time line that the President outlined.

Q. One more. Iraq says it has no weapons of mass destruction. Everyone in this administration, from the President on down, says it does. Will you wait until this analysis is complete? Or is there a real-time transfer of intelligence data, as in today or tomorrow, from the United States government to the inspectors saying, they say they have none, it is a lie, here's the proof, go look?

Mr. Fleischer. Well, we're going to continue to work with the inspectors to help to get them the information so they can do their job. And we want the inspectors to be successful in doing their job.

Of course, at the same time, we want to make certain that sources and methods are not compromised in any information that can be conveyed to the inspectors. I think that's very well-known and the inspectors understand that.

Q. But they say they were not getting this information prior to the Iraqi declaration. Are they getting it now, or will you wait until this analysis is complete?

Mr. Fleischer. As you can imagine, I'm not at liberty to discuss conveyance of intelligence information in any great detail. But it's in the United States interest for the inspectors to be successful.

Q. Ari, if the President is going to commit American lives, those of young men and women, to a war, isn't there a higher obligation to come up with affirmative proof than simply asserting a charge on past behavior?

Mr. Fleischer. Well, again, there are reasons the President and the Vice President, members of the President's administration, foreign leaders—I remind you that Vice President Gore, just as recently as July of this year, himself, categorically, based on what he knew when he was Vice President, said, Iraq has weapons of mass destruction. Former President Clinton said the identical thing.

There's a reason that all these people in both parties have said it. They've said it because they have reporting to let them know that it's true.

To your first question, the burden on the President—and on that score, you're absolutely right. Of course, there is. And this President does not engage in any discussion of war lightly. I want to remind you, he's the person who's had, because of the attack on our country on September 11th, the burden and the duty to hug the widows and the children of those who have lost their lives already in combat. Combat is the last thing this President wants to engage in.

In the event it ever gets to the point of combat, you can be assured the President will communicate with the American people and explain the reasons why to the American people, that this choice would become an unavoidable choice. That is not to say that the President will release intelligence information that will compromise sources or methods or abilities to win a war, if that were to be the only way to go. But, yes, the President would talk more to the American people. We are not at that point. The President hopes to avoid that point.

Q. Ari, two questions on Iraq. Would you clarify one thing for me? As I understand it, the Iraqis not only have to say whatever it is they have, but also prove that they destroyed what they used to have. Is that, in fact, the case? And, secondly, there have been concerns expressed that the Iraqis would lay something out in their declaration—this is the reason for the talks over the weekend about making it available to everyone—that they would somehow lay out the means to make weapons of mass destruction. Where does that concern come from, and is that a concern of the U.S.?

Mr. Fleischer. On your second point, I would refer you to the statement that was issued by the President of the Security Council in this regard. I will read from it. It begins, "After consulting with members of the Security Council, the Presidency decided to allow access to the Iraqi declaration to those members with the expertise to assess the risks of proliferation and other sensitive information to begin its immediate review."

There are proliferation concerns, of course, and so those concerns will be dealt with as the Presidency of the United Nations Security Council indicates, in a way that makes sure our mutual international goals of nonproliferation are in no way endangered by this process.

Remarks by United Nations Secretary-General Annan, December 9, 2002

Q. Mr. Secretary-General. What are your impressions initially here of the Declaration, from what you are hearing from Vienna, and from New York, as far as Iraqi cooperation, and their willingness to reveal now to the world their WMD program?

Secretary-General Annan. I think the documents have just arrived, and as you all know, the inspectors will have to review them, analyze them, and report to the [Security] Council. And I think that's going to take a while. And until they've done that, I don't think I will have much to tell you.

Q. Mr. Secretary-General, would you say the United States is putting too much pressure, too little pressure or just enough pressure on Mr. Blix?

Secretary-General Annan. Well, I have always maintained that the inspectors have work to do, and we should allow them to do a professional job. And I have indicated they should be given the time and the space to do it, and I hope all Member States will do that. And don't forget, the Resolution was passed unanimously, and I do expect the Council to support the inspectors as they do a professional job.

Q. The Administration in Washington keeps insisting that the Iraqis cannot be trusted and that this Report, like previous reports, will not be truthful. Are you concerned that this will lead to hostilities, to clashes?

Secretary-General Annan. I will wait for the inspectors to finish their analysis and report to the Council before we get to that hurdle.

Q. Mr. Secretary, the Americans are saying they have evidence, solid evidence— the Resolution 1441 demands that Member States cooperate with the inspectors— give them the information they need. Are you being told by the Administration why aren't they playing ball, why aren't they giving the evidence to the inspectors?

Secretary-General Annan. Well, Mr. Blix has indicated that he would appreciate sharing of intelligence, and he would like governments who have information to give him and the inspectors that information, particularly with regard to sites where they may find hidden material.

Q. Sir, Mr. Secretary-General, the United States agreed on Friday in the Security Council to allow Dr. Blix to redact the document, and now they seem to have changed their mind and would like a full copy. Is it your concern that this process is somewhat being hijacked by the U.S. policy, U.S. foreign policy?

Secretary-General Annan. Well, the President of the Council seems to have a new sense of the Council, a new sense that the document should be given to certain members of the Council, and has worked that out with Blix. If that is the wish of the Council I have no problem with that.

Q. Mr. Secretary, the decision to give a copy to the permanent five [members of the Security Council] and not to the non-permanent ten, does that strike you as a democratic decision?

Secretary-General Annan. I think the Council is a master of its own deliberations. If the Council decided to do that, it is their right and I will not quibble with that.

Q. Mr. Secretary-General, do you think that Saddam Hussein is now seriously trying to avoid war, judging from the fact that they presented the documents in time, as they promised?

Secretary-General Annan. I have maintained that war is not inevitable, and it is up to President Saddam Hussein to disarm, to cooperate fully with the inspectors, and honor all his obligations to the United Nations. If that were to be done I would see no reason for war.

Q. Mr. Secretary-General, do you have a reaction on the Iraqi statement to the Kuwaiti people over the weekend?

Secretary-General Annan. I haven't studied the full text; apparently it was a long text. I know that there was an apology to the people and the government of [Kuwait], which is a positive development. But I will have to analyze the text to see what the rest of the statement says. There are indications that some of the things that were said may not be that helpful, but I will have to study the full text.

White House Press Briefing, December 10, 2002

[Today] the President met with the Chairman of Turkey's AK party, Chairman Erdogan, to talk about regional security vis-a-vis the United States and Turkey, and a variety of issues dealing with economic conditions in Turkey and Turkey's ascension potentially into the European Union. It was a very cordial and positive meeting.

Q. To what extent did the President talk with his Turk counterpart about either Iraq or U.S. use of military bases in Turkey?

Mr. Fleischer. The two did discuss the situation in Iraq. they both agreed that Iraq is a threat to peace, and the importance of Saddam Hussein disarming. They discussed the United Nations process, which is—both recognized as a very constructive process in terms of making certain that Saddam Hussein conforms to his international obligations. We have a variety of mutual interests with Turkey as we work closely on how to address this threat.

As you know, my longstanding policy is not to get into any operational specifics. They did discuss ways that we could cooperate, and I leave it at that.

Q. You said cooperative and agreed to cooperate and so forth in terms of the talks with Turkey. Does that mean that Turkey has agreed to allow the U.S. to use Turkish soil to bomb Iraq?

Mr. Fleischer. No, I said nothing about any outcome of that nature. It would not be in my position to describe anything—

Q. Your said the meeting was very positive—

Mr. Fleischer. It was.

Q. And that's what we're asking.

Mr. Fleischer. That's correct. But I would not say anything more concrete than that. It is not my place to report for other nations.

Q. You didn't. But I'm asking you, is this what you mean?

Mr. Fleischer. And I'm not answering the question, Helen. It was a positive meeting. And I don't want you to read into that. But the fact of the matter is—

Q.—positive, and agreed to cooperate. We know why—

Mr. Fleischer. Because I'm not giving you the specificity of what cooperation means in that context.

Q. Wasn't he invited here to twist his arm?

Mr. Fleischer. Helen, I know you have seen diplomatic relations for many years, but often countries look at issues and want to work together because they have mutual agreement about policy. Do not presume that I am indicating what Turkey may or may not do. That is for Turkey, a sovereign government, to decide. And I give you no inclination one way or another about any future decisions that Turkey may or may not make.

But certainly, the President makes very clear in his meetings the threat that he believes the world faces from Saddam Hussein. And the President also believes very strongly that the stronger the world is, the greater the chance of averting war, because Saddam Hussein will indeed react to that strength of pressure to disarm.

Q. On Iraq, can you tell us where we are in the evaluation process, what the administration is doing to pore over these thousands of pages from Iraq, how you're approaching this task?

Mr. Fleischer. The United States government is carefully reading through the declaration that Iraq has sent. It is voluminous. Much of it is in Arabic, and there are a team of translators, a team of government officials are looking at the information, making their way through it very carefully. Experts who are versed in the particular areas that have been released are dedicating themselves to the area of their expertise as the report is divided up within the intelligence community.

They are just in the beginning of that process. I anticipate this is a process that is going to take some considerable period of time. And this process will be thoughtful, it will be deliberative, and it will be careful. It will be careful to make certain that we thoroughly and completely understand what it is that Iraq is purporting to declare, as well as what they have failed to declare in this rather large document.

Q. So you think it will be several more days before you have any sort of judgment about the extent to which they're being genuine?

Mr. Fleischer. I think that's a very good possibility. And I hesitate to guess how many several more days. Whatever the proper period of time is that it will take will be the proper time that it takes, because it's important to have a careful and through understanding of what Iraq is saying, and that way we can judge it in its entirety.

Q. Ari, does that mean that you're not going to release any preliminary, step-by-step reaction? Is there anything—

Mr. Fleischer. No, I really don't anticipate any step-by-step reactions to it. That's why I said that we want to take a look at this in its entirety and see what it is that has been declared by Iraq, as well as to understand what may be not included in this document.

Remarks by United Nations Secretary-General Annan and UNMOVIC Chairman Blix, December 10, 2002

Secretary-General Annan. Good afternoon. We have just had a very frank discussion with the Council members on the way forward as the inspectors analyze the Iraqi Declaration. And I think what is important is that there is a clear understanding of how to proceed and there was also a very strong support for the work of the inspectors and for Mr. Blix and Dr. [Mohamed] ElBaradei and their teams. I think Mr. Blix may want to say something.

Dr. Blix. Perhaps I should tell you that, as of today, we now have [43 inspectors from UNMOVIC and 27] from the IAEA, so we are up to 70 inspectors all in all. We have a helicopter in place and we have inspected quite a few sites well in advance of the 45-day limit that the Security Council has given. As to the declaration, you know that it has arrived, and we are working on it—both here and our colleagues in Vienna are working on the nuclear part of it.

I told the Council that we hope that we will have been through the main part of the document, which is about 3,000 pages, by Friday. The bottleneck, frankly, is translation; we have about 500 pages in Arabic which need to be translated. But nevertheless, by Friday we think we will have a view of that, and we have asked the P5, who have got the text also and who have the experts on proliferation-sensitive matters, to advise us by Friday, and we are ready to share with them our conclusions.

So in the best case, by Monday, we will be able to have a working version of the text of the main part, which we can share with all the members of the Council. And so far the timetable is still holding, that by Thursday next week, on the 19th, we would come to the Council then and have some preliminary views on the substance, a very preliminary assessment of the substance. What we are now dealing with was only to take out of the declaration things that could be risky from the point of view of proliferation.

Q. On the substance, I know that it is still very early on at this stage, but what can you tell us about what the Iraqis are claiming relative to their weapons program? Are they denying any existence of a weapons program?

Dr. Blix. I don't think I want to get into the substance, because that relates to next week. What we are now focusing upon are the things that could be risky to have spread out, and sort of, as you call it, "cookbooks" for proliferation. This is what we are focusing upon, and we will give the advice and be ready on that by Friday. By next week, we will have some views on the substance, with a preliminary assessment on the whole thing.

* * * *

Q. Are there any cookbooks so far?

Dr. Blix. Yes, there are some.

Q. Dr. Blix, have you asked the Iraqis for a list of the Iraqi scientists that have, and have they complied with that request?

Dr. Blix. No, we have not yet. I have put them on notice that we will ask them for names of people who were active in the different programs. That is all in conformity with the Security Council [resolution]. But we have not asked for specific experts yet.

Q. Why have you not done that?

Dr. Blix. We haven't. We haven't. Many other things to do.

Q. Dr. Blix, does your team need the support of the P-5 to evaluate the report?

Dr. Blix. Well, the idea is that we will coordinate and consult with them, and that's precisely what we talked about, how do we achieve that now, and that we hope will come about by Friday. But obviously those who are far away, like the Chinese and the Russians, they are sending their copies I think today, and it might be difficult for them to have a very detailed comment by Friday. Nevertheless, there is still the hope that it will be managed by Monday.

Q. Are you going to leave in the name the name of foreign suppliers or are you going to edit them?

Dr. Blix. Well, foreign suppliers used to be something that they called sensitive, for the reason that they [UNSCOM] had sometimes been obtaining information through the foreign suppliers about the Iraqi program, and if they were to give their names publicly, then they would never get another foreign supplier giving you information. So that was the main reason for it. There were also those who did not know; they [suppliers] might have exported things quite legally, and they were not aware of where it was going to. So there are some guidelines from the past on this that we will (practice?) But it's subject to the agreement of the Security Council.

Q. Can you tell us a little bit about the mechanism that you've set up now for the future consultations on the Declaration. The fact that the Americans got a copy of the declaration first caused a little bit of confusion. Have you sorted that out? The other members of the Security Council, will they consult among themselves through you, or without you, before going to the Security Council?

Dr. Blix. Well, this is actually more a question for the relations between the elected 10 and the P-5 [of the Security Council], and we will come out with what we propose to be the working version of it all, and I think that discussion that you relate to, that's for them and not for us.

Q. Prior to the declaration being handed over, the Iraqis were claiming they had no weapons program. How was that sort of statement handled, from what you've seen so far?

Dr. Blix. I think that Dr. Al Saadi still maintains that attitude. We will come back to that next week.

Q. Dr. Blix, can you take one more please? About something new, is your assessment that there is nothing new, and it doesn't include any evidence of what has been destroyed?

Dr. Blix. They cover also the period up to the present time or practically the present time; they haven't done that before. So evidently there will be something new. But for the rest, whether any revisions of the past, I will not talk.

Q. But just about the evidence that you have asked for in terms of the destruction of weapons, did you get anything on that?

Dr. Blix. Well, that relates to the past. We will come back to that.

Remarks by Secretary of Defense Rumsfeld, December 11, 2002

Secretary Donald Rumsfeld delivered his remarks after meeting with officials in Qatar.

We have just had a meeting, and I thank the minister for the wonderful cooperation between our two countries in the global war on terrorism. It's a broad coalition of some 90 countries, and certainly Qatar has been significant in its contributions, and we value that.

The implementing agreement that we're—have just signed is certainly an indication of what we consider to be an important and valued defense partner. There is no question but that the agreement will enable us to strengthen our long-term strategic cooperation and to engage in some upgrades here in the country that will work to our mutual benefit. And certainly General Franks, who is here with me, has worked long and hard on this subject with the officials of the government.

Q. Can you give us some idea of what the agreement is that you signed? And secondly—

Secretary Rumsfeld. Well, the agreement that we signed is something that will improve our mutual readiness and military capabilities; it will permit a variety of upgrades, some of which are quality of life upgrades. Others will provide state-of-the-art capabilities for the forces here in the country.

With respect to the situation on the vessel, the situation is that a vessel was stopped by a multinational naval force. You're quite right; there were questions about its flag, questions about its cargo and questions about its destination. The operation was conducted peacefully; no one was injured. And it turns out that there—the contents of the ship was not what was manifested on the cargo list.

I have been en route here, and I don't consider myself to be up to date, up to the minute in terms of the communications that may be taking place between various countries. And I think I'll leave it to the folks in Washington to handle the rest of the details.

* * * *

Q. We can see that as the U.S. continues mobilizing and massing troops in the region. Don't you think that you are ignoring U.N. efforts and resolutions?

Secretary Rumsfeld. That's quite a question. I suppose the short answer is no. How could you even ask that question when it was the Iraqi regime that ignored 16 resolutions of the United Nations over a period of many, many years? Second, how could you even ask that question given the fact that it was the United States that went to the United Nations and received a unanimous vote in the Security Council? Not one vote opposing it. So a question that is premised that the United States is ignoring the United Nations is obviously misplaced.

Q. One last question, please. What are the details of your new bilateral agreement with the Qataris filed today? Can you tell us some of the details about it?

Secretary Rumsfeld. I think I answered that for the previous questioner.

Q. A two-tiered question. First of all, how do you justify the United States getting the copy of Iraq's declaration before the rest of the permanent members of the Security Council?

And the second part of the question is, how do you view Iraq's cooperation so far with the work of the inspectors? And is this enough to defuse the crisis or not?

Secretary Rumsfeld. Well, let me say this about that. My understanding is that the United Nations made a decision that they needed to reproduce the declaration, and they asked the United States to reproduce it. The United States did that. And then all of the five P-5 countries received the document at the same time, is my understanding.

So I don't think I have to justify a decision by the United Nations, because it was a decision by the United Nations as to how they wanted to have the documents reproduced. I believe I'm correct on that. These are matters that are not in the Department of Defense of the United States, they're matters that are handled by the United Nations.

The second question is how do we view the cooperation by Iraq thus far. The resolution, the unanimous resolution of the United Nations stated that Iraq was in material breach of the United Nations' resolutions. It then stated a series of additional things that Iraq ought to do and ought not to do. One of the things that they asked Iraq to do was to supply this declaration, which was to have been full and complete. It is, I think, 20,000 pages long. People are just beginning to read it and to study it and to analyze it, and we won't know the extent to which Iraq has or has not complied with the unanimous U.N. resolution until all the various countries take the time and have the patience to read it and consider it and analyze it.

The only other indication—there are two other indications of cooperation or the lack thereof. One is that inspectors have been allowed into Iraq, as the United Nations requested. A second is that the resolution suggests that it's not appropriate for Iraq to interfere with inspectors or to interfere with member states. And Iraq has continued to fire on coalition aircraft that are conducting Operation Northern Watch and Southern Watch.

Q. A question for Mr. Rumsfeld. Sir—[*brief audio break*]—the nuclear option, should President Saddam Hussein use weapons of mass destruction. How does this differ from what the former secretary of defense, now Vice President Dick Cheney, said about a dozen years ago when he said all options were on the table? And why has this come out at this particular point in time?

Secretary Rumsfeld. Well, it's very interesting to me when I get asked a question like that. It begins by saying, "It's been reported," and then the question is, well, why did it come out at this time?

To my knowledge, that subject's not been raised by people in the United States government. If you have information to the contrary, I'd be curious to hear it.

Q. But does that policy differ from what Dick Cheney said 12 years ago, when he said all options would be on the table?

Secretary Rumsfeld. You know, I would have to go back and read what Defense Minister Cheney said a decade ago.

But the policy of the United States has been, generally, to not rule things out.

Whatever that might mean in a given situation, I don't know. But to my knowledge, the president of the United States, the vice president, the secretary of defense or secretary of state, not one of us have commented on the subject you're raising.

Q. [Once you were] actively engaged in helping Iraq during the Iran-Iraq war; now, you're probably the most proactive person within the administration who is calling for not only the disarmament of Iraq, but the change of regime. How do you justify this change in your position between then and now?

Secretary Rumsfeld. And the question is to me, and it's to me because of my personal activities over the years? Is that—

Q. No, when you were a member of the administration during the '80s.

Secretary Rumsfeld. Right, okay. I'd be happy to respond to that. In the early 1980s, Iran and Iraq were in a war. President Reagan was president, and I was a private citizen. 241 marines were killed in Beirut, Lebanon, in a terrorist attack. President Reagan and Secretary of State George Shultz asked me if I would take a leave of absence from my business and come in and assist them for a period of months with respect to the problems in the Middle East.

I met with Saddam Hussein during that period. And the purpose was to attempt to see if the Iraqi regime could be at all helpful in our efforts in the Middle East with respect to terrorism. In fact, I had nothing to do with helping Saddam Hussein and his regime against Iran. We had, I think, one or two meetings. The United States then did provide intelligence information, as I understand it—but I was back in private business at the time—to that regime. So that's the first part of the question.

You say how do you justify that. I justify it because 241 Marines were killed and the president of the United States asked me to do that. And I did it. And it was a perfectly responsible and appropriate thing for us to do.

Second. You say now the United States is active, or I am active, against the Saddam Hussein regime, and how do I justify that. First of all, I work for the president of the United States. I don't make these decisions, I serve the president. He has gone to the Congress of the United States, which voted overwhelmingly in favor of the president's position with respect to Iraq, namely that they represent a danger to the region and a danger to the world because it has long been listed as a terrorist state and it has relationships with terrorist networks. Indeed, I don't even need to enumerate them.

The president then decided to go to the United Nations. And I keep hearing this about war with Iraq and all of this, but the fact is the president has not made a decision with respect to that. People are poring over this declaration to see what it says, what they've acknowledged, and the extent to which they have decided to cooperate with the United Nations. And at some point, nations—this nation, other nations—will be able to make a judgment as to whether or not they believe Iraq is being cooperative with the United Nations.

Remarks by Secretary of State Powell, December 12, 2002

Secretary Colin Powell was interviewed by Kahled Al-Shami of Al Quds Al Arabi.

Q. Okay. So if we can move to Iraq and the question everybody is asking in the Arab world now, whether the U.S. still needs to obtain approval from the Security Council to launch war in Iraq in response to what it unilaterally may view as material breach.

Secretary Powell. The United States is not looking for a way to launch war. The United States is looking at a way to launch peace with a disarmed Iraq. And so we are studying the declaration that Iraq submitted. Other members of the Security Council are studying the declaration, as is UNMOVIC and IAEA, and I would not make a judgment as to whether or not the declaration will be found deficient and whether or not that might lead to a material breach and whether or not, if it did, that would lead to action on the part of the United Nations.

We want to approach this in a multilateral way, talking with our friends, consulting with our Security Council colleagues in the United Nations, hoping to find a way to solve this peacefully, but at the same time recognizing that unless the threat of military force is there, Iraq will not disarm.

The person who will decide whether or not there will be war or peace is Saddam Hussein, and all he has to do is give up these terrible weapons that he has used to kill fellow Arabs, fellow Muslims in that part of the world, and to step away from his past behavior which invaded neighboring countries. It was not the United States who invaded Kuwait; it was Iraq. It was not the United States that went to war with Iran; it was Iraq. It was not the United States that fired chemical weapons at Iran; it was Iraq. And it was not the United States that murdered innocent Iraqi citizens with chemical weapons; it was Iraq.

And so I think all of the attention of the world, to include the attention of the Arab world, should be on Saddam Hussein and whether or not he is prepared to give up the weapons of mass destruction that he has used to terrorize the region.

Q. And with due respect, sir, it seems to us that almost everyone's opinion in the Arab world, that even the Iraqi cooperation with the U.N. will continue, the U.S. will still go to war to remove Saddam next month. How accurate is this, and will you allow him to stay in power if he is proven disarmed by the inspectors?

Secretary Powell. It is not an accurate assessment. Nobody has ever said in the United States Government that we are going to war next month. No decision has been made by the President because, as he said to the United Nations, he wants the United Nations to live up to its responsibilities and he wants Saddam Hussein to cooperate.

The President has said repeatedly that the purpose of this is to disarm. And if he cooperates, not just cooperate to see how much he can get away with, but cooperate fully to turn over all the documents necessary, all the people who could be interviewed to get to the truth, and turn over all his capacity to develop weapons of mass destruction, if he does all that to the satisfaction of the international community, then there will be no war and the people of Iraq can decide who their leader should be.

Q. Okay. In the name of the Iraqi opposition—

Secretary Powell. But there's no doubt in my mind, though, that the Iraqi people would be better off with a different leader who did not waste their oil on weapons, as opposed to education, as opposed to healthcare, as opposed to food, as opposed to roads, as opposed to clean water. It is really sinful, a crime, what Saddam Hussein has done with the wealth of the Iraqi people over the last 30 years.

Q. I mean, we take it as what President Bush repeatedly said earlier this year, that it is a U.S. policy that the regime in Iraq has to go. So is this a change of policy now?

Secretary Powell. It was President Clinton and the United States Congress in 1998 which said that the regime has to be changed because the regime would not give up its weapons of mass destruction. We came into office in 2001 and kept that policy because Saddam Hussein had not changed.

We now believe it is appropriate for Saddam Hussein to be forced to change, either by the threat of war, and therefore that compels him to cooperate. If he cooperates, then the basis of changed regime policy has shifted because his regime has, in fact, changed its policy to one of cooperation. So if he cooperates, then that is different than if he does not cooperate.

Q. So removing Saddam, in itself, is no longer a U.S. policy as we take it?

Secretary Powell. It remains our policy to change the regime until such time as the regime changes itself. So far, we cannot be sure that he is cooperating or he is acting in a way that could give us comfort, or should give the international community comfort, that he is giving up his weapons of mass destruction. He continues to give us statements that suggest he is not in possession of weapons of mass destruction when we know he is.

So the burden is on him, not on us. The burden is on Saddam Hussein. And our policy, our national policy—not the U.N. policy but our national policy—is that the regime should be changed until such time as he demonstrates that it is not necessary to change the regime because the regime has changed itself. But we are not at that point, therefore I am not advocating, nor am I suggesting to you, that United States policy has changed.

Q. In light of the Iraqi opposition conference here in London, do you think that they can present a real alternative to Saddam? And who is going to be in power, as far as you are concerned, in Baghdad after Saddam goes?

Secretary Powell. It is not our place to decide who should lead the Iraqi people. If Saddam leaves or has to be forced out of power and a new regime brought in, a new leadership brought in, I am confident it will be some combination of people inside the country and outside the country.

I am pleased that the conference is taking place, but I would not presume from this distance, nor would America presume to say who should be the leader of the Iraqi nation.

What we would be committed to would be a representative government where all the Iraqi people decide who should lead their nation, and lead it in a way that keeps it together as a single nation and where all parts of the nation—Shia, Sunni and Kurds—are able to live free and in peace and believe that their interests are represented by the government.

Q. It seems that the Iraqi opposition enjoys varied degrees of credibility, even inside Washington. So as far as you are concerned, do you think they can provide reliable alternative to Saddam's regime, and would you rule out American military ruling of Iraq after Saddam?

Secretary Powell. It is not possible to rule out anything because we don't know what will happen. You know, I can't answer that because if military force is necessary, then military force will go in. But it is the U.S. Government's desire for the Iraqi people to lead themselves, not for any outside power to be the leadership for Iraq in the future. There may be some transition period where the international community would have to help the Iraqi people put in place a representative government. But that is the goal, not for the United States, or any other nation, for that matter, who might be in such a coalition, if one is formed, to serve as the leader of the Iraqi nation.

Remarks by Secretary of Defense Rumsfeld, December 12, 2002

Secretary Rumsfeld was interviewed by Dana Lewis on NBC's "Today" while visiting Qadar.

Q. Good morning, Matt. Defense Secretary Rumsfeld, at the end of a four-day, four-nation tour; as you say, I had the chance to sit down with him this morning, and he had this warning for any nation, including Iraq, that might threaten the United States with biological or chemical weapons.

Secretary Rumsfeld. Let there be no doubt that I and the president and others have let it be known, publicly and privately, to the Saddam Hussein regime that anyone who is involved in using weapons of mass destruction will wish they hadn't.

Q. And reports now suggest the U.S. has information Iraq may have supplied extremists connected to al Qaeda with chemical weapons.

Secretary Rumsfeld. I think what I can say publicly is that, as has been said by the Central Intelligence Agency and the president, there are al Qaeda connected to Iraq who have used that country, just as there are al Qaeda in Iran and Pakistan and the United States and other countries. And we also know that the al Qaeda and other terrorist networks have actively sought to gain access to chemical and biological and radiation weapons.

Q. No decision yet on war, says the Defense secretary. But the buildup of forces continues in the Gulf. In Qatar, a major war exercise to test Central Command's new mobile headquarters manned by a thousand troops normally stationed in Florida, today in one of 33 air-conditioned hangars to meet the Defense secretary and General Tommy Franks.

Washington says more and more Arab nations welcoming an American military presence.

Secretary Rumsfeld. We have been going out to countries believing that the credible use of force or the potential use of force would be a way to encourage the Iraqi regime to behave and to cooperate with the inspectors. We have gone out to countries across the globe and asked for their support in the event that it becomes necessary to have a coalition of countries disarm Iraq. And the response has been excellent. The numbers of countries coming in and offering assistance is very encouraging.

Remarks by Secretary of Defense Rumsfeld and U.S. Central Command Commander Franks, December 12, 2002

Secretary Donald Rumsfeld and General Tommy Franks delivered their remarks at Central Command Headquarters in Doha, Qatar.

Secretary Rumsfeld. It has been an excellent trip. There's no question but that in each stop the growing support for the global war on terrorism has been manifested. We have had excellent cooperation from each of those countries. And I was privileged last evening to join the foreign minister in signing an implementing agreement here that General Franks and his team have been working on.

I also, and I would say particularly, have had an opportunity to meet with U.S. and coalition forces, both here and in Djibouti. It has been a treat for me to be able to tell them how much they're appreciated and what a wonderful job those from the United States and those from coalition countries are doing for the cause of freedom. Their morale is high, and their capabilities are excellent.

One aspect of the stop here has been the opportunity to join General Franks in observing the Exercise Internal Look. It is an indication, I would say, of the readiness and the new capabilities that exist. And certainly General Franks and his team are doing an absolutely superb job, and we appreciate it.

General Franks. Well, Mr. Secretary, in fact it's a great honor for all of us—myself certainly, but also for these great men and women—to have you visit. And so I would say thank you for that.

You know, for more than two years now, we have talked a lot about transformation, and we have thought a lot about what transformation means. And we have thought about the way we field our assets, the way we train our people, the sorts of technologies we use and a great many other things.

The power of this exercise, Internal Look, in my view, has been that—or is that it is giving us an opportunity to get out at all those points.

You know, the doctrines that existed for our armed forces several years ago really don't apply to the first war of the 21st century. The fact is that we have the assets we have and what we are able to build, and we have the responsibility to train our people, to get the highest readiness that we can. And so we have had an opportunity here in Qatar to begin this Internal Look exercise, and have a chance to study our readiness, have a chance to look at our state of training. And I just have to tell you that up to this point, I'm very, very pleased with what I see.

And with that, sir, I guess I would offer that the secretary is ready to answer your questions.

Q. Mr. Secretary, can you comment on a published report today that said that an al Qaeda-linked group managed to get a chemical weapon inside Iraq in the past few months that may have been VX gas. This morning you suggested that you may have

seen information to that regard. Is there credible evidence that this happened and is this report accurate?

Secretary Rumsfeld. I am inclined not to discuss intelligence information.

Q. I have a question for General Franks. It's four days into Internal Look. Can you say today what the assessment is of that new forward command—[*inaudible*]?

General Franks. Yeah, thanks. I mentioned that 21st century and what we're look-ing at with the global war on terrorism means we have to think about the way we do our work in the military a bit differently.

What we know for sure is that enhanced flexibility provides my boss, and provides the president of the United States additional options with respect to where we're able to deploy, what the time lines for deployment look like. And so in fact, a bit more than a year ago, we started building this deployable command post. And being able to bring it into Qatar for Exercise Internal Look has given us an opportunity to do several things. One, it's given us an opportunity to pack up this brand new set of technology, which is absolutely cutting edge, state of the art, and move it several thousand miles, set it up again, and then train ourselves on how to use that.

I don't know about you, but each time we go from Microsoft something to Microsoft something else, you know, I go through a little training process. And so that's what this exercise continues, by the way, to be all about. We're just at the begin-ning of the exercise now. And as I said, I like what we see, I like the reaction of our peo-ple to the technology, and I like the performance of the technology.

Q. Secretary, notwithstanding the fact that Internal Look has been in the offing for some time, the activities of the U.S. military here in the Gulf in general have been thrown open to the media in the last week or 10 days, rather more than they were before. Are you pretty anxious to send a strong message to Iraq at this time?

Secretary Rumsfeld. I think that first of all, I didn't know that the activities had been thrown open to the press in an unusual way. So if anyone's trying to read signals from me, don't.

The—I think it's important to think of the setting six months ago. Six months ago, the Iraqis refused to have inspectors in their country; they were ignoring 16 resolu-tions of the United Nations.

Because of the potential for the use of force, and because of the initiative of the president of the United States going to the Congress and getting and overwhelming votes in both houses, and then going to the United Nations and getting a unanimous resolution from the Security Council, because of those activities and only because of those activities there now are inspectors in Iraq.

And it is the mix of diplomacy with a recognition, one would think, on the part of the Iraqis that—(music begins to play)—that's very nice—on the part of the Iraqis that has persuaded them that it is in their best interest to fulfill this request for a dec-laration, which they now have done, and to allow inspectors in. And only time will tell the extent to which they really are or are not going to cooperate.

But I think that it is very clear to me that had the president not gone to the Congress, and had he not gone to the United Nations, and had the United Nations not acted and had the Iraqis continue to believe that they could ignore 16 or 17 resolutions of the United Nations, that they would have had they believed that was possible. They now believe it is not possible, which is why you're beginning to see at least a declaration and inspectors in their country.

Q. I have two questions, one for Mr. Secretary. You talked about—you talked many times about the connection between Iraq and [*al Qaeda ?*]. Do you have real evidence about that?

Secretary Rumsfeld. The truth is, I have not talked many times about that. What I did do some weeks back was, because I was being asked questions by people like you about that linkage, and I thought, my goodness, I will see if I can provide some unclassified information that might be helpful on that question. So I contacted the Central Intelligence Agency and received a single sheet of paper with four or five points on it. In response to a question, not at my initiation, I responded, and I read precisely what the Central Intelligence Agency had declassified. I happen to know a lot of classified information, but I don't talk about classified information. And literally, the sum total of anything I have ever said on the subject is in that one piece of paper.

Q. Last week President Bush said that Iraq is already in violation—[*inaudible*] by firing on U.S. planes in the no-fly zones. You said this morning that we needed to give it time. Has the U.S. softened its position on Iraq?

Secretary Rumsfeld. No. The position of the president is the position of the United States. The reason the president said what he said—because that's what the resolution says. The resolution, if you'll go back and read the U.N. resolution, cited a series of things that could be considered further material breach, not an initial material breach, but a further material breach. Just in plain English, that means that they stand in material breach the day the resolution was passed. So I don't think there was anything distinctive about what the president said, except to reiterate what the resolution said.

And what I have said is—I said—you say I said, "Be patient." That's not my nature—to be patient. But the truth is that a declaration that is in thousands of pages, in two languages, has just arrived in the early part of this week in the hands of the members of the Security Council. It seems to me not unreasonable to allow people to look at it, read it, analyze it and see what we think about it. And if that means be patient, it—I think I would characterize it, I suppose, as it means being reasonable.

This thing has been served up. It is now in many countries, being examined and looked at and thought about. And I suspect that the people that are doing that—I'm obviously not one of them doing it. There's an interagency committee in the United States that's working on it. I'm here, so I don't know what it says. And I don't think it's really possible to know, in a matter of hours or days, what that document represents, whether it represents a degree of cooperation or whether it's another example of a lack of cooperation. And I just simply don't know.

Q. Secretary, last month the Arab League voted against any use of force in Iraq. However, many Gulf states are specifically hosting military bases. Do you think that specifically the Gulf nations are caught in a Catch-22 where they're appeasing the Arab League and appeasing the United States?

Secretary Rumsfeld. Oh, goodness, I wouldn't put it that way. It seems to me that each country is a sovereign country that can make up their own judgments as to how they want to conduct themselves. And we have excellent cooperation from any number of states here in the Gulf and from around the world. If you think about it, the global war on terrorism now has over 90 countries involved. If you further think about it, the resolution that passed in the United Nations was unanimous, and there were countries in that unanimity that would fit into the description you've just indicated.

Remarks by Secretary of Defense Rumsfeld, December 12, 2002

Secretary Donald Rumsfeld delivered his remarks at a Town Hall Meeting with American troops in Doha, Qatar.

Clearly one of the best parts of my job as Secretary of Defense is to be able to get out of that office, come to places like this and have a chance to look folks in the eye and say personally how much we appreciate what you're doing.

There's no question but that the folks in this room, this hall, and others who are standing and defending freedom all across the globe are people who weren't drafted, you weren't conscripted, you volunteered. You stepped forward and said that this calling is important and that you want to be a part of it. And indeed, it is important.

The attack on September 11th that killed thousands of innocent men, women and children from dozens of countries of all religions was a jolt to the United States. They were devastating to be sure, those attacks, yet if one thinks about it what took place was unconventional in its approach but conventional in what was done. What we face today is something far worse. That is the connection between terrorist states and terrorist networks and weapons of mass destruction. Weapons capable of killing not just hundreds or thousands of people, but literally tens of thousands or hundreds of thousands of people.

It means that the 21st Century is a different time. It is a distinctly different security environment. Our Department of Defense, our country is in the process of transforming itself to fit those new threats and those new capabilities that exist in the world.

The objective, indeed your mission in the global war on terror, is to see that attacks of that magnitude, of that lethality don't happen.

Our task is to disrupt the terrorist networks, to deal with states that are providing haven for terrorists and terrorist networks, to do everything humanly possible to see that they do not get their hands on chemical, biological, radiation or nuclear weapons.

So let there be no doubt. You are what stands between our people, the American people, free people all over the world, and an evil that cannot be appeased, that cannot be ignored, and must not be allowed to win. You're doing a great job at it. It's appreciated. It's appreciated by me and it's recognized by the American people, you can be sure of that.

It certainly is not easy to be this far from home during a holiday season—at any time, but particularly during the holiday season. It's tough on some of you to be sure, it's also tough on your families and we recognize that. They suffer the same distance, they suffer the same separation, and it's important for all of us to recognize that they sacrifice and in a very real way they serve as well. So our gratitude goes to you, it goes to your families.

The President made a promise to the nation shortly after September 11th. He said that after the attacks on September 11th that we will not waiver, we will not tire, we will not falter, and we as a people will not fail.

And you're the ones that are delivering on that promise that the President made. Looking at each of you, I know that that promise will be kept.

So thank you for all you do. You have my best wishes.

What I'd like to do now is to see if I can persuade General Franks to come back up here so that the two of us can respond to questions that you might have.

What I will do as an ex-professional politician is respond skillfully to those I can answer, and I'll defer to General Franks the tough ones that I can't.

Q. History will recall that the OPEC Cartel is not the best friend of the United States and the Western world. The oil-producing nations of the local region vastly profit from U.S. agenda and energy interests on astronomical terms. The United States [*inaudible*] foreign policy towards this part of the world as the [boss] of international terrorism, inadvertent as that may be.

Secretary Rumsfeld. Let me walk around the second part of that question sideways.

There are a lot of people in the world who think that our interest in the Middle East is oil and that there's a great deal going on in connection with the war on terrorism that relates to oil, and I'm not one of them.

My view is fairly simplistic on the subject. Oil is a commodity. Countries that have it are going to want to sell it because they can make money off of it. And we as a country can have a foreign policy that fits our values, that fits our relationships around the world, that fits our economic interests and it need not be rooted in oil. The fact of the matter is that when the dust settles, whoever owns oil is going to want to sell it and oil-using countries will want to buy it, and there will be a world price and a world market and I think it's a misunderstanding to think that the United States interests in this part of the globe begins and ends with oil because it isn't true and it doesn't fit the economics.

Q. We saw on the news today about President Bush ordering the smallpox vaccination for the military. About when are these vaccinations expected to begin and when can we expect to have them completed?

Secretary Rumsfeld. The answer is that I approved the use of a smallpox vaccine some days ago and they're in the process of implementing a program which will make it available first to first responders—medical-type people who would be handling any sort of an outbreak with respect to smallpox. And then it will be made, in fairly close proximity to that it will be made available to people who are in the parts of the world where there is a possible risk of a smallpox epidemic. In terms of the actual number, weeks and days, I can't tell you. But it is being tracked and it will be moving along through the armed forces.

Simultaneously the President is addressing the matter from the civilian standpoint, working with the Department of Health and Human Services and they will have a program there to make the smallpox vaccine available to the American people as well.

Q. What are your respective assessments thus far of Iraq's level of cooperation in the ongoing weapons inspection.

Secretary Rumsfeld. This is off the record.

Let me say this about that. Comma.

We are at an early stage. If you think back a few weeks and months no one was interested in the problems in Iraq and the development of weapons of mass destruction in the United Nations. The President called it to the world's attention. Went to the Congress, received overwhelming support. Went to the United Nations and received a unanimous vote in the United Nations on the new resolution.

And as a result of that we find that there are inspectors going back into Iraq and Iraq is in the process of responding to one of the stipulations in that resolution, namely filing a declaration with the United Nations. It arrived last weekend, as I recall. It is lengthy. It could be anywhere from 12,000 to 24,000 pages including annexes. It's partly in Arabic, partly in English. There is an interagency team in Washington that's in the process of translating it and examining it. There also are interagency efforts taking place in several other countries to do exactly the same thing.

As this plays out, very likely what will happen is the United States will begin discussions with other members of the Security Council that have been examining that declaration to determine what they think about it. To what extent has it or has it not fulfilled the obligation in the unanimous U.N. Resolution? Is it inclusive? Does it in fact set forth all of the WMD activities and programs and capabilities that Iraq currently has, or does it not?

I think just in fairness to the process, it would be kind of out of line for me to opine as to what I think it might prove to be. Time will tell. In a relatively short period of weeks, I suspect, people will have had enough to look at it, think about it, analyze it, and then discuss it with other countries and then come to some conclusions. That is one indication of cooperation or lack of cooperation.

A second indication of cooperation or lack of cooperation is the fact that there are some inspectors currently in the country.

A third indication would be the provision in the Resolution that said that the inspectors may take Iraqis out of the country with their families so that they will be free to talk and say what they know about Iraq's weapons of mass destruction program. That has not yet happened. That, needless to say, will be an indication of cooperation or lack of cooperation.

Most of what has been discovered in prior inspection regimes has been provided to the inspectors not by a discovery process on the ground in Iraq, but rather by defectors, people who got out of the country and knew where the weapons were, knew what the capabilities were, knew where the documentation was, and told the outsiders that that's the case.

The two most prominent defectors were sons-in-laws of Saddam Hussein who when they returned to Iraq were brutally murdered.

A third example of cooperation or lack of cooperation might be considered whether or not the Iraqis continue to fire on coalition airplanes and air crews in the Northern and Southern No-Fly Zones, and as all of you know, they are continuing to fire on coalition air crews in both the North and the South.

White House Press Briefing, December 13, 2002

Q. U.N. officials, diplomats who have gone over the declaration, again a preliminary assessment, are saying that there are some pretty glaring omissions. Do you view this as more game playing, more deception by Iraq? And if so, how long does the administration intend to let it go on?

Mr. Fleischer. Well, we've always said that we want to carefully review the document in terms of reviewing not only what is in it, but what is not in it. That review is still going on, and I think that, given the President's desire to have this in totality and to address this in a more comprehensive way and in a very thoughtful and deliberative way, I don't think it would be appropriate for me to comment on these preliminary reports that you're hearing from others, including the United Nations.

Q. I have two questions, one a follow. Given that the world does seem to be speaking out, saying there are holes in this report, you say you need to complete your own review. But is this speeding up the time frame, do you think, in which the U.S. will respond, rather than taking as long to perhaps act now while others are saying there's a lot of holes here in this document?

Mr. Fleischer. On your first question, because this is such a serious matter and because the content of what Iraq says in this declaration and what they don't say in this declaration has important implications for war and peace, the United States will take as much time as necessary to do it right, and we will continue to be deliberative and to be thoughtful as we review this document.

And the President will, as I indicated, at the appropriate time in his judgment, share with the United States and people of the world what he thinks about Iraq's declaration. But because of the importance of this, the President will await. And while others are free to speak out as they see fit, and to give preliminary judgments, the President looks forward to, at the appropriate time, giving a more comprehensive judgment based on all the information, not just the preliminary information.

Q. But isn't time of the essence here? Like the quicker you can get moving in a winter time frame if, indeed, the U.S. decides to act, isn't it better to get going rather than taking—

Mr. Fleischer. The President is going to be guided by a time line that allows for the greatest deliberation and the greatest thought. That's the guideline that will direct the President.

Q. Ari, there have been reports that Iraq has been able to obtain several million doses of atropine over the last several months through the U.N. Oil for Food Program, as it's properly known. Is the White House concerned about this? Are you checking into how it happened and who's responsible?

Mr. Fleischer. Well, I think the reason it happened is there's a goods review list and the goods review list is being continually reviewed itself to make certain that it's as tight as can be, recognizing the dual use nature of many of the products that do get bought for legitimate purposes. And if something is not covered on the dual use list, the reason is because the world, through the United Nations, which imposes the sanctions on Iraq, has made the decision or the determination that it should not be a prohibited product. That's how it was able to be purchased.

We do have concerns about this, and this is something we continue to talk to the United Nations about as the periodic reviews of the goods review list come up.

Q. Can I continue just one little second? Given what atropine is used for, as a counter to chemical weapons, what does—does this have any message, you think? Or does this underline our concerns that Iraq does, indeed, have—

Mr. Fleischer. It does. Its purchase gives us reason to be concerned about Iraq's development of chemical weapons or biological weapons. And that's why we have concerns about this.

Q. Administration officials—Dr. Rice, Ambassador Negroponte—have been talking with Hans Blix in recent days about using the provision of the Security Council resolution that allows interviews out of Iraq of Iraqi scientists. Are you confident you have convinced him to utilize that provision of the resolution? And have you dealt with his concerns, all of his concerns about doing so?

Mr. Fleischer. We will continue to work productively with the inspectors and with Hans Blix and General ElBaradei. It's very important that the United States and the international community work together to address the problems inside Iraq. And history has shown that one of the most effective ways to judge what Iraq is up to is by talking to the people who are involved in the weapons development programs.

And history has also shown that there are Iraqis who want to talk. And that's why the resolution passed by the United Nations includes a provision that facilities the ability of Iraqis to leave the country with their families to talk to the United Nations so that peace can be kept. And this provision was put in there because experience has shown that the Iraqi regime does not want people to talk and that, when they find people who talk, they kill them. And that is why the provision was put in, to allow people and their families to leave Iraq. And that is often one of the best ways to obtain information from people who want to provide information so that we can keep the peace. So it's an important provision.

Q. Dr. Blix has substantial concerns about it. Are you confident that these interviews will take place?

Mr. Fleischer. Well, again, I have never since the inspectors went back into Iraq tried to analyze every day's activities. The United States has focused on this in a very fundamental way to make certain that the entire regime is effective and working. And we are confident that, in working with the United Nations, and working through the international community, the resolution will be enforced.

White House Press Briefing, December 16, 2002

Q. On Iraq, how would you characterize where they are at the moment? And would you clarify what responsibility we believe the Iraqis have, not just to disclose what they have, but to prove what happened to the stuff they used to have?

Mr. Fleischer. Well, the administration is continuing to take a look at the declaration that Iraq has provided. And I think other nations will also be weighing in on their views of what Iraq has provided. Hans Blix will be talking about what Iraq has provided. And this is all appropriately so, under the terms of the resolution 1441, which sent the inspectors back into Iraq.

The declaration Iraq prepared was for the use of the members of the United Nations Security Council, and they will all be making their thoughts known shortly. The United States is continuing to review it. And as I indicated this morning, at the appropriate time, if we have something to say you'll be advised of when that would be.

The President thinks it's very important at this time for Iraq to show the world that it is serious about peace, and that at this time they take their determination from the United Nations Security Council clearly, and that they do, indeed, produce a document that is full, complete and accurate.

Q. But isn't there a greater responsibility than just saying, here's what we've got or what we don't have. Don't they also have to prove to the inspectors what happened to the things that they once had that were declared and to make sure that everyone knows how it is that they eliminated the WMD—if, in fact, they did—the WMD capability that they had?

Mr. Fleischer. This is one of the issues that the declaration will shed light upon. It will be part of the review of the declaration to see what is not in it, and to match it up against previous declarations, particularly the United Nations—the UNSCOM report in 1999, which right before they were thrown out or right after they were thrown out they did the final reporting on what they knew at the time that they were thrown out of Iraq. And it will be important and it will shed some light on whether Iraq is telling the truth or not, to see what Iraq has said in this declaration and compare it to their past promises for what they have indeed destroyed.

Q.—Hans Blix may be in New York this week to brief on the status of the inspections. Do you anticipate that he will also brief the U.S. separately, or he'll come and talk to the President about how things are going?

Mr. Fleischer. Well, he has repeatedly talked to many of the nations on the Security Council, especially the P-5. If there is something, we'll obviously report it to you. But I'm not aware of any meeting at this point.

Q. And after he briefs the Council this week—I guess he said mid-week—is there some anticipation that moving through the next stage in the process of some sort of diplomatic consultations after that, or what happens after that?

Mr. Fleischer. Well, I don't want to make any guesses or predictions yet. We're still, as the United States, in the process of still looking at the document. And so I think we want to come to our assessments about what is in it and what is not in it before we can anticipate what the next step would possibly be.

* * * *

Q. Ari, is the United States receiving any cooperation from the government of Iran regarding Saddam Hussein? And also, what are your thoughts on the Iraqi dissidents meeting in London? They haven't exactly been unified in their—

Mr. Fleischer. On the Iraqi dissidents meeting in London, as you know, the legislation passed by the Congress several years ago for regime change did call for the United States to work very closely with the Iraqi groups that are dedicated to a different type of leadership in Iraq. The conference took place this weekend, and the United States has sent a very clear message to people in this conference, as well as to people around the world, and that is that we support a democratically oriented Iraq, an Iraq that is whole, that's borders and integrity remains intact—the integrity of the borders remain intact. And we look forward to working with Iraqis both inside and outside the government to make this reality.

Q. What is a democratically oriented country?

Mr. Fleischer. Democratically inclined, is what I said, and that means we understand that the way to make progress in the world is by representing the will of the people, and not through dictatorships, not people who are autocratic and dictatorial. So when I say that, democratically inclined, it means a leadership that is respectful of the will of the people.

Q. But not necessarily democratically elected?

Mr. Fleischer. Well, obviously, that is always the ideal around the world. Ultimately, the President believes that every nation in the world should be democratically elected. That is the best measure of serving the will of the people. But there's also a reality to the world, and we recognize that. But our goals and our vision, of course, remain the same about the President's ideals.

Q. Also about Iran—is Iran helping at all?

Mr. Fleischer. I'd have to ask specifically on that topic. That's a very broad question, so let me ask specifically on that topic for you.

Q. Is the White House still confident that Iraqi scientists will be interviewed outside of the country? And is Hans Blix cooperating in that effort?

Mr. Fleischer. We continue to have fruitful conversations with—we continue to have fruitful conversations with the United Nations about the full implementation of Resolution 1441. That is an important part of Resolution 1441, as passed unanimously by all members of the Security Council. The reason the United States feels so strongly about this is because this often is the best way to find out what Iraq is really up to.

There are people inside Iraq who are dedicated to peace, who would like to talk, have knowledge that they would like to share, and it's in the interests of the world to hear their facts.

Remarks by Secretary of State Powell and Japanese Foreign Minister Kawaguchi, December 16, 2002

Secretary Colin Powell and Minister Yoriko Kawaguchi delivered their remarks after meeting in Washington, DC.

Q. Mr. Secretary, can you offer an evaluation of the 12,000-page document that the Iraqis gave to the U.N. based on the U.S. assessment of these documents? And if Iraq isn't forthcoming in providing lists of scientists or access to scientists, is this a redline issue for this government?

Secretary Powell. We have been analyzing the declaration for a week now, and we have received some preliminary reports, but the analysis is continuing and I will wait for the task force working on it to complete their work before making a definitive statement.

We said at the very beginning that we approached it with skepticism, and the information I have received so far is that that skepticism is well founded. There are problems with the declaration. We are sharing the problems we see with UNMOVIC and IAEA and we are in discussions with the other permanent members of the Security Council.

But we will withhold making a final judgment or final statement until we have completed our analysis, completed our discussions with UNMOVIC and IAEA and our colleagues on the permanent membership of the Security Council, and then statements will be forthcoming, I expect, toward the end of the week after Dr. Blix makes his presentation to the Security Council on Thursday.

The Resolution 1441 provides for those who need to be interviewed to be made available, and if Iraq does not comply with that requirement of the resolution, I'm sure the international community will take note and decide what action is appropriate. But I would not like to characterize what might or might not happen in the future at this point.

Q. A question for all of you. My question is as follows, and that is Japan's coordination regarding the Iraqi situation. The four of you, in your respective initial remarks, did refer to Iraq. In case new international cooperation is needed vis—vis Iraqi situation, I understand you confirmed in your meeting that Japan and U.S. will engage in close coordination. When you speak of new international cooperation, I believe you envisage military action against Iraq.

If that military action against Iraq becomes inevitable, Japan has various legal constraints, and therefore cannot have its self-defense forces participate in combat action. So I wonder what sort of assistance U.S. considers would be appropriate by Japan or what sort of assistance the U.S. would hope to get from Japan, and I wonder what sort of support Japan considers it possible to provide.

Secretary Powell. President Bush, and I think all world leaders, hope that this matter can be resolved peacefully. But if Iraq does not cooperate and, once again, violates a U.N. resolution, then I believe the international community has an obligation to act and do whatever is necessary to disarm Iraq of its weapons of mass destruction, and that includes the use of military force.

It remains to be seen whether Iraq will cooperate. It remains to be seen what the U.N. will do in the absence of cooperation.

With respect to what Japan might or might not do, consistent with their basic laws and their constitution, that's an issue I really must yield to my colleague to address and I would not speculate other than to say that we are in the closest coordination and it is up to the Government of Japan and the people of Japan to determine how they might respond in the face of a mandate from the international community to do something about Iraq's lack of cooperation.

Foreign Minister Kawaguchi. In our meeting today, as I mentioned earlier, we exchanged our views on Iraq, and of course a peaceful resolution is most desirable, but if further action by the international community would become necessary in accordance with the Security Council resolution, then our two countries will engage an even closer coordination. That is what we said.

As far as Japan is concerned, should there be material breach of the U.N. resolution, and military action becomes inevitable, then what response would Japan take? Now, in the first place, we have to remember that the problem is caused by the weapons of mass destruction of Iraq and the proliferation of weapons of mass destruction. So Japan sees this as a challenge for the entire international community. Japan, as a responsible member of the international community, needs to consider what action, what response will be appropriate for Japan as a responsible member of the international community. And we have to decide on that with our own initiative, support for refugee, support for the neighboring countries around Iraq. These are possible areas we will have to take into consideration—these and other options. And we are, in fact, currently considering all sorts of possibilities.

We communicated this to the U.S. side. A special envoy of the Prime Minister visited neighboring countries of Iraq. At that time, the special envoy explained that in case there is military action, refugee assistance and assistance for the neighboring countries would be necessary, or rather, these were the points raised by the neighboring countries. So we'll keep in mind various possibilities.

White House Press Statement, December 17, 2002

We applaud the results of the conference that concluded today. This was a broad-based gathering of free Iraqis opposed to the tyrannical regime in Baghdad. Free Iraqis came together in this conference to accomplish two objectives: to agree on a statement setting forth their vision of the future of Iraq; and to form a follow-up advisory committee. They accomplished both these objectives. The conference represents a strong statement of aspirations of Iraqis inside Iraq and throughout the world for a better future. We support these aspirations, and we look forward to working together with all Iraqis to achieve them.

White House Press Briefing, December 17, 2002

Q. Has the President issued an unlawful order to the CIA to commit assassinations?

Mr. Fleischer. Helen, are you saying has the President issued an unlawful order? The answer is, no.

Q. Do you see a story on Sunday about assassinations?

Mr. Fleischer. I heard your question about has the President done something that's against the law.

Q. Okay, the question is, has he issued an order on assassinations?

Mr. Fleischer. I do not discuss any of the directives that the President may issue.

Q. So you won't answer the question?

Mr. Fleischer. I never discuss intelligence directives and whether or not they exist or don't exist.

Q. Well, it would it be unlawful if it were an order on assassinations.

Mr. Fleischer. I assure you the President would not do anything that is against the law.

Q. Just a quick follow-up, does the executive order President Ford signed prohibiting the United States from assassinations stand?

Mr. Fleischer. Yes, it does.

Q. Okay, one quick question on Iraq. You talked about this being a success, the meeting of the opposition. As I understand it, though, some of the groups actually walked out, saying they were not represented and were not wanted. What can you tell us about that?

Mr. Fleischer. I think if you take a look at what was done in the conference, that you will see that this conference represented a strong statement of Iraqi aspirations for a better future. We support those aspirations and we look forward to working with Iraqis both inside and outside Iraq to achieve those objectives.

Q. You have to judge that. The LA Times today published a poll that found that 72 percent of Americans, including 60 percent of Republicans, said the President has not provided enough evidence to justify starting a war with Iraq. Is the President losing the public relations battle here in the United States?

Mr. Fleischer. Well, one, I think that I'll just state what is well known. The President will not make any decision about war and peace and the possibility of putting some of our nation's best men and women in harm's way on the basis of a poll. He will do it on the basis of his judgment as Commander-in-Chief and what it will take to save and protect American lives in the event that he reaches the conclusion Saddam Hussein will indeed engage in war against the United States or provide terrorists with weapons to engage in war against the United States, just like on September 11th with the attack. And if he reaches that judgment, he will do so because the information he has and the judgment he makes suggest that, not because of a poll.

I think it's also fair to say that when you take a look at a variety of ways to measure public opinion, you will see different things out there in the public. The Pew Research Institution has done work on this topic and has come to very different conclusions. So the President will not make judgments based on polls, he'll make judgments based on what he believes is right.

Remarks by United Nations Secretary-General Annan, December 17, 2002

Q. A quick question, Sir. How serious a problem will it be if, in their declaration, the Iraqis do not resolve some of the outstanding questions that UNSCOM and former weapons inspectors still say remain?

Secretary-General Annan. Well, I think as I've said before, we need to give Mr. Blix and [Mr.] ElBaradei time to analyze these documents. They will be giving on to the [Security] Council the cleaned-up versions of the documents. And then they will analyze it, synthesize it, and brief the Council. I think we should all wait for that. I don't want to speculate as to what UNSCOM did or did not do or which gaps UNSCOM had. UNMOVIC has a mandate and they should carry on with it.

Q. On the subject of Iraqi scientists, what should happen if they are not forthcoming with the names, or don't allow them to be interviewed outside the country?

Secretary-General Annan. That will be up to the Council to decide. I know that Mr. Blix and [Mr.] ElBaradei, who is joining him here this week, are thinking through that problem, and obviously, would want to interview Iraqi scientists either in Iraq or if they decide to come out—they will interview them out—outside the country. But I would say we should leave them to determine how to proceed. I know there's lots of debate on this. And we should not speculate as to what the government will do or not do. If they do ask to see the scientists and want to interview them, I hope they'll be able to do it inside or outside. But of course, this is something that the inspectors will have to resolve on the ground.

Q. Sir, are you satisfied that the Americans are providing to the U.N., evidence that they say that would show that there is significant holes in the document?

Secretary-General Annan. The information is not being given to me directly. They have to give it to the inspectors. And I think, again, I will wait to hear what [Messrs.] Blix and ElBaradei have to report.

Q. May I just ask a follow-up to that, of how critical Thursday becomes in your mind? This is the first time for UNMOVIC and IAEA to give some sort of initial analysis or judgement. How critical is Thursday?

Secretary-General Annan. I think it's important in the sense that they are giving these documents to all the 15 members. But I think the actual analysis is going to come later.

Remarks by Secretary of Defense Rumsfeld, December 18, 2002

Secretary Donald Rumsfeld was interviewed on CNN's "Larry King Live."

Q. And the question everyone—well, senior administration officials are saying, Mr. Secretary, that the president is poised to say that Iraq has failed to provide a complete and accurate accounting of weapons. Is that true?

Secretary Rumsfeld. Well, I think I'll let the president make the announcement that he may or may not make, Larry. But I think it is pretty clear from the people who have had a chance to take a look at the documents that they are still trying to find things in them that they expected to be there that weren't there, but—

Q. What are they saying in 12,000 pages?

Secretary Rumsfeld. Well, I have not seen it. I've been out of the country in the Horn of Africa and in the Gulf—the Persian Gulf, and I just came back very recently. But there's an interagency team that's been looking at it, and Secretary of State Powell has made some comments about what he has heard from the people who've been seeing it through and trying to find out what, in fact, they've declared.

My guess is that the United States will take some time and will talk to some of our friends and allies around the world about the declaration and share ideas and thoughts about what's in it and what may not be in it.

Q. Will—Mr. Secretary, will the public be told before action commences what exactly we know they have?

Secretary Rumsfeld. The [— first of all, the president has made no decision about—but] it's important to emphasize that, because I think there is so much talk about Iraq that one doesn't want to get ahead of the facts.

I think that there's a dilemma there, and it is this: That you have a variety of sources who gather intelligence. Some are from human beings, some are from other technical means. And to the extent you reveal something that you know through intelligence gathering, you run the risk of compromising the human beings who gave you that information, and people can get killed if it's traceable back to them.

And you also can compromise—that is to say reduce the value of—the technical methods you're using, because people can—the Iraqis can say, well, if they know that, they must know it's through these means. And in which case, your access to that information is closed off or other types of information.

The second problem with it is that if there were to be a conflict, those—you would need to use those means of intelligence gathering and to the—

Q. Further.

Secretary Rumsfeld.—further, and to the extent they were closed off. So, one has to exercise great care about what is said and what is not said.

Q. So, that requires on the part of the public total trust.

Secretary Rumsfeld. No, not at all. There's a great deal of information that's available, and I think that most people who've spent any time thinking about this and looking at what the Iraqis have done and revealing how they handled themselves in previous inspection situations, and read the U.K.'s—the United Kingdom's dossier which was released by Tony Blair, Prime Minister Tony Blair, knows pretty well that the Iraqis have had very active weapons of mass destruction programs.

Q. Honestly, Mr. Secretary, what do they have to do? What do they have to do to stop this?

Secretary Rumsfeld. The Iraqis?

Q. Yes.

Secretary Rumsfeld. Well, it's a wonderful question, and it's the right question. There's a certain way that things get skewed around, suggesting that somebody has to prove that they have these. The U.N. resolution says they have to prove they don't. That is what the resolution said. It said, look, we've got enough evidence to know that you've been developing nuclear and chemical and biological weapons. And the United Nations has passed these previous resolutions, and you've agreed not to do that, Iraq, but here you are continuing to do it.

Now, we're giving you a final opportunity to show us what you've got, admit what you've got, declare what you have, allow inspectors in so that they can see what you have, and give them freedom to roam throughout the country. But that only works if there's a cooperative country, if Iraq is cooperative and decides, yes, the game's up. We're going to let them come in, we're going to show them what we have and we want the world to know that. That's when you invite inspectors in. But if it's cat and mouse and hide and seek, it will never work.

Q. So, they have to turn over a new leaf.

Secretary Rumsfeld. Indeed. The other option they have is to leave the country. I mean, Saddam Hussein and his family could—

Q. Exile.

Secretary Rumsfeld. Why sure. I mean, if he doesn't care to give up his weapons of mass destruction, then he's got the choice of leaving.

Q. Is there an end game to this?

Secretary Rumsfeld. Well, the end game that the United Nations expressed in that unanimous Security Council resolution was that the Iraqi regime disarm, and that they prove that they have disarmed.

Q. And then, Saddam stays?

Secretary Rumsfeld. Well, that's a separate issue, I guess. The position of the Congress of the United States and the United States has been for four, five, six years—four or five years, I guess, that the only way you can achieve disarmament, given his past record is if there is a regime change.

Q. Now, this is an if, but General Richard Myers yesterday—I want to quote him correctly—said that it's very difficult to know how Iraqi troops will behave this time, don't go on the Gulf War previously, and that we could be—this will not be a cake walk. True?

Secretary Rumsfeld. He was asked in a press briefing with me that if he thought it was going to be a cake walk, and he properly said, look, war is not a cake walk. War is tough, people get killed, and it's dangerous and things happen. And we know he has weapons of mass destruction, we've known he's used those weapons on his own people and on the Iranians in previous periods.

And his answer was correct, this is not 1991 or '90, it's not the Gulf War. It's the year 2002. In some ways, the Iraqi regime is much weaker militarily and conventional capability. In weapons of mass destruction, one has to believe they are much stronger. So, it is a dangerous business, and he is engaged in a dangerous game.

Q. You going to take a smallpox vaccination?

Secretary Rumsfeld. Sure.

Q. Is every major official going to?

Secretary Rumsfeld. No.

Q. (inaudible) the president, but you are.

Secretary Rumsfeld. Well, I certainly intend to, simple because it's hard to ask people to do something that you're not willing to yourself. But, no, I mean, we've got people here who have no reason to be using up vaccination serum unless they prefer to.

Q. But the fear is logical to you, too.

Secretary Rumsfeld. I've spent a lot of time thinking this through, and a smallpox epidemic is so vicious and kills so many people so rapidly and spreads far and wide that after a great deal of thought, I concluded that the U.S. military people who have vulnerability—potential vulnerability—ought to take it. And unless a person has some weakened immune system, the statistics are such that I think that the balance is appropriate and that the men and women in uniform who might be deployed in areas of vulnerability will be doing it.

Q. If they had enough and spread it enough, could they change the course of a war with smallpox?

Secretary Rumsfeld. There was an unclassified exercise done by Johns Hopkins, I believe, and it had been a year or two or three, called I believe Dark Winter. And they postulated a smallpox attack in three cities in America, and within a relatively short period of months, the numbers of people to be killed were up in the hundreds of thousands.

Q. The *Washington Post* says the chiefs of two United States ground forces are challenging belief of some senior Pentagon civilians that Saddam would fall almost immediately upon being attacked. They're calling for more attention to worst-case scenarios. Where do you balance this?

Secretary Rumsfeld. I've not heard a senior Pentagon official—civilian or military—suggest that there would be that kind of initial collapse. Every conceivable option is looked at, and two service chiefs who were cited in the article, I've met with them, the president has met with them, the chairman and the vice chairman have met with, and they are fully aware without any question or ambiguity and have told the president precisely what they think and told me precisely what they think. And the implication in that story I think is simply not accurate.

Q. When a free country is preparing for what might be action, how many things do you read or hear or see that are wrong?

Secretary Rumsfeld. Oh, my goodness, you can't imagine the number of things you see and hear that are wrong. It is just breathtaking how much misinformation floats around. I guess it's part of our free society—

Q. Are you surprised by it?

Secretary Rumsfeld. Well—

Q. Is there more of it now?

Secretary Rumsfeld. Oh, sure. We've got 24-hour news. Back 25 years ago when I was in this Pentagon, we didn't have anything like this all-day, constant, the numbers of newspapers, the numbers of editions, the numbers of radio and television stations, the numbers of hours and the appetite for information. So, it's not surprising. It is. Think of the number of people that are talking and heard and writing and on television.

Q. Daily.

Secretary Rumsfeld. Daily, every day, every hour. And of course, their access to information is modest for the most part in terms of classified information.

I must say, it just amazes me when I look at the newspaper once in a while and think, my goodness, here are all of these wonderful people out there reading that, thinking that's true. It isn't so.

Q. Well, as a servant of the public, taxpayers pay you, what do you owe them?

Secretary Rumsfeld. You owe them—the—you owe them an investment of time, which I try to do. I'm here with you.

Q. Correct.

Secretary Rumsfeld. And I think it's important. There's no question that the people who serve the public have a responsibility to do the best they can to provide information to the American people and to the world. I need to communicate with the men and women in uniform. I need to communicate with the civilians in the Department of Defense, with the Congress, with the executive branch.

So, we have an obligation to do that, and we owe them the truth, and we owe them as much information that does not jeopardize military activities.

Q. And how much access—they complain, many in the press complain that this— under your administration of the Department of Defense, less access is provided than any other.

Secretary Rumsfeld. I think that's—first of all, it's not clear to me that people— that if you dropped a plumb line through the press that they would say that. I don't believe they would say that.

White House Press Briefing, December 19, 2002

Q. Ari, do you have any sense yet of the tenor of Hans Blix's briefing to the Security Council? And is the administration satisfied with the content of his briefing?

Mr. Fleischer. The Security Council meeting continues at—in New York. And once the portion of the meeting is concluded, Mr. Blix, I am advised, will go out and discuss with the press that which he said in the private meeting. So I think I have to yield and allow Mr. Blix to speak. Then the United States Ambassador to the United Nations Negroponte and then Secretary Powell will speak.

Q. But certainly, you've got some sense of what he's going to say. Is the administration convinced that he—that he shares the administration position on the declaration?

Mr. Fleischer. Let me put it this way to be as helpful as I can while being respectful of the fact that Mr. Blix deserves the right to make his remarks known, I think that it will become increasingly clear that the world community—including the United Nations—sees omissions in the Iraqi document. At a time when the United Nations Security Council and the United States and all member states of the Security Council were looking to Iraq to provide a full complete and accurate description of their weapons programs. There is a wide recognition that Iraq has not done that. There are omissions and there are problems.

Q. One more on this. Do you feel, does the administration feel like the weapons inspectors do have a larger role to play when it comes to disproving this declaration? Or, is the burden not on them at all? Is their primary function, in the President's mind, to recruit Saddam's weapons scientists at this point?

Mr. Fleischer. The President feels very strongly that the burden is on Saddam Hussein. Saddam Hussein must cooperate with the inspectors. The President believes, as the inspectors themselves have often said, that they have a very difficult task, particularly if Iraq does not cooperate, particularly if Iraq does not declare full information, and if Iraq hides the information they have, or if Iraq omits information from the declaration.

The President thinks the mission of the inspectors includes both inspections to find whatever can be found, given Iraq's attempts to deceive and to hide, as well as to interview scientists and people involved in the weapons program. Those are both part of their mission, in the President's judgment.

Q. Ari, back to Iraq and the process that you've spoken about. You seem to be giving a fairly substantial role to the inspectors in trying to have them interview Iraqi scientists. A, what is that? And, B, is there any indication—are you having to press the inspectors to do this, or are they resisting you in some fashion?

Mr. Fleischer. Two points. One, the reason that the United States thinks it's important for scientists and people involved in the weapons program of Iraq to be interviewed is because this is about making sure that peace can be protected by Saddam Hussein disarming.

One of the best ways to know if he is disarming is to talk to the people who are involved in making the arms in the first place. If he hasn't included his arms in the declaration, obviously he's got something he's hiding. One of the best ways to know what he's hiding is to talk to the people who are more deeply involved in it than the people who have produced their declarations.

So the purpose of talking with them is to preserve the peace by knowing what Saddam Hussein is developing and hopefully to ascertain as much information as possible about where it may be and what the extent of it is. History has shown that that often is the best and most effective way to catch Saddam Hussein in his lies and to determine the truth about what Saddam Hussein is doing.

I think if you take a look at some of the statements that have come from the inspectors, they, too, believe that that is part of their mission. It is part of their charge under

Resolution 1441 and the U.N. resolution, and we anticipate that they will use all the tools at their disposal to carry out their mission.

Q. Soon? Immediately?

Mr. Fleischer. Well, the exact modalities of it are to be determined by the inspectors on the ground. But we do anticipate that they will do so. It is part of their charge, given to them by the 15 members of the Security Council.

Q. So if an admission is not an material breach, is that the next level then that we're going to, in order to catch Iraq in material breach, is to have these scientists give us the information? Or have the inspectors somehow—

Mr. Fleischer. Whether it is or is not a material breach, it is important for the inspectors to use every tool at their disposal, including the interview of scientists and people involved in the weapons program. That's per the U.N. resolution.

Q. Yes. It's actually a process question, would that constitute a material breach then? Seeing as the information that's out there now seems to suggest that an omission from the report would not be a material breach we're looking for. So what's the next level of material—what would constitute a material breach?

Mr. Fleischer. I don't know that this is a matter of gradations and levels. This is a matter of whether Saddam Hussein is going to disarm and whether the inspectors have the tools they need to do their jobs. And clearly, talking to scientists is one of the tools.

Mr. Fournier, you didn't—well, you did have a question in the first round.

Q. The President has been saying all along he has zero tolerance for Iraq, and what I want to know—since you're not going to be able to come back to us later, if material breach is declared that is—that can be used as justification for war under U.N. resolution, why don't we just go in now? Why wait another six weeks and try to get support?

Mr. Fleischer. Again, this will be something that Secretary Powell and Ambassador Negroponte will get into a little bit later. But what is important here is ascertaining whether or not Iraq has made the strategic decision to disarm. And we want to make certain that he is not engaged in further acts of defiance.

If you want to know how the President approaches this process, I recommend go back and take a look at exactly what the President said in Prague on this question. And let me read this to you. The President said, "Should he again deny that his arsenal exists, he will have entered his final stage with a lie." And the President looks at this as a stage. The President looks at this as a process. And the President will look at this in a very deliberative fashion and in a fashion in consultation with our allies.

Make no mistake, the President has said if that happens, Saddam Hussein is entering his final stage with a lie. The exact time period of this final stage will be determined by Saddam Hussein, because Saddam Hussein must disarm.

Q. Are we in the final stage?

Mr. Fleischer. The President will be the one to make that determination and we will see exactly what Saddam Hussein does. But clearly the President has said—

Q. There are omissions and problems. Based on that quote, we're in the final stage with a lie.

Mr. Fleischer. I think once you are advised of whether or not the United States has come to the conclusion that Saddam Hussein is in material breach, that would mean that the final stage is beginning with a lie.

Chapter 6

December 19, 2002–February 4, 2003
The U.S. Declares Iraq to be in "Material Breach" of U.N. Security Council Resolution 1441; France and Germany Lead Opposition to Military Action as Divisions Among NATO Allies Sharpen

CHRONOLOGY

2002

December 19. UNMOVIC Chairman Hans Blix tells UNSC members that the Iraqi weapons declaration filed on December 7 "is essentially a reorganized version" of information Iraq provided UNSCOM in 1997, and that it "is not enough to create confidence" that Iraq has abandoned its WMD efforts.

2003

January 18. Global protests against war on Iraq take place in cities around the world, including Tokyo, Moscow, Paris, London, Montreal, Ottawa, Toronto, Cologne, Bonn, Goteborg, Istanbul, and Cairo, as well as U.S. cities including Washington D.C. and San Francisco.

January 27. The chairmen of the inspections effort, Hans Blix and Mohammed ElBaradei, report to the U.N. Security Council that, while Iraq has provided some access to facilities, concerns remain regarding undeclared material, their inability to interview Iraqi scientists, and their inability to deploy aerial surveillance during inspections.

January. Turkey invites at least five other regional countries to a "'last-chance' meeting to avert a U.S.-led war against Iraq." According to U.S. intelligence officials, France secretly sells prohibited spare parts to Iraq for its fighter jets and military helicopters.

January. A statement released to various newspapers and signed by the leaders of Britain, Spain, Italy, Portugal, Hungary, Poland, Denmark and the Czech Republic shows support for the U.S., saying that Saddam should not be allowed to violate U.N. resolutions.

Sources: Chronology entries are drawn from www.abc.com, www.bbc.com, www.nytimes.com, www.reuters.com, www.washingtonpost.com, www.wikipedia.com, and staff research.

DOCUMENTS

Remarks by Secretary of State Powell, December 19, 2002

Well, good afternoon, ladies and gentlemen. On November 8th, the United Nations Security Council responded to the challenge issued by President Bush in his 12 September speech to the United Nations General Assembly. On that day, the Security Council unanimously passed Resolution 1441, requiring Iraq to disarm itself of its weapons of mass destruction and to disclose all of its nuclear, chemical, biological and missile programs.

Resolution 1441 was the latest in a long string of Security Council resolutions since Iraq's invasion of Kuwait. Previous resolutions, which included requirements to disarm and to end the cruel repression of the Iraqi people, have all been defied or ignored by Iraq.

Resolution 1441 recognized that Iraq "has been and remains in material breach of its obligations," but gave the Iraqi regime, again, a final opportunity to comply with its disarmament obligations.

Iraq's answer came on December 7th in a 12,200-page document submitted to the Security Council.

Resolution 1441 required Iraq to submit a declaration on all its mass weapons program of destruction, a declaration that was "currently accurate, full and complete," in the words of the resolution.

The inspectors told the Security Council this morning that the declaration fails to answer many open questions. They said that in some cases they even have information that directly contradicts Iraq's account.

Our experts have also examined the Iraqi document. The declaration's title echoes the language of Resolution 1441. It is called, "Currently Accurate, Full and Complete Declaration." But our experts have found it to be anything but currently accurate, full or complete. The Iraqi declaration may use the language of Resolution 1441, but it totally fails to meet the resolution's requirements.

The inspectors said that Iraq has failed to provide new information. We agree. Indeed, thousands of the document's pages are merely a resubmission of material it gave the United Nations years ago, material that the U.N. has already determined was incomplete.

Other sections of the Iraqi declaration consists of long passages copied from reports written by the United Nations and the International Atomic Energy Agency. The only changes the Iraqi regime made were to remove references critical to its own conduct. The declaration totally fails to address what we had learned about Iraq's prohibited weapons programs before the inspectors were effectively forced out in 1998.

And let me just touch on a few examples, and we'll be giving out a fact sheet later with additional examples.

Before the inspectors were forced to leave Iraq, they concluded that Iraq could have produced 26,000 liters of anthrax. That is three times the amount Iraq had declared. Yet, the Iraqi declaration is silent on this stockpile, which, alone, would be enough to kill several million people.

The regime also admitted that it had manufactured 19,180 liters of a biological agent called botchulinum toxin. U.N. inspectors later determined that the Iraqis could have produced 38,360 additional liters. However, once again, the Iraqi declaration is silent on these missing supplies.

The Iraqi declaration also says nothing about the uncounted, unaccounted precursors from which Iraq could have produced up to 500 tons of mustard gas, sarin gas and VX nerve gas.

Nor does the declaration address questions that have arisen since the inspectors left in 1998. For example, we know that in the late 1990s, Iraq built mobile biological weapons production units. Yet, the declaration tries to waive this away, mentioning only mobile refrigeration vehicles and food-testing laboratories.

We also know that Iraq has tried to obtain high-strength aluminum tubes which can be used to enrich uranium in centrifuges for a nuclear weapons program. The Iraqi regime is required by Resolution 1441 to report those attempts. Iraq, however, has failed to provide adequate information about the procurement and use of these tubes.

Most brazenly of all, the Iraqi declaration denies the existence of any prohibited weapons programs at all. The United States, the United Nations and the world waited for this declaration from Iraq. But Iraq's response is a catalogue of recycled information and flagrant omissions. It should be obvious that the pattern of systematic holes and gaps in Iraq's declaration is not the result of accidents or editing oversights or technical mistakes. These are material omissions that, in our view, constitute another material breach.

We are disappointed, but we are not deceived. This declaration is consistent with the Iraqi regime's past practices. We have seen this game again and again—an attempt to sow confusion and buy time, hoping the world will lose interest. This time, the game is not working. This time, the international community is concentrating its attention and increasing its resolve as the true nature of the Iraqi regime is revealed again.

On the basis of this declaration, on the basis of the evidence before us, our path for the coming weeks is clear.

First, we must continue to audit and examine the Iraqi declaration to understand the full extent of Iraq's failure to meet its disclosure obligations.

Second, the inspections should give high priority to conducting interviews with scientists and other witnesses outside of Iraq, where they can speak freely. Under the terms of Resolution 1441, Iraq is obligated—it is their obligation—to make such witnesses available to the inspectors.

Third, the inspectors should intensify their efforts inside Iraq. The United States, and I hope other Council members, will provide the inspectors with every possible assistance, all the support they need to succeed in their crucial mission. Given the gravity of the situation, we look forward to frequent reports from Dr. Blix and Dr. ElBaradei.

Finally, we will continue to consult with our friends, with our allies, and with all members of the Security Council on how to compel compliance by Iraq with the will of the international community.

But let there be no misunderstanding. As Ambassador John Negroponte said earlier today, Saddam Hussein has so far responded to this final opportunity with a new lie. The burden remains on Iraq. Not on the United Nations. Not on the United States. The burden remains on Iraq to cooperate fully and for Iraq to prove to the international community whether it does or does not have weapons of mass destruction. We are convinced they do until they prove to us otherwise.

Resolution 1441 calls for serious consequences for Iraq if it does not comply with the terms of the resolution. Iraq's noncompliance and defiance of the international community has brought it closer to the day when it will have to face these consequences. The world is still waiting for Iraq to comply with its obligations. The world will not wait forever. Security Council Resolution 1441 will be carried out in full. Iraq can no longer be allowed to threaten its people and its region with weapons of mass destruction. It is still up to Iraq to determine how its disarmament will happen. Unfortunately, this declaration fails totally to move us in the direction of a peaceful solution.

And now I'd be prepared to take some questions.

Q. I'm a little confused because this was to have been Iraq's last chance and you've just laid out four additional things, including interviewing scientists, and you're still saying that Iraq has the opportunity to so-and-so and so-and-so. I don't know if you're saying an airtight case hasn't been made or somehow you have some slim hope it can be turned around by Iraq.

Secretary Powell. It remains to be seen. The resolution was its last chance and there were obligations for Iraq in that resolution: one, to accept the resolution; two, to provide a declaration. We have begun our analysis of that declaration and we find so far that it has failed to do what it was supposed to do.

But we will continue to work with UNMOVIC and IAEA and we'll consult with other members of the Council to see what conclusions the Council members arrive at, and to see whether or not more evidence can be brought forward to make the case to the Council that Iraq has totally missed its opportunity.

But so far, with respect to complying with the conditions and the terms of 1441, Iraq is well on its way to losing this last chance.

Q. Mr. Secretary, you've used the expression "material breach." Can you tell us why you've chosen to use this? And how would you answer those who have been saying this morning that by using this without taking action you are, in fact, devaluing the expression?

Secretary Powell. "Material breach." I think, perhaps, too much has been made of the term. Material breach is a term that comes from the law that says a party to a commitment has failed in meeting the terms of that commitment. Iraq has done that repeatedly in the past. That's why 1441 begins with that statement of past material breach on many occasions by Iraq, still in material breach, and this is a new material breach.

I don't think we are devaluing the term. I think we are using the term to make it clear to the world that, once again, we have a breach on the part of Iraq with respect to its obligations and therefore the spots have not changed.

Now, I'll let the other members of the Council make their own judgment as to whether they wish to characterize it as such right now. The important point, I think, is that from what we heard from Dr. Blix and Dr. ElBaradei this morning, and what I heard from other members of the Council who have spoken, is that there is no question that Iraq continues its pattern of noncooperation, its pattern of deception, its pattern of dissembling, its pattern of lying. And if that is going to be the way they continue through the weeks ahead, then we're not going to find a peaceful solution to this problem.

Q. Mr. Secretary, is there a deadline by which Iraq has to show this compliance, and will the United States return to the Security Council and seek another resolution authorizing military action toward the end of next month if Iraq does not comply?

Secretary Powell. There is no calendar deadline, but obviously there is a practical limit to how much longer you can just go down the road of noncooperation and how much time the inspectors can be given to do their work.

In the weeks ahead, we expect both the IAEA and UNMOVIC to give regular reports as they get deeper into their inspection work, and as they analyze the declaration further. There are still long sections of the annexes that came with the declaration that have to be carefully examined. So I would not put a timeline on it, but obviously it is not indefinite. This situation cannot continue.

A body of evidence is slowly building since the passage of Resolution 1441, and that body of evidence shows that Iraq is still not cooperating. It is Iraq's obligation to cooperate and they are the ones who are supposed to be coming forward under this resolution to demonstrate to the international community what they have done in the past, what they might still be holding, and to come clean. And what we have seen in this declaration is they still have not made a decision to come clean. And the inspectors will not be able to do their work until Iraq demonstrates that they are cooperating and they are coming clean and bringing forward the information. And until that happens, we should be very skeptical, and I'm afraid we should be very discouraged, with respect to the prospects of finding a peaceful solution.

Q. Mr. Secretary, when is the U.S. planning to share its intelligence with the inspectors, if at all? I think we were told they were waiting until after the initial assessment. Is now the right time to do that?

Secretary Powell. We have, of course, been sharing our evaluation of the declaration with the inspection teams of both IAEA and UNMOVIC with respect to providing them additional forms of support that would make the inspection effort perhaps more targeted and effective. We are prepared to start doing that and we'll be in contact with them.

Q. Mr. Secretary, as you know, the Vice President, in particular, has been very skeptical about inspections. So far, the inspectors have not turned up anything. Are you not concerned that if another month elapses and the inspectors are not able to

find any of these weapons that you say are hidden, that that's going to undermine your case to the world that there is, in fact, violations?

Secretary Powell. We have all been skeptical of inspections because we are basically distrustful of Saddam Hussein and the Iraqi regime, and for good reason, and so, the President took the case to the international community.

The declaration, I think, is further evidence of Iraq's unwillingness to comply with the requirements of the international community. And I don't want to prejudge what the inspectors might or might not find and it is not clear, exactly, what they have found or not found yet. They are getting up to speed. The number of inspectors has increased. Bits and pieces of information will come together. I hope that when members of the Council provide more support to the inspectors, it may make their work even that much more effective. But I wouldn't prejudge. The President has said repeatedly, he is interested in the disarmament of Iraq peacefully, if possible, but if that is not possible, it will be done by force.

Q. Thank you. Mr. Secretary, if the U.S. goes to war with Iraq, what kind of war would it be? Will it be swift, or will it be bloody? How will it differ from Desert Storm?

Secretary Powell. We are doing everything we can to avoid war. The President has made that clear. But if war comes, the only thing I would say about the nature of that conflict is that it will done in a way that would minimize the loss of life, and it would be done to be accomplished is as swift a manner as possible, and for the purpose of getting rid of weapons of mass destruction and liberating the Iraqi people. But I wouldn't go any further right now.

Q. Mr. Secretary, are you satisfied with the Turkish cooperation on this Iraq subject?

Secretary Powell. We have been in very close touch with the Turkish Government at all levels, and the new Turkish Government as well, and we are satisfied with the level of dialogue. And in the days ahead, now that some political issues are behind us with respect to EU accession, I think the new Turkish Government will be able to focus more on consultation with us with respect to Turkish actions and Turkish interests in what we are doing.

Q. The Iraqi declaration helped to clarifications or more additions, would the United States be ready and willing to accept more qualifications of what they already said? Would you take into consideration that they said, "Oh, yes, we forgot this year what we actually have done with this"? Will that be possible to prevent a war?

Secretary Powell. Let's see what happens in the days ahead. I can't hypothesize on that because I have little confidence that the Iraqis will do anything but try to—see, we answered your question here, but we're not answering all these other questions that perhaps you haven't even asked us yet.

The resolution was clear: currently accurate, full and complete. It means the burden is on them to come forward and say, "You know we've been doing this. You know we've done it in the past. We have now changed, turned over a new leaf, and we're giving you all the information you need to see that we are giving this up, or anything we still are doing we will not do and we are demonstrating to you where this is so it can be destroyed, and we are in compliance."

But that has not been the attitude of the Iraqi Government for the past 12 years, it is not the attitude of the Iraqi Government today, and the world should view this with great skepticism, keep the pressure on, make sure Iraq knows that it will be disarmed one way or the other, and hope that the Iraqi people and Iraqi leaders, besides Saddam Hussein, realize that they are going to disarm one way or the other.

Q. Mr. Secretary, Mr. Blix said today that he had asked for lists of Iraqi scientists who had worked on these programs. He said that there were no efforts yet to try and work on modalities for access to these people. Are you going to push them harder to—I mean, getting access, after all, is what you're after.

Secretary Powell. We are working on modalities now and we are putting in place, working with Dr. Blix and Dr. ElBaradei, putting in place means by which one could accomplish this interview task. It has some complex aspects to it.

And there will be names that will be made available. And let us remember this. Under the resolution, when those names are presented to the Iraqi Government, they are required to provide these individuals for interview, and for interview in a safe place, and for their families to be in a safe place where they will not be in danger of losing their lives for telling the truth.

And so we are hard at work on all of these modalities.

White House Fact Sheet, December 19, 2002

Illustrative Examples of Omissions From the Iraqi Declaration to the United Nations Security Council

Anthrax and Other Undeclared Biological Agents

The U.N. Special Commission concluded that Iraq did not verifiably account for, at a minimum, 2160kg of growth media. This is enough to produce 26,000 liters of anthrax—3 times the amount Iraq declared; 1200 liters of botulinum toxin; and, 5500 liters of clostridium perfrigens—16 times the amount Iraq declared. Why does the Iraqi declaration ignore these dangerous agents in its tally?

Ballistic Missiles

Iraq has disclosed manufacturing new energetic fuels suited only to a class of missile to which it does not admit. Iraq claims that flight-testing of a larger diameter missile falls within the 150km limit. This claim is not credible. Why is the Iraqi regime manufacturing fuels for missiles it says it does not have?

Nuclear Weapons

The Declaration ignores efforts to procure uranium from Niger. Why is the Iraqi regime hiding their uranium procurement?

VX

In 1999, U.N. Special Commission and international experts concluded that Iraq needed to provide additional, credible information about VX production. The declaration provides no information to address these concerns. What is the Iraqi regime trying to hide by not providing this information?

Chemical and Biological Weapons Munitions

In January 1999, the U.N. Special Commission reported that Iraq failed to provide credible evidence that 550 mustard gas-filled artillery shells and 400 biological weapon-capable aerial bombs had been lost or destroyed. The Iraqi regime has never adequately accounted for hundreds, possibly thousands, of tons of chemical precursors. Again, what is the Iraqi regime trying to hide by not providing this information?

Empty Chemical Munitions

There is no adequate accounting for nearly 30,000 empty munitions that could be filled with chemical agents. Where are these munitions?

Unmanned Aerial Vehicles (UAV) Programs

Iraq denies any connection between UAV programs and chemical or biological agent dispersal. Yet, Iraq admitted in 1995 that a MIG-21 remote-piloted vehicle tested in 1991 was to carry a biological weapon spray system. Iraq already knows how to put these biological agents into bombs and how to disperse biological agent using aircraft or unmanned aerial vehicles. Why do they deny what they have already admitted? Why has the Iraqi regime acquired the range and auto-flight capabilities to spray biological weapons?

Mobile Biological Weapon Agent Facilities

The Iraqi declaration provides no information about its mobile biological weapon agent facilities. Instead it insists that these are "refrigeration vehicles and food testing laboratories." What is the Iraqi regime trying to hide about their mobile biological weapon facilities?

Summary

None of these holes and gaps in Iraq's declaration are mere accidents, editing oversights or technical mistakes: they are material omissions.

Remarks by President Bush, December 20, 2002

Q. Mr. President, your administration concluded yesterday that Saddam Hussein pretty much blew his last chance to come clean on his weapons of mass destruction. Are we now on a path to war?

President Bush. One thing is for certain; we will fulfill the terms and conditions of 1441.

The world spoke clearly that we expect Mr. Saddam Hussein to disarm. Yesterday's document was not encouraging. We expected him to show that he would disarm. And as the Secretary of State said, it's—it's a long way from there. And we're serious about keeping the peace. We're serious about working with our friends in the United Nations so that this body, ably led by Kofi Annan, has got relevance as we go into the 21st century. And yesterday was a disappointing day for those who have longed for peace.

White House Press Briefing, December 20, 2002

Q. Ari, yesterday the United States accused Iraq of a material breach with its weapons declaration, and yet there appears to be some difference of opinion within even the P-5 on the Security Council about whether that constitutes Iraq being in material breach of Security Council Resolution 1441. Can you clear this up? Can one member state declare a country to be in material breach? Does it take action by the Security Council to achieve that?

Mr. Fleischer. Well, I think that nothing precludes either the Security Council or individual member states of the Security Council from making their judgments known. Clearly, if it's a collective action—or it's not a question of action, but if it's a collective judgment, the United Nations Security Council has the right to convene and enter into anything it deems collective. But nothing, because the United Nations Security Council has the right to do things collectively, prohibits individual member states from offering their individual judgments.

Q. So it's a judgment—it's an accusation as put forth by the United States, but it's not an established fact yesterday that Iraq is in material breach?

Mr. Fleischer. You've heard the Secretary of State assert it, and I'm not going to get into the semantic game of whether it's a judgment or a fact. Obviously, the judgment that the facts support calling it material breach would not have been made if it wasn't based on the facts.

Q. I'm not sure I want to call it a semantic game or agree that it's a semantic game. There could be differences within the P-5, with Russia, even with the French, about whether or not Iraq is in breach of the resolution, or whether the weapons inspectors would have to find proof that Iraq's declaration was false to put them in breach.

Mr. Fleischer. I remind you that under the declaration, voted 15 to nothing, Iraq, according to that declaration, is in material breach. So they're in material breach in the present, and I'm not aware that the fact that they submitted a declaration that has been judged universally to be lacking in totality and has not fully complied with the United Nations requests means they've gotten themselves out of material breach.

Q. My [question] has to do with Hans Blix, the director of the inspectors, the U.N. inspectors, who I believe has said publicly that he would like to get more or better intelligence from Washington and London to aid his inspection. Is that a possibility?

Mr. Fleischer. Well, we continue to meet with and talk to Hans Blix about all matters of how the world can cooperate to make the job of the inspectors easier. It is entirely in the interest of the United States of America for the inspectors to have every tool and resource necessary to help them to be as effective as they can to do their jobs. And the United States will do that. It is in our interests for the inspectors to be able to find whatever can be found, dispute Saddam Hussein's effort to hide everything he can hide. It is in our interest to see the inspectors continue to apply themselves with additional tools, such as the helicopter that only arrived into Iraq in the last week for the inspector's use. The inspectors themselves are ramping up with our help and our support.

So we will continue to work with them to provide them information. The one thing we won't do is do anything that, around the world, not just in Iraq, but around the world, could compromise sources or methods.

Q. I wanted to follow up on a question earlier about the inspectors. You were talking earlier about the U.S. concern about compromising sources and methods and being very deliberate about providing information to the inspectors. For those members of the Security Council who are asking the United States to provide them the intelligence information that the United States is saying is persuasive, the United States' answer is, no; is that correct?

Mr. Fleischer. No, the United States' answer is, yes. We continue to provide information and to share intelligence and to make means available to the inspectors so they can do their job. It is in our interest to do so.

Q. But to the members of the Security Council and to our allies—

Mr. Fleischer. I think you've got an issue—let me ask you if you have this issue. There was a different issue where the President of the Security Council made a determination in the longstanding traditions of the Security Council dealing with proliferation information, that in an effort to make certain that there are no proliferation impacts from the release of an Iraqi report that was rather explicit on some of their nuclear programs, that information that could be proliferation-sensitive was shared only with the P-5 nations, all of which are nuclear nations. The non P-5 nations or the E-10, the information was not shared with, which is a procedure and a tradition of the Security Council.

I'm aware there has been some discussion of that from the E-10, but this is a decision made by the United Nations Security Council along the lines of making certain that proliferation concerns are addressed.

Q. Just to make sure that I have this straight. The United States is willing to give all the intelligence that we have to the inspectors—

Mr. Fleischer. In keeping with what I said earlier about sources and methods. And that's not just an issue for the inspectors. The United States, as I said, has every interest in wanting to make sure the inspectors are able to do their job. But around the world, we won't have any sources or methods if around the world people think the United States is willing to just share sources and methods everywhere. And so I think that's generally accepted and expected.

Q. And the P-5 also? The P 5

Mr. Fleischer. The P-5 are not the inspectors; the inspectors are the ones who are doing the work.

Q. But you're talking about—the P-5 members are not able to get the same intelligence that the inspectors would have?

Mr. Fleischer. I think you need to ask the P-5 nations. But the United States is sharing information with the inspectors. And we have close collaboration around the world with various nations on sharing of information on the intelligence front. And, of course, I'm not going to describe to you what is shared.

Q. Ari, this morning Tony Blair issued, I guess, a Christmas message to the troops whose gist was, be ready. Does the President have a similar holiday message for the troops?

Mr. Fleischer. The President's radio address is going to be aimed at the country and it's going to be a message of greetings for the Christmas season, and I encourage you to listen to that.

Q. But in a larger sense, does the President have any thoughts to share with the troops as, you know, the possibility of war with Iraq looms?

Mr. Fleischer. Let me put it to you this way. The President's message to America's men and women around the world is that the job that they do and the duty they fulfill helps keep our nation strong and free. It keeps us the pride of the world, and it keeps us the great nation, the strong nation that we are. He has tremendous gratitude for the sacrifices that people are making in serving our country.

Q. But nothing specific to Iraq and the potential sacrifices that may be yet to come?

Mr. Fleischer. No. I think again, I've addressed it as I can. That's what the President's message is.

Remarks by Secretary of Defense Rumsfeld and Chairman of the Joint Chiefs of Staff Myers, December 23, 2002

Secretary Rumsfeld. On Thursday of last week the administration set forth the inadequacies of the Iraqi declaration, which is described as "failing to meet the U.N. resolution's requirements," unquote. The U.S. is continuing to discuss with members of the Security Council how to gain Iraq's compliance with its international obligations. Thanks to President Bush's leaderships, the U.N. passed a unanimous resolution giving Iraq an opportunity to comply with its disarmament obligations, and inspectors are back in the country for the first time in many years. We've arrived at this point because of the growing international diplomatic and military pressure.

The moment Saddam and his ruling clique seem to feel that they're out of danger, they will undoubtedly see no incentive to comply with their international obligations. That is why, after the passage of Resolution 1441, the U.S. and coalition countries are continuing to take steps to keep pressure on the regime. Among other things, we've continued patrolling the skies over the north and south no-fly zones. We've continued developing a humanitarian relief and reconstruction plan for a post-Saddam Hussein Iraq. We've continued working with the Iraqi opposition. We've taken steps to prepare for a post-Saddam transition. And we're continuing to work with friends and allies to keep the military pressure on Iraq. For example, the recent Internal Look exercise in Qatar tested the new Central Command's deployable headquarters. I was there week before last. General Myers was there last week. And it should indicate to Iraq that the U.S. and its coalition partners are prepared to act if necessary.

Similarly, we're taking prudent and deliberate steps with respect to alerts and mobilizations and deployment of U.S. forces—active, Guard and Reserve. These include alerting Reserve combat, combat support and combat service support forces, deployment of combat and combat support forces needed to pave the way for future deployments in the event that that becomes necessary, activating mobilization bases for processing of Reserve components. I expect that we and others could continue to make prudent force-flow decisions in the weeks and months ahead, depending on the degree of Iraqi cooperation.

None of these steps reflect a decision by the president or the United Nations or anyone else, to my knowledge, to use force. The president has not made such a decision. Rather, they are intended to support the diplomatic efforts that are under way, to enhance force protection in the region and elsewhere in the world, including the United States, and to make clear to the Iraqi regime that there need—that they need to comply with their U.N. obligations.

In the period ahead, we'll continue to work with the United Nations member states to encourage Iraqi compliance. As the president said, the use of force is the last choice. The goal is for Iraq to comply with U.N. resolutions.

This is our last scheduled briefing this year. It's been an eventful one for military and media alike. Reporting can indeed be difficult and dangerous, as we saw last week.

I salute you and your colleagues for your professionalism, and I wish you and your families a safe and happy holiday.

Last, I want the men and women in uniform to know how much we appreciate the sacrifice, especially those who are serving far from home and loved ones during this special time of year. All Americans know that our country can celebrate this season of peace only because the armed forces of the United States voluntarily stand ready to defend freedom and defeat terror. And we are grateful to each one of them.

General Myers. Good morning, and thank you, Mr. Secretary. I just got back this morning from a troop visit to Qatar, Afghanistan and Kuwait, and I can tell you that our young men and women on the front lines of this global war on terrorism are doing a superb job. They are highly motivated, despite being away from families during this holiday season. And they're ready to take on any mission that our nation may ask of them.

As the secretary said, we are continuing our deliberate and steady force build-up in the region. It's important to posture or forces appropriately to complement our diplomatic efforts. We want to ensure we can act quickly should it be necessary.

Q. General Myers, do you see today's action by an Iraqi aircraft to shoot down this drone, penetrating the southern no-fly zone, as an escalation of things we've been seeing in the no-fly zone with the recent firings?

General Myers. Brett, I don't. They have—I think we've lost two other Predators, I believe, to hostile fire in southern Iraq. They've been attempting—they attempt to shoot down all our aircraft that fly over southern and northern Iraq in support of the U.N. Security Council resolutions. And they got a lucky shot today and they brought down the Predator. But I don't see—I do not see it as an escalation. It's been something they've been doing for literally the last couple of years.

Q. Your thoughts on the fact that there have been these increased firings and this firing today, as the Iraqis are saying that they are completely complying on all fronts with the U.N. resolution?

Secretary Rumsfeld. Well, they obviously aren't. And they've been making a strenuous, energetic effort to shoot down U.S. aircraft for many, many, many months now—manned and unmanned.

Q. Mr. Secretary, both you and General Myers mentioned it vaguely, but I wondered if you could elaborate a little bit on the deployment, the massive buildup of air, land and sea forces in the next month, and what sort of message—

Secretary Rumsfeld. I don't know that we've said anything about massive buildups of air, land and sea forces in the next month. I don't think you did or I did.

General Myers. Sir, I didn't—

Q. Are you going to do that?

Secretary Rumsfeld. First of all, we don't announce alerts or activations or deployments. Never have. I doubt if we ever will, unless it's for some domestic emergency of some type, like a forest fire. [The Department of Defense does not acknowledge alert or deployment orders in advance, however, once an individual unit receives an alert or deployment order, that unit may acknowledge it in accordance with standing DoD public affairs guidance.]

We—what I did do was to specify that no decision has been made with respect to the use of force. It is the president's last choice, not the first choice.

However, there wouldn't be inspectors back in Iraq had there not been and were there not now the possibility of the use of force. And as a result, the United States and, I presume, some other countries will, from time to time, be making decisions with respect to how to manage that capability on our part in a way that is consistent with the diplomacy and with our—the world's desire to have Iraq comply with the U.N. resolutions.

If you think about it, a decision was made a number of years ago for the United States military to put in the Reserves and the Guard, as opposed to the active forces, a whole set of capabilities that are necessary if you are going to in fact be engaged in the use of force. That means that you cannot do the things you normally would do with active forces—to prepare ports and prepare airfields and to train people and to begin that process of being able to respond—in the event the president makes such a decision, without activating Reserve and Guard. So we're doing that. It's a shame that we're organized that way, and we intend to see that we're no longer organized that way in the future. But at present, we are organized that way.

Second, there are, in the case of Guard and Reserve, some instances where they need 30, 60, 90 days notice. They have to get their teeth fixed. They have to fill out papers. They have to get training. They have to get a whole series of equipment up to speed. And as a result, unless you want to wait 30, 60, 90 days, if and when the president were to make such a decision, you have to take steps now. And as a result, what we're doing is, in some instances, we're not even alerting. What we're doing is, we're saying, "Here's an alert order, not that we intend to activate you or mobilize you or deploy you, but we intend to give you an alert so that you can get all that stuff done, get your paperwork through, get your teeth fixed, do the—get your medical exams, do the kinds of things that need to be done so that it won't take 30, 60, 90 days in the event we need your services."

So that is the process that's taking place, and it is in a very orderly and deliberate and prudent way. Dick Myers and I have spent many, many hours with the individuals who manage this. At the present time, the Department of Defense is mal-organized to deal with something like this. We tend to be organized to either be—do everything or do nothing. And what we're trying to do is to—here we've got the control over the activation of Guard and Reserve in the services, the three services, the four services. We have—the Joint Forces Command has a voice in all of this. And in some cases, there are capabilities in the combatant commanders' hands. So you've got all of these six or eight or different places where you may want to bring forces to a different state of readiness. So we're working with all of them and trying to get those threads up through the needlehead so that the—it remains clear to the Iraqis that it's in their best interests to disarm. And in the event that the president does make such a decision, he has the ability to do it in some reasonable period of time. It is not a simple thing to do. But we're working very hard trying to do it in a way that doesn't unduly inconvenience a group of people by activating them before they're needed. So it's a process that's going to be going forward as we move ahead.

Q. General Myers, would you also say it might put a little—this might also put a little bit of pressure on Saddam Hussein and ratchet up diplomacy?

General Myers. Well, I think we've also said that this is going to complement the other diplomacy that's going on. Certainly he has to know that the world is serious about the UNSCR 1441. And after all, it becomes his decision then how he wants to respond.

Secretary Rumsfeld. There wouldn't be any inspectors in there now if he weren't concerned about that, that's for sure.

Q. Over the weekend there were some statements from Saddam's regime inviting U.S. government personnel or the CIA along on the inspection. Do you have any response to that? Do you think it's a good idea?

Secretary Rumsfeld. I have no idea what the decision will be with respect to that. I read the same statements. I have no—I'm not sure if they are accurate or if they were actually given by responsible people there. And I don't know quite what the United States might consider doing. I suppose the—they invited intelligence people in, as I recall, and I suppose the intel community is thinking about that at the present time.

Q. Mr. Secretary, I have a question to you and one to General Myers. To you, sir: Do you think it's theoretically possible that the inspectors would stay for a long time in Iraq and prevent any development of weapons of mass destruction by their very presence and the alert they might get from satellites from the U.S?

Secretary Rumsfeld. I don't know. The—as we've said, the purpose of inspectors, U.N. inspectors, is not to go into a discovery process, and it's not a deterrent or a preventative technique historically, as your question suggests it conceivably could be. In fact, what it's been is only—it has only worked in situations where the country has decided to cooperate and the country says, "I want to prove to the world that we do not have these things, and if we do have them, we'll destroy them." And they invite the inspectors in so that the international community can say, "Aha! You're right. They're cooperating. They're doing exactly what we wanted them to do, and isn't that a good thing?"

Inspectors have never been successful in terms of a discovery process. It's an enormous country. You know, it's bigger than Texas, or as big, I guess. I haven't looked lately, but it is a very big place. And they've got enormous—miles and miles and miles of underground tunneling. I mean, I don't know how inspectors on the surface of the

Earth can know—even know what's going on in the underground facilities that the Iraqis have. So I just don't know the answer to your question.

Q. General Myers, can I ask you to go back over one thing you said. You said that the United States is continuing its deliberate and steady build-up, and that you want to ensure you can act quickly if necessary. Do you have some indication or any reason or do you have any concerns at the moment that Saddam Hussein could suddenly make some aggressive move in this period of time? Are you now posturing to deal with any aggressive move that he might make?

And my other questions is, given all of that, is the United States, has the Bush administration made the commitment to let the inspectors get out of Iraq before any hypothetical military action would take place?

General Myers. On the first part, and I think the secretary covered it in his statement, and I covered it in mine, I believe, that I think we remain postured. You know, one of the reasons we conduct Operation Northern Watch and Southern Watch under the previous United Nations Security Council resolutions is to ensure that the Iraqi regime can't attack the Kurdish population, as it has done in the past, to make sure they can't attack the Shi'ia population, as it has done in the past. That's part of what we're doing over there.

So we are—yes, we're ready and postured and have been for some time to know when that might be happening, and then take appropriate action. And I don't think we're worried, particularly worried one way or the other. This has been—this has been a potential from—for the last 10 years anyway. I might remind you that he also—in the north, also used chemical weapons on the Kurdish population. And so that's part of the reason we're over there.

This build-up—

Secretary Rumsfeld. It's one of the reasons for the Northern and Southern No-fly Zone.

Q. Well, I guess my confusion—and I do want to also ask about the question of inspectors—is—

General Myers. I was just going to say that, as we said in our opening statements, of course, now we're under a new U.N. Security Council resolution, 1441. We think by posturing our forces over there, as the secretary said, we probably wouldn't have a 1441, and we wouldn't have the compliance, as poor as it's been up to this date, by the Iraqis if it hadn't been for the fact that we have forces postured in the region to be ready to take whatever action is necessary. So we'll continue that deliberate force flow that we've been conducting now for several months.

Q. [*Off mike*]—commitment to let the inspectors get out before any hypothetical military action would begin.

Secretary Rumsfeld. We're in close touch with the inspectors on deconfliction on all kinds of things. When they go south of the 36—33, and they go north of 36, we know it, and we work with them.

Q. But do you have a commitment to let them get out?

Secretary Rumsfeld. We don't have commitments to do anything. I said we are in very close coordination with the inspectors and we deconflict. And obviously, that is something that we do just in the normal course of things. It doesn't have anything to do with commitments or lack of commitments; it has to do with just orderly good business.

Q. Mr. Secretary, some Iraqi opposition members have been vocal, saying that should President Bush order some military action in Iraq, asking that the Iraqi army soldiers be spared from an initial attack because if it happened, they believe large numbers of them would turn on Saddam immediately. Is that something that you believe would happen should an attack come to fruition?

Secretary Rumsfeld. I guess I don't really get into the "believes," "might," "should," hypotheticals. The fact of the matter is, in Gulf War, 70—80,000 of the Iraqi Army surrendered almost instantaneously, in a matter of hours and days. I would—I think it's not unreasonable to suspect that the same might occur in even larger numbers in this instance, but it's not knowable.

So, one, the combatant commander, needless to say, has to be prepared for both contingencies. He has to be prepared to cope with a situation where they do not surrender, and by the same token, he has to be prepared—from a humanitarian standpoint, to be prepared for a situation where they might very well, in which case you have to suddenly switch what it is your task is. And I can assure you that General Franks has thought these things through very carefully, and there's a good deal of evidence that suggests that not everyone is terribly enthusiastic about Saddam Hussein and his regime.

White House Press Briefing, December 27, 2002

Q. Is the United States satisfied with the cooperation it's getting from the Iraqis, in terms of the interviews of Iraqi scientists?

Mr. McClellan. Well, that's part of the process that is spelled out in the U.N. resolution. I refer you back to OP-5 and the U.N. resolution, where it calls on the regime in Iraq to provide immediate, unimpeded, unrestricted and private access to all officials and other persons who UNMOVIC or the IAEA wish to interview. And it says that UNMOVIC and the IAEA may, at their discretion, conduct interviews inside or outside of Iraq, may facilitate the travel of those interviewed and family members outside of Iraq, and that its sole discretion such interviews may occur without the presence of observers from the Iraqi government. So this goes back to—again, there must be full compliance with the U.N. resolution from Iraq.

There has been a number of indications that they continue to be unwilling to change their past behavior. We still have not seen the evidence that Iraq is willing to change, and that they are willing to comply with all aspects of the U.N. resolution which seeks disarmament. And, again, the regime in Iraq will disarm—it is there choice how they will disarm, but they will disarm.

And so this is all part of the process, but it goes back to what Secretary Powell said as recently as last week, that they appear to be unwilling to change their past behavior. And we have yet to see evidence that they will change their past behavior.

Q. So are you saying they're not complying in this specific aspect of the interviews of the scientists?

Mr. McClellan. Well, I'm talking about their overall objective here, which is to disarm, for the Iraqi regime to disarm. And, again, I think I just addressed it by saying that there are a number of indications that they appear to be unwilling to change their past behavior and comply in full with the U.N. resolution.

Q. Is this one of those indications?

Mr. McClellan. Well, again, it calls for—in OP-5. We'll see. This is a process that— it was the President that directed the United States to seek disarmament through the U.N. And that's what we are doing. This is part of the process, and they must comply fully with the U.N. resolution. This is one part of that.

Q. Is the United States satisfied with the cooperation it's getting from the Iraqis, in terms of the interviews of Iraqi scientists?

Mr. McClellan. Well, that's part of the process that is spelled out in the U.N. resolution. I refer you back to OP-5 and the U.N. resolution, where it calls on the regime in Iraq to provide immediate, unimpeded, unrestricted and private access to all officials and other persons who UNMOVIC or the IAEA wish to interview. And it says that UNMOVIC and the IAEA may, at their discretion, conduct interviews inside or outside of Iraq, may facilitate the travel of those interviewed and family members outside of Iraq, and that its sole discretion such interviews may occur without the presence of observers from the Iraqi government. So this goes back to—again, there must be full compliance with the U.N. resolution from Iraq.

There has been a number of indications that they continue to be unwilling to change their past behavior. We still have not seen the evidence that Iraq is willing to change, and that they are willing to comply with all aspects of the U.N. resolution which seeks disarmament. And, again, the regime in Iraq will disarm—it is there choice how they will disarm, but they will disarm.

And so this is all part of the process, but it goes back to what Secretary Powell said as recently as last week, that they appear to be unwilling to change their past behavior. And we have yet to see evidence that they will change their past behavior.

Q. So are you saying they're not complying in this specific aspect of the interviews of the scientists?

Mr. McClellan. Well, I'm talking about their overall objective here, which is to disarm, for the Iraqi regime to disarm. And, again, I think I just addressed it by saying that there are a number of indications that they appear to be unwilling to change their past behavior and comply in full with the U.N. resolution.

Q. Is this one of those indications?

Mr. McClellan. Well, again, it calls for—in OP-5. We'll see. This is a process that—it was the President that directed the United States to seek disarmament through the U.N. And that's what we are doing. This is part of the process, and they must comply fully with the U.N. resolution. This is one part of that.

Q. Is the United States satisfied with the cooperation it's getting from the Iraqis, in terms of the interviews of Iraqi scientists?

Mr. McClellan. Well, that's part of the process that is spelled out in the U.N. resolution. I refer you back to OP-5 and the U.N. resolution, where it calls on the regime in Iraq to provide immediate, unimpeded, unrestricted and private access to all officials and other persons who UNMOVIC or the IAEA wish to interview. And it says that UNMOVIC and the IAEA may, at their discretion, conduct interviews inside or outside of Iraq, may facilitate the travel of those interviewed and family members outside of Iraq, and that its sole discretion such interviews may occur without the presence of observers from the Iraqi government. So this goes back to—again, there must be full compliance with the U.N. resolution from Iraq.

There has been a number of indications that they continue to be unwilling to change their past behavior. We still have not seen the evidence that Iraq is willing to change, and that they are willing to comply with all aspects of the U.N. resolution which seeks disarmament. And, again, the regime in Iraq will disarm—it is there choice how they will disarm, but they will disarm.

And so this is all part of the process, but it goes back to what Secretary Powell said as recently as last week, that they appear to be unwilling to change their past behavior. And we have yet to see evidence that they will change their past behavior.

Q. So are you saying they're not complying in this specific aspect of the interviews of the scientists?

Mr. McClellan. Well, I'm talking about their overall objective here, which is to disarm, for the Iraqi regime to disarm. And, again, I think I just addressed it by saying that there are a number of indications that they appear to be unwilling to change their past behavior and comply in full with the U.N. resolution.

Q. Is this one of those indications?

Mr. McClellan. Well, again, it calls for—in OP-5. We'll see. This is a process that—it was the President that directed the United States to seek disarmament through the U.N. And that's what we are doing. This is part of the process, and they must comply fully with the U.N. resolution. This is one part of that.

Remarks by Secretary of State Powell, December 29, 2002

Secretary Colin Powell was interviewed on NBC's "Meet the Press" by Tim Russert.

Q. You have said that Saddam Hussein is in material breach in Iraq.

Secretary Powell. The declaration was.

Q. His declaration of what he possessed in terms of weapons of mass destruction. How long will we allow him to be in material breach before taking action?

Secretary Powell. He has been in material breach from the very beginning, from back in 1991. The false declaration, or the inadequate declaration, if I can put it that way, is another material breach, in our judgment, and therefore it just adds to the case against him that he is not yet cooperating fully when you look at that declaration. And so we will wait to get additional reports from Dr. Blix and Dr. ElBaradei, the head of UNMOVIC and the International Atomic Energy Agency in January and wait to see what report we get from them in a more definitive way at the end of January.

Q. Is time running out for Saddam Hussein?

Secretary Powell. I think that this can't go on indefinitely. We are anxious to see the results of the inspectors' work and the President has not made a decision yet with respect to the use of military force or with respect to going back to the United Nations, but it's a situation, of course, we're monitoring closely, and, of course, we're positioning ourselves and positioning our military forces for whatever might be required.

Q. But if he disarms completely, he could stay in power?

Secretary Powell. We will wait and see what happens. If he disarms completely to the satisfaction, complete satisfaction, of the international community, that would suggest that the nature of that regime is changing. We just have to wait and see.

Q. A final question. If we do go into Iraq, what happens to the oil fields?

Secretary Powell. The oil fields are the property of the Iraqi people and if a coalition of forces goes into those oil fields, we would want to protect those fields and make sure that they are used to benefit the people of Iraq and are not destroyed or damaged by a failing regime on the way out the door. And you can be sure that they would be protected and the revenue generated from any such oil fields would be used in accordance with international law and to benefit the people of Iraq.

Remarks by Secretary of State Powell, December 29, 2002

Secretary Colin Powell was interviewed on Fox News Sunday by Tony Snow.

Q. Iraq now is permitting some scientists to be interrogated by the United Nations, but they're doing it in the Al Rasheed Hotel. I've stayed in that hotel. It's bugged. Can one credibly hold such interviews in a bugged hotel?

Secretary Powell. Well, whether it's bugged or not is not the issue, so much as whether or not the individual is free to talk. The first one who came in had a minder with him, somebody with him. That's why we believe it is important that for those key people that we believe have knowledge that would be useful and who might have a willingness to share such knowledge, such interviews would be better held outside of the country, and also with protections for their family, protection for their families. And that's why we have pushed that and that's why it is part of the U.N. resolution.

Q. Iraq has supplied a list of 500 names of scientists involved in various weapons development programs. Do we think that's a legitimate list?

Secretary Powell. I haven't seen the list and I don't think our intelligence community has had enough time to analyze the list. But it's a list that Dr. Blix had asked for and Iraq made the deadline in providing the list.

Q. Final question. Has the President decided to use force against Iraq?

Secretary Powell. He has not. He hopes for a peaceful solution. But at the same time, we are taking prudent actions, positioning our forces so that they will be ready to do whatever might be required.

Remarks by President Bush, January 3, 2003

President Bush delivered his remarks to troops at Fort Hood in Texas.

The Iraqi regime is a grave threat to the United States. The Iraqi regime is a threat to any American and to threats who are friends of America.

Why do I say that? Well, first of all, the leader in Iraq has publicly proclaimed his hatred for our country and what we stand for. The Iraqi regime has a record—a record of torturing their own people, a brutal record and a record of reckless aggression against those in their neighborhood.

The Iraqi regime has used weapons of mass destruction. They not only had weapons of mass destruction, they used weapons of mass destruction. They used weapons of mass destruction on people in other countries, they have used weapons of mass destruction on their own people. That's why I say Iraq is a threat, a real threat.

Four years ago, U.N. inspectors concluded that Iraq had failed to amount— account for large stockpiles of chemical and biological weapons, weapons capable of killing millions. In last month's declaration, Iraq again failed to account for those weapons.

The Iraqi dictator did not even attempt to submit a credible declaration. We can now be certain that he holds the United Nations and the U.N. Security Council and its resolutions in contempt. He really doesn't care about the opinion of mankind. Saddam Hussein was given a path to peace; thus far, he has chosen the path of defiance.

The fate of the Iraqi regime is being determined by its own decisions. Saddam Hussein knows precisely what he can and must do to avoid conflict. We have made that clear. The world has spoken with one voice.

And even now, he could end his defiance and dramatically change directions. He has that choice to make. We certainly prefer voluntary compliance by Iraq. You see, the use of military force is this nation's last option, its last choice.

Yet, if force becomes necessary to disarm Iraq of weapons of mass destruction and enforce the will of the United Nations; if force becomes necessary to secure our country and to keep the peace, America will act deliberately, America will act decisively, and America will prevail because we've got the finest military in the world.

We are ready. We're prepared. And should the United States be compelled to act, our troops will be acting in the finest traditions of America, should we be forced to act. Should Saddam Hussein seal his fate by refusing to disarm, by ignoring the opinion of the world, you will be fighting not to conquer anybody, but to liberate people.

See, we believe in freedom. No matter what their oppressors may say, the people of Iraq have no love for tyranny. Like all human beings, they desire and they deserve to live in liberty and to live in dignity. America seeks more than the defeat of terror. We seek the advance of human freedom in a world at peace. That is the charge history has given us, and that is the charge we will keep.

In crucial hours, the success of our cause will depend upon you. As members of our military, you serve this nation's ideals and you demonstrate those ideals in your code and in your character. As Commander-in-Chief, I have come to know the men and women who wear America's uniform. I have seen your love of country and your devotion to a cause larger than yourself. I have seen your discipline, your idealism, and your sense of honor. I know that every order I give can bring a cost. I also know without a doubt that every order I give will be carried out with skill and unselfish courage.

Some crucial hours may lie ahead. We know the challenges and the dangers we face. If this generation of Americans is ready, we accept the burden of leadership, we act in the cause of peace and freedom. And in that cause, we will prevail.

Address by Iraqi President Hussein, January 6, 2003

Iraqi President Saddam Hussein delivered the following address to the Iraqi nation on the anniversary of the founding of the Iraqi army.

In the Name of Allah,

The Merciful, The Compassionate,

Remember thy Lord inspired the angels (with the message): "I am with you: give firmness to the Believers: I will instill terror into the hearts of the Unbelievers: smite ye above their necks and smite all their finger tips off them. "This is because they contended against Allah and His Messenger: if any contend against Allah and His Messenger, Allah is strict in punishment." Thus (will it be said): "Taste ye then of the (punishment): for those who resist Allah, is the penalty of the Fire." O ye who believe! when ye meet the Unbelievers in hostile array, never turn your backs to them. If any do turn his back to them on such a day-unless it be in a stratagem of war, or to retreat to a troop (of his own)—he draws on himself the wrath of Allah, and his abode is Hell, an Evil refuge (indeed)! It is not ye who slew them; it was Allah: when thou threwest (a handful of dust), it was not thy act, but Allah's: in order that He might test the Believers by a gracious trial from Himself: for Allah is He Who heareth and knoweth (all things). That, and also because Allah is He Who makes feeble the Plans and stratagems of the Unbelievers. (O Unbelievers!) if ye prayed for victory and judgment, now hath the judgment come to you if ye desist (from wrong), it will be best for you: if ye return (to the attack), so shall We. Not the least good will your forces be to you even if they were multiplied: for verily Allah is with those who believe! (Allah's is the Word of Truth)

Our great people,

The valiant men of our Armed forces,

On previous occasions, we have said that our view of our history in Iraq, which is also our view of our history as a nation, is that it is tantamount to faith. This is because history, to our nation and people, is not merely a register of contextual activities. It is rather a record of sacrifices made in blood in order for the nation to preserve its qualities and maintain its role, and in order for our people as well to remain as such. What raises history and elevates it to the status of belief is the fact that the sacred blood shed in the most crucial situations for our nation to assert its traits, and its mission to augment its everlasting contribution to humanity, has been the blood of the Mujahideen who loved Allah and would therefore not hesitate to carry out, their missions as designated by Allah, the Almighty, along with the honor they had in carrying the Call of the Message of Heaven to mankind as a whole, after spreading it in their own great nation.

This is how the faithful people of our nation view history, and this is how we have read our history and believed in its meanings, and have hence stressed that our history is not merely a series of events, as in the case in the history of a lot of activities and situations in life for other nations and peoples. History is rather the reservoir in which exist, and from whose depth we derive, the laws that elevate the nation to assume its great mission for humanity, having attained the sublime status of communication with Allah, as a nation of loving, chosen believers, who are confident and obedient to the commands of the Almighty; a nation conscious of its great mission of faith both nationally and on the level of humanity, which is extended from the essence of the tenets established throughout its eternal history and the wealth of values adorning the landmarks of distinction along its mission.

After an absence from the fields, arenas and objectives of the Almighty, when He Has Willed it to be extended, your role returns again to you, Iraqi men and women of valour and sacrifice, the heroes of our valiant armed forces under all your titles—your role is regained, now that you have snatched the opportunity to re-assume it deservedly with your special traits which emanate from your great faith in all that brings satisfaction to Allah and gratification to the homeland and the nation. On the arenas of this role of yours and its eternal mission, you have presented scores of martyrs, which keeps your picture bright and unblemished, as you have evinced no reluctance whatsoever in taking the stand of faith and dignity with which you have responded to the call of history, blessed with the spirit and fragrance of Heaven. History, which you have treated as a glorious faith, returns now carrying all the values and requirements of faith and generous sacrifice in order to strengthen its principles and the edifice of your glorious community on the basis of those principles.

History is the doctrine of the present that is linked to the spirit and values of the glorious past. Its spirit and high effect exist in you, valiant men and women. Hence our celebration of the 6th of January every year, as a historic mission of the struggle and Jihad of our heroic armed forces and faithful people, on the basis of the same values already referred to, now that you have reaffirmed these meanings through your faith and stands, through the blood shed by those martyred or wounded amongst us, and through the suffering and resilience of our prisoners of war. So this has become a day for us to recall all these meanings as we celebrate and honor the day every year. The celebration is unlike any other, because this one of honor and renewal of our pledge to the Almighty before ourselves, our people and armed forces, and our nation and humanity, as a people and army of Mujahideen, men and women who have established the foundation for this faith in the depth of our blood and suffering, and in our treatment of the spirit of history, whereby we recall history in our sacrifices and our readiness as followers of a rich and glorious Faith at present and in the future as well.

On this basis, Great people and Army of valiant Mujahideen, when we celebrate and honor the 6th of January, we take another look at, and ponder, in a spirit both pure and full of faith, unstained by treason to the principles or abandonment of the pledge we made to Allah, the nation and humanity, not only the difficulties which we have been through or which have been imposed on us, difficulties through the claws of which we have derived all that would bring dignity and pride to our nation, but also the role and stand awaiting us. This will ensure our continued adherence to the great values and mission entrusted to our nation and people on the basis of our history, rather than make our celebration of the day isolated occasion. It is indeed the basic situation. It is the road and agenda with all that is linked to it of our recent past during thirty years of glorious history and the extensions made to, or from, it. This is going to be the doctrine of faith for our coming generations, our children and grandchildren in Iraq, in the same way as it is the doctrine of the present. It is a source of pride for the Mujahideen and freedom-fighters of our nation. It is their reservoir of experience and values, together with what is derived from the struggle of our brothers in Palestine and in all other arenas and situations of honor for the people of our nation .To them, it is an example to follow and emulate, once they recall it along with the depth of the nation's history and glorious faith .It will be a torch of light linked to that ancient history of the nation, the voice of a strong lesson in the nation, scented by the blood of sacrifice,in order that our posterity will remain on the right path,son after father,regardless of the size and value of the sacrifices made, until victory is achieved over the forces of evil and injustice which mean our nation ill ;infringe upon its rights and harbor greedy intentions against it.

When you, the valiant people of Iraq, renew your pledge to Allah,to yourselves,to the nation and to humanity at large,that you will continue the march of jihad,you do not only strengthen your adherence to your belief and your sacrifices for the Faith, whose meanings have been eloquently expressed, in your sacred blood, as well as in your suffering, sacrifice and perseverance, but you also ensure final victory over the enemies of Allah, your enemies .Allah loves those who rely on Him and who remain strong and honest believers. Allah does not like weaklings.If Allah blesses you with His satisfaction, for victory comes only from Him, the Almighty, Yours will be an assured triumph at the outset, and in the end when the defeat of your enemies will bring them contempt ; for they have done themselves, as well as others, wrong through misjudgment and misconduct when they deviated from all honorable values on the basis of which fair-minded people come together to achieve understanding and cooperation.

But if the aggressors choose a way other than this, then, after thanking Allah, we shall all be even happier than the others. Indeed, we shall thank the Almighty if He guides the enemies to the right path, in the same way as we shall be grateful when He destroys them and brings shame to their arrogance.

Oh, Allah, pray guide the along the road of righteousness if You so decide. Otherwise, smite them with Your wrath and smash them with Your destruction blow, for they are a group of criminals

If anyone attempts to intimidate you, the people of Iraq, repel him and tell him that he is a small midget while we belong to a nation of glorious Faith, a great nation and an ancient people who have, through their civilization, taught the human race as a whole what man was yet to know.

We are the offsprings of the sword and the pen; and, in the Name of Allah, we shall fear no one in defending our right, and shall continue our march on the path drawn by Allah, in order to achieve the tasks assigned to us by the Almighty. Our right is a clear right, as clear as is their falsehood; and we shall not be intimidated by their falsehood. Allah shall drown them in shame.

Allah is our God, and He is the Greatest. Theirs is an abject shame, while ours is an elevated status with values that will ensure Allah's content and the appreciation of free-minded humanity.

He, whose hoisted banner is adorned with the call: "Allah is the Greatest", fluttering on its post, and who keeps his pledge to Allah, to the martyrs and to the faithful, shall fear no tyrants.

Our chests are filled with the great conviction in our victory, whose fruit will be in our hands and whose banners will be all over our heads as a great people in a glorious nation, God willing.

Shame, and more shame, with defeat will go to your opponent.

And may every new year bring happiness and well-being.

We salute the Palestinian people of heroic mujahideen as well as every hero and heroine amongst the champions of self-sacrifice who confront the zionist aggression with their lives and thus foil the wrong ideas of the American administrations which have acted in alliance with their artificial zionist creation in the crimes they perpetrate and the shame they reap .

Glorious and sublime are our martyrs in Palestine, Iraq and the nation as a whole.

Long live Palestine, free and Arab, from the sea to the river.

Long live Great Iraq and its valiant army of Mujahideen.

Long live our glorious Arab nation.

Greetings to every valiant hero and noble heroine in our nation as they repel and resist injustice. Courageous Men and Women of our great people, and our valiant Armed forces,

We know you and trust the pledge that you have taken upon yourselves on several occasions .We are confident,as we rely on Him, the Great, Keeper of all Power,the Merciful,the Compassionate,that you will be with every new dawn for a new day,better and better until you attain the best state,with Allah Grace,to the disappointment of your desperate enemies,the friend and wicked assistants of Satan,the inhabitants of night and the dark.

The moon, the stars and the sun will,with Allah's Grace expose all the schemes that they hide in the darkness of their minds and chests .Their arrows will go astray,while your arrows will hit them,now that Allah has deemed your struggle to be a driving force in the march of every mujahid and freedom-fighter in your nation and in the peoples of the world at large against injustice and its perpetrators spearhead by their master: Their Tyrant.

Be aware, then Brothers, that victory is yours now, in the past and on the Day of final harvesting, in spite of all the hysterical hubbub and clamor which the enemy has been making; for the enemy has many objectives behind this uproar and self-defeating pandemonium .Iraq is not the only target in this confusion,even if the noise is meant to intimidate us and to cover the aggression to be decided by the enemy whenever the devil so instructs him. The objective is rather to subject the Arab Gulf area to a full,complete and physical occupation through which to achieve many goals .These include political interference and military intervention in the countries of the region in a manner unaccustomed before, with a view to securing complete control over their resources. The fragmentation of some of these countries, which has been a dream declared by the enemy since the early 1970s, and about which various enemy scenarios have been published, may have gone some way towards being achieved now, including the occupation of land, at the lowest cost possible. But the enemy will pay dearly later, on top of what it is paying at present for its reckless policies of greed and expansionism. Through its noise and rumblings, coupled with the ongoing aggression and blockade inflicted on Iraq, the enemy is providing cover for the heinous crimes perpetrated by the zionist entity against our people in Palestine.

In this respect, the enemy has achieved a lot of the objectives desired by zionism; for now public opinion is diverted completely towards the enemy's noise and mobilization against Iraq and the confusion it has created about the Gulf, leaving very little room for the zionist aggression to be attended to, condemned and confronted. The enemy is preparing now to control entry to the Red Sea and the gate-ways to the Arab Sea, with a view to ensuring enemy interest's and security for the zionist entity, while securing transport lines for oil and military shipments there. The enemy is in full coordination with the zionist entity in this respect, and has achieved a lot of what it wanted to see achieved in order to cover the weaknesses of its agencies,as exposed before the U.S. public opinion, vis-a-vis the events of the 11th of September 2001 and the weakness, or indeed near-collapse, of the United States economy. The enemy has been trying to divert the American people's attention from these facts,the details of which are being sought by many conscientious people there. This includes the failure of the policy of the United States towards the Palestinian question and the rights of the people of Palestine, the failure of U.S. policies in the world in general, with anger and hatred being generated amongst peoples everywhere against those policies, as well as the failure of the U.S. military policy in Afghanistan in the face of local resistance there. One of the objectives of the enemy's continued aggression and pressure on Iraq is to provide psychological support, in a climate of saber-rattling, in order to intimidate the people of the Middle East and the world, and to make the inspection teams go beyond the declared objectives of the Security Council, even in the bad resolution issued in its name. So, now, instead of looking for the so-called weapons of mass destruction, in order to expose the distortion and lies propagated by those who endeavor, in vain, to deceive public opinion, the inspection teams are interested in collecting names and making lists of Iraqi scientists, addressing employees with questions that carry hidden agendas, giving special attention to military camps, to unproscribed military production, and to other matters, all or most of which constitute purely intelligence work.

The covers used to camouflage the subjects which we have mentioned, or say the largest part of them, are required for those subjects, which also need the sound of weapons and the perpetuation of crises in the Arab homeland and its periphery. In the meantime, the enemy's occupation of the Gulf and the Red Sea will have been established, which will enable the enemy whose lines of communication and transport will now have become shorter, to launch aggression and cause damage in any direction it chooses, including expanding its aggression against Iraq on the basis of strategic and tactical objectives. Nothing will therefore be more disappointing and discouraging to the enemy than for our people to be prepared, after relying on Allah, for any further confrontation expected with the enemy in addition to the aggression already perpetrated on a daily basis, while maintaining our life for the present and the future, building, building and building—with great optimism and conviction that the future is secured by firm adherence to Faith. The light of truth belongs to us, while our enemy has the darkness of the present and the darkness of distant horizons. We are fully prepared for everything and for any eventuality. Our success is in the hands of Allah, and Allah shall repel the schemes of the infidels. In any case, we are in our country; and whoever is in his own homeland with truth on his side, and is force to face an enemy that stands on the side of falsehood and comes as an aggressor from beyond seas and oceans, will no doubt emerge triumphant, because victory always belongs to those who stand by truth in their own home while defeat certainly belongs to their enemies.

On this basis, and not under any other consideration, we conduct ourselves as we watched the hissing of the snakes and the barking dogs together with the aggression being continually inflicted on the north and south of our country. Our behavior reflects the confidence of capability which requires no hasty or perturbed behavior, but is based on the necessary calculation and consideration of which we have accumulated such experience as would make every Iraqi man and woman, everyone in our people and every soldier in our armed forces, as well as every official and community leader, well-aware of his or her task and indeed his or her position in the battle of reconstruction and the arena of confrontation, if the devil pushes those who ignite it to a precipice.

On the basis of this experience and the preparedness that rests on a solid and unshakable base of faith and conviction, it is the enemy that is confused, and it is the enemy that should seek a way out of what is regarded a mess in which the enemy has thrown itself. The enemy ought to remember the terrible end of all empires that committed aggression against our people and nation in the past.

As for the people of Iraq, their victory, with reliance on Allah, is at hand, having already existed in their chests; and it is up to the enemies to trace the echoes of their trumpets.

Allah is the Greatest.

Allah is the Greatest. And the wretched aggressors shall be repelled.

Remarks by Secretary of State Powell, January 7, 2003

Secretary Colin Powell was interviewed on Public Radio International's "World Radio Program."

Q. What do you need to hear to satisfy you and the administration that war with Iraq is not necessary?

Secretary Powell. You know, the President is anxious to find a peaceful solution to this problem. The international community is looking for a peaceful solution. That's why the President took it to the United Nations.

What we would like to hear, not just the U.S., but what the whole international community would like to hear, that Saddam Hussein fesses up, cooperates fully with Dr. Blix, the head of the UNMOVIC inspection group, and Dr. ElBaradei, the head of the International Atomic Energy Agency, and provides them full and complete information on all the programs that Iraq has had over the years and that Iraq continues to have. And if he would turn it all over and not try to deceive, not try to hide, then we'd be on our way to a peaceful solution.

And so we are supporting the inspectors in every way that we can, providing them information, providing them other materials that might be useful to their efforts, and hope that they continue to do the kind of job they're doing now and intensify their work.

And we will wait and see what they report first on the 9th of January later this week and then the formal report that they will provide on the 27th of January, which is not a final report but it's a formal presentation of their first two months' work.

Q. So if they say they have found nothing, then does that mean there will be a peaceful solution and no war?

Secretary Powell. No, it depends on what they say they have found and how much more work they have to do. They may have found nothing to that point. The question is what else are they going to have to do to ascertain whether Iraq does or does not have these weapons of mass destruction, as we believe they do.

I would be surprised if they would come up with a clean bill of health after just two months. They can certainly come up with a bad bill of health after two months if there is no cooperation or if we see the kind of action such as was evidenced when Saddam Hussein put forward that flawed declaration a few weeks that the whole world saw was flawed. That was certainly not an indication that he is cooperating fully.

Q. To that end, we've been hearing a lot of hint that the United States has compelling evidence of illicit programs in Iraq. Has the U.S. yet shared that intelligence with the inspection team?

Secretary Powell. We have put out a number of papers, both classified and unclassified, to a variety of audiences, and we've put out unclassified information to the American people and the international community, and we are providing information to UNMOVIC and to IAEA that will help them do their work. So we are working closely with them and sharing with them. We want them to be able to do their work and we're trying to help them every way we can.

Q. I want to talk a little bit about a post-Saddam Iraq. A lot of people—some people say that if the rampant lawlessness and the warlordism of Afghanistan right now, at least outside of Kabul, the capital, is any indication, then a post-Saddam Iraq is not a very promising one despite U.S. assurances right now.
Can the U.S. ensure a different outcome for Iraq?

Secretary Powell. Well, first of all, let me tell you your premise. Afghanistan is not quite the way you describe it. While there is a problem out in the countryside and we haven't totally solved the problem, increasingly President Karzai is extending his control over the country. We don't have rampant warlordism. Most of the country is reasonably stable, by Afghanistan standards. We have a problem in some parts of the country. A national army is being created, a national police force is being created, the judicial system is being created. And in just about one year, we have gone from nothing back then to a government that is now starting to function.

So, the glass may not be full yet in Afghanistan, but it certainly isn't empty, and I think we should be proud of our accomplishment.

In Iraq you have a different situation where you wouldn't be working with a country that has absolutely nothing going for it at the beginning, having been run by something like the Taliban, but you have an educated population, there is a middle class in Iraq, and above all, there is a source of income for the people in the country, a source of income that comes from oil, oil money that would no longer be wasted on weapons and threatening one's neighbors, but on improving the country.

So I think the circumstances are quite different and the international community would have a different time of it, and I suspect an easier time of it, than we had in Afghanistan.

Q. Tony Blair, the British Prime Minister, today gave another supportive speech about the relationship between the U.S. and Britain. Perhaps you heard some of that.

Secretary Powell. I did.

Q. But he also urged the U.S. to adopt a broader agenda to include the Middle East peace process, poverty in the Third World, and global warming. Do you expect the United States eventually to give greater priority to these issues as a kind of payback for Europe's support for any kind of war against Iraq?

Secretary Powell. We give greater priority, not as a payback but because it's the right thing for the United States to do. When you say we ought to do more on poverty, the United States contributes more than any other nation on the face of the earth right now with respect to aid programs assisting countries around the world.

President Bush put forward about a year ago the Millennium Challenge Account which will increase our aid funding to developing nations by some 50 percent. We are the largest provider of food to the World Food Program. We are feeding people all over the world. In fact, the need is even greater than ever and we are encouraging our European friends to give more than they're currently giving.

With respect to the Middle East peace process, we certainly are engaged and wish we could find a solution more quickly than we have been able to in the past two years and, in fact, years before that. And we are working with the British and other friends to do more.

So I don't think the Prime Minister was suggesting that we are not involved in these issues, but that we all have to do more, and I am in constant touch with the British Foreign Secretary on that.

With respect to climate, there is a different view between those who felt that the Kyoto Protocol was the way to go and the United States position and the position of a number of countries that that was not the economically viable way to go. And so those who believe in Kyoto are ratifying and bringing themselves under that protocol and we are looking for other ways to achieve this common purpose that all nations have, and that's to reduce the emissions from our industrialized and industrializing countries that create global warming.

Remarks by Secretary of State Powell and IAEA Director General ElBaradei, January 10, 2003

Secretary Powell. Well, good afternoon, ladies and gentlemen. Dr. ElBaradei just had a good conversation over a number of key issues that are before the world today. We've talked about the situation with respect to Iraq, with respect to North Korea and also some of the nuclear activities that are taking place within Iran.

With respect to Iraq, we reviewed the report that he gave to the Security Council yesterday, and he briefed me on his forthcoming trip with Dr. Blix to Iraq to present to Iraqis their need for additional cooperation, better cooperation, the kind of cooperation we've seen so far, and to fill in the gaps that have been noted in the information they have been providing. And I look forward to the Director General's presentation to the Security Council on the 27th of January. That'll be a very important presentation, the first official presentation after several months of inspection work.

* * * *

Dr. ElBaradei. Thank you very much, Secretary Powell. As the Secretary just said, we had very good and useful meeting reviewing many issues of international concern in the area of nonproliferation or proliferation of nuclear weapons.

In the case of Iraq, I've told the Secretary that we are inching forward but not as fast as we would like to be, and we still would like to see more proactive cooperation on the part of Iraq. Iraq has been cooperating well in the area of process but not as much in the area of substance. We'd like to see more evidence, more documentations, more interviewing of people, more physical evidence of destruction of item they've said they have disposed of.

We are going, Dr. Blix and I, to Iraq on the 19th and 20 of this month basically to impress on the Iraqi that we cannot continue to have open questions, that this process has to come to a closure as soon as we can, that the international community is pretty much fed up with the process of Iraq disarmament which have lasted for almost 12 years, and we will then be reporting to Security Council on the 27th of January, updating the Council on where we are at this time.

* * * *

Q. Mr. Secretary, if the inspectors come back on January 27th with the same assessment, like the one they provided yesterday, will you still be willing to move ahead with your military plans? And to Dr. ElBaradei, do you see under any circumstances Iraq being capable of producing nuclear bombs while the inspectors are doing their work there?

Secretary Powell. Well, since I don't know what the inspectors will say on the 27th, I think it would not be appropriate for me to make a judgment as to what we would say at that time, what actions we might take. But let there be no question in anyone's mind, I think the international community, through Resolution 1441, has spoken clearly.

Iraq must be disarmed of its weapons of mass destruction. And I think the United States Government, President Bush, both the government and President Bush and the American people, and I think the people of the world have spoken that this has to be accomplished. And if it isn't accomplished peacefully under the provisions of 1441, then I think the Security Council has to take the action that's indicated and determine whether or not force is appropriate.

And President Bush has also made it clear that we reserve the right, the United States reserves the right, in the absence of international action to disarm Iraq, to act with like-minded nations to disarm Iraq. And we are positioning ourselves for whatever eventuality might occur. And as the President has also said, he hopes for a peaceful solution, but we will be ready to act otherwise if that is what is required to make sure that Iraq is disarmed of its weapons of mass destruction.

Dr. ElBaradei. On Iraq nuclear capability, we have been out of Iraq for four years. We have just started our inspection seven weeks ago. We still have a lot of work to do. As I've just mentioned, the more Iraq cooperate actively with us, the better we will be able to provide positive assurances to the Security Council. So we still—it's still work in progress and we are not yet able to come to a conclusion on that issue.

Q. Mr. Secretary, are you concerned by reports that Russia may have provided GPS jammers to Iraq, that this is a matter that could be subject to sanctions or not, and have you contacted the Russians about these concerns?

Secretary Powell. I am aware of the various reporting, but I have nothing that I want to say about it or add to the story right now. We would be—we, of course, would be concerned.

* * * *

Q. Interviewing the Iraq scientists, how can you see? Do you believe the Iraqi will accept to send them to Cyprus, the Iraqi scientists, to interview them for Dr. ElBaradei.

Secretary Powell. The U.N. resolution is clear that they should be made available and we are working with the inspection teams to work out modalities where people can give the information they have that might lead to the truth in a way that they can do so safely. And one way to do that safely is to remove them from the country so that they're not subject to threats and intimidation, nor are their family members. And we're working with both the Director General and with Dr. Blix to work out the modalities of how that might be possible.

Remarks by United Nations Secretary-General Annan, January 14, 2003

Q. I would like to ask you if you think that the Security Council has got its priorities out of order. As you noted yourself—well, perhaps you did not note it, but this house is at this moment obsessed with the issue of Iraq, which at present seems in no position to threaten anyone with weapons of mass destruction. Nevertheless, the drive to war continues. As you yourself mentioned, there are dangerous new developments in the Korean Peninsula. In the Middle East, the bloodbath of the Israeli occupation and Palestinian suicide bombers continues. And yet, we see that we are focusing on Iraq the whole time. Has the Security Council got its priorities wrong?

Secretary-General Annan. Let me say that, from my own remarks, it is obvious that the world is facing many challenges. The Security Council, by the nature of its remit, is focused on peace and security issues. But the other parts of the United Nations and the international community should be focusing on some of the other issues that I raised. This is an issue not for the United Nations alone, but for the entire international community. I think the Council is seized with Iraq because it has been on its agenda for quite a while. Now, of course, the inspectors are back in and have resumed their work. Mr. Blix will give an update on 27 January.

But I am not sure that it is only the Council that is responsible for this emphasis and focus on the Iraq issue. I am afraid that you ladies and gentlemen also have something to do with it, because I have given you a whole list of issues that are—or should be—very high on the international agenda. Why is it that we focus on only one?

Q. Let me ask you about a topic that you do not really hear about often with regard to Iraq. In the past, you have said that Iraq must face its responsibilities. You have also said you have been opposed to the war and any type of military offensive. Right now, with regard to the state of play, what is your opinion? Should there be a military attack on Iraq—if a country such as the United States goes ahead—especially if no weapons of mass destruction are found?

Secretary-General Annan. I do not think, from where I stand, that we are at that stage yet. The inspectors have a responsibility in Iraq. The Council has asked them to pursue the disarmament program and report back, and then the Council will make a determination—if Iraq has performed or not. If there is a breach, the Council will then have to take the decision. I think the inspectors are just getting up to full speed. They are now quite operational and able to fly around and get their work done. I think we should wait for the update that they will give to the Council on the twenty-seventh, and hear what further instructions the Council gives them. But the inspectors are carrying on with their work, and I think the resolution is very clear that it is when the inspectors report back, either at the critical stages in their work or if there are unforeseen developments that they bring back to the Council that makes the Council determine that there has been a breach, and therefore there should be serious consequences. I do not think we are there yet. So I really do not want to talk about war. Nor is the Council talking about war.

Q. Although you say that you would prefer that there not be a war, in the event that there is a war, what sort of humanitarian consequences do you see the Iraqi people facing, and is the United Nations prepared to respond?

Secretary-General Annan. We have been doing some contingency planning on that and we are extremely worried about the humanitarian fallout and consequences of any such military action. Obviously we do not want to be caught unprepared. So we have gone ahead and made contingency plans, and we are in touch with Governments that can provide some financial assistance for us to move our preparedness to the next level. But we are worried. The consequences for the population and the refugees who may have to leave can be quite substantial and negative.

Q. There has been some debate about what cooperation actually entails in terms of the Iraqi Government's relationship with the United Nations weapons inspectors. Are you of the mind that the Iraqis are fully cooperating, as set out in resolution 1441 (2002)? Or is there a need for what is now being termed "proactive" cooperation?

Secretary-General Annan. I think the inspectors who are working with the Iraqis have been very clear, and in their own analysis of the Iraqi declaration they have determined that there are major gaps which need to be filled. They have indicated that they would prefer—and they would expect—Iraq to be proactive in its cooperation. And I suspect that that would be one of the main topics of discussion when Mr. ElBaradei and Mr. Blix go to Iraq next week. They will press for the gaps to be filled in; they will press for Iraq to be more proactive in its cooperation; and they will do whatever needs to be done for them to fulfill their mandate. So it is not perfect. It is better than it used to be, but I think the inspectors are pressing for the gaps to be filled in.

Q. Mr. Hans Blix gave an interview yesterday to the BBC in which he said that he did not know how long the American Government was willing to wait for them to complete their searches. He also said that it could be that one day it will say, "Move aside, boys; we're coming in". Can you explain to us what the procedure is for pulling the inspectors out? Can he take instructions from a Member State, or does he have to have clear instructions from the Security Council to pull inspectors out of Iraq? There was a controversial decision made by Mr. Butler in the past. Will there be a repeat of that in the future?

Secretary-General Annan. I think that Security Council resolution 1441 (2002) is quite clear that the Council will have to meet based on reports from the inspectors to determine what action the Council should take. I would expect that if the inspectors find anything, they will report to the Council and the Council will take a decision. And depending on that decision we will all see where we go from there.

* * * *

Q. You mentioned that the issue of Iraq is not an issue that relates only to the Security Council, but the whole world is interested in it. Are you planning, or have you thought about, using your moral authority in a last salvation initiative to help the region—at least concerning this issue—and to send some kind of political adviser to underline the urgency of the situation to the Iraqis?

Secretary-General Annan. I have been in touch with quite a lot of the leaders in the region about the region. The leaders in the region remain engaged in the process of convincing President Saddam Hussein and the Iraqi leadership to disarm and to cooperate fully with the inspectors. If they do disarm and comply with the demands of the Security Council, the region may not have to go through another military confrontation. This is a message that I have sent to them, and I keep repeating it. I hope the [Iraqi] leadership is listening. All the leaders of the countries in the region, including Turkey, are sending the same message to Iraq. I hope they will heed the request.

Q. What is your opinion on the debate as to whether or not the United States should be requesting a second resolution in the Security Council before declaring war against Iraq, if that comes to pass? Do you think that a second resolution should be requested?

Secretary-General Annan. I think that it has been envisaged in Security Council resolution 1441 (2002) that the Council will take the matter up a second time to discuss the question of Iraq if the inspectors inform the Council either that Iraq is not cooperating or that they have found weapons. If that is the case, I think the Council is obliged to debate the matter and take the necessary decision.

Q. In your view, do you believe there is going to be a second Security Council meeting? That is, is there going to be a second resolution?

Secretary-General Annan. I think normally there can be a second resolution when the Council discusses these things, especially on such an urgent matter. They are supposed to take a decision.

Q. Mr. Secretary-General, your name has become attached to the idea of humanitarian intervention—that the world cannot stand by and watch a genocide occur within borders. Some have argued that the new United States concept of pre-emptive action is simply an expansion of the "Kofi doctrine" of humanitarian intervention. Do you believe there is a case for pre-emptive military action, especially in the case of incipient terrorism?

Secretary-General Annan. That is an interesting question. But I would want to distinguish the two. I think the basis on which I argued for intervention, which eventually also led to the establishment of a commission by the Canadian Government, which issued a wonderful report that I would recommend to all of you: "The Responsibility to Protect". It argues that sovereignty is not just privilege; it also carries responsibilities. Governments do have responsibilities to protect their citizens. If they fail to do so, in a situation where their human rights are systematically and grossly being violated, the international community may have to step in, because a Government has failed to protect the people. We should not allow them to use their sovereignty as a shield behind which to commit these gross violations.

If I understand the Washington doctrine properly, that is focused on terrorists or groups or countries that may be planning attacks against them. Therefore the pre?emptive action is, if you wish, an extended doctrine of self?defense. But it is a difficult issue to deal with, because one can talk of war of prevention, where you see a force arrayed against you, with a visible threat, ready to attack, and you make a preemptive strike to stop that attack. There are instances of this in history. Beyond that, where the threat is not imminent and the evidence is not obvious, it becomes a very murky area to deal with. So one will have to be very careful when moving into these areas of pre-emptive strike. Of course, the evidence is usually only with the one who is making the strike. Often, others may claim that it is not verifiable or that the evidence is not convincing.

So, except for those situations where the evidence is clear, where there is imminent threat, where it is obvious and so forth, it can lead to lots of confusion and set precedents that others can use.

* * * *

Q. You are in touch with Secretary of State Powell; you are in touch with Iraqi officials. Is there any message on the looming crisis that you are giving them that you can
share with us?

Secretary-General Annan. Now, I think we are all aware in the work going on in
the Council. We are all aware—particularly those of you in this room—of Council resolution 1441 (2002) and the legislative climate surrounding the passage of that resolution. We will have to assume, and I will have to assume, that the members of the
Council acted in good faith; that the issue is disarmament and that they will do whatever it takes to disarm; and that if the disarmament were to succeed and we were to
agree that Iraq has been stripped of its weapons of mass destruction, then that should
be the end of the story. If, on the other hand, it were to come out that Iraq continues
to defy, and that disarmament has not happened, as I have said, the Council will have
to face up to its responsibilities and take the necessary action. But, of course, this is the
understanding and the spirit of the resolution, which I hope we will all respect.

* * * *

Q. Do you believe it would be a mistake for the United States to take the holes and
gaps in the 7 December declaration by Iraq and add to that this idea of a lack of
proactive cooperation—in other words, if the inspectors do not find anything, that is
a sign that Iraq does not cooperate—and put those two things together and use that
as an excuse for going to war without the authorization of the Security Council?

Secretary-General Annan. I really cannot speak for Washington, and I do not
know how these decisions would be made. But I think, if I can judge from the Council discussion last week, that the Council members are not looking to go in that direction at this stage.

* * * *

Q. I was interested in your answer about a clear case for when pre-emption might be
necessary—forces arraigned against you, a visible threat ready to attack. Given the
build-up of U.S. forces in the Gulf, I was wondering if that is actually helpful towards
reaching a diplomatic, peaceful solution in Iraq.
    If I could just follow up a bit on the possible role for the United Nations—assum-
ing, of course, that all peaceful means will be pursued, what sorts of scenarios are you
looking at in terms of a U.N. role in a post-conflict Iraq?

Secretary-General Annan. On your first question—whether the presence of U.S.
troops is helpful for the solution—I think I would want to make a distinction between
pressure and the threat of use of force and the actual use of force; when do you cross
that threshold. I think there is no doubt in anyone's mind that the pressure has been
effective, that it has worked. Without that pressure I don't think the inspectors would
be back in Iraq today. It took us four years to try to get them in there. Four days after

President Bush spoke at the U.N. and challenged the world and Iraq, Iraq accepted to get them in. So there is not doubt that the pressure has had an effect.

On your other question, regarding what scenarios the U.N. is looking at when we look at post-conflict Iraq, at this stage we focus mainly on the humanitarian aspects. We are doing some preliminary thinking on the political and administrative areas. We have no definite thoughts, and I would prefer not to be drawn into speculation at this stage.

White House Press Release, January 15, 2003

President Bush will welcome British Prime Minister Blair to Camp David on January 31, 2003. The United Kingdom is one of America's closest allies and a strong and valuable partner in the war on terrorism and the effort to eliminate Iraqi weapons of mass destruction. They will discuss a range of issues in a meeting and an informal working dinner.

Remarks by Secretary of Defense Rumsfeld and Chairman of the Joint Chiefs of Staff Myers, January 15, 2003

Secretary Rumsfeld. Good afternoon. After United Nations (U.N.) inspectors briefed the Security Council last week, a number of the observers seemed to seize on the inspectors' statement that they found "no smoking gun" as yet. Conversely, if the inspectors had found new evidence, the argument might then have been that inspections were in fact working and, therefore, they should be given more time to work. I guess for any who are unalterably opposed to military action, no matter what Iraq may do, there will be some sort of an argument.

Another way to look at it is this; that the fact that the inspectors have not yet come up with new evidence of Iraq's WMD program could be evidence in and of itself of Iraq's non-cooperation. We do know that Iraq has designed its programs in a way that they can proceed in an environment of inspections, and that they are skilled at denial and deception.

The president has repeatedly made clear—and it bears repeating—that the burden of proof is not on the United States, it's not on the United Nations or the international community to prove that Iraq has these weapons. The burden of proof is on the Iraqi regime to prove that it is disarming, and to show the inspectors where the weapons are.

As the president said, "The inspectors do not have the duty or the ability to uncover weapons hidden in a vast country. The responsibility of inspectors can only be to confirm the evidence of voluntary and total disarmament by a cooperative country. It is Saddam Hussein who has the responsibility to provide that evidence, as directed and in full." Unquote.

Thus far, he has been unwilling to do so. We continue to hope that the regime will change course and that Iraq will disarm peacefully and voluntarily. No one wants war. The choice between war and peace will not be made in Washington or, indeed, in New York; it will be made in Baghdad. And the decision is facing the Iraqi regime.

This is a test for them, to be sure, but it is also a test for the U.N.. The credibility of that institution is important. Iraq has defied some 16 U.N. resolutions without cost or consequence. The Security Council unanimously approved a new resolution, which required that Iraq, quote, "provide a currently accurate, full and complete declaration," unquote, of its WMD programs, which asserted that any false statement or omissions in the declaration submitted by Iraq shall constitute a further material breach of Iraq's obligations, and which declared that this was Iraq's final opportunity to comply with its disarmament obligations, unquote. That is what the resolution said.

When the U.N, makes a statement like that, it puts its credibility on the line. To understand what's at stake, it's worth recalling the history of the U.N.'s predecessor, the League of Nations. The league collapsed because member states were not willing to back up their declarations with consequences. When the league failed to act after the invasion of Abyssinia, it was discredited. And the lesson of that experience was summed up by Canadian Prime Minister Mackenzie King, who declared at that time, quote: "Collective bluffing cannot bring about collective security," unquote. The lesson is as true today as it was at the start—as it was back in the 20th century. The question is the—whether or not the world has learned that lesson.

General Myers. Thank you, Mr. Secretary. And good afternoon.

I'd like to begin by speaking briefly of Iraq's recruitment of human shields and the International Law of Armed Conflict.

As many of you know from news reports in Reuters and AFP, the London Observer, and in many other newspapers around the world, Iraq announced in late December that it will recruit and receive volunteers from Arab and Western countries to serve as human shields who would be deployed to protect sensitive sites. This is a deliberate recruitment of innocent civilians for the purpose of putting them in harm's way should a conflict occur. The last time Iraq used people as human shields was in December of 1998, when Iraq failed to comply with U.N. arms experts and coalition forces began Operation Desert Fox. A year earlier, the Iraqi encouraged hundreds of Iraqi families to put themselves at risk as voluntary human shields at palaces and strategic facilities in Iraq when Iraq refused to allow U.N. inspectors access to government sites.

I'd like to note that it is illegal under the international law of armed conflict to use non-combatants as a means of shielding potential targets. And Iraq action to do so would not only violate this law, but also be considered a war crime in any conflict. Therefore, if death or serious injury to a non-combatant resulted from these efforts, the individuals responsible for deploying any innocent civilians as human shields would be guilty of grave breaches of the Geneva Convention.

Let me also give you a quick update on where we stand with the Iraqi opposition training. Several hundred U.S. Army trainers arrived in Hungary late last week to prepare for the training of Iraqi opposition who have volunteered for possible action in Iraq. The training task force led by Major General Dave Barno is located at Taszar Air Base in Hungary. He is there to coordinate with the Hungarian Ministry of Defense prior to the arrival of any potential volunteers. And I'd like to take this opportunity to publicly thank our friends in Hungary for use of their facilities. The use of Taszar Air

Base emphasizes a rather long-standing relationship between the U.S. and Hungary, and we thank them very much.

Q. Mr. Secretary, NATO officials said today in Brussels that the United States has now formally asked NATO for support in any possible conflict with Iraq, in such areas as, oh, the possible use of bases, refueling, and—and other non-combat areas: air support, that kind of thing, perhaps refueling. And that also—that you want NATO to provide some help to—and support for Turkey, perhaps protection from Scud attack. I wonder if you might comment on that, on—on the request—

Secretary Rumsfeld. Well, sure. We were asked when we were over there for the—I guess the Prague meeting what—by NATO nations what role anyone might envisage for NATO, and we responded that we'd be happy to come back to them. And the U.S. ambassador to NATO did in fact recently go in to the North Atlantic Council and say that here are a series of things that might or might not be appropriate, and opened that dialogue.

In any case, obviously, we have to begin with the fact that the president has made no decision to use force. But it does take time to plan. And just as we're planning with individual countries, it seemed appropriate to, to the extent NATO wished to, to begin that planning process. And there were various things like force protection, and as you point out, some others, including AWACS and a number of things that apparently are under consideration.

Q. So these would be non-combat—this would be non-direct combat support?

Secretary Rumsfeld. I wouldn't prejudge it.

Q. And how about—how about security support from Turkey?

Secretary Rumsfeld. I guess the definition of what is or is not combat is one problem in answering that question. And, of course, we already know that there are countries that have indicated they want to participate individually in ways that I think would be characterized as combat.

Q. How about support from Turkey? How about—

Secretary Rumsfeld. Well, Turkey is a member of NATO.

Q. How about security support from Turkey?

Secretary Rumsfeld. Sure. Turkey is a member of NATO, and if there's a conflict in that part of the world, that's an appropriate issue for them to address.

* * * *

Q. Mr. Secretary, you talked about Iraqis are skilled at denial and deception. Wouldn't it make sense for the inspectors to burrow into the concealment mechanisms of the regime, particularly its special security organization, going into their headquarters? That apparently hasn't been done yet. Is that something you think they should be doing?

Secretary Rumsfeld. I tell you, I'm not inclined to give advice to the inspectors. We're giving assistance. We're providing intelligence assistance. We're giving sites that they ought to look at—the Central Intelligence Agency is. And I'm so distant from what they're actually doing on the ground that for me to be telling them what they ought to be doing...

The one thing I will say is what we've said from the beginning and which is in their resolution: we do continue to believe that it's terribly important for them to take people, knowledgeable people—scientists, technicians, people who have been in involved in weapons of mass destruction programs—and get them out of the country, with their families, so that they can speak honestly and tell the truth, because the success that inspectors have had in the past is not as finders, not as discoverers, not running around peeking under every rock, but by talking to knowledgeable people, defectors, people who will talk to them, and then being cued as to where they can, in fact, go find something. And it strikes me that if that was the magic formula the last time, it's very likely to be the formula this time that would work.

* * * *

Q. Mr. Secretary, you've said many times from the podium here that you'd like to see Saddam Hussein just pack up and leave Iraq and it would be a nice thing for everybody. If that indeed happened and someone else in the regime stepped up to take over, and they continued to say that they didn't have weapons of mass destruction, would the situation change at all?

Secretary Rumsfeld. Indeed, it would. The—were that the case, then we'd be exactly where we are now, just with a different leader. If a new—if somebody takes over that country, whether because Saddam Hussein leaves, or because he's displaced by somebody in that country, or somebodies, plural, the same principles that we've indicated would pertain. Number one, we would expect the ability to get in on the ground and assure that weapons of mass destruction have been located and destroyed. And that the new government would agree that it would not have weapons of mass destruction, that it would not threaten its neighbors, that it would maintain a single country and not divide it up into parts, whether ethnically or religiously, and that it would have put in place a process so that to—there would be a path towards something like representative government, so that there would be assurances for the elements within that country that they would be able to participate in the governing of that country. No particular template or formula. We're not talking about U.S.-style democracy. We're— look what's happened in Afghanistan with the loya jirga—it's distinctive to that country. So it would—my guess is that what I've just said is probably what would happen.

* * * *

Q. Mr. Secretary, you talked at the beginning about how you need to be prepared and in position for military action, and that was your explanation for your consultations with NATO. I wonder if you could extend that to the deployment issue a bit. You've signed a number of deployment orders in the last few weeks. How are you thinking about how urgent it is to get large numbers of forces deployed there, versus what issues might arise if they end up having to wait a long time?

Secretary Rumsfeld. Well, you know, there's no perfect model for what we're trying to do. What we're trying to do is to support the diplomacy. And the process of working—the State Department sent out, you know, three or four or five dozen cables asking for countries that are interested in cooperating and getting involved in the planning process so that in the event force has to be used, that planning will have taken place. The same thing's true with NATO. We are proceeding to flow forces in an orderly way. We're doing some herding, we're doing some mobilizing, and we're doing some deploying.

We also recognize that the timing of the decision-making is not in our hands. So what we have to do is to try to do what we're doing in a way that gives the president and the world options to use force if, in fact, that becomes necessary, while at the same time recognizing that you—one can't pick a date certain, or even a time frame certain. And, therefore, what you must do is also have back-up plans so that you don't over-stress the force and that you manage it in a way that's appropriate. And we're doing the very best we can. And so far, so good.

Q. How close are you to the point where you'll need to go to Congress for supplemental funding to deal with the costs of these movements?

Secretary Rumsfeld. Well, I have my opinion, and the executive branch, the White House and the OMB are currently wrestling with my opinion and the opinion of other agencies that are in a similar circumstance.

There's no question but that if you think back, we asked for an additional $10 billion for the global war on terrorism, excluding anything involving Iraq. The Congress didn't decide to provide that. Therefore, our budget was passed absent that $10 billion, even though the global war on terrorism is going on. It involves forces in the United States, force protection overseas, a variety of things are going on, as you know, in six, eight countries.

Now, what does all that mean? It means that we are—we've gone through October, we've gone through November, gone through December, we're now going through January. That's four months. That's roughly a third of a year, if my memory serves me correctly. And what do you do? You're conducting the government's business, the business of our country, at the request of the Congress and the president, and you're doing it without having your budget approved for those particular activities: the global war on terrorism. Nor, despite the resolution in the Congress on Iraq, have we received funds for the Iraq component of the global war on terrorism, which is a part of it.

That means that we're robbing Peter to pay Paul. It's a terrible way to manage your affairs. I think it was a mistake that we didn't have the $10 billion approved. We knew we were going to spend it. We knew the global war on terrorism wasn't going to go away. And yet it wasn't approved. So that means we need a supplement. And the question is, when do you need it? Well, obviously, we shouldn't have needed it because it should have been appropriated in the first place. Therefore, every month that goes by, you're robbing Peter to pay Paul in a way that's not good management practice, it's not good business practice, and it's not something that we like to do. And there is a point where you can't do it anymore.

Q. How much?

Secretary Rumsfeld. It's up to the president.

* * * *

Q. Mr. Secretary, whether or not there is a war, will you say—will Saddam Hussein still be in power a year from today?

Secretary Rumsfeld. Oh, my goodness. That's not for me to say. I think that—I can take you through a logic—a brief logic chain. He is a vicious dictator who is repressing his people. He has had in the past weapons of mass destruction, and he used them against his own people, and he used them against his neighbors. He's fired ballistic missiles at two, three or four countries in the past. He has challenged the legitimacy of most of his neighbors at one time or another. He has demonstrated in the past an unwillingness to cooperate with 16 U.N. resolutions.

   The United Nations has now said that they want him to disarm and they want him to reveal his weapons of mass destruction capabilities to the inspectors. I think the—if you drop a plumb line through everything that's happened since the passage of that latest resolution, one would have to conclude that he has not been forthcoming.

   What will happen next, I can't say. That's well above my pay grade.

Q. You seem to be indicating—

Secretary Rumsfeld. But the president of the United States did take the time yesterday, I believe, to say something like, quote, "time is running," unquote.

* * * *

Q. But the world keeps talking about "Well, we need some evidence. We need some"—

Secretary Rumsfeld. Well, the world doesn't talk. The media talks, and people talk.

Q. Various leaders of various governments—

Secretary Rumsfeld. Yes, yes. Let me go back to what's been going on up on the Hill. They have been trying to connect the dots about September 11th. What did somebody know? How did it happen? Was there some way to stop and save the lives of those 3,000 people?

In the case of Iraq, the task is to connect the dots before there's a smoking gun. If there's a smoking gun, and it involves weapons of mass destruction, it is a lot of people dead, not 3,000, but multiples of that.

And that is what the world is going through. The world is doing it at a time in a new century, with a new set of facts, where the power, the lethality of these weapons, is so vastly greater than conventional weapons and as has historically been the case.

And what the world is doing is it is wrestling with a dilemma. The dilemma is that, historically, we've tended to not do things until attacked. That has been generally the pattern. Not always. There have been plenty of people in the history of warfare who have seen people massing on their border and decided that that was a target of opportunity and went after the massing force near their border before they could attack. We'll call that a preemptive action. The United States did not wait for al Qaeda and Taliban in Afghanistan to keep continuing attacking us; we went after them.

Now, what the world is trying to get comfortable is if—if we behave like we behaved in the 20th century, and we said "Fair enough. We don't believe in attacking other countries. We believe we should wait and be attacked." And if that attack were to involve a biological weapon—or a nuclear weapon—the price to be paid for waiting would be enormous. Therefore, in trying to connect the dots before the fact, you have to do it in an environment that's not comfortable with that, that hasn't really been through this much. And it isn't surprising that there's a debate. It isn't surprising that people are weighing these things and giving them a value and an importance and a significance that they merit. These are big issues.

Q. Many leaders are arguing they want clearer evidence—from U.N. inspectors, from the United States—

Secretary Rumsfeld. Right.

Q.—before any preemptive action should be taken, and that they accuse—
Secretary Rumsfeld. Exactly.

Q.—some are accusing the U.S. of thinking of taking the law into its own hands, which is—

Secretary Rumsfeld. The right of self-defense is inherent in the sovereign state. So that—that issue is, it seems to me, clear and self-evident.

There isn't anybody who wouldn't love to have all the dots connected. Why—why isn't it—it—wouldn't it be wonderful if someone came down, walked in the room right now, and said, "Gee, here are all the dots. Let's connect them for everybody so life is simple." Life isn't simple. Life is complicated. You're dealing with a very tough apple. He's been in power a whale of a long time. He has killed a pile of people. He's attacked a number of nations. He's used chemical weapons on his own people and on his neighbors. And he's got a very effective denial and deception program. And if some-one is sitting here thinking, "Well, wouldn't it be nice if somebody walked up and handed you a chemical or a biological weapon, or physical evidence that they're with-in 15 minutes of having a nuclear weapon," that would be wonderful. It isn't going to happen! It will only happen if he decides to do it.

Q. Well, why not release more intelligence that you have, so people can connect the dots?

Secretary Rumsfeld. The United States is cooperating fully with the inspectors. We're offering intelligence capabilities in the air, we're offering specific information as to sites. Those sites are being inspected.

And this is a country that is enormous. This is a country that has vast underground capabilities to deceive and deny. It is a country where the people are intimidated and frightened to death that they'll be killed, if in fact they cooperate at all with those inspectors. It is a country where we have not yet gotten scientists and technicians and knowledgeable people to either defect or to leave the country, which the resolution called for, with the approval of Saddam Hussein. It isn't for us to grab those people and abduct them. His job, under that resolution, was to offer them up, to volunteer them so that the inspectors could take them and their families outside the country, to Cyprus, and talk to them.

Q. But the inspectors have said you've only just started releasing intelligence to them. I mean, do you feel under pressure to release a lot more intelligence or are you afraid those sources and methods—

Secretary Rumsfeld. It's not my decision. It's the Central Intelligence Agency that's been assigned by the government to work with the inspectors.

Q. Surely you must have an opinion on this.

Secretary Rumsfeld. I have both opinions and knowledge. And what I just said is correct; that they are—the United States government, the Central Intelligence Agency, is in fact giving site locations and specific information to the inspectors. They are doing that.

Q. And what is the status of that offer to provide overhead surveillance for the inspectors?

General Myers. We've offered the U-2 and Predator to the U.N. To date, they have accepted the use of the U-2; it would be under U.N. auspices—flown under U.N. aus-pices. And we—any time. We're ready to go. We've got the modalities in place. We've talked to UNMOVIC about all that.

But it was interesting that the Iraqi regime sent a letter to UNMOVIC, to Dr. Blix, and said, gee, we'd have a real problem with a U-2 flying over central Iraq because we'd have trouble deconflicting from all those other aircraft that are flying around that we're shooting at currently.

Remarks by Secretary of Defense Rumsfeld, January 15, 2003

Secretary Donald Rumsfeld was interviewed by Dan Rather of CBS News.

Q. Earlier today, I talked exclusively with Secretary of Defense Donald Rumsfeld. I asked his opinion on the possibility that Saddam Hussein might choose exile instead of war.

Secretary Rumsfeld. History suggests that people do, in fact, if they make a judgment that the game is up, and it's over, and they've run their string, do on occasion leave. Whether this particular individual will do it, I don't know.

Q. Mr. Secretary, you have dealt with Saddam Hussein since the mid-1980s, been face to face with him, very few people have done that. Is it your judgment that there's some possibility he would go into exile? Is it your judgment he would fight to the finish?

Secretary Rumsfeld. If he sees that it's over, and he's not going to keep his country, he may very well decide to leave, and that would be a very good thing for the world. The last thing anyone wants is a war.

Q. Mr. Secretary, about the possibility, if there is any real possibility, of Iraqi scientists going outside the country to be interviewed, is it realistic to believe that a thousand or more people, keeping in mind the families who would want to go for safety reasons, that this can actually happen?

Secretary Rumsfeld. Oh, indeed. I think it can happen, Dan. Most of the people in that country don't like Saddam Hussein, they know he's a vicious dictator. And if they were offered an opportunity to get out of the country, I think that they would be willing to do that. There are people willing to do that, if we can find them, and if he'll allow them to leave.

Q. Of any number of Iraqi citizens, including a number of university students, say to me, Secretary Rumsfeld keeps saying that Iraq has the possibility of developing nuclear weapons. North Korea says it's already developed nuclear weapons. What would you say to those people if you faced them eyeball to eyeball?

Secretary Rumsfeld. The difference with Iraq is that Iraq for the better part of a decade has been subject to U.N. resolutions. Everything has been tried. The world community has pretty well run out the string. This is a regime that has—it's punched every single ticket of being an irresponsible member of the world community.

Remarks by Secretary of State Powell, January 16, 2003

Secretary Colin Powell was interviewed by a panel of journalists representing member countries newly elected to the United Nations Security Council.

It's a great pleasure to welcome you as representing the new elected members of the Security Council countries. And, as you know, the United States works very closely with the Security Council and I think that was evidenced in the work we did to produce Resolution 1441 and other work that we do.

Very often you hear about the permanent five members of the Security Council, but I always remember that there are 15, and the ten elected members are just as important. Even though they don't have veto rights, they bring the hopes and aspirations of the people of their country and they are sovereign nations who have to be dealt with as sovereign nations with their own points of view, their own principles to uphold and their own public positions.

And it is for that reason that I welcome this opportunity to speak to those publics through you and I look forward to working with the new members in the months ahead.

Q. If I can key off, sir, do you regret now having gone to the United Nations? Was it a mistake? And I think in the context of the insistence from, at the moment, all of your allies that there needs to be a second resolution and the resistance at this moment to giving you authorization to go off to Iraq. If you hadn't gone to the U.N., you could go ahead and do it, maybe you would already have done it by now.

Secretary Powell. We have absolutely no regrets. The problem that was before the international community was one that had to be dealt with by the international community. And that's why the President felt it was important for him to go before the United Nations on the 11th (sic) of September and remind the United Nations of its responsibilities to enforce its resolutions—many resolutions over a period of a dozen years that Iraq had systemically ignored, Iraq had thrown out or caused to be thrown out or made it impossible for the UNSCOM inspectors to remain in Iraq in 1998, and nobody knew what Iraq had been doing since 1998, but certainly there was no question that they were working on weapons of mass destruction but there were no inspectors in there to see what was going on.

So it was a United Nations problem and this President, anxious to work with the international community, took it to the United Nations. But we have no regrets. When you are dealing with a international body like that, different countries have different opinions, and Resolution 1441 is still playing out. On the 27th of January, the chief inspectors, Dr. Blix and Dr. ElBaradei, will report to the Security Council and each of the 15 members of the Security Council will be there to receive that report and make a judgment about that report. The United States has not asked for a resolution, a second resolution. It has not done anything right now but say that it waits for Dr. Blix's report.

We believe, however, that based on what we have seen so far, Iraq is failing to meet the mandate of 1441. Iraq has failed to cooperate. It has failed to put forward a believable declaration, as required. It is not making people available. It is not making documents available. It is deceiving the inspectors. It is trying to make it harder for the inspectors to do their work.

What the United States will be looking for on the 27th of January and what every member of the Security Council should be looking for on the 27th of January is a simple—is a simple proposition: Is Iraq cooperating, as was intended under 1441? And is it cooperating in a way that would satisfy the demands of the international community for Iraq to disarm? And that's a judgment that the Council will have to make.

We cannot get ourselves into a situation where the Council just, in the presence of this kind of non-cooperation, just wants to not do anything and let it continue forever.

Q. What's the level of proof for a judgment?

Secretary Powell. The level of proof is what will persuade the Council whether or not Iraq is or is not disarmed or being disarmed. So it is not a legal level of proof before a court of law. It's a judgment that will have to be made by the 15 members of the Council. Is Iraq cooperating in a way that will allow the inspectors to get to the truth? So far, we do not believe Iraq is. If Iraq wanted to get to the truth and wanted to satisfy the mandate, they would be not waiting to have information pulled out of them, pried out of them, dug out of holes. They'd be putting it all forward. Here's what we did. Here are all the people who used to participate in the programs that we no longer have. That's what we are looking for.

And if that is not the spirit of cooperation, I think, that is present, then I think the Security Council has to take a hard look at it. There's a lot of debate of whether it's 1441 or 1284. That is really—there are two resolutions, but that isn't the major question before us. The major question before us is how to get implementation under 1441 and the Council will receive this report on the 27th of January and the Council will, in due course, sometime after that, make its judgment as to what the inspectors should do. Dr. Blix said today, I think, or yesterday, that he will await the instructions of the Security Council, which is quite correct. That's what he should—

Q. But, Mr. Secretary, it looks like this administration is rushing for a war that they don't want to give the inspectors more time. As Mr. Blix said, they could do a better job if they had all been presented a report on March the 27th. And so far, outside Washington all the capitals of the world are waiting for the proof that the Iraqi regime has weapons of mass destruction and so far we haven't seen anything, just your word and the word of the President of the United States.

Secretary Powell. I think we have presented information to members of the Council over time. If you want proof that Iraq has weapons of mass destruction and has used them in the past, I can show you pictures of them using them in the past. We know they have used them in the past against their own people, against others. And there is no doubt that they were developing nuclear weapons before the Gulf War, and the IAEA did a good job of bringing that to a halt. But we are not yet satisfied that we know what they have been doing since the IAEA was asked to leave the country some four years or so ago.

And so it seems to me that a regime that has the intent to develop weapons of mass destruction, the capacity to do so, and we believe has been doing so, the burden is on them to prove that they do not have weapons of mass destruction. That's the problem. It is not—you know, we believe and we believe that we will be presenting information in the days ahead, more than we have in the past, that will give you our impression and our evidence, and we are waiting to see what the inspectors turn up. That's why we're waiting for the first official report from Dr. Blix on the 27th of January.

There are also many people who don't want to see the evidence. They don't want to know anything about it. We just don't want to have to deal with this problem. The reason the inspectors are back in Iraq now is because the President of the United States and other nations made it clear that Iraq was going to be disarmed one way or the other.

And so the American buildup that you're seeing and other buildup—buildups by other nations that you see taking place, is part of supporting the diplomatic pressure to make Iraq perform, to make Iraq comply with the resolution. The President has not made a decision for war. The President has said he would like to see this resolved peaceably. But if it isn't resolved peacefully—peacefully—then, he believes the international community has an obligation to disarm Iraq forcefully. And he believes if the international community isn't willing to do it, then the United States, with likeminded nations, may have that obligation so that the world does not face an Iraq with weapons of mass destruction.

And so the 27th of January is an important date. We will get this report from Dr. Blix and Dr. ElBaradei and then we can make collective, as well as individual, judgments. Each country can make its judgment.

Q. Can we just get back on the issue of the second resolution? Will you seek a second resolution? Do you need a second resolution?

Secretary Powell. If we want the entire Security Council to act as a body, the international community, the U.N., to act as a body, then that would suggest a second resolution. But we have always made it clear that even in the absence of a second resolution, if the United States feels strongly that Iraq still has weapons of mass destruction and trying to develop new ones, the United States reserves the right and believes there is sufficient authority within international law, based on many acts of noncompliance, many material breaches in the past and continuing material breaches into the present, that would give us a basis for undertaking whatever might be required to disarm Iraq.

But the question of whether or not there is going to be a second resolution and who'll introduce it and what might it look like and what will the vote be for it, it's premature for me to speculate on this.

Q. Sir, if I may—

Secretary Powell. I'm well aware that many nations around the world would like to see a second resolution as the legal basis for action and we are taking their concerns very much to mind and to heart. We have been patient. We have not rushed to judgment, but at the same time, you can't keep judgment from occurring just because you're afraid that the judgment might lead to actions that you would just as soon not support or not see undertaken.

The thing that is absolutely clear, that the President has spoken to it, Prime Minister Blair has spoken to it, many nations have spoken to it, even those nations who are anxious to see a second resolution, and that is that Saddam Hussein must be disarmed. And so far, he was given a last final chance under 1441 and the evidence so far is that he has failed to take the opportunity that's been presented to him.

Q. Sir, may I say that all along the atmosphere, the attitude of the U.S. administration has been very hostile, very belligerent and very strong, and denunciatory language has been used, and there is a feeling that all over the world that the United States has made up its mind in any case to invade Iraq and also, the U.S. has failed to establish to the satisfaction of the world that Iraq poses a clear and present physical threat to the United States.

Secretary Powell. The international community has engaged in diplomacy with Iraq for the last dozen years. That's what all those many U.N. resolutions were all about. This is not a court proceedings. This is a reluctant witness and a reluctant provider of evidence that has taken every effort to hide what it is doing and to distract the inspectors from their work and to deceive the inspectors and to keep the information hidden in a very large country, and at the same time saying they have no weapons of mass destruction. If they have no weapons of mass destruction, and we believe that evidence has been provided over the years that they do have weapons of mass destruction, then I certainly believe the obligation is on them to say, "Okay, here is why we make the claim that we have no weapons of mass destruction."

We're not dealing with a misdemeanor. We're dealing with a felonious state that has used these weapons of mass destruction and has done everything to hide them for the last 15 years. If you look at what the inspectors were doing in the early '90s after the Gulf War and Iraq was saying, "We don't have anything, we don't have anything," and then suddenly a defector gets out and says, "Well, let me tell you what they have." And suddenly we have this piece of information and we go back and say, "You do you have biological weapons," and they say, "Oh, yeah, well, we forgot to tell you about that." This is not the kind of assurance you should take from this kind of a regime.

And I'm saying to you right now that if they do have biological weapons, as they finally had to admit, that is a threat not only to the nations immediately around Iraq, that is a threat to the world. And anybody who would be complacent and say you Americans are picking on this terrible regime, which is developing biological weapons that are no threat to anybody, I think that is a wrong way to look at it.

* * * *

Q. Let me get back to the question of proof. Iraq has—if Iraq behaves as we know it used to behave and would not disclose, then the world still expects some kind of proof or some better feeling of the kind of threat you now perceive to share that intensity to confront that threat. And you always mention these kinds of proofs you want to disclose within the next days. We haven't seen anything yet. More things are

coming. Where is it? It's like sort of the secret weapon, you know, from history. Surely you'll be able to elaborate on that.

Secretary Powell. No, there is—you know, there will not be a—I don't know of a secret weapon that we're suddenly pulling out of a vault or out of an office somewhere. But we believe that as this debate unfolds, beginning on the 27th, the information that we have available to us and we'll be providing to the world, and what the inspectors say with respect to lack of cooperation, and what the inspectors might have been able to find that would satisfy somebody as concrete evidence, they may or may not between now and the 27th. We believe a persuasive case will be there at the end of the month that Iraq is not cooperating.

Now, we will have to look at that case at the time and then the Council will have to make a judgment as to what the Council should do at that time. And the United States separately, and each nation separately, will have to make its own judgment as to what it should or should not do.

Q. So why the rush? I work—my office is at the United Nations. I can tell you a lot of diplomats there ask me that question all the time. Why the rush? Why can't we have another year? Why not give us the time to find the evidence? Kofi Annan himself had a press conference the day before yesterday, and in answer to a question of mine said, "I see no evidence that we're there yet in terms of the war. Give the process time." Blix has been talking about using 1284 which spells out the processes of a year. But is it purely being the domestic American political calendar that requires it to happen—

Secretary Powell. It's not—what part of our domestic political calendar do you have in mind? The election is over and there's not another one coming for—

Q. Well, I guess the idea is that people have to start pitting the hustlings in New Hampshire in the year's time.

Secretary Powell. No, no, that has got nothing to do with American domestic politics. It has to do with the threat that has been left un-dealt-with for all these many, many months, and these many, many years for that matter.

And what we don't want to see happen is for the Iraqis to suddenly play this game on us again where the world says, "Oh, gee. Let's just leave them alone. They're not bothering anybody. And let's not put any military forces into play. Let's not show them any forceful determination on the part of the international community, and all will be well again."

And we'll be right back here, and if a year or two years from now we were to follow such a course of action and suddenly one day Saddam Hussein pops up and said, "Surprise, you didn't get it. But here it is." Then we'll all be staring at each other wondering why we didn't do something.

So it is not that we are in a rush to judgment. We think that it has been a rather slow movement to justice over the last—or judgment, over the last 12 years. And now that we have started it with 1441, it is time to move rapidly to get to the bottom of the case with this regime.

1284 was done in 1999 for another time and another place, and it essentially talks about coming up with a list of uncompleted tasks, I think, or something like that is the term of [*inaudible*]. Well, how do you make a solid determination of what uncompleted tasks are if you're not getting the kind of cooperation you need to determine what the full set of tasks are in the beginning, to begin with?

And so I think there will be a debate, a discussion that we'll have to enter into, as to how Blix and ElBaradei should move forward after they have reported on the 27th of January. As you well know, that's the only report called for under 1441. But that is not to say that the Council might not instruct both of them, "Come back in two weeks and give us a report." And that's a debate that will have to take place within the Council.

Q. Do you think it's fair, that perception of you as the loyal opposition inside the White House? I suppose that every time you are—if you are risking five dollars for every time you are portrayed as the dissident in residence of this administration, you will be as rich as Bill Gates.

Secretary Powell. No, I don't think so. We have strong members of this administration in the national security part of the administration, and we present our views to the President. We are blessed to have a strong President who can hear these views and make a decision.

But the policy of this government is not set by the Secretary of State or the Secretary of Defense or anyone but the President. And when you say I am a dissident, I feel like I should go, you know, find asylum somewhere.

But I certainly don't feel that way. I feel that the President values the advice he receives from all of his national security associates and all of us feel absolutely free to argue with each other, debate with each other and provide our best advice to the President.

And, you know, the President is the one who decided that he should take this to the international community, to the United Nations. The President is the one who decided rather than look for another crisis in Northeast Asia—rather than find a—create a crisis atmosphere in South—in Northeast Asia, we should try to find a diplomatic solution.

These are, I think, multilateral approaches of the kind that we are constantly asked to pursue. And multilateralism doesn't mean, however, getting so wrapped up in the process that nothing comes out the other end.

The U.N. has been given a challenge by Iraq. For 12 years, Iraq said to the most important international organization on earth, one that was created to deal with problems like this, "We don't care what you think or what resolutions you pass. We don't care and we no longer want the inspectors here. We're going to make it impossible for them to act and we're going to try to hide things." Anybody who thinks they're not hiding things is not looking at reality.

* * * *

Q. You're talking to the new members of the Security Council and there are a lot in there which have doubts following you in this, especially Germany which might have the Security Council at that point. Governments might break apart during the course of that political action. Would you do it alone, pay that price, risking international solidarity or risking sort of alliances in the course of action against Iraq?

Secretary Powell. We are not out to cause fissures within governments. We are out to do one thing, and that is to disarm Iraq. And the 15 members of the Security Council who met on the morning of the 7th of November . . . fifteen of them said, "Here is a tough resolution that we all have agreed to unanimously that calls for Iraq to cooperate in getting to the truth and to let the inspectors back in." If the Council had not spoken that clearly at that time, not a single inspector would be there today. There would be nothing going on but more Iraqi intransigence. It is pressure, not a willingness to cooperate, that has brought us to this point. That pressure has to be maintained.

I hope that as we go into these discussions my colleagues in the Security Council and the capitals represented by the Security Council and the nations represented by the Security Council will meet their responsibilities with respect to the disarmament of Iraq and I hope that they will be able to convey to their people why this is important. It's important for not just the safety and security of the United States.

The United States is not just off looking for a war to get into. It is important that regimes like this do not have these kinds of weapons of mass destruction and this is a regime that has been working on it for more than 12 years, 15 years, since before the Gulf War, long before, wasted its people's treasure, and that the United Nations has to remain a relevant body. And if you're passing all these resolutions over the years, and then passing unanimously 1441 by a 15-0 vote, you then walk away from 1441 without what you were seeking. That would be a terrible blow to the United Nations.

But I do recognize—I'm not unmindful of the positions of the individual governments you represent here today and the fact that there are countries where the public opinion is very definitely against any military action to compel Iraqi compliance. Everybody has hope that Iraq will comply peacefully. Well, everybody then should be putting pressure on Iraq.

* * * *

Q. Are you disturbed by the level of anti-Americanism? And linked to that, the word—the "I" word is making its appearance increasingly frequently—imperialism. We saw it in The New York Times Magazine the other day, U.S. News and World Report. Al Gore himself used it the other day. Does the anti-Americanism worry you?

Secretary Powell. There is a degree of anti-Americanism out there. It comes in waves and then it goes. I think that we can persuade the international community that what we are doing is not some form of American imperialism. America has not been an imperialistic nation. We have had possessions over the years and what we've done with most of them is get rid of them. Those are the ones that wanted to be free and independent. We are not the ones who colonized or imposed imperialistic regimes on the world.

Address by Iraqi President Hussein, January 17, 2003

Iraqi president Saddam Hussein delivered the following address to the Iraqi nation.

In the Name of God, the Compassionate, the Merciful

There are those who, on being told: "Your enemy has mustered a great force against you and so fear them," they grew more tenacious in their faith and replied: "Allah's help is all- sufficient for us. He is the best Protector." Thus they earned Allah's grace and bounty and no harm befell them. For they had striven to please Allah, whose, bounty is infinite. It is Satan that prompts men to fear his followers. But have no fear of them. Fear Me, if you are true believers. Do not grieve for those that quickly renounce their faith. They will not harm Allah in the least. He seeks to give them no share in the hereafter. Their punishment shall be terrible indeed.

God speaks the truth

Great people in Iraq, the land of faith, Jihad, bravery and glory..

Brave members of the gallant armed forces..

Sons of our glorious Arab nation..

Men of goodwill in the world, wherever you are.. From the bright light of dawn, from the ray of sun which has risen after a long absence, from its horizon, from the lids of the eyes which were wounded by heavy tears for people, dear for all of us, who can no more be seen, but who can become visible with the new sun, and from the horizon which God has ordained to be vast, with a new birth and life in whose skies exist green birds and a strong newborn which God has decided to be faithful to its nation, from all this your glorious Revolution and march, a new Iraq, was born. Its faith has been increased and deepened after the Grand Confrontation on the night of 16/17 1991, the grand military phase of the eternal battle of Um Al-Maarik, by the flagrance of the generous blood, suffering and commendable patience. A new Iraq was born with firm resolution, great power of vision and a heart, which has been increased in strength by a determination for ascent and for overcoming difficulties. It was firm in its love for its nation. Its faith, which God has given it and which the situation and banner was perfumed by generous blood from its sons, has been deepened by a scarifies which God has accepted in compensation for the negligence which took over those who ruled Baghdad, and therefore the foreigners with the horny feet of their horses, found their way towards it. The radiation of its eyes over the nation and humanity has set down, after the water of Tigris was dyed with plentiful blood along with the ink of its books which were filled with science and knowledge, and which were thrown into the water in the year 1258, as a punishment for a history whose soul departed its body and for a civilization whose faith and guards disappeared. Hence, the ravens croaked in it, showing impudence to its eyes through which humanity saw its way to raise in culture after it had played its role and into enlighten those who could see that and accepted from it as a means from God to them as a reward for its faith and fear.

The new Iraq was born on such a view, and was born with it, its rifle in place of the arrow, spear and sword, to be armed so that the ravens could not be so covetous as to venture its palms and the eyes of its children.

A strong, believing and healthy Iraq was born. But the birth, as all other births which came before it in the horizon of humanity and in our nation, was not able to render ineffectual the croak of ravens, nor the hissing of snakes or the crossing of far crocodiles from the seas of their family in order to help the beasts of earth in their attack against the sun, in a desperate hope to obscure its light which radiated from Baghdad or to shed the blood of its people in a fake hope and out of an imagination that the generous blood shed on the soil of Baghdad and on the soil of Iraq could hinder the plants and trees from becoming green, from blossoming and from carrying with its fragrance pollens which might tempt the appetite of butterflies, and thus be able to carry with the news of new faith and resolution, with the dew and tears, a pollen to every tree whose branches and leaves become dry or ceased to give fruits now that the water ceased to reach its roots and was confident that no one could take care of its fruits and guard its plants, trees and growth.

With the new birth, there was Satan and his companion, the lizards of this time, who spit out their fire on the healthy body. But, as the birth of Baghdad was now healthy and proper, blessed by heaven by order of its God, and that its guard were putting their hands on their rifles during the dawn prayer on the day of birth, with great confidence in their breasts, on the night of 16/17 January 1991 and afterwards, Baghdad, in the name of Iraq, kept defending itself along with every faithful valiant and noble woman in defense of the command which God has so decided to their new birth. Their will of determination never bent . They defeated all evil troops of more than thirty states together with those who supported them. The number of the army, which the jihadists in the Iraq army had confronted, mounted to twenty-eight. The state of Iraq stood in the face of the aggression of forty-two countries on the night of 16 / 17 January. The confrontation and the battle lasted for a month and a half with such momentum. Afterwards, the sanctions and aggression continued for thirteen years until the present day. Such was the defense of the Iraqis on that day and the days that followed. Others, in their turn, defended the seeds which they sowed and elevated what they had built, to the point that their fields were mixed with the spacious gardens. Plants covered the land of Iraq reminding of its past when the land of Iraq was described as the land of the black for the multitude of its plants which disappeared from Baghdad, its countryside and towns, until it appeared as if they did not exist before as one sign of its health. It had mixed with the lofty constructions, dear and visible, and was dominated by the high minarets, domes and signs of the houses of worship. And with every exaltation of "Allah is the greatest" on the battlefields, the same gratification rose high in the mosques together with the voices of worship in their places, each in accordance with his own religion and manner. A visitor could tell that he was in Baghdad even though his eyes were shut, in an attempt that a traveler could hardly recognize his feet on the map—Was there a place much better than Baghdad, where religions and racial tolerance together with constructive views being born, on the side and direction of every constructive thing of other views—?

The new birth brought back once again the spirit of Baghdad, and with the birth a stand, a sword, a pen and a banner were born. The call of "Allah is the greatest" blessed the stand, the sword and the pen. The birth whose threats were knitted by the dawn and blessed by the call for prayer, was an impregnable birth to every malicious, perfidious and greedy—It could not deserve, nor could Allah and the people accept for it, but the life chosen for it by its pioneers after they asked the permission of their Lord, the Merciful. The scheming of the attackers backfired in that aggression and in the ongoing aggression which they make longer to the present day. Everyone who tries to climb over its wall, be it an aggressor, an insolent, a wicked, a perfidious and an oppressor will fail in his attempt.

Is not this your description and position for the men of Iraq, the believer and loyal jihadists, and for the noble women as well? Or is there anyone who might delude himself into believing to say, after treading down his luck, that Saddam Hussein is speaking about his wishes and not about a description of a condition in which he lives and gets to know, with heart and soul, its comprehensive and detailed nature? By God, this is your description and attitude, or even a reward for your suffering, sacrifices, and patience, o brave men and women.. The evil ravens and evil crocodiles, still foster wickedness and would never cease their communication with their disappointed hopes, despite the fact that their deep wounds and disgrace can not be rubbed out with the passage of time. The lizards which breathed out fire on our lord, Ibrahim (peace be upon him), as is often related by people, still give birth and still assign for every birth the task of breathing out fire, out of their belief that they are capable of burning away, in defiance of God's will which He chose to be cool and safe.

Hence, with the flying banner, raise high your swords and rifles, oh our dear people, and remind anyone who may still be under a delusion, so that he might not be deluded of your stand in the (Greatest March), on the day of the Grand Allegiance and in other attitudes, but if he does so, let your guns waiting in ambush for him, preceded and guided by the radiation and light of your faith necessary for safeguarding your eyes. This is because, if their ravens have a fancy and find no one to deter them, God forbid, then they would peck up the eyes and devour the hearts and brains of faith, virtue and innovation. Hold fast to your banner, the banner of (Allah is the Greatest)..There is nothing but it that can help motivate the resolution to rise and give to defense its profound connotation.

Say :God is the greatest, oh brothers and sons. Remember the meanings of this great call in accordance with the profundity of your faith, so that its echo, along with your words and support, could be sounded by all towns and rural areas, by mountains and by plains. And with the help of the waters of Tigris and Euphrates and the water of the Gulf, your voice can reach not only every brave man and woman in the land of faith and Jihad, but also every loyal man and woman in the nation, every fair-minded and everyone who has an honorable stance in humanity.

When birth is associated with a stance, a determination, a pen, a sword and a banner, then birth can assume its proper role in our nation, God willing.

When we say that history is tantamount to doctrine, and is remembered by those who inherit it with contemplation, consideration and responsibility, this is because everything right is born with it and from it, and becomes a new and constant history after it gives a new birth with each glory and construction. A firm belief is its safe foundation . It becomes a doctrine carried from the past, still possesses the condition of the true birth when so remembered by its sons with the responsibility of the present, and with the due ambition for the future.

Such was the labor of the past. From its womb it begets a doctrine; new in its spirit, in dress and colour and its special path —And with the new doctrine, a strong flagpost and hand has been born bearing our pride and our guidance to faith: Allahu Akbar, to stand firm in the face of every violent wind, God willing, or evil attempt. Yes, Allahu Akbar—

Allahu Akbar—

Brothers :

The saying that (history repeats itself) means, among other things, that aspects of the past could be repeated though they assume the colors and names of their stages— They repeat themselves should they be re-analyzed, revived and dissolved into their primary elements and ingredients as to their strength and weakness, ascent and descent, climbing and falling into abyss , good and bad, climbing to peaks and falling into abyss, pursuit of good will and virtue against pursuit of evil and vice, those who hate people and bring harm to them against those who love people and work for their welfare, the destroyers and the constructors and the like in the series of the images and their contrasts, up and down, bad and good.

Yes, it is true that history repeats itself but not on the basis of an uncontested premise of the ability to go up, as compared with the past without faith, consciousness, attitude and determination, or to give up to a descent case, as compared with the past also, except when all its items in life, man and nature are repeated to the point that it can hardly be conceived. Yet, a conscientious faith in portraying of how the role of man can be effective and ascending, of how can that faith be maintained together with its factors and causes and how can one reject any condition that may have an adverse impact on the faith, of the role of the believing and vanguard man in it and in its movement, or the denouncing of all this, is the decisive case in which history may repeat itself in the same form, here and there, whether negatively or positively.

Brother..

Baghdad in its known history , had played the role of the Arabs' and Muslims' pure eye. It was God's spear on earth, the Arabs' skull, the reservoir of their wisdom and glorious heritage, the focal point of their civilization and great radiation. That was with other supporting roles in other centers in conformity of what had happened in Baghdad or before that time. When the Mongols and Tatars reached the zenith of their strength and occupied China, India, Persia and other countries, they were unable to convert their ascent to strength by backwardness and destruction into a force capable of bringing construction, civilization and culture. The destroying force found its complex in Baghdad; the abode of civilization and peace, and made it its target for destruction which was rendered feeble because of the weakness of those who did not hold firm to the factors of ascent, its causes and results, and also of the weakness of its rulers and the betrayal of the traitors—Hulago and his troops occupied Baghdad for forty days and destroyed every live thing in it.. And because the people of Baghdad, I mean the rulers in it, were not quite prepared when the Mongols and Tatars invaded the territory of China, India, Persia and the surroundings, their invasion of Baghdad was in agreement of what history had described, and which later include Syria and the parts connected to it.

But Baghdad was not in a position to defend itself properly, and therefore the eyes of Hulago's army were not gouged out on its walls nor was it extinguished in its face the venture of trespassing it, or even to deny it the chance of going ahead to others from the nation to attack them as it attacked Baghdad, till Hulago's eyes were gouged out at the hands of the Mameluke dynasty in Egypt at the famous battle of (Ain Jalut),after they were able to get prepared for it and learnt lessons from the war before them and after Hulago's intent and methods were revealed—History tells us that western peoples and circles had played, for their own reasons, a role in directing Hulago to the east, indeed to the Arab world in particular. The Jews and their supporters played a remarkably malicious role against Baghdad in the past and this conspiratorial, aggressive and wicked role is today reverting to them, to the Zionist Jews and to the Zionists who are not of Jewish origin, particularly those who are in the U.S. administration and around who stood in opposite front of our nation and Iraq . The force in America proved itself to be incapable of educating itself. It was not able to change itself into a capability, so that its impact would be humanitarian and instructive. Zionism and prejudicial people had pushed it to search for a role through a devastating brutal instinct instead of ascending to a position of responsible ability and to its civic, cultural role which suits this age and suits the role of balanced nations and their construction role in the collective milieu and work.

Yet, Baghdad today, brothers, has its eyes pure, its mind and conscious clear of any rust or cover, and are proud of the nation and for it, in the name of God, after they have put their trust in the Owner of Potency and gets prepared to the role.

Although some eyes and minds in our nation and humanity are still incapable of seeing or perceiving the pros and cons in the nation and humanity, the people and rulers of Baghdad have resolved to compel the Mongols of this age to commit suicide on its walls and make the confrontation, in terms of meaning and sacrifice, to rise to a level which could lead other eyes and minds to be wide open of what is going around it and get elevated to its role, and make the force which it possesses after or before anyone may take this risk and is deceived by its Satan to trespass the walls of Baghdad, to be effective in the human milieu, capable of converting it into an ascent force in the milieu of constructive competition and not a brute force based on brutal devastating instinct.

Acting upon this, brothers and friends in our nation and humanity, we give our promise and make the Capable and the Great, our witness for our promise.

And acting upon this also, we have prepared our plans and muster our strength at the level of armies, people and leadership after placing our reliance on God . All success is from God.

Allah is the greatest

Allah is the greatest

Brothers..

The rulers of Baghdad in the past grew old. They renounced the role so commanded for them by God and deterred those who were responsible for their subjects from introducing innovations in their life affairs and defense of it when Hulago came to the walls of Baghdad in the year 1258. Thus Hulago came with the sunset and the rule passed to him with Baghdad as its capital. The Mongols succeeded and the sun set down from Baghdad at that time.

But now, despite Hulago's spirit has settled in whomsoever it has settled; in their actions, in what they did, or in what they are now doing, or in what they intend to do, of those who have been incited by the criminal Zionists in more than a place in the world, they have come to confront our nation at a time when the sons of our nation are embracing inside their souls and breasts, a great faith and a great state of consciousness of their role and of how it should be in order that they attain what it must be attained, and thus the nation could revert to its true belief, and could, with its Jihad and struggle, realize a true ascent to its great, faithful, pan-Arab and humanitarian role.

Hulago's army has now come at this age to confront Baghdad after it has born anew with the sunrise, to record, with its new youth, a level of ascent which suits it well after it has abandoned its leading role for about seven hundred years.

O Iraqis, you have indeed brought the sun back to Baghdad, and have shined in it at the time the city has been illuminated by you. But oh, how can a new Hulago destroy the city or the great Iraq, and how can the brutal, the perfidious and the greedy, after God has ordained this nation to rise again, defeat the will of determination of your brothers in Palestine as well or wherever the will of truth, steadfastness and resistance has ripened or blossomed in the breast of every believer who embraces a great confidence. Oh people..

You know that the first human civilization in history was grown, blossomed and bore fruits in Iraq . From that civilization, the air carried its seeds to reach to whomever it could reach, who, according to his own personal opinion, added colour to it to suit his own country. For this reason, it is the mother of civilization of Iraq which Hulago of this age wants to attack.. So, tell him in a clear, loud voice, oh evil, halt your evil-doings against the mother of civilization, its museum and basic witness, the cradle and the birthplace of prophets and messengers. Tell him to let people, each in accordance with his human choice, to build, and to build and to build which is necessary for rising high the construction, for work, for fruitful cooperation and for the dissemination of love among people. Tell him to avoid provoking hatred and evil doings so that every one can enjoy his rights, full and complete, in such a manner that might please God and bring happiness for him in the two worlds..

Everyone in whose body the Hulago' intent and action has settled down will commit suicide at the walls of Baghdad and Iraq towns, as was the case with those who died at the walls of Jenin and Palestinian towns. The entire nation will rise up in defense of its right to life, of its role and of anything it holds sacred —Their arrows will be on the wrong track or will recoil to their breasts, God willing —The martyrs of the nation will turn into green birds in paradise as the Merciful has promised. Let evil be on he who thinks evil..

Long live our glorious nation.

Long live Iraq.

Long live Iraq with its brave jihadist armyr—

Long live Palestine, free and Arab from the sea to the river—Long live Palestine's freedom fighters and jihadists together with its heroic people—

Glory and heaven be for martyrs—

Glory and heaven be for the martyrs of Iraq, Palestine and the nation—

Allah is the greatest.

Allah is the greatest.

Allah is the greatest.

Remarks by Secretary of State Powell, January 19, 2003

Secretary Colin Powell was interviewed on CNN's Late Edition by Wolf Blitzer.

Q. A quick question everybody in the country, people around the world, want to know: Will there be a war with Iraq?

Secretary Powell. We're still hoping for a peaceful solution, but it is up to Saddam Hussein and Iraq to make that decision. Dr. Blix and Dr. ElBaradei are in Baghdad today. I hope they will make it clear to Saddam Hussein that he is running out of time, he has got to cooperate; moreover, he has got to disarm and he has got to do it in a way that the inspectors don't have to go hunt-and-peck looking for things, but that Iraq comes forward and meets the will of the international community that it must disarm of its weapons of mass destruction. If they do that, there is still a chance for a peaceful solution.

Q. How much time do the Iraqis have?

Secretary Powell. Well, we'll see. I think time is running out. We can't keep this up forever. And we'll all look forward to receiving the report from Dr. Blix and Dr. ElBaradei next Monday, the 27th of January, at the United Nations. And after that, the Security Council will have an opportunity to make its judgment as to what should happen next, and the President of the United States will also make his judgment as to what he thinks should happen next.

Q. Well, you're quoted as saying earlier in the week, you said, "We believe a persuasive case will be there at the end of the month that Iraq is not cooperating."

Secretary Powell. I think there is a persuasive case there now. Iraq has given us a false declaration in December, still has not accounted for stocks of various biological and chemical agents that we know they had. And there is a discrepancy between what they had and what they are now reporting they have, and they have not solved those discrepancies. And we simply can't walk away from that kind of discrepancy.

So there is a case now. And we will see how strong that case looks when Dr. Blix and Dr. ElBaradei report, but I think it's fairly persuasive that they are not cooperating, and I hope they understand as a result of the visit of the two chief inspectors today that time is running out on them.

Q. It's one thing not to cooperate. It's another thing to find a smoking gun. The inspectors say so far they have not found a smoking gun. Is not cooperating enough of a smoking gun, if you will, to justify war?

Secretary Powell. That will be a matter for the Council to decide, and the President will make his own decision. But, you know, look at what we have found. We have found false declarations. There are all sorts of toxic agents that are unaccounted for.

And then this week, the inspectors found chemical rockets. Now, those rockets are not just laying benignly around. What are they doing there? Why—

Q. But they were—

Secretary Powell. What difference does it make? The point is that they are designed for a unique purpose, and that is to carry a chemical agent. And so they should have been declared. They should have been destroyed. This is the kind of weapon that Iraq says it no longer has, and yet there it is.

Now, whether that constitutes one person's smoking gun or some other person's smoking gun, I think it contributes to a body of evidence that suggests Iraq is not disarming and is not cooperating with efforts of the United Nations inspectors to get them to disarm. And that's what we're looking for, and I hope that message comes through clearly today when they meet with the Iraqi officials.

Q. Well, the Iraqis say it was simply a slip, they made a mistake.

Secretary Powell. Yeah. Well, how many other slips are there out there? They are laying there. They are in a facility. It's not a slip. They knew they were there. Somebody knew they were there. The inspectors found them. They didn't have a chance to hide these. How many other slips are there?

And when you look at the declaration, when you look at the efforts they have been taking to hide things, when you see the documents that are relevant—relevant to knowing the truth—are being squirreled away in the homes of scientists, when scientists are not allowed to come forward, then you can't say that they are participating in the effort to make sure they have no weapons of mass destruction.

And so I think their record so far, since the passage of U.N. Resolution 1441, is not a good record. And they have very little time left to make it a good record. And everybody knows what they have to do: come forward, tell the truth, give an accurate declaration, tell us what happened to these stocks of biological and chemical agents, tell us what you've got and put it out there for the inspectors to see. If you say you don't have them, if you say you're clean, then come clean.

And time is running out and we just can't keep hunting and pecking and looking and trying to see if we can capture something or discover something. Iraq is supposed to be cooperating in this effort. Iraq is supposed to be disarming. And they have not established, to my satisfaction anyway, and I think to the satisfaction of the international community, that they are moving in good faith to disarm, which is what they're supposed to do under the resolution.

Q. You keep saying time is running out. How much time do they have?

Secretary Powell. I'm not prepared to give a time here today, Wolf, because I think it's important that we continue this deliberative process that was set out in U.N. Resolution 1441. Dr. Blix and Dr. ElBaradei will report next Monday. The Council will hear their report, take their report into account. So will the President of the United

States and his advisors. And then we'll see what happens next or what steps are appropriate after that.

Q. You have heard the chief U.N. inspector Hans Blix say that after January 27, a week from tomorrow, they still need 60 days thereafter to come up with another review before any action necessarily could be taken. Do you accept that argument?

Secretary Powell. I heard Dr. Blix, and what he's referring to, of course, is another U.N. Resolution, 1284, which has another deadline to it.

Q. That was back in 1998.

Secretary Powell. Right. Well, 1999, if I'm not mistaken. Early 1999.

But the real issue is how the Council views this. 1441, the latest resolution, was rather specific. We want an accurate, complete and full declaration of what you're doing. We want cooperation with inspections. We don't want you to frustrate their efforts. Iraq is making it hard for us to perform aerial reconnaissance in support of the U.N. inspectors. And so far, they have not acted in a way that suggests they're serious about disarming. And if they're not serious about disarming, the Council should recognize that next week and start to decide what to do, and not just say let's just keep going and slip into the 1284, the other resolution, route.

And so I know Dr. Blix is operating under two resolutions, but the fact of the matter, it will be up to the Council to decide what happens next after Dr. Blix reports and Dr. ElBaradei reports.

Q. Some of the allies—the French, other permanent members of the Security Council, the Russians—say they need a second resolution before there can be any war. You disagree with them. Why?

Secretary Powell. I'm saying that there is more than enough evidence, and frankly there is more than enough authority in previous resolutions, if it becomes necessary to act unilaterally or with likeminded nations.

But there are a number of nations who say they would like to see a second resolution. Well, the United States will examine the evidence that is before us after the two inspectors report next week. We'll consult with our friends and allies. And it is up to the Security Council to decide whether or not they want a referral to Council to see whether or not a second resolution is appropriate at this time.

And if that is what the Council wants to do, the United States would certainly participate in that debate. But the President has always said, from the very beginning, that the object is to disarm Iraq, and if the U.N. is not willing to do it and is not willing to be relevant in a situation such as this, the United States reserves the option, if it feels it must do so, to act with likeminded nations to disarm Iraq.

Q. But as you well know, being a former Chairman of the Joint Chiefs of Staff, you can't keep tens of thousands, hundreds of thousands of U.S. troops in the Persian Gulf region forever in an unlimited capacity, 50- or 60- or 70,000 Marines aboard

amphibious assault ships under a hot sun in the Persian Gulf. How long can you keep them there? So there is a sort of deadline that's created by the deployment.

Secretary Powell. The President has not made a decision. These are deployments with the purpose of supporting diplomacy and making sure there is no doubt in Saddam Hussein's mind that we're going to keep the pressure on. If we had not shown a willingness to put in place a military force, the inspectors would never have gotten in. Iraq isn't doing this as, you know, a cooperative effort. They still don't understand that they must comply with the requirements of 1441 or they're going to face military action.

And therefore, it is very prudent of the United States and other nations to begin deploying armed forces to the region. Now, how long they would stay and how long you can maintain a particular level, I will let my colleague Don Rumsfeld talk to that. But the President has made it clear that we will position ourselves to do whatever might be necessary in the absence of Saddam Hussein disarming under the terms of 1441.

Q. If you take a look at this proposal apparently out there, the Saudis, the Turks, others, that want to see some Iraqi generals overthrow Saddam Hussein or get Saddam Hussein to leave, to go into exile someplace.

Do either of these proposals, in your estimate, have a chance of succeeding?

Secretary Powell. Well, I'm not familiar with all of these proposals that are being talked about in the press. I don't know how real any of them are. I think the Iraqi people would be a lot better off and this whole situation would be resolved if Saddam Hussein and all of those around him who think like him—his sons and the top leadership of the regime—would leave so that others could step forward who would understand the importance of disarming and how a better future awaits the Iraqi people if they disarmed and cooperated with the U.N. and used their oil wealth for the benefit of the people, as opposed to developing weapons of mass destruction to threaten their neighbors and to threaten the world.

And so if that were to happen, I think that would be just fine, from my standpoint. But I don't know how much merit there is to these various so-called proposals.

Q. Are you open to supporting a U.N. Security Council resolution that would give amnesty to these generals, these military officers, if they were to rise up against Saddam Hussein?

Secretary Powell. Well, I would certainly consider it. I can't say in the abstract whether or not we would support such a resolution or not. If this happens or there is a possibility of it happening, I'd be more than willing to talk to my colleagues in the U.N. about it. But I'm not going to say today in a hypothetical sense what we might or might not do.

Q. Five years ago, you were on his program, the first year that I was hosting this program, and we spoke about Iraq. You were then in the private sector. I want you to listen to what you said:

"Perhaps we should communicate to the Iraqis that we're not going to get into this "Perils of Pauline" exercise every few months. Once you have denied us access to a particular facility, we're going to put that on the target list and take it out at a time of our choosing, and not have to create large armadas every 4 months to impose our will."

That was a little younger Colin Powell, 5 years ago, in April 1998. But those words probably still ring true today.

Secretary Powell. Well, they tried it with Desert Fox, I think later that year, and it didn't persuade the Iraqis to disarm. And so a policy was adopted at the end of the Clinton administration and continued under this administration, toward the end of the Clinton administration, that said regime change seems to be the only thing these people understand.

And so, once again, they are being given a last chance by the United Nations, under 1441, to disarm, change the nature of this regime, disarm, participate in the disarmament, cooperate with your disarmament, come forward, be honest. You say you don't have them? Then let's establish the facts that you don't have. But we think you do have them. And if that is not the solution you choose, then it is not going to be pinpricks; it's going to be a military operation that will remove the regime.

Q. Like me, you lived through the anti-war demonstrations during Vietnam. Yesterday, a big demonstration here in Washington, elsewhere around the country. How concerned are you that this anti-war movement seems to be growing across the United States?

Secretary Powell. Well, people are free to express their concerns and there's always a great deal of anxiety when it looks like military action may be coming. But I think most American people understand that if we have to undertake military action, it will be for good reason, and that is to disarm a regime that is threatening its neighbors and threatening the United States, and they would support the President if it becomes necessary to undertake military action.

Remarks by Secretary of Defense Rumsfeld, January 19, 2003

Secretary Donald Rumsfeld was interviewed by George Stephanopoulos on ABC's "This Week."

Q. The chief U.N. weapons inspectors are in Baghdad this morning with very tough words for Iraq. But they've also said in recent days that they need more time, perhaps several months, to finish their job. And French president Jacques Chirac has backed that call. Is there any harm in taking that time?

Secretary Rumsfeld. Well, you know, it's interesting. It would be logical to take time if one actually believed that we were sending in not inspectors, but finders, discoverers, people who were going to go out and go through that vast country and climb through tunnels and catch things that someone didn't want them to see.

Q. But isn't that what they're doing?

Secretary Rumsfeld. Oh, no. My goodness, no! The test here is not whether they can find something. The test is whether or not Iraq is going to cooperate. The reason—only reason for inspections is if a country is willing to say "yes, we're ready to go along with what the world community wants and show you what we have and you can come in and we'll destroy it." Now, think of it, South Africa did that. Kazakhstan did that. Ukraine did that. We know what an inspection operation looks like.

Q. But Iraq isn't doing that?

Secretary Rumsfeld. Of course not. They've submitted a fraudulent declaration. There are great gaps between their records with respect to anthrax and botulism and sarin and VX. They are not submitting the list of scientists that could be taken out of the country. They have systematically not done things in a cooperative way. Now, the inspectors have every right in the world to be concerned about that.

Q. But as a practical matter, if there is no "smoking gun," can you get the coalition you need to fight this war?

Secretary Rumsfeld. Oh, it's already there. There are a large number of countries that have already said they're willing to participate in a coalition of the willing. And there will be more at that point in the event that cooperation is not there from Iraq.

I mean, the hope is that—the last thing anyone wants is to use force. War is your last choice, not the first choice. The hope is that Iraq will be cooperative. If they're not, the hope is that Saddam Hussein will leave the country. And there are countries in that region that is hoping that's the case. If not, the hope is that the people of the country will take back their country and their government from this vicious regime.

Q. How about the argument that with the inspectors there right now, U.S. forces in the region, Saddam Hussein is effectively contained, so you don't need to take quick military action?

Secretary Rumsfeld. Well, what we know is that containment hasn't worked. If you think of what the international community has done for a decade—they have tried economic sanctions, we've tried diplomacy, they've tried the use of limited military force in the northern and southern no-fly zones, they have now gone to the U.N. to get a resolution, and the only reason there are inspectors in there at all is because of the threat of the use of force. I mean, that is what's supporting the diplomacy that exists.

Q. In the last few days, the inspectors have come across some finds. A dozen

empty chemical warhead shells. A cache of nuclear documents. What do you make of these findings?

Secretary Rumsfeld. Well, if you think of the fact that there have been no inspectors there for four years, I guess it's been, three or four years, that you've got a country and a regime that is very skillful at denial and deception—they are actively trying to deceive the inspectors and the world. One has to almost think that anything that's found, quote, "discovered," has to be something that Saddam Hussein was not uncomfortable having be found. I mean, how else would it be found? The country's enormous.

Q. You don't think it could have just been by mistake? That's what they say.

Secretary Rumsfeld. It's serendipity. You could make a mistake. Sure, that's possible. But I can't believe that—if you think back to inspections, the way people have learned things that the regime did not want was almost always from a defector, someone who got outside the country, like his two sons-in-law did, and then meet with the inspectors, told them what's going on. Now, of course, Saddam Hussein killed his two sons-in-law. So that's the threat against any inspector—correction, any scientist that an inspector might talk to.

Q. You know, you say that keeping the inspections going might not do any good. But I guess my question is, is there any military disadvantage to taking this extra time? Is there a time when the window for military action closes? Say by late March-April?

Secretary Rumsfeld. Well, you know, not really, if you think about it. The flow of forces by the United States and the preparations by other countries—there's a good deal of planning going on by other countries with the United States, and the United Kingdom has made some alert decisions and mobilization decisions—that process costs money. And it is not something one wants to do unless there's a value in doing it. And so we've been trying to be careful and measured in how we did it, and the numbers people, and the flow, the pattern that we've done it. But the United States Armed Forces are prepared to do what the president asks them to do.

Q. At any time?

Secretary Rumsfeld. There's obviously better times than others.

Q. What's the best time?

Secretary Rumsfeld. Oh, I don't think I want to get into it.

Q. Okay. Let's turn to diplomacy. The Saudis and other Arab nations have moved this week with a plan. They're floating a plan that would offer Saddam Hussein exile or, alternatively, isolate him by providing amnesty to up to several hundred senior

Iraqi officials. Do you think that's a good idea?

Secretary Rumsfeld. Oh, I think war is your last choice. I would be delighted if Saddam Hussein threw in the towel, said "the game's up, the international community has caught me, and I'll just leave."

Q. And if he did that, would the United States be willing to give him immunity, say, from war crimes prosecutions?

Secretary Rumsfeld. Well, I'm not in the Justice Department or in the White House and those are questions for them. But if—to avoid a war, I would be, personally, would recommend that some provision be made so that the senior leadership in that country and their families could be provided haven in some other country. And I think that that would be a fair trade to avoid a war.

Q. Do you have much hope that a plan like that can work?

Secretary Rumsfeld. I'm always hopeful. I think that the people in his country know what a vicious regime he runs. And they may decide to throw him out. He and his family may decide that they've run their string and that they'll leave. I just don't know. Certainly, either of those courses would be preferable to the use of force.

Q. Meanwhile, you have to prepare for war. I want to show up on the screen some guidelines you wrote for yourself that you think you have to think about before you commit forces to combat. They were printed in "The New York Times." Let me show it for our viewers right now.
It says: "If there is a risk of casualties, that fact should be acknowledged at the outset, rather than allowing the public to believe an engagement can be executed antiseptically, on-the-cheap, with few casualties." What should the public know right now about what a war with Iraq would look like and what the costs would be?

Secretary Rumsfeld. Cost in dollars or cost in lives?

Q. Dollars and human costs.

Secretary Rumsfeld. Well, the lesser important is the cost in dollars. Human life is a treasure. The Office of Management and Budget estimated it would be something under 50 billion dollars.

Q. Outside estimates say up to 300 billion.

Secretary Rumsfeld. Baloney. How much of that would be paid by the United States, how much by other countries is an open question. But if you think about it, September 11th, besides the 3,000 lives, cost this country hundreds of billions of dollars. So, yes, measure the risk of acting, but also the risk of not acting. And if we suffered a biological September 11th, the cost would just be many, many, many multiples of any conflict.

Q. But do you think the risk of an attack like that, another attack on the United States is increased by taking military action against Iraq?

Secretary Rumsfeld. It is clearly decreased, because every day that Iraq continues with its chemical, biological, and nuclear programs, they get that much more mature and that much closer to—in the case of nuclear—to his having a nuclear weapon.

Q. But might not an attack inspire other terrorists to try to attack the homeland?

Secretary Rumsfeld. I don't think the other terrorists need inspiration to attack us. They already have. They're trying to do it now. We're frustrating it all across the globe by arresting people and putting pressure on them.

In terms of human life, the other part of your question—first of all, war is always unpredictable. It never plays out. We know he has chemical and biological weapons. Might he use them? Yes, he might.

Q. And we're prepared for that?

Secretary Rumsfeld. Our forces are prepared.

Q. How—he's also said, he had a speech the other day, I'm going to show a segment from that, Saddam Hussein did, and in that speech he said, "Baghdad, its people and leadership is determined to force the Mongols of our age to commit suicide at its gates." I guess that means he's saying if you want to come here, you're going to have to fight in the streets of Baghdad. What kind of challenges does that pose to the military?

Secretary Rumsfeld. Well, first, Saddam Hussein is a liar. He lies every single day. He's putting weapons systems right next to mosques, next to schools, next to hospitals, next to orphanages. He's talking about "human shields." He is still claiming that he won the war. His people are being told every day that they won. It was a great victory in 1991 when he was thrown out of Kuwait and chased back to Baghdad.

Now, it seems to me that almost every time you quote something from him, you should preface it by saying "here's a man who has lied all the time and consistently."

Q. So you think he might not fight in Baghdad?

Secretary Rumsfeld. I have no idea what he'll do, but he is only one man. He may very well want to use weapons of mass destruction. But his people are going to have to carry that out, his military. And we have let his military know that anyone who is anyway connected with weapons of mass destruction, and if they are used in a conflict, if force is used, that they will be held personally accountable. And they will be.

Q. But even without weapons of mass destruction, urban warfare itself is a dirty business.

Secretary Rumsfeld. All warfare is a dirty business. I don't know what the people of Baghdad would do. There's a large population of Shi'ia that are no fans of Saddam Hussein in Baghdad. They could revolt. There have been indications that he's—he's used chemicals on his own people before, as well as on his neighbors. It's entirely possible he could do something like that.

So, I think to try to predict what kind of a, this "Fortress Baghdad" concept, to predict how that might play out, I think, is probably not possible.

Q. There seems to be some increasing restlessness about the possibility of war here at home. Demonstrations across the country yesterday, including here in Washington, estimates anywhere from fifty to five hundred thousand people. I know that's a wide range of estimates.

Secretary Rumsfeld. Come now!

Q. How many do you think were there?

Secretary Rumsfeld. I have no idea.

Remarks by Secretary of State Powell, January 20, 2003

Secretary Colin Powell delivered his remarks after a U.N. Security Council Ministerial Session.

We've just, just concluded a Security Council meeting and I was quite pleased at the commitment that my colleagues showed to campaign against terrorism and I'd like to thank my colleague from France, Minister de Villepin, for coming up with this idea and for leading it as presidency of the Council. You have followed the proceedings and you will see the resolution, so I'll take whatever questions you might have.

Q. Mr. Secretary, do you think the United States has to come back to the Security Council for another resolution to act militarily, and if I can ask a second question—

Secretary Powell. No, let's do one at a time. As 1441 lays out clearly, Iraq has an obligation to provide to the inspectors all the information that they need to do their job. Iraq has an obligation to have submitted a complete, accurate declaration. Iraq has an obligation to create conditions within Iraq so the inspectors can do their work and not guess at where things might be. And so far, Iraq is not complying with the obligations it has under 1441.

I noted that today that Dr. Blix and Dr. ElBaradei have made a statement that they've gotten a little more from Iraq, but it's just more of the same. Only under pressure does Iraq respond. And so we will anxiously await the chief inspectors' report next Monday, and then I think the Council has to examine Iraq's behavior against the requirements of 1441 and make a judgment as to what should happen next. I will not say now, I will not prejudge now what the Council might do with respect to a second resolution, or what have you. Let's wait and see what the inspectors say.

* * * *

Q. Your words in front of the Security Council today sounded like an ultimatum to the members of the Security Council, sort of fish or cut bait. Are you telling everyone that the U.S. will go unilaterally, and did you mean to make an ultimatum to the Council members?

Secretary Powell. What I was responding to were some comments that have been made by other Security Council members in the course of the debate, and the point I was making was that the Security Council has a responsibility under 1441 to bring Iraq into compliance with its obligations to the international community. And I wanted there to be no mistake about this, and time is running out.

There's no question that Iraq continues not to understand the seriousness of the position that it is in, and this is the time for it to realize that we will not just allow Iraq to frustrate the will of the United Nations, of the international community. If the United Nations is going to be relevant, it has to take a firm stand with respect to Iraq's continuing disregard of its obligations under 1441 and other resolutions.

Q. Mr. Secretary, Mr. Blix and some other Council members, and today the Chinese Foreign Minister, said that this is just the beginning that today's finding of more chemical warheads, this agreement and the 27th report is just the beginning. How do you reconcile this with—

Secretary Powell. It's very easy to reconcile. This is not the beginning. They have known for years how many chemical weapons, warheads they have. And so we had to discover, the inspectors had to discover, another cache of them last week. And then suddenly today or yesterday, the Iraqis say, "Oh by the way, we found four more." They know what they have. It is their obligation to come forward. And we cannot let them dribble this information, and dribble these items out for as long as they choose to in an effort to thwart the will of the international community.

* * * *

Q. [*Inaudible*] a few months ago, when President Bush came to the United Nations, to what extent is your department under pressure from other parts of the administration to take a more stringent line on Iraq now?

Secretary Powell. We are unified within the administration. We made it clear; the international community said bring this to the United Nations. President Bush did that. He did that in a powerful speech in September that was followed by Resolution 1441. The pressure is on Iraq. Iraq has the responsibility right now to avoid a conflict, to avoid a war. It would be a very simple matter for this regime to come clean, recognize that we will not be deterred from our obligations to the world to disarm this regime from of its weapons of mass destruction. So all of the eyes of the world should be on what Saddam Hussein and Iraq does in order to comply with the will of the United Nations. There is no disagreement within the American administration.

Q. There seems to be a lot of disagreements here among you, Mr. Foreign Secretary of Germany, of France, about second resolution, about compliance from Iraqis. How are you going to deal with this? And a second question—

Secretary Powell. Let's take one, because there's a lot of people here. No, no, one. Let me answer that question. We will deal with it in the matter that we have laid out in the resolution and in our discussions. Next Monday, the two chief inspectors will report to the Council. The Council will consider what they present to the Council and then there will be a debate beginning that day and then another debate, or a continuation of the debate, on the 29th. And I can assure you that in the days after that there will be many conversations between me and my colleagues in the Security Council and I suspect between heads of state and government to determine what the next step should be and to make a judgment as to whether or not Iraq is disarming.

If Iraq is disarming then there may be a solution to this crisis without conflict. But if Iraq is not disarming, the United Nations cannot simply turn its head away and ignore this lack of respect that Iraq has for the United Nations and the international community and we must not be afraid to meet the challenges that are ahead.

Remarks by Secretary of State Powell, January 21, 2003

Q. What is the danger in allowing more time, even a couple of months more, for the inspections to progress and for more evidence to accumulate?

Secretary Powell. The danger is that people would just allow the process to drag on and there will be no resolution. They have had a lot of time. They have had 12 years. They have had since 1441 was passed in early November. And what we have been looking for is a serious effort on Iraq's part to comply with the will of the community, the international community, as expressed in 1441.

And to give them an early test and to give us an early test of whether they would comply or not, we fought for and got into the resolution the declaration that was required, in early December, you will recall. And that was an early test as to whether we were going to be playing the same old game or a new game where, instead of us looking for the needle in the haystack, they would say, "Here's the haystack. We're taking the hay out of the way. There's the needle. You can verify that it is there. And that's where a needle used to be and we can prove why it isn't there any longer."

It's not the attitude we're getting. We got a false declaration, full of gaps, full of holes, and ever since, they've been playing the same game and stringing things out.

And so suddenly we find 12 missiles, or rockets, last week. Oh, where'd they come from? And then Dr. Blix and Dr. ElBaradei go in and start to let them know this is your last chance. And, oh well, we just found four more, and now we're going to send people all over the country looking for things. And yes, we will give you more information. Oh yes, we will now think about passing a law that they should have passed long ago.

And so the question isn't how much longer do you need for inspections to work. Inspections will not work. It's the skepticism that we have had all along to give Iraq one last chance for inspections to work if Iraq would work. And what Iraq has to do is come clean, stop it, stop the nonsense, stop the cheat and retreat, stop trying to figure out where the inspectors are going tomorrow morning, stop frustrating the reconnaissance that we're trying to use to help the inspectors, the air reconnaissance. We know the gaps that exist between how much anthrax you could have made and what you reported as having destroyed. A lot of the items that Deputy Secretary Armitage used in his speech today, those are easily quantifiable things, if they wanted to do it, if they weren't trying to hide things. We all know that they have some mobile capability with respect to their weapons of mass destruction. They know what we're talking about. Produce them.

And so unless we see that kind of change in attitude on the part of Iraq, then how much longer should inspections go on? One month, two months, three months? What will be the difference if they are simply trying to get time in order to frustrate the purpose of the inspections? The purpose of the inspections is not to find a needle in a haystack. The purpose of the inspections if for the haystacks to be identified because Iraq says there's nothing in the haystacks. That's what they're saying.

And so this is the time for them to come clean and cooperate fully, and without any more games or reservations and ten-point plans with Dr. Blix and Dr. ElBaradei. I'm pleased that the two inspection teams have gotten more access than they have had previously, but let's remember why they're getting that access. It's not because the Iraqis have suddenly changed their way of doing business, which we had hoped they would do, but because they are feeling the heat. They are feeling the pressure of the international community and they're feeling the pressure of military force that may be brought to bear.

Q. To encourage Saddam Hussein to go into exile, as has been talked about the last couple of days, would you be prepared to give an explicit promise that he and top members of his regime would not be pursued for war crimes prosecution?

Secretary Powell. It's not for the United States to excuse anyone from international prosecution, but I'm not sure what the whole international community might be willing to do. I think we would be receptive to anything that would get him and his family and his cohorts, the immediate group around him, out of power. But I can't say now what the actual conditions might be or what protection he might be given. I just can't—I can't get into that hypothetical a discussion, although I could tell you there would be a lot of enthusiasm for such a deal, and enthusiasm tends to produce opportunities to encourage such an action.

But I see nothing that suggests that there is any such real proposal on the table. I'm not aware of anybody who's gone in and said, "Oh, Great Leader, here's a deal for you from various people who were mentioned as being involved in this." In fact, I think the Saudi Foreign Minister, if I'm not mistaken, earlier today, specifically said—and I wasn't watching that closely, but said that they have not been conducting any such activity.

But the world would be better served if this regime would step down, step down right away, and we would have to take a look at what replaced it. And if what replaced it was led by somebody who immediately stood up and said, "We're coming into compliance and we're going to tell you everything you want to know. We're going to make available to you every scientist. You give us the name, and you will be able to talk to that person in the next day or so without any minders, without any tape recorders, without any threats to their family. And we want to cooperate with you fully to get rid of this stuff which is doing us no good except about to bring disaster down upon our country."

Q. Why do you think, though, all these anti-war protesters in our country and the French Government, for instance, and the Germans, have such a different view of this? What is it that the administration is not getting across to them?

Secretary Powell. You'll have to speak to them because I think the case is rather clear. This is a regime that has ignored the will of the international community for all these years. And we stood together as a body on the 8th of November, I think it was. And by a vote of 15 to 0, said come into compliance. And there was a reason for that resolution. The resolution recognized that they had been ignoring the will of the international community and that there was sufficient evidence that should have convinced anybody that this was a regime that was pursuing these weapons of mass destruction and, even more frightening, it was regime that has demonstrated in the past it would use them.

Q. But what happened—what's happened between the resolution passing and now? I mean, Prime Minister Blair took a bit of a grilling today from lawmakers in England about his commitment to the United States and, you know, throw that in with what happened with the French at the U.N.. There does seem to be a shift somewhat.

Secretary Powell. Nobody wants war. The President doesn't want war. I don't want a war. War is to be avoided if at all possible. And there's great unease—it goes to your question. There is great unease in many places, and there's some unease within the United States as well, about war and the consequences of war.

But sometimes, force is necessary to achieve a worthwhile purpose and to protect our country and to protect the world. And the United Nations, with the United States leadership, made a judgment that this was one of those circumstances where Iraq presents that kind of danger and that kind of threat to the world and it has to be disarmed. We have a joint resolution of Congress that says that, and we have 1441 that says that.

Now, what has changed between 1441 and today? We have now seen several months of the same pattern of behavior that we have seen for the previous years, 12 years or so, that didn't get us a solution to this problem. And the United Nations, and the international community as represented by the United Nations, cannot simply say, "Well, you know, we passed this resolution, but we don't want to go down the road that was called for in this resolution if Saddam Hussein does not disarm." It is a chilling prospect for many nations, but the United States clearly understood that a day might come when we would have to take those steps in the absence of Saddam Hussein disarming. And we are reaching, we are getting closer to that moment of truth. And I am confident that with more presentations of the kind that Secretary Armitage made today and the documentation that went out today, it will be clear to the people in the world that this is a problem that has to be dealt with.

Q. But how—

Secretary Powell. I have worked very hard in my two years as Secretary of State and worked under the President's guidance and leadership to have smart sanctions, to contain them and to hopefully move them in the right direction. We have worked with friends and allies around the region trying to get the message through to Saddam Hussein. The President has tried diplomacy and gone to the international community. But we believe that this is a threat to the people of Iraq, to the people of the region, and ultimately to the people of other parts of the world and to the United States.

Q. Getting back to Mark's original question, actually, with French leaders being so public, coming out so public and saying that, you know, why don't we just give it a little more time, I mean, what kind of message can you give to their leaders that we can't wait this amount of time? I mean, is it a message—is it a message—

Secretary Powell. What did they say? I mean, what they said is we should let this process continue. But it's not clear to me how long they want it to continue or whether they're serious about bringing it to a conclusion at some time.

The United States has not made a decision yet as to what should happen after the 27th. We are all going to watch and listen carefully on the 27th when the inspectors present the results of their work. I will then consult with my colleagues in the Security Council and other nations around the world. The President will consult. Prime Minister Blair will be coming over. It will be a chance for further consultations. And then the United States will make its decision. We have not made a decision as to what will happen after the inspectors present on the 27th.

It's almost as if people want to make a decision before the 27th. We haven't made a decision.

Q. Let me ask you about oil, which is of interest people—

Secretary Powell. Oil?

Q. Oil, from Houston. There has been some reports there's a dissension in the administration over what to do, say, after a war with the oil fields, with some people, such as yourself, saying, well, it should be under a U.N. guidance and—

Secretary Powell. I said that?

Q. Well, there have been some reports that you were on that side versus Eliot Abrams and others who want the U.S. to take control and privatize them.

Secretary Powell. No, no, no. There is no disagreement. This is speculation that has no foundation. If there is a conflict with Iraq and we and the leadership of the coalition take control of Iraq, the oil of Iraq belongs to the Iraqi people. And whatever form of custodianship there is, initially in the hands of, you know, the power that went in, or under international auspices at some point, it will be held for and used for the people of Iraq. It will not be exploited for the United States' own purpose. We will follow religiously international law, which gives clear guidance with respect to the responsibilities of an occupying power, if it comes to that. Everybody speculates about what my views are, what Eliot's views are, what somebody else's views are. What I've just told you, you can take to the bank.

Q. So it can't be used to pay for the war?

Secretary Powell. You mean to reimburse us?

Q. Correct.

Secretary Powell. I don't know of anybody who's made that suggestion. It'll be held in trust for the Iraqi people and it will benefit the people of Iraq.

Q. Who would hold it? I mean, it would be under—

Secretary Powell. That I cannot answer, if that's your specific question.

Q. But it would not be—

Secretary Powell. Hmm? Let me answer the question this way, and this is the best answer you're going to get. It will be held and it will be used in accordance with international law that lays out specific responsibilities of an occupying power.
And at this point I can't get into, you know, who's got title, how is it sold—

Q. Could we go in and privatize it?

Secretary Powell. I can't get into that. Privatizing?

Q. You know, or separating—I mean, it's now pretty much state-controlled. I mean, could we go in and, I don't know, sell it off to various—[*laughter*].

Secretary Powell. I think they've answered the question.

Q. Who would operate the oil fields, I guess he's asked?

Secretary Powell. Well, I don't—

Q. Chevron-Texaco, or would the Iraqi National Oil Company continue?

Secretary Powell. We don't have an answer to that question yet. It will be held. If we are the occupying power, it will be held for the benefit of the Iraqi people and it will be operated for the benefit of the Iraqi people. How will we operate it? How best to do that? We are studying different models. But the one thing I can assure you of is that it will be held in trust for the Iraqi people, to benefit the Iraqi people. That is a legal obligation that the occupying power will have.

Q. Has any decision been made about the occupation, what form it would take? Would it be our Army Civil Affairs units? Would it be under U.N. trusteeship? Would it be military?

Secretary Powell. There are a variety of models and they're all being examined. In the first instance, of course, if it's a military occupation, the military is initially in charge. But there is no desire for the United States Armed Forces to remain in charge or to run a country for any length of time beyond that which is necessary to make sure that there is an appropriate form of government to take over from the initial military occupation. I don't know how long and nobody can tell you how long that period of time is.

Q. Could oil revenues be used to finance some of the costs of the occupation?

Secretary Powell. In order not to split hairs or pretend that I'm an expert, let me just rest on the argument, on the simple statement, that whatever we do will be consistent with international law with respect to the responsibilities of an occupying power.

And the oil belongs to the Iraqi people. How it will be used, how the funds generated by the oil will be fed back into the Iraqi economy, I can't get into all of those issues. Whether or not it can be used to assist the occupying power in conducting activities that support the Iraqi people—for example, their humanitarian relief efforts, what it might cost us to deliver humanitarian relief to them—these are all issues that I just don't have the expertise to get into.

But I know that in our conversations, and a lot of work is being done, in our conversations the overarching, guiding principle is we will be consistent with the requirements of international law.

Q. At this stage—I think [Deputy] Secretary Armitage used the phrase today "wishful thinking" to describe the French attitude toward continued inspections. At this stage, with the report coming up on the 27th, do you see anything that could change the attitude of our—the French and the German allies?

Secretary Powell. I can't speculate as to what might change their attitudes. I think what we have to do now is to be patient, wait and see the report on Monday, see what Dr. Blix and Dr. ElBaradei think are the prospects for achieving the goals of 1441. And then the President will consult with his fellow heads of state and government, I will consult with my foreign minister colleagues, and there will be debate within the Council beginning that afternoon, I am sure there will be some discussion, but, really, the discussion of the report begins on the 29th.

* * * *

Q. One more? Do you feel as though you were sandbagged by de Villepin on yesterday, and had you known what was in store for you from the French, would you have gone to participate in that meeting?

Secretary Powell. Well, I think that might be a bit much. The conference was about terrorism. And frankly, the 15 presentations were pretty good and all focused on terrorism, and our need to do more. And there was only one comment in there that kind of got off into another direction, and that was when my colleague Joschka Fischer said something which caused me to respond. I did not know that Minister de Villepin was going to go out and sort of let his press conference get totally devoted to this. And of course, when I made my press conference I wasn't aware exactly what happened at his. And so that drove all the headlines.

Unfortunately, it overwhelmed what the purpose of the conference was all about, and so it might have been better for the French to have not focused it that way. That's why I'm late. He and I have just had a conversation.

Q. Was it pleasant?

Secretary Powell. It was a candid and honest forthright exchange of views.

Q. In very undiplomatic speak—

Secretary Powell. It's a blip. I mean, everybody knows the French position and we'll have more conversations with the French. But I'll let them speak for their position. Our position is that Saddam Hussein must be disarmed and he can either do it peacefully or he can step down and let someone else do it or it will be done for him. And I hope the French will come to the understanding of the need for such a strategy and the importance of such a strategy, and that the United States will stick with that strategy.

Excerpts from Remarks by Secretary of Defense Rumsfeld and Chairman of the Joint Chiefs of Staff Myers, January 22, 2003

Secretary Donald Rumsfeld and Chairman, Joint Chiefs of Staff, General Richard Myers, spoke with reporters at the Foreign Press Center, the Pentagon.

Secretary Rumsfeld. Thank you very much. Good afternoon.

Starting today, the Department of Defense will be broadcasting the Pentagon weekly press briefing to the Iraqi people through Commando Solo radio broadcasts. We're doing so because the truth matters, and it's important, we believe, that the Iraqi people know the truth and hear the truth.

To all Iraqis who are listening today for the first time, I say that this is democracy in action, it is freedom in action. Every week, General Myers and I stand in the Pentagon in front of independent journalist professionals and answer their questions—try to answer their questions. Some of the questions are tough, some of the questions—many of the questions are insightful and all of them add to the information available to the American people and the people of the world. And when they leave, none of these journalists will worry at all about what will happen to them for what they said or what they asked. They know that they and their families will not be threatened and that no one will be beaten or punished. The truth is important; it matters; it is the foundation of justice.

By contrast, Saddam Hussein's regime is built on terror, intimidation and lies. A decade ago, Saddam Hussein promised to give up his weapons of mass destruction, weapons he has used to kill thousands of innocent Iraqis. At the end of the Gulf War, he agreed to disarm. Yet, for more than a decade, his regime has refused to live up to its promises. Instead, they have fed the world a steady diet of untruths and deception.

Last year, the countries of the United Nations came together to give Saddam Hussein one last chance to come clean, to give up his chemical, biological weapons and his nuclear weapon programs and to prove to the world that he was doing so by inviting inspectors in. The United Nations passed a unanimous resolution requiring Saddam Hussein to submit to—a currently accurate, full and complete declaration of his WMD programs. He again said he would comply, but when he submitted his declaration it was not complete. There were numerous omissions, and it was characterized by many who reviewed it as fraudulent.

It's a strange situation. You know, in real life if someone in your community is caught lying over and over and over again, at some point that person develops a reputation for not telling the truth, and eventually, that person's no longer believed. And when someone says, "Well, Liar Joe just came around the corner but you can't believe him," people don't believe him. The same should be true in international affairs. The burden of proof is not on the United States or the United Nations to prove that Iraq has these weapons. We know they do. The United Nations put the burden of proof on Saddam Hussein's regime to prove that it is disarming and to show the inspectors where the weapons are. Thus far, he has not done so.

Contrary to what Saddam Hussein told the Iraqi people, America is not the enemy. Our goal is peace, not war. We continue to hope that the Iraqi regime will change course and disarm peacefully and voluntarily. But the choice between war and peace will not be made in Washington, D.C. It will not even be made at the United Nations. It will be made in Baghdad by Saddam Hussein. Either he decides to cooperate or he decides to continue not cooperating. We hope he will choose wisely.

General Myers?

General Myers. Good afternoon. And thank you, Mr. Secretary.

I just returned Monday from a trip that began in Stuttgart, Germany, to participate in the change-of-command ceremonies for the U.S. European Command commander and the Supreme Allied Commander Europe, General Joe Ralston, who gave—passed the command on to General Jim Jones, former commandant of the Marine Corps.

While in the region, I took the opportunity to visit my Italian counterpart in Rome, General Moschini, and to visit some of our troops in Vicenza, Italy.

After that, I had the opportunity to visit our forces at Incirlik Air Base in Turkey and to reciprocate a November visit with my Turkish counterpart, General Ozkok, in Ankara. While in Ankara, I had very good meetings with the chief of defense and with senior members of his staff, as well as a very good meeting with the minister of defense.

Turkey has long been a trusted ally, and the friendship continues in these difficult times. The relationship with Turkey has been an important one for both our countries, as well as for the region and NATO, and it's been that way for decades.

In both Rome and Ankara meetings, we discussed a wide variety of important military issues that are on all of our plates. It was also an opportunity to thank both of these allies for their support of our operation against terrorism, Operation Enduring Freedom. This cooperation has proven invaluable to our overall effort on this war on terrorism.

With that, I think we're ready to take questions.

* * * *

Q. Mr. Secretary, Jesus—[last name inaudible]—from the Mexican News Agency. I have a question regarding the foreign media. Why do you think that the majority of the foreign media is not getting the message of the United States in terms that—to see that really what you say is the real truth, that Saddam Hussein is a threat for the rest of the world? We haven't seen any proof of the arguments. You say that he has weapons of mass destruction.

And secondly, why is the U.S. government trying to have a dichotomy on foreign policy in terms of North Korea—

Secretary Rumsfeld. I'm sorry, I didn't understand. Why is the U.S. government—

Q. A dichotomy. Yeah, I mean—

Secretary Rumsfeld. Oh, a dichotomy.

Q. Yeah, with North Korea.

Secretary Rumsfeld. Okay.

Q. They have a nuclear weapon, and they say, "We have it." And you are going—we went to diplomacy with this country, and we want war with Iraq.

Secretary Rumsfeld. Good. I'd like to overrule the gentleman who opened the meeting and suggest there are so many people here. The second questions are second questions instead of follow-up questions. And it seems to me that we'll get a lot more people included if we have a question, and then, if it's appropriate, a follow-up question that follows up, as opposed to being on a totally different subject. Seems reasonable to me.

But the—first of all, I don't know that you're correct. The premise of your question was why is the majority of the foreign media x, y or z? I don't know that you or I are in a position to judge what the foreign media says. Maybe in your country. But there are many, many countries that are very supportive of the United States. There are 90 nations supporting the global war on terrorism. There are many, many handfuls of countries who have come to us, told us they are ready, willing and able to participate in the use of force, in the event that it becomes necessary and Iraq is not cooperative.

If one looks across the globe, I think that it's very difficult to make the case that you made that the foreign media is x, y or z. I think the foreign media tends to be all across the lot, just like people are. They have different opinions in different parts of the world for different reasons.

We don't see it as a dichotomy between the approaches that have been taken for Iraq and North Korea. In the case of North Korea, we're at a—in a diplomatic path. The United States, working with China and Russia and South Korea and Japan, are attempting to persuade North Korea that it ought not to go forward with its nuclear programs. Whether they'll be successful on the diplomatic path, I don't know.

Conversely in the case of Iraq, it's been 10 or 11 years. The world community has, in fact, been using every conceivable approach. They've used diplomacy. They've used economic sanctions. They've used carrots, with the oil-for-food program. They've used limited military activity, in the Northern and Southern no-fly zones. They've had 16 resolutions. Here's a country that has used chemical weapons against its own people, used chemical weapons against its neighbors, fired ballistic missiles into three or four countries. This is a distinctively different situation.

Here is a—both have weapons of mass destruction. Both are dictatorial regimes. Both are treating their people in a way that anyone who's interested in human rights has to feel a great deal of compassion for those people. But there are distinctive differences.

General Myers. May I?

Secretary Rumsfeld. You bet.

General Myers. On the first part of your question, on the rest of the world aligning with U.S. opinion on this, it's not U.S. opinion, it's the United Nations opinion. They're the ones that came—15 to zero, Security Council voted on 1441 that says,

"Iraq, this is your last chance to come clean with weapons of mass destruction." I mean, the facts are pretty clear on that. And so this is—I would say it's world opinion, it's not U.S. opinion. Now the rest of it, I guess, is up to your judgment, but those are the facts as I see them.

* * * *

Q. Has there been progress recently in your military talks about Turkish-U.S. military cooperation on Iraq, and are you happy with the level of Turkish support regarding your request to base or deploy troops on Turkish territory? Thanks.

Secretary Rumsfeld. Well, I'll just—Dick Myers, General Myers was just there. But we have—two things I would say. One is we think it's best, and, in fact, we know it's best, to let other countries characterize specifically what it is they're doing with respect to cooperation with the United States. From my standpoint, I think Turkey's been quite cooperative.

General Myers. Absolutely. We had—we had good discussions, my discussions with my counterpart, General Ozkok, later—earlier this week were very frank and very open. One of the things we do share is a common vision of wanting an Iraq that is peaceful and without weapons of mass destruction. Again, I'll go back to the secretary's comments; we'll let Turkey characterize the sort of support that they're willing to provide. But it was described to me that, "Gee, General Myers, you're impatient. We're told the United States is impatient about Turkey's help," and so forth. That's not the case.

We've been a strategic ally, as I mentioned in my earlier remarks, for a long time, and we've been allies because we have a common vision of what kind of security and stability we want not only in NATO, but in the region that Turkey lives in. And that will continue.

* * * *

Q. Sir, a question about the mood among European allies. You were talking about the Islamic world a second ago. But now the European allies. If you look at, for example, France, Germany, also a lot of people in my own country—I'm from Dutch public TV, by the way—it seems that a lot of Europeans rather give the benefit of the doubt to Saddam Hussein than President George Bush. These are U.S. allies. What do you make of that?

Secretary Rumsfeld. Well, it's—what do I make of it?

Q. They have no clerics. They have no Muslim clerics there.

Secretary Rumsfeld. Are you helping me? Do you think I need help?
What do I think about it? Well, there isn't anyone alive who wouldn't prefer unanimity. I mean, you just always would like everyone to stand up and say, Way to go!

That's the right to do, United States.

Now, we rarely find unanimity in the world. I was ambassador to NATO, and I—when we would go in and make a proposal, there wouldn't be unanimity. There wouldn't even be understanding. And we'd have to be persuasive. We'd have to show reasons. We'd have to—have to give rationales. We'd have to show facts. And, by golly, I found that Europe on any major issue is given—if there's leadership and if you're right, and if your facts are persuasive, Europe responds. And they always have.

Now, you're thinking of Europe as Germany and France. I don't. I think that's old Europe. If you look at the entire NATO Europe today, the center of gravity is shifting to the east. And there are a lot of new members. And if you just take the list of all the members of NATO and all of those who have been invited in recently—what is it? Twenty-six, something like that?—you're right. Germany has been a problem, and France has been a problem.

Q. But opinion polls—

Secretary Rumsfeld. But—just a minute. Just a minute. But you look at vast numbers of other countries in Europe. They're not with France and Germany on this, they're with the United States.

Now, you cite public opinion polls. Fair enough. Political leaders have to interest themselves in where the public is, and talk to them, and think about that, and then—and provide leadership to them. And you're quite right. You can find polls—

I can remember a poll—I won't—it was back in 1964. I watched it over something like a three-month period. It went from zero in favor of a certain topic to 55 percent in favor of it, down to 13 percent, all in three months. Now, does that suggest that polls can be fickle and rise and fall, depending on facts, depending on circumstances? Of course they can.

And that's—that's what political leaders are supposed to do, is to lead. And they—they're responsible for engaging facts and making assessments and then going out before their people and telling them their honest conviction as to what their country ought to do. And if a country doesn't agree with us, heck, that's happened lots of times in history.

Excerpts from Statements by German Chancellor Schroeder and French President Chirac, January 22, 2003

President Chirac and Chancellor Schroeder delivered their statements at a joint session of the French and German parliaments in Versailles marking the 40th anniversary of the friendship treaty between the two countries.

Chancellor Schroeder. Ladies and gentlemen, the goal of a stronger European security identity is not directed against anybody. In this way we assume our responsibility for the stability of the continent, but we also offer our European experiences concerning peace and development to other peoples. German and French soldiers are doing this side by side in Afghanistan, in the Balkans, and in other places. And we are cooperating side by side in the settlement of international crises—the North Korean or

Iraqi crisis, for example. We have agreed to cooperate particularly closely in the U.N. Security Council, where four European states are currently holding global responsibility for peace and international security. This seems of fundamental importance to me, particularly in this difficult period. Jointly we want to ensure that the U.N. Security Council can really fulfill its central task of safeguarding international peace also in this conflict.

* * * *

President Chirac. It is also urgent that Europe asserts itself as an international player. It is now an example for all those who refuse the fatality of war. Its dream is not a vain glory, about which illusions have been dispelled, but to use its power at the service of peace. It personifies an ambition for humanity, a Europe capable of acting, including in the military field, and which is necessary to the world's balance.

Armed with such a conviction, Germany and France have proposed to the European Convention the creation of a European Union of security and defense, which, in the face of risks and threats of all kinds, would provide for common security and solidarity in a constitutional treaty.

* * * *

This union will also contribute to strengthening the European pillar of the [North Atlantic] Alliance, thus illustrating the complementary and compatibility of our commitments to the European Union and to the Atlantic Alliance.

* * * *

The world is confronted with situations of crisis, alas, on all continents. I am of course thinking about Iraq. This is a major challenge. War is not inevitable. The only framework for a legitimate solution is that of the United Nations. France and Germany, successive holders of the presidency of the Security Council, are engaged in close and exemplary consultations to give peace all its chances.

I am also thinking about Afghanistan where our forces are involved, side by side, to contribute to the stability and security of this country and thus make its reconstruction possible.

Finally, this new Europe must establish with its new eastern neighbors and Mediterranean neighbors, in particular North Africa, relations of privileged partnership providing for their increased participation in our policies and real sharing in our cooperation.

Remarks by Secretary of State Powell, January 22, 2003

Secretary Colin Powell was interviewed on the NewsHour with Jim Lehrer.

Q. Is it correct to conclude from the statements of President Bush and others in the last few days that the U.S. has decided military action is justified against Iraq now?

Secretary Powell. The President hasn't come to a conclusion that military action is appropriate yet. The President is in consultation with leaders around the world and we are anxiously awaiting the report of the two chief inspectors, Dr. Blix and Dr. ElBaradei, on Monday. And we'll study those reports carefully. There will be a debate within the Security Council as to the implications and the meaning of those reports. And then the President will make his decision after that.

But certainly we are not encouraged by what we have seen in recent weeks. We are not encouraged by Saddam Hussein's performance. He continues to cheat. He continues to deceive. You know, it's a question of whether or not we're looking for a needle in a haystack or whether he was supposed to open up the haystack and show us the needle. And the right answer: He was supposed to come forward, give a full, accurate, complete declaration. He has not done that. He is not letting our reconnaissance planes fly. He is not providing the basic information the inspectors need to do their job.

What happened to all the anthrax? All the botulinum? To the chemical warheads? Things keep getting discovered that he should have brought forward earlier. And so we are certainly not satisfied with his performance at this time. We'll see what the inspectors say on Monday. And then he'll be in consultation with his colleagues and will make appropriate decisions as we move forward.

Q. Do you see this report on Monday as a final report or an interim report, which is what the inspectors call it?

Secretary Powell. Well, technically, it is an interim report from the inspectors. But the question of how much longer should the inspectors work is really a function of what they're able to achieve in the presence of this kind of performance on the part of the Iraqi regime to deny them what they need to do their job—to follow them around, to have more people following them than are inspectors inspecting.

And so the question is: Do we do that for a few more weeks, a few more months? It doesn't make any difference if he is not coming forward, if he is not letting it be—making it possible for the inspectors to do what the resolution calls for.

The resolution does not call for them to go snooping all over Iraq to see what they can find. The resolution puts the burden not on the inspectors, but on Saddam Hussein to come forward—complete declaration, full cooperation, and telling us everything that has been going on in Baghdad and throughout Iraq for, lo, these many years with respect to weapons of mass destruction.

If he were to do that, if he had done it over the years, but especially in the weeks since 1441—here's what we used to do, we're not doing it now, you can audit it, here's what we have left that we haven't told you about before but we're telling you now, here's the difference between what you think we have and what we actually have, and here's how we account for those differences—if that had been his attitude, we'd be in a different situation. That has not been his attitude. He still thinks that he can string out this process and escape the judgment of the international community. And the international community cannot allow that to happen.

Q. The conclusion that you just spoke of, is this a United States conclusion on its own, or is this based on debriefings from Mr. Blix and Mr. ElBaradei and others involved in the U.N. inspecting process itself?

Secretary Powell. I think it is a judgment that we have come to by watching the process unfold over the last couple of months, but also what we have heard from the inspectors. Dr. Blix was heard on television earlier today complaining about the fact that Iraq will not let reconnaissance planes assist in the effort. They're slow-rolling it. They're making it impossible for us to assist the inspectors in that regard.

We also saw the declaration that the Iraqis put forward. You know, we had a specific reason for inserting the requirement for a declaration in 30 days and insisting that the resolution call for the declaration to be full, accurate and complete—because we wanted to test the Iraqis. Are you serious? Are you really going to start telling the truth or are you not? And it is obvious that that declaration was not anything that we could have confidence in and the United States declared it a material breach at that time in December. Other nations did not do so, but not one nation stood up and said this is a good declaration and they're serious this time. And that's the problem we have.

So we have enough to make a judgment, but we're going to wait and see what the inspectors say on Monday. And then the President will be in consultation with other heads of state and government, I'll be in consultation with my colleagues on the Security Council, and Ambassador Negroponte will be participating in the discussions that will take place in New York.

Q. Well, it appears, you know, to an outside observer that a huge collision is about to come about as a result of this report on Monday. The position of France, Germany, Russia and China, among others, are saying give the inspectors more time; military action is not justified.

How do you explain that?

Secretary Powell. Well, there are those who feel that if the inspectors just had more time, they would find everything. We have a view—and I think others have a view quite similar to ours—that says, in the absence of cooperation, the inspectors will not find everything; they will not find that which is most troubling to us, weapons of mass destruction, and the capacity to make those weapons.

And so in order for inspectors to do their work, they have to have full Iraqi cooperation. But it's just more than cooperation. What the resolution called for was not just Iraqi cooperation. It demanded that Iraq be disarmed, Iraq disarm itself. And the inspectors were supposed to verify or ascertain that disarmament.

And in the absence of Iraq stepping up to its responsibilities and saying to the international community, "Not only am I claiming I am free of weapons of mass destruction, I will give you all the evidence you need to prove that fact," and that's what they have not done. And they have said they don't have any weapons of mass destruction. If that is the truth, come forward with the evidence for that truth and lay it out before the world, lay it out before the inspectors to verify, and there will be no war. But Iraq has not taken that step.

Q. Are we confronted with a situation here where the United States and France and Germany and China and the rest of the world are looking at the same information and interpreting it differently? Or does the United States have knowledge about something that the rest of the U.N. Security Council and the rest of the world doesn't know about?

Secretary Powell. I think it's a combination of the two, Jim. I believe that we have more information and knowledge, much of it highly classified, that others do not have access to, or at least say they are not aware of, of things that have gone on inside of Iraq. And I hope that we will have the opportunity to present this in the debate that's coming up.

We will be making more statements in the days ahead after the inspectors have given their report. My deputy, Deputy Secretary Armitage, gave a powerful presentation yesterday on some of the discrepancies that have not been dealt with, and Deputy Secretary Wolfowitz of the Defense Department will be making a similar statement tomorrow, and I'll be making a statement at Davos this coming weekend. So I think we'll be putting out more information.

But, frankly, Jim, there are some nations in the world who would like to simply turn away from this problem, pretend it isn't there. They are troubled by the consequences of going down this road to the requirements of 1441, which is ultimately the use of force if Iraq does not comply. The United States fully understood that when we went down the path of 1441, we were hoping for the best, but we were preparing for the worst.

And let's also be clear about something else. The only reason the Iraqis are participating in this inspection process now, the only reason they allowed the inspectors to come back in in the first instance, was because of the threat of force. And as my colleague, Don Rumsfeld, said on another show earlier today, the deployments that are now underway, those wonderful young men and women who are now deploying to the region, are still supporting diplomacy. The President has not yet made a decision for war, and that decision can be avoided if something happens in the very near future on the part of the Iraqi regime to come into compliance with their obligations under all these resolutions.

But the one thing that we have also made clear is that time is running out. We cannot let them stretch this game out until the world loses interest in this issue. The United States will not lose interest in this issue.

Q. As you know, support for the U.S. position seems to be dropping among nations around the world. Also, recent opinion polls among the American people show the same thing. They want unified action with the U.N.. They're less enthusiastic about the U.S. going alone.

Does that concern you at all?

Secretary Powell. Certainly, it does. We watch these polls, of course, but we have to do what we believe is right. And we believe that if we can make our case to the American people, to the world, that support can be generated; it can be turned around.

And I also think that people will understand that if we have to take military action, the United States will not be doing it alone. There will be other nations that will be joining us, whether part of a U.N.-approved action under a second resolution or, if that's not possible, and we believe military action is appropriate, there will be other nations that will be joining us. It'll not just be the United States and the United Kingdom.

I am also confident that it would be a successful operation, and in the aftermath of that operation the Iraqi people will be better off, as we would work with coalition partners and international organizations to put in place a new government in Iraq that would be responsive to its people and use the treasure that it has for the benefit of its people, and not to threaten its people or to threaten its neighbors or to threaten the world.

Q. Was it a correct reading of your response Monday to what happened at the U.N.—I won't go through the whole thing—but that you were a little annoyed with the French and their attitude about this?

Secretary Powell. Well, the meeting was called at the request of the French presidency to discuss terrorism, and we had a good, full discussion of terrorism within the Security Council, and in private meetings we also talked about Iraq and North Korea and other issues. And so the French decided to focus on Iraq and we kind of, frankly, trampled the purpose of the meeting. And so I responded to that. And we're in touch with our French colleagues and to make sure that we all understand each other's position as we go forward.

But the meeting was called to deal with terrorism, recognizing that Iraq is in the background and everybody wants to talk about Iraq, but 15 foreign ministers came together to talk about terrorism in general.

Q. So you thought you were sandbagged on Iraq?

Secretary Powell. Well, I wouldn't say "sandbagged" is the word. I just think that my colleague, Foreign Minister de Villepin, found it necessary to talk about Iraq. And when it came my turn for a press conference following the Security Council meeting, I also spoke about Iraq. It was the issue of the day. But it's unfortunate that we didn't spend as much time in our press conferences getting the press conference back to the subject of the day, which was terrorism.

Q. As you probably know, both French President Chirac and Mr. Schroeder of Germany met together and had a joint news conference in Brussels [*sic*] and said, essentially, that they're going to do everything they can to prevent military action against Iraq.
What do you think of that?

Secretary Powell. Well, I have heard that, and perhaps they should wait and see what the inspectors have to say on Monday. The United States is preparing itself for military action if it's called for. The President still hopes for a peaceful resolution of this matter. But that is in the hands of the Iraqi regime.

But what we are determined to see happen is that Iraq be disarmed, disarmed peacefully; and if that turns out not to be possible, then disarmed through the use of force. And I think all of the nations of the world and all of the members of the Security Council should wait and see what the inspectors have to tell us on Monday. And that's certainly what the United States is waiting for.

Column by National Security Advisor Rice, January 23, 2003

The following column titled "Why We Know Iraq is Lying" originally appeared in the New York Times.

Eleven weeks after the United Nations Security Council unanimously passed a resolution demanding yet again that Iraq disclose and disarm all its nuclear, chemical and biological weapons programs, it is appropriate to ask, "Has Saddam Hussein finally decided to voluntarily disarm?" Unfortunately, the answer is a clear and resounding no.

There is no mystery to voluntary disarmament. Countries that decide to disarm lead inspectors to weapons and production sites, answer questions before they are asked, state publicly and often the intention to disarm and urge their citizens to cooperate. The world knows from examples set by South Africa, Ukraine and Kazakhstan what it looks like when a government decides that it will cooperatively give up its weapons of mass destruction. The critical common elements of these efforts include a high-level political commitment to disarm, national initiatives to dismantle weapons programs, and full cooperation and transparency.

In 1989 South Africa made the strategic decision to dismantle its covert nuclear weapons program. It destroyed its arsenal of seven weapons and later submitted to rigorous verification by the International Atomic Energy Agency. Inspectors were given complete access to all nuclear facilities (operating and defunct) and the people who worked there. They were also presented with thousands of documents detailing, for example, the daily operation of uranium enrichment facilities as well as the construction and dismantling of specific weapons.

Ukraine and Kazakhstan demonstrated a similar pattern of cooperation when they decided to rid themselves of the nuclear weapons, intercontinental ballistic missiles and heavy bombers inherited from the Soviet Union. With significant assistance from the United States warmly accepted by both countries disarmament was orderly, open and fast. Nuclear warheads were returned to Russia. Missile silos and heavy bombers were destroyed or dismantled once in a ceremony attended by the American and Russian defense chiefs. In one instance, Kazakhstan revealed the existence of a ton of highly enriched uranium and asked the United States to remove it, lest it fall into the wrong hands.

Iraq's behavior could not offer a starker contrast. Instead of a commitment to disarm, Iraq has a high-level political commitment to maintain and conceal its weapons, led by Saddam Hussein and his son Qusay, who controls the Special Security Organization, which runs Iraq's concealment activities. Instead of implementing national initiatives to disarm, Iraq maintains institutions whose sole purpose is to thwart the work of the inspectors. And instead of full cooperation and transparency, Iraq has filed a false declaration to the United Nations that amounts to a 12,200-page lie.

For example, the declaration fails to account for or explain Iraq's efforts to get uranium from abroad, its manufacture of specific fuel for ballistic missiles it claims not to have, and the gaps previously identified by the United Nations in Iraq's accounting for more than two tons of the raw materials needed to produce thousands of gallons of anthrax and other biological weapons.

Iraq's declaration even resorted to unabashed plagiarism, with lengthy passages of United Nations reports copied word-for-word (or edited to remove any criticism of Iraq) and presented as original text. Far from informing, the declaration is intended to cloud and confuse the true picture of Iraq's arsenal. It is a reflection of the regime's well-earned reputation for dishonesty and constitutes a material breach of United Nations Security Council Resolution 1441, which set up the current inspections program.

Unlike other nations that have voluntarily disarmed and in defiance of Resolution 1441 Iraq is not allowing inspectors "immediate, unimpeded, unrestricted access" to facilities and people involved in its weapons program. As a recent inspection at the home of an Iraqi nuclear scientist demonstrated, and other sources confirm, material and documents are still being moved around in farcical shell games. The regime has blocked free and unrestricted use of aerial reconnaissance.

The list of people involved with weapons of mass destruction programs, which the United Nations required Iraq to provide, ends with those who worked in 1991 even though the United Nations had previously established that the programs continued after that date. Interviews with scientists and weapons officials identified by inspectors have taken place only in the watchful presence of the regime's agents. Given the duplicitous record of the regime, its recent promises to do better can only be seen as an attempt to stall for time.

Last week's finding by inspectors of 12 chemical warheads not included in Iraq's declaration was particularly troubling. In the past, Iraq has filled this type of warhead with sarin a deadly nerve agent used by Japanese terrorists in 1995 to kill 12 Tokyo subway passengers and sicken thousands of others. Richard Butler, the former chief United Nations arms inspector, estimates that if a larger type of warhead that Iraq has made and used in the past were filled with VX (an even deadlier nerve agent) and launched at a major city, it could kill up to one million people. Iraq has also failed to provide United Nations inspectors with documentation of its claim to have destroyed its VX stockpiles.

Many questions remain about Iraq's nuclear, chemical and biological weapons programs and arsenal and it is Iraq's obligation to provide answers. It is failing in spectacular fashion. By both its actions and its inactions, Iraq is proving not that it is a nation bent on disarmament, but that it is a nation with something to hide. Iraq is still treating inspections as a game. It should know that time is running out.

Remarks by Deputy Secretary of Defense Wolfowitz, January 23, 2003

Deputy Secretary Paul Wolfowitz delivered his remarks at the Council for Foreign Relations in New York City.

As terrible as the attacks of September 11th were, however, we now know that the terrorists are plotting still more and greater catastrophes. We know they are seeking more terrible weapons-chemical, biological, and even nuclear weapons. In the hands of terrorists, what we often call weapons of mass destruction would more accurately be called weapons of mass terror. The threat posed by the connection between terrorist networks and states that possess these weapons of mass terror presents us with the danger of a catastrophe that could be orders of magnitude worse than September 11th. Iraq's weapons of mass terror and the terror networks to which the Iraqi regime are linked are not two separate themes—not two separate threats. They are part of the same threat. Disarming Iraq and the War on Terror are not merely related. Disarming Iraq of its chemical and biological weapons and dismantling its nuclear weapons program is a crucial part of winning the War on Terror. Iraq has had 12 years now to disarm, as it agreed to do at the conclusion of the Gulf War. But, so far, it has treated disarmament like a game of hide and seek-or, as Secretary of State Powell has termed it, "rope-a-dope in the desert."

But this is not a game. It is deadly serious. We are dealing with a threat to the security of our nation and the world. At the same time, however, President Bush understands fully the risks and dangers of war and the President wants to do everything humanly possible to eliminate this threat by peaceful means. That is why the President called for the U.N. Security Council to pass what became Resolution 1441, giving Iraq a final opportunity to comply with its disarmament obligations and, in so doing, to eliminate the danger that Iraq's weapons of mass terror could fall into the hands of terrorists. In making that proposal, President Bush understood perfectly well that compliance with that resolution would require a massive change of attitude and actions on the part of the Iraqi regime. But history proves that such a change is possible. Other nations have rid themselves of weapons of mass destruction cooperatively in ways that were possible to verify. So let's talk for a moment about what real disarmament looks like: There are several significant examples from the recent past-among them South Africa, Ukraine and Kazakhstan. In South Africa, for example, President De Klerk decided in 1989 to end that country's nuclear weapons program and, in 1999 [1990], to dismantle all their existing weapons. South Africa joined the Nonproliferation Treaty in 1991 and later that year accepted full scope safeguards by the U.N.'s atomic energy agency. South Africa allowed U.N. inspectors complete access to both operating and defunct facilities, provided thousands of current and historical documents, and allowed detailed, unfettered discussions with personnel that had been involved in their nuclear program. By 1994, South Africa had provided verifiable evidence that its nuclear inventory was complete and its weapons program was dismantled. In the 1990s, President Kravchuk of Ukraine and President Nazarbayev of Kazakhstan ratified the Nuclear Nonproliferation and START Treaties, committing their countries to give up the nuclear weapons and strategic delivery systems that they had inherited with the dissolution of the Soviet Union. Kazakhstan and Ukraine both went even further in their disclosures and actions than was required by those treaties. Ukraine requested and received U.S. assistance to destroy its Backfire bombers and air-launched cruise missiles. Kazakhstan asked the United States to remove more than 500 kg. of highly enriched uranium. Given the full cooperation of both governments, implementation of the disarmament was smooth. All nuclear warheads were returned to Russia by 1996, and all missile silos and heavy bombers were destroyed before the START deadline. Each of these cases was different but the end result was the same: the countries disarmed while disclosing their programs fully and voluntarily. In each case, high-level political commitment to disarmament was accompanied by the active participation of national institutions to carry out that process. In each case, the responsible countries created a transparent process in which decisions and actions could be verified and audited by the international community.

In Iraq's case, unfortunately, the situation is the opposite. U.N. Security Council Resolution 1441 gave Saddam Hussein one last chance to choose a path of cooperative disarmament, one that he was obliged to take and agreed to take 12 years ago. We were under no illusions that the Baghdad regime had undergone the fundamental change of heart that underpinned the successes I just mentioned. Nevertheless, there is still the hope—if Saddam is faced with a serious enough threat that he would otherwise be disarmed forcibly and removed from power—there is still the hope that he might decide to adopt a fundamentally different course. But time is running out.

The United States entered this process hopeful that it could eliminate the threat posed by Iraq's weapons of mass terror without having to resort to force. And we've put more than just our hopes into this process. Last fall, the Security Council requested member states to give, quote, "full support," unquote, to U.N. inspectors.

The United States answered that call and President Bush directed departments and agencies to provide, I quote, "material, operational, personnel, and intelligence support," unquote, for U.N. inspections under Resolution 1441. Such assistance includes a comprehensive package of intelligence support, including names of individuals whom we believe it would be productive to interview and information about sites suspected to be associated with proscribed material or activities. We have provided our analysis of Iraq's nuclear, chemical, biological and missile programs, and we have suggested an inspection strategy and tactics. We have provided counterintelligence support to improve the inspectors' ability to thwart Iraqi attempts to penetrate their organizations.

The United States has also made available a wide array of technology to support the inspectors' efforts, including aerial surveillance support in the form of U-2 and Predator aircraft. So far, Iraq is blocking U-2 flights requested by the U.N., in direct violation of Resolution 1441, which states that inspectors shall have free and unrestricted use of manned and unmanned reconnaissance vehicles.

Let's consider for a moment what inspectors can do and what they can't. As the case of South Africa and the other success stories demonstrate, inspection teams can do a great deal to verify the dismantling of a program if they are working with a cooperative government that wants to prove to the world it has disarmed. It is not the job of inspectors to disarm Iraq; it is Iraq's job to disarm itself. What inspectors can do is confirm that a country has willingly disarmed and provided verifiable evidence that it has done so. If a government is unwilling to disarm itself, it is unreasonable to expect the inspectors to do it for them. They cannot be charged with a "search and destroy" mission to uncover so-called smoking guns, especially not if the host government is intent on hiding them and impeding the inspectors' every move. Inspectors cannot verify the destruction of weapons materials if there are no credible records of their disposition.

Think about it for a moment. When an auditor discovers discrepancies in the books, it is not the auditor's obligation to prove where the embezzler has stashed his money. It is up to the person or institution being audited to explain the discrepancy. It is quite unreasonable to expect a few hundred inspectors to search every potential hiding place in a country the size of France, even if nothing were being moved. And, of course, there is every reason to believe that things are being moved constantly and hidden. The whole purpose, if you think about it, for Iraq constructing mobile units to produce biological weapons could only have been to be able to hide them. We know about that capability from defectors and other sources, but unless Iraq comes clean about what it has, we cannot expect the inspectors to find them.

Nor is it the inspectors' role to find Saddam's hidden weapons when he lies about them and conceals them. That would make them not inspectors, but detectives, charged with going through that vast country, climbing through tunnels and searching private homes. Sending a few hundred inspectors to search an area the size of the state of California would be to send them on a fool's errand or to play a game. And let me repeat: this is not a game.

David Kay, a former chief UNSCOM inspector, has said that confirming a country's voluntary disarmament is a job that should not take months or years. With cooperation, it would be relatively simple because the real indicators of disarmament are readily apparent. They start with the willingness of the regime to be disarmed, the commitments communicated by its leaders, the disclosure of the full scope of work on weapons of mass destruction, and verifiable records of dismantling and destruction.

Unfortunately, though not surprisingly, we have seen none of these indications of willing disarmament from Iraq.

So let's discuss what disarmament does not look like. Despite our skepticism about the intentions of the Baghdad regime, we entered the disarmament process in good faith. Iraq has done anything but that.

Instead of a high-level commitment to disarmament, Iraq has a high-level commitment to concealing its weapons of mass terror. Instead of charging national institutions with the responsibility to dismantle programs, key Iraqi organizations operate a concealment effort that targets inspectors and thwarts their efforts. Instead of the full cooperation and transparency that is evident in each of those disarmament success stories, Iraq has started the process by openly defying the requirement of Resolution 1441, and I quote, "to provide a currently accurate, full and complete" declaration of all of its programs.

Indeed, with its December 7th declaration, Iraq resumed a familiar process of deception. Secretary Powell has called that 12,200-page document a catalogue of recycled information and brazen omissions that the secretary said, "totally fails to meet the resolution's requirements. Most brazenly of all"—I'm still quoting Powell—"the Iraqi declaration denies the existence of any prohibited weapons programs at all," unquote.

Among those omissions are large quantities of anthrax and other deadly biological agents and nuclear-related items that the U.N. Special Commission concluded Iraq had not accounted for. There are also gaps in accounting for such deadly items as 1.5 tons of the nerve gas VX, 550 mustard-filled artillery shells, and 400 biological weapons-capable aerial bombs that the U.N. Special Commission concluded in 1999—and this is the U.N.'s conclusion—Iraq had failed to account for.

There is no mention of Iraqi efforts to procure uranium from abroad. Iraq fails to explain why it's producing missile fuel that seems designed for ballistic missiles it claims it does not have. There is no information on 13 recent Iraqi missile tests cited by Dr. Blix that exceeded the 150-kilometer limit. There is no explanation of the connection between Iraq's extensive unmanned aerial vehicle program and chemical or biological agent dispersal. There is no information about Iraq's mobile biological-weapons production facilities. And, very disturbingly, Iraq has not accounted for some two tons of anthrax growth media.

When U.N. inspectors left Iraq in 1998, they concluded, and I quote: "The history of the Special Commission's work in Iraq has been plagued by coordinated efforts to thwart full discovery of Iraq's programs," unquote. What we know today from the testimony of Iraqis with first-hand knowledge, from U.N. inspectors and from a variety of other sources, about Iraq's current efforts to deceive inspectors suggests that Iraq is fully engaged today in the same old practices of concealment and deception. Iraq seems to be employing virtually all of the old techniques that it used to frustrate U.N. inspections in the past.

At the heart of those techniques, of course, is hiding things, and moving them if they're found. In the past, Iraq made determined efforts to hide its prohibited weapons and to move them if inspectors were about to find them. In 1991, in one of the first, and only, instances where the inspectors found prohibited equipment, they came upon some massive calutrons, devices used for enriching uranium, at an Iraqi military base. Even at that early stage, Iraq had begun to make provisions to move its illegal weapons in case inspectors stumbled across them. As the inspectors appeared at the front gate, the Iraqis moved the calutrons out the back of the base on large tank transporters.

Today, those practices continue, except that over the last 12 years, Iraqi preparations for concealing their illegal programs have become more extensive and sophisticated. Iraq's national policy is not to disarm but rather to hide its weapons of mass terror. That effort, significantly—the effort of concealment—is led by none other than Saddam's own son, Qusay, who uses a Special Security Organization under his control for that purpose. Other security organizations contribute to these "anti-inspection" activities, including the National Monitoring Directorate, whose ostensible purpose is to facilitate inspections. Instead, it provides tip-offs of sites that are about to be inspected and uses "minders" to intimidate witnesses. Iraqi security organizations and a number of government agencies provide thousands of personnel to hide documents and materials from inspectors, to sanitize inspection sites and to monitor the inspectors' activities. Indeed, the "anti-inspectors" vastly outnumber the couple of hundred of U.N. personnel on the ground in Iraq.

Already, we have multiple reports and other evidence of intensified efforts to hide documents in places where they are unlikely to be found, such as private homes of low-level officials and universities. We have reports and other evidence of prohibited material and documents being relocated to agricultural areas and private homes or hidden beneath mosques and hospitals. Furthermore, according to these reports, the material is moved constantly, making it difficult to trace or find without absolutely fresh intelligence. It is a shell game played on a grand scale with deadly serious weapons.

Those efforts at concealment are assisted by active surveillance and penetration of the inspectors. In the past, Iraq systematically used its intelligence capabilities to support efforts to conceal its illegal activities. Former inspector David Kay recalled that in 1991, the inspectors came across a document warning the chief security official of the facility they were about to inspect, that David Kay would lead the U.N. team. That warning had been issued less than 48 hours after the decision had been made for Kay to lead the team, and at that time, fewer than 10 people within the inspection organization were supposed to know the operational plan.

In the 1990s, there were reports that Iraqi intelligence recruited U.N. inspectors as informants. And it was known that Iraqi scientists were fearful about the confidentiality of their interviews. Recent reports that Iraq continues these kinds of efforts are a clear sign that it is not yet serious about disarmament.

Today, we also anticipate that Iraq is likely to target U.N. computer systems through cyber intrusions to steal inspections, methods, criteria, and findings. And we know that Iraq has the capability to do that. According to Khidhir Hamza, a former senior official in the Iraqi nuclear program, Iraq's Babylon Software Company was set up to develop cyber warfare capabilities on behalf of the Iraqi Intelligence Service in the early 1990s. Some people assigned to Babylon were segregated into a highly compartmented unit and tasked with breaking into foreign computers to download sensitive data. Some of the programmers reported that they had accumulated sufficient expertise to break into moderately protected computer systems, such as those that the inspectors depend upon.

Further technique is intimidation and coercion, both of the inspectors and of the people they're inspecting. In the past, Iraq did not hesitate to use pressure tactics to obtain information about the inspectors. Sometimes the pressure was quite crude. During the UNSCOM period, one inspector was reportedly filmed in a compromising situation and blackmailed.

Sometimes the pressure was more subtle. Richard Spertzel, a former inspector in the biological warfare unit, recalled the case of an Iraqi official who coyly asked a member of Spertzel's team, "Just how far is it from Salt Lake City to Minnesota?" Since this woman had just moved from Salt Lake City to Minneapolis a few days prior to her arrival in Iraq, you can imagine that she was unnerved by the comment.

More recently Iraq has again begun referring to the inspectors as spies, clearly hoping to make them uncomfortable at best and afraid at worst, and to intimidate Iraqis from interacting with them.

For Iraqis, there is nothing subtle about the intimidation. As President Bush stated so correctly, and as numerous reports by Human Rights Watch and other organizations confirm, "The dictator of Iraq is a student of Stalin, using murder as a tool of terror and control, within his own cabinet, within his own army, and even within his own family."

Today we know from multiple sources that Saddam has ordered that any scientist who cooperates during interviews will be killed, as well as their families. Furthermore, we know that scientists are being tutored on what to say to the U.N. inspectors and that Iraqi intelligence officers are posing as scientists to be interviewed by the inspectors.

And finally, of course, there's obstruction, and obstruction concealed by lying. In the past, U.N. inspectors faced many instances of delay, with excuses that ranged from, "We can't find the keys," to "You can't come in here because only women are allowed." When all else fails, lying becomes a standard technique.

Richard Butler, the former head of the U.N. Special Commission, reported, and I quote, "Iraqi leaders had no difficulty sitting across from me and spontaneously changing a reported fact or figure." For example, he said, six previously reported warheads could suddenly become 15, or vice versa, with no explanation or apology about a previous lie. Butler reports that actions taken to obstruct inspectors were often explained away with excuses that were as credible as "the dog ate my homework." One example that Butler quotes, literally: "A wandering psychopath cut some wires to the chemical plant monitoring camera. It seems he hadn't received the medicine he needed because of the U.N. sanctions." And here's another: "The wicked girlfriend of one of our workers tore up the documents in anger."

During the UNSCOM period, Richard Spertzel on one occasion confronted Dr. Rihab Taha, still a principal and sinister figure in Iraq's biological weapons program. He said to her, and I quote, "Dr. Taha, you know that we know that you're lying, so why are you doing it?" Dr. Taha drew herself up and replied, "Dr. Spertzel, it is not a lie when you are ordered to lie." Lying was more than a technique. It was, and it remains, a policy.

Today, Iraqi obstruction continues on large issues as well as small ones. Authorities that Resolution 1441 confers unconditionally on the inspectors are constantly subject to conditions by the Baghdad regime. For example, the resolution requires that the U.N. inspectors shall have, quote, "free and unrestricted use and landing of fixed- and rotary-winged aircraft, including manned and unmanned reconnaissance vehicles," unquote. But Iraq has objected to U-2 flights and shoots at our Predators. Even more serious, Iraq has yet to make a single one of its scientists or technical experts available to be interviewed in confidential circumstances free of intimidation as required by the U.N. resolution.

Long ago Iraq became accustomed to the fact that even when caught, the consequences could be negligible. And hence a new game entered the lexicon: cheat and retreat. This happened on issue after issue. For example, as Butler reports—I'm quoting again—"Initially Iraq had denied ever having manufactured, let alone deployed, VX. But this was not true." Confronted with evidence of VX in soil samples, the Iraqis then admitted they had manufactured, but claimed a quantity of no more than 200 liters. Subsequent probing showed they'd made far more. So Iraq's initial complete lie had been replaced by a false statement about the quantity. Iraq then reached for a third lie: they'd never weaponized VX. This, it turned out, was yet a third falsehood.

The same pattern was repeated with Iraq's nuclear and biological weapons. Baghdad revised its nuclear declaration to the IAEA four times within 14 months of the initial submission in April 1991. During the UNSCOM period, Iraq submitted six different biological warfare declarations, each one of which the U.N. inspectors rejected. Following the defection of Saddam's son-in-law, Husayn Kamil, Iraq dramatically disclosed more than half a million pages of biological weapons-related documents. But, in fact, sparse relevant information was buried within a massive volume of extraneous data, all of which was intended to create the appearance of candor and to overwhelm the U.N. inspectors' analytical resources.

A process that begins with a massive lie and proceeds with concealment, penetration, intimidation and obstruction cannot be a process of cooperative disarmament. The purpose of Resolution 1441, I repeat, was not to play a deadly game of hide-and-seek or cheat-and-retreat for another 12 years. The purpose was to achieve a clear resolution of the threat posed by Iraq's weapons of mass terror.

If Iraq were to choose to comply with the requirement to dismantle its weapons of mass terror, we would know it. We would know it from their full and complete declaration of everything that we know that they have, as well as by revelations of programs that our intelligence has probably not yet discovered. Recall that after the Gulf War, we were stunned by the magnitude of Iraq's nuclear program, despite all of our intelligence efforts and those of our allies, including Israel, and even though Iraq had been subject to IAEA inspections for many years.

We would know it if we saw an attitude on the part of the Iraqi government that encouraged people to cooperate with inspectors, rather than intimidated them into silence and lies. We would know it when inspectors were able to go about their work without being spied on or penetrated. And we would know it most of all when Iraqi scientists and others familiar with the program were clearly speaking freely.

But in the absence of full cooperation, particularly in the absence of full disclosure of what Iraq has actually done, we cannot expect that the U.N. inspectors have the capacity to disarm an uncooperative Iraq, even with the full support of American intelligence and the intelligence of other nations.

American intelligence capabilities are extraordinary, but they are far from the omniscient, all-seeing eye depicted in some Hollywood movies. For a great body of what we need to know, we are dependent on traditional methods of intelligence—that is to say, human beings, who either deliberately or inadvertently are communicating to us.

It was only after Saddam Hussein's son-in-law, Husayn Kamil, defected in 1995 that U.N. inspectors were led to a large cache of documents, on a chicken farm, that contained important revelations about Iraq's biological weapons. In contemplating the magnitude of the task of finding such hidden sites, one might ask: How many farms are there in Iraq? How many structures are there in which important documents could be stored? How many garages in that big country are large enough to hold the tractor- trailers that make up an Iraqi mobile biological weapons factory?

And we need to be worried. Even when inspectors were in Iraq before, the Baghdad regime was building and retaining weapons of mass terror. It would be folly to think that those efforts stopped when the inspectors left.

Consider that in 1997, U.N. inspectors found Iraq had produced and weaponized at least 10 liters of ricin. In concentrated form, that quantity of ricin is enough to kill more than 1 million people.

Baghdad declared to the U.N. inspectors that it had over 19,000 liters of botulinum toxin, enough to kill tens of millions; and 8,500 liters of anthrax, with the potential to kill hundreds of millions. And consider that the U.N. inspectors believe that much larger quantities of biological agents remained undeclared. Indeed, the inspectors think that Iraq has manufactured two to four times the amount of biological agents it has admitted to and has failed to explain the whereabouts of more than two metric tons of raw material for the growth of biological agents. Despite 11 years of inspections and sanctions, containment and military response, Baghdad retains chemical and biological weapons and is producing more. And Saddam's nuclear scientists are still hard at work.

As the President put it, and I quote, "The history, the logic and the facts lead to one conclusion: Saddam Hussein's regime is a grave and gathering danger. To suggest otherwise is to hope against the evidence. To assume the regime's good faith is to bet the lives of millions and the peace of the world in a reckless gamble. And this is a risk we must not take."

So, we come back to the imperative: Baghdad must disarm, peacefully if at all possible, but by force if necessary. The decision on whether Iraq's weapons of mass terror will be dismantled voluntarily or whether it will have to be done by force is not up to us, it is not up to the inspectors, it is not up to the United Nations. The decision rests entirely with Saddam Hussein. So far, he has not made the fundamental decision to disarm, and unless he does, the threat posed by his weapons programs will remain with us, and, indeed, it will grow.

Yes, there are real dangers in confronting a tyrant who has and uses weapons of mass terror and has links to terrorists. But those dangers will only grow. They are far greater now than they would have been five or 10 years ago, and they will be much greater still five or 10 years from now. President Bush has brought the world to an extraordinary consensus and focus on this problem; it is time to see it resolved, voluntarily or by force, but resolved one way or another. And time is running out.

On a happier note, if one thinks about it, once freed from Saddam's tyranny, it is reasonable to expect that Iraq's educated, industrious population of more than 20 million could build a modern society that would be a source of prosperity, not insecurity, for its neighbors.

Barham Salih, a very brave and distinguished Iraqi Kurdish leader, spoke recently of the dream of the Iraqi people, and I quote. He said, "In my office in Suleymaniyah, I meet almost every day some traveler who has come from Baghdad or other parts of Iraq. Without exception, they tell me of the continuing suffering inflicted by the Iraqi regime, of the fearful hope secretly nurtured by so many enslaved Iraqis for a free life, for a country where they can think without fear and speak without retribution."

We may someday look back on this moment in history as the time when the West defined itself for the 21st Century, not in terms of geography or race or religion or culture or language, but in terms of values, the values of freedom and democracy.

For people who cherish freedom and seek peace, these are indeed difficult times. But such times can deepen our understanding of the truth. And this truth we know: the single greatest threat to peace and freedom in our time is terrorism. So this truth we must also affirm: the truth does not belong to tyrants and terrorists. The truth belongs to those who dream the oldest and noblest dream of all—the dream of peace and freedom.

White House Document, "What Does Disarmament Look Like", January 23, 2003

Introduction

On September 12, 2002, President Bush called on the United Nations to live up to its founding purpose and enforce the determination of the international community—expressed in 16 U.N. Security Council resolutions—that the outlaw Iraqi regime be disarmed of its weapons of mass destruction.

On November 8, the Security Council unanimously passed UNSCR 1441, which gave the Iraqi regime "a final opportunity to comply with its disarmament obligations" (OP 2). Recognizing that genuine disarmament can only be accomplished through the willing cooperation of the Iraqi regime, the resolution called for the reintroduction of weapons inspectors into Iraq, to test whether or not the regime had made a strategic decision to give up its mass destruction weapons.

The world knows what successful cooperative disarmament looks like. When a country decides to disarm, and to provide to the world verifiable evidence that it has disarmed, there are three common elements to its behavior:

The decision to disarm is made at the highest political level;

The regime puts in place national initiatives to dismantle weapons and infrastructure; and

The regime fully cooperates with international efforts to implement and verify disarmament; its behavior is transparent, not secretive.

Examples of Cooperative Disarmament

In recent years, there have been several notable examples of countries that have chosen to give up mass destruction weapons, and willingly cooperated with the international community to verify its disarmament. These countries include:

- South Africa
- Ukraine
- Kazakhstan

High level Political Commitment

President de Klerk decided in 1989 to end South Africa's nuclear weapons production and in 1990 to dismantle all weapons. South Africa joined the Nuclear Nonproliferation Treaty (NPT) in 1991 and later that year accepted full scope International Atomic Energy Agency (IAEA) safeguards.

Under the leadership of President Kravchuk and President Nazarbayev, Ukraine and Kazakhstan, respectively, ratified the Nuclear Nonproliferation and START Treaties. This created high- level political commitments to give up the nuclear weapons and strategic delivery vehicles they inherited upon the dissolution of the Soviet Union.

National Initiatives to Dismantle Weapons of Mass Destruction

South Africa, Ukraine, and Kazakhstan each charged high-level organizations with implementing disarmament. In South Africa it was the Atomic Energy Commission and ARMSCOR. In Kazakhstan it was primarily the Ministries of Defense and Atomic Energy. In Ukraine it was mainly the Ministry of Defense. Each of these organizations worked cooperatively with outside organizations—for example, the IAEA in South Africa and the United States and Russia in Ukraine and Kazakhstan—to implement disarmament.

Full Cooperation and Transparency

The true measure of cooperation is to answer questions without being asked. In each of these examples, weapons programs were disclosed fully and voluntarily.

South Africa began its disclosure with a declaration to the IAEA on its nuclear program, which was expanded over time. South Africa allowed the IAEA complete access to operating and defunct facilities, provided thousands of current and historical documents, and allowed detailed, unfettered discussions with personnel involved in the South African program.

An IAEA article from 1994 sums up the cooperative South African approach to nuclear disarmament and IAEA verification:

"In the case of South Africa, the results of extensive inspection and assessment, and the transparency and openness shown, have led to the conclusion that there were no indications to suggest that the initial inventory is incomplete or that the nuclear weapon program was not completely terminated and dismantled. However, in the future, and without prejudice to the IAEA's rights under the safeguards agreement, the IAEA plans to take up the standing invitation of the South African Government—under its reiterated policy of transparency—to provide the IAEA with full access to any location or facility associated with the former nuclear weapons program and to grant access, on a case-by-case basis, to other locations or facilities that the IAEA may specifically wish to visit."

Given the full cooperation of both governments, implementation of the disarmament decision was smooth. All nuclear warheads were returned to Russia by 1996, and all missile silos and heavy bombers were destroyed before the December 2001 START deadline. The United States had full access, beyond Treaty requirements, to confirm silo and bomber destruction, which were done with U.S. assistance.

Both countries have also gone farther in disarmament than the NPT and START Treaty require. For example, Kazakhstan no longer has strategic missiles and Ukraine is well on the way to giving up its strategic missiles. Ukraine asked for U.S. assistance to destroy its Backfire bombers and also air-launched cruise missiles.

In the early 1990s, Kazakhstan revealed to us a stockpile of more than 500 kg. of HEU, and asked that we remove it to safety in the United States. It has also shut down its plutonium- producing reactor and is using U.S. assistance to ensure the long-term safe storage of the spent fuel. Finally, Kazakhstan used U.S. assistance to destroy all nuclear test tunnels and bore holes—a total of almost 200—at the former Soviet test site there.

Iraqi Non-cooperation

The behavior of the Iraqi regime contrasts sharply with successful disarmament examples.

Instead of high-level commitment to disarm, highly organized concealment efforts, staffed by thousands of Iraqis, are led from the very top of the Iraqi regime.

Iraq's concealment activities are run by the Special Security Organization (SSO), under the control of Qusay Saddam Hussein, Saddam Hussein's son.

Instead of charging organizations to work with outside groups to disarm, the regime tasks key institutions with thwarting the inspectors.

The National Monitoring Directorate—whose stated function is to facilitate inspections—actually serves as an "anti- inspections" organization that:

Provides tip-offs to inspection sites; and

Uses "minders" to intimidate witnesses.

The minders are often former engineers and scientists with direct WMD experience, and first-hand knowledge of what needs to be protected from the inspectors when they arrive at a facility.

Thousands of personnel from Iraqi security agencies provide manpower for hiding documents and materiel from inspectors, policing inspection sites, and monitoring the inspectors' activities.

Such organizations include the Military Industrialization Organization, the SSO, the Special Division for Baghdad Security, the Iraqi Intelligence Service (IIS), the Special Republican Guard, the Republican Guard, and the Directorate of General Security.

These "anti-inspectors" vastly outnumber the 200 UNMOVIC and the IAEA personnel on the ground in Iraq.

Instead of cooperation and transparency Iraq has chosen to conceal and to lie.

Iraq's declaration is not "currently accurate, full, and complete." It is inaccurate and incomplete.

Anthrax and Other Undeclared Biological Agents

The U.N. Special Commission concluded that Iraq did not verifiably account for, at a minimum, 2160kg of growth media. This is enough to produce 26,000 liters of anthrax—3 times the amount Iraq declared; 1200 liters of botulinum toxin; and, 2200 liters of aflatoxin, a carcinogen.

Ballistic Missiles

Iraq has declared its attempt to manufacture missile fuels suited only to a type of missile which Iraq's declaration does not admit to developing.

Iraq claims that its designs for a larger diameter missile fall within the U.N.-mandated 150km limit. But Dr. Blix has cited 13 recent Iraqi missile tests which exceed the 150km limit.

Nuclear Weapons

The Declaration ignores efforts to procure uranium from abroad.

VX

In 1999, U.N. Special Commission and international experts concluded that Iraq needed to provide additional, credible information about VX production. UNSCOM concluded that Iraq had not accounted for 1.5 tons of VX, a powerful nerve agent. Former UNSCOM head Richard Butler wrote that "a missile warhead of the type Iraq has made and used can hold some 140 liters of VX . . . A single such warhead would contain enough of the chemical to kill up to 1 million people."

The declaration provides no information to address these concerns.

Chemical and Biological Weapons Munitions

In January 1999, the U.N. Special Commission reported that Iraq failed to provide credible evidence that 550 mustard gas- filled artillery shells and 400 biological weapon-capable aerial bombs had been lost or destroyed.

The Iraqi regime has never adequately accounted for hundreds, possibly thousands, of tons of chemical precursors.

Empty Chemical Munitions

There is no adequate accounting for nearly 30,000 empty munitions that could be filled with chemical agents.

If one of those shells were filled with the nerve agent Sarin, which Iraq is known to have produced, it would contain over 40,000 lethal doses.

Unmanned Aerial Vehicles (UAV) Programs

Iraq denies any connection between UAV programs and chemical or biological agent dispersal. Yet, Iraq admitted in 1995 that a MIG-21 remote-piloted vehicle tested in 1991 was intended to carry a biological weapon spray system.

Iraq already knows how to put these biological agents into bombs and how to disperse biological agent using aircraft or unmanned aerial vehicles.

Mobile Biological Weapons Agent Facilities

The Iraqi declaration provides no information about its mobile biological weapon agent facilities.

Iraq continues its tactics of "cheat and retreat" that defeated prior inspections efforts, and Iraq continues its efforts to hide prohibited WMD programs.

This fall, satellite photos revealed activity at several suspected WMD facilities, apparently in anticipation of the resumption of inspections.

We have multiple reports of the intensified efforts to hide documents in spaces considered unlikely to be found, such as private homes of low level officials and universities. On January 16, 2003, a joint UNMOVIC/IAEA team found a significant cache of documents related to Iraq's uranium enrichment program in the home of Iraqi scientist Faleh Hassan.

We have many reports of WMD material being buried, concealed in lakes, relocated to agricultural areas and private homes, or hidden beneath Mosques or hospitals. In one report such material was buried in the banks of the Tigris river during a low water period. Furthermore, according to these reports, the material is moved constantly, making it difficult to trace or to find without absolutely fresh intelligence.

The regime routinely conducts well-organized surveillance of inspectors.

The SSO tracks the number, expertise, equipment, vehicles, location, and heading of inspectors.

Iraq has in the past used, and is likely again to use, cyber attack methods in its efforts to collect intelligence.

Computer systems used to store, process, or communicate UNMOVIC and IAEA inspection schedules, methods, criteria, or findings will be particularly high-value targets.

At a minimum, Iraq can apply tools and methods readily available from publicly accessible Internet sources, many of which are quite effective and require only moderate skill to implement.

According to Iraqi defector Dr. Khidhir Hamza, Iraq's Babylon Software Company was developing cyber warfare capabilities on behalf of the Iraqi Intelligence Service as early as the 1990s. People assigned to Babylon initially worked on information security technologies and techniques, but some of the programmers were segregated into a "highly compartmented unit" and tasked with breaking into foreign computers in order to download sensitive data or infect the computers with viruses. Some of the programmers reported that they had accumulated enough expertise to break into moderately protected computer systems.

Yet the Iraqis accuse the inspectors of being spies—the gravest accusation that a totalitarian government can make.

In mid-January Iraqi Vice President Taha Yassin Ramadan said "We know they [the inspectors] are playing an intelligence role. The way they are conducting their inspections and the sites they are visiting have nothing to do with weapons of mass destruction. But we are cooperating with inspection teams in a positive way in order to expose the lies of those who have bad intentions."

Iraq has not provided "immediate, unimpeded, unrestricted and private access to witnesses."

Instead inspectors have been expected to interview Iraqis with minders under unsecure conditions.

The regime has resisted allowing interviews outside the country.

Iraq's list of WMD scientists together with their associated work places and dates ends in 1991 although UNSCOM proved that the programs did not.

Iraq refuses to provide key documents, some of which have been demanded by inspectors for years.

Iraq has impeded the inspectors' demand to begin aerial surveillance.

Conclusion

Iraq's behavior contrasts sharply with successful disarmament stories.

Instead of a high-level commitment to disarm, Iraq's concealment efforts are led by Saddam's son Qusay. The inspectors are labeled spies and treated as the enemy, not as a partner in disarmament.

Instead of national initiatives to disarm, Iraq's SSO and National Monitoring Directorate are national programs involving thousands of people to target inspectors and thwart their duties.

Instead of cooperation and transparency, Iraq has chosen concealment and deceit best exemplified by a 12,000 page declaration which is far from "currently accurate, full, and complete," as required by the United Nations Security Council.

Remarks by Secretary of State Powell, January 23, 2003

Secretary Colin Powell was interviewed by the Financial Times.

Q. If I could begin, last September you made and won the argument that the U.N. route was the best for the United States in disarming Iraq, and you successfully got the resolution you wanted unanimously. Since then, the transatlantic alliance seems less stable than it was. Clearly, in the last few days, those differences are emerging.

What would be your advice now to the President on seeking a second resolution after the weapons inspectors present their report?

Secretary Powell. Well, I usually give my advice to the President directly and first before I give to even as august of a— So I hope you won't feel offended if I don't say that.

But let me go back to how you started to roll out your question. The President decided to take it to the international community in September because he believed it was a problem for the international community.

We are often accused of being unilateralist. We are often accused of going off on our own. And this was a case where Iraq had been in complete violation of the will of the international community for all these years. And the President was deeply concerned about it and we think that all nations should be concerned about the behavior of Iraq, not only what it has but what it might have in the future, and, frankly, its arrogance with respect to U.N. mandates and U.N. resolutions.

So he took it to the U.N. and, in a powerful speech, he challenged the U.N. to meet its responsibilities. And some oh, seven weeks later, after much debate and much discussion, 15 nations of the Security Council—all of them, to include principal European actors as well, within the perm five—came together and passed U.N. Resolution 1441.

1441 put the burden on Iraq, not on the inspectors. 1441 said to Iraq you have one last chance. You have been in breach before, you continue to be in material breach, and the burden is now on you to demonstrate that you are disarmed, or will disarm. And it also made clear that after a period of time the Security Council would consider, in the absence of Iraqi disarmament, further actions that might be taken.

It was a tough resolution to get, as you all followed day by day, but that's what the Security Council said. And we have now seen, since the 8th of November when it was passed, several months of activity on the part of the inspectors. Let there be no doubt that if it wasn't for the President's speech and this resolution, there would be no inspectors in Iraq. Iraq would still be going its merry way, completely oblivious to the will of international community, completely oblivious to what its obligations are.

And so it is the pressure that came from the resolution and the willingness to use force at the end of the day on the part of not only the United States, but it is implied in the resolution itself. That is what caused Iraq to let the inspectors in and to undertake some passive activities with respect to their obligations to disarm.

But what we have also seen in the last several months is that Iraq continues to try to do it their way. They continue to deceive. They continue to practice deception. They are not answering the most fundamental questions that, in the last several days, we have been putting before the world in very stark terms. What happened to the anthrax? What happened to the chemical weapons? What happened to the artillery shells? What happened to the botchulinum toxin? Why aren't you letting the reconnaissance planes fly freely? Why aren't you coming clean? Why do you continue to act as if nothing has really changed? 1441 changed the terms of this debate and it is an obligation of Iraq to disarm and the inspectors are there to verify it and to assure the community that that is what has happened.

The President has made it clear, and it seems to me to be clear from the resolution, that if Iraq does not do this, then the Security Council must consider other means to make it happen.

The Security Council will meet on Monday in a permanent representative session to hear from Dr. Blix and Dr. ElBaradei. There is no question that the United States is positioning forces and leaning forward in order to support diplomacy, as my colleague, Don Rumsfeld, said yesterday, but also to make it clear to Iraq that this is not a game that can continue forever, and that if it does not disarm itself in the manner expected by 1441, then force remains an option.

Notwithstanding all the reporting that is around, the President has not made a decision. Other nations, particularly in Europe, may have made a decision before seeing what the inspectors have to say and hearing what the inspectors have to say, but the United States has not made a decision.

And so we will all be listening carefully. We will be commenting on what we see. We will be very candid and direct in our interrogatories back to Dr. Blix and Dr. ElBaradei—and also to the Iraqis—as to what they have to do to avoid conflict. There is still the possibility of a peaceful solution, but time is running out.

And what we are concerned about is that there are some who would say, "Well, let's just keep inspecting forever." But inspecting forever, or for some very long, extended period of time, in the presence of continued Iraqi limited passive cooperation, as opposed to saying, "Here's what we had. Here's how we got rid of it. Here's what we have now. We're turning it in. There are no more chemical rockets laying around for you to trip over or find. We are no longer asking the inspectors or expecting the inspectors to catch us by looking for a needle in the haystack. Here's the haystack. We're opening it up. There's the needle. Go verify it's the needle. Destroy it if you want. There's a blank spot where a needle used to be and here's what we did with the needle." And so that's what Iraq has to do—assist in its disarmament—if it wishes to find a peaceful solution.

And what we must not do, cannot do, for the safety of our people and for the safety of especially the region and for the credibility of the United Nations, is to essentially just let this dribble out and dribble down without a resolution. And so I believe we have some challenging days ahead. The United States remains firmly committed to the

disarmament of Iraq, one way or the other, and we hope it can be achieved peacefully.

Q. The French and the German leaders yesterday made sort of quite a big show of
apparent unity. But if you—but talking to people behind the scenes, it does appear as
though the French at least seem—and indeed, if you take their public remarks, seem
a little bit more other than what you've described as people who want inspections just
to go on and on.

That certainly seems to describe the German position, but it doesn't necessarily
seem to describe the French position. And from what, you know, we've heard, it's possible, you know, that the French have left open the possibility that they would agree
to something which would have a very firm, set, determinative deadline. Perhaps, you
know, perhaps it can be as short as a month. They might prefer longer.

Is that something now—I mean, is that what you—is there room there for agreement between the United States and France, or a very firm, fixed deadline now after
this next round of discussions?

Secretary Powell. Well done, Gerry. I will do many things today, but characterize
the French position is not one of them.

But certainly, I've heard the same reports. I've had very direct conversations with
Dominique earlier in the week, as you know, both privately as well as public
exchanges. And France, I am sure, is examining all of this. They have made it clear that
they believe more time is necessary, but they also say things like, "We can contain him."
Containment is not the issue. The issue is disarmament. Contain him until what? Circumstances arrive in the future when he could pop out of containment? We did containment. And I didn't have any problem with containment. You know, that containment would eventually solve the problem. It hasn't. The problem is still there. So the
issue is disarmament.

And I have yet to hear from any of my European colleagues as to when they would
be satisfied with respect to inspections. And the trouble with this is the point I made
earlier. The issue is not the inspectors. The issue is Iraq.

Iraq—and let me remind you that we pressed to put that 30-day declaration in
there. There was a big, big debate, as you'll recall. And it was a big debate within the
administration as to whether or not we should try to sell this point. But we succeeded. And the real reason for that was to get an early indication of Iraqi behavior. And it
was a disappointment and we saw it all in December when the declaration came in.

So that we wouldn't wait six months, eight months, nine months, to see if they
were playing the same old game. We knew it when the declaration came in. We
declared it a material breach. I did. The other nations did not declare it a material
breach. And that's fine. That's their judgment to make. But not one of them, not one
of the Security Council members or any other nation, with the exception of perhaps
one or two that I might be able to think of, said that it was a full, accurate and complete declaration, as it was supposed to be.

And so that's the fundamental issue. If Iraq understood the seriousness of this and
knew that the international community remained unified on this issue, then they
would have responded to 1441 by saying, you know, there's no longer the expression,

"Glad you asked." You know, "Glad you asked. Here it is." They could have come forward immediately with complete access. They could have come forward immediately with all the documentation. They would not have been hiding documents in scientists' homes and digging in back yards and moving things around, trying to play the same game on UNMOVIC that they played on UNSCOM.

And we have not seen that yet. And so the burden remains on Iraq. And the question is not how much time the inspectors should be given, but how much time should Iraq be given.

Q. But if they said let's give them another 30 days—

Secretary Powell. Well, yes, I can't hypothesize on that point. But I'll wait to see if that's what the French say. I haven't heard that from them.

The Germans, they made their decision before we even had a speech to the United Nations or 1441. And so, you know, they're consistent. And that's—I can't comment on—you know, I can't go off on the German angle that you presented me, Gerry, because they've made their decision long before the President even went to the U.N..

The French, I will—we'll see what they say after the Monday presentation, just as everybody will see what we say after the Monday presentation.

Q. But if the—the inspectors have already said they would like more time. And [*inaudible*] Bush at war, there's this comment from the President that he said at one point, maybe in two years time it'll just be us and the British in the coalition. If the inspectors do ask formally for more time, and clearly there are nations like France and Germany that support our position, would you be prepared to reduce the transatlantic alliance to just Britain in order to go ahead with military action?

Secretary Powell. One, let's see what they actually do ask for. But it's not so much what they ask for. It's what they say to us Monday about the circumstances under which they're doing their work and how Iraq is behaving. That's what I'm interested in hearing.

The judgment as to whether they get more time or not is not for the inspectors to make, but for the Security Council to make. And that's the discussion and debate we'll be having.

I believe that the danger presented by this regime in the form of its weapons of mass destruction, the terrorism that it sponsors, the abuse of the human rights of its own people, its record of invading its neighbors and gassing its own people, the record of this regime is such, and the need for the international community's will to be followed in this instance, especially after 1441 at 15-0, require that we act if Iraq does not act.

And I'm confident that if there is agreement to act with a U.N.—another resolution, if that comes to pass, I think it will be a strong coalition and it will be more than just the U.S. and U.K.. And if the U.N. finds it impossible to act and it is a coalition of the willing, I'm fairly confident it will be more than the United States and the United Kingdom.

And we have been in touch with many countries around the world who see the problem in the same terms that we do, in the same terms that the resolution did, and I think they would be a significant coalition. I can't tell you everybody who might be in it.

But I don't view this in cataclysmic terms of breaking up the transatlantic relationship. There are a lot of things that keep this partnership, this relationship, together. This is a difficult issue. I am very familiar with the public opinion polls in all the countries of Europe, as well as here in the United States. It is better if this is solved by the international community. But the international community should recognize, everybody should recognize, that the person that is keeping it from being solved by the international community in a peaceful way is Saddam Hussein.

Q. What is—the question in Europe is why the hurry. What is the outcome, as you see it, if we go the German-French route, if we give the inspectors several more months?

Secretary Powell. I can't tell what the outcome is. That's the point. They don't tell in their presentations what the outcome is. What will they—what will we know in two or three months' time in the face of continued Iraqi non-cooperation, which you most likely will get, if they think they can just, you know, okay, it's two or three months' time. Isn't it time to suspend sanctions? Then another two or three months' time. And if you were merely chasing around the countryside looking for things, rather than assisting Iraq and verifying Iraqi disarmament. The United Nations and the resolution does not call for the inspectors to disarm Iraq. It calls for Iraq to disarm and for the inspectors to assist in that process. That's what I think is fundamentally different.

And so if there are those who suggest more time should be given, then let's hear what they're talking about. More time for what to happen? For the inspectors to do what? And what progress would you expect the inspectors to make in that period of time in the face of the kind of behavior and performance we've seen from Iraq so far?

Q. Yeah. I mean, if we go to war, it would be the biggest and most important war, I suppose, since—certainly since 1991 with the U.S. [*inaudible*] in terms of, you know, ground forces or however you measure it. You know, as President Chirac said the other day, war is, in a sense, a failure.

Do you think you have absolutely made the case, explained to the American people and to the people of the world, why war, which is always the last resort, why we have got to this point, to this result? Have you done that yet, explained to them why this war may be necessary?

Secretary Powell. I think we have to do more. I think we have been making the case. Obviously, there is—I can't deny that we have to do more, because I can see the reaction around the world. And the President will do more. We will all do more with the President. We've started to make that case, I think, more fully now, just not in anticipation of war but in doing a better job of educating, with the speech that Rich Armitage made on Tuesday, Paul Wolfowitz is speaking today, I'll say something in Davos on Sunday.

And so you will see us talking clearly and directly about this, not for the sake of getting ready for war, but for the sake of making sure everybody understands what the stakes are, what the risks are, and why this is an important issue for the safety of the region, for the betterment of the lives of the people of Iraq, and for the United Nations and the relevance of the United Nations.

This was not a trivial resolution and I will never forget those early days of debate right after the President's speech when I said to my colleagues in the Council, "Do not vote for a first resolution if you know that you will never vote for a second if it comes to you." Let's be straight as to what we are facing here. Let's make sure we have all signed up. It took seven weeks to go from that conversation I'm describing now to the end of a negotiations on the resolution. But let's be clear what we're signing up for. We're not signing up for inspections forever. We're not signing up for containment. We're not signing up for, you know, a permanent group of inspectors forever. We're signing up for the disarmament of Iraq.

And the whole thrust of the resolution is to give who one last chance? The inspectors? No. Give Iraq one last chance. And everybody knew what they were signing up for. And as I said at the U.N. earlier today, the road ahead may be very difficult, and will be very difficult militarily if it comes to this, and the President still hopes it does not come to this. It may difficult politically. It may be difficult with respect to, you know, how the publics react to it.

But things may change rather markedly once success comes, this threat is removed, and the Iraqi people face a better future. And so don't underestimate the effect that success might have. And if it is a military operation—and I repeat, the President has not made that judgment. He is waiting until he hears on Monday and then he will be consulting broadly with his fellow heads of state and government.

As you know, Prime Minister Blair is here next Friday, and so there's a lot of consultation will take place and a lot of discussion. But should, at the end of the day, whenever that day approaches, comes, military action is required, it will be challenging. It will be controversial, no doubt. But we will be successful, and from that success new opportunities will arise.

Remarks by Secretary of State Powell and British Foreign Secretary Straw, January 23, 2003

Secretary Colin Powell and Foreign Secretary Jack Straw delivered their remarks after meeting in Washington.

Secretary Powell. We will be having more conversations after this press conference, but we have spent some time talking about the situation in North Korea as well as the situation with respect to Iraq.

We are looking forward to the report of the chief inspectors on Monday to the Security Council with respect to Iraq's compliance with the requirements of U.N. Resolution 1441. As the President has repeatedly said, he is hopeful for a peaceful solution, but we must not mistake the will of the international community to see this matter is resolved.

Resolution 1441, which was voted unanimously by the Security Council 15-0 does not deal with inspectors as much as it deals with Iraq. It gives Iraq one last opportunity to come into compliance with its obligations under the various previous U.N. resolutions, and it also makes clear that if Iraq does not act in a responsible manner and disarm itself with the inspectors assisting in that process, then it is the responsibility of the Security Council, the same 15 members, with new membership now, of course, since it changed over at the beginning of the year, to consider what should be done about this.

And so this is a process that is unfolding, and we will listen carefully to the inspectors' reports on Monday and then be in consultation with our friends and allies around the world, and participate in the discussions within the Security Council. And then decisions will be forthcoming from those consultations and that discussion.

But let's not lose sight of the fact that the issue is the disarmament of Iraq, not how much more time the inspectors need, but how much more time should we give Iraq when they have not used the time they have already been given to do what is required of them, and that is to disarm.

There are questions that must be asked. Why are they trying to deceive the inspectors? Why are they not allowing reconnaissance to take place? Why are they hiding documents in the homes of individuals? Why are we just starting to discover things that should have been declared? Why was the declaration so false?

All of these are relevant questions that we will put to the two inspection chiefs and put to our Council colleagues as the debate continues next week and until we determine what the appropriate actions should be. And this will be a judgment that the Security Council will have to make, and of course each member of the Security Council, including the United States, reserves the right to act in a way that's consistent with its international obligations as well as its own national interests.

We hope it can be resolved peacefully, but, once again, we must understand that it may require the use of force. It is the deployments that we have made and the United Kingdom has made in recent weeks that we think have put pressure on Iraq to get even this passive cooperation, but flawed and incomplete and inadequate cooperation that has been received so far. And we'll continue to our discussions about this and other issues after this press conference, but I would invite my colleague to say a few words.

Foreign Secretary Straw. Thank you very much, and it's a great pleasure for me to be with my good friend and colleague, Secretary Powell, here this morning. Secretary Powell has described the issues we've been discussing. I just wanted to say this about Iraq. As Secretary Powell has said, we negotiated 1441 it was a U.S./U.K. draft. There was a high degree of skepticism in some quarters when we started negotiating it that there would ever be any level of consensus; still less unanimity in the international community.

But as we negotiated it, because people saw the strength of the case against Iraq, they came together to pass 1441. And again, as Secretary Powell has just said, 1441 imposes obligations on Iraq. One of the things that's happened because of Iraq's continuing record of deceit and delay over many years is that the onus of proof has shifted from the international community to Iraq. And the resolution itself makes that very clear.

People sometimes say, "Why Iraq? What are the inspectors going to find?" And some suggest this is some kind of hype game of hide-and-seek that only if the inspectors find something dramatic is there proof that Iraq has "failed to comply." It's not like that. What the last lot of inspectors, UNSCOM, said to the United Nations in February, 1999, just after they had been forced out by Saddam Hussein, was that amongst other things unaccounted for were 3,000 tons of precursor chemicals; 360 tons of bulk chemical warfare agents, including one and a half tons of the deadly VX nerve agent; 30,000 special munitions for delivery of chemical and biological agents; and 550 mustard gas shells. Any of those sets of munitions could cause lethal damage across the region and could be used in terrorism across the world.

Saddam Hussein has not yet explained where these are. He has, yes, ensured that traffic inspectors allow U.N. inspectors' vehicles through "on red." But that is not compliance. And time is running out for him to comply fully with the terms of 1441.

As I've said, we don't see January the 27th as a deadline, and it was never set down as a deadline when we were negotiating 1441. But it is an important moment at which the United Nations needs to signal the determination which it set out very clearly on the 8th of November about the necessity of resolving this issue.

Q. Secretary Straw, can I ask you, sir, about your government's position? How long might Britain be willing to string along with the Security Council considering, as you have noticed, French, German, et cetera, opinion, or abandon that approach and stand with the United States and a handful of other allies that want to do something about this without further delay?

Foreign Secretary Straw. Well, I'm afraid I don't see the dichotomy in that way. I was in the United Nations General Assembly when the President of the United States made that wonderful speech on September the 12th setting out his faith in the United Nations. And that faith was, as it turned out, well- placed on November the 8th when 1441 was passed.

That sets out obligations on Iraq and responsibilities for the United Nations. And our position, I think, is exactly the same as that of the United States Government, which is that we wish to maintain that faith in the United Nations but there has to be a reciprocal responsibility shown by the United Nations. And both Prime Minister Blair and I and the British Government have always said that, given that we can't predict the final outcome of discussions inside the U.N., we have to reserve the position as to what decisions we will take if there is no clear resolution within the U.N..

Q. The kind of disagreements between Paris and Berlin, on the one hand, and Washington on the other, to what extent do you think that affects Britain's position in Europe, whether negatively or positively?

Foreign Secretary Straw. Well, look, you can always write these things up in that way. What I know about 1441 was that it was supported actively by France. They voted for it. They were involved in its negotiation. And I also know, because I was in the room when it happened, that Germany fully supported the terms of 1441, including explicitly its final paragraph saying that Iraq would have to accept serious consequences from a failure to comply at the Prague NATO summit in November. And that was a position of the German Government as well.

We've known since the summer that Germany was not going to be willing to take part under any circumstances in military action, and that, of course, is a decision for them. But I don't know any representative within the European Union who does not accept the overwhelming need to take positive and effective action about Iraq.

Q. Mr. Secretary, both Secretaries, please. If I could ask you, why do you think it has been so difficult to persuade principally the French and others that the onus, the burden of proof, should be on Iraq, not on this coalition to produce a smoking gun? And what do you think, down the road, the impact would be on the United Nations if the coalition of the willing were to proceed without the backing of the United Nations?

Secretary Powell. I think France and Germany do understand that the obligation is on Iraq and if there is any confusion about that, I'm sure we will clear it up in the days ahead in our conversations with them. There are different ideas right now as to how to proceed. And the United States believes that the best way to proceed is to keep showing determination, political determination, and military determination with our deployments, deployments, which as Secretary Rumsfeld said the other day, support diplomacy.

And now let's wait and see what the inspectors say on Monday with respect to the degree of cooperation they have received or not received, what they believe the situation is, and then we'll have a debate.

And so, I do not rule out that a solution would be found either, for a peaceful way to do it, or the use of military force that would draw the strong support of the Council. This is a beginning debate, not the end of the debate. And even though there are sharp differences now, as reported in the press, and clearly there are sharp differences, there were sharp differences when we also started with 1441 at the beginning. But 1441 is clear, and everybody signed up to it, to include the Germans by extension at the NATO Summit, as Secretary Straw said. And that was clear.

They are in material breach now. They have been in the past. They have a chance to fix the situation by disarming themselves. It's very clear what they had to do. The inspectors were a means to help them disarm. And if they did not disarm, if they did not meet the terms of 1441, then they were subject to serious consequences. And that was the final part of 1441, which was signed up on by the French as well as 14 other nations at the time.

Foreign Secretary Straw. All countries come at these important issues from slightly different perspectives. And it's no different today than it was, in a sense, has been. But as Secretary Powell has said, 1441 was a unanimous decision. My own view is that one of the reasons why it took such time and attention to negotiate was because everybody in the room knew that what they were signing up to in that resolution was the consequences of the resolution, as well.

Indeed, the consequences could not have been more clearly spelled out. In the last paragraph, paragraph 13, where it says "if Iraq fails to comply, serious consequences will follow." And everybody knew, too, that serious consequences means only one thing: force. President Chirac is on record, himself, as accepting that force may have to be used in order to enforce the will of the United Nations.

So yes, as the Secretary said, there are varying reports of different opinions at the moment, but everybody has agreed of the seriousness of the deceit and delay of Saddam Hussein and the threat that he poses and of the need for it to be dealt with.

Secretary Powell. Let me add, yes—I want to talk to the second point. The United Nations came together and responded to the challenge that President Bush laid down on the 12th of September. And that resulted in 1441, 15-0. The international community spoke clearly in that resolution. For the international community now to say, "Nevermind. I'll walk away from this problem," or ignore it, or allow it to be strung out indefinitely with no end, I think would be a defeat for the international community and a serious defeat for the United Nations process.

Foreign Secretary Straw. Perhaps I could just add that—because I often read stuff about exceptionalism and isolationism here. I was in the General Assembly on the 12th of September when the President made his speech. And he opened the speech, in a sense, by renewing his commitment to the United Nations by announcing that the United States would be rejoining UNESCO. And you could hear and feel the sense around the room that he was a President really committed to this route. And by your deeds shall you judge them. This administration has shown real commitment to the United Nations, but as ever, commitments have to be reciprocal.

Q. Mr. Secretary, you have spoken about your optimism about getting the agreement of the Security Council for the next steps forward. Does that mean you want another resolution if the use of force should become necessary?

Secretary Powell. I think that's an open question right now. I think we have always held the position that there is probably sufficient authority in earlier resolutions, or in 1441. But we know that many of our colleagues in the Security Council would prefer to see a second resolution if it comes to the use of military force.

What will happen next week is the inspectors will report and there will be debate that day, there will be debate again on the 29th. I'm sure all of the heads of state and government will be talking to one another, and then a judgment will be made as to how to proceed from that point on. But I would not rule anything in or anything out at this point. We will see how it unfolds.

Q. What do you both believe are the risks of going into war against Iraq without the full approval of the U.N.?

Foreign Secretary Straw. Look, we've currently got the full approval of the United Nations. We've made it clear in the United Kingdom Government that we would much prefer a second resolution. But for reasons that are well rehearsed and understood, we've had to reserve the position if achieving a second resolution is not possible.

There are consequences for the whole of the international community if we cannot follow through the resolve that was shown on the 8th of November. That's what's at stake here. What's at stake is the authority of the whole of the U.N.. Because it was the U.N. which backed the military action to stop the gratuitous invasion of Kuwait by Iraq, the U.N. which put in the weapons inspectors, the U.N. which had very patiently to put up with four years of monumental lying and deceit from Saddam Hussein, saying they had nothing at all, we only discovered things when we had defectors, the U.N. which had to suffer the humiliation of having those inspectors effectively kicked out, and then four years of limbo. So it is the authority of the U.N., of the international order, that is at stake, which is why we have to follow this through.

And to repeat a point made by Secretary Powell, we in the United Kingdom Government are in exactly the same position as the United States Government, and I think the whole rest of the world. We want to see this resolved peacefully, but we also know, to quote Kofi Annan, that sometimes—and this, by God, is one occasion—you have to back effective diplomacy with a credible threat of force.

Q. You have spoken a lot about the endgame here at the U.N. and your optimism that it will succeed. But I'm just wondering how—I'm having problems with the microphone. I can't help but wonder as you're standing here, both of you, underneath a portrait of someone who paid a great deal of attention to what some might call "Old Europe," whether you, as you say, who are going to weigh very carefully what the inspectors say on Monday, are willing to give the same opportunity and listen to the concerns so loudly expressed over the last couple of days by the French and the Germans.

Secretary Powell. Of course, I am. We're all part of an alliance, the NATO alliance. We're all part of the Euroatlantic Partnership. You see two nations represented before you that are democracies with public opinions and with sovereign points of view. And I enter into all of these issues with a desire to hear from the others and recognizing that they have points of view and they have principles they believe in. And that's the greatness of our alliance, this great democratic alliance, where we listen to others and we find a way forward.

And I think we have demonstrated since the President's speech on the 12th of September that there is a way forward. It's a way forward if we remain united, if we don't take our eye off the ball, and if we recognize the problem is not what the inspectors can find or not find, the problem is not the United States, the problem is not the United Kingdom; the problem is Saddam Hussein and his willingness to disarm and the obligation he has to disarm, in the eyes of the world and in front of the international community.

And let us not have any illusions about why this is important. As you heard the Secretary say earlier: He has materials. He has weapons. He has the intention to create more weapons of mass destruction. This isn't just for bragging purposes. He has used this kind of weaponry in the past against his own people, against his neighbors. He has invaded his neighbors. And this is a serious challenge for the region, for the world. And that's what the United Nations is all about, and this is a challenge that must be met.

Q. Do you take it as a given that the British will be there if the President goes the military route, goes to war? Or as you watch obvious divides in Europe now and

opposition to this war, do you countenance the idea seriously that the administration goes it alone?

Secretary Powell. Oh, I don't think we'll have to worry about going it alone. I think that the case is clear. I think that as we move forward, if it can't be solved peacefully, and if the U.N. should fail to act—and I hope that is not the case—then the United States reserves the right to do what it thinks is appropriate to defend its interests, the interests of its friends and to protect the world. And I am quite confident if it comes to that we'll be joined by many nations. Many nations have already expressed a willingness to serve in a coalition of the willing. And I would let the representative of Her Majesty's Government speak for the United Kingdom, but I am sure it will be a strong coalition. And we have had examples of this in the not too distant past where the international community wasn't able to act through the Security Council, but nevertheless action was taken by a coalition of the willing.

Foreign Secretary Straw. Look, no decisions have been made about military action, certainly in the United Kingdom and, I believe, in the United States. Yes, we're having to increase the credible threat of force to maintain its credibility, and that is why we in the United Kingdom are now committing up to 30,000 U.K. forces alongside the larger number of U.S. forces in the region. And they are there to be used if necessary and if we make the decisions.

But I'll repeat again that we're doing this, first of all, to enforce the law of the United Nations in whatever circumstances it is done. That's why it's being done. Secondly, we would much prefer a second resolution, but that requires cooperation from our colleagues and partners inside the United Nations. But there is still a way in which this can be resolved peacefully. To pick up the point the Secretary said right at the opening, this is not about inspectors, it's not about the U.S. or the U.K. or France or Germany; it's about Saddam Hussein and the Iraqi regime and the fact that it has been violating international law; holding stocks of poisons, of viruses, of deadly diseases; trying to rebuild its nuclear capacity to make nuclear weapons in complete defiance of international law. That's the issue and that's why this matter has to be resolved.

Remarks by Secretary of State Powell, January 24, 2003

Secretary Colin Powell delivered his remarks en route to Davos, Switzerland.

Q. Can you talk about your meeting with Jack Straw yesterday and whether you discussed the option of giving the inspectors a little bit more time in order to bring France and Germany around, some sort of compromise?

Secretary Powell. No, I can't discuss my personal conversations with Mr. Straw. I saw reports this morning as to what we were supposed to have spoken about, but it wasn't a very accurate report about what we did speak about. Our plan is very straightforward, and a lot of the commentary all week long should be put in context with what our plan is. I think you've heard me go through this before. The President has made no decisions. He said he is waiting for the 27th of January to receive the inspectors' report, along with other members of the Security Council and the world. Once we have received that report, those reports, we'll comment on it, we'll study them.

I'm sure that the President will speak to the issue at the State of the Union, but I would not expect to see any dramatic announcements at the State of the Union, if anybody's waiting for that, with respect to this issue. I think that the President will lay out the U.S. position carefully, and then there will be a debate in the Council on the 29th. Prime Minister Blair will be at Camp David on the 31st to meet with the President. And then after I've had a chance to consult with my colleagues in the Security Council, all of them, and the President has had a chance to, as I'm sure he will, consult with heads of state and government, we'll make a judgment about what we've heard and what we see then ahead.

The bottom line is that 1441 called for Iraq to perform and for the inspectors to help Iraq perform, not for the inspectors to perform in the absence of Iraq performing. It was not a search mission, it was a mission to assist Iraq into coming into compliance with U.N. resolutions. We wouldn't be this far along, and I don't think it's that far along yet, but inspectors have been able to get in, they have been able to set up. But Iraq has not cooperated in the way that I had hoped they would, but I didn't have great expectations that they would, but we gave them one last chance, as the resolution says. They wouldn't have done what they've done at this point if it had not been for the power behind diplomacy, the military power behind diplomacy.

The President has made it clear that Iraq has to be disarmed, through its own efforts, with the assistance of the inspection teams, and with the mandate of the international community, or it will have to be disarmed by force. So a lot of the commentary, really, all week long, about where everybody stands and what's going to happen is a little premature.

Q. It seems quite likely that this level of cooperation will continue, in much the same way as it has done for the last three weeks. If that happens, how much longer can you wait?

Secretary Powell. If that happens, I think that it will be an indication that it doesn't depend how long the inspectors stay there, they will not be able to fully do their jobs. I'm not going to prejudge what the President might decide. I'm not going to prejudge that tonight. There are steps that we plan to go through, methodically, deliberately, just as we did when we took the case to the Security Council, just as we did for the seven weeks that we negotiated the resolution, and just as we have done for the last couple of months, just a we did when the declaration was submitted in December.

So we are doing this deliberately, wholeheartedly, patiently, but there will be ultimately an end, I believe, to the patience of the international community, and we're doing it in full consultation and coordination with our friends and allies, some of whom have a different perspective on it than we do. None of which surprises me. There wasn't anything said this week in public that I hadn't heard privately, so I wasn't shocked.

Q. Sandbagged?

Secretary Powell. It's hard to be—well, let me put it this way. The conference was supposed to be on terrorism, but what was said in lieu of talking about terrorism was not the least bit of a surprise to me because we had talked about it the night before privately and we talked about it at lunch after the meeting.

Q. In your speech on Sunday, do you plan to give any new information?

Secretary Powell. Will I have any new information in my speech on Sunday? I don't know what's new to you, my dear. I'll have to wait and look at it again and see if there's anything in there that we have not already said within the last several days, between what Paul Wolfowitz did in a very comprehensive lay down yesterday and what Rich Armitage did on Tuesday. So I don't want to mislead you. Nothing that would be beyond the kind of cataloguing of, yeah, pretty much like that. There may be something you haven't heard before, but don't expect that there's some grand new element or announcement if that's what you're looking for.

* * * *

Q. To the extent that the premise would be that if there is action, you'd rather have U.N. support, how confident are you that if within the next few weeks you can pull together a majority either for a resolution or at least for support for action?

Secretary Powell. It of course would be most desirable to have the whole community, the whole Security Council, behind it. We'll have to see whether or not that is a possibility, as time unfolds, and as President Bush and others make their decisions.

If the Security Council rallied behind the need for the use of force, lots of countries would fall under that resolution. If they don't, and it's still deemed appropriate by the President and other leaders, world leaders, that military action needs to be taken, there are quite a number of countries that have already indicated that they would like to have another resolution, but without that other resolution, they will be with us. I don't want to give names or to give you a count, because I think that each country should speak for itself on a matter as important as this, but we would not be alone. That's for sure. I could rattle off at least a dozen off memory, and I think that there will be more.

Q. Mr. Secretary, don't you worry what that would do to the U.N. Security Council, and the U.N. system? I mean, in a way it will be Iraq's choice, and other's choice, but it's also your choice if you go outside of the Security Council framework.

Secretary Powell. I do worry, and that's why we have said to the Security Council. Don't shirk from your responsibilities. We believe this is a responsibility to take this to conclusion. The President, I think, made that clear in his speech on 12 September. I kind of talked to that point when I responded in the Security Council this past Monday. You can't be afraid to go down this road because the going's going to get tough or hard. You should have realized that was a possibility when you signed on and you became a party to 1441.

We were hoping for the best. We were hoping for a peaceful solution. We're still hoping for a peaceful solution. That remains the President's hope and wish, that remains our policy. But we also knew, the day may come when that wouldn't be the case and we would have to use force, and the force that is being assembled now, as Don Rumsfeld noted the other day and says regularly, is designed to support diplomacy but it is also designed, if necessary, to be built up to do what is necessary to do.

Remarks by Secretary of State Powell, January 25, 2003

Secretary Powell delivered his remarks from Davos, Switzerland.

Q. Mr. Secretary, what do you think of the Swiss offer to hold talks here in Switzerland between the United States and Iraq in Davos?

Secretary Powell. The foreign minister just made a reference to the fact that talks had been held here in the past and that was the extent of the reference but no talks are planned.

Q. Are you willing to have such talks, Mr. Secretary?

Secretary Powell. We have lots of venues in which one could hold talks. She made a gracious passing reference to the fact that talks had been held here previously and that was the extent of her comment. I thanked her for the offer.

Remarks by Secretary of State Powell, January 26, 2003

Secretary Colin Powell delivered the following address at the World Economic Forum in Davos, Switzerland.

Now, I'm aware, as everyone in this room is aware, that Americans and Europeans do not always see things the same way in every instance. I would quickly point out that this is hardly a new development. Henry Kissinger, decades ago, wrote a book on the Atlantic alliance, and he called it, "The Troubled Partnership." I am told that later Henry had second doubts about the title when he found that some bookstores were placing it on the shelf reserved for books about marriage counseling. But maybe the bookstore owners knew what they were doing, because problems with some of our friends across the Atlantic go back a long time, more than two centuries by my count. In fact, one or two of our friends we have been in marriage counseling with for over 225 years nonstop, and yet the marriage is intact, remains strong, will weather any differences that come along because of our mutual shared values.

Differences are inevitable, but differences should not be equated with American unilateralism or American arrogance. Sometimes differences are just that—differences. On occasion, our experiences, our interests, will lead us to see things in a different way. For our part, we will not join a consensus if we believe it compromises our core principles. Nor would we expect any other nation to join in a consensus that would compromise its core principles. When we feel strongly about something, we will lead. We will act even if others are not prepared to join us. But the United States will always work, will always endeavor, to get others to join in a consensus. We want to work closely with Europe, home of our closest friends and partners. We want to work closely with Europe on challenges inside Europe and beyond, and you can trust us on that.

When we talk about trust, let me use that as a bridge to one of the major issues of the day, Iraq. Let me try to explain why we feel so strongly about Iraq and why we are determined that the current situation cannot be allowed to continue. We are where we are today with Iraq because Saddam Hussein and his regime have repeatedly violated the trust of the United Nations, his people and his neighbors, to such an extent as to pose a grave danger to international peace and security.

The United Nation's Security Council recognized this situation and unanimously passed Resolution 1441, giving Iraq one last chance to disarm peacefully after 11 years of defying the world community. Today, not a single nation, not one, trusts Saddam and his regime. And those who know him best trust him least: his own citizens, whom he has terrorized and oppressed; his neighbors, whom he has threatened and invaded. Citizens and neighbors alike have been killed by his chemical weapons.

That is why Resolution 1441 was carefully crafted to be far tougher and far more thorough than the many resolutions that preceded it. 1441 places the burden squarely on Iraq to provide accurate, full and complete information on its weapons of mass destruction.

1441 is not about inspectors exposing new evidence of Iraq's established failure to disarm. It is about Iraq disclosing the entire extent of its illicit biological, chemical, nuclear and missile activities, and disarming itself of them with the help of inspectors to verify what Iraq is doing.

This is not about inspectors finding smoking guns. It is about Iraqis failure—Iraq's failure to tell the inspectors where to find its weapons of mass destruction.

The 12,200-page declaration Iraq submitted to the United Nations Security Council on December 7th utterly failed to meet the requirements of the resolution, utterly failed to meet the requirements of being accurate, full and complete. Iraq attempted to conceal with volume what it lacked in veracity. Not one nation in the Security Council rose to defend that declaration. Not one person in this room could do so. The requirement for a declaration was put in as an early test of Iraq's intent to change its behavior. It failed the test.

This past week, United Nations Inspector Blix and International Atomic Energy Agency Inspector ElBaradei went to Baghdad to deliver the message that Iraq's cooperation has been inadequate. Iraq's response did nothing to alter the fact that Baghdad still is not providing the inspectors with the information they need to do their job. There is no indication whatever that Iraq has made the strategic decision to come clean and to comply with its international obligation to disarm.

The support of U.S. intelligence and the intelligence of other nations can take the inspectors only so far. Without Iraq's full and active cooperation, 100 or so inspectors would have to look under every roof and search the back of every truck in a country the size of California to find the munitions and programs for which Iraq has failed to account for.

After six weeks of inspections, the international community still needs to know the answers to key questions. For example: Where is the evidence—where is the evidence—that Iraq has destroyed the tens of thousands of liters of anthrax and botulinum we know it had before it expelled the previous inspectors? This isn't an American determination. This is the determination of the previous inspectors. Where is this material? What happened to it? It's not a trivial question. We're not talking about aspirin. We're talking about the most deadly things one can imagine, that can kill thousands, millions of people. We cannot simply turn away and say, "Well, never mind." Where is it? Account for it. Let it be verified through the inspectors.

What happened to nearly 30,000 munitions capable of carrying chemical agents? The inspectors can only account for only 16 of them. Where are they? It's not a matter of ignoring the reality of the situation. Just think, all of these munitions, which perhaps only have a short range if fired out of an artillery weapon in Iraq, but imagine if one of these weapons were smuggled out of Iraq and found its way into the hands of a terrorist organization who could transport it anywhere in the world.

What happened—please, what happened—to the three metric tons of growth material that Iraq imported which can be used for producing early, in a very rapid fashion, deadly biological agents?

Where are the mobile vans that are nothing more than biological weapons laboratories on wheels? Why is Iraq still trying to procure uranium and the special equipment needed to transform it into material for nuclear weapons?

These questions are not academic. They are not trivial. They are questions of life and death, and they must be answered.

To those who say, "Why not give the inspection process more time?", I ask: "How much more time does Iraq need to answer those questions? It is not a matter of time alone, it is a matter of telling the truth, and so far Saddam Hussein still responds with evasion and with lies.

Saddam should tell the truth, and tell the truth now. The more we wait, the more chance there is for this dictator with clear ties to terrorist groups, including al-Qaida, more time for him to pass a weapon, share a technology, or use these weapons again.

The nexus of tolerance and terror, of terrorists and weapons of mass destruction, is the greatest danger of our age. The international community knows what real disarmament looks like. We saw it in Kazakhstan. We saw it take place in the Ukraine. We saw it in South Africa. We see none of the telltale signs of real disarmament, honest disarmament, in Iraq. Instead of a high-level determination to work with inspectors, we have continued defiance. Instead of a transparent disarmament process, we get the same old tactics of deceit and delay, documents hidden in private homes, denial of reconnaissance flights, denial of access to people and facilities, the kind of access that must be unimpeded and unrestricted in order to be successful.

Tomorrow, Chief Inspectors Blix and ElBaradei will make their report to the United Nations Security Council. My government will study their report carefully, will study it with gravity, and we will exchange views on its findings that were presented with other members of the Council.

We are in no great rush to judgment tomorrow or the day after, but clearly time is running out. There is no longer an excuse for Iraqi denial of its obligation. We must have Iraq participate in the disarmament or be disarmed.

We should not (sic) understand what is at stake here. Saddam Hussein's hidden weapons of mass destruction are meant to intimidate Iraq's neighbors. These illegal weapons threaten international peace and security. These terrible weapons put millions of innocent people at risk.

It is more than that. Saddam's naked defiance also challenges the relevance and credibility of the Security Council and the world community. When all 15 members of the Council voted to pass U.N. Resolution 1441, they assumed a heavy responsibility to put their will behind their words. Multilateralism cannot become an excuse for inaction. Saddam Hussein and others of his ilk would like nothing better to see the world community back away from this resolution, instead of backing it with their solemn resolve.

We will work through these issues patiently and deliberately with our friends and with our allies. These are serious matters before us. Let the Iraqi regime have no doubt, however, if it does not disarm peacefully at this juncture, it will be disarmed down the road.

The United States believes that time is running out. We will not shrink from war if that is the only way to rid Iraq of its weapons of mass destruction.

We continue to reserve our sovereign right to take military action against Iraq alone or in a coalition of the willing. As the President has said: "We cannot defend America and our friends by hoping for the best. History will judge harshly those who saw a coming danger but failed to act."

It is our hope, however—it is our will—that we can do this peacefully. It is our hope, if we will it to happen, that Iraq would participate in its disarmament. If it does not, it is also our hope that the international community will stand behind the elements of 1441, and as a great coalition, we will deal with this problem once and for all.

Remarks by Secretary of State Powell, January 26, 2003

Secretary Colin Powell was interviewed by European journalists in Davos, Switzerland.

Q. I'm a Turkish journalist. My name is Hasan Cemal. I'm from Istanbul. Are you satisfied with the military cooperation of Turkey? And in the meantime, to what extent Turkey is helping U.S. opening the northern front?

Secretary Powell. We are satisfied with the cooperation we are receiving from Turkey. Turkey is a great friend and, of course, a great ally of the United States and we have tried to be very helpful to Turkey in recent years as they have worked their way through economic difficulties.

I had good meetings yesterday with the Prime Minister and with Mr. Erdogan. And among the things we discussed were the military preparations we are trying to make to support diplomacy to make sure that Saddam Hussein does not mistake our determination, and also to position ourselves should it be necessary to use military force.

Turkey is aware of what we would like to be able to do in Turkey and they are responding to us in a measured way. We have already gotten some answers back. But we also understand that it is a complex political environment for Turkey with a changing government, a parliament that must be consulted, and we are being patient as our Turkish colleagues examine the requests that we have made of them, and as they consult with each other—with the Turkish General Staff, with the President of the Republic, and with both the Prime Minister and Mr. Erdogan—but we're satisfied with the level of cooperation. I can't, obviously—I obviously can't go into the details of the specific requests or specific responses to specific requests, but I'm satisfied with the cooperation. They know what we would like to have and they have all of our requests under consideration and they have to work it through their own system, political system, to include the parliament. And we are just waiting for them to take the necessary action.

Q. From the, in the same respect, I mean, do you think that Turkey could play some small—what kind of concrete role for a peaceful solution to this [*inaudible*]?

Secretary Powell. I think Turkey is trying, as all nations are trying, to find a peaceful solution. You know they held a meeting in Istanbul the other day of leaders from the region and came out with a declaration asking Saddam Hussein to take seriously his obligations. That's a helpful role. And I think Turkey has a significant interest in seeing if a peaceful solution can be found. So we appreciate Turkish efforts and encourage those efforts.

* * * *

Q. You referred to the fact, yourself, there is a gap in understanding and it came to light here at this meeting very much. And I think in the end it will turn on the point mentioned by the Dutch banker, at the point of evidence. I think you could still convince the majority of Europeans, including of Germans—maybe not our administration but the people—if you put the—could put any evidence on the table.

And when I say "put it on the table" I'm thinking of the 26 photographs Adlai Stevenson showed at the Security Council back in '62.

Secretary Powell. Yeah.

Q. Is there any such thing? Can we expect anything like that? Or is it just conclusions and inferences?

Secretary Powell. I think some of them are hard conclusions. I touched on a few of them. But they really don't satisfy the public yet because we say there's a gap, but you can't see the gap, and it doesn't have the same power as if I was able to suddenly produce a building and inside the building are the missing chemicals. So I very much understand what you mean by a "Stevenson moment." We talk about it a lot.

We do have a number of intelligence products that convince us that what we are saying is correct, convince us that they are doing these things, and we hope in the next week or so to make as much of this available in public as possible. Whether there will be a "Stevenson" photo or "Stevenson" presentation that would be as persuasive as Adlai Stevenson was in 1962, that I can't answer.

Stevenson had a much easier task, I think. I mean, all he had to prove was that there were Russian missiles in Cuba, and viola, there were Russian missiles in Cuba. And we all remember the famous exchange when the Russian Ambassador responded, "I am not in an American court, Mr. Stevenson." But the fact of the matter is he was in something worse than an American court; he was in the court of public opinion and everybody could see it.

I would love to have that kind of material to present, and we are seeing what we can do, what we might find in the next couple of weeks.

Q. But in a sense, you were saying that, in your speech that that kind of material is, in a sense, irrelevant because what you seemed to be saying was that we know that there were weapons there, and everybody agrees on that, and it is now up to Iraq actively to demonstrate what it has done with those weapons which undeniably were there. So you're saying that, really, he has got to produce the evidence to justify himself, which seemed a very reasonable statement when you expressed it.

Secretary Powell. I think it's very reasonable, yeah.

Q. But do you think that is the kind of position that—

Secretary Powell. I would—

Q.—the European [*inaudible*] will find—will ultimately find acceptable?

Secretary Powell. No, that's my question to ask you guys.

Well, I don't know. But I think it is a reasonable proposition to say that it is his obligation to come forward with everything he has done over the years. It seems to me to be powerful to see inspectors coming out of the home of a scientist carrying documents that have to do with nuclear weapons development. What are they doing in his house? How many other houses have documents that have been squirreled away?

One thing we do know for a fact is that they have an active program of hiding material. Why are they hiding? If they have no weapons, why are they hiding this stuff? Why don't they come clean if they have no weapons? And if they have no weapons and they also say they want to comply with the will of the international community, then why don't they act like they want to comply with the will of the international community? Why is it necessary to have ten people follow every inspector? Why are they trying to get inside the inspection team's work so that they know where they're going?

There's an old expression in the Army, and it says, "Glad you asked." You know, when something bad is going on, I want to tell you the truth, so, "Glad you asked." Iraq should be saying: "Glad you asked. We don't want a war. We don't have any weapons of mass destruction. I have no intent to use weapons of mass destruction. Ask any question you want and it will be answered. Ask for access to anybody you want to talk to, we'll make them available. And we'll tell them to tell you what they did in the past and you can ask them anything you want about what they're doing now. And they don't need any minders and they don't need to take tape recorders with them, and their families are in no danger and they know that."

That's not what we're seeing. We're seeing people who are not speaking because they know of the risks that they're putting their family in. And so it's that attitude that seems to me to be—is evidence of continued lack of cooperation, and they're hiding things, second piece of evidence of the kinds of things that I said today, that Deputy Secretary Wolfowitz laid out in great detail on Thursday, and Deputy Secretary

Armitage also laid out in great detail last Tuesday.

Now, what I would also love to see, love to have, but do not at the moment have, are some concrete things. You know, I'd like to have Exhibit A on the ground. Shall we say, a CNN moment? But perhaps that will—

Q.—ask a supplementary. But let's settle, now that you've made this perhaps much clearer than before that what you need is active cooperation in the sense that, it wasn't clear enough even to us, so maybe it wasn't clear enough to him. If he turned round and said, "Glad you asked," and started offering some of this cooperation, how would you then be able to—wouldn't you then be back in the gray area of is this enough cooperation? How do you react then? How long do you give the cooperation?

Secretary Powell. I would love to have to answer that question, if he would start to move in that direction. I think that's—he's had since the first week of November to act that way. And instead of acting that way we got this stream of—this stream of invective and all these diatribes coming out of Baghdad accusing the United States of, you know, being responsible for all these terrible things. He spent the first 30 days that he had coming up with a 12,000-page piece of junk.

I wondered, when we heard it was 12,000 pages, if it's 12,000 pages, it's junk. Because how could he have come up with an honest 12,000 pages in 30 days? All he's going to do is send us stuff that's already there. In fact, he took old U.N. reports, took out the most damning parts with respect to his behavior, and submitted it as part of the declaration.

And there was a reason that declaration was in there. It was put in there at the insistence of the United States, and we debated it strongly. We had a hot debate within the administration as to whether it should be in there. We all agreed, you know, on balance, it ought to be in there. Why? To give an early test of whether or not he is going to be serious about his obligations and whether or not he's going to cooperate. And that's why I called it, on behalf of the United States Government, a material breach the day it came out.

Q. You emphasized today that time is running out, time is running out—

Secretary Powell. Yeah.

Q. How soon is it?

Secretary Powell. Well, I can't answer your question. And if I knew the answer, I still wouldn't answer your question because I don't know the answer. It is a judgment that will have to be made by President Bush and by other leaders. Every nation represented here is a sovereign nation with its own democratic constituency and leadership. But it's not something that can go on indefinitely, so I think we are in the final phases of this.

Q. You talked about a delay for the inspectors. Does this mean that you expect from this delay a better comprehension between you and European governments?

Secretary Powell. Well, you're taking me down a path that I, with all due respect, choose not to go down yet. There is an issue in the press about delay, meaning give more time to Iraq and give more time to the inspectors. We understand that some nations think this is a good idea. We also know that the inspectors may propose such an idea when they report tomorrow.

And our plan is pretty straightforward and it's a matter of record. We will listen to the inspectors tomorrow. We will have an initial reaction to what they say, both on the part of our Ambassador in the Security Council and I may make a statement once I see what they say.

And then on Tuesday, the President will reflect on all of this, and I am sure he will talk to it in his State of the Union Address on Tuesday night. But the State of the Union Address is not going to be a declaration of war. It will be mostly on domestic policy and this situation.

And then there will be a debate in the Council on Wednesday. The President will be spending part of next week talking to heads of state and government. "Well, what was your impression? What do you think? What do you think the next step should be?" Prime Minister Blair is coming next Friday. There may be other leaders who will be visiting Washington over the next week or so.

And then I think we'll be making a determination as to what the next step should be. And so I'm choosing my words rather precisely: "what the next step should be." And I can't tell you yet what that next step will be or when we will decide to take it.

Q. We have your personal judgment on the presentation of the Resolution 1441, but how do you understand it?

Secretary Powell. The presentation?

Q. I mean the content of the Resolution 1441.

Secretary Powell. It had several important elements to it. The first important element is that we all agreed that Hussein is in violation of his obligations. He was in material breach. He still is in material breach of his obligations under previous resolutions.

This was an important point during the debate for 1441. There were some who said let's not talk about the past, let's just talk about the future. And some of us insisted, no, you can't just say that we wipe the board clean. He was in breach, he remains in breach, and we're giving him one last chance to get out of breach. That's the second element. This is a final chance for Saddam Hussein to remove the basis of his material breach, and we laid out what it is we're expecting from him: a full, accurate, complete declaration. We gave some specific criteria that will allow the inspectors to do their job if they got back in and if Saddam was cooperating.

And then finally, and this also was a major point of debate for seven weeks. What happens if there are new breaches and he doesn't cooperate? There were some who wanted to say, well, let's just see what happens if that happens. And there were others who said, no, for this resolution to have any force, any effect, any utility, and not to be just like all other resolutions, there have to be consequences associated with this resolution. There must be consequences for continued misbehavior.

And at the end, this was the most contentious part of the negotiation, and that's why the last part of the resolution, OP paragraphs, I think it's 12 and 13, or 11 and 12—I forget—that's why it specifically says if he does not cooperate, if there are further material breaches, it will be referred to the Council and the Council will decide what to do, and made specific references to serious consequences. Serious consequences means that he'll have to be disarmed forcibly. Nobody had any confusion as to what that meant.

And we also recognized that there would be many members who would want to come back for a second resolution and we understood that. But we would not commit ourselves to be solely, to be bound solely by the need for a second resolution, so we preserved our right, in light of his previous material breaches and continuing material breach, to take unilateral action with other likeminded nations, if that turned out to be the case.

And so this is the judgment that will be made in the near future.

Q. Is there now—do you now have a different idea about a second resolution? Time has progressed. Even the coalition [*inaudible*] there, also.

Secretary Powell. Obviously, if a judgment is made that we really do have to take military action, it would be much better if military action were taken by the whole international community, consistent with the intent of 1441. And if a resolution could come out of the Council that would repeat the elements of 1441 and give further authority for all available means, that would make it a lot easier for some nations to join such an effort. You would have a broader coalition. I'm also sure—

Q. You would welcome it?

Secretary Powell. We'd welcome it. But we would not find it a precondition if we felt it was necessary to go. And if we go in the absence of additional U.N. action, I've been in touch with enough countries, and we have had enough consultations with nations in Europe as well as nations elsewhere, that it would not just be the United States going alone, even in the absence of a U.N. resolution.

* * * *

Q. Can I ask you a different question on this, if it's possible? You didn't think that France, Germany of the old Europe while Italy, Spain and some countries of the Eastern Europe will join the European Union, now the new Europe, as Defense Secretary Rumsfeld said [*inaudible*].

(Inaudible) But then, in fact, a [*inaudible*] the second question. "Because a more effective role do you expect from Europe, and in particular from Italy, that is in a strategic position [*inaudible*]?

Secretary Powell. Europe has many nations within that grand continent. Each is a sovereign nation. Each is a democracy, thank heavens. And each has to be responsive to—each government has to be responsive to its people. And each nation will make its own independent judgment.

Often, they can make that judgment through the EU, and therefore it becomes a collective judgment. I've been in touch with the presidency of the EU in the person of Mr. George Papandreou, and I've been in touch with Javier Solana, and they'll be meeting tomorrow and Tuesday. And I hope that whatever statement comes out of the EU will include the strongest condemnation of what Saddam Hussein has been doing and will recognize the burden is on him to avoid war and him to come into compliance.

In the case of Germany, they made a decision, a political decision, even before 1441 as to what their position would be. I mean, it was part of the campaign, the political campaign that went on during the summer and I guess into the fall.

France feels strongly that more time should be given. They haven't ruled out what they might do at the end of the day, I don't think. And I understand that position.

I have had straightforward, honest, candid conversations with my colleague Dominique de Villepin and my colleague Joschka Fischer and my colleague in just about every other European country. And I think I have a good understanding of European attitudes. And I think they have a good understanding of our attitude.

I, you know, much is made of friction between the United States and Europe. And then you have to break it down. Is it between the United States and U.K.? Well, no. The United States and Germany? Sometimes. The United States and France? The United States and Italy? The United States and Spain?

You see, you have a continent with—how many nations on it?

Q. Who's counting?

Secretary Powell. We have a continent with three nations. Much easier. It's much easier.

Q. Between 25 and 40.

Secretary Powell. Between 25 and 40?

Q. If we enlarge the EU, it would be about 27, 28.

Secretary Powell. Yes, yes. And even then, you don't have everybody.

And so to get to the second part of your question, what would we expect? If it comes to conflict, obviously I would hope that each European nation would recognize the need for military action and would support us in any way that they could. But that will be a judgment made by each country based on its own sovereign responsibilities, its obligation to its own parliament and legislature, or legislature, and to its own people. And it would be presumptuous of me to say to any country what they should or should not do.

Q. Coming from Sweden, I have to ask you about my countryman, Mr. Blix. Do you think he would become a problem to you or do you trust him?

Secretary Powell. I trust Hans Blix. I've spent many hours with him. He is an honest man doing a difficult job and he will be fair in his presentation, I'm sure. He will not be fooled by Saddam Hussein and he will not be pressured by anyone else to say something that he does not believe to be the truth.

And Dr. Rice has spent time with him. President Bush has met with Hans Blix and Mohamed ElBaradei, and we have confidence in them.

Q. Yes, do you—from new Europe, you are seen as the one who sees—understands our differences, the differences between. How far do you understand those differences between Europe and the United States? And do you understand that a misunderstanding is growing between European public opinions and your government? Maybe it is also because American doctrine has changed. We were used—we were used and—as containment, and containment was the basis of a strong coalition between Europe and the United States.

And now your doctrine is the doctrine of preemptive action, and isn't it the cause of the, how do you say, in a way the [*inaudible*] divergence and the States are growing apart?

Secretary Powell. Yeah, there's no question that there has been some divergence. I think it is bridgeable. I mean, the United States has been very active in the work that we did together to expand NATO. We have tried to be supportive and helpful in what Europe did to expand the EU. We're working actively with Europe in finding a—hoping to find a solution for the problem in Cyprus.

One little joke I use with my staff, you know, if America is in this, you know, this awkward position of everybody, you know, sort of resenting us, so then why was I the one they called to solve this problem between Morocco and Spain on this little island? You know? I didn't want to do this, but we were called upon.

Because I think we are still a nation that is trusted and looked to for the role that we can play in the world. Europe and the United States cannot be separated. We can have our differences. We can have our debates. We can have our disagreements. I have been in public life at a senior level for 20 years, and I can go year by year and tell you what they were, every single year. Would you like to go back to Crookham and Greenham Commons, sir?   Would you like to go back to what it took to get the missiles and the Pershing IIs into various parts of Europe? Would you like to go to some of the basing problems we had in—with Italy? It was France who, in—let me see if my memory serves me correctly—kicked NATO out of Paris.

Q. In '66.

Secretary Powell. Yes. So, I mean, it is not as if these differences have not come along and nations at one time or another have acted, how shall we say, unilaterally, as France did in 1966. These things come and go. They are part of a thriving, vibrant alliance.

But to suggest that somehow it's breaking up, I have been listening to this for 20 years. It is not breaking up. Because that which pulls us together on any one day is far stronger than the issue that may be causing some division.

Now, you say we have come up with a new strategy. If you look at the National Security Strategy that we published, you will find one paragraph or two on preemption. It is not a strategy of preemption. Preemption is a tool within a strategy. We've always had a strategy—a tool of preemption. There is no nation that does not have the right to preempt a threat that is coming at it is that so real and pressing. It's like a police officer seeing somebody running down a street with a gun getting ready to shoot somebody. Do you preempt it or don't you preempt? You preempt.

So what we did in our National Security Strategy was elevate that concept, that tool of preemption, to a higher level. And I'll come back to why we did that. But if you read the whole document, you will see that the document talks about economic development, it talks about partnerships, it talks about a Europe whole and free, it talks about health issues, it talks about how America has to work with its friends and allies. Two elements got highlighted. Preemption, which became a strategy, which is it is not. And our strategy remains one of working with our friends and partners. Containment is always better than war if you really can contain something.

And the other thing that got a lot of attention is America says that it wants to be stronger than anybody else. Well, this is not necessarily a bad thing because America uses its military strength wisely. And, excuse me, during the entire period of the Cold War, we all spent a lot of money to make sure that we were stronger than Russia. And when you're stronger than evil forces around the world, you tend to contain and deter them. And so having powerful military forces is, at least in our concept, and especially in the hands of the United States, is stabilizing and not destabilizing.

The reason containment doesn't have the same relevance and the reason we had to lift preemption a little higher—how do you contain Osama bin Laden? How do you contain al-Qaida? You can contain a state—

Q. There's no question on terrorism and al-Qaida. The problem in Europe and the States is for European opinions the fight against terrorism is the number one danger and nobody understand why Iraq has become the number one in your preoccupations.

Secretary Powell. Terrorism is still number one in our preoccupation; the President spends more time on terrorism. If he was here, he would talk to you about—every morning he goes through his list of threats that have been presented by the intelligence and law enforcement community. So he is—terrorism is his number one priority.

But he also sees that Iraq is a serious danger to the region and to the world. It is a state that has sponsored terrorism over the years. It is a state in which we find these horrible weapons still being developed. There are other states that are doing it, but none has had the sort of unremitting dedication to the creation of these weapons and has been willing to remain isolated for all these years and to be under sanctions for all these years in order to keep trying to develop these evil weapons for the purpose of getting power.

And because of the connection that exists between Iraq and certain terrorist organizations, we have to be concerned that these weapons can ultimately fall into the hands of terrorists.

Q. You referred in your speech to the links between al-Qaida and Iraq. Now, even some of our secret service chiefs say publicly there is no evidence of that.

Secretary Powell. We do have evidence of it. We are not suggesting that there is a 9/11 link, but we are suggesting—we do have evidence—of connections over the years between Iraq and al- Qaida and other terrorist organizations.

Q. But isn't there more evidence of—because I think this is another thing that has really perplexed public opinion, as Mr. Colombani says, everybody is behind the U.S. on terrorism, I think, in every country. But what has perplexed public opinion is that Iraq did seem to be a change of subject, now partly because there's no evident link, but there may be some link; but secondly also, because there are other nations in the region which seem to be much more closely linked with the terrorist threat, either through financing, whatever, or Saudi, or, as in the case of Pakistan, through the fact that, you know, everybody believes that bin Laden is actually in Pakistan, most likely. So why the focus on Iraq in those circumstances?

Secretary Powell. There is a focus on Iraq. There is also a focus on Pakistan. I spend a good bit of my time dealing with the problems in Pakistan with respect to, you know, the Pakistan- India situation and cross-border terrorism, hostile acts across the line of control after President Musharraf has said that they would stop it, and I have to remain in close touch with Pakistan to ensure that they take every effort to stop that kind of activity. We are also working with Pakistan to round up terrorists in Pakistan and we're working with them to track down al-Qaida remnants in the remote sections of western Pakistan along the Afghan border. We're doing that.

We're also keeping our eyes on Afghanistan, as I mentioned this morning. And we are also examining our policies constantly with respect to Iran. And we also have not lost sight of other nations in the region and other places in the world. And so it is not impossible for us to do all of these things without neglecting any one of them.

Q. How are you going to make use of bases in Turkey and the ports in Turkey against [*inaudible*] strike?

Secretary Powell. I really don't think it would be appropriate for me to comment on what our military options and plans might be. I think that's something that would be better just to continue to discuss privately. I'm sorry.

* * * *

Q. How about the criticism that's levied at you from the Arab and Islam world that you have your priorities wrong, that you really should be looking at the Israel-Palestine conflict? And even if that argument doesn't have any merit, don't you think this

is, if you like, poisoning the relationship between the West and the Arab world?

Secretary Powell. We are doing everything we can to see if we can get movement and traction in the Middle East. That's why I spent a lot of time with the Quartet. We've come up with a new roadmap. The two sides each have sets of objections to the roadmap, but I think it is a good way forward.

And we are waiting for the Israeli election to be concluded, which is now taking place, and as soon as that's behind us and the situation politically stabilizes within the region, the President is determined to move forward with the roadmap.

This has been one of the most challenging problems we've faced and the most frustrating, frankly, to get your hands around. It's not because we haven't tried. But we need reform within the Palestinian community. We need the end of terror, the end of violence, the end of bombings. In the absence of that, it is very difficult to get movement on the Israeli side when the Israelis are faced with violence and they have an obligation to protect their people.

* * * *

Q. What is your post-Saddam vision of Iraq?

Secretary Powell. A country that lives in peace with its neighbors; a country that cooperates in getting rid of weapons of mass destruction; a country that will be one country and not break up into parts; a country that will, with the help of the international community, use the resources that this nation has. What makes Iraq different from a number of other countries, which might be in this kind of circumstance, is that it has—it will have money. It has the wealth of its oil. And so it has the potential to deal with the needs of its people and not waste the money on weapons. And a country that with the help of the international community can hopefully form a representative form of government that will represent all the people of Iraq in an honest, balanced, fair way.

Q. What will happen in Iraq the day after, the day after military action? What will happen? What will happen to the Iraqi oil?

Secretary Powell. On the second question, if conflict comes—and we still hope it can be avoided—the oil of Iraq belongs to the people of Iraq. And the United States, if we are the leader of this coalition, would respect international law as to how a nation that is temporarily in charge of another nation, how it would protect and preserve the resources of that nation for its people.

And any suggestion that the United States is doing this for oil or to take control of the oil of Iraq or to sell the oil of Iraq for our own purposes or to dole it out to friends is nonsense. We will do it in accordance with international law and it'll be done for the benefit of the Iraqi people. It's their oil. It's not our oil. We would act responsibly. And suggestions that the United States would not act responsibly goes against the history of the United States in similar situations over the course of the last 50 years.

Q. Are you in favor of invasion forces?

Secretary Powell. Now, did I get—with respect to what the day after will look like, so much depends on what happens the day before and the day of, and so I would just be fantasizing with you.

But don't—war is a complex, difficult thing. One never knows how it will unfold. There are always unintended consequences. But the people of Iraq may welcome a new regime that is cooperating with the world, rather than fighting the world.

Q. Are you in favor of invasion forces—invasion in Iraq? Also,—

Secretary Powell. We're in favor of one Iraq.

Q. One Iraq.

Secretary Powell. Now, what it looks like, I think this is something for the people of Iraq, all the people of Iraq—Kurds, Shias, Sunnis—

Q. Exactly. You want one Iraq, but the Iraqi opposition is working very hard for a federation, including the Iraqi Kurds.

Secretary Powell. I understand that there are many different points of view, but our position is that we do not want to see Iraq splinter in any way.

Q. I raised the following question that—the answer was what happens to the oil after, not what happens to oil during the military operation, but what happens to the oil fields, what happens to the oil transports, what happens to that part of the world oil consumption which still comes from Iraq?

Secretary Powell. While the military operation is going on, or after?

Q. Yeah. During.

Secretary Powell. I can't answer that question because I don't know how the military operation will unfold, so I can't answer that question. There are fields in the north, there are fields in the south, and I hope the military operation would proceed at a rate, a fast enough rate so that we could bring those fields under protection, and recognizing that it will have an impact on the overall oil market. But I'm not about to get into speculation as to, you know, what the situation will be. It would be much too hypothetical for me to jump in and guess about.

Q. You keep repeating, "if conflict can be avoided," and you've made very clear in your speech that that is your preference for—

Secretary Powell. It is the President's preference.

Q. And the President makes it clear in his speeches, too. And I'd like to ask two questions related to that. Given that fact, why do you think it is that the view seems to be extremely widespread that, in fact, a war is inevitable and that actually that America's preference is actually for war? I mean, I'd to reflect, if you like, on the way this has come across to public opinion, whether it's the media's role, whether you, perhaps, have not expressed yourselves as clearly or as precisely as you should have done, or whatever.

And the second related thing is, now you say, "if conflict can be avoided." Could you lay out for us a sort of step-by-step guide as to how conflict, you know, might be avoided? What would have to happen over the next few weeks to make the avoidance of conflict a real possibility?

Secretary Powell. The President often says to people who visit him in the Oval Office that he's the one who has to go look in the faces of the mothers and fathers of young men and women who might be lost in conflict, so he has no desire to see a war. But he also recognizes that we will not get a solution from Iraq if you do not demonstrate that you're willing to fight to achieve our purpose of disarmament.

And so I think some people often overlook the first point that he makes and go right to the second point, the Americans want a war. Why do we want a war? You know, look at our tradition and history. It's not our tradition. It's not our history. It's not our proclivity. In fact, I can argue, if you want to look at the whole history of the American Republic over the last 220 years, we've always been kind of slow to anger, and then sometimes to our regret. But when war comes, and if there's no other choice, we're going to do it and we're going to do it well.

But the President has been trying to find a peaceful solution. But he knows no peaceful solution will come if it doesn't also appear that we are prepared to back our words and our desire for a peaceful solution with the threat of force. All of this business about, well, the inspectors are in and they're doing fine and everything's terrific, why are they in? Are they in because Saddam Hussein woke up one morning and said, "You know what? I'll let them in. I'll show everybody what I got."

And this will go to the other question. Why, suddenly, on the Monday after the President's speech did they come in with, oh, we're going to let the inspectors in? Oh, gosh, we didn't know until President Bush spoke that they wanted the inspectors to come in. No, because President Bush made it clear that this time there had to be consequences. And that's what he said in his speech. Suddenly, the Iraqis let them in.

And then they started to back out, and then they started to change what the inspectors could do, and then they started to play the usual games. They did everything they could to try to keep 1441 from ever coming into being. This wasn't an open, cooperative effort on the part of Iraq. It was an effort to frustrate, to deny, to deceive, to keep out the international community—not to comply rather than to comply.

But guess what? They got 1441 anyway. And they had one more chance with 1441 to demonstrate that they were going to comply, and they haven't done it, which gets to the second question: What do they have to do? What they have to do—

Q. [*Inaudible.*]

Secretary Powell. I'm still answering the question. What they have to do is all of these gaps that we're talking about, fill the gaps, answer the questions. And if there are still some elements in their programs that we don't know about—this is not brain surgery.

If they want to comply, they would turn over every document, they would make available every scientist, they would take us to every site where this kind of activity has been going on or went on in the past, and say, "Look." They would not be having haystacks everywhere with us to go find the needle. They would be saying, "We are changing our policy and the nature of our regime. Here were the haystacks, here are the haystacks. Here's where they were. There is the needle. Go verify it's there. Destroy it. That's where a needle used to be. It's gone. You can look at it. We'll tell you what happened to it."

Now, that may be too much to ask for, but that's the right question to ask and that's the right thing to ask for. And this isn't brain surgery. That would avoid a war.

* * * *

Q. Do you consider what's happened in Afghanistan a good example of what will happen in Iraq after the war? You said you are proud of what happened in—

Secretary Powell. I'm proud of what we did in Afghanistan.

Q.—in Afghanistan, but there is a large part of the country that is not under the control of the Alliance, and—

Secretary Powell. Wait a minute. You know, everybody loves to say Afghanistan is still, you know, it's a mess and there are warlords running all everywhere, and why don't we have armies everywhere. It's just not the case. There is a degree of stability in Afghanistan that it has not seen in decades. It has a central government that is slowly getting itself organized, slowly extending its reach.

With the help of the international community, with the ISAF force and with America's Operation Enduring Freedom, we are now spreading out our young men and women to many locations throughout Afghanistan to work with the Afghans. They're getting control of their finances. A new ring road is going in that will enhance commerce and connect the country.

One million refugees returned.

Q. One million?

Secretary Powell. Yes, one million refugees returned. And I think it's more than one million now. But, I mean, these are people who voted with their feet to come back to this country. And we're slowly working with the Afghans to incorporate these people back into the country.

* * * *

When you look at what our casualties have been for the past year, for an operation of this size and with the continuing danger from al-Qaida remnants, mostly down in the southeast section along the Pakistan border, which has always been a problem area for many, many years, there are still problems in the country. But a lot has been accomplished.

And so I think we should be proud of what we have been able to do. Children are going to school. Women are being integrated into the society. They have had a Loya Jirga. They have formed in an Afghan style, not an American style, an Afghan way, formed a government. They will have elections in the not too distant future.

We should be very proud of what we've done in Afghanistan and we will stay there, not go racing off to Iraq because we can't do both. We will stay in Afghanistan with whatever else we might have to do elsewhere in the world.

Q. How long will you stay in Iraq?

Secretary Powell. As long as necessary. We have—you know, we have demonstrated our willingness to put our treasure to the task for the time that it takes. We've done it repeatedly. We did it in Japan. We did it in Europe. Memories are short. And we have had a history of going to places that were in need and satisfying that need and using the treasure of the American people—their financial treasure, their political treasure, and their most precious treasure, their men and women—to stay the course when we run into difficult situations and we help nations that are in need. And we're going to do it in Afghanistan and we have demonstrated that.

And if we take on this awesome responsibility to lead a coalition of the willing or to lead the international community into Iraq, if that cannot be avoided, we understand the obligations that we pick up and what our responsibilities will be to keeping one country intact, taking care of the humanitarian needs, as the lady from Amnesty International questioned me, and leaving the country in a better situation than we found it.

Remarks by United Nations Secretary-General Annan, January 27, 2003

I suspect you are all here to listen to [Messrs. Hans] Blix and [Mohamed] ElBaradei. They will be giving their report today. And I think we are all lucky to have two able leaders leading the inspection teams, Blix and ElBaradei, who are determined to do a professional job. They are independent-minded and last week they had the chance to go to Iraq and tell the Iraqis what they expect of them and have asked them what to do. They expect a more pro- active engagement, and I hope the Iraqis will do what the inspectors have asked them to do. It's not just the inspectors, but the leaders in the region have also come together, all the neighbors, asking them to work with the inspectors and disarm. And of course, today we will hear from the inspectors what they have to report to the [Security] Council.

Q. Mr. Secretary-General, do you believe that the inspectors should be given more time to do their job? And do you feel that if the United States goes it alone with a U.S.-led coalition, as it says it will if necessary, that this would hurt the United Nations, the Security Council and multilateralism?

Secretary-General Annan. I think the inspectors will report to the Council what they have achieved, the state of their work and what more needs to be done for them to come to certain conclusions. And they will be able to give the facts to the Council and the Council will have to determine how to proceed next. But I think if they do need time, they should be given the time to do their work and all of us, the Council when they sent them, must have realized that time will be necessary—a reasonable amount of time. I'm not saying forever, but they do need time to get the work done. And I suspect the Council will allow for that time to be done. The Council has acted unanimously on this issue. It spoke with one voice in Resolution 1441, and I think the unity of the Council and the international community working together is extremely important. And I'm sure all countries will do whatever they can to keep that unity.

Q. What impact do the U.S. threats have, Sir, on the process? And do you fear that the U.S. acting alone, as Edie has asked, will destroy basically the multilateral approach that the U.N. has forged with the —?

Secretary-General Annan. I hope, as I have said, that this unity will be maintained. We have, in my own speech to the General Assembly on the 12th of September, I stressed the need for multilateralism, the need for Council action, the need for Council legitimacy, and that position has not changed. I really hope that Iraq will comply and we will be able to get and disarm Iraq peacefully. I have not given up on peace and you shouldn't either.

Remarks by UNMOVIC Chairman Blix and IAEA Director General ElBaradei, January 27, 2003

Dr. Hans Blix and Dr. Mohammed ElBaradei delivered the following reports before the United Nations Security Council.

Dr. Blix. Resolution 1441 (2002), adopted by the Security Council on Iraq in November last year, asks the United Nations Monitoring, Verification and Inspection Commission (UNMOVIC) and the International Atomic Energy Agency (IAEA) to "update" the Council 60 days after the resumption of inspections. This is today. The updating, it seems, forms part of an assessment by the Council and its members of the results, so far, of the inspections and of their role as a means to achieve verifiable disarmament in Iraq.

As this is an open meeting of the Council, it may be appropriate briefly to provide some background for a better understanding of where we stand today. With the Council's permission, I shall do so.

I begin by recalling that inspections as a part of a disarmament process in Iraq started in 1991, immediately after the Gulf War. They went on for eight years, until

1998, when inspectors were withdrawn. Thereafter, for nearly four years there were no inspections. They were resumed only at the end of November last year.

While the fundamental aim of inspections in Iraq has always been to verify disarmament, the successive resolutions adopted by the Council over the years have varied somewhat in emphasis and approach. In 1991, resolution 687 (1991), adopted unanimously as a part of the ceasefire after the Gulf war, had five major elements. The first three related to disarmament. They called for declarations by Iraq of its programs of weapons of mass destruction and long-range missiles, verification of the declarations through the United Nations Special Commission (UNSCOM) and the IAEA, and supervision by these organizations of the destruction or the elimination of proscribed items and programs. After the completion of the disarmament, the Council would have the authority to proceed to a lifting of the sanctions and the inspecting organizations would move to long-term ongoing monitoring and verification.

Resolution 687 (1991), like the subsequent resolutions to which I shall refer, required cooperation by Iraq, but this was often withheld or given grudgingly. Unlike South Africa, which decided on its own to eliminate its nuclear weapons and welcomed inspection as a means of creating confidence in its disarmament, Iraq appears not to have come to a genuine acceptance—not even today—of the disarmament that was demanded of it and that it needs to carry out to win the confidence of the world and to live in peace.

As we know, the twin operation "declare and verify", which was prescribed in resolution 687 (1991), too often turned into a game of hide-and-seek. Rather than just verifying declarations and supporting evidence, the two inspecting organizations found themselves engaged in efforts to map the weapons programs and to search for evidence through inspections, interviews, seminars, inquiries with suppliers and intelligence organizations. As a result, the disarmament phase was not completed in the short time expected. Sanctions remained and took a severe toll until Iraq accepted the oil for food program and the gradual development of that program mitigated the effects of the sanctions.

The implementation of resolution 687 (1991) nevertheless brought about considerable disarmament results. It has been recognized that more weapons of mass destruction were destroyed under this resolution than were destroyed during the Gulf War: large quantities of chemical weapons were destroyed under UNSCOM supervision before 1994. While Iraq claims—with little evidence—that it destroyed all biological weapons unilaterally in 1991, it is certain that UNSCOM destroyed large biological weapons production facilities in 1996. The large nuclear infrastructure was destroyed and the fissionable material was removed from Iraq by the IAEA.

One of three important questions before us today is how much might remain undeclared and intact from before 1991 and, possibly, thereafter; the second question is what, if anything, was illegally produced or procured after 1998, when the inspectors left; and the third question is how we can prevent any weapons of mass destruction from being produced or procured in the future.

In December 1999—after one year without inspections in Iraq—resolution 1284 (1999) was adopted by the Council, with four abstentions. Supplementing the basic resolutions of 1991 and of the following years, it provided Iraq with a somewhat less ambitious approach: in return for "cooperation in all respects" for a specified period of time, including progress in the resolution of "key remaining disarmament tasks", it opened the possibility, not for the lifting, but for the suspension of sanctions. For nearly three years, Iraq refused to accept any inspections by UNMOVIC. It was only after appeals by the Secretary-General and Arab States, and pressure by the United States and other Member States, that Iraq declared, on 16 September last year, that it would again accept inspections without conditions.

Resolution 1441 (2002) was adopted on 8 November last year and emphatically reaffirmed the demand on Iraq to cooperate. It required this cooperation to be immediate, unconditional and active. The resolution contained many provisions that we welcome as enhancing and strengthening the inspection regime. The unanimity by which it was adopted sent a powerful signal that the Council was of one mind in creating a last opportunity for peaceful disarmament in Iraq through inspection.

UNMOVIC shares the sense of urgency felt by the Council to use inspection as a path to attain, within a reasonable time, verifiable disarmament of Iraq. Under the resolutions I have cited, it would be followed by monitoring for such time as the Council feels would be required. The resolutions also point to a zone free of weapons of mass destruction as the ultimate goal.

As a subsidiary body of the Council, UNMOVIC is fully aware of and appreciates the close attention that the Council devotes to the inspections in Iraq. While today's "updating" is foreseen in resolution 1441 (2002), the Council can and does call for additional briefings whenever it wishes. One was held on 19 January, and a further such briefing is tentatively set for 14 February.

I turn now to the key requirement of cooperation and Iraq's response to it. Cooperation might be said to relate to both substance and process. It would appear from our experience so far that Iraq has decided in principle to provide cooperation on process, notably access. A similar decision is indispensable to provide cooperation on substance in order to bring the disarmament task to completion through the peaceful process of inspection and to set the monitoring task on a firm course. An initial minor step would be to adopt the long-overdue legislation required by the resolutions.

I shall deal first with cooperation on process. This relates to the procedures, mechanisms, infrastructure and practical arrangements to pursue inspections and seek verifiable disarmament. While inspection is not built on the premise of confidence but may lead to confidence if it is successful, there must nevertheless be a measure of mutual confidence from the very beginning in running the operation of inspection. Iraq has, on the whole, cooperated rather well so far with UNMOVIC in this field. The most important point to make is that access has been provided to all sites we have wanted to inspect, and, with one exception, it has been prompt. We have further had great help in building up the infrastructure of our office in Baghdad and the field office in Mosul.

Arrangements and services for our plane and our helicopters have been good. The environment has been workable. Our inspections have included universities, military bases, presidential sites and private residences. Inspections have also taken place on Fridays, the Muslim day of rest; on Christmas Day; and on New Year's Day. These inspections have been conducted in the same manner as all other inspections. We seek to be both effective and correct.

In this updating, I am bound, however, to register some problems, the first relating to two kinds of air operations. While we now have the technical capability to send a U-2 plane placed at our disposal for aerial imagery and for surveillance during inspections and have informed Iraq that we planned to do so, Iraq has refused to guarantee its safety unless a number of conditions are fulfilled. As these conditions went beyond what is stipulated in resolution 1441 (2002) and what was practiced by UNSCOM and Iraq in the past, we note that so far Iraq is not complying with our request. I hope this attitude will change.

Another air operation problem, which was solved during our recent talks in Baghdad, concerned the use of helicopters flying into the no-fly zones. Iraq had insisted on sending helicopters of its own to accompany ours. This would have raised a safety problem. The matter was solved by an offer on our part to take the accompanying Iraqi minders in our helicopters to the sites, an arrangement that had been practiced by UNSCOM in the past.

I am obliged to note some recent disturbing incidents and harassment. For instance, for some time, far-fetched allegations have been made publicly that questions posed by inspectors were of an intelligence character. While I might not defend every question that inspectors might have asked, Iraq knows that they do not serve intelligence purposes, and Iraq should not say so.

On a number of occasions, demonstrations have taken place in front of our offices and at inspection sites. The other day, a sightseeing excursion by five inspectors to a mosque was followed by an unwarranted public outburst. The inspectors went without United Nations insignia and were welcomed in the kind manner that is characteristic of the normal Iraqi attitude to foreigners. They took off their shoes and were taken around. They asked perfectly innocent questions and parted with the invitation to come again. Shortly thereafter, we received protests from the Iraqi authorities about an unannounced inspection and about questions not relevant to weapons of mass destruction. Indeed, they were not.

Demonstrations and outbursts of this kind are unlikely to occur in Iraq without initiative or encouragement from the authorities. We must ask ourselves what the motives may be for these events. They do not facilitate an already difficult job, in which we try to be effective, professional and, at the same time, correct. When our Iraqi counterparts have some complaint, they can take it up in a calmer and less unpleasant manner.

The substantive cooperation required relates above all to the obligation of Iraq to declare all programs of weapons of mass destruction and either to present items and activities for elimination or else to provide evidence supporting the conclusion that nothing proscribed remains.

Paragraph 9 of resolution 1441 (2002) states that this cooperation shall be "active". It is not enough to open doors. Inspection is not a game of catch as catch can. Rather, as I noted, it is a process of verification for the purpose of creating confidence. It is not built upon the premise of trust. Rather, it is designed to lead to trust, if there is both openness to the inspectors and action to present them with items to destroy, or credible evidence about the absence of any such items.

On 7 December 2002, Iraq submitted a declaration of some 12,000 pages in response to paragraph 3 of resolution 1441 (2002), and within the time stipulated by the Security Council. In the fields of missiles and biotechnology, the declaration contains a good deal of new material and information covering the period from 1998 and onward. This is welcome.

One might have expected that in preparing the declaration, Iraq would have tried to respond to, clarify and submit supporting evidence regarding the many open disarmament issues, with which the Iraqi side should be familiar from the UNSCOM document S/1999/94 and the so-called Amorim report of March 1999 (S/1999/356). These are questions that UNMOVIC, Governments and independent commentators have often cited.

While UNMOVIC has been preparing its own list of current unresolved disarmament issues and key remaining disarmament tasks in response to requirements in resolution 1284 (1999), we find the issues listed as unresolved in the two reports that I mentioned professionally justified. These reports do not contend that weapons of mass destruction remain in Iraq, nor do they exclude that possibility. They point to a lack of evidence and to inconsistencies, which raise question marks and which must be straightened out if weapons dossiers are to be closed and confidence is to arise.

Those issues deserve to be taken seriously by Iraq, rather than being brushed aside as evil machinations of UNSCOM. Regrettably, the 12,000 page declaration, most of which is a reprint of earlier documents, does not seem to contain any new evidence that would eliminate the questions or reduce their number. Even Iraq's letter sent, in response to our recent discussions in Baghdad, to the President of the Security Council on 24 January does not lead us to the resolution of those issues.

I shall only give some examples of issues and questions that need to be answered, and I turn first to the sector of chemical weapons.

The nerve agent VX is one of the most toxic ever developed. Iraq has declared that it only produced VX on a pilot scale, just a few tons, and that the quality was poor and the product unstable. Consequently, it was said that the agent was never weaponized. Iraq said that the small quantity of agent remaining after the Gulf War was unilaterally destroyed in the summer of 1991.

UNMOVIC, however, has information that conflicts with this account. There are indications that Iraq had worked on the problem of purity and stabilization and that more had been achieved than has been declared. Indeed, one of the documents provided by Iraq even indicates that the purity of the agent, at least in laboratory production, was higher than declared. There are also indications that the agent was weaponized.

In addition, there are questions to be answered concerning the fate of the VX precursor chemicals, which Iraq states were lost during bombing in the Gulf War or were unilaterally destroyed by Iraq. I would now like to turn to the so-called Air Force document that I have discussed with the Council before. This document was originally found by an UNSCOM inspector in a safe in Iraqi Air Force headquarters in 1998 and taken from her by Iraqi minders. It gives an account of the expenditure of bombs, including chemical bombs, by Iraq in the Iraq-Iran war. I am encouraged by the fact that Iraq has now provided this document to UNMOVIC.

The document indicates that 13,000 chemical bombs were dropped by the Iraqi Air Force between 1983 and 1988, while Iraq has declared that 19,500 bombs were consumed during this period. Thus, there is a discrepancy of 6,500 bombs. The amount of chemical agent in these bombs would be in the order of about 1,000 tons. In the absence of evidence to the contrary, we must assume that these quantities are now unaccounted for.

The discovery of a number of 122 millimeter chemical rocket warheads in a bunker at a storage depot 170 kilometer southwest of Baghdad was much publicized. This was a relatively new bunker, and therefore the rockets must have been moved there in the past few years, at a time when Iraq should not have had such munitions.

The investigation of these rockets is still proceeding. Iraq states that they were overlooked from 1991 from a batch of some 2,000 that were stored there during the Gulf War. That could be the case. They could also be the tip of a submerged iceberg. The discovery of a few rockets does not resolve, but rather points to, the issue of several thousands of chemical rockets that are unaccounted for.

The finding of the rockets shows that Iraq needs to make more effort to ensure that its declaration is currently accurate. During my recent discussions in Baghdad, Iraq declared that it would make new efforts in this regard and had set up a committee of investigation. Since then it has reported that it has found four more chemical rockets at a storage depot in Al-Taji.

I might further mention that inspectors have found at another site a laboratory quantity of thiodiglycol, a mustard gas precursor.

While I am addressing chemical issues, I should mention a matter, which I reported on 19 December 2002, concerning equipment at a civilian chemical plant at Al Fallujah. Iraq has declared that it had repaired chemical processing equipment previously destroyed under UNSCOM supervision and had installed it at Fallujah for the production of chlorine and phenols. We have inspected this equipment and are conducting a detailed technical evaluation of it. On completion, we will decide whether this and other equipment that has been recovered by Iraq should be destroyed.

I turn to biological weapons. I mentioned the issue of anthrax to the Council on previous occasions and I come back to it, as it is an important one. Iraq has declared that it produced about 8,500 liters of this biological warfare agent, which it states it unilaterally destroyed in the summer of 1991. Iraq has provided little evidence of that production and no convincing evidence of its destruction.

There are strong indications that Iraq produced more anthrax than it declared and that at least some of this was retained after the declared destruction date. It might still exist. Either it should be found and be destroyed under UNMOVIC's supervision, or convincing evidence should be produced to show that it was indeed destroyed in 1991.

As I reported to the Council on 19 December last year, Iraq did not declare a significant quantity, some 650 kilograms, of bacterial growth media, which was acknowledged, as reported in Iraq's submission to the Amorim panel in February 1999. As part of its 7 December 2002 declaration, Iraq resubmitted the Amorim panel document, but the table showing this particular import of media was not included. The absence of this table would appear to be deliberate, as the pages of the resubmitted document were renumbered.

In the letter of 24 January of this year to the President of the Security Council, Iraq's Foreign Minister stated that "all imported quantities of growth media were declared". This is not evidence. I note that the quantity of media involved would suffice to produce, for example, about 5,000 liters of concentrated anthrax.

I turn now to the missile sector. There remain significant questions as to whether

Iraq retained SCUD-type missiles after the Gulf War. Iraq declared the consumption of a number of SCUD missiles as targets in the development of an anti-ballistic missile defense system during the 1980s. Yet no technical information has been produced about that program or data on the consumption of the missiles.

There has been a range of developments in the missile field during the past four years, presented by Iraq in the declaration, as non-proscribed activities. We are trying to gather a clear understanding of them through inspections and on-site discussions. Two projects in particular stand out. They are the development of a liquid-fuelled missile, named Al Samoud 2, and a solid propellant missile, called Al Fatah. Both missiles have been tested to a range in excess of the permitted range of 150 kilometers, with the Al Samoud 2 being tested to a maximum of 183 kilometers and the Al Fatah to 161 kilometers. Some of both types of missiles have already been provided to the Iraqi Armed Forces, even though it is stated that they are still undergoing development.

The Al Samoud's diameter was increased from an earlier version to the present 760 millimeters. This modification was made despite a 1994 letter from the Executive Chairman of UNSCOM directing Iraq to limit its missile diameters to less than 600 millimeters. Furthermore, a November 1997 letter from the Executive Chairman of UNSCOM to Iraq prohibited the use of engines from certain surface-to-air missiles for use in ballistic missiles.

During my recent meeting in Baghdad, we were briefed on these two programs. We were told that the final range for both systems would be less than the permitted maximum of 150 kilometers.

These missiles might very well represent prima facie cases of proscribed systems. The test ranges in excess of 150 kilometers are significant, but some further technical considerations need to be made before we reach a conclusion on this issue. In the meantime, we have asked Iraq to cease flight tests of both missiles.

In addition, Iraq has refurbished its missile production infrastructure. In particular, Iraq reconstituted a number of casting chambers, which had previously been destroyed under UNSCOM supervision. They had been used in the production of solid-fuel missiles. Whatever missile system these chambers are intended for, they could produce motors for missiles capable of ranges significantly greater than 150 kilometers.

Also associated with these missiles and related developments is the import, which has been taking place during the last few years, of a number of items, despite the sanctions, including as late as December 2002. Foremost among these is the import of 300 rocket engines that may be used for the Al Samoud 2. Iraq has also declared the recent import of chemicals used in propellants, test instrumentation and guidance and control systems. These items may well be for proscribed purposes; that is yet to be determined. What is clear is that they were illegally brought into Iraq; that is, Iraq or some company in Iraq circumvented the restrictions imposed by various resolutions.

I have touched upon some of the disarmament issues that remain open and that need to be answered if dossiers are to be closed and confidence is to arise. Which are the means at the disposal of Iraq to answer these questions? I have pointed to some during my presentation of the issues. Let me be a little more systematic. Our Iraqi counterparts are fond of saying that there are no proscribed items, and if no evidence is presented to the contrary, they should have the benefit of the doubt, be presumed innocent. UNMOVIC, for its part, is not presuming that there are proscribed items and activities in Iraq, but nor does it or anyone else, after the inspections between 1991 and 1998, presume the opposite—that no such items and activities exist in Iraq. Presumptions do not solve the problem. Evidence and full transparency may help. Let me be specific.

Information provided by Member States tells us about the movement and concealment of missiles and chemical weapons and mobile units for biological weapons production. We shall certainly follow up any credible leads given to us and report what we might find, as well as any denial of access.

So far, we have reported on the recent find of a small number of empty 122-millimeter warheads for chemical weapons. Iraq declared that it appointed a commission of inquiry to look for more. Fine. Why not extend the search to other items, declare what may be found and destroy it under our supervision?

When we have urged our Iraqi counterparts to present more evidence, we have all too often met the response that there are no more documents. All existing relevant documents have been presented, we are told. All documents relating to the biological weapons program were destroyed together with the weapons.

However, Iraq has all the archives of the Government and its various departments, institutions and mechanisms. It should have budgetary documents, requests for funds and reports on how they have been used. It should also have letters of credits, bills of lading and reports on production and losses of material.

In response to a recent UNMOVIC request for a number of specific documents, the only new documents Iraq provided was a ledger of 193 pages, which Iraq stated included all imports from 1983 to 1990 by the Technical and Scientific Importation Division, the importing authority for the biological weapons program. Potentially, it might help to clear some open issues.

The recent inspection find in the private home of a scientist of a box of some 3,000 pages of documents, much of them relating to the laser enrichment of uranium, supports a concern that has long existed that documents might be distributed to the homes of private individuals. This interpretation is refuted by the Iraqi side, which claims that research staff sometimes may bring home papers from their work places. On our side, we cannot help but think that the case might not be isolated and that such placements of documents is deliberate to make discovery difficult and to seek to shield documents by placing them in private homes.

Any further sign of the concealment of documents would be serious. The Iraqi side committed itself at our recent talks to encourage persons to accept access also to private sites. There can be no sanctuaries for proscribed items, activities or documents. A denial of prompt access to any site would be a very serious matter.

When Iraq claims that tangible evidence in the form of documents is not available, it ought at least to find individuals, engineers, scientists and managers to testify about their experience. Large weapons programs are moved and managed by people. Interviews with individuals who may have worked in programs in the past may fill blank spots in our knowledge and understanding. It could also be useful to learn that they are now employed in peaceful sectors. These are the reasons why UNMOVIC asked for a list of such persons, in accordance with resolution 1441 (2002).

Some 400 names for all biological and chemical weapons programs, as well as for their missile programs, were provided by the Iraqi side. This can be compared to over 3,500 names of people associated with those past weapons programs that UNSCOM either interviewed in the 1990s or knew from documents and other sources. At my recent meeting in Baghdad, the Iraqi side committed itself to supplementing the list, and some 80 additional names have been provided.

In the past, much valuable information came from interviews. There were also cases in which the interviewee was clearly intimidated by the presence of, and interruption by, Iraqi officials. This was the background of the provision of resolution 1441 (2002) for a right for UNMOVIC and the IAEA to hold private interviews "in the mode or location" of our choice, in Baghdad or even abroad.

To date, we have asked 11 individuals for interviews in Baghdad. The replies have invariably been that the individual will speak only at Iraq's monitoring directorate or, at any rate, in the presence of an Iraqi official. This could be due to a wish on the part of the invited to have evidence that they have not said anything that the authorities did not wish them to say. At our recent talks in Baghdad, the Iraqi side committed itself to encouraging persons to accept interviews "in private"—that is to say, alone with us. Despite this, the pattern has not changed. However, we hope that, with further encouragement from the authorities, knowledgeable individuals will accept private interviews, in Baghdad or abroad.

I must not conclude this update without some notes on the growing capability of UNMOVIC.

In the past two months, UNMOVIC has built up its capabilities in Iraq from nothing to 260 staff members from 60 countries. This includes approximately 100 new UNMOVIC inspectors, 60 air operations staff, as well as security personnel, communications, translation and interpretation staff, medical support, and other services at our Baghdad office and Mosul field office. All serve the United Nations and report to no one else. Furthermore, our roster of inspectors will continue to grow as our training program continues—even at this moment we have a training course in session in Vienna. At the end of that course, we shall have a roster of about 350 qualified experts from which to draw inspectors.

A team supplied by the Swiss Government is refurbishing our office in Baghdad, which had been empty for four years. The Government of New Zealand has contributed both a medical team and a communications team. The German Government will contribute unmanned aerial vehicles for surveillance and a group of specialists to operate them for us within Iraq. The Government of Cyprus has kindly allowed us to set up a field office in Larnaka. All of these contributions have been of assistance in quickly starting up our inspections and enhancing our capabilities. So has help from the United Nations in New York and from sister organizations in Baghdad.

In the past two months, during which we have built up our presence in Iraq, we have conducted about 300 inspections to more than 230 different sites. Of these, more than 20 were sites that had not been inspected before. By the end of December, UNMOVIC began using helicopters both for the transport of inspectors and for actual inspection work. We now have eight helicopters. They have already proved invaluable in helping to "freeze" large sites by observing the movement of traffic in and around the area.

The setting up of a field office in Mosul has facilitated rapid inspections of sites in northern Iraq. We plan to establish soon a second field office in the Basra area, where we have already inspected a number of sites.

We now have an inspection apparatus that permits us to send multiple inspection teams every day all over Iraq, by road or by air. Let me end by simply noting that that capability, which has been built up in a short time and which is now operating, is at the disposal of the Security Council.

Dr. ElBaradei. For the past 60 days, the inspectors of the International Atomic Energy Agency (IAEA) have been engaged in the process of verifying the existence or absence of a nuclear- weapon program in Iraq. Today, pursuant to paragraph 5 of resolution 1441 (2002), I have submitted to the President of the Security Council an update report on our progress since we resumed our nuclear-verification activities in Iraq—in terms of the approach we have adopted, the tools we have used, the specific results achieved, the degree of cooperation we have received, and, finally, our view on how we should proceed. Copies of the report are available in this Chamber. Let me in this statement outline the key aspects of this report.

To understand the approach of IAEA inspections over the past two months, it is important first to recall what was accomplished during our inspections from 1991 to 1998, in fulfillment of our Security Council mandate to eliminate Iraq's nuclear-weapon program. In September 1991, the IAEA seized documents in Iraq that demonstrated the extent of its nuclear-weapon program. By the end of 1992, we had largely destroyed, removed or rendered harmless all Iraqi facilities and equipment relevant to nuclear-weapon production. We confiscated Iraq's nuclear-weapon- usable material—highly enriched uranium and plutonium—and by early 1994 we had removed it from the country. By December 1998, when the inspections were brought to a halt with a military strike imminent, we were confident that we had not missed any significant components of Iraq's nuclear program.

While we did not claim absolute certainty, our conclusion at that time was that we had neutralized Iraq's nuclear-weapon program and that there were no indications that Iraq retained any physical capability to produce weapon-usable nuclear material.

During the intervening four years of our absence from Iraq, we continued our analytical work to the best of our ability, using satellite imagery and other information. But no remote analysis can replace on-site inspection, and we were therefore not able to reach any conclusions about Iraq's compliance with its Security Council obligations in the nuclear field after December 1998.

Against this backdrop, when Iraq agreed last September to reopen its doors to inspection, and following the subsequent adoption by the Security Council of resolution 1441 (2002), which strengthened the IAEA's authority and the inspection process, the first goal of our inspection activities was reconnaissance. In this phase, we sought to re-establish rapidly our knowledge base of Iraq's nuclear capabilities, to ensure that key facilities had not been reopened, to verify the location of nuclear material and relevant non-nuclear material, and to identify and begin interviewing key Iraqi personnel.

Over these first two months of inspection, we have made good progress in our knowledge of Iraq's nuclear capabilities, with a total of 139 inspections at some 106 locations to date. The bulk of these inspections have taken place at State-run or private industrial facilities, research centers and universities—either at locations where Iraq's significant technical capabilities were known to have existed in the past, or at new locations suggested by remote monitoring and analysis. All inspection activities have been carried out without prior notification to Iraq, except where notification was needed to ensure the availability of required support. IAEA inspectors have taken— and will continue to take—full advantage of the inspection authority granted by resolution 1441 (2002). In doing so, the inspectors have been instructed to make every effort to conduct their activities with appropriate professionalism and sensitivity.

While we are continuing to some extent with this reconnaissance work, our inspections are now well into the investigative phase—with particular emphasis on determining what, if anything, has occurred in Iraq over the past four years that is relevant to the re-establishment of Iraq's nuclear capabilities. These investigative inspections focus on areas of concern identified by other States; facilities identified through satellite images as having been modified or constructed since 1998; and other inspection leads identified independently by the IAEA.

In parallel with these inspection activities, the IAEA has been conducting an exhaustive analysis of supporting information obtained from various sources. In this context, we have integrated the new information submitted by Iraq, including the declaration submitted on 7 December in response to resolution 1441 (2002), with the records we had accumulated between 1991 and 1998 and the additional information we had compiled through remote monitoring since 1998. The Iraqi declaration was consistent with our existing understanding of Iraq's pre-1991 nuclear program; however, it did not provide any new information relevant to certain questions that have been outstanding since 1998, in particular regarding Iraq's progress prior to 1991 related to weapons design and centrifuge development. While these questions do not constitute unresolved disarmament issues, they nevertheless need further clarification.

In addition to on-site inspection and offsite analysis, IAEA inspectors have employed a variety of tools to accomplish their mission. Taking advantage of the signature of radioactive materials, we have resumed the monitoring of Iraq's rivers, canals and lakes to detect the presence of certain radioisotopes. A broad variety of environmental samples and surface swipe samples have been collected from locations across Iraq and taken to IAEA laboratories for analysis, and we have reinstituted routine car-borne and hand-held gamma surveys for the detection of undeclared nuclear material.

The inspectors have also conducted a great number of interviews of Iraqi scientists, managers and technicians—primarily in the workplace in the course of unannounced inspections—as a valuable source of information about past and present programs and activities. The information gained has been helpful in assessing the completeness and accuracy of Iraq's declarations.

Resolution 1441 (2002) also clearly gave IAEA and the United Nations Monitoring, Verification and Inspection Commission the authority to determine the modalities and venues for conducting interviews with Iraqi officials and other persons. The first two individuals whom the IAEA requested to see privately declined to be interviewed without the presence of an Iraqi Government representative. This has been a restricting factor. Although the Iraqi Government recently committed itself to encouraging Iraqi officials and other personnel to be interviewed in private when requested, regrettably the third request, made two days ago, for a private interview was again turned down by the interviewee.

The IAEA will continue to determine the modalities and locations of the interviews, including the possibility of interviewing Iraqi personnel abroad. We will continue to report to the Security Council on our efforts to conduct interviews according to our preferred modalities and venues and our degree of success in that regard.

Let me summarize briefly a number of the findings that have resulted from our inspection activities thus far.

First, we have inspected all of those buildings and facilities that were identified, through satellite imagery, as having been modified or constructed over the past four years. IAEA inspectors have been able to gain ready access and to clarify the nature of the activities currently being conducted in these facilities. No prohibited nuclear activities have been identified during these inspections.

A particular issue of focus has been the attempted procurement by Iraq of high-strength aluminum tubes and the question of whether these tubes, if acquired, could be used for the manufacture of nuclear centrifuges. Iraqi authorities have indicated that their unsuccessful attempts to procure the aluminum tubes related to a program to reverse engineer conventional rockets. To verify this information, IAEA inspectors have inspected the relevant rocket production and storage sites, taken tube samples, interviewed relevant Iraqi personnel and reviewed procurement contracts and related documents. From our analysis to date, it appears that the aluminum tubes would be consistent with the purpose stated by Iraq and, unless modified, would not be suitable for manufacturing centrifuges. However, we are still investigating this issue. It is clear, however, that the attempt to acquire such tubes is prohibited under Security Council resolution 687 (1991).

Another area of focus has been to determine how certain other dual-use materials have been relocated or used—that is, materials that could be used in nuclear-weapons production but also have other legitimate uses. A good example is the Iraqi declaration concerning high-explosive HMX, which states that, of the HMX under IAEA seals in Iraq at the end of 1998, some had been supplied to cement plants as an industrial explosive for mining. The whereabouts and final use of the removed material are matters that will require further investigation, although it will be difficult to verify the disposition of the HMX that is declared to have been used.

A fourth focal point has been the investigation of reports of Iraqi efforts to import uranium after 1991. The Iraqi authorities have denied any such attempts. The IAEA will continue to pursue this issue. At this stage, however, we do not have enough information and we would appreciate receiving more.

We are also making progress on a number of other issues related, for example, to the attempted importation of a magnet production facility.

In addition to the new authorities granted by resolution 1441 (2002), I believe that the unified resolve of the Council to support the inspection process has been a vital ingredient and must remain so if we are to achieve a peaceful resolution of the situation in Iraq. I trust that the Council will continue its unified and unequivocal support for the inspection process in Iraq.

Over the next several months, inspections will focus ever more closely on follow-up of specific concerns as we continue to conduct visits to sites and interviews with key Iraqi personnel. We have begun helicopter operations, which increase the inspectors' mobility and their ability to respond rapidly to new information and allow wide-scale radiation detection surveys. Laboratory analysis of environmental samples is continuing and we will be reinstalling air samplers for wide-area environmental monitoring. We also will reintroduce surveillance systems with video cameras in key locations to allow near-real-time remote monitoring of dual-use equipment.

By its very nature, the inspection process, both in Iraq and elsewhere, is based not on trust, but on a thorough process of fact-finding supported by access to all available information. Where applicable, this should include information available to States that may be relevant to the purpose of the inspection. We have begun in the last few weeks to receive more actionable information from States—that is, information of direct and current value for inspection follow-up. I would continue to call on States that have access to such information to provide it to the inspecting organizations so that the inspection process can be accelerated and additional assurances can be generated.

Finally, we have urged Iraq once again to increase the degree of its cooperation with the inspection process. In support of the IAEA inspections to date, the Iraqi authorities have provided access to all facilities visited, including presidential compounds and private residences, without conditions and without delay. The Iraqi authorities also have been cooperative in making available additional original documentation in response to requests by IAEA inspectors.

In our discussions with Iraqi officials last week in Baghdad, we emphasized the need to shift from passive support—that is, responding as needed to inspectors' requests—to proactive support—that is, voluntarily assisting inspectors by providing documentation, people and other evidence that will assist in filling in the remaining gaps in our information.

One example of how Iraq could be more proactive was illustrated by the inspection of a private residence just two weeks ago, which resulted in the retrieval of a sizeable number of documents, some of which were classified and related, in part, to Iraq's pre-1991 efforts to use laser technology for enriching uranium. While these documents do not appear to reflect new or current activities related to nuclear weapons in Iraq, they may enhance our detailed understanding of certain aspects of Iraq's pre-1991 nuclear program. It is urgent and essential, therefore, that Iraq, on its own initiative, identify and provide any additional evidence that would assist the inspectors in carrying out their mandate.

This proactive engagement on the part of Iraq would be—as we have told them—in its own best interest and is a window of opportunity that may not remain open for very much longer. Iraq should make every effort to be fully transparent—with a demonstrated willingness to resolve issues rather than requiring pressure to do so. The international community will not be satisfied when questions remain open with regard to Iraq's weapons of mass destruction; the world is asking for a high level of assurance that Iraq is completely free from all such weapons and is already impatient to receive it. The sooner such assurance can be provided by the inspecting organizations, the sooner the prospects that a peaceful resolution will translate into a plausible reality.

Inspections are time-consuming. I should mention that even in the case of South

Africa, where full and active cooperation was forthcoming, it took the IAEA approximately two years to complete the process in that country. However, if inspection is successful, it can ensure disarmament through peaceful means. It is worth recalling that in our past experience in Iraq, the elimination of its nuclear weapons program was accomplished mostly through intrusive inspections. It is also worth recalling that the presence of international inspectors in Iraq today continues to serve as an effective deterrent to, and insurance against, resumption of programs to develop weapons of mass destruction, even as we continue to look for possible past activities.

To conclude, we have to date found no evidence that Iraq has revived its nuclear weapons program since the elimination of the program in the 1990s. However, our work is steadily progressing and should be allowed to run its natural course. With our verification system now in place, barring exceptional circumstances and provided there is sustained, proactive cooperation by Iraq, we should be able within the next few months to provide credible assurance that Iraq has no nuclear weapons program. These few months, in my view, would be a valuable investment in peace because they could help us avoid a war. We trust that we will continue to have the support of the Council as we make every effort to verify Iraq's nuclear disarmament through peaceful means and to demonstrate that the inspection process can and does work as a central feature of the international nuclear arms control regime.

Remarks by Secretary of State Powell, January 27, 2003

Well, good afternoon, ladies and gentlemen. Earlier today, in accordance with U.N. Resolution 1441, Doctors' Blix and ElBaradei provided the United Nations Security Council their 60-day reports on inspection activity in Iraq.

We listened carefully as the inspectors reported that Iraq has not provided the active, immediate and unconditional cooperation that the Council demanded in U.N. Resolution 1441.

As Dr. Blix said, "Iraq appears not to have come to a genuine acceptance, not even today, of the disarmament that was demanded of it." Let me repeat, because this is the essence of the problem. Dr. Blix said, "Iraq appears not to have come to a genuine acceptance, not even today, of the disarmament that was demanded of it." 1441 is all about the disarmament demanded of Iraq.

The inspectors' findings came as no surprise. For 11 years before 1441, Saddam Hussein's regime refused to make the strategic decision, the political decision, to disarm itself of weapons of mass destruction and to comply with the world's demands.

To this day, the Iraq regime continues to defy the will of the United Nations. The Iraqi regime has responded to 1441 with empty claims, empty declarations and empty gestures.

It has not given the inspectors and the international community any concrete information in answer to a host of key questions: Where is the missing anthrax? This is not just a question of historical curiosity. It is essential for us to know what happened with this deadly material.

Where is the VX? Also not just a trivial question. We must know what happened to this deadly material.

Where are the chemical and biological munitions? Where are the mobile biological laboratories? If the Iraqi regime was truly committed to disarmament, we wouldn't be looking for these mobile labs. They'd drive them up and park them in front of UNMOVIC headquarters for inspection.

Why is Iraq violating the restrictions on ballistic missiles? Why is it violating the ban on missiles with a range of more than 150 kilometers? Where are the credible, verifiable answers to all of the other disarmament questions compiled by the previous inspectors?

Today, we heard that the inspectors have not been able to interview any Iraqi in private. We heard that the inspectors have not been allowed to employ aerial surveillance. Why not? If Iraq was committed to disarmament, if Iraq understood what 1441 was all about, they would willingly allow this kind of surveillance, they would willingly allow people to be interviewed without minders, without fear of retribution.

We have heard that the inspectors have still not received, a full list of Iraqi personnel involved with weapons of mass destruction. If Iraq no longer has weapons of mass destruction, they should willingly give the names of all who were involved in their previous programs to the inspectors for examination and interview.

The inspectors told us that their efforts have been impeded by a swarm of Iraqi minders. Why, if Iraq was committed to disarmament, would they be going to these efforts to deceive and to keep the inspectors from doing their work? Passive cooperation is not what was called for in 1441.

The inspectors have also told us that they have evidence that Iraq has moved or hidden items at sites just prior to inspection visits. That's what the inspectors say, not what Americans say, not what American intelligence says, but we certainly corroborate all of that. But this is information from the inspectors.

And the inspectors have caught the Iraqis concealing "top secret" information in a private residence. You all saw the pictures of that information being brought out. Why? Why, if Iraq was committed to disarmament, as required under 1441, would we be finding this kind of information squirreled away in private homes, for any other reason than to keep it away from the inspectors?

The list of unanswered questions and the many ways Iraq is frustrating the work of the inspectors goes on and on. Iraq's refusal to disarm, in compliance with Resolution 1441, still threatens international peace and security. And Iraq's defiance continues to challenge the relevance and credibility of the Security Council.

The international community's goal was, is and remains Iraq's disarmament. The Security Council and the international community must stand behind Resolution 1441. Iraq continues to conceal quantities, vast quantities, of highly lethal material and weapons to delivery it. They could kill thousands upon thousands of men, women and children if Saddam Hussein decides to use these against those men, women and children, or, just as frightening, to provide them to others who might use such weapons.

Iraq must not be allowed to keep weapons of mass terror and the capacity to produce more. The world community must send a clear message to Iraq that the will of the international community must be obeyed.

Last September, the United Nations acted at the request of the United States. We acted through 1441 with the hope—the President had the hope, the other members of the Security Council who voted unanimously for this resolution had the hope—that

Iraq would take this one last chance presented to it by the international community to disarm peacefully.

And remember the key elements of that resolution. Iraq has been and continues to be in material breach of all of its earlier obligations. We are giving, the resolution said, one more chance to Iraq. We put a firm list of conditions for Iraq to meet and what they should allow the inspectors to do to assist them in that disarmament. And let's not forget a vital part of the resolution that comes toward the end: there would be serious consequences for continued Iraqi violation of its obligation. Those serious consequences are the lever that was needed to get the inspectors in to get the inspectors to be able to do their work, which was to assist Iraqi in disarmament.

Iraqi intransigence brings us to a situation where we see that regime continuing to confront the fundamental choice between compliance with 1441 and the consequences of its failure to disarm.

Even at this late date, the United States hopes for a peaceful solution. But a peaceful solution is possible only if Iraq disarms itself with the help of the inspectors. The issue is not how much more time the inspectors need to search in the dark. It is how much more time Iraq should be given to turn on the light and to come clean. And the answer is not much more time. Iraq's time for choosing peaceful disarmament is fast coming to an end.

Thank you, and I am prepared for your questions.

Q. It's my understanding that although you guys believe—well, are convinced that Iraq is neither cooperating nor complying with the resolution, you're not yet prepared to go to the Security Council with the serious consequences part. Is that correct? And if it is, can you explain why there are—

Secretary Powell. Our plan is straightforward. We passed 1441 with a unanimous vote in the Security Council. Fifteen nations acted. Now that we have received this report from the two chief inspectors, I think it is important for us to ask questions of the inspectors. That is happening this afternoon in New York and it will also happen on Wednesday as members of the Security Council pose questions to Dr. Blix and to Dr. ElBaradei. The President will be in touch with fellow heads of state and government about this matter. I will be in touch with my colleagues in the Security Council.

And after these consultations are completed, and you know Prime Minister Blair is coming on Friday, Mr. Berlusconi is coming this week as well to see President Bush, and after we have had these consultations and considered the entire situation, and have a little time pass, Security Council members need time to consult with their capitals on what they have heard and seen today, and when those consultations are through and the President has had a chance to discuss this with his fellow heads of state and government and I've done my consultations, we will determine what the next steps are.

Q. I thought you sort of laid it out pretty clearly, but I wondered, does this report—which I'm sure you anticipated—does this move the administration closer to a showdown with Iraq? And if you care to, and I'd understand if you chose not to,

have you got a response to the Iraqi Foreign Minister who doesn't think you tell the truth?

Secretary Powell. With respect to the first part of your question, time is running out. We've made it clear from the very beginning that we could not allow the process of inspections to string us out forever. There are some who would like to take months. Dr. ElBaradei made a reference today that he needed a few more months.

But make careful note of the context in which he was making that observation; and that is, if there was active cooperation on the part of the Iraqis. If there isn't that kind of active cooperation, you can be sitting on the things you know and looking at the things you know about, but there may be many other things that you don't know about that you are unable to get information on.

And so inspections only work in the presence of cooperation, active cooperation, and a willingness on the part of the other side to participate in the disarmament. And we have examples of this, in South Korea and Kazakhstan, Ukraine and other nations that have gone down this road.

With respect to the Iraqi Foreign Minister calling me a liar, this will not cause me any distress or loss of sleep.

Q. Mr. Secretary, you have spoken, in Davos most recently, about a connection between Iraq and terrorist groups, including al-Qaida. Are you saying there is evidence that that has happened in the past, or is there evidence currently that there's still a connection?

Secretary Powell. I think we have said consistently all along, through last fall and into this year, that we have seen contacts and connections between the Iraqi regime and terrorist organizations, to include al-Qaida. As we have been able to focus on this more and look back in time, I think we're more confident of that assessment and we see no reason not to believe that such contacts and the presence of al-Qaida elements or individuals in Iraq is a reasonable assumption, and we have some basis for that assumption. And the information that we can divulge in greater detail, we will be divulging in the days ahead.

Yes, Betsy.

Q. Mr. Secretary, can you say whether you are willing, whether the U.S. is willing to give the inspectors a couple of more weeks, maybe a month, but no more than that, in order to complete their work?

Secretary Powell. We are going to do exactly what I described earlier: consult with leaders around the world. President Bush has been on the phone this morning with President Aznar. He'll be on the phone and he'll be meeting with others. I'll be doing likewise. And when all these consultations are finished, we will let it be known what our next steps are going to be.

Q. I have a two-part question for you, sir. Up until a week ago yesterday, you were a strong advocate for a diplomatic solution to the Iraqi situation.

Secretary Powell. I still am.

Q. In fact, to the point where many of my brethren even labeled you a dove.

Secretary Powell. I've been labeled many things over the years.

Q. But as of the talk shows a week ago yesterday, last Sunday, you started talking tough, and you've been talking very tough ever since, in Switzerland and again today.
Now, one, what changed your mind? And then I have a follow-up question, if I may.

Secretary Powell. It has been clear from the very beginning—you know, I am one of the principal authors of 1441, and for better or worse, I can take some credit for having been one of its champions as we drove it through the United Nations Security Council process for a period of seven and a half weeks.

And we always insisted on three elements to that: one, Iraq is in material breach; two, this is their last chance; there have to be serious consequences. And those serious consequences meant the use of force. And you've heard me say that repeatedly, repeatedly. And I've also said that if the international community through the U.N., when the time comes, does not wish to use force, the United States reserves its right as a sovereign nation to make a judgment within this clear record of violation to use force alongside likeminded nations who might wish to be part of such a coalition.

So I have been consistent throughout this entire process. And as I've watched the process unfold, I have watched Iraq go by every exit ramp—diplomatic exit ramp—that was put there for them. They could have made a full, complete and accurate declaration in December, which would have given us some confidence that they were serious about disarmament. Instead, they gave us 12,200 pages of nothing very useful.

The inspectors said that today. There was nothing new. They added nothing to the body of knowledge. They tried to deceive the inspectors. They tried to deceive us. One ramp gone by.

We have watched subsequently as they have kept reconnaissance planes from doing the work that could be helpful to the inspectors. They have done all of the things that I have described and you have heard other of my colleagues describe—Deputy Secretary Armitage, Deputy Secretary Wolfowitz, last week. And so we are getting closer and closer to the point where the Security Council is going to have to look at the options that it had anticipated it would have to look at when 1441 was originally passed.

And so hang any label you want on me. I am a great believer in diplomacy and a great believer in finding a peaceful solution. But I also recognize that when somebody will not accept a peaceful solution by doing their part of creating a peaceful solution, one must never rule out the use of force to implement the will of the international community, but more importantly, to protect our people and to protect the world.

* * * *

Q. Whether it's a few weeks or it's a month, what do you think of the idea of one final deadline? One final exit ramp for Iraq to answer the questions that you laid out at the start?

Secretary Powell. Iraq could answer this this afternoon, if it chose to. Rather, the Iraqi Foreign Minister spent his time calling me a liar.

I will stick with what I said earlier. We will have our discussions and consultations this week and then we will announce next steps at an appropriate time.

Q. Regarding the Wednesday debate at the Security Council, what are the objectives of your delegation going to be going into the debate?

Secretary Powell. It's a consultation, really, and it began, to some extent, this afternoon. But our delegation, Ambassador Negroponte, and I think, the other delegations, will be putting questions to the inspectors. We have a number of issues that we want to raise with the inspectors that perhaps might indicate areas they want to look in and give us answers to questions we have about the work they've done so far.

That is really the purpose of these consultations. These consultations this week are not for the purpose of determining what the next steps should be, I think. We'll need more work and heads of state and government talking to one another and foreign ministers talking to each other before one would make a judgment as to what those next steps should be. So I think this is an opportunity for the 15 members of the Council to learn more about what the inspectors have found out.

Keep in mind there are new members on the Council. Not—there's been some changeover since 1441 was passed, and it gives these new elected members an opportunity to learn more about the process, about the spirit and intent of 1441, and to ask questions of Dr. Blix and Dr. ElBaradei.

Q. Thanks. The Germans are calling—as president next month, they're calling for another report on February 14th. Do you think this is just a waste of time? Do you think it's another delaying tactic by the Germans, by the French, to say that they're not ready to make such a decision?

Secretary Powell. No, I wouldn't characterize it that way. It was always part of the process that Dr. Blix and Dr. ElBaradei report on a regular basis to the Council. They reported in early December. They were there not too long ago. The 27th of January was the first report really required directly by 1441, and I think it's quite appropriate for the new president of the Council, Germany, that takes over on the 1st of February, to call for reports as the presidency or other members of the Council see fit.

But what we can't do is just keep kicking the can down the road in the absence of a change in policy and attitude and go from passive to more than active cooperation, not cooperation alone, but a demonstrated willingness on the part of Iraq to participate in the disarmament and not try to frustrate the disarmament effort.

* * * *

Q. Secretary Powell, as impassioned as you are and as adamant as you are that you see in 14—in the inspectors' reports examples of Iraq noncompliance, many of your colleagues on the Security Council feel equally as strong that there are cases of compliance. The French, the Germans, the Russians have all come out today saying that they think the inspectors should be given more time.

How are you and the President planning to convince your colleagues and dissuade them—persuade them to—

Secretary Powell. What we're going to do is consult with our colleagues, and I'm sure that the President will be talking to leaders of all these countries, and I'll be talking to the ministers. We will consult, just as we did when 1441 was put together in the first instance, and try to come to a collective judgment as to what should be the next steps.

And as I'll say for about the fifth time, in due course those next steps will be announced. Yes, there are disagreements. There are some who are satisfied with passive cooperation at this point. Passive cooperation is not what 1441 was all about.

Dr. Blix, it seems to me, made it rather clear today that he is not getting the kind of cooperation and Iraq has not made the fundamental choice it has to make that it is going to be disarmed.

Excerpts from the President's State of the Union Address, January 28, 2003

The following is an excerpt from the President's State of the Union address.

Our nation and the world must learn the lessons of the Korean Peninsula and not allow an even greater threat to rise up in Iraq. A brutal dictator, with a history of reckless aggression, with ties to terrorism, with great potential wealth, will not be permitted to dominate a vital region and threaten the United States.

Twelve years ago, Saddam Hussein faced the prospect of being the last casualty in a war he had started and lost. To spare himself, he agreed to disarm of all weapons of mass destruction. For the next 12 years, he systematically violated that agreement. He pursued chemical, biological, and nuclear weapons, even while inspectors were in his country. Nothing to date has restrained him from his pursuit of these weapons—not economic sanctions, not isolation from the civilized world, not even cruise missile strikes on his military facilities.

Almost three months ago, the United Nations Security Council gave Saddam Hussein his final chance to disarm. He has shown instead utter contempt for the United Nations, and for the opinion of the world. The 108 U.N. inspectors were sent to conduct—were not sent to conduct a scavenger hunt for hidden materials across a country the size of California. The job of the inspectors is to verify that Iraq's regime is disarming. It is up to Iraq to show exactly where it is hiding its banned weapons, lay those weapons out for the world to see, and destroy them as directed. Nothing like this has happened.

The United Nations concluded in 1999 that Saddam Hussein had biological weapons sufficient to produce over 25,000 liters of anthrax—enough doses to kill several million people. He hasn't accounted for that material. He's given no evidence that he has destroyed it.

The United Nations concluded that Saddam Hussein had materials sufficient to produce more than 38,000 liters of botulinum toxin—enough to subject millions of people to death by respiratory failure. He hadn't accounted for that material. He's given no evidence that he has destroyed it.

Our intelligence officials estimate that Saddam Hussein had the materials to produce as much as 500 tons of sarin, mustard and VX nerve agent. In such quantities, these chemical agents could also kill untold thousands. He's not accounted for these materials. He has given no evidence that he has destroyed them.

U.S. intelligence indicates that Saddam Hussein had upwards of 30,000 munitions capable of delivering chemical agents. Inspectors recently turned up 16 of them—despite Iraq's recent declaration denying their existence. Saddam Hussein has not accounted for the remaining 29,984 of these prohibited munitions. He's given no evidence that he has destroyed them.

From three Iraqi defectors we know that Iraq, in the late 1990s, had several mobile biological weapons labs. These are designed to produce germ warfare agents, and can be moved from place to a place to evade inspectors. Saddam Hussein has not disclosed these facilities. He's given no evidence that he has destroyed them.

The International Atomic Energy Agency confirmed in the 1990s that Saddam Hussein had an advanced nuclear weapons development program, had a design for a nuclear weapon and was working on five different methods of enriching uranium for a bomb. The British government has learned that Saddam Hussein recently sought significant quantities of uranium from Africa. Our intelligence sources tell us that he has attempted to purchase high-strength aluminum tubes suitable for nuclear weapons production. Saddam Hussein has not credibly explained these activities. He clearly has much to hide.

The dictator of Iraq is not disarming. To the contrary; he is deceiving. From intelligence sources we know, for instance, that thousands of Iraqi security personnel are at work hiding documents and materials from the U.N. inspectors, sanitizing inspection sites and monitoring the inspectors themselves. Iraqi officials accompany the inspectors in order to intimidate witnesses.

Iraq is blocking U-2 surveillance flights requested by the United Nations. Iraqi intelligence officers are posing as the scientists inspectors are supposed to interview. Real scientists have been coached by Iraqi officials on what to say. Intelligence sources indicate that Saddam Hussein has ordered that scientists who cooperate with U.N. inspectors in disarming Iraq will be killed, along with their families.

Year after year, Saddam Hussein has gone to elaborate lengths, spent enormous sums, taken great risks to build and keep weapons of mass destruction. But why? The only possible explanation, the only possible use he could have for those weapons, is to dominate, intimidate, or attack.

With nuclear arms or a full arsenal of chemical and biological weapons, Saddam Hussein could resume his ambitions of conquest in the Middle East and create deadly havoc in that region. And this Congress and the America people must recognize another threat. Evidence from intelligence sources, secret communications, and statements by people now in custody reveal that Saddam Hussein aids and protects terrorists, including members of al Qaeda. Secretly, and without fingerprints, he could provide one of his hidden weapons to terrorists, or help them develop their own.

Before September the 11th, many in the world believed that Saddam Hussein could be contained. But chemical agents, lethal viruses and shadowy terrorist networks are not easily contained. Imagine those 19 hijackers with other weapons and other plans—this time armed by Saddam Hussein. It would take one vial, one canister, one crate slipped into this country to bring a day of horror like none we have ever known. We will do everything in our power to make sure that that day never comes.

Some have said we must not act until the threat is imminent. Since when have terrorists and tyrants announced their intentions, politely putting us on notice before they strike? If this threat is permitted to fully and suddenly emerge, all actions, all words, and all recriminations would come too late. Trusting in the sanity and restraint of Saddam Hussein is not a strategy, and it is not an option.

The dictator who is assembling the world's most dangerous weapons has already used them on whole villages—leaving thousands of his own citizens dead, blind, or disfigured. Iraqi refugees tell us how forced confessions are obtained—by torturing children while their parents are made to watch. International human rights groups have catalogued other methods used in the torture chambers of Iraq: electric shock, burning with hot irons, dripping acid on the skin, mutilation with electric drills, cutting out tongues, and rape. If this is not evil, then evil has no meaning.

And tonight I have a message for the brave and oppressed people of Iraq: Your enemy is not surrounding your country—your enemy is ruling your country. And the day he and his regime are removed from power will be the day of your liberation.

The world has waited 12 years for Iraq to disarm. America will not accept a serious and mounting threat to our country, and our friends and our allies. The United States will ask the U.N. Security Council to convene on February the 5th to consider the facts of Iraq's ongoing defiance of the world. Secretary of State Powell will present information and intelligence about Iraqi's legal—Iraq's illegal weapons programs, its attempt to hide those weapons from inspectors, and its links to terrorist groups.

We will consult. But let there be no misunderstanding: If Saddam Hussein does not fully disarm, for the safety of our people and for the peace of the world, we will lead a coalition to disarm him.

Tonight I have a message for the men and women who will keep the peace, members of the American Armed Forces: Many of you are assembling in or near the Middle East, and some crucial hours may lay ahead. In those hours, the success of our cause will depend on you. Your training has prepared you. Your honor will guide you. You believe in America, and America believes in you.

Sending Americans into battle is the most profound decision a President can make. The technologies of war have changed; the risks and suffering of war have not. For the brave Americans who bear the risk, no victory is free from sorrow. This nation fights reluctantly, because we know the cost and we dread the days of mourning that always come.

We seek peace. We strive for peace. And sometimes peace must be defended. A future lived at the mercy of terrible threats is no peace at all. If war is forced upon us, we will fight in a just cause and by just means—sparing, in every way we can, the innocent. And if war is forced upon us, we will fight with the full force and might of the

United States military—and we will prevail.

And as we and our coalition partners are doing in Afghanistan, we will bring to the Iraqi people food and medicines and supplies—and freedom.

Many challenges, abroad and at home, have arrived in a single season. In two years, America has gone from a sense of invulnerability to an awareness of peril; from bitter division in small matters to calm unity in great causes. And we go forward with confidence, because this call of history has come to the right country.

Americans are a resolute people who have risen to every test of our time. Adversity has revealed the character of our country, to the world and to ourselves. America is a strong nation, and honorable in the use of our strength. We exercise power without conquest, and we sacrifice for the liberty of strangers.

Americans are a free people, who know that freedom is the right of every person and the future of every nation. The liberty we prize is not America's gift to the world, it is God's gift to humanity.

We Americans have faith in ourselves, but not in ourselves alone. We do not know—we do not claim to know all the ways of Providence, yet we can trust in them, placing our confidence in the loving God behind all of life, and all of history.

May He guide us now. And may God continue to bless the United States of America.

Remarks by Secretary of State Powell, January 29, 2003

Secretary Colin Powell was interviewed by TF-1 Television of France.

Q. President Bush said yesterday that the United States course doesn't depend on orders. Does it mean that the United States could go to war without the approval of the Security Council of the U.N.?

Secretary Powell. The President has always said that he believes the danger from the Iraqi regime is such that we have to preserve the option of using military force with likeminded nations—other nations would join us in such a cause—even in the absence of additional U.N. authority. We believe, frankly, that in 1441, that resolution, and in earlier resolutions, there is more than adequate authority to make the case that Saddam's continued violation of international law is sufficient cause to go to war.

But because the world was so interested in unifying, seeing if we could unify behind this, we took it back to the U.N. last fall. And after seven weeks of very tough negotiations, we came out with Resolution 1441, giving Saddam Hussein one more chance to get out of the breach that he is already in.

And that resolution is very important because everybody who signed up for that resolution, all 15 nations, to include France, said he is in material breach, we're giving him one last chance, the inspectors help him take that one last chance, and it if he doesn't comply, then serious consequences will follow. And those serious consequences, everybody who signed up, everybody who voted for that resolution, understood that serious consequences meant the likelihood of war.

Q. And next week, you're going to go to the Security Council. What kind of proof, what kind of intelligence, are you going to provide?

Secretary Powell. I will be bringing information and intelligence, some of which has not been seen before, that will help make the case that Dr. Blix was presenting the other day that Saddam Hussein is trying to deny the inspectors access to weapons of mass destruction capacity within Iraq, and I will also be presenting information and intelligence that describes some of these programs and some of these weapons.

Q. Like what?

Secretary Powell. Well, would you be kind enough to wait till next Wednesday?

Q. And in France, at the moment, 60%—more than 70% of the population is against the war. Do you think that France could use its veto at the Security Council, and did you think about this importance?

Secretary Powell. France is a sovereign nation and I would not presume to suggest what President Chirac might decide to do. I hope that whatever decision France makes, it will be in light of the seriousness of this problem, in light of the danger posed by Saddam Hussein and these weapons of mass destruction.

France fully understands and the French leadership fully understands the danger. They participated in the preparation of 1441. They were one of the leaders in shaping 1441. And my French colleagues, and especially my colleague Dominique de Villepin, clearly understood that serious consequences might flow.

I understand that there is strong public opposition, but I hope that as we go forward in this next period of time and more information is presented and Saddam Hussein continues to essentially disregard the will of the international community, that the people of France will understand that there comes a time when this kind, this kind of behavior cannot simply be ignored and looked away from; one must take action.

And when that time comes, I hope France will look at its situation carefully and will be able to support whatever action is required. But I fully understand the French position at the moment.

Q. How much time are you ready to give to the inspectors?

Secretary Powell. It's not how much time for the inspectors. People keep saying give the inspectors more time. More time to do what? Search in the dark? More time to be deceived by Saddam Hussein? That's not the right question.

The right question is: How much more time do we give Saddam Hussein? If he were to come out this afternoon and say, "I'm now going to tell the truth, here's where the biological weapons are, here are where the chemical rounds are, here is the rest of my nuclear program, here are the documents, here are all the people you want to interview," if he were to do that, then how much time the inspectors need almost doesn't make any difference. Give them as much time as they say they need to verify that they have destroyed all this material.

But the problem is he is not doing that. He continues to deceive. He continues to deny. And my colleague—

Q. Do you have the proof—do you have the proof that he has everything—

Secretary Powell. Mr. Blix said so. Mr. Blix said so. It's not the United States. Mr. Blix said so on Monday that he is not cooperating. He's had some passive cooperation, but he continues to not accept the responsibility to disarm.

And so my friends on the Security Council and elsewhere in the world who keep saying give the inspectors more time, give the inspectors more time, what's wrong with more time for the inspectors, the answer to that question simply is more time for the inspectors has to be linked to positive action on the part of the Iraqis to show what they've got, and not just have the inspectors wandering around in the dark looking for things. Turn on the lights. Show us what you have. Be serious.

And for those who say, well, we'll just look away and ignore this danger, I think it is a danger that cannot be ignored. As the President said last night, we would be devastated years from now, next year, the year after, if one day, in Paris or in Washington, D.C., or in London or in Cairo—anywhere—suddenly one of these chemical rounds showed up as a terrorist weapon and we wondered why we didn't deal with it in the year 2003.

Remarks by Secretary of State Powell, January 29, 2003

Secretary Colin Powell was interviewed by ZDF Television of Germany.

Q. Mr. Secretary, your presentation next week at the United Nations, is this the last effort to convince members of the Security Council that the use of force is inevitable?

Secretary Powell. No. I think my presentation next week will be for the purpose of presenting to my colleagues in the Council more information, more intelligence, to back up what Dr. Blix has been saying about lack of performance on the part of the Iraqis in coming forward and disarming themselves.

We will also illustrate some of the things they have done to deceive the inspectors. We will also show information concerning the programs they have had over the years to develop chemical weapons, biological weapons and nuclear weapons and why it is so important that the world must insist that Saddam Hussein disarm, and that the inspectors are there to help him do that and to verify that he is doing it.

Q. You are trying to convince your partners. Are you going to seek a resolution of the United Nations authorizing the use of force?

Secretary Powell. Well, we haven't made a judgment yet as to what we will do at that point. I mean, this is just the beginning of a period of intense diplomatic activity.

We had the Blix report and the ElBaradei report two days ago. The President gave his State of the Union address last night. The President will be consulting with his fellow heads of state and government over the next period of time. I'll make my presentation on the 5th of February. And then we'll make a judgment after this consultation as to what the next steps should be, whether it's another resolution before the U.N. or whether it is some other action that we might feel obliged to take.

The President, as always, is approaching this patiently. He is being very deliberative about it. He understands the consequences of going to war. But he also understands the consequences of not disarming Saddam Hussein.

It's still a wonderment to us why more people don't recognize that chemical weapons, chemical weapons that this person, Saddam Hussein, has used in the past are still in his possession; that he has been trying to develop biological weapons, and we think he has biological weapons. That's what the inspectors are asking for. Where is the anthrax? Where is the botulinum? And he has been trying to develop nuclear weapons.

And this is not just an American claim. The inspectors have put this claim before the world; not just these inspectors, the last group of inspectors. And so it seems to me the whole world should be outraged that an individual such as this continues to move in this direction, and the United Nations has said, "Stop. Stop. Stop. Stop," and he has not stopped.

And then finally we came together and passed a powerful resolution, 15-0. And that resolution said he is in breach of his obligations, two, we give him a chance to get out of breach, we give him a chance to disarm, and we'll let the inspectors help him. And three, if he doesn't disarm, if he continues to ignore the international community, then he has to face serious consequences. And if it wasn't for that third part, serious consequences, we wouldn't see anything going on now—no inspectors would have gotten back in.

But we cannot let him use the presence of the inspectors as a way to deceive us again. He must face serious consequences if he does not disarm.

Q. The policy of the German Government is contradictory to what you've just said and to the American position. Do you feel this is a difference of opinion among friends that happens, or is it more serious?

Secretary Powell. It's a very strong difference of opinion between and among friends. Germany is a friend of the United States. As you may know, I began my military career in Germany. I've lived in Germany. I think I know Germany, and I have the warmest feelings toward Germany and the German people. But we have an honest disagreement on this issue. And Germany has taken a very strong position even before the U.N. Resolution 1441, before we even thought about what we should do to fix this, Germany had a strong position against the use of military force under any set of circumstances that they see out there right now.

I understand that position. We disagree with that position. We hope that in the days ahead as we discuss this issue in the Council that perhaps Germany, its leaders and the German people will look at this in a different light and understand that as difficult as war is, as unpleasant as war is—something we want to avoid—and I, more than anyone else do everything I can to avoid war, sometimes it's not possible when you're faced with the kind of evil represented by Saddam Hussein and the kind of evil weapons that he is trying to keep in his possession.

Remarks by Secretary of Defense Rumsfeld, January 29, 2003

In the State of the Union remarks last evening, the President made clear that Saddam Hussein poses a "serious," to quote him, "and mounting threat to our country, [and] our friends and our allies" that cannot be ignored. As the President pointed out, the Iraqi regime has not accounted for some 38,000 liters of botulism toxin, 500 tons of Sarin, mustard gas, VX nerve agent, upwards of 30,000 munitions capable of delivering chemical weapons, and a number of mobile biological labs designed to produce biological weapons while evading detection. His regime has the design for a nuclear weapon; it was working on several different methods of enriching uranium, and recently was discovered seeking significant quantities of uranium from Africa. The regime plays host to terrorists, including al Qaeda, as the President indicated. Saddam's regime hides military equipment in or near mosques, hospitals, civilian homes and has a history of using innocent civilians as human shields. That is why, as he said, our nation and the world must not allow a brutal dictator with a history of reckless aggression and ties to terrorism to dominate a vital region and threaten the United States.

For those who counsel more time for inspections, the President responded that we have given Saddam Hussein more than a decade to give up chemical, biological and his nuclear weapon program. Yet nothing to date has restrained him: Not economic sanctions, not diplomacy, not isolation from the civilized world, not even cruise missile strikes on his military facilities. He's now refusing to cooperate with the 17th U.N. Security Council resolution. As Mr. Blix's report pointed out, at what point do reasonable people conclude that we know his answer as to whether or not he intends to cooperate and voluntarily disarm? As the President made clear, the dictator of Iraq is not disarming; to the contrary, he is deceiving. His time to do so is running out. It's up to Iraq to prevent the use of force. And let's hope that they do so.

* * * *

Q. Mr. Secretary, I realize that intelligence is a touchy issue, but there are major questions about the information that Secretary Powell will provide to the Security Council next week, I believe it's February 5th. People in this building, including you, have said that you have proof that Iraq is still cheating the inspectors in even the most recent inspections. Will the information that you provide, including perhaps satellite photographs, will it be more directed to show that the Iraqis are still cheating the inspectors? Or, will it provide direct information of weapons—that the Iraqis still have these weapons? Can you give us some information on this?

Secretary Rumsfeld. Well, the President outlined a good portion of the case yesterday evening. The agency, Central Intelligence Agency, is in the process of developing the final materials that will be used by Secretary Powell. I do not—and they're in the process of declassifying certain things, and I do not know what that final draft will look like; I've seen earlier iterations, but there is—there certainly will be information that will be provided as they go through that declassification process.

I think the way to think about it is this; there's two... there's one threshold issue, and that's the issue of preemption. It is difficult for all of us who have grown up in this country and believed in the principle that unless attacked, one does not attack—other countries have had different approaches, but for the most part, our country has had a view that that was the way we did things; it was other countries that have attacked us, for the most part, and initiated conflicts.

The question, though, is, in the 21st century, with biological weapons, for example, that could kill hundreds of thousands of people, what does one do? Does one wait until they're attacked, or does one look at a pattern of behavior and a pattern—a fact pattern, and draw a conclusion?

And so that key threshold issue is one that our country, the people of our country and the world, have engaged. And because it's new and because it's difficult and not easy, and we have not—we've had September 11th and some 3,000 human beings, innocent men, women and children of all nationalities and religions lost their lives. A biological attack that killed 300,000 or more would affect people's judgment about whether or not they would prefer that their government act before the fact. And there is no doubt in my mind but that the overwhelming majority of the American people would prefer that their government take the kinds of steps necessary to prevent that type of attack. So that's the first issue.

The second issue is people are kind of looking for a photograph or a thing that they can hold up and say, 'Aha! That proves something.' As I've said here, the Congress spent months trying to connect the dots after September 11th, trying to figure out what happened. How did all of those things go along, and how could we not know it and stop it? And wouldn't we have acted preemptively to stop it, had we been able to figure out how to stop it?

It's hard to connect the dots even after the fact, these many months, with going over thousands of documents up there on the Hill. Now they've appointed another commission to look at it. It's even harder to connect the dots before something happens.

But if you think of this fact pattern, you have a country that had chemical and biological weapons and an active nuclear program, according to the U.N. inspectors who were in there, and according to information and documents that were found. You have a country that was asked by the United Nations in the 17th resolution to declare what they have—after lengthy diplomacy, lengthy economic sanctions—to declare what they have, bring it forward so that they can be disarmed. You have a country that agreed to do that. And then you have a country that declined to do it, by filing a declaration that was fraudulent, by taking steps to inhibit the inspectors from doing their work in a reasonable way, by behaving totally differently than South Africa or Ukraine or Kazakhstan, which invited inspectors in, showed the world what they had, had them dismantled and disarmed, totally opposite. They're telling their people to lie to the inspectors, they're telling their people to hide things. They are taking documentation and putting it in multiple locations. You have a country that is out in the world buying things that are necessary for the development and progress in their chemical, biological and nuclear programs. And they're doing it not openly and saying it's dual use material and we're doing it innocently, but clandestinely, and paying more money than they need to.

So if you work your way down there, and then you say to yourself, 'this is a country that's not a normal country.' This is not Canada, or Australia, or some country that behaves as a good citizen of the world. This is a country that has used chemical weapons against its own people, that's used chemical weapons against its neighbors, that fired ballistic missiles into four countries in the region, that's threatened the United States of America, that has relationships with terrorist networks.

Now, what does all that force a person to think? It seems to me that at some point one has to say, 'what ought a person to think about all of that?' And that's—that to me is evidence as hard as a photograph. And indeed, it is critically important for people to engage it in that fact pattern and come to their own conclusion about how do they feel about that.

Open Letter from Leaders of Bulgaria, the Czech Republic, Denmark, Italy, Hungary, Spain, Portugal, the United Kingdom, January 30, 2003

The real bond between the United States and Europe is the values we share: democracy, individual freedom, human rights and the Rule of Law. These values crossed the Atlantic with those who sailed from Europe to help create the USA. Today they are under greater threat than ever. The attacks of 11 September showed just how far terrorists—the enemies of our common values—are prepared to go to destroy them. Those outrages were an attack on all of us. In standing firm in defense of these principles, the governments and people of the United States and Europe have amply demonstrated the strength of their convictions. Today more than ever, the transatlantic bond is a guarantee of our freedom.

We in Europe have a relationship with the United States which has stood the test of time. Thanks in large part to American bravery, generosity and far-sightedness, Europe was set free from the two forms of tyranny that devastated our continent in the 20th century: Nazism and Communism. Thanks, too, to the continued cooperation between Europe and the United States we have managed to guarantee peace and freedom on our continent. The transatlantic relationship must not become a casualty of the current Iraqi regime's persistent attempts to threaten world security.

In today's world, more than ever before, it is vital that we preserve that unity and cohesion. We know that success in the day-to-day battle against terrorism and the proliferation of weapons of mass destruction demands unwavering determination and firm international cohesion on the part of all countries for whom freedom is precious. The Iraqi regime and its weapons of mass destruction represent a clear threat to world security. This danger has been explicitly recognized by the United Nations. All of us are bound by Security Council Resolution 1441, which was adopted unanimously. We Europeans have since reiterated our backing for Resolution 1441, our wish to pursue the U.N. route and our support for the Security Council, at the Prague Nato Summit and the Copenhagen European Council.

In doing so, we sent a clear, firm and unequivocal message that we would rid the world of the danger posed by Saddam Hussein's weapons of mass destruction. We must remain united in insisting that his regime is disarmed. The solidarity, cohesion and determination of the international community are our best hope of achieving this peacefully. Our strength lies in unity.

The combination of weapons of mass destruction and terrorism is a threat of incalculable consequences. It is one at which all of us should feel concerned. Resolution 1441 is Saddam Hussein's last chance to disarm using peaceful means. The opportunity to avoid greater confrontation rests with him. Sadly this week the U.N. weapons inspectors have confirmed that his long-established pattern of deception, denial and non-compliance with U.N. Security Council resolutions is continuing. Europe has no quarrel with the Iraqi people. Indeed, they are the first victims of Iraq's current brutal regime. Our goal is to safeguard world peace and security by ensuring that this regime gives up its weapons of mass destruction. Our governments have a common responsibility to face this threat. Failure to do so would be nothing less than negligent to our own citizens and to the wider world. The United Nations Charter charges the Security Council with the task of preserving international peace and security. To do so, the Security Council must maintain its credibility by ensuring full compliance with its resolutions. We cannot allow a dictator to systematically violate those Resolutions. If they are not complied with, the Security Council will lose its credibility and world peace will suffer as a result. We are confident that the Security Council will face up to its responsibilities.

José Maria Aznar, *Spain*
José Manuel Durao Barroso, *Portugal*
Silvio Berlusconi, *Italy*
Tony Blair, *United Kingdom*
Vaclav Havel, *Czech Republic*
Peter Medgyessy, *Hungary*
Leszek Miller, *Poland*
Anders Fogh Rasmussen, *Denmark*
Embassy of Bulgaria

Remarks by President Bush and Italian Prime Minister Berlusconi, January 30, 2003

President Bush and Prime Minister Silvio Berlusconi delivered their remarks after meeting at the White House.

President Bush.   I will make an opening statement; Silvio will make an opening statement; we'll have one question from the Americans, one question from the Italians. We're running a little late—we'd like to spend hours answering your questions, but the problem is we've got other matters to work on.

First, it's my honor to welcome Silvio Berlusconi back, he is a personal friend. Italy is a great friend of America, America is a great friend of Italy. The Prime Minister and I will of course be talking about a lot of matters, the most significant matter will be how to keep the peace, how to make the world a peaceful place.

I am most grateful that the Prime Minister signed a letter, along with other leaders of European countries, which clarified the issue that we're dealing with—and that is that Saddam Hussein is a clear threat to peace. It was a strong statement. It also was a statement of solidarity with the United States, and I appreciated that very much.

Prime Minister Berlusconi. Thank you.

President Bush. I appreciate your friendship. I welcome you back to the Oval Office and look forward to having a long and fruitful discussion.

Prime Minister Berlusconi. We are here for good work, for a just cause and for everybody, I think. And I am here with a friend, with a country, that is the best friend of my country.

* * * *

Q. Sir, are you open to giving Saddam a final deadline, and you willing to let him slip into exile—this, a man who recently said he wants to break the neck of our country?

President Bush. First, let me echo the comments of my National Security Advisor, who the other day in commenting about this process said this is a matter of weeks, not months. In other words, for the sake of peace, this issue must be resolved. Hopefully, it can be done peacefully. Hopefully the pressure of the free world will convince Mr. Saddam Hussein to relinquish power. And should he choose to leave the country, along with a lot of the other henchmen who have tortured the Iraqi people, we would welcome that, of course.

I will tell my friend, Silvio, that the use of military troops is my last choice, not my first. The commitment of young men and Americans into battle is a difficult decision, because I understand the cost of war. But I also understand the cost of inaction. There is a high price to be paid for the civilized world by not enforcing the opinion of the world, which was for Saddam Hussein to disarm.

There's a reason why leaders around the world believe he ought to disarm. There's a reason why the Security Council of the United Nations voted 15-0 to say to Saddam, disarm—and that's because he's dangerous.

Prime Minister Berlusconi. In Italy, I already said it, I have the opportunity to say that we have always been the faithful ally country of United States, we are close friends of the United States, also in this case.

I believe that the moment has arrived to find out where all the weapons of mass destruction that Saddam Hussein said he had, where they ended up. We really fear that after the series of terrorist attack, which culminated with the attacks on September 11th, there is the intention of the terrorists is to really come to a terrible disaster. And to do so, they have to avail themselves of the biological, chemical weapons that we know were available as Saddam Hussein.

Therefore, on the basis of the United Nations Security Council Resolution 1441, Saddam Hussein has to reveal and account for the weapons that we know he has. So the decision on face rests in his hands. We all want peace.

And I'm here today to help my friend, President Bush, to convince everybody that this is in the interest of everybody. And if we are all united, the European Union, the United States, the Federation of Russia, everybody, all the other states under the United Nations, then Saddam Hussein will understand that he will have no other option but to reveal the arms and to destroy them.

President Bush. Along those lines, let me make one clarification on my statement. I think that no matter how Mr. Saddam is dealt with, the goal of disarming Iraq still stays the same, regardless of who is in charge of the government. And that's very important for the Iraqi people to know.

And I also want to assure Silvio that should we require military action, shortly after our troops go in, will go food and medicine and supplies to the Iraqi people. We will, of course, win militarily, if we have to. But we'll also want to make sure that we win the peace, as well.

Q. Mr. Prime Minister, I just had a question. You expressed your sentiment to friendship for the United States, and loyalty. Now, will you be ready to commit Italy to go along with the United States should the United States put together a coalition of the willing, as the President has said?

Prime Minister Berlusconi. We will never forget that we owe our freedom—our freedom—our wealth to the United States of America. And our democracy. And we also will never forget there have been many American young lives that were lost and sacrifice themselves for us.

So for us, the United States is not only our friend, but they are the guarantee of our democracy and our freedom. And I already has the opportunity to say this to President Bush, every time I see the U.S. flag, I don't see the flag only representative of a country, but I see it as a symbol of democracy and of freedom.

Remarks by Secretary of State Powell and Canadian Foreign Minister Graham, January 30, 2003

Secretary Colin Powell and Foreign Minister William Graham delivered their remarks after meeting in Washington, DC.

Secretary Powell. Then we talked about the multilateral international issues of the day. We had a good and full discussion about Iraq and North Korea. And I value the opportunity to hear from Minister Graham with respect to the Canadian position and I gave him a foretaste of what's coming up in the next few weeks with my presentation at the Security Council next Wednesday, and then continuing consultations after that to see what action the Security Council chooses to take. And then of course the two chief inspectors will be back before the Council on the 14th of February.

* * * *

Foreign Minister Graham. As you say, we discussed other issues. Primarily that was Iraq, for obvious reasons. And I want to express to you, Mr. Secretary, the admiration of Canada and Canadians of the way you've been—you brought, with the President, this matter to the United Nations and made a clear determination that we're going to work through the United Nations as the way in which we can ensure the security of the world in the future, and also the best security for the United States. And we understand that you intend to keep to that path. I want to encourage you to keep to that path.

Canada has made it clear that if there is a United Nations authorization, the Prime Minister has said we, of course, have always supported that multilateral approach, we would be there. We will be watching. We are working on this. We had a debate in our House of Commons last night—all parties, a frank exchange amongst Canadians as to how we feel about this. There's very clearly a recognition that 1441 is the way to go—1441 speaks of a process which is still ongoing and of consequences if that process demonstrates certain things. It isn't over yet because that process isn't complete and a demonstration has yet to be made, but we look forward to you doing that on February the 14th. We look forward to hearing what Dr. Blix has to say on the 14th, and we will remain engaged with you to make sure that this is brought to a conclusion in a way that strengthens the international institutions and strengthens our chances for peace in the world.

Q. Secretary Powell, do you believe that Canada will end up backing the U.S. if it goes to war without the United Nations endorsement?

Secretary Powell. Oh, I would not wish to speak for Canada. Minister Graham can do that.

I do know that Canada will do just as the Minister said, and as the Prime Minister has said over the weeks and months: "study this very carefully, recognize the significance and the importance of this issue." I think Canada is committed to the disarmament of Iraq of weapons of mass destruction and we all hope it can be done with the full support of the international community. And we'll stay in close touch in the weeks ahead to make sure that we have a complete understanding of each other's views.

Q. Mr. Minister, is Canada still opposed to using force? It sounds like you're not ready to join any coalition to use force.

Foreign Minister Graham. No—

Q. What are you—can you tell us what you're waiting for?

Foreign Minister Graham. What the Prime Minister has said was that if there is a coalition directed by the United Nations, and as the Secretary has said, Resolution 1441 speaks of a process which is going to determine whether or not Iraq is failing to disarm, and if that is determined, that there will be consequences of that. That is something that is yet being determined in a framework of the United Nations. It's an ongoing process. We are watching that. We are engaged. We will be there to support that process. We do believe that Iraq has to be disarmed and we will work with the Secretary, with the United States and with other countries, through the U.N., to achieve that goal.

* * * *

Q. Mr. Minister, in America we have long cherished our relationship with the Canadians, but there is a feeling among many Americans that the Canadians have perhaps gone a bit wobbly on the United States over the issue of Iraq. What would you say to those Americans to give them reassurance?

Foreign Minister Graham. I would say to them that as the Secretary of State has said and as the President has made clear by his actions, by going to the United Nations, that the United States itself recognizes that its long-term security and the security of the world means working with coalitions of parties; that if one party, one state, acts by itself, it takes the responsibility by itself, it risks consequences in a complicated area like the Middle East, which would be very serious.

And the United States has made it very clear that it does not intend to do that. It intends to work within a coalition. And the best way to ensure the security of the world and to ensure the security of the United States is through the United Nations because, ultimately, that is the world saying to Saddam Hussein, "You have failed to act, here are the consequences, and we are delivering it. This is not the United States acting unilaterally or arbitrarily. This is the world judgment."

That is where Canada has stood with the United States. The Secretary has often said to me "we appreciate the fact where we constantly said you need a strong resolution. We support you in that." We support the United States in that.

And we support the United States in its determination to work through multilateral institutions because we believe that our joint long-term security is best served there. And I believe Americans, at their heart, believe that too, and that's why this government in the United States has been so firm in working in the way it has.

So thank you all very much. I have to go now myself, but I'll be seeing, I think, some of you later. Thank you very much.

Remarks by United Nations Secretary-General Annan, January 30, 2003

Q. Yesterday, a very large majority of the [Security] Council [members] indicated that they wanted inspections to continue and to try and get peaceful disarmament—I think it was 11 out of 15. What's your reaction to the debate, which I'm sure you kept close track of?

Secretary-General Annan. I think you're right that was the sense of the Council yesterday. And of course the discussions continue and everyone is looking forward to [U.S.] Secretary [of State Colin] Powell's visit here next week. And I suspect many of the Foreign Ministers are going to come for that meeting. And this issue will be discussed further following the evidence he puts before the Council. Whether that will change the minds of some members of the Council will depend on the material he puts before them. So we will have to wait and see.

Q. Would you expect any evidence then to be taken by the inspectors in the field and be checked by them?

Secretary-General Annan. I think the inspectors have made it clear for quite some time that they would appreciate receiving actionable information from all governments who have them. They have received some and I hope they would also use whatever information that is given next week that will be helpful for their work.

Remarks by President Bush and British Prime Minister Blair, January 31, 2003

President Bush and Prime Minister Tony Blair delivered their remarks after meeting at the White House.

President Bush. It's my honor to welcome Tony Blair back to the White House. We just had a wide-ranging discussion on a lot of issues. I appreciate my friend's commitment to peace and security. I appreciate his vision. I appreciate his willingness to lead. Most importantly, I appreciate his understanding that after September the 11th, 2001, the world changed; that we face a common enemy—terrorists willing to kill innocent lives; that we now recognize that threats which gather in remote regions of the world must be dealt with before others lose their lives.

Tony Blair is a friend. He's a friend of the American people, he's a friend of mine. I trust his judgment and I appreciate his wisdom.

Welcome.

Prime Minister Blair. First of all, can I say how delighted I am to be back in the White House and to see President Bush. And as he's just described to you, we had an excellent discussion, covering all the key issues of the day. And I would like to praise his leadership in the world since September the 11th, particularly, on what I think are the two key issues that face our world today—which are issues of international terrorism and weapons of mass destruction. And I think both of those issues come together because they threaten the peace and the order and the stability of the world.

And what is essential is that in every respect, in every way that we can we mobilize international support and the international community, in order to make sure that these twin threats that the world faces are dealt with. And I have no doubt at all that we can deal with them. But we should realize those two threats—terrorism, weapons of mass destruction—are not different, they're linked. And dealing with both of them is essential for the future peace and security and prosperity of the world.

Q. Thank you, sir. First, quickly to the Prime Minister, did you ask President Bush to secure a second U.N. resolution and to give the inspectors more time? And, President Bush, the U.N. says—the U.N. inspectors say Saddam is not complying, you say

Saddam is not complying, why wait a matter of weeks? What's—why hold up on the decision?

President Bush. First of all, you violated the two-question rule—as usual. He's had a bad habit of this. I'll start.

Saddam Hussein is not disarming. He is a danger to the world. He must disarm. And that's why I have constantly said and the Prime Minister has constantly said this issue will come to a head in a matter of weeks, not months.

Prime Minister Blair. The whole point about the present situation is that when President Bush made his speech to the United Nations, when we went down the United Nations route, we passed Resolution 1441. And I think it really repays reading that, because we said very clearly that Saddam had what we said was a final opportunity to disarm, and that he had to cooperate fully in every respect with the U.N. weapons inspectors.

As Dr. Blix said in his report to the Security Council earlier this week, he's not doing that. And therefore, what is important is that the international community comes together again and makes it absolutely clear that this is unacceptable. And the reason why I believe that it will do that is precisely because in the original Resolution 1441, we made it clear that failure to disarm would lead to serious consequences.

So this is a test for the international community. It's not just a test for the United States or for Britain. It's a test for the international community, too. And the judgment has to be, at the present time, that Saddam Hussein is not cooperating with the inspectors, and therefore is in breach of the U.N. resolution. And that's why time is running out.

Q. A question for the President, if I may. What is the status, in your view, of any second resolution? Is it something that you think it's worth spending time and energy trying to assemble and, if so, why?

President Bush. First, let me reiterate what I just said. This is a matter of weeks, not months. Any attempt to drag the process on for months will be resisted by the United States. And as I understand the Prime Minister—I'm loath to put words in his mouth—but he's also said weeks, not months.

Secondly, I want to remind you, I was the guy that went to the United Nations in the first place. I said, why don't we come together as a world to resolve this issue, once and for all. Why doesn't the United Nations stand up as a body and show the world that it has got the capacity to keep the peace.

So, first of all, in answer to one part of your question, this just needs to be resolved quickly. Should the United Nations decide to pass a second resolution, it would be welcomed if it is yet another signal that we're intent upon disarming Saddam Hussein. But 1441 gives us the authority to move without any second resolution. And Saddam Hussein must understand that if he does not disarm, for the sake of peace, we, along with others, will go disarm Saddam Hussein.

Q. Thank you, sir. Mr. President, is Secretary Powell going to provide the undeniable proof of Iraq's guilt that so many critics are calling for?

President Bush. Well, all due in modesty, I thought I did a pretty good job myself of making it clear that he's not disarming and why he should disarm. Secretary Powell will make a strong case about the danger of an armed Saddam Hussein. He will make it clear that Saddam Hussein is fooling the world, or trying to fool the world. He will make it clear that Saddam is a menace to peace in his own neighborhood. He will also talk about al Qaeda links, links that really do portend a danger for America and for Great Britain, anybody else who loves freedom.

As the Prime Minister says, the war on terror is not confined to just a shadowy terrorist network. The war on terror includes people who are willing to train and to equip organizations such as al Qaeda.

See, the strategic view of America changed after September the 11th. We must deal with threats before they hurt the American people again. And as I have said repeatedly, Saddam Hussein would like nothing more than to use a terrorist network to attack and to kill and leave no fingerprints behind. Colin Powell will continue making that case to the American people and the world at the United Nations.

Q. One question for you both. Do you believe that there is a link between Saddam Hussein, a direct link, and the men who attacked on September the 11th?

President Bush. I can't make that claim.

Prime Minister Blair. That answers your question. The one thing I would say, however, is I've absolutely no doubt at all that unless we deal with both of these threats, they will come together in a deadly form. Because, you know, what do we know after September the 11th? We know that these terrorists networks would use any means they can to cause maximum death and destruction. And we know also that they will do whatever they can to acquire the most deadly weaponry they can. And that's why it's important to deal with these issues together.

Q. Mr. President and Prime Minister, if I could, sir, the arms inspectors made their report on Monday this week. You've both made clear that it's a question of weeks, not months. And here we are at the end of the week and the Iraqis are suddenly inviting the arms inspectors back to Baghdad for further consultations. Could I ask both of you what you make of that?

President Bush. Let's see if I can be polite. Saddam Hussein has had 12 years to learn how to deceive, and I would view this as more deception on his part. He expects to be able to convince 108 inspectors that he is open-minded. The only way that he can show that he is truly a peaceful man is to not negotiate with inspectors, is not to string the inspectors along, but to disarm in front of inspectors. We know what a disarmed regime looks like. We know what it means to disarm. There's no negotiations. The idea of calling inspectors in to negotiate is a charade. If he is going to disarm, he must start disarming. That's the only thing he needs to talk to the inspectors about, is, here, I'm disarming.

Prime Minister Blair. That's absolutely right. If you look back at the history of this, for 12 years, he's played these games. And that's why it's so important to realize what the U.N. inspectors were put back in to do. The U.N. inspectors—and this is the crucial point, because it's on this basis that the whole issue of the U.N. authority rests— the U.N. inspectors did not go back into Iraq to play a game of hide-and-seek with Saddam. They didn't go back in as a detective agency. They went back in under an authority that said that they had to cooperate fully, in every respect: the interview of witnesses, not just access to sites; honest, transparent declarations in the material they had. They're not doing that.

Now, why are they calling back the inspectors? I think it's fairly obvious. It's because as the pressure grows, they want to play the same games as they've been playing all the way through. That's why it's important we hold to the path that we've set out. They have to disarm. They have to cooperate with the inspectors. They're not doing it. If they don't do it through the U.N. route, then they will have to be disarmed by force.

Q. Mr. President, an account of the White House after 9/11 says that you ordered invasion plans for Iraq six days after September the 11th—Bob Woodward's account. Isn't it the case that you have always intended war on Iraq, and that international diplomacy is a charade in this case?

President Bush. Actually, prior to September the 11th, we were discussing smart sanctions. We were trying to fashion a sanction regime that would make it more likely to be able to contain somebody like Saddam Hussein. After September the 11th, the doctrine of containment just doesn't hold any water, as far as I'm concerned.

I've told you the strategic vision of our country shifted dramatically, and it shifted dramatically because we now recognize that oceans no longer protect us, that we're vulnerable to attack. And the worst form of attack could come from somebody acquiring weapons of mass destruction and using them on the American people, or the worst attack could come when somebody uses weapons of mass destruction on our friends in Great Britain.

Recently, Tony Blair's government routed out a poison plot. It should say to the people of Great Britain, there is a present danger, that weapons of mass destruction are a danger to people who love freedom. I want to congratulate you on your fabulous job of using your intelligence and your law enforcement to protect the people of Great Britain.

Today, Italy rounded up yet another cell of people who are willing to use weapons of mass destruction on those of us who love freedom.

And so, no, quite the contrary. My vision shifted dramatically after September the 11th, because I now realize the stakes. I realize the world has changed. My most important obligation is to protect the American people from further harm. And I will do that.

Email from U.S. National Security Agency Chief of Staff ("Regional Targets" Division) Koza, January 31, 2008

The following email communication was allegedly sent by Frank Koza, Chief of Staff in the "Regional Targets" Division of the National Security Agency, to undisclosed recipients. The email was identified as classified (top secret). The source of the leaked email was identified in the British media as Katharine Gun, a translator for British intelligence's Government Communications Headquarters (GCHQ). The document was first published in The Observer.

Subject: Reflections of Iraq Debate/Votes at UN-RT Actions + Potential for Related Contributions
Importance: HIGH (Top Secret//COMINT//X1)

All,
As you've likely heard by now, the Agency is mounting a surge particularly directed at the U.N. Security Council (UNSC) members (minus US and GBR of course) for insights as to how to membership is reacting to the on-going debate RE: Iraq, plans to vote on any related resolutions, what related policies/ negotiating positions they may be considering, alliances/ dependencies, etc.—the whole gamut of information that could give U.S. policymakers an edge in obtaining results favorable to U.S. goals or to head off surprises. In RT, that means a QRC surge effort to revive/ create efforts against UNSC members Angola, Cameroon, Chile, Bulgaria and Guinea, as well as extra focus on Pakistan U.N. matters.

We've also asked ALL RT topi's to emphasize and make sure they pay attention to existing non-UNSC member U.N.-related and domestic comms for anything useful related to the UNSC deliberations/ debates/ votes. We have a lot of special U.N.-related diplomatic coverage (various U.N. delegations) from countries not sitting on the UNSC right now that could contribute related perspectives/ insights/ whatever. We recognize that we can't afford to ignore this possible source.

We'd appreciate your support in getting the word to your analysts who might have similar, more in-direct access to valuable information from accesses in your product lines. I suspect that you'll be hearing more along these lines in formal channels—especially as this effort will probably peak (at least for this specific focus) in the middle of next week, following the SecState's presentation to the UNSC.

Remarks by British Prime Minister Blair, February 3, 2003

Prime Minister Tony Blair delivered his remarks to the British Parliament.
With permission, Mr Speaker, I shall make a statement on my visit to Washington.

* * * *

The immediate focus of the visit was Iraq. Over the last week, in addition to meeting President Bush, I have seen Prime Minister Aznar, President Mbeki, Prime Minister Berlusconi and Prince Saud. Today, I have spoken to President Chirac. After this

Statement, I will be speaking to President Putin and I have also spoken to the Prime Ministers of Turkey, Canada, Greece, Poland, Portugal and Australia. I shall meet President Chirac tomorrow. In addition, my Right Honorable Friend the Foreign Secretary is in regular contact with his opposite numbers from countries on the U.N. Security Council, in the European Union and in the Middle East, and will be in New York for U.N. meetings later this week.

We are entering the final phase of a 12 year history of the disarmament of Iraq. The duty on Saddam to destroy all his weapons of mass destruction was a central part of the ceasefire agreement at the end of the Gulf War in 1991. In a series of 17 resolutions since then the U.N. Security Council has put Saddam under 27 separate and categorical obligations: to give full, final and complete declarations on its weapons programs; to give inspectors unconditional and unrestricted access; to cease the concealment of Iraq's weapons of mass destruction; and to cooperate fully with the inspectors in the disarmament of all its weapons of mass destruction. He has consistently flouted these obligations which is why for years there has been a sanctions regime in place against Iraq, which because of the way Saddam has applied it, has caused wholly unnecessary suffering to the Iraqi people.

Last November the U.N. Security Council concluded unanimously that Iraq was still in material breach of U.N. resolutions. Saddam was given and I quote "a final opportunity" to comply with his disarmament obligations. Resolution 1441 imposed on Saddam a duty to give "a currently accurate, full and complete declaration of all aspects of its programs to develop chemical, biological and nuclear weapons, ballistic missiles, and other delivery systems"; and to provide "immediate, unimpeded, unrestricted and private access" to all people the inspectors wish to interview "in the mode or location" of the inspectors' choice; and also to cooperate actively and fully with all the inspectors' demands.

Failure by Iraq at any time to comply with and cooperate fully in the implementation of the resolution was said in terms to constitute a further material breach.

Mr Speaker, eight weeks have now passed since Saddam was given his final chance. Six hundred weeks have passed since he was given his first chance.

The evidence of cooperation withheld is unmistakable. He has still not answered the questions concerning thousands of missing munitions and tons of chemical and biological agents unaccounted for. Rocket warheads with chemical weapons capacity have been found by the inspectors: they should have been declared. Classified documents of relevance to Iraq's past nuclear program have been discovered in a scientist's private house: they should have been handed over. Of the first eleven documents specifically requested by the inspectors, only three have been produced. Not a single interviewee has come to an appointment with the inspectors without official minders.

As the report we published at the weekend makes clear, and which I have placed in the library of the House, there is a huge infrastructure of deception and concealment designed to prevent the inspectors from doing their job. U.S. Secretary of State Colin Powell will report further to the U.N. on this on Wednesday.

As Dr Blix, the U.N. Chief Inspector reported last week, "Iraq appears not to have come to a genuine acceptance—not even today—of the disarmament which was demanded of it." He said that Iraq's declaration seemed to contain no new evidence; that there are indications that Iraq has weaponised the nerve agent VX, one of the most toxic ever developed; that there are strong indications that Iraq produced more anthrax than it has declared; and that the discovery of chemical rocket warheads could be the tip of an iceberg.

The situation could not therefore be clearer. There is a duty on Saddam to co-operate fully. At present he is not co-operating fully. Failure to do so is a material breach of Resolution 1441. Should Dr Blix continue to report Iraqi non-cooperation, a second Resolution should be passed confirming such a material breach. President Bush and I agreed we should seek maximum support for such a Resolution, provided, as ever, that seeking such a Resolution is a way of resolving the issue not delaying or avoiding dealing with it at all. I continue to believe the U.N. is the right way to proceed. There is an integrity in the process set out in 1441 and we should follow it.

We, of course, discussed the fact that WMD is not the only threat we face and Iraq is not the only country posing a risk in respect of WMD. Over the past few weeks, we have seen powerful evidence of the continuing terrorist threat: the suspected ricin plot in London and Manchester; Al Qaeda experiments in Afghanistan to develop chemical, biological and radiological weapons; the arrests of those linked to Al Qaeda in Spain and France; and further arrests in Italy.

What is more, many of these arrests show the terrorist groups actively seeking to use chemical or biological means to cause as much death and injury and suffering as they can. We know from 11 September that these terrorists have no demands that could ever be negotiated upon, no constraint in terms of finance and numbers to carry out terrorists acts, no compunction in taking human life.

At the same time, we know too that Iraq is not alone in developing WMD; that there are unstable, fiercely repressive states either proliferating or trying to acquire WMD, like North Korea.

I repeat my warning: unless we take a decisive stand now, as an international community, it is only a matter of time before these threats come together. That means pursuing international terrorism across the world in all its forms. It means confronting nations defying the world over WMD.

That is why a signal of weakness over Iraq is not only wrong in its own terms. Show weakness now and no-one will ever believe us when we try to show strength in the future. All our history—especially British history—points to this lesson. No-one wants conflict. Even now, war could be avoided if Saddam did what he is supposed to do. But if having made a demand backed up by a threat of force, we fail to enforce that demand, the result will not be peace or security. It will simply be returning to confront the issue again at a later time with the world less stable, the will of the international community less certain, and those repressive states or terrorist groups who would destroy our way of life, emboldened and undeterred.

Mr Speaker, even now I hope that conflict with Iraq can be avoided. Even now, I hope Saddam can come to his senses, co- operate fully and disarm peacefully, as the U.N. has demanded.

But if he does not, if he rejects the peaceful route, then he must be disarmed by force. If we have to go down this route, we shall do all we can to minimize the risks to the people of Iraq and we give an absolute undertaking to protect Iraq's territorial integrity. Our quarrel has never been with the Iraqi people but with Saddam.

But Saddam's weapons of mass destruction and the threats they pose to the world must be confronted. In doing so, this country, and our armed forces, will be helping the long-term peace and security of Britain and the world.

Op-ed in the *Wall Street Journal* by Secretary of State Powell, February 3, 2003

President Bush warned in his State of the Union address that "the gravest danger facing America and the world is outlaw regimes that seek and possess nuclear, chemical and biological weapons." Exhibit A is Saddam Hussein's Iraq. As the president said, we need only look at how Saddam has terrorized, oppressed, and murdered his own people to understand his methods. And, perhaps most critically, the President confirmed that Iraq has open channels and ties to terrorist organizations, including al Qaeda.

Last November, the U.N. Security Council unanimously passed Resolution 1441, giving Iraq one last chance to disarm peacefully or "face serious consequences." However, instead of disarming, Iraq has responded to Resolution 1441 with empty claims, empty declarations, and empty gestures. Just a week ago, U.N. chief weapons inspector Hans Blix told the Security Council that "Iraq appears not to have come to a genuine acceptance, not even today, of the disarmament that was demanded of it." Indeed, the Iraqi regime is going to great lengths to conceal its weapons of mass destruction. It has removed material from sites it knew were likely to be inspected. The regime also has an active program of coaching scientists before they talk to inspectors and only permits interviews when minders are present. On top of that, thousands of pages of sensitive weapons-related documents have been found in private homes.

Resolution 1441 established two key tests: a full and accurate disclosure of Iraq's weaponry and a requirement to cooperate immediately, unconditionally, and actively with the inspectors. Iraq has failed both tests. Iraq's declaration of its weapons holdings is incomplete and inaccurate and provides no substantive information on the disposition of its weapons of mass destruction. Not surprisingly, the U.N. inspectors have found it woefully deficient. In his report to the Security Council, Mr. Blix noted that Iraq has failed to account for its production of the deadly nerve agent VX, some 6,500 chemical bombs, and about 1,000 metric tons of chemical agent. Iraq also previously acquired the materials to make much more anthrax than it declared.

In their inspections, Mr. Blix's team discovered a number of chemical warheads not previously acknowledged by Iraq. Iraq also continues to acquire banned equipment, with proscribed imports arriving as recently as last month. The inspectors also reported that Iraqi activity is severely hampering their work. For example, Iraq has refused the inspectors' request to use a U-2 reconnaissance aircraft, a critical tool for inspections. Inspectors are accompanied everywhere by Iraqi minders, are slandered by Iraqi officials as spies, and face harassment and disturbing protests that would be unlikely to occur without the encouragement of the authorities.

On Wednesday, I will present to the Security Council U.S. intelligence showing further evidence of Iraq's pattern of deception. Our evidence will reinforce what the inspectors told the Security Council last week—that they are not getting the cooperation they need, that their requests are being blocked, and that their questions are going unanswered. While there will be no "smoking gun," we will provide evidence concerning the weapons programs that Iraq is working so hard to hide. We will, in sum, offer a straightforward, sober and compelling demonstration that Saddam is concealing the evidence of his weapons of mass destruction, while preserving the weapons themselves. The world must now recognize that Iraq has not complied with the will of the international community as expressed in Resolution 1441. Iraq has failed the resolution's two tests—to disclose and to cooperate—in a manner that constitutes a further material breach of the resolution.

In response, the U.S. will begin a new round of full and open consultation with our allies about next steps. Much has been made of the friction between the U.S. and some of its traditional partners over how to proceed with Iraq. We will work to bridge our differences, building on the bedrock of our shared values and long history of acting together to meet common challenges. The fruits of our partnership are evident all around the globe, from Western Europe to Japan, Korea, Bosnia, and Afghanistan.

Together we must face the facts brought to us by the U.N. inspectors and reputable intelligence sources. Iraq continues to conceal deadly weapons and their components, and to use denial, deception and subterfuge in order to retain them. Iraq has ties to and has supported terrorist groups. Iraq has had no compunction about using weapons of mass destruction against its own people and against its neighbors.

President Bush's message has been clear from the beginning. The President eloquently and persuasively set forth the U.S. position at the U.N. on Sept. 12: A peaceful outcome to this situation is possible if Iraq cooperates with the U.N. and disarms. Unfortunately, Saddam seems to be leading his nation down another path. The U.S. seeks Iraq's peaceful disarmament. But we will not shrink from war if that is the only way to rid Iraq of its weapons of mass destruction.

Remarks by French President Chirac and British Prime Minister Blair, February 4, 2003

President Jacques Chirac and Prime Minister Tony Blair delivered their remarks at a press conference after meeting in Le Touquet, France.

President Chirac. Ladies and Gentlemen, as we start this press conference, I would like to say how happy we have been, we the French, to welcome the Prime Minister of Britain. We are here with my government and I would like to thank very warmly, on my behalf and the Prime Minister's behalf, the French authorities, especially the Mayor of Le Touquet. This place is a symbol of our friendship between our two countries.

A word to begin with to stress, as we have had long experience of bilateral meetings both of us, also of multilateral meetings, so I would like to emphasize the very warm character of our meetings, and I have to stress this because some commentators in the media in the cultural world may have raised this point. And I have never met such a warm gathering, there is a very warm feeling coming from our talks, and this is the truth, very simply put.

We have raised a number of matters, first of all the topical international issues, Iraq to begin with. On this our approach is not quite identical, but I must say something to begin with, because I have heard a number of comments, initially among political leaders. We represent two ancient civilizations, two old nations, two old cultures. For centuries now we have been side by side and sometimes we have been fighting each other. But we have forged also links and had interests that were not always the same. There is no surprise in this. And now today in the European context we have to have the will, the determination and the imagination to pare down all our differences and strengthen what unites us. But of course there is no magic bullet and it is natural to see that today we have made some progress, some substantial progress in our cooperation, but unfortunately there are still some differences, but the point is to manage these differences in a friendly way, and not in an aggressive way.

On the matter of Iraq our approach is different, but to start with we have two main beliefs that we share. The main belief is that we have to disarm Iraq, and the second one is that this move, these actions must be pushed within the organization of the United Nations. That is the very essence and on this we completely agree. Starting from this line, we may have a different approach on the Consequences But these differences are minor, much less than what might appear. I am giving my point of view, and the British Prime Minister will give his in a moment, but as I see things today, the essential thing is to leave the inspectors to do their work. We have to take into consideration all the elements that ... them and with the statements that are expected from Colin Powell tomorrow. We shall expect the consequences drawn by Mr Blix and Mr Baradei in the Security Council in a few days and we believe that everything has to be done to give the inspectors all possible resources that they may need in order to come up with the result that we seek, which is to disarm Iraq, and we believe that it is possible to do this by these means.

* * * *

Prime Minister Blair. Thank you. And first of all can I express my warm appreciation to the people of Le Touquet for their kindness in welcoming us here, and thank President Chirac and Prime Minister Raffarin and their colleagues for what has been a summit with a tremendous spirit of cooperation and friendship. And as the President said, of course there are differences on certain issues, but I think what was remarkable was the degree to which we were able to come together around a whole set of common themes and undertakings that I think auger very well for the future.

* * * *

And finally, on the issue of Iraq, of course there are the differences that are familiar to people, but I think it is important to emphasize again the two common points that the President alluded to—support for the notion of disarming Iraq of weapons of mass destruction and the belief that this is best pursued through the United Nations. And as the President indicated, of course we have the presentation that will be made by Colin Powell tomorrow, we have then the report of Dr. Blix, the Chief Inspector, on 14 February and we will make our judgments then.

I want to conclude by saying one word about the entente cordiale. There will be a celebration of this, as you know, next year. There will be of course much that is symbolic in that celebration. But I think what we have achieved today is very clear evidence of substance. And I know of course there will be all sorts of questions that you will pose to us, perhaps to elicit the differences—maybe I do you an injustice. But I think it is just worth emphasizing yet again, not just what we agreed today, but the spirit in which we agreed it, which I welcome very greatly.

Q. Mr. President, one of the great thinkers of our time, Mr. Donald Rumsfeld, stated that France was part of old Europe, in other words a Europe looking back over its shoulder at the past, and we understand your reluctance to support war in the Middle East, therefore might I ask you if you are going to be able to maintain this position after this Franco-British Summit but remain in tune with the majority of public opinion both in France and in Britain rather than towing the Rumsfeld line? And Mr Blair, Nelson Mandela, a gentleman whom you have held in much esteem, has suggested that you are now fulfilling the function of Minister of Foreign Affairs of the United States of America. How do you react to this observation? And if it were to have any accuracy, would it not impede the ambitions of those who wish to see you as the future President of Europe?

President Chirac. On your first question, I would simply say that when there are very important grave issues at stake, it is very important to stand by one's principles, but also to respect other people and their principles. So do not expect me to open heaven knows what Pandora's box or get into an argument with anybody.

Prime Minister Blair. I am very happy being British Prime Minister, thank you.

Q. Mr President, do you think there needs to be a time limit set on U.N. inspections? If not, in a country the size of Iraq with just over 100 inspectors and indifferent cooperation from Saddam Hussein, couldn't the operation just simply go on forever?

President Chirac. Well I note that the inspection system is something that in the past proved to be very effective. I would recall that in the first round of inspections they destroyed more arms, the inspectors did, than had been destroyed during the war of the Gulf war. I just note that point. So the inspectors system is very effective. My second point is that you asked me to judge on whether these present inspectors are effective, well I am in no position to do so. It is for them to tell us whether or not they have the ways and means, or if they need further means to do their job. And it is also for them to tell us what level of cooperation they are getting and what assistance they need. I have full confidence in them in that respect. And I would add that France will approve, without reservation, any request from them for staff or for material support that the inspectors come up with, anything that Mr Blix or Mr Baradei ask for, we will give them unreservedly.

Q. Prime Minister, first of all I would like to ask you, you have often said that you would not want to have to choose between America and Europe. Last week when you signed the letter of the 8, did you choose America over Europe? And Mr President, is

it possible for France to accept or support military intervention in Iraq, and if it is yes, on what conditions?

Prime Minister Blair. Well first of all I think it is important to recognize that every-one actually came together around Resolution 1441 which demands the complete and total disarmament of Iraq of weapons of mass destruction, and I would simply point out that the letter of course was signed by the European leaders. But the common position of Europe, as I said a moment or two ago, was set out on 27 January at the General Affairs Council.

President Chirac. As to our position, I repeat, it is well known to one and all, namely that there is still a lot that can and needs to be done in terms of disarmament by and through peaceful means. Therefore we would only adopt a position after such time as we believe, and when we believe, that nothing further can be achieved there.

* * * *

Q. Wouldn't France's position be stronger if alongside all these diplomatic negotiations France were not actually stepping up its military pressure on Iraq?

President Chirac. Well it would not appear that there is a paucity or dearth of military means or military equipment being built up in the region.

Q. Mr President, the British and the Americans have said that there are only weeks, and not months, for Iraq to cooperate with the weapons inspectors and implied that means that war is weeks, not months away, unless there is a miracle. Would you use France's veto to veto a resolution in those circumstances?

President Chirac. Firstly I feel that war is always the worst possible solution and would add that in that region, above all others, we don't need any more wars. Having said that, I repeat, I feel that we need to wait. We have adopted a strategy of using inspectors. We need to have confidence in the inspectors—I do, I do, not everybody does—and we need to give those inspectors the amount of time they need to carry out the work we have entrusted to them. That is my position. As for the rest, well France will view its responsibilities as it sees fit at the appropriate time and in the light of the circumstances at that time.

Q. President Chirac, you have never specifically ruled out the possibility that in some circumstances at the end of the day France might be willing to join military action against Saddam Hussein. You are saying for the moment that such a decision can be postponed until the inspectors' work has finished, but can you say in what circumstances you would ever join military action? And has today's meeting changed your mind in any little way at all?

President Chirac. I would have no comment to make on this question and you will understand why I say this, as a Permanent Member of the Security Council I am not going to prejudge any possible decision and therefore adopt ahead of time a public position on the matter. So I have no comment to make.

Q. Could the Americans bring pressure to bear on the French and the Russians in the form of economic threats were we not to tow the Bush line, of course vis a vis Iraq?

President Chirac. Look, this is something which seems to be pie in the sky as far as I am concerned. I have never heard of any retaliation of any sort, retaliatory action that might be taken by the Americans. While we may not have a convergence of views with the Americans on this, but nonetheless given the excellent nature of our relations with the Americans there is absolutely no question of any retaliation on the part of the Americans.

Q. Mr President, do you agree with the British and the American governments that Saddam Hussein is already in material breach of the United Nations resolutions? And if you do agree with that, do you accept the consequence that force may have to be used against him?

President Chirac. This is just one more way of asking the same question over and over again, and I really wonder sometimes whether this is a game or that you think I am somebody who understands nothing and you have got to ask the same question in different ways that finally maybe it might get to my brain, but it still doesn't get there I have to tell you. I have told you what I have to say and I have nothing further to add, regardless of how you formulate your questions.

One point in conclusion before I give the final, final word to the Prime Minister. I fully understand that the main problem at the present time is Iraq because it involves war or peace are at stake and these are major issues. And of course I fully understand that that is what is foremost in all your minds, it certainly is foremost in my mind and I am sure in Mr Blair's as well. But I want to highlight the fact that when you look at things with a bit more perspective, when you take account of the past and you look to the future and you look to the way in which we are building Europe, which are huge challenges in front of us and challenges which we are facing progressively, when you look at all of that, when as I say you take a bit of perspective on the issue, we note that that which unites us at the European level, and in particular that which unites the United Kingdom and France, is increasingly important and far more important than anything that divides us, and that is the message I want to highlight here and that is the way forward. Our successors will not be dealing with the same issues as we have to deal with here today, at least I hope they won't have to deal with them, I hope they won't have to face problems of war and peace as we do. On the other hand, they will judge us on whether or not we were capable of making progress towards enhancing understanding and dialogue amongst people, among our peoples, concerted action between us, joint efforts to the benefit of what is the most important of all in the world, namely peace, democracy and development, and that is how we will be judged and that is what we have joined together in tackling and that is at the core of our concerns. And of course around all of that, pulled hither and thither, nevertheless we do feel that little by little we are moving forward in the right direction. From time to time the little destabilisation here or there, a little movement here or there, which is a bit out of step with our general move forward, but these movements are rarer and rarer and we are able to control them and that is where our ambitions lie. We need to manage this through respect for the other partner, respect for areas where we are separated and accentuating those areas where we can unite, for us, the United Kingdom and France and in the context of our ambition for the future of Europe.

This meeting here today from that point of view has in my view been extremely positive and so I am very happy at that and I am grateful to the British Prime Minister and his Ministers and officials for their efforts, my Ministers and my colleagues who have done excellent work, and that which in the historical perspective is important. And I will now give the final word to the Prime Minister.

Prime Minister Blair. And that is that there are far more things that unite us than that divide us. That is all I have to say.

February 5–March 5, 2003
Secretary of State Powell Brings the Case Against Saddam Hussein to the U.N. Security Council

CHRONOLOGY

2003

February 5. At the United Nations, U.S. Secretary of State Colin Powell presents the U.S. government's case with regard to Iraq's programs of weapons of mass destruction (WMD). The presentation includes tape recordings, satellite photographs and other intelligence data, and aims to prove WMD production, evasion of weapons inspections, and a link to Al-Qaida.

February 7. The chief United Nations arms inspector, Hans Blix, says Iraq appears to be making fresh efforts to cooperate with U.N. teams searching for weapons of mass destruction.

February 8. Sections of a "dossier" issued by the U.K. government, which purported to present the latest British intelligence about Iraq, and which had been cited by Tony Blair and Colin Powell as evidence for the need for war, are criticized as having been plagiarized. Reports allege that sections of the report were copied without permission from a number of sources including *Jane's Intelligence Review* and work from a 12-year-old doctoral thesis that had been published in the U.S. journal *Middle East Review of International Affairs*.

February 10. France and Belgium break the NATO procedure of silent approval concerning the timing of protective measures for Turkey in case of a possible war with Iraq. Germany says it supports the veto. The procedure was put into operation on February 6 by NATO Secretary General George Robertson. In response Turkey calls upon Article 4 of the NATO Treaty, which stipulates that member states must deliberate when asked to do so by another member state if it feels threatened.

February 12. An audio tape attributed to Osama bin Laden is released by al-Jazeera television. It recounts the battle of Tora Bora and urges Muslims to fight the United States and to overthrow the Iraqi regime of Saddam Hussein.

February 14. A large demonstration, estimated at 150,000 to 200,000 people, takes place in Melbourne to protest against the Australian government's support for the U.S. policy on Iraq. UNMOVIC chief weapons inspectors Hans Blix and Mohamed ElBaradei present their second report to the United Nations Security Council. They state that the Iraqis had been co-operating well with the inspectors and that no weapons of mass destruction had been found, but that Saddam Hussein's regime had still not accounted for many banned weapons believed to be in his arsenal. Mr. Blix also expresses doubts about some of the conclusions in Secretary of State Colin Powell's Security Council presentation of February 5, and specifically questions the significance of some of the photographic evidence presented by Secretary Powell.

February 15. People around the world demonstrate against the planning of the war against Iraq. In Rome and London crowds number one million. In Berlin half a million people take part in the largest demonstration in decades. Protest marches also take place all over France; in other smaller European cities; in South Africa, Syria, India, Russia, and Canada; and in various cities in the United States.

February 18. Hours before the first ships transporting heavy United States military equipment to Turkey are supposed to reach port, the Turkish government announces that it will withhold approval to dock unless the United States increases a reciprocal $6 billion foreign aid grant to $10 billion. The Bush administration indicates that no substantial changes will be made to the proposed aid package.

February 24. Secretary of State Colin Powell states at a meeting in Beijing that "[i]t is time to take action. The evidence is clear ... We are reaching that point where serious consequences must flow." His speech appears to imply that military action is likely to follow within weeks, based on previous briefings from the Pentagon.

February 25. The United States, Britain and Spain present to the U.N. Security Council a much-anticipated second resolution stating that Iraq "has failed to take the final opportunity" to disarm, but does not include deadlines or an explicit threat of military force. Meanwhile, France, Germany, and Russia offer a counter-proposal calling for peaceful disarmament through further inspections. Both major parties of Kurdistan, an autonomous region in Northern Iraq, vow to fight Turkish troops if they enter Kurdistan to capture Mosul or interfere in Kurdish self-rule. Between them the two parties can mobilize up to 80,000 guerrillas—most likely no match for the modern Turkish army, but a severe blow to the unity of U.S. allies on the Northern front expected in the U.S. plan to invade Iraq.

February 26. Hans Blix states that Iraq still had not made a "fundamental decision" to disarm, despite recent signs of increased cooperation. Specifically, Iraq had refused to destroy its al-Samoud 2 long range missiles—a weapon system that was in violation of the U.N. Security Council's resolutions and the U.S. treaty with Iraq. Also, an R-400 aerial bomb was found that could possibly contain biological agents. Given this find, the U.N. Inspectors requests access to the Al-Aziziyah weapons range to verify that all 155 R-400 bombs can be accounted for and proven destroyed. Blix also expresses skepticism over

Iraq's claims to have destroyed its stockpiles of anthrax and VX nerve agent. Blix says he found it "a bit odd" that Iraq, with "one of the best-organized regimes in the Arab world," would claim to have no records of the destruction of these illegal substances. "I don't see that they have acquired any credibility," Blix states. George Bush commits publicly to a post-invasion democracy in Iraq, saying it will be "an example" to other nations in the region. Tony Blair passes a motion in the British House of Commons supporting a new resolution at the U.N. Security Council. One hundred and twenty U.K. Labor Party MPs dissent and vote against it—double the number who opposed the previous such motion—but the U.K. Conservative Party backs the government's motion. Saddam Hussein, in an interview with Dan Rather, rules out exile as an option.

February 27. A U.N. Security Council meeting on Iraq ends without forming an agreement on a timeline for further weapons inspections or future reports.

February 28. Hans Blix refers to Iraq's stated intention to begin destroying Al Samoud 2 missiles as "a very significant piece of real disarmament." However, White House Press Secretary Ari Fleischer declares that Iraq's commitment to destroy these missiles is a fraud foreseen by President Bush, and indicates that the United States insists on a total and complete disarmament of Iraq. He also repeats that if the United Nations does not act to disarm Baghdad, the United States will lead a coalition of voluntary countries to disarm Saddam Hussein.

March 1. Under U.N. supervision, Iraq begins destroying four of its Al Samoud 2 missiles. The Turkish speaker of Parliament voids the vote accepting U.S. troops involved in the planned invasion of Iraq into Turkey on constitutional grounds: 264 votes for and 250 against accepting 62,000 U.S. military personnel do not constitute the necessary majority under the Turkish constitution, due to 19 abstentions. The United Arab Emirates calls for Iraqi president Saddam Hussein to step down to avoid war. The sentiment is later echoed by Kuwait.

March 2. The country of Bahrain becomes the third Arab country to call for Iraqi president Saddam Hussein to step down. *The Observer* publishes what it claims is a leaked memo dated January 31, 2003, requesting intelligence gathering focused on U.N. Security Council members, with a focus on members from Angola, Cameroon, Chile, Mexico, Guinea, and Pakistan; the purported objective is to determine how the members intend to vote. Iraq destroys six more Al Samoud missiles, bringing the total destroyed to 10 out of an estimated 100 missiles ordered eliminated by the United Nations. The White House continues to dismiss Iraq's actions as "part of its game of deception." Iraq indicates that it may halt destruction of the missiles if the U.S. indicates it will go to war anyway. *The Sun* reports that military action against Iraq could begin as soon as March 13, hours after the U.N. is likely to vote on the proposed second resolution put forth by the United States, Britain, and Spain.

March 3. Turkey indicates that its Parliament will consider a second vote on whether to allow U.S. troops to use Turkish bases for a military attack on Iraq. Iraqi technicians use bulldozers to crush six more of the banned Al-Samoud 2 missiles, bringing to 16 the number destroyed in three days.

March 4. Iraq destroys three more Al Samoud 2 missiles, bringing to 19 the number Baghdad destroys out of the 100 ordered by the U.N. to be eliminated. Iraq also destroys a launcher and five engines in a rush to prove it is disarming before a crucial U.N. report on March 7. U.N. Secretary-General Kofi Annan calls the new actions "a positive development" while the White House remains unconvinced saying that "despite whatever limited head-fakes Iraq has engaged in, they continue to fundamentally not disarm."

March 5. Pope John Paul II calls on Catholics to commemorate Ash Wednesday by fasting and praying for peace. He sends an envoy, Cardinal Pio Laghi, to President Bush, to urge him not to go to war. Laghi tells Bush that the Pope believes that a war would be a "defeat for humanity" and would be neither morally nor legally justified. Two days before his scheduled update to the United Nations on Iraqi cooperation with inspection, Hans Blix credits Iraq with "a great deal more of cooperation now," although still expressing some skepticism as to whether or not the cooperation will continue. Among the examples of cooperation that he cites are Iraq's destruction of Samoud 2 missiles, which he calls "the most spectacular and the most important and tangible." He adds that "here weapons that can be used in war are being destroyed in fairly large quantities." In general, he states, "you have a greater measure of cooperation on interviews in general." These statements help to harden the opposition to the U.S.-led war by several other Security Council members. Secretary of State Colin Powell says that U.S. intelligence indicates that Hussein had ordered the production of more Al Samoud 2 missiles parts and engines. The Iraqi government does not deny the claim, simply reiterating their view that the missiles are legal. He also points out that Iraq had delivered "some documents that have not been found before." Iraq destroys nine more Al Samoud 2 missiles, bringing to 28 the total number of missiles scrapped.

Sources: Chronology entries are drawn from www.abc.com, www.bbc.com, www.nytimes.com, www.reuters.com, www.washingtonpost.com, www.wikipedia.com, and staff research.

Documents

Excerpts from United Nations Security Council Ministerial Meeting on Iraq, February 5, 2003

United States Secretary of State Colin Powell. Mr. President and Mr. Secretary General, distinguished colleagues, I would like to begin by expressing thanks for the special effort that each of you made to be here today. This is an important day for us all as we review the situation with respect to Iraq and its disarmament obligations under U.N. Security Council Resolution 1441.

Last November 8, this Council passed Resolution 1441 by a unanimous vote. The purpose of that resolution was to disarm Iraq of its weapons of mass destruction. Iraq had already been found guilty of material breach of its obligations stretching back over 16 previous resolutions and 12 years.

Resolution 1441 was not dealing with an innocent party, but a regime this Council has repeatedly convicted over the years.

Resolution 1441 gave Iraq one last chance, one last chance to come into compliance or to face serious consequences. No Council member present and voting on that day had any illusions about the nature and intent of the resolution or what serious consequences meant if Iraq did not comply.

And to assist in its disarmament, we called on Iraq to cooperate with returning inspectors from UNMOVIC and IAEA. We laid down tough standards for Iraq to meet to allow the inspectors to do their job.

This Council placed the burden on Iraq to comply and disarm, and not on the inspectors to find that which Iraq has gone out of its way to conceal for so long. Inspectors are inspectors; they are not detectives.

I asked for this session today for two purposes. First, to support the core assessments made by Dr. Blix and Dr. ElBaradei. As Dr. Blix reported to this Council on January 27, "Iraq appears not to have come to a genuine acceptance, not even today, of the disarmament which was demanded of it." And as Dr. ElBaradei reported, Iraq's declaration of December 7 "did not provide any new information relevant to certain questions that have been outstanding since 1998."

My second purpose today is to provide you with additional information, to share with you what the United States knows about Iraq's weapons of mass destruction, as well as Iraq's involvement in terrorism, which is also the subject of Resolution 1441 and other earlier resolutions.

I might add at this point that we are providing all relevant information we can to the inspection teams for them to do their work.

The material I will present to you comes from a variety of sources. Some are U.S. sources and some are those of other countries. Some of the sources are technical, such as intercepted telephone conversations and photos taken by satellites. Other sources are people who have risked their lives to let the world know what Saddam Hussein is really up to.

I cannot tell you everything that we know, but what I can share with you, when combined with what all of us have learned over the years, is deeply troubling. What you will see is an accumulation of facts and disturbing patterns of behavior. The facts and Iraqis' behavior, Iraq's behavior, demonstrate that Saddam Hussein and his regime have made no effort, no effort, to disarm, as required by the international community.

Indeed, the facts and Iraq's behavior show that Saddam Hussein and his regime are concealing their efforts to produce more weapons of mass destruction.

Let me begin by playing a tape for you. What you're about to hear is a conversation that my government monitored. It takes place on November 26th of last year, on the day before United Nations teams resumed inspections in Iraq. The conversation involves two senior officers, a colonel and a brigadier general from Iraq's elite military unit, the Republican Guard.

[*The tape is played.*]

Let me pause and review some of the key elements of this conversation that you just heard between these two officers.

First, they acknowledge that our colleague, Mohammed ElBaradei is coming, and they know what he's coming for and they know he's coming the next day. He's coming to look for things that are prohibited. He is expecting these gentlemen to cooperate with him and not hide things.

But they're worried. We have this modified vehicle. What do we say if one of them sees it? What is their concern? Their concern is that it's something they should not have, something that should not be seen.

The general was incredulous: "You didn't get it modified. You don't have one of those, do you?"

"I have one."

"Which? From where?"

"From the workshop. From the Al-Kindi Company."

"What?"

"From Al-Kindi."

"I'll come to see you in the morning. I'm worried you all have something left."

"We evacuated everything. We don't have anything left."

Note what he says: "We evacuated everything." We didn't destroy it. We didn't line it up for inspection. We didn't turn it into the inspectors. We evacuated it to make sure it was not around when the inspectors showed up. "I will come to you tomorrow."

The Al-Kindi Company. This is a company that is well known to have been involved in prohibited weapons systems activity.

Let me play another tape for you. As you will recall, the inspectors found 12 empty chemical warheads on January 16th. On January 20th, four days later, Iraq promised the inspectors it would search for more. You will now hear an officer from Republican Guard headquarters issuing an instruction to an officer in the field. Their conversation took place just last week, on January 30.

[*The tape was played.*]

Let me pause again and review the elements of this message.

"They are inspecting the ammunition you have, yes?"

"Yes. For the possibility there are forbidden ammo."

"For the possibility there is, by chance, forbidden ammo?"

"Yes."

"And we sent you a message yesterday to clean out all the areas, the scrap areas, the abandoned areas. Make sure there is nothing there. Remember the first message: evacuate it."

This is all part of a system of hiding things and moving things out of the way and making sure they have left nothing behind.

You go a little further into this message and you see the specific instructions from headquarters: "After you have carried out what is contained in this message, destroy the message because I don't want anyone to see this message."

"Okay."

"Okay."

Why? Why? This message would have verified to the inspectors that they have been trying to turn over things. They were looking for things, but they don't want that message seen because they were trying to clean up the area, to leave no evidence behind of the presence of weapons of mass destruction. And they can claim that nothing was there and the inspectors can look all they want and they will find nothing.

This effort to hide things from the inspectors is not one or two isolated events. Quite the contrary, this is part and parcel of a policy of evasion and deception that goes back 12 years, a policy set at the highest levels of the Iraqi regime.

We know that Saddam Hussein has what is called "a Higher Committee for Monitoring the Inspection Teams." Think about that. Iraq has a high-level committee to monitor the inspectors who were sent in to monitor Iraq's disarmament—not to cooperate with them, not to assist them, but to spy on them and keep them from doing their jobs.

The committee reports directly to Saddam Hussein. It is headed by Iraq's Vice President, Taha Yasin Ramadan. Its members include Saddam Hussein's son, Qusay.

This committee also includes Lieutenant General Amir al-Sa'di, an advisor to Saddam. In case that name isn't immediately familiar to you, General Sa'di has been the Iraqi regime's primary point of contact for Dr. Blix and Dr. ElBaradei. It was General Sa'di who last fall publicly pledged that Iraq was prepared to cooperate unconditionally with inspectors. Quite the contrary, Sa'di's job is not to cooperate; it is to deceive, not to disarm, but to undermine the inspectors; not to support them, but to frustrate them and to make sure they learn nothing.

We have learned a lot about the work of this special committee. We learned that just prior to the return of inspectors last November, the regime had decided to resume what we heard called "the old game of cat-and-mouse."

For example, let me focus on the now famous declaration that Iraq submitted to this Council on December 7th. Iraq never had any intention of complying with this Council's mandate. Instead, Iraq planned to use the declaration to overwhelm us and to overwhelm the inspectors with useless information about Iraq's permitted weapons so that we would not have time to pursue Iraq's prohibited weapons. Iraq's goal was to give us in this room, to give those of us on this Council, the false impression that the inspection process was working.

You saw the result. Dr. Blix pronounced the 12,200-page declaration "rich in volume" but "poor in information and practically devoid of new evidence." Could any member of this Council honestly rise in defense of this false declaration?

Everything we have seen and heard indicates that instead of cooperating actively with the inspectors to ensure the success of their mission, Saddam Hussein and his regime are busy doing all they possibly can to ensure that inspectors succeed in finding absolutely nothing.

My colleagues, every statement I make today is backed up by sources, solid sources. These are not assertions. What we are giving you are facts and conclusions based on solid intelligence. I will cite some examples, and these are from human sources.

Orders were issued to Iraq's security organizations, as well as to Saddam Hussein's own office, to hide all correspondence with the Organization of Military Industrialization. This is the organization that oversees Iraq's weapons of mass destruction activities. Make sure there are no documents left which would connect you to the OMI.

We know that Saddam's son, Qusay, ordered the removal of all prohibited weapons from Saddam's numerous palace complexes. We know that Iraqi government officials, members of the ruling Ba'ath Party and scientists have hidden prohibited items in their homes. Other key files from military and scientific establishments have been placed in cars that are being driven around the countryside by Iraqi intelligence agents to avoid detection.

Thanks to intelligence they were provided, the inspectors recently found dramatic confirmation of these reports. When they searched the homes of an Iraqi nuclear scientist, they uncovered roughly 2,000 pages of documents. You see them here being brought out of the home and placed in U.N. hands. Some of the material is classified and related to Iraq's nuclear program.

Tell me, answer me: Are the inspectors to search the house of every government official, every Ba'ath Party member and every scientist in the country to find the truth, to get the information they need to satisfy the demands of our Council?

Our sources tell us that in some cases the hard drives of computers at Iraqi weapons facilities were replaced. Who took the hard drives? Where did they go? What is being hidden? Why?

There is only one answer to the why: to deceive, to hide, to keep from the inspectors.

Numerous human sources tell us that the Iraqis are moving not just documents and hard drives, but weapons of mass destruction, to keep them from being found by inspectors. While we were here in this Council chamber debating Resolution 1441 last fall, we know, we know from sources that a missile brigade outside Baghdad was dispersing rocket launchers and warheads containing biological warfare agent to various locations, distributing them to various locations in western Iraq.

Most of the launchers and warheads had been hidden in large groves of palm trees and were to be moved every one to four weeks to escape detection.

We also have satellite photos that indicate that banned materials have recently been moved from a number of Iraqi weapons of mass destruction facilities.

Let me say a word about satellite images before I show a couple. The photos that I am about to show you are sometimes hard for the average person to interpret, hard for me. The painstaking work of photo analysis takes experts with years and years of experience, poring for hours and hours over light tables. But as I show you these images, I will try to capture and explain what they mean, what they indicate, to our imagery specialists.

Let's look at one. This one is about a weapons munition facility, a facility that holds ammunition at a place called Taji. This is one of about 65 such facilities in Iraq. We know that this one has housed chemical munitions. In fact, this is where the Iraqis recently came up with the additional four chemical weapons shells.

Here you see 15 munitions bunkers in yellow and red outlines. The four that are in red squares represent active chemical munitions bunkers.

How do I know that? How can I say that? Let me give you a closer look. Look at the image on the left. On the left is a close-up of one of the four chemical bunkers. The two arrows indicate the presence of sure signs that the bunkers are storing chemical munitions. The arrow at the top that says "security" points to a facility that is a signature item for this kind of bunker. Inside that facility are special guards and special equipment to monitor any leakage that might come out of the bunker. The truck you also see is a signature item. It's a decontamination vehicle in case something goes wrong. This is characteristic of those four bunkers. The special security facility and the decontamination vehicle will be in the area, if not at any one of them or one of the other, it is moving around those four and it moves as needed to move as people are working in the different bunkers.

Now look at the picture on the right. You are now looking at two of those sanitized bunkers. The signature vehicles are gone, the tents are gone. It's been cleaned up. And it was done on the 22nd of December as the U.N. inspection team is arriving, and you can see the inspection vehicles arriving in the lower portion of the picture on the right.

The bunkers are clean when the inspectors get there. They found nothing.

This sequence of events raises the worrisome suspicion that Iraq had been tipped off to the forthcoming inspections at Taji. As it did throughout the 1990s, we know that Iraq today is actively using its considerable intelligence capabilities to hide its illicit activities. From our sources, we know that inspectors are under constant surveillance by an army of Iraqi intelligence operatives. Iraq is relentlessly attempting to tap all of their communications, both voice and electronics. I would call my colleagues' attention to the fine paper that the United Kingdom distributed yesterday which describes in exquisite detail Iraqi deception activities.

In this next example, you will see the type of concealment activity Iraq has undertaken in response to the resumption of inspections. Indeed, in November of 2002, just when the inspections were about to resume, this type of activity spiked. Here are three examples

At this ballistic missile site on November 10th, we saw a cargo truck preparing to move ballistic missile components.

At this biological weapons-related facility on November 25th, just two days before inspections resumed, this truck caravan appeared—something we almost never see at this facility and we monitor it carefully and regularly.

At this ballistic missile facility, again, two days before inspections began, five large cargo trucks appeared, along with a truck-mounted crane, to move missiles.

We saw this kind of housecleaning at close to 30 sites. Days after this activity, the vehicles and the equipment that I've just highlighted disappear and the site returns to patterns of normalcy. We don't know precisely what Iraq was moving, but the inspectors already knew about these sites so Iraq knew that they would be coming.

We must ask ourselves: Why would Iraq suddenly move equipment of this nature before inspections if they were anxious to demonstrate what they had or did not have?

Remember the first intercept in which two Iraqis talked about the need to hide a modified vehicle from the inspectors. Where did Iraq take all of this equipment? Why wasn't it presented to the inspectors?

Iraq also has refused to permit any U-2 reconnaissance flights that would give the inspectors a better sense of what's being moved before, during and after inspections. This refusal to allow this kind of reconnaissance is in direct, specific violation of operative paragraph seven of our Resolution 1441.

Saddam Hussein and his regime are not just trying to conceal weapons; they are also trying to hide people. You know the basic facts. Iraq has not complied with its obligation to allow immediate, unimpeded, unrestricted and private access to all officials and other persons, as required by Resolution 1441. The regime only allows interviews with inspectors in the presence of an Iraqi official, a minder. The official Iraqi organization charged with facilitating inspections announced publicly and announced ominously, that, "Nobody is ready" to leave Iraq to be interviewed.

Iraqi Vice President Ramadan accused the inspectors of conducting espionage, a veiled threat that anyone cooperating with U.N. inspectors was committing treason.

Iraq did not meet its obligations under 1441 to provide a comprehensive list of scientists associated with its weapons of mass destruction programs. Iraq's list was out of date and contained only about 500 names despite the fact that UNSCOM had earlier put together a list of about 3,500 names.

Let me just tell you what a number of human sources have told us. Saddam Hussein has directly participated in the effort to prevent interviews. In early December, Saddam Hussein had all Iraqi scientists warned of the serious consequences that they and their families would face if they revealed any sensitive information to the inspectors. They were forced to sign documents acknowledging that divulging information is punishable by death.

Saddam Hussein also said that scientists should be told not to agree to leave Iraq; anyone who agreed to be interviewed outside Iraq would be treated as a spy. This violates 1441.

In mid-November, just before the inspectors returned, Iraqi experts were ordered to report to the headquarters of the Special Security Organization to receive counter-intelligence training. The training focused on evasion methods, interrogation resistance techniques, and how to mislead inspectors.

Ladies and gentlemen, these are not assertions. These are facts corroborated by many sources, some of them sources of the intelligence services of other countries.

For example, in mid-December, weapons experts at one facility were replaced by Iraqi intelligence agents who were to deceive inspectors about the work that was being done there. On orders from Saddam Hussein, Iraqi officials issued a false death certificate for one scientist and he was sent into hiding.

In the middle of January, experts at one facility that was related to weapons of mass destruction, those experts had been ordered to stay home from work to avoid the inspectors. Workers from other Iraqi military facilities not engaged in illicit weapons projects were to replace the workers who had been sent home. A dozen experts have been placed under house arrest—not in their own houses, but as a group at one of Saddam Hussein's guest houses.

It goes on and on and on. As the examples I have just presented show, the information and intelligence we have gathered point to an active and systematic effort on the part of the Iraqi regime to keep key materials and people from the inspectors, in direct violation of Resolution 1441.

The pattern is not just one of reluctant cooperation, nor is it merely a lack of cooperation. What we see is a deliberate campaign to prevent any meaningful inspection work.

My colleagues, Operative Paragraph 4 of U.N. Resolution 1441, which we lingered over so long last fall, clearly states that false statements and omissions in the declaration and a failure by Iraq at any time to comply with and cooperate fully in the implementation of this resolution shall constitute—the facts speak for themselves—shall constitute a further material breach of its obligation.

We wrote it this way to give Iraq an early test, to give Iraq an early test. Would they give an honest declaration and would they, early on, indicate a willingness to cooperate with the inspectors? It was designed to be an early test. They failed that test.

By this standard, the standard of this Operative Paragraph, I believe that Iraq is now in further material breach of its obligations. I believe this conclusion is irrefutable and undeniable.

Iraq has now placed itself in danger of the serious consequences called for in U.N. Resolution 1441. And this body places itself in danger of irrelevance if it allows Iraq to continue to defy its will without responding effectively and immediately.

This issue before us is not how much time we are willing to give the inspectors to be frustrated by Iraqi obstruction. But how much longer are we willing to put up with Iraq's non-compliance before we, as a Council, we as the United Nations say, "Enough. Enough."

The gravity of this moment is matched by the gravity of the threat that Iraq's weapons of mass destruction pose to the world. Let me now turn to those deadly weapons programs and describe why they are real and present dangers to the region and to the world.

First, biological weapons. We have talked frequently here about biological weapons. By way of introduction and history, I think there are just three quick points I need to make. First, you will recall that it took UNSCOM four long and frustrating years to pry, to pry an admission out of Iraq that it had biological weapons. Second, when Iraq finally admitted having these weapons in 1995, the quantities were vast. Less than a teaspoon of dry anthrax, a little bit—about this amount. This is just about the amount of a teaspoon. Less than a teaspoonful of dry anthrax in an envelope shut down the United States Senate in the fall of 2001.

This forced several hundred people to undergo emergency medical treatment and killed two postal workers just from an amount, just about this quantity that was inside of an envelope.

Iraq declared 8500 liters of anthrax. But UNSCOM estimates that Saddam Hussein could have produced 25,000 liters. If concentrated into this dry form, this amount would be enough to fill tens upon tens upon tens of thousands of teaspoons. And Saddam Hussein has not verifiably accounted for even one teaspoonful of this deadly material. And that is my third point. And it is key. The Iraqis have never accounted for all of the biological weapons they admitted they had and we know they had.

They have never accounted for all the organic material used to make them. And they have not accounted for many of the weapons filled with these agents such as their R-400 bombs. This is evidence, not conjecture. This is true. This is all well documented.

Dr. Blix told this Council that Iraq has provided little evidence to verify anthrax production and no convincing evidence of its destruction. It should come as no shock then that since Saddam Hussein forced out the last inspectors in 1998, we have amassed much intelligence indicating that Iraq is continuing to make these weapons.

One of the most worrisome things that emerges from the thick intelligence file we have on Iraq's biological weapons is the existence of mobile production facilities used to make biological agents.

Let me take you inside that intelligence file and share with you what we know from eyewitness accounts. We have first-hand descriptions of biological weapons factories on wheels and on rails.

The trucks and train cars are easily moved and are designed to evade detection by inspectors. In a matter of months, they can produce a quantity of biological poison equal to the entire amount that Iraq claimed to have produced in the years prior to the Gulf War.

Although Iraq's mobile production program began in the mid- 1990s, U.N. inspectors at the time only had vague hints of such programs. Confirmation came later, in the year 2000. The source was an eyewitness, an Iraqi chemical engineer who supervised one of these facilities. He actually was present during biological agent production runs. He was also at the site when an accident occurred in 1998. 12 technicians died from exposure to biological agents.

He reported that when UNSCOM was in country and inspecting, the biological weapons agent production always began on Thursdays at midnight, because Iraq thought UNSCOM would not inspect on the Muslim holy day, Thursday night through Friday.

He added that this was important because the units could not be broken down in the middle of a production run, which had to be completed by Friday evening before the inspectors might arrive again.

This defector is currently hiding in another country with the certain knowledge that Saddam Hussein will kill him if he finds him. His eyewitness account of these mobile production facilities has been corroborated by other sources.

A second source. An Iraqi civil engineer in a position to know the details of the program confirmed the existence of transportable facilities moving on trailers.

A third source, also in a position to know, reported in summer, 2002, that Iraq had manufactured mobile production systems mounted on road-trailer units and on rail cars.

Finally, a fourth source. An Iraqi major who defected confirmed that Iraq has mobile biological research laboratories in addition to the production facilities I mentioned earlier.

We have diagrammed what our sources reported about these mobile facilities. Here you see both truck and rail-car mounted mobile factories. The description our sources gave us of the technical features required by such facilities is highly detailed and extremely accurate.

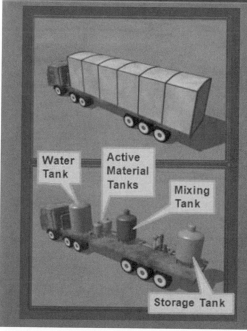
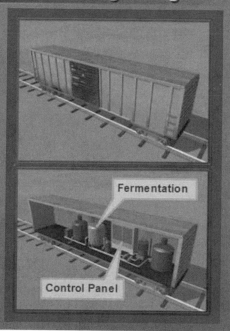

Presentation by Secretary of State Colin Powel ll to the United Nations Security
Council Ministerial Meeting on Iraq, February 5, 2003, slides 19 and 20.

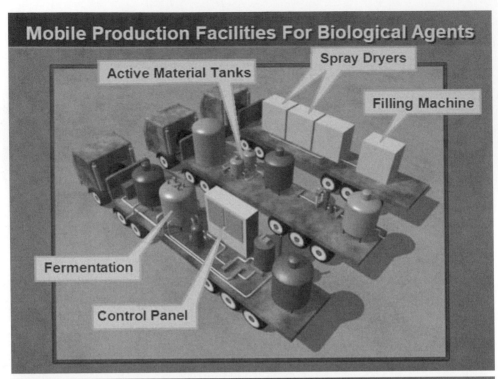

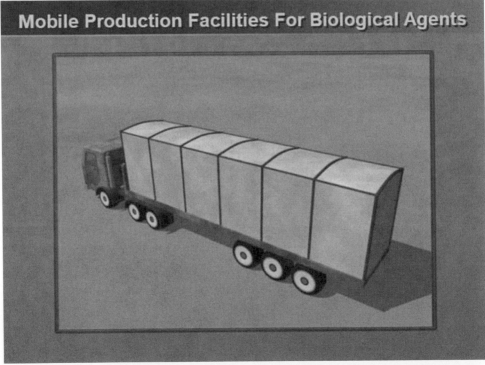

Presentation by Secretary of State Colin Powel ll to the United Nations Security Council Ministerial Meeting on Iraq, February 5, 2003, slides 21 and 22.

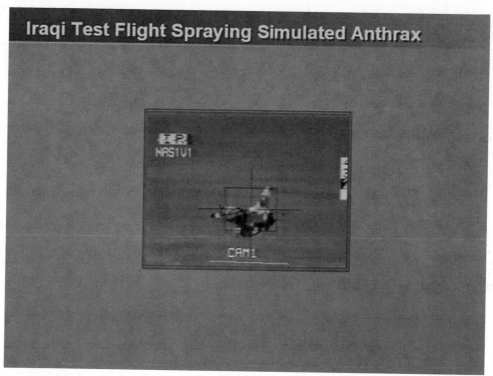

Iraqi Test Flight Spraying Simulated Anthrax

Presentation by Secretary of State Colin Powel ll to the United Nations Security
Council Ministerial Meeting on Iraq, February 5, 2003, slide 23.

As these drawings, based on their description show, we know what the fermentors
look like. We know what the tanks, pumps, compressors and other parts look like. We
know how they fit together, we know how they work, and we know a great deal about
the platforms on which they are mounted.

As shown in this diagram, these factories can be concealed easily—either by moving ordinary looking trucks and rail-cars along Iraq's thousands of miles of highway
or track or by parking them in a garage or a warehouse or somewhere in Iraq's extensive system of underground tunnels and bunkers.

We know that Iraq has at least seven of these mobile, biological agent factories. The
truck-mounted ones have at least two or three trucks each. That means that the mobile
production facilities are very few—perhaps 18 trucks that we know of. There may be
more. But perhaps 18 that we know of. Just imagine trying to find 18 trucks among
the thousands and thousands of trucks that travel the roads of Iraq every single day.

It took the inspectors four years to find out that Iraq was making biological agents.
How long do you think it will take the inspectors to find even one of these 18 trucks
without Iraq coming forward as they are supposed to with the information about
these kinds of capabilities.

Ladies and gentlemen, these are sophisticated facilities. For example, they can produce anthrax and botulinum toxin. In fact, they can produce enough dry, biological
agent in a single month to kill thousands upon thousands of people. A dry agent of
this type is the most lethal form for human beings.

Presentation by Secretary of State Colin Powel ll to the United Nations Security Council Ministerial Meeting on Iraq, February 5, 2003, slides 24 and 25.

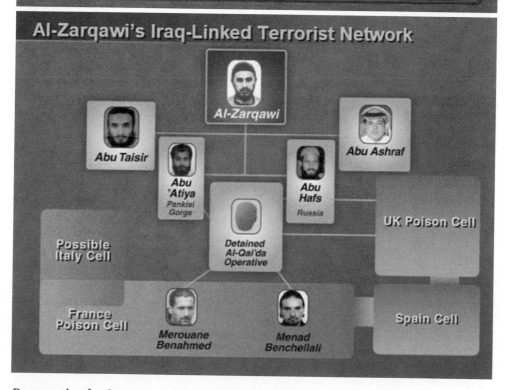

Presentation by Secretary of State Colin Powell ll to the United Nations Security Council Ministerial Meeting on Iraq, February 5, 2003, slide 26 and 40.

By 1998, U.N. experts agreed that the Iraqis had perfected drying techniques for their biological weapons programs. Now Iraq has incorporated this drying expertise into these mobile production facilities.

We know from Iraq's past admissions that it has successfully weaponized not only anthrax, but also other biological agents including botulinum toxin, aflatoxin and ricin. But Iraq's research efforts did not stop there.

Saddam Hussein has investigated dozens of biological agents causing diseases such as gas gangrene, plague, typhus, tetanus, cholera, camelpox, and hemorrhagic fever. And he also has the wherewithal to develop smallpox.

The Iraqi regime has also developed ways to disperse lethal biological agents widely, indiscriminately into the water supply, into the air. For example, Iraq had a program to modify aerial fuel tanks for Mirage jets. This video of an Iraqi test flight obtained by UNSCOM some years ago shows an Iraqi F-1 Mirage jet aircraft. Note the spray coming from beneath the Mirage. That is 2,000 liters of simulated anthrax that a jet is spraying. (VIDEO)

In 1995, an Iraqi military officer, Mujahid Saleh Abdul Latif told inspectors that Iraq intended the spray tanks to be mounted onto a MiG-21 that had been converted into an unmanned aerial vehicle, or UAV. UAVs outfitted with spray tanks constitute an ideal method for launching a terrorist attack using biological weapons.

Iraq admitted to producing four spray tanks, but to this day, it has provided no credible evidence that they were destroyed, evidence that was required by the international community.

There can be no doubt that Saddam Hussein has biological weapons and the capability to rapidly produce more, many more. And he has the ability to dispense these lethal poisons and diseases in ways that can cause massive death and destruction.

If biological weapons seem too terrible to contemplate, chemical weapons are equally chilling. UNMOVIC already laid out much of this and it is documented for all of us to read in UNSCOM's 1999 report on the subject. Let me set the stage with three key points that all of us need to keep in mind. First, Saddam Hussein has used these horrific weapons on another country and on his own people. In fact, in the history of chemical warfare, no country has had more battlefield experience with chemical weapons since World War I than Saddam Hussein's Iraq.

Second, as with biological weapons, Saddam Hussein has never accounted for vast amounts of chemical weaponry: 550 artillery shells with mustard, 30,000 empty munitions and enough precursors to increase his stockpile to as much as 500 tons of chemical agents.

If we consider just one category of missing weaponry, 6500 bombs from the Iran-Iraq War, UNMOVIC says the amount of chemical agent in them would be on the order of a thousand tons.

These quantities of chemical weapons are now unaccounted for. Dr. Blix has quipped that, "Mustard gas is not marmalade. You are supposed to know what you did with it." We believe Saddam Hussein knows what he did with it and he has not come clean with the international community.

We have evidence these weapons existed. What we don't have is evidence from Iraq that they have been destroyed or where they are. That is what we are still waiting for.

Third point, Iraq's record on chemical weapons is replete with lies. It took years for

Iraq to finally admit that it had produced four tons of the deadly nerve agent VX. A single drop of VX on the skin will kill in minutes. Four tons. The admission only came out after inspectors collected documentation as a result of the defection of Hussein Kamel, Saddam Hussein's late son-in-law.

UNSCOM also gained forensic evidence that Iraq had produced VX and put it into weapons for delivery, yet to this day Iraq denies it had ever weaponized VX. And on January 27, UNMOVIC told this Council that it has information that conflicts with the Iraqi account of its VX program.

We know that Iraq has embedded key portions of its illicit chemical weapons infra-structure within its legitimate civilian industry. To all outward appearances, even to experts, the infrastructure looks like an ordinary civilian operation. Illicit and legiti-mate production can go on simultaneously or on a dime. This dual-use infrastructure can turn from clandestine to commercial and then back again.

These inspections would be unlikely, any inspections at such facilities, would be unlikely to turn up anything prohibited, especially if there is any warning that the inspections are coming. Call it ingenious or evil genius, but the Iraqis deliberately designed their chemical weapons programs to be inspected. It is infrastructure with a built in alibi.

Under the guise of dual-use infrastructure, Iraq has undertaken an effort to recon-stitute facilities that were closely associated with its past program to develop and pro-duce chemical weapons. For example, Iraq has rebuilt key portions of the Tareq State Establishment. Tareq includes facilities designed specifically for Iraq's chemical weapons program and employs key figures from past programs.

That's the production end of Saddam's chemical weapons business. What about the delivery end? I'm going to show you a small part of a chemical complex called "Al Musayyib", a site that Iraq has used for at least three years to transship chemical weapons from production facilities out to the field. In May 2002, our satellites pho-tographed the unusual activity in this picture.

Here we see cargo vehicles are again at this transshipment point, and we can see that they are accompanied by a decontamination vehicle associated with biological or chemical weapons activity. What makes this picture significant is that we have a human source who has corroborated that movement of chemical weapons occurred at this site at that time. So it's not just the photo and it's not an individual seeing the photo. It's the photo and then the knowledge of an individual being brought together to make the case.

This photograph of the site taken two months later, in July, shows not only the pre-vious site which is the figure in the middle at the top with the bulldozer sign near it, it shows that this previous site, as well as all of the other sites around the site have been fully bulldozed and graded. The topsoil has been removed. The Iraqis literally removed the crust of the earth from large portions of this site in order to conceal chemical weapons evidence that would be there from years of chemical weapons activity.

To support its deadly biological and chemical weapons programs, Iraq procures needed items from around the world using an extensive clandestine network. What we know comes largely from intercepted communications and human sources who are in a position to know the facts.

Iraq's procurement efforts include: equipment that can filter and separate microorganisms and toxins involved in biological weapons; equipment that can be used to concentrate the agent; growth media that can be used to continue producing anthrax and botulinum toxin; sterilization equipment for laboratories; glass- lined reactors and specialty pumps that can handle corrosive chemical weapons agents and precursors; large amounts of thionyl chloride, a precursor for nerve and blister agents; and other chemicals such as sodium sulfide, an important mustard agent precursor.

Now, of course, Iraq will argue that these items can also be used for legitimate purposes. But if that is true, why do we have to learn about them by intercepting communications and risking the lives of human agents?

With Iraq's well-documented history on biological and chemical weapons, why should any of us give Iraq the benefit of the doubt? I don't. And I don't think you will either after you hear this next intercept.

Just a few weeks ago we intercepted communications between two commanders in Iraq's Second Republican Guard Corps. One commander is going to be giving an instruction to the other. You will hear as this unfolds that what he wants to communicate to the other guy, he wants to make sure the other guy hears clearly to the point of repeating it so that it gets written down and completely understood. Listen.

[*Transmission.*]

Let's review a few selected items of this conversation. Two officers talking to each other on the radio want to make sure that nothing is misunderstood. "Remove." "Remove." "The expression." "The expression." "The expression. I got it." "Nerve agents." "Nerve agents." "Wherever it comes up." "Got it, wherever it comes up." "In the wireless instructions." "In the instructions." "Correction, no, in the wireless instructions." "Wireless, I got it."

Why does he repeat it that way? Why is he so forceful in making sure this is understood? And why did he focus on wireless instructions? Because the senior officer is concerned that somebody might be listening. Well, somebody was.

"Nerve agents." "Stop talking about it." "They are listening to us" "Don't give any evidence that we have these horrible agents." But we know that they do and this kind of conversation confirms it.

Our conservative estimate is that Iraq today has a stockpile of between 100 and 500 tons of chemical weapons agent. That is enough agent to fill 16,000 battlefield rockets. Even the low end of 100 tons of agent would enable Saddam Hussein to cause mass casualties across more than 100 square miles of territory, an area nearly five times the size of Manhattan.

Let me remind you that—of the 122 mm chemical warheads that the U.N. inspectors found recently. This discovery could very well be, as has been noted, the tip of a submerged iceberg.

The question before us all, my friends, is when will we see the rest of the submerged iceberg?

[*Video.*]

Saddam Hussein has chemical weapons. Saddam Hussein has used such weapons. And Saddam Hussein has no compunction about using them again—against his neighbors and against his own people. And we have sources who tell us that he recently has authorized his field commanders to use them. He wouldn't be passing out the orders if he didn't have the weapons or the intent to use them.

We also have sources who tell us that since the 1980s, Saddam's regime has been experimenting on human beings to perfect its biological or chemical weapons.

A source said that 1,600 death-row prisoners were transferred in 1995 to a special unit for such experiments. An eyewitness saw prisoners tied down to beds, experiments conducted on them, blood oozing around the victims' mouths, and autopsies performed to confirm the effects on the prisoners.

Saddam Hussein's humanity—inhumanity has no limits.

Let me turn now to nuclear weapons. We have no indication that Saddam Hussein has ever abandoned his nuclear weapons program. On the contrary, we have more than a decade of proof that he remains determined to acquire nuclear weapons.

To fully appreciate the challenge that we face today, remember that in 1991 the inspectors searched Iraq's primary nuclear weapons facilities for the first time, and they found nothing to conclude that Iraq had a nuclear weapons program. But, based on defector information, in May of 1991, Saddam Hussein's lie was exposed. In truth, Saddam Hussein had a massive clandestine nuclear weapons program that covered several different techniques to enrich uranium, including electromagnetic isotope separation, gas centrifuge and gas diffusion.

We estimate that this illicit program cost the Iraqis several billion dollars. Nonetheless, Iraq continued to tell the IAEA that it had no nuclear weapons program. If Saddam had not been stopped, Iraq could have produced a nuclear bomb by 1993, years earlier than most worst case assessments that had been made before the war.

In 1995, as a result of another defector, we find out that, after his invasion of Kuwait, Saddam Hussein had initiated a crash program to build a crude nuclear weapon, in violation of Iraq's U.N. obligations. Saddam Hussein already possesses two out of the three key components needed to build a nuclear bomb. He has a cadre of nuclear scientists with the expertise and he has a bomb design.

Since 1998, his efforts to reconstitute his nuclear program have been focused on acquiring the third and last component: sufficient fissile material to produce a nuclear explosion. To make the fissile material, he needs to develop an ability to enrich uranium. Saddam Hussein is determined to get his hands on a nuclear bomb.

He is so determined that has made repeated covert attempts to acquire high-specification aluminum tubes from 11 different countries, even after inspections resumed. These tubes are controlled by the Nuclear Suppliers Group precisely because they can be used as centrifuges for enriching uranium.

By now, just about everyone has heard of these tubes and we all know that there are differences of opinion. There is controversy about what these tubes are for. Most U.S. experts think they are intended to serve as rotors in centrifuges used to enrich uranium. Other experts, and the Iraqis themselves, argue that they are really to produce the rocket bodies for a conventional weapon, a multiple rocket launcher.

Let me tell you what is not controversial about these tubes. First, all the experts who have analyzed the tubes in our possession agree that they can be adapted for centrifuge use.

Second, Iraq had no business buying them for any purpose. They are banned for Iraq.

I am no expert on centrifuge tubes, but this is an old army trooper. I can tell you a couple things.

First, it strikes me as quite odd that these tubes are manufactured to a tolerance that far exceeds U.S. requirements for comparable rockets. Maybe Iraqis just manufacture their conventional weapons to a higher standard than we do, but I don't think so.

Second, we actually have examined tubes from several different batches that were seized clandestinely before they reached Baghdad. What we notice in these different batches is a progression to higher and higher levels of specification, including in the latest batch an anodized coating on extremely smooth inner and outer surfaces.

Why would they continue refining the specifications? Why would they continuing refining the specification, go to all that trouble for something that, if it was a rocket, would soon be blown into shrapnel when it went off?

The high-tolerance aluminum tubes are only part of the story. We also have intelligence from multiple sources that Iraq is attempting to acquire magnets and high-speed balancing machines. Both items can be used in a gas centrifuge program to enrich uranium.

In 1999 and 2000, Iraqi officials negotiated with firms in Romania, India, Russia and Slovenia for the purchase of a magnet production plant. Iraq wanted the plant to produce magnets weighing 20 to 30 grams. That's the same weight as the magnets used in Iraq's gas centrifuge program before the Gulf War.

This incident, linked with the tubes, is another indicator of Iraq's attempt to reconstitute its nuclear weapons program.

Intercepted communications from mid-2000 through last summer showed that Iraq front companies sought to buy machines that can be used to balance gas centrifuge rotors. One of these companies also had been involved in a failed effort in 2001 to smuggle aluminum tubes into Iraq.

People will continue to debate this issue, but there is no doubt in my mind. These illicit procurement efforts show that Saddam Hussein is very much focused on putting in place the key missing piece from his nuclear weapons program, the ability to produce fissile material.

He also has been busy trying to maintain the other key parts of his nuclear program, particularly his cadre of key nuclear scientists. It is noteworthy that over the last 18 months Saddam Hussein has paid increasing personal attention to Iraq's top nuclear scientists, a group that the government-controlled press calls openly his "nuclear mujaheddin." He regularly exhorts them and praises their progress. Progress toward what end?

Long ago, the Security Council, this Council, required Iraq to halt all nuclear activities of any kind.

Let me talk now about the systems Iraq is developing to deliver weapons of mass destruction, in particular Iraq's ballistic missiles and unmanned aerial vehicles, UAVs.

First, missiles. We all remember that before the Gulf War Saddam Hussein's goal was missiles that flew not just hundreds, but thousands, of kilometers. He wanted to strike not only his neighbors, but also nations far beyond his borders.

While inspectors destroyed most of the prohibited ballistic missiles, numerous intelligence reports over the past decade from sources inside Iraq indicate that Saddam Hussein retains a covert force of up to a few dozen Scud-variant ballistic missiles. These are missiles with a range of 650 to 900 kilometers.

We know from intelligence and Iraq's own admissions that Iraq's alleged permitted ballistic missiles, the al-Samoud II and the Al-Fatah, violate the 150-kilometer limit established by this Council in Resolution 687. These are prohibited systems.

UNMOVIC has also reported that Iraq has illegally imported 380 SA-2 rocket engines. These are likely for use in the al-Samoud II. Their import was illegal on three counts: Resolution 687 prohibited all military shipments into Iraq; UNSCOM specifically prohibited use of these engines in surface-to-surface missiles; and finally, as we have just noted, they are for a system that exceeds the 150-kilometer range limit. Worst of all, some of these engines were acquired as late as December, after this Council passed Resolution 1441.

What I want you to know today is that Iraq has programs that are intended to produce ballistic missiles that fly over 1,000 kilometers. One program is pursuing a liquid fuel missile that would be able to fly more than 1,200 kilometers. And you can see from this map, as well as I can, who will be in danger of these missiles.

As part of this effort, another little piece of evidence, Iraq has built an engine test stand that is larger than anything it has ever had. Notice the dramatic difference in size between the test stand on the left, the old one, and the new one on the right. Note the large exhaust vent. This is where the flame from the engine comes out. The exhaust vent on the right test stand is five times longer than the one on the left. The one of the left is used for short-range missiles. The one on the right is clearly intended for long-range missiles that can fly 1,200 kilometers.

This photograph was taken in April of 2002. Since then, the test stand has been finished and a roof has been put over it so it will be harder for satellites to see what's going on underneath the test stand.

Saddam Hussein's intentions have never changed. He is not developing the missiles for self-defense. These are missiles that Iraq wants in order to project power, to threaten and to deliver chemical, biological—and if we let him—nuclear warheads.

Now, unmanned aerial vehicles, UAVs. Iraq has been working on a variety of UAVs for more than a decade. This is just illustrative of what a UAV would look like. This effort has included attempts to modify for unmanned flight the MiG-21 and, with greater success, an aircraft called the L-29.

However, Iraq is now concentrating not on these airplanes but on developing and testing smaller UAVs such as this. UAVs are well suited for dispensing chemical and biological weapons. There is ample evidence that Iraq has dedicated much effort to developing and testing spray devices that could be adapted for UAVs.

And in the little that Saddam Hussein told us about UAVs, he has not told the truth. One of these lies is graphically and indisputably demonstrated by intelligence we collected on June 27th last year.

According to Iraq's December 7th declaration, its UAVs have a range of only 80 kilometers. But we detected one of Iraq's newest UAVs in a test flight that went 500 kilometers nonstop on autopilot in the racetrack pattern depicted here.

Not only is this test well in excess of the 150 kilometers that the United Nations permits, the test was left out of Iraq's December 7th declaration. The UAV was flown around and around and around in this circle and so that its 80-kilometer limit really was 500 kilometers, unrefueled and on autopilot—violative of all of its obligations under 1441.

The linkages over the past ten years between Iraq's UAV program and biological and chemical warfare agents are of deep concern to us. Iraq could use these small UAVs which have a wingspan of only a few meters to deliver biological agents to its neighbors or, if transported, to other countries, including the United States.

My friends, the information I have presented to you about these terrible weapons and about Iraq's continued flaunting of its obligations under Security Council Resolution 1441 links to a subject I now want to spend a little bit of time on, and that has to do with terrorism.

Our concern is not just about these illicit weapons; it's the way that these illicit weapons can be connected to terrorists and terrorist organizations that have no compunction about using such devices against innocent people around the world.

Iraq and terrorism go back decades. Baghdad trains Palestine Liberation Front members in small arms and explosives. Saddam uses the Arab Liberation Front to funnel money to the families of Palestinian suicide bombers in order to prolong the Intifadah. And it's no secret that Saddam's own intelligence service was involved in dozens of attacks or attempted assassinations in the 1990s.

But what I want to bring to your attention today is the potentially much more sinister nexus between Iraq and the al-Qaida terrorist network, a nexus that combines classic terrorist organizations and modern methods of murder. Iraq today harbors a deadly terrorist network headed by Abu Musab al-Zarqawi an associate and collaborator of Osama bin Laden and his al-Qaida lieutenants.

Zarqawi, Palestinian born in Jordan, fought in the Afghan war more than a decade ago. Returning to Afghanistan in 2000, he oversaw a terrorist training camp. One of his specialties, and one of the specialties of this camp, is poisons.

When our coalition ousted the Taliban, the Zarqawi network helped establish another poison and explosive training center camp, and this camp is located in northeastern Iraq. You see a picture of this camp.

The network is teaching its operatives how to produce ricin and other poisons. Let me remind you how ricin works. Less than a pinch—imagine a pinch of salt—less than a pinch of ricin, eating just this amount in your food, would cause shock, followed by circulatory failure. Death comes within 72 hours and there is no antidote. There is no cure. It is fatal.

Those helping to run this camp are Zarqawi lieutenants operating in northern Kurdish areas outside Saddam Hussein's controlled Iraq. But Baghdad has an agent in the most senior levels of the radical organization Ansar al-Islam that controls this corner of Iraq. In 2000, this agent offered al-Qaida safe haven in the region.

After we swept al-Qaida from Afghanistan, some of those members accepted this safe haven. They remain there today.

Zarqawi's activities are not confined to this small corner of northeast Iraq. He traveled to Baghdad in May of 2002 for medical treatment, staying in the capital of Iraq for two months while he recuperated to fight another day.

During his stay, nearly two dozen extremists converged on Baghdad and established a base of operations there. These al-Qaida affiliates based in Baghdad now coordinate the movement of people, money and supplies into and throughout Iraq for his network, and they have now been operating freely in the capital for more than eight months.

Iraqi officials deny accusations of ties with al-Qaida. These denials are simply not credible. Last year, an al-Qaida associate bragged that the situation in Iraq was "good," that Baghdad could be transited quickly.

We know these affiliates are connected to Zarqawi because they remain, even today, in regular contact with his direct subordinates, include the poison cell plotters. And they are involved in moving more than money and materiel. Last year, two suspected al-Qaida operatives were arrested crossing from Iraq into Saudi Arabia. They were linked to associates of the Baghdad cell and one of them received training in Afghanistan on how to use cyanide.

From his terrorist network in Iraq, Zarqawi can direct his network in the Middle East and beyond. We in the United States, all of us, the State Department and the Agency for International Development, we all lost a dear friend with the cold-blooded murder of Mr. Laurence Foley in Amman, Jordan, last October. A despicable act was committed that day, the assassination of an individual whose sole mission was to assist the people of Jordan. The captured assassin says his cell received money and weapons from Zarqawi for that murder. After the attack, an associate of the assassin left Jordan to go to Iraq to obtain weapons and explosives for further operations. Iraqi officials protest that they are not aware of the whereabouts of Zarqawi or of any of his associates. Again, these protests are not credible. We know of Zarqawi's activities in Baghdad. I described them earlier.

Now let me add one other fact. We asked a friendly security service to approach Baghdad about extraditing Zarqawi and providing information about him and his close associates. This service contacted Iraqi officials twice and we passed details that should have made it easy to find Zarqawi. The network remains in Baghdad. Zarqawi still remains at large, to come and go.

As my colleagues around this table and as the citizens they represent in Europe know, Zarqawi's terrorism is not confined to the Middle East. Zarqawi and his network have plotted terrorist actions against countries including France, Britain, Spain, Italy, Germany and Russia. According to detainees Abu Atiya, who graduated from Zarqawi's terrorist camp in Afghanistan, tasked at least nine North African extremists in 2001 to travel to Europe to conduct poison and explosive attacks.

Since last year, members of this network have been apprehended in France, Britain, Spain and Italy. By our last count, 116 operatives connected to this global web have been arrested. The chart you are seeing shows the network in Europe.

We know about this European network and we know about its links to Zarqawi because the detainees who provided the information about the targets also provided the names of members of the network. Three of those he identified by name were arrested in France last December. In the apartments of the terrorists, authorities found circuits for explosive devices and a list of ingredients to make toxins.

The detainee who helped piece this together says the plot also targeted Britain. Later evidence again proved him right. When the British unearthed the cell there just last month, one British police officer was murdered during the destruction of the cell.

We also know that Zarqawi's colleagues have been active in the Pankisi Gorge, Georgia, and in Chechnya, Russia. The plotting to which they are linked is not mere chatter. Members of Zarqawi's network say their goal was to kill Russians with toxins.

We are not surprised that Iraq is harboring Zarqawi and his subordinates. This understanding builds on decades-long experience with respect to ties between Iraq and al-Qaida. Going back to the early and mid-1990s when bin Laden was based in Sudan, an al-Qaida source tells us that Saddam and bin Laden reached an understanding that al-Qaida would no longer support activities against Baghdad. Early al-Qaida ties were forged by secret high-level intelligence service contacts with al-Qaida, secret Iraqi intelligence high-level contacts with al-Qaida.

We know members of both organizations met repeatedly and have met at least eight times at very senior levels since the early 1990s. In 1996, a foreign security service tells us that bin Laden met with a senior Iraqi intelligence official in Khartoum and later met the director of the Iraqi intelligence service.

Saddam became more interested as he saw al-Qaida's appalling attacks. A detained al-Qaida member tells us that Saddam was more willing to assist al-Qaida after the 1998 bombings of our embassies in Kenya and Tanzania. Saddam was also impressed by al- Qaida's attacks on the USS Cole in Yemen in October 2000.

Iraqis continue to visit bin Laden in his new home in Afghanistan. A senior defector, one of Saddam's former intelligence chiefs in Europe, says Saddam sent his agents to Afghanistan sometime in the mid-1990s to provide training to al- Qaida members on document forgery.

From the late 1990s until 2001, the Iraqi Embassy in Pakistan played the role of liaison to the al-Qaida organization.

Some believe, some claim, these contacts do not amount to much. They say Saddam Hussein's secular tyranny and al-Qaida's religious tyranny do not mix. I am not comforted by this thought. Ambition and hatred are enough to bring Iraq and al-Qaida together, enough so al-Qaida could learn how to build more sophisticated bombs and learn how to forge documents, and enough so that al-Qaida could turn to Iraq for help in acquiring expertise on weapons of mass destruction.

And the record of Saddam Hussein's cooperation with other Islamist terrorist organizations is clear. Hamas, for example, opened an office in Baghdad in 1999 and Iraq has hosted conferences attended by Palestine Islamic Jihad. These groups are at the forefront of sponsoring suicide attacks against Israel.

Al-Qaida continues to have a deep interest in acquiring weapons of mass destruction. As with the story of Zarqawi and his network, I can trace the story of a senior terrorist operative telling how Iraq provided training in these weapons to al-Qaida. Fortunately, this operative is now detained and he has told his story. I will relate it to you now as he, himself, described it.

This senior al-Qaida terrorist was responsible for one of al- Qaida's training camps in Afghanistan. His information comes firsthand from his personal involvement at senior levels of al- Qaida. He says bin Laden and his top deputy in Afghanistan, deceased al-Qaida leader Muhammad Atif, did not believe that al- Qaida labs in Afghanistan were capable enough to manufacture these chemical or biological agents. They needed to go somewhere else. They had to look outside of Afghanistan for help.

Where did they go? Where did they look? They went to Iraq. The support that this detainee describes included Iraq offering chemical or biological weapons training for two al-Qaida associates beginning in December 2000. He says that a militant known as Abdallah al-Iraqi had been sent to Iraq several times between 1997 and 2000 for help in acquiring poisons and gasses. Abdallah al-Iraqi characterized the relationship he forged with Iraqi officials as successful.

As I said at the outset, none of this should come as a surprise to any of us. Terrorism has been a tool used by Saddam for decades. Saddam was a supporter of terrorism long before these terrorist networks had a name, and this support continues. The nexus of poisons and terror is new. The nexus of Iraq and terror is old. The combination is lethal.

With this track record, Iraqi denials of supporting terrorism take their place alongside the other Iraqi denials of weapons of mass destruction. It is all a web of lies.

When we confront a regime that harbors ambitions for regional domination, hides weapons of mass destruction, and provides haven and active support for terrorists, we are not confronting the past; we are confronting the present. And unless we act, we are confronting an even more frightening future.

And, friends, this has been a long and a detailed presentation and I thank you for your patience, but there is one more subject that I would like to touch on briefly, and it should be a subject of deep and continuing concern to this Council: Saddam Hussein's violations of human rights.

Underlying all that I have said, underlying all the facts and the patterns of behavior that I have identified, is Saddam Hussein's contempt for the will of this Council, his contempt for the truth, and, most damning of all, his utter contempt for human life. Saddam Hussein's use of mustard and nerve gas against the Kurds in 1988 was one of the 20th century's most horrible atrocities. Five thousand men, women and children died. His campaign against the Kurds from 1987 to '89 included mass summary executions, disappearances, arbitrary jailing and ethnic cleansing, and the destruction of some 2,000 villages.

He has also conducted ethnic cleansing against the Shia Iraqis and the Marsh Arabs whose culture has flourished for more than a millennium. Saddam Hussein's police state ruthlessly eliminates anyone who dares to dissent. Iraq has more forced disappearance cases than any other country—tens of thousands of people reported missing in the past decade.

Nothing points more clearly to Saddam Hussein's dangerous intentions and the threat he poses to all of us than his calculated cruelty to his own citizens and to his neighbors. Clearly, Saddam Hussein and his regime will stop at nothing until something stops him.

For more than 20 years, by word and by deed, Saddam Hussein has pursued his ambition to dominate Iraq and the broader Middle East using the only means he knows: intimidation, coercion and annihilation of all those who might stand in his way. For Saddam Hussein, possession of the world's most deadly weapons is the ultimate trump card, the one he must hold to fulfill his ambition.

We know that Saddam Hussein is determined to keep his weapons of mass destruction, is determined to make more. Given Saddam Hussein's history of aggression, given what we know of his grandiose plans, given what we know of his terrorist associations, and given his determination to exact revenge on those who oppose him, should we take the risk that he will not someday use these weapons at a time and a place and in a manner of his choosing, at a time when the world is in a much weaker position to respond?

The United States will not and cannot run that risk for the American people. Leaving Saddam Hussein in possession of weapons of mass destruction for a few more months or years is not an option, not in a post-September 11th world.

My colleagues, over three months ago, this Council recognized that Iraq continued to pose a threat to international peace and security, and that Iraq had been and remained in material breach of its disarmament obligations.

Today, Iraq still poses a threat and Iraq still remains in material breach. Indeed, by its failure to seize on its one last opportunity to come clean and disarm, Iraq has put itself in deeper material breach and closer to the day when it will face serious consequences for its continue defiance of this Council.

My colleagues, we have an obligation to our citizens. We have an obligation to this body to see that our resolutions are complied with. We wrote 1441 not in order to go to war. We wrote 1441 to try to preserve the peace. We wrote 1441 to give Iraq one last chance.

Iraq is not, so far, taking that one last chance.

We must not shrink from whatever is ahead of us. We must not fail in our duty and our responsibility to the citizens of the countries that are represented by this body.

* * * *

Chinese Foreign Minister Tang Jiaxuan. I also wish to thank Secretary Powell for his presentation.

I would now like to share the following views on Iraq. First, the fact that the Foreign Ministers of most Council members are present at today's meeting shows the importance that all parties attach to the authority and role of the Security Council and their support for a resolution of the Iraqi issue within the framework of this world body. The Security Council has basically maintained unity and cooperation on this issue. That is of crucial importance to its appropriate resolution and represents the desire of the international community.

Secondly, China welcomes the United States move to provide the United Nations with its information and evidence on weapons of mass destruction in Iraq, which we believe is consistent with the spirit of resolution 1441 (2002) and could help increase transparency. We hope that various parties will hand over their information and evidence to the United Nations Monitoring, Verification and Inspection Commission (UNMOVIC) and to the International Atomic Energy Agency (IAEA). That will help make their inspections more effective. And, through their on-the-spot inspections, that information and evidence can also be evaluated. The two agencies should report their findings to the Security Council in a timely manner.

Thirdly, the inspections have been going on for more than two months now. The two agencies have been working very hard, and their work deserves our recognition. It is their view that they are not now in a position to draw conclusions, and they have suggested continuing with the inspections. We should respect the views of the two agencies and support the continuation of their work. We hope that the upcoming trip to Iraq by Chairman Blix and Director General ElBaradei on the 8th will yield positive results.

Not long ago, the two agencies pointed out some problems in the inspections. We urge Iraq to adopt a more proactive approach, to make further explanations and clarification as soon as possible and to cooperate with the inspection process.

Fourthly, the Security Council has a common stand on the elimination of weapons of mass destruction in Iraq. This is fully reflected in the relevant Council resolutions, particularly 1441 (2002), which was adopted unanimously. The most important aspect at present remains the full implementation of this resolution. As for the next step to be taken, the Council should decide this through discussions among all members, based on the results of the inspections.

Fifthly, it is the universal desire of the international community to see a political settlement to the issue of Iraq, within the United Nations framework, and to avoid war. This is something to which the Security Council must attach due importance. As long as there is still the slightest hope for a political settlement, we should exert our utmost efforts to achieving it. China is ready to join others in working in this direction.

* * * *

U.K. Foreign Secretary Jack Straw. May I, as the Foreign Minister of China has done, congratulate Germany on taking over the presidency of the Security Council and congratulate you personally on assuming the Chair this morning.

We have just heard a most powerful and authoritative case against the Iraqi regime set out by United States Secretary of State Powell. The international community owes him its thanks for laying bare the deceit practised by the regime of Saddam Hussain—and worse, the very great danger which that regime represents.

Three months ago we united to send Iraq an uncompromising message: cooperate fully with weapons inspectors, or face disarmament by force. After years of Iraqi deception, when resolutions were consistently flouted, resolution 1441 (2002) was a powerful reminder of the importance of international law and of the authority of the Security Council itself.

United and determined, we gave Iraq a final opportunity to rid itself of its weapons of mass terror, of gases which can poison thousands in one go; of bacilli and viruses like anthrax and smallpox, which can disable and kill by the tens of thousands; of the means to make nuclear weapons, which can kill by the million.

By resolution 1441 (2002), we strengthened inspections massively. The only missing ingredient was full Iraqi compliance—immediate, full and active cooperation. But the truth is—and we all know this—without that full and active cooperation, however strong the inspectors' powers, however good the inspectors, inspections in a country as huge as Iraq could never be sure of finding all Iraqi weapons of mass destruction.

Sadly, the inspectors' reports last week, and Secretary Powell's presentation today, can leave us under no illusions about Saddam Hussain response. Saddam Hussain holds United Nations Security Council resolution 1441 (2002) in the same contempt as all previous resolutions in respect of Iraq. Let us reflect on what that means: Saddam is defying every one of us, every nation here represented. He questions our resolve and is gambling that we will lose our nerve rather than enforce our will.

Paragraph 1 of resolution 1441 (2002) said that Saddam was and remained in "material breach" of Security Council resolutions. Paragraph 4 of that same resolution then set two clear tests for a further material breach by Iraq. The first test was that Iraq must not make "false statements" or "omissions" in its declaration. But the Iraqi document submitted to us on 7 December, as we have heard from Secretary Powell, was long on repetition but short on fact. It was not full, nor accurate, nor complete. By anyone's definition, it was a "false statement". Its central premise—that Iraq possesses no weapons of mass destruction—is a lie. This outright lie was repeated yesterday on television by Saddam Hussain.

The declaration also has obvious omissions, not least in a failure to explain what has happened to the large quantities of chemical and biological weapons materiel and munitions unaccounted for by United Nations weapons inspectors in 1998. And there is no admission of Iraq's extensive efforts to develop weapons of mass destruction since the last round of United Nations Special Commission (UNSCOM) inspections ended in December 1998.

Paragraph 4 goes on to set a second test for a further material breach—namely, a "failure by Iraq at any time to comply with, and cooperate fully in the implementation of" resolution 1441 (2002). Following the presentation by the inspectors last week, and today's briefing by Secretary Powell, it is clear that Iraq has failed this test. These briefings have confirmed our worst fears, that Iraq has no intention of relinquishing its weapons of mass destruction, no intention of following the path of peaceful disarmament set out in Security Council resolution 1441 (2002). Instead of open admissions and transparency, we have a charade, where a veneer of superficial cooperation masks wilful concealment, the extent of which has been devastatingly revealed this morning by Secretary Powell.

In his report last week, Mr. Blix set out a number of instances in which Iraqi behavior reveals a determination to avoid compliance. Why is Iraq refusing to allow the United Nations Monitoring, Verification and Inspection Commission (UNMOVIC) to use a U-2 plane to conduct aerial imagery and surveillance operations? When will Iraq account for the 6,500 bombs that could carry up to 1,000 tonnes of chemical agent? How will Iraq justify having a prohibited chemical precursor for mustard gas? And how will Iraq explain the concealment of nuclear documents and the development of a missile program in clear contravention of United Nations resolutions?

There is only one possible conclusion from all of this, which is that Iraq is in further material breach, as set out in United Nations Security Council resolution 1441 (2002). I believe that all colleagues here, all members, will share our deep sense of frustration that Iraq is choosing to spurn this final opportunity to achieve a peaceful outcome.

Given what has to follow, and the difficult choice now facing us, it would be easy to turn a blind eye to the wording of resolution 1441 (2002) and hope for a change of heart by Iraq. Easy, but wrong, because if we did so we would be repeating the mistakes of the past 12 years and empowering a dictator who believes that his diseases and poison gases are essential weapons to suppress his own people and to threaten his neighbors, and that by defiance of the United Nations he can indefinitely hoodwink the world.

Under the French presidency two weeks ago, we had a special meeting on the dangers of international terrorism—a meeting which I greatly welcomed—and the grave danger to the world of terrorists acquiring weapons of mass destruction through the connivance of rogue States. Secretary Powell has today set out deeply worrying reports about the presence in Iraq of one of Osama bin Laden's lieutenants, Al-Zarqawi, and other members of Al Qaeda and their efforts to develop poisons.

It defies the imagination that all of this could be going on without the knowledge of Saddam Hussain. The recent discovery of the poison ricin in London has underlined again that this is a threat which all of us face.

Saddam must be left in no doubt as to the serious consequences and the serious situation which he now faces. The United Kingdom does not want war. What we want is for the United Nations system to be upheld. But the logic of resolution 1441 (2002) is inescapable. Time is now very short. The Council will have further reports from the inspectors on Friday week, 14 February. If non-cooperation continues, the Council must meet its responsibilities.

Our world faces many threats, from poverty and disease to civil war and terrorism. Working through this great institution, we have the capacity to tackle these challenges together. But if we are to do so, then the decisions we have to take must have a force beyond mere words.

This is a moment of choice for Saddam and for the Iraqi regime. But it is also a moment of choice for this institution, the United Nations. The pre-war predecessor of the United Nations—the League of Nations—had the same fine ideals as the United Nations. But the League failed because it could not create actions from its words. It could not back diplomacy with a credible threat and, where necessary, the use of force, so small evils went unchecked. Tyrants became emboldened, and then greater evils were unleashed.

At each stage, good men said, "Wait. The evil is not big enough to challenge". Then, before their eyes, the evil became too big to challenge. We slipped slowly down a slope, never noticing how far we had gone until it was too late.

We owe it to our history, as well as to our future, not to make the same mistake again.

Russian Foreign Minister Igor Ivanov. Russia views today's meeting in the context of the consistent efforts of the Security Council to find a political settlement to the situation surrounding Iraq, on the basis of complete and scrupulous compliance with the relevant resolutions.

The unanimous adoption of Security Council resolution 1441 (2002) and the deployment of international inspectors in Iraq have demonstrated the ability of the international community to act together in the interests of attaining a common goal. We are convinced that maintaining the unity of the world community, primarily within the context of the Security Council, and our concerted action, in strict compliance with the Charter of the United Nations and the resolutions of the Security Council, are the most reliable means of resolving the problem of weapons of mass destruction in Iraq through political means.

There is no doubt that we all want to resolve this problem. It was with that in mind that we listened very closely to the presentation given by Secretary of State Powell. Russia continues to believe that the Security Council—and, through it, the entire international community—must have all of the information it needs in order to determine whether or not there are remaining weapons of mass destruction in Iraq.

The information given to us today definitely will require very serious and thorough study. Experts in our countries must immediately begin to analyze it and then draw the appropriate conclusions. The main point is that this information must immediately be handed over for processing by the United Nations Monitoring, Verification and Inspection Commission (UNMOVIC) and the International Atomic Energy Agency (IAEA), including through direct on-site verification during the inspections in Iraq.

Baghdad must give the inspectors answers to the questions that we heard in the presentation given by the United States Secretary of State. We appeal once again to all States immediately to hand over to the international inspectors any information that can help them discharge their responsible mandate.

The information provided today by the United States Secretary of State once again convincingly indicates that the activities of the international inspectors in Iraq must be continued. They alone can say to what extent Iraq is complying with the demands of the Security Council. They alone can help the Security Council work out and adopt carefully balanced decisions—the best possible decisions.

The statements made by Mr. Blix and by Mr. ElBaradei in this very Chamber on 27 January show that a unique inspection mechanism has been deployed in Iraq which has everything it needs to ensure compliance with resolution 1441 (2002) and other Security Council resolutions. This great potential must be used to the fullest.

The Security Council and all its members must do everything they can to support the inspection process. Russia, for its part, intends to continue actively to promote the creation of the best possible conditions for the work of the international inspectors in Iraq. In particular, we are prepared to provide an aircraft for aerial monitoring and, if need be, additional inspectors as well.

Russia welcomes the continuation of dialogue between the Executive Chairman of UNMOVIC and the Director General of the IAEA with Iraq on outstanding unresolved issues. We hope that this dialogue will be extremely concrete and productive. It is facilitated, inter alia, by the fact that work has been carried out according to the timetable set out in resolution 1284 (1999), which should make the international inspections and monitoring even more systematic and effective, especially with respect to clarifying key disarmament tasks by the end of March of this year.

It is perfectly obvious that the work of UNMOVIC and the IAEA can be effective only with full cooperation in good faith from Iraq. Iraq should be the first to be concerned about providing definitive clarity on the question of weapons of mass destruction and their delivery systems. That is the only way to reach a political settlement, including the lifting of the sanctions on Iraq. Baghdad should fully realize how crucial this is and do everything in its power so that the international inspectors can carry out their mandate.

Recently, we have often heard the expression that time is running out for a settlement to the question of Iraq. Of course, resolution 1441 (2002) aims to quickly achieve practical results, but it does not set out any concrete time frame. The inspectors alone can advise the Security Council on how much time they need to carry out the tasks entrusted to them. In this respect, we cannot rule out the possibility that at some stage the Security Council may need to adopt a new resolution, or perhaps more than one resolution. The main point is that our efforts should continue to be aimed at doing everything possible to facilitate the inspection process, which has proven its effectiveness and which makes it possible to implement Council decisions by peaceful means.

Unfortunately, the current situation concerning Iraq is far from being the last problem whose solution we will all still have to work on. The international community of the twenty-first century is confronting new global threats and challenges requiring a unified response from all States. A graphic example of that approach was the creation of the broad coalition to combat the primary and most dangerous threat of our time: international terrorism. It is precisely because of the unity of the world community that initial success has been achieved in combating that scourge. However, it is perfectly obvious that we are only beginning a very difficult battle with terrorism. And the information from the United States Secretary of State about the activities of Al Qaeda is further corroboration of that fact.

The unity of the world community will continue to be the principal guarantee of the effectiveness of the world's action. It is precisely unity that is essential in our approach to all problems, however complicated they may be. Tactical differences may arise, it is true. And probably there will be quite a few of them, given the complexity of the tasks we need to resolve. But they must not overshadow the strategic goals that are in the interests of our common security and stability.

* * * *

French Foreign Minister Dominique Galouzeau de Villepin. I congratulate the German presidency of the Security Council on having organized this meeting, and I thank Colin Powell, Secretary of State of the United States, for having taken the initiative of convening it. I listened with much attention to the elements that he shared with us. They contained information, indications and questions that deserve further exploration. It will be up to the inspectors to assess the facts, as envisaged in resolution 1441 (2002). Already, his presentation has provided new justification for the approach chosen by the United Nations; it must strengthen our common determination.

By unanimously adopting resolution 1441 (2002), we chose to act through the path of inspections. That policy rests on three fundamental points: a clear objective on which we cannot compromise—the disarmament of Iraq; a method—a rigorous system of inspections that requires Iraq's active cooperation and that affirms the Security Council's central role at each stage; and finally, a requirement—that of our unity. It gave full force to the message that we unanimously addressed to Baghdad. I hope that today's meeting will enable us to strengthen that unity.

Important results have already been achieved. The United Nations Monitoring, Verification and Inspection Commission (UNMOVIC) and the International Atomic Energy Agency (IAEA) are working. The deployment on the ground of more than one hundred inspectors, with 300 visits a month on average, an increase in the number of sites inspected and full access to the presidential sites, in particular, are all major achievements. In the nuclear domain, these first two months have enabled the IAEA to make—as Mr. ElBaradei emphasized—good progress in its knowledge of Iraq's capacity, and that is a key element.

In the areas covered by UNMOVIC, the inspections have provided us with useful information. For example, Mr. Blix has indicated that no trace of biological or chemical agents has thus far been detected by the inspectors, either in the analyses of samples taken on the inspected sites or in the 12 empty warheads discovered on 16 January at Ukhaider.

There are still grey areas in Iraq's cooperation. The inspectors have reported real difficulties. In his 27 January report, Mr. Blix gave several examples of unresolved questions in the ballistic, chemical and biological domains. These uncertainties are not acceptable. France will continue to pass on all the information it has so they can be better defined.

Right now, our attention has to be focused as a priority on the biological and chemical domains. It is there that our presumptions about Iraq are the most significant. Regarding the chemical domain, we have evidence of its capacity to produce VX and yperite. In the biological domain, the evidence suggests the possible possession of significant stocks of anthrax and botulism toxin, and possibly a production capability. Today the absence of long-range delivery systems reduces the potential threat of these weapons, but we have disturbing signs of Iraq's continued determination to acquire ballistic missiles beyond the authorized 150-kilometer range. In the nuclear domain, we must clarify in particular any attempt by Iraq to acquire aluminum tubes.

So it is a demanding dmarche, anchored in resolution 1441 (2002), that we must take together. If this path were to fail and lead us into a dead end, then we rule out no option, including in the final analysis the recourse to force, as we have said all along.

In such a hypothesis, however, several answers will have to be clearly provided to all Governments and all peoples of the world to limit the risks and uncertainties. To what extent do the nature and scope of the threat justify the recourse to force? How do we make sure that the considerable risks of such intervention are actually kept under control? This obviously requires a collective dmarche of responsibility on the part of the world community. In any case, it must be clear that, in the context of such an option, the United Nations will have to be at the centre of the action to guarantee Iraq's unity, ensure the region's stability, protect civilians and preserve the unity of the world community.

For now, the inspections regime favored by resolution 1441 (2002) must be strengthened, since it has not been explored to the end. Use of force can only be a final recourse. Why go to war if there still exists an unused space in resolution 1441 (2002)? Consistent with the logic of that resolution, we must therefore move on to a new stage and further strengthen the inspections. With the choice between military intervention and an inspections regime that is inadequate for lack of cooperation on Iraq's part, we must choose to strengthen decisively the means of inspection. That is what France is proposing today.

To do this, we must define with Mr. Blix and Mr. ElBaradei the requisite tools for increasing their operational capabilities. Let us double or triple the number of inspectors and open up more regional offices. Let us go further: Why not establish a specialized body to keep under surveillance the sites and areas already inspected? Let us substantially increase the capabilities for monitoring and collecting information on Iraqi territory. France is ready to provide full support; it is ready to deploy Mirage IV observer aircraft. Let us collectively establish a coordination and information-processing centre that would supply Mr. Blix and Mr. ElBaradei, in real time and in a coordinated way, with all the intelligence resources they might need. Let us list the unresolved disarmament questions and rank them by importance. With the consent of the leaders of the inspection teams, let us define a demanding and realistic time frame for moving forward in the assessment and elimination of problems. There must be regular follow-up to the progress made in Iraq's disarmament.

This enhanced regime of inspections and monitoring could be usefully complemented by having a permanent United Nations coordinator for disarmament in Iraq, stationed in Iraq and working under the authority of Mr. Blix and Mr. ElBaradei.

Iraq must cooperate actively, however. The country must comply immediately with the demands of Mr. Blix and Mr. ElBaradei, in particular by permitting meetings with Iraqi scientists without witnesses; agreeing to the use of U2 observer flights; adopting legislation to prohibit the manufacture of weapons of mass destruction; and immediately handing over to the inspectors all relevant documents on unresolved disarmament questions, in particular in the biological and chemical domains. Those handed over on 20 January constitute a step in the right direction. The 3,000 pages of documents discovered at the home of a researcher show that Baghdad must do more. Absent documents, Iraq must be able to present credible testimony. The Iraqi authorities must also provide the inspectors with answers to the new elements presented by Colin Powell.

Between now and the inspectors' next report, on 14 February, Iraq will have to provide new elements. The upcoming visit to Baghdad by the leaders of the inspectors will have to be the occasion for clear results to that end.

This is the demanding dmarche that we must take together towards a new stage. Its success presupposes, today as yesterday, that the international community will remain united and mobilized. It is our moral and political duty first to devote all our energy to Iraq's disarmament in peace and in compliance with the rule of law and justice. France is convinced that we can succeed on this demanding path so long as we maintain our unity and cohesion. This is option of collective responsibility.

Spanish Foreign Minister Ana Palacio Vallelersundi. I would also like to associate myself with those who have expressed their gratitude for the information provided by Secretary of State Colin Powell. But I would first of all like to say how important it is that he has brought that information to the Security Council. This once again represents recognition by the United States of America of the importance of keeping the question of Iraq within the framework of the United Nations. Similarly, this reminds us that we are dealing with a responsibility that belongs to the entire international community.

The Secretary of State has put before us compelling data that point to the existence of weapons of mass destruction and to the consequences of their possible use. Those data also confirm that Iraq is deceiving the international community and that it is not cooperating. Legally speaking, and in the context of the United Nations and of resolution 1441 (2002) in particular, that information leads to the legal conclusion that there has been a flagrant violation of the obligations established in resolution 1441 (2002).

The Secretary of State has also given us information on the links between Saddam Hussein regime and terrorism. The international community cannot allow a country to acquire components, develop production lines, possess clandestine mobile production units and laboratories or acquire stocks of weapons of mass destruction. We cannot tolerate such a violation of international law, as it endangers international peace and security and undermines the very foundations of non-proliferation regimes that it has taken many decades to establish. Such a violation also jeopardizes the very existence of an international community that is able to organize peaceful coexistence in our global society.

There is only one explanation for the lack of cooperation by Saddam Hussein regime with the work of verifying his programs of weapons of mass destruction: that Saddam Hussain has not renounced his plan to use such weapons as he has undoubtedly used them in the past. As a Spaniard, I am particularly concerned that biological and chemical weapons still under Iraqi control, such as the ones shown to us today by Secretary of State Colin Powell, could end up in the hands of terrorists.

The International Atomic Energy Agency (IAEA) and the United Nations Monitoring, Verification and Inspection Commission (UNMOVIC) have our full confidence and support. But inspections are not an end in themselves. Rather, they are the means of verifying that Iraq is carrying out effective and complete disarmament of its arsenal of weapons of mass destruction. Inspections will only bear fruit if Iraq cooperates actively. To date, it has not done so.

Time does not mean time for the inspectors. On the contrary, it means an ultimatum to Saddam Hussein regime that it must disarm voluntarily. As Secretary of State Colin Powell said, the inspectors are not detectives. The inspectors should be the proxies for the international community in witnessing voluntary disarmament. We can consider all the mechanisms, offices, additional inspections and minders we want. But the issue will still be the same: the lack of will on the part of Saddam Hussein regime to fulfill its disarmament obligations. We will only be deceiving ourselves if we ignore that fact. Therefore, we can, and must, demand a change of political will: full cooperation with regard to disarmament, without delay or subterfuge. What is at stake is the credibility of the Security Council, which the Charter of the United Nations established as the most valuable instrument for the maintenance of peace. The Council is the key to our collective security.

However, for 12 years we have witnessed systematic non- compliance with Security Council resolutions by Saddam Hussein regime. Spain therefore reiterates that it is imperative to send Saddam Hussein regime an unequivocal message that noncompliance with the resolutions of the Council and the proliferation of weapons of mass destruction and longrange missiles pose a threat to peace and that, consequently, preserving international peace and security means, as the Council has underscored, the immediate and complete disarmament of Iraq.

A fundamental element of Spain's actions in the current Iraqi crisis is respect for international law, of which Security Council resolutions are an essential part. My Government believes that in spite of Iraq's continued non-compliance with its obligations—which has been made patently clear from the disturbing information just presented to us by Secretary of State Powell—there is still is a chance for peace if Iraq radically modifies its lack of compliance.

Saddam Hussein regime must understand that if it does not comply with its obligations, then it must confront the grave consequences called for in resolution 1441

(2002). But it should also understand that the full responsibility falls solely upon Saddam Hussain and his willingness to cooperate with the obligations imposed by the international community. That cooperation has heretofore been conspicuously absent. The international community urges him to take advantage of the last chance that has been given to him under resolution 1441 (2002). For the sake of peace in the world, I hope that Saddam Hussein regime will not miss that opportunity.

* * * *

German Foreign Minister Joschka Fischer. I would like to thank Secretary of State Colin Powell for the information he has just given us. The place and timing of this detailed account underline once more that the Security Council is and remains the centre of decision-making on the Iraq crisis. Germany supports this approach. Given the implications they could have for future decisions, the findings have to be examined carefully. We can already see that they coincide in part with information that we also have. They are based on a close exchange of information.

It is now decisive that the United Nations inspectors also be provided with this extensive material, insofar as that has not yet happened. They have to work with this information to be able to clarify the unresolved questions quickly and fully. And Iraq has to answer the elements which were provided today by our colleague Colin Powell to the Security Council. The more expert information the inspection teams have at their disposal, the more targeted their work can be. Thus, from the outset, Germany, too, has passed on the information to Hans Blix, Mohamed ElBaradei and their teams.

The Security Council has been dealing with Iraq for 12 years. As a matter of principle, the unity of the Council is of central importance in this context. Baghdad has time and again violated the obligations laid down in the relevant Council resolutions. Nor do we hold any illusions on the inhumane and brutal nature of Saddam Hussein dictatorship. Under his rule, Iraq has attacked its neighbors Kuwait and Iran, fired missiles at Israel and deployed poison gas against Iran and its own Kurdish population. The regime is terrible for the Iraqi people. That is why a policy of containment, sanctions and effective military control of the no-fly zones has been implemented since the Gulf War. Iraq must comply with all relevant Security Council resolutions in their entirety and completely disarm its weapons of mass destruction potential.

The presence of the inspectors in Iraq has already effectively reduced the danger of that potential. Nevertheless, the aim of resolution 1441 (2002) is the full and lasting disarmament of Iraq. In his latest report, Hans Blix listed many open questions. The regime in Baghdad must give clear answers to all these concrete questions without delay.

Despite all the difficulties, United Nations efforts to disarm Iraq in the past were not without success. In the 1990s, the inspectors were able to destroy more weapons of mass destruction capacities than did the Gulf War. The threat potential of Iraq to the region was thus clearly reduced. The current basis for the inspections is laid down in resolutions 1284 (1999) and 1441 (2002). The weapons inspectors from the United Nations Monitoring, Verification and Inspection Commission (UNMOVIC) and the International Atomic Energy Agency (IAEA) have powers that reach further than ever before. They have to be given a real chance and the time they need to fully exhaust the possibilities.

Chief Inspector Blix and IAEA head ElBaradei will travel to Iraq again next weekend and thereafter update us. The success of that trip will be of paramount importance. It will depend crucially on the full cooperation of Baghdad. Quite a few States suspect that Saddam Hussein regime is withholding relevant information and concealing military capabilities. This strong suspicion has to be dispelled beyond any doubt. That is exactly why resolution 1441 (2002) provides for the instrument of inspections in Iraq by UNMOVIC and the IAEA.

The dangers of a military action and its consequences are plain to see. Precisely because of the effectiveness of the work of the inspectors, we must continue to seek a peaceful solution to the crisis.

In the world of the twenty-first century, the United Nations is key to conflict prevention, crisis management and peace building. On the basis of resolution 1441 (2002) and in the light of practical experience, we need to enhance the instruments of inspection and control. We need a tough regime of intensive inspections that can guarantee the full and lasting disarmament of Iraq's weapons of mass destruction. By tightening inspections, we are creating an opportunity for a peaceful solution. Such a tough system of inspections could also be effectively applied by the Security Council in other cases. Our French colleague made some very interesting proposals on this matter which deserve our further consideration.

Moreover, we ought to support all endeavors of States in the region that are currently engaging in considerable diplomatic efforts to bring the Iraqi Government to fully implement the resolutions. Iraq has to disarm openly, peacefully and in cooperation with the inspectors without any delay.

Iraqi Representative Aldouri. My delegation congratulates you, Sir, on your assumption of the presidency of the Council for this month. We wish you success in your work amid these extraordinarily difficult international circumstances.

We should have liked to have been granted sufficient time, commensurate with the gravity of the statement made by the United States Secretary of State in his presentation, and not just a few minutes to rebut a statement that lasted 90 minutes. Nevertheless, Iraq will provide detailed and technical explanatory answers to the allegations made in that statement. I shall be polite and brief.

The pronouncements in Mr. Powell's statement on weapons of mass destruction are utterly unrelated to the truth and the reality on the ground. No new information was provided; mere sound recordings cannot be confirmed as genuine. Council members may have seen me smile when I heard some of those recordings; they contain certain words that I will not attempt to translate here. However, those incorrect allegations, unnamed and unknown sources, schemes and presumptions are all in line with United States policy, which is directed towards one known objective.

In the interview that he granted yesterday to former British Minister Tony Benn, President Saddam Hussain reiterated that Iraq is completely free from weapons of mass destruction—a statement repeated by numerous Iraqi officials for more than a decade.

Mr. Powell could have spared himself, his team and the Security Council a great deal of effort by presenting those allegations directly to the United Nations Monitoring, Verification and Inspection Commission (UNMOVIC) and the International Atomic Energy Agency (IAEA), in accordance with the provisions of paragraph 10 of Security Council resolution 1441 (2002). He could have left the inspectors to work in peace and quiet, to investigate without media pressure. At any rate, the forthcoming visit of Mr. Blix and Mr. ElBaradei on 8 and 9 February will provide another opportunity to test the validity of those allegations. Ongoing inspections have shown that previous allegations and reports from the United States and Britain were false.

Iraq submitted an accurate, comprehensive and updated 12,000- page declaration that included detailed information about previous Iraqi programs, as well as updated information about Iraqi industries in various fields.

The inspectors began their activities intensively in Iraq on 27 November 2002, with more than 250 UNMOVIC and IAEA staff, including more than 100 inspectors. As of 4 February 2003, the inspection teams had conducted 575 inspections throughout Iraq, covering 321 sites. The sites singled out by President Bush on 12 September 2002 and by British Prime Minister Tony Blair in the same month, as well as in the United States Central Intelligence Agency (CIA) report of October 2002, were at the top of the list of sites inspected by the inspection teams. Inspectors discovered that none of the allegations contained in those reports was true. Thus, the truth and accuracy of Iraq's declaration that it was free from weapons of mass destruction have been documented by the two technical agencies entrusted by the Security Council with undertaking that task.

It is well known that inspection teams took samples of water, soil, plants, air and factory and production remnants from vast areas, including cities, villages, highways, farms, factories and universities throughout Iraq—north, south, east and west. UNMOVIC and IAEA analyses of those samples concluded that there was no indication of proscribed chemical, biological or radiological agents or, indeed, of any other proscribed activities in any part of Iraq.

Mr. Blix confirmed in his statement to The New York Times on 30 January 2003 that the inspections did not support any of the scenarios alleged by Mr. Colin Powell—that Iraqi officials were moving proscribed material within or out of Iraq with the goal of concealing it. He confirmed that he did not find sufficient reason to believe that Iraq was sending scientists out of Iraq to prevent them from being interviewed and that he had no reason to believe that President Bush was correct in saying in his State of the Union address that Iraqi intelligence agents were posing as scientists for the interviews. We would like to reiterate that Iraq encourages its scientists to submit to interviews requested by UNMOVIC and the IAEA.

As for the existence of the mobile laboratories alleged by Secretary Powell this morning, just yesterday Mr. Blix stated that to date UNMOVIC had found no proof of the presence of such mobile units.

As regards the U-2 overflights and the controversy that has developed in that connection, Iraq does not object to such flights for the purpose of conducting inspection activities. Rather, the objection is that United States and British warplanes are imposing illegal no-fly zones, contrary to Security Council resolutions. To overcome that obstacle, it would be enough for such warplanes to suspend their flights during U-2 flights. Iraq cannot be held responsible for those flights.

The allegation that trucks leave sites prior to the arrival of inspection teams is false.

Inspections occur suddenly, without prior notification to the Iraqi side. Furthermore, UNMOVIC and the IAEA have their own sources that provide satellite imagery, and they also use helicopters for surveillance and inspection activities. We therefore believe that those two agencies are very well informed about what takes place on the ground in Iraq. It is important to remind the Council that weapons of mass destruction programs are not like an aspirin pill—something that can be easily hidden. Rather, they require huge production facilities for research and development, weaponization and deployment. Such facilities cannot be concealed. Inspectors have crisscrossed all of Iraq and found no evidence of that.

As regards the sound recordings, suffice it to say that scientific and technical progress has reached a level that would allow for the fabrication of such allegations and for their presentation in the way that Mr. Powell presented them. Anyone can be recorded, at any time and anywhere in the world.

As for the supposed relationship between Iraq and the Al Qaeda organization, I would like to note what President Saddam Hussain has said:

"If we had a relationship with Al Qaeda and we believed in that relationship, we would not be ashamed to admit it. We have no relationship with Al Qaeda".

I would like now to refer to a recent statement by a United States official as reported in The New York Times three days ago. He stated that analysts at the CIA have complained that Administration officials have exaggerated reports on weapons of mass destruction in Iraq, and particularly on Iraq's presumed relationship with Al Qaeda, in order to bolster their case for war.

I would like to add that Mr. Jack Straw has ignored intelligence reports from his own Government stating that there is no relationship between Iraq and Al Qaeda.

Mr. Powell's assertion that Iraq used chemical weapons against its own people particularly surprised me, given that a CIA official unmasked the truth on 31 January—just a few days ago—in The New York Times. He stated that the United States Administration has known since 1988 that Iraq did not use chemical weapons against its own people for one simple reason: it does not have the chemical weapon that was used in the Halabja incident.

In conclusion, I want to say that the obvious goal behind the holding of this meeting and the presentation of false allegations by the Secretary of State of the United States was to sell the idea of war and aggression against my country, Iraq, without providing any legal, moral or political justification. This was primarily an attempt to sway United States public opinion—and world public opinion generally—in favor of launching a hostile attack against Iraq.

In return, Iraq offers security and peace and reiterates before the members of the Security Council our commitment to continue our proactive cooperation with the inspection teams in order to make it possible for them to complete their tasks as soon as possible so as to verify that Iraq is free of weapons of mass destruction, lift the unjust sanctions imposed against us, ensure respect for our national security and guarantee regional security by ridding the whole Middle East of weapons of mass destruction, including Israel's huge arsenal of weapons of mass destruction, in accordance with the provisions of paragraph 14 of Security Council resolution 687 (1991).

Statement by the Foreign Ministers of Albania, Bulgaria, Croatia, Estonia, Latvia, Lithuania, Macedonia, Romania, Slovakia and Slovenia (the Vilnius Group Countries), February 5, 2003

Earlier today, the United States presented compelling evidence to the United Nations Security Council detailing Iraq's weapons of mass destruction programs, its active efforts to deceive U.N. inspectors, and its links to international terrorism. Our countries understand the dangers posed by tyranny and the special responsibility of democracies to defend our shared values. The trans-Atlantic community, of which we are a part, must stand together to face the threat posed by the nexus of terrorism and dictators with weapons of mass destruction.

We have actively supported the international efforts to achieve a peaceful disarmament of Iraq. However, it has now become clear that Iraq is in material breach of U.N. Security Council Resolutions, including U.N. Resolution 1441, passed unanimously on November 8, 2002. As our governments said on the occasion of the NATO Summit in Prague: "We support the goal of the international community for full disarmament of Iraq as stipulated in the U.N. Security Council Resolution 1441. In the event of non-compliance with the terms of this resolution, we are prepared to contribute to an international coalition to enforce its provisions and the disarmament of Iraq." The clear and present danger posed by the Saddam Hussein's regime requires a united response from the community of democracies. We call upon the U.N. Security Council to take the necessary and appropriate action in response to Iraq's continuing threat to international peace and security.

Remarks by United Nations Secretary-General Annan, February 5, 2003

Q. When are you going to Baghdad, Sir?

Secretary-General Annan. Let me say that, we have had a very good discussion followed by a working lunch and I still believe that war is not inevitable but a lot depends on President Saddam Hussein and the Iraqi leadership. I think the message today has been clear—everyone wants Iraq to be proactive in cooperating with the inspectors and fulfill the demands of the international community. I think if they do that, we can avoid a war. The inspectors are going back over the weekend, carrying the message of the international community to the Iraqi authorities, and I urge them to listen and follow through on the demands, as I have said, for the sake of their own people, for the region and for the sake of world order.

As far as my own visit to Baghdad is concerned—as you know the question was posed in the [Security] Council today and has been floating around for a while—let me say that the message that has been given to Iraq is very clear. That message has come from the united Security Council, it has come from the Arab League, it has come from its neighbors and the inspectors are going back in the next few days to give them the same message in the name of a united international community. And they [Iraq] should listen to them. If I were to go I would not carry a different message. I would be carrying the same message and they should listen to Drs. [Hans] Blix and [Mohammed] ElBaradei, and I hope they do so.

Q. Can you give us your reaction to the U.S. presentation today?

Secretary-General Annan. I think the Council members all reacted and we followed up with discussions at lunch. It is expected that the inspectors will take up the new information that the Secretary of State has given. Some of it may be familiar with them. They will factor that into their work and when they are in Iraq they will pursue the leads that they have been given.

Q. When are you going to go to Baghdad exactly?

Secretary-General Annan. I have just said I'm not going. I am not going. I am not going to Baghdad. But the inspectors are going and they should be listened to.

Q. After today's presentation , are you convinced by the Americans' argument that Iraq is in material breach of [operative paragraph 4 of Resolution 1441]?

Secretary-General Annan. I just indicated that at the discussions this morning the inspectors have been asked to follow through and they will report back as part of their work.

Q. Did you find the Secretary's presentation persuasive, convincing?

Secretary-General Annan. I think Secretary of State [Colin Powell] made a strong presentation to the Council members. He was thorough and he took his time to do it.

Q. The last time Mr. Blix and ElBaradei came to the Security Council each one of them presented his report, and each one of those two reports was received in a positive light and in a negative light at the same time, depending on who was looking at it. Is there a mechanism that the U.N. can set in place whereby it would not be interpreted according to who is interpreting it?

Secretary-General Annan. Obviously, the report the inspectors brought back to the Council was not black and white. If you wish, as somebody said, it was grey. And that was to be expected given the nature of their work. But as they keep presenting their reports to the Council, depending on what they come up with, the Council will have to make a judgement at some stage as to whether Iraq is performing, is cooperating, or is not and they should declare material breach. But the judgement has to come some day. It is not up to the inspectors to declare material breach. They will present the facts and it is up to the Council to make that judgement.

Q. How crucial will the Blix and ElBaradei reports on 14 February become in light of today?

Secretary-General Annan. I think, given the developments since their last report on 27 January, this would also be an important report. Members will be looking to see if there have been any further developments, any changes in the Iraqi attitude and mindset.

* * * *

Q. You expressed the view before that was pretty much the majority of the Council, that the new information should be given to the inspectors to facilitate their work. Did you have a sense that the United States expected a different outcome, that this information actually should have led to force.

Secretary-General Annan. I think the United States officials have said all along that they do not believe that war is inevitable provided Iraq complies. So even at this stage, they are not saying peace is out.

Q. If that were the case, they could have given that information to Blix in private.

Secretary-General Annan. Well, I think it could have been done but they chose to do it this way and Blix and ElBaradei have been urged to factor into their work the information that has been given and the Americans have indicated that they will give them the information and any further information they have.

Q. Is there any talk of a U.N. role beyond a possible conflict? Is there any talk at all of that?

Secretary-General Annan. Well, I think it is, particularly for those of you in this house, it is clear that if it were to come to that, and I don't think we are there yet, when you look back, whether it is Kosovo or Afghanistan, or everywhere, if it comes to that the U.N. has always had a role to play.

It has not been discussed. As you know, we are doing some contingency planning on the humanitarian side. This is also something that we have given some preliminary thought to, but we are not there at all.

Remarks by Secretary of State Powell, February 5, 2003

Secretary Colin Powell was interviewed on CBS's "60 Minutes II" by Dan Rather.

Q. Listened closely to you today. Impossible to come away with any other conclusion: We're going to war.

Secretary Powell. Well, we hope we don't have to go to war, but I must say that unless there is a change on the part of Saddam Hussein and the Iraqi regime, I think the Security Council will have to deal with this, and I think they will stand up to the challenge of a dictator who doesn't understand that the will of the international community cannot be ignored in this way.

Q. Is it or is it not your expectation that Saddam Hussein will offer some kind of compromise, maybe allow the U-2 flights or something such as that? Be enough to get a delay?

Secretary Powell. It wouldn't surprise me if he offered some token to the inspectors and made some offer with respect to process. But that's not what we're looking for. We're looking for a substantive change in the policy of his government, not just another way to play cat-and-mouse with the inspectors.

So, in my judgment, it will not be enough for him to simply say, "Okay, I'll now start to allow the U-2 flights." That's not the issue. The issue is him making people available so we can find out what they know about these weapons of mass destruction, without monitors being around, so that he starts to turn over equipment that we know he has and he's hiding, that he comes clean. He needs to come clean.

Q. Mr. Secretary, in addition to being a diplomat, you're a lifetime soldier. Why wouldn't Saddam Hussein say, "Look, if they're going to strike me, I'm going to unload what anthrax or some other chemical or biological weapon now," or, at the very least, use them against our troops when they go in?

Secretary Powell. I faced this question before in the Gulf war, and he could have done it then. We made sure that he and his subordinate leaders understood that there would be consequences for such action, and those officers who would actually execute such orders would be held to account after the conflict. They weren't used then.

But even in anticipation that they might be used, we did everything to protect our soldiers and we did not let the threat of that kind of capability stopping us from what needs to be done, and we cannot let that kind of a threat now stop us from what might need to be done.

Q. And the possibility, some would say the probability, that even as we speak he's getting some of these chemical and biological weapons in the hands of terrorists, al-Qaida and otherwise?

Secretary Powell. I don't know if he is or he is not, but that's a chance that we don't want to take. That's why I was so strong in making that case today about the danger of the nexus between terrorism and weapons of mass destruction.

Q. Mr. Secretary, you have to be aware a lot of people are saying Colin Powell has changed, that for a long time he was at least the one strong voice in the Bush administration saying diplomacy, go with the U.N., we can't go it alone; and now you make this appearance before the U.N. and people say, "Listen, he's gone to the other side."

Secretary Powell. I haven't gone anywhere. I am right where I have always been.

These silly labels that people like to hang on various individuals in government are just those: silly labels.

I said clearly at the beginning that we should try the diplomatic route. The President agreed with that. The President decided to go the diplomatic route.

But when we passed Resolution 1441 there was a hammer in 1441. It said you have been in breach; Saddam Hussein and Iraq, we are giving you a chance to get out of breach by coming clean; and if you don't come clean, there are serious consequences. And everybody who worked on that resolution and all of us who passed it on the 8th of November last year understood that serious consequences meant the use of force.

Unfortunately, Saddam Hussein and the Iraqi regime are slowly going by all the off ramps for peace, all the off ramps for diplomacy to solve this problem.

Q. So, unless something dramatic changes, we're going to war?

Secretary Powell. I wouldn't answer it that way, Dan, because I always like to keep hope alive that one can avoid war. We'll see what happens when the two chief inspectors go to Baghdad this weekend and whether they bring back anything of use for Security Council deliberations.

And then, next Friday, both of them, Dr. Blix and Dr. ElBaradei, will report again to the Security Council. I think that will be a very important meeting.

Q. Mr. Secretary, I want to read you what the Iraqi official spokesman said after you appeared before the United Nations today, and I quote directly about what you presented: "A collection of stunts, special effects and unnamed sources." That was one quote. Another: "Utterly unrelated to the truth."
Your reaction to those?

Secretary Powell. I spent most of the last 4 days going over every sentence in my statement and making sure that when people raised questions about every one of those statements we could support those statements.

There are no doctored tapes. There are no doctored photos. What you see is the truth and it is reality, and we are very, very confident in what we presented today.

Q. And to those who say, "Well, there's no smoking gun," would you argue with that?

Secretary Powell. What do you mean by a smoking gun? How about lots of smoke? I think I put forward a case today that said there's lots of smoke.

There are many smoking guns. When we say that he has had thousands of liters of anthrax, and we know it—he's admitted it, it's a matter of record, there's evidence, there's no question about it—is that a smoking gun? Is it a smoking gun that he has this horrible material somewhere in that country and he's not accounted for it? And the very fact that he has not accounted for it, I say could be a smoking gun. It's been a gun that's been smoking for years.

Remarks by Secretary of Defense Rumsfeld and General Myers, February 5, 2003

Secretary Donald Rumsfeld and General Richard Myers responded to questions during hearings on the National Defense Authorization Act for Fiscal Year 2004 (H.R. 1588) before the House Committee on Armed Services.

Congressman Marty Meehan (D-MA). Mr. Secretary, in 1998, as a member of the Project for the New American Century, you sent a letter to then-President Clinton, calling for regime change in Iraq through military means if necessary. And I would like to read a portion of that letter.

"We believe that the United States has the authority under existing U.S. resolutions to take the necessary steps, including military steps, to protect our vital interests in the Gulf. In any case, American policy cannot continue to be crippled by a misguided insistence on unanimity in the U.S. Security Council."

Do you believe that working through the United Nations Security Council with regard to disarming Iraq is a misguided and crippling policy?

Secretary Rumsfeld. No. I support the President's decision to go through the United Nations.

Congressman Meehan. The——

Secretary Rumsfeld. I would add, however, that in life it is rare when one gets unanimity. It seems that almost anything anyone proposes, somebody is not going to like. And so I think the process of going to the United Nations is a useful thing, has been a useful thing. But I think that we probably ought not to expect that in life that we are going to get unanimity.

Congressman Meehan. Sure. Mr. Secretary, today in the Washington Post it highlighted the fact that Saddam Hussein has armed anywhere between 1 and 8 million civilians with semiautomatic rifles, rocket launchers and other military weapons. This militia appears to be designed to fight in cities and towns, street by street. What is being done now to ensure that if we go to war with Iraq, that these civilians will not take arms against our troops; and assuming for a moment that our troops do have to militarily engage armed civilians in the streets of Baghdad, are there any plans currently to use nonlethal technologies to kind of disarm and disperse?

Secretary Rumsfeld. Congressman, you are right. There are reports that that is what Saddam Hussein said. That does not make it so. He announced to the world that everything Colin Powell was going to say was a lie before he even knew what he was going to say. He announced that the pictures that were going to be shown were doctored, which is false. He lies just about on every single thing he says. And believing him would be a big mistake.

I do not know whether or not he has done what he said he is doing. General Franks has a plan that addresses a host of very unpleasant contingencies, and there are a lot of things like that that can go wrong, that can be unpleasant, that can make the task much more complex.

With respect to the use of nonlethal riot agents, I regret to say that we are in a very difficult situation. There is a treaty that the United States signed, and there are existing requirements that, without getting into details, require—well, let me put it this way. Absent a Presidential waiver, in many instances our forces are allowed to shoot somebody and kill them, but they are not allowed to use a nonlethal riot control agent under the law. It is a very awkward situation. There are times when the use of nonlethal riot agents is perfectly appropriate, when transporting dangerous people in a confined space; in an airplane, for example; when there are enemy troops, for example, in a cave in Afghanistan, and you know that there are women and children in there with them and they are firing out at you, and you have the task of getting at them, and you would prefer to get at them without also getting at women and children, and noncombatants as you point out.

The difficulty of writing a rule of engagement so that a soldier, a single human being, a private, a sergeant, knows what to do in that enormously complex—is he going to break the law or not? And we have tangled ourselves up so badly in this issue—Dick Myers and I spent this week, if I am not mistaken, probably an hour, an hour and a half, trying to fashion rules of engagement that would be simple enough so that people who have the task on the front line in a few instances, in a second or two, can make a decision what they can do and what they can't do. And it is very complex, and it is unfortunate in my humble opinion.

Congressman Meehan. Is there any way, Mr. Secretary, we can untangle this I guess within the next month or so?

Secretary Rumsfeld. We are doing our best to live within the straitjacket that has been imposed on us on this subject, and trying to find ways that people can—that we can write things in a way that people can understand them and function and not break the law and still, in certain instances, be able to use nonlethal riot agents.

Do you want to—is that roughly right?

General Myers. I think that is roughly right. And then I think to get to the question about combatants and noncombatants, if people take up arms and become combatants then they are subject to the laws of armed conflict. And on the other hand, if they are noncombatants, if the regime were to use civilians as human shields and so forth, a different matter, and you would have to address that differently. And I think we ought to keep that in mind. If they pick up arms and become combatants, then they are combatants and they will be treated as such.

Human shields, General Franks has thought, tried to think through that very hard, and has worked very diligently with the ground forces and the air forces and those involved to think about ways to handle those situations where you have minimum impact on noncombatants. That is always the goal.

And I think the other thing is that the people of Iraq, my belief is, from the information I am getting, prefer—will not fight in this way; that the average person will not fight, because they will see this for what it is—and that is to get whatever regime that makes food distribution a problem and a reward in some cases, that prevents medical care across the population in general, and that treats minority pieces of the population in ways that are not right—and I think they will see it in that way.

And certainly we have been trying to advertise if conflict is called for, that will be the goal. And hopefully those people that will be tempted to pick up arms will say we are not going to do that.

* * * *

Congressman Robert Andrews (D-NJ). The question I have for you is the far more immediate question. And within the balance of what propriety and respect for classified information would let you do, I think it is very important that we dissuade this notion we hear in the popular media that, quote, going it alone in Iraq is even a remote possibility.

I am confident that Secretary Powell's powerful presentations today at the United Nations will yield a formal declaration of support from the U.N. should conflict be necessary. But, I wonder if you could outline for us the activities for military cooperation that are already in place, that are already committed by allies of the United States, to the extent that concerns about confidentiality and classified information let you do that.

Secretary Rumsfeld. Congressman, you are certainly right. We have a nontrivial number of countries that have already agreed, quite apart from any second resolution, that are willing to participate with military combat and support capabilities. We have a number of countries two or three times that that are close to that.

We have a very large number that have agreed to participate as part of a coalition of the willing, by providing access, basing, overflight and that type of thing. We have another group of countries that are willing to do it only if there is a second resolution at the UN. They say, although the political cover, if you will, that they would get by knowing the number of countries and the names of the countries, that are able to participate or willing to participate would certainly I think bring some of them in regardless of whether there is a second resolution.

And then there is another pretty good group of countries that are indicating that they want to help in a post-Saddam Hussein Iraq in the coalition to assist in reconstruction.

Then there are three or four countries that have said they won't do anything. I believe Libya, Cuba and Germany are ones that have indicated they won't help in any respect, I believe.

* * * *

Congressman Jim Marshall (D-GA). I am one who thinks that if we are going to go into Iraq, sooner is better than later for many reasons, take more than five minutes for me to explain my justification for that. Certainly don't want to do it too soon, and don't want to do it without our allies in tow and without Security Council approval, et cetera.

I think that having allies in tow and Security Council approval is something that is important to the overall war on terrorism.

Mr. Secretary, you mentioned that a larger objective, a long-term objective is to have those kids in the Madrassas learning math instead of hatred of the United States, that in the long-run, cutting off the supply of terrorists is something that is strategically very important to us. And yet, I understand that last week, if I understood the exchange earlier correctly, you and General Myers spent an hour and a half trying to figure out rules of engagement because you were troubled by the use of nonlethal force when the enemy is engaged.

To me, at least, I have to believe that one of the things that you are thinking about is how to do this in Iraq causing the least damage to the long-term strategic objective of not fomenting more angry terrorists and kids that want to kill Americans.

And so I have to assume that one of the things you are considering is how to do this with the least force, as the military always does, and using nonlethal force from time to time. Am I correct about that?

Secretary Rumsfeld. Your phraseology suggested that we were troubled by the use of nonlethal force. That would be a terrible misunderstanding. But what we were trying to do, is to find ways that nonlethal force, that is to say, riot agents, for example, could be used within the law and within the treaty.

And that is a difficult thing to do given the treaty that has been signed by the—it is a treaty, is it not?

General Myers. Yes.

Secretary Rumsfeld. That has been signed by the United States and the other addendum or attachments or agreements or understandings that attach thereto.

We agree with you that it is important that the—that force be measured, force be proportionate, force be designed in a way that it enables you to achieve your military goals with the least conceivable interference with innocent people and noncombatants.

Remarks by President Bush, February 6, 2003

The Secretary of State has now briefed the United Nations Security Council on Iraq's illegal weapons programs, its attempts to hide those weapons, and its links to terrorist groups. I want to thank Secretary Powell for his careful and powerful presentation of the facts.

The information in the Secretary's briefing and other information in our possession was obtained through great skill, and often at personal risk. Uncovering secret information in a totalitarian society is one of the most difficult intelligence challenges. Those who accept that challenge, both in our intelligence services and in those of our friends and allies, perform a great service to all free nations. And I'm grateful for their good work.

The Iraqi regime's violations of Security Council resolutions are evident, and they continue to this hour. The regime has never accounted for a vast arsenal of deadly biological and chemical weapons. To the contrary; the regime is pursuing an elaborate campaign to conceal its weapons materiels, and to hide or intimidate key experts and scientists, all in direct defiance of Security Council 1441.

This deception is directed from the highest levels of the Iraqi regime, including Saddam Hussein, his son, the Vice President, and the very official responsible for cooperating with inspectors. In intercepted conversations, we have heard orders to conceal materiels from the U.N. inspectors. And we have seen through satellite images concealment activity at close to 30 sites, including movement of equipment before inspectors arrive.

The Iraqi regime has actively and secretly attempted to obtain equipment needed to produce chemical, biological and nuclear weapons. Firsthand witnesses have informed us that Iraq has at least seven mobile factories for the production of biological agents, equipment mounted on trucks and rails to evade discovery. Using these factories, Iraq could produce within just months hundreds of pounds of biological poisons.

The Iraqi regime has acquired and tested the means to deliver weapons of mass destruction. All the world has now seen the footage of an Iraqi Mirage aircraft with a fuel tank modified to spray biological agents over wide areas. Iraq has developed spray devices that could be used on unmanned aerial vehicles with ranges far beyond what is permitted by the Security Council. A UAV launched from a vessel off the American coast could reach hundreds of miles inland.

Iraq has never accounted for thousands of bombs and shells capable of delivering chemical weapons. The regime is actively pursuing components for prohibited ballistic missiles. And we have sources that tell us that Saddam Hussein recently authorized Iraqi field commanders to use chemical weapons—the very weapons the dictator tells the world he does not have.

One of the greatest dangers we face is that weapons of mass destruction might be passed to terrorists, who would not hesitate to use those weapons. Saddam Hussein has longstanding, direct and continuing ties to terrorist networks. Senior members of Iraqi intelligence and al Qaeda have met at least eight times since the early 1990s. Iraq has sent bomb-making and document forgery experts to work with al Qaeda. Iraq has also provided al Qaeda with chemical and biological weapons training.

We also know that Iraq is harboring a terrorist network, headed by a senior al Qaeda terrorist planner. The network runs a poison and explosive training center in northeast Iraq, and many of its leaders are known to be in Baghdad. The head of this network traveled to Baghdad for medical treatment and stayed for months. Nearly two dozen associates joined him there and have been operating in Baghdad for more than eight months.

The same terrorist network operating out of Iraq is responsible for the murder, the recent murder, of an American citizen, an American diplomat, Laurence Foley. The same network has plotted terrorism against France, Spain, Italy, Germany, the Republic of Georgia, and Russia, and was caught producing poisons in London. The danger Saddam Hussein poses reaches across the world.

This is the situation as we find it. Twelve years after Saddam Hussein agreed to disarm, and 90 days after the Security Council passed Resolution 1441 by a unanimous vote, Saddam Hussein was required to make a full declaration of his weapons programs. He has not done so. Saddam Hussein was required to fully cooperate in the disarmament of his regime; he has not done so. Saddam Hussein was given a final chance; he is throwing that chance away.

The dictator of Iraq is making his choice. Now the nations of the Security Council must make their own. On November 8th, by demanding the immediate disarmament of Iraq, the United Nations Security Council spoke with clarity and authority. Now the Security Council will show whether its words have any meaning. Having made its demands, the Security Council must not back down, when those demands are defied and mocked by a dictator.

The United States would welcome and support a new resolution which makes clear that the Security Council stands behind its previous demands. Yet resolutions mean little without resolve. And the United States, along with a growing coalition of nations, is resolved to take whatever action is necessary to defend ourselves and disarm the Iraqi regime.

On September the 11th, 2001, the American people saw what terrorists could do, by turning four airplanes into weapons. We will not wait to see what terrorists or terrorist states could do with chemical, biological, radiological or nuclear weapons. Saddam Hussein can now be expected to begin another round of empty concessions, transparently false denials. No doubt, he will play a last-minute game of deception. The game is over.

All the world can rise to this moment. The community of free nations can show that it is strong and confident and determined to keep the peace. The United Nations can renew its purpose and be a source of stability and security in the world. The Security Council can affirm that it is able and prepared to meet future challenges and other dangers. And we can give the Iraqi people their chance to live in freedom and choose their own government.

Saddam Hussein has made Iraq into a prison, a poison factory, and a torture chamber for patriots and dissidents. Saddam Hussein has the motive and the means and the recklessness and the hatred to threaten the American people. Saddam Hussein will be stopped.

Statement by NATO Secretary General Robertson, February 6, 2003

Secretary General Robertson spoke with reporters at NATO Headquarters, Brussels, Belgium.

The Council met this afternoon to consider proposals to task planning for prudent deterrent and defensive measures in relation to a possible threat to Turkey.

As I have said previously, there is complete agreement among NATO countries about their commitment to defend Turkey, and on the substance of the planning measures.

That remains the case. The Washington Treaty imposes responsibilities on all NATO members. These responsibilities will be met.

Where there has been a disagreement is over when to formally task this military planning. Not whether to plan but when to plan.

The Council this afternoon examined the arguments in great detail. We did not reach a final conclusion. But we have put a set of decisions under a silence procedure for agreement early next week.

Does that mean that there is continuing disagreement on the timing issue in NATO? Yes it does. But I am confident that we will reach a decision early next week.

To conclude, I should emphasis that there is no linkage between the timing of NATO's decision and the debate about Iraq at the U.N.. We are not reacting to that debate but to a request that we should begin planning to deal with a threat to Turkey's territory and people.

NATO's solidarity with Turkey is not in doubt.

Remarks by President Bush, February 7, 2003

Q. Sir, can you tell us what you plan to do to win over France, Germany, China, Russia, other allies that are still skeptical about your need to confront Saddam?

President Bush. The Security Council unanimously passed a resolution, called 1441, that said Saddam Hussein must completely disarm. Saddam Hussein has not disarmed. Colin Powell made that case very clear. And now the members of the Security Council can decide whether or not that resolution will have any force, whether it means anything. This is a defining moment for the U.N. Security Council.

President Announces Combat Operations Have Ended President Discusses Future of Iraq Life Under Saddam Hussein

If the Security Council were to allow a dictator to lie and deceive, the Security Council would be weakened. I'm confident that when the members assess their responsibilities and the responsibilities of the U.N., that they will understand that 1441 must be upheld in the fullest.

* * * *

Q. Mr. President, given the facts as Secretary Powell laid them out at the U.N. the other day, do you really see any means of disarming Saddam other than, at this point, using military force?

President Bush. That's up to Saddam Hussein. I mean, the record is poor, at best. The man has been told to disarm for 12 long years. He's ignored the demands of the free world. And then we passed another resolution, and for 90 days he's—the best way I can describe it is—played a game with the inspectors. So the U.N. Security Council has got to make up its mind soon as to whether or not its word means anything.

And, you know, I've never felt we needed a resolution; 1441 speaks very clearly. It talks about serious consequences if he doesn't disarm. However, I said yesterday that it would be helpful to have a resolution so long as it demands compliance with 1441, confirms the spirit of 1441. But Saddam Hussein is—he's treated the demands of the world as a joke up to now, and it was his choice to make. He's the person who gets to decide war and peace.

Q. Do you have any confidence in him at all, given his track record, that he will change his ways?

President Bush. This is a guy who was asked to declare his weapons, said he didn't have any. This is a person who we have proven to the world is deceiving everybody—I mean, he's a master at it. He's a master of deception. As I said yesterday, he'll probably try it again. He'll probably try to lie his way out of compliance or deceive or put out some false statement. You know, if he wanted to disarm, he would have disarmed. We know what a disarmed regime looks like.

I heard somebody say the other day, well, how about a beefed- up inspection regime. Well, the role of inspectors is to sit there and verify whether or not he's disarmed, not to play hide- and-seek in a country the size of California. If Saddam Hussein was interested in peace and interested in complying with the U.N. Security Council resolutions, he would have disarmed. And, yet, for 12 years, plus 90 days, he has tried to avoid disarmament by lying and deceiving.

Yes, John, last question, then we've got to go swear the man in.

Q. Sir, if the Security Council doesn't go along with you, what happens then?

President Bush. I have said that if Saddam Hussein does not disarm, we will lead a coalition to disarm him. And I mean it.

Remarks by Secretary of Defense Rumsfeld, February 7, 2003

Secretary Donald Rumsfeld delivered his remarks at a Town Hall Meeting at Aviano Air Force Base in Italy.

Q. My question is regarding what happens after Iraq. You've already pointed out a pretty good end state, what we want to see happen in Iraq. What's the next step? What do you see the Department of Defense doing to combat terrorism?

Secretary Rumsfeld. The—Iraq or no Iraq, the global war on terrorism will go on, and it will go on because our country and in fact our friends and allies really were never arranged to deal with this. We were organized, trained and equipped to fight armies, navies and air forces, and instead we're facing shadowy enemies that don't have armies, navies or air forces. And they're getting increasingly more powerful weapons and they—terrorist networks have relationship with terrorist states. Now that's an enormous danger we face.

And what the department's going to have to do is to work with the other elements of national power—the Treasury Department, where they're drying up bank accounts; the law enforcement, where they're arresting people—and keep putting pressure on terrorists, so that it's more difficult for them to recruit, more difficult for them to retain people, more difficult for them to move money, more difficult for them to move between countries, and over time create enough disincentives for terrorists that they end up doing something else.

We're going to have to find ways to see that the money that's flowing into these schools that are training young people to be terrorists—that that money is dried up.

We're going to have to find ways to see that those schools teach people mathematics and things that they can use in their lives.

This department is going to have a big responsibility. Iraq is a problem, but so too are other countries, countries that have these terrible weapons. And right now in the news is North Korea. And when people read about what's taking place there, one can't worry—help but worry but that they could then sell those nuclear materials to some other country, a terrorist state, for example, and then that danger is one we have to face.

It's interesting, with the end of the Cold War, people kind of relaxed, took a deep breath and said, "Well, that took care of that." Fifty years we were steady, the Western Europeans were steady, we defeated that danger that existed on the face of the Earth, and it was an enormous accomplishment. And with a deep breath, everyone said, "Well, that takes care of that." And here we are, a decade later—plus, and we recognize that we still live in a dangerous world, we live in an untidy world, we live in a new security environment. And we can live in that world, we can. We can do it. We can't do it without paying attention, we can't do it without a terrific armed force that we have here, we can't do it without working closely with our allies because we do live in a world that's increasingly interdependent, but we can do it, and by golly, we will. Thank you very much.

Remarks by Secretary of Defense Rumsfeld, February 7, 2003

Secretary Donald Rumsfeld was interviewed on the Sabine Christiansen Show on German ARD TV.

Q. Mr. Secretary, You put Germany in one category with Cuba and Libya in remarks this week that have outraged many Germans. What's the point of such blunt characterization of one of your allies?

Secretary Rumsfeld. Well, I didn't put Germany there. I was testifying before a congressional committee and I was asked the question as to which countries are opposed to the President's position with respect to Iraq and I answered the question.

Q. I heard the question.

Secretary Rumsfeld. Yeah, and the answer to the question was that those countries are the ones that have been publicly indicating their opposition. Each of those countries are sovereign countries. Each of those countries are perfectly able to make up their decision. The German government made a decision and those governments have made a decision. All I was doing was accurately representing what they have said publicly. I can't imagine why someone would be so sensitive to be concerned about it.

Q. We are very sensitive, I think, as a democratic state and as an ally of the American people, that we are standing in one line suddenly with Libya or Cuba, with totalitarian states.

Secretary Rumsfeld. Obviously, the German people are wonderful people. My relatives came from here. I still have relatives in this country. I love to come to this country. But the German government made a decision on this issue, which is their right. And they are a sovereign state. They were elected. They can do that. And that's the decision they made. It isn't for me to suggest that what they say publicly is not their position. It is their position.

Q. But it was and seemed to be-sounded to us very hard-and what were you trying to achieve when you said that?

Secretary Rumsfeld. I was trying to answer the Congressman's question. He asked me the question: What are the countries? I said, look, there are a lot of countries that are for the President's position on Iraq. They believe that Iraq should be disarmed. Indeed you saw the letter of eight European countries. You've seen the letter from ten more European countries. That's eighteen European countries who have taken that position. I mentioned those. I then said there are a group of countries that have indicated they would like to help, but only if there is a second resolution in the United Nations. I then said there were a group of countries that have said they would prefer only to help after Saddam Hussein was gone, in a coalition of the willing on a multinational basis. And then I said there is a group of countries who have opposed the President's position. And they said, "who are they?" And I said this is who they are.

Q. But you know that we are helping already quite a lot. We have about two thousand six hundred soldiers that are taking care here on U.S. bases

Secretary Rumsfeld. There's been no question. Indeed, and Germany has been excellent with respect to the Operation Enduring Freedom and the global war on terrorism. Germany has been participating in the ISAF, the International Security Assistance Force in Afghanistan.

It seems to me that if you are asked a question and you answer it before a congressional committee, that that's a very reasonable thing to do.

Q. Would you say Germany is a really reliable ally to the United States?

Secretary Rumsfeld. Well, my goodness. Germany has been a part of the North Atlantic Treaty Organization for many, many years. We've had a long-standing relationship. It's been a good relationship. There have been many times, however, in the NATO environment where one or another country has not agreed with each other. And that's fair enough. That happens. I think each country, each sovereign nation, can make those decisions for themselves; and they do. And I understand that. I don't expect every country to agree with every other country on every issue.

Q. Is that all in the moment, that you say we are just not agreeing with each other? I mean, how would you describe the relationships, America and Germany, in the moment? Our foreign minister, Mr. Fischer, says, well, the relationship is excellent. Would you describe it the same way? Or is it not so excellent?

Secretary Rumsfeld. Oh, I'm not going to get into these adjectives about the relationship. The relationship has been over the decades, a very strong relationship and at this particular moment, obviously in the United Nations, the German government has taken a position that is different from the United States government. And has that ever happened before? Sure. Has it happened with most every country on the face of the earth at one time or another? Sure. Is it likely to happen again sometime? Sure. Can we live with that? You bet.

Q. But if you listen to every word which is exchanged in the moment, then it seemed that the relationship is not really good at the moment.

Secretary Rumsfeld. Well, there are a lot of people in the media who like a good fight and they want to stir it up and they keep pressing this and pressing that. Well, you know, that's what sells newspapers. They like to look for some difference and highlight it and emphasize it.

Q. Okay, President Bush is pressing the Security Council to force Iraq to disarm and to agree on a second resolution authorizing to use force. When can we expect a second resolution?

Secretary Rumsfeld. I didn't know that President Bush was doing that. Since I left the United States has a decision been made to announce, I should say, to put forward a second resolution?

Q. No, he said he would like to have a second, he would like to, um, he did that last night.

Secretary Rumsfeld. I'm just not knowledgeable about it. I've been on an airplane flying across the ocean and so I'm not in a position to comment on that. There may very well be any number of countries who would offer a second resolution, and they could vary considerably, some could suggest the use of appropriate force; others might just simply validate what the world has found, namely, that the declaration was false and that the inspectors have not been cooperated with by Iraq, and leave it there.

Q. But you would favor...

Secretary Rumsfeld. Or you may not have one at all. I mean—Kosovo—there was no resolution for example.

Q. But you would favor a second resolution...

Secretary Rumsfeld. No, it is not for me...

Q. ...because Germany, Russia and France already reacted on that and said that they don't see the need for a second resolution.

Secretary Rumsfeld. I didn't know that. I'm without an opinion on it. That's a matter for the President to decide as to whether or not he wants to have a second resolution. And I just don't know what his decision will be.

Q. If there would be a second resolution, would you count on support from France then for that resolution? Would you count on the majority on the Security Council?

Secretary Rumsfeld. I just don't know. France will decide what it wants to decide. And it not only has a vote like all the other members, but it has a veto and I have no idea what they might finally decide to do. They've clearly been associated with the German government as opposed to the U.S. government on this, and they've been the two countries that have taken the strongest position against the U.S. position. Where they will end up, I suppose, is a function of what kind of a resolution seems to be moving along, and then they will make their judgments, and I just can't predict the outcome.

Q. The Pope is just one of many who say we haven't exhausted all means for a peaceful solution. But President Bush seems convinced that it is now time to act. Do you still give diplomatic efforts a chance?

Secretary Rumsfeld. Well, certainly the President has made that conscious decision. He has said that he wanted to go to the Congress and he wanted to go to the United Nations, and as we have seen, what's been taking place is the momentum supporting his position has been growing. There are countries that are opposed, to be sure. On the other hand, there are dozens of countries that are supporting the President's decision.

Now, what does time do? If time is meant to provide more opportunity for the inspectors to go in and try to find things that Saddam Hussein doesn't want them to find, then there is no amount of time that one could have. Because he has got a country the size of France; he has all kinds of people hiding things. As Secretary Powell presented, he has got people who are actively deceiving and denying. So you could have years and not accomplish anything. On the other hand, if time is to determine whether or not Saddam Hussein wants to cooperate with the United Nations, that doesn't take very long. We've had 12 years. We've had 17 resolutions that he has violated. We've tried diplomatic efforts. We've tried economic sanctions. We've tried limited military activity in the northern and southern no-fly zones. So, each person is going to have to make a judgment on that, and say how much time? Do you want another 12 years, or is one more year, or one more month, and what makes sense? And I think that's something that people are wrestling with in the world. And I think that's a legitimate question.

Q. How much time does Saddam still have?

Secretary Rumsfeld. Well that's a call for the President and the United Nations. It's not for me to say. The President has asked us and others to flow forces and to try to demonstrate to the Iraqi regime that the string has run out and that they should coop-erate, and clearly they wouldn't even have inspectors in there if there hadn't been the threat of force. They've been diddling the United Nations along for years. But if you think back what's been done-a great many things, diplomatic, economic. The effort has been significant by the international community to get them to cooperate.

Q. Monday morning is the deadline at the NATO in Brussels. Do you expect Ger-many to contribute in the defense efforts for Turkey and for further NATO measures concerning Iraq?

Secretary Rumsfeld. I don't know what Germany will do. Turkey is a valued mem-ber of NATO. The issue before the house is: should NATO engage in planning to think about the possibility of providing Turkey with Patriot missile defense capability, with, I believe, NATO AWACS, and possibly one or two other things. I can't imagine any country in this circumstance with a NATO ally, with that neighbor not allowing plan-ning to go forward, so that Turkey, a member of NATO, would conceivably...that NATO would be prepared in the event it was necessary to provide Patriots.

Now, if it is blocked in NATO, I am sure the countries will do it bilaterally. But it would be an amazing thing to me that a country would carefully consider the matter and then oppose that. I just can't imagine a country doing that.

Q. Can you think of German-American relations getting back to where they were with this government? With this German...

Secretary Rumsfeld. Oh, I'm not going to make a comment about this government or that government. The German people vote and it is a democratic country and they elect who they want. And it is not for another country to opine what they think about this government or that government. I've been around so long that I think back-right now people are dramatizing what's going on in the Alliance. But I remember back

Q. Are they dramatizing?

Secretary Rumsfeld. Sure, I remember going back to the Kennedy and Johnson era, President Kennedy and President Johnson. And there was an issue over the Sky Bolt. And it tore everything apart and the Alliance was in shatters and so forth, and we walked our way through it. There was the Mansfield Amendment when I was in Con-gress in the 60's and 70's. And it was going to withdraw forces from Europe and what's it mean—a disengagement, and so forth—and we managed our way through it. There was Michel Jobert the foreign minister of France and Henry Kissinger, the U.S. Secre-tary of State, and they were at each other every day and we worked our way through it. There was the gas line from Russia that was being proposed and that was a big issue. There has been an enormous issue like that practically every four or five or six years of my adult life. And I think that people who are looking at this and thinking, oh my goodness the sky is falling, don't understand history. You are never going to have that many nations finding themselves in full agreement all the time. That's the nature of life.

Q. We hope so, that German-American relations will get back to where they were. Thank you so much.

Secretary Rumsfeld. I think the relationship between Germans and Americans as people is excellent.

Remarks by President Bush, February 8, 2003

President Bush delivered the following radio address to the nation.

Good morning. On Wednesday, Secretary of State Powell briefed the United Nations Security Council on Iraq's illegal weapons program, its attempts to hide those weapons, and its links to terrorist groups.

The Iraqi regime's violations of Security Council Resolutions are evident, they are dangerous to America and the world, and they continue to this hour.

The regime has never accounted for a vast arsenal of deadly, biological and chemical weapons. To the contrary, the regime is pursuing an elaborate campaign to conceal its weapons materials and to hide or intimidate key experts and scientists. This effort of deception is directed from the highest levels of the Iraqi regime, including Saddam Hussein, his son, Iraq's vice president and the very official responsible for cooperating with inspectors.

The Iraqi regime has actively and secretly attempted to obtain equipment needed to produce chemical, biological and nuclear weapons. Firsthand witnesses have informed us that Iraq has at least seven mobile factories for the production of biological agents—equipment mounted on trucks and rails to evade discovery.

The Iraqi regime has acquired and tested the means to deliver weapons of mass destruction. It has never accounted for thousands of bombs and shells capable of delivering chemical weapons. It is actively pursuing components for prohibited ballistic missiles. And we have sources that tell us that Saddam Hussein recently authorized Iraqi field commanders to use chemical weapons—the very weapons the dictator tells us he does not have.

One of the greatest dangers we face is that weapons of mass destruction might be passed to terrorists who would not hesitate to use those weapons. Saddam Hussein has longstanding, direct and continuing ties to terrorist networks. Senior members of Iraqi intelligence and al Qaeda have met at least eight times since the early 1990s. Iraq has sent bomb-making and document forgery experts to work with al Qaeda. Iraq has also provided al Qaeda with chemical and biological weapons training. And an al Qaeda operative was sent to Iraq several times in the late 1990s for help in acquiring poisons and gases.

We also know that Iraq is harboring a terrorist network headed by a senior al Qaeda terrorist planner. This network runs a poison and explosive training camp in northeast Iraq, and many of its leaders are known to be in Baghdad.

This is the situation as we find it—12 years after Saddam Hussein agreed to disarm and more than 90 days after the Security Council passed Resolution 1441 by a unanimous vote. Saddam Hussein was required to make a full declaration of his weapons programs. He has not done so. Saddam Hussein was required to fully cooperate in the disarmament of his regime. He has not done so. Saddam Hussein was given a final chance. He is throwing away that chance.

Having made its demands, the Security Council must not back down when those demands are defied and mocked by a dictator. The United States would welcome and support a new resolution making clear that the Security Council stands behinds its previous demands. Yet, resolutions mean little without resolve. And the United States, along with a growing coalition of nations, will take whatever action is necessary to defend ourselves and disarm the Iraqi regime.

Remarks by Secretary of Defense Rumsfeld, February 8, 2003

Secretary Donald Rumsfeld delivered his remarks at the Munich Conference on European Security Policy.

As to Iraq, we still hope that force may not be necessary to disarm Saddam Hussein. If it comes to that; however, we already know that the same will hold true-some countries will participate, while others may choose not to. The strength of our coalition is that we do not expect every member to be a party of every undertaking.

The support that has already been pledged to disarm Iraq, here in Europe and across the world, is impressive and it's growing. A large number of nations have already said they will be with us in a coalition of the willing-and more are stepping up each day.

Last week, the leaders of Britain, the Czech Republic, Denmark, Hungary, Italy, Poland, Portugal, Spain, issued a courageous statement declaring that "the Iraqi regime and its weapons of mass destruction represent a clear threat to world security," and pledging that they would "remain united in insisting that his regime be disarmed."

Their statement was followed this week by an equally bold declaration by the "Vilnius 10"-Estonia, Latvia, Lithuania, Slovakia, Slovenia, Bulgaria and Romania, Albania, Croatia and Macedonia. They declared: "Our countries understand the dangers posed by tyranny and the special responsibility of democracies to defend shared values... We are prepared to contribute to an international coalition to enforce [Resolution 1441] and the disarmament of Iraq."

Clearly, momentum is building-momentum that sends a critically important message to the Iraqi regime-about the seriousness of purpose and the world's determination that Iraq disarm.

Let me be clear: no one wants war. No, war is never a first or an easy choice. But the risks of war to be balanced against the risks of doing nothing while Iraq pursues the tools of mass destruction.

It may be difficult for some to fully understand just how fundamentally September 11th transformed our country. Americans saw the attacks on the Pentagon and World Trade Towers as a painful and vivid foreshadowing of far more deadly attacks to come. We looked at the destruction caused by the terrorists, who took jetliners, turned them into missiles, and used them to kill 3,000 innocent men, women and children-and we considered the destruction that could be caused by an adversary armed with nuclear, chemical or biological weapons. Instead of 3,000 to be killed, it could be 30,000, 300,000.

Konrad Adenauer once said that "history is the sum total of things that could have been avoided." With history, we have the advantage of hindsight. But we must use that advantage to learn. Our challenge today is even more difficult. It is to try to connect the dots before the fact-to prevent an attack before it happens-not to wait and then hope to try to pick up the pieces after it happens.

To do so, we must come to terms with a fundamental truth-we have reached a point in history when the margin for error that we once enjoyed is gone. In the 20th century, we, all of us here, were dealing, for the most part, with conventional weapons that could kill hundreds or thousands of people. If we miscalculated- or underestimated or ignored a threat-it could absorb an attack, recover, take a deep breath, mobilize, and go and defeat an attacker. In the 21st century, that's not the case; the cost of underestimating the threat is unthinkable.

There is a momentous fact of life that we must come to terms with and it is the nexus between weapons of mass destruction, terrorist states and terrorist networks. On September 11th, terrorist states discovered that missiles are not the only way to strike Washington-or Paris, or Berlin or Rome or any of our capitals. There are other means of delivery-terrorist networks. To the extent a terrorist state transfers weapons of mass destruction to terrorist groups, they could conceal their responsibility for an attack.

To this day, we still do not know with certainty who was behind the 1996 bombing of the Khobar Towers in Saudi Arabia. We still do not know who was responsible for the anthrax attacks in the United States. The nature of terrorist attacks is that it is difficult, and sometimes impossible, to identify those responsible. And a terrorist state that can conceal its responsibility for an attack certainly would not be deterred.

We are all vulnerable to these threats. As President Bush said in Berlin, "Those who despise human freedom will attack it on every continent." We need only to look at the recent terrorist bombings in Kenya or Bali, or the poison cells that have recently been uncovered and disclosed here in Europe, to see that is the case.

Last week, President Bush spoke to the world about the threat posed by Saddam Hussein. This week, Secretary Powell presented additional information in the Security Council:

Intercepted communications between Iraqi officials, Satellite images of Iraqi weapons facilities, and Human intelligence-from agents inside Iraq, defectors and detainees captured in the global war on terror. He presented not opinions, not conjecture, but facts demonstrating:

Iraq's ongoing pursuit of nuclear, chemical and biological weapons; Its development of delivery systems, including missiles and unmanned aerial vehicles; Its tests of chemical weapons on human beings; Its ongoing efforts to deceive U.N. inspectors and conceal its WMD programs; and Its ties to terrorist networks, including al-Qaeda-affiliated cells operating in Baghdad. It is difficult to believe there still could be question in the minds of reasonable people open to the facts before them. The threat is there to see. And if the worst were to happen-and if we had done nothing to stop it- not one of us here today could honestly say that it was a surprise. It will not be a surprise. We are on notice, each of our nations, each of us individually. Really the only question is: what will we do about it?

We all hope for a peaceful solution. But the one chance for a peaceful solution is to make clear that free nations are prepared to use force if necessary-that the world is united and, while reluctant, is willing to act.

There are those who counsel that we should delay preparations. Ironically, that approach could well make war more likely, not less likely-because delaying preparations sends a signal of uncertainty, instead of a signal of resolve. If the international community once again shows a lack of resolve, there is no chance that Saddam Hussein will disarm voluntarily or flee his country- and thus little chance of a peaceful outcome.

There is another reason to prepare now: NATO member nations have an Article V commitment to defend Turkey, should it come under attack by Iraq. Those preventing the Alliance from taking even minimum measures to prepare to do so, risk undermining the credibility of the NATO Alliance.

The stakes are high. Iraq is now defying the 17th U.N. Security Council resolution. The Council voted to warn Iraq that this was its "final opportunity to comply with its disarmament obligations." Quote, unquote. The resolution, which passed unanimously, did not say the "next to final opportunity." It said the "final opportunity." And those who voted for it, and they voted unanimously, knew what it said. They were explicitly reminded what it said. The question is did the U.N. mean it? Did they mean it? We will soon know.

Seventeen times the United Nations has drawn a line in the sand-and 17 times Saddam Hussein has crossed that line. As last week's statement by the eight European leaders so eloquently put it, quote: "If [those resolutions] are not complied with, the Security Council will lose its credibility and world peace will suffer as a result."

Let me add these sad thoughts about the state of the United Nations. An institution that, with the support and acquiescence of many of the nations represented in this room, that would permit Iraq, a terrorist state that refuses to disarm, to become soon the chair of the United Nations Commission on Disarmament, and which recently elected Libya-a terrorist state-to chair the United Nations Commission on Human Rights of all things, seems not to be even struggling to regain credibility.

That these acts of irresponsibility could happen now, at this moment in history, is breathtaking. Those acts will be marked in the history of the U.N. as either the low point of that institution in retreat, or the turning point when the U.N. woke up, took hold of itself, and moved away from a path of ridicule to a path of responsibility.

To understand what is at stake, it is worth reminding ourselves of the history of the U.N.'s predecessor, the League of Nations. When the League failed to act after the invasion of Abyssinia, it was discredited as an instrument of peace. It was discredited properly. The lesson of that experience was best summed up at the time by Canadian Prime Minister Mackenzie King, who declared: "Collective bluffing cannot bring about collective security."

That lesson is as true today, at the start of the 21st century, as it was in the 20th century. The question before us is-have we learned it?

There are moments in history when the judgment and the resolve of free nations are put to the test. This is such a moment. The security environment we are entering is the most dangerous the world has seen. The lives of our children and grandchildren could well hang in the balance.

When they look back at this period, what will they say of us? Have we properly recognized the seriousness of the threat, the nexus between weapons of mass destruction, terrorist states and terrorist networks? Will they say we stood still-paralyzed by a straightjacket of indecision and 20th century thinking-while dangers gathered? Or will they say that we recognized the coming danger, united, and took action before it was too late?

The coming days and weeks will tell.

Remarks by President Bush, February 9, 2003

President Bush delivered his remarks at a retreat for Republicans in White Sulphur Springs, West Virginia.

The world changed on September the 11th. Obviously, it changed for thousands of people's lives for whom we still mourn. But it changed for America, and it's very important that the American people understand the change. We are now a battle ground. We are vulnerable. Therefore, we cannot ignore gathering threats across the ocean. It used to be that we could pick or choose whether or not we would become involved. If we saw a threat, it may be a threat to a friend, in which case we would be involved, but never did we realize the threat could be directed at the American people.

And that changed. And therefore, when we hear of stories about weapons of mass destruction in the hands of a brutal dictator, who hates America, we need to take that seriously, and we are. And when we find out there's links between Baghdad and a killer who actually ordered the killing of one of our fellow citizens, we've got to realize the—what that means to our future.

And that's why this administration and this country is holding the U.N. Security Council and the world to its demands that Saddam Hussein disarm. It is important for the country to realize that Saddam Hussein has fooled the world for 12 years, is used to fooling the world, is confident he can fool the world. He is—wants the world to think that hide and seek is a game that we should play. And it's over.

You see, our country recognizes, and a lot of other countries now recognize as well, the role of the inspector is to show up and verify whether Saddam Hussein is disarming. That's the role of the inspector. The inspectors—there's 104 of them—the role of the inspector is not to go into a state the size of—a country the size of California and try to find out where this guy has hid things over a 12 year period of time.

And the inspectors have gone to Iraq, and it is clear that not only is Saddam Hussein deceiving, it is clear he's not disarming. And so you'll see us over the next short period of time, working with friends and allies and the United Nations to bring that body along. And it's a moment of truth for the United Nations. The United Nations gets to decide, shortly, whether or not it is going to be relevant, in terms of keeping the peace, whether or not its words mean anything.

But one thing is certain, for the sake of peace and for the sake of security, the United States and our friends and allies, we will disarm Saddam Hussein if he will not disarm himself. (Applause.)

And so we've got a lot to do—we've got a lot to do to leave behind a safer country and a better country and a safer and better world. But I'm glad history has called this country into action at this point in time, because there's no doubt in my mind, when we make our mind up, we can achieve a lot.

And there's no doubt in my mind, when the United States acts abroad and home, we do so based upon values—particularly the value that we hold dear to our hearts, and that is, everybody ought to be free. I want to repeat what I said during my State of the Union to you. Liberty is not America's gift to the world. What we believe strongly, and what we hold dear, is liberty is God's gift to mankind. And we hold that value precious. And we believe it is true.

And as we work to make the world a safer place, we'll also work to make the world a freer place. And as we work to make America a freer place, we'll work to make it a more compassionate place. Big obstacles have been placed in our way. Working together, we will achieve what we need to achieve to cross those obstacles.

Remarks by Secretary of State Powell, February 9, 2003

Secretary Colin Powell was interviewed on NBC's "Meet the Press" by Tim Russert.

Q. How close are we to war with Iraq?

Secretary Powell. I do not know. I hope that we can avoid war. There is still the opportunity to avoid war. The President prefers a peaceful solution, but it is in the hands of Saddam Hussein. What he has to do is comply, as required by the U.N. Resolution 1441, and turn over all the documents, make available all the scientists and engineers for interview, show us everything that he has been doing for these many years with respect to weapons of mass destruction.

[Resolution] 1441 was not a confusing document. It was very clear. Saddam is in material breach, he has been in material breach. We give him a chance to come clean. He takes that chance or not. If he does not take the chance, then serious consequences follow.

So far, he has ignored the will of the United Nations, the will of the Security Council, as expressed in 1441. So we are running out of time and he has only got a short period of time left to demonstrate compliance or force will have to be used to bring him into compliance.

Q. Hans Blix, the Chief U.N. weapons inspector, is in Iraq today. He is reporting to the U.N. Security Council on Friday— Valentine's Day, ironically. If he says that Saddam is still not cooperating, how many days does Saddam have left?

Secretary Powell. I think if he says that, then the Security Council will have to sit in session immediately and determine what should happen next. But I do not want to put a timeline on it, nor do I want to prejudge what Dr. Blix and Dr. ElBaradei may say.

But Friday is going to be an important day for the Security Council and if we still find the kind of noncompliance that we have seen for the past several months, then I think it is time for the Security Council to start considering a resolution that says Iraq is in material breach and it is time for serious consequences to follow. That was the intent behind 1441. Everyone who voted for 1441 last November 8 understood that.

Q. The Germans and the French have a proposal, which they talked about again today, which would put United Nations troops in Iraq, triple the number of inspectors, and give inspections a longer time. Could you accept that proposal?

Secretary Powell. First of all, I do not know what the proposal is. There have only been press reports on the proposal. But I suspect it is a variation of what the French Foreign Minister said at the Security Council on Wednesday, and it is the wrong issue. The issue is not more inspectors; the issue is compliance on the part of Saddam Hussein. If he complies, if he does what he is supposed to do and tells us where the anthrax went, where did the botulinum toxin go, where did all the missiles go, where is the mustard gas, where are all of the documents you have been hiding—if he complies, then that can be done with a handful of inspectors. But if he is not complying, tripling the numbers of inspectors does not deal with the issue.

This idea of more inspectors or a no-fly zone or whatever else may be in this proposal that is being developed is a diversion, not a solution.

Q. If, in fact, Mr. Blix says Saddam is still not complying, but the French and the Russians and the Chinese and the Germans say let's give them more time, will the United States go forward without the United Nations?

Secretary Powell. If he is not complying, then what is more time for? For what purpose, if he is not going to comply? He can do that today, he can do that tomorrow— more time is not the issue. Compliance is the issue. And how much longer are we to wait? The resolution was passed on the 8th of November. We are now into February. It is three months—November, December, January—February. And so it is time for him to comply. And so far, he has not complied and he has had these months to comply.

Q. We would go forward without the U.N., if need be?

Secretary Powell. If the U.N. does not face up to its responsibilities as clearly laid out in Resolution 1441, then it would be necessary for the United States to act with a willing coalition. And there are many nations that have stepped forward. You saw the statement from a group of 8 European nations and another statement a few days later from another group of 10 European nations. And so there will be many members in this coalition who see the danger as clearly as we do, as clearly as the United Nations did when it passed U.N. Resolution 1441. This is not the time for the United Nations to step back from the clear statement it made in U.N. Resolution 1441.

Q. When you went before the United Nations on Wednesday, you produced this slide from November 10 talking about Iraqi ballistic missiles and said that it showed activity there. The Iraqis then brought out news people to that site and said Powell's all wrong, nothing illegal was going on there. Do you stand by your accusations?

Secretary Powell. Yes. And when we were preparing that material, we knew that Iraq would be instantly preparing its dog- and-pony shows for reporters to be taken to sites. And I could have told you as that slide was going up that the very next day there would be activity at that site for reporters to go see.

It is not just what we saw on that particular day; it is a pattern of activity we look at over an extended period of time. And on the particular day that that shot was taken, there was a pattern of activity that was out of the normal, it was not what we usually see at that site. So it is not just what you see at one day; it is a pattern of activity that builds up over time, and it is other sources building on what we see in the photographs. And everything that I laid out that day is multi- sourced and I am quite sure will stand the test of time.

Q. As you remember in 1991, the Persian Gulf war, the Kuwaiti Ambassador to the U.S.'s daughter came forward with a fake story. There were suggestions of satellite photos showing 250,000 Iraqi troops on the Saudi border which the St. Petersburg Times demonstrated was not correct, and now this headline about Britain's intelligence dossier. Britain admits that much of its report on Iraq came from magazines, in fact, a "cut-and-paste" job of magazines—something you called a fine report.

Are you concerned that there's a sloppiness with evidence and a rush to war?

Secretary Powell. No, I do not think so. I think Britain stands behind its document. They have acknowledged that they use other sources that they did not acknowledge or attribute, but I think the document stands up well because it describes a pattern of deceit on the part of the Iraqis that is not just a pattern of deceit that exists today, but has existed for many years and has been documented in many, many ways. I do not think it was presented as an intelligence document. It was presented as a document, a 19-page document, if my memory serves me correctly, that demonstrates how the Iraqis, over time, have deceived inspectors, have tried to send them down the wrong path. And it is a pattern that continues to this day.

Q. You stand by every word?

Secretary Powell. It is not my document. I will let the British—

Q. Of your presentation?

Secretary Powell. Oh, yes.

Q. Let me show you another slide you put up, and this is the tape and how you described it:

"Here you see 15 munitions bunkers in yellow and red outlines. The four that are in red squares represent active chemical munitions bunkers."

If we know those are active chemical bunkers, why not just send the inspectors there?

Secretary Powell. Well, the inspectors eventually did go there, and by the time they got there, they were no longer active chemical bunkers. And if you note, I think—I do not have the pictures right in front of me, but we took the pictures before the inspectors arrived, and the second picture I showed or the third picture I showed had the inspectors arriving with more than enough notice that this was a likely place to be inspected, so that we believe, and I think the evidence shows clearly, that the Iraqis had sanitized the sites.

Q. You also mentioned a terrorist camp in Northern Iraq which has been there for at least 8 months. Why don't we just take it out?

Secretary Powell. Well, there are lots of places that one could say why don't we just take out, but we examine all of these things. We are constantly reviewing what our military options are and we are constantly reflecting how a particular action might play in diplomatic terms as well. But we have taken none of our options off the table and we have been able to monitor these sites and these activities and form a pattern of behavior that is troubling. But we have considered various options over time, but I would not like to get into a discussion of any particular option or why we did or did not execute it.

Q. But that camp is in Kurdish-controlled Iraq. Why don't you tell the Kurds to have it broken down, rather than blame Saddam?

Secretary Powell. The Kurds are aware of the site. There is tension up in that area. There is not complete control over the Kurds of the site and we do know that there are connections between Iraqi intelligence officers and the people who are responsible for that site. And we can see these connections and we can see material that comes out of that site and then gets into transit lanes that deliver such material into parts of Western Europe, and we have been rolling up the network.

Q. Let me show you a CIA analysis that was from October 7, 2002:
"Baghdad, for now, appears to be drawing a line short of conducting terrorist attacks with conventional or chemical- biological weapons against the U.S. Should Saddam conclude a U.S.-led attack could no longer be deterred, he probably would become much less constrained in adopting terrorist actions. Saddam might decide that the extreme step of assisting Islamic terrorists in conducting any weapons of mass destruction attack against the U.S. would be his last chance to exact vengeance by taking a large number of victims with him."
Do you agree with that?

Secretary Powell. He might and he might not. It is not a statement of fact. It is a statement of opinion on the part of the analyst saying this is what he might do. He might also have done that during the Gulf war, but we made it clear to Iraq and to all of Iraq's generals and other leaders that anybody participating in such an act or delivering such weapons would be held very much to account after a conflict.

And it is a risk that I think we have to take because we cannot be terrified into inaction because they might use these kinds of weapons. But we are making it clear in all of our declarations and what we are communicating to Iraq that it would not be wise for any military leader or political leader currently in this Iraqi regime to take such action in the event of a conflict or in anticipation of a conflict because they would be held very much personally to account.

Q. Would we pledge not to use nuclear weapons under any circumstances in Iraq?

Secretary Powell. Our declaratory policy with respect to all of the weapons available to the President of the United States is we do not rule any in or any out. It does not mean we are going to use nuclear weapons. You know, we have quite a capability in the Armed Forces of the United States. But as a matter of declaratory policy, we do not say what we might or might not do with any particular weapon that is in the inventory of the Armed Forces of the United States.

Q. But if he uses chemical, we could respond with nuclear?
Secretary Powell. I have answered the question, and it is always wiser to just leave that declaratory policy as I have stated it, Tim.

Q. Let me take you back to your biography of 1995, My American Journey:
"—we should not commit military force until we had a clear political objective. My advice would always be that the tough political goals had to be set first."

Secretary Powell. Yes.

Q. And let's apply those to Iraq. And I refer you to Bob Woodward's book, Bush at War, where he talks about conversations you had with President Bush talking about Iraq and the complication. And here's one:
"Powell told Bush that as he was getting his head around the Iraq question he needed to think about the broader issues, all the consequences of war. Powell said the President had to consider what a military operation against Iraq would do in the Arab world. The entire region could be destabilized. Friendly regimes in Saudi Arabia, Egypt, Jordan, could be put in jeopardy or overthrown. Anger, frustration in America abounded. War could change everything in the Middle East."
Could the entire Middle East become destabilized if we go into Iraq?

Secretary Powell. Or more stabilized. It is not known at this point. We do not know how it will unfold. But I think that if conflict comes we would hope to do it quickly, we will hope to do it with a minimum of destruction and a minimum loss of civilian life, and we would remove a despotic regime. And that might well set up circumstances for a more stable Middle East and Persian Gulf region.

But as President Bush was considering all of this, he thought of everything. We put all the considerations on the table before the President: the difficulty we would have in the region with disturbances and some transient problems we would have, and some of the risks of destabilization. And I think that is what makes this a good national security team. Everything was taken into consideration as we worked out way through this problem last summer and fall.

Q. And what about the expense? How much would it cost? How long will we be there?

Secretary Powell. I do not know how much it would cost and I just cannot tell you in terms of dollar amounts how much this would cost. But it would not be an inexpensive operation. But it is a cost that I think we have to bear.

How long the United States Armed Forces might be there also is a question we cannot answer at this time. A lot would depend on the nature of the conflict and how quickly we are able to put in place a representative form of government that would be better for the region and better for the people of Iraq. But we should not be under any illusions as to the simple reality that it will take a significant investment of the United States and the United States Armed Forces, but I think we will be joined in this effort by many other nations, even those who are at the moment objecting to any military action whatsoever.

Joint Declaration by Russia, Germany, and France, February 10, 2003

Russia, Germany and France, in close coordination, reaffirm that the disarmament of Iraq, in accordance with the relevant U.N. resolutions since UNSCR 687, is the common aim of the international community, and that it must be pursued to its conclusion within the shortest possible period. There is a debate over the means to achieve this. This debate must continue in the spirit of friendship and respect that characterizes our relations with the United States and other countries. Any solution must be inspired by the principles of the United Nations Charter, as stated recently by Mr Kofi Annan. UNSCR 1441, adopted unanimously by the Security Council, provides a framework whose possibilities have not yet been thoroughly explored. The inspections conducted by UNMOVIC and the IAEA have already yielded results. Russia, Germany and France favor the continuation of the inspections and the substantial strengthening of their human and technical capabilities by all possible means and in consultation with the inspectors, within the framework of UNSCR 1441. There is still an alternative to war. The use of force could be only a last resort. Russia, Germany and France are determined to give every chance to the peaceful disarmament of Iraq. It is up to Iraq to cooperate actively with UNMOVIC and the IAEA so that they can complete the inspections. The Iraqi regime must face up to its responsibilities in full. Russia, Germany and France note that the position they express reflects that of a large number of countries, particularly within the Security Council.

Statement by NATO Secretary General Robertson, February 10, 2003

Secretary General Robertson spoke with reporters at NATO Headquarters, Brussels, Belgium.

As you all know, silence on the technical issue of tasking the NATO Military Authorities to undertake prudent contingency planning to deter or defend against a possible threat to Turkey was broken by three NATO countries this morning.

In parallel, Turkey has requested consultations under Article 4 of the North Atlantic Treaty.

Article 4 states that NATO's members will consult together whenever, in the opinion of any of them, the territorial integrity, political independence or security of any NATO country is threatened.

These consultations began this morning and will resume this afternoon, at a meeting of the NATO Council at 4.30 p.m.

This is undoubtedly a difficult situation. But Allies have had differences before and will have more in the future. What matters is to arrive at a consensus. And we will.

We are united in our commitment to the security of all NATO's members. The question still is not "if" but "when" to begin the planning.

We have a difficult issue in front of us. It is an issue which concerns solidarity with one ally—Turkey. It is *not* related to any possible participation by NATO in a military operation against Iraq.

I am not trying to minimize the issue. It is serious. The NATO nations take it seriously—hence the debate—and Allies will act responsively and collectively.

Questions and Answers

Spokesman: Thank you. I will now invite questions. Could you please ask your questions in a short way and, also, avoid asking multiple and sub-questions, so everyone has a chance. Thank you very much. We'll start with Klaus Pompers, ZDF.

Q. Klaus Pompers. Very short question, Secretary General: Who is to blame?

Secretary General Robertson. I don't allocate blame. Three countries have broken silence. Therefore, 16 countries agree with the tasking. But the differences of opinion that exist today are no different to differences that have existed. They're just slightly more serious at this time. But I don't allocate blame or praise. We have to work to get a consensus. That's difficult. It's sometimes very painful. But we've done it before and I'm confident that we can do it again.

Q. Secretary General, Judy Dempsey, Financial Times. Did Turkey ask for Article Four in 1991?

Secretary General Robertson. The discussions in 1991 were complicated and we're not actually sure whether they asked for those consultations under Article Four, or whether that was avoided by the deployments that took place. But I'm pretty certain that this is most likely to be the first time that a nation has asked for formal consultations under Article Four.

Q. Michael Thurston, AFP. It's been over three weeks, now, that you haven't come to an agreement. How long do you think it's going to take for an agreement? Is it possible to reach an agreement within days, weeks, or...? How long is it going to take?

Robertson. Well, I'm confident that we will reach agreement, but I can't say when that's going to happen. Three nations have yet to be persuaded. But we're going to meet today. We are probably, if necessary, going to meet tomorrow or the next day, and we will eventually get an agreement, because that's the way the alliance works and everybody this morning, including the countries who have broken silence, have emphasized the unity that there is in terms of defending Turkey and of achieving an alliance consensus.

So there's a lot of work going on in this building, but also in a lot of capitals as well, to try and find the formula that will allow the taskings to go ahead.

* * * *

Q. Mag News. I'm sorry you'll not be able to see me. Anyhow, do you still plead that there is no argument among the NATO members?

Secretary General Robertson. Well, there's still an argument. I've never denied that there was an argument. I think that would be foolish. There is a very heated argument inside NATO about the timing. But that what it's about. It is about the timing. And clearly, if we haven't achieved agreement after three weeks of discussion, then that argument is of a serious nature.

But at the same time, I think people are focusing on it now in a very determined way, that Turkey has asked for consultations under four, and many of the countries concerned believe that that now focuses it in an invaluable way on Turkey and its defense and that that may well lead, or help to lead to a solution to the present problems, the existing difficulties.

Remarks by President Bush and Australian Prime Minister Howard, February 10, 2003

President Bush and Prime Minister Howard delivered their remarks during their meeting at the White House.

President Bush. Prime Minister Howard is a close, personal friend of mine; a person whose judgment I count on; a person with whom I speak quite frequently. I believe he's a man of clear vision. He sees the threats that the free world faces as we go into the 21st century. I'm proud to—I'm proud to work with him on behalf of a peaceful world and a freer society. He's a man grounded in good values and I respect him a lot, and I'm glad he's back here in the Oval Office.

Prime Minister Howard. Well, thank you very much, Mr. President. I'm delighted to be back in the United States, where talk is naturally about Iraq and other related matters. I want to say that from the very beginning, the President has shown very strong leadership on a difficult issue. He's been prepared to go out and argue a very strong case. It's not been an issue that's been free of criticism for any of those who've advocated a particular point of view.

Australia's position concerning Iraq is very clear. We believe a world in which weapons of mass destruction are in the hands of rogue states, with the potential threat of them falling into the hands of terrorists, is not a world that Australia—if we can possibly avoid it—wants to be part of. And that is the fundamental reason why Australia has taken the position she has.

And it's the fundamental reason why we believe the goals that the United States set of disarming Iraq are proper goals and they are goals that the entire world should pursue. We all hope that they might—despite the apparent unlikelihood, we all hope that there might be a peaceful solution. The one real chance of a peaceful solution is the whole world saying the same thing to Iraq.

And that's why we believe the closest possible cooperation and unity of—objective unity of advocacy is very important.

Q. Iraq has agreed to allow U-2 flights and also private interviews with some scientists. Does this make it harder for you to argue that Saddam Hussein is not—is not cooperating?

President Bush. No, Iraq needs to disarm. And the reason why we even need to fly U-2 flights is because they're not disarming. We know what a disarmed country looks like. And Iraq doesn't look like that. This is a man who is trying to stall for time, trying to play a diplomatic game. He's been successful at it for 12 years. But, no, the question is, will he disarm.

I notice somebody said the other day, well, we need more inspectors. Well, a disarmed—a country which is disarming really needs one or two inspectors to verify the fact that they're disarming. We're not playing hide-and-seek. That's what he wants to continue to play. And so, you know, Saddam's got to disarm. If he doesn't, we'll disarm him.

Q. Sir, can I ask an Australian question?

President Bush. Please.

Q. Could you tell us whether you count Australia as part of the coalition of the willing?

President Bush. Yes, I do. You know, what that means is up to John to decide. But I certainly count him as somebody that understands that the world changed on September the 11th, 2001. Ironically enough, John Howard was in America that day, in Washington, D.C., the day the enemy hit.

In our country it used to be that oceans could protect us—at least we thought so. There was wars on other continents, but we were safe. And so we could decide whether or not we addressed the threat on our own time. If there was a threat gathering from afar, we could say, well, let's see, it may be in our interest to get involved, or it may not be. We had the luxury. September the 11th, that changed. America is now a battle-ground in the war on terror.

Secondly, the Secretary of State made it very clear that there are connections between Saddam Hussein and terrorist networks. And, therefore, it is incumbent upon all of us who love freedom to understand the new world in which we live. John Howard understands that.

Q. In addition to being among the some people who are calling for inspections, the French today blocked NATO from helping Turkey. And President Chirac said, nothing today justifies a war.

President Bush. Yes.

Q. Given what Americans and the French went through in the last century, are you upset by their attitude now?

President Bush. I wouldn't—"upset" isn't the proper word. I am disappointed that France would block NATO from helping a country like Turkey prepare. I don't under-stand that decision. It affects the alliance in a negative way.

Q. You think it does?

President Bush. I think it affects the alliance in a negative way, when you're not able to make a statement of mutual defense. I had a good talk with Jacques Chirac recently. I assured him that, you know, that we would continue to try to work with France as best we can. France has been a long time friend of the United States. We've got a lot in common. But I think the decision on NATO is shortsighted in my judg-ment. Hopefully, they'll reconsider.

Q. Mr. President, there are many Australians—there are many Australians and others who are still not convinced that they should be going with you to war. At this late stage what's your personal message to them?

President Bush. My personal message is that I want to keep the peace and make the world more peaceful. I understand why people don't like to commit the military to action. I can understand that. I'm the person in this country that hugs the mothers and the widows if their son or husband dies. I know people would like to avoid armed conflict. And so would I. But the risks of doing nothing far outweigh the risks of what-ever it takes to disarm Saddam Hussein.

I've thought long and hard about this issue. My job is to protect the American peo-ple from further harm. I believe that Saddam Hussein is a threat to the American peo-ple. I also know he's a threat to our friends and allies.

The second thing—my message is, and I started speaking about this today, I also have got great compassion and concern for the Iraqi people. These are people who have been tortured and brutalized, people who have been raped because they may disagree with Saddam Hussein. He's a brutal dictator. In this country and in Australia people believe that everybody has got worth, everybody counts, that everybody is equal in the eyes of the Almighty. So the issue is not only peace, the issue is freedom and liberty.

I made it clear in my State of the Union—and the people of Australia must understand this—I don't believe liberty is America's gift to the world; I believe it is God's gift to humanity.

Remarks by Secretary of Defense Rumsfeld and Australian Prime Minister Howard, February 10, 2003

Prime Minister Howard. Well, thank you very much, Mr. Secretary. I'm delighted to be back at the Pentagon. The relationship between Australia and the United States has many facets. One of those has been our constant cooperation in military conflicts over the years. We value very much that association. Australians, particularly the older generation, remember the vital help rendered to us during World War II by the United States. And together we have fought on many battlefields and done many things in pursuit of the values that we share.

We face as close friends the threat around the world of weapons of mass destruction in the hands of rogue states and the frightening possibility that those same weapons could fall into the hands of international terrorists. That is a new dimension of instability, replacing some of the older threats. And that's the motivation for what Australia has been doing, in partnership with the United States, concerning Iraq.

We hope that military conflict can be avoided. It can only be avoided—if there's a faint hope of it being avoided—that can only happen if you get the entire world, through the United Nations, saying the one thing to Iraq: The game is up. You must disarm.

If that were to happen, and we were to see the Arab states energized to say the same thing, we may be able to avoid a conflict. And that is why we believe, not as a matter of international law, but a matter of accumulating international political pressure and diplomatic pressure, that a further resolution is desirable.

I've had a very good discussion with the secretary about the predeployment. The basis of ours is understood by the United States. There's yet to be a final decision taken, if military conflict becomes the ultimate option, and that is one that will be dealt with in accordance with the constitutional processes of Australia. We have, nonetheless, along with the United Kingdom, predeployed forces. Australia does not believe that all of the heavy lifting on something like this should be done by the United States and United Kingdom alone, albeit our contribution is a much smaller one, commensurate with the different size of our country. But you are sending a new and sharper signal when you predeploy, and that's what we've done, and we've been very willing to do that in cooperation with our American and British friends. And as always, the Australian military is very happy to work in close harmony and cooperation with the United States military. It's been a long association and a very positive one.

* * * *

Q. Mr. Secretary, France, Germany and Belgium today vetoed NATO protection for Turkey, saying that that would simply make it easier for the United States to invade Iraq. Could NATO begin disintegrating over decisions like this?

Secretary Rumsfeld. Oh, I think not. NATO's been around a long time, and I suspect it'll be around a long time ahead.

I think that technically what they did was not veto, but I think the phrase is they broke silence on a—what otherwise would have been a planning process for NATO. And I have not heard precisely what they said as to what their reasons were, but NATO very likely will end up engaged in that subject through a different route. It's my understanding that the next step very likely would be Turkey coming back in, as is the right of any member nation, and having the subject engaged again through a different mechanism of NATO.

I think the—it was—it's unfortunate that they are in stark disagreement with the rest of their NATO allies. There's three countries. There are 19 countries in NATO. So it's 16 to 3. I think it's a mistake. And what we have to do for the United States is make sure that that planning does go forward, preferably within NATO, but if not, bilaterally or multiple bilaterals. And we are already going about that task.

As you'll recall, what—all that was asked for was that planning begin for AWACS, which—and for chemical and biological detection units and for Patriot capability, all of which are defensive. And it seems to me that NATO will end up doing that, and the time that's lost will be made up because we'll start to do it bilaterally. And in the event that the three stand out at the end, my guess is that the other 16 nations of NATO would form a coalition to provide that kind of assistance.

Q. Could any delay for such protection delay a possible attack on Iraq were President Bush to make such a decision?

Secretary Rumsfeld. Well, no, because the planning's going to go forward outside of NATO if necessary, the plan to see that Turkey's circumstance is at it should be. It's an important ally in NATO. It's a moderate Moslem state. And it seems to me that those three countries taking that position prevents NATO from fulfilling its obligation to a NATO ally. And I'm sure that they'll find—NATO will find a way to do it eventually.

Q. Mr. Secretary, you just have come back from Germany, and you've spoken over the weekend to so many of the United States allies. What is your real sense of what is going on in Europe at the moment? If Germany and France, two of our most traditional allies, plus Belgium, are now taking this view, aside from the fact the U.S. is going to go forward, as you say, what does it really say to you about U.S. relations with Germany? I mean, what do you take from all of this? What does all of this really mean?

Secretary Rumsfeld. Well, there have been differences within NATO my entire life-time—adult lifetime. I could list six or eight of them: the natural gas pipeline, the Sky-bolt back in the Kennedy and McNamara era. I mean, there's always been something. And that's—that's the nature of it. When you've got that many countries going togeth-er, everyone's not always going to agree on everything.

And what's the meaning of it? I guess time will tell. But at the moment, what it means is that three European countries are isolated from the rest of the NATO alliance: 16 countries—two North American and 14 in Europe—don't agree with them, with those three countries. That's what it means.

Remarks by Secretary of State Powell, February 10, 2003

Secretary Colin Powell was interviewed by the Los Angeles Times Editorial Board.

Q. You, of course, have been known to put forth what's been called now "The Powell Doctrine," which has to with now how you're getting in and know how you're getting out. So what exactly, then, is the objective in getting in to Iraq? Is it to disarm and/or nation-build, both? And what's the short-term and long-term strategy in terms of getting in and getting out?

Secretary Powell. First of all, we don't want to "get in" if it can be avoided. We've been trying, and I've been working very hard, the President's been working very hard, to see if we can find a peaceful solution. But it became clear in the first year and a half of the administration that even with smart sanctions, even with no-fly zones and the like, and even with 16 previous resolutions, Saddam Hussein was not showing any intention to disarm himself of weapons that we knew he had and the whole world knew he had.

And so we took it to the U.N. looking for a peaceful solution. Could have avoided the U.N. and just say, "That's it, we're going to attack." Went to the U.N. because it was an international problem, not just a U.S. problem, and 3 months ago, on the 8th of November, passed a resolution, 1441, as you're all familiar with, that did several things. One, you're guilty. That's what the resolution said. You are in material breach, you have been in material breach, you remain in material breach. And you can generate new material breaches if you don't cooperate and if you don't give us an honest declara-tion. That's what the resolution said. We will send the inspectors in to help you dis-arm, but this is your last chance. You've already been found guilty.

And if you don't take this last chance, then all of this has to come back to the Secu-rity Council for the consideration of serious consequences. Every member of the Council who voted that morning, to include Syria, France and all the other 13, knew exactly what the resolution meant. We want a peaceful solution, we're giving you one last chance, the inspectors will help you seize that chance, but serious consequences flow.

And we have been waiting now for 3-plus months for a satisfactory answer and we have continued to get unsatisfactory responses. The declaration, the fooling around he's doing, the deception, the deceiving, the slipping out a little bit to see if that'll keep everybody quiet and away from him. And we're reaching a moment of truth where this can't continue and therefore military force may be required.

But it is a last resort, and consistent with what is sometimes called "The Powell Doctrine," you try to find other ways to solve a problem. But when you can't solve it in other ways and you use force, you use it in a decisive manner.

If a peaceful way cannot be found and force is used, it is preferable to do it within the context of the international community. But if that is not possible, the President has made it clear from the very beginning that he's prepared to act with a willing coalition, even if it isn't under U.N. authority. We think it still would be under U.N. authority because 1441 and earlier resolutions, we believe, gives sufficient authority to such action.

And there are a number of countries who are willing to go with us. The Prime Minister of Australia is here today and he's made a commitment. His troops are moving. The Prime Minister of the United Kingdom, Spain, Italy, the Vilnius 10, the group of eight from last week. So we're not in this alone.

Now, to get to the heart of your question, to what we want to do. One, if military action was required, we would want to conduct a military operation that would be over as quickly as possible and would be for the purpose of removing this regime that has defied the international community for 12 years, and helping the Iraqi people put in place a responsible regime that would be committed to disarmament. We would then also make sure that the country is disarmed of its weapons of mass destruction.

We would do everything we could to preserve infrastructure, to make sure that civilians are not injured during this operation, and start to redirect the energies of that nation and the wealth of that nation and the great talent that exists in that nation in a more positive direction. Twenty billion dollars a year of oil revenue is available to the people of Iraq. We would protect that treasure, make sure that that oil is used for the benefit of the people, and hopefully we could go home as quickly as we have established something that is stable, keeps the country intact, is representative of all the people.

We would hopefully do this with the assistance of many other nations, the United Nations and with the European Union and a number of other nations that have expressed a willingness to help. And I think we will have fundamentally changed the political situation in that part of the world. No longer a Saddam Hussein threatening neighbors, shooting rockets at neighbors or shooting gas at people. Stopped proliferation at least in that part of the world and that country, and perhaps that would be an example to others.

And then the United States would want to disengage as quickly as we can and as safely as we can, but making sure we haven't left instability in our wake. How long would that take? Probably a while. I've got no illusions.

Q. A while, meaning?

Secretary Powell. I can't tell. I don't know. A lot will depend on how quickly the Iraqis are able to come together. It's a complex political problem because you've got Shi'as, you've got Kurds, you've got the Sunnis, and you have experts in this room who know this region very, very well. And we've got to find a model that would cause them to come together in some form of government. And I think there will be a role for somebody for some extended period of time to assist them. It might be international, through the U.N. in some manner, or it might be a leadership on the part of a coalition of the willing.

But I can tell you that all of the incentive will be there for us to finish the job and then leave, but not leave before the job is finished. But I cannot tell you at this point whether that would be months or years. I'd have a better idea immediately after when we see the kind of response we get from the people and we see the kind of reaction to those who have been outside the country and those who are still inside the country and are in leadership positions and willing to participate in the rebuilding of a political system.

But it is going to be a very demanding task and there should be no illusions about it, and it is not going to be something that's a matter of weeks. I think it's going to be an extended period. I just don't want to put an X—I don't want to fill in the X because I don't know what to tell you that would not be misleading.

Q. As you see it now, then, is U.S. action in Iraq, attack on Iraq, inevitable?

Secretary Powell. Nothing is inevitable, but I think the likelihood of us finding a peaceful solution is becoming diminished with each passing day in the face of continued Iraq noncompliance and non-cooperation. And they keep trying to play games. The inspectors went there this weekend, the two chief inspectors, and at this late date you would have thought Iraq, if they were serious, would have said, "Here is every document we own. You can speak to anybody, take them anywhere you want. You can go take them to L.A. and talk to them. You can see anything. And by the way, here's some things you don't even know about. But we want to come clean so we're bringing it out for you to see."

Now, that is the kind of attitude that we are looking for and hoped for when Resolution 1441 passed and Iraq was finally faced with serious consequences for ignoring the will of the international community. There were never real teeth in the previous resolutions. This one has real teeth in it and the President is deadly serious, and there are tens upon tens of thousands of United States troops and British troops and Australian troops on the move to put the pressure on in the name of diplomacy and to take military action if diplomacy does not find a way forward.

And one would think that Iraq, seeing all this, would realize that you can come clean now or you can be removed.

Q. Mr. Secretary, today the Iraqis have said that they'll allow U-2 flights and they provided documents yesterday. Do you have any—

Secretary Powell. They immediately then qualified it within 2 hours to say only if the United States and the United Kingdom did this or did that or didn't do this or that with respect to the no-fly zones. So they—they always do this.

Q. Even today?

Secretary Powell. Yeah, today. I mean, in one breath they said we're going to let the U-2 flights begin, and then the latest wire service thing I saw just a few moments ago said but there's some things that the U.S. has to do.

The question isn't—isn't getting a U-2 flight up there. If they were cooperating, we wouldn't need any U-2 flights. If they were doing what the clear intent of the resolution is, you don't need 300 or 500 or 1,000 more inspectors—the French-German, now I guess Russian diversionary tactic. If they were doing what they were supposed to do under the resolution, you could probably do it with half the number of inspectors that are there now.

Q. What about the new initiative? Is—how much is that derailing, diverting attention? How difficult is it going to be to pull together the Security Council again?

Secretary Powell. It, of course, takes attention away as people have to respond to what these three leaders have said. But we're not getting knocked off course or off point. We will continue to move forward, waiting anxiously to see what Dr. Blix and Dr. ElBaradei say on Friday, and then we will consult with other members of the Council, to include these three members of the Council, veto-bearing—two of the three are veto-bearing members of the Council—and see what the next step should be.

But it is simply not, in my judgment, not an adequate response to the challenge to say, oh, let's just send in two or three times as many inspectors and some more technical means. We've suggested two to three times as many inspectors, you will recall, I think, Robin, at the beginning of this whole process. Blix did not respond because it's hard to get—would he go get two or three times as many inspectors. So they did not ramp up as much as we had encouraged them to do in the beginning, and now—and I didn't hear the French and the Germans and the Russians sort of joining in at that time. But now, suddenly, this is a solution. But it really isn't a solution.

Three months have gone by and we have not seen the kind of progress, anything like the kind of progress. Blix and ElBaradei said they have not seen the kind of progress that they had hoped for. What they have been getting is passive cooperation, to quote them. And to quote the famous Blix statement of 27 January, even at this late date, Iraq doesn't understand it has to disarm.

Q. Can I play devil's advocate, though? Then I'll hand it back to you.

Secretary Powell. Sure. No, but it will make the—it does complicate things, to answer your question.

Q. And if you need to go off the record, fine. I'd just be interested in, I mean, clearly this is, particularly after your quite powerful presentation at the Security Council last week, this is kind of stunning that the—that three of the five members of the Security Council would take such an outspoken and determined position at this juncture.

You know, what do you do behind the scenes to try to get them back on board? And related to that, do you send a message that, look, those who are going to participate in ousting Saddam will also have a role in the post-war process, and those who aren't part of it may not have a role afterwards?

Secretary Powell. After my presentation last Wednesday, I met with 13 of the 15 members of the Council. I didn't have to meet with myself, though some people suggest one of these days I should. And, of course, Jack Straw I had been talking all morning. But I met with all the other 13—I'm sorry. The Syrians. Right. I didn't have a bilateral with the Syrians, so that's 12. Plus Papandreou. That's 13. So 13 people, 12 of whom are members of the Council. And we had good, straightforward conversations and they know the direction that we are moving in. They understand that direction. Each of them a sovereign nation that will have to make up their own mind. And it's not yet time for making up their mind.

And even though three of them today, two of them speaking out and then Germany from the other day, believe the way forward is with additional inspectors and that more time should be given to the inspectors, that is the position they hold. We'll see what Blix and ElBaradei say on Friday, and then next week we will get into consultations with those three and the other 11 and see what the various positions are, and then decide whether or not it's appropriate to put down a resolution that captures the situation that we see exists. Or maybe somebody else wants to put down a resolution.

Q. Can Britain now go without material breach?

Secretary Powell. Can Britain go without another resolution?

Q. Go with—on another resolution, can it go—move forward without the term "material breach" in it.

Secretary Powell. I don't know. You'd have to ask Britain. I wouldn't want to speak for the United Kingdom.

Q. Has there been—do you feel there's been proper discussion led by the administration about the possible consequences of this involvement? When you look back, obviously Vietnam and the sorts of involvements that demoralized and damaged U.S. prestige. Has there been the discussion that there needs to be with the American people about the implications of this, whether it be not just the best possible scenario, but the worst possible scenarios, which of course could mean increased terrorism in this country, the U.S. being seen as the world's bully, et cetera? Do you feel that there's been a proper discussion of what we may be getting ourselves into?

Secretary Powell. I know that we have discussed it extensively within the administration, and I think the American people understand. You know, you look at the polling and you look at all of the coverage that there has been on this issue in television and newspapers and elsewhere, and I don't think the President has been misleading in any way to the nation by saying we've got a major challenge ahead of us.

And if you look at the coverage for the last couple of months, I think everybody understands there is the risk of increased terrorism, there is the risk of disturbances in the Middle East and in Muslim countries. We have been trimming down in some of our embassies with authorized departures, letting some of our dependents come home, kind of battening down the hatches. I can assure you that all the reservists who have been called up, their families, their communities, are following all this very closely. And it is a time of high anxiety and I think the President is speaking to that high anxiety within the country.

I don't think we should ignore the alternative, or an alternative, that says if we are successful, a lot of the naysaying that's going on and a lot of the criticism that we are receiving could turn very quickly to support for our efforts. If we are seen as having to go to war and prosecuting that war in the way America knows how to prosecute a war—and that is, do it quickly, do it decisively, do it surgically, with minimum loss of civilian life or collateral damage, and swift moves, and take over a country and then quickly demonstrate that our sole goal in being in that country is to help the country—then I think opinion might change very, very quickly, and all of the risks that we are taking could quickly dissipate.

There is no love lost for Saddam Hussein in the region. I mean, he is not running for Soldier of the Month in any of the Arab countries that I'm in touch with. And, in fact, one could even make the case there that some people are saying time to get this over with. Nevertheless, we are hopeful, but limited hope in the time remaining, for a peaceful solution.

But I've been through a number of crises and conflicts during my career where that same kind of anxiety level was there, and then once it was done and you dealt with it and you put something in place that is better, the anxiety goes away and some of the problems that had been anticipated that didn't occur go away, and some of the problems that did occur tend to also dissipate with respect to their effect.

* * * *

Q. And that one of the important things is finding a model for Iraq to follow in forming a government. And that model would seem to be, perhaps, a difficult thing. Is it Afghanistan? Is it Kosovo?

Secretary Powell. No, it's Iraq. And it's unlike any of the others. It's going to be very difficult and we are looking at a variety of modes—a trusteeship model for an extended period of time under international trusteeship of some kind. Or is it going to take a military leader to manage it for a while? Or can we find a solution where those who are coming from outside the country and those inside the country can find an accommodation that would put in place a political system that is representative of its people and has the confidence of its people?

But it's tough. I mean, Mesopotamia is not—you know, it's not tiddly-winks. And they've never had such a system. And you've got Kurds who want to—you know, may have a different goal ultimately in life than the Shi'as in the South or the mixed population in the middle, with Baghdad being a city that is mostly Shi'a, not Sunni, but the leadership and the intelligentsia and the power has heretofore been mostly Sunni.

So it is not going to be easy, but it's not as if we haven't faced difficult challenges like this in different parts of the world over the last 50 or 60 years. It's not an insurmountable task.

Q. But if you have—what—

Secretary Powell. I don't know what the model is.

Q. I'm sorry. If you would accept a military leader, then, does that mean accepting a Ba'athist government again?

Secretary Powell. A what?

Q. The ruling party.

Secretary Powell. No. What I had in mind there was—I'm an old infantryman, and if there is a war, one day there's going to be an infantry general, perhaps armored, standing up in Baghdad saying, "We now have taken control of this country." And when that general does that, at that moment we are the occupier and we have sovereignty over that country, and it may take a while before we can release that sovereignty to civilian authorities.

And we have experience with that model, as well. Until we got in place an interim government in Afghanistan, for example, until the Bonn conference and got all that sorted away, it was commanders we had on the ground, just as it was in Japan and Germany for a period of time.

Q. The period of time being a good number of years in both Japan and Germany.

Secretary Powell. But I don't—

Q. Would that be a possibility?

Secretary Powell. I don't—I can't answer that. I just—it's not knowable to me at this point. I would not be trying to use that model because I think it's different now. It's not 1945 and we're not trying to conquer and devastate a country. Germany and Japan were conquered and devastated. This is a country that will be intact. Its institutions will still be there. We don't expect that we'll have to be putting in place a new health and human service system, but will certainly improve that which is there.

But the institutions, if we do this right, the institutions will fundamentally be intact, and it's a matter of making sure that those institutions have now been purged of the kind of dictatorial leadership that was pursuing weapons of mass destruction and abusing human rights.

Q. Once Iraq has been—let's say it's been occupied. Where do you see relations with Saudi Arabia headed, particularly given that they took this woman back who is under subpoena here, they profess to be working with the United States in the war

against terrorism, yet at the same time you read in The New York Times they're talking about getting rid of—or not having the American troops based in there post-war?
What is your read on Saudi Arabia?

Secretary Powell. I think Saudi Arabia is starting to—is starting to enter a period
of change and transformation. The Crown Prince has been making statements recently that suggest that. And in the aftermath of a conflict with Iraq, with a new Iraq on its
border, it's a different strategic equation. Some of the smaller Gulf states around Saudi
Arabia have started to make changes. Kuwait, Bahrain come to mind.

Saudi Arabia, I think, is coming to the realization that you cannot continue to deny
opportunity to half your population on the basis of gender. They are coming to the
realization that they need to educate their young people. It's a very young population.
They need to educate the young people of Saudi Arabia for the jobs that are going to
be out there and for the needs that the society has.

And with respect to military presence, a good reason, the reason we have most of
the military presence in Saudi Arabia that we do have, is because of Iraq. And if Iraq
is no longer the issue, then obviously we could talk to the Saudis about readjusting our
footprint.

And so I think we will have excellent relations with Saudi Arabia in the aftermath
of this with one huge problem and irritant removed from the region. Don't underestimate the different situation that will be there when nobody is afraid of Saddam Hussein any longer and when everybody can look north or south or east or west and see a
different situation in their neighborhood where people are now just building their
society and not threatening their neighbors.

Q. Do you anticipate, then, putting greater pressure on Syria? Because Lebanon is
a training base for—continues to be a training base for terrorists.

Secretary Powell. We would certainly—we put a lot of pressure on Syria now, and
I think in the aftermath of an Iraq conflict new opportunities open up with respect to
the Middle East peace process, with respect to terrorism in general.

And to come back to the question that you touched on earlier, Janet, maybe it isn't
such a bad idea that people be a little fearful of, you know, acting in a way that is
inconsistent with international norms and standards.

Q. But then, to follow that up, if you have a situation where you say, well, okay, if
people aren't so afraid of what Saddam Hussein is going to do, then we'll have a different template there, but what about if the world is more afraid of the United States?
I mean, what if part of what's driving this.

But I'm wondering how much people within your own administration have
undercut some of your diplomatic efforts. I mean, when you have intemperate language like "pygmy" and "axis of evil" and "old Europe," and you have people sort of
throwing out these things which seem to only feed the paranoia that's already there
about—for the United States, what do you do in a situation like this where you actually do have some, some members of the international community who say, "You
know what? We're more worried about you guys than we are about Iraq. He's a small-

time guy you guys are trying to turn into Hitler. We're more worried about the only superpower that's throwing its weight around."

Secretary Powell. There is nobody who wants to be a friend of ours who has anything to worry about from us. And most of my days are spent with foreign leaders— I've had two heads of state here so far today, the President of Ecuador and the Prime Minister of Australia, and my days are spent with foreign ministers and prime ministers and presidents—other leaders from every continent on the face of the earth.

And for those who do not wish us ill, they come here and they want to talk about— they want to talk about trade, they want to talk about economic development, they want to talk about assistance. They want to talk about how they can have a strategic relationship with the United States. They want to talk about how they can have a better partnership with the United States. And the number of nations that are threatened or quivering or terrified because of American—what did my buddy, Vedrine call it?— hyperpower status are quite few. And frankly, some of them, perhaps, I don't mind if they're all that nervous.

* * * *

Q. Yeah. How are you going to get the allies on board? You pulled out all stops last week and that wasn't enough. What's your strategy?

Secretary Powell. You're saying I don't have them aboard. You know, before I spoke, the Group of Eight put out a statement. An hour after I spoke, another 10— small countries, I know they are small countries.

Q. The calculation is you don't even have the nine, though.

Secretary Powell. That's your calculation, not mine.

Q. Well, it's what they say up at the United Nations, but all right. How are you going to bring the three very important permanent members of the Security Council on board? What are you going to do this week?

Secretary Powell. Lots.

* * * *

We're going to work. And, one, there's nothing to bring them on board for yet. I mean there's nothing—all, all—what's happened since last Wednesday, really?

I gave a speech last Wednesday. I met with lots of people. Everybody had been making statements. The President has spoken to a lot of people. In the last five days he's spoken to Jiang Zemin, he's spoken to Putin, he's spoken to Chirac, he's spoken to Blair, had a meeting with Howard, he's spoken to Berlusconi, received Berlusconi. There is a lot going on.

Q. But the French say that conversation was very inconclusive and they agreed to disagree, that they didn't make any progress and there was no agreement that they shared anything, any position in common except they want disarmament.

Secretary Powell. That's a position in common. Yeah. That is a position in common. And so there is a lot going on and there are a lot of statements being made, there are a lot of negotiations taking place, there are a lot of discussions taking place, there are lot of people choosing up sides, there are a lot of people talking about one resolution or another, people talking about monitors, talking about this, talking about that, but there is really nothing before the Council right now for them to decide.

And so we'll hear from Blix and ElBaradei and then, I suspect, in the very near future, after Friday, there will be something for the Council to consider. And then we'll see after some serious discussions and consultation and negotiations who votes yes, who votes no, and who abstains and who—

Remarks by Secretary of State Powell, February 10, 2003

Secretary Colin Powell was interviewed by Al-Ahram.

Q.—they stated that their opposition to war at this particular time. Why isn't the United States putting these views into consideration?

Secretary Powell. We are taking all views into consideration. Nobody wants war. The United States does not want war. Egypt does not want war. The solution to the possibility of war is very straightforward. Iraq should disarm.

The international community came together in New York last November 8 at the Security Council and passed a strong resolution, 1441; and in that resolution everybody acknowledged that Iraq had been guilty of hiding its weapons of mass destruction, that Iraq was being given one more chance to come into compliance and to get rid of these weapons of mass destruction, that the inspectors would help Iraq, but that if Iraq, once again, failed to answer the international community, then Iraq must face serious consequences.

We cannot have an international system that functions when you have a nation such as this that continues to develop weapons that he has used against his own people and against his neighbors. He has invaded his neighbors.

The United States did not invade Iran, Iraq did. The United States did not invade Kuwait, Iraq did. Iraq used chemical weapons against Iran and chemical weapons their own people and fired missiles at neighbors during the Gulf war. So the problem is not with the United States, the problem is with Iraq. We would be pleased at a peaceful solution, but the President is determined, and I think the international community is determined, that Iraq must be disarmed of its weapons of mass destruction. And if it is not done peacefully, the President believes strongly, and I think many other nations believe strongly, that a coalition would then have to use force to disarm Iraq.

There are many nations that believe as we do: the United Kingdom, Spain, Italy, the Group of Eight that put out the statement last week, and then the Vilnius Ten that put out a statement last week. And we hope that people will understand that if force is used, it will be done in the most measured way, and it'll be done not for the purpose of hurting the Iraqi people, but for the purpose of dealing with a regime that simply is irresponsible.

And in the aftermath of such a conflict the United States and its coalition partners would do everything we could to help the Iraqi people, to give them a better life, to help them use the $20 billion a year that they get from oil revenue to build hospitals, to build schools, to build roads, to improve agriculture, to take care of poverty, to do all the things that are possible in Iraq if Iraq was not spending this money on weapons of mass destruction.

Q. What about the stiff opposition of Moscow, of France and Germany just yesterday and today? And they are really, quite very tough in their position.

Secretary Powell. Russia—they are. They have a strong view. Russia and France voted for Resolution 1441, which calls for serious consequences if Iraq did not comply. Iraq has not complied.

Russia, France and Germany, which is a member of the Security Council, and many others believe that there should be more time given and that there should be more inspectors added. We are sensitive to those concerns, and we listen to them. They are our friends, they are our allies.

But it is not how many more inspectors should be put in, it is will Iraq comply? And if Iraq complies then you don't need more inspectors. There are more than enough inspectors. But if Iraq does not comply, if it is not cooperating, if it is not turning over documents, if it is not letting people speak freely about what they know, if they are not bringing in the missiles we know they have, if they are not telling us what they did with the anthrax and the botulinum toxin, then more inspectors does not solve that problem. The problem is Iraq is not complying and not cooperating. And more inspectors, in and of itself, is not the answer in the absence of Iraqi cooperation and compliance.

Q. But the Blix and Baradei yesterday, I mean, declared that the Iraqis were very positive and they understand and even today they declared that they permit the U-2 on [*inaubible*].

Secretary Powell. Well, there's a statement today that said they would start letting the U-2s fly, but the U-2s are not the answer if they are still going to try to hide everything on the ground from the U-2s. The U-2s might be able to assist in the disarmament, but the U-2s, in and of itself, are not the answer, nor are more inspectors.

We're pleased if they are letting the U-2s fly, but what happens is, every time the inspectors go and visit, Iraq gives a little bit more—a few more documents. Okay, why didn't they give them the U-2 on Saturday or Sunday? No, they wait until Monday, and maybe it can start Wednesday. So the Iraqis are playing a game that we are all familiar with.

We have watched this game for 12 years. And the region would be better off if this game comes to an end one way or another. If Iraq truly wanted peace and did not want to see war in the region, they would be saying, "Here are all the documents, here are all the facilities, you don't need a U-2, here it is, we'll show it to you. You don't have to take a picture from the sky. You can come take a picture right up close."

We would not be playing this game of detective. We would be playing a game of "You wanted to know? Here it is. Come look." And they still are hiding. They still are deceiving. They still are not showing their willingness to comply.

Q. Would you be ready to receive an Arab delegation to seek a last-minute compromise that could avoid a war?

Secretary Powell. Us receive a delegation?

Q. We're hoping a voluntary resignation of President Saddam and major changes in the system.

Secretary Powell. I think the Arab nations have been playing a very important role by supporting the position that said Saddam Hussein must disarm. President Mubarak, especially, has been playing a very, very active and important role in suggesting to the Iraqis that they comply and avoid a conflict, and in his position of leadership within the Arab world, making that case to other Arab leaders.

If the Arab leaders wanted, as a group, to approach Saddam Hussein, certainly that is their prerogative and we would welcome such an approach, but it has to be an approach that says to Saddam Hussein, "You must comply." And of course, I would always be willing to receive any delegation from the Arab world or from any—

Q.—would Saddam's resignation be enough?

Secretary Powell. Excuse me. Or from any representative of the Egyptian Government if that's the question. I'm sorry. Go ahead.

Q. Would Saddam's resignation be enough or what else would you demand?

Secretary Powell. What we need to see is a regime that is changed or a changed regime that is gone. And it isn't just one person.

We need to see a change. The United States has no desire in the event of conflict of going in and pulling Iraq apart or breaking all of its institutions. Those institutions are needed to take care of the people, to run the systems. It is the regime that's at the top that is causing all of this trouble in the region and for the Iraqi people and for the world. And if that regime down to some level, I don't know how many, were gone and responsible leaders stood up and said to the world, "Look, they are gone. We are now here. We are in control of this country. We invite the U.N. to come in. We invite others to come in, a coalition to come in to work with us on finding where all of these weapons all, and we will tell you everything we know. We will give you all the documents, you can interview all the scientists. Here's what we know about what happened to the anthrax. Here's what happened to the VX." We should not take lightly the dangerous nature of these weapons.

And it is not the United States accusing without evidence. Iraq admitted, they admitted years ago, that they had anthrax, that they were working on nuclear weapons, but they admitted it only after they were caught—not voluntarily. And so we have got to see a change in attitude where they are now voluntarily telling us everything they have done.

And if a new leadership would do that and would work with the international coalition to come in and help them, peacefully, then that would be a significant, significant step.

Q. Why did the United States refuse to even consider the, the reported proposal from Russia and the France to deploy U.N. peacekeeper—

Secretary Powell. Because the proposal, one, there is no proposal yet. The only thing we know about is additional monitors and some technical material.

Q. No one's proposing 12,000 U.N. soldiers?

Secretary Powell. No. Nobody's proposed that. Nobody has proposed that. Have you—where did you see that proposal? In a paper? In a German newspaper called Der Spiegel.

Q. Yes.

Secretary Powell. But it was immediately discounted by both the French and the Germans. I know of no proposal for peacekeepers or blue helmets except in this newspaper article.

Q. There are seven, seven conditions what made the [*inaubible*] radio of any country.

Secretary Powell. What President Chirac said today in his press conference with President Putin was more monitors and technical means, which is pretty much what Foreign Minister deVillepin was talking about at the U.N. last week.

So if they were just talking about an additional number of inspectors and maybe some additional technical means, that is interesting. The United States proposed that when we first passed 1441. Let's have three times as many inspectors. If he's going to cooperate, let's do it fast.

But now it is not for the purpose of helping them, it is for the purpose of slowing down the momentum to deal with this matter once and for all. So the issue is not more inspectors or more technical capability. The issue is Iraq compliance and Iraq cooperation and Iraq coming forward in the way I described a moment ago.

* * * *

Q. Last question. How would you consider Arab public opinion fears that Iraq will be the first in the U.S. hate list of Arab and Muslim nations?

Secretary Powell. The U.S. has no hate list. The U.S. does not look for countries to hate. The U.S. looks for friends and partners and most of the nations in the Arab world are our friends and partners. Most Muslim nations in the world are our friends and partners.

And I must say that if you'll look at our history, our record of the last 12 years, when Kuwait, a Muslim nation, was invaded by a neighbor, Iraq, who came and restored Kuwait to its legitimate government? Did we make Kuwait the 51st state of the United States or did we restore Kuwait to its legitimate leadership?

We did what we always do. We gave it back to its people. We are a partner of Kuwait. Do you we have troops there, yes. For our purpose? No. For security in the region.

When Kosovo was in danger, the Muslim population of Kosovo, who led the coalition that went and fought for those Muslims? And Kosovo is now moving forward. It still has a difficult road ahead. And in Afghanistan, when Afghanistan became the center of terrorism with the Taliban supporting al-Qaida, and something had to be done about it after 9/11, the United States did that working with the Muslim nation, Pakistan, as our partner and friend.

And we went and we removed the Taliban regime and we're now searching out the remaining elements of al-Qaida. And what are U.S. troops doing in Afghanistan now? Going after terrorists and helping rebuild a country. Our Congress is putting billions of dollars in to help the Muslim population of Afghanistan. We have helped President Karzai go back into a position of authority. We have helped with the creation of institutions in Afghanistan.

Are we new imperialists who want to run Afghanistan? No. We want to help the Afghans determine their own future and help them. We're rebuilding schools, we've created conditions so that a million Muslims have been able to return to their homes in Afghanistan. So this suggestion that the United States has nations on its hate list is just ludicrous.

We want friends and partners around the world, and we have shown ourselves over the years to be a friend and partner, solid friend and partner, of every nation that wishes to be a friend and partner with us in the region.

Q. So once you achieve your goals in Iraq and post-Saddam era you leave or are you going to ask for bases or facilities?

Secretary Powell. Of course we leave. We want to do what is necessary if conflict comes, and we hope conflict won't come. We still hope for peace—a peaceful resolution. But if conflict comes and we have to go into Iraq, it is our goal, our simple goal, to find a solution quickly to put in place a government in Iraq to help Iraqis put in place a government in Iraq that would be responsible to the needs of all the people of Iraq that will keep the country together and will dedicate itself to the elimination of weapons of mass destruction, to proper standards of human rights, and we will help fix all of the systems that are now broke with respect to healthcare, with respect to education, with respect to institutions that rest on, you know, responsible leaders, and then we want to go.

We have lots of demands on the United States.

Q. What do you ask from Egypt?

Secretary Powell. Egypt, we ask, as always, from Egypt for their support and their friendship. President Mubarak is a strong leader. He is a leader that we—he's a leader whose wisdom we value and then we stay in close touch with President Mubarak. President Mubarak is also a leader of his own nation and has to be responsive to the needs of his own nation and to the will of his people.

These are difficult times and we will find ways through these difficult times. It is also a time where there is a need for all of us to be respectful of each other, to be respectful of each others' religions. This is the time when we see hatred coming forth, those of us in positions of leadership should speak against that hatred, whether it's hatred manifested by anti- Semitism, or hatred manifested by anti-Muslim comments or activities.

We can leave this room right now and I can take you to, within five minutes, I can take you to a mosque, a temple, a synagogue, a Catholic Church, Orthodox Church. You know we know what diversity is. We know what the strength of all the religions of the world are when they harness together in peace in the manner in which we've done here in the United States.

Q. Mr. Secretary, are you going to respond in kind if Iraq uses weapons of mass destruction? What is your doctrine?

Secretary Powell. We never discuss that. Why aren't you worried about Iraq using weapons of mass destruction rather than, "Would you respond if Iraq uses weapons of mass destruction?" Will you scream bloody murder if Iraq uses these terrible weapons that Iraq says it does not have. How could they use them if they don't have them?

Now, if they use them, the United States, we have no, no intention of doing anything that would hurt the people of Iraq, but we will do what is necessary to defend ourselves. But I hope before everybody asks what the United States would do, somebody would say, "My God, they did have them. They were lying."

Remarks by United Nations Secretary-General Annan, February 10, 2003

Q. Hi, Mr. Secretary-General. The Iraqis today agreed to U2 flights; they said they were going to pass legislation. The French, Germans and Russians called for more inspections, but the United States keeps saying the game is over. Do you believe that the game is over?

Secretary-General Annan. Let me say that we all have to wait for the report of the inspectors. They should be in the [Security] Council on Friday to hear what they have to say. I know that, at the moment, there appear to be differences of opinion as to how we should proceed. But I am confident that the Member States will be able to find a way out of this.

Q. Do you think that Iraq is complying 100 per cent with what you have seen so far?

Secretary-General Annan. I would not want to speculate. As I said, I am waiting for the report of the inspectors and then the Council will have to make that judgement.

Q. Do you find what they did today, the announcement on the U2s and on the legislation, encouraging? Is this a good sign?

Secretary-General Annan. It is encouraging. In fact, both [Chief Inspectors Hans] Blix and [Mohammed] ElBaradei said they are beginning to see a change, a certain change in their attitude, and he doesn't describe it as a breakthrough and he hoped this would be sustained. But since I haven't spoken to him and I haven't seen his report, you can understand I am hesitant to jump in and comment.

Q. Could you answer one more question about why you've called a meeting of the Security Council to discuss contingency planning on humanitarian issues?

Secretary-General Annan. First of all, let me say, as Secretary-General I have made it very clear that I hope this issue can be resolved peacefully. But of course we are also realistic, and we have handled previous crises before, and we are doing contingency planning, and I stress contingency planning, without any expectation, any decision one way or the other, so that we will not be caught unprepared if things were to go the military way. We have had enough experience in other crises to understand that we should make some arrangements and preparations, and we know what happened in '91, and we are not taking anything for granted. We hope it will be resolved peacefully but we just want to share with the Council members our thinking, our basic planning, and the information we have through the research we have done.

Remarks by President Bush, February 13, 2003

President Bush delivered the following remarks to troops at the Mayport Naval Station in Jacksonville, Florida.

The world changed on September the 11th, 2001. You see, we learned that oceans no longer protect us; that a threat that gathers on the other side of the Earth can strike our own cities, can kill our own people. That's what we learned. And I'm not going to forget that lesson. You see, we saw what terrorists could do, with four airplanes as weapons. We're not going to wait and see what they can do with even deadlier weapons.

Today the gravest danger in the war on terror—the gravest danger facing America and the world—is outlaw regimes that seek and possess nuclear, chemical and biological weapons. These regimes could use such weapons for blackmail, terror, mass murder. They could also give or sell those weapons to terrorist allies who would use them without the least bit of hesitation. That's the reality of the world we live in, and that's what we're going to use every ounce of our power to defeat.

We have an obligation to protect America and the Americans. We understand our responsibility, and jointly we'll do just that—we'll protect America and our friends and allies from these thugs.

The civilized world has awakened to the growing danger posed by the Iraqi regime. Twelve years ago, Saddam Hussein agreed to disarm as a condition of suspending the Gulf War. Three months ago, the United Nations Security Council gave him a final chance to meet that obligation. Saddam Hussein is not disarming, he's deceiving.

America has laid out the facts for the world to see. Saddam Hussein has chemical weapons programs, and the means to use them. Saddam Hussein has a biological weapons program, and the means to deliver those weapons. He has secretly attempted to obtain materials needed to produce nuclear weapons. Saddam Hussein aids and protects terrorists, including members of al Qaeda. He harbors a senior al Qaeda leader who ordered the assassination of an American diplomat—the same man who plotted against Spain and Italy in the Republic of Georgia, and Russia, and Great Britain, and France, and Germany. The Iraqi regime is engaged in a massive campaign to conceal its weapons of mass destruction, and its ties to terrorists. And that deception continues today.

At any moment during the last 97 days—and during the last 12 years—Saddam Hussein could have completely and immediately disarmed himself. Instead, he's used all this time to build and to hide weapons. He must be hoping that by stalling he'll buy himself another 12 years. He's wrong. This country will not accept a serious and mounting threat to our nation, our people, and our friends and allies.

Military force is always this nation's last option. Yet if force becomes necessary to disarm Iraq and enforce the will of the United Nations, if force becomes necessary to secure our country and to keep the peace, America will act deliberately, America will act decisively, and America will act victoriously with the world's greatest military.

America will also be acting with friends and allies. An overwhelming majority of NATO members oppose the threat of Iraq, and understand that tough choices may be necessary to keep the peace. Many nations have offered to provide forces or other support to disarm the Iraqi regime. Every nation of the Gulf Cooperation Council has agreed to help defend and protect Kuwait. And now the world's most important multilateral body faces a decision.

The decision is this for the United Nations: When you say something does it mean anything? You've got to decide, if you lay down a resolution, does it mean anything? The United Nations Security Council can now decide whether or not it has the resolve to enforce it's resolutions.

I'm optimistic that the U.N. Security Council will rise to its responsibilities, and this time ensure enforcement of what it told Saddam Hussein he must do. See, I believe when it's all said and done, free nations will not allow the United Nations to fade into history as an ineffective, irrelevant debating society. I'm optimistic that free nations will show backbone and courage in the face of true threats to peace and freedom.

If there is a conflict, American forces will act in the honorable traditions of our military, and in the highest moral traditions of this country. Our military will be fighting the oppressors of Iraq, not the people of Iraq. America's military fights not to conquer, but to liberate.

In case of conflict, this great nation is already putting plans and supplies into place, so that food and other humanitarian relief will flow quickly to the Iraqi people. You see, we seek more than the defeat of terror; we seek an advance of freedom and a world at peace. That is the charge that history has given us—and that is a charge we will keep.

In crucial hours, the success of our cause will depend on the men and women of our military. You serve this nation's ideals, and you live out those ideals in your code and in your character. I've seen your love of country, and your devotion to a cause larger than yourself. I've seen your discipline, your idealism, and your sense of honor. I know that every mission you are given will be carried out with skill and unselfish courage.

Excerpts from United Nations Security Council Ministerial Meeting on Iraq, February 14, 2003

UNMOVIC Chairman Dr. Hans Blix. Since I reported to the Security Council on 27 January, the United Nations Monitoring, Verification and Inspection Commission (UNMOVIC) has had two further weeks of operational and analytical work in New York and active inspections in Iraq. That brings the total period of inspections so far to 11 weeks. Since then, we have also listened, on 5 February, to the presentation to the Council by the United States Secretary of State and to the discussion that followed. Lastly, Mr. ElBaradei and I have held another round of talks in Baghdad with our counterparts and with Vice President Ramadan, on 8 and 9 February.

Let me begin today's briefing with a short account of the work being performed by UNMOVIC in Iraq.

We have continued to build up our capabilities. The regional office in Mosul is now fully operational at its temporary headquarters. Plans for a regional office at Basra are being developed. Our Hercules L-100 aircraft continues to operate routine flights between Baghdad and Larnaca. The eight helicopters are fully operational. With the resolution of the problems raised by Iraq for the transportation of minders into the no-fly zones, our mobility in those zones has improved. We expect to increase utilization of the helicopters. The number of Iraqi minders during inspections had often reached a ratio as high as five per inspector. During the talks in January in Baghdad, the Iraqi side agreed to keep the ratio to about one to one. The situation has improved.

Since we arrived in Iraq, we have conducted more than 400 inspections covering more than 300 sites. All inspections were performed without notice and access was almost always provided promptly. In no case have we seen convincing evidence that the Iraqi side knew in advance that the inspectors were coming.

The inspections have taken place throughout Iraq at industrial sites, ammunition depots, research centers, universities, presidential sites, mobile laboratories, private houses, missile production facilities, military camps and agricultural sites. At all sites which had been inspected before 1998, rebaselining activities were performed. This included the identification of the function and contents of each building, new or old, at a site. It also included verification of previously tagged equipment, application of seals and tags, taking samples and discussions with the site personnel regarding past and present activities. At certain sites, ground-penetrating radar was used to look for underground structures or buried equipment.

Through the inspections conducted so far, we have obtained a good knowledge of the industrial and scientific landscape of Iraq, as well as of its missile capability, but, as before, we do not know every cave and corner. Inspections are effectively helping to bridge the gap in knowledge that arose due to the absence of inspections between December 1998 and November 2002.

More than 200 chemical and more than 100 biological samples have been collected at different sites. Three quarters of these have been screened using our own analytical laboratory capabilities at the Baghdad Centre. The results to date have been consistent with Iraq's declarations.

We have now commenced the process of destroying approximately 50 liters of mustard gas declared by Iraq that was being kept under UNMOVIC seal at the Muthanna site. One third of the quantity has already been destroyed. The laboratory quantity of thiodiglycol, a mustard gas precursor, which we found at another site, has also been destroyed.

The total number of staff in Iraq now exceeds 250 from 60 countries. This includes about 100 UNMOVIC inspectors, 15 International Atomic Energy Agency (IAEA) inspectors, 50 aircrew and 65 support staff.

In my 27 January update to the Council, I said that it seemed from our experience that Iraq had decided in principle to provide cooperation on process, most importantly prompt access to all sites and assistance to UNMOVIC in the establishment of the necessary infrastructure. This impression remains and we note that access to sites has so far been without problems, including to those that had never been declared or inspected, as well as to presidential sites and private residences.

In my last updating, I also said that a decision to cooperate on substance was indispensable in order to bring, through inspection, the disarmament task to completion and to set the monitoring system on a firm course. Such cooperation, as I have noted, requires more than the opening of doors. In the words of resolution 1441 (2002), it requires immediate, unconditional and active efforts by Iraq to resolve existing questions of disarmament, either by presenting remaining proscribed items and programs for elimination or by presenting convincing evidence that they have been eliminated.

In the current situation, one would expect Iraq to be eager to comply. While we were in Baghdad, we met a delegation from the Government of South Africa. It was there to explain how South Africa gained the confidence of the world in its dismantling of the nuclear-weapons program by a wholehearted cooperation over two years with IAEA inspectors. I have just learned that Iraq has accepted an offer by South Africa to send a group of experts for further talks.

How much, if any, is left of Iraq's weapons of mass destruction and related proscribed items and programs? So far, UNMOVIC has found no such weapons, only a small number of empty chemical munitions which should have been declared and destroyed. Another matter—and one of great significance—is that many proscribed weapons and items are not accounted for. To take an example, a document which Iraq provided suggested to us that some 1,000 tons of chemical agent were unaccounted for. One must not jump to the conclusion that they exist. However, that possibility is also not excluded. If they exist, they should be presented for destruction. If they do not exist, credible evidence to that effect should be presented.

We are fully aware that many governmental intelligence organizations are convinced and assert that proscribed weapons, items and programs continue to exist. The United States Secretary of State presented material in support of this conclusion. Governments have many sources of information that are not available to inspectors. Inspectors, for their part, must base their reports only on evidence that they can themselves examine and present publicly. Without evidence, confidence cannot arise.

In my earlier briefings, I noted that significant outstanding issues of substance were listed in two Security Council documents from early 1999 and should be well known to Iraq. I referred, as examples, to the issues of anthrax, the nerve agent VX and longrange missiles, and said that such issues "deserve to be taken seriously by Iraq, rather than being brushed aside" (S/PV.4692, p. 5). The declaration submitted by Iraq on 7 December, despite its large volume, missed the opportunity to provide the fresh material and evidence needed to respond to the open questions. This is perhaps the most important problem we are facing. Although I can understand that it may not be easy for Iraq in all cases to provide the evidence needed, it is not the task of the inspectors to find it. Iraq itself must squarely tackle this task and avoid belittling the questions.

In my January update to the Council, I referred to the Al Samoud 2 and the Al Fatah missiles, reconstituted casting chambers, construction of a missile-engine test stand and the import of rocket engines, which were all declared to UNMOVIC by Iraq. I noted that the Al Samoud 2 and the Al Fatah could very well represent prima facie cases of proscribed missile systems, as they had been tested to ranges exceeding the 150-kilometer limit set by the Security Council. I also noted that Iraq had been requested to cease flight tests of these missiles until UNMOVIC completed a technical review.

Earlier this week, UNMOVIC missile experts met for two days with experts from a number of Member States to discuss these items. The experts concluded unanimously that, based on the data provided by Iraq, the two declared variants of the Al Samoud 2 missile were capable of exceeding 150 kilometres in range. This missile system is therefore proscribed for Iraq pursuant to resolution 687 (1991) and the monitoring plan adopted under resolution 715 (1991). As for the Al Fatah, the experts found that clarification of the missile data supplied by Iraq was required before the capability of the missile system could be fully assessed.

With respect to the casting chambers, I note the following: UNSCOM ordered and supervised the destruction of the casting chambers that had been intended for use in the production of the proscribed Badr-2000 missile system. Iraq has declared that it has reconstituted these chambers. The experts have confirmed that the reconstituted casting chambers could still be used to produce motors for missiles capable of ranges significantly greater than 150 kilometres. Accordingly, these chambers remain proscribed.

The experts also studied the data on the missile engine test stand that is nearing completion and have assessed it to be capable of testing missile engines with thrusts greater than that of the SA-2 engine. So far, the test stand has not been associated with a proscribed activity.

On the matter of the 380 SA-2 missile engines imported outside of the export/import mechanism and in contravention of paragraph 24 of resolution 687 (1991), UNMOVIC inspectors were informed by Iraq during an official briefing that these engines were intended for use in the Al Samoud 2 missile system, which has now been assessed to be proscribed. Any such engines configured for use in this missile system would also be proscribed.

I intend to communicate these findings to the Government of Iraq.

At the meeting in Baghdad on 8 and 9 February, the Iraqi side addressed some of the important outstanding disarmament issues and gave us a number of papers, for instance regarding anthrax and growth material, the nerve agent VX and missile production. Experts who were present from our side studied the papers during the evening of 8 February and met with Iraqi experts in the morning of 9 February for further clarifications. Although no new evidence was provided in the papers and no open issues were closed through them or the expert discussions, the presentation of the papers could be indicative of a more active attitude focusing on important open issues.

The Iraqi side suggested that the problem of verifying the quantities of anthrax and two VX precursors, which had been declared unilaterally destroyed, might be tackled through certain technical and analytical methods. Although our experts are still assessing the suggestions, they are not very hopeful that it could prove possible to assess the quantities of material poured into the ground years ago. Documentary evidence and testimony by staff who dealt with the items still appear to be needed.

Not least against this background, a letter of 12 February from Iraq's National Monitoring Directorate may be of relevance. It presents a list of names of 83 participants "in the unilateral destruction in the chemical field, which took place in the summer of 1991". As the absence of adequate evidence of that destruction has been and remains an important reason why quantities of chemicals have been deemed unaccounted for, the presentation of a list of persons who can be interviewed about the actions appears useful and pertains to cooperation on substance. I trust that the Iraqi side will put together a similar list of names of persons who participated in the unilateral destruction of other proscribed items, notably in the biological field.

The Iraqi side also informed us that the commission that had been appointed in the wake of our finding 12 empty chemical weapons warheads had had its mandate expanded to look for any still existing proscribed items. This was welcomed.

A second commission, we learned, has now been appointed with the task of searching all over Iraq for more documents relevant to the elimination of proscribed items and programs. It is headed by the former Minister of Oil, General Amer Rashid, and is to have very extensive powers of search in industry, administration and even private houses.

The two commissions could be useful tools to come up with proscribed items to be destroyed and with new documentary evidence. They evidently need to work fast and effectively to convince us, and the world, that this is a serious effort.

The matter of private interviews was discussed at length during our meeting in Baghdad. The Iraqi side confirmed the commitment, which it made to us on 20 January, to encourage persons asked to accept such interviews, whether in or out of Iraq. So far, we have only had interviews in Baghdad. A number of persons have declined to be interviewed unless they were allowed to have an official present or were allowed to tape the interview. Three persons who had previously refused interviews on UNMOVIC's terms subsequently accepted such interviews, just prior to our talks in Baghdad on 8 and 9 February. These interviews proved informative. No further interviews have since been accepted on our terms. I hope this will change. We feel that interviews conducted without any third party present and without tape recording would provide the greatest credibility.

At the recent meeting in Baghdad, as on several earlier occasions, my colleague Mr. ElBaradei and I urged the Iraqi side to enact legislation implementing the United Nations prohibitions regarding weapons of mass destruction. This morning we had a message that a presidential decree containing prohibitions with regard to importation and production of biological, chemical and nuclear weapons has now been issued. We have not yet had time to study the details of the text of the decree.

I should like to make some comments on the role of intelligence in connection with inspections in Iraq. A credible inspection regime requires that Iraq provide full cooperation on process, granting immediate access everywhere to inspectors, and on substance, providing full declarations supported by relevant information and material and evidence. However, with the closed society in Iraq of today and the history of inspections there, other sources of information, such as defectors and government intelligence agencies are required to aid the inspection process.

I remember how, in 1991, several inspections in Iraq that were based on information received from a Government helped to disclose important parts of the nuclear weapons program. It was realized that an international organization authorized to perform inspections anywhere on the ground could make good use of information obtained from Gwith eyes in the sky, ears in the ether, access to defectors, and both eyes and ears on the market for weapons-related material. It was understood that the information residing in the intelligence services of Governments could come to very active use in the international effort to prevent proliferation of weapons of mass destruction. This remains true, and by now we have a good deal of experience in the matter.

International organizations need to analyze such information critically and especially benefit when it comes from more than one source. The intelligence agencies, for their part, must protect their sources and methods. Those who provide such information must know that it will be kept in strict confidence and be known to very few people. UNMOVIC has achieved good working relations with intelligence agencies, and the amount of information provided has been gradually increasing. However, we must recognize that there are limitations and that misinterpretations can occur.

Intelligence information has been useful for UNMOVIC. In one case, it led us to a private home where documents mainly relating to laser enrichment of uranium were found. In other cases, intelligence has led to sites where no proscribed items were found. Even in such cases, however, inspection of these sites was useful in proving the absence of such items and in some cases the presence of other items—conventional munitions. It showed that conventional arms are being moved around the country and that movements are not necessarily related to weapons of mass destruction.

The presentation of intelligence information by the United States Secretary of State suggested that Iraq had prepared for inspections by cleaning up sites and removing evidence of proscribed weapons programs. I would like to comment only on one case, with which we are familiar, namely, the trucks identified by analysts as being for chemical decontamination at a munitions depot. This was a declared site, and it was certainly one of the sites Iraq would have expected us to inspect. We have noted that the two satellite images of the site were taken several weeks apart. The reported movement of munitions at the site could just as easily have been a routine activity as a movement of proscribed munitions in anticipation of an imminent inspection. Our reservation on this point does not detract from our appreciation for the briefing.

Yesterday, UNMOVIC informed the Iraqi authorities of its intention to start using the U-2 surveillance aircraft early next week under arrangements similar to those UNSCOM had followed. We are also in the process of working out modalities for the use of the French Mirage aircraft starting late next week and for the drones supplied by the German Government. The offer from Russia of an Antonov aircraft with night vision capabilities is a welcome one and is next on our agenda for further improving UNMOVIC's and IAEA's technical capabilities. These developments are in line with suggestions made in a non-paper recently circulated by France, suggesting a further strengthening of the inspection capabilities.

It is our intention to examine the possibilities for surveying ground movements, notably by trucks. In the face of persistent intelligence reports, for instance about mobile biological weapons production units, such measures could well increase the effectiveness of inspections.

UNMOVIC is still expanding its capabilities, both in terms of numbers of staff and technical resources. On my way to the recent Baghdad meeting, I stopped in Vienna to meet 60 experts who had just completed our general training course for inspectors. They came from 22 countries, including Arab countries.

UNMOVIC is not infrequently asked how much more time it needs to complete its task in Iraq. The answer depends upon which task one has in mind: the elimination of weapons of mass destruction and related items and programs which were prohibited in 1991—the disarmament task—or the monitoring that no new proscribed activities occur. The latter task, though not often focused upon, is highly significant, and not controversial. It will require monitoring, which is ongoing—that is, open-ended, until the Council decides otherwise.

By contrast, the task of disarmament foreseen in resolution 687 (1991) and the progress on key remaining disarmament tasks foreseen in resolution 1284 (1999), as well as the disarmament obligations which Iraq was given a final opportunity to comply with under resolution 1441 (2002), were always required to be fulfilled in a shorter time span. Regrettably, the high degree of cooperation required of Iraq for disarmament through inspection was not forthcoming in 1991. Despite the elimination, under UNSCOM and IAEA supervision, of large amounts of weapons, weapons-related items and installations over the years, the task remained incomplete when inspectors were withdrawn almost eight years later, at the end of 1998.

If Iraq had provided the necessary cooperation in 1991, the phase of disarmament under resolution 687 (1991) could have been short, and a decade of sanctions could have been avoided. Today, three months after the adoption of resolution 1441 (2002), the period of disarmament through inspection could still be short if immediate, active and unconditional cooperation with UNMOVIC and IAEA were to be forthcoming.

IAEA Director General Mohamed ElBaradei. My report to the Council today is an update on the status of the nuclear verification activities of the International Atomic Energy Agency (IAEA) in Iraq, pursuant to Security Council resolution 1441 (2002) and other relevant resolutions. Less than three weeks have passed since my last update to the Council, on 27 January, a relatively short period in the overall inspection process. However, I believe it is important for the Council to remain actively engaged and fully informed at this critical time.

The focus of the IAEA's inspections has now moved from the reconnaissance phase into the investigative phase. The reconnaissance phase was aimed at re-establishing rapidly our knowledge base of Iraq's nuclear capabilities, ensuring that nuclear activities at known key facilities had not been resumed, verifying the location of nuclear material and relevant non- nuclear material and equipment, and identifying the current workplaces of former key Iraqi personnel. The focus of the investigative phase is achieving an understanding of Iraq's activities over the last four years, in particular in areas identified by States as being of concern and in those identified by IAEA on the basis of its own analysis.

Since our 27 January report, IAEA has conducted an additional 38 inspections at 19 locations, for a total of 177 inspections at 125 locations. Iraq has continued to provide immediate access to all locations. In the course of the inspections, we have identified certain facilities at which we will be re-establishing containment and surveillance systems in order to monitor, on a continuous basis, activities associated with critical dual-use equipment. At this time, we are using recurrent inspections to ensure that this equipment is not being used for prohibited purposes.

As I mentioned in my last report to the Council, we have a number of wide-area and location-specific measures for detecting indications of undeclared past or ongoing nuclear activities in Iraq, including environmental sampling and radiation detection surveys. In this regard, we have been collecting a broad variety of samples, including water, sediment and vegetation, at inspected facilities and at other locations across Iraq, and analyzing them for signature of nuclear activities.

We have also resumed air sampling at key locations in Iraq. Three of the four air samplers that were removed in December 2002 for refurbishing have been returned to Iraq. One of these has been installed at a fixed location, and the other two are being operated from mobile platforms. We intend to increase their number to make optimum use of this technique.

We are also continuing to expand the use of handheld and car- borne gamma surveys in Iraq. The gamma survey vehicle has been used en route to inspection sites and within sites, as well as in urban and industrial areas. We will start helicopter-borne gamma surveys as soon as the relevant equipment receives its final certification for use on the helicopter model provided to us for use in Iraq.

IAEA has continued to interview key Iraqi personnel. We have recently been able to conduct four interviews in private, that is, without the presence of an Iraqi observer. The interviewees, however, have taperecorded their interviews. In addition, discussions have continued to be conducted with Iraqi technicians and officials as part of inspection activities and technical meetings. I should note that, during our recent meeting in Baghdad, Iraq reconfirmed its commitment to encourage its citizens to accept interviews in private, both inside and outside of Iraq.

In response to a request by IAEA, Iraq has expanded the list of relevant Iraqi personnel to over 300, along with their current work locations. The list includes the higher-level scientists known to IAEA in the nuclear and nuclear-related areas. We will continue, however, to ask for information about Iraqi personnel of lesser rank whose work may be of significance to our mandate.

I would like now to provide an update on a number of specific issues that we are currently pursuing. I should mention that, shortly before our recent meeting in Baghdad, and based on our discussions with the Iraqi counterpart, Iraq provided documentation related to these issues: the reported attempt to import uranium, the attempted procurement of aluminum tubes, the procurement of magnets and magnet production capabilities, the use of the high explosive HMX, and those questions and concerns that were outstanding in 1998. I will touch briefly on each of those issues.

Iraq continues to state that it has made no attempt to import uranium since the 1980s. IAEA recently received some additional information relevant to this issue, which will be further pursued, hopefully with the assistance of the African country reported to have been involved.

IAEA is also continuing to follow up on acknowledged efforts by Iraq to import high-strength aluminum tubes. As members will know, Iraq has declared these efforts to have been in connection with a program to reverse-engineer conventional rockets. The IAEA has verified that Iraq had indeed been manufacturing such rockets. However, we are still exploring whether the tubes were intended rather for the manufacture of centrifuges for uranium enrichment. In connection with this investigation, Iraq has been asked to explain the reasons for the tight tolerance specifications that it had requested from various suppliers. Iraq has provided documentation related to the project of reverse engineering and has committed itself to providing samples of tubes received from prospective suppliers. We will continue to investigate the matter further.

In response to IAEA inquiries about Iraq's attempts to procure a facility for the manufacture of magnets, and the possible link with the resumption of a nuclear program, Iraq recently provided additional documentation, which we are now examining.

In the course of an inspection conducted in connection with the aluminum tube investigation, IAEA inspectors found a number of documents relevant to transactions aimed at the procurement of carbon fibre, a dual-use material used by Iraq in its past clandestine uranium enrichment program for the manufacture of gas centrifuge rotors. Our review of these documents suggests that the carbon fibre sought by Iraq was not intended for enrichment purposes, as the specifications of the material appear not to be consistent with those needed for manufacturing rotor tubes. In addition, we have carried out follow-up inspections, during which we have been able to observe the use of such carbon fibre in non-nuclear-related applications and to take samples. IAEA will, nevertheless, continue to pursue this matter.

We have also continued to investigate the relocation and consumption of the high explosive HMX. As I reported earlier, Iraq has declared that 32 tons of HMX previously under IAEA seal has been transferred for use in the production of industrial explosives, primarily to cement plants as a booster for explosives used in quarrying.

Iraq has provided us with additional information, including documentation on the movement and use of this material, and inspections have been conducted at locations where the material is said to have been used. However, given the nature of the use of high explosives, it may well be that IAEA will be unable to reach a final conclusion on the end use of this material. While we have no indication that this material was used for any application other than that declared by Iraq, we have no technical method of verifying, quantitatively, the declared use of the material in explosions. We will continue to follow this issue through a review of civilian mining practices in Iraq and through interviews of key Iraqi personnel involved in former relevant research and development activities.

We have completed a more detailed review of the 2,000 pages of documents found on 16 January at the private residence of an Iraqi scientist. The documents relate predominantly to lasers, including the use of laser technology to enrich uranium. They consist of technical reports; minutes of meetings, including those of the Standing Committee for Laser Applications; personal notes; copies of publications and student research project theses; and a number of administrative documents, some of which were marked as classified. While the documents have provided some additional details about Iraq's laser enrichment development efforts, they refer to activities or sites already known to IAEA and appear to be the personal files of the scientist in whose home they were found. Nothing contained in the documents alters the conclusions previously drawn by IAEA concerning the extent of Iraq's laser enrichment program. We nevertheless continue to emphasize to Iraq that it should search for and provide all documents, personal or otherwise, that might be relevant to our mandate.

Last week, Iraq also provided IAEA with documentation related to questions and concerns that, since 1998, have been in need of further clarification, particularly as regards weapons and centrifuge design. However, no new information was contained in that documentation.

It is to be hoped that the new commissions established by Iraq to look for any additional documents and hardware relevant to its programs for weapons of mass destruction will be able to uncover documents and other evidence that could assist in clarifying these remaining questions and concerns, as well as other areas of current concern.

Finally, as Mr. Blix mentioned earlier, I was informed this morning by the Director General of Iraq's National Monitoring Directorate that national legislation prohibiting proscribed activities was adopted today. The resolution of this long- standing legal matter is, in my view, a step in the right direction if Iraq is to demonstrate its commitment to fulfilling its obligations under Security Council resolutions.

In the coming weeks, IAEA will continue to expand its inspection capabilities in a number of ways, including its already extensive use of unannounced inspections at all relevant sites in Iraq. To strengthen and accelerate our ability to investigate matters of concern, and to reinstate and reinforce our ongoing monitoring and verification system, which came to a halt in 1998, we intend to increase the number of inspectors and support staff. We will also be adding more analysts and translators to support analysis of documents and other inspection findings. We intend to augment the number of customs and procurement experts for the monitoring of imports by Iraq. We will also intensify and expand the range of technical meetings and private interviews with Iraqi personnel, in accordance with our preferred modalities and locations, both inside and outside Iraq.

In addition, we intend to expand our capabilities for near real-time monitoring of dual-use equipment and related activities and to implement several additional components of wide-area environmental monitoring aimed at identifying fingerprints left by nuclear material and nuclear-related activities.

We hope to continue to receive from States actionable information relevant to our mandate. Now that Iraq has accepted the use of all of the platforms for aerial surveillance proposed by supporting States to the United Nations Monitoring, Verification and Inspection Commission (UNMOVIC) and IAEA—including U-2s, Mirage IVs, Antonovs and drones—we plan to make use of them to support our inspection activities, in particular with a view to monitoring movements in and around sites to be inspected.

The Government of Iraq reiterated last week its commitment to comply with its Security Council obligations and to provide full and active cooperation with the inspecting organizations. Subject to Iraq's making good on this commitment, the measures to which I have referred will contribute to the effectiveness of the inspection process.

As I have reported on numerous occasions, by December 1998 IAEA concluded that it had neutralized Iraq's past nuclear program and that therefore no unresolved disarmament issues remained at that time. Hence, our focus since the resumption of our inspections in Iraq two and a half months ago has been verifying whether Iraq revived its nuclear program in the intervening years.

We have to date found no evidence of ongoing prohibited nuclear or nuclear-related activities in Iraq. However, as I have just indicated, a number of issues are still under investigation and we are not yet in a position to reach a conclusion about them, although we are moving forward with regard to some of them. To that end, we intend to make full use of the authority granted to us under all relevant Security Council resolutions to build as much capacity into the inspection process as necessary.

In that context, I would underline the importance of information that States may be able to provide to help us in assessing the accuracy and completeness of the information provided by Iraq.

IAEA's experience in nuclear verification shows that it is possible, particularly with an intrusive verification system, to assess the presence or absence of a nuclear weapons program in a State even without the full cooperation of the inspected State. However, prompt, full and active cooperation by Iraq, as required under resolution 1441 (2002), will speed up the process. More importantly, it will enable us to reach the high degree of assurance required by the Security Council in the case of Iraq, in view of its past clandestine programs for weapons of mass destruction and its past pattern of cooperation. It is my hope that the commitments made recently in Baghdad will continue to translate into concrete and sustained actions.

* * * *

French Foreign Minister Dominique Galouzeau de Villepin. I would like to thank Mr. Blix and Mr. ElBaradei for the information they have just given us on the ongoing inspections in Iraq. I would like to reiterate to them France's confidence in and complete support for their work.

One knows the value France has placed on the unity of the Security Council from the outset of the Iraqi crisis. Today this unity is based on two fundamental elements.

Together we are pursuing the objective of effectively disarming Iraq, and therefore we are obligated to achieve results. We must not call into question our common commitment in this regard. Collectively we bear this onerous responsibility that must leave no room for ulterior motives or assumptions. Let us be clear: none of us feels the least indulgence towards Saddam Hussein and the Iraqi regime.

In unanimously adopting resolution 1441 (2002) we collectively expressed our agreement with the twostage approach proposed by France: disarmament through inspections and, if this strategy should fail, consideration by the Security Council of all the options, including resorting to force. Clearly, it was in the event that inspections failed, and only in that case, that a second resolution could be justified.

The question today is simple: do we believe in good conscience that disarmament via inspections missions is now a dead end, or do we believe that the possibilities regarding inspections made available in resolution 1441 (2002) have not yet been fully explored?

In response to this question, France believes two things. First, the option of inspections has not been exhausted, and it can provide an effective response to the imperative of disarming Iraq. Secondly, the use of force would have such heavy consequences for the people, the region and international stability that it should be envisaged only as a last resort.

What have we just learned from the reports by Mr. Blix and Mr. ElBaradei? We learned that the inspections are producing results. Of course, each of us would like more, and we will continue, together, to put pressure on Baghdad in order to obtain more. But the inspections are producing results.

In previous reports to the Security Council, on 27 January 2003, the Executive Chairman of the United Nations Monitoring, Verification and Inspection Commission (UNMOVIC) and the Director General of the International Atomic Energy Agency (IAEA) identified with precision the areas in which progress was expected. Significant gains have now been made on several of these fronts.

The Iraqis have provided the inspectors with new documents regarding chemical and biological weapons and also announced they are establishing commissions of inquiry led by former officials of weapons programs, in accordance with the requests of Mr. Blix. In the ballistic area, the information provided by Iraq has also enabled the inspectors to make progress. We now know exactly the real capabilities of the Al Samoud 2 missile. Dismantling of unauthorized programs must now begin, in accordance with Mr. Blix's conclusions. In the nuclear domain, useful information has been given to IAEA on the important points discussed by Mr. ElBaradei on 27 January: the acquisition of magnets that could be used to enrich uranium and the list of contacts between Iraq and the country that may have provided it with uranium.

We are now at the heart of the logic of resolution 1441 (2002), which must ensure effective inspections through precisely identifying banned programs and then eliminating them. We are all well aware that the success of the inspections presupposes that we get full and complete cooperation from Iraq, something France has consistently demanded.

We are starting to see real progress. Iraq has agreed to aerial reconnaissance over its territory. It has allowed Iraqi scientists to be questioned by inspectors without witnesses. A draft legislative bill barring all activities linked to programs for weapons of mass destruction is being adopted, in accordance with a long-standing request from the inspectors. Iraq is providing a detailed list of the experts who witnessed the destruction of military programs in 1991.

Naturally France expects these commitments to be verified. Beyond that we must maintain strong pressure on Iraq so that it goes further along the path of cooperation.

Progress like this strengthens us in our conviction that the inspections can be effective, but we must not close our eyes to the amount of work that remains to be done. Questions remain to be clarified, verifications must be made, and installations or equipment undoubtedly remain to be destroyed.

In order to do this we must give the inspections every opportunity to succeed. On 5 February I made proposals to the Council. Since then we detailed those proposals in a working document addressed to Mr. Blix and Mr. ElBaradei and distributed to Council members. What is the spirit of those proposals? They are practical and concrete proposals that can be quickly implemented and are designed to enhance the efficiency of inspection operations. They fall within the framework of resolution 1441 (2002) and consequently do not require a new resolution by the Council. These proposals support the efforts of Mr. Blix and Mr. ElBaradei, who are the best to tell us which ones they wish to accept to ensure maximum effectiveness in their work.

Mr. Blix and Mr. ElBaradei have already made useful and operational comments in their reports. France has already announced it has additional resources to make available to Mr. Blix and Mr. ElBaradei, starting with our Mirage IV reconnaissance aircraft.

Yes, I hear the critics: there are those who think that, in principle, inspections cannot be at all effective. But I recall that they are the very foundation of resolution 1441 (2002) and that the inspections are producing results. One may judge them to be insufficient, but they are there. Then there are those who believe that continuing the inspection process would be a kind of delaying tactic aimed at preventing military intervention. That naturally raises the question of the time allotted to Iraq. Here, we are at the centre of the debate. What is at stake is our credibility and our sense of responsibility. Let us have the courage to see things plainly.

There are two options. The option of war might seem, on the face of it, to be the swifter. But let us not forget that, after the war is won, the peace must be built. And let us not delude ourselves: that will be long and difficult, because it will be necessary to preserve Iraq's unity and to restore stability in a lasting way in a country and a region harshly affected by the intrusion of force. In the light of that perspective, there is the alternative offered by inspections, which enable us to move forward, day by day, on the path of the effective and peaceful disarmament of Iraq. In the end, is that not the surer and the swifter choice?

No one can maintain today that the path of war will be shorter than the path of inspections; no one can maintain that it would lead to a safer, more just and more stable world. For war is always the outcome of failure. Could it be our sole recourse in the face of today's many challenges?

Therefore, let us give the United Nations inspectors the time that is necessary for their mission to succeed. But let us together be vigilant and ask Mr. Blix and Mr. ElBaradei to report regularly to the Council. France, for its part, proposes another meeting at ministerial level, on 14 March, to assess the situation. Thus we would be able to judge the progress made and what remains to be accomplished.

In that context, the use of force is not justified at this time. There is an alternative to war: disarming Iraq through inspections. Moreover, premature recourse to the military option would be fraught with risks. The authority of our action rests today on the unity of the international community. Premature military intervention would call that unity into question, and that would remove its legitimacy and, in the long run, its effectiveness. Such intervention could have incalculable consequences for the stability of a scarred and fragile region. It would compound the sense of injustice, would aggravate tensions and would risk paving the way for other conflicts.

We all share the same priority: fighting terrorism mercilessly. That fight requires total determination; since the tragedy of 11 September 2001, it has been one of the main responsibilities of our peoples. And France, which has been struck hard several times by that terrible scourge, is wholly mobilized in this struggle, which involves all of us and which we must pursue together. That was the sense of the Security Council meeting held on 20 January at France's initiative.

Ten days ago, the United States Secretary of State, Mr. Powell, cited alleged links between Al-Qaeda and the Baghdad regime. Given the present state of our research and information, gathered in liaison with our allies, nothing enables us to establish such links. Moreover, we must assess the impact that a disputed military action would have on that level. Would not such an intervention be likely to deepen divisions among societies, among cultures, among peoples—divisions that nurture terrorism?

France has always said that we do not exclude the possibility that, one day, we might have to resort to force if the inspectors' reports concluded that it was impossible for inspections to continue. Then the Council would have to take a decision, and its members would have to shoulder all of their responsibilities. In such a scenario, I want to recall here the questions that I stressed at our last debate, on 5 February, to which we must respond. To what degree do the nature and the extent of the threat justify immediate recourse to force? How do we ensure that the considerable risks of such an intervention can actually be kept under control?

In any case, in such an eventuality it is the unity of the international community that would guarantee its effectiveness. Likewise, it is the United Nations that, whatever may happen, will remain tomorrow at the centre of the peace to be built. To those who ask with anguish when and how we will yield to war, I should like to say that nothing will be done in the Security Council, at any time, in haste, out of a lack of understanding, out of suspicion or out of fear. In this temple, the United Nations, we are the guardians of an ideal; we are the guardians of a conscience. The heavy responsibility and the immense honor that are ours must lead us to give priority to disarmament through peace.

It is an old country, France, of an old continent such as mine, Europe, that speaks before the Council today, that has known war, occupation, barbarity—a country that does not forget and that is aware of all it owes to the fighters for freedom who came from America and elsewhere. And yet France has always stood upright in the face of history and before mankind. Faithful to its values, it wants to act resolutely with all the other members of the international community. We believe in our ability to build a better world together.

* * * *

Chinese Foreign Minister Tang Jiaxuan. Let me begin by thanking Mr. Blix and Mr. ElBaradei for reporting to the Security Council on their inspection work in Iraq. Last November, this Council adopted resolution 1441 (2002) by consensus, reiterating the firm determination of the international community to verify and destroy weapons of mass destruction in Iraq's possession. Now the Iraqi issue has reached its most critical juncture. The international community shares the universal hope to see a political resolution of this issue within the United Nations framework and places tremendous expectations on the inspection work of the United Nations Monitoring, Verification and Inspection Commission and the International Atomic Energy Agency. Here, I wish to share some of my views with the Security Council.

First, Iraq must implement the relevant Security Council resolutions strictly, comprehensively and earnestly. We urge the Iraqi side to recognize fully the importance and urgency of the inspections and to provide greater cooperation in a more proactive way. The latest visit to Baghdad by the two chief United Nations inspectors has achieved some positive results. The Iraqi side has made some commitments. We request Iraq to make good on those promises as soon as possible and to provide clarifications and explanations as soon as possible regarding the questions raised by the two chief inspectors in their briefings earlier.

Secondly, it is necessary for the inspection work in Iraq to continue. Resolution 1441 (2002) provides explicit authorization and specific requirements for the inspections.

Pursuing the implementation of this resolution remains an important task for us. In that respect, a great deal of work still needs to be done by the Security Council and by the two inspection bodies. Judging from what has been done in the recent past, the inspection work has made progress and has clarified quite a number of issues. However, new elements have also been discovered in that process. The two bodies are dutybound and justified to further the inspections with the aim of finding out the truth and fulfilling the mission conferred on them by the Security Council. Thus, in agreement with the majority opinion among Council members, China believes that the inspection process is working and that the inspectors should continue to be given the time they need so as to implement resolution 1441 (2002).

Thirdly, the Security Council has to step up its efforts with regard to the inspections. The Iraqi issue bears on peace and stability in the Gulf region and on the credibility and authority of the Security Council. The Council should deal with this complex situation appropriately and responsibly, in accordance with the purposes and principles of the Charter, in order to carry out its important task of maintaining international peace and security. Top priority must now be given to strengthening its guidance of and support for the inspection work and to facilitating a productive political settlement. Intensifying inspections is aimed at seeking a peaceful solution to the Iraqi issue. China stands ready to continue to provide the two bodies with personnel and the necessary technical assistance, thereby continuing our efforts towards a political settlement of the Iraqi issue.

China is an ancient civilization. Our ancestors proposed long ago the idea of peace being the best option. At present, peace and development are common aspirations of all peoples around the world. Sitting on the Security Council, we simply have no reason not to make every effort to reach that goal, and we are obliged to try our best, and to use all possible means to avert war. Only by pursuing a political settlement can we truly live up to the trust and hope that the international community places in the Security Council.

* * * *

British Foreign Secretary Jack Straw. I speak on behalf of a very old country, founded in 1066 by the French. In opening, I would like to thank Mr. Blix and Mr. ElBaradei for their reports and to express my very great appreciation to them and to their inspection teams for their great efforts in the face of what I think is still very clear: Iraq's failure fully and actively to comply with resolution 1441 (2002).

The issue before us could not be graver. It is about the authority of the United Nations and about the responsibility of the Security Council for international peace and security. Just three months ago, on 8 November, we unanimously adopted resolution 1441 (2002), submitted by the United States and ourselves. We said then that Iraq's proliferation of weapons of mass destruction and of long-range missiles and its non- compliance with Council resolutions were a threat to international peace and security.

We all knew—and we all know—that they have had these weapons. It is why we said that Iraq had them, why all 5 permanent members and all 10 elected members said the same thing. We knew that the issue was not whether Iraq had them, but whether Iraq was actively cooperating to get rid of them. We emphasized that Iraq had been found guilty 12 years ago by the world community.

It is worth just reminding ourselves that Iraq is the only country in the world that has launched missile attacks on five of its neighbors, invaded two of its neighbors—both Muslim—and killed without any justification hundreds of thousands of innocent people in Iran, in Kuwait and in Iraq itself.

In his report, Mr. Blix referred to the decisions that were made in 1991, and he said that regrettably the high degree of cooperation required by the Council of Iraq for disarmament through inspection was not forthcoming in 1991. It is worth reminding ourselves, when we discuss this issue of time scales, that on 3 April 1991, this Council gave Iraq 90 days to disarm—by 2 July 1991. In the 11 years, 7 months and 12 days—quite a lot of time—since the Council's deadline to Iraq ran out, what is it they have done?

Well, they have lied; they have concealed; they have played games—the game of catch as catch can, as Mr. Blix told us on 27 January. Saddam said for four years that he had no biological weapons program, no anthrax bacillus, no smallpox virus, no VX nerve agent. And indeed, the inspectors found absolutely nothing. It took the defection of Saddam's own son-in-law to uncover Saddam's biological weapons program, more terrible than anybody had thought.

To bring us up to date, as Mr. Blix and Mr. ElBaradei spelled out in their report on 27 January, Iraq has failed to account for thousands of tons of chemical weapons and precursor chemicals, of shells and bombs for anthrax, for mustard gas and for VX nerve agent. They have failed to make a full and complete disclosure, as required of them, on 7 December. They have failed to cooperate fully and actively on substance, as well as on process, with the inspectors. And they have failed substantively to meet the obligations imposed on them.

I have listened with very great care to my colleagues who have spoken so far. We all agree on the importance of resolution 1441 (2002), and it is striking that nobody who has spoken so far—and, I warrant, nobody who speaks after me—has suggested for a second that Iraq is fully and actively complying with the obligations that we imposed on them on 8 November of last year. So, Iraq's material breaches, which we spelled out on 8 November, are still there.

In that regard, I would be glad to put the following questions to the inspectors: Why did Mr. Blix think that Iraq has refurbished equipment like the engine casting chambers at Al Mamoun and the chemical processing equipment at Al Falujah, both of which were destroyed by the United Nations Special Commission (UNSCOM) because they were prohibited? Since the last report, how many interviews have taken place with the officials that the inspectors have asked to interview, and how many in places to which the inspectors are sure are not subject to electronic interception and bugging by Iraq? Has any of the outstanding material identified by UNSCOM in early 1999—the missing 8,500 liters of anthrax, the 1.5 tons of VX nerve agent, the 6,500 chemical bombs—been satisfactorily dealt with by Iraq? Do recent documents provided by Iraq give any serious evidence of this? As for the nuclear dossier, how many of its open issues has the International Atomic Energy Agency (IAEA) been able to close through Iraq's cooperation?

I thought that the most significant point made by Mr. Blix in his report, which has subsequently been echoed by everyone who has spoken so far, was in his closing remarks, when he said that three months after the adoption of resolution 1441 (2002), the period of disarmament through inspection could still be short if the immediate, active and unconditional cooperation with the United Nations Monitoring, Verification and Inspection Commission (UNMOVIC) and IAEA were to be forthcoming.

I take those words to mean that Iraq has yet to be forthcoming with that immediate, active and unconditional cooperation. I would like to ask Mr. Blix, picking up a phrase from his report of 27 January, whether he believes that Iraq has yet come to a genuine acceptance of the disarmament that has been demanded of it.

The issue before us is of the authority of the United Nations and of the defiance of United Nations resolutions. On 8 November, we said unanimously that Saddam was to have a final opportunity. Can anyone say—does anyone truly believe here—that he has yet taken that final opportunity? Like every other member of this Council, and, I believe, of the international community, I hope and believe that a peaceful solution to this crisis may still be possible. But this will require a dramatic and immediate change by Saddam, and that will be achieved only if we, the Security Council, hold our nerve in the face of this tyrant, give meaning to our words and to the decisions that we have already collectively taken, and make ourselves ready to ensure that Iraq will face the serious consequences that we all decided would have to happen if Iraq's defiance did not end.

I want to close by saying this. The period of 12 years since resolution 687 (1991) was adopted on 3 April 1991 has, frankly, been a period of humiliation for this body— the Security Council—and for the United Nations, as games have been played with the Council's authority. And the period after the inspectors were effectively kicked out by Iraq at the end of 1998 until 8 November will hardly be described as the best in the Security Council's history, because Iraq was in open defiance of the United Nations and nothing effectively was being done about its weapons of mass destruction.

I am proud that, with the United States, the United Kingdom took the initiative on this issue and tabled what became resolution 1441 (2002). I am glad to note the progress on process that has been made. I am glad to note that, notwithstanding the clear statement by the Government of Iraq on 10 September last year that inspectors would never go back into Iraq, inspectors have now gone back into Iraq. We note the progress on process that has been made.

But I also say this: in our efforts to secure a peaceful conclusion to this crisis, as we must, I know, and I think everybody else here knows, that we have reached this stage only by doing what the United Nations Charter requires of us, which is to back a diplomatic process with a credible threat of force and also, if necessary, to be ready to use that threat of force. If we back away from that—if we decide to give unlimited time for little or no cooperation on substance—then the disarmament of Iraq and the peace and security of the international community, for which we are responsible, will get not easier, but very much harder.

This issue is not just about Iraq—it is about how we deal with proliferators elsewhere across the globe. If we send out the message to proliferators the world over that defiance of the United Nations pays, it will not be peace that we will have secured.

Secretary of State Colin Powell. It is a great pleasure to be here again to consider this very important matter. I am very pleased to be here as the Secretary of State of a relatively new country on the face of the Earth. But I think I can take some credit sitting here as the representative of the oldest democracy represented here around this table. I am proud of that. It is a democracy that believes in peace, a nation that has tried in the course of its history to show how people can live in peace with one another. But it is a democracy that has not been afraid to meet its responsibilities on the world stage when it has been challenged and, more importantly, when others in the world have been challenged, when the international order has been challenged or when the international institutions of which we are a part have been challenged. That is why we joined, and have been an active member of, institutions such as the United Nations and a number of others that have come together for the purpose of peace, the purpose of mutual security and the purpose of letting other nations that pursue a path of destruction, that pursue a path of developing weapons of mass destruction and that threaten their neighbors know that we will stand tall, that we will stand together to meet these kinds of challenges.

I want to express my appreciation to Mr. Blix and Mr. ElBaradei for their statements this morning. They took up a difficult challenge when they went back into Iraq last fall in pursuit of disarmament, as required by resolution 1441 (2002). I listened very attentively to all they said this morning, and I am pleased that there have been improvements with respect to process. I am pleased that there have been improvements with respect to not having five minders with each inspectors, but fewer than five minders with each inspector. But I think they are still being minded; they are still being watched; they are still being bugged. They still do not have the freedom of access around Iraq that they need in order to do their job well.

I am pleased that a few people have come forward for interviews. But not all the people who should be coming forward for interviews are doing so, or have the freedom to interview in such a way that their safety and the safety of their families can be protected, as required by resolution 1441 (2002). I am glad that access has been relatively good.

But that is all process—it is not substance. I am pleased to hear that decrees have now been issued that should have been issued years and years ago. But does anyone really think that a decree from Saddam Hussain—directed to whom?—is going to fundamentally change the situation? And it comes out on a morning when we are moving forward down the path laid out by resolution 1441 (2002). These are all process issues. These are all tricks that are being played on us.

They say that new commissions are being formed that will go and find materials that they claim are not there in the first place. Can anybody honestly believe that either one of those two new commissions will actively seek out information that they have been actively trying to deny to the world community, to the inspectors, for the past 11-plus years?

I commend the inspectors. I thank them for what they are doing. But at the same time I have to keep coming back to the point that the inspectors have repeatedly made. They have made it again here this morning; they have been making it for the past 11-plus years. What we need is not more inspections, not more immediate access; what we need is immediate, active, unconditional, full cooperation on the part of Iraq. What we need is for Iraq to disarm.

Resolution 1441 (2002) was not about inspections. Let me say that again: resolution 1441 (2002) was not about inspections. Resolution 1441 (2002) was about the disarmament of Iraq. We worked on that resolution for seven weeks, from the time of President Bush's powerful speech here in the General Assembly on 12 September until the resolution was adopted on 8 November. We had intense discussions. All of you are familiar with that; you participated in those discussions. That was about disarmament.

The resolution began with the clear statement that Iraq had been in material breach of its obligations for the previous 11 years, and remained to that day—the day the resolution was adopted—in material breach. The resolution said that Iraq must now come into compliance; it must disarm. The resolution went on to say that we wanted to see a declaration from Iraq, within 30 days, of all of its activities. "Put it all on the table; let us see what you have been doing. Give us a declaration that we can believe in that is full, complete and accurate"—that is what we said to Iraq on 8 November. And some 29 days later we got 12,000 pages. Nobody in this Council can say that that was a full, complete or accurate declaration.

Now it is several months after that declaration was submitted, and I have heard nothing to suggest that they have filled in the gaps that were in that declaration, or that they have added new evidence that should give us any comfort that we have a full, complete and accurate declaration. You will recall that we put that declaration requirement into the resolution as an early test of Iraq's seriousness. Are they serious? Are they going to disarm? Are they going to comply? Are they going to cooperate? The answer, with that declaration, was, "No—we are going to see what we can get away with. We will see how much we can slip under your nose. And everybody will clap, and say 'Isn't that wonderful; they provided a declaration'"—a declaration that was not of any particular use.

We then had some level of acceptance of the fact that inspectors were going back in. Recall that Iraq tried to use that gambit right after the President's speech in September to try to keep resolution 1441 (2002) from ever coming down the pipe. Suddenly, on the Monday after the President's speech, they said, "Oh! We'll let inspectors back in". Why? Because when the President spoke, and when Iraq saw that the international community was now coming together with seriousness and with determination, it knew it had better do something. It did not do it out of the goodness of its heart, or because it suddenly discovered that it had been in violation for all those years. They did it because of pressure. They did it because this Council stood firm. They did it because the international community said, "Enough! We will not tolerate Iraq continuing to have weapons of mass destruction to be used against its own people, to be used against its neighbors—or worse, if we find a post-11 September nexus between Iraq and terrorist organizations that are looking for just such weapons." And I would submit—and will provide more evidence—that such connections are now emerging. We can establish that they exist.

We cannot wait for one of these terrible weapons to show up in one of our cities and wonder where it came from after it has been detonated by Al-Qaeda or somebody else. This is the time to go after this source of this kind of weaponry.

And that is what resolution 1441 (2002) was all about. To this day we have not seen the level of cooperation that was expected, anticipated and hoped for—I hoped for it. No one worked harder than the United States. And I submit that no one worked harder—if I may humbly say so—than I did to try to put forward a resolution that would show the determination of the international community to the leadership in Iraq so that they would now meet their obligations and come clean and comply. And they did not. Notwithstanding all of the discussion that we have heard so far this morning about, "Give inspections more time; let's have more airplanes flying over; let's have more inspectors added to the inspection process"—Mr. Blix noted earlier this week that it is not more inspectors that are needed. What is needed is what both Mr. Blix and Mr. ElBaradei have said, what has been needed since 1991: immediate, active, unconditional compliance and cooperation.

I am pleased that Iraq is now discussing this matter with South Africa. But it is not brain surgery. South Africa knows how to do it. Anybody knows how to do it. If we were getting the kind of cooperation that we expected when resolution 1441 (2002) was passed and that we hoped for when resolution 1441 (2002) was passed, these documents would be flooding out of homes, flooding out of factories. There would be no question about access. There would be no question about interviews. If Iraq were serious in this matter, interviewees would be standing up outside the offices of the United Nations Monitoring, Verification and Inspection Commission (UNMOVIC) and the International Atomic Energy Agency (IAEA), in Baghdad and elsewhere, waiting to be interviewed because they would be determined to prove to the world, to give the world all the evidence needed that these weapons of mass destruction are gone.

Notwithstanding all of the lovely rhetoric, the questions remain. Some of my colleagues have talked about them. We have not accounted for the anthrax. We have not accounted for the botulinum, the VX, bulk biological agents, growth media, 30,000 chemical and biological munitions. These are not trivial matters one can just ignore and walk away from and say "Well, maybe the inspectors will find them, maybe they won't". We have not had a complete, accurate declaration. We have seen the reconstitution of casting chambers for missiles. Why? Because they are still trying to develop these weapons. We have not seen the kind of cooperation that was anticipated, expected and demanded by this body. And we must continue to demand it; we must continue to put pressure on Iraq and to put force upon Iraq to make sure that the threat of force is not removed, because resolution 1441 (2002) was all about compliance, not inspections. The inspections were put in as a way, of course, to assist Iraq in coming forward and complying: in order to verify; in order to monitor, as the chief inspector noted.

But we still have an incomplete answer from Iraq. We are facing a difficult situation. More inspectors? Sorry, that is not the answer. What we need is immediate cooperation. Time? How much time does it take to say, "I understand the will of the international community, and I and my regime are laying it all out for you" and not playing "guess", not forming commissions, not issuing decrees, not getting laws that should have been passed years ago suddenly passed on the day when we are meeting. These are not responsible actions on the part of Iraq. These are continued efforts to deceive, to deny, to divert, to throw us off the trail, to throw us off the path.

The resolution anticipated this kind of response from Iraq. That is why in all of our discussions about that resolution we said, "They are in material breach. If they come into a new material breach with a false declaration or are not willing to cooperate and comply, as operative paragraph 4 says, then the matter has to be referred to the Council for serious consequences." I submit that notwithstanding the improvements in process that we have noted—and I welcome this, and thank the inspectors for their hard work—these improvements in process do not move us away from the central problem that we continue to have. And more inspections and a longer inspection period will not move us away from the central issue, the central problem we are facing. And that central problem is that Iraq has failed to comply with resolution 1441 (2002).

The threat of force must remain. Force should always be a last resort. I have preached this for most of my professional life as a soldier and as a diplomat. But it must be a resort. We cannot allow this process to be endlessly strung out, as Iraq is trying to do right now: "String it out long enough and the world will start looking in other directions. The Security Council will move on. We will get away with it again."

My friends, they cannot be allowed to get away with it again. We are now in a situation where Iraq's continued non-compliance and failure to cooperate, it seems to me in the clearest terms, require this Council to begin to think through the consequences of walking away from this problem or the reality that we have to face this problem and that in the very near future we will have to consider whether or not we have reached that point where this Council must face this issue—as distasteful as it may be and as reluctant as we may be. So many of you would rather not have to face this issue, but it is an issue that must be faced. And that issue is whether or not it is time to consider serious consequences of the kind intended by resolution 1441 (2002). The reason we must not look away from it is because these are terrible weapons. We are talking about weapons that will kill not a few people, not 100 people, not 1,000 people, but could kill tens of thousands of people if these weapons got into the wrong hands.

The security of the region, the hopes for the people of Iraq themselves, and our security rest upon us meeting our responsibilities and, if it comes to it, invoking the serious consequences called for in resolution 1441 (2002). Resolution 1441 (2002) is about disarmament and compliance and not merely a process of inspections that goes on forever without ever resolving the basic problem.

Russian Foreign Minister Igor Ivanov. Our meeting today is in its way a unique occasion in the history of the United Nations. The Security Council is meeting again as an urgent matter at the level of Ministers for Foreign Affairs to seek a solution to a most acute problem: a settlement of the situation concerning Iraq. This fact is further evidence that the world community sees the United Nations as the most suitable mechanism for settling the most burning issues facing the world today.

For it is precisely within the United Nations and the Security Council that all States have an opportunity, on an equal footing, to seek solutions to problems involving the interests of general security. That is why, with each additional meeting of the Security Council, the international community is further engaging hopes for strengthening the unity and solidarity of States in the face of common threats and challenges.

The reports today by Mr. Blix and Mr. ElBaradei, whom we welcome and whom we thank for the enormous amount of useful work that they are doing, have shown very clearly that in Iraq a unique potential has been established in the area of inspections and monitoring. I think that, in our discussions and conclusions, we should be guided not by feelings, emotions, sympathies or antipathy with respect to any particular regime. Rather, we should be guided by the actual facts and, on the basis of those facts, should draw our conclusions. This is why we supported the inspectors' return to Iraq and why we must continue to provide them with all necessary assistance. It is only on the basis of the professional data they provide us with that we can, without making a mistake, come to a correct conclusion.

The international inspections, carried out daily, are proceeding smoothly with Iraqi cooperation. There is unimpeded access to all sites, including the most sensitive sites, as required under resolution 1441 (2002).

During the last visit of Mr. Blix and Mr. ElBaradei to Baghdad, substantial progress was made, and we cannot disregard that. Now there is no obstacle to aerial monitoring of Iraqi territory, using the American U-2, the French Mirage IV and the Russian Antonov.

The situation is improving with regard to interviews with Iraqi scientists. They are now being held without minders. The Iraqis have provided to UNMOVIC a number of new documents about past military programs and have also set up two commissions to search for additional materials.

We simply cannot ignore these facts. We can think back to our meeting of 5 February, when these matters were discussed as pending, and we asked Iraq to resolve them. Thanks to the last visit by Mr. Blix and Mr. ElBaradei these matters have now been resolved. In fact there is forward movement which, I repeat, we must not ignore.

We strongly urge Baghdad to further increase its cooperation with the international inspectors. After all, this is first and foremost in its own interest. Clearly, UNMOVIC and IAEA have the necessary conditions to carry out the tasks assigned to them. As far as we know, nobody is proposing changing the mandate of UNMOVIC or IAEA or introducing any changes into the unanimously adopted resolution 1441 (2002). But all States—or at least the overwhelming majority of States in the world—are saying the United Nations Security Council must continue to provide the inspectors with all the support they need.

At the same time, however, the work of the inspectors must be made more systematic and focused. It is necessary to set clear tasks and then consistently monitor their implementation. In this connection I would like to recall the responsibilities of the inspectors as enshrined in resolution 1284 (1999), according to which UNMOVIC and IAEA are to submit for Security Council approval their work program, including the list of key disarmament tasks. The adoption of such a program would provide us with objective criteria, not only for assessing the degree of Baghdad's cooperation with the United Nations, but, most importantly, for helping us answer whether Iraq is today a threat to international peace and security, and, if so, what specifically must be done to remove that threat. This work program must be submitted as soon as possible.

Mr. Blix and Mr. ElBaradei may be asked small questions of clarification. But there is one point of principle we must all answer: must the UNMOVIC and IAEA inspectors continue their work in Iraq in the interest of a political settlement, and have all the necessary conditions to that end been met? Russia answers "yes" to that question. Yes, the conditions are there; yes, the inspectors must continue their inspections. This position is shared by the overwhelming majority of States in the world, including within the Security Council.

We have a unique opportunity to reach agreement on how to solve this most urgent international problem through political means, in strict accordance with the United Nations Charter. This is a real opportunity, and it must not be missed. Force may be resorted to, but only when all other remedies have been exhausted. As may be seen from today's discussion, we have not yet reached that point. I hope we will not reach that point.

We are all fully aware of the exceptional responsibility placed on us by the international community in accordance with the United Nations Charter. Our energies today must therefore be directed not to competing against each other, but rather to uniting our efforts.

It is symbolic that today's meeting is being held on St. Valentine's Day. This is a day when people get engaged, cementing their greatest hopes. It is our hope we will be able to do likewise.

German Foreign Minister Joschka Fischer. I would like to thank Mr. Blix and Mr. ElBaradei for their update on the inspections in Iraq. They have briefed us on the substantial progress of their work, but also on deficits in the Iraqi regime's cooperation with the inspectors. Those deficits must be rectified by Baghdad without delay. Iraq must not be allowed to possess any weapons of mass destruction and must disarm completely. Baghdad must actively and fully cooperate with the United Nations Monitoring, Verification and Inspection Commission (UNMOVIC) and the International Atomic Energy Agency (IAEA) and must comply unconditionally with the requirements of the relevant resolutions.

The inspectors have reported on headway that they have made. The first private interviews with Iraqi experts have taken place without official escorts. The problem of U-2 aerial surveillance has been resolved. Helicopters, drones and Mirage and Antonov aircraft are to be put at UNMOVIC's disposal to ensure comprehensive surveillance from the air. The inspectors have thus been able to score some successes. Already today their presence on the ground has substantially diminished the danger emanating from Iraq. The need now is to gain experience with the new measures in place and to evaluate them in the light of our common goal of ensuring Iraq's complete disarmament. Why should we now turn away from that path? Why should we now halt the inspections? On the contrary, the inspectors must be given the time they need to successfully complete their mission.

How we proceed from here is laid down by resolutions 1441 (2002) and 1284 (1999). What is crucial are the resolutions' three core elements: full cooperation, inspection and verification.

First, Iraq must cooperate fully, unconditionally and actively with the inspectors if the looming tragedy is to be averted.

Secondly, the inspection regime must be made more efficient. France has made very concrete proposals on how this can be done. These envisage increasing the number of inspection teams and improving the technical resources at their disposal. In addition, the inspectors' capacities for coordination, surveillance and concrete action need to be spelled out precisely and strengthened. We strongly support these proposals, for they help ensure a response more appropriate to the size of the task.

Thirdly, and in parallel with the inspections, the verification and monitoring mechanisms called for in resolution 1284 (1999) need to be developed and expanded. An ongoing, long- term monitoring regime must prevent any future rearmament. We need structures that guarantee Iraq's disarmament and containment on a permanent basis. That is of immense importance for the whole region. Such a reinforced inspection and verification regime could also be of service to the United Nations in other crises involving weapons of mass destruction.

All possible options for resolving the Iraq crisis by peaceful means must be thoroughly explored. Whatever decisions need to be made must be taken by the Security Council alone. It remains the only body internationally authorized to do so.

Military action against Iraq would, in addition to the terrible humanitarian consequences, above all endanger the stability of a tense and troubled region. The consequences for the Near and Middle East could be catastrophic. There should be no automatism leading us to the use of military force. All possible alternatives need to be exhaustively explored. That was once again reaffirmed by the Governments of Russia,

France and Germany in a joint declaration issued on Monday. Diplomacy has not yet reached the end of the road.

Iraqi Permanent Representative Mohammed Aldouri. I thank you, Sir, and the Security Council for granting Iraq the opportunity to participate in this meeting and to address the Security Council within the time allotted to us.

I listened very carefully to the presentations by Mr. Blix, Executive Chairman of the United Nations Monitoring, Verification and Inspection Commission (UNMOVIC), and Mr. ElBaradei, Director General of the International Atomic Energy Agency (IAEA), as well as to the statements of members of the Security Council. I should like to make a number of observations.

Iraq agreed to act on resolution 1441 (2002), based on the fact that it provided a means to reach a solution to the so- called issue of the disarmament of Iraqi weapons of mass destruction. Following three rounds of technical negotiations with the United Nations and the return of inspectors to Iraq, Iraq provided everything that might fall within the concept of proactive Iraqi cooperation.

I should like to note that Iraq submitted the declaration required under paragraph 3 of resolution 1441 (2002) in record time. The declaration contained many documents on previous Iraqi programs in the nuclear, chemical, biological and ballistic fields. We continue to believe that those documents require in-depth study by the relevant authorities because they contain updated information responding to many questions. We have the right to wonder whether the declaration has been studied with due diligence and thoroughness, or should the declaration be reconsidered as a whole by the relevant parties? We should like the file to be reconsidered in its entirety.

Secondly, Iraq opened its doors to the inspection teams without imposing restrictions or conditions. The entire world was surprised at that unprecedented level of cooperation. We know that some States were not very happy about that cooperation. In fact, some would have wished that Iraq had obstructed inspections or locked some doors. However, that did not and will not happen because Iraq has genuinely decided to prove that it is free of weapons of mass destruction and to dispel all doubts in that regard.

Let me recall what Mr. Blix and Mr. ElBaradei stated this morning. So far, 675 inspections have taken place within Iraq in this short period of time. The inspectors have found no evidence contradicting Iraq's declarations or confirming the allegations made by the United States and the United Kingdom on the presence of proscribed weapons programs or of the weapons whose presence was alleged by the representative of the United Kingdom this morning.

Thirdly, with respect to the interviews with Iraqi scientists, the Government continues to encourage scientists to agree to interviews. Lists of the names of additional scientists have been submitted at the request of Mr. Blix and Mr. ElBaradei. Other lists are on the way, as they know.

Fourthly, Iraq has agreed to overflights by U-2, Mirage and Antonov II aircraft in Iraqi airspace for surveillance purposes. While these aircraft are undergoing their missions, it is logical and reasonable for British and United States aeroplanes to cease air strikes because these would affect the security of those missions. Thus, inspectors have six levels of aerial surveillance: satellites, high-altitude U-2 surveillance aircraft, medium-level Mirage aircraft, low-level Antonov II aircraft, and helicopters and other means of aerial surveillance.

With respect to the Iraqi legislation that some have considered to be among the important elements of Iraq's cooperation, Iraq did not take a negative stance in this regard. We had technical and legislative considerations. At any rate, the decree was enacted today in order to put an end to the controversy surrounding this matter. I was surprised to hear some say that the decree was unimportant or late in coming.

With respect to other issues, UNMOVIC, following its establishment, adopted a process that includes assimilating outstanding disarmament issues into the reinforced monitoring system; this was referred to in the organizational plan it submitted to the Security Council in document S/2000/292. However, in order to facilitate UNMOVIC's mission to identify and resolve these issues, Iraq, in its full, comprehensive and updated declaration of 7 December 2002, provided full, important details on these outstanding issues and on the means to resolve them.

Nevertheless, Iraq has begun to cooperate proactively with UNMOVIC, which has recently agreed to discuss these issues with Iraq; we have provided 24 documents concerning many of the outstanding issues. Two commissions of high-ranking Iraqi officials and scientists have been created to consider these issues and provide the information, as requested by Mr. Blix and Mr. ElBaradei on more than one occasion.

After all that, we hear allegations by some not only that has Iraq not cooperated, but that it is in material breach of resolution 1441 (2002). Our question is, where is this material breach? Does it lie in the allegations made by the United States of America at the previous meeting—with which many States worldwide did not agree—or is the matter related to the notion of the proactive cooperation required of Iraq?

Many in this forum have called for proactive cooperation. What is proactive cooperation? If it means that Iraq must show weapons of mass destruction, we would respond with the Arabic proverb that an empty hand has nothing to give. You cannot give what you do not have. If we do not possess such weapons, how can we disarm ourselves? How can such weapons be dismantled when they do not exist?

We agree with those who believe that the best way to resolve these issues is through continuing proactive cooperation with the inspectors. We do not stand with those who want the inspections to fail. I refer to an article The Washington Post quoting members of the United States Senate as saying that "We [the U.S. Government] have undermined the inspectors."

With regard to the issue of missiles that has been referred to by many speakers today, I would like to note, for those who are unaware of it, that Iraq declared those missiles in its biennial declaration as well as in its full declaration to the Security Council. The missiles were not discovered by the inspectors. Iraq continues to stress that these missiles, delivered to our armed forces, do not have a range exceeding 150 kilometres. The issue was recently discussed with UNMOVIC experts. Iraq believes that this issue can be resolved with a technical solution. It is therefore illogical to accuse Iraq of having gone beyond the permitted range, as long as Iraq is addressing the issue in a completely transparent manner and as long as its installations and test sites are open and subject to monitoring. In this regard, Iraq would suggest that test firings could be undertaken of a random choice of missiles, in order to ascertain the range. There is ample opportunity for open dialogue between technical parties in Iraq and in UNMOVIC in order to reach a satisfactory solution to this issue.

With regard to the subject of VX and anthrax, which were also mentioned, Iraq has put forward practical proposals to resolve these issues, among other outstanding issues related to VX, anthrax and certain chemical precursors, as well as to information on growth media. Iraq has suggested that one could ascertain the amount of VX and anthrax that has been destroyed by measuring the dissolved quantities of VX and anthrax at sites where unilateral destruction took place at the beginning of 1991, and that it is possible to extrapolate the quantity destroyed by scientific investigation and by comparing the result with Iraq's declaration. The issue, therefore, needs strenuous effort and persistence, because this is a difficult subject.

At a time when voices worldwide are calling on the United States and the United Kingdom to listen to reason and respect international legitimacy and peace, the United States of America and the United Kingdom continue to mass forces against Iraq and to threaten war in disregard of international law and human rights.

We stress that Iraq has chosen the path of peace. We have opted for solutions that would satisfy the international community. We are prepared to provide all means to assist in making clear the true picture, in order to avoid the objections of those who are ill-intentioned, who wish to start a war in Iraq and the region, and whose clear political and economic objectives would result in incalculable consequences.

We hope that the Security Council will heed the desire of the vast majority of States Members of the United Nations, and allow the inspectors to fulfill their role and carry out their tasks through dialogue and proactive cooperation. That will certainly lead to peace and not war. We also seriously call upon the Security Council to consider lifting the unjust embargo imposed on Iraq and to rise to its commitments by respecting Iraq's sovereignty, independence and territorial integrity. We call upon the Council to continue to work towards the elimination of all weapons of mass destruction in the entire Middle East, in implementation of paragraph 14 of resolution 687 (1991).

Remarks by Secretary of State Powell, February 14, 2003

Secretary Colin Powell delivered his remarks following the United Nations Security Council meeting in New York City.

Q. How did the tone of today's meeting come across to yourself? And given the tone of the meeting, which many people thought was against proceeding with a second resolution right now, giving the inspectors more time, how does that come to you in terms of your work on a second resolution? Are you planning to ahead with one?

Secretary Powell. Well, I think it was a very good, spirited debate which continued in our private session, and I found it very useful and helpful. We all, of course, congratulated Dr. Blix and Dr. ElBaradei and their teams for the work that they are doing under very challenging conditions.

What it came down to is the following proposition that we discussed this morning, and more in the private session, and that is that robust inspections have to be matched by cooperation and compliance. And no matter how robust you make the inspections, no matter how many inspectors you put in, unless there is compliance and coopera-tion on the part of the Iraqi regime, they really haven't accomplished anything.

And while we noted some progress on process, frankly, I was not satisfied that we have seen anything with respect to real progress on substance. A few more people have been interviewed. We still have them coming with tape recorders—and guess who gets a copy of the tape when they leave. We heard this morning about a decree from Sad-dam Hussein that says everybody is supposed to cooperate. Isn't that very convenient the morning of our meeting?

So it's more of the same game-playing, in my judgment, that's going on. Two com-missions that have been formed that are going to go look for things that they should have been producing for the inspectors all along. More of the games being played.

And so I think we have to take that all into account as we make a judgment as to whether or not they are complying, are they cooperating, and in my judgment, they still are not complying or cooperating. And I think both inspectors, at the end of their statements, indicated clearly that they have not yet seen the kind of level of coopera-tion that would bring this matter to a conclusion.

And so we will continue to debate this issue within the Council, among Council members. And with respect to action on another resolution, will go back to Washing-ton, consult with my colleagues, consult with the President, and talk to other members of the Council and make a judgment in the not too distant future.

But I have not yet seen what we all hoped to see when Resolution 1441 was passed, and that is Iraq coming forward, cooperating and complying with the demands of the Council that it disarm itself of its weapons of mass destruction and allow the inspec-tors to do their work in verifying and monitoring that disarmament.

I'll give you a perfect example. I talked about the declaration, which was a failed declaration, in December. Nobody defended that declaration. And when it was the Iraqi Perm Rep's opportunity to respond, his answer to all of the gaps, all the things that were missing: Read it again. That's what he said. This is not what we were looking for.

Q. Mr. Secretary, Dr. Blix challenged quite a bit of the American intelligence infor-mation, including information about the overhead satellite images, said that this shell game of components moving around the base, see no evidence that this is hap-pening.

Is this sort of—I mean, one gets the sense that this presentation tend to make it much more difficult for you to make a case that there is a need to move towards a mil-itary response.

Secretary Powell. No. I don't think Dr. Blix challenged a great deal. What he said was on the satellite photo that I used last week that highlighted four spots in that large complex that we believed chemical weapons were stored in, he said, based on his analysis, there could be an alternative explanation to the activity that I highlighted, and that is certainly his judgment to make.

I have quite a bit of information in addition to the one satellite photo that I showed which at least convinces us that there were prohibited munitions at that site and the place was sanitized.

Betsy.

Q. Mr. Secretary, are you going to agree to a March 14th meeting and have you shared with Mr. Blix the information that convinces you that that photograph is indeed as you interpreted it.

Secretary Powell. We will provide as much information as we can to Dr. Blix since it seems to be a matter in contention, although it's historic now because they have been there and they have not seen anything and see no evidence of the presence of those weapons. And so I could certainly share more information with him, but it would be of a historic nature.

With respect to another meeting on the 14th, as proposed by my colleague Dominique deVillepin, the Council decided to not make a decision on that at this point and let us all go back to capitals, reflect on it.

As you know, the inspectors will be reporting again to the Council, probably in permanent representative session, not minister session, on the 1st of March. So we did not make a conclusion or reach a conclusion with respect to another foreign ministers meeting.

Yes.

Q. The applause at the end of the Villepin spot, speech were interpreted by some as anti-American applause. How did you feel when everybody started applauding at the end of his speech?

Secretary Powell. Well, everybody, you know, people are free to express their emotion, and they did. And I listened carefully to what Dominique said and I'm quite sure that he listened carefully to what I said. We are friends, we agree on many, many things and we often have strong disagreements. And as you can only do with a friend of 225 years, you do it with respect and you do it with the understanding that sooner or later we'll find a way forward and the friendship will continue as it has for the last 225 years.

None of this is personal. We're trying to get to the right answer. Both of us are trying to get to the right answer, and often this produces fireworks and disagreements which have to be argued out and debated. And that's what the United Nations was created for and what alliances are created for.

Q. Mr. Secretary, thank you very much. Did the events of the day make you more willing to negotiate a compromise or more determined to go it alone, and is there any truth to the possibility of accepting to buy consensus, if you will, through a two-week wait with an ultimatum to Saddam Hussein?

Secretary Powell. We didn't talk about a compromise. We listened to the inspectors, which was the purpose of the meeting, and people commented on what they heard and the current state of play with respect to this matter and how 1441 is being implemented. And now we will retire back to our capitals, talk to our heads of state and government, and we'll be in touch with each other in the days ahead and decide what next steps are appropriate.

Q. When you said that you have more evidence regarding the links between Iraq and terrorist organizations, were you referring to new evidence and evidence that you may yet present in a new format, or is this something that's already been presented?

And one other thing. Could you comment on the—

Secretary Powell. No, one. We have a lot of information. We are not trying to overstate the case, but we think that we have sufficient information, intelligence information, that suggests that there are linkages. But I don't want to overstate the case. I think I gave an accurate presentation of the material that we have, that which we could make available, last Wednesday when I spoke before the Council.

Remarks by Secretary of State Powell, February 14, 2003

Secretary Colin Powell was interviewed on CNN by Andrea Koppel.

Q. Considering what you heard both in the public session that we were all listening to and then behind closed doors, under the present circumstances, would you recommend to President Bush to go for a second resolution?

Secretary Powell. Well, I've got to get back to Washington and talk to my colleagues in the administration and speak to the President, so I think I will withhold my recommendation to the President and give it to him, but it was a very good debate, both in the open session and in the private session and it comes down to the following issue when you shred out all of the different points of view. Robust inspections have to be something that goes hand in hand with cooperation and compliance on the part of the Iraqi regime. No matter how robust the inspection regime—you make the inspection regime, if Iraq is not cooperating, if Iraq is not complying with the resolution, you're not going to get to the right answer which is the disarmament of Iraq.

And that's the point I tried to make: Let's not lose sight of the issue. The issue is disarmament and compliance and cooperation, not the inspection regime. And what I heard today from the inspectors and what I heard from the Iraqi Permanent Representative was that they have done some things with respect to process. Suddenly, Saddam Hussein issues a decree today, suddenly the legislature finally takes action—a new law, but these are just process items. We still don't have a substantive change in thinking on the part of the Iraqi regime. They haven't made a strategic decision yet to cooperate. And so robust inspections or more inspectors or more technical features to the inspection won't compensate, in my judgment, for a lack of cooperation and a failure of Iraq to understand they must comply.

Q. U.S. officials have been sitting down with their British counterparts this week trying to figure out what kind of language could be in a second U.N. resolution. Why is this? We know why it's important to the U.K.. Why would this be important to the U.S.?

Secretary Powell. We believe that a second resolution, if we go for one and if one is passed, would once again express the intent of the Security Council that Iraq come into compliance and if it hasn't come into compliance at this point then serious consequences should follow. That was the whole logic behind 1441. So it would be consistent with 1441 to go for such a resolution, but the President's made it clear all along that in the absence of a second resolution, if Iraq still has not disarmed, then the United States is willing to lead a coalition of nations that would be willing to join the United States in the disarmament.

And obviously a second resolution would provide political support to all the many heads of state and government, all those countries who think as we do, that Iraq must be disarmed one way or the other.

Q. We heard all of the statements made by the foreign ministers in public, the French, the Germans, the Russians, the Chinese—all in opposition to moving ahead with a second resolution or war. Did they match those words privately, or did you hear something different?

Secretary Powell. We had a number of conversations over a brief lunch period and in the private session we had with all of the same ministers, lots of questions were directed to Dr. Blix and to Dr. ElBaradei, and we had a good, healthy discussion that expanded on the morning discussion. I also heard Bulgaria, Spain and the United Kingdom speak strongly in support of the need for Iraq to comply.

And so even though there are a lot of different opinions expressed, and they were strong opinions, it comes down to what judgment do you make with respect to Iraq's understanding of the nature of 1441. Are they complying? Are they disarming? And I think, in my judgment anyway, the answer to that question still remains no, they don't understand, they are not taking it seriously. We see a lot of process. We see people showing up for interviews who have tape recorders. Guess where a copy of that tape is going. Do you think anybody is going to honestly answer questions with a tape recorder that they have to come out of that building and give the tape to who—their minder?

And so we still need a lot more work to be done. And, frankly, one of the major items of discussions in the private session—

Q. I'm sorry—

Secretary Powell.—were interviews, interviews. We need to do a better job of getting people into an environment where they can speak honestly and truthfully, without minders, without tape recorders, without bugged rooms. Both of the inspectors focused on this in our private session.

Q. You said we need a lot more work to be done. I mean, that really is the point that the French, the Chinese and the others are saying with inspections. You don't mean in that regard, do you?

Secretary Powell. No, no. We need a lot more work to be done. The inspectors are doing their work. We didn't say stop the inspections. What we said is no matter what you do with the inspections, in the absence of compliance we need a lot more work to be done with respect to compliance. Iraq needs to do a lot more work to convince us that it is complying. It has not provided any real evidence that it is complying with the demand of the United Nations.

Q. Not that long ago, you were saying inspections will not work. Are you saying that maybe they will?

Secretary Powell. No, I'm saying the only thing that counts is compliance. If Iraq starts to comply and cooperates, and starts turning over all documents, not forming commissions to go look for documents. I mean, just consider—

Q. How much more time? How much more time, Mr. Secretary?

Secretary Powell. Just consider what the Iraqi Permanent Representative said after we all have said the declaration they submitted in December was inadequate, it was not full, it was not complete. And I hit it again today. I hit it last week. What was his answer today? Read it again, it's all in there. It isn't all in there. The chief inspectors know that. We all know it.

And so this is further evidence of Iraq just trying to rope-a- dope this along, to keep it going until people lose interest and walk away.

Q. So how much more time? The President has said weeks. Are we still talking weeks or are we talking days?

Secretary Powell. We're talking weeks.

Q. The French and others have made clear that they think the inspections should go on longer. Why do you think they're pushing that line?

Secretary Powell. Well, I don't know. You'll have to ask them. My own judgment is that there are some members of the Council who don't want to face up to the obligations that we undertook when that resolution was passed, and that was, in the presence of a bad declaration, which we had, in the presence of noncompliance, which we have, lack of cooperation, which we have, we are obliged to look at serious consequences. Serious consequences could mean the use of armed force.

One member of the Council has made it clear that war is not a last resort; war is no resort, according to Germany. Germany has said so. And so there are some nations that will try to do everything to avoid the consequences required of the Council to impose its will upon Iraq. And that mean the use of armed force.

Q. One of the things the French and others have said who are opposed to war is that they are concerned about the consequences and what will happen the day after, the months after, the years after. How can the U.S. be sure that the region will not suffer the consequences of a post-Saddam Iraq?

Secretary Powell. The United States has one terrific record over the last almost 100 years of leaving places better off after we have conducted a military operation. I can make that case with respect in just the last ten or twelve years to Kuwait, Kosovo and to Afghanistan.

People are worried about consequences, and I understand that anxiety. But there are also going to be positive consequences. This regime, if we have to go in and use military force, will no longer be there threatening the world. Those weapons of mass destruction will be gone. The neighbors will not have to worry about this any more, nor will the rest of the world. And we can then re-adjust our military footprint, which is a source of some concern in the region.

And I think one of the consequences of a military operation, if it comes to that— and we're trying to avoid it—was that the people of Iraq will start to benefit from the oil of Iraq; the wealth of the nation will now go to benefit the people of the nation, and not to weapons of mass destruction, not to threatening your neighbors. That's one of the consequences that could also come out of such a conflict, if it comes to a conflict.

Q. When you say adjust the footprint, you mean withdrawing troops, withdrawing American troops from Saudi Arabia, from Kuwait?

Secretary Powell. A lot of our presence, a lot of our presence in the region—we didn't have a large presence in the region before the Gulf War. One of the reasons that our presence increased significantly after the Gulf War was because of Iraq. And so, in the absence of that kind of regime that we've seen for all these years in Iraq, a new regime that is responsible to its people, has been put in place by its people and is reflective of its people and is living in peace with its neighbors and is trying to build up schools and hospitals and not chemical and biological weapons, you change the entire situation in the region for the better, and obviously the kind of presence that we have there now would be changed accordingly.

Q. One presence that would be there, some of your colleagues on the Hill this week said that there would be an American general who would likely be in place there for about two years. Why—

Secretary Powell. Nobody said that. What we said was that obviously, if you have a military operation and the military operation is successful, the commander of that operation would initially be in charge, and that would be—

Q. But we don't know for how long?

Secretary Powell. We don't know for how long, but it would be for the shortest possible period of time until it can be transitioned over to a civilian administrator and then any international body that has a role to play and rapidly transition into the hands of the Iraqi people, as fast as we can make that happen.

We have no desire to have an American general running a country, or running, especially, a Muslim country. The two-year comment came in response to a question to one of my associates in the State Department about how long does an AID program usually last, and the answer was, a program like that usually takes two years for an AID program and that got mixed up with another comment about generals into we plan to have a general there for two years. We've never said any such thing.

Q. Before we end, I just have to ask you, from what you have heard so far today, is it your sense as a former military man that war with Iraq is more inevitable than it was going into today's session.

Secretary Powell. No, I wouldn't say that. I would say there's still a chance for peace. But, you know, we will not—we will not realize that peace if we ever back off on the pressure, if we ever make it look like we do not have the will to take this to conflict if necessary to disarm Iraq.

But the question of war and peace is up to Saddam Hussein and the Iraqi regime. The Council has spoken. The Council spoke clearly in 1441. We had a good, spirited debate today after hearing from the two chief inspectors. The burden now is on Saddam Hussein with respect to the question of whether there will be war or peace.

Joint Statement by Belgium, France, and Germany, February 16, 2003

Belgium, France and Germany reaffirm their determination to honor their obligations under the North Atlantic Treaty with regard to all allies, notably Turkey, as well as the importance which they attribute to the transatlantic relationship. They stress that their objective is full and effective disarmament of Iraq within the scope of U.N. Security Council resolution 1441. In particular, they underline that the use of force can only be the last resort and that not all options offered by UNSCR 1441 have, as yet, been fully exploited. They recall that it is up to Iraq to cooperate actively, immediately and unconditionally with UNMOVIC and IAEA. Following Turkey's recourse to article 4 of the North Atlantic Treaty, Belgium, France and Germany note that all Member States wishing to do so can contribute with adequate measures in order to respond to the concerns expressed by Turkey. Belgium and Germany who are integrated into the military structure of NATO have agreed to the proposal by the Secretary General of NATO to invite the military authorities to provide military advice on prudent defensive contingency planning in support of Turkey. The implementation of measures proposed by the military authorities will require a new decision. The decision by NATO does not in any way prejudge the ongoing efforts by Belgium, France and Germany to continue to work within the framework of UNSCR 1441.

Statement by NATO Secretary General Robertson, February 16, 2003

Secretary General Robertson spoke with reporters following the meeting of the NATO Defense Planning Committee at NATO Headquarters, Brussels, Belgium.

Good evening ladies and gentlemen and thank you for your patience. It's been a long day for all of us. But we have come to a conclusion.

Ambassadors of 18 NATO nations, members in the Defense Planning Committee of NATO, came to this building this morning confident that we had the elements necessary to provide the basis for a consensus decision.

The discussions today were both arduous but constructive. One country—Belgium—proposed amendments to a draft decision sheet which were discussed and considered at some length.

I am happy to announce that we have been able—collectively—to overcome the impasse we have faced for the past few days.

We agree on substance, we agree on timing and we agree on how to integrate our collective solidarity with Turkey in the wider context.

A political decision backed by consensus has always been the preferred choice of this Alliance. The search for consensus remains a cornerstone of how the North Atlantic Alliance operates.

It is therefore with great personal satisfaction that I can now confirm that the 18 NATO Allies, members of the integrated military structure, agreed today to task military planners to begin their work and advise Allies with military advice on the following possible missions:

• preventive deployment of AWACS aircraft;
• NATO support for the deployment of theatre missile defences for Turkey;
• NATO support for possible deployment of Allied chemical and biological defense capabilities.

The military authorities will also review contingency plans related to the reinforcement of Turkey in the context of the current situation, and update these plans as needed.

These measures are intended to provide Turkey solely with defensive assistance.

Alliance solidarity has prevailed. NATO nations have assumed their collective responsibility towards Turkey, a nation at the moment under threat.

In closing, I wish to say that my choices were always taken having in mind the greater interest of the Alliance as a whole. My job as Secretary General of NATO is to lead the nations towards consensus. And that is what I've done today. Thank you very much.

Q. You got a decision here today on the base of 18. Do you believe you would have got the decision if all 19 had been around the table, if this was done at the NAC?

Secretary General Robertson. Well, we would have preferred to have a decision by the North Atlantic Council with all 19 members present. France is by its own choice not a member of the integrated military structure, and therefore not a member of the Defense Planning Committee. We reached consensus today. I think that's a good thing.

France has got its own position and can answer for itself. But today was a remarkable day with an important decision and a very firm and clear signal by the Alliance that we will stand by an Ally if that Ally is under threat.

Q. I have one question for Lord Robertson and another one for Mr. Kujat, please. Lord Robertson, you said on Wednesday that France, Belgium and Germany are destroying NATO. Why are they doing that, and how far does this perception of yours go?

Secretary General Robertson. I did not say that. I don't know where you heard it from, I certainly did not say that. I represent all of the nations in NATO. Those who are in the majority and those who are in the minority. My job—and it's pretty painful at times, and it takes a long time, on occasion—is to get consensus amongst the allies because we operate by consensus, and by unanimity, and that is what we've done today. One nation was not... is not part of the... the Defense Planning Committee and that is their choice. But we have consensus among the 18 allies, and therefore the military defensive and contingency planning can now go ahead.

But I make no accusations against the good faith or the loyalty, or the reliability of any of the nations in NATO. I haven't done it, I wouldn't do it, and I certainly have not done it.

Statement by the NATO Defense Planning Committee (DPC), February 16, 2003

At the Prague Summit, the NATO Allies committed themselves to take effective action to assist and support the efforts of the United Nations to ensure full and immediate compliance by Iraq, without conditions or restrictions, with U.N. Security Council Resolution 1441. This remains our policy.

Following Turkey's request for consultations within the framework of Article 4 of the North Atlantic Treaty, as expressed in its letter of 10 February 2003, and pursuant to Article 4 of the Treaty which states that "the Parties will consult whenever, in the opinion of any of them, the territorial integrity, political independence or security of any of the Parties is threatened", Allies have begun consultations.

As part of these consultations, the Chairman of the Military Committee briefed the North Atlantic Council on 10 February 2003, assessing the potential threat against Turkey and informing about planning requirements for the reinforcement of Turkey's defense, including relevant timelines.

In this context, the DPC:

• notes the Turkish request for consultations within the framework of Article 4 of the North Atlantic Treaty;

• notes that all Allies have reaffirmed their determination to fulfill all of their obligations deriving from the spirit and the letter of the North Atlantic Treaty towards Turkey;

• recalls the provisions of Article 1 of the North Atlantic Treaty, and in particular the undertaking of Allies to refrain in their international relations from the threat or use of force in any manner inconsistent with the purposes of the United Nations;

• notes the actions taken by Allies to support Turkey;

• agrees that, as a consequence of the Turkish request, the NATO Military Authorities should provide military advice to the DPC on the feasibility, implications and timelines of the following possible missions:

a. preventive deployment to Turkey of NATO AWACs and supporting logistics, under SACEUR command, for defensive purposes, as required for surveillance, early warning and maintaining the integrity of Turkish airspace;

b. NATO support for possible deployment by Allies of theatre missile defences to Turkey and their incorporation into the NATO Integrated Extended Air Defense System;

c. NATO support for possible deployment by Allies of chemical and biological defense capabilities to Turkey;

• agrees that, as a further consequence of the Turkish request:

a. SACEUR is authorized to liaise directly with national military authorities with respect to these possible defensive missions;

b. the NMAs should review contingency plans related to the reinforcement of Turkey in the context of the current situation, update the plans as needed, and report to the Council.

Our Heads of State and Government at Prague pledged our full support for the implementation of UNSCR 1441, and this decision to approve the planning of protection measures for Turkey is fully consistent with the deliberations and efforts in the United Nations.

We continue to support efforts in the United Nations to find a peaceful solution to the crisis. This decision relates only to the defense of Turkey, and is without prejudice to any other military operations by NATO, and future decisions by NATO or the U.N. Security Council.

The DPC will decide on the implementation of the defensive measures as a matter of urgency; will continue to consult in the context of the Turkish request under Article 4; and will continue to follow closely discussion in the U.N. Security Council and the implementation of UNSCR 1441.

Excerpts from Time Interview of French President Chirac, February 16, 2003

President Jacques Chirac was interviewed for Time Magazine by James Graff and Bruce Crumley.

Q. Do last week's U.N. inspectors' reports mark a turning point in the debate over Iraq?

President Chirac. In the preceding two days, I received phone calls from several heads of state, both members and nonmembers of the Security Council, and I came to the conclusion that a majority of world leaders share our determination to search for a peaceful solution to disarming Iraq.

Q. If there is a war, what do you see as the consequences for the Middle East?

President Chirac. The consequences of war would be considerable in human terms. In political terms, it would destabilize the entire region. It's very difficult to explain that one is going to spend colossal sums of money to wage war when there may be another solution yet is unable to provide adequate aid to the developing world.

Q. Why do you think fallout from a war would be so much graver than Tony Blair and George Bush seem to?

President Chirac. I simply don't analyze the situation as they do. Among the negative fallout would be inevitably a strong reaction from Arab and Islamic public opinion. It may not be justified, and it may be, but it's a fact. A war of this kind cannot help giving a big lift to terrorism. It would create a large number of little bin Ladens. Muslims and Christians have a lot to say to one another, but war isn't going to facilitate that dialogue. I'm against the clash of civilizations; that plays into the hands of extremists. There is a problem-the probable possession of weapons of mass destruction by an uncontrollable country, Iraq. The international community is right to be disturbed by this situation, and it's right in having decided Iraq should be disarmed. The inspections began, and naturally it is a long and difficult job. We have to give the inspectors time to do it. And probably-and this is France's view-we have to reinforce their capacities, especially those of aerial surveillance. For the moment, nothing allows us to say inspections don't work.

Q. Isn't France ducking its military responsibilities to its oldest ally?

President Chirac. France is not a pacifist country. We currently have more troops in the Balkans than the Americans. France is obviously not anti-American. It's a true friend of the United States and always has been. It is not France's role to support dictatorial regimes in Iraq or anywhere else. Nor do we have any differences over the goal of eliminating Saddam Hussein's weapons of mass destruction. For that matter, if Saddam Hussein would only vanish, it would without a doubt be the biggest favor he could do for his people and for the world. But we think this goal can be reached without starting a war.

Q. But you seem willing to put the onus on inspectors to find arms rather than on Saddam to declare what he's got. Are there nuclear arms in Iraq?

President Chirac. I don't think so. Are there other weapons of mass destruction? That's probable. We have to find and destroy them. In its current situation, does Iraq-controlled and inspected as it is-pose a clear and present danger to the region? I don't believe so. Given that, I prefer to continue along the path laid out by the Security Council. Then we'll see.

Q. What evidence would justify war?

President Chirac. It's up to the inspectors to decide. We gave them our confidence. They were given a mission, and we trust them. If we have to give them greater means, we'll do so. It's up to them to come before the Security Council and say, "We won. It's over. There are no more weapons of mass destruction," or "It's impossible for us to fulfill our mission. We're coming up against Iraqi ill will and impediments." At that point, the Security Council would have to discuss this report and decide what to do. In that case, France would naturally exclude no option.

Q. But without Iraqi cooperation, even 300 inspectors can't do the job.

President Chirac. That's correct, no doubt. But it's up to the inspectors to say so. I'm betting that we can get Iraq to cooperate more. If I'm wrong, there will still be time to draw other conclusions. When a regime like Saddam's finds itself caught between certain death and abandoning its arms, I think it will make the right choice. But I can't be certain.

Q. If the Americans were to bring a resolution for war before the U.N., would France use its veto?

President Chirac. In my view, there's no reason for a new resolution. We are in the framework of (U.N. Security Council Resolution) 1441, and let's go on with it. I don't see what any new resolution would add.

Q. Some charge you are motivated by anti-Americanism ?

President Chirac. I've known the U.S. for a long time. I visit often, I've studied there, worked as a forklift operator for Anheuser-Busch in St. Louis and as a soda jerk at Howard Johnson's. I've hitchhiked across the whole United States; I even worked as a journalist and wrote a story for the New Orleans Times-Picayune on the front page. I know the U.S. perhaps better than most French people, and I really like the United States. I've made many excellent friends there, I feel good there. I love junk food, and I always come home with a few extra pounds. I've always worked and supported transatlantic solidarity. When I hear people say that I'm anti-American, I'm sad-not angry, but really sad.

Q. Do you think America's role as the sole superpower is a problem?

President Chirac. Any community with only one dominant power is always a dangerous one and provokes reactions. That's why I favor a multipolar world, in which Europe obviously has its place. Anyway, the world will not be unipolar. Over the next 50 years, China will become a global power, and the world won't be the same. So it's time to start organizing. Transatlantic solidarity will remain the basis of the world order, in which Europe has its role to play.

Q. Haven't tensions over Iraq poisoned transatlantic relationships?

President Chirac. I repeat: Iraq must be disarmed, and for that it must cooperate more than it does now. If we disarm Iraq, the goal set by the Americans will have been fulfilled. And if we do that, there can be no doubt that it will bex due in large part to the presence of American forces on the spot. If there hadn't been U.S. soldiers present, Saddam might not have agreed to play the game. If we go through with the inspections, the Americans will have won, since it would essentially be thanks to the pressure they exercised that Iraq was disarmed.

Q. Don't you think it would be extremely difficult politically for President Bush to pull back from war?

President Chirac. I'm not so sure about that. He would have two advantages if he brought his soldiers back. I'm talking about a situation, obviously, where the inspectors say now there's nothing left, and that will take a certain number of weeks. If Iraq doesn't cooperate and the inspectors say this isn't working, it could be war. If Iraq is stripped of its weapons of mass destruction and that's been verified by the inspectors, then Mr. Bush can say two things: first, "Thanks to my intervention, Iraq has been disarmed," and second, "I achieved all that without spilling any blood." In the life of a statesman, that counts-no blood spilled.

Q. Yet Washington may well go to war despite your plan.

President Chirac. That will be their responsibility. But if they were to ask me for my friendly advice, I would counsel against it.

Remarks by United Nations Secretary-General Annan, February 17, 2003

Secretary-General Kofi Annan delivered his remarks after meeting with European Union leaders in Brussels, Belgium.

I've just had an important exchange with leaders of the European Union countries in what I believe is a defining moment for international co-operation.

I told them that we must keep the focus on Iraq and on its obligations to disarm. On that critical point, I think we all agree that Iraq must disarm and do it proactively and immediately. And I think it is important that we focus on that principal task and avoid the tendency of turning on each other.

I also believe we should approach this issue positively and what is required at this stage is co-operation, persistence and constant pressure. It is imperative that the Iraqi leadership understand the gravity and urgency of the situation. I urge the Iraqi leadership to choose compliance over conflict. If they were to continue their defiance under Security Council Resolution 1441 the Members may have to make a grim choice—a grim choice of whether to declare further material breach and the serious consequences that should follow.

But I hope that will not be necessary and I believe, I have always believed, that it is possible to resolve this issue peacefully and that war is not inevitable.

Finally, I believe that if the Security Council manages to resolve this crisis successfully and effectively, its credibility and influence will be considerably enhanced. If on the other hand, the international community fails to agree on a common position, and action is taken without the authority of the Council, then the legitimacy and support for that action will be seriously impaired.

I also expressed my concern about the tensions that are emerging among nations and the tensions in the transatlantic relationship. I believe that if the Council were to come to a decision and were to be able to resolve this, these tensions would diminish considerably. But we live in a difficult world and we cannot afford to have such tensions or have them sustained over a long period.

And this is why I hope that Member States will come together and argue their case out in a patient, persuasive diplomacy that is required to produce a common front.

We must all remember that when we started working on Resolution 1441, most people did not believe that the Members could agree. In the end, they did not only agree, it was passed unanimously, but it took difficult and patient negotiations and persuasion, together, and I hope that lesson will guide us as we move ahead in our search for a common solution.

Let me also say that what is happening in Iraq, or what happens in Iraq, will not happen in a vacuum. The broader our consensus on Iraq, the better the chance we can come together again as an international community and deal effectively with all the burning conflicts in the world. And that is extremely important because when you look around you, we have many, many difficult issues to tackle.

Q. Mr. Secretary-General, I will ask my question in English. I wonder whether you have informed the 15 leaders if Iraq is already in material breach of previous U.N. resolutions. My first question and then...

Secretary-General Annan. May I ask you to just ask one. There are lots of other people...

* * * *

Q. Mr. Secretary-General, I am a Kurdish journalist and I would like to ask you whether the United Nations is prepared on the eve of war to safeguard the Kurdish people because they are in the middle of that and in Turkey and Northern Iraq they fear a war in this area.

Secretary-General Annan. I think we are worried about the fallout of the war and the humanitarian implications. And this is why we have doing contingency planning, not that we take it for granted that a war will come, but we do not want to be caught unprepared. As far as protecting the Kurdish people, as you indicate, first of all if there were to be a war, the U.N. will not be on the ground running the operation. And whoever are involved will have to respect international humanitarian law and laws of war and protect innocent civilians as they wage war. Of course, we would insist on respect for human rights and international humanitarian law, but I hope it will not come to that.

Remarks by United Nations Secretary-General Annan and Italian Prime Minister Berlusconi, February 18, 2003

Secretary-General Kofi Annan and Prime Minister Silvio Berlusconi delivered their remarks after meeting in Rome, Italy.

Prime Minister Berlusconi. Good afternoon, I am pleased to welcome today the Secretary General of the United Nations with whom I have been able to discuss the problems that in the present moment are afflicting the entire world. Naturally, the most important being those concerning Iraq and Saddam Hussein, and everyone's desire to find a solution that is one of peace. I believe it important to underline this. No one should think that the hope is to be forgotten, we are all convinced, as resulted yesterday evening at meeting of the European Council, that there is still a way to work towards a peaceful solution and for a peaceful way for Iraq to comply with solution 1440 of the Security Council.

I would also add my feeling of admiration for the Secretary General, who honors me with his friendship, and also gratefulness for what he did yesterday. He spoke at the European Council, and his speech was extremely useful, an important contribution to Europe's effort at unity, which was transformed into a common declaration.

Secretary-General Annan. Thank you very much, Mr. Prime Minister. And let me thank you for receiving me once again here. It's always a pleasure for me to come to Italy to have this kind of discussion. We've had a very fruitful discussion, and as you heard from the Prime Minister, we did focus on Iraq. And yesterday, I was privileged to join the European Heads of State Summit in Brussels.

As the Prime Minister said, the Summit came up with a very good communique, a communique that made clear what the European position is, including the fact that Iraq must disarm and act immediately and work proactively with the inspectors to disarm. But as he has also repeated, we all felt that war is not inevitable and we should press our efforts to find a peaceful solution. But that also demands that Iraq meets its obligation and fulfills the requirements imposed on it by the Security Council.

Europe has a key role to play in this crisis, not just on the political and other aspects but also on the possible humanitarian consequences of the conflict. And yesterday, last night, I had the opportunity to brief them on our own contingency planning—on the needs of the population, during and immediately after the war, the possible refugee flows, the internally displaced, the vulnerable children and the needs that we will require, the money we will require, to look after their needs. And here I expect Europe to play a key role.

And let me conclude by telling my friend Silvio and the European leaders that I share their hope that we can find a peaceful solution.

Q. You will meet the Holy Pope this afternoon. What are your expectations from this meeting?

Secretary-General Annan. It is difficult to talk about a meeting which hasn't taken place yet, but let me say that I would obviously expect to talk to him about Iraq. His envoy Cardinal Etchegaray whom he sent to Iraq has just got back and I hope they'll be able to brief me on their findings and share with me their own impressions on the situation.

Q. Mr. Secretary-General, you mentioned in your comments yesterday in Brussels that inspections can't go on forever and that at some point the Security Council might have to face the grim choice of deciding whether Iraq is in material breach. How long do you think is politically realistic for inspections to continue and do you support some kind of a time frame or time line that maps out what Iraq must accomplish by a certain date as has been suggested by Britain?

Secretary-General Annan. I think on the question of how long the inspections go on, it is an issue the Council will have to tackle. As it stands now, there is no time limit in these resolutions. The inspectors are carrying on their work, but of course the debate going on in the Council, where some members have indicated that this has gone on long enough and others believe that it should continue, is how long do we go on? There are some who believe that as long as the inspectors are doing reasonable work and there are those who believe that whatever the inspectors do they may not be able to get full cooperation of the Iraqis.

As far as the inspectors are concerned, they're carrying on with their work until the Council decides otherwise. If the Council were to decide that there had been a material breach and that serious consequences were to follow and to determine that, the inspectors may have to suspend or stop their work. Until that judgment is made, they will have to go on. And I would hesitate to give you in terms of months or weeks how much time they need. That is a judgment for the Council. And I think I've been around long enough not to usurp their responsibilities and their authority.

Statement by President Bush, February 19, 2003

I welcome today's decision by NATO's Defense Planning Committee to approve the deployment of AWACS aircraft, Patriot missiles, and biological and chemical defense equipment to Turkey. This is an important demonstration of the solidarity of NATO allies in view of a potential threat to an Alliance member. It follows the decision taken on Sunday, by the same committee, to request military planning for such deployments.

Today's decision is a direct response to the request by Turkey for consultations under Article 4 of the Washington Treaty, as well as the commitment by all NATO Heads of State and Government, stated at Prague on November 21, 2002, "to take effective action to assist and support the efforts of the U.N. to ensure the full and immediate compliance by Iraq, without conditions or restrictions, with UNSCR 1441."

I am grateful for the resolute leadership of NATO Secretary General Lord Robertson in bringing the Alliance discussions to a successful conclusion. I also appreciate the efforts of all the members of the Defense Planning Committee to fulfill their responsibilities as Alliance members in exceptionally difficult circumstances.

Remarks by President Bush and NATO Secretary General Robertson, February 19, 2003

President Bush and Secretary General George Robertson delivered their remarks after meeting at the White House.

President Bush. George, welcome. I'm honored to have you here. You represent our nation's most important alliance, NATO. Today, this alliance is providing equipment to Turkey to help protect our Turkish ally from a potential attack from Iraq.

I want to thank you for your leadership. You've done a fantastic job of keeping this alliance together, moving it forward—by not only addressing the current threats that we face, but preparing NATO to address threats into the future. And I congratulate on a great leadership and welcome you back to the Oval Office.

Secretary General Robertson. Thanks, Mr. President. On the 12th of September, NATO passed a declaration of Article V of the Washington Treaty. We came to the aid of an ally, the United States, under threat, under attack.

And today we've sent AWACS aircraft and Patriot missiles and chem, bio and defensive equipment to Turkey, another ally, in trouble, under threat, asking for help. That's what the alliance of free nations is all about.

Sometimes we—you know, we can take a bit of time to do it. It reminded me of Winston Churchill, whose bust is over there, who once famously said of the United States of America: The United States can always be counted on to do the right thing, after it's exhausted every other alternative.

Well, you can say exactly the same thing about NATO, but when we get there, we're strong and we stand for the values that unite a great alliance.

Remarks by Secretary of State Powell, February 19, 2003

Secretary Colin Powell was interviewed on Radio France.

Q. The question is, only today President Bush made a statement about a second resolution. Why and when is he going to lay down a second resolution, Mr. Secretary?

Secretary Powell. We haven't made a decision yet, but we are examining the possibility of a second resolution. We believe that one is certainly appropriate. Iraq, in our judgment, clearly is in material breach, and, because it is in material breach, one should consider serious consequences.

But there are other nations that disagree, to include France and Germany, and so we will discuss it with our colleagues at the Security Council and make a judgment as to when it might be appropriate to lay down a second resolution and what purpose it would serve. But we haven't made a decision yet, to answer your question specifically.

Q. And what you are saying here, the second resolution will be—what will it constitute? What will constitute it?

Secretary Powell. Well, I can't really say yet because we are still discussing it here within our Administration and discussing it with various friends and partners on the Security Council. So it would be premature for me to say what is in it until we actually have a resolution that we are ready to put forward.

Let me just say that we are looking at the possibility of a second resolution, as the President said, but the actual content and timing for putting down a resolution is still under consideration.

Q. Do you intend to lay down this resolution before or after March the 1st?

Secretary Powell. Well, it is the same question and I have to give the same answer, and that is we haven't decided yet what the content of such a resolution should be or when we would lay it down.

Q. It sounds as if the French are definitely out of the game or is there still a chance they could come aboard, or what—what do you expect from the consultation with France?

Secretary Powell. We stay in close touch with the French. We had, obviously, discussions with them last Friday in New York when we had the debate, both the open debate as well as the private debate, and then we had other opportunities to discuss the issue with the French.

I take note of the European Commission statement yesterday that once again reaffirmed that Iraq must comply with the will of the U.N.. Iraq must disarm. There is a question as to how much time Iraq should be given to disarm. We believe time is running out. It is not a matter of more inspectors or a longer inspection process. Our French colleagues suggest that is the issue. That is not the issue, in our judgment. The issue is: Is Iraq complying? Are they taking action on the specific issues we have brought to their attention—the destruction of prohibited missiles, accounting for the anthrax and the VX and the botulinum toxin and all the other horrible weapons that they had in their possession?

This isn't speculation on the part of the United States. We know they had these weapons. The previous inspection regime said they had those weapons. They have acknowledged having had those weapons, but they won't tell us what has happened to all of that material.

I think we owe it to the international community, we owe it to the world, to get the right answers, to get the correct answers, and Iraq must comply. And it cannot be a satisfactory solution for inspections just to continue forever because some nations are afraid of stepping up to the responsibility of imposing the will of the international community.

I might also add that the only reason Iraq has participated in any inspection activity has been the threat of force, and it has been the United States, the United Kingdom, and very few others, who have been willing to put their soldiers on the line to convey that threat of force in order to get Iraq to do what little it has already done.

And so we are working with our friends and allies to see about the content of a second resolution and when one would table such a resolution.

I would also point out that many of us believe, the United States certainly believes, that there is probably enough authority in Resolution 1441 to take action if Iraq does not comply and does not cooperate.

Q. What do you think about the date of March the 14th or the 15th, suggested by the French, in order for Hans Blix to report again before the Security Council?

Secretary Powell. Well, we already have a date for him to report again. He will be reporting at the end of the month, and we can see where we are at that point. My colleague, Dominique de Villepin, suggested another meeting of the Foreign Ministers on the 14th of March, but I was reluctant at this point to agree to such a meeting until we had seen what progress we have made with Iraq and also heard from Dr. Blix and Dr. ElBaradei at the end of the month.

We can't just keep meeting as foreign ministers to listen to reports about how Iraq is thinking about cooperating or is cooperating on process. It is not process that we are looking for; it is compliance. And compliance will come about when Iraq decides, when Iraq decides, that it must disarm, and we will know that very quickly. They will start to tell us where the nerve agent went. They will tell us where the missiles are. They will cooperate. They will give people to the inspectors to be interviewed freely and openly, without minders, without tape recorders taking down their words.

This is what we need, not more inspections that are an excuse for not taking action, as opposed to compliance, which will satisfy the international community that Iraq is truly disarmed. The inspectors tell us repeatedly that Iraq is not yet taking the actions that suggests it understands it must comply and disarm.

Q. Right. But what is the gap, according to you, between the French and—France and the United States? What is the gap that we need to breach and the [*inaubible*] understanding, and what is your feeling about the anti-Americanism and the anti-French movement these days? What is your commentary about this? It's such a pity.

Secretary Powell. France believes that more time should be given to the inspectors and that there should be more robust inspections, more inspectors, more technical assistance to the inspectors. That is not objectionable, except the real issue is not more inspectors or more inspections, but compliance. And that is what we have not seen.

And last Friday, France argued strongly for more inspectors, and I argued back and others of my colleagues argued back that what we need to see is compliance, not just more inspections, and we can't use more inspections as an excuse for taking action. France says that that is not its position, but it is pressing now for more inspectors and more time for the inspectors, and we believe that time is running out. We cannot allow Iraq to continue to play a game of hide-and-seek and essentially escape the judgment of the international community while we are conducting inspections forever or trying to recruit more inspectors.

This is not a trivial matter. The materials that we believe Iraq has, and Iraq has admitted that it has, are dangerous materials, dangerous for the people of the region, dangerous for the people of the world, especially in this modern world after 9/11 where we see that these kinds of weapons in the hands of a terrorist organization are deadly and could affect any nation in the world, not just the United States, not just the region of the Middle East, but could affect France and other European nations.

There is debate now between France and the United States, but I am confident that France and the United States will remain close, will remain friends. We have been friends for 225 years, through many difficult times, and we will find a way through this difficult time.

Q. Yet there have been some damages already.

Secretary Powell. Well, certainly there have been some problems in the relationship with rhetoric on both sides, but, you know, democracies are free to express their views, and we have always found that we are able to resolve our differences; and the alliance, the NATO alliance will continue and the transatlantic alliance, and especially the friendship and partnership that exists between France and the United States will continue, even in the midst of this disagreement and after this disagreement.

Q. Mr. Secretary, my last question will be the following one. Do you have some more evidence that you are ready to give to the inspectors?

Secretary Powell. We have given the inspectors a great deal of information and we are giving them more and always examining new information that comes in to make available to the inspectors.

I have to also point out, however, that we should not think Iraq is not guilty because people say, "Show us more evidence, give us more information." Iraq is guilty by its own admission. It has these weapons. It has acknowledged that it has these weapons. We are trying to find out what happened to them. What did they do with them? Where did the bombs go? Where did the missiles go? Where did the rockets go? Where did the nerve agents go? Where did the biological agents go?

So Iraq is already convicted. It is already guilty. The evidence is overwhelming. And all nations in the Security Council, to include France, agreed with that when we passed Resolution 1441. We all unanimously agreed that Iraq was in breach of its obligations and we were giving it one last, final chance.

Our position, the United States position, is that Iraq is not taking that one last, final chance, and we cannot just keep inspecting or adding more inspectors forever where the challenge is: Are they complying? And so far, our judgment is that they are not complying.

Remarks by Secretary of State Powell, February 19, 2003

Secretary Colin Powell was interviewed on Phoenix TV.

Q. We're privileged to be speaking with you prior to your trip to Asia.

The war with Iraq looks imminent. Why do you choose this particular time for your Asia trip?

Secretary Powell. Well, I am looking forward to the Korean inauguration of a new president on the 25th of February, and since I was in the region, it was useful to stop in and spend time with my Chinese colleagues. I have excellent relations with my Chinese colleagues, especially with Foreign Minister Tang.

And it will give us another opportunity—it will be the fourth time in the last month—for he and I to discuss issues having to do with Asia—the situation between the region and the D.P.R.K. and its nuclear programs. We will talk about our bilateral relationship and, of course, we will talk about Iraq.

The United States and China are unified in our desire to find a peaceful solution to the situation with Iraq, but the United States and China are also unified in U.N. Resolution 1441, which we both voted for as permanent members of the Security Council to see that Iraq gets rid of its weapons of mass destruction, that it is disarmed. And so far Iraq has not complied with the terms of 1441. Even though the inspectors have been able to go back in, Iraq continues not to provide the inspectors what they need to do the job and disarm Iraq, so this will be an opportunity for me to discuss this once again with my Chinese colleagues and point out to them that the United States feels strongly that we cannot just allow inspections to continue forever, and the answer is not more inspectors, the answer is Iraq compliance. And if Iraq does not comply, then the United Nations Security Council must consider whether or not other action is appropriate. And this will be a subject of discussion with my Chinese colleagues.

Q. Let me ask you this question, which is being asked by everybody in this whole world, is the war with Iraq in weeks? End of February or early March?

Secretary Powell. Well, you are assuming there is going to be a war with Iraq. We are hoping for a peaceful solution, but we cannot just wait forever. The President has made it clear that he feels the international community must come together to see that Iraq is disarmed.

Remarks by Secretary of State Powell, February 19, 2003

Secretary Colin Powell was interviewed by Middle East Broadcasting.

Q. Recently, during a meeting on the Hill, you spoke—that in case the war takes place and after the guns fall silent, you talked about a military administrator for Iraq. This did not sit well with some of the Iraq opposition. It did not sit well with some of your friends who said that, you know, Iraq is not Grenada, that this reminds them of the days of the British viceroys or what not. Could you please address these concerns because you said you don't want to stay in Iraq for long time?

Secretary Powell. Yes. It is quite the contrary. Grenada—when you have a military operation, there is going to be a military commander in charge. But how long did that military commander remain in Grenada? A very short period of time.

It is our desire if there is a conflict in Iraq, and we still hope one can be avoided, but if there is a conflict, then a military commander will initially be in charge; not only to run the military operation, but to make sure that right after the operation things are secure, that the people are protected, that humanitarian supplies come in. You need some central authority initially.

It is not our goal to destroy Iraq. It is our goal to remove a regime that we believe has wasted the people's treasure on weapons of mass destruction. So we are not going to destroy Iraq and we think once the regime has been eliminated there will be institutions that remain in place. As soon as we can, we would want to get the military commander to transfer real authority to a civilian leadership, perhaps initially of an international character as one develops a new Iraqi leadership consisting of people who are outside the country right now in the opposition, as well as those who are inside the country who are responsible and who are committed to the same values that those outside the country are.

I think to have a new leadership in Iraq, you have to have a combination of both. And I think all of my colleagues agree with that and I think the opposition would agree with that, so we are going into Iraq not to destroy a place, but to make it better. People worry about the negative consequences. There will be positive consequences if it is necessary to go into Iraq.

Q. Sir, you spoke about regime change in Iraq will probably help the United States to reshape the region. Again, this probably is misunderstood or interpreted differently by people in the region who relied on commentators in this country who say that maybe the United States should establish some sort of a new imperium in the region, a new design for the region, address those concerns.

Secretary Powell. The United States has the best record of any major power for not establishing imperiums, for not taking over countries. Kuwait—did we take over Kuwait? No. Have we taken over Afghanistan? No. We gave it back to its Muslim leaders. Did we take over Kosovo when we bombed it and made it safer for the Muslim population? No. Did we take over Japan? Germany? Italy? No.

The United States' record is not one of imperialism. It is one of doing the job, bringing peace, restoring order and getting a responsible government in place. And when we said we were going to do that in Iraq if it becomes necessary to have a conflict, it is all for the purpose of making Iraq a good neighbor that is not developing weapons, that is not threatening its neighbors, that is committed to the welfare of its people. That will change the region. That's what we meant.

Q. Sir, you have been engaging the EU, NATO, and the Turks and others, but we haven't seen you in the region recently.

Secretary Powell. Oh, I want to come back very soon. I have been quite busy at the U.N. and other places, so my travels have been difficult and there have been some other crises I've had to deal with—India and Pakistan, which caused me to travel there a bit—

Q. Sure.

Secretary Powell.—but I'm anxious to return to the region.

Q. Before diplomacy runs its course?

Secretary Powell. Well, it is all a function of schedule. I have to go to Asia this week, but I hope to return to the region at the earliest opportunity.

Remarks by Secretary of Defense Rumsfeld and Chairman of the Joint Chiefs of Staff Myers, February 19, 2003

Secretary Rumsfeld. As we continue in the diplomatic phase with Iraq, it's useful to recall the nature of the regime that we're dealing with. The best way of judging what one might do in the future is to look at what they've done in the past. For decades, Saddam Hussein has demonstrated that he does not hesitate to take life, even on a massive scale, when it serves his purposes. One of the ways Saddam Hussein has demonstrated this is through his use of civilians as human shields. It is a practice that reveals contempt for the norms of humanity, the laws of armed conflict, and, I am advised, Islamic law, practice and belief.

International law draws a clear distinction between civilians and combatants. The principle that civilians must be protected lies at the heart of international law of armed conflict. It is the distinction between combatants and innocent civilians that terrorism, and practices like the use of human shields, so directly assaults.

Saddam Hussein makes no such distinction. During Operation Desert Shield, he held hundreds of non-Iraqi civilians at government and military facilities throughout Iraq and described them as human shields. He deliberately constructs mosques near military facilities, uses schools, hospitals, orphanages and cultural treasures to shield military forces, thereby exposing helpless men, women and children to danger. These are not tactics of war, they are crimes of war. Deploying human shields is not a military strategy, it's murder, a violation of the laws of armed conflict, and a crime against humanity, and it will be treated as such. Those who follow his orders to use human shields will pay a severe price for their actions.

We hope to provide a more detailed briefing on human shields at a later date.

General Myers. Thank you, Mr. Secretary. And good afternoon.

I'd just like to add some comments to the secretary's comments on human shields. Press reports, I think today, say that a hundred human-shield volunteers from London have arrived in Baghdad.

And I want to note, again, it is a violation of the law of armed conflict to use non-combatants as a means of shielding potential military targets—even those people who may volunteer for this purpose. Iraqi actions to do so would not only violate this law but could be a—could be considered a war crime in any conflict. Therefore, if death or serious injury to a noncombatant resulted from these efforts, the individuals responsible for deploying any innocent civilians as human shields could be guilty of grave breaches of the Geneva Conventions.

Q. Mr. Secretary, Turkey would be a key ally in any invasion of Iraq that were ordered. Yet Turkey is pressing for more aid in return for use of its bases. The United States—the White House made clear that the United States has told Turkey to take it or leave it on what you've offered them. Have you given them any deadline? And what do you do if Ankara says no? What do you do militarily? Would that make it much more difficult to invade Iraq?

Secretary Rumsfeld. Well, obviously the more assistance one gets, the easier it is. The less assistance one gives, the more difficult it is. But nonetheless, it's doable, and there are work-arounds.

I don't know that—I think what you have to remember is that Turkey is a democracy, and it's a democracy in a region where there are relatively few democracies. And they are going through a democratic process, which is a healthy thing. And there's a lot of debate and discussion taking place. What they'll ultimately decide, of course, is a function of how the parliament decides to address it. And they've been a long-standing ally and friend and NATO ally as well to the United States. And they're cooperating at the present time with respect to Operation North Watch, and I suspect that in one way or another—a variety of ways, probably—they'll end up cooperating in the event that force has to be used in Iraq.

Q. But you have military equipment at sea now from the 4th Infantry Division headed for Turkey, and the Turkish leaders said today there's no vote in parliament planned this week. Do you have a deadline of when you must know from Turkey, so that you could make other plans for forces that might go there?

Secretary Rumsfeld. We don't discuss deployments.

Q. Will the use of human shields, if it occurs, affect the operation? Would it affect the tactics that your commanders use?

Secretary Rumsfeld. Those are judgments that they'll have to make at the time, and certainly the crime of war which would be committed by the use of human shields is something that would be dealt with post-conflict—

* * * *

Q. Mr. Secretary, there are rumors floating around now, as there have been on a few occasions in the past, that a senior—one of Saddam's senior lieutenants has been put under house arrest. I think it's Qusay Hussein's father-in-law. And the suspicion was that he may have been planning some kind of coup. This raises again the question of how you would—how the United States would view a coup that removed Saddam from power but perhaps one that was orchestrated by his senior henchmen.

Secretary Rumsfeld. Unfavorably. There is not much point in having Saddam Hussein remove himself and substitute something of a kind in his place. So it wouldn't have any effect.

Q. Wouldn't have any effect on war planning or [*inaubible*].

Secretary Rumsfeld. Not that I can think of. You know, one dictator who wants weapons of mass destruction and wants to ignore 17 U.N. resolutions for another who is a dictator who wants weapons of mass destruction and wants to continue violating some 17 U.N. resolutions is not a very happy trade.

Q. Mr. Secretary, how do you view the rising tide of anti-war sentiment in Europe? It is becoming massive and difficult to ignore, I would think. From the point of view of the administration, help to put that in perspective.

Secretary Rumsfeld. Well, it is a(n) indication of democracies. That's the way democracies do things. There are differences of views. People are allowed to express themselves in a variety of different ways. We can note that in dictatorships, that doesn't happen; you're not seeing massive demonstrations of any type in Baghdad or Iraq. And so, I suppose, what one can take away from it is that there are a great many people who support and who recognize the seriousness of the issue and are in support. And there are some people in the streets who are not. And that is as it's always been.

I think the thing I would come back to is something I've said on a number of occasions, and I feel very deeply. These are tough issues. These are not easy issues. They are complicated. It's relatively simple when there is an attack on Pearl Harbor or when Germany occupies two or three countries in World War II. It is not simple in this case because what we're dealing with is something that is a 21st century phenomenon. It is weapons of vastly greater power in the hands of people who have demonstrated their willingness to use them and have threatened their neighbors and us and others. So, the threat that exists is a very serious one. And I think that we ought not to be surprised that there are difference of views and that it's going to take a while for people to get comfortable with this new century and recognize the seriousness of the threats.

Q. There are some who say the comments that you have made from the podium and in interviews have been decidedly unhelpful to the campaign to try to bring more members into the coalition. Can you address the kind of comments that you have made about Germany and France, which may have been intended to be humorous but have caused offense over there, and your role as a spokesman for trying to bring these nations into the coalition?

Secretary Rumsfeld. Well, I think if one goes back and looks at the precise words that I've used, they're—they are what they are. And the impression that is left often in news articles that Europe is opposing the United States, I think, is belied by the facts. The facts are that the vote in NATO was 16, including the United States, to three. And therefore the implication that there's some sort of a transatlantic problem, I think, is— misses the mark. What's taking place is, there are differences of views, to be sure, within Europe and in the world and—as well as within countries. And as I say, that is not surprising to me, given the difficulties of the issues.

* * * *

Q. Just to follow up on an earlier question, is war, in your view, inevitable at this point? And if not, could you tell us a couple of scenarios that to you seem to—or would seem to be able to avert a war?

Secretary Rumsfeld. Sure. It's not inevitable. The—although, as the president has said, time is running out. The ways it could end other than through the use of force are that the Iraqi regime could decide to leave the country and the new leadership would adhere to and agree with and practice the basic principles that are involved. Number one, it would be a single country. Number two, it would not have weapons of mass destruction, it would yield up everything it has, it would not threaten its neighbors, and it would provide the people of Iraq an opportunity to—a voice in their government in a way that protected the rights of ethnic or religious minorities in the country. That's one way.

A second way would be that someone in the country decided that he should leave involuntarily. A third is that the Iraqi regime should suddenly, after 11, 12 years, decide it wants to cooperate with the United Nations and adhere to the resolutions.

* * * *

Q. Mr. Secretary, in Europe it seems it's not just a matter of divided opinions, but public survey after public-opinion survey in our strongest allies shows strong majorities opposing the U.S. posture with Iraq. Even in Britain, Tony Blair has acknowledged that the vast majority of people are against him, and he's in political trouble because of it. Why do you think there is so much opposition to our posture?

Secretary Rumsfeld. I thought I answered that. I really—first of all, it is not our posture; there are a large number of nations that support the position of President Bush and the United States of America. It is not a—the view of a single country. There are a large and growing number of countries that agree with the position that the president has taken. That's fact number one.

The implication that because a few countries are opposing or because some publics are opposing—I would go back to what I said earlier: these are tough issues. This is a new period. We've not gone through this before. This is hard stuff. And it's not easy for anyone, including me and the people in this building, to think that through and make a calculation as to what the risks to our people are. And the president of the United States is the person who ultimately has that responsibility. And it's a big responsibility.

Q. There didn't seem to be as much opposition with regard to Afghanistan. I'm wondering what you think about the notion that the administration's handling of not only this issue, but its willingness recently to go its own way when it suited its pur-

poses, on treaty after treaty, has hurt it in this case, when it now needs other nations. I'm wondering what you think about that.

Secretary Rumsfeld. The president went to the Congress, got an overwhelming vote. He went to the United Nations and got a unanimous vote of the Security Council that said, as we all know, that Iraq was in material breach of the preceding U.N. resolutions and that this was its, quote, "final opportunity," unquote, and if it failed in this final opportunity, that it would face "serious consequences," I believe is the direct quote from Resolution 1441.

A unanimous vote in the Security Council is not, quote, "going it alone." I keep reading these words: unilateral, go it alone. They get mouthed and written over and over again—and some sort of breach between the United States and Europe. The fact of the matter is there are people within every country, and within Europe, that are on different views on this. And that is understandable because these are tough, tough issues.

Q. Mr. Secretary, as you're preparing for possible war with Iraq, you're also preparing to allow hundreds of journalists to accompany U.S. troops, not just from the United States, but also more than a hundred from other countries as well. To what extent is this policy a reaction to some of the bad publicity you got in the international press concerning the war in Afghanistan? And are you confident that an organization such as Al-Jazeera, which you've complained about their accuracy in the past, who has been offered slots to accompany some U.S. forces, won't broadcast information that could compromise the mission?

Secretary Rumsfeld. Well, let me start and then Dick can talk about the latter portion of the question.

First of all, it's not a reaction to anything.

Second, my impression of the press reaction to the handling of the press with respect to Afghanistan was that it was not negative, it was—compared to previous circumstances, 1991 and other times. There's always going to be people in the press who prefer this or prefer that. In fact, I'm told that at the present time, with respect to the decision that's been made to embed press in, that there are people who disagree with that. In other words, if you do something, somebody's not going to agree with it. That's life.

Now—so I wouldn't characterize the Afghan—the reaction to the way the department dealt with the press as negative on a relative basis. There's always someone complaining about something, but I would say it was not net negative compared to prior situations.

* * * *

Q. Mr. Secretary, we're about less than two months now away from mid-April, when the Iraqi desert becomes very hot and it would be difficult for U.S. forces and other forces to operate in protective suits. If we have much further delay in the United Nations in discussions on possible resolutions, et cetera, how long can we go on this before we're forced to defer to sometime in the fall before any action would be possible?

Secretary Rumsfeld. You know, how long the president will go—the thing to keep in mind about the United Nations process, it's not how long should you go to try to have the inspectors find and discover weapons of mass destruction in the country; that's not what they're there for. The question is how long does it make sense to wait to determine the extent to which the Iraqi government is cooperating? And the answer, according to both of those gentlemen thus far, is that their cooperation has been somewhere well short of what the resolution called for.

Remarks by Secretary of State Powell and NATO Secretary General Robertson, February 20, 2003

Secretary Colin Powell and Secretary General George Robertson delivered their remarks after meeting in Washington, DC.

Secretary Powell. Well, good morning, ladies and gentlemen. I have had the pleasure once again to receive the Secretary General of NATO, Lord George Robertson, and we've had a very good discussion following on the discussions that Lord Robertson had with President Bush last evening.

I had the chance this morning to again thank George for the superb work that he and his team, working with the United States team, and, frankly, the teams of many of the NATO nations, most of the NATO nations, in finding a solution to the problem we had with respect to providing support to a fellow NATO member, Turkey.

And I think we had a good outcome and I know that the Turks are pleased and we are certainly pleased, and it shows the vitality of the alliance and how we can find solutions to the most vexing, difficult problems. But what you need to find such solutions is a good leader, and George Robertson is such a good leader, and I thank him again for the hard work he and his staff put into this effort.

I also briefed the Secretary General on where we are with respect to Iraq and other issues. We also talked about Afghanistan, noting the work that has been done there over the past year plus in putting a society and a country and a government back together, and the continuing need there is now, will be, for military presence in the form of not only OEF, Operation Enduring Freedom forces, but the International Security Assistance Force.

And we noted that perhaps NATO can play a more active role as an alliance and not just member-nations of the alliance participating in ISAF. And so in the weeks ahead, we'll be exploring with Lord Robertson and his staff how best to accomplish this, and I'm very pleased that NATO is willing to play this more forward leaning role. And it's, once again, a sign of the vitality of the alliance and the continuing relevance of the alliance.

And so, George, it's a great pleasure to welcome you here, sir, and I invite you to say a word.

Secretary General Robertson. Thanks very much, Colin. It's good to be here in the State Department and I like compliments and praise as much as anybody in politics or out of politics, but I want to place on record my thanks to you and to your people, both here and in Brussels, for the efforts that they put in, and indeed to those of the other nations who were determined to find a solution.

After some pretty tough talking and some strong opinions being raised, we got a result on Sunday night, late Sunday night, and we made a decision that led to a deployment yesterday of the protective measures for Turkey, and within a week the AWACS planes that defended America after the 11th of September will be flying over Turkey defending another ally under threat. That's what the alliance is about: strong and powerful in defense of the common interests and common values that we stand for. And I'm assuring everybody in the United States that the transatlantic link remains as strong as possible, that we can repair any damage to NATO's public reputation quite easily by the comments that are made and especially the deeds that are done.

As you say, Colin, Afghanistan is an area where NATO is now helping Germany and the Netherlands to mount the International Security Assistance Force, helping to bring peace and stability to that troubled part of the world, and the countries that are there just now, the Netherlands and Germany and to be followed on by Canada, are looking for more NATO support and that is something that the alliance will look to because we're interested in stability. And of course, Afghanistan has been for too long an exporter of trouble, instability, drugs and trafficking, and if we can help to reduce that threat to the whole of Europe, then NATO will play its part and do it strongly, too.

Q. Mr. Secretary, is the aid package for Turkey still at an impasse? Has there been any give on either side since we last saw you?

Secretary Powell. Well, as you know, we spent a lot of time over the weekend with our Turkish colleagues. I was with them till midnight last Thursday night and the President saw them on Friday, and then I reaffirmed to them yesterday morning in a phone call to the Prime Minister that our position was firm with respect to the kind of assistance we could provide with respect to the level. There may be some other creative things we can do, but the level was our ceiling.

And I know that they are in consultation now within their government, within their council of ministers, and I expect to hear back from them before the day is out. But I have nothing further to report, Barry.

Q. Mr. Secretary, when do you expect a second resolution to be put forward, roughly what shape do you think it will take, and will it set any explicit deadline for Iraqi compliance?

Secretary Powell. We are in close consultation with our friends in the Security Council and other nations around the world about continued Iraqi noncompliance with 1441. There was an article in the paper this morning that illustrated once again that they will take process and convert process into a way of avoiding their obligations under 1441, and we view this with great seriousness. It's the case we made last Monday at the United Nations that's what is wanted is compliance, and not necessarily more inspectors or more monitoring, because Iraq knows how to thwart those kinds of efforts.

And in the absence of such compliance, we believe that it is appropriate to put down a resolution in the very near future. I can't tell you exactly when we will do it, but it is not going to be in the far distant future, but in the near future.

And I think I will not discuss what the elements of the resolution will be until I've completed the consultation with our friends, and the same goes with respect to any timelines associated with a resolution.

Q. Mr. Secretary, have you heard from Dr. Blix on what he is asking of the Iraqis vis-á-vis the al-Samoud II missile and other components related to it?

Secretary Powell. No, I haven't heard anything today. As you know, the al-Samoud is—he identified it and components such as engines and test stands and casting machinery and casting chambers and things of that nature—are all prohibited items. They're not supposed to have them. And they are in the process, I think, of being positively identified and tagged. And I will wait to see whether Dr. Blix directs Iraq to take any action with respect to those specific items, but I haven't heard anything today.

Q. Secretary Powell, as you know better than the rest of us, right now, the U.S. does not have the nine votes that would be necessary to pass a resolution. Is it a definite that the U.S. will submit a resolution, even if you think you don't have the votes? And how do you intend to win over at least nine, if not more members of the Security Council to persuade them that Iraq is not in compliance?

Secretary Powell. Well, there's no resolution down so whether we have the votes or not is something of an academic question. We still believe that a resolution is appropriate. We're working on such a resolution. And we don't put a resolution down unless we intend to fight for that resolution, unless we believe we can make the case that a resolution is appropriate. And when we put a resolution down, we will then convey the argument to all the members of the Security Council as to why it is a proper resolution to support, and I hope we'll be able to achieve the support needed to pass it.

Q. Mr. Secretary, today in the paper, some representatives of smaller countries on the Security Council are saying they actually wish they weren't in those seats right now because of the extreme pressure that the U.S. and other people are putting on. What can you say to that?

And I'm also interested in whether you agree with Lord Robertson that the sort of breaks and tensions in NATO can be easily overcome.

Secretary Powell. With respect to the latter part of your question, I certainly do agree with George. I've been around this business for many years and I don't know how many times I have gone through wither NATO, the end of NATO, what comes next, the Warsaw Pact has gone away, why hasn't NATO? And voila, it's still here.

And I remember when I was Chairman of the Joint Chiefs of Staff, all the Russian generals would say to me, "Well, we got rid of the Warsaw Pact. When are you going to get rid of NATO?" I said, "How can we get rid of an organization where people keep applying to join?" And so it has gone from the 16 nations that we had, heading now to 26 nations, and it's a vibrant alliance which can deal with the kinds of problems that it just dealt with and it continues to be the single, the single organization that links the transatlantic community, North America with Europe. And it will continue to have value far into the future, and these problems come, they get dealt with by democratic nations working together, and they get put behind us and the alliance continues to move forward.

With respect to the elected members of the Security Council, there are always tough issues before the Council. All I ask of each of these nations is to weigh the facts, the weight the evidence, read Resolution 1441 again, and come to a considered judgment when it's time to vote. I believe that we should put trust in these countries, whether they are big or small. They all have sovereign rights to decide. We present our case. We don't threaten. We don't suggest that blackmail is in order. We present our case, and hopefully the power of our argument will persuade them to vote with us. But there are always difficult issues before the Council and this certainly is one of them.

Remarks by Secretary of State Powell, February 20, 2003

Secretary Colin Powell was interviewed on Spain's Antena 3.

Q. The U.S. and U.K., they are working now on a draft for a new resolution. Can you share with us some details? There's going to be some deadline in the text? A deadline? Some details on the new resolution?

Secretary Powell. Well, we're still working on the new resolution. We're also in contact with our Spanish colleague, Ana Palacios, and discussing the matter with her. And I think the new resolution will contain language that points out Iraq's failure to comply with its obligations under 1441 and earlier resolutions and it will bring this to the attention of the Security Council for something to be done, to be considered for action.

But I don't know that there will be a deadline in the resolution, but clearly time is running out. The problem is that Iraq is not complying. We have press reports in our newspapers today about how the inspectors are not able to do the work that Iraq said they could do. So the issue isn't more inspectors, the issue isn't more robust inspections or time for inspections; the issue is compliance, and in the absence of compliance, I think the Security Council has to consider another resolution and make a judgment as to how much more time Iraq should be given.

Q. What could happen if, at the end, France is going to use its right to veto?

Secretary Powell. Well, France has a right to veto, as does any other permanent member of the Security Council. But I hope that when all the facts are put before the Security Council and they see that Iraq is not complying, not really cooperating with the inspectors, that a lot of the things that were said at the United Nations last week about Iraqi compliance have turned out not to be the case, that sooner or later the Council will say enough is enough, in the absence of compliance, we are obliged under the Resolution 1441 to take action.

That is certainly the position of the United States and I think Prime Minister Aznar has been in the forefront of those leaders who understand our obligations to the safety of the world, our commitment to the people of the world to do something about these terrible weapons.

Q. Mr. Secretary, I ask you now as a former military, there is the perception out there the war beyond the second week of March is going to be a bad scenario for the American Army in Iraq. I cannot believe that the weather and the moon phases are killing the diplomacy and the passions.

Secretary Powell. They are not. The weather and the moon phases have nothing to do with the diplomacy. The diplomacy is something that stands by itself. But the reality is that Iraq has not taken this last opportunity given to it by 1441. The United States, the United Kingdom and others have been sending forces to the region to support diplomacy; to make sure Iraq understands the seriousness of this matter. And if it weren't for those forces that are deployed in the area and moving to the area, Iraq wouldn't be doing anything at all.

But what it is doing is not enough and we always knew when we passed Resolution 1441 that the day might come when the Security Council had to take a look and say this isn't working, Iraq is not complying, they are not cooperating; longer inspections, more inspectors are not the answer; we must use military force. And I hope that the members of the Security Council and the other nations in the world that might join in a coalition are prepared to do their duty when the moment comes.

Q. Mr. Powell, what if, at the end, at the last moment, Saddam Hussein chooses exile to avoid the war, to avoid defeat? Is going the U.S. prosecute him? Is going the U.S. Army in any way enter in Iraq?

Secretary Powell. I think if Saddam Hussein and his top leadership were to leave the country, go into exile, I think this would be a very positive step. And at that time, the United Nations could take a look at the leadership that emerges, that follows Saddam Hussein, and if that leadership says we want to disarm of all these weapons of mass destruction, we want nothing to do with any of this, we want to cooperate fully with the United Nations, then inspectors would have something to work with, and, frankly, it may be possible for the U.S. to provide direct assistance to that new leadership.

The United States has no desire to invade a country or take over a country. That's not our history. That's not our tradition. We do have a desire to protect ourselves and protect our friends and to protect the world from these kinds of dangerous weapons. But the world will be better served if Saddam Hussein would go off into exile with the key members of his family and of the leadership group that has brought such tragedy to the people of Iraq.

Q. Mr. Powell, if the real goal of the administration is to implement the will of the international community, why to put military government in Baghdad after the war, American? Why not an international?

Secretary Powell. We would only have military government until such time as we can transition to international presence, to international authority, or to the people of Iraq. But when you're conducting a military operation, a military commander is in charge. But as soon as his work is done, we want to transition. We don't want a military government of the type we had in Germany or in Japan after World War II that went on for years. We want to transition authority back to civilian authority and then to the Iraqi people with some international presence.

The United States does not want to be in charge of a country such as Iraq for any length of time. We have to be there long enough to make sure that we are taking care of the people, that they are being provided food, and that we have provided stability in the country, and then turn it over to international organizations and turn it over to the people of Iraq. The United States record is quite clear on this. We want to do the job, do it well, preserve peace, and then transition back to civilian authority under the leadership of Iraqis.

Remarks by Secretary of State Powell, February 20, 2003

Secretary Colin Powell was interviewed on Russia's RTR Television.

Q. Mr. Secretary, during the last days, Baghdad took many steps about the United Nations demand. Baghdad let U-2 aircrafts fly over the territory of Iraq. Saddam Hussein officially banned production of weapons of mass destruction.

Did it make any changes to the situation and do you think the necessity of war is postponed?

Secretary Powell. No, I think these changes have been minor and not that serious. I am pleased that the U-2s are now flying. But the decree he put out banning weapons of mass destruction was a decree put out to private citizens who don't have them in the first place. It didn't apply to the government. So it's this kind of game that he plays all the time.

What he needs to do is comply, to bring forward all the documents that he has, to fix all the errors in the declaration that he submitted, to bring forth all the missiles that the inspectors keep finding and tagging, to account for what happened to the nerve agents and the biological agents and all of the other terrible things that he's had for these years. He should be coming forward with that, and not just grudgingly, every few days slipping out something to see if he can keep the United Nations from acting, to see if he can just keep the inspections going on and on and on, but never really complying.

The challenge that we have before us now, and my colleague and I, Foreign Minister Igor Ivanov, and I have spoken about this many times. The challenge we have now is not just how long the inspections should be or how many inspectors there should be assigned to the task, but is Iraq complying. And I'm sorry, the evidence before us is that Iraq still tries to deceive, to divert attention, and is not yet complying. And unless there is compliance in the near future, I think the Security Council has to meet and decide whether or not serious consequences are called for.

Q. Last weekend, there were huge demonstration all over the world, including New York City and San Francisco, voices of dissent. What impact do the demonstrations have on your decision in the administration?

Secretary Powell. We watch these demonstrations carefully. We know that there is great anxiety, that there are many, many people who do not want to see war. We don't want to see war. They don't think war is the right answer.

War must always be a last resort, but it must be a resort. If the international community is to have any standing, if the United Nations is to have any meaning, it must be able to impose its will when faced with a nation like Iraq that simply ignores the will of the international community.

And so I understand that people are hoping that war can be avoided. I hope it can be avoided. But the one who has the power in his hands to decide whether there will be war or peace is Saddam Hussein. If he complies, or if he leaves the country tomorrow, there will be no war. The problem is he has shown no signs of leaving the country and he still shows no signs of complying by coming forward with the documents, with people to be interviewed, with the materials that we know he has, with the mobile biological laboratories, with all these things that have been documented and are facts, not speculation. He still has not come forward and said here they are, I no longer want to have anything to do with these kinds of weapons, I'm changed. He's not changed, unfortunately, so far.

Remarks by Secretary of State Powell, February 20, 2003

Secretary Colin Powell was interviewed on BBC's NewsNight.

Q. Colin Powell, how close are you to agreeing a text for a second resolution with the British?

Secretary Powell. I think we're very close. I've been in close consultation with Foreign Secretary Straw and members of my team have been in close touch with members of his team, so I would expect in the very near future we'll be putting down a resolution, more likely next week.

Q. Have you agreed that it will contain explicit authorization for military action?

Secretary Powell. Well, I'm not sure that it will. I think it will be a resolution that summarizes the situation as it exists, shows that Iraq is not in compliance, however much inspectors may be moving around the country, and that's good; but if there is no compliance, if there is no cooperation of the kind we expected, then that's not good, and I think the resolution will point out that lack of cooperation and point to the fact that the United Nations Security Council is supposed to act in the presence of this lack of cooperation.

A lot of arguments about more inspectors, keep the inspections going, but we must not lose sight of the basic issue. The basic issue is Iraqi compliance, and that's not what we're getting.

Q. But without the actual term "military action" or authorization of military action, isn't it going to be less likely that you'll be able to launch military action quickly?

Secretary Powell. Well, you know, right now, an argument can be made, and it's an argument we would make, that 1441, Resolution 1441, provides more than enough authority. This next resolution need not say "military action" to provide the authority for the use of force if that's what is decided is appropriate.

And so we're looking at the language to come up with language that the Security Council will receive in a positive way and recognize that it is time for them to meet their responsibilities to the international community.

But this is not a rush to war, as some say. This issue has been lingering for 12 years and it has been months since the inspectors got started and months since 1441 was passed, and Iraq is still not in compliance. And so we'll see what the language of the resolution looks like and the whole world will see it in the not too distant future.

Q. Will it contain a deadline or a series of deadlines for Saddam?

Secretary Powell. I don't think the resolution will, but clearly time is running out. We can't just allow this matter to drag along and to allow those who are not prepared to use military force, as was the intent of 1441 in the presence of Iraqi noncooperation, we can't allow it to just be drug out with requests for more inspectors, for more process, for more actions on the part of the Iraqis which are not intended to comply but intended to deceive.

For example, much was made last week of Saddam Hussein's issuing a decree telling everybody to turn in or have nothing to do with weapons of mass destruction. Now that we've read the decree, we see that it applies to private citizens, and not to the government. So it's another act of disingenuousness on the part of Saddam Hussein. More people are going to be made available for interview, but we see in our press this morning that more people have not been made available for interview. No more documents have been forthcoming.

Last week at the Security Council, I clearly pointed out that the declaration that Iraq provided in December was flawed, it was incomplete. And the response of the Iraqi Permanent Representative at the Security Council last week was, well, read it again, we're not giving you anything more. We can't accept answers like that. This is a serious matter. Weapons of mass destruction are in Iraq, 1441 says so, and Iraq must come into compliance.

Q. But what is your response to President Chirac, who said that the inspectors are doing their work, there is no need for a second resolution now, and France would have no choice but to oppose?

Secretary Powell. Well, I certainly appreciate President Chirac's point of view. I appreciate the points of view expressed by all the members of the Security Council and we'll listen to them carefully. But we believe that the inspectors are not yet able to do their work in the presence of Iraqi noncompliance, and the inspectors essentially have said that.

Q. But the evidence you've brought so far has failed to convince a majority of people in Britain that war is required. Opinion polls and public demonstration show that, indeed, church leaders this very day have said that Tony Blair has not made the moral argument for war.

How much does it matter to you, and do you understand the political risk that he is running?

Secretary Powell. Of course I do. And of course we watch the demonstrations that have taken place in the United Kingdom and elsewhere around Europe, and we take them very much into account. But the simple facts, the simple reality, is that the case is clear: Iraq has weapons of mass destruction. The previous inspection regime said so as a result of their work from 1991 to 1998, when they were forced out of the country. And 1441 begins with the opening premise that Iraq remains in material breach of its obligations. Where is the anthrax? Where is the botulinum toxin? These are not just simple medications or chemicals that we can ignore knowing what happened to these items. These are deadly organisms and deadly chemicals. Where are the missiles that we know exist? The mobile biological warfare labs?

It's easy to say we haven't seen enough evidence, therefore we must not act. But it seems to me the evidence is clear, the evidence has been there for the past 11 to 12 years, and the United Nations must not step back from its responsibilities, and I am pleased that there are leaders such as Prime Minister Blair that even in the presence of dissension within the United Kingdom he recognizes the responsibility that we have as an international community not to step back from this challenge, not to avoid the difficult days and difficult steps that may be ahead.

Remarks by Secretary of Defense Rumsfeld, February 20, 2003

Secretary Donald Rumsfeld was interviewed by Jim Lehrer on PBS's NewsHour.

Q. No breakthrough yet on the Turkish bases situation; is that right?

Secretary Rumsfeld. That's correct.

Q. What's the problem? Is it money?

Secretary Rumsfeld. Well, no. It's the fact that Turkey is a democracy. It has a relatively new government. It is wrestling with a whole set of issues, and the reality is that what the United States has asked of Turkey is significant. And so they need time to think it through and talk to their parliament and give consideration to it. I suspect in the day or two immediately ahead, why we'll have some sort of an answer, and in the last analysis, Turkey is our ally in NATO. Turkey is participating now in Operation

Northern Watch, where we have coalition aircraft in Turkey that monitors the northern portion of Iraq. And they have been helpful in a number of ways.

Q. What would not having access to their bases do to a potential military action against Iraq?

Secretary Rumsfeld. Well, I don't think that's really the issue, whether we'll have access to their bases, and whether we'll be able to overfly and those types of things. We already have that for Operation Enduring Freedom, the global war on terror. I think the real issue they're considering now is the extent to which they want to increase that to permit larger numbers of heavier troops to come in from the north in the event that the decision is made that force is necessary to disarm Saddam Hussein.

Q. But if you don't have the 40,000 troops, what I've been reading, there's 40,000 troops that the U.S. wants to put into the northern boundary through Turkey for potential conflict with Iraq, if you can't do it that way, what I'm asking is—

Secretary Rumsfeld. We'll do another way.

Q. You'll do it another way. And it still can be done, and it's not going to upset things. I just—did you read the New York Times? The New York Times quoted a White House spokesman, a White House person this morning as saying that this was extortion in the name of alliance, that's what Turkey was up to. Do you agree with that?

Secretary Rumsfeld. No. I don't. I mean, I think what it is, is a democratic country going through the whole series of questions as to what they think their role ought to be. And I think that's fair. These are tough issues that countries are wrestling with. I think that's not the way I would characterize it.

Q. The Turkey problem aside, is the U.S. military ready to go against Iraq?

Secretary Rumsfeld. Yes.

Q. In general terms, I know you don't like to talk specifics, but in general terms, what is the force that's ready to go?

Secretary Rumsfeld. I would characterize it as ample. The United States at the president's request decided that as the diplomacy took place in the world, and in the United Nations, that it was important to begin flowing forces to support that diplomacy. And we've had many, many weeks now to do that. The United Kingdom has had many, many weeks to do that. Other countries have taken steps to deploy various types of assets. NATO did this last week, deployed some capability to Turkey, for example. Other countries have been deploying things like chemical and biological detection units to Kuwait. So a number of countries have been flowing capabilities and forces into that region. And there has been a good deal of time, so we are at a point where, if the president makes that decision, the Department of Defense is prepared and has the capabilities and the strategy to do that.

Q. In general terms of the figures, 150,000 troops, five aircraft battle groups, and heavy bombers, is that roughly it from the U.S. point of view?

Secretary Rumsfeld. I won't do numbers.

Q. Okay. That's the conventional wisdom that's in every story.

Secretary Rumsfeld. That doesn't make it so.

Q. I know.

Secretary Rumsfeld. You know the old rule. People who don't know talk, and people who know don't talk.

Q. Okay. But, are these—are there limits to how long these American forces can remain ready to go?

Secretary Rumsfeld. Well, there's obviously a preference. You don't ramp up to a high level and sustain it for a long period easily. What you have to do is rotate capabilities in and out over time.

Q. We keep hearing that the time is running out to keep these forces ready. Is that true?

Secretary Rumsfeld. Well, the way to think of it, it seems to me, is the way the president put it, and that is that it's been 12 years, and what's being tested now is not whether or not inspectors can go in and find weapons of mass destruction, that's not what inspectors are for. They're not finders or discoverers. What's being tested now is whether or not Saddam Hussein is going to cooperate. And it doesn't take a lot of time to determine whether or not Saddam Hussein is going to cooperate. So, once the construct of that issue is placed properly before the world, it seems to me the answer gets increasingly clear. We've now had 17 resolutions. It's been 12 years. They've tried diplomacy. The world has tried economic sanctions. The world has tried military activity in the northern and southern no fly zones. At some point, why the time runs out. And that's what the president has said.

Q. I didn't make my question clear. I meant, is there a time element involved in keeping those thousands of troops, how many ever there are, and bombers and hardware, at a state of readiness before they have to stand down, that's what I meant?

Secretary Rumsfeld. Well, as I say, it costs money. It keeps people away from their homes and families, and their jobs in the case of Guard and Reserve. So, obviously, your first choice is not to flow forces and then sustain them there for one, two, three, four years, whatever, another 12. There has to be some end to these things. Either you use them or you bring them back.

Q. Well, let's talk about that a moment. Do you feel that just having this large force that you outlined in general terms is a momentum for war in and of itself, just because they're there, they must be used?

Secretary Rumsfeld. No, I don't. What I think of them as, Saddam Hussein was ignoring the United Nations for the past period of years. Saddam Hussein is not ignoring the United Nations today. He's not cooperating, but he's not ignoring them. Inspectors are back in there. They're not being cooperated with, so they're not finding much. But the only reason Saddam Hussein has changed at all is because of the flow of forces, and the threat of force.

Q. What would be your, as Secretary of Defense, what would be your position on pulling those troops back and bringing them back home? In other words, if there was a peaceful solution to this, I've heard what you said that you don't think that's going to happen, he isn't cooperating, but if something pulls, if somebody pulls something out of a hat, is it—what's the downside of bringing all those people back home and all that equipment?

Secretary Rumsfeld. Well, I think there—I still—I mean, everyone agrees, the last choice is to use force and have a war. They are dangerous things, people get killed. Unforeseen things happen. There still is at least a remote possibility that he could decide to leave the country at some point. To the extent he is persuaded that it's inevitable, that he's going to lose his position, and his regime is going to be cast out, it's at least possible. Was it 1 percent? I don't know. But it's not zero percent that he might leave. The second possibility is that the people in Iraq might decide he should leave and help him. So that's a possibility.

If that happens, if that were to happen, as remote as it may be, it would only happen because the people in Iraq, he or the people around him who decide they prefer he not be there, were persuaded that it was inevitable that he was going to go either voluntarily or involuntarily.

Q. And would it be your positions that, hey, look, we won a war without having to fight it?

Secretary Rumsfeld. Oh, my goodness, that would be—everyone's first choice would be to not have to have a conflict.

Q. You do understand that people believe there is not a—as you know, this is a matter of public debate, that people think, oh, my goodness, President Bush and Secretary Rumsfeld have all these forces there now, and they feel obligated to use them. You're saying that is not the case?

Secretary Rumsfeld. No, the president's determination, and I work for the president, his determination is that Iraq be disarmed. His first choice is that it be done voluntarily. The Iraqi regime refuses to cooperate with the inspectors, and with the United Nations. They have for many, many years.

Your second choice would be that the regime leaves, voluntarily or involuntarily.

The last choice would be that the regime has to be thrown out, and the president is determined that if that's necessary, he will lead a coalition of a large number of countries and do that.

Q. Let's talk about that option. How would you describe the mission? If in fact it comes to military action, and those people, those Americans and the others who are standing by have to actually take military action, what's the goal, what's the mission?

Secretary Rumsfeld. The mission would be to invade the country, make it very clear that the purpose was, number one, to change that regime, and disarm the country. That the purpose is to disarm the country of weapons of mass destruction, and it would be done in a certain way, adhering to certain principles. And the principles would be that when that regime was gone, the new government of Iraq, and it would be an Iraq that would be for the Iraqi people. It wouldn't be a regime, you know, determined from outside of Iraq.

But it would be a single country, it would be a country with no weapons of mass destruction. It would be a country that did not threaten its neighbors. It would be a country where the people of that country, the ethnic minorities and the religious minorities, would have a voice in their government. And that there would be some process, and the sooner the better, that Iraqi people could govern themselves. The oil is the oil of the Iraqi people. And this speculation around that somebody is interested in their oil is nonsense. That oil belongs to the Iraqi people, and it will be important for the Iraqi people.

Q. On the combat itself, are you planning, are you and your folks planning for a ferocious war where—I mean, an all-out defense by the Iraqi military when the U.S. comes in, and when the others come in?

Secretary Rumsfeld. The task of war planners is to plan for every conceivable contingency. And they are doing that, from the most pessimistic to the most optimistic.

Q. Is it likely that—the Gulf War spoiled everybody, of course, most of the Iraqi military threw down their arms and surrendered. Are you expecting that to happen again?

Secretary Rumsfeld. Oh, I would expect that there would be Iraqi forces that would surrender rather rapidly. Their morale is not high. They also have lived under Saddam Hussein, and know what kind of a person he is.

Q. Is that a central part of your planning? Does that have to happen for this to be successful?

Secretary Rumsfeld. No, no. Absolutely not. No, as I say, General Franks and his planners have developed plans that will address the wide variety of contingencies.

Q. What about the use of chemical and biological weapons—

Secretary Rumsfeld. Including that.

Q.—including against our folks.

Secretary Rumsfeld. They've looked at the risk that Saddam Hussein, which says they have no chemical and biological weapons, of course, would use biological and chemical weapons against U.S. forces, he could use them against neighboring countries, like Kuwait, or Jordan, or Turkey, or Israel. They could also use them against their own population, and blame them on the United States and coalition forces, they've done that before. So there are a variety of ways they could use chemical or biological weapons.

Q. Do you expect them to do it?

Secretary Rumsfeld. What we expect is that it's our job to be prepared for any conceivable contingency. And, therefore, all the way from that unhappy thought, and dangerous thought, all the way over to catastrophic success, where so many people surrender so fast that the task becomes very quickly humanitarian assistance, and medical assistance, and water, and those types of things. So, they have developed contingency plans for the full spectrum of contingencies.

Q. What do you expect the Iraqi civilians to do? To treat American troops as liberators or as conquerors?

Secretary Rumsfeld. Well, I suppose we'll get that across the spectrum as well. Certainly the people that are close in to Saddam Hussein would know that their future is not bright. The people who are engaged in managing or using weapons of mass destruction would have to know that their future would be bleak.

On the other hand, people who surrender, and people who recognize that resistance is not wise, that it's inevitable that the United States and the coalition forces would prevail, and acquiesce in that would be treated quite differently.

Q. Do you expect the invasion, if it comes, to be welcomed by the majority of the civilian population of Iraq?

Secretary Rumsfeld. There's obviously the Shia population in Iraq and the Kurdish population in Iraq have been treated very badly by Saddam Hussein's regime, they represent a large fraction of the total. There is no question but that they would be welcomed. Go back to Afghanistan, the people were in the streets playing music, cheering, flying kites, and doing all the things that the Taliban and the Al-Qaeda would not let them do. Saddam Hussein has one of the most vicious regimes on the face of the earth. And the people know that.

Now, is there a risk when that dictatorial system isn't there that there could be conflicts between elements within the country, get even type things, yes. And we've got to be careful to see that that doesn't happen.

Q. What about just the basic idea that they've been told for years that the Americans are the infidels. I mean, it would be like welcoming Hitler into Chicago if he had taken over. I mean, is that not—

Secretary Rumsfeld. Jim.

Q. No, no, I'm just saying, we're the enemy.

Secretary Rumsfeld. My goodness. That's a terrible thought.

Q. I know, I know. But isn't that—

Secretary Rumsfeld. If a politician had said that, they'd get in trouble.

Q. I know. But, I'm just saying, is your planning, the war plan based on the idea that the Iraqi people are going to welcome American troops and American invasion?

Secretary Rumsfeld. Contingency planning is based on a full spectrum of possibilities, and that is one, and there are others at the other end of the spectrum that are less happy. And the plans have been prepared to deal with that full range of possibilities. But, to suggest that a war plan depends on one of them happening would be wrong.

Q. It's been suggested that you are emphasizing only the upside of this, and that you haven't talked publicly about, hey, wait a minute, they may not—they may resist, they may do this, they may do that, thousands and thousands of people could die, including a lot of Americans. Do you feel that this has been—that the American people have been told enough about the possibilities for the downside of this kind of conflict?

Secretary Rumsfeld. I think the downsides have been widely discussed. I mean, I prepared a list of things that could be very unpleasant back in September or October, and I've added to the list. And everyone who works with me has seen the list, including the president, and the National Security Council, and they know that there are a full range of things that can be unfortunate, and make life very difficult. And we've heard them all, the use of weapons of mass destruction, the possibility of firing ballistic missiles and chemical weapons into neighboring countries, the possibility that one ethnic group in the country could take advantage of disorder and attack another ethnic group, the possibility of using chemicals against his own people, the possibility of fortress Baghdad, and urban conflict. It goes on and on, flooding, the possibility of flooding. There are any number of things that can go wrong. Now, there are also a number of things that can go right, and what one has to do is to look at them all with a cold eye, and be very clear that you've simply got to be prepared to deal with all of them. And that is what General Franks and his team have been doing. And he's doing a superb job for the country.

Q. You mentioned yourself the possibility of a humanitarian crisis that could come. Does your—is the intelligence been saying—it's been written up in the papers that Saddam Hussein may intentionally try to starve his people, may intentionally set the oil fields afire, may intentionally do all kinds of things to create a humanitarian crisis, a chaos for his own people. Are we prepared to deal with that?

Secretary Rumsfeld. We are certainly organized, and have thought through what we would do in each instance where we have either imagined or seen intelligence that suggests that that regime might do one or more of those things.

Q. And there are a lot of what they call—the private aid groups have been on this program and elsewhere saying that there has been very little coordination with them from the U.S. government, they're prepared to help out and all that, and they're waiting for the calls. Are you all talking to them, are your folks talking to them?

Secretary Rumsfeld. Yes, there are interagency groups in the United States government who have been planning the civil side, a post Saddam Hussein Iraq. That is to say, what do you do about food, what do you do about water, what do you do about medicine. And they have been working for weeks, and they have been coordinating with international groups. Indeed, there have been stockpiles of various types of humanitarian assistance that have already begun to flow into the region, and there's no question but that the United States military is prepared to participate and help international organizations, including the United Nations are already storing materials, and I think probably the information you have is out of date.

Q. Okay. All right. Are you concerned about how just the prospect of going to war is dividing the world?

Secretary Rumsfeld. Well, you always would want unanimity in anything, and of course, the president is not decided to go to war. So—

Q. I'm saying, just the prospect of it.

Secretary Rumsfeld. I understand. You'd always prefer that everyone agree, and yet, you say, dividing the world. I don't know that I would say that. I think that if I were to look at the globe and countries on earth, I would find people in almost every country who agree, and people who didn't agree. And you'd find in Europe the eight countries signed a letter supporting the president, then ten countries signed a letter supporting the president. The U.N. Security Council voted unanimously to support the resolution, 17th Resolution on Iraq, Resolution 1441. So to say that it's dividing the world, I think is a bit of an overstatement. There are an awful lot more people who didn't demonstrate than who demonstrated. And demonstrations occur in democracies, that's what we do. We have free speech, and that's fine, and that's fair. And these are tough issues. These are not easy issues. The idea of having to think about the prospects of the use of chemical or biological weapons by a terrorist state, or by a terrorist network, killing hundreds of thousands of people is not a nice thing to think about. And it's not something that people immediately say, well, we have to avoid that. We have to think about that a while.

Q. But, it has not given you any pause at all to consider whether or not, the numbers you just laid out, that aside, that the message as to why this military action may have to be taken has not gotten through to everyone. You feel it so strongly, clearly, so does the president, so do a lot of other people, Tony Blair, others, and yet it hasn't gotten through to a lot of other folks. Does that not concern you, bother you?

Secretary Rumsfeld. Of course, you always would prefer everyone agree. But, I've never seen a situation where everyone agreed. In democracies everyone never agrees. And it doesn't mean that someone is right, and someone is wrong, it means that in my mind, at least, it means that in this instance these are difficult issues for people to wrap their heads around. And yet, the risk of being wrong, the risk of inaction, there's risks to action, and you've been discussing them at length here, there are also risks to inaction, 3,000 people were killed in the United States on September 11th in a very conventional, unconventionally delivered, but a conventional attack. If that had been chemical weapons or biological weapons it might not have been 3,000, it could have been 30,000, or 300,000, or a million, and we know that, and the world has to think about that. Now, there's a big effort going on in the Congress to try to connect the dots, who knew what before September 11th, what could you have known, a phone call here, a credit card there, someone taking flying lessons, how do you connect those dots. How many countries would have anticipated in trying to stop that before it happened, based on that fragmentary information? And yet, we had Secretary Powell's powerful presentation to the United Nations, laying out the case as to what the Iraqi government has been doing.

Q. As you know, they're all over you in Europe and elsewhere, because of remarks you made about Germany, and France, and all of that, and they're suggesting that you, above a lot of others, really are not that concerned about what the governments—

Secretary Rumsfeld. I am concerned. I mean, I just went over to Munich and spoke to their Kunde conference, the security conference, and met with all of those folks. Needless to say you're concerned. You want as many people as possible to agree with you. And the president has taken it to the United Nations. I keep reading things like, unilateral, I can't make a prediction, but I'll bet anything there is at least a 50/50 chance that there would be more countries, if the decision is made, that there would be more countries supporting the United States and the coalition of the willing, with the United Kingdom and other countries in this coalition than there were in the Gulf

War in 1991. So the charge of unilateral just isn't right. The allegation that the United States has an issue with Europe isn't right. The issue in Europe is between Europeans. It's basically between France, Germany, and the rest of Europe.

Q. What's your own view about the positions of France and Germany on this?

Secretary Rumsfeld. I think they're democracies, they have to decide what they want to decide. They're sovereign countries. People elected those people to office, that's what they think, and that's life. But, the idea that therefore there is a split between the United States and Europe I think is a misunderstanding. There is a split between most of the European countries, the eight and the ten, and France and Germany.

Q. But, there's also a split between the United States and France, and Germany, as well.

Secretary Rumsfeld. But, not with the 18 countries of Europe.

Q. No, but there is with France and Germany.

Secretary Rumsfeld. On this issue, and we're allies in NATO.

Q. Do you think that's all it is, is this issue?

Secretary Rumsfeld. Well, certainly that's all it is today. I mean, I think they made a mistake on Turkey, and I think they've corrected it now. They opposed sending defensive capabilities, chemical and biological detection units to Turkey, in the North Atlantic Council, and since then they've permitted it to happen, and they've since been deployed. So I think they've changed their position on that, which is a good thing.

Q. Do you think eventually they could even change their position on military action?

Secretary Rumsfeld. I don't know. I wouldn't want to predict. Of course, you know, things change, times change, if the inspectors found something that was disturbing to them, I just don't know what will happen. We would much prefer that Germany and France were in agreement.

Q. But, it's not necessary?

Secretary Rumsfeld. Well, you'd prefer it. The president has indicated that he will—if Saddam Hussein doesn't cooperate, and he doesn't flee, and he isn't removed, and he is—the president is determined to see that he is disarmed, then he will lead, as he said, a coalition of willing countries, and it will be a large coalition. There will be a lot of countries.

Remarks by Secretary of State Powell, February 21, 2003

Q. I'd like to change subjects for just a minute. Do you know if the Blix letter on the missiles, on whether the missiles would be destroyed, has come out yet? And what it says?

Secretary Powell. I don't know and I would really have to refer that to Blix himself. I don't think it has, but don't take that for the record. I'll have Richard check. I don't know what might have happened today, but I can't answer the question.

Q. What would your choice be? Do you want the missiles destroyed or do you want them disabled in some way?

Secretary Powell. We believe they are prohibited, we believe the test stand was designed for a prohibited purpose, we believe all of the engines that have been brought in are prohibited, and therefore believe they ought to be destroyed.

Q. Could you give us an update on Turkey and the negotiations?

Secretary Powell. I think we've made some progress. The information I have, which I was talking to you about this morning, I'll give you now for the record. We have been contacted by the Turkish authorities through our Ambassador and they say there are some outstanding issues with respect to the three documents we were discussing with them and on some of the ideas that we had for flexibility with respect to economic assistance.

Our teams will be working intensively over the next 2 to 3 days to resolve these issues. They're difficult, but they should be resolvable. And if they are resolved, then we believe the possibility exists for the Turkish government to take this to their parliament early next week. It is not yet a done deal, but there has been progress in the last 12 hours. The next question I think will be, has 6 billion dollars remained the number? The answer is yes. We're trying to see how much flexibility there is in the use of that 6 billion dollars, in order to assist them in the months ahead.

Remarks by President Bush and Spanish President Aznar, February 22, 2003

President Bush and President Jose Maria Aznar delivered their remarks while meeting in Crawford, Texas.

President Bush. I welcome my good friend, President Jose Maria Aznar, to Crawford. We're especially pleased that Ana is with him, as well. I visited his ranch on my first visit to Europe as the President. I'm very pleased to return the hospitality.

Spain is a strong and trusted ally. Our two nations have drawn closer than ever before in fighting terrorism across Europe and beyond. Spain has apprehended members of al Qaeda and continues to share vital information—intelligence information. President Aznar is a strong fighter in the war against terror, and I value his advice.

I respect and appreciate his leadership in the U.N., the EU and NATO, to meet the new threats of this new century. For the Spanish people and for their leader, the cause of liberty is more than a phrase; it is a fundamental commitment expressed in resolute action.

President Aznar and I agree that the future of peace depends on the disarmament of Iraq. We agree that Saddam Hussein continues to be in violation of U.N. Security Council Resolution 1441. We agree that the terms of that resolution must be fully respected. By Resolution 1441, the Security Council has taken a clear stand, and it now faces a clear choice. With all the world watching, the Council will now show whether it means what it says.

Early next week, working with our friends and allies, we will introduce an additional Security Council resolution that will set out in clear and

simple terms that Iraq is not complying with Resolution 1441. For the record, this would not be a second resolution on Iraq's weapons of mass destruction, it would only be the latest in a long series of resolutions, going back 12 years.

We will discuss this resolution with members of the Security Council, and we will hear again from Chief Inspector Blix. During these final deliberations, there is but one question for the Council to address, is Saddam Hussein complying with Resolution 1441. That resolution did not ask for hints of progress or minor concessions. It demanded full and immediate disarmament. That, and that alone, is the issue before the Council. We will not allow the Iraqi dictator, with a history of aggression and close ties to terrorist groups, to continue to possesses or produce weapons of mass destruction.

Our coalition draws its strength from the courage and moral clarity of leaders like President Aznar. In times of testing, we discover who is willing to stand up for the security of free peoples and the rights of mankind.

Mr. President, you are clearly a man willing to take this stand. I thank you for your leadership. I thank you for your friendship.

President Aznar. Well, good morning, good day to everyone. I would firstly like to thank, on behalf of my wife and for myself, I would like to thank Laura Bush and George Bush for their invitation to visit the ranch. And this is a time to work, to rest, to talk in truly marvelous surroundings.

Spain is an EU member and a non-permanent member of the U.N. Security Council. Spain is very clearly in favor of the strength of the transatlantic link. In these three extremely important dimensions, Spain is committed with an active role in contributing to an appropriate response to the threat that Saddam Hussein's regime entails for international peace and security. We've worked very hard, and with good results, to forge consensus within the European Union that it is necessary to maintain. We share the efforts and the needs within the Security Council that the international community has to maintain to guarantee peace and security in the world.

Precisely, it is in the Security Council that the international community has laid the responsibility of maintaining world peace and security. Our responsibility is precisely to work so that the Security Council can exercise its responsibilities, working in order to achieve in agreement the firm compliance of international legality.

I cannot but underline the importance of that relationship in our struggle against terrorism. We free societies are the targets of terrorists, and they must be fought unconditionally, with no reservations and not being allowed to be blackmailed by them. And we cannot be kidnapped by this fear that—we cannot be the hostages of the terrorists, and we will not be.

And allow me to say two things in this regard. Cooperation between the United States and Spain against terrorism is total. And I would like to thank President Bush for his resolve and his commitment in this regard. And secondly, I would like to express how satisfied I am in the—again having arrested important terrorists today in Spain, people who only think of murdering and committing crimes.

Spain is a democratic and European voice, and we know that there cannot be peace without law, and that peace cannot be separate from security. And in these international law and—the disarmament obligations that Saddam Hussein has been subject to for the last 12 years must be implemented. And this has to be based on the will and everyone's commitment and our capacity to do so.

We have expressly reaffirmed Resolution 1441. Resolution 1441 and the usefulness of the military capabilities deployed in order to achieve Saddam's disarmament. We are committed to peace, and peace is our horizon. But if we are unable to combat aggressive dictators, tyrannic regimes, this is something that endangers the very existence of international peace and harmony. And if we are incapable of guaranteeing this peace, international peace would become senseless rhetoric. And we honestly do not want to get into rhetoric when we're speaking of international order, weapons of mass destruction, terrorist groups, lives in danger, or threats that we have to confront.

Thus, my position in my talks with President Bush can be summarized as follows. Expressly, we are ready to fight together against weapons of mass destruction and terrorism—that is, for a world in peace and for a safe world. And we are working in order that the U.N. Security Council, in its role based on the U.N. Charter, may work towards peace and security in the world through a new resolution that has the greatest support, and majority support.

Our aim is for Iraq to disarm and for Saddam to comply with his obligations. And international legality has to be credible and we have to strengthen our efforts, we have to continue with our pressure on Saddam Hussein, and do all this in unity and in agreement within the framework of the Security Council. Of course, time is not indefinite; we don't have much time.

And lastly, as I already talked about with President Bush, we have to work towards peace and security in the region. And this requires quick action on our part to solve the Palestinian- Israeli conflict. In that scenario, we are also ready and willing to work jointly.

Q. Mr. President, you need nine votes in the Security Council, and no vetoes. And yet, as of this point, only four countries have spoken out in favor of moving forward and no minds seem to have been changed. Are you ready to move ahead now with this new resolution, even if you don't have the votes to pass it?

And to the Prime Minister—President Aznar—you've been making many calls yourself to world leaders and members of the Security Council. Have you been able to change anyone's mind? And if not, why not?

President Bush. There's not even a resolution put on the table yet. There will be one soon. And so the people will be able to see what they're asked to vote on. We just got off a phone call with Tony Blair and Silvio Berlusconi. It was a four-way conversation to talk about the resolution and the strategy.

This discussion sounds vaguely familiar. I think I remember getting asked the same questions prior to the last resolution, the Resolution 1441 that passed 15 to zero; where the Security Council said, with a unanimous voice, Saddam must disarm. He hasn't disarmed. And so the clarity of vision that took place four months ago I'm confident will be in place after the Security Council takes a good look at the facts. And so we're just beginning, is my point.

President Aznar. I hear many messages on unilateral actions. But what I must say is that President Bush, the U.S. government and all the allies are all working together in the framework of the United Nations. And that's how Resolution 1441 came out. And that's how the new resolution we're working on has to come out.

It's difficult to ask for an agreement on something that doesn't exist yet. We'll ask for people's agreement when it does exist. We hope it's soon. We hope it's good. And we hope it assembles the greatest possible supporters. Because what we cannot forget is that our aim is disarmament and to avoid the threat that weapons of mass destruction, a possible use by Saddam Hussein, the threat that this poses to the world.

Q. My question is for the Spanish President of the government. Regarding this new proposal for a new resolution, we know it will bear the seal of the United States and of Great Britain. But will it also bear the Spanish seal? Will Spain be considered or will it be a co-author of that resolution?

President Aznar. Well, we're working on it, and we devoted some time last night and this morning to precisely that. And we want to be as clear as possible in that it has as many possible supporters in the Security Council. And as I said, our commitment is a very active commitment, and it's also very active in supporting this resolution. We know very much and very well what we're handling here and what's at stake. And what we want for the world is peace and security, and that's what we're working for with our best will, in order not to be submitted to blackmail of any kind. We're not thinking of our comfort, but of our responsibility. We want peace, freedom and prosperity for all.

Q. It took almost two months to get Resolution 1441 out of the Security Council. Are you willing to wait that long this time, and is this the really last chance for the United Nations to prove its relevancy?

President Bush. Yes. Si. Last chance.

Q. Are you going to wait that long?

President Bush. No. As the President said, time is short. And this is a chance for the Security Council to show its relevance. And I believe the Security Council will show its relevance, because Saddam Hussein has not disarmed.

President Aznar. What I want to say is that if Resolution 1441 states that it's Saddam's last opportunity, that means that time cannot be long, because the last opportunity has already been given to him. What we have to verify now is whether he has disarmed, or not. If we now said that time was infinite, it would be a laugh. It would be very difficult for anyone to take us seriously, beginning with the United Nations. That would be the worst possible message we could send for peace.

Q. My question is addressed to both Presidents. I would like to know whether in your proposed resolution you are going to be talking about the al-Samoud long-range missiles and whether you are going to be—because Iraq has today mentioned that it was ready to start destroying them—and whether in your resolution you're going to be speaking about an ultimatum, a deadline, or a threat for the use of force. What do you think this is going to be—what are you going to contain?

President Bush. We're in the process of discussing the language. If Iraq decides to destroy the weapons that were long- range weapons, that's just the tip of the iceberg. My question is, why don't they destroy every weapon—illegal weapon.

Saddam Hussein wants time. And after all, he thinks he will get time, because he has done so—he has deceived the world for 12 years. He'll play like he's going to disarm; he has no intention of disarming. Otherwise, he would have done so. He'll say words that encourage—that sound encouraging. He's done so for 12 years. And so the idea of destroying a rocket or two rockets or however many he's going to destroy says to me that he's got a lot more weapons to destroy, and why hadn't he destroyed them yet?

In terms of language, that's exactly why we—that's exactly why Jose Maria and I are talking. And we'll let you know what's in the resolution when we put it down.

President Aznar. Well, what I want to say is that we cannot designate Saddam Hussein as the manager of international peace and security. We've been with this item on the agenda for 12 years. And what we cannot do is play this game in which you have inspectors are handed over something, everything is going well, but if it isn't, well, that means they're hiding weapons.

So the world can make these mistakes, but the mistake we cannot make is to let Saddam Hussein being the one managing peace and a threat. And that's why we're working so intensely towards a new resolution. And that's why I'm convinced and that's why we're all working towards these common aspirations of peace, security and freedom for the world.

Remarks by Secretary of State Powell, February 23, 2003

Secretary Colin Powell delivered his remarks while visiting Tokyo, Japan.

In my conversations with the Prime Minister and with the Foreign Minister, as you might expect, we spent a considerable amount of time discussing the situation in Iraq and the challenge that will be facing the United Nations in the days ahead. I indicated to the Prime Minister that the United States, working with the United Kingdom and other nations, would be tabling a resolution sometime early next week that will ask the United Nations to take note of the fact—as the Security Council to take note of the fact—that Iraq still is not complying—that Iraq is not taking advantage of the one last chance given to it by U.N. Resolution 1441. The resolution that will be tabled will be a simple resolution, directly to the point, and once it has been tabled there will be a period of consultation among Security Council members—among international leaders around the world—before a judgment is made with respect to bringing that resolution to a vote or whatever other action the Security Council might consider.

The bottom line, however, is that time is running out for Iraq. We cannot sit by and idly let Iraq continue to thwart the will of the international community. The issue is not more inspectors. The issue is not more time for inspections. The issue is disarmament. The issue is Iraq complying with the will of the international community and participating in its disarmament and allowing the inspectors, or those who are there to monitor their activities, get on with their work—give them everything they need to do their work. Iraq still has not identified the errors in their declarations and how to fix those errors in their declaration. They keep saying: "Just read the declaration again." We've read it again; it still fails. It is an inaccurate declaration that does not comply with the requirements of 1441.

Iraq's still not accounted for the terrible materials that we know they have: anthrax, boutulinum toxin, the missiles that they have, the other weapons that we know they have, the programs that they have had underway over the years. It is these programs that Iraq must come forward and let the monitors and the inspectors know the disposition of or what happened to them. It's not a matter of the inspectors wandering all over Iraq looking for these materials, looking for these programs. So we face the same problem that we faced at the beginning when we first put 1441 forward, and that is Iraq is still not complying and time is drawing to a close when the international community—the Security Council—must show its relevance by insisting that Iraq disarm or that Iraq be disarmed by a coalition of forces that will go in and do it.

* * * *

Q. Mr. Secretary, the people in Japan have been watching the Iraqi situation with great seriousness. Despite our government's basic support for the U.S. position on Iraq, the evidence that you presented to the Security Council has failed to convince the majority of the Japanese people that you need to go to war now. So do you have anything new, anything different, that you can present to the Japanese people, and could you please try again here today and explain to us why a war is necessary right now?

Secretary Powell. To go to the last part of the question: A war is not necessary. It is Saddam Hussein who is putting in place conditions that will perhaps result in war. It is Saddam Hussein who has accumulated these horrible weapons. The presentation that I gave to the Security Council on the 5th of February was a summary of evidence that we have and it was a summary, really, of evidence that has been known for a long period of time. I tried to put it all together in a way that people could see it. But it is not just an idle accusation or a lack of evidence; the evidence is there. If the evidence was not there in the beginning, Resolution 1441 wouldn't have passed in the first place. If you read the resolution, the resolution begins saying that Iraq is in material breach of its obligations—remains in material breach—and for years it has been denying the truth. We know that they have been experimenting with weapons of mass destruction of a nuclear kind. We had to catch them in lies to prove that they had certain chemical facilities and chemical materials available. We had to catch them in a lie to show back in the mid-nineties that they had biological materials—they were working with anthrax and boutulinum toxin. All of these have a singular purpose, and that is to destroy large numbers of human beings. So this evidence is not new evidence. What more evidence does one need? We know they have this material. This issue before us is they have not accounted for the material—they won't tell us what has happened to it. We have evidence that, and I tried to put forward some of that evidence on the 5th of February, that this material remains within Iraq—and we must assume it is there until they can demonstrate to us that it's not there.

If they were serious about disarmament—and this is right to the Japanese people—if Iraq was serious about disarmament, if they were not trying to deceive us as they have for the past twelve years, they would be doing everything in their power to bring forth all the documentation, all the information, let us interview anybody that we wanted to interview, and interview them anywhere that we wanted to interview them to make sure they were not being intimated. If Iraq was serious, they would be showing us where all the missiles are and not wondering whether the inspectors would find something or not find something. If Iraq was serious, this matter could be over in a short period of time. We would see full cooperation. If I was in the position of Saddam Hussein and I was trying to persuade the United Nations that I had no weapons of mass destruction, you would not have to ask me to bring forward scientists and engineers. I would bring them all forward; I'd line them all up in front of UNMOVIC headquarters and say: "Here they are. Take them anywhere you want. Ask them any questions you want. We will have nobody minding them. We will have no tape recorders so that we could get retribution later. Go take them and find out all you want. What documents do you need? We will bring back documents from all the places we've sent them in the homes of scientists."

We would not see this continued pattern of deception, which has not changed in twelve years. And it's time for us to stop saying, "Well, gosh, give us new evidence." The evidence is there. The evidence is clear. The evidence has been there for these past dozen years, and especially we have evidence up to 1998 when they threw out the inspectors. And so, it is not enough any longer to say, "We don't want to take action because we don't see enough evidence or more evidence." It is time to take action. The evidence has been clear. They are guilty; 1441 says they are guilty, and 1441 said if they don't fix this, if they don't comply now, if they don't cooperate now, then serious consequences must flow. We are reaching that point, where serious consequences must flow.

Q. You know, just following up that question for a moment, after 9/11, the whole world turned to us and said, "We're Americans like you," including the French. Last weekend we saw the largest series of antiwar, anti-American protests—in London certainly in its entire history. This follows what you have talked about at the Securi-

ty Council; it follows what's happened with the inspectors; it follows what's happening in Iraq. There seems to be a disconnect, I guess, between what America believes it should do, and what the rest of the world is perceiving. And I wonder why that is and if it isn't just a touch frustrating for you, since you're the man who is presenting and preparing this policy, and you've stood in front of the Security Council and tried to convince the world.

Secretary Powell. Yeah, I would prefer it if there were rallies saying that Iraq must disarm, but I have also seen previous situations in my professional career where on the eve of potential conflict there was a strong outpouring of support against that conflict. Nobody wants to see conflict. And when conflict is potentially in the near future, there will always be an outpouring that says, "Isn't there some other way?" I wish there were some other way. I have worked hard throughout my career to find ways other than conflict to solve problems, but sometimes you can't avoid it, and you must continue to do what you believe is the correct thing to do and the correct policy, even in the presence of demonstrations. People are free to demonstrate, and they don't see the danger the way we see the danger. We've studied this information for years. We've studied the evidence for years, and we continue to see Iraqi deception, Iraqi diversion of inspectors, Iraqi efforts to hide, Iraqi efforts to confuse. And all that does is persuade us that they continue to have these weapons and they are trying to hang onto them, and they have lost none of their intention to develop these kinds of weapons. And even though it might not be in all places the most popular thing to do, there are a number of world leaders who have stood up—such as Prime Minster Blair, such as Mr. Aznar of Spain, Mr. Berlusconi of Italy—a number of leaders who have stood up in many, many nations of Europe. Yes, there is public resistance in Europe and elsewhere. It's a difficult call for many people, but these leaders are standing up because they know they don't want to wonder a couple of years from now, when Iraq suddenly pops out and demonstrates in a way that can convince everybody that they had these weapons. They don't want to be in the position, and President Bush has made this clear—he doesn't want to be in the position of saying, "Why didn't we do something about this when we had mobilized the whole world?"

I also need to point out that 15 members of the Security Council sitting in session on the 8th of November, knowing what they were doing, said that Iraq is guilty, Iraq has to come into compliance, and if it doesn't, Iraq must face serious consequences. And that was not an idle statement on their part. We debated that statement for seven weeks, in the knowledge that the day might come when we have to make a judgment that Iraq has not complied, is not cooperating, and it is time for serious consequences.

Q. I think you'll put the resolution on the table Monday or Tuesday, but how long can you wait for the vote? Can you wait for a matter of weeks, or it's a matter of days? That's the first question. And what kind of support are you looking for from the Japanese government? Are you asking Mr. Koizumi to support or push or put pressure on the [*inaubible*] countries? That's the second part of the question, thank you.

Secretary Powell. On the second part of your question, the Prime Minister and I discussed this last night, as I did also with the Foreign Minister, and we hope that the

Prime Minister and the Foreign Minister, because they have been supporting our efforts, will continue to support those efforts. And as part of that support, in their conversations—normal diplomatic and head- of-government/state conversations—they will continue to support our efforts. And I hope that once they see the resolution, they would find it the appropriate thing to do to show support for that and to contact members who might be voting one way or another and express their support. That's part of diplomatic effort. There will be other nations, I'm sure, that will be calling around with a different message. And so, yes, we are into a period of intense diplomacy beginning after the tabling of the resolution next week, and we would hope that those who support our efforts would use their good offices to show that support. It isn't going to be a long period of time from the tabling of the resolution until a judgment is made as to whether the resolution is ready to be voted on or not. And I don't want to speculate as to how long that period of time might be, but one can see that Dr. Blix will be reporting to the Council on the 7th of March, and I would assume that once he has made that report, everybody will have one last opportunity to make a judgment. And shortly after that judgment will have to be made as to what the Security Council should do.

Remarks by National Security Advisor Rice, February 24, 2003

Today, as you probably heard, the United States and the United Kingdom and Spain today put down a draft resolution—a resolution before the Security Council that is an affirmation of the Council's willingness to uphold 1441, a resolution that was passed in November. The purpose of this resolution is to clearly state what we believe to be obvious, which is that Saddam Hussein, having been given one final opportunity to comply with the disarmament obligations that he undertook back in 1991 in order to end a war of aggression which he began, that he has, as the resolution says, "decides that Iraq has failed to take the final opportunity afforded to it in Resolution 1441."

That's really the critical line. It simply states that he failed to take the opportunity afforded to him in 1441, and in that sense, is an affirmation of the willingness of the Council to enforce its own resolutions and to stand up for its own resolutions.

We expect that over the next period of time there will be discussion of this resolution. I'm sure it's already being discussed, and it will be discussed among members. People will talk to capitals. And Hans Blix will report on March 7th, as you know, and we would expect that not too long after that, there will need to be a decision about the resolution.

So, with that, I will—

Q. Dr. Rice, if the resolution is passed, would the United States government interpret it as being an authorization for military action?

Dr. Rice. As you know, we believe that the authorization to enforce the United Nations Security Council resolutions exist already in a number of resolutions, going all the way back to 1991. And I would just remind everybody that 1441 makes very clear that further material breach by Saddam Hussein's failure to comply with 1441 would bring serious consequences. So we believe the authorization is already there.

Q. What does that one line actually mean? And why did you decide to do a resolution that has—that's one page long and has only one new sentence in it?

Dr. Rice. Resolution 1441 is a very powerful resolution. And Resolution 1441 says all that there is about the need for Iraq to comply, about the obligations that Iraq undertook when it ended the war—when the war was ended in 1991, and the new obligations that were placed on Iraq were full and complete compliance with 1441, back in November when it was passed. So it wasn't necessary to have a long resolution; it was just important to reference 1441, which is a very powerful resolution in its own right.

And I might just note that the "whereas" clauses preceding that last line point, for instance, to the important operative paragraphs like the importance of filing a full and complete declaration, and then providing full cooperation to UNMOVIC, neither of which Iraq has done.

Q. But you didn't—I mean, you could have said in that sentence, for instance, that they are now and continue to be in material breach, but did not. It appears that this was an effort to get a resolution that would be as small a target as possible for those who were inclined not to make a decision at this point.

Dr. Rice. I would call it an efficient resolution, in that it is very clearly linked to everything that everybody agreed to in 1441. And so if you agreed to 1441, and you have to agree that Iraq did not file a full and complete declaration, which I think is now common wisdom, and if you have to agree that Iraq is not fully cooperating and complying with the obligations that it undertook in 1441—for instance, refusing—still refusing to have scientists interviewed privately, still refusing to make available documentation for a whole variety of past programs that are unaccounted for, negotiating with the inspectors about how the U-2 will fly—if you accept that, then you have to accept that they're not in full compliance. You have to accept that they failed to take their final opportunity. And I would think it would be hard to vote against this.

Q. If this did not pass, you would then be in the position of having everybody in agreement on 1441, but having the Security Council on the record as not having approved the resolution that he was—had turned down his final chance. That would seem to make it more difficult for you to do what you said many times you would do, which is go ahead and enforce it with a coalition of the willing. Are you willing to be in a position where you are running contrary to the Security Council if you did lose? And what would constitute victory here? Nine votes and a veto? Nine votes and no veto?

Dr. Rice. Well, obviously, we would like to have the Security Council uphold the obligations that it undertook when it passed 1441 unanimously. Again, if he's not filed a full, complete, and fair declaration—which he did not on December 8th—and if he is not fully cooperating in his own disarmament, if he's trying to turn the inspectors, instead, into detectives, then he's not in compliance with 1441. And this resolution simply notes in the language of 1441 that that will have meant that he has passed on his final opportunity to comply.

We will see what people do. But again, it's hard for me to understand how you can vote for 1441, witness what has gone on from December—or from November until now, and argue the converse of this, that he has taken advantage of his final opportunity to comply.

Q. I'm not sure that was responsive to the question, though. The question is, if you don't have a victory—first of all, if you can define victory—but if you don't have a victory, are you ready to be—to run counter to a vote—

Dr. Rice. Well, the President has made very clear that the Security Council needs to act and that, if the Security Council is unable to act, then we will have to act with a coalition of the willing. It's—again, David, the language of this says he's not taken advantage of his final opportunity to comply. It's going to be awfully hard to argue that he has taken advantage of his final opportunity to comply. And so the Security Council is, I think, now on—is now there and must really take a decision to see whether or not it's going to enforce its own resolutions.

And I can't define victory for you. Victory will be if the—victory for the Security Council will be if it is able to carry out its obligations to enforce its resolutions.

Q. The President at one point didn't think a second resolution was necessary; now that's the argument that France and Germany have taken up. So I have two questions. First of all, what argument now does the U.S. make to sort of get around that argument, that we don't need this? And then, secondly, if Iraq turns over the missiles for destruction before this is—how much higher is your mountain then to try to get this resolution passed, because then France and Germany could argue, see, some weapons have been destroyed?

Dr. Rice. It's been the position of the United States all along that we didn't need a second resolution. But as the President said, it would be welcome to have a second resolution that would once again affirm that the Security Council is prepared to enforce its own resolutions. And so that's the purpose of this.

It was also, of course, important for a number of other countries that we seek a second resolution. I think you know that for a number of our closest allies it was an important step to take. And so, while we still don't believe that it was necessary—all the authorization necessary was in 1441 and previous resolutions—it seemed a wise thing to do, and it does give people a chance to affirm, one more time, not the second resolution, but you know, depending on how you count, the 18th resolution that calls on Saddam Hussein's regime to comply.

As to missile destruction, it would be a good thing if he destroyed these missiles, because 687 requires that he does. It's obvious that the inspectors have decided that they are proscribed, they are beyond the prohibited—the proscribed range. But that's just the tip of the iceberg. That's just the beginning of a long list of things that would constitute disarmament. Because, after all, we're talking about missing anthrax and missing botulinum toxin and missing VX and missing sarin gas. We're talking about a long list of documents that are missing to give any confidence to the world as to what happened to all of those deadly—we're talking about biological—mobile biological weapons labs that have—now we have confirmation from several sources exist that Saddam Hussein continues to hide. So there's a long list of disarmament tasks.

Q. But wouldn't it give the momentum to the other side, though, if the—now maybe they'll get the anthrax.

Dr. Rice. I think the problem—and we can just expect this to happen over the next couple weeks, I can absolutely predict that it's going to happen over the next couple weeks—that Saddam Hussein will do what he's done over the last 12 years. Whenever he's under tremendous pressure, he puts forward a little cooperation in hopes that he can release the pressure. And then he goes back to cheating and retreating and deceiving again. And then, when things get a little hot again, he puts forward a little bit more cooperation.

What 1441 says is full and complete compliance with his disarmament obligations; 1441 says one final opportunity to comply. It does not say, one final opportunity to cooperate a little bit, or final opportunity to make a little bit of progress, or final opportunity to offer up one of your weapons programs. It says, total and complete. And so, it's not going to be acceptable this time, this game.

Q. Condi, a little bit about the fact that CBS is reporting based on an interview that, in fact, this is maybe a moot point because he's saying that he's not going to destroy the Al Samoud missiles. What's—

Dr. Rice. Well, he's been in contempt for the last 12 years. I guess he intends to continue to be in contempt on that issue, as well as the many, many others in which he's in contempt.

Q. Dr. Rice, pass or fail, will the vote on this resolution signal the end—the exhaustion of all diplomatic options here? How is your work over the next three weeks complicated by the resolution—or the package that the French and the Germans put on the table today, and the Chinese have apparently supported? And in terms of final opportunities for diplomacy, will it be helpful for the President to meet face to face with some of these leaders in the interim?

Dr. Rice. Well, I've not seen the package that the other parties put on the table. I've seen reports of some elements of it. But what it says to me is that it's a strong admittance that what is happening now is not working; that the inspectors are not getting the kind of cooperation that they need; that Saddam Hussein is not disarming; that he is not voluntarily complying and that somehow more inspectors or monitors or more effort is somehow going to make him comply. And I just think it's illogical to believe that he is going to somehow comply in the face of more monitors when he isn't complying, given the pressures of 1441, given the force buildup in the region.

It seems to me that you have the worst of both worlds. You've admitted that the—that 1441 is not being complied with, but you're trying to somehow alter and play with

1441 to make him more capable of complying with it. I don't think it's going to work, and I don't—and it's certainly is not of interest. What we need here is for the Iraqis to fully and completely disarm, or for the Security Council to do what it needs to do and enforce it's own resolutions.

Q. Will he be meeting face to face with some of these leaders?

Dr. Rice. The President has met face to face with a lot of people recently. Just with President Aznar,; and he's, of course, been with Prime Minister Blair, and Prime Minister Berlusconi. I'm sure he's open to meeting with anybody. But he's been on the telephone a lot with a lot of leaders, as well as has Secretary Powell. I have, and a number of people have. So the diplomacy will be very intense in this period of time, and we'll see what we think may be effective.

Q. I'm sorry, can I just follow up?

Dr. Rice. Yes.

Q. You describe this second resolution as efficient. Could it also be described as artful in this sense that it is, in your view, boxing in those opponents to this resolution? They're boxing in, in the sense that they are linked to 1441 which they approved, and therefore, if they veto it, as David raises, that you feel like you've got a ready-made argument to say, what are you vetoing? Are you vetoing yourself?

Dr. Rice. I just think that that's the case. The case is that 1441 was a resolution—was unanimously approved, and Saddam Hussein has, by nobody's calculation, complied with 1441. He didn't file a complete and fair declaration. He isn't cooperating actively with the inspectors. He's making some faint cooperation on process, but on substance there remain myriad unanswered questions. So you can't argue that he's complying. This says he's not complying with 1441. It seems to me that if you voted for 1441, it's hard to vote against this.

Q. Dr. Rice, I'm sorry, could I ask you to come back to Bob's first question whether the vote, pass or fail, represents the exhaustion of the last diplomatic option—

Dr. Rice. Yes, I'm sorry, I didn't answer that. There may be other options that people will want to explore, but the focus has to be now on disarming Saddam Hussein and making certain that he can no longer threaten international peace and security. Anything that does not achieve that, the world should not be willing to settle for.

Q. But there may be other—

Dr. Rice. Well, there have been those who have talked about his leaving, and I don't know if that is a possibility. But there are those who have talked about his leaving. But what I can assure you is that there are no deals to be struck here with the Iraqi leadership. There are no deals to be struck here about just a little bit of compliance or a schedule for compliance, or something along those lines. And the sorts of things that he was able to do in '96, I think there's no room for those.

Q. So when you say, talk about the focus shifting—talking about your focus shifting to forcibly disarming him if he's still there?

Dr. Rice. It is hard to imagine any other way, if he has failed to voluntarily disarm, to disarm him except forcibly.

Q. What is your strategy for getting up to nine votes? Do you hope to pick off Russia and China and isolate France, or some other strategy? What are you—

Dr. Rice. Well, we're going to work with everybody. We aren't counting votes and saying, well, that one is off limits, or that vote can't be won. Since people voted 15-0 for 1441, the logic of it is that we ought to be able to get votes for this resolution, as well, because this resolution is so clearly in support of 1441.

So we'll have an all-out diplomatic effort—we and the British and the Spanish and others will have an all-out diplomatic effort to talk to various parties about the logic of this resolution, and hopefully to bring people around to vote for it. But I wouldn't, at this point, say that we believe any vote is off limits.

Q. It seems clear to the Americans and the British that 1441 is not being complied with, and you have a majority of the members of the Council, at this point, seem willing to let the inspections continue. Is there a sense that you're being too artful in your language here? You're getting resolutions that, in the case of 1441, all of the members of the Security Council can agree with, and yet all don't agree on whether Iraq is complying with it. Blair had the same problem with the newest resolution.

Dr. Rice. I don't hear very many people saying he's complied with 1441. I've heard arguments about more time, or more inspectors. The paper that was put down today—if it contains what I've been told it contains—again suggests that 1441 isn't working; therefore, we have to try something different. So I don't think anybody is saying he's complying with 1441.

Our point is, and the point of the British and others, and the reason that we believe it was time to bring this now, is that he should not be allowed to play this game for an infinite amount of time, trying to split the Council, trying to play public opinion, continuing to cheat and retreat like he's done since 1991.

And if there's a difference, I think it's about the timing. But I don't think anybody would argue that that declaration was full and fair and complete, or that he is complying. All you have to do is look at the reports that Drs. Blix and ElBaradei have made, that talk about the need for more active cooperation, that talk about the need for the Iraqis to actually comply, that if the Iraqis were actually complying, then this job could get done. But the Blix and ElBaradei reports don't talk about an Iraq that is fully complying with 1441.

Q. So if the difference is about the timing, then why doesn't the resolution address that, set a deadline?

Dr. Rice. Because Saddam Hussein has had plenty of deadlines in his life. The main thing here is to get everybody focused on bringing this to a conclusion, because the world has waited not three months or four months, it has waited 12 years. The Iraqi people continue to live under sanctions in an abnormal condition because for 12 years the international community has been unable to deal with Saddam Hussein's defiance.

We all continue to live under the threat of continued programs of weapons of mass destruction linked to someone who's got links to terrorism. It's time to deal with this problem. And so it should be very clear by now that when the President said, weeks, not months, he really did mean, weeks, not months.

Q. All that diplomatic effort you talk about, some of the countries whose votes you need are either very dependent on American friendship, or particularly benefit from it. What are the consequences for a Mexico, a Chile, or an Angola voting against this resolution? What are you telling them?

Dr. Rice. Well, we're going to try to convince people that their responsibilities as members of the Security Council necessitate a vote that will strengthen the role of the Security Council in international politics, not weaken it. Because we've got a lot of tough issues ahead of us. As you know, North Korea was just referred to the Security Council. There are going to be a lot of difficult issues. The IAEA is trying to make sense of what's going on is Iran. The international community has a lot of hard work to do on weapons of mass destruction. And so we're going to try to convince people that the Security Council needs to be strong here.

This is an important issue, a critically important issue for the United States, because the President of the United States believes very strongly that the American people are under threat, that American security interests are under threat, and that world peace and security is threatened by Saddam Hussein. So no one should underestimate the importance of this issue for the United States and the importance of America's resolve in getting this done.

But we'll talk to people, and we'll make both the case about the U.N. Security Council and the importance of this issue to the United States.

Q. Two very quick questions. One is, have you got any readout from Russia, I guess, your ally in this process, about Mr. Primakov's visit to Baghdad? And, secondly, I'm not clear about the timing issue. As you say, you identify that's the big issue for the Europeans, and you are effectively setting a deadline by saying you would like to get this addressed in the U.N. the week after March the 7th. Why not do what you did in 1441, which was allow it to string out for a few extra weeks, and bring the whole world on board?

Dr. Rice. Well, 1441 was a different kind of resolution. There was, frankly, a lot to discuss and negotiate about 1441: what would be the precise character of the weapons inspections, how were you strengthening the weapons inspectors. There were just a lot of issues that had to be dealt with in 1441. But this is not a resolution that lends itself to that kind of discussion. This is really now an up or down on whether or not the Security Council is going to enforce Resolution 1441. And so it doesn't lend itself to the same kinds of discussions.

But we're perfectly willing—over the next period of time, we'll have the Blix report, and then shortly after we would hope to have a vote. But the diplomacy here is of a different character than what had to go into 1441, which was really constructing a new inspections regime in order to give Saddam Hussein one final opportunity to comply.

Resolution 1441 was a big departure from the way that the inspections regimes had been structured in the past. In the past they really had been trying to give the inspectors the ability to hunt and see what they could find, and to go into this palace or that palace. Resolution 1441 was designed as a very intensive test of Saddam Hussein's willingness to disarm. It was a test of whether or not he was going to behave like South Africa or Kazakhstan, and actually voluntarily disarm. And in that sense, there was a lot of work to be done on how to put together that kind of regime. This is a very different kind of resolution.

Q. And Primakov?

Dr. Rice. I've not gotten a readout. He's, I'm sure, reporting to Moscow. But we went through this in 1991. I was the Soviet specialist in 1991.

Q. Dr. Rice, you were talking about exile as a one last possible diplomatic resolution. If we did see an exile situation, would the United States want to see Saddam Hussein tried before an international court?

Dr. Rice. Look, I think that the—this is something that the international community will have to discuss and come to terms with. My only point is that if—if he wanted to leave and give his people a chance to build a better life, I think that is something that the world would applaud at this point.

Q. Would we help him?

Dr. Rice. Something the international community would need to discuss. But there are several things that would still need to be done. And a post-Saddam Iraq, however that happens, has to deal with the weapons of mass destruction and the disarmament of the country; has to deal—has to ensure the territorial integrity of Iraq; has to ensure that sectarian violence does not break out; and needs to put the Iraqi people on a path toward a more democratic future. And those goals remain, however one gets to a post-Saddam Iraq, if we do.

Q. On exile, do you have any more indication that it is a viable possibility than you all had in the past couple of weeks?

Dr. Rice. No.

Remarks by Secretary of State Powell, February 24, 2003

Secretary Colin Powell delivered his remarks in Beijing, China.

Let me begin by saying it is a great sight to be back in China. This is my third visit to Beijing since becoming Secretary and my fourth visit to China, which I think illustrates the importance that we attach to this relationship. And in this visit so far I've had excellent meetings with Vice President Hu and Foreign Minister Tang, and I am looking forwarding to meeting right after this brief press conference with President Jiang Zemin.

Vice President Cheney will further our high level dialogue during his visit this spring. Our relations with China have really moved to a new dimension. In addition to three meetings in 18 months, President Bush and President Jiang have had frequent phone calls and I meet with my counterpart, Foreign Minister Tang, almost every other week now. In between, we two communicate by phone on a regular basis. The U.S. and China are now addressing, through these many ways of dialogue, issues of worldwide concern, not just to us bilaterally, but issues that affect the entire world.

As a fellow permanent member of the Security Council, we work closely with our Chinese colleagues to ensure for example that Iraq cannot continue to threaten international peace and security. I discussed with Foreign Minister Tang and with Vice President Hu earlier today the need for us to take action in the near future with respect to Iraq and noted that early this week, we and the United Kingdom will be tabling a new resolution that will make clear that time is running out on Iraq and that Iraq has so far not taken the opportunity given to it under U.N. Resolution 1441 to come into compliance with its international obligations.

The United States believes strongly, and I conveyed this to my Chinese interlocutors today, that it is time for Saddam to disarm or depart, and for the Security Council to get ready to live up to its responsibilities if Saddam does not meet his responsibilities.

* * * *

Q. Over the past few weeks you have had frequent contact with Mr. Tang Jiaxuan. I wonder how the United States makes sure that China's interests will not be harmed in Iraq after the war against Saddam Hussein.

Secretary Powell. Yes, I have had quite a number of opportunities to meet with Minister Tang. We have been doing everything we can to avoid a war. We have been using the United Nations, both the United States and China and other members of the Security Council. We're working hard to see if we can get Iraq to comply and avoid a war and there is still time to avoid a war. We must not be afraid of a conflict, if a conflict is what it takes to remove weapons of mass destruction from Iraq. We are not talking to any of our friends and colleagues about "slicing up the pie" so to speak after the conflict. If there is a conflict and the United States leads a coalition into Iraq, everything we do during that conflict and after that conflict will be for the purpose of providing a better life for the Iraqi people. And with respect to such issues as oil and their other natural assets, those assets belong to the Iraqi people and everything we do would preserve those assets and make sure they serve the Iraqi people and not anyone else. And so, I am sure that China shares that same point of view if a conflict comes, but China is working just as hard as the United States to see if such a conflict can be avoided. But the Security Council must meet its responsibilities if Iraq does not comply. That was the clear intent of U.N. Resolution 1441 when it was passed in November. We now have four months of experience, almost, with that resolution, and so far Iraq continues to play games, continues to deceive, continues to let out a little bit here, a little bit there, but has not answered the basic questions: What happened to the anthrax? Where is the botulism toxin? What have you done with the missiles? Why aren't you getting us the documents that are needed? Why can't people be interviewed without having minders and tape recorders present? Stop the game. But the game continues because that is Saddam Hussein's intent, to try to hang onto these weapons of mass destruction, and that must not be allowed. That was the clear intent of Resolution 1441. To end his possession, to make sure that weapons of mass destruction no longer exist in Iraq and that it will happen one way or the other—peacefully or through the use of force.

* * * *

Q. My question is also about Iraq. Just as you mentioned the resolution of United Nations, if the United Nations does not produce a resolution which permits the United States to take military action towards Iraq, what will United States do next step? In the opinion of the United States, what is role of United Nations? That's all, thank you.

Secretary Powell. We hope that Iraq will comply. That is the reason why we went to the United Nations in the first place to get a strong Resolution 1441, that made it clear that the international community was unified and that Iraq had to disarm. If Iraq does not comply and the United Nations, in the presence of that noncompliance refuses to act, I think it would be a bad day for the United Nations—not willing to step up to its responsibilities. And, as President Bush has said all along, he reserves the right to lead a coalition of the willing to disarm Iraq if the United Nations is not willing to provide a coalition to do so. We believe that there is sufficient authority in Resolution 1441, 678 and 687 and earlier resolutions for such action, but it is also clear that if Iraq is not complying, a second resolution would be very, very helpful in order to make the case to the international community. And so let us hope that a peaceful solution can be found. But let's also not lose sight of the fact that the only reason that Iraq has done anything—anything—in the last four to six months is because of the threat of force and because of the unity of the international community. This is not the time to step away from this responsibility. This is the time to disarm Iraq, one way or the other.

Q. What does China stand to gain if it were to support the new resolution that you will propose at the United Nations? If it were to support the new resolution that you plan to table in the U.N.?

Secretary Powell. That's not the right question. The right question is, the whole world, what the whole world stands to gain? What we stand to gain is a rogue regime such as Iraq not having weapons of mass destruction, chemical, biological, or nuclear weapons with which to threaten their neighbors, or perhaps even become a source of such weaponry to terrorists. We should focus on that regime and what it has done and how it has tried to deceive the world for these past twelve years about its weapons of mass destruction and its intent to develop even more weapons of mass destruction. The burden for this crisis rests squarely with Iraq and with Saddam Hussein.

Q. So, I want to ask you two questions. The first: You showed yourself to the world as a dove in the Afghanistan war, but you now become a hawk in Iraqi issues and speak words just like Rumsfeld, so why you change? The second question is, you want to persuade China to don't give their veto to Iraq resolutions and you want China to give more pressure to North Korea. What's the exchange, what do you give some gift to China, for example: Taiwan issues.

Secretary Powell. It's very unwise to stereotype people with one-word labels. I have always advocated peaceful solutions to international crises. I've been a soldier. I've fought in wars. I've lost friends in wars. I've sent men and women to die in battle. So, I hate war. And anything that can be done to avoid a war should be done. But when a war cannot be avoided, fight it and fight it well. Now, what does that make me? You pick. But that is my personal philosophy. Avoid war, but if you have to fight it, do it well, get it over with and get back to building the peace. And that remains our philosophy and we have tried in every way possible to prevent there being a conflict with Iraq. But it is Iraq that is denying the world the opportunity for a peaceful solution.

CBS News Interview of Iraqi President Hussein, February 24, 2003

Iraqi President Saddam Hussein was interviewed by Dan Rather of CBS News. Text and translation from the Iraqi Permanent Mission to the United Nations.

Q. [On destroying the Sumoud Missiles.]

President Hussein. We are committed to dealing and implementing Resolution 1441 as demanded by the United Nations. It is on this basis that we have acted and shall continue to act. As you know, Iraq is allowed under U.N. resolutions, to develop land-to-land missiles of a range of 150 kilometers. And we are committed to complying to these specifications. We have no missiles exceeding this range, and the inspection teams have searched everywhere. Indeed I think you should seek an answer to this question from them.

I believe that the U.S. and the world should know by now that Iraq does not possess any of the weapons claimed by top-ranking officials in the U.S. and the U.K..

I think that part of this fabricated campaign, together with the military build-up underway, is meant to cover the huge lie that Iraq is in possession of nuclear, chemical and biological weapons of mass destruction, and it is on this basis that resolution

1441 was adopted. Although Iraq is absolutely certain that it is void of any WMDs, as indeed has been confirmed by all officials concerned, and in order that Iraq's position may not be misinterpreted, Iraq has accepted resolution 1441 so that the facts are made clear. This is why, missiles such as the ones you are referring to, which exceed in range the limits set under U.N. resolutions, do not exist in Iraq any longer, because they have all been destroyed in the past as announced at the time.

Q. [On core-issues.]

President Hussein. In all divine religions, God has stressed to mankind in all scriptures, that the tow most important things in life, after the creation of man and Faith, are food and peace. This is true of Islam, Christianity and other religions. So peace, i.e. security, is an issue most fundamental to one's life and to the lives of others. Add to this man's right to live, not only in the sense of having food, but also in exercising his role vis-á-vis his own humanity and the humanity of others. I believe this is the core issue.

Q. [On expecting U.S. war or invasion.]

President Hussein. We hope it will not happen; but we are bracing ourselves to such an eventuality. You have, no doubt, observed the noramalcy prevailing in public life in Iraq. People are getting married, making friends, maintaining normal relations with neighbors and relatives, travelling around the country, and enjoying life as much as they can. Yet, they are preparing themselves at the same time for this eventuality which is being talked about by U.S. officials. Therefore, our people will continue be prepared, while we pray God Almighty to spare the Americans the experience of going down this road, and to spare the Iraqis the evil of those who ride the band-wagen of evil to launch aggression against Iraq.

Q. [On possibility of being killed or captured.]

President Hussein. We, as believer, accepts God's will, whatever it may be. There is no value for life without faith. A true believer accepts his fate while taking precautions at the same time not to fall in an precipice of death, or any such precipice which his enemy may try dig for him. Prior to the revolution of July 1958, we were ordinary citizens in a people many of whom found it difficult to purchase shoes to wear, not only in the countryside, but in the cities as well, and many in fact were deprived of the simplest necessities of life. At that time, we had placed ourselves at the service of our people, having first relied on God Almighty, with all the dangers that we had to face in those days, the kind of dangers that are well known; and I do not want here to indulge in these details.

At that time, we never asked whether we were going to live or die. We had put our faith in God because what was essential to us was the kind of virtues of service to the people that would please God. Now that we have become leaders, with positions in the government, as President, Vice-President, Ministers, etc, it cannot be morally acceptable for us to change our stance. When we were fighters for freedom, our people believed us and followed the banner of the Revolution until victory. In spite of the great difficulties faced by our people along that course, difficulties well-known to the world, our people remained true to their principles.

So, I believe it is not right for a leader to ask himself whether he is going to live or die. Indeed, the basic question should be, to what extent will he remain true to his people and to humanity at large. There and then, God's will shall prevail unimpeded; for I believe that no power on earth can do anything contrary to God's desire.

Q. [On ties with Osama bin Laden.]

President Hussein. Is this the basis of concern amongst U.S. officials? Or is it the basis of concern for the American people only?

Q. Mr. President. I can confirm to Your Excellency accurately and sincerely that this question is a main concern in the minds of the American people.

President Hussein. This subject emerged only recently amongst the concerns of U.S. officials, that is after they had realized that their allegations about Iraq acquiring WMD after 1998 may be exposed at the U.N. for what they really are (i.e. mere allegations), which would be embarrassing to them, so they began talking about the possibility of some connections between Iraq and Mr. Osama bin Laden. By the way, the same subject was also raised with me by Mr. Tony Benn, and I gave him my unequivocal answer which I shall repeat to you just as clearly now: Iraq has no relations whatsoever with Mr. Osama bin Laden, and I believe that Osama bin Laden himself answered this question in a recent speech by him.

Q. Do you agree or disagree, in principle, with the attacks of 11 September?

President Hussein. Our principles are not only nationalist and Pan-Arab, but they are humane as well. We believe that the world must seek opportunities for peace, not opportunities for fighting, war, inflicting harm or vengeance. We had believed in these principles long before we became leader, and have made them our practice with our people since we assumed leadership. But we believe, on the basis of God's teachings to us, as He also instructed mankind at large, under other religions, that there must be a law governing the conduct of humanity, a law which does not allow an aggressor to commit aggression while others remain silent, a killer to perpetrate murder while other applaud his deed, or an invader to occupy other countries while others make no move. In sum, we believe in the principles enshrined in the Charter of the United Nations, which stipulate that when one is aggressed against one has the right to repel aggression. The U.N. Charter was not drafted by Muslims yet, we believe in it.

Q. [On asylum.]

President Hussein. I take Mr. Rather's motive in this question to excitement, which is an American way of interviewing which some people may not like; but, as far as I am concerned, I can understand it; however, I shall answer your question: I was born here in Iraq. And I was born as a true Arab believer. I am proud, and I have taught my children to be proud, of the value of Arab history in all it human dimensions, and of all the stances of Faith which every believer, man or woman, should take. I also taught my children the importance and value of patriotism and the homeland, and to be true to their honor and their people. And now I am teaching this to my grandchildren. This is how we have been talking to the people of Iraq since the days of our struggle underground. I believe that it shall not be acceptable for any leader who talks to his people and to mankind at large about principles in a manner that sound genuine before coming to power, and then change his discourse when he is in power. As for us, we do not change, because our basic premise is that we were born in Iraq as part of a great and glorious nation, and have live n Iraq, blessed by God Almighty to be, through the will of the Iraqi people, in our present status and position. Therefore, we shall die here in Iraq, or on the soil of our nation, according to the will of God.

As for the question of asylum, we think that only he who forsakes his nation will seek to save himself. But he who is committed to the honor of defending his country and people, children men and women, shall abide by the same moral values that he has talked about to his people, never abandoning these values. Indeed, let me say again, maybe Mr. Rather, is after excitement in this question. But what ought to be said here is that whoever asks Saddam Hussein to take asylum in his country is a man without morals, because what his offer mean would be an insult to the people of Iraq. He would be saying to the Iraqis:" Your unanimous decision to choose Saddam Hussein as your leader is of no value. Which is why I will ask him, or convince him, to relinquish power and leave you to the mercy of beasts without a leadership. So rest assured that this matter is alient to the ethics of Saddam Hussein. Then, again, as a journalist, you raise questions such as this one for purposes of excitement, and for some an answer as well; and I can understand that. But I believe that he who speaks about destiny of a country as if it can be determined by another country, would be committing a grave sin. We believe that destiny is determined by God; for however powerful, tyrannical or capable of destruction a particular country may be, it cannot coerce the will of a people resolved to live in freedom and dignity and to defend it honor, integrity, homeland and sanctities.

You remember that in 1991, Mr. Tariq Aziz, then our foreign minister, met Mr. James Baker who wanted Mr. Aziz to convey to the Iraqi leadership the threat of pushing Iraq back into the pre-industrial age. So the attack on Iraq continued for one month and a half, during which time 3000 warplanes were used against Iraq, together with missiles and some 2700 helicopter gunships, with troops from 28 countries. Nevertheless, Iraq was not pushed back to the pre-industrial age. True, a lot of destruction was brought to our bridges, churches, mosques, temples, universities, palaces, plants and factories, and a lot of killing was inflicted on our children, women and the elderly. But the Iraqis, driven by their resolve after relying on God Almighty, have rebuilt everything, in the light of which U.S. officials started claiming that, the withdrawal of UNSCOM (which by the way—was done upon U.S. instructions, may have enabled Iraq to develop weapons of mass destruction. Then they began saying that they had intelligence to the effect that Iraq had developed such weapons. We, on the other hand, say that we do not have such weapons. But what does all this mean? It means that Baker's threat of 1991 had not come true. So any talk about the possibilities of metamorphosing Iraq is unfair both to God Almighty, Who doesn't need the fairness from those whom He creates, but expects only their devotion, as well as to the Iraqis and to their potential as a people in confronting adversity with talent, creativity and productive work.

We hope and pray that war will not take place; but if it were to happen, Iraq will still be there. A country, such as our, with 8000 years of civilization behind it, which was indeed the cradle of man first civilization, cannot be imagined to simply diminish simply because an external power wants or imagines, for some reason, to put an end to its role.

Q. [On the belief in victory.]

President Hussein. You know that in both situations(that is in 1990-91 and now), we did not cross the Atlantic to commit aggression against the United States. We, as people, armed forces and leadership, are here at home in Iraq when U.S. officials are declaring their intentions to perpetrate aggression against Iraq, Is it not part of our responsibility and the basic meaning of our patriotism, moral commitment and faith to say to the coming aggressor: " If you commit aggression against us, we shall not succumb." And if we were to reserve this question by putting it to any honest U.S. citizen, in his own country of the USA, including Mr. Rather, and said to him: Let us suppose that at any time in the future, power will revert to a country other than the USA, and then this power decides to cross the Atlantic to occupy you, will you surrender or will you resist? Let me answer by saying to all good Americans, if you happen to face any such situation in the future, do not succumb, but resist and defend your country and your honor as a people. But you ought not to commit aggression on others.

As you know, we have not committed aggression against the USA, while the U.S. government is inflicting death on our children, our women and the elderly, burning our crops and destroying our property on a daily basis. Even now, as I am sitting with you here, U.S. warplanes may be raiding the northern or southern parts of Iraq to drop their lethal cargo on our population and our property which, be it private or public, belongs to the people in all circumstances.

So, when if the world is governed by the law of the strong: a law according to which the weak must accept being hegemonized by the strong who possess the supremacy of destructive force, then such a law will be void of the most basic elements of morality and of the simplest meanings of faith, regardless who you are and what faith you believe in. this means capitulation to the law of the jungle; and we, as true believers, refuse to surrender to the law of the jungle. It is our duty, under the rules of the honor of responsibility, that we defend our country, our children and our people. We shall never surrender, neither to the USA, nor to any other power, even if the U.S. power of destruction were to become many many times its present size, we shall continue to resist aggression, and shall fight with honor, and victory can come only from God Almighty.

Let me, however, make a correction about history, which should be important to you and to the American people. In 1991 Iraq was not defeated. We withdrew from Kuwait by our own decision. True we were under bombardment; but once we were inside Iraq, neither the army, nor the people, of Iraq was defeated. You must remember this fact, or have seen in the writings which have since appeared about what actually took place in the tank-battle near Basrah, and how Mr. Bush, the father, delivered a speech declaring an unconditional ceasefire, except for when their forces are fired at, in which case they would retaliate. So Iraq was not defeated in 1991

Let me also explain to you, Mr. Rather, why I refer to former President Bush as (Mr.) Bush. It is because I respect people. When Khumeini died (May his soul rest in peace), and I received the news of his death, I told our Minister of information at that time: Don't gloat over his death, for this is the law of God. Interestingly enough, let me tell you that I hadn't used to refer to President George Bush, Sr., as (Mr.) Bush when he was in office. But from the day he left office, I began calling him Mr. Bush whenever his name came up. In any case, the law of faith says this: you must respect even your enemy as a human being.

Q. [On confirming that 1991 was a defeat to Iraq.]

President Hussein. Let me answer this question. You know goals of Bush, the father, and why he repeated his attacks later. Why did he come back to repeat his military strikes against us when he was President of the USA if we had been defeated. So when a military conflict takes place, the war includes advance and retreat. Mr. Bush, Sr., had mobilized 28 armies and 42 countries against us at the time; and when we saw the world collaborating in a military operation on the field against our country and our armed forces, we withdrew our armies from Kuwait, without losing more than 10% of our hardware in one and a half months of fighting on the battle field; so we withdrew in order to be able to carry on fighting inside Iraq. And we did fight on, and defeated the tanks that came to fight us on the outskirts of Basrah. This has been written about in the books published by American military experts.

So, in actual fact, the ceasefire declaration was issued by Mr. Bush, the father, without having consulted his allies to announce that the military offensive had achieved its objectives which was why they wanted to stop the war unconditionally.

So we lost a battle, but were not defeated. You know that the war between our country and Iran had last eight years during which Iran lost battles to us and we lost others to them. But how are things measured. They are measured on the basis of the final outcome. The United States can inflict destruction, but the question remains: Why keep destroying? Why make the world your enemy? Did the Americans develop their weapons in order to destroy the world? Or, Did their scientists and tax-payers work and pay for weapons for the defense of the United States? I believe that when American scientists developed weaponry, and when American tax-payers paid, and continue to pay for the weapons, then what they had in mind must have been the defense of the United States. But is it wise for anyone, any official, in possession of military supremacy, to commit aggression on others, destroy them, kill their people and their children simply because they say Allah is our God and we believe in Him, and we shall defend our freedom and our right to independence and dignity and to make our own choices in life while respecting others? What does Iraq threaten the United States with? Iraq has not committed aggression against the USA. Neither the people, nor the officials, of this country have said at any time that they are enemies of the United States, or enemies of the American people and their national choices. Is it right for any superior power to aggress against others? Is it right to do that because of ambitions coveted or desired by companies of special interests?

Mr. Rather, you are an experienced man and must know that the battle will no be over only when the guns are silent, or when the national will bows to the aggressor. It is not enough to have supremacy in the air or in missile capacity; for it is the guns that will remain to tell the tale of a great people's resistance against occupation and the defeat of the aggressors. This is not because Iraq wants to enter into confrontation with others. The United States or any other country, but this is a general principle. The people of Iraq have decided to re-assume their great patriotic and nationalist role of faith in human civilization, and will persist in this role of self-respect and respect to other peoples and to their will and right to free choice.

So let us pray for the good of all peoples, asking God to give them faith and spare them both from bringing harm to, or being harmed by others.

Q. Mr. President, U.S. Vice-President Richard Cheney has stated that when the Us forces enter Iraq, they will be welcomed with greetings and music as an army of liberation. Do you think the American people should believe this sort of thing?

President Hussein. If the Iraqi army, or any other army for that matter, were to cross the Atlantic and occupy America, will the people of America receive this army with music. I don't think any man in a position of responsibility should say this, because when he does say this sort of thing, it's as if he is preparing his own people to welcome any occupying force invading their country with music and festivities.

I don't believe that. In fact I am absolutely certain that not a single Iraqi citizen will welcome any American, if the latter comes as an invader. But all Iraqis will welcome any American citizen who comes as a friend. So you see yourself that you, who have come from a country threatening to destroy Iraq, have been received with the respect and warmth to which you are entitled from all officials and people who know where you come from. What does this mean? Our citizen knows that you come as a guest and should be able to wonder about in Iraq in freedom. But if you had come as a trooper in an occupying force, you would not have been able to move freely in the country. So, as long as you are here, moving about in freedom, this means that you are here as a guest, and it is the duty of the people of Iraq to host you in welcome as a guest, because they are committed to such a duty.

If Americans or others want to know the true situation in Iraq, they should ask themselves a specific question. The people of Iraq chose Saddam Hussein in a public referendum in 1995 and again in 2002, by giving him 99.6% and 100% of the vote on the two occasions respectively. I can understand that such high voting figures may seem strange to you; but whatever you take out of them, the figures big. Consider also the circumstances under which the Iraqi people gave Saddam Hussein this kind of vote. They elected him under circumstances of war and embargo. What does this mean? It means that the people of Iraq decided to take a patriotic stance under these circumstances as a statement to foreigners saying: It is we who choose our way and you will not draw our path for us.

If the referendum had taken place at a time after than the time of the embargo and the war, may be Saddam Hussein would not have obtained the same percentage of the vote of the Iraqi people. If you want to see an indication on the way Iraqis act if attacked by a foreign power that wants to occupy their land and usurp their dignity, freedom, and honor, look at the outcome of the referendum.

You probably know that nothing negative was said in the west about the organization of the referendum of 2002, for many reporters from all over the world were present . some of the reporters stood by the ballot box to make sure that it was true that the Iraqis said (yes) to Saddam Hussein.

Q. [On the possible new U.N. resolution and would it change Iraq's stance.]

President Hussein. The basic constants do not change. The basic thing that we are committed to the security council resolutions which we have accepted. The inspectors have come to Iraq, and have seen that we had been telling the truth and that we have not developed weapons of mass destruction as was said by some parties . so, what would any new resolutions be about now ?

The constants of our stance are clear: we do not bargain over our independence, dignity and freedom. At the same time we comply with what has been adopted by the Security Council. If new resolutions that en fringe upon our dignity, freedom and independence, are adopted, our position will be clear and built on our previous position.

Q. [On developing El-Soumod missiles.]

President Hussein. Do you mean the EL-Soumod missiles that are with the U.N. limits and of a 150 Km range ? Iraq has not violated any U.N. resolution, but if anyone wants to reconsider the past Security Council resolution with which we have complied, including the allowed 150 Km range missiles, the issue would be put into a completely new framework, i.e. the U.N. would be relinquishing its own resolutions, and that the basic issue has become not implementing Security Council resolutions, but inflicting harm on Iraq. (on burning oil wells, and destroying dams): I have answered the hypothesis, but to indulge in the details: One does not burn his own resources, nor is not to insinuate that they destroy Iraqi dams in their possible invasion. As for Iraq, it does not destroy its property or petrol. On the contrary it protects them and uses them to maintain its life.

Q. [On what H.E. wants to say to the American people.]

President Hussein. First of all convey to them that the people of Iraq are not the enemy of the American people, but the enemy of the aggressive policy adopted by the American Administrations against of the nations including Iraq. Iraqis want and work for living in peace. They wish that all the nations of the world, including the American people, live in peace, and respect the will and rights of the other nations. If the American people wants to know more facts through a direct televised dialogue, Iam ready to enter into a dialogue with Mr. Bush, the president of USA on TV before the entire world, so that I speak out my remarks regarding U.S. policies, and he can say his remarks about Iraqi policies. Thus the Americans and the rest of the world would know who is right and who is wrong. I do not mind Mr. Dan Rather conducting the debate which can be made by satellite, with Mr. Bush in Washington and myself here in Baghdad, in fair way.

We have seen in movies, the American people are courageous, and like the Arabs, when challenged for a duel, they would not refuse. We are not asking for a duel with weapons, but a live debate on TV between Mr. Bush and me. If he is convinced with his position regarding going to war, this would be an opportunity for him to convince the world of his reasons for opting for war, if he has already decided to go to war. It is also an opportunity for us to explain our views that we have a right to live in peace. I think it is the American and the Iraqi peoples as well as the world at large have the right to hear us clearly explain our positions so that they can judge where right and wrong are.

Don't you call for facts in us ? we have heard and read in American writings of philosophers, novels and even seen in movies that they do. So why should we hide away from the people and not let the facts be seen by all the people concerned ? This is what I am calling for: either we both go for peace, which is what we want and wish, to avoid our people any harm, or he who opts for no peace, convince his people of his reasons.

Of course this not a joke. I propose this as a sign of respect on my side to the American public opinion, to my people, and to the entire world. I call for this because the war is not a joke. He who considers the war as the first option in his life is not a normal person. If a dialogue could bring on opportunity for peace, why shouldn't we go for it, and thus show respect to our peoples and put the facts before the centers of decision making in both countries ? in Iraq, the final decision is taken, after consulting the people, by the higher leadership in the country, and from our knowledge of the American constitution, in the U.S., it is the president who makes the decision. So why do not we seize this opportunity to have alive debate on the TV? Then everyone can chose his own way and means. If president Bush, has another proposal on the basis of the same idea, we are ready to hear it.

The important thing is that the debate should be heard in a normal and correct way, but in the U.N. the voice of people are not always heard. I do not mean, by the debate, that Mr. Bush and I deliver speeches; we should sit together as we are doing now with you, with the difference that each one of us would be in a different location, and I would ask him questions he would ask me questions. I would explain Iraq's position, and he the U.S. position. He would explain why does he want to go to war, and I would explain why do we hold on peace and defend

Our dignity, sovereignty, and rights, in away that the American, Iraqis and other peoples would hear us in a direct and honest way and without pre-written speeches. The citizens want to see a direct and live dialogue. I think this applies to the psychology of American just as it does for Iraqis. The peoples do not want to listen to speeches, but to a dialogue where each party presents his reasons and counter reasons. The debate should air live and in its totality from American and Iraqi TV.

Q. [On the possibility that this will be the last interview.]

President Hussein. What I believe in is that man's destiny is basically determined by God Almighty. But as God also tells us that man should take the necessary preparations on Earth, I feel as if we will meet again no matter what is going to happen. We hope that the Iraqi people and the American people live in security and peace, and that they have ties between them in a way that expresses the national interest without anyone of them inflicting harm on the other.

Q. [On the danger of the troops and fleets going toward Iraq.]

President Hussein. I understand, hear and see everything, but the final result will be determined by God Almighty, and by the Iraqis, here in Iraq , and in Baghdad. I don't mean the fate of the Americans but that of the Iraqis in Iraq, and the fate of any aggression against the Iraqis who are living peacefully in the country.

Q. [On being the champion of the Arab street.]

President Hussein. I do not seek to be so (champion of the Arabs), for what we work for is not a personal matter. What we want to achieve is, after God's blessings, is to be true to our conscience and obtain its satisfaction along with the satisfaction of our Iraqi people and Arab nation by serving them and the satisfaction of humanity when the world understands our principles as they are and not as people of falsehood present them. The basic thing for us, is to please our people in Iraq and our Arab nation. It is not to be described as champion or not. The important thing for us is to be described as the faithful son of the this nation, and I think this is a legitimate right for every citizen in his nation.

Q. [On agreeing or not agreeing that bin Laden is the champion of the Arabs.]

President Hussein. What do you think? According to the principles in which Arabs believe, I am happy when a thousand champions appear in the nation; champions in the sense of loyalty to the nation and its principles, and not seeking personal interests. So, we become happy, just as you do in America, if the number of champions of peace, work, and production increases. We think that the basic thing is to lift the injustice inflicted on our Arab nation and Iraqi people who are part of our Arab nation. You see how the Palestinian are killed and their property destroyed, without anyone trying to set them free from the chains that are lied to their hands. If you consider Osama bin Laden a champion in America, we are not jealous of him, for jealousy is for women in some of their specific interests in life. Men should not be jealous of each other in any work they compete in, if their competition is in the interest of the nation and humanity at large.

Mr. Rather is a clever man and he means to get to the facts, for I do not think that his questions are not merely for the purpose of excitement of pulling someone to say things that will be counted on him.

Guidelines for a U.N. Security Council Resolution on Iraq Proposed by France and Russia, February 24, 2003

1. Full and effective disarmament in accordance with the relevant (U.N. Security Council) resolutions remains the imperative objective of the international community. Our priority should be to achieve this peacefully through the inspection regime. The military option should only be a last resort. So far, the conditions for using force against Iraq are not fulfilled:

While suspicions remain, no evidence has been given that Iraq still possesses weapons of mass destruction or capabilities in this field;

Inspections have just reached their full pace; they are functioning without hindrance; they have already produced results;

While not yet fully satisfactory, Iraqi cooperation is improving, as mentioned by the chief inspectors in their last report.

2. The Security Council must step up its efforts to give a real chance to the peaceful settlement of the crisis. In this context, the following conditions are of paramount importance;

The unity of the Security Council must be preserved;

The pressure that is put on Iraq must be increased.

3. These conditions can be met, and our common objective—the verifiable disarmament of Iraq—can be reached through the implementation of the following proposals:

A. Clear program of action for the inspections:

According to resolution 1284, UNMOVIC and IAEA have to submit their program of work for approval of the Council. The presentation of this program of work should be speeded up, in particular the key remaining disarmament tasks to be completed by Iraq pursuant to its obligations to comply with the disarmament requirements of resolution 687 (1991) and other related resolutions.

The key remaining tasks shall be defined according to their degree of priority. What is required of Iraq for implementation of each task shall be clearly defined and precise.

Such a clear identification of tasks to be completed will oblige Iraq to cooperate more actively. It will also provide a clear means for the Council to assess the cooperation of Iraq.

B. Reinforced inspections:

Resolution 1441 established an intrusive and reinforced system of inspections. In this regard, all possibilities have not yet been explored. Further measures to strengthen inspections could include, as exemplified in the French non-paper previously communicated to the chief inspectors, the following: increase and diversification of staff and expertise; establishment of mobile units designed in particular to check on trucks; completion of the new system of aerial surveillance; systematic processing of data provided by the newly established system of aerial surveillance.

C. Timelines for inspections and assessment:

Within the framework of resolution 1284 and 1441, the implementation of the program of work shall be sequenced according to a realistic and rigorous timeline:

The inspectors should be asked to submit the program of work outlining the key substantive tasks for Iraq to accomplish, including missiles/delivery systems, chemical weapons/precursors, biological weapons/material and nuclear weapons in the context of the report due March 1;

The chief inspectors shall report to the Council on implementation of the program of work on a regular basis (every three weeks);

A report of UNMOVIC and IAEA assessing the progress made in completing the tasks shall be submitted by the inspectors 120 days after the adoption of the program of work according to resolution 1284;

At any time, according to paragraph 11 of resolution 1441, the executive chairman of UNMOVIC and the director general of the IAEA shall report immediately to the Council any interference by Iraq with inspections activities as well as failure by Iraq to comply with its disarmament obligations;

At any time, additional meetings of the Security Council could be decided, including at high level.

To render possible a peaceful solution, inspections should be given the necessary time and resources. However, they cannot continue indefinitely. Iraq must disarm. Its full and active cooperation is necessary. This must include the provision of all the additional and specific information on issues raised by the inspectors as well as compliance with their requests, as expressed in particular in Mr. Blix' letter of Feb. 21, 2003. The combination of a clear program of action, reinforced inspections, a clear timeline and the military build up provide a realistic means to reunite the Security Council and to exert maximum pressure on Iraq.

Remarks by British Prime Minister Blair, February 25, 2003

Prime Minister Tony Blair delivered his remarks to the British Parliament.

With permission, Mr Speaker, I will make a further statement on Iraq.

Let me again briefly recap the history of the Iraqi crisis. In 1991 at the conclusion of the Gulf War, the true extent of Saddam's WMD program became clear. We knew he had used these weapons against his own people, and against a foreign country, Iran, but we had not known that in addition to chemical weapons, he had biological weapons which he had denied completely and was trying to construct a nuclear weapons program.

So on 3 April 1991, the U.N. passed the first U.N. Resolution on Saddam and WMD, giving him 15 days to give an open account of all his weapons and co-operate fully with the U.N. inspectors in destroying them. 15 days later he submitted a flawed and incomplete declaration denying he had biological weapons and giving little information on chemical weapons. It was only four years later after the defection of Saddam's son-in-law to Jordan, that the offensive biological weapons and the full extent of the nuclear program were discovered . In all, 17 U.N. Resolutions were passed. None was obeyed. At no stage did he co-operate. At no stage did he tell the full truth.

Finally in December 1998 when he had begun to obstruct and harass the U.N.

inspectors, they withdrew. When they left they said there were still large amounts of WMD unaccounted for. Since then the international community has relied on sanctions and the No Fly Zones policed by U.S. and U.K. pilots to contain Saddam. But the first is not proof against Saddam's deception and the second is limited in its impact.

In 2001 the sanctions were made more targeted. But around $3 billion a year is illicitly taken by Saddam, much of it for his and his family's personal use. The intelligence is clear: he continues to believe his WMD program is essential both for internal repression and for external aggression. It is essential to his regional power. Prior to the inspectors coming back in he was engaged in a systematic exercise in concealment of the weapons.

That is the history. Finally last November U.N. Resolution 1441 declared Saddam in material breach and gave him a "final opportunity" to comply fully immediately and unconditionally with the U.N.'s instruction to disarm voluntarily. The first step was to give an open, honest declaration of what WMD he had, where it was and how it would be destroyed. On 8 December he submitted the declaration denying he had any WMD, a statement not a single member of the international community seriously believes. There have been two U.N. inspectors reports. Both have reported some cooperation on process. Both have denied progress on substance.

So: how to proceed? There are two paths before the U.N.. Yesterday the U.K. along with the U.S. and Spain introduced a new Resolution declaring that "Iraq has failed to take the final opportunity afforded to it in Resolution 1441".

But we will not put it to a vote immediately. Instead we will delay it to give Saddam one further final chance to disarm voluntarily. The U.N. inspectors are continuing their work. They have a further report to make in March. But this time Saddam must understand. Now is the time for him to decide. Passive rather than active co-operation will not do. Co-operation on process not substance will not do. Refusal to declare properly and fully what has happened to the unaccounted for WMD will not do. Resolution 1441 called for full, unconditional and immediate compliance. Not 10 per cent, not 20 per cent, not even 50 per cent, but 100 per cent compliance. Anything less will not do. That is all we ask; that what we said in Resolution 1441 we mean; and that what it demands, Saddam does.

There is no complexity about Resolution 1441. I ask all reasonable people to judge for themselves:

After 12 years is it not reasonable that the U.N. inspectors have unrestricted access to Iraqi scientists—that means no tape recorders, no minders, no intimidation, interviews outside Iraq as provided for by Resolution 1441? So far this simply isn't happening.

Is it not reasonable that Saddam provides evidence of destruction of the biological and chemical agents and weapons the U.N. proved he had in 1999? So far he has provided none.

Is it not reasonable that he provides evidence that he has destroyed 8,500 liters of anthrax that he admitted possessing, and the 2,000 kilos of biological growth material, enough to produce over 26,000 liters of anthrax?

Is it not reasonable that Saddam accounts for up to 360 tonnes of bulk chemical warfare agent, including 1 tonnes of VX nerve agents, 3,000 tonnes of precursor chemicals, and over 30,000 special munitions?

To those who say we are rushing to war, I say this. We are now 12 years after Saddam was first told by the U.N. to disarm; nearly 6 months after President Bush made his speech to the U.N. accepting the U.N. route to disarmament; nearly 4 months on from Resolution 1441; and even now today we are offering Saddam the prospect of voluntary disarmament through the U.N..

I detest his regime. But even now he can save it by complying with the U.N.'s demand. Even now, we are prepared to go the extra step to achieve disarmament peacefully.

I do not want war. I do not believe anyone in this House wants war. But disarmament peacefully can only happen with Saddam's active co-operation.

12 years of bitter experience teaches that. And if he refuses to co-operate—as he is refusing now and we fail to act, what then? Saddam in charge of Iraq, his WMD intact, the will of the international community set at nothing, the U.N. tricked again, Saddam hugely strengthened and emboldened—does anyone truly believe that will mean peace? And when we turn to deal with other threats, where will our authority be? And when we make a demand next time, what will our credibility be? This is not a road to peace but folly and weakness that will only mean the conflict when it comes is more bloody, less certain and greater in its devastation.

Our path laid out before the U.N. expresses our preference to resolve this peacefully; but it ensures we remain firm in our determination to resolve it.

I have read the memorandum put forward by France, Germany and Russia in response to our U.N. Resolution. It is to be welcomed at least in these respects. It accepts that Saddam must disarm fully. And it accepts that he is not yet co-operating fully. Indeed not a single member of the EU who spoke at the Summit in Brussels on 17 February disputed the fact of his non-co-operation.

But the call is for more time, up to the end of July at least. They say the time is necessary "to search out" the weapons. At the core of this proposition is the notion that the task of the inspectors is to enter Iraq to find the weapons, to sniff them out as one member of the European Council put it. That is emphatically not the inspectors' job. They are not a detective agency. And even if they were, Iraq is a country with a land mass roughly the size of France. The idea that the inspectors could conceivably sniff out the weapons and documentation relating to them without the help of the Iraqi authorities is absurd. That is why 1441 calls for Iraq's active co-operation.

The issue is not time. It is will. If Saddam is willing genuinely to co-operate then the inspectors should have up to July, and beyond July; as much time as they want. If he is not willing to co-operate then equally time will not help. We will be just right back where we were in the 1990s.

And, of course, Saddam will offer concessions. This is a game with which he is immensely familiar. As the threat level rises, so the concessions are eked out. At present he is saying he will not destroy the Al-Samud missiles the inspectors have found were in breach of 1441. But he will, under pressure, claiming that this proves his co-operation. But does anyone think that he would be making any such concessions, that indeed the inspectors would be within a 1,000 miles of Baghdad, were it not for the U.S. and U.K. troops massed on his doorstep? And what is his hope? To play for time, to drag the process out until the attention of the international community wanes, the troops go, the way is again clear for him.

Give it more time, some urge on us. I say we are giving it more time. But I say this too: it takes no time at all for Saddam to co-operate. It just takes a fundamental change of heart and mind.

Today the path to peace is clear. Saddam can co-operate fully with the inspectors. He can voluntarily disarm. He can even leave the country peacefully. But he cannot avoid disarmament.

One further point. The purpose in our acting is disarmament. But the nature of Saddam's regime is relevant in two ways. First, WMD in the hands of a regime of this brutality is especially dangerous because Saddam has shown he will use them. Secondly, I know the innocent as well as the guilty die in a war. But do not let us forget the 4 million Iraqi exiles, the thousands of children who die needlessly every year due to Saddam's impoverishment of his country—a country which in 1978 was wealthier than Portugal or Malaysia but now is in ruins, 60 per cent of its people on food aid. Let us not forget the tens of thousands imprisoned, tortured or executed by his barbarity every year. The innocent die every day in Iraq victims of Saddam, and their plight too should be heard.

And I know the vital importance in all of this of the Middle East peace process. The European Council last week called for the early implementation of the Roadmap. Terror and violence must end. So must settlement activity. We welcomed President Arafat's statement that he will appoint a Prime Minister, an initiative flowing from last month's London conference on Palestinian reform. I will continue to strive in every way for an even-handed and just approach to the Middle East peace process.

At stake in Iraq is not just peace or war. It is the authority of the U.N.. Resolution 1441 is clear. All we are asking is that it now be upheld. If it is not, the consequences will stretch far beyond Iraq. If the U.N. cannot be the way of resolving this issue, that is a dangerous moment for our world. That is why over the coming weeks we will work every last minute we can to reunite the international community and disarm Iraq through the U.N.. It is our desire and it is still our hope that this can be done.

Remarks by Secretary of Defense Rumsfeld, February 25, 2003

Secretary Donald Rumsfeld delivered his remarks at the Hoover Institution in Washington, DC.

Q. There have been a lot of reports in the last 24 hours on TV in regard to these small aircraft, I mean very small aircraft, that are pilotless, that potentially could deliver biological things. Can you comment, to the extent you're allowed to, in regard to how we're looking at that; what is the degree of equipment that they have, in our assessment, et cetera.

Secretary Rumsfeld. They come in a variety of sizes and shapes and capabilities. They are perfectly capable of being equipped with spraying and aerosol type capabilities. They—today with the global position systems, GPS, and the kinds of maps that one can buy readily, these types of things can be purchased and used and guided and directed with great precision, and capable of dispensing those kinds of weapons.

They do exist. We know that Iraq has a number of so-called UAVs, unmanned aerial vehicles, of different types; that they train with them and exercise them.

Q. What's the typical range that they have?

Secretary Rumsfeld. They vary dramatically in their range. But in some cases, they've taken—countries have taken regular manned aircraft and equipped them for unmanned flight, so they would have the type of typical range depending on the speed and circumstance of the aircraft that they converted. Of the smaller types that are made directly for the purpose as opposed to being first made as a manned aircraft, we've seen them go hundreds of kilometers. And they can be done—it can be done two ways. It can be done on a guided basis, or it can be done on a pre-programmed basis. And as I say, with great precision.

Q. Let me just ask whether—could you speculate for us what is going to be the event that will trigger the decision to go to war, and do you think that event will have an impact on the support that you have in the—from the U.S. population as well as countries that should be a part of our coalition but aren't yet there?

Secretary Rumsfeld. You know, who knows what's going to happen in the U.N., who knows what could happen on the ground? There are so many different things that could happen. You know, as we're meeting he could decide to leave the country. It's a nice thought. Someone could decide to help him leave the country. Not a bad thought. I just don't know. There are so many things that could happen, and these are decisions that are made, of course, by the president of the United States and by other countries' leaders. And I just simply wouldn't want even to begin to speculate. We have aircraft flying around in that region, as you know, in the northern and southern no-fly zones. And we have U-2 aircraft that are assisting the U.N. inspectors. And I suppose something could happen to one of those aircraft that could cause a problem. There's any number of things, and it's just not possible to speculate on it.

Q. What do you see as Iraq's military capability?

Secretary Rumsfeld. The—if you go to organizations like Jane's and others that look at militaries in various countries, they—you know, and drop a plumb line through everyone's best guess—first of all, it's a closed society, so there's a great deal that people don't know. But the guess is that it's somewhere, something under 50 percent of what its capability was in 1991 during the Gulf war in terms of conventional capability: full stock. With respect to chemical, biological capabilities that one knows that they have advanced—and they are, in my judgment, probably more lethal and dangerous today than they would have been back in '91, but I don't know that for sure. I don't think anyone does, except the Iraqis.

* * * *

Q. How much support do you think Saddam truly has from the Iraqi people? How do their sentiments break down?

Secretary Rumsfeld. It's awfully hard to know; in fact, it's impossible to know, unless one just speculates. I don't know how many people who live in an exceedingly repressive regime actually like it. So one has to believe that to the extent people prefer not to be repressed and not to live in fear that they would prefer to have a different regime.

Because it is such a repressive regime, however, people are afraid to say what they think. And until at some moment they see that it is inevitable that that regime is not going to be there, I would suspect that it would be very difficult to come up with any accurate speculation. We have a lot of intelligence and a lot of anecdotal information that, needless to say, is encouraging. But I think, you know, placing your hopes in it is a stretch. I think you just have to wait and see what happens, in the event that that would be the case.

They've lived under a—that repressive regime for a very long time, and it can't be easy. If one looks at the size of their prison population, and looks at the number of people that the regime kills each year, and reads the various non-governmental organizations' reports on their human rights violations and the way they treat people, it's hard to believe that there would be an awful lot of support; to say nothing of the fact that there's a relatively small minority of Sunni that pretty much run the country, and there's a large Shi'a population and a large Kurdish population that probably is—holds that with a minimum of high regard.

* * * *

Q. There has been commentary, primarily in the European press, to some extent in the American press, about three Iraqi ships sailing under radio silence, operating without visiting ports. Do you have any information you can share with us as to whether they are carrying weapons of mass destruction or whether they represent any other kind of threat?

Secretary Rumsfeld. I can't. I see that speculation and—but there's really nothing that's definitive that I could add.

* * * *

Q. There's been a lot of speculation that the window of opportunity for an attack on Iraq is getting narrower and narrower in the sense that the weather will hinder any operations. I've been to Baghdad, and 110 degrees is regarded as a cool morning.

What is going to happen if you keep waiting and waiting and waiting and waiting for the U.N. to pass or not to pass something, and it eventually gets to be April and May? Can you invade at that time?

Secretary Rumsfeld. The—any time one—the force flows that have taken place by the United States and several other countries have really been designed to demonstrate a seriousness of purpose on the part of the U.N. Resolution 1441 and to support the diplomacy. And it has had a very favorable effect. There's no question. It has not caused that regime to cooperate fully in a manner that is required by 1441, as yet, but there's no question but that there wouldn't be any inspectors doing anything if those force flows had not taken place.

It is very clear that once you flow forces, it's stressful to maintain them for long periods of time. Second, as you suggest, it is clearly preferable to be engaged in Iraq in a period other than the summer. There's always going to be a whole host of considerations that the political leadership of a country has to take into account, and that's part of it, but so too are the implications that are being discussed and debated up in the United Nations.

Q. Yeah. I have a mike here. There's been a lot of discussion in some of the opposition to the war about our interest going into Iraq with respect to the oil resources that are there. And I'm wondering if you could comment on any postwar plans we have for redistributing the assets or—for the benefit of the Iraqi people.

Secretary Rumsfeld. Yes, sir. Thank you for asking that.

There's been a lot of speculation in the world—and I suppose it's understandable—suggesting that the interest of the United States and the coalition countries that are concerned about Iraq relates to oil. It does not relate to oil. I mean, it just plain doesn't.

There are a lot of market folks here who understand markets, and the reality is that if you own oil, you want to sell it. That's why it's valuable to have it. And if you sell it, it doesn't matter who you sell it to; it's going to go into a world market. And oil's fungible and money's fungible. And it's going to get purchased by somebody, and the United States will have plenty of oil, as will other, Western European countries, in my view.

The short answer is that the oil belongs to the Iraqi people. It is—the full intention is that in the event there is a post- Saddam Hussein regime in Iraq, that the oil would be operated and sold for the benefit of the Iraqi people, I suppose initially by the coalition forces or some international group of some sort, and then shortly thereafter by some legitimate Iraqi operation that would be managing that important natural resource. But it is clearly not something that anyone in the coalition thinks is for any purpose other than the benefit of the Iraqi people.

* * * *

Q. Given all the time, the deliberation in the process, the global media coverage, and the helpfulness of the element of surprise—there's also a lot of discussion about strategy going on and maybe there's been an evolution of strategy during these international discussions—can you tell us anything about the extent to which surprise will play a role here should we have a war? And to what extent can you disclose whether there has been an evolution, or, let's say, a more—a refinement of the strategy that would be used in Iraq?

Secretary Rumsfeld. Well, there's strategic surprise and tactical surprise. And clearly, you give up strategic surprise when you decide you want to flow forces over a prolonged period of months. You do not necessarily give up tactical surprise. So it seems to me that the answer's kind of yes and no. I—to go back to Bob's question, what could conceivably precipitate it could be surprising to anyone, because at the moment we're still on the diplomatic track and the—what's being—has been tested—

It's just fascinating to me that—I suppose they never should have called them "inspectors". They should have been called "verifiers", because once we used the word and the U.N. used the word "inspector" people began to think of them as discoverers and finders. And, in fact, they're not. There isn't any way in the world that a country that size that these handfuls of people could go in and find things that the Iraqi government was determined to have them not find. What that process really was a process to determine whether or not the Iraqi government was going to cooperate with the United Nations resolution. And that's what's being measured and tested. So when people say they need—inspectors need more time to find things, it seems to me that that construct leads to the answer, Gee, it's a big country, let's give them more time to find things. But if, in fact, the test is not whether or not they're going to be able to discover something—which is very, very difficult, absent defectors who have their families outside the country and are—feel free to actually talk to a U.N. person. So I think that the test really is, is whether or not they're going to cooperate. And that's something that is yet to be seen.

Remarks by Secretary of Defense Rumsfeld, February 25, 2003

Secretary Donald Rumsfeld was interviewed on Al Jazeera Television.

Q. I would like to put it to you straight away the issue between you, the Bush Administration, and Iraq is not weapons of mass destruction. It is for you—how to get rid of Saddam Hussein and his regime.

Secretary Rumsfeld. Well, wrong. It is about weapons of mass destruction. It is unquestionably about that. And the fact that for many years now the Iraqi regime led by Saddam Hussein has not been willing to cooperate with the United Nations resolutions. And the issue you cast as between the Bush Administration and the Iraqi government is really not the right construct. This is a matter that the world community has addressed. That is why there have been 16, now 17 resolutions by the United Nations Security Council. The last one was unanimous.

This is not a U.S.-Iraqi issue. This is an issue between the United Nations and the international community and a government that has consistently refused to stop its weapons of mass destruction program.

Q. Fair enough. If that is the case and let us suppose that the U.N. inspectors, weapons inspectors would come up and say right, we declare Iraq free from weapons of mass destruction. Would you be satisfied and would you let Saddam Hussein alone after that?

Secretary Rumsfeld. First of all it's not me. It's the United States of America and it's the United Nations. The United Nations resolution has found Iraq to be in material breach of their obligations under those resolutions. The Iraqi regime has not cooperated with the inspectors and the idea that the inspectors could come up and say that is just beyond imagination because the inspectors have said quite the contrary that in fact they're not cooperating.

If Iraq were to do that obviously then they would have fulfilled the U.N. resolution.

Q. People hear from perhaps you, from President Bush saying that if Saddam Hussein goes it will be all to the good of the world, of that region. The implication is that you would like Saddam Hussein to, would like to get rid of Saddam Hussein and his—

Secretary Rumsfeld. Oh, I see your point, sure. There's no question but that you have Saddam Hussein who's been there and has not responded to political diplomacy and they've not responded to the economic oil for food sanctions, they've not responded to the limited military activity in the Northern and Southern No-Fly Zones. They stand in material breach. His choice—choices, plural. One is to cooperate and he hasn't done it. We wish he would. A second choice is to do nothing and lead to a potential conflict, which is everyone's last choice. A third choice is to leave the country and have someone in that country that the Iraqi people want that will not have weapons of mass destruction, will not repress the Iraqi people, will not threaten their neighbors. That clearly would be the first choice, would be for him to just leave, go to another country, and allow that country to have a government that's representative of the people of that country and that is respectful of the various ethnic and religious minorities in that country and doesn't invade Kuwait and doesn't make weapons of mass destruction and doesn't traffic with terrorist networks.

Q. About trafficking with terrorist networks, I'll come to that later if I may. But if we look back, we find that three American Administrations—George Bush, Sr., first Clinton, second Clinton—when they were asked about the purpose of the sanctions regime against Iraq, whether it is to get rid of Saddam Hussein and change the regime in Iraq, they almost swore on the Bible saying that the purpose is not that, it is only for weapons of mass destruction. Now you say that you would like to see Saddam Hussein gone.

Secretary Rumsfeld. I think the world would like to see him gone. What happened in the second Clinton Administration, I think you're factually a little off, in the second Clinton Administration the Congress passed legislation that favored regime change in Iraq and the President signed it. So President Clinton and the United States government in toto decided that the only way to get Iraq to cooperate would be for Saddam Hussein to leave and his behavior in the intervening period has suggested that that was correct, and President Bush has followed on the policy of President Clinton.

Q. What is the legitimacy of the principle of changing a regime in a country, which is a member of the United Nations? Is that an acceptable way of dealing with things?

Secretary Rumsfeld. The United Nations a few months ago passed a unanimous resolution, Security Council Resolution 1441, and in it cited the preceding 16 resolutions that the Iraqi regime has disobeyed. It then said that Iraq stands, as of that moment, in material breach. It asked for a declaration of their weapons of mass destruction and said that if it was not a complete declaration they would stand in further material breach. They did not submit an appropriate full declaration. And they then said that if they did not cooperate with the inspectors they would be in further material breach.

And then it said that in the event that it is determined that they are in further material breach that they should recognize that this was a, I believe the quote was a "final opportunity." This is a unanimous resolution of the United Nations. A final opportunity and that there would be serious consequences, or words of that type.

Now what does that mean? It means that the United Nations has decided that if 17 resolutions are ignored by Iraq that the unanimous voice of the Security Council was that at some point that final opportunity will have been missed and that serious consequences would result. It seems to me that the legitimacy is that the risk of allowing that process to go forward and the development of those weapons and the ignoring of the United Nations—17 resolutions—puts in jeopardy the Security Council and the international community.

Q. I'm not trying to sort of find excuses or defend the regime of Saddam Hussein. There are so many regimes in the world that are hated, disliked, if you like dictatorial and so on. In Africa, in your backyard in South America and in Asia. Does this mean that in order to make life better for people you go and get rid of all these regimes?

Secretary Rumsfeld. Well, it was a United Nations resolution. It was a unanimous resolution of the international community.

Second, if the United States does anything we won't do it alone. It would be with a large coalition of countries. There are already more countries involved with the United States in the global war on terror than there were during the Gulf War. It would be a large number of nations that would have decided that the threat from that regime is so great—Here's a country that invaded a neighbor, Kuwait. It's a country that's used chemical weapons on its neighbor Iran. It's a country that's used chemical weapons on its own people. It's a country that has fired ballistic missiles into three of its neighbors. It is a country that is repressing its people. It is a country that, as Secretary Powell indicated, has relationships with terrorist networks and there's the risk of transferring some of those lethal weapons to terrorists. So it's a problem not for the United States alone but a problem for the United Nations and the international community.

Q. What do you think is logical to get rid of the weapons of mass destruction even if you would want to wage war on Iraq afterwards? Instead of getting exposed to their use, you attack now while you say those weapons exist in Iraq.

Secretary Rumsfeld. Well they do exist. The evidence was laid out for the world by Secretary Powell. It's a fact. The regime keeps denying that they exist and keeps denying and deceiving the international community.

Some people have argued that well, the inspectors are in. Why not give them more time? And of course the inspectors aren't there to find anything. The inspectors are there to work with, theoretically, a cooperative country, but the country isn't being cooperative. There's no way the inspectors can find anything. They could be there for years and not find anything because it's a country the size of France. It's an enormous place. The WMD programs have been designed to be conducted in an inspections environment.

So all time does is allow them to continue developing those weapons, to continue dealing with terrorist networks and put in jeopardy the neighbors and the world.

Q. Going back to the point about Saddam Hussein being, peddling with terrorist networks and so on. You haven't produced convincing or compelling evidence that this was the case, especially with Osama bin Laden.

Secretary Rumsfeld. Secretary Powell did in fact make the assertions and he presented some evidence. It is possible to present additional evidence, to be sure. To the extent one does that, you then lose your means of collection of that intelligence and defeat the efforts you're trying to make to be able to predict what they might do.

So you're correct, there has been not all the evidence, but some of the evidence has been presented, but there's some evidence that has been reserved because it would be so helpful to the Iraqis to know exactly what we knew.

Q. I want to put this to you, even if you want to send me to Guantanamo, and that is—

Secretary Rumsfeld. Not likely.

Q. That is that Osama bin Laden and Saddam Hussein, either you created them or you helped them. I mean Osama bin Laden fought the Soviet occupiers in Afghanistan on your behalf, I suppose. And also you went and, I mean you offered help to Saddam Hussein in the darkest hours of his war with Iran. I think you also met him as a representative of the President, of the American President.

Secretary Rumsfeld. Well for you to say that the United States created Osama bin Laden of course would not be correct. He is what he is. There's no question but that there was a period when he was opposing the Soviet invasion of Afghanistan and the United States was also opposing the Soviet invasion of Afghanistan. That does not mean that the United States—A lot of countries were opposing the Soviet invasion of Afghanistan. In fact there were very few countries that liked it besides the Soviet Union. The Afghanistan people didn't like it, we didn't like it. Most of the countries of the world that don't like to see a nation get attacked didn't like it. And it happens also that Osama bin Laden didn't like it. So that commonality of interests led to that coincidence of being on the same side but it would be a misunderstanding to say that therefore the United States or the United Nations or a coalition of countries created him. He is what he is. He's a terrorist. He's proud of it.

* * * *

Q. If you go to Iraq, your forces, how long do you envisage staying on there?

Secretary Rumsfeld. If we went, it would not be with our forces it would be with a large coalition that would be involved. And in the event that it happened there would be a still larger coalition of countries from the region and elsewhere who would be participating in a post-Saddam Hussein Iraq.

The United States is not interested in the oil in that region from Iraq. That's just utter nonsense. It is not interested in occupying any country. We are interested in having our forces go home. But we recognize that a coalition might be necessary for a short period until a government of Iraq could be created by the Iraqis. Look at Afghanistan as a model. We don't want to stay in Afghanistan. What did we do? We assisted the Afghan people with a security environment so that they could have a Loya Jurga and create their own government. That's what they've done. They've created a transitional government.

The United States with obviously the coalition would help with humanitarian assistance, we would help provide stability, we would look for the weapons of mass destruction, we would hope to see an Iraqi government evolve soon that would not have weapons of mass destruction, that wouldn't try to invade Kuwait, that wouldn't use chemical weapons on its neighbors or its own people, that would set itself on a path towards representation for the various minorities and ethnic and religious elements in the country, and that they'd have a voice in that government. Our choice would be to stay as long as we needed to do that, but not one minute longer.

Q. If I understand, some people say you are targeting Iraq because it is the weakest side of the axis of evil, and that you want to cover your failures in Afghanistan, you still have unfinished job.

Secretary Rumsfeld. The failures of Afghanistan. Did you see the people when the coalition forces and the Northern Alliance and the forces on the ground liberated Kabul? They were singing, they were flying kites, they were happy.

Two million refugees have come back into that country. Is that a failure? People are voting with their feet. Individual people. Neither you or I will ever meet them, but they're making a conscious decision to go back to Afghanistan because they know of certain knowledge that it's better there today than it was before. That is not a failure. That is an enormous success.

There are no longer al Qaeda training camps in that country. They are no longer flying airplanes into U.S. buildings from that country, with people trained from that country. The people have picked a transitional government. It's their government. There are men and women going to school. There are people out driving cars. There's humanitarian assistance being provided. They're training an Afghan National Army. This is no failure. This is a success.

Q. Do you think that Iraqi opposition are going to be a reliable partner in after, let us say, the Saddam Hussein regime?

Secretary Rumsfeld. Oh, I think there are—

Q. They are fractious; it is very well known that they are not united.

Secretary Rumsfeld. That's the way it is with democracies. That's the way it is with people who are free to say what they think. They have different views.

What will happen, I would predict that in the event that Saddam Hussein is not there and a new regime evolved, what will happen is there will be people from the Iraqi opposition to be sure, there will be people, Iraqi expatriates, to be sure. There will be more people from inside Iraq who want to participate in that government and it will be a mixture. You will find a uniquely Iraqi solution to whatever that government ought to be and there isn't anybody in the world, in the United States or any other country, that is smart enough to craft a model or a template and say that's what it will be because we don't know what it will be. It will be something that's uniquely Iraqi, just as it was in Afghanistan.

Lots of people ask why is the United States of America the only super power in the world targeting Iraq. They say well, Iraq is a pot of black gold and it is in a strategic position which would facilitate for you the next stage of your agenda for the region. Perhaps Iran is on your list of targets. People speculate about other countries. And also there is the continued Israeli problem.

Q. What is your idea for the region?

Secretary Rumsfeld. Well the only idea we have for the region is that it not be producing weapons of mass destruction and it not be invading neighbors, and that it be peaceful, and that it be, that the Iraqi people figure out how they want to run their country free of a dictator like Saddam Hussein and that he no longer threatens the neighbors and threatens others.

There is no master plan. We don't run around the world trying to figure out how other people ought to live. What we want is a peaceful region.

You used the word black gold. I've seen the same kinds of articles and suggestions that that's the case.

You know, I've been around economics long enough to know that if somebody owns oil they're going to want to sell it. If they want to sell it, it's going to end up in the market. And it doesn't matter if they sell it to Country A or Country B. If they sell it, it's going to be in the market and that's going to affect the world price. Money is fungible and oil is fungible. This is not about oil, and anyone who thinks it is, is badly misunderstanding the situation.

Q. But it depends on who controls the oil.

Secretary Rumsfeld. Anyone who controls it wants to sell it. It doesn't matter. That is not a problem. If you own—If a bad person owns the oil and a good person owns the oil—different oil—and the bad person doesn't want to sell it to you but the good person is willing to, it doesn't matter because then the good person sells it to you.

You're not going to be buying this person's oil but this person's going to be selling it to somebody else. And the world price will be the same. Everyone will have the oil they need. They aren't going to horde it, they're not going to keep it in the ground. They need the money from the oil. So it's not a problem.

Q. Would it worry you if you go by force into Iraq that this might create the impression that the United States is becoming an imperial, colonial power?

Secretary Rumsfeld. Well I'm sure that some people would say that, but it can't be true because we're not a colonial power. We've never been a colonial power. We don't take our force and go around the world and try to take other people's real estate or other people's resources, their oil. That's just not what the United States does. We never have and we never will. That's not how democracies behave. That's how an empire-building Soviet Union behaved but that's not how the United States behaves.

What have we done? We've gone into help Bosnia be free. We've helped Kosovo—Moslem countries. We've helped Kuwait get free. We helped free the world from Hitler and from the Japanese imperial aggression in Asia in World War II. We didn't keep any real estate. We didn't keep any resources. In fact we gave money. We were the biggest donors of food aid in Afghanistan before September 11th. Before we were ever attacked it was the United States—not a Muslim country, but a country that cared enough about the people of Afghanistan that we provided food for them.

Think of the people in Iraq today. If Saddam Hussein were gone the sanctions would be gone. The sanctions would be gone. The U.N. imposed economic sanctions and the people there would be better off.

Q. Would you still think that the United Nations is a viable channel to solve this problem at this hour, which seems—

Secretary Rumsfeld. We hope so. We certainly hope so. It's important I think not only for the people of Iraq and ending the weapons of mass destruction, but I think it's also important for the United Nations.

When Abyssinia was invaded the League of Nations did nothing and the League of Nations fell because of that. They had resolution after resolution and they couldn't act. The result was that people lost confidence in it. People are now saying the people are going to introduce a second resolution. It's not the second resolution, it's the 18th resolution. The United Nations is going to have to look itself in the mirror and say how do we feel about that? What are we going to do? At what point ought a country like Iraq to begin to believe that the United Nations resolutions mean something?

Q. How do you gauge the efficiency of the United Nations when you, for instance, face the French position and their possible use of the veto, also the division within NATO, and with the European Union? These are your allies.

Secretary Rumsfeld. Well the division in NATO was 16 with us and three against. Is that a division? No. What it is it's the normal thing. Free sovereign countries come together, look at an issue, and come to somewhat different views. Sixteen agreed with the United States, 14 from Europe, Canada was one; and three didn't agree. There were eight countries who signed one letter and ten countries in Europe who signed another. That's 18 countries in Europe have supported the U.S. position on Iraq.

I think that, how do I feel about it? One would always like unanimity. One would always prefer that everyone agreed with everything you said and everything you did. Life would be easy. It's unrealistic. There's never been unanimity on tough issues, and these are tough issues. They're very difficult issues, and I understand that.

Q. Does it surprise you that the largest demonstrations happened in the capitals and the cities of those people who are supportive of your position now vis-á-vis Iraq?

Secretary Rumsfeld. Well, it doesn't really because if you think about it, today with the Internet people can organize very quickly and get lots of people to demonstrate, but if you take the population of Western Europe, of those three countries for example. I think you mentioned three countries that have the largest. You take their populations and compare it to the number of people who demonstrated, it's a very small fraction. Even though it was a large number of people, it's a very small fraction of the people. In democracies that's what people do. You don't see people demonstrating in Iraq. You don't see people demonstrating against the government in Iraq because they'll be killed.

Remarks by President Bush, February 26, 2003

In Iraq, a dictator is building and hiding weapons that could enable him to dominate the Middle East and intimidate the civilized world—and we will not allow it. This same tyrant has close ties to terrorist organizations, and could supply them with the terrible means to strike this country—and America will not permit it. The danger posed by Saddam Hussein and his weapons cannot be ignored or wished away. The danger must be confronted. We hope that the Iraqi regime will meet the demands of the United Nations and disarm, fully and peacefully. If it does not, we are prepared to disarm Iraq by force. Either way, this danger will be removed.

The safety of the American people depends on ending this direct and growing threat. Acting against the danger will also contribute greatly to the long-term safety and stability of our world. The current Iraqi regime has shown the power of tyranny to spread discord and violence in the Middle East. A liberated Iraq can show the power of freedom to transform that vital region, by bringing hope and progress into the lives of millions. America's interests in security, and America's belief in liberty, both lead in the same direction: to a free and peaceful Iraq.

The first to benefit from a free Iraq would be the Iraqi people, themselves. Today they live in scarcity and fear, under a dictator who has brought them nothing but war, and misery, and torture. Their lives and their freedom matter little to Saddam Hussein—but Iraqi lives and freedom matter greatly to us.

Bringing stability and unity to a free Iraq will not be easy. Yet that is no excuse to leave the Iraqi regime's torture chambers and poison labs in operation. Any future the Iraqi people choose for themselves will be better than the nightmare world that Saddam Hussein has chosen for them.

If we must use force, the United States and our coalition stand ready to help the citizens of a liberated Iraq. We will deliver medicine to the sick, and we are now moving into place nearly 3 million emergency rations to feed the hungry.

We'll make sure that Iraq's 55,000 food distribution sites, operating under the Oil For Food program, are stocked and open as soon as possible. The United States and Great Britain are providing tens of millions of dollars to the U.N. High Commission on Refugees, and to such groups as the World Food Program and UNICEF, to provide emergency aid to the Iraqi people.

We will also lead in carrying out the urgent and dangerous work of destroying chemical and biological weapons. We will provide security against those who try to spread chaos, or settle scores, or threaten the territorial integrity of Iraq. We will seek to protect Iraq's natural resources from sabotage by a dying regime, and ensure those resources are used for the benefit of the owners—the Iraqi people.

The United States has no intention of determining the precise form of Iraq's new government. That choice belongs to the Iraqi people. Yet, we will ensure that one brutal dictator is not replaced by another. All Iraqis must have a voice in the new government, and all citizens must have their rights protected.

Rebuilding Iraq will require a sustained commitment from many nations, including our own: we will remain in Iraq as long as necessary, and not a day more. America has made and kept this kind of commitment before—in the peace that followed a world war. After defeating enemies, we did not leave behind occupying armies, we left constitutions and parliaments. We established an atmosphere of safety, in which responsible, reform-minded local leaders could build lasting institutions of freedom. In societies that once bred fascism and militarism, liberty found a permanent home.

There was a time when many said that the cultures of Japan and Germany were incapable of sustaining democratic values. Well, they were wrong. Some say the same of Iraq today. They are mistaken. The nation of Iraq—with its proud heritage, abundant resources and skilled and educated people—is fully capable of moving toward democracy and living in freedom.

The world has a clear interest in the spread of democratic values, because stable and free nations do not breed the ideologies of murder. They encourage the peaceful pursuit of a better life. And there are hopeful signs of a desire for freedom in the Middle East. Arab intellectuals have called on Arab governments to address the "freedom gap" so their peoples can fully share in the progress of our times. Leaders in the region speak of a new Arab charter that champions internal reform, greater politics participation, economic openness, and free trade. And from Morocco to Bahrain and beyond, nations are taking genuine steps toward politics reform. A new regime in Iraq would serve as a dramatic and inspiring example of freedom for other nations in the region.

It is presumptuous and insulting to suggest that a whole region of the world—or the one-fifth of humanity that is Muslim—is somehow untouched by the most basic aspirations of life. Human cultures can be vastly different. Yet the human heart desires the same good things, everywhere on Earth. In our desire to be safe from brutal and bullying oppression, human beings are the same. In our desire to care for our children and give them a better life, we are the same. For these fundamental reasons, freedom and democracy will always and everywhere have greater appeal than the slogans of hatred and the tactics of terror.

Success in Iraq could also begin a new stage for Middle Eastern peace, and set in motion progress towards a truly democratic Palestinian state. The passing of Saddam Hussein's regime will deprive terrorist networks of a wealthy patron that pays for terrorist training, and offers rewards to families of suicide bombers. And other regimes will be given a clear warning that support for terror will not be tolerated.

Without this outside support for terrorism, Palestinians who are working for reform and long for democracy will be in a better position to choose new leaders. True leaders who strive for peace; true leaders who faithfully serve the people. A Palestinian state must be a reformed and peaceful state that abandons forever the use of terror.

For its part, the new government of Israel—as the terror threat is removed and security improves—will be expected to support the creation of a viable Palestinian state—(applause)—and to work as quickly as possible toward a final status agreement. As progress is made toward peace, settlement activity in the occupied territories must end. And the Arab states will be expected to meet their responsibilities to oppose terrorism, to support the emergence of a peaceful and democratic Palestine, and state clearly they will live in peace with Israel.

The United States and other nations are working on a road map for peace. We are setting out the necessary conditions for progress toward the goal of two states, Israel and Palestine, living side by side in peace and security. It is the commitment of our government—and my personal commitment—to implement the road map and to reach that goal. Old patterns of conflict in the Middle East can be broken, if all concerned will let go of bitterness, hatred, and violence, and get on with the serious work of economic development, and political reform, and reconciliation. America will seize every opportunity in pursuit of peace. And the end of the present regime in Iraq would create such an opportunity.

In confronting Iraq, the United States is also showing our commitment to effective international institutions. We are a permanent member of the United Nations Security Council. We helped to create the Security Council. We believe in the Security Council—so much that we want its words to have meaning.

The global threat of proliferation of weapons of mass destruction cannot be confronted by one nation alone. The world needs today and will need tomorrow international bodies with the authority and the will to stop the spread of terror and chemical and biological and nuclear weapons. A threat to all must be answered by all. High-minded pronouncements against proliferation mean little unless the strongest nations are willing to stand behind them—and use force if necessary. After all, the United Nations was created, as Winston Churchill said, to "make sure that the force of right will, in the ultimate issue, be protected by the right of force."

Another resolution is now before the Security Council. If the council responds to Iraq's defiance with more excuses and delays, if all its authority proves to be empty, the United Nations will be severely weakened as a source of stability and order. If the members rise to this moment, then the Council will fulfill its founding purpose.

I've listened carefully, as people and leaders around the world have made known their desire for peace. All of us want peace. The threat to peace does not come from those who seek to enforce the just demands of the civilized world; the threat to peace comes from those who flout those demands. If we have to act, we will act to restrain the violent, and defend the cause of peace. And by acting, we will signal to outlaw regimes that in this new century, the boundaries of civilized behavior will be respected.

Protecting those boundaries carries a cost. If war is forced upon us by Iraq's refusal to disarm, we will meet an enemy who hides his military forces behind civilians, who has terrible weapons, who is capable of any crime. The dangers are real, as our soldiers, and sailors, airmen, and Marines fully understand. Yet, no military has ever been better prepared to meet these challenges.

Members of our Armed Forces also understand why they may be called to fight. They know that retreat before a dictator guarantees even greater sacrifices in the future. They know that America's cause is right and just: liberty for an oppressed people, and security for the American people. And I know something about these men and women who wear our uniform: they will complete every mission they are given with skill, and honor, and courage.

Much is asked of America in this year 2003. The work ahead is demanding. It will be difficult to help freedom take hold in a country that has known three decades of dictatorship, secret police, internal divisions, and war. It will be difficult to cultivate liberty and peace in the Middle East, after so many generations of strife. Yet, the security of our nation and the hope of millions depend on us, and Americans do not turn away from duties because they are hard. We have met great tests in other times, and we will meet the tests of our time.

We go forward with confidence, because we trust in the power of human freedom to change lives and nations. By the resolve and purpose of America, and of our friends and allies, we will make this an age of progress and liberty. Free people will set the course of history, and free people will keep the peace of the world.

Remarks by Secretary of Defense Rumsfeld, February 26, 2003

Secretary Donald Rumsfeld delivered his remarks following a briefing of U.S. Senators on Iraq.

Q. Mr. Secretary, can you tell us about your meeting with the members?

Secretary Rumsfeld. Well, it started and it ended, and it was a good one. There were a lot of important questions, and we had a good discussion. General Pace and I made practically no opening remarks and simply answered questions for—I don't know what it was—better than an hour.

Q. Did it focus around the price tag on the war, or around post-Saddam Iraq?

Secretary Rumsfeld. Both of those were discussed, and the situation in the United Nations. And we discussed Afghanistan and President Karzai's visit; the provincial reconstruction teams that we're developing for Afghanistan, and which—two of which are deployed; one is deployed tomorrow, and others are in the works.

Q. Can you talk about the price tag for this war, I mean the $95 billion reported today? And how are you going to ask for that from Congress?

Secretary Rumsfeld. The—first of all, no decision has been made by the president to use force. The hope still is that force wouldn't be necessary; that Iraq would cooperate or that Saddam Hussein would leave the country, recognizing that the time had come.

In the event force has to be used, it's not knowable how long it would last, what kinds of weapons would be used, how many other countries would be participating, although there are a large number of countries that have indicated they would be participating. And cost would be a function of what it cost minus what other countries provided. So there are so many variables, to pretend that someone can even marginally usefully speculate on that when no decision has been made is obviously not, I don't think, a very useful exercise.

Q. With people moving into place to become human shields now, what are you telling them? And would they be ultimately charged with—

Secretary Rumsfeld. It's a war crime.

Q. They'd be charged with war crimes?

Secretary Rumsfeld. It is a war crime to use human shields.

Q. But they are voluntarily putting themselves in that position. What do you say to those people?

Secretary Rumsfeld. Well it's clear that people who put themselves in dangerous positions put themselves in dangerous positions.

Q. If we do attack Iraq, would that have any impact on the targets, where these people are?

Secretary Rumsfeld. I don't know that I'd want to suggest that. I think that—then all you would have to do, if you were Iraq, would be to take a human shield and put them on all your weapons of mass destruction locations and all the places you didn't want somebody to hit, obviously.

Q. Do you think that there's a possibility that our—that the U.S. policy regarding assassinations of foreign leaders will change?

Secretary Rumsfeld. Not to my knowledge. I've never heard it discussed in that context.

Q. If we were to get near enough to Saddam Hussein—if the U.S. Army, our U.S. military—

Secretary Rumsfeld. I've never heard that subject discussed in—that there's any plan at all to change the policy. That's just not something that I've ever heard.

Remarks by Secretary of State Powell, Greek Foreign Minister Papandreou, European Union High Representative Solana, and European Union Commissioner Patten, February 27, 2003

Secretary Powell. On Iraq we all share the same objective—Iraq's disarmament as required under U.N. Security Council 1441, Resolution 1441. The United States and some of our European friends do have some differences with regard to the next steps that should be taken and we are exploring those differences in an open, honest and candid fashion.

I was pleased to see the European Council's statement of February 17th which reinforced the need for Saddam Hussein to comply and to disarm. We are all hopeful for a peaceful solution, but we also understand that 1441 provided for serious consequences if Saddam Hussein did not comply. We and the European Union agree that it is important to keep the focus on Saddam and on his obligations to disarm. The responsibility and the decision to comply with the demands of the international community rest with him, and we believe it is time for him to come clean.

Foreign Minister Papandreou. Thank you very much, Colin. Here with both Javier Solana and Chris Patten, I think we can also say we value very much this opportunity to exchange views and discuss our cooperation on a very large number of very important issues. And certainly today was a very constructive and useful discussion.

Obviously, Iraq is on our minds, and we do stand united in purpose, that is, for full compliance by Saddam Hussein of 1441 and full disarmament of Iraq. We are very concerned, not only in Iraq but around the world, on the issue of weapons of mass destruction and proliferation. And this, of course, is why we also are ready to help in any way we can on the North Korean issue.

On Iraq, we were able to, again, bring the EU discussions we've had amongst my colleagues and also the heads of states and government to the discussion today where we have, again, as I said, reiterated we are at common purpose. We also have said that we need to—we don't exclude the use of force, but we need to use all possible diplomatic means, every window of opportunity, in trying to resolve this crisis, even at the last moment, peacefully; and of course the importance of the U.N. role in this whole process.

Q. Mr. Foreign Minister, can you tell us how you manage as the presidency to bridge the differences between the two important countries, Germany and France, inside the European Union and some other European countries with the United States?

Foreign Minister Papandreou. Well, again, I would stress we are united in purpose of disarming Iraq and for full compliance of 1441. Secondly, I think it's very important to again stress that we are democratic countries and that we have a very open public debate in Europe, in the United States, on all these issues with a wide range of views on how one deals with situations such as the one in Iraq, and obviously you'll be getting different views.

But that should not undermine the common will that we have for solving this problem. And secondly, this democratic debate is, in the end, our strength. This is what represents us. This is the value, these are the values we cherish as democratic societies. So we should not see this as a weakness, but we should see it as our basic strength. In the end, the international community, of course, will have to decide the U.N. Security Council, how it will move. But I think we will be enriched by the debate we've had.

Q. Mr. Secretary and the other gentlemen as well, if you could comment on this. Hans Blix's report, which has been filed, reportedly does not come down either way. It has something for everyone and no real ammunition for any side. If Iraq proceeds to destroy the Al Samoud missiles in the next day or so and begins to meet that deadline, how will the United States and Great Britain persuade the rest of the Security Council that there shouldn't be more time before facing serious consequences and taking military action?

Secretary Powell. I think I'll wait and actually see the Hans Blix report in due course and not only see it, but I'm looking forward to watching and hearing what he has to say when he and Dr. ElBaradei report on the 7th.

With respect to the missiles, it doesn't change our view of the situation in the slightest. Those missiles were prohibited in the first place. They should have been destroyed long ago. They were told to destroy them some days ago and they've been stringing it out until the very last minute, and we will see what this letter they are going to send in within 48 hours actually says they're going to do. It's not entirely clear yet. But I think it's just more indication of the reality that we have been trying to convey to the world that Saddam Hussein is trying to string it out, trying to divert attention, trying to pretend he is cooperating when he is not cooperating, trying to use process as an excuse for not cooperating, and not complying with the will of the international community. It is just further chaff that he is throwing into the system to try to divert attention. And that is our view right now and that's the argument that we would take into the Security Council when we have the next debate on the resolution.

Q. May I ask Mr. Solana or any of our other European visitors to comment on that?

Representative Solana. I'd be glad to, but we do have, we do share our responsibilities here. I can say just something that, we obviously will be following the reports and what Hans Blix will be handing over to the Security Council. It's not the European Union per se that is going to make the decision, it's the Security Council. We have members of the Security Council that are members of the European Union, and we do exchange views and discuss amongst ourselves—sometimes agree, sometimes disagree.

But what we have said as a European Union is that first of all, we want to exhaust all means. I think all 15 would prefer, if possible, a peaceful solution. Then there are different approaches as to how you, when that limit is exhausted, of course, different ideas on this. But we have also said that this is an issue for the Security Council. So we will have to wait to see what the Security Council says.

Q. Mr. Secretary, is there a role for the presidents of the European Union and the Arab world, in this last moment, to do something before the inevitable war? And I'm saying that because, in the weekend we are having an Arab League summit, and actually the Greek Foreign Minister will be visiting Cairo for that. Is there something the Europeans in conjunction with the Arab world can do to avoid, maybe get a message to Saddam Hussein?

Secretary Powell. I never see war as inevitable. But time clearly is running out. Saddam Hussein is trying to use time to his advantage to avoid the consequences of his failure to comply. And I would encourage the European Union, I would encourage the Arab League, I spoke to the Secretary General of the Arab League this morning, and I would encourage them to issue the strongest possible statement to Saddam Hussein that he must comply, and time is running out in which he can comply.

He's, frankly, running out of time. Or suggest to him that perhaps to avoid what might flow in terms of serious consequences, it might be in his best interest to step down and get out of the way and let some responsible leadership take over in Baghdad and allow the international community to help that responsible leadership disarm itself of its weapons of mass destruction as required by 1441, and work with the international community to provide a better life for the people of Iraq. And I hope that's one of the messages that might come out of the summit meeting. With respect to the European Union, the Minister can speak for the Union.

Foreign Minister Papandreou. Well, I just don't have to add much to that than other that we will be there and that certainly we'll be conveying the discussions we've had here in Washington. And I think that the Arab world has a very major role to play as being part of the region, neighboring Iraq, and of course, a number of other countries, Turkey also has taken initiatives vis- á-vis Iraq with a regional initiative. We're in touch with both these initiatives, and I think it's, it is important and it, there is an opportunity to get a very strong message to Baghdad and if it's understood, to possibly have a full compliance, and therefore, as the Secretary said, war is not, in the end, inevitable.

Commissioner Patten. Can I just add this, that the Foreign Minister and I were at, in Cairo for the Arab League Foreign Minister's meeting almost a fortnight ago. And we sent both the Arab League Foreign Ministers and the European Union sent very clear and strong messages to Baghdad. The problem is, I'm not sure whether Saddam Hussein has the radio switched on.

Q. Mr. Secretary, a question involving diplomatic math. We may have, perhaps, a week or two to get—for the U.S. and Britain to get nine votes. Do you think you can

get the remaining votes needed, perhaps five at a minimum? And do you think you can persuade those with vetoes not to use them?

Secretary Powell. Well, we are in contact with all of the members of the Security Council, both the permanent members as well as the elected ten. We're presenting our point of view why we felt it was necessary to put down a second resolution. And depending on what Dr. Blix and Dr. ElBaradei report, and depending on what the Iraqis do over the next week or two, we will see where we are with respect to support for such a resolution.

I think we have a good case, a solid case, and it's all, frankly ad ref until we do hear from Dr. Blix and Dr. ElBaradei, but I'm confident that if we don't see the kind of improvement that I think we must see in the form of compliance, in the form of full cooperation, in the form of answering all the questions that have been there for years; we don't need a new list of questions, we don't need new benchmarks. Everybody knows what Saddam Hussein should be doing.

And if he isn't doing it and shows no indication he's doing it, I think we can present a strong enough argument for the second resolution that we put down that will be able to get the support needed to pass it.

Remarks by Secretary of State Powell, February 28, 2003

Secretary Colin Powell was interviewed by Anwar Khalil of Radio Pakistan.

Q. Well, sir, as perhaps you already know, there is a growing concern among Pakistani people that a military action against Iraq will adversely affect the whole region, including Pakistan, and that war should be avoided at all cost.

How do you propose to address this concern, sir?

Secretary Powell. We believe that war should be avoided and we have been trying to avoid a war. For 12 years, Iraq has been in violation of its obligation—a simple obligation—get rid of chemical, biological and nuclear weapons and weapons programs for peace and security in the region. Iraq has said no, we will not respond, we will not obey.

And then we came together several months ago and passed Resolution 1441 in the United Nations, which said you must do this or face serious consequences. And so far, Iraq continues to not comply. And therefore, as much as we have wanted peace, and we still hope for peace, we simply cannot allow Iraq to continue to have biological weapons which kill people by the hundreds and thousands, or chemical weapons of the kind that they have used against their own people and have used against their neighbors.

The United States does not want to go to war. It is Iraq who is the problem. It is Saddam Hussein who is keeping these weapons. What purpose would these weapons serve in that part of the world? All we want to see is a leadership in Iraq, a regime in Iraq, that gets rid of these weapons and lives in peace with its neighbors. And I hope that our Pakistani friends will understand that it is important for the world not to shrink from this responsibility. We know that there may be difficult days ahead if a conflict is necessary, but we also know that such a conflict would be conducted in a way to minimize any damage or loss of life as much as possible, considering it is a conflict; and in the aftermath of that conflict, we can build a better regime that is responsive to its people and I think will live in peace with its neighbors. And that is something we should all hope for. But we still hope to avoid war.

Q. Well, sir, here is my second question about what people in Pakistan generally believe, and they believe that the proposed war against Iraq will result in loss of innocent life, mostly Muslims, and also in the disintegration of Iraq. Would you agree, sir?

Secretary Powell. No, we are committed to the integrity of Iraq. We do not want to see Iraq break up into pieces, and that has been our commitment to anybody who asks us about it, and to the United Nations and to the neighbors in the region of Iraq.

We don't want to see life lost anywhere—Muslim, Christian, Jew or any other life lost. But we must remember that the weapons we are talking about have already taken Muslim lives. They have been used to take the lives of Iraqis, used against their own people. Saddam Hussein has used these weapons against their own people.

We must not see him as some kind of benevolent figure who is just sitting there being persecuted by the United States. He has persecuted his own people, deprived them of their human rights, fired these terrible weapons outside of his own country against Iran and against other nations in the region.

And so that is what we are trying to deal with, not go after Muslims. If you look at what the United States has done over the past 12 years, we have gone into Kuwait—to conquer Kuwait? No. But to free Kuwait from a Muslim invasion that came from Iraq. We did that and we went home. We didn't go to Baghdad in 1991. We came home, hoping that Baghdad would comply with the law, the United Nations.

We went to Kosovo to help Kosovo Albanians, who were Muslims. And we went to Afghanistan, as you know, your neighbor—not for the purpose of suppressing it and keeping it under our foot or to claim it. Instead, we defeated the Taliban and we have put in place a responsible government, elected by its own people through a Loya Jirga process, a full election next year, and we are pouring hundreds of millions of dollars into Afghanistan—not to rearm it, but to rebuild it.

And this is America's history with respect to its activities in the Muslim world. We come to help. We come to protect. We do not come to take life. We come to give a better life to the people of the nations that we have found it necessary to go and help.

Remarks by Secretary of State Powell, February 28, 2003

Secretary Colin Powell was interviewed by Anne Toulouse of Radio France International.

Q. The French Foreign Minister Dominique de Villepin said today in an interview, and I quote him, "The U.S. strategy on Iraq is sliding from disarmament towards remodeling of the Middle East." How do you respond to that?

Secretary Powell. Well, I disagree categorically with my colleague Dominique de Villepin's comment. 1441, which we are trying to implement, had one goal, and that was to disarm Iraq of its weapons of mass destruction. France voted for the resolution, as did the United States of America. And that is all we have been insisting on.

And if Iraq had disarmed itself, gotten rid of its weapons of mass destruction over the past 12 years, or over the last several months since 1441 was enacted, we would not be facing the crisis that we now have before us.

I must say, however, that if we are unable to get Iraq to comply and military action is necessary to remove this regime and to get rid of the weapons of mass destruction, it's quite clear to me that a new regime would be more responsive to the needs of its people, would live in peace with its neighbors, and perhaps that would assist the region in finding more peace, prosperity and stability for other nations in the region.

But the suggestion that we are doing this because we want to go to every country in the Middle East and rearrange all of its pieces is not correct, and I think Minister de Villepin is wrong.

Q. Now, about Africa, you have—what have you said or will you say to countries such as Cameroon and Guinea to pressure them to vote for your resolution at the Security Council?

Secretary Powell. Each of those three nations who are on the Security Council will have to make their own judgment. They are free, independent nations capable of making their own judgment.

What we will be doing is presenting the argument to them, showing them that these weapons of mass destruction are dangerous, Iraq has ignored its obligations, and we believe it is time for the Security Council to take action. And we hope that we can make a persuasive case to vote for our resolution when our resolution finally comes to the floor to be voted on.

We have not asked for a vote yet because we are still looking for a peaceful solution. We are giving more time to the inspection process, as many people have requested. But ultimately, time has to end. You cannot keep doing this for an extended period of time, beyond 12 years since we started, or four months since Resolution 1441 was passed.

And we hope that if Iraq does not comply, the three African countries will join the other members of the Security Council, we hope, in voting for a resolution that says it is time for the will of the international community to be obeyed, one way or the other.

Q. Mr. Secretary, during the first Gulf War, several African nations were a part of the military operation, and now it seems you have some difficulties to get some on board, even if in a diplomatic offensive. How do you explain that?

Secretary Powell. Well, we are still contacting nations around the world. And, you know, there is no war yet. We haven't started a war. We don't want a war. But I am confident that if it becomes necessary to go into action, the United States will be joined by many nations around the world. A number of them have already indicated their support, and I suspect that once action is deemed necessary, many other nations, to include nations of Africa, will support the United States.

We have heard expressions of support from a number of African nations, but I would leave it up to them individually to express publicly the level of support they will provide to coalition efforts.

Letter from Iraqi General Al-Saadi on behalf of Iraqi President Hussein to United Nations Monitoring, Verification, and Inspection Commission (UNMOVIC) Executive Chairman Blix, February 28, 2003

General Amir Al-Saadi addressed his letter to Dr. Hans Blix, Executive Chairman, UNMOVIC, New York, NY.

I would like to refer to your letter dated 21 February, 2003, regarding your request to submit the al-Samoud 2 missile and its attachments to UNMOVIC for the purpose of starting verifiable destruction and I would like to inform you of the following:

1. Our acceptance in principle of your request, despite our belief that the decision to destroy was unjust and did not take into consideration the scientific facts regarding the issue, as well as the timing of this request (which) seems to us to be one with political aims, especially that those missiles, production and testing facilities are declared fully and are subject to ongoing monitoring and their issue is not considered urgent in comparison with other technical tasks related to verifying remaining unresolved issues of previous programs, as well as ascertaining the ill claims you receive regarding the existence of proscribed and undeclared activities in Iraq that requires your verification and declaring the facts to the world because they are used to justify an aggression against Iraq.

2. We regret to note that your request did not take into consideration the recommendations of the technical team included at the end of the Missiles Experts Committee's report held in UNMOVIC on 12 February, 2003, which noted the need to establish criteria to ensure that the missiles do not pass the range of 150 km, which we previously requested holding technical talks about them in accordance with our letter dated 19 February, 2003, and prior to your writing of the above-mentioned letter to which we have not yet received an answer.

3. In order to establish a framework and timetable and other technical and procedural criteria required for implementation, we suggest dispatching a technical team urgently for this purpose.

Remarks by President Bush, March 1, 2003

President Bush delivered the following radio address to the nation.

Good morning. America is determined to enforce the demands of the United Nations Security Council by confronting the grave and growing danger of Saddam Hussein and his weapons of mass destruction. This dictator will not be allowed to intimidate and blackmail the civilized world, or to supply his terrible weapons to terrorist groups, who would not hesitate to use them against us. The safety of the American people depends on ending this threat.

But America's cause is always larger than America's security. We also stand for the advance of freedom and opportunity and hope. The lives and freedom of the Iraqi people matter little to Saddam Hussein, but they matter greatly to us.

Saddam Hussein has a long history of brutal crimes, especially in time of war—even against his own citizens. If conflict comes, he could target civilians or place them inside military facilities. He could encourage ethnic violence. He could destroy natural resources. Or, worst of all, he could use his weapons of mass destruction.

In order to minimize the suffering of Iraq's people, the United States and our coalition partners stand ready to provide vital help. We will deliver medicine to the sick, and make sure that Iraq's 55,000 food distribution sites, operating with supplies from the oil-for-food program, are stocked and open as soon a possible. We are stockpiling relief supplies, such as blankets and water containers, for one million people. We are moving into place nearly three million emergency rations to feed the hungry. The United States and Great Britain are providing tens of millions of dollars to the U.N. High Commissioner for Refugees, and to such groups as the World Food Program and UNICEF, so they will be ready to provide emergency aid to the Iraqi people.

We will also lead in carrying out the urgent and dangerous work of destroying chemical and biological weapons. We will provide security against those who try to spread chaos, or settle scores, or threaten the territorial integrity of Iraq. And we will seek to protect Iraq's natural resources from sabotage by a dying regime, and ensure they are used for the benefit of Iraq's own people.

The United States has no intention of determining the precise form of Iraq's new government. That choice belongs to the Iraqi people. Yet we will ensure that one brutal dictator is not replaced by another. All Iraqis must have a voice in the new government, and all citizens must have their rights protected.

Rebuilding Iraq will require a sustained commitment from many nations, including our own. We will remain in Iraq as long as necessary, and not a day more. America has made and kept this kind of commitment before—in the peace that followed World War II. After defeating enemies, we did not leave behind occupying armies; we left constitutions and parliaments. We did not leave behind permanent foes; we found new friends and allies.

There was a time when many said that the cultures of Japan and Germany were incapable of sustaining democratic values. They were wrong. Some say the same of Iraq today. They, too, are mistaken. The nation of Iraq—with its proud heritage, abundant resources and skilled and educated people—is fully capable of moving toward democracy and living in freedom.

It will be difficult to help freedom take hold in a country that has known three decades of dictatorship, secret police, internal divisions, and war. Yet the security of our nation and the hopes of millions depend on us, and Americans do not turn away from duties because they are hard. We have met great tests in other times, and we will meet the tests of our time.

White House Press Statement, March 1, 2003

The United States believes the just-concluded meeting of the Iraqi opposition Advisory Committee in Salahudeen, Northern Iraq was a welcome opportunity for many courageous Iraqis to continue planning for a future democratic Iraq.

The U.S. delegation—headed by Presidential Special Envoy for Free Iraqis Zalmay Khalilzad—reaffirmed America's commitment to a democratic, representative, broad-based future Iraqi government that respects the principles of justice, the rule of law, and the human rights of Iraq's people; maintains Iraq's territorial integrity; is at peace with Iraq's neighbors; forswears weapons of mass destruction; fights terrorism; and fulfills its international obligations.

The United States is committed to working in partnership with the people of Iraq to bring this vision to life. We will continue this work in the days ahead, both with those represented at Salahudeen as well as others from throughout the broad community of free Iraqis, and with those Iraqis who have yet to be freed. Iraq's people are ready to begin the challenging road toward democracy. We salute the brave members of the Iraqi opposition and all Iraqis now suffering in silent captivity. Many freedom-loving nations throughout the world look forward with them to the day of their liberation.

Remarks by Secretary of State Powell, March 3, 2003

Secretary Colin Powell was interviewed on the United Kingdom's ITN.

Q. Thanks for seeing us. When you're seeing the Iraqis come up with information, it seems, on anthrax, VX nerve gas, we've seen Saddam destroy missiles over the weekend, Dr. Blix is telling us quite this is significant disarmament. Is he wrong?

Secretary Powell. Well, things are being destroyed, and perhaps documents are coming forward. I haven't seen them yet. But why didn't they do it four months ago? Why didn't they do it four years ago? Why didn't they do it 12 years ago when they were supposed to? Why are they kind of doling it out now?

They're not doing it because the inspections have suddenly become effective or they're suddenly threatened by a U.N. resolution. They're doing it because a powerful allied force is assembling in the region, consisting, for the most part, of the U.S., the U.K. and some other nations participating in it.

Q. Nevertheless, it changes the propaganda battle.

Secretary Powell. It changes the propaganda battle but it doesn't change reality. Reality is that they are still trying to deceive, they are still trying to send us down ratholes. Realty is they have not made a strategic decision to comply with 1441.

They were given a last chance to do so and they have not complied. The inspectors are not the means of getting them to comply. They were supposed to comply. And if they haven't complied, then they've lost their last chance and they should face the serious consequences that were called for in 1441.

Q. You're a military man. We all remember you as a four star general. I mean, you know the battle plan now. How much of a setback is not having Turkey, not having access to Turkish—

Secretary Powell. It's a disappointment. It will require readjustment of our plans. I don't know whether or not the Turkish parliament will have an opportunity to reconsider this in a time frame that—

Q. But you're putting on serious pressure for them to—

Secretary Powell. Well, we are talking to them. We are, of course, in constant contact with our Turkish colleagues. But even if we aren't able to persuade the Turkish parliament in the necessary time available to us to change their minds, our military authorities have options that will still make it absolutely certain that we'll be able to perform this military mission in an efficient, effective way and achieve our objective.

Q. Diplomacy. I mean, the word is today that you're not going to push a second resolution if you don't have the votes next week. Everything we're hearing is that you'll go to war regardless of whether you have a second resolution, that key word "regardless."
Secretary Powell. Well—

Q. And Tony Blair will be with you. Is that how you see it?

Secretary Powell. Well, the word—I don't know whether this is the revealed world or out of all your newspapers, but, in fact, we are going to listen to Dr. Blix and Dr. ElBaradei on Friday when they make their report, we'll consult with our friends and colleagues over the weekend, and then we'll make a judgment as to how to pursue a second resolution. We want to push for a second resolution and we are—

Q. And Tony Blair will be with you regardless of a second resolution?

Secretary Powell. We are pushing for a second resolution, and I won't speak for Prime Minister Blair. But we understand the importance and usefulness of a second resolution, not only to Prime Minister Blair but to all of us. We'd like to see a second resolution. But President Bush has made it clear from the very beginning that if there is not compliance, he believes the U.N. should act, and through the second resolution is one way, but there is sufficient authority in 1441 and earlier resolutions if willing nations and members of a willing coalition feel it is necessary to act to protect the stability of the region to get rid of these weapons of mass destruction. And, frankly, we're going to be creating a better life for the Iraqi people once they are through with this problem and through with Saddam Hussein.

Q. The price of this war is already high, isn't it? I mean, if you look out there— divided U.N., I mean, bitter divisions in Europe. You've got Tony Blair's government in London probably seeing the most serious crisis of confidence arguably since he came to power. I mean, this is serious collateral damage, isn't it, already?

Secretary Powell. It's not—

Q. Do you see it that way?

Secretary Powell. It is a serious situation and I won't make light of it, but at the same time, what we are doing and what Prime Minister Blair is doing and President Bush is doing, what Prime Minister Aznar is doing, what Mr. Berlusconi is doing, and so many other European nations are doing, is stepping up to this challenge of leadership. Either the international community's will has meaning or it does not have meaning, and in 1441 a clear standard was laid down and it said Iraq is in violation, it is guilty, it's been guilty for 12 years, it must come into compliance, if it doesn't come into compliance, serious consequences must flow. Everybody knew that that meant. It means military action would be required. And leader after leader has stood up to stand behind the meaning of that resolution, to include President Bush and Prime Minister Blair.

And even though I understand the political difficulties that they are all facing, and President Bush has his own set of political issues here, if it is clear that this is something that has to be done, and we do it and we do it well and efficiently, as I'm quite sure we will, and weapons of mass destruction are removed from Iraq and the Iraqi people realize there's a better life for them with the removal of this dictator, I think public opinion will quickly shift in the other direction and it will be seen as wise, enlightened, bold leadership, and all political leaders will benefit from it.

Q. Last one, very briefly. What does your instinct tell you? How long are you going to wait?

Secretary Powell. I would say that time is running out. We'll wait and see what they say on Friday and then I will say in—

Q. Days?

Secretary Powell.—in the not too distant future. We're not talking a long period of time. I don't want to get pinned down on days or weeks or a week, but certainly I think next week we would have to give very serious consideration as to what the next step should be.

Remarks by Secretary of State Powell, March 3, 2003

Secretary Colin Powell was interviewed on Russia's ORT.

Q. Thanks for this opportunity. And what now, Mr. Secretary? What are the chances for peace and war now, after the latest developments?

Secretary Powell. Well, I think there is always a chance for peace, and peace will come if Saddam Hussein and the Iraqi regime do what they have been asked to do by the international community for the last 12 years, and that is to completely comply with all their obligations to disarm, to get rid of their weapons of mass destruction, to make the strategic decision to disarm. They haven't done that.

They keep doling out little pieces of weapons. They keep reluctantly responding to the demands of the U.N.. They keep pretending that they are disarming, that they are doing things for the inspectors, when, in fact, they are doing the minimum necessary to try to keep the pressure off.

They're now destroying some missiles. Well, there's nothing wrong with destroying those missiles, but we know why they're being destroyed. It's because there are large American and United Kingdom and other forces assembling in the region, not because suddenly they have decided they have to comply and they realize they've made a mistake for all these years. It is simply military pressure and the threat of force that is causing them to do what they are doing now.

What we would like to see them do is to come clean, let everybody come out to be interviewed that need to be interviewed, give all the documents over, account for everything, not try to game this every day with a little bit more, a little bit less, a little bit more, a little bit less. One day, we'll destroy the missiles. The next day, well, maybe we won't destroy the missiles. This is the game they have been playing for so many years, and the game has now come to an end, and it must come to an end soon.

Q. What about the position of Russia? How do you account for the fact that Russia, together with France and China, just say that more time should be given to inspectors?

Secretary Powell. We talk to our Russian colleagues regularly. I speak to Foreign Minister Ivanov every few days, and President Putin and President Bush are in very close contact with each other. And we understand the Russian position and of course we respect the Russian position, but there is a disagreement. We believe that the issue is not more time for the inspectors or more inspectors; the issue is: Has Saddam Hussein made a strategic decision to come to into compliance with the United Nations resolutions? And we have seen nothing to suggest that he has made such a decision.

There is also a disagreement between us and Russia as to how serious the threat is. Are these weapons of mass destruction a threat to the United States, a threat to the Russian Federation, a threat to the region? We sincerely believe these weapons are a threat and the intention of this man, Saddam Hussein, to deploy such weapons is a threat to the region and to the world at large, especially after 9/11 when we are deeply concerned that terrorist organizations are looking for these kinds of weapons of mass destruction to conduct horrible attacks throughout he world, attacks that are not just directed at America but could be directed at Russia, as well. Russia has been forced to deal with terrorism, just like the United States has been forced to deal with terrorism, right in our own capitals.

Q. What about the second resolution in the Security Council? Are you going to push with this? And what are your instructions to Mr. Negroponte?

Secretary Powell. Well, I always try to keep my instructions to Mr. Negroponte somewhat private, but I think it is no secret that we believe this resolution is appropriate. We are now waiting for Dr. Blix and Dr. ElBaradei to report to the Council on Friday. And after we have heard their reports and consulted with our friends on the Council, our colleagues on the Council, and I'm sure I'll be consulting with my Russian colleagues, then I believe in the very near future after the 7th of March a judgment should be made as to whether or not it is time to seek a vote on this resolution.

Q. Yeah, well, I have one minute, sir. What can you say to the Russian viewers? March is a time for war or April for time for war, or no time for war?

Secretary Powell. We would prefer not to have a war. Nobody wants war. President Bush does not want war. President Putin does not want war. No sensible person wants war.

But sometimes, when you have a regime like Saddam Hussein's, which has essentially said, I don't care, I don't care for the past 12 years what I have been told to do. I am a dictator, I am a despot, I do terrible things to my people, I'm developing these weapons of mass destruction and I don't care what the rest of the world thinks. When you're faced with that kind of a situation and when you have laid down the rule in Resolution 1441 that he must comply, and he still does not comply, then, unfortunately, war becomes an option. This man must be disarmed for the safety of the region and for the safety of the world, and he will be disarmed—peacefully, hopefully, but, if necessary, the United States is prepared to lead a coalition of the willing, a coalition of willing nations, either under U.N. authority or without U.N. authority, if that turns out to be the case, in order to disarm this man. And it will be a peaceful world, a less threatened world, if he is disarmed and it'll be a better future for the people of Iraq if that's what it comes—if that's what comes in their future.

Remarks by Secretary of State Powell, March 3, 2003

Secretary Colin Powell was interviewed on Germany's RTL.

Q. Secretary of State Powell, there is word that the U.S. intends to push the resolution to a vote next week, even if you don't have the nine votes yet. Is this accurate? Can you confirm it?

Secretary Powell. Well, we are going to wait and see what Dr. Blix and Dr. ElBaradei report to the Security Council on Friday, and then over the weekend we'll consult with our friends and colleagues on the Security Council. I'm sure I'll be talking to my colleague, Joschka Fischer. And then early next week, we'll make a judgment on what we have heard, make a judgment on whether it's time to put the resolution up to a vote, and nobody really knows who has the votes until the votes are actually taken.

This is not an easy vote for those nations on the Security Council, but the United States feels that it is appropriate to move forward with a vote in the absence of compliance on the part of Saddam Hussein and the Iraqi regime. We have not seen the kind of compliance that we expected when 1441 was passed. We believe that he has missed his last chance to comply. And it is not clear that he can do anything in the next several days or week or so that would give us and give the world any assurance that he is truly trying to get rid of these weapons of mass destruction.

Q. What is your strategy towards Turkey now? Are you still expecting a change of mind there?

Secretary Powell. Well, we don't know. Turkey faced a very difficult situation in their parliament. Turkey and the United States have been close friends for many years and we'll be close friends for many years in the future.

If we make a judgment in the next several days that the Turkish parliament really is not in a position to deal with the requests that we have made to it in a second parliamentary session, then we have alternative plans that will allow us to conduct any military operations that the President might order. We'll still be able to accomplish our mission.

Q. In general, has the time for diplomacy run out yet?

Secretary Powell. It's getting toward the end. We have had diplomacy with Saddam Hussein for 12 years. We have been waiting for 12 years and we have passed resolution after resolution after resolution. They were simple resolutions: Please give up weapons of mass destruction, use the wealth of the Iraqi people to benefit the Iraqi people, not to develop weapons of mass destruction.

And time after time, resolution after resolution, he ignored the will of the international community. When the inspectors were starting to get close in 1998, he created conditions so that they had to leave. And finally, in the fall of 2002, the international community came together, a 15-0 vote for the Security Council. Resolution 1441 said this is your last chance, disarm, come into compliance, and if not, there will be serious consequences.

Now the debate before us is, well, shouldn't we have more inspectors? The inspection teams have not asked for more inspectors. Should we not give inspections more time? How much more time would be necessary if he's still not complying and cooperating? The only reason he's doing these small steps that you see is not because of inspections or because of the resolution; it's because there is a powerful force assembling and he's trying to keep that force from being used.

Q. Speaking about Germany, the German position is well known. What could our government else to do ease the tensions a bit?

Secretary Powell. Well, I don't know. Germany feels strongly that military force should not be used in this situation under any circumstances. I regret that position. I think it is not the correct position. But it is nevertheless the strong position of Chancellor Schroeder and the German Government and it reflects the will of the German people, and I respect that. Germany is a democracy that makes its own judgment as to what its position will be.

But I hope that Germany will understand our position and that if it is necessary that there be a conflict in order to disarm Iraq, I hope that Germany can assist in the aftermath in helping the Iraqi people build a brighter future. There will be a brighter future for the Iraqi people once they have disarmed themselves, one way or another, of these weapons of mass destruction.

And so Germany still has a role to play. This has been a difficult issue between the United States and Germany, but we have been through so many things together over the years that the relationship will survive this problem. We have German troops in Afghanistan. We are cooperating with Germany in so many different ways. And they are, of course, one of our strongest friends and allies and will remain so.

Q. Still, some people in Germany are concerned that the Americans might be reducing the military as an outcome of these tensions.

Secretary Powell. No, nonsense, nonsense. We are constantly looking at our presence in Europe, where our bases are, where should they be, what makes sense. And so General Jones, the new Supreme Allied Commander in Europe and the Commander of our forces in Europe, is examining the disposition of our bases and forces. This is perfectly understandable. It will be done in full consultation with the German Government. But it is not in response to this issue. This is something that has been underway for some time. And we are constantly reviewing our base structure in Germany. As you may recall after the Cold War ended, we reduced our presence in Germany by, oh, I guess, 60 or 70 percent, which was appropriate. So that's all. That is part of our regular restructuring and transformation study activities.

Remarks by Secretary of State Powell, March 3, 2003

Secretary Colin Powell was interviewed on France's TF-2.

Q. Mr. Secretary, can you tell us if you are confident that the U.S. will get a majority of votes at the U.N. next week?

Secretary Powell. Well, as you know, we are talking to our friends on the Security Council and I am increasingly optimistic that if it comes to a vote, we will be able to make a case that will persuade most of the members of the Security Council to vote for the resolution.

Of course, there are permanent members of the Council who have the option of vetoing such a resolution, but as you know and as your watchers and listeners know, there is a great deal of diplomacy taking place, there are great debates taking place as to how to move forward. But I hope that if we take the vote for a resolution, we'll be successful in getting the necessary votes to pass it.

Q. President Chirac was in Algeria yesterday and he said that thanks to the U.S. pressure, military pressure, Saddam was starting slowly, but starting to disarm. Are you concerned with the possibility of so, that the war was not necessary? Are you concerned over the possibility of a veto from France at the U.N.?

Secretary Powell. Well, first of all, I agree very much with President Chirac that it has only been through the threat of military force that Saddam Hussein has done anything. The limited cooperation we have seen is only the result of force, political force under Resolution 1441, and the threat of force by U.S. and United Kingdom forces moving into the region.

Trust me, if he did not see that threat of war, there would be no cooperation. He would be doing what he has been doing all of these years: ignoring the United Nations.

For 12 years, and especially since 1998, saying, I don't care what you think, pass all your resolutions, what do I care? I'm going to develop weapons of mass destruction to threaten the region, to threaten my own people, to keep a tight dictatorial rule over my country, and I don't care whether you like it or not.

And then finally, this past fall, the United Nations once again met and passed a resolution and this time said you must comply or face serious consequences. He's still not complying and therefore the choice is before us as to whether he should face serious consequences and whether the U.N. is irrelevant.

Now, France will have to make its own judgment as to how it will deal with this resolution. France is a sovereign nation. I understand the feelings of the people in France with respect to war. We don't want to see a war, but we also know that if it hadn't been for the threat of war, nothing would have been accomplished over the last four months; and if it is still not possible to get a strategic change in the mind of Saddam Hussein, then war may be necessary to compel him to disarm. And it will be a better region and a better world and a less threatened world once he is disarmed, one way or the other.

Q. You've said several times that time is running out for Saddam Hussein. President Bush has said the same thing. We get the impression, from a European perspective, that time is also running against the United States, that the more you wait, the more you get in trouble at the U.N., with the Turkish. Can you answer this, please?

Secretary Powell. We are prepared to do what is necessary militarily, if it comes to that. And although we were disappointed in the Turkish vote, I can assure you that our plans are flexible enough to handle this decision on the part of the Turkish parliament.

Obviously, you cannot keep a force like this, this large, just sitting around for a long period of time, as some have suggested. And that's not the right solution anyway, just to keep a force sitting around. The right solution is for him to comply, for him to disarm. And if he would disarm, this force would go away. But he has not made that strategic choice.

You can see it in what he has been doing with these missiles he's been destroying. One day, he says, no, I will not destroy them, I don't have to, they are not a violation. And the next day, he sends a letter to the inspectors, a very nasty letter, saying, well, I'll let you know in 48 hours what I'm going to do. And then he destroys one, then another.

But he is keeping in place the infrastructure to make them all over again once the pressure is off. We have the pressure on. This is the time to use that pressure, and, if necessary, use force to solve this problem once and for all so that it will not be a problem next year or the year after. Saddam Hussein must be disarmed and he must be disarmed now, one way or the other.

Q. My last question, Mr. Secretary. You say that war is not inevitable and you know that European political opinion thinks that war is—will happen because the United States will need force to remove Saddam Hussein from power. What can you tell them about that?

Secretary Powell. The issue is Saddam Hussein disarming. He has chosen to try not to disarm. He has chosen to divert our attention. He has chosen to deceive us once again. And unfortunately, my French colleagues believe that more inspectors will be the answer. But the inspection team has not asked for more inspectors. The inspector teams say that they want to see Saddam Hussein comply so that the inspectors can do their work.

My French colleagues say let the inspections just keep going. But we know from history that if Saddam Hussein sees that all he has to do is play with the inspectors for a long period of time and not truly make the decision to comply, those kinds of inspections will not work. And if they ever get close to getting his weapons of mass destruction, he'll do what he did in 1998; he makes it impossible for them to do their job and they will leave the country.

Don't underestimate the ability of this dictator to play to the desire for peace in the international community as a way of keeping his weapons of mass destruction. And we are determined that this time he must be disarmed and the world will be better off once he is disarmed, and I think European public opinion at that point will say hmm, maybe this is something we should have supported. We saw the same kind of reaction and public opinion before the Gulf War, but after the Gulf War when we had restored Kuwait, then people realized that maybe that was the right thing to have done.

Remarks by United Nations Secretary-General Annan, March 4, 2003

Q. The recent activities by the Iraqis to destroy the Al Sammoud missile and to come forward more on the issues of VX and anthrax—does that constitute cooperation in your opinion?

Secretary-General Annan. I think Inspector [Hans] Blix has indicated it's a positive development. He has indicated there's much more to be done, but this is a positive development. And he will be reporting to the [Security] Council on Friday, and I expect he will have more to say.

Q. What is your view, sir? And also, I have a follow-up.

Secretary-General Annan. No, this is a judgement for the Council. The inspectors are to report the facts and, as I've indicated, it is a positive development. And I think when the Inspector reports, the Council will make its own judgement.

Q. Do you think, Sir, that this can avoid military action by the U.S., and if it cannot, what could and should avoid military action?

Secretary-General Annan. Please, can you repeat the question? Sorry.

Q. Do you think that these recent moves can and should avoid military action by the U.S.? And if not, what could avoid military action?

Secretary-General Annan. I think the Council's decision will be based on the totality of the presentation by the inspectors and the information they have in front of them. Let's not forget that, in accordance with Resolution 1441, the Council has the right to declare further material breach at any time based on the reports of the inspectors and then move on to serious consequences. So let's give the process time. Let the inspectors report on Friday and see where the Council goes from there.

Q. Sir, good morning. I know that on previous occasions you rejected the idea of travelling to Baghdad. I just want to ask you again if that is still your position. That's number 1. And number 2, now there are many different initiatives floating around. There's the French-Russian-German memorandum; there's the British-Spanish-American draft resolution; there's the Canadian proposal. What do you make of all those and do you think the international community has something there to work with to avert war at this stage?

Secretary-General Annan. I think that is part of the democratic process in the Council. We are trying to resolve a very difficult issue and various members have put forward proposals to try and resolve the differences in the hope that one can bring the Council together for them to work in unity. I've always maintained it is when they work in unity that they are their most effective. So all these proposals that you say are on the table is an attempt to see if they can find a common ground and work together to deal with the problem. I'm in touch with most of these governments, both here and at their capitals, with their Presidents and Foreign Ministers, trying to see how we can all work together to deal with this issue.

On the question of my own visit to Iraq, I have indicated that, obviously as Secretary-General, my good offices are always available. But in the present circumstances, I'm not sure what a visit to Iraq would achieve and what message one would take to Iraq. Because I think that we've had a very open and active communication through the inspectors, through neighboring governments, and through the Arab League and a whole range of people. So at this stage, I maintain my position, I have no plans to travel to Iraq.

Q. The British and Russian Foreign Secretaries are meeting right now to discuss Iraq. How confident are you that their differences can be resolved?

Secretary-General Annan. The British and the —?

Q. The [British and the] Russian Foreign Secretaries.

Secretary-General Annan. Well obviously, it is good that they're getting together to discuss their differences. Whether they will be able to resolve them at one sitting, I do not know. But I think it's a healthy sign that they've come together to discuss how we move forward.

Q. Can you think of Japan and Germany being a permanent members of the Security Council in the near future?

Secretary-General Annan. Let's try and deal with this urgent matter first—the question of Iraq. But I think the question of Germany's and Japan's membership in the Security Council is something that has to be part of a broader Security Council reform. Until we achieve that reform, I don't see Germany or Japan getting in alone.

Q. The U.S. announced that they're going to rush to vote on their resolution after hearing [Mr.] Blix's report. Do you think the Security Council is ready for this vote?

Secretary-General Annan. Well, the Council is a master of its own deliberations. And the Council will have to decide whether they vote or not, whether they are ready for a vote or they want to postpone it for a future date. But they can vote and they can postpone it. It is their right.

Q. Mr. Annan, I was going to ask you what you thought of the Iranian statement this morning calling for free elections in Baghdad as a way to bridge the gap.

Secretary-General Annan. I read the press report and I think, obviously, elections are something that is in the future of any reform process. But I'm not sure that we are there yet. Thanks.

Q. Secretary-General, the President of the U.S. has called this a moment of testing the credibility of the United Nations in terms of its effectiveness in seeing through resolutions. Others say it's a crisis of credibility in terms of the U.N. to maintain consensual decisions in the face of the super power's desire. NGOs say that there's a crisis in a sense of living up to humanitarian responsibilities of the U.N.. To what extent do you see this as a profound moment facing this organization, and what do you understand to be the credibility of the United Nations in this situation?

Secretary-General Annan. I think this is a critically important stage for the United Nations. Obviously, whenever we discuss issues of war and peace, it is something that consumes all of us because of the human implications. And, as I have indicated, war is always a human catastrophe and we should only consider it when all possibilities for peaceful settlement have been exhausted. And I think this is what you've seen in the Council. They are trying to overcome this difficulty.

There are suggestions that if the Security Council does not vote for action, then its credibility would be mortally wounded. I tend to believe that if the Council were to manage to come together and resolve this crisis effectively and successfully, the credibility and the influence of the Council will be enhanced.

On the other hand, if the action were to be taken outside Council authority, the support for that action—popular and otherwise—would also be diminished. I also believe that to state that if the Council does not vote one way, it is going to go the way of the League of Nations, is overstating the case. I think the Council and the U.N. will not go the way of the League of Nations. And I think the historical comparisons are not as simple as it appears. The U.N. is much, much larger than the Iraqi crisis. The Iraq crisis is one of the issues we're dealing with. Yes, it's the most important one today. But we are much more than that. We're dealing with economic, social, humanitarian, and other issues. We're dealing with many other crises around the world. And I hope we are able to handle this effectively, bearing in mind the interest and the needs of the Iraqi population and their humanitarian concerns that you mentioned earlier.

Remarks by Secretary of State Powell, March 4, 2003

Secretary Colin Powell was interviewed on Spain's TVE.

Q. Mr. Secretary, thank you for visiting us. What's more important, the unity in the Security Council or a deadline?

Secretary Powell. I would like to see unity in the Security Council maintained, but the most important thing is to see Saddam Hussein disarmed. The Security Council came together when they passed Resolution 1441 last fall and they said that Saddam Hussein must now disarm, he must come into compliance, this is his last chance. That's what the resolution says. And if he does not come into compliance, if he does not take this last chance, he must face serious consequences.

I hope that there will be unity in the Security Council, or as much unity as we can generate, when the vote comes, if that vote does come, to say, you know, Saddam Hussein has lost his last chance. So I would like to see unity in the Security Council and I hope that the Security Council members will realize that they must keep the pressure on Saddam Hussein, and if he has not complied, they must be willing to step up to the task, as difficult as it may be and as unpleasant as it may be and unappreciated as it may be in European public opinion, to take the necessary military action to disarm Saddam Hussein. He cannot be allowed to walk away from the will of the international community after 12 years of ignoring the will of the international community.

Q. Are you pressing for a vote, even in the case where you have not the nine votes?

Secretary Powell. Well, we don't know whether we have nine votes or ten votes, or more. Over the next week or so, I think there will be very intense diplomatic discussions with all of the members of the Security Council and we will see what each of us thinks the vote count is, and then a judgment will be made as to when the resolution should be brought to a vote.

We are all waiting to see what Dr. Blix and Dr. ElBaradei say on Friday, and then over the weekend we'll be consulting to get a collective judgment of where the different nations on the Security Council stand.

Each nation on the Security Council is a sovereign nation, free to make its own choice, respond to its own political dynamic and listen to its own people. But leadership sometimes means that you listen to the people but sometimes you have to do something that doesn't enjoy public opinion at the moment but it is nevertheless the right thing to do for improving the stability of a particular region, in this case the Gulf region, or for protecting the people. Strong leaders sometimes have to make these kinds of difficult decisions in order to try to achieve a better world, in order to try to achieve the chances for peace and to put down the potential for terrorism and to put dictators in their place.

Q. There is still a chance for peace in two or three days? Do you believe that Saddam Hussein would change his mind?

Secretary Powell. I think it's unlikely. He has demonstrated for 12 years that he doesn't care what the rest of the world thinks. He intends to have weapons of mass destruction. He will manipulate public opinion. He will manipulate the world's opinion. He will do everything to make it look like he is cooperating and complying, when it is obvious that he is not cooperating and complying.

The issue is not more inspectors, the issue is not longer inspections, the issue is has he made a decision that we all can see and understand that says I'm going to provide anybody you need to be interviewed, I'm going to provide all the documents you need to find out what I did with my chemical and biological weapons, I'm going to destroy all of this infrastructure, I don't want any more weapons of mass destruction, I'm turning it all in, I will tell you everything you need to know. That's what he has not done. That is what I was hoping, praying he would do after 1441 was passed. But that is not what he has done. He continues to deceive. He continues to hide things. He continues to pretend he's destroying something here while he's protecting the ability to make more somewhere else. This is not what we are expecting from Saddam Hussein, but, unfortunately, it's what we got, and we must not step back from the difficult choices that may be ahead to disarm this dictatorial regime.

Q. But has he time in two, three days or one week—

Secretary Powell. He has time, but I think it is—you know, it is—your guess is as good as mine. I have not seen anything to suggest that he understands the seriousness of this issue or the determination of the international community. So I don't know that he can make a choice that would prevent the international community from facing the difficult issue of should we use force.

Remarks by Secretary of Defense Rumsfeld and Central Command Commander Franks, March 5, 2003

Q. One, are you still optimistic Turkey will allow U.S. forces to use its soil to open a northern frontier or a northern offensive? And second, part of the same question, if Turkey does not, the ships that are waiting to unload and the 4th Infantry Division, are they necessary to you conducting war if we should be so ordered ahead of time, or would you have to wait till all of those assets come around and get in place in the Persian Gulf?

General Franks. If I could, I'll take the second part of the question. And I think that it may be the secretary who would want to comment on optimism or with respect to what the government of Turkey might decide to do.

It is—it's been recognized that we have a number of ships in the eastern Mediterranean that we have the capability with ground forces in order to introduce those ground forces into Turkey. And one would not want to make a decision about where those ground forces might be introduced publicly, actually. And, you know, one of the things that we always do is we protect our planning effort, because as the combatant commander and as the operator for this, I actually am interested in security, and I am interested in secrecy. And in some cases what that does is it puts me in a position to permit others to speculate. We're going to protect our forces. We're going to protect our plan. And when the timing is right to make decisions like the destination of the 4th Infantry Division, then we'll be prepared to do that.

Secretary Rumsfeld. With respect to Turkey, Turkey's an ally, it's a friend, it's also a democracy. And they're working their way through a democratic process with a new government that's not ever governed before and through their parliamentary process. What they may ultimately decide remains to be seen. In any event, as the general indicates, we have workarounds.

Q. Does the general need the 4th Infantry Division? Do you need it to wage war now or could they be a reserve force?

General Franks. As I think the secretary and others have indicated—I think Dick Myers indicated yesterday—if the president of the United States decides to undertake action, we are in a position to provide a military option.

Q. Mr. Secretary, I'd like—you mentioned the briefing on targeting that was done here today. I'd like to ask General Franks, that briefer and other military officers have said recently that you would expect fewer civilian casualties this time around than in the '91 Gulf War because of a greater use and reliance on precision-guided weapons. I'm wondering first whether you agree with that. And secondly, how would you explain to those who would doubt that, given the fact that we believe that Baghdad is where the regime is and that that would be the focus of the attention?

General Franks. As you know, neither the secretary nor I heard the briefing, and so I don't know exactly what that briefing included. But I do know this: Anytime a nation undertakes a war, there are some fixed quantities and there are variables. I believe that it is true that the variables for this particular effort, if a decision is made to undertake it, will be different than the variables that we have seen in warfare in the past. And I can give you a couple of reasons for that, one of which is simply precision, the types of weapons that are used. And so one would expect to see a reduction in variables. That does not necessarily mean that one would expect to see a reduction in civilian casualties, and I think it's a key point, and I'll tell you why.

We have seen in the past the regime in Baghdad position intentionally military equipment close to hospitals, close to schools, close to mosques, close to other civilian infrastructure, and we certainly are not in a position to prevent the regime from doing that again. And so, my personal view is that one should not ever put a stake in the ground and say there will be more or less casualties, either friendly or enemy, because while we can reduce the variables, we also recognize that a very ruthless regime that sits in Baghdad will make his own decisions about where to position the lives of his own people.

* * * *

Q. General Franks, could you give us your assessment of the situation or the possibility of conflict between the Turks and the Kurds in northern Iraq? I'm particularly interested if you have extracted any promises from either side not to fight or not to try to seize the oil fields, what you feel the U.S. responsibility is in keeping those two sides apart and not fighting, and whether this is complicated by the possibility that you won't be able to base a lot of ground troops in Turkey.

General Franks. A wise man said once upon a time, once upon a time that prediction is extremely difficult, especially if it has to do with the future.

Q. Your assessment, then, not your prediction, but your assessment of the level of conflict.

General Franks. But what I—what I can say is historically, and all recognize that there have been frictions between the Kurds and the Turks up in northern Iraq, we certain believe that that is a factor. We, in fact, work representatives with both the Kurds and with the Turks and will continue to do that. And actually I would not—I wouldn't be willing to predict what might happen up there. We're aware of history, and so we'll be working in order to mute whatever problem may arise.

Q. To go back, you said at the start that if there's a war, there's no doubt that we'll prevail. And I think that most Americans probably want to know how—what is the cost going to be in American lives and how long might it take. Now I know you can't answer those questions precisely, but I wonder if you could share your thoughts about it. You know, are we looking at a conflict of weeks, months? In the Gulf War, there were 148 Americans killed. Would you hope to be able to keep U.S. casualties to that sort of level?

General Franks. It's a fair question, but it's unknowable, actually. You'll recall what I said a minute ago about noncombatant—we talked civilian—but noncombatant casualties. And I think one doesn't know.

I think one doesn't know the duration that we may face. I may have an opinion, the secretary may have an opinion, but it is in fact unknowable. And since we can't know what the duration will be, we can't predict, using some formulation, some mathematical model, what casualties might look like—you'll all remember that there was an effort to do that some 11 or 12 years ago, and you'll recall the results of that effort, how the facts wound up matching against the predictions.

And so what—so since we don't know the answer to that, what we do on the operational side, where our youngsters are out there on the ground, is we work very, very hard to balance the mission against the potential gain and the risk.

And so I won't predict numbers of casualties, but I will say that we'll continue to work to do the job at the least cost in terms of lives, both our own and Iraqi, and the least cost in terms of treasure.

Secretary Rumsfeld. When you think about anyone who tried to predict the cost of World War I or World War II or Korea or Vietnam or Afghanistan, it—their guesses would be embarrassing to be compared with the facts. Same thing with casualties—to guess the casualties of any of those. To guess the length of any of those. War is an uncertain business, and as the general says, there's so many variables that it's really more of a misservice to speculate on those things.

I will say this: I'll make one speculation, and that is that the—we don't know precisely what the total cost of September 11th was in dollars—we know lives: some 3,000 people—but in dollars. It had such a violent impact on our economy, on business and the economics, not just of New York City or Washington, D.C., but of the entire country, that it—very likely anything that one ends up with, an unknowable number today, in the event that force has to be used with respect to Iraq, would be a fraction of what September 11th cost.

Q. Well, Mr. Secretary, to use one of your favorite words, can you promise it won't be a quagmire?

Secretary Rumsfeld. I can almost promise you that someone in this room will SAY it's a quagmire. Quite apart from the facts.

Q. Mr. Secretary and General Franks, a few days ago we heard the president say once again that regime change in Iraq is one of the U.S. objectives. Is it your understanding that the military objective, then, in any possible action against Iraq would be to kill or capture Saddam Hussein? And could there be a victory without either one of those things occurring?

General Franks. It depends on one's personal view of the definition of regime. If one looks at regime as the control of diplomacy, the control of borders, the control of economic infrastructure, the control and security of population, then one would find that certainly to be within my mission statement. And so I won't go with you to the point of the personalities; I will simply say that the mission statement that the president has asked us to look at, has asked us to plan for is precisely clear, exactly determined, and there is no doubt in my mind about what the expectation of my bosses or the United States of America may be if this is required.

Q. Does the name "Saddam Hussein" appear in the mission statement?

General Franks. Mr. Secretary?

Secretary Rumsfeld. The answer to the question is that in the event force has to be used—and that decision has not been made—it will be made because of a failure on the part of Saddam Hussein and his regime to cooperate with the 17 U.N. resolutions.

Therefore, clearly the goal of the use of force would be unambiguously to have the people who did not cooperate not there.

Q. Including Saddam Hussein, I presume.

Secretary Rumsfeld. No longer in charge of that country.

Q. Mr. Secretary, if your goal is primarily to disarm Iraq, what concretely could Saddam Hussein do to prevent a war? Like giving evidence on the missing CW/BW; would that be enough?

Secretary Rumsfeld. Those are not issues for me to respond to. Those are questions that the president and the United Nations and Secretary Powell and others are wrestling with as they try to make a judgment as to what the prospects are.

Q. General Franks, a couple of armored division got deployment orders just this week. And if you look at how long it would take for them to get there and get hooked up with their equipment, you know, you're looking at a few weeks. You've already said you have what you need for the military option. Are we now getting some clues into your thinking about what kind of follow-on course requirements might be needed? You probably know there's some dispute in town about that issue.

General Franks. Actually, what I would say is let me correct just the first part of the question. I didn't say that I'd given the secretary or that the secretary had passed to the president the option. What I said was that we are in a position at this point in time where the secretary and the president of the United States have options. In order for me to talk about the units which have been alerted, you referred to, would be about the same thing as me answering a question that says, "What's your plan?" And none of us actually expect that we're going to talk about that, so I really won't.

Q. Well, can you talk about your thoughts about what kind of force would be needed to secure Iraq in the post-war period?

General Franks. I could, but I believe right now is not the time to do that, especially to reinforce the point the secretary made a minute ago: The president of the United States has not made a decision to do this. But I think it's fair to say that one would expect a great deal of planning and thought to be going into that.

Q. Mr. Secretary, you keep talking about a growing coalition, and it's difficult for us to perceive that.

Secretary Rumsfeld. Well, that's very clear. The reason for that—that it's difficult to perceive—is because no decision has been made to use force. And clearly, until that decision is made, countries have to look at the circumstance when it's made and then make their judgment. What we do know is that there is a large and growing number of countries that have said to us on a variety of differing basis that they would like to participate. There are already a number of countries that are doing military planning with General Franks; there's a number of countries who have already said that you're going to have overflight rights and basing and various other things; there are a number of countries who have said they want to participate in a post-Saddam Hussein stabilization activity. But until a decision is made, it shouldn't be surprising that that's not public.

Q. I see two other countries, Australia and Britain, that have committed ground forces and one other country that has said they will send sniffer equipment to detect chemical and biological weapons.

Secretary Rumsfeld. If you were a neighbor of Saddam Hussein and you did not know of certain knowledge whether he would be there in six months, I think you'd be cautious about discussing the subject publicly, as well.

Q. So we should not be misled by the fact that the coalition appears to have two other countries and the United States that are willing to commit ground forces at this point?

Secretary Rumsfeld. I think that your visibility into it is, understandably, not great because the countries involved do not care at this stage to prejudge whether or not force is going to be used.

Remarks by Secretary of State Powell, March 5, 2003

Secretary Colin Powell delivered the following remarks at the Center for Strategic and International Studies in Washington, DC.

Let me put the question to you directly and clearly in the simplest terms that I can. The question simply is: Has Saddam Hussein made a strategic political decision to comply with the United Nations Security Council resolutions? Has he made a strategic political decision to get rid of his weapons of mass destruction? That's it, in a nutshell. The question is not how much more time should be allowed for inspections. The question is not how many more inspectors should be sent in. The question simply is: Has Saddam Hussein made a strategic decision, a political decision, that he will give up these horrible weapons of mass destruction and stop what he's been doing for all these many years?

That's the question. There is no other question. Everything else is secondary or tertiary. That's the issue. It's an issue that's been on the table for 12 years. It's the issue that was put to Saddam Hussein in 1991 after the Gulf War. And over a period of years, and resolution after resolution after resolution, the same question was put to him, the same challenge was given to him, the same instruction was given by the international community, by the Security Council, to Saddam Hussein: Disarm, give up these weapons of mass destruction, stop threatening your people, let your neighbors live in peace, no longer fearful of these kinds of weapons. And for 12 years, Saddam Hussein has given the same answer back repeatedly: No, I will not.

On September 12th of last year, President Bush took the issue, once again, to the United Nations, and before the General Assembly on that day, the 12th, he challenged

the world community to act, to act in a definitive way to deal with this threat to international peace and security that was being posed and had been posed for so many
years by Saddam Hussein and his regime.

We then went into a spirited debate for the next seven weeks after the President's
speech to come up with a resolution that would lay it out clearly once and for all. It's
interesting to note that as soon as this debate began and Saddam Hussein recognized
that something might come out of it, he started to respond. Within a few days after the
President's speech, he said, oh, I'll let the inspectors in, after years of saying, no, you
can't come back in, after he caused them to leave in 1998.

Was he doing that because he had suddenly made a strategic decision to comply or
disarm? No. He was doing it because he began to feel the pressure. And once again, he
started to play the game that he had been playing for the last 11 or so years, to divert
attention, to distract, to throw chaff up, to confuse, to cause us to lose our way in
applying our will.

Nevertheless, the debate went forward, even though there were people who said,
well, gosh, why do we need a new resolution? We have all these other resolutions, and
he's now going to let the inspectors back in. But we went right ahead. We ignored all
of that. We ignored the letters that went back and forth between he and the United
Nations and the inspectors as he tried to see if he could derail a new resolution. And
he failed.

And after some seven weeks of the most intense negotiations, intense diplomacy
imaginable, last November, the Security Council unanimously, 15 to zero—people
thought it couldn't be done—15 to zero, the Security Council unanimously passed
Resolution 1441.

And let's be clear what Resolution 1441 is all about. It's not just a bunch of meaningless words. Every one of those words was fought over. It's not about inspectors. It's
not about an inspection regime. It is about Saddam Hussein, in the first instance, in
the first part of that resolution, being found guilty again, reaffirming his guilt over the
preceding 11 years of possessing and developing with the intention of having and
potentially using weapons of mass destruction.

That resolution, in the first instance, was about Saddam Hussein continuing to be
in material breach of multiple previous resolutions, 16 of them, that demanded his
disarmament. It was about giving Saddam Hussein, in the next instance, one last
chance to come clean and disarm. That was the clear purpose of the resolution. One
last chance. You have been in material breach. You have been guilty. You still are guilty.
We're giving you one last chance to make that strategic choice, make that political
decision to give up these horrible weapons that threaten humanity, to give them up,
come into compliance. Once again, join with your neighbors in trying to build a better neighborhood. Come into compliance, one last chance. But the drafters of that resolution and all of the ministers and ambassadors who worked on it knew who we were
dealing with. We have seen the record of the past 11 years.

So we made it clear that there had to be certain other elements in the resolution.
One of the other elements had to be an inspection regime that would be tough,
demanding, that would allow the inspectors to go anywhere, anytime, anyplace. It also
said that Hussein had to provide them everything they needed to do their job, had to
cooperate, provide people for interviews, all the other things that you have heard dis-

cussed. That was an essential part of the resolution.

And then the final element of that resolution, so that there could be no doubt about what would follow in the absence of compliance, it made it clear that if he missed this one last chance, if he committed new material breaches, then serious consequences would follow.

Nothing we have seen since the passage of 1441 indicates that Saddam Hussein has taken a strategic and political decision to disarm; moreover, nothing indicates that the Iraqi regime has decided to actively, unconditionally and immediately cooperate with the inspectors. Cooperate for the purpose of showing everything they have, not cooperate for the purpose of seeing how little we can show them.

Process is not performance. Concessions are not compliance. Destroying a handful of missiles here under duress, only after you're pressed and pressed and pressed and you can't avoid it, and you see what's going to happen to you if you don't start doing something to deceive the international community once again, that's not the kind of compliance that was intended by U.N. Resolution 1441. Iraq's too little, too late gestures are meant not just to deceive and delay action by the international community, he has as one of his major goals to divide the international community, to split us into arguing factions. That effort must fail. It must fail because none of us wants to live in a world where facts are defeated by deceit, where the words of the Security Council mean nothing, where Saddam and the likes of Saddam are emboldened to acquire and wield weapons of mass destruction.

Saddam's response to Resolution 1441 is consistent with his answers to all the previous resolutions. He has met each one of them with defiance and deception, with every passing year since 1991 and with every passing day since the adoption of Resolution 1441. Saddam, as a result, has taken Iraq deeper and deeper into material breach of its international obligations.

It was precisely because of his long history of defiance and deception when the Security Council's members voted to pass Resolution 1441, we were expecting to see this all again. And we carefully included in the resolution some early tests to see whether or not we were wrong. Maybe he had changed. Maybe this time it would be different.

One of those early tests was 30 days after the passage of the resolution we wanted to see from Saddam Hussein something we were supposed to have seen back in 1991, but didn't, and that was a current, accurate, full and complete declaration of its banned programs. The Iraqi regime was to give inspectors immediate, unimpeded and unrestricted access to any site and any person to help them do their job of verifying whether Iraq was disarming. In that first 30 days, wait for the declaration, see if this kind of access was granted.

1441 spelled out very clearly that false statements or omissions, and failure to cooperate with these inspectors, as they started to do their work, these two elements combined, would constitute a further material breach, a further finding of guilty, not complying.

No one has seriously claimed that Iraq provided a currently accurate, full and complete declaration on December 8th when they met the 30-day schedule. No one has stood up to defend them. So many of my colleagues, unfortunately, on the Security Council don't even want to remember that. Well, that was back in December. We know we don't have to think about that now. Well, that was December. That's not worry about that now. Let's not discuss that at our next meeting. Let's just let bygones by bygones. Let's see what we can get him to do today that might make us feel a little better.

It's not going to work. We cannot ignore it. The things that are not in the declaration are things that we have to know about. Instead, we got a mixture of lies and deceit, falsities. Chief U.N. Inspector Blix and International Atomic Energy Head ElBaradei both told the Council on December 19th that there was not much new in that Iraqi declaration, and we shouldn't have been surprised. Indeed, the 12,000-page document that they tried to pass off as the whole truth was nothing but a rehash of old and discredited material, with some new lies thrown in for good measure to make it look fresh. Fresh lies on top of the old lies.

It repeated the biggest lie of all, the claim that Iraq has no weapons of mass destruction, thereby setting the stage for further deception of the inspectors as they went about their business.

You know, it's illustrative just to look at a couple of examples. You take VX nerve agent. VX nerve agent is the most deadly chemical weapon imaginable. Horrible to contemplate. As a soldier, I had to contemplate it, both as a battlefield commander, as Chairman of the Joint Chiefs of Staff, and it was a weapon that I never wanted to see used in battle, I would never like to see used in a terrorist operation, I would never like to see used against any human being. A few drops and you're dead.

Back in 1991, Iraq was required then to declare and destroy its arsenal of all these kinds of materials and VX. And what did Iraq do back in 1991? It denied it had any. And it stuck to that denial for four long years, all the way through 1995. Inspectors were all over the country. Inspectors were there looking. Inspectors were doing what inspectors are supposed to do: verify what they have been told. And they were told there was no VX.

In 1995 or thereabouts, Saddam Hussein's son-in-law, who knew a lot, defected, and he spilled the beans. He let it be known that the Iraqi regime had VX. And as a result of what he told the international community, what he told the inspectors, the Iraqi regime was forced to admit it. Forced to admit that it had produced large amounts of this terrible, terrible poison.

If it hadn't been for that cueing from his son-in-law, who subsequently paid with his life when he foolishly went back home, if you have any doubts about the nature of this regime, if it hadn't been for the cueing that he provided, who knows where Saddam Hussein might be today with VX? The fact of the matter is, we don't know where he is today with VX because the latest declaration is still inadequate.

Even now, eight years after that discovery, he continues his deception. He still claims that Iraq has never weaponized its VX stocks. He wants us to believe that while he has had some VX, he can't use it.

The inspectors aren't buying it. Dr. Blix reported to the Security Council on January 27th that there are indications the Iraqis have made more progress on weaponizing VX than they have admitted.

Just a few days ago now, the Iraqis suddenly have come forward and said they will provide a report on their VX, where he's going to look for a new report to come in a week or so, they said. I'm not going to hold my breath. We've been waiting for these reports to come for years and they have not come. Why do they come now? They are trying to get out of the glare of the light. They're trying to get off the stove. They're trying to, once again, put us off the case. How many lives would you risk, innocent lives would you risk on the veracity of such a report coming from Saddam Hussein? He still hasn't made the strategic choice to comply and disarm.

The saga of Iraq's prohibited missile programs offers another example of how he weaves his web of deceit. Missiles in and of themselves are not weapons of mass destruction, but they can deliver such warheads. Shortly after the end of the Gulf War, in order to contain Saddam Hussein and as part of that early series of resolutions, missiles with ranges of more than 150 kilometers were banned, were banned from Iraq by Security Council Resolution 687. He's not supposed to have missiles that will go beyond 150 kilometers, but he does.

In its voluminous declaration of December 8th, Iraq flatly stated that it had no such missiles. We don't have any. But data from flight tests for two missiles, the al-Samoud II and the al- Fatah, showed that they traveled more than 150 kilometers. They were clearly trying to upgun these missiles so that they go far beyond their prohibited range. And why would one want to do that? To reach out, that's why they wanted to do it.

So Iraq quickly shifted tactics and said, well, you know, that's really not the case, let's talk about this, let's show you why you've got the wrong data, and they tried to throw the inspectors off the track. But the inspectors insisted, Dr. Blix insisted, that these missiles be destroyed.

You should see the first letter that came back from the Iraqis, when Dr. Blix's letter went to them. It was an attack, once again, saying well, you know, you shouldn't be doing this, it's wrong, we're innocent. Once again, denial. Once again, trying to deceive. Once again, only going along with the destruction because they were trying to keep us divided, keep us confused, and try to delay what might well be heading their way.

Nobody should be quick to declare a victory for compliance in the missile department. And from recent intelligence, we know that the Iraqi regime intends to declare and destroy only a portion of its banned al-Samoud inventory and that it has, in fact, ordered the continued production of the missiles that you see being destroyed. Iraq has brought its machinery that produces such missiles out into the daylight for all to see. But we have intelligence that says, at the very same time, it has also begun to hide machinery it can use to convert other kinds of engines to power al-Samouds II.

Once again, he plays the double game. Even as he orders some to be destroyed, he is continuing with activities that will allow more to be produced. We can see no real improvement on substance. Iraq is far from disarming.

But what about process? People talk about process. Shouldn't we be pleased about the cooperation we have seen with the inspectors? Unfortunately, we don't find Baghdad's performance much better in that regard.

Since my presentation to the Security Council on February 5th, we have received further intelligence from multiple sources showing that Iraq is continuing in its efforts to deceive the inspectors. Much of this intelligence from a variety of sensitive sources, many of these sources I cannot share with anyone in any greater detail than I am here today, but it's reliable and shows that the Iraqi regime is still moving weapons of mass destruction materials around the country to avoid detection.

Why should we be surprised? This has been his pattern. This has been what he's been doing for 12 years. For example, we know that in late January, the Iraqi Intelligence Service transported chemical and biological agents to areas far away from Baghdad, near the Syrian and Turkish borders, in order to conceal them, and they have concealed them from the prying eyes of inspectors.

In early February, fearing that UNMOVIC had precise intelligence about storage locations, the Iraqis were moving prohibited materials every 12 to 24 hours. And in mid-February, concerned about the surveillance capabilities of the U-2 overflights that they finally were going to permit, Iraq was transferring banned materials in old vehicles and placing them in poor, working class neighborhoods outside the capital.

If Baghdad really were cooperating, if they really wanted to comply, if it really was disarmament that they were interested in, they would be bringing all of these materials out, not scattering them for protection.

We also know that senior Iraqi officials continue to admit in private what they continue to deny in public, that Iraq does, indeed, possess weapons of mass destruction. A senior official stated in late January that Baghdad could not answer UNMOVIC's questions honestly without causing major problems for Iraq.

Another senior official said that allowing UNMOVIC to question Iraqi scientists outside of Iraq would prove disastrous. Why? Because free of intimidation, free from the risk of loss of life, they might tell the truth. And we also know that Saddam Hussein has issued new guidance to key officials saying everything possible must be done to avoid discovery of Iraq's weapons of mass destruction.

If Iraq was serious about disarming, it would encourage, it would order, it would tell all of its scientists: Step forward, those of you who know anything about what we have been doing for the last 10 years. come forward so that information can be made available so we can convince the international community of our claims.

That is not what is happening. Instead, Saddam's security officials have been working aggressively to discourage or to control interviews between Iraqi scientists and inspectors and we should not be deceived because a few, a few have made themselves available without minders.

Last month, a senior Iraqi official told an Iraqi scientist not to cooperate with the U.N. inspectors. He threatened the scientist with grave misfortune if the scientist did not obey. Iraqi security officials have required scientists who have been invited to interviews with the inspectors to wear concealed recording devices. Hotels where the interviews are being conducted have been bugged.

Resolution 1441 was meant to end this kind of action. It was intended to end 12 years of deceit and manipulation. It was intended to give him one last chance to comply. And that's why the Security Council demanded full and immediate compliance, not piecemeal gestures of cooperation, not more documents of deception, not more half-measures and half-truths.

The inspectors are very, very dedicated professionals. I've gotten to know Dr. Blix and Dr. ElBaradei very, very well and I've met with some members of their teams. These are terrific people. We should be so thankful that there are international civil servants such as they who are willing to undertake these kinds of missions under difficult circumstances, and I give them all the credit for their willingness to do this. None of this that I am talking about is of any fault of theirs.

They are working hard. But unfortunately, the inspection effort isn't working. Why? Because it was never intended to work under these kinds of hostile circumstances. It was intended to help the Iraqis comply. They were not intended to be detectives that went around seeking out things in the absence of genuine Iraqi cooperation. Inspections cannot work effectively as long as the Iraqi regime remains bound and determined to hold on to its weapons of mass destruction instead of divesting itself of these terrible items.

In recent weeks, we have seen a dribbling out of weapons—a warhead there, a missile there—giving the appearance of disarmament, the semblance of cooperation. And in recent days, they have promised more paper, more reports. But these paltry gestures and paper promises do not substantially reduce Saddam's capabilities, they do not represent a change of heart on his part, and they do not eliminate the threat to international peace and security.

Nor do they come because Saddam is worried about hordes of additional inspectors being sent into Iraq armed with work plans and benchmarks. They have everything to do, these process efforts on their part, they have everything to do with the fact that Saddam faces an ever nearer prospect of defeat by overwhelming military force. It is the threat of force—and no one will deny this—it is the threat of force that is causing him to comply, not the threat of inspections or the threat merely of resolutions. In the absence of his willingness to do what he has to do, it is only the threat of force that is getting him to do anything at all.

If, at this late date, Saddam were truly to decide to come clean and comply with 1441, the current number of inspectors could do the job of verifying Iraq's disarmament and they wouldn't need an enormous amount of time in which to do it. Inspectors have said so. The amount of time needed to verify all this is a function of how much cooperation and the willingness there is to comply with the resolutions, not the number of inspectors. What is now needed is that strategic and political decision which we have not seen over the past 12 years.

Inspections will amount to little more than casting at shadows unless Iraq lifts the fog of denial and deception that prevents inspectors from seeing the true magnitude of what they're up against. It is for Iraq to prove to the Security Council and to the world that it has disarmed.

We know that true disarmament looks like. We saw it with South Africa. We saw it with the Ukraine. The leaders of both of those countries made solemn political commitments to disarm and they worked with the international community. And even then it took a lot of time, but at least you knew that they were in union with you to disarm. Those two nations did everything possible to ensure complete cooperation with inspectors, and an expeditious, rigorous, transparent disarmament process was put in place.

What would it look like in Iraq? Instead of letting the inspectors grope for answers in the dark, Iraq would bring all of its documents out and all of its scientists into the light to answer the outstanding questions. Indeed, Iraq would be besieging the inspectors with information. Mobile labs would be driven up and parked outside of UNMOVIC headquarters. All of the missiles of the al-Samoud variety would be destroyed immediately. They wouldn't be hesitating. They would go and find the infrastructure for these missiles and what machinery they have hidden to produce more and make them available for destruction.

I return to the fundamental question: Is he complying? That's it. Is Iraq complying with 1441? And the only reasonable answer is no.

Last November, when 1441 was passed, the international community declared Saddam Hussein a threat. In four months since, that has not changed; he is still a threat. He was given one last chance to avoid war. If Iraq complies and disarms, even at this late hour, it is possible to avoid war.

He is betting, however, that his contempt for the will of the international community is stronger then the collective resolve of the Security Council to impose its will. Saddam Hussein is betting that some members of the Council will not sanction the use of force despite all the evidence of his continued refusal to disarm. Divisions among us—and there are divisions among us—if these divisions continue, will only convince Saddam Hussein that he is right. But I can assure you, he is wrong.

So those who say that force must always be a last resort, I say that I understand the reluctance to use force. I understand the hesitation to undertake human—human—to take human life. I have seen the horrors of war. I have been where the dying is done. I agree with those who say that lives must only be sacrificed for the greatest of causes. We should do everything possible to avoid war. We have done that, and no one believes that more deeply than President Bush. That's why he went to the United Nations. That's why he persuaded all 15 of us on the Security Council to give Saddam Hussein one last chance.

It is always a hard thing for citizens to accept the prospect of war, and it should be. But consider the chilling fact that Saddam Hussein also knows what war is like. He has used war and weapons of mass destruction against his neighbors and against thousands of his own citizens. And in this post-September 11th world, getting those appalling weapons out of his hands is the only way to guarantee that he won't use them again, or he won't make common cause and pass them on through his terrorist connections for use practically anywhere in the world.

Consider what could happen if Saddam Hussein, a tyrant who has no scruples and no mercies, concludes that the governments of the world will not condone military action under any circumstances, even as a last resort, as at least one member of the Security Council feels. Under those circumstances, he will never comply with his obligations. All he has to do is wait us out. And a terrible message will go far and wide to all those who conspire to do harm, to all those who seek to acquire weapons of mass destruction. It is now for the international community to confront the reality of Iraq's continued failure to disarm.

The Security Council resolution put forward last week by the United Kingdom, Spain and the United States says precisely that: "Iraq has failed to take the final opportunity afforded it in Resolution 1441." That is a simple statement of fact, as well. Iraq has refused to disarm and cooperate. It serves the interest of no one for Saddam to miscalculate. It doesn't serve the interest of the United States or the world or Iraq for Saddam to miscalculate our intention or our willingness to act. By passing this new resolution, the Council will remove any doubt that it will accept anything less than

Iraq's complete disarmament of its weapons of mass destruction and full cooperation with the inspectors to verify its compliance.

If Saddam leaves us no choice but to disarm him by force, the United States and our coalition partners will do our utmost to do it quickly, do it in a way that minimizes the loss of civilian life or destruction of property. We will do our utmost in such circumstances, should they be forced upon us, to meet the humanitarian needs of the Iraqi people. And we would take responsibility for the post-war stabilization of that country. We would be responsible for establishing and maintaining order, destroying Iraq's weapons of mass destruction once and for all.

Dismantling terrorist networks with nodes in Iraq would also be a priority.

And soon after these immediate needs are met and internal security is established, we would want to move as quickly as possible to civilian oversight of the next stages in the transformation of Iraq, working with the many coalition partners we will have, working with all the elements of the international community that would be willing to play a role in such an effort. Then, legitimate Iraqi institutions representing all Iraqis, representing the people, can be raised up; institutions created and a formal government put in place that will make sure the nation does not rearm, that the treasure that exists in Iraq in the form of its oil is used for the benefit of the people of Iraq. The United States has a superb record over the past 50 or 60 years of helping countries that we found it necessary to do battle with or in, put themselves on a better footing for a brighter future.

To be sure that there will be lots of work to do. The work of reconciliation and rehabilitation and reconstruction will be a long and hard one, but we are up to the task. But the true test of our collective commitment to Iraq will be our efforts to help the Iraqi people build a unified Iraq that does not threaten international peace, one that is a welcome presence among the nations of the world, not an international pariah.

For 30 years, Saddam has fed off the blood, sweat, and tears of his people. He has murdered, tortured, and raped to stay in power. He has squandered Iraq's vast oil wealth on lavish palaces and secret police and weapons programs.

The United States and the international community want to help free the Iraqi people from fear, freedom from want. We in the world community desire to help Iraqis move their country toward democracy and prosperity. We want to help the Iraqi people establish a government that accepts principles of justice, observes the rule of law and respects the rights of all citizens. In short, we want to see an Iraq where people can look to the future with hope, and not be seen as a pariah on the world stage.

We aren't just thinking about that famous day after. We know it's not going to be just one day after, but many days after a long, formidable challenge that will lie ahead of us and our coalition partners, until such time as Iraqis are prepared to govern their own land.

Even as the Iraqi people are liberated, we are determined to do all we can to renew hope in other parts of the region. To strive for peace between Israelis and Palestinians. President Bush has recently again emphasized his own personal commitment to achieving the vision of two states, Israel and Palestine, living side by side in peace, security and dignity, and to implementing the roadmap, the Quartet roadmap, that will help make that vision a reality.

We stand ready to lead the way to this better future. To get there, all those in the region who yearn for peace—the Palestinians, the Israelis, and their Arab neighbors—will have to fulfill deep commitments and make difficult compromises. But the tough choices will be worth it. While the process of peacemaking poses obligations for all, the benefits of peace will be felt for generations to come by millions of people.

But if the international community wants the hopeful prospects for the days, months and years ahead to materialize for Iraq, we must confront the reality of Saddam Hussein's intransigency. We must confront that reality here and now. We must face the reality that Saddam's Iraq is Exhibit A of the grave and growing danger that an outlaw regime can supply terrorists with the means to kill on a massive scale.

Last November, the entire Security Council declared his weapons of mass destruction to be that threat to international peace and security. And if that threat existed last November when we voted for 1441, it certainly exists now. If the international community was resolute then, it must be resolute now.

Resolution 1441 was not just President Bush and the United States saying Saddam is a menace to the world. It was France, Britain, Russia, China, Syria and all the rest of the Security Council going on record saying so. We spent seven weeks working over and weighing every single word of that resolution. All of the members of the Council knew when they passed 1441 that the time might come when we would have to meet our responsibility to use force in the absence of Saddam Hussein's strategic decision to disarm and comply.

For the past four months, he's been trying to avoid the consequences of his non-compliance, to escape the moment of truth. Now is the time for the Council to come together once again to send a clear message to Saddam that no nation has been taken in by his transparent tactics. Now is the time for the Council to underscore its unanimous conclusion that Saddam remains in material breach of his obligations.

Now is the time to tell Saddam once and for all that the clock has not been stopped by his machinations, that the clock continues to tick, and that the consequences of his continued refusal to disarm will be very, very real.

The goal of the United States remains the Security Council's goal: Iraq's disarmament. One last opportunity to achieve it through peaceful means remains open to Saddam Hussein, even at this late hour. What we know for certain, however, is that Saddam Hussein will be disarmed. The only question before us now is how. The question remains as it was at the beginning: Has Saddam Hussein made that strategic choice? He has not and we will see in the next few days whether or not he understands the situation he is in and he makes that choice. And that is the argument we will be taking to the Security Council.

Q. Sir, if the case was that you wanted to make the Security Council resolution as you said, now what the Security Council is saying, they do not see this suitable. So why don't you want to respect the will of the Security Council in this?

Secretary Powell. At this point, we are respecting the will of the Security Council. There's a lot of speculation about what the Council might or might not do when it meets next week. I think that's when it is more than likely that action will be taken on a resolution, if that seems like the appropriate step after we hear from Dr. Blix and Dr. ElBaradei.

But at the same time, we have also made clear that we believe that the threat is so great that if the Security Council is unable to take action, despite our best efforts to work with it, we must, in the interest of our own safety and, we believe, the safety of the region and the world, reserve the option to act with a coalition of willing nations if the Council does not act.

We believe the situation is that clear and the situation is that dangerous.

Q. Mr. Secretary, you said at the beginning, you pointed out that 1441 demonstrated in its 15-0 vote a common perspective on what needs to be done to disarm Iraq. Yet right now we seem to be perceiving a completely different sense of the imminence of the threat between those very same members of the Security Council. How do you explain the difference in the perception of the imminence of the threat that seems to have emerged right now?

Secretary Powell. There was always a difference in the perception of the threat. Some of my colleagues in the Council have never quite seen it as strongly as we have seen it and that was the case during the seven weeks of the debate and before the debate. There are even some members of the Council who argue most vociferously now for delay or something else, who were anxious to see sanctions go away years ago when it was clear there was something still going on in Iraq.

The one thing that we all agree upon is that there is no doubt that Iraq has weapons of mass destruction and the capability to develop them, or else I don't think we would have gotten a 15-0 vote. The debate really is, well, how much should we be concerned it, how much should we worry about it?

What we came together and said in 1441 is that they're in breach, continue to be in breach, they have not accounted for so much of this horrible material that they have, they have not allowed the inspectors in to verify the claims that they have made, and that this is a threat to the security of the region.

We believe what highlights the threat, at least in our eyes, is the nexus that now exists in the post-9/11 world that it was one thing, and it was a bad enough thing for Saddam Hussein to have these weapons of mass destruction available to him, but if, per chance, he also served as a source for these weapons of mass destruction, either accidentally or deliberately putting them in the hands of terrorists, we would all look back on this moment in time and feel awful if, at some future moment in time, a horrible attack took place and we discover one of these weapons was used, and when we had the chance to do something about it and we had the obligation to do something about it, we didn't do something about it.

But there certainly is a difference in perspective among the members, some of the members, as to the seriousness of this threat. And many of my colleagues agree with us on this issue. Some of my colleagues, three of whom I was watching on television earlier today, believe that the problem is there, the threat is there, but the solution to it is just, oh, let the inspectors keep going.

What I didn't hear in their press conference today is for how long, and how many more inspectors do you think will do, will do what the number of inspectors there are unable to do. And there was very little comment from them today or in earlier days about the basic fact that you still don't have somebody who is complying. He is not— he has not made that strategic choice. And I don't think any one of them would argue that he has.

One final, then I do have to go.

Q. You just said that you didn't hear your colleagues be very concrete on what needs to be done. Suppose they were to agree with you and others to set a series of very specific benchmarks with very specific deadlines, almost in the form of ultimatum, focusing on specific items, such as the VX, or the anthrax, or the biological labs, with the presumption that if there is not a concrete response on these specific items, as to some extent there has been on the rockets, then there would be common action for the purpose of disarming Iraq?

Secretary Powell. I'm not sure that even some of them would find that, or if we laid out such a series of benchmarks now, and a month or two or three months later we found some of them had been met and others had not been met, we'd be right back in the same boat, in my judgment. Let's give them some more time.

I don't think it's a question of additional benchmarks. All of these benchmarks have been out there for years. Some of the benchmarks that are spoken of and some of the elements that I'm sure we'll be hearing about later in the week are not new elements. They have been there all along. They have been the basis of previous resolutions. They've been there all along.

And it is not the need for new specific benchmarks to measure Saddam Hussein. I think we have a lot to measure with—against—with him—to measure him with already. As a result of his lack of performance on the declaration, his lack of answering the basic questions that people have been asking repeatedly with respect to VX, with respect to botulinum toxin. He doesn't need to have these benchmarks repeated. He knows what they are, and he has not demonstrated a willingness to answer the questions that have been out there for so many, so many years.

And that's our—that's the reason we are reluctant to yet see another resolution come forward that starts listing benchmarks in that resolution as a new measure of merit. We've given him enough measures of merit and I think we can pretty much judge now that he is not compliant, not made that decision, and is not cooperating in a way that would verify if he had made that decision.

Joint Statement by the Foreign Ministers of France, Germany, and Russia, March 5, 2003

Foreign Ministers de Villepin, Ivanov and Fischer delivered their joint statement in Paris.

Our common objective remains the full and effective disarmament of Iraq, in compliance with Resolution 1441.

We consider that this objective can be achieved by the peaceful means of the inspections.

We moreover observe that these inspections are producing increasingly encouraging results:
  • The destruction of the Al-Samoud missiles has started and is making progress,
  • Iraqis are providing biological and chemical information,
  • The interviews with Iraqi scientists are continuing.

Russia, Germany and France resolutely support Messrs Blix and El-Baradei and consider the meeting of the Council on 7 March to be an important step in the process put in place.

We firmly call for the Iraqi authorities to co-operate more actively with the inspectors to fully disarm their country. These inspections cannot continue indefinitely.

We consequently ask that the inspections now be speeded up, in keeping with the proposals put forward in the memorandum submitted to the Security Council by our three countries. We must:
  • Specify and prioritize the remaining issues, program by program,
  • Establish, for each point, detailed timelines.

Using this method, the inspectors have to present without any delay their work program accompanied by regular progress reports to the Security Council. This program could provide for a meeting clause to enable the Council to evaluate the overall results of this process.

In these circumstances, we will not let a proposed resolution pass that would authorize the use of force.

Russia and France, as permanent members of the Security Council, will assume all their responsibilities on this point.

We are at a turning point. Since our goal is the peaceful and full disarmament of Iraq, we have today the chance to obtain through peaceful means a comprehensive settlement for the Middle-East, starting with a move forward in the peace process, by:
  • Publishing and implementing the roadmap;
  • Putting together a general framework for the Middle-East, based on stability and security, renunciation of force, arms control and trust building measures.

Remarks by Secretary of Defense Rumsfeld, March 6, 2003

Secretary Donald Rumsfeld was interviewed on CNBC's "Capital Report."

Q. Mr. Secretary, thank you so much for being with us here on Capital Report. The first question is are we days away from war?

Secretary Rumsfeld. Well, that's a call that of course is one for the president and the United Nations, and really it's not so much for them as much as it is Saddam Hussein. I mean, the whole test was not whether inspectors could discover anything, but whether or not he would cooperate, and he clearly has not been cooperating to the extent that he would need to to have fulfilled the U.N. Resolution 1441. Whether he will in the days, the period ahead I just don't know.

Q. But you now have Russia, France, Germany all saying—but in particular Russia and France, who have veto, saying they would oppose any resolution that gives us the go-ahead to conduct war against Saddam Hussein. Do you think it was a mistake to go to the U.N. and get embroiled in this?

Secretary Rumsfeld. Well, no, I don't. I think the president made the right call. It— he went to the Congress first and received a very strong vote, and he went to the United Nations and received a unanimous vote in the Security Council.

You gain something and you give up something. You give up freedom of action for a period; and on the other hand, you've gained a period where the important, tough issues are being discussed and debated, and that's important. I mean, democratic systems have people who need to get familiar with facts and with circumstances, and with our new security environment. We need a debate like that. It's a good thing to have that kind of a debate.

Q. Do you expect that, if it looks like we're going to lose a U.N. vote, that we would ask for a U.N. vote in the Security Council?

Secretary Rumsfeld. Well, first of all, people say a lot of things that they ultimately don't do, and whether someone would veto it, I just don't know. I don't even know what the language will ultimately be or what the proposal will be.

We do know that all of those countries voted for Resolution 1441 of the United Nations Security Council, and we do know that it said that they're in material breach, and we said if they didn't—it said if they didn't supply a declaration that was honest, they would be in further material breach, and if they didn't cooperate, they'd be in still further material breach, and that there would be serious consequences, and that this was not their next-to-last chance, but it was their final opportunity—was I think the language. Pretty clear language, and they all knew what they were voting for. These are people who can read.

* * * *

Q. Mr. Secretary, there are reports that the British have asked the United States to hold off on any use of force between 72 hours and a week after any action in the United Nations. Is that something that you could live with?

Secretary Rumsfeld. It's not for me; it's for the president, and I'm sure that the president is anxious to find ways to accommodate the needs of the various countries, particularly countries like represented by the prime minister, Tony Blair. He has been so supportive and so helpful, and I'm sure that Secretary Powell, who is dealing with all of these issues up in New York, is worrying all those things through. It's not something that the Department of Defense is engaged in.

Q. Do you think that it's a real possibility that Saddam Hussein could strike Israel preemptively if we do not strike Iraq first? Does that worry you?

Secretary Rumsfeld. Saddam Hussein has used chemical weapons on his own people, he has used them on his neighbors, the Iranians. He has fired missiles—ballistic missiles into four of his neighboring countries, and then your question is do I think that he could strike preemptively at Israel.

* * * *

Q. You mentioned the propaganda war. That seems to be, at the moment, a war we're not doing that well in, if you look at public opinion polls, et cetera. I mean, that— that—we've gotten a lot of viewer e-mail on this casualty question, which is why I'm pressing it. Is there a real danger that if you have a bad strike that you're really going to turn a lot of people against us?

Secretary Rumsfeld. Well, you're quite right that we're not doing that well, and of course, the reason is it's not an even playing field. We're a democracy and they're a dictatorship, so they control their ground, and they manage the press, and they lie repeatedly. And we don't manage the press, we don't lie—

Q. You'd like to sometimes.

Secretary Rumsfeld. No, we don't at all. We've got a free press, and it's one of our great strengths. But to the extent that he lies and then it's carried worldwide, repeated over and over and over again—and we know that happened in Afghanistan. We saw instances where people were taken out of hospitals, moved over to a non-hospital building that had been hit, and pretended that they were killed and hurt in a hospital, which is just flat, absolutely false.

Now that carries all over the world, and on the other hand, we don't do that in the United States. We tell the truth, as we should, and so the imbalance in what the world sees is a direct result of that.

Q. But are you saying we've lost the PR battle against Saddam Hussein? How could that be?

Secretary Rumsfeld. I wouldn't say we've lost it. I think that the comment was correct. We seem to not do as well as he does. He's an accomplished liar, and every time he lies, it's carried in televisions all across the globe, and no one says that this is a man who has repeatedly lied, and when you listen to him, you should be on notice—he's a liar. He doesn't tell the truth. He's got a history of denying and deceiving and tricking people, and so listener, we're going to show it to you, but be on notice, it's probably not true. No one says that.

Q. But we've lost the PR battle with our allies, as well, it seems to me.

Secretary Rumsfeld. But does it really?

Q. With the leaders of Russia, France, Germany.

Secretary Rumsfeld. Well, my goodness, now let's—if you want to start counting, go back and take the eight nations that signed the letter supporting President Bush and then go take the ten European nations that in addition supported President Bush. The number of people that will be involved in a coalition in the event that force has to be used will be in big double digits. It very likely will be close to or the same as, or somewhat more than the coalition that existed during the Gulf War. In the global war on terror, President Bush has put together a coalition of 90 nations. It's the largest coalition in the history of mankind.

Now is here unanimity? No. Did anyone ever expect unanimity? No. Life isn't like that. Everyone does not just line up.

Q. You must have expected a little bit better than this.

Secretary Rumsfeld. I don't know that I did. I think you go back to the Gulf War. The vote passed in the Congress by a couple of votes. This one was overwhelming.

The last U.N. resolution was unanimous. Think of it. And simply because one or two or three countries stand up and say we don't agree with this, does that mean that the world is against it? No. It means that there is an absence of unanimity, and I understand that. These are tough issues, they're important issues. They ought to be debated and discussed.

Q. Do you expect the world to be with you for the rebuilding of Iraq, post-war?

Secretary Rumsfeld. I expect a large number of countries to be involved in the event force is used, let alone afterwards—of course.

Q. Let me just switch back to Saddam Hussein—

Secretary Rumsfeld. But when you said the world, the answer is no. There is never going to be unanimity. I would guess Cuba, no matter what we did, wouldn't agree. I would guess North Korea, no matter what we did, wouldn't agree.

Q. We're going to talk about North Korea, but one more question on Saddam. What about the hunt for Saddam Hussein? Is it dead or alive, like Osama bin Laden?

Secretary Rumsfeld. The goal is to disarm that country and see that they have weapons of mass destruction destroyed. It is to see that there is a regime in place that does not threaten its neighbors. It's to see that it remains a single country.

Saddam Hussein, if he's not there, is a blessing for the Iraqi people—that's for sure. Now if he's replaced by another person of his type, that wouldn't be helpful at all, either, so the real task is to see that the weapons of mass destruction are destroyed and that we have—there's a regime there that doesn't threaten their neighbors.

Q. What is there going to be in this war, as opposed to the one 12 years ago, that would prevent Saddam Hussein from using chemical or biological weapons, which we know he has developed?

Secretary Rumsfeld. Probably nothing. That is to say that in the last conflict he correctly assessed that he could remain in power. In this instance, if force has to be used because he won't cooperate and disarm, he would probably correctly assess that he will not be there, and therefore he might even have a greater incentive to use weapons of mass destruction, one would think. On the other hand, he can't use them, which is a wonderful thing.

Q. Why not?

Secretary Rumsfeld. Because he's hiding somewhere in an underground bunker. He has to get people to do that, and what we need to do is to persuade the people around him that would have to implement those kinds of terrible orders that it's not in their interest to do so, and if they do they would become war criminals and that they would be hunted down and found and held accountable for doing something that is that beyond the pale.

Q. Colleen Rowley, the whistleblower at the FBI, is quoted in the papers this morning saying that if we go to war against Saddam Hussein, she is expecting—and many people at the FBI are expecting terrorist attacks here in the United States as a result.

Secretary Rumsfeld. I'm not familiar with what she may have said. There is no question but that anyone who looks at the threat matrix every day knows that there are threats all over the world, and fortunately, because the global war on terror is succeeding and President Bush has put together that worldwide coalition, we have had a great deal of success in putting pressure on terrorist networks and disrupting a great many potential terrorist acts.

* * * *

Q. So won't there be a manhunt for Saddam as well?

Secretary Rumsfeld. I would think so, sure, but I don't think that the world necessarily has to hold baited breath to find either one. The task is to disrupt their capability to do great damage to innocent people.

* * * *

Q. What would you like to say to the American people on the eve of what may be a war?

Secretary Rumsfeld. Well, I think that I would say this: that we're in a new century, we're in a new security environment. The connection between weapons of mass destruction and terrorist states and terrorist networks has created a security circumstance that is probably one of the most dangerous the world has seen. These weapons are not weapons that can kill simply hundreds or even a few thousand; they are weapons that can kill tens of thousands and potentially hundreds of thousands of people.

That means that we have to think anew about these issues, and therefore the debate and discussions and, quite honestly, the differences that are being expressed in the Congress, in the press, is not a bad thing; it's a good thing. It's forcing us all to think about those issues and understand them better and understand the risks and the dangers. Now, it's very clear that there are risks to acting. What we have to understand is there are also risks to not acting, and the risk to not acting can in fact put at risk large numbers of innocent men, women and children in this country and in the countries of our friends and allies around the world.

Q. And to those people who say that if we have to go in there unilaterally and do this, that the risks will become much greater because we isolate ourselves as kind of the enemy for radicalized elements in that part of the world, how do you respond?

Secretary Rumsfeld. Well, I'd respond in two ways. First, we don't have to do anything to be the target in the world. We already were attacked on September 11th. We already know that as the country that has a distinctive position in the world, that we are the target—Western countries, Western culture. So you don't need to do anything more. And second, I would say that this mantra that's being repeated over and over and over on television and in the press and in foreign countries about U.S. acting unilaterally and going it alone is so false and so inaccurate that it is breathtaking. How it can keep being repeated by intelligent people? We have a 90-nation coalition in the global war on terrorism. It's the biggest coalition in the history of mankind. We will have a large number of countries if force has to be used. The U.N. resolution passed unanimously. There are countries lining up to be helpful with military assistance in the event force has to be used, with respect to basing and over- rights, with respect to intelligence cooperation and with respect to assistance in a post-Saddam Hussein Iraq.

Now, how anyone can say that that's going it alone, how anyone can say it is unilateral, is absolutely beyond me. It isn't, and it's repeated every single day over and over. Why? Because one or two or three or four countries have stood up and opposed it, and that is considered the world by people, for some unknown reason to me. It's utter nonsense. That's not the world. Those are important countries, many of them are good friends of ours, and they have a different opinion, and that's fair enough, and God bless them; they ought to say what they think and they ought to do what they think, but they are not the world. There are lots of countries in the world, and a lot of countries have been enormously supportive and helpful.

Q. What do you say to the anti-war protesters who have been here in Washington, hundreds of thousands?

Secretary Rumsfeld. Sure.

Q. Yeah.

Secretary Rumsfeld. Well, isn't it a wonderful thing that we have a democracy and that they can say what they think? You don't see anti-war protesters—you don't see anti-Saddam Hussein protesters in Iraq. You don't see them in dictatorships; you don't see them in repressive regime countries. We've always had people who had differences of opinion. If you go back to pre- World War II—I'm from Chicago. The America First Group was there, and they used to fill stadiums. They filled Madison Square Garden over and over again with people, saying we must not get engaged in a war in Europe, and Hitler can be dealt with, and not to worry. Now, were they good people? You bet. Were they sincere people? Yes. I've known some of them very, very well, personally. Charles Lindbergh was one. He would speak to these organizations, and he was a fine man—the man who flew across the Atlantic the first time in the Spirit of St. Louis. But is it possible to be sincere and be wrong? Yes, it is. And we've always had, in a free country, people who have different views, and we expect that.

March 6–19, 2003

The U.S. and U.K. Put Forth, Then Withdraw, a Draft U.N. Security Council Resolution Authorizing War; Bush Issues a 48-Hour Ultimatum

CHRONOLOGY

2003

March 6. United States intelligence reports that the Iraqi government has ordered U.S. military uniforms with plans of carrying out attacks on Iraqi citizens which would then be blamed on U.S. soldiers. Iraqi exiles testify in Washington about the brutal crimes committed against Iraqi citizens by the Hussein regime. Iraq flattens six more Al Samoud 2 missiles, meaning the country has now destroyed 34 of its known stock of 100 of the banned rockets. China joins France, Russia, and Germany in putting itself officially on record as opposing a U.S.-led war. Jiang Zemin is quoted as saying, "The door of peace should not be closed." U.S. President George W. Bush holds a live, televised press conference on the latest developments in the War on Terrorism, the situation with North Korea and the standoff with Iraq.

March 7. The *Washington Times* publishes a report detailing recent U.S. intelligence showing that France has been secretly selling spare parts to Iraq for its fighter jets and military helicopters during the past several months. Other intelligence reports indicate that Iraq has succeeded in acquiring French weaponry illegally for years.

March 9. Near the Iraq/Kuwait border, a dozen Iraqi soldiers attempt to surrender to British paratroopers testing their weapons during a routine exercise. The stunned soldiers from the 16 Air Assault Brigade are forced to tell the Iraqis that they were not firing at them, informing them further that it is too early to surrender.

March 11. Iraqi fighters threaten two U.S. U-2 surveillance planes forcing them to abort their mission and return to base. Iraqi officials describes the incident as a "technical mistake" by the U.N. inspectors. Ewen Buchanan, spokesman for UNMOVIC, says that Iraqi officials had been notified about the flight beforehand. According to Arab media, Saddam Hussein opens training camps in Iraq for Arab volunteers willing to carry out suicide bombings against U.S. forces, if an attack on Iraq takes place.

March 12. British prime minister Tony Blair proposes an amendment to the possible 18th resolution which would call for Iraq to meet certain benchmarks to prove that it was disarming. The benchmarks include a televised speech from Hussein declaring the country's intentions to disarm, and accounting for Iraq's chemical weapons stockpiles and unmanned drones. France once again threatens to veto even if a majority of the council votes in favor of the resolution.

March 13. Reports claim that a large portion of the Iraqi military is ready to surrender if a war begins. Defense Secretary Donald Rumsfeld admits that the U.S. government is communicating with Iraqi soldiers.

March 16. The leaders of the United States, Britain, Portugal and Spain meet at a summit in the Azores Islands. President Bush calls Monday, March 17th the "moment of Truth," meaning that the "coalition of the willing" would make its final effort to extract a resolution from the U.N. Security Council that would give Iraq an ultimatum to disarm immediately or to be disarmed by force. The United States orders all non-essential diplomats out of Kuwait, Syria, and Israel. Anti-Saddam Iraqi groups begin defacing and vandalizing posters of the dictator all over Iraq. Demonstrations also take place in Kirkuk, where an estimated crowd of 20,000 marches on the Ba'ath party's main administrative headquarters demanding the overthrow of Saddam's government. Marches destroy posters of the Iraqi leader and throw a grenade at a government building. Some reports indicate that one senior Ba'ath party official is killed in the attack.

March 17. The U.K.'s ambassador to the U.N. says the diplomatic process with Iraq has ended. In a televised speech, George Bush gives Saddam Hussein 48 hours to go into exile or face war. U.S. Intelligence reports that Iraqi soldiers in Southern Iraq have been armed with chemical weapons. France announces that it would support U.S. troops if Iraq launches chemical weapons against U.S. forces.

March 18. Saddam Hussein rejects the option of his exile from Iraq to avoid war.

DOCUMENTS

Remarks by President Bush, March 6, 2003

Good evening. I'm pleased to take your questions tonight, and to discuss with the American people the serious matters facing our country and the world.

This has been an important week on two fronts on our war against terror. First, thanks to the hard work of American and Pakistani officials, we captured the mastermind of the September the 11th attacks against our nation. Khalid Sheikh Mohammed conceived and planned the hijackings and directed the actions of the hijackers. We believe his capture will further disrupt the terror network and their planning for additional attacks.

Second, we have arrived at an important moment in confronting the threat posed to our nation and to peace by Saddam Hussein and his weapons of terror. In New York tomorrow, the United Nations Security Council will receive an update from the chief weapons inspector. The world needs him to answer a single question: Has the Iraqi regime fully and unconditionally disarmed, as required by Resolution 1441, or has it not?

Iraq's dictator has made a public show of producing and destroying a few missiles—missiles that violate the restrictions set out more than 10 years ago. Yet, our intelligence shows that even as he is destroying these few missiles, he has ordered the continued production of the very same type of missiles.

Iraqi operatives continue to hide biological and chemical agents to avoid detection by inspectors. In some cases, these materials have been moved to different locations every 12 to 24 hours, or placed in vehicles that are in residential neighborhoods.

We know from multiple intelligence sources that Iraqi weapons scientists continue to be threatened with harm should they cooperate with U.N. inspectors. Scientists are required by Iraqi intelligence to wear concealed recording devices during interviews, and hotels where interviews take place are bugged by the regime.

These are not the actions of a regime that is disarming. These are the actions of a regime engaged in a willful charade. These are the actions of a regime that systematically and deliberately is defying the world. If the Iraqi regime were disarming, we would know it, because we would see it. Iraq's weapons would be presented to inspectors, and the world would witness their destruction. Instead, with the world demanding disarmament, and more than 200,000 troops positioned near his country, Saddam Hussein's response is to produce a few weapons for show, while he hides the rest and builds even more.

Inspection teams do not need more time, or more personnel. All they need is what they have never received—the full cooperation of the Iraqi regime. Token gestures are not acceptable. The only acceptable outcome is the one already defined by a unanimous vote of the Security Council—total disarmament.

Great Britain, Spain, and the United States have introduced a new resolution stating that Iraq has failed to meet the requirements of Resolution 1441. Saddam Hussein is not disarming. This is a fact. It cannot be denied.

Saddam Hussein has a long history of reckless aggression and terrible crimes. He possesses weapons of terror. He provides funding and training and safe haven to terrorists—terrorists who would willingly use weapons of mass destruction against America and other peace-loving countries. Saddam Hussein and his weapons are a direct threat to this country, to our people, and to all free people.

If the world fails to confront the threat posed by the Iraqi regime, refusing to use force, even as a last resort, free nations would assume immense and unacceptable risks. The attacks of September the 11th, 2001 showed what the enemies of America did with four airplanes. We will not wait to see what terrorists or terrorist states could do with weapons of mass destruction.

We are determined to confront threats wherever they arise. I will not leave the American people at the mercy of the Iraqi dictator and his weapons.

In the event of conflict, America also accepts our responsibility to protect innocent lives in every way possible. We'll bring food and medicine to the Iraqi people. We'll help that nation to build a just government, after decades of brutal dictatorship. The form and leadership of that government is for the Iraqi people to choose. Anything they choose will be better than the misery and torture and murder they have known under Saddam Hussein.

Across the world and in every part of America, people of goodwill are hoping and praying for peace. Our goal is peace—for our nation, for our friends and allies, for the people of the Middle East. People of goodwill must also recognize that allowing a dangerous dictator to defy the world and harbor weapons of mass murder and terror is not peace at all; it is pretense. The cause of peace will be advanced only when the terrorists lose a wealthy patron and protector, and when the dictator is fully and finally disarmed.

Tonight I thank the men and women of our armed services and their families. I know their deployment so far from home is causing hardship for many military families. Our nation is deeply grateful to all who serve in uniform. We appreciate your commitment, your idealism, and your sacrifice. We support you, and we know that if peace must be defended, you are ready.

Q. Let me see if I can further—if you could further define what you just called this important moment we're in, since you've made it clear just now that you don't think Saddam has disarmed, and we have a quarter million troops in the Persian Gulf, and now that you've called on the world to be ready to use force as a last resort. Are we just days away from the point of which you decide whether or not we go to war? And what harm would it do to give Saddam a final ultimatum? A two- or three-day deadline to disarm or face force?

President Bush. Well, we're still in the final stages of diplomacy. I'm spending a lot of time on the phone, talking to fellow leaders about the need for the United Nations Security Council to state the facts, which is Saddam Hussein hasn't disarmed. Fourteen forty-one, the Security Council resolution passed unanimously last fall, said clearly that Saddam Hussein has one last chance to disarm. He hasn't disarmed. And so we're working with Security Council members to resolve this issue at the Security Council.

This is not only an important moment for the security of our nation, I believe it's an important moment for the Security Council, itself. And the reason I say that is because this issue has been before the Security Council—the issue of disarmament of Iraq—for 12 long years. And the fundamental question facing the Security Council is, will its words mean anything? When the Security Council speaks, will the words have merit and weight?

I think it's important for those words to have merit and weight, because I understand that in order to win the war against terror there must be a united effort to do so; we must work together to defeat terror.

Iraq is a part of the war on terror. Iraq is a country that has got terrorist ties. It's a country with wealth. It's a country that trains terrorists, a country that could arm terrorists. And our fellow Americans must understand in this new war against terror, that we not only must chase down al Qaeda terrorists, we must deal with weapons of mass destruction, as well.

That's what the United Nations Security Council has been talking about for 12 long years. It's now time for this issue to come to a head at the Security Council, and it will. As far as ultimatums and all the speculation about what may or may not happen, after next week, we'll just wait and see.

Q. Are we days away?

President Bush. Well, we're days away from resolving this issue at the Security Council.

* * * *

Q. Mr. President, you have, and your top advisors—notably, Secretary of State Powell—have repeatedly said that we have shared with our allies all the current, up-to-date intelligence information that proves the imminence of the threat we face from Saddam Hussein, and that they have been sharing their intelligence with us, as well. If all these nations, all of them our normal allies, have access to the same intelligence information, why is it that they are reluctant to think that the threat is so real, so imminent that we need to move to the brink of war now?

And in relation to that, today, the British Foreign Minister, Jack Straw, suggested at the U.N. that it might be time to look at amending the resolution, perhaps with an eye towards a timetable like that proposed by the Canadians some two weeks ago, that would set a firm deadline to give Saddam Hussein a little bit of time to come clean. And also, obviously, that would give you a little bit of a chance to build more support within the members of the Security Council. Is that something that the governments should be pursuing at the U.N. right now?

President Bush. We, of course, are consulting with our allies at the United Nations. But I meant what I said, this is the last phase of diplomacy. A little bit more time? Saddam Hussein has had 12 years to disarm. He is deceiving people. This is what's important for our fellow citizens to realize; that if he really intended to disarm, like the world has asked him to do, we would know whether he was disarming. He's trying to buy time. I can understand why—he's been successful with these tactics for 12 years.

Saddam Hussein is a threat to our nation. September the 11th changed the strategic thinking, at least, as far as I was concerned, for how to protect our country. My job is to protect the American people. It used to be that we could think that you could contain a person like Saddam Hussein, that oceans would protect us from his type of terror. September the 11th should say to the American people that we're now a battlefield, that weapons of mass destruction in the hands of a terrorist organization could be deployed here at home.

So, therefore, I think the threat is real. And so do a lot of other people in my government. And since I believe the threat is real, and since my most important job is to protect the security of the American people, that's precisely what we'll do.

Our demands are that Saddam Hussein disarm. We hope he does. We have worked with the international community to convince him to disarm. If he doesn't disarm, we'll disarm him.

You asked about sharing of intelligence, and I appreciate that, because we do share a lot of intelligence with nations which may or may not agree with us in the Security Council as to how to deal with Saddam Hussein and his threats. We have got roughly 90 countries engaged in Operation Enduring Freedom, chasing down the terrorists.

We do communicate a lot, and we will continue to communicate a lot. We must communicate. We must share intelligence; we must share—we must cut off money together; we must smoke these al Qaeda types out one at a time. It's in our national interest, as well, that we deal with Saddam Hussein.

But America is not alone in this sentiment. There are a lot of countries who fully understand the threat of Saddam Hussein. A lot of countries realize that the credibility of the Security Council is at stake—a lot of countries, like America, who hope that he would have disarmed, and a lot of countries which realize that it may require force—may require force—to disarm him.

Q. Thank you, Mr. President. Sir, if you haven't already made the choice to go to war, can you tell us what you are waiting to hear or see before you do make that decision? And if I may, during the recent demonstrations, many of the protesters suggested that the U.S. was a threat to peace, which prompted you to wonder out loud why they didn't see Saddam Hussein as a threat to peace. I wonder why you think so many people around the world take a different view of the threat that Saddam Hussein poses than you and your allies.

President Bush. Well, first, I—I appreciate societies in which people can express their opinion. That society—free speech stands in stark contrast to Iraq.

Secondly, I've seen all kinds of protests since I've been the President. I remember the protests against trade. A lot of people didn't feel like free trade was good for the world. I completely disagree. I think free trade is good for both wealthy and impoverished nations. But that didn't change my opinion about trade. As a matter of fact, I went to the Congress to get trade promotion authority out.

I recognize there are people who—who don't like war. I don't like war. I wish that Saddam Hussein had listened to the demands of the world and disarmed. That was my hope. That's why I first went to the United Nations to begin with, on September the

12th, 2002, to address this issue as forthrightly as I knew how. That's why, months later, we went to the Security Council to get another resolution, called 1441, which was unanimously approved by the Security Council, demanding that Saddam Hussein disarm.

I'm hopeful that he does disarm. But, in the name of peace and the security of our people, if he won't do so voluntarily, we will disarm him. And other nations will join him—join us in disarming him.

And that creates a certain sense of anxiety; I understand that. Nobody likes war. The only thing I can do is assure the loved ones of those who wear our uniform that if we have to go to war, if war is upon us because Saddam Hussein has made that choice, we will have the best equipment available for our troops, the best plan available for victory, and we will respect innocent life in Iraq.

The risk of doing nothing, the risk of hoping that Saddam Hussein changes his mind and becomes a gentle soul, the risk that somehow—that inaction will make the world safer, is a risk I'm not willing to take for the American people.

Q. Thank you, Mr. President. How would—sir, how would you answer your critics who say that they think this is somehow personal? As Senator Kennedy put it tonight, he said your fixation with Saddam Hussein is making the world a more dangerous place. And as you prepare the American people for the possibility of military conflict, could you share with us any of the scenarios your advisors have shared with you about worse-case scenarios, in terms of the potential cost of American lives, the potential cost to the American economy, and the potential risks of retaliatory terrorist strikes here at home?

President Bush. My job is to protect America, and that is exactly what I'm going to do. People can ascribe all kinds of intentions. I swore to protect and defend the Constitution; that's what I swore to do. I put my hand on the Bible and took that oath, and that's exactly what I am going to do.

I believe Saddam Hussein is a threat to the American people. I believe he's a threat to the neighborhood in which he lives. And I've got a good evidence to believe that. He has weapons of mass destruction, and he has used weapons of mass destruction, in his neighborhood and on his own people. He's invaded countries in his neighborhood. He tortures his own people. He's a murderer. He has trained and financed al Qaeda-type organizations before, al Qaeda and other terrorist organizations. I take the threat seriously, and I'll deal with the threat. I hope it can be done peacefully.

The rest of your six-point question?

Q. The potential price in terms of lives and the economy, terrorism.

President Bush. The price of doing nothing exceeds the price of taking action, if we have to. We'll do everything we can to minimize the loss of life. The price of the attacks on America, the cost of the attacks on America on September the 11th were enormous. They were significant. And I am not willing to take that chance again, John.

Q. Thank you, sir. May I follow up on Jim Angle's question? In the past several weeks, your policy on Iraq has generated opposition from the governments of France, Russia, China, Germany, Turkey, the Arab League and many other countries, opened a rift at NATO and at the U.N., and drawn millions of ordinary citizens around the world into the streets in anti-war protests. May I ask, what went wrong that so many governments and people around the world now not only disagree with you very strongly, but see the U.S. under your leadership as an arrogant power?

President Bush. I think if you remember back prior to the resolution coming out of the United Nations last fall, I suspect you might have asked a question along those lines—how come you can't get anybody to support your resolution. If I remember correctly, there was a lot of doubt as to whether or not we were even going to get any votes, much—well, we'd get our own, of course. And the vote came out 15 to nothing, Terry. And I think you'll see when it's all said and done, if we have to use force, a lot of nations will be with us.

You clearly named some that—France and Germany expressed their opinions. We have a disagreement over how best to deal with Saddam Hussein. I understand that. Having said that, they're still our friends and we will deal with them as friends. We've got a lot of common interests. Our transatlantic relationships are very important. While they may disagree with how we deal with Saddam Hussein and his weapons of mass destruction, there's no disagreement when it came time to vote on 1441, at least as far as France was concerned. They joined us. They said Saddam Hussein has one last chance of disarming. If they think more time will cause him to disarm, I disagree with that.

He's a master at deception. He has no intention of disarming—otherwise, we would have known. There's a lot of talk about inspectors. It really would have taken a handful of inspectors to determine whether he was disarming—they could have showed up at a parking lot and he could have brought his weapons and destroyed them. That's not what he chose to do.

Secondly, I make my decisions based upon the oath I took, the one I just described to you. I believe Saddam Hussein is a threat—is a threat to the American people. He's a threat to people in his neighborhood. He's also a threat to the Iraqi people.

One of the things we love in America is freedom. If I may, I'd like to remind you what I said at the State of the Union: liberty is not America's gift to the world, it is God's gift to each and every person. And that's what I believe. I believe that when we see totalitarianism, that we must deal with it. We don't have to do it always militarily. But this is a unique circumstance, because of 12 years of denial and defiance, because of terrorist connections, because of past history.

I'm convinced that a liberated Iraq will be—will be important for that troubled part of the world. The Iraqi people are plenty capable of governing themselves. Iraq is a sophisticated society. Iraq's got money. Iraq will provide a place where people can see that the Shia and the Sunni and the Kurds can get along in a federation. Iraq will serve as a catalyst for change, positive change.

So there's a lot more at stake than just American security, and the security of people close by Saddam Hussein. Freedom is at stake, as well, and I take that very seriously.

Q. Mr. President, good evening. If you order war, can any military operation be considered a success if the United States does not capture Saddam Hussein, as you once said, dead or alive?

President Bush. Well, I hope we don't have to go to war, but if we go to war, we will disarm Iraq. And if we go to war, there will be a regime change. And replacing this cancer inside of Iraq will be a government that represents the rights of all the people, a government which represents the voices of the Shia and Sunni and the Kurds.

We care about the suffering of the Iraqi people. I mentioned in my opening comments that there's a lot of food ready to go in. There's something like 55,000 oil-for-food distribution points in Iraq. We know where they are. We fully intend to make sure that they're—got ample food. We know where their hospitals are; we want to make sure they've got ample medical supplies. The life of the Iraqi citizen is going to dramatically improve.

Q. Sir, I'm sorry, is success contingent upon capturing or killing Saddam Hussein, in your mind?

President Bush. We will be changing the regime of Iraq, for the good of the Iraqi people.

Q. Mr. President, to a lot of people, it seems that war is probably inevitable, because many people doubt—most people, I would guess—that Saddam Hussein will ever do what we are demanding that he do, which is disarm. And if war is inevitable, there are a lot of people in this country—as much as half, by polling standards—who agree that he should be disarmed, who listen to you say that you have the evidence, but who feel they haven't seen it, and who still wonder why blood has to be shed if he hasn't attacked us.

President Bush. Well, Bill, if they believe he should be disarmed, and he's not going to disarm, there's only one way to disarm him. And that happens to be my last choice—the use of force.

Secondly, the American people know that Saddam Hussein has weapons of mass destruction. By the way, he declared he didn't have any—1441 insisted that he have a complete declaration of his weapons; he said he didn't have any weapons. Secondly, he's used these weapons before. I mean, this is—we're not speculating about the nature of the man. We know the nature of the man.

Colin Powell, in an eloquent address to the United Nations, described some of the information we were at liberty of talking about. He mentioned a man named Al Zarqawi, who was in charge of the poison network. He's a man who was wounded in Afghanistan, received aid in Baghdad, ordered the killing of a U.S. citizen, USAID employee, was harbored in Iraq. There is a poison plant in Northeast Iraq. To assume that Saddam Hussein knew none of this was going on is not to really understand the nature of the Iraqi society.

There's a lot of facts which make it clear to me and many others that Saddam is a threat. And we're not going to wait until he does attack. We're not going to hope that he changes his attitude. We're not going to assume that he's a different kind of person than he has been.

So, in the name of security and peace, if we have to—if we have to—we'll disarm him. I hope he disarms. Or, perhaps, I hope he leaves the country. I hear a lot of talk from different nations around where Saddam Hussein might be exiled. That would be fine with me—just so long as Iraq disarms after he's exiled.

Q. Thank you, Mr. President. As you said, the Security Council faces a vote next week on a resolution implicitly authorizing an attack on Iraq. Will you call for a vote on that resolution, even if you aren't sure you have the vote?

President Bush. Well, first, I don't think—it basically says that he's in defiance of 1441. That's what the resolution says. And it's hard to believe anybody is saying he isn't in defiance of 1441, because 1441 said he must disarm. And, yes, we'll call for a vote.

Q. No matter what?

President Bush. No matter what the whip count is, we're calling for the vote. We want to see people stand up and say what their opinion is about Saddam Hussein and the utility of the United Nations Security Council. And so, you bet. It's time for people to show their cards, to let the world know where they stand when it comes to Saddam.

Q. Mr. President, are you worried that the United States might be viewed as defiant of the United Nations if you went ahead with military action without specific and explicit authorization from the U.N.?

President Bush. No, I'm not worried about that. As a matter of fact, it's hard to say the United States is defiant about the United Nations, when I was the person that took the issue to the United Nations, September the 12th, 2002. We've been working with the United Nations. We've been working through the United Nations.

Secondly, I'm confident the American people understand that when it comes to our security, if we need to act, we will act, and we really don't need United Nations approval to do so. I want to work—I want the United Nations to be effective. It's important for it to be a robust, capable body. It's important for it's words to mean what they say, and as we head into the 21st century, Mark, when it comes to our security, we really don't need anybody's permission.

Q. Thank you, Mr. President. Even though our military can certainly prevail without a northern front, isn't Turkey making it at least slightly more challenging for us, and therefore, at least slightly more likely that American lives will be lost? And if they don't reverse course, would you stop backing their entry into the European Union?

President Bush. The answer to your second question is, I support Turkey going into the E.U. Turkey's a friend. They're a NATO ally. We will continue to work with Turkey. We've got contingencies in place that, should our troops not come through

Turkey—not be allowed to come through Turkey. And, no, that won't cause any more hardship for our troops; I'm confident of that.

Q. Mr. President, as the nation is at odds over war, with many organizations like the Congressional Black Caucus pushing for continued diplomacy through the U.N., how is your faith guiding you? And what should you tell America—well, what should America do, collectively, as you instructed before 9/11? Should it be "pray?" Because you're saying, let's continue the war on terror.

President Bush. I appreciate that question a lot. First, for those who urge more diplomacy, I would simply say that diplomacy hasn't worked. We've tried diplomacy for 12 years. Saddam Hussein hasn't disarmed, he's armed.

And we live in a dangerous world. We live in new circumstances in our country. And I hope people remember the—I know they remember the tragedy of September the 11th, but I hope they understand the lesson of September the 11th. The lesson is, is that we're vulnerable to attack, wherever it may occur, and we must take threats which gather overseas very seriously. We don't have to deal with them all militarily. But we must deal with them. And in the case of Iraq, it is now time for him to disarm. For the sake of peace, if we have to use our troops, we will.

My faith sustains me because I pray daily. I pray for guidance and wisdom and strength. If we were to commit our troops—if we were to commit our troops—I would pray for their safety, and I would pray for the safety of innocent Iraqi lives, as well.

One thing that's really great about our country, April, is there are thousands of people who pray for me that I'll never see and be able to thank. But it's a humbling experience to think that people I will never have met have lifted me and my family up in prayer. And for that I'm grateful. That's—it's been—it's been a comforting feeling to know that is true. I pray for peace, April. I pray for peace.

Q. Thank you, Mr. President. As you know, not everyone shares your optimistic vision of how this might play out. Do you ever worry, maybe in the wee, small hours, that you might be wrong and they might be right in thinking that this could lead to more terrorism, more anti-American sentiment, more instability in the Middle East?

President Bush. Hutch, I think, first of all, it's hard to envision more terror on America than September the 11th, 2001. We did nothing to provoke that terrorist attack. It came upon us because there's an enemy which hates America. They hate what we stand for. We love freedom and we're not changing. And, therefore, so long as there's a terrorist network like al Qaeda, and others willing to fund them, finance them, equip them—we're at war.

And so I—you know, obviously, I've thought long and hard about the use of troops. I think about it all the time. It is my responsibility to commit the troops. I believe we'll prevail—I know we'll prevail. And out of that disarmament of Saddam will come a better world, particularly for the people who live in Iraq.

This is a society, Ron, who—which has been decimated by his murderous ways, his torture. He doesn't allow dissent. He doesn't believe in the values we believe in. I believe this society, the Iraqi society can develop in a much better way. I think of the risks, calculated the cost of

inaction versus the cost of action. And I'm firmly convinced, if we have to, we will act, in the name of peace and in the name of freedom.

Q. Mr. President, if you decide to go ahead with military action, there are inspectors on the ground in Baghdad. Will you give them time to leave the country, or the humanitarian workers on the ground or the journalists? Will you be able to do that, and still mount an effective attack on Iraq?

President Bush. Of course. We will give people a chance to leave. And we don't want anybody in harm's way who shouldn't be in harm's way. The journalists who are there should leave. If you're going, and we start action, leave. The inspectors—we don't want people in harm's way. And our intention—we have no quarrel with anybody other than Saddam and his group of killers who have destroyed a society. And we will do everything we can, as I mentioned—and I mean this—to protect innocent life.

I've not made up our mind about military action. Hopefully, this can be done peacefully. Hopefully, that as a result of the pressure that we have placed—and others have placed—that Saddam will disarm and/or leave the country.

Q. Mr. President, good evening. Sir, you've talked a lot about trusting the American people when it comes to making decisions about their own lives, about how to spend their own money. When it comes to the financial costs of the war, sir, it would seem that the administration, surely, has costed out various scenarios. If that's the case, why not present some of them to the American people so they know what to expect, sir?

President Bush. Ed, we will. We'll present it in the form of a supplemental to the spenders. We don't get to spend the money, as you know. We have to request the expenditure of money from the Congress, and, at the appropriate time, we'll request a supplemental. We're obviously analyzing all aspects. We hope we don't go to war; but if we should, we will present a supplemental.

But I want to remind—remind you what I said before. There is a huge cost when we get attacked. There is a significant cost to our society—first of all, there is the cost of lives. It's an immeasurable cost—3,000 people died. This is a significant cost to our economy. Opportunity loss is an immeasurable cost, besides the cost of repairing buildings, and cost to our airlines. And so, the cost of an attack is significant.

If I thought we were safe from attack, I would be thinking differently. But I see a gathering threat. I mean, this is a true, real threat to America. And, therefore, we will deal with it. And at the appropriate time, Ed, we will ask for a supplemental. And that will be the moment where you and others will be able to recognize what we think the dollar cost of a conflict will be.

You know, the benefits of such a—of such a effort, if, in fact, we go forward and are successful, are also immeasurable. How do you measure the benefit of freedom in Iraq? I guess, if you're an Iraqi citizen you can measure it by being able to express your mind and vote. How do you measure the consequence of taking a dictator out of—out of power who has tried to invade Kuwait? Or somebody who may some day decide to lob a weapon of mass destruction on Israel—how would you weigh the cost of that? Those are immeasurable costs. And I weigh those very seriously, Ed. In terms of the dollar amount, well, we'll let you know here pretty soon.

Q. Thank you, Mr. President. If I can follow on Steve's question, on North Korea. Do you believe it is essential for the security of the United States and its allies that North Korea be prevented from developing nuclear weapons? And are you in any way growing frustrated with the pace of the diplomacy there?

President Bush. Well, I think it's—I think it's an issue. Obviously, I'm concerned about North Korea developing nuclear weapons, not only for their own use, but for—perhaps they might choose to proliferate them, sell them. They may end up in the hands of dictators, people who are not afraid of using weapons of mass destruction, people who try to impose their will on the world or blackmail free nations. I'm concerned about it.

We are working hard to bring a diplomatic solution. And we've made some progress. After all, the IAEA asked that the Security Council take up the North Korean issue. It's now in the Security Council. Constantly talking with the Chinese and the Russians and the Japanese and the South Koreans. Colin Powell just went overseas and spent some time in China, went to the inauguration of President Roh in South Korea; spent time in China. We're working the issue hard, and I'm optimistic that we'll come up with a diplomatic solution. I certainly hope so.

Q. Thank you, sir. Mr. President, millions of Americans can recall a time when leaders from both parties set this country on a mission of regime change in Vietnam. Fifty thousand Americans died. The regime is still there in Hanoi, and it hasn't harmed or threatened a single American in the 30 years since the war ended. What can you say tonight, sir, to the sons and the daughters of the Americans who served in Vietnam to assure them that you will not lead this country down a similar path in Iraq?

President Bush. That's a great question. Our mission is clear in Iraq. Should we have to go in, our mission is very clear: disarmament. And in order to disarm, it would mean regime change. I'm confident we'll be able to achieve that objective, in a way that minimizes the loss of life. No doubt there's risks in any military operation; I know that. But it's very clear what we intend to do. And our mission won't change. Our mission is precisely what I just stated. We have got a plan that will achieve that mission, should we need to send forces in.

Last question. Let's see who needs one. Jean.

Q. Thank you, Mr. President. In the coming days, the American people are going to hear a lot of debate about this British proposal of a possible deadline being added to the resolution, or not. And I know you don't want to tip your hand—this is a great diplomatic moment—but from the administration's perspective and your own perspective, can you share for the American public what you view as the pros and cons associated with that proposal?

President Bush. You're right, I'm not going to tip my hand.

Q. But can you help us sort out the—

President Bush. Thank you for—thank you. Anything that's debated must have resolution to this issue. It makes no sense to allow this issue to continue on and on, in the hopes that Saddam Hussein disarms. The whole purpose of the debate is for Saddam to disarm. We gave him a chance. As a matter of fact, we gave him 12 years of chances. But, recently, we gave him a chance, starting last fall. And it said, last chance to disarm. The resolution said that. And had he chosen to do so, it would be evident that he's disarmed.

So more time, more inspectors, more process, in our judgment, is not going to affect the peace of the world. So whatever is resolved is going to have some finality to it, so that Saddam Hussein will take us seriously.

I want to remind you that it's his choice to make as to whether or not we go to war. It's Saddam's choice. He's the person that can make the choice of war and peace. Thus far, he's made the wrong choice. If we have to, for the sake of the security of the American people, for the sake of peace in the world, and for freedom to the Iraqi people, we will disarm Saddam Hussein. And by we, it's more than America. A lot of nations will join us.

White House Press Statement, March 6, 2003

Continuing to deceive Inspections not working Concessions are not compliance United Nations Resolution 1441 was meant to end 12 years of lies and manipulation. Nothing we have seen since the passage of 1441 indicates that Iraq has decided to disarm or decided to actively,unconditionally, and immediately cooperate with the inspectors.

Intelligence from multiple sources shows that Iraq is continuing efforts to deceive inspectors by moving weapons of mass destruction material around the country to avoid detection. Baghdad is also working to discredit intelligence information being provided to the inspection teams by the United States and our allies.

The inspections are not working. Dribbling out of a warhead here, a missile there, may give the appearance of disarmament, but it is not reducing Saddam's capabilities. It is not eliminating the threat. He gives a little to save a lot, but we've caught on to this game.

Iraq has had more than a decade to decide to disarm. Iraq could have made the decision on November 8 when 1441 was passed. It could make the decision today.

Process is not performance. Concessions are not compliance. Destroying a handful of missiles is not disarmament. Saddam Hussein is betting that his contempt for the will of the Security Council is stronger than our collective resolve. Division among us will only convince Saddam that he is right.

If Saddam leaves us no choice but to disarm him by force, the United States and our coalition partners will do our utmost to minimize the loss of civilian life, meet the humanitarian needs of the Iraqi people, and take responsibility for the post-war stabilization of the country.

We want an Iraq whose people are free from fear and can look to the future with hope. The hard work of rehabilitation and reconstruction will begin at the first possible moment, but our collective, long-term commitment to Iraq will be our efforts to help the Iraqi people build a unified Iraq that does not pose a threat to international peace and a welcome presence among nations.

Remarks by United Nations Secretary-General Annan, March 6, 2003

Q. Mr. Secretary-General, do you think there is still a chance to get the [Security] Council unified and avoid a war with Iraq?

Secretary-General Annan. Well I think, as you know, the Ministers are coming tomorrow—some of them will be here today—and we will all have a chance to discuss this calmly. The positions are very hard now. But of course there are already several proposals on the table. You have the resolution; you have the Canadian idea; you have the French-German-Russian idea, and there may be others. And so, until there is an actual vote one cannot tell what will happen.

Q. Are you planning to use your good offices to reunify the Council?

Secretary-General Annan. I am working very hard. I am encouraging people to strive for a compromise, to seek a common ground, and to make concessions, you get concessions.

Draft U.N. Security Council Resolution Proposed by the U.S., U.K. and Spain, March 7, 2003

Recalling all its previous relevant resolutions, in particular its resolutions 661 (1990) of 6 August 1990, 678 (1990) of 29 November 1990, 686 (1991) of 2 March 1991, 687 (1991) of 3 April 1991, 688 (1991) of 5 April 1991, 707 (1991) of 15 August 1991, 715 (1991) of 11 October 1991, 986 (1995) of 14 April 1995, 1284 (1999) of 17 December 1999 and 1441 (2002) of 8 November 2002, and all the relevant statements of its president,

Recalling that in its resolution 687 (1991) the council declared that a cease-fire would be based on acceptance by Iraq of the provisions of that resolution, including the obligations on Iraq contained therein,

Recalling that its resolution 1441 (2002), while acknowledging that Iraq has been and remains in material breach of its obligations, afforded Iraq a final opportunity to comply with its disarmament obligations under relevant resolutions,

Recalling that in its resolution 1441 (2002) the council decided that false statements or omissions in the declaration submitted by Iraq pursuant to that resolution and failure by Iraq at any time to comply with, and cooperate fully in the implementation of, that resolution, would constitute a further material breach,

Noting, in that context, that in its resolution 1441 (2002), the council recalled that it has repeatedly warned Iraq that it will face serious consequences as a result of its continued violations of its obligations,

Noting that Iraq has submitted a declaration pursuant to its resolution 1441 (2002) containing false statements and omissions and has failed to comply with, and cooperate fully in the implementation of, that resolution,

Reaffirming the commitment of all member states to the sovereignty and territorial integrity of Iraq, Kuwait, and the neighboring states,

Mindful of its primary responsibility under the Charter of the United Nations for the maintenance of international peace and security,

Recognizing the threat Iraq's noncompliance with council resolutions and proliferation of weapons of mass destruction and long-range missiles poses to international peace and security,

Determined to secure full compliance with its decisions and to restore international peace and security in the area,

Acting under Chapter VII of the Charter of the United Nations,

1. Reaffirms the need for full implementation of resolution 1441 (2002);

2. Calls on Iraq immediately to take the decisions necessary in the interests of its people and the region;

3. Decides that Iraq will have failed to take the final opportunity afforded by resolution 1441 (2002) unless, on or before March 17, 2003, the Council concludes that Iraq has demonstrated full, unconditional, immediate and active cooperation in accordance with its disarmament obligations under resolution 1441 (2002) and previous relevant resolutions, and is yielding possession to UNMOVIC and the IAEA of all weapons, weapon delivery and support systems and structures, prohibited by resolution 687 (1991) and all subsequent relevant resolutions, and all information regarding prior destruction of such items;

4. Decides to remain seized of the matter.

Excerpts from United Nations Security Council Ministerial Meeting on Iraq, March 7, 2003

UNMOVIC Chairman Hans Blix. For nearly three years, I have been coming to the Security Council to present the quarterly reports of the United Nations Monitoring, Verification and Inspection Commission (UNMOVIC). They have described our many preparations for the resumption of inspections in Iraq. The twelfth quarterly report (S/2003/232, annex) is the first that describes three months of inspections. They come after four years without inspections. The report was finalized 10 days ago, and a number of relevant events have taken place since then. Today's statement will supplement the circulated report on these points in order to bring the Council up to date.

Inspections in Iraq resumed on 27 November 2002. In matters relating to process, notably prompt access to sites, we have faced relatively few difficulties—and certainly far fewer than those that were faced by the United Nations Special Commission

(UNSCOM) in the period 1991 to 1998. This may well be due to the strong outside pressure.

Some practical matters which were not settled by the talks that Mr. ElBaradei and I had with the Iraqi side in Vienna prior to inspections or in resolution 1441 (2002) have been resolved at meetings which we have had in Baghdad. Initial difficulties raised by the Iraqi side about helicopters and aerial surveillance planes operating in the no-fly zones have been overcome. That is not to say that the operation of inspections is free from friction but at this juncture we are able to perform professional no-notice inspections all over Iraq and to increase aerial surveillance.

American U-2 and French Mirage surveillance aircraft already give us valuable imagery, supplementing satellite pictures, and we expect soon to be able to add night vision capability through an aircraft offered to us by the Russian Federation. We also expect to add low-level, close-area surveillance through drones provided by Germany. We are grateful not only to the countries which place these valuable tools at our disposal, but also to the States, most recently Cyprus, which have agreed to the stationing of aircraft on their territory.

Iraq, with a highly developed administrative system, should be able to provide more documentary evidence about its proscribed weapons programs. Only a few new documents of this type have come to light so far and been handed over since we began inspections. It was a disappointment that Iraq's declaration of 7 December 2002 did not bring new documentary evidence. I hope that efforts in this respect, including the appointment of a governmental commission, will give significant results. When proscribed items are deemed unaccounted for, it is, above all, credible accounts that are needed—or the proscribed items, if they exist.

Where authentic documents do not become available, interviews with persons who may have relevant knowledge and experience may be another way of obtaining evidence. UNMOVIC has names of such persons in its records, and they are among the people whom we seek to interview. In the past month, Iraq has provided us with the names of many persons who may be relevant sources of information, in particular persons who took part in various phases of the unilateral destruction of biological and chemical weapons and proscribed missiles in 1991.

This provision of names prompts two reflections. The first is that, with such detailed information existing regarding those who took part in the unilateral destruction, surely there must also remain records regarding the quantities and other data concerning the various items destroyed.

The second reflection is that, with relevant witnesses available, it becomes even more important to be able to conduct interviews in modes and locations which allow us to be confident that the testimony provided is given without outside influence. While the Iraqi side seems to have encouraged interviewees not to request the presence of Iraqi officials—so-called minders—or the taping of the interviews, conditions ensuring the absence of undue influences are difficult to attain inside Iraq. Interviews outside the country might provide such assurance. It is our intention to request such interviews shortly. Nevertheless, despite remaining shortcomings, interviews are useful. Since we started requesting interviews, 38 individuals have been asked for private interviews, of which 10 have accepted under our terms—seven of them during the past week.

As I noted on 14 February, intelligence authorities have claimed that weapons of mass destruction are moved around Iraq by trucks and, in particular, that there are mobile production units for biological weapons. The Iraqi side states that such activities do not exist. Several inspections have taken place at declared and undeclared sites in relation to mobile production facilities. Food-testing mobile laboratories and mobile workshops have been seen, as well as large containers with seed-processing equipment. No evidence of proscribed activities has so far been found. Iraq is expected to assist in the development of credible ways to conduct random checks of ground transportation.

Inspectors are also engaged in examining Iraq's program for remotely piloted vehicles. A number of sites have been inspected, with data being collected to assess the range and other capabilities of the various models found. Inspections are continuing in that area.

There have been reports, denied from the Iraqi side, that proscribed activities are conducted underground. Iraq should provide information on any underground structure suitable for the production or storage of weapons of mass destruction. During inspections of declared or undeclared facilities, inspection teams have examined building structures for any possible underground facilities. In addition, ground-penetrating radar equipment was used in several specific locations. No underground facilities for chemical or biological production or storage have been found so far.

I should add that, both for the monitoring of ground transportation and for the inspection of underground facilities, we would need to increase our staff in Iraq. I am not talking about a doubling of staff. I would rather have twice the amount of high-quality information about sites to inspect than twice as many expert inspectors to send.

On 14 February I reported to the Council that the Iraqi side had become more active in taking and proposing steps which potentially might shed new light on unresolved disarmament issues. Even a week ago, when the current quarterly report was finalized, there was still relatively little tangible progress to note; hence the cautious formulations in the report before the Council.

As of today, there is more. While the Iraqi side tried to persuade us during our meetings in Baghdad that the Al Samoud 2 missiles that they have declared fall within the permissible range set by the Security Council, the calculations of an international panel of experts led us to the opposite conclusion. Iraq has since accepted that these missiles and associated items must be destroyed and has started the process of destruction under our supervision. The destruction undertaken constitutes a substantial measure of disarmament—indeed, the first since the middle of the 1990s. We are not watching the breaking of toothpicks. Lethal weapons are being destroyed. However, I must add that the report I have today tells me that no destruction work has continued today. I hope that this is a temporary break.

Until today, 34 Al Samoud 2 missiles—including four training missiles, two combat warheads, one launcher and five engines—have been destroyed under UNMOVIC supervision. Work is continuing to identify and inventory the parts and equipment associated with the Al Samoud 2 program. Two "reconstituted" casting chambers used in the production of solid propellant missiles have been destroyed and the remnants melted or encased in concrete. The legality of the Al Fatah missile is still under review, pending further investigation and measurement of various parameters of that missile. More papers on anthrax, VX and missiles have recently been provided. Many have been found to restate what Iraq has already declared, and some will require further study and discussion.

There is a significant Iraqi effort under way to clarify a major source of uncertainty as to the quantities of biological and chemical weapons that were unilaterally destroyed in 1991. A part of this effort concerns a disposal site that was deemed too dangerous for full investigation in the past. It is now being re- excavated. To date, Iraq has unearthed eight complete bombs, comprising two liquid-filled intact R-400 bombs and six other complete bombs. Bomb fragments have also been found. Samples have been taken. The investigation of the destruction site could, in the best case, allow a determination of the number of bombs destroyed at that site. It should be followed by a serious and credible effort to determine the separate issue of how many R-400-type bombs were produced. In this, as in other matters, inspection work is moving forward and may yield results.

Iraq proposed an investigation using advanced technology to quantify the amount of unilaterally destroyed anthrax dumped at a site. However, even if the use of advanced technology could quantify the amount of anthrax said to be dumped at the site, the results would still be open to interpretation. Defining the quantity of anthrax destroyed must, of course, be followed by efforts to establish what quantity was actually produced.

With respect to VX, Iraq has recently suggested a similar method to quantify a VX precursor stated to have been unilaterally destroyed in the summer of 1991.

Iraq has also recently informed us that, following the adoption of the presidential decree prohibiting private individuals and mixed companies from engaging in work related to weapons of mass destruction, further legislation on the subject is to be enacted. That appears to be in response to a letter from UNMOVIC requesting clarification of the issue.

What are we to make of these activities? One can hardly avoid the impression that, after a period of somewhat reluctant cooperation, there has been an acceleration of initiatives from the Iraqi side since the end of January. This is welcome, but the value of these measures must be soberly judged in the light of how many question marks they actually succeed in straightening out. This is not yet clear.

Against this background, the question is now asked whether Iraq has cooperated "immediately, unconditionally, and actively" with UNMOVIC, as required under operative paragraph 9 of resolution 1441 (2002). The answers can be seen from the factual descriptions that I have provided. However, if more direct answers are desired, I would say the following. The Iraqi side has tried on occasion to attach conditions, as it did regarding helicopters and U-2 planes. Iraq has not, however, so far persisted in attaching these or other conditions for the exercise of any of our inspection rights. If it did, we would report it.

It is obvious that, while the numerous initiatives that are now being taken by the Iraqi side with a view to resolving some longstanding open disarmament issues can be seen as active or even proactive, these initiatives, three to four months into the new resolution, cannot be said to constitute immediate cooperation, nor do they necessarily cover all areas of relevance. They are nevertheless welcome, and UNMOVIC is responding to them in the hope of solving presently unresolved disarmament issues.

Members of the Council may relate most of what I have said to resolution 1441 (2002), but UNMOVIC is performing work under several resolutions of the Security Council. The quarterly report before members is submitted in accordance with resolution 1284 (1999), which not only created UNMOVIC, but also continues to guide much of our work. Under the timelines set by that resolution, the results of some of this work is to be reported to the Council before the end of this month. Let me be more specific.

Resolution 1284 (1999) instructs UNMOVIC to "address unresolved disarmament issues" and to identify "key remaining disarmament tasks", and the latter are to be submitted for approval by the Council in the context of a work program. UNMOVIC will be ready to submit a draft work program this month, as required.

UNMOVIC, UNSCOM and the Amorim panel did valuable work to identify the disarmament issues that were still open at the end of 1998. UNMOVIC has used this material as starting points but has analyzed the data behind it and data and documents since 1998 to compile its own list of unresolved disarmament issues, or, rather, clustered issues. It is the answers to these issues that we seek through our inspection activities. It is also from the list of these clustered issues that UNMOVIC will identify key remaining disarmament tasks. As noted in the report before members, this list of clustered issues is ready.

UNMOVIC is required to submit only the work program with the key remaining disarmament tasks to the Council. As I understand, several Council members are interested in the working document with the complete clusters of disarmament issues, and we have declassified it and are ready to make it available to members of the Council on request. In this working document—which may still be adjusted in the light of new information—members will get a more up-to-date review of the outstanding issues than in the documents of 1999, to which members usually refer. Each cluster in the working document ends with a number of points indicating what Iraq could do to solve the issue. Hence, Iraq's cooperation could be measured against the successful resolution of issues.

I should note that the working document contains much information and discussion about the issues that existed at the end of 1998, including information that came to light after 1998. It contains much less information and discussion about the period after 1998, primarily because of a paucity of information. Nevertheless, intelligence agencies have expressed the view that proscribed programs have continued or restarted in this period. It is further contended that proscribed programs and items are located in underground facilities, as I mentioned, and that proscribed items are being moved around Iraq. The working document does contain suggestions on how these concerns may be tackled.

Let me conclude by telling members that UNMOVIC is currently drafting the work program that resolution 1284 (1999) requires us to submit this month. It will obviously contain our proposed list of key remaining disarmament tasks; it will describe the reinforced system of ongoing monitoring and verification that the Council has asked us to implement; it will also describe the various subsystems that constitute the program—for instance, for aerial surveillance, for information from Governments and suppliers, for sampling and for the checking of road traffic.

How much time would it take to resolve the key remaining disarmament tasks? While cooperation can, and is, to be immediate, disarmament and, at any rate, the verification of it, cannot be instant. Even with a proactive Iraqi attitude induced by continued outside pressure, it would still take some time to verify sites and items, analyze documents, interview relevant persons and draw conclusions. It would not take years, nor weeks, but months. Neither Governments nor inspectors would want disarmament inspection to go on forever. However, it must be remembered that, in accordance with the governing resolutions, a sustained inspection and monitoring system is to remain in place after verified disarmament, to give confidence and to sound an alarm if signs were seen of the revival of any proscribed weapons programs.

IAEA Director General Mohamed ElBaradei. My report to the Council today is an update on the status of the International Atomic Energy Agency's (IAEA) nuclear verification activities in Iraq pursuant to Security Council resolution 1441 (2002) and other relevant resolutions.

When I last reported to the Council, on 14 February, I explained that the Agency's inspection activities had moved well beyond the reconnaissance phase—that is, reestablishing our knowledge base regarding Iraq's nuclear capabilities—and into the investigative phase, which focuses on the central question before the IAEA relevant to disarmament: whether Iraq has revived, or attempted to revive, its defunct nuclear weapons program over the last four years.

At the outset, let me state one general observation, namely, that during the past four years, at the majority of Iraqi sites, industrial capacity has deteriorated substantially due to the departure of the foreign support that was often present in the late 1980s, the departure of large numbers of skilled Iraqi personnel in the past decade and the lack of consistent maintenance by Iraq of sophisticated equipment. At only a few inspected sites involved in industrial research, development and manufacturing have the facilities been improved and new personnel taken on. This overall deterioration in industrial capacity is of course of direct relevance to Iraq's capability for resuming a nuclear weapons program.

The IAEA has now conducted a total of 218 nuclear inspections at 141 sites, including 21 that had not been inspected before. In addition, IAEA experts have taken part in many joint inspections of the United Nations Monitoring, Verification and Inspection Commission (UNMOVIC) and the IAEA.

Technical support for nuclear inspections has continued to expand. The three operational air samplers have collected weekly air particulate samples from key locations in Iraq that are being sent to laboratories for analysis. Additional results of water, sediment, vegetation and material sample analyses have been received from the relevant laboratories.

Our vehicle-borne radiation survey team has covered some 2,000 kilometers over the past three weeks. Survey access has been gained to over 75 facilities, including military garrisons and camps, weapons factories, truck parks, manufacturing facilities and residential areas.

Interviews have continued with relevant Iraqi personnel, at times with individuals and groups in the workplace during the course of unannounced inspections, and on other occasions in pre- arranged meetings with key scientists and other specialists known to have been involved with Iraq's past nuclear program. The IAEA has continued to conduct interviews, even when conditions were not in accordance with the IAEA's preferred modalities, with a view to gaining as much information as possible— information that could be cross-checked for validity with other sources and which could be helpful in our assessment of areas under investigation.

As the Council may recall, when we first began to request private unescorted interviews, the Iraqi interviewees insisted on taping the interviews and on keeping the recorded tapes. Recently, upon our insistence, individuals have been consenting to being interviewed without escorts and without taped records. The IAEA has conducted two such private interviews in the last 10 days, and hopes that its ability to conduct private interviews will continue unhindered, including possibly interviews outside Iraq.

I should add that we are looking into further refining the modalities for conducting interviews to ensure that they are conducted freely and to alleviate concerns that interviews are being listened to by other Iraqi parties. In our view, interviews outside Iraq may be the best way to ensure that interviews are free. We therefore intend to request such interviews shortly. We are also asking other States to enable us to conduct interviews with former Iraqi scientists that now reside in those States.

In the last few weeks Iraq has provided a considerable volume of documentation relevant to the issues I reported earlier as being of particular concern, including Iraq's efforts to procure aluminum tubes, its attempted procurement of magnets and magnet production capabilities and its reported attempt to import uranium. I will touch briefly upon the progress made on each of those issues.

Since my last update to the Council, the primary technical focus of IAEA field activities in Iraq has been on resolving several outstanding issues related to the possible resumption of efforts by Iraq to enrich uranium through the use of centrifuges. For that purpose, the IAEA assembled a specially qualified team of international centrifuge-manufacturing experts.

With regard to aluminum tubes, the IAEA has conducted a thorough investigation of Iraq's attempts to purchase large quantities of high-strength aluminum tubes. As previously reported, Iraq has maintained that those aluminum tubes were sought for rocket production. Extensive field investigation and document analysis have failed to uncover any evidence that Iraq intended to use those 81mm tubes for any project other than the reverse-engineering of rockets.

The Iraqi decision-making process with regard to the design of those rockets was well documented. Iraq has provided copies of design documents, procurement records, minutes of committee meetings and supporting data and samples. A thorough analysis of that information, together with information gathered from interviews with Iraqi personnel, has allowed the IAEA to develop a coherent picture of attempted purchases and intended usage of the 81mm aluminum tubes, as well as the rationale behind the changes in the tolerances.

Drawing on that information, the IAEA has learned that the original tolerances for the 81mm tubes were set prior to 1987, and were based on physical measurements taken from a small number of imported rockets in Iraq's possession. Initial attempts to reverse engineer the rockets met with little success. Tolerances were adjusted during the following years as part of ongoing efforts to revitalize the project and improve operational efficiency. The project languished for long periods during that time and became the subject of several committees, which resulted in specification and tolerance changes on each occasion.

Based on available evidence, the IAEA team has concluded that Iraq's efforts to import those aluminum tubes were not likely to have been related to the manufacture of centrifuges and, moreover, that it was highly unlikely that Iraq could have achieved the considerable re-design needed to use them in a revived centrifuge program. However, this issue will continue to be scrutinized and investigated.

With respect to reports about Iraq's efforts to import high- strength permanent magnets—or to achieve the capability for producing such magnets—for use in a centrifuge enrichment program, I should note that, since 1998, Iraq has purchased high-strength magnets for various uses. Iraq has declared inventories of magnets of 12 different designs. The IAEA has verified that previously acquired magnets have been used for missile guidance systems, industrial machinery, electricity meters and field telephones. Through visits to research and production sites, reviews of engineering drawings and analyses of sample magnets, IAEA experts familiar with the use of such magnets in centrifuge enrichment have verified that none of the magnets that Iraq has declared could be used directly for centrifuge magnetic bearings.

In June 2001, Iraq signed a contract for a new magnet production line, for delivery and installation in 2003. The delivery has not yet occurred, and Iraqi documentation and interviews of Iraqi personnel indicate that this contract will not be executed. However, they have concluded that the replacement of foreign procurement with domestic magnet production seems reasonable from an economic point of view. In addition, the training and experience acquired by Iraq in the pre-1991 period makes it likely that Iraq possesses the expertise to manufacture high-strength permanent magnets suitable for use in enrichment centrifuges. The IAEA will therefore continue to monitor and inspect equipment and materials that could be used to make magnets for enrichment centrifuges.

With regard to uranium acquisition, the IAEA has made progress in its investigation into reports that Iraq sought to buy uranium from the Niger in recent years. The investigation was centered on documents provided by a number of States that pointed to an agreement between the Niger and Iraq for the sale of uranium between 1999 and 2001.

The IAEA has discussed these reports with the Governments of Iraq and of the Niger, both of which have denied that any such activity took place. For its part, Iraq has provided the IAEA with a comprehensive explanation of its relations with the Niger, and has described a visit by an Iraqi official to a number of African countries, including the Niger, in February 1999, which Iraq thought might have given rise to the reports. The IAEA was able to review correspondence coming from various bodies of the Government of the Niger, and to compare the form, format, contents and signatures of that correspondence with those of the alleged procurement-related documentation.

Based on a thorough analysis, the IAEA has concluded, with the concurrence of outside experts, that these documents—which formed the basis for the reports of recent uranium transactions between Iraq and the Niger—are, in fact, not authentic. We have therefore concluded that these specific allegations are unfounded. However, we will continue to follow up any additional evidence, if it emerges, relevant to efforts by Iraq illicitly to import nuclear materials.

Many concerns regarding Iraq's possible intention to resume its nuclear program have arisen from Iraqi procurement efforts reported by a number of States. In addition, many of Iraq's efforts to procure commodities and products, including magnets and aluminum tubes, have been conducted in contravention of the sanctions controls specified under Security Council resolution 661 (1990) and other relevant resolutions.

The issue of procurement efforts remains under thorough investigation, and further verification will be forthcoming. In fact, an IAEA team of technical experts is currently in Iraq. It is composed of customs investigators and computer forensic specialists, and it is conducting a series of investigations, through inspections at trading companies and commercial organizations, aimed at understanding Iraq's patterns of procurement.

In conclusion, I am able to report today that, in the area of nuclear weapons—the most lethal weapons of mass destruction—inspections in Iraq are moving forward. Since the resumption of inspections a little over three months ago—and particularly during the three weeks since my last oral report to the Council—the IAEA has made important progress in identifying what nuclear-related capabilities remain in Iraq, and in its assessment of whether Iraq has made any efforts to revive its past nuclear program during the intervening four years since inspections were brought to a halt. At this stage, the following can be stated.

First, there is no indication of resumed nuclear activities in those buildings that were identified through the use of satellite imagery as having been reconstructed or newly erected since 1998, nor any indication of nuclear-related prohibited activities at any inspected sites.

Secondly, there is no indication that Iraq has attempted to import uranium since 1990.

Thirdly, there is no indication that Iraq has attempted to import aluminum tubes for use in centrifuge enrichment. Moreover, even if Iraq had pursued such a plan, it would have encountered practical difficulties in manufacturing centrifuges out of the aluminum tubes in question.

Fourthly, although we are still reviewing issues related to magnets and magnet production, there is no indication to date that Iraq imported magnets for use in a centrifuge enrichment program.

As I stated earlier, the IAEA will naturally continue further to scrutinize and investigate all of these issues.

After three months of intrusive inspections, we have to date found no evidence or plausible indication of the revival of a nuclear-weapon program in Iraq. We intend to continue our inspection activities, making use of all the additional rights granted to us by resolution 1441 (2002) and all additional tools that might be available to us, including reconnaissance platforms and all relevant technologies. We also hope to continue to receive from States actionable information relevant to our mandate.

I should note that, in the past three weeks, possibly as a result of ever-increasing pressure by the international community, Iraq has been forthcoming in its cooperation, particularly with regard to the conduct of private interviews and in making available evidence that could contribute to the resolution of matters of IAEA concern. I hope that Iraq will continue to expand the scope and accelerate the pace of its cooperation.

The detailed knowledge of Iraq's capabilities that IAEA experts have accumulated since 1991, combined with the extended rights provided by resolution 1441 (2002), the active commitment by all States to help us fulfill our mandate, and the recently increased level of Iraqi cooperation—should enable us in the near future to provide the Security Council with an objective and thorough assessment of Iraq's nuclear-related capabilities. However credible this assessment may be, we will endeavor—in view of the inherent uncertainties associated with any verification process, and particularly in the light of Iraq's past record of cooperation—to evaluate Iraq's capabilities on a continuous basis as part of our long-term monitoring and verification program, in order to provide the international community with ongoing and real-time assurances.

German Foreign Minister Joschka Fischer. The aim of the international community remains the complete disarmament—and only the disarmament—of Iraq to finally eliminate the international threat posed by Iraqi weapons of mass destruction. That is what all the relevant Security Council resolutions state.

What is at stake now is the unity of the international community. We have taken a forceful stance in our common fight against international terrorism. We fight together against the proliferation of weapons of mass destruction. We stand united in our condemnation of the Iraqi regime. Where we have different views is on our strategy of how to achieve the effective and total disarmament of Iraq. The Security Council must not spare any effort to find a joint approach to attain our common goal.

The briefings by Mr. Blix and Mr. ElBaradei have made clear once more that Iraq's cooperation with the United Nations Monitoring, Verification and Inspection Commission (UNMOVIC) and the International Atomic Energy Agency (IAEA) does not yet fully meet United Nations demands. Baghdad could have taken many of its recent steps earlier and more willingly. In recent days, cooperation has, nevertheless, notably improved. That is a positive development, which makes it all the less comprehensible why that development should now be abandoned.

There is real progress to be noted on the implementation of relevant Security Council resolutions in all fields. In the sphere of missile technology, there has been clear progress. Thus, Iraq informed the inspectors of its Al Samoud missiles. After examination by UNMOVIC, it was established that their range was too long. After Mr. Blix had set for the regime in Baghdad a deadline for their destruction, Iraq began to destroy the missiles within the prescribed time frame. That is important progress. It shows that peaceful disarmament is possible and that there is a real alternative to war. That positive development also shows that Hans Blix's approach of giving the regime in Baghdad concrete time frames is successful. This method also ought to be used for other unresolved problems.

As far as Iraq's nuclear potential is concerned, we can note great progress. Mr. ElBaradei has just confirmed that. The accounts presented by Iraq are plausible and verifiable. Cooperation on inspections is good. The IAEA is confident about reaching final conclusions soon.

Turning to biological weapons, there has also been progress in individual spheres; for example, in the excavation of many R-400 aerial bombs which are now being assessed by UNMOVIC. Baghdad has announced the presentation of a comprehensive report on open questions in the field of biological and chemical weapons. The interviews with Iraqi scientists are now taking place without monitoring or recording. Preparations are being made to conduct interviews abroad.

France, Russia and Germany presented a memorandum to the Security Council on 24 February proposing a tough regime of intensive inspections (S/2003/214, annex). On the basis of those proposals, the inspections should be stepped up and accelerated. For that to happen, each remaining problem has to be specified and priorities have to be set. A time frame should thereby be prescribed for every single problem.

Therefore, Mr. Blix and Mr. ElBaradei should present us with a detailed, comprehensive working program that clarifies how they and their teams intend to tackle the complete disarmament of Iraq, as called for by the United Nations. It is very important that that working program be presented to the Security Council without delay. We would like to hear today a statement by the inspectors on the remaining key disarmament issues in the cluster report that has been drawn up.

The inspections cannot go on forever. The aim of disarming Iraq has to be pursued energetically and systematically. The Iraqi Government has to fully cooperate with the inspectors. But given the current situation and the ongoing progress, we see no need for a second resolution. Why should we leave the path that we have embarked on now that the inspections, on the basis of resolution 1441 (2002), are showing viable results?

The Security Council is now meeting for the third time within a month at ministerial level to discuss the Iraq crisis. This shows the urgency we attach to the disarmament of Iraq and to the threat of war. The crisis in Iraq troubles our Governments. It troubles the people in our countries. It troubles the entire region of the Near and Middle East. Precisely because the situation is so dramatic, we have to keep firmly reminding ourselves what a war would mean, what the endless suffering it would bring to countless innocent people and what catastrophic humanitarian consequences it would entail. Are we really in a situation that absolutely necessitates the ultima ratio, the very last resort? I think not, because peaceful means are far from having been exhausted.

The Security Council faces—in fact, we all face—an important decision, probably a historic turning point. The alternatives are clear: the disarmament of Iraq by war or its disarmament by exhausting all peaceful means. The risks of a military option are evident to us all. There is good reason to believe that the region would not become more stable, but rather more unstable, through a war, and, what is more, that in the long term international terrorism would be strengthened, not weakened, and that our joint efforts to resolve the Middle East conflict would be hindered.

Then there is the alternative. If we succeed in implementing the effective and complete disarmament of Iraq with peaceful means, we will improve the framework conditions for a regional process of stability, security and cooperation, based on the renunciation of the use of force, on arms control and on a cooperative system of confidence-building measures.

Resolutions 1441 (2002) and 1284 (1999) point a clear way forward for the Security Council. They have to remain the basis of our action. The progress of the last few days has shown that we have efficient alternatives to war in Iraq. By taking this path, we will strengthen the relevance of the United Nations and the Security Council.

* * * *

Secretary of State Colin Powell. It seems to me that we are meeting today with one very, very important question before us. Has the Iraqi regime made the fundamental strategic and political decision to comply with United Nations Security Council resolutions and to rid itself of all of its weapons of mass destruction and all of the infrastructure for the development of weapons of mass destruction? It is a question of intent on the part of the Iraqi leadership. The answer to that question does not come from how many inspectors are present or how much more time should be given or how much more effort should be put into the inspection process. It is not a question of how many clusters of unanswered questions there are or whether more benchmarks are needed or enough unresolved issues have been put forward to be examined and analyzed and conclusions reached. The answer depends entirely on whether Iraq has made the choice to actively cooperate in every possible way, in every possible manner, in the immediate and complete disarmament of itself—of its prohibited weapons. That is what resolution 1441 (2002) calls for.

I would like to thank Mr. Blix and Mr. ElBaradei for their reports this morning, which shed more light on this difficult question. I listened to them very carefully to see if I would hear that, finally, Iraq had reached the point at which it understood that the will of the international community must now be obeyed. I was pleased to hear from both of those distinguished gentlemen that there has been some continuing progress on process and even some new activity with respect to substance. But I was sorry to learn that all of it is still coming in a grudging manner, that Iraq is still refusing to offer what was called for by resolution 1441 (2002): immediate, active and unconditional cooperation—not later, but immediate; not passive, but active; not conditional, but unconditional in every respect.

Unfortunately, in my judgement, despite some of the progress that has been mentioned, I still consider what I heard this morning to be a catalogue of noncooperation. If Iraq genuinely wanted to disarm, we would not have to be worrying about setting up means of looking for mobile biological units or any units of that kind—they would be presented to us. We would not need an extensive program to search for underground facilities that we know exist. The very fact that we must make these requests seems to me to show that Iraq is still not cooperating. The inspectors should not have to look under every rock, go to every crossroads and peer into every cave for evidence, for proof. We must not allow Iraq to shift the burden of proof onto the inspectors. Nor can we return to the failed bargain of resolution 1284 (1999), which offered partial relief for partial disclosure. Resolution 1441 (2002) requires full and immediate compliance, and we must hold Iraq to its terms.

We also heard this morning of an acceleration of Iraqi initiatives. I do not know whether we should call these things "initiatives". Whatever they are, Iraq's small steps are certainly not initiatives. They are not something that came forward willingly and freely from the Iraqis. They have been pulled out—or pressed out—by the possibility of military force, by the political will of the Security Council. These initiatives—if that is what some would choose to call them—have been taken only grudgingly; rarely unconditionally; and primarily under the threat of force.

We are told that these actions do not constitute immediate cooperation. But that is exactly what is demanded by resolution 1441 (2002). And even then, progress is often more apparent than real. I am very pleased that some Al Samoud 2 missiles are now being broken up, although perhaps the process of breaking them up has paused for a moment. And I know that they are not toothpicks, but real missiles. But the problem is that we do not know how many missiles there are and how many toothpicks there are. We do not know whether or not the infrastructure to make more has been identified and broken up. We have evidence that shows that the infrastructure to make more missiles continues to remain within Iraq and has not yet been identified and destroyed.

There is still much more to do and, frankly, it will not be possible to do what we need to do unless we get the full and immediate cooperation that resolution 1441 (2002) and all previous resolutions demanded. It seems to me that the intention of the Iraqi regime to keep from turning over all of its weapons of mass destruction has not changed. It is not cooperating with the international community in the manner intended by resolution 1441 (2002). If Iraq had made that strategic decision to disarm, cooperation would be voluntary—even enthusiastic. It would not be coerced and pressured. That is the lesson we learned from South Africa and Ukraine, where officials did everything possible to ensure complete cooperation with inspectors.

I also listened to Mr. ElBaradei's report with great interest. As we all know, in 1991 the International Atomic Energy Agency (IAEA) was just days away from determining that Iraq did not have a nuclear program. We soon found out otherwise. The IAEA is now reaching a similar conclusion. But we have to be very cautious. We have to make sure that we keep the books open, as Mr. ElBaradei said he would. There is dispute about some of these issues and some of the specific items. Mr. ElBaradei talked about the aluminum tubes that Iraq has tried to acquire over the years. We also know that, notwithstanding the report today, new information is available to us and, I believe, to the IAEA, about a European country where Iraq was found shopping for these kinds of tubes. That country has provided information to us and to the IAEA that the material properties and manufacturing tolerances required by Iraq are more exact by a factor of 50 per cent or more than those usually specified for rocket motor casings. Its experts concluded that the tolerances and specifications that Iraq was seeking cannot be justified for unguided rockets. I am very pleased that we will keep this issue open.

I also welcome the compilation of outstanding issues that Mr. Blix and his staff have provided to some of us and will make available to all of us. The United Nations Monitoring, Verification and Inspection Commission (UNMOVIC) put together a solid piece of research that, when one reads the entire 167 pages, adds up fact by chilling fact to a damning record of 12 years of lies, deception and failure to come clean on the part of Iraq. That document is, in fact, a catalogue of 12 years of abject failure—

not by the inspectors, but by Iraq. We looked carefully at the draft given to the UNMOVIC commissioners, which will be available more widely after this meeting, and we found nearly 30 instances of Iraq's refusal to provide credible evidence substantiating its claims. We have counted 17 examples of the previous inspectors actually uncovering evidence contradicting Iraqi claims. We see instance after instance of Iraq lying to the previous inspectors and planting false evidence—activities which we believe are still ongoing.

As members read the document, they will be able to see, page after page, how Iraq has obstructed the inspectors at nearly every turn over the years. By way of example, we have talked about the R-400 bombs. The report says that, during the period around 1992, Iraq several times changed its declaration about the quantity of bombs it had produced. In 1992 it declared that it had produced a total of 1,200 of those bombs, with the admission, finally, in 1995, after it was pulled out of them, of an offensive biological warfare program. This number was subsequently changed to a total of 1,550 such bombs. Given the lack of specific information from Iraq, the United Nations Special Commission (UNSCOM) could not calculate the total number of R-400 bombs that Iraq had produced for its programs. Thus, the report says, it has proved impossible to verify the production and destruction details of R-400 bombs. UNMOVIC cannot discount the possibility that some R-400 bombs filled with chemical weapons and biological weapons remain in Iraq.

In this document, UNMOVIC refers to actions that Iraq could take to help to resolve this question: present any remaining R- 400 bombs and all relevant moulds, provide more supporting documentation on production and inventory relating to the R-400 and R-400A bombs it manufactured, provide further documentation explaining the coding system that it used with the R-400-type bombs, including the coding assigned to specific chemical and biological weapons agents, and provide credible evidence that the R-400 bomb production line stopped after September 1990.

This is just one example of the kind of documentation that the Council will be seeing. What leaps out is that these actions that Iraq is being asked to take, they could have taken many times over the preceding 12 years. We are not talking about "immediately"; we are talking about why it has not been done over the past 12 years, and about how can we now rely on assurances in the presence of this solid record of lying and deceit over the years.

These questions could easily have been cleared up in Iraq's 7 December declaration; there should not be these kinds of outstanding issues to work on. But there are, and we will all examine them carefully. The point is that this document conclusively shows that Iraq had and still has the capability to manufacture these kinds of weapons; that Iraq had and still has the capability to manufacture not only chemical but also biological weapons; and that Iraq had and still has literally tens of thousands of delivery systems, including increasingly capable and dangerous unmanned aerial vehicles. These are not new questions being presented for our consideration; these are old questions that have not been resolved and that could have been resolved in December with the declaration, or that could have been fully resolved over the past four months if Iraq had come forward and done what resolution 1441 (2002) wanted it to do.

In his report this morning, Mr. Blix remarked on the paucity of information on Iraq's programs since 1998. We have all been working hard to fill that gap, but Iraq is the one that could fill that gap if it were truly complying with resolution 1441 (2002). It would be inundating the inspectors with new information, not holding it back and providing it begrudgingly. The draft document that we reviewed today in preparation for this meeting was 167 pages long. If Iraq were genuinely committed to disarmament, Mr. Blix's document would not be 167 pages of issues and questions; it would be thousands upon thousands of pages of answers about anthrax, about VX, about sarin, about unmanned aerial vehicles; it would set out in detail all of Iraq's prohibited programs. Then, and only then, could the inspectors really do the credible job they need to do of verification, destruction and monitoring.

We have been down this road before. In March 1998, Saddam Hussein was also faced with the threat of military action. He responded with promises—promises to provide inspectors at that time with immediate, unconditional and unrestricted access. The then chief inspector reported to the Council a new spirit of cooperation, along with his hope that the inspectors could move very quickly to verify Iraq's disarmament. We know what happened to that hope: there was no progress on disarmament, and nine months later the inspectors found it necessary to withdraw.

I regret that not much has changed. Iraq's current behavior—like the behavior chronicled in Mr. Blix's document—reveals a strategic decision to continue to delay, to deceive, to try to throw us off the trail, to make it more difficult, to hope that the will of the international community will be fractured, that we will go off in different directions, that we will get bored with the task, that we will remove the pressure, that we will remove the force. And we know what has happened when that has been done in the past. We know that the Iraqis still are not volunteering information and that, when they do, what they are giving is often partial and misleading. We know that, when confronted with facts, the Iraqis are still changing their story to explain those facts, but not enough to give us the truth.

So, has the strategic decision been made to disarm Iraq of its weapons of mass destruction by the leadership in Baghdad? My judgement—I think, our judgement— has to be, clearly not. And this is now the reality that we, the Council, must deal with. Security Council membership carries heavy responsibility: a responsibility to the community of nations to take hard decisions on tough issues such as the one we are facing today. Last November, the Council stepped up to its responsibilities. We must not walk away; we must not find ourselves here this coming November with the pressure removed and with Iraq once again marching down the merry path to weapons of mass destruction, threatening the region, threatening the world.

If we fail to meet our responsibilities, the credibility of the Council and its ability to deal with all the critical challenges we face will suffer. As we sit here, let us not forget the horrors still going on in Iraq. Let us spare a moment to remember the suffering Iraqi people, whose treasure is spent on these kinds of programs and not for their own benefit—people who are being beaten, brutalized and robbed by Saddam and his regime. Colleagues, now is the time for the Council to send a clear message to Saddam that we have not been taken in by his transparent tactics. Nobody wants war, but it is clear that the limited progress we have seen, the process changes we have seen, and the slight substantive changes we have seen come from the presence of a large military force—nations that are willing to put their young men and women in harm's way in order to rid the world of these dangerous weapons. It does not come simply from resolutions, it does not come simply from inspectors: it comes from the will of the Council—the unified political will of the Council—and from the willingness to use force, if it comes to that, to make sure that we achieve the disarmament of Iraq.

Now is the time for the Council to tell Saddam that the clock has not been stopped by his stratagems and machinations. We believe that the draft resolution that has been put forward for action by the Council is appropriate and that in the very near future we should bring it before the Council for a vote. The clock continues to tick, and the consequences of Saddam Hussein continued refusal to disarm will be very, very real.

Russian Foreign Minister Igor Ivanov. The Iraq problem has many aspects. On the one hand, we all agree that we must achieve the full and effective disarmament of Iraq, in conformity with Security Council resolution 1441 (2002). On the other hand, it is quite clear that the way in which we resolve this problem will determine not only the future of Iraq: in essence, we are now laying the foundations for ensuring peace and security in our time.

Therein lies the special responsibility that is now ours and the choice that we shall have to make. If, through our joint efforts, we succeed in resolving the Iraqi crisis in accordance with the Charter of the United Nations, it will certainly have a positive effect on our efforts to settle other conflicts. Most significant, it will be an important step towards a new, just and secure world order. That is why Russia has consistently and resolutely sought to solve the Iraq problem on the basis of international law and of Security Council resolutions. Today, more than ever before, we have reason to state that this is not only the proper, but also the most reliable, way.

The report submitted by Mr. Blix demonstrates that, thanks to our united, energetic efforts and to the pressure that has been brought to bear on Baghdad from all sides, including through the buildup of a military presence, we have been able to achieve essential progress in implementing resolution 1441 (2002).

Let us take a look at the facts. There is an ongoing enhanced inspections regime in Iraq. International inspectors are being given immediate, unimpeded, unconditional and unrestricted access to any site. Active use is being made of helicopters and aircraft for the purpose of aerial surveillance during the course of inspections. On the whole, the Iraqi authorities' level of cooperation with inspectors is thoroughly different from the practice we saw previously under the United Nations Special Commission (UNSCOM).

Mr. Blix and Mr. ElBaradei have repeatedly pointed out, including in their latest reports, problems in conducting interviews with Iraqi specialists. We agree with the view that the Iraqi leadership must more energetically encourage its citizens to take part in those interviews without minders. Judging from the latest reports, such interviews are gradually beginning to become the norm.

Qualitatively new changes with regard to carrying out concrete tasks have taken place during the inspection process. There is a real disarmament process in Iraq for the first time in many years. Weapons banned by resolutions of the Security Council are being eliminated. Those weapons include the Al Samoud 2 missiles, which were officially declared by the Iraqi side and which are now being destroyed under the supervision of the United Nations Monitoring, Verification and Inspection Commission (UNMOVIC). Those weapons also include the discovered 122mm shells, which can carry poisonous chemical substances. The Iraqis have turned over fragments from R-400 aerial bombs to the inspectors for analysis. The experts are working on the possibility of analyzing ground soil in areas where VX gas and anthrax growth media have been destroyed. Baghdad has also turned over to inspectors several dozen new documents, which are now being analyzed. I repeat that these are two facts that demonstrate that the inspectors' activities are developing.

We agree in principle with Mr. Blix's view that if the latest positive steps taken by Baghdad had been undertaken earlier, the results would be more convincing today. But it is nevertheless important that those steps were taken. As the heads of UNMOVIC and the International Atomic Energy Agency (IAEA) have pointed out, those steps open up the way to resolving outstanding problems. I wish once again to emphasize that they open up the way to resolving outstanding problems. This is important in principle.

Furthermore, I would like to draw the Council's attention to yet another aspect highlighted by Mr. Blix, namely, the long-term monitoring of Iraq's non-production of weapons of mass destruction. This is yet another important safety mechanism to ensure that Iraq will not produce weapons of mass destruction in the future.

In that connection, the question arises as to whether it is now reasonable to halt inspections, thereby halting the momentum achieved in the process of Iraq's disarmament. Let us take another look.

What is really in the genuine interest of the world community—continuing the albeit difficult but clearly fruitful results of the inspectors' work or resorting to the use of force, which will inevitably result in enormous loss of life and which is fraught with serious and unpredictable consequences for regional and international stability? It is our deep conviction that the possibilities for disarming Iraq through political means do exist. They really exist, and that cannot but be acknowledged. What we need now is not new Security Council resolutions; we have enough of those. We now need active support for the inspectors to carry out their tasks.

Russia is firmly in favor of continuing and strengthening inspection activities and of making them more focused in nature. That goal would be furthered by the speedy submission—in the days to come—of an UNMOVIC program of work for the approval of the Security Council, a program that includes a list of key remaining disarmament tasks. Such tasks should be formulated with the utmost clarity; and they should be realizable. That would enable us to evaluate objectively Iraq's level of cooperation and, most importantly, to provide an exhaustive answer to all the remaining open questions regarding banned Iraqi military programs.

Of course, we all face a difficult choice. Hardly anyone among us could claim to be in possession of the absolute truth. It is therefore quite natural for different points of view to be expressed during the course of our discussion. But such differences should not lead to a rift among us. We are all standing on the same side of the barricade. We all share common values. Only by acting in solidarity will we effectively face up to new global threats and challenges. We are certain that the Security Council has to emerge united and strong from the Iraq crisis, not weakened and divided. Russia will continue to work towards that goal.

French Foreign Minister Dominique Galouzeau de Villepin. I would like to thank Mr. Blix and Mr. ElBaradei for the presentation they have just made. Their reports testify to the regular progress in the disarmament of Iraq.

What have the inspectors told us? They have told us that Iraq has been actively cooperating with them for a month; that, with the progressive destruction of Al Samoud 2 missiles and their equipment, substantial progress has been made in the area of ballistics; and that new prospects are opening up with the recent questioning of several scientists. Significant evidence of real disarmament has now been observed. That, indeed, is the key to resolution 1441 (2002).

I would solemnly like to ask a question in this body, the same question being asked by the people of the world: Why should we today engage in a war with Iraq?

I would like also to ask: Why smash instruments that have just proved their effectiveness? Why choose division, when our unity and our resolve are leading Iraq to rid itself of its weapons of mass destruction? Why should we wish to proceed by force, at any cost, when we can succeed peacefully?

War is always an acknowledgement of failure. Let us not resign ourselves to the irreparable.

Before making our choice, let us weigh the consequences; let us consider the effects of our decisions.

Indeed, it is clear to all that in Iraq, we are resolutely moving towards the complete elimination of weapons of mass destruction programs.

The method that we have chosen works. The information supplied by Baghdad has been verified by the inspectors and is leading to the elimination of banned ballistic equipment.

We must proceed the same way with all the other programs—with information, verification, destruction. We already have useful information in the biological and chemical domains. In response to the inspectors' questions, Iraq must give us further information in a timely fashion, so that we may obtain the most precise knowledge possible about any existing inventories or programs. On the basis of that information, we will destroy all the components that are discovered, as we are doing for the missiles, and we will determine the truth of the matter.

With regard to nuclear weapons, Mr. ElBaradei's statements confirm that we are approaching the time when the International Atomic Energy Agency (IAEA) will be able to certify the dismantlement of the Iraq program.

What conclusions can we draw? That Iraq, according to the very terms used by the inspectors, represents less of a danger to the world than it did in 1991, and that we can achieve the objective of effectively disarming that country.

Let us keep the pressure on Baghdad. The adoption of resolution 1441 (2002); the assumption of converging positions by the vast majority of the world's nations; diplomatic actions by the African Union, the League of Arab States, the Organization of the Islamic Conference and the Non-Aligned Movement—all of these common efforts are bearing fruit.

The American and British military presence in the region lends support to our collective resolve. We all recognize the effectiveness of the pressure that is being exerted by the international community. We must use it to achieve our objective of disarmament through inspections. As the European Union noted, these inspections cannot continue indefinitely. The pace must therefore be stepped up.

That is why France wishes today to make three proposals.

First, let us ask the inspectors to establish a hierarchy of disarmament tasks and, on that basis, to present us, as quickly as possible, with the work program provided for by resolution 1284 (1999). We need to know immediately which priority issues could constitute the key disarmament tasks to be carried out by Iraq.

Secondly, we propose that the inspectors submit a progress report every three weeks. That will make the Iraqi authorities understand that under no circumstances may they interrupt their efforts.

Finally, let us establish a schedule for assessing the implementation of the work program. Resolution 1284 (2002) provides for a time frame of 120 days. We are willing to shorten it, if the inspectors consider it feasible.

The military agenda must not dictate the calendar of inspections. We agree to accelerated timetables, but we cannot accept an ultimatum as long as the inspectors are reporting progress in terms of cooperation. That would mean war. That would lead to the Security Council's being stripped of its responsibilities. By imposing a deadline of a few days, would we merely be seeking a pretext for war?

I will say it again: as a permanent member of the Security Council, France will not allow a resolution to be adopted that authorizes the automatic use of force.

Let us consider the anguish and the expectations of people all over the world, in all our countries, from Cairo to Rio, from Algiers to Pretoria, from Rome to Jakarta. Indeed, the stakes go beyond the fate of Iraq alone.

Let us be clear-sighted. We are defining a method for resolving crises. We are choosing how to define the world we want our children to live in.

This is true in the case of North Korea, and in the case of south Asia, where we have not yet found the path towards a lasting resolution of disputes. It is true in the case of the Middle East. Can we continue to wait while acts of violence multiply?

These crises have many roots—political, religious and economic. Their origins lie deep in the turmoil of history. There may be some who believe that these problems can be resolved by force, thereby creating a new order. But this is not what France believes. On the contrary, we believe that the use of force can give rise to resentment and to hatred, and fuel a clash of identities and of civilizations—something that our generation has a prime responsibility to avert.

To those who believe that war would be the quickest way to disarm Iraq, I can reply that it would create divisions and cause wounds that will be long in healing. How many victims will there be? How many grieving families?

We do not subscribe to what may be the other objectives of a war. Is it a question of regime change in Baghdad? No one underestimates the cruelty of that dictatorship or the need to do everything possible to promote human rights. But that is not the objective of resolution 1441 (2002), and force is certainly not the best way of bringing about democracy. In this case and in others, it would encourage a dangerous instability.

Is it a question of fighting terrorism? War would only increase it, and we could then be faced with a new wave of violence. Let us beware of playing into the hands of those who want a clash of civilizations or a clash of religions.

Finally, is it a question of reshaping the political landscape of the Middle East? In that case, we run the risk of exacerbating tensions in a region already characterized by great instability. Furthermore, the large number of communities and religions in Iraq itself increases the danger of a potential break-up.

We all have the same demands. We want more security and more democracy. But there is another logic besides that of force. There is another path; there are other solutions.

We understand the profound sense of insecurity with which the American people have been living since the tragedy of 11 September 2001. The entire world shared the sorrow of New York and of America, struck at the heart. I say this in the name of our friendship for the American people and in the name of our common values: freedom, justice, tolerance.

But there is nothing today to indicate a link between the Iraqi regime and Al Qaeda. Will the world be a safer place after a military intervention in Iraq? Let me state my country's conviction: it will not.

Four months ago, we unanimously adopted a system of inspections to eliminate the threat of potential weapons of mass destruction and guarantee our security. Today we cannot accept, without contradicting ourselves, a conflict that might well weaken it.

Yes, we, too, want more democracy in the world. But we can achieve this objective only within the framework of a true global democracy based on respect, sharing, and the awareness of genuinely common values and a common destiny. Its core is the United Nations.

Let us make no mistake. In the face of multiple and complex threats, there is no single response, but there is a single requirement: we must remain united.

Today we must together invent a new future for the Middle East. Let us not forget the immense hope created by the efforts of the Madrid Conference and the Oslo Agreement. Let us not forget that the Middle East crisis represents our greatest challenge in terms of security and justice. For us, the Middle East, like Iraq, represents a priority commitment.

This calls for even greater ambition and even greater boldness. We should envision a region transformed through peace, and civilizations that, through the courageous act of reaching out to each other, can rediscover their self-confidence and an international prestige that is equal to their long history and their aspirations.

In a few days, we shall solemnly fulfill our responsibility through a vote. We will be facing an essential choice: disarming Iraq through war or through peace. This crucial choice includes others. It includes the international community's ability to resolve the many current or future crises. It carries with it a vision of the world, a concept of the role of the United Nations.

France therefore believes that to make this choice, to make it in good conscience in this forum of international democracy, before their peoples and before the world, heads of State or Government must meet again here, in New York, in the Security Council.

This is in everyone's interest. We must rediscover the fundamental vocation of the United Nations: to allow each of its Members to assume its responsibilities in the face of the Iraqi crisis, but also to seize together the destiny of a world in crisis and thus recreate the conditions for our future unity.

Chinese Foreign Minister Tang Jiaxuan. Four months ago, in this Chamber, the Council unanimously adopted resolution 1441 (2002) in a spirit of unity and cooperation. The adoption of that resolution fully manifested the determination of the Council to destroy the weapons of mass destruction possessed by Iraq and truly reflected the desire of the international community for a political settlement of the Iraqi issue. It is precisely for that reason that the resolution has been widely welcomed and supported by all countries the world over.

Undoubtedly, it is an arduous task for us to ensure the implementation of the relevant Council resolutions and the full and comprehensive destruction of Iraq's weapons of mass destruction. However, it is gratifying to note that much progress has been made in the weapons inspections, thanks to the unremitting efforts of the United Nations Monitoring, Verification and Inspection Commission (UNMOVIC) and the International Atomic Energy Agency (IAEA). Judging from today's reports by the two inspection bodies, resolution 1441 (2002) has been implemented smoothly on the whole, with progress made and results achieved. It is true that there are also problems and difficulties in the inspection process. That is exactly why it is highly necessary to continue the inspections. We believe that, as long as we keep to the road of political settlement, the goal of destroying Iraq's weapons of mass destruction could still be attained.

Resolution 1441 (2002) did not come easily. Given the current situation, we need resolve and determination and, more important, patience and wisdom. The Council therefore needs to maintain its unity and cooperation more than ever so as to preserve its authority. We believe that the Council should provide strong support and guidance to the two inspection bodies in their work, let them continue inspections and seek the truth until they have fulfilled the mandate of resolution 1441 (2002). At the same time, we also urge the Iraqi Government to take further effective measures in earnest to strengthen its cooperation with the inspectors on matters of substance and to the creation of conditions necessary for political settlement. Under the current circumstances, there is no reason to shut the door to peace. Therefore, we are not in favor of a new resolution, particularly one authorizing the use of force.

The Iraqi issue bears on peace and development in the Gulf region and in the world at large. With a view to finding a solution to that issue, we must take into full account the shared interests of all nations and the long-term interests of human development. Now that we have entered the twenty-first century, peace and development still remain the major themes of our times. All countries in the world, faced with the common tasks of maintaining peace and achieving development and prosperity, desperately need a stable and peaceful international environment.

Among all things in the universe, human beings are of paramount importance, and peace is the most precious. Over the past months, right in this Chamber, we have heard many times, from many United Nations Member States, strong appeals to resolve the Iraqi issue politically. Outside this Chamber, we have also heard justified cries of "peace, not war" from the peoples of many countries. The power of the Security Council derives from all United Nations Member States and from the peoples of all nations. We have no reason to remain indifferent to those strong demands and outcries. In order for the Security Council to be responsible to history and to safeguard the common interests of all peoples in the world, the Chinese Government strongly appeals to the Council to shoulder its responsibility and to do all it can to avoid war and to maintain its efforts to achieve a political settlement.

* * * *

Spanish Foreign Minister Ana Palacio. On 14 February, I opened my statement by pointing out that, along with millions of citizens of the world, I was hoping to hear just one sentence from the inspectors: that Saddam Hussein was fully, unconditionally and actively complying with resolution 1441 (2002).

I did not hear it on that day, nor have I heard it today. I also have the feeling today that we run the risk of not seeing the forest for the trees. The concrete progress achieved by the inspectors in their commendable work, to which I pay tribute on behalf of Spain, and the gestures made by Saddam Hussein are distracting us from the objective defined by the international community 12 years ago: the complete disarmament of the Iraqi regime.

We have been marking time for 12 years. I have two questions to raise that I believe are fundamental for us all: Are we discharging our obligations as members of the Security Council? What message are we sending to the world? According to the United Nations Charter, the mission of the Security Council is to maintain international peace and security, to identify threats thereto and to define action to be taken.

I can only say that the threat remains and that Saddam Hussein has yet to comply with the resolutions of this Council. This is happening 12 years after the adoption of resolution 687 (1991) and four months after the adoption of resolution 1441 (2002), which, as the Council will remember, constituted the final opportunity.

So, 12 years later, we still find ourselves in the same situation as in 1991. Twelve years later, the principal actor is the same: Saddam Hussein. Twelve years later, the threat is the same: his weapons of mass destruction. Twelve years later, his attitude is identical: a profound contempt for international law and the clear intention to divide us. Twelve years later, his strategy remains the same: to deceive us. How much longer? How much time is needed to take the strategic decision to collaborate fully, actively and unconditionally? I am afraid that we are facing a question whose answer everyone knows but which many prefer to ignore.

Instead of sending a solid and cohesive message, the Council runs the risk of becoming a media platform showcasing our differences and making our work even harder.

Through continuous and systematic misrepresentation of the facts, Saddam is achieving something extraordinarily dangerous. He has managed to get many to identify the Security Council—the guarantor of international legitimacy—as the aggressor, while he identifies himself as the victim. He has managed to divide the international community, as the Foreign Minister of Mexico said so well a moment ago. He has also managed to reverse the burden of proof, shifting onto us a responsibility that is his alone.

How could we have come to a situation where a dictator that has provoked wars, invaded countries, gassed his own population, trampled all existing human rights and flouted the law for 12 years is now putting the credibility of the Council in jeopardy?

My second question is, what message are we sending? It is impossible not to realize that only maximum pressure and the credible threat of force make an impression on the Iraqi regime. Let me recall that this is the underlying logic of resolution 1441 (2002) and of the draft resolution sponsored by the United States, the United Kingdom and Spain, which will soon be submitted to the Council.

I welcome and appreciate the progress that has been achieved by the inspectors, in particular the destruction of the Al Samoud missiles. But all of a sudden proof of the existence of programs of weapons of mass destruction, whose existence was denied until now, appears as if by magic—because of the 300,000 soldiers deployed in the region. Or we suddenly hear of the existence of missiles and motors that are banned under international law. That conduct confirms our fears. Those weapons exist. They have not been destroyed. They can be used again.

As Secretary of State Powell said, if Saddam Hussein was lying before when he was hiding those weapons, why should we believe him now when, after revealing their presence, he claims that he has destroyed all remaining weapons, without our being able to detect a genuine will to disarm.

Given those questions, what message should the Council send? First, we will not tolerate any more of Saddam Hussein games. He did not comply in 1991. He deceived the United Nations Special Commission in 1995. He remained free of inspections for almost four years. And now, even when resolution 1441 (2002) indicates that it represents the final opportunity, he is once again trying to prevent its implementation.

The Council has to state also that we cannot encourage, through action or failure to act, those possessing weapons of mass destruction who feel that they can systematically violate international law with impunity. The Council should send the clear message that it is very aware that the threat looming over us is more serious than ever and that it concerns the confluence of the existence of weapons of mass destruction, their possible use by terrorist groups and the criminality of political leaders who make use of both those weapons and terrorists.

The Security Council has to send a clear message that it considers that the time has come to stop being a hostage to those, who in seeking their own objectives, mistakenly interpret our aspiration to peace as a sign of weakness. The Council must make it clear that it has always advocated not Iraq's containment or its partial disarmament but its complete disarmament of weapons of mass destruction, in particular chemical and bacteriological weapons, and that this should be done peacefully, which requires full Iraqi cooperation. And if such cooperation is lacking, Iraq alone will be responsible for the consequences.

Finally, it must be made very clear that the Council must assume its responsibility before the entire world to respond to this situation.

Disarming Iraq is not a question of more inspectors or more time. That, to paraphrase a French thinker, is merely the strategy of impotence. With respect to nuclear material and missiles, we can envisage the possibility of achieving results without the regime's willingness to disarm or even its proactive collaboration. But that is not true for chemical and bacteriological weapons. We all know that. It is particularly in the area of the disarmament of chemical and bacteriological weapons that disarmament can be achieved only if there is political will on the part of the Iraqi regime. Inspectors will naturally have to continue for the time that is necessary and with the means that are necessary. But it must be done on the basis of a radical change in the willingness of Saddam Hussein regime to disarm. So far, Iraq has given no credible signs of possessing the will to disarm.

I have listened to those who consider that decisions the Council may adopt will provoke a great loss of human lives and great damage in Iraq. They criticize that and hold us responsible for it. No, it is others such as Saddam Hussein who are responsible for the deaths of millions through their wars, invasions, actions and decisions. It is others such as Saddam Hussein who use chemical weapons. It is others such as Saddam Hussein who destroy entire families, peoples, nations. It is not the Security Council that is responsible. We are seeking international peace and security, because we all want peace. But we want a peace that is safe and that ensures that those weapons will not be used by Iraq and that they will not fall into the hands of terrorist groups, which could use them to achieve their own ends. To act otherwise is to harbor false hopes and to look for arrangements that could only seriously undermine the credibility and effectiveness of the Council and even the international peace and stability that we all seek.

British Foreign Secretary Jack Straw. I have listened with very great care to what my colleagues speaking before me have said. We are all agreed that Iraq must be fully disarmed of weapons of mass destruction and that Iraq's failure to cooperate immediately, unconditionally and actively with the inspectors has to be dealt with. As we negotiated resolution 1441 (2002), the evidence was there for all to see that Iraq had been and remained in material breach. All 15 members voted to give the Iraqi regime a final opportunity to comply with its obligations.

The first question before the Council, therefore, is this: has Iraq taken this final opportunity to disarm? I was very much struck, while listening with care to all the statements—and of course people have different points of view—by the fact that nobody—not one minister in the Council—said, in my hearing, that Iraq is now fully, actively and immediately in compliance with resolution 1441 (2002). It has not so far taken this final opportunity. If anybody in the Chamber or outside has any doubt about that conclusion, then I commend to them the so-called clusters report on the outstanding issues concerning Iraq's proscribed weapons program, which, as a member of the commission behind the United Nations Monitoring, Verification and Inspection Commission, I have already had the privilege of reading. As Mr. Blix knows, I have read all 167 pages of that report in every particular. It is a painstaking piece of work and I thank Mr. Blix for publishing it. But it is also a chilling read about the failure of Iraq to comply with successive resolutions of the Council each day of the past 12 years.

There has not been active cooperation in the areas which matter. As a result, UNMOVIC has not been able to resolve any substantive issues outstanding from 1998. As we all know—this is a point to which I shall return shortly—Iraq refused to admit inspectors for three years after resolution 1284 (1999) was adopted, agreeing to them only under threat of enforcement action and in an attempt to frustrate resolution 1441

(2002). Iraq has dragged its feet on as many elements of procedural and substantive cooperation as possible.

I would like to draw attention to just one aspect, which is often overlooked. Mr. Blix referred to the fact that Iraq recently informed us that following the adoption of a presidential decree prohibiting private individuals and mixed companies from engaging in work related to weapons of mass destruction, further legislation on this subject is to be enacted. No one should be taken in by that as a concession. Iraq was ordered on 2 October 1991—I have here the instruction from the Council—to enact legislation, in conformity with international law, to do precisely what it is now saying it intends to do. What is more, what it has so far done covers not the operations of the State but only those of private individuals and mixed companies. So 12 years on, 12 years after the world saw that Iraq had developed, under the world's nose, weapons of mass destruction and delivery systems—nuclear systems, biological systems, chemical systems—Iraq is still refusing to pass a law saying that such activity by members of State Government authorities is illegal.

This is not something for which they needed to search. It is not something for which they need the assistance of inspectors or ground-penetrating radar. It is something they could and should have done back in October 1991 and that, notwithstanding all the pressure, they are still refusing to do.

Then we come to the issue of interviews. As Mr. Blix and Mr. ElBaradei have reported, Iraq has done everything possible to prevent unrestricted, unrecorded interviews. There have now been 12 private interviews between the United Nations Monitoring, Verification and Inspection Commission and the International Atomic Energy Agency against a United Nations Special Commission list of 3,500 people previously associated with weapons of mass destruction programs. We know for a fact that all of those 12—and all prospective interviewees—were threatened and intimidated by the Iraqi regime beforehand and told that their exchanges were being recorded. The interviewees were not being recorded by bugs and tape recorders that they were told to take into the meetings. But they were told that they were going to be recorded in any event by bugs placed in the walls of the recording halls. I understand that scientists most likely to have the most incriminating evidence have been locked away by the Iraqi security services. There have been no interviews in the safe havens outside Iraq—not one. And the restrictions placed on the interviewees is itself the most incriminating evidence that Saddam has something to hide.

The Al Samoud 2 episode further confirms Iraq's familiar tactics. Iraq under-declared the number of missile engines it—illegally—imported. It declared 131 engines but imported 380. Iraq also falsely declared that the missile had a maximum range of 150 kilometers when it was designed—it was not an accident—to fly considerably in excess of that. We know that Iraq's agreeing to the destruction process, necessary as it is, is a calculation that it can satisfy the Council with a partial response in only one of the 29 categories of unresolved disarmament questions.

I must say, with all due respect to good colleagues, that it defies experience to believe that continuing inspections with no firm end date, as I believe has been suggested in the French, German and Russian memorandum, will achieve complete disarmament if—as the memorandum acknowledges—Iraq's full and active cooperation is not immediately forthcoming. The memorandum is not even a formula for containment, given Iraq's proven ability to exploit the existing sanctions regime to continue to develop weapons of mass destruction. We knew nothing about the missile engines. We knew nothing about the rest of this—imported under our noses in breach of the sanctions regime—until we passed resolution 1441 (2002).

To find a peaceful solution to the current crisis, the Council must not retreat from the demands it set out clearly in resolution 1441 (2002). What we need is an irreversible and strategic decision by Iraq to disarm; a strategic decision by Iraq to yield to the inspectors all of its weapons of mass destruction and all relevant information, which it could and should have provided at any time in the past 12 years; a strategic decision like that taken by South Africa when it decided freely to abandon its secret nuclear program.

I greatly welcome the progress the inspectors have reported. My earnest wish, and that of my Government, has all along been to achieve the disarmament of Iraq's weapons of mass destruction, if humanly possible by peaceful means. But if we are to achieve that, we have to recognize that the progress which has been reported represents only the tip of a very large iceberg of huge unfinished business required of Iraq.

Just as I welcome the progress about which we have heard, I say to the Council that there are very serious lessons for us to draw from what has been reported. Let us consider what has changed. Why has there been this sudden bout of activity when there was no progress at all for weeks before, and when for months and years before that, Saddam Hussein was rearming under our noses?

It is not our policy which has changed. It is not international law which has changed—there have been from the beginning the clearest instructions to Saddam to disarm. No, what has changed is one thing and one thing only: the pressure on the regime. Mr. Blix said in his opening remarks that the changes may well be due to strong outside pressure. That is absolutely right. In his remarks, Dominique de Villepin described a lot of diplomatic pressure by the Non-Aligned Movement, the European Union, the Arab League and many others. I greatly welcome all of that diplomatic pressure.

Dominique went on to say that the forces of the United States and of the United Kingdom lend support to that pressure. With due respect for my good friend, I think it is the other way around. What has happened is that all that pressure was there for every day of 12 years. In Mr. Blix's carefully chosen words, the strong outside pressure is—and let us be blunt about this—the presence of more than 200,000 young men and women of the United States and of the United Kingdom, willing to put their lives on the line for the sake of this body, the United Nations.

Dominique also said that the choice before us was one between disarmament by peace and disarmament by war. That is a false choice. I wish it were that easy, because then we would not be obliged to have this discussion; we could all put up our hands for disarmament by peace and go home. The paradox we face is that the only way we are going to achieve disarmament by peace of a rogue regime that, all of us know, has been in defiance of the Council for the past 12 years—the only way that we can achieve its disarmament of weapons mass destruction, which, the Council has said, pose a threat to international peace and security—is by backing our diplomacy with the credible threat of force.

I wish that we lived in a different world where this was not necessary, but, sadly, we live in this world, and the choice is not ours as to how this disarmament takes place—the choice is Saddam Hussein. Would that it were ours, because it would be so easy, but sadly, it is not. And there is only one possible, sensible conclusion that we can draw: we have to increase the pressure on Saddam Hussein. We have to put this man to the test. He has shown this week that he does not need more time to comply, he can act with astonishing speed when he chooses to. What is more, he knows exactly what has to be done. He knows this because he is the originator of the information. The Iraqis do not need a Mr. Hans Blix and all his staff to produce 167 pages of forensic questions; they have the answer book already. Look how fast they acted to produce 13,000 pages of a declaration, albeit much of it irrelevant. It may take time to fabricate further falsehoods, but the truth takes only seconds to tell.

And I should just like to make something clear on the issue of automaticity, which, again, my good friend Dominique raised. Nothing has ever been automatic about the threat of force or the use of force; it has always been conditional. It would be utterly irresponsible and in defiance of our solemn duties to the Council for us to walk into a situation where force was used automatically. And, although the canard has been around that some of us were in the business of using force automatically, the truth is that it is not being used automatically, it should not be used automatically, it will not be used automatically, and nothing to which my Government has ever put its name has ever suggested that that would be the case.

What we seek is compliance by Saddam Hussein with resolution 1441 (2002). And I make this point: we are not suggesting that, in a matter of days, Mr. Blix and Mr. ElBaradei would be able to complete all their work—that they would be able to verify the disarmament of Iraq. No one is suggesting that. But what we are suggesting is that it is perfectly possible, achievable and necessary for Saddam Hussein and the Iraqi regime to bring themselves into compliance so that, instead of us all admitting—either by our words or by our silence, as we have today—that Saddam is not in full compliance, that he has not taken a further opportunity and the final opportunity, we can say the reverse and can celebrate the achievement of the fine ideals of the United Nations and the upholding of one of the central points of the work program of the United Nations—that we back our diplomacy, if necessary, with the credible threat of force.

As founding members of the United Nations and permanent members of the Security Council, we remain committed to exploring every reasonable option for a peaceful outcome and every prospect of a Council consensus. In the light of that and of what I have said, I shall tell the Council that, on behalf of the sponsors of our draft resolution—the Kingdom of Spain, the Government of the United States and the Government of the United Kingdom—I am asking the Secretariat to circulate an amendment, which we are introducing, that will specify a further period beyond the adoption of a resolution for Iraq to take the final opportunity to disarm and to bring itself into compliance. But the Council must send Iraq the clear message that we will resolve this crisis on United Nations terms: the terms that the Council established four months ago when we unanimously adopted resolution 1441 (2002).

* * * *

Iraqi Permanent Representative Mohamed Aldouri. I would like to thank Mr. Blix and Mr. ElBaradei for their efforts and for their briefings. Let me underline our pledge to continue proactive cooperation with them.

Iraq's actions are based on a deep sense of responsibility and on a clear vision of the nature of the very difficult international situation, which is inauspicious not only for Iraq and its people but for the region and the entire world, including the United Nations. The entire world, with the exception of a few States, wishes to see the United Nations continue to fulfill the tasks entrusted to it in the area of international peace and security.

It seems that a possible war of aggression against Iraq has become imminent, regardless of any decision by the Security Council and despite the fact that official and public international opinion strongly rejects aggression and war and demands a peaceful solution. The French, German, Russian and Chinese position makes it clear that there is no need for a second resolution to be adopted by the Security Council. It demands that the work of the inspectors continue and that they be given enough time to complete their tasks by peaceful means.

The position of the Arab countries is also clear, particularly the position taken at the latest Arab Summit, which unanimously rejected an attack on Iraq as a threat to Arab national security. The Summit called for a peaceful resolution of the Iraqi crisis within the framework of international legitimacy. The Summit affirmed the Security Council's responsibility to preserve the independence, security and territorial integrity of Iraq. The Summit also declared that it is time to lift the sanctions imposed on Iraq.

The latest summit of the 116-member Non-Aligned Movement, held in Kuala Lumpur, condemned the use or threat of military action, considering it to be aggression and a flagrant violation of the principle of non-interference.

The heads of State and Government and other representatives of 57 Islamic countries, who recently met at the Doha Summit, also declared their absolute rejection of any aggression against Iraq, considering it to be a threat to the security of all Islamic States.

Here, I would like to recall the position of the African Union, which has clearly and categorically rejected war and called for a peaceful solution. I should like also to express my appreciation for the efforts being made by churches throughout the world in stressing the importance of peace, in particular the efforts being made by His Holiness Pope John Paul II in advocating peace and denouncing war, which he considers to be lacking any moral basis or legitimacy.

On behalf of the people of Iraq, I salute all peoples of the world, in particular the peoples of the United States of America, the United Kingdom and Spain, who took to the streets by the millions to express their devotion to peace and their rejection of war.

The United States Administration, together with that of the United Kingdom, continues to fabricate "facts" and "evidence" suggesting Iraq's possession of weapons of mass destruction. However, they have not managed to convince the international community. The inspectors have proven that there are no such weapons and that such allegations are false. Secretary of State Powell spoke of the lack of a strategic political decision by Iraq to demonstrate its commitment to complying with the resolutions of international legitimacy and to ridding Iraq of weapons of mass destruction.

Let me affirm that in 1991 Iraq did indeed take the strategic decision to rid itself of weapons of mass destruction. Accordingly, the United Nations Special Commission (UNSCOM) worked in Iraq for eight years. Iraq handed over many of those weapons to UNSCOM for destruction in the period from 1991 to 1994. UNSCOM did in fact undertake the destruction of those weapons. That was in addition to the weapons unilaterally destroyed by Iraq in the summer of 1991, which included proscribed biological material. Those are the basic facts of the matter. Since then, nothing that contradicts those facts has been unearthed.

All weapons that have been proscribed fall into one of two categories: they have been either declared or unilaterally destroyed by Iraq. All the declarations that Iraq has been repeatedly asked to present concerned the details and verification of that unilateral destruction and nothing—nothing—else. It is for the accusers to prove otherwise, if they possess any evidence.

With respect to what Secretary of State Powell stated about Iraq's VX program, the fact is that Iraq had no VX weapons to declare. No VX agent remained for Iraq to declare. Iraq has never produced stable VX and has never weaponized VX. No one has any evidence to prove the contrary. Mr. Powell should not jump to hasty conclusions as he has done in the past on the issue of the aluminum tubes and with his claims of uranium imports. Today the Council heard exactly the opposite directly from Mr. ElBaradei.

With respect to the statements on Iraq's cooperation that I heard this morning from many members of the Council, allow me to refer to the statement by Mr. Blix, not today but two days ago in a press conference. At that press conference, Mr. Blix stated that Iraq is cooperating proactively—I stress that he used the word "proactively". He stated that real disarmament is taking place on the ground. He stated that the efforts being undertaken by Iraq and the inspectors represent steps towards the actual verification of Iraq's unilateral destruction of its previous proscribed programs.

When asked whether Iraq represents a threat now, he replied that all agree that Iraq possesses very limited military capacities in comparison with 1991, and that Iraq is being very closely monitored by the inspectors.

On the issue of interviews, Mr. Blix stated that his experts have made it clear that those interviews are yielding important and beneficial results in terms of data. In this regard, he pointed out the importance of Iraq's submitting the names of those who had participated in the destruction of proscribed programs, which would surely facilitate the verification of such destruction. He added that he did not agree with those who say that resolution 1441 (2002) is a disarmament resolution and not an inspection resolution.

The statements of the United States and the United Kingdom, as well as those of some other speakers today, show that there is a state of confusion. Officials in the United States and the United Kingdom, as well as those standing at their side, are unable to provide any evidence proving the existence of weapons of mass destruction in Iraq. Furthermore, they have been unable to conceal their own private agenda in the region and the rest of the world.

This all started with the issue of Iraq's possession and development of weapons of mass destruction. Then they demanded that Iraq accept the return of inspectors. They then moved on to the issue of proactive cooperation with the inspectors, followed by demands for the submission of evidence proving that Iraq was free from weapons of mass destruction. At the most recent meeting, they concentrated on the need to destroy Al Samoud 2 missiles. The discussion then moved on to the claim that Iraq is destroying such missiles on the one hand and manufacturing new ones on the other. Talk then began about an alleged link with terrorism and about regime change. Finally, here we are hearing that Iraq is a threat to the national security of the United States—that is the claim made by President Bush—although earlier we had heard that Iraq was a threat to its neighbors.

This is an attempt to confuse the issue. It is an attempt to mask the real agenda of the United States of America and the United Kingdom with regard to Iraq. It is a very simple agenda. The objective is the complete takeover of Iraq's oil and the political and economic domination of the entire Arab region. It is the implementation of what is being called a new Sikes-Pico plan for the Middle East—the redrawing of the region once more.

When Iraq accepted Security Council resolutions it was hoping for justice from the Council, and it continues to do so. The introduction of the new draft resolution and the most recent amendment do not relate to disarmament. The aim is to drag the Security Council into taking actions that will have detrimental consequences, not only for Iraq, but for the very credibility of this international Organization.

I should like at this point to express Iraq's gratitude to all those who oppose the draft resolution. Let me repeat to them that Iraq will not waver in its continuing proactive and rapid cooperation with the United Nations Monitoring, Verification and Inspection Commission and the International Atomic Energy Agency.

We call upon the Security Council to shoulder its historical responsibility, especially today, by thwarting aggression against Iraq and preventing a new crime from being committed in its name—a crime whose impact would far surpass that of any crime of the past century. In conclusion, let me add that war against Iraq will wreak destruction, but it will not unearth any weapons of mass destruction, for one very simple reason: there are no such weapons, except in the imagination of some. All those who assist in the commission of such a war, without a direct interest in it, will be sorry indeed.

Remarks by Secretary of State Powell, March 7, 2003

Secretary Colin Powell was interviewed on ABC's World News Tonight by Peter Jennings.

Q. So many people don't understand why you shouldn't let the inspections continue if they are accomplishing anything.

Secretary Powell. When you see how Iraq has avoided answering these questions for year after year after year, you don't come away with a great deal of confidence that, in the absence of a strategic change on his part, that the inspectors will ever get to the bottom of it all.

Q. Most people think they're doing a reasonably effective job at the moment.

Secretary Powell. I think they are doing a reasonably effective job in light of what they are able to do, and they are only able to do what the Iraqis are really allowing them to do. And Iraq is clearly still bugging the rooms in which people are being interviewed. We're quite confident they're still moving things around the countryside. We are not—

Q. The inspectors didn't agree with you on that this morning.

Secretary Powell. Well, they didn't agree, but I think I have better information than the inspectors. I think I have more assets available to me than the inspectors do.

Q. But if you have better assets available to you than the inspectors, why don't you tell the inspectors what's going on so that they can catch the Iraqis in the process?

Secretary Powell. We are giving them as much as we can that is actionable, that really can cue them to something.

Q. Mr. Secretary, many people think that your dismissal again today of the inspection process is because your administration keeps moving the goal posts, that it is not just about disarming Saddam Hussein; it is, as the President said, about getting rid of Saddam Hussein. So the Security Council is left in the position of either agreeing with you completely, or else.

Secretary Powell. If our sole goal was to get rid of Saddam and we didn't care about weapons of mass destruction and we didn't care about the views of the Security Council, the President could have done that any time in the past year. But the issue that he brought to the Security Council last September was the issue of weapons of mass destruction and how to get rid of them, and he challenged the Security Council to make Saddam Hussein live up to the commitments and the obligations he had as a result of all the previous resolutions.

Q. Do you, in retrospect, think it was a mistake to support the inspections? I think it was Vice President Cheney who said in August that these renewed inspections were a trap.

Secretary Powell. No, I don't think it was a mistake. I think it was an essential part of determining whether or not Saddam Hussein was serious.

Q. March the 17th. Is this the magic date, or are we actually talking about ten days, or possibly more, from the time this U.N. British resolution is tabled?

Secretary Powell. It's ten days from today. It seemed like a reasonable period of time to put forward this proposition to the Security Council and to the world, and see whether or not there is a way to avoid a solution by force of arms and is there a way to find a peaceful solution. But we had to draw a line. This just can't continue this way.

Q. Just to be clear, are we talking about absolute compliance here, or are we talking about cooperation?

Secretary Powell. We did not say that we would expect them to turn in everything on the 17th. That would be a bit much. But I think the language is clear as to the kind of performance we are expecting to see.

Remarks by President Bush, March 8, 2003

President Bush delivered the following radio address to the nation.

[T]he Chief United Nations Weapons Inspector reported yesterday to the Security Council on his efforts to verify Saddam Hussein's compliance with Resolution 1441. This resolution requires Iraq to fully and unconditionally disarm itself of nuclear, chemical and biological weapons materials, as well as the prohibited missiles that could be used to deliver them. Unfortunately, it is clear that Saddam Hussein is still violating the demands of the United Nations by refusing to disarm.

Iraqi's dictator has made a public show of producing and destroying a few prohibited missiles. Yet, our intelligence shows that even as he is destroying these few missiles, he has ordered the continued production of the very same type of missiles. Iraqi operatives continue to play a shell game with inspectors, moving suspected prohibited materials to different locations every 12 to 24 hours. And Iraqi weapons scientists continue to be threatened with harm should they cooperate in interviews with U.N. inspectors.

These are not the actions of a regime that is disarming. These are the actions of a regime engaged in a willful charade. If the Iraqi regime were disarming, we would know it—because we would see it; Iraq's weapons would be presented to inspectors and destroyed. Inspection teams do not need more time, or more personnel—all they need is what they have never received, the full cooperation of the Iraqi regime. The only acceptable outcome is the outcome already demanded by a unanimous vote of the Security Council: total disarmament.

Saddam Hussein has a long history of reckless aggression and terrible crimes. He possesses weapons of terror. He provides funding and training and safe haven to terrorists who would willingly deliver weapons of mass destruction against America and other peace-loving countries.

The attacks of September the 11, 2001 showed what the enemies of America did with four airplanes. We will not wait to see what terrorists or terror states could do with weapons of mass destruction. We are determined to confront threats wherever they arise. And, as a last resort, we must be willing to use military force. We are doing everything we can to avoid war in Iraq. But if Saddam Hussein does not disarm peacefully, he will be disarmed by force.

Across the world, and in every part of America, people of goodwill are hoping and praying for peace. Our goal is peace—for our own nation, for our friends, for our allies and for all the peoples of the Middle East. People of goodwill must also recognize that allowing a dangerous dictator to defy the world and build an arsenal for conquest and mass murder is not peace at all; it is pretense. The cause of peace will be advanced only when the terrorists lose a wealthy patron and protector, and when the dictator is fully and finally disarmed.

Remarks by Secretary of State Powell, March 9, 2003

Secretary Colin Powell was interviewed on NBC's Meet the Press by Tim Russert.

Q. This Tuesday or Wednesday, the United States and Great Britain will move a resolution before the United Nations which will set March 17th as a firm deadline for Saddam Hussein to cooperate fully on disarmament. Do we have the nine votes in the Security Council to pass that resolution?

Secretary Powell. That's not clear yet. We'll have to wait and see when the vote is taken sometime this week. But I am encouraged by the discussions I've been having with a number of members of the Council.

There are some members of the Council among the permanent membership of the Council that are firmly against such a vote. You know France's position, certainly. But I think most of the elected ten members are making up their judge—their minds over this weekend, and I've been in close contact with them.

So I think we have a chance to get, a strong chance, and I am encouraged that we might get the nine or ten votes needed for passage of the resolution, and we'll see if somebody wants to veto it. But I will have to wait and see. We'll all have to wait and see.

Q. France has already said that even if it passes, they will veto.

Secretary Powell. They haven't used the word "veto" but they have certainly indicated that they would use their veto. They said they would not support such a resolution and would do everything they could to stop it.

Q. What about the Chinese and Russians?

Secretary Powell. The Chinese and Russians, I think, are making their own judgments on it. They haven't used the veto word, either. I think the Russians have expressed strong opposition to it and the Chinese, I'm not entirely sure what they might do. But yes, there is resistance.

Q. Has President Putin of Russia told President Bush that he would not veto it?

Secretary Powell. No. He has had good conversations with President Bush over the past week and I have had a number of conversations in person and on the phone, of course, with my Russian colleague, Igor Ivanov. And there are strong and different points of view, but we will see what the Russian Federation does when the vote is taken.

Q. Mr. Secretary, if the resolution does not pass, or if you do get the nine or ten votes but the French veto it, will the deadline of March 17th still hold for Saddam Hussein?

Secretary Powell. Well, that, of course, is a deadline that is a part of the resolution, so if the resolution doesn't pass, March 17th, as a matter for the U.N., is not relevant. But at least in our own mind, and thinking in the American administration, time is running out, time has just about run out. And I think the President, in the presence of such a vote in the U.N., would then make his determination as to whether it is time for us to use American force with a willing coalition that would go in.

But we are still looking at the 17th as enough time to have made a judgment that he is not complying, he is not cooperating. I mean, just look at what he said yesterday in the presence of the debate: everything's fine, I'm clean, everything's okay, get rid of all the sanctions; ignore the paper that Dr. Blix is putting out listing page after page of unresolved issues that have been unresolved for years, and Saddam Hussein just wants to ignore them all.

Q. But if it doesn't pass, then the 17th is no longer operative? We could have military action before that?

Secretary Powell. It depends on what the President's decision is after we have seen what happens in the U.N. this week.

Q. The situation we're in now has been described as a failure of American diplomacy—some say enormous, some say colossal—and people point to how we got where we are now. This is an article in The Washington Post. I want to give you a chance to respond:

"Months of painstaking efforts by Secretary of State Colin Powell to win international consensus for military action against Iraq have been complicated by a growing resentment over what many foreign diplomats regard as the Bush Administration's heavy- handed and bullying tactics of the last two years. `There have been really aggressive battles that have got people's backs up,' said a diplomat who is supporting the U.S. The U.S. team often acts like thugs. People feel bullied. They can affect the way you respond when someone makes a request. Foreign officials say anger over the administration's style say that almost from the moment President Bush took office, the administration's rejection of the Kyoto Treaty with global warming, the whole policy on South Korea, North Korea and sunshine, and the ABM Treaty, and on and on and on."

Is there some validity to that?

Secretary Powell. I don't think so, Tim. We came in as an administration that was strongly committed to principled stands. We took a principled stand with respect to Kyoto. Others did not agree with our stand. I understand that. Other nations went down the Kyoto route. We are finding other ways to deal with the problem of greenhouse emissions.

We have tried to cooperate with the international community on the expansion of

NATO, on encouraging the expansion of the European Union. We do support the Sunshine Policy in South Korea but we believe it is important to not deceive ourselves as to the nature of the North Korean regime or what they've been doing. And we found in the first two years we were in office that that was a sound position when we discovered that the North Koreans were still developing nuclear weapons even though they were supposed not to be developing nuclear weapons.

So we have taken strong positions. We have worked hard on globalization. We have started initiatives for dealing with HIV/AIDS around the world. We have gotten the Doha trade round extended. There are many things we have done that demonstrate our commitment to international organizations, and we listen carefully to the views of our friends.

But at the same time, sometimes we can't reconcile our views with those of our friends. And when that is the case, we believe it is important for us to stand on the principle that we believe in.

Q. But as you know, the U.S. image in the world is being held up to ridicule in many quarters. There are people now expressing grave reservations about the war. I remember when John Kennedy went to Berlin, hundreds of thousands of Germans screaming and cheering Kennedy in the street, and now 50 percent of Germans say that our President, President Bush, is a warmonger. What happened?

Secretary Powell. I think people are not willing to face up to what we are willing to face up to, and that is that in the case of Iraq we have a dictator who, for 12 years, has denied the legitimacy of the United Nations. People are talking about us, you know, somehow affecting the United Nations in a negative way. It is Saddam Hussein who ignored the legitimacy of the United Nations for 12 years and some 16 resolutions, when finally the President of the United States, not taking unilateral action but going to the United Nations, said we must deal with this, we must not let him get away with this. And it was the President of the United States, with his diplomatic efforts and the diplomatic efforts of the entire administration team, that got Resolution 1441 passed with a 15-0 vote. That was a triumph of American diplomacy.

Unfortunately, there are some members of the Council and many people in the world who thought that 1441 was just words. It wasn't. It was a statement of principle. Saddam Hussein is guilty. We're giving him one last chance to disarm. Will he take it? And if he doesn't take, serious consequences would follow.

And everybody who voted for 1441 knew that. Well, he hasn't taken it, as evidenced just yesterday with his essentially placing demands on the U.N. while we're placing demands on him, and it's outrageous and it is time to take him to account. And I regret that not all nations understand that and all peoples understand that in those nations. At the same time, the United States enjoys strong support from most European nations and the President is determined that this matter has to be dealt with for the safety of the region, the safety of the world, the safety of the American people.

Q. But in terms of world opinion, how was it that we have lost a battle of public relations to a tyrant like Saddam?

Secretary Powell. Well, I don't know that I can fully answer that question, except that I have been in a number of crises before, and it's a matter of war and peace. Most people would prefer to be on the side of peace. I would prefer to be on the side of peace. And it is always unpopular—I've seen it in a number of crises, whether it was going into Panama or whether it was the Gulf War—where public opinion is against you until the time of truth comes, the moment of truth comes, when you go in and you find out what they really have been doing and you liberate a people and you bring a better life to that country for the people of that country, and then you'll see that public opinion will change.

Q. The President talks about Saddam being a threat to his neighborhood, and let me show you Iraq and its neighborhood, surrounded by Iran, Kuwait, Saudi Arabia, Jordan, Syria and Turkey. Other than Kuwait, none of those other countries have expressed publicly support for a military action against Saddam Hussein. If he's such a threat to his neighborhood, why are those countries so silent?

Secretary Powell. They have their own domestic political reasons for silence, but at the same time, we are getting the kind of support that we need in the event that military action is required.

Q. From those countries?

Secrctary Powell. We are getting the kind of support that we will need. Now, there are some difficulties with respect to each of the countries. In Turkey, for example, the government, which is still forming, took the issue to parliament. I mean, we had intense discussions with the Turks. I met with them in Davos, in Switzerland, a few weeks ago. The Prime Minister and the new Prime Minister. I've had the Foreign Minister and the Finance Minister to Washington, to my home recently. And they went forward to their parliament. They weren't able to succeed in the first vote.

Now, I know they are forming their government now and they are committed to take that issue back to the parliament. So Turkey is supportive. Even though they have internal domestic political problems, they wish to be supportive of our effort. Other nations in the region are supporting in ways that are consistent with what they are able to do with respect to their domestic constituencies.

Q. Your testimony before the United Nations has now been directly challenged by members at the United Nations. This is what the head of the International Atomic Energy Agency, Mohamed ElBaradei, said, that, "In recent months, the administration and Britain have alleged Iraq illegally sought high-strength aluminum tubes for a centrifuge-based uranium enrichment program and had sough uranium from Niger." He said experts had concluded the tubes were for a rocket engine program, as Iraq had said, and that documents used to allege the connection between Iraq and Niger were fabricated. Overall, he concluded there is no evidence that Iraq has revived a nuclear weapons program.

Mr. ElBaradei saying that you and the President misled the world on the aluminum tubes and that the documents, in terms of Niger and Iraq, were fabricated. Those are very serious charges.

Secretary Powell. Well, with respect to the aluminum tubes, we still believe the case is out. The CIA has done a great deal of analysis on those tubes. They are not persuaded they were just for rockets. And, in fact, another nation this week, a European nation, came forward with some additional information that still, I think, leaves it an open question as to what the purpose of those tubes was.

With respect to the uranium, it was the information that we had. We provided it. If that information is inaccurate, fine. We're continuing to examine this issue. And as Dr. ElBaradei said, it's still an open issue to be looked at.

But we have to be a little careful about nuclear weapons programs. We saw the IAEA almost give Iraq a clean bill of health in the early '90s, only to discover that they had a robust nuclear weapons program that they had not discovered. And if you just look at Iran this week, right now, the IAEA is discovering, as a result of information and intelligence made available, that Iran has a far more robust program for the development of nuclear weapons than the IAEA thought.

So while I respect Dr. ElBaradei's opinion, he's a very dedicated international civil servant, I think we have to keep an open book on this as more information comes forward.

Q. Another rationale provided by the administration for action against Saddam is his connection to al-Qaida. Tom Friedman, in The New York Times, wrote this:

"I am also very troubled by the way Bush officials have tried to justify this war on the grounds that Saddam is allied with Osama bin Laden, or will be soon. There is simply no proof of that, and every time I hear them repeat it, I think of the Gulf of Tonkin resolution from the Vietnam times. You don't take the country to war on the wings of a lie."

Secretary Powell. I don't think it's a lie. I think there is information and evidence that there are connections. We have talked about Mr. al-Zarqawi and some of the people who are in Baghdad who are linked with al-Qaida and Osama bin Laden and who were there with the certain knowledge of the Iraqi regime. We have seen connections and we are continuing to pursue those connections.

We are not resting our whole case on this linkage. We are resting our case for the necessity perhaps of going to war on the fact that Saddam Hussein has developed weapons of mass destruction, has them in his possession, and for 12 years he has violated the will of the international community. It is the international community that has been violated here, not Saddam Hussein. He is the one who has stuck his finger in the eye of the international community. He is the one who has been deceiving and telling the lies all these years. And the fact that there is also an al-Qaida connection, I think certainly adds to the case, but we are not resting the whole case on that connection.

Q. And for us to succeed in terms of our policy towards Iraq, one, Iraq must be disarmed of weapons of mass destruction; and Saddam Hussein must go?

Secretary Powell. I think the region would be a lot better off, and certainly the Iraqi people would be a lot better off, if Saddam Hussein were no longer there. We have said clearly, though, that within the U.N. context it was getting rid of the weapons of mass destruction. It was the previous administration, President Clinton's Administration, and the American Congress in 1998 that made it an American position that regime change seemed to be the only way to get rid of the weapons of mass destruction and to get Saddam Hussein out of the place so that the Iraqi people would no longer suffer under that kind of leadership.

What we have said is: Can the regime change itself? Can there be a changed regime, if it was the full force and pressure, political pressure of the U.N. and the threat of force? And what we have seen so far is that regime has not yet indicated it would change itself, and time is running out. And when that time elapses, then the regime must be changed.

Q. But if Saddam Hussein came forward on a deathbed conversion and said, all right, I give it all up, take it all, I'm completely disarmed, complete cooperation, he could then stay?

Secretary Powell. That deal has been out there for 12 years. That deal has been out there since 1441 was passed in early November. It was clear that 1441 said Saddam Hussein is guilty, there are consequences for this guilt; now, one last chance. What we are interested in is getting rid of the weapons of mass destruction. One last chance. Let's see all the people who were involved in these programs, for them to be interviewed, interviewed without threat, out of the country. Let's see all the documents. Let's see all the equipment. Let's see all the facilities.

He could have done this the day after by bringing forward all that material, all the documents. These folks are master documenters. They are bureaucrats. They have records. And as Dr. Blix has said and as he has put out in the document released Friday, they simply have not answered Questions, vital Questions, about what happened to anthrax, what happened to botilinum toxin. They have not answered these Questions for the last 10 to 12 years. And it is not acceptable now to keep asking the Questions and not getting the answers.

Q. But if we commence military action, that operation would not be successful unless Saddam is killed or captured?

Secretary Powell. At this point, if military action is required, it's because the regime has not changed itself, it is not complying with the demands of the international community, and therefore the regime has to be changed.

Q. And no one would emerge as an alternative to Saddam until they knew that he was dead or captured?

Secretary Powell. Well, I can't speculate what somebody might or might not do, but it seems to me once the regime is changed, I know that there are many Iraqis, both inside the country and outside the country, who are standing ready to help the Iraqi people toward a better life, a life where the oil treasure of Iraq, the wealth that that country has, will be used to benefit its people, not to threaten its neighbors, not to keep dictators in power, and not to essentially waste its wealth on weapons of mass destruction.

Q. This week, before Congress, you said that we would be in Iraq for some time.

Secretary Powell. Yes.

Q. During the campaign, in the presidential debate, the President was emphatic about nation-building. Let's just listen to this quickly: "Well, I don't think our troops ought to be used for what's called nation-building."
Isn't that exactly what we'd have to do in Iraq?

Secretary Powell. In Iraq, I think what we would have to do, if military action is required, is to remove this regime and, as quickly as possible, get international organizations involved, get the international community totally involved. We would have to make sure that we maintained stability and that the country didn't break up. We'd be there for a while and we would help with the nation-building. There's no question about that.

But we hope that the Iraqis can build their own nation under new leadership and with the wealth that comes to them in the form of $20 billion a year in revenue.

Q. Many people across the country still step back and say, "Mr. Secretary, why would we invade a country that has not yet attacked us?" What's the answer?

Secretary Powell. I think 9/11 changes the calculus that one uses for this. Saddam Hussein has been a threat to the region and we believe that his development of weapons of mass destruction and his intent toward his neighbors and the hostility he holds toward us; and in the post-9/11 period, where you have this potential nexus between weapons of mass destruction and terrorist organizations, non-state actors who are trying to get such weapons, suggests that this kind of threat has to be dealt with. And he has been in violation not only of, you know, our desire to see him be disarmed and get rid of these weapons of mass destruction, he's been in violation of international obligations for 12 years.

And so this is a case where we believe the international community should act to protect itself, and, in protecting itself, protect the United States and protect the neighbors of Iraq.

Q. Do you think it will be war?

Secretary Powell. I don't know, Tim. I think the window is closing rapidly. I think if we do not see a rather remarkable and unexpected change after what Saddam Hussein said yesterday—I'm not expecting—then I think the probably of war is rapidly increasing.

Q. Are we prepared for all the risks and ramifications, the insurrection in the Arab street, the potential difficulties in Pakistan, the environmental hazards, the refugees, and on and on and on, when we open that bottle?

Secretary Powell. All of those issues have been examined and looked at, and we are making all of the contingency plans one might expect. And we are also looking at the real possibility that after such an action there will be very positive consequences that flow from a military victory, which there will be, positive consequences that suggest that we now have a country willing to live in peace with its neighbors, that is disarmed of its weapons of mass destruction, and a dictator that does not cause the kind of turmoil in the region that Saddam Hussein has caused in that region for the last 29 years.

Remarks by Secretary of State Powell, March 9, 2003

Secretary Colin Powell was interviewed on Fox News Sunday by Tony Snow.

Q. Mr. Secretary, let's first begin with the prospect of a vote in the United Nations Security Council. It's going to take place this week?

Secretary Powell. Yes.

Q. And it is the resolution that says that by March 17th Saddam must comply fully with Resolution 1441?

Secretary Powell. It says that if by March 17th he hasn't complied, and there are some terms in the resolution that describe what compliance means, he will be seen to have lost his last chance to comply. And I think everybody knows what that means: it's time to force compliance through the use of military force.

Q. Is there any wiggle room on that date, or is March 17th going to be the date?

Secretary Powell. Well, that's the date in the resolution and I have no plans to change it, and no one has suggested to me it be changed, although I'm sure there are a lot of people who would just like to see this drag on and on and on.

Q. Do you think you may be able to get nine or ten votes in the Security Council?

Secretary Powell. Yes, I think we're in striking distance of that. We'll be in intense negotiations over the next couple of days. A lot of diplomacy will be taking place. But I think we're in striking distance of nine or ten. But we'll just have to wait and see what individual nations, who will have to make up their minds, actually vote for on the day of the vote.

Q. Do you believe, if you get nine or ten votes, that France will veto?

Secretary Powell. I will not speculate on that. I think it's—

Q. Would you be surprised?

Secretary Powell. I would not be surprised if they veto, because they've been pretty clear that they want to stop that resolution. I don't think they've hidden their hand on this one. They've been out front saying they don't think is the way to go. But we'll wait and see what they actually do. But right now, I would expect the French to do everything they can to stop it, to include possibly the use of a veto, although they haven't used the veto word.

Q. You don't believe Saddam Hussein will comply with the terms of this resolution by the 17th, do you?

Secretary Powell. I think it's very unlikely, and what he said yesterday is further evidence of the kind of individual and regime we're dealing with. In the midst of all of this, with Dr. Blix giving a mixed report on Friday, and with Dr. Blix issuing a document of almost 200 pages showing all of his misbehavior, Saddam's misbehavior over the years, and all the unanswered questions that have been there for years, for Saddam Hussein to stand up and say, I've complied now, get rid of the sanctions, and him start placing demands on the United Nations, this is outrageous. And it seems to me every member of the Security Council should be offended this morning that Saddam Hussein, once again, shows his brazen attitude toward the international community.

Q. So, unlikely that he's going to make the moves by March 17th; at that point, there's one option left?

Secretary Powell. At that point, I think if there is a resolution passed and he hasn't done what is required by the 17th, then he's lost his last chance, and at that point I think there is a high likelihood that military force is what's going to disarm Saddam Hussein by changing the regime.

Q. Isn't it the case that that's likely to happen regardless of what the U.N. Security Council does?

Secretary Powell. If the U.N. Security Council does act in a positive way, and we hope it will, then clearly military force will be appropriate and there will be international support for that through the U.N.. If the U.N. Security Council fails to act, does not pass this resolution, well, that's the choice the Council has to make. But the President has always said he reserves his option and he believes there is a sufficient basis in international law, and certainly in the congressional resolution that was passed here last fall, for him to act with a willing coalition to disarm Saddam Hussein by removing the regime.

Q. We've been led to believe the vote will take place Tuesday. Is that your understanding?

Secretary Powell. It will take place sometime this week. I don't want to be precise with respect to a particular day. It won't be tomorrow, Monday.

We put the resolution down in a modified fashion on Friday, and we have to give members of the Council a little bit of time to get back home and reflect on it.

Q. Suppose there is military action. A couple of practical questions. First, will the government give public notice to journalists and others saying, okay, you need to get out?

Secretary Powell. If military action is coming, there will have to be some, I think, prudent notice given to people who might not want to be in Iraq.

Q. What do you say to human shields?

Secretary Powell. I think it would be wise for them to remove themselves, as well, if it appears that military action is imminent.

Q. And if they don't?

Secretary Powell. We are going to fight this battle, if it is necessary to fight this battle, and we still hope it will not be necessary, but if it becomes necessary, we'll do it in the way we have always done it—with utmost care, with respect to targeting with utmost care to minimize collateral damage, and to make sure that we are not doing anything that puts civilians unnecessarily in harm's way. That is always a risk.

Q. But they're on their own?

Secretary Powell. Yes. I don't know where they will all be and I don't know what positions they would be at. As for my understanding of the situation, many of those human shields have started to depart Iraq and some have actually been evicted by the Iraqi regime.

Q. President Carter, former President Carter, had an op-ed piece in The New York Times today. I want to read a quote from that piece and then get your reaction. Here is what former President Carter had to say:

"Increasingly unilateral and domineering policies have brought international trust in our country to its lowest level in memory. American stature will surely decline further if we launch a war in clear defiance of the United Nations."

Do you think the United States is held in lower esteem today than when Jimmy Carter was President?

Secretary Powell. I won't compare it to President Carter's presidency. Let me just say that there are a number of nations in the world that are fully supporting our efforts, and you heard a number of them speak at the Security Council the other day: Spain, the United Kingdom, Bulgaria, Italy, Portugal, the newly independent nations of the former Soviet Union. So we need to knock down this idea that nobody is on our side and we're totally isolated. Australia. So many nations recognize this danger. And they do it in the face of public opposition.

And I have been in a number of crises over my career in public service where, when it's a choice between peace and war, people will generally vote for peace. They want peace. I want peace. But sometimes, conflict is necessary. And if you do it right, if you do it well, if you demonstrate that you are leaving something better in place after the conflict, then attitudes change and people, frankly, respect what you have done.

Q. Let's talk about the United Nations a bit. The United States, the administration, decided to go before the United Nations and seek ratification of a series of policies designed to get Saddam Hussein to disarm. During that time, the President's ratings have slipped precipitously in the United States. Our polls show that his ratings have gone from 77 percent to 55 percent in the course of just one year. In addition, European nations that were singing our praises after September 11th, now are demonstrating in the streets.

So what have we gained?

Secretary Powell. What we gained by going to the United Nations was Resolution 1441, which was unanimously approved by the Security Council, that said Saddam Hussein is guilty and there's only one way for him to get out of that state of guilt, and that's to come clean immediately, unconditionally, without any reservations, or he'd face serious consequences. Everybody knew when we voted for that resolution what it meant.

He has not done it unconditionally. He hasn't done it. He hasn't complied. That's a simple fact he hasn't changed. Therefore, it is becoming time for serious consequences to kick in. But a lot of our friends don't like facing that reality of serious consequences. Many people in the world, unfortunately, don't see the danger as clearly as I think we do, the Brits do, the Spaniards do, the Australians do, so many others do. Weapons of mass destruction, chemical, biological weapons, the potential to develop nuclear weapons in this day and age, with a nexus between rogue states and the potential for terrorists to get their hands on that kind of material, seems to me create a new strategic dimension, a new strategic environment, that this President is not willing to just step back from.

He was asked to be multilateral. The President was asked to take the case to the U.N.. He did. And it's going to be very unfortunate if the U.N. uses 1441 as a way to wiggle away from their responsibilities, as opposed to step up to their responsibilities.

Q. Is that not what Hans Blix has done already? In his testimony the other day— and you caught this—he switched from talking about Resolution 1441 to Resolution to Resolution 1284, which was negotiated some time ago and is considerably weaker, he changed the goal posts, did he not?

Secretary Powell. Well, he tried to shift to 1284, and he is operating under 1284. Hans Blix is a decent, honest man, and nobody made 1284 go away. But 1441 said immediately, unconditional, now. 1284 was a more deliberate process, partial results for partial progress. Interestingly, France delayed 1284 for seven months and then abstained from voting for 1284.

And so, you know, it's kind of curious to find myself in this position where France has been against active efforts to disarm Saddam Hussein, and I was hoping that with their support of 1441, which took seven weeks to achieve, they now have understood that disarmament must come, and 1441 was a means for that disarmament if Iraq didn't comply, not a means to kick the can down the street longer and allow Saddam Hussein to achieve his objective, which is to stretch this out long enough so that we lose interest, we go away, the troops go home, and nothing has changed with respect to his desire to have these weapons.

Q. Which gets us back to the U.N. process. It has, in fact, dragged things out. People do not have the same sense of urgency they had before. Is it not the case that going through all this, as respectful as it of the United Nations, has actually made it more difficult to go after Saddam Hussein and given him more time to dig in so that war is more likely, and blood war is more likely?

Secretary Powell. Well, it certainly has given him more time to do whatever it is he's going to do, whatever he is going to do. But at the same time, I think it was essential for the President to take the case to the United Nations. And in terms of our own preparations, it takes to put in place the kind of force necessary, not only to give pressure to diplomatic efforts, but also to be ready to use force. And so I don't think much time was lost with respect to our military preparations and it was an important step to take.

We always recognized that it was a risky step, but the President, in response to, you know, some of the pressures we hear from overseas, he brought it to the United Nations, where it should have been brought.

Q. If France were to veto, what do you think that would do to French credibility?

Secretary Powell. Well, I think it would be unfortunate if France decided to veto this resolution in the presence of a positive vote that would pass the resolution, and I think France would not be looked upon favorably in many parts of the world. And certainly, even though France has been a friend of ours for many, many years and will be a friend in the future, I think it will have a serious effect on bilateral relations, at least in the short term.

Q. Let's talk a bit about Friday's drama before the United Nations Security Council. As you mentioned, Hans Blix delivered a mixed report. What he said before everybody was that, as a matter of fact, there have been a series of things that he had investigated and found no evidence.

As a matter of fact, I want to focus preliminarily on one thing that you've talked about, mobile biological laboratories. Here is what Mr. Blix had to say to the Security Council about that:

"Food testing mobile laboratories and mobile workshops have been seen, as well as large containers with seed processing equipment. No evidence of proscribed activities have so far been found."

When he talks about those mobile food laboratories and places where people grow things and that there was no evidence there, this is the second time that he's taken direct issue with something you raised before the Security Council on February 14th. Is he getting it wrong?

Secretary Powell. No. What he said was he hasn't found any yet. It doesn't mean they're not there. We have solid evidence that they are there. We have firsthand defector information that there are mobile biological laboratories.

He also said, well, maybe one way to do it would be to put roadblocks out and to sort of blanket the country with traffic cops, seeing if we can catch one of these things on the road. I think it's unlikely that that would work.

If Saddam Hussein was really intent on complying with the resolutions, I think he would be bringing forward evidence, he would be bringing forward all of these programs, he would be bringing forward weapons. We wouldn't be searching for them, we wouldn't be tripping over them, we wouldn't suddenly discover something like R-400 bomb fragments. These are master bureaucrats in Iraq. They keep records on everything. The evidence is there somewhere, and they're not presenting the evidence.

Q. And Hans Blix has put together so-called cluster reports that apparently are pretty, as you point, they're damning. Does it bother you that he did not make more of Iraqi noncompliance during the course of his remarks?

Secretary Powell. I think he could have done a lot more with respect to noncompliance. When you look at his cluster report, when you look at page after page of what the Iraqis have done over the years to hide, to deceive, to cheat, to keep information away from the inspectors, to change facts to fit the latest issue, and once they put that set of facts before you, when you find out those facts are false, they come up with a new set of facts. It's a constant pattern.

And when you read his clusters, you see a series of questions at the end that the Iraqis could have answered anytime over the last 12 years to make this problem go away. The problems are still there. The lies are still there.

Q. Does it bother you that he did not talk publicly before the Security Council—

Secretary Powell. I think—

Q. Go ahead.

Secretary Powell. I think he could have made more of the deficiencies within that, within the cluster document, but I don't write his script.

Q. What about an addendum where he mentions that drones could fly over and inflict serious damage on our troops? That was submitted after he had given his testimony.

Secretary Powell. Yes. And there is a drone, as they call it, or a UAV program that they came upon that they discovered that they're not supposed to have, looks like it is a prohibited item.

Q. Well, is that—

Secretary Powell. And that's the kind of thing we're going to be making some news about in the course of the week and point this out. And there are other things that have been found that I think more can be made of.

Q. You said on the 14th of February that you have more information to deliver about al-Qaida cooperation with Iraq. When are we going to see that?

Secretary Powell. I think the CIA and other intelligence agencies of the government are hard at work in generating more information that suggests there is a nexus between al-Qaida and Iraq. We are not trying to overstate this case and we're not trying to force any conclusions with respect to 9/11, but we think there's a pretty good case that, with the al-Zarqawi presence that we have seen in Baghdad, with other things that have gone on, the Baghdad regime is witting of the presence of al-Qaida in Iraq and it is certainly a place where they can find some opportunity to perform, to act, to find haven. And so we don't want to overstate the case, but we're not going to listen to the case that says there is no connection, because that isn't accurate.

* * * *

Q. Final question. Time also is reporting that the United States has offered repeatedly intelligence—this follows on what we were just talking about—to Mohamed ElBaradei, Hans Blix and others, and they haven't been using it. I've been hearing the same thing. Is it true?

Secretary Powell. They have been using the information that we have been giving them that is actionable. Sometimes we have information that they really can't use; it's not something that inspectors can use to go look at a particular place, but it helps condition their activities and their thinking so they have an idea of what the Iraqis are trying to do to deceive them.

And so I think the inspectors are trying to use the actionable information that we give them, but there is other information that we have that is not actionable. And so we shouldn't expect that all the information we give them is usable to them, and so I don't want to be critical of the inspectors in this regard. We will continue to try to provide them as much information for as long as these inspections can continue.

Q. A week?

Secretary Powell. Well, it remains to be seen. But it is a tough problem that they are working on.

Here's the problem in a nutshell, Tony. The inspectors are dedicated international civil servants. They've got tough jobs. Hans Blix and Mohamed ElBaradei have very tough jobs. Their jobs would be made so much easier, and we wouldn't be in this crisis mode, if Iraq would do what Iraq was obliged to do since 1991: come clean; comply; cooperate unconditionally, actively; do it now; turn over the evidence; bring in the equipment; point out everything; don't do silly things like Saddam Hussein did yesterday by placing demands on the U.N. while rather than responding to the demands of the U.N.. It was an outrageous statement. We ought to see it for what it is and realize this is a man who has not changed his fundamental intent to thwart the will of the international community.

And if he succeeds in doing that because we don't get a vote, a satisfactory vote, on this resolution, the President will still meet his obligations to the American people, and I believe his obligations to the world, and if we have to do that through the use of military force, we will do it well, and I think in retrospect people will look back and say that was the right thing to do in the absence of full compliance on the part of Saddam Hussein.

Remarks by Secretary of State Powell, March 9, 2003

Q. Mr. Secretary, are you planning on flying overseas for any last-minute diplomacy?

Secretary Powell. No, I'm in constant touch with all of the members of the Council and I have some overseas visitors over the next 24 to 36 hours that will give me assurance that I am contacting the highest level individuals in the various countries that we're interested in. And I saw many of the key players on Friday at the U.N..

And so diplomacy is a combination of personal visits, overseas trips, as well as phone calls. And I've also deployed a number of my assistant secretaries and ambassadors to help us with this effort, as well.

Q. Mr. Secretary, there is a report out this morning that there is a new CIA threat assessment that says that al-Qaida may actually participate in attacks in Iraq if the United States goes to war.

Secretary Powell. I haven't seen that report, so I can't comment on it.

Q. Secretary Powell, do you think France would definitely veto?

Secretary Powell. Well, I would let the French use the veto word, and they haven't, but it's clear that they have expressed strong opposition to another resolution and said they would do everything they could to stop it. So we will have to see what they actually do when the vote comes, but they're certainly signaling veto.

Q. Mr. Secretary, how firm is the March 17th deadline?

Secretary Powell. It's in the resolution and we have no plans to change it, and nobody has directly suggested to us that we change it, although there are a lot of people who would just as soon not see a second resolution at all.

We tabled it on Friday afternoon, the United Kingdom did, and we have to give our friends a couple of days to study it, reflect on it. And I expect to be hearing back from members of the Council as early as this afternoon and a good part of tomorrow.

Remarks by French President Chirac, March 10, 2003

President Jacques Chirac was interviewed by TF1 and France 2 Television.

Q. Firstly, given that this is your first interview since the beginning of this crisis, let's go back a bit to the start. Can you explain to us why, from the outset, France has so firmly opposed war?

President Chirac. We want to live in a multipolar world, i.e. one with a few large groups enjoying as harmonious relations as possible with each another, a world in which Europe, among others, will have its full place, a world in which democracy progresses, hence the fundamental importance for us of the United Nations Organization which provides a framework and gives impetus to this democracy and harmony. We want a world where the inevitable crises—regional crises, or what we call proliferation crises—can be managed as effectively as possible. Finally, we want a world which attaches special importance to respect for the Other, the dialogue of cultures, dialogue of civilizations, and tries to avoid clashes.

In this context, we have from the outset found ourselves up against a problem, an Iraq which obviously possessed weapons of mass destruction, which were in the hands of an indisputably dangerous regime and consequently posed a definite threat to the world. So it was essential to disarm that regime, that country, to eliminate its weapons of mass destruction.

Q. Precisely, has Iraq cooperated properly on this?

President Chirac. There were two ways to disarm her. There was war, of course, but there was also the method of inspections and exerting pressure, the one which consisted in going over there, with the U.N.'s authority, to control these weapons, find and then destroy them. And the international community, by adopting UNSCR 1441 unanimously, took the decision which consisted in saying: "we are going to disarm Iraq peacefully, i.e. through the inspections. We are going to appoint inspectors, and they will tell us whether or not this method is possible".

Q. But after 1441, can one say that Iraq is still, this evening for example, a dangerous country?

President Chirac. A country which has Iraq's past and political structure is always a dangerous country. But the country is genuinely dangerous only if it has the capabilities to commit aggression, if it has the capabilities to attack.

Q. And for you it doesn't have them today?

President Chirac. The problem was to make sure that it no longer had those capabilities or, at any rate, that those capabilities could be controlled and destroyed. So the U.N. sent the inspectors. I'd like to remind you that this isn't a technique which is being tried out for the first time. From 1991 until 1998, there was an inspections regime which, regrettably, was halted as a result of blunders. There was an inspections regime which destroyed more weapons in Iraq than were destroyed throughout the Gulf War and which, in particular, resulted in the complete, almost complete eradication in all likelihood—at any rate according to what the inspectors say—of Iraq's nuclear program...

Q. Weapons are still being found today...

President Chirac. There are some certainly. Missiles with a longer than permitted range are being destroyed. There are probably other weapons.

Q. Once Saddam Hussein can no longer be trusted, isn't the quest to disarm through inspections a never-ending one? That's what the United States is saying.

President Chirac. Firstly, I don't believe that. I think that the inspectors, who are skilled experts in whom we can have total confidence, consider today that if they are given the necessary time and resources—that's what Mr Blix said at the last Security Council meeting, he said that he considers today, if Iraq steps up her cooperation, which is, of course, never sufficient but which has improved, the set objective could be achieved, i.e. the elimination of the weapons of mass destruction.

Q. But isn't 100% cooperation a sine qua non?

President Chirac.—Certainly.

Q. Yet today it isn't 100%. The inspectors are saying this.

President Chirac. No, the inspectors say that cooperation has improved and that they are today in a position to pursue their work. And this is what is of paramount importance. It's not for you or me to say whether the inspections are effective, whether Iraq is sufficiently cooperative. In fact, she isn't, I can tell you that straightaway.

Q. Not sufficiently.

President Chirac. Not sufficiently. But it isn't for you or for me to decide that, that's for the inspectors to whom the U.N. has entrusted the responsibility of disarming Iraq to say. The inspectors have to tell us: "we can continue and, at the end of a period which we think should be of a few months"—I'm saying a few months because that's what they have said—"we shall have completed our work and Iraq will be disarmed". Or they will come and tell the Security Council: "we are sorry but Iraq isn't cooperating, the progress isn't sufficient, we aren't in a position to achieve our goal, we won't be able to guarantee Iraq's disarmament". In that case it will be for the Security Council and it alone to decide the right thing to do. But in that case, of course, regrettably, the war would become inevitable. It isn't today.

Q. Some people are arguing: rather than disarm Saddam, couldn't his regime simply be toppled, because after all he's a dictator who has been cruel to his country, we've seen that?

President Chirac. Yes, that's another problem. There are other regimes to which that could also apply.

Q. You mean the list is too long?

President Chirac. I'm not today going to draw up a list but, anyway, the North Korean regime naturally comes to mind, it's in no way better than Iraq's and has weapons of mass destruction, in particular nuclear ones which aren't hypothetical, but, regrettably, definitely exist.

Q. Some people are saying "why not start with Iraq?"

President Chirac. We have to say what we want. We could have said: "we want first and above all to change the Iraqi regime". That would have been a different argument, a different problem, one which would nevertheless have needed, as you will recognize, consultation, particularly at United Nations level.

We have said: "we want to disarm Iraq". We unanimously chose the path of disarming him. Today, nothing tells us that this path is a dead end and, consequently, it must be pursued since war is always a final resort, always an acknowledgement of failure, always the worst solution, because it brings death and misery. And we don't consider we are at that point. That's why we are refusing to embark on a path automatically leading to war so long as the inspectors haven't told us: "we can't do any more". And they are telling us the opposite.

Q. France has proposed that the heads of State themselves go to the meeting, tomorrow or the day after, when the vote is taken. Will you yourself go to New York to voice, defend the French position at the Security Council?

President Chirac. I myself proposed that the next Security Council meeting be held at head-of-State and government level. Why? First of all for one essential reason. It's that, when it comes to deciding on war or peace, with all the consequences that entails at the human, economic and political levels, and with all the risks it simultaneously presents for men, women, children in the region, it seemed to me legitimate for the decision to be taken by the heads of State and government themselves. That seemed to me to be their responsibility.

We shall see, discussions are under way and we'll see what's decided.

There was [also] a second reason which, in my view, makes a Security Council discussion at summit level inevitable, it's that, as I told you just now, there are other crises in the world. Regional crises, like the Middle East with the Israeli-Palestinian problem, and proliferation crises like that of North Korea. And there are regrettably others. It seems to me important and useful for this problem of how to resolve crises to be assessed at the highest level.

Q. And if you go to the U.N., it's to say what? It's to vote "no", possibly use your veto or to abstain?

President Chirac. What's involved here? Today, we are following a course of action laid down by UNCSR 1441. This means that the international community, expressing its view through the unanimous adoption of this resolution by the fifteen Council members, particularly at the suggestion of France who played a very active part in drafting it, has decided to disarm Iraq, through inspections, detection then destruction of the weapons of mass destruction...

Q. Now, we're moving on to a second resolution...

President Chirac. And in our view, the inspectors' reports confirm that there are no grounds for changing, that we must pursue this path and that the goal can be achieved by pursuing it. Some of our partners, who have their reasons, consider that we need to finish the task fast and by taking another approach, that of war.

Q. With an ultimatum?

President Chirac. That led to the proposal of a new resolution setting an ultimatum. To start with, there was talk of 17 March, then of a possibility of a British amendment to postpone the date of the ultimatum a bit, it's of little consequence. In other words, we move from a course of action involving the pursuit of the inspections in order to disarm Iraq to a different one consisting of saying: "in so many days, we go to war".

Q. And you don't want that?

President Chirac. France won't accept it and so will refuse that solution.

Q. If need be, she will threaten to exercise her veto?.. That way you will scupper the resolution.

President Chirac. I repeat: France will oppose that resolution. Now what does that mean? There are fifteen members of the Security Council. Five permanent members and ten members who change every two years. For a resolution to be adopted, it must have a majority of nine members. So the first scenario which is today, this evening, the most probable, is that this resolution won't get a majority of nine members.

Q. The Americans are saying the opposite. Colin Powell thinks he will get it.

President Chirac. I'm telling you what I feel. I firmly believe, this evening, that there isn't a majority of nine votes in favor of that resolution including an ultimatum and thus giving the international green light to war.

Q. In other words, France wouldn't need to use her veto?

President Chirac. In this scenario, that's exactly right. In this scenario, France will, of course, take a stand. There will be nations who will vote "no", including France. Some will abstain. But, in any case, there won't, in this scenario, be a majority. So there won't be a veto problem.

Q. And if the opposite happens?

President Chirac. Then, the second scenario: what I believe this evening to be the views of a number of people change. If this happens, there may indeed be a majority of nine votes or more in favor of the new resolution, the one authorizing war, to put things simply. If that happens, France will vote "no". But there is one possibility, what's called exercising a veto, it's when one of the five permanent members—the United States, Britain, Russia, China and France—votes "no", and then even if there is a majority in favor of it, the resolution isn't adopted. That's what's called exercising a veto.

Q. And, this evening, this is your position in principle?

President Chirac. My position is that, regardless of the circumstances, France will vote "no" because she considers this evening that there are no grounds for waging war in order to achieve the goal we have set ourselves, i.e. to disarm Iraq.

Q. So, exercising this veto—in fact, some people call the veto the diplomatic atom bomb -, some people, including some members of the governing party, have said this would be firing a bullet in our allies' back...

President Chirac. Don't let yourself by influenced by polemics. I repeat: war is always the worst solution. And France which isn't a pacifist country, who doesn't refuse war on principle, who is in fact proving this by currently being the leading contributor of troops to NATO, particularly in the Balkans, France isn't a pacifist country. France considers that war is the final stage of a process, that all possible means must be used to avoid it because of its tragic consequences.

Q. At the end of the day, wouldn't using your veto be committing a practically unprecedented act vis—vis the United States?

President Chirac. First of all, it's been done quite often.

Q. But not against the U.S., except in 1956.

President Chirac. Vetoes have been used very often. All in all, France has used it eighteen times, the last time in 1989, at the time of the Panama crisis. Britain has used it thirty-two times and the United States seventy-six times. So what you call using the veto, i.e. going against a majority isn't exceptional, it happens, it's allowed under international rules, under international law.

Q. You will use this veto regardless of the position of the Russians or the Chinese who can also use it? Will it be a common position?

President Chirac. I believe today that the Russians and Chinese, who are in the same situation as France regarding the possibility of saying a definitive "no", are, I think, prepared, if there's a resolution authorizing war, to adopt the same attitude as France.

Q. Colin Powell was saying that that veto would have very serious consequences, a very serious impact on bilateral relations between France and the United States. Wouldn't it trigger a crisis with our allies?

President Chirac. I told you that France wasn't a pacifist country. Nor is she anti-American, it's absurd to think that. We have two centuries of common history, of sharing the same values. We have always been together at difficult moments, hand in hand, and our relations and our friendship have deep roots in our peoples, going far beyond isolated events. So there's no risk of the United States and France, of the American and French peoples quarreling or falling out.

Q. But don't you fear reprisals, for example an economic embargo on a number of our products?

President Chirac. That doesn't make any sense. First of all, because I know the Americans too well to imagine them using that type of method...

Q. They've already done so in the past...

President Chirac. The U.S. is a free-market country and, above all, we're no longer in the 1960s or 1970s, we're in a globalized world with international organizations. Trade today is governed by the rules of the World Trade Organization, of the European Union. If the Americans wanted to take measures vis—vis France, they would have to take them vis-a-vis the whole of Europe, including Britain. So that's not serious.

* * * *

Q. ...Franco-American relations will, nevertheless be affected for a long time...

President Chirac. I'm absolutely convinced of the contrary. In fact, I note that President George Bush has said so very clearly, and to my mind speaking from the bottom of his heart. Two days ago, talking about his difference of views on the Iraq problem with the French and the Germans, he said with the utmost clarity: "the French and Germans are our friends and will remain so". Of course! We have a difference of views, but don't let's get blinded by the problems of this particular moment. Let's not sacrifice our principles and our values because, at a given moment, there's a crisis.

Q. And if the Americans don't get this majority, some way or other, at the Security Council, do you think they will nevertheless wage war?

President Chirac. I can't give an opinion on that point since it's not my decision or my place to interfere in the one the Americans will take. There are almost daily telephone contacts between us and we have told them to take care, that one couldn't be a standard bearer for democracy, dialogue and not use every possible method to avoid a war. And if the international community didn't give its approval, a dangerous precedent would be set if the United States bypassed the U.N.. You will tell me: "they have deployed 200,000 men". But they have already won! I had the chance to tell President Bush this not long ago. It's highly probable that, had the Americans and British not deployed such significant forces, Iraq wouldn't have provided the more active cooperation the inspectors demanded, which they have found and has probably been obtained because of that pressure. So, it can be said that in actual fact, through their strategy of disarming Iraq, the Americans have achieved their goal. They have won.

Q. So they wouldn't lose face?
President Chirac. I don't see how they would lose it. You know, you can't lose face if you achieve your goal without waging war.

Q. If there is war, if the United States decide to wage war regardless of whether there's a U.N. mandate, if it's without a U.N. mandate, will France take any part at all in that war?

President Chirac. We aren't involved and won't be if there's no U.N. decision, of course.

Q. No aircraft carrier, base, or deployment of men or soldiers?

President Chirac. No military capability.

Q. Overflying national territory, if the request is made?

President Chirac. That goes without saying. It's part of the normal relations between allies. The Americans are our allies. We don't agree with them on an immediate war in that part of the world, in Iraq, that doesn't mean we aren't allies. If the

Americans need to overfly our territory, it goes without saying [they can], that's normal between allies.

Q. If a war were triggered without a U.N. mandate, could France, not being involved in the armed operations, be involved in rebuilding Iraq?

President Chirac. No one can say in advance what the results of a war will be. It's rare for them to be positive. There are first of all dead women, men and children and subsequently, in this specific case, the risk of the country breaking up, with all that means in the way of uncertainty. Then a bit of calm will have to be recreated in a region which has, regrettably, been traumatized for a long time, is vulnerable and really doesn't need an extra war. So we don't know exactly what the consequences of a war will be. But what is certain is that after a war things do indeed have to be repaired.

Q. And France will ask to participate in that reconstruction?

President Chirac. She will be asked to do so! There will have to be reconstruction both at the structural and political levels. And that reconstruction can be done only through the U.N.. One can't imagine anyone taking on alone the responsibility of restoring a viable situation in that country and that region, and that also applies to the United States.

Q. Even with an American protectorate?

President Chirac. That's a risky hypothesis.

Q. You don't believe in it?

President Chirac. I don't know what the Americans want to do, but I'm saying that's a risky hypothesis. On the other hand, what is certain is that we shall all have to join together to repair, if I may say so, the damage. Quite obviously, France will have her part to play there and will shoulder her responsibilities. But we would prefer, I repeat it once again, to achieve the goal the international community has set itself, i.e. to disarm Iraq. And Iraq's disarmament, make no mistake about it, will bring about the end of the regime. Since disarmament requires transparency. And dictators don't withstand scrutiny for long.

Q. In the United States, Richard Perle was saying that, at the end of the day, in this crisis, France is seeking to establish her position in the world by opposing Washington. Is the opposite true, do you yourself get the impression that this crisis is revealing hegemonic designs on the part of the United States vis-a-vis the organization of the world?

President Chirac. There you're indulging in polemics and I don't do that. Above all, I don't wish to do so with the Americans. But here we're getting to a problem of principle. We're in no way in conflict with the United States, we have no reason for having a conflict with the United States. But here we are faced with a problem of principle, I would say a moral problem. Are we going to wage war when there's perhaps a means of avoiding it? In line with her tradition, France is saying: "if there's a way to avoid it, it must be avoided". And we shall do our utmost to do so.

Q. But they're saying it's a moral problem and Tony Blair too is saying: "there's the axis of evil and that axis of evil must be destroyed"...

President Chirac. Let's take care to avoid extreme language.

Q. Does that seem uncalled for to you?

President Chirac. I didn't approve of it.

Q. Whatever happens, there will, nevertheless, be a loser in this crisis: Europe.

President Chirac. I don't believe so. Firstly, because I've never thought that Europe was a bed of roses. The European path is difficult, steep and full of pitfalls. And you will note that, ever since we've pursued it, we've always made progress, regardless of the difficulties and pitfalls. And whenever there's been a crisis, we've emerged from it with a stronger Europe. Take the example we're dealing with today. We made efforts, in the wake of the single market, a number of other reforms and the single currency, to embark on the path of establishing a common foreign and defense policy. Here again, we knew very well that we would have difficulties. They have surfaced with the Iraq issue. Let me remind you, to give you an example, that at a time when we were obviously taking two different positions, we—the British and ourselves—met for our latest Franco-British summit at Le Touquet, and ... while noting our difference of view on the Iraq issue, made very significant progress on a whole range of decisions, which went somewhat unnoticed because of the Iraq crisis, but allowed us to make headway on the path towards a common defense.

* * * *

Q. Even so, Europe is deeply divided...

President Chirac. No, don't you believe it! You know, I have long experience of Europe. I know Europe well. I know how it works. (...) It won't be at all divided once the crisis is over. And the remorse felt at having been unable to form a single position will give it new strength to achieve the goal it has set itself. That's the whole story of Europe. Europe's history is punctuated by crises from which, in every case, it has emerged stronger. And this will happen again. Quite simply because everyone is aware that, if we want (...) a multipolar world in which Europe counts for something and exists, it must be genuinely united. And it will be.

Q. Our compatriots are worried about two or three things. If there is war, first of all, the risk of a possible resurgence of terrorism. Secondly, that there could be antag-

onism between the different communities which make up this country, that there could be clashes between them. And, thirdly, about the economy which, finally, has slowed down a great deal recently. And people tend to think it's due to these threats of war. Can you reassure them on these subjects?

President Chirac. Terrorism first of all. It's certain that, if there's war, the first victors will probably be those seeking confrontation, the clash of civilizations, cultures and religions. In my opinion, a war of this nature can lead only to increased terrorism. In any event it's highly likely.

Q. Including France?

President Chirac. France has suffered painfully from terrorism, she has experienced it. And consequently she is perhaps a bit more on her guard than others. At any rate, what I can tell you is that, in this sphere, it seems to me that war is something which will break up the world coalition against terrorism. Since, after all, we mustn't forget that a very great majority of the world's countries and peoples are against this war, a very, very great majority of them. France isn't isolated, far from it. So if there's war there is indeed a risk of a new upsurge in terrorism. What I can [also] tell you is that the French government has taken a set of the most effective measures possible to combat what is an extremely unpredictable development, to prevent terrorism growing. I note, moreover, that, over the past two or three months a number of spectacular operations, most of which have in fact been made public, have neutralized some really dangerous terrorist rings. At least those have been neutralized.

Q. On inter-community tension?

President Chirac. France is a country which has always aimed to integrate her children and doesn't want to accept the separation of communities along ethnic lines. And so everything which can worsen this problem must be combated. We are trying to do the utmost to ensure that, in France and elsewhere in the world, understanding, respect for the Other—regrettably too often ignored—dialogue, particularly between religions, communities and cultures, prevents these fruitless, dangerous and cruel clashes.

Finally, you referred to the economy. Certainly the sound of boots, so to speak, doesn't help the economy. We can clearly see that growth is falling, with the tragic consequences this entails for employment, that investment is being postponed, that there's an absence of confidence, consumption is suffering and that, consequently, admittedly, the economy is today having problems. It's to a large extent due to the international situation and the prospects of war.

Here too we have to try to act as efficiently as possible. And I believe that the government, from this point of view, has not just taken the right path, but the only possible one, i.e. the one which consists in combining a policy to promote employment, for social reasons, with one to encourage the economy and particularly investment and consumption.

Q. Just one word about yourself, President Chirac. There's a lot of talk about your adopting a Gaullist position. Does this please you? Are you drawing inspiration from Gaullism, particularly when it comes to opposing the United States?

President Chirac. Hold on, General de Gaulle never opposed the United States. General de Gaulle was even the first to stand at the United States' side whenever there was a crisis.

Q. Let's say, if you like, that he didn't hesitate to express his opposition?

President Chirac. No he never opposed the United States.

Q. He slammed NATO'S door, for example.

President Chirac. Yes, he asserted France's interests.

Q. You don't think about that today? Do you feel that connection? Or don't you ever have such thoughts?

President Chirac. I can but be flattered, at all events, with the comparison you want to make. But I try to find my own inspiration.

Q. I have one final question to ask you. What today are the odds on avoiding war? People feel it's inevitable.

President Chirac. I don't know at all. What I know is that even if they are one in a thousand or a million, that wouldn't in any way lessen my determination to do my utmost to enable us to resolve the Iraq problem without waging war.

Remarks by United Nations Secretary-General Annan, March 10, 2003

One of the difficulties we have had to face, in this latest phase of the search for a Cyprus settlement, is that our work has been overshadowed by the atmosphere of crisis and great anxiety that is affecting the whole world. The question of Iraq's disarmament has brought the international community to a dangerous point of division and discord. I'm sure you will understand if I devote the remainder of my remarks to that issue.

Let me start by repeating something which must be obvious: all peoples today feel the threat of weapons of mass destruction. It is an issue of the utmost gravity—by no means confined to Iraq. The whole international community needs to act together to curb the proliferation of these terrible weapons, wherever it is happening.

The determination of the Security Council to disarm Iraq of such weapons is the most urgent issue—because Iraq has actually used such weapons in the past, and because it has twice committed aggression against its neighbors. That is why the Security Council, ever since 1991, has passed successive resolutions requiring Iraq to disarm. On this critical question, there are no divisions, no grounds for doubt, dispute or delay.

All around the globe, people want to see this crisis resolved peacefully. There is widespread concern about the long-term consequences of war in Iraq for the fight against terrorism; for the Middle East peace process; and for the world's ability to address common concerns in the future if deep divisions are sowed today between nations and between peoples of different religions.

Indeed, one must have no illusions about what war means. In certain circumstances the use of force may be necessary to secure a lasting peace. But the reality is that it would cause great human suffering, whether it is long or short; that it may lead to regional instability and economic crises; and it can—as it often has before—lead to unintended consequences producing new threats and new dangers.

War must always be a last resort—arrived at only if and when every reasonable avenue of achieving Iraq's disarmament by peaceful means has been exhausted. The United Nations—founded to save succeeding generations from the scourge of war—has a duty to search till the very end for the peaceful resolution of conflicts.

Ladies and Gentlemen,

The members of the Security Council now face a great choice. If they fail to agree on a common position, and action is taken without the authority of the Security Council, the legitimacy and support for any such action will be seriously impaired. If, on the other hand, they can come together, even at this late hour, to address this threat in a united manner and ensure compliance with their previous resolutions, then the Council's authority will be enhanced, and the world will be a safer place.

Indeed, Iraq does not exist in a vacuum. What happens there will have profound implications—for better or worse—for other issues of great importance to the surrounding region, and to the world. The broader the consensus on Iraq, the better the chance that we can come together again and deal effectively with other burning conflicts in the world, starting with the one between Israelis and Palestinians. Only a just resolution of that conflict can bring real hope of lasting stability in the region.

Even beyond the Middle East, the success or failure of the international community in dealing with Iraq will crucially affect its ability to deal with the serious situation developing on the Korean Peninsula—not to mention the conflicts which are causing such terrible suffering in Africa, and setting back the prospects for stability and development, from Cote d'Ivoire to the Democratic Republic of the Congo.

And there are many other scourges that the world has to face, besides war. Whether they are protecting themselves against terrorism or struggling against the grim triad of poverty, ignorance and disease, States need to work together, and they can do so through the United Nations. However this conflict is resolved, the United Nations will remain as important as it is today.

We have seen in recent months what an immense significance States and peoples around the world attach to the legitimacy provided by the United Nations Security Council, and by the United Nations, as the common framework for securing the peace. As they approach their grave decision, I must solemnly urge all members of the Security Council to keep this in mind, and to be worthy of the trust in them that the world's peoples have shown.

Q. Mr. Secretary-General, as you know there does not appear to be much unity on the Council. The Russian Foreign Minister today said he would veto a resolution. How badly damaged would the Security Council, as an institution, by this lack of unity?

Secretary-General Annan. I think obviously there are divisions and this is why they need to come together and seek a compromise and work together. It may be late or it may still be possible but one has to try and I will say that the Council has been divided before and yet has managed to come together and find a common basis for moving forward. We saw this when we were discussing resolution 1441. Many thought it would not be possible that the Council could not come together. I think with good will and determination and a real focus we should be able to resolve this one as well. But if we are not able to resolve it, as I have indicated, whichever way this conflict is resolved, we must be clear.

The United Nations will be important and [it] will have important roles to play, regardless of how this issue is resolved. We went through this with regard to Kosovo where action was taken outside of the Council and yet those who took action had to return to the Council to be able to deal with the aftermath. Here it is not just dealing with the aftermath of Iraq but also with all the broader issues that I have referred to and I hope that the Council members will be able to come together and deal with the burning issues of the day.

* * * *

Q. Mr. Secretary-General, tomorrow you will be at the inauguration of the ICC, do you see a parallel in America's behavior on the Iraq question and their attitude towards the ICC—which they did not only decline to join but are fighting against it?

Secretary-General Annan. Well, I think it is the sovereign right of a government to decide when to sign onto a treaty and when not to. And obviously, the U.S. has decided not to sign onto the Rome Treaty. And the other members states, over 80 of them, who have agreed are pressing ahead, with the formation of this Court, which I welcome and I think my presence here indicates a strong support, I have for that Court and I have been able to take time out despite the Iraqi crisis to join those who are launching the Court and I think it is [an] important development in the Rule of Law and a development of International Law, and I believe that in time all nations are going to need the Court. And so I have not given up on those who have not yet acceded to this Treaty of Rome. I hope that, once the Court is launched and demonstrates what it can do, they will sign on.

Q. Mr. Secretary-General, you said that an attack on Iraq without a second Council resolution would not be legitimate. Would you consider it as a breach of the U.N. Charter?

Secretary-General Annan. I think that under today's world order, the Charter is very clear on circumstances under which force can be used. I think the discussion going on in the Council is to ensure that the Security Council, which is master of its own deliberations, is able to pronounce itself on what happens. If the U.S. and others were to go outside the Council and take military action it would not be in conformity with the Charter.

Remarks by Secretary of State Powell, March 10, 2003

Q. Mr. Secretary, have you made many phone calls today?

Secretary Powell. I've made quite a few phone calls, and I'm looking forward to having a nice meeting and discussion with my colleague.

Q. How's the vote count?

Secretary Powell. You can make your vote count, and we'll make our vote count. We're just having a good exchange of views today.

Remarks by Secretary of State Powell, March 10, 2003

Q. Mr. Secretary, can you say how concerned you were that the report of the drones that the Iraqis have been trying to get that can disseminate biological and chemical weapons, that they were not in the report?

Secretary Powell. I think we should be concerned. It seems to me that this information on the drones, which I know UNMOVIC was evaluating, but it was information that was available last week, and should be of concern to everyone.

Iraq continues to demonstrate that it has not really changed its strategic intent, which is the case we've been making all along. So we're concerned about that, and I think other information will be coming forward that suggests Iraq has really not changed.

Q. Mr. Secretary, are you feeling like you're in a bit of a competition with the French, the French Foreign Minister? He's in Africa trying to persuade those undecided votes. Do you feel as if—

Secretary Powell. I'm in no competition with Dominique de Villepin. He does what he has to do, and I do what I have to do. We are both working for causes we believe in, we are both trying to consult with all the members of the Council, and as you see, I have been in touch today at some length with the Foreign Minister of Guinea and I have been on the phone most of the morning with nations around the world. It's a combination of phones, visits and means of that type that allow you to make your point. And so I'm not in competition with anybody. I'm trying to do my job the way I think I can do it best.

Excerpts from Remarks by Secretary of Defense Rumsfeld, March 11, 2003

Secretary Rumsfeld. The president made clear that he is determined to confront the threat posed by Saddam Hussein and that if he does not disarm, he will be disarmed by a coalition of willing countries. And I believe that if such a decision were to be made, it would prove to be a large coalition. We hope to see the United Nations act. The credibility of the U.N. is important to the world. But if the Security Council fails this test of resolve, a coalition will be ready to act nonetheless.

The question before the United Nations is clear: Is Saddam Hussein taking this final opportunity that was offered by Resolution 1441 to disarm or not? And the answer to the question, it strikes me, is increasingly obvious. He makes a show of destroying a handful of missiles; missiles which he claimed in his declaration did not violate U.N. restrictions, but now admits that they do violate U.N. restrictions. Yet even as he destroys those missiles, he's ordered the continued production of the very same types of missiles. He claims to have no chemical or biological weapons, yet we know he continues to hide biological and chemical weapons, moving them to different locations as often as every 12 to 24 hours, and placing them in residential neighborhoods.

He is an accomplished deceiver, or else why would so many in the world community continue to be deceived so long? If it becomes necessary to use military force, we know he will stop at nothing to deceive the world by spreading lies. We are taking extraordinary measures to prevent innocent casualties. Hussein, by contrast, will seek to maximize civilian deaths and create the false impression that coalition forces target innocent Iraqis, which of course is not the case.

Before any conflict begins, we should look back and recall his history of deception: What he said and what he did during the Gulf War conflict. During that war, the Iraqi regime went to great lengths to convince the world that coalition forces had targeted innocent civilians and Muslim holy sites.

For example, on February 13th, 1991, coalition forces fired precision guided bombs at the Amiriyah bunker in Baghdad. The bunker had originally been constructed as an air raid shelter during the Iran-Iraq war. But when—the latter was converted into a military command and control center.

Unbeknownst to coalition forces, the Iraqi regime had told civilians that it was an air raid shelter, and admitted them to the top floors in the evening. Right beneath them was a military command and control center that was being used by senior Iraqi officials for military communications. We later learned that Saddam Hussein had decreed that all Iraqi military bunkers would also house civilians.

Another example. During the gulf war on February 11th, 1991 the Iraqi regime deliberately removed the dome of the al-Bushra mosque and dismantled it in an attempt to make it appear that coalition forces had deliberately struck a mosque. Which was not the case. Satellite photos later revealed that while the dome was gone, there was no damage to the minaret, the courtyard buildings, or the dome foundation, which would have been the case had coalition forces struck the building.

There are many other examples. But the point is this: he does not tell the truth, he lied during the Gulf war, and if there is to be another war, he will lie again. Indeed, he already is. The only question is whether he will be believed despite his record.

We know from recent intelligence that he has ordered uniforms that are virtually identical to those of U.S. and British forces for his Fedayeen Saddam troops, who would theoretically wear them while committing atrocities against innocent Iraqis. His regime may be planning to use weapons of mass destruction against its own citizens, and then blame coalition forces. When his regime begins claiming once again that coalition forces have targeted innocent Iraqi civilians, if that's to be the case, we need to keep his record in mind.

* * * *

Q. Sir, support for a possible war is shrinking rapidly in Great Britain. Would the—two questions. Would the United States go to war without Great Britain? And two, would the role of the British in an initial assault be scaled back?

Secretary Rumsfeld. This is a matter that most of the senior officials in the government discuss with the U.K. on a daily or every- other-day basis. And I had a good visit with the Minister of Defense of the U.K. about an hour ago. Their situation is distinctive to their country, and they have a government that deals with a parliament in their way, distinctive way. And what will ultimately be decided is unclear as to their role; that is to say, their role in the event that a decision is made to use force. There's the second issue of their role in a post- Saddam Hussein reconstruction process or stabilization process, which would be a different matter. And I think until we know what the resolution is, we won't know the answer as to what their role will be and to the extent they're able to participate in the event the President decides to use force, that would obviously be welcomed. To the extent they're not, there are workarounds and they would not be involved, at least in that phase of it.

Q. We would consider going to war without our closest ally, then?

Rumsfeld. That is an issue that the President will be addressing in the days ahead, one would assume.

Remarks by United Nations Secretary-General Annan, March 11, 2003

Q. I would like to ask a question about Iraq. What do you think about extending the deadline of March 17th and what do you think about the possible veto of Russia and France?

Secretary-General Annan. I heard yesterday that there may be further amendments to the resolution. I don't have the details of it but some governments believe that the 17 March deadline is too short. Whether it is an issue for the Member States, whether they will be able to extend the date and for how long, is something that I am waiting to see evolve.

On the question of possible veto by France and the Russian Federation, this is a right of individual Members to vote whichever way that they deem fit. They have indicated that if the issue were to come to a vote they may vote "no" but of course it depends what sort of resolution is going to be on the table if indeed there are further discussions on the resolution. But if they were to cast a negative vote, it is their right.

Q. It is not very good for the unity you would like to see.

Secretary-General Annan. Not very good for the unity but we have seen this before. Many vetoes have been cast, I hope we will be able to come together on this one but to be able to come together on this one and avoid the vetoes implies that we need to come with a compromise that everybody can rally around and say this is the direction we are going to go and put pressure on the Iraqi authorities to disarm. If we are not able to find that compromise and the divisions remain then we are likely to have these vetoes.

* * * *

Q. Is it true that France has the right to veto the decision of the Security Council? The Dutch Government has stated that France will blow up the United Nations if they will do so. Do you disagree in this point with the Dutch Government?

Secretary-General Annan. First of all, when it comes to voting in the Security Council, the Permanent Members have veto rights and have used them in the past. As I have indicated, on this issue, I myself have always pleaded for unity of the Council and for them to get a common position compromising and move forward together and put on their collective pressure, because it is when they work together that they are most effective and have the greatest impact. If that were to fail and France, and maybe other countries, were to exercise their veto, I don't think that would be the end of the United Nations. Obviously, we've all indicated that it would be better if they had worked together as they worked on [resolution] 1441 but what I would want to say is that no matter how this issue is resolved at the end of the day the U.N. is going to be as important as ever and the U.N. will have an important role, the Security Council that is, in how we handle the situation in Iraq, and in the region, regardless of how the conflict is resolved.

Statement by U.K. Foreign Secretary Straw, March 12, 2003

Four months ago, in Resolution 1441, the United Nations gave Iraq a final opportunity to disarm by co-operation, or face serious consequences. We have been working flat out in recent days for agreement on a second resolution. That process is now coming to a conclusion. A decision will have to be taken by the end of this week.

In order to seek the widest consensus, Sir Jeremy Greenstock is now discussing further amendments to our draft with Security Council partners. And he is circulating six tests by which Iraqi compliance would be measured. Each of those tests is demanding, but deliverable. They are:

• a statement by Saddam Hussein admitting that he has concealed weapons of mass destruction, but will no longer produce or retain weapons of mass destruction;

• deliver at least 30 scientists for interview outside Iraq, with their families;

• surrender all anthrax, or credible evidence of destruction;

• complete the destruction of all Al Samoud missiles;

• account for all unmanned aerial vehicles, including details of any testing of sparying devices for chemical and biological weapons;

• surrender all mobile chemical and biological production facilities. These tests are not traps. Every one of them could be met promptly, if only Saddam Hussein were to make the strategic choice to co-operate with the U.N..

All of us involved in this—the Prime Minister, Sir Jeremy Greenstock in New York, and myself—will continue to devote all our energies, every waking minute, to our efforts to reach agreement in the Security Council.

Throughout this process, our objective has been to work through the U.N., and to strengthen the U.N. system by showing that it can handle a crisis of this gravity. Despite the threats to veto our resolution, whatever the circumstances, we still think this is the right approach. It is in the U.K.'s national interest, and in the interests of the U.N. as a whole.

It can only damage the U.N.'s authority if the Security Council fails to carry out what it said it would do in Resolution 1441. We will continue to do all we can to avoid that outcome.

Remarks by Secretary of State Powell, March 13, 2003

Secretary Colin Powell was interviewed by Richard Wolffe of Newsweek.

Q. Now, this piece is not about the second resolution or where we're at; it's supposed to be the bigger view, your view over the last few months of diplomacy, and your take on how it's played out. But if I don't ask this question, my office will think I'm a complete Euro-wimp. So, you mentioned on the Hill today there may be no chance of a vote, maybe it won't come to a vote. Is that really where we stand or are people reading too much in to your testimony?

Secretary Powell. I was trying to lay out a range of alternatives that are before us, and that is certainly one of them. And I felt it was important to make sure nobody misunderstood the range of alternatives that are before us. Ana Palacios did something similar yesterday. I can't remember if Jack Straw did or not. But it certainly is an option. And I wasn't trying to make news; I was just trying to set up the full range of options. Because everybody this morning was pushing toward, you know, a vote. And everybody was handicapping us. I started to call Las Vegas to see what the handicap was this morning on what the boot count was.

And you'll notice I also said that our strategy, what we're doing, is pushing ahead, working hard, trying to get the most support we can for a second resolution, which I think would be the best thing to do or achieve. But unfortunately it's still going to face a French veto.

Q. Let me get straight in, because I know we're going to be short on time here. In the weeks after 9/11, you argued with the principals that Iraq shouldn't be top of the threat list, that Saddam wasn't going anywhere and that, in fact pursuing Iraq may even break up the coalition against terror. Obviously, the President decided something else after, Afghan style. What changed things for you?

Secretary Powell. It wasn't weeks after, it was at that very next Saturday that we debated this in front of the President, as has been well reported and recorded, and the President decided in that first week that we had to go after the enemy that had just struck us. And it was Osama bin Laden, it was al-Qaida, and then when the Taliban wouldn't turn him over, it became the Taliban. And he announced that to the nation the following Thursday, if I'm not mistaken—that nine days in there.

So it was a decision that was pretty straightforward and, I thought, rather obvious. But a case was made, as you well know, and it was a very legitimate case, that there are other terrorist organizations and there are nations that are havens and support the terrorist groups, such as Afghanistan was. And this is all presented to the President. These weren't revelations. We all knew this. We had been worrying about Iraq since we came in here.

And the debate that we had was should we go after Iraq at the same time as Afghanistan. I argued that Afghanistan, everybody will understand, al-Qaida everybody will understand. We've got several thousand dead Americans and 80 other nations—or it's 90 now—nations of casualties. And we pulled everybody together behind this, NATO, the U.N., OIC, you name it, they were all behind us in this. This is what the American people are expecting. Let's do this and we can take care of the others in due course.

Would we have gone after Iraq if there hadn't been a 9/11 at that time? No. And so should 9/11, in and of itself have been the precipitating reason to go after Iraq? No. Did it change the prism through which we viewed Iraq? Yes, definitely. And that's why the President said we'll look at this in I think he said the next phase, or subsequent phases. And so we did that.

Meanwhile, however, we finished work on smart sanctions, which was a year's worth of work, but we finally got them. The Pentagon kept reviewing its plans, kept waiting to see whether we had changed attitudes on the part of Saddam Hussein, and there was none. And so in the course of last spring and summer, as we debated this, as we got Afghanistan not fixed but up and running, Karzai is there, we have an interim authority, we are starting to do other things on the war on terrorism, Abu Sayyaf. We work with a number of countries around the world, Yemen and other places, and we realize the comprehensive nature of the assault that will be required, going after financial systems, intelligence systems. You know all that; I won't belabor it.

Q. Right.

Secretary Powell. And then, finally, what about these other countries that are a problem, the nexus between weapons of mass destruction and terrorist organizations. So, naturally, we have turned our attention to Iraq. As we looked at Iraq and realized how we were fighting a war against terror through a terrific coalition, it seemed—to me, anyway—that we would want something approaching that level of support if we were going to do Iraq. We needed people who would be in on this.

And we discussed this and debated this through the summer. And I think definitely what happened in August, and the President made the decision in August to go to the U.N. in September. I wasn't expecting as exciting an August as it turned out to be, because he had decided it the first week of August that he was going to do that on the 12th of September. Which was a given, because we knew he was going to the U.N.. He was going to speak on something on the 12th of September, and this had become the pressing issue of the day. You all were writing about nothing else even then.

Q. Exactly. Nothing's changed.

But people like Tony Zinni have said, you know, Iraq still isn't the biggest threat facing America. Again, has your opinion of the threat really changed that much?

Secretary Powell. My opinion has always been that Iraq is a dangerous country, it's a dangerous regime. It is developing weapons of mass destruction. And it was something that had to be dealt with sooner or later. It was always on our agenda. It moved up and down the agenda, depending on what else was going on in the world. But it was always there, lurking.

And so the post-9/11 period highlighted it in a way that it hadn't been highlighted before with this potential nexus. Does it mean that they're coming after us tomorrow morning? No, but this is clearly a guy who never changed his fundamental intent and has never modified his decision to pursue these kinds of technologies, these kinds of weapons. And, you know, some people have been committed to that proposition since the very beginning, when I was out of the government.

And so the approach that I took to it was that we should try to get as much support for this as we can and we should work to give the Iraqis one more opportunity to change their mind, and to realize a better life awaited the Iraqi people, and perhaps some form of survival for the regime. It would have to be a different regime, a changed regime from the one we talked about, which got us into all those tautologies about regime change and change in regime.

Q. Right.

Secretary Powell. Which really mean the same thing, if you go back to what Clinton said in '98: "This regime won't change, therefore we will change it. If it changes itself"—you can change it forever. (Inaudible). But, in any event, so the diplomatic approach was, I think, a very sound one. The President took it and he asked for a second resolution, or he asked for a resolution. And we got the whole Security Council unified behind that. And before anyone forgets anything, the last act of the Security Council on this issue was 1441.

Q. Did you think the diplomatic process could effectively avert the war?

Secretary Powell. Before 1441?

Q. 1441 itself, that fulsome [*inaudible*]—it comes back to this question, was there ever a realistic chance. Realistic, not Saddam turning into a diplomatic—a democratic leader, but a realistic chance that that could have worked?

Secretary Powell. I think there was a realistic chance that it could have worked, if he realized the seriousness of the President's intent. And certainly, in words and deeds, as the President spoke and as he started to give direction and build up the force, there shouldn't have been any doubt in Saddam Hussein's mind. So there was a chance it might have worked. Others would say, no, there never was. Just look back in the Gulf War. He saw that built up and it didn't deter him or cause him to leave Kuwait. But that buildup was not intended to go to Baghdad but this one was and is. And that might have changed.

And if it wasn't a realistic effort, or a realistic possibility of that happening and you had to use force, this was a useful way to go about it, getting international support for the use of force. And whatever happens next week, we have 1441.

Q. Right. Does—you know, the neo-conservative critics who have said all along that you had another agenda, about war at all costs, I'm just wondering if you did think there was a potential for a different outcome from what seems to be—

Secretary Powell. No, if I didn't think there was a potential, and frankly the President didn't think the potential was there, I don't think he would have gone down that road. The President has said repeatedly that he wanted to avoid war. He says it in a very human way: I'm the one who has to go see these mothers and dads of people who have lost their lives. And why would I want that, why would I welcome that?

But he also knows, as Commander-in-Chief, he has to show the determination necessary to take the nation to war, if that's what it takes to achieve the objective that he's set before him. Now lots of people call me "the reluctant warrior" or "the dove." And I say, fine. Would you like to tattoo it on me? I don't mind.

I've seen war, I've been in war, I've led men in battle. I did two years in Vietnam, I served on the line in Korea and I've commanded corps in Europe. I have sent men into battle in Panama, I've stopped coups in the Philippines. I've gone to Desert Storm. I've stopped—I talked generals out of power in Haiti. So I've been around the track a little bit and I don't have to demonstrate my toughness or my credentials to anyone. I don't like war, and I will work hard to avert war. But I think I know how to fight a war very well and I've had experience doing it.

Q. Some people have told us that the uniform guys at DOD have brought their concerns about war plans to you and that you have raised some of those issues, questions about the war plans, in principals' meetings. Does—is that true?

Secretary Powell. I keep in my own lane. I am not blindfolded—obviously, that's my profession; they're my associates of 35 years. But I do not bring people over here that Don does not know or sent to brief me. And I sit in at all—not all of the meetings, but most of the meetings at which General Myers and Tommy Franks briefs the plans. So I'm very mindful of what the plans are. Any concerns I've had about those plans, I've expressed in those meetings or with Secretary Rumsfeld or General Franks or General Myers.

Q. But you have raised them in those meetings directly with—

Secretary Powell. Yes, we have big, open meetings. Right. Well, not too big and not too open—

No, I was a former Chairman and I was in the Gulf War.

Q. Right.

Secretary Powell. And so I think I have made useful contributions, appropriate to my experience but also appropriate to my current position.

Q. I would like to just go back to something Senator Biden has said. He suggested you may have been outflanked in terms of the military buildup, because it happened so quickly, there were so many troops out in the region that it effectively curtailed the diplomatic window, the timeframe you had to negotiate in. Is that—

Secretary Powell. To negotiate 1441, or the current situation?

Q. No, the current situation.

Secretary Powell. No, I knew what the buildup was. I've known it all along. I knew the numbers as they grew, and I also knew the—the time windows, if I could put it that way. And if there was going to be a diplomatic solution, it wasn't a question of time, it was a question of intent on the part of Hussein and have we given the inspectors a reasonable period of time to go in there and test compliance and cooperation. And they had since the 27th of November. And even before then they were working not directly on the ground, but they were working with Hussein.

So we have been able to watch from, frankly, roughly the 15th of September, when the Iraqis first said—not in response to any change of heart but to the President's speech, "Hey, let the inspectors in." Why? Because they didn't want a resolution. And they did everything they could to finesse a resolution for those seven weeks that it took to get the resolution, took us to create a resolution. And that certainly wasn't an indication of changed attitude on their part.

And then we got the resolution on the 8th of November and watched for another three weeks until the inspectors went in. No change in attitude. And now we see in four months—four months of inspectors. So how many more months of this?

Q. Timing is kind of interesting as well, because there are some things British officials have told me. They said, you know, if the administration had gone out in September and said, we're going to be patient, wait six months for the inspections to work, that's even more than the French want in terms of 120 days or whatever. If the administration had taken a different line with the rhetoric back in September, it may

not have seemed like a rush to war to the rest of the world, would we be looking at a different outcome? Do you think that—

Secretary Powell. No, I don't think so. I think that's a dodge. It's easy here in March to go back and say, if only in September you had said, they have exactly six months, where would the French be at the six month point in 58 days from now—if that's what six months is—well, it is six months, isn't it?

The question—you see, there are those who—and it's not evil intent in all cases. It's that people naturally don't want to go to war. It's not a natural state, and therefore people will try to do everything to avoid war. Sometimes you can't avoid it. I've done everything to avoid war and to prevent war—and I stand proudly on that effort. But sometimes, you have to take it to the test of arms. And there are those who just don't want to face that. So as a way of not facing it, they say, well, why didn't you give him six months instead of four months? Why don't you give him 120 days? And why aren't you supporting inspectors? And shouldn't we have three times as many inspectors?

That's not the issue. You've heard my every Friday speech at the U.N..

Q. I have.

Secretary Powell. Poor lad.

Q. I think it's worse for you.
The French tactics, did they mislead you through 1441? Did you just [*inaudible*], did people take away different things from it?

Secretary Powell. We struck a compromise. We arrived at a 1441, unanimous solution. We made it clear that we do not view 1441 as requiring a second resolution. There is sufficient authority in 1441 that all of our lawyers will stand up and say that is the case. And the French will probably—not the French—others might say—the French and others might say, no, because you have to come back to the Council for it to consider serious consequences, that kind of sets up a second resolution. We never accepted that argument.

In fact, there isn't a word in there that wasn't negotiated to death. And you'll notice that the word—if I'm not mistaken, Richard—is "consider," "the Council will consider." Well, we've done that every Friday for the last few weeks. We've considered it. We believe that the time for compliance and consideration is drawing to a close.

Now, the French—we made clear at the very beginning the fact that one of my—the afternoon of the President's speech or the next day, it was the 13th when I had lunch with the foreign ministers, the five perm reps?

The President spoke in the morning. No, it must have been the next day Richard. I am pretty sure it was Friday the 13th. And we were all discussing what were we going to do now that we had the President's speech at Kofi Annan's luncheon table. And the French were kind of expounding, and talking about the need for a second resolution. And we went on and on and on about the second resolution.

And I said to everybody at the table, and especially to Dominique de Villepin, I understand you're thinking about a second resolution; let's chat about it. The concern

I have is, we must make sure there is nobody here who is expressing a willingness to vote for a first resolution when, at the time you're expressing your willingness to vote for a first resolution, you know that you will never vote for a second one. And so what we did was not let 1441 be written in a way that would put us into that trap.

Now, the French clearly demonstrated over the succeeding months since then that they were prepared to give inspectors a lot more time and, frankly, be a lot more tolerant of Saddam Hussein and what he was doing and grabbing on to process—process issues and process progress, if I can put it that that way—as real progress. And we made it clear this wasn't going to do it for us.

And so the French were pretty up front from the beginning, and we were up front from the beginning. And we have now come into this period where we went for a second resolution because some of our friends need it; the British were particularly threatened. Otherwise, we didn't need it. We were doing it for—to spread the support, because there is widespread disagreement within the Council and among the publics, especially. And some of our political friends are in trouble in other countries. So that's why we tried to get a second resolution.

But that's why we also said that we feel our interests remain threatened and under 1441 we have the authority and reserve the right to use that authority in the absence of a second resolution.

Q. Okay. Can I just do two more?
De Villepin's kind of ambush before your presentation, I heard it was preceded by a dispute over, again, 1441. Was there a promise to go for a second step? The French thought they had a promise that there would be a second step but—suddenly there wasn't going to be. And then that leads to—

Secretary Powell. No. Dominique contacted me in early January. He contacted me in I think either—early January, it was early in the year, and said he felt strongly that we should have a counter-terrorism conference in the Security Council to talk about foreign relations, and I said, why? He just felt, the beginning of the new year, the importance of the issue, led him to believe that such a conference would be useful.

We talked about it among the ministers, particularly in the Perm 5 and thought it might be useful with the French presidency—which is why they were doing it—felt it was important.

Q. [*Inaudible.*]

Secretary Powell. Can't go wrong with something like that.

We were very mindful, as I was, that the 27th, seven days later, is when we were going to get the first Blix report. And so we weren't unaware of that. And in our conversations with the French, we made clear the conference had to focus on counter-terrorism; we did not want to get into an Iraq situation and start talking about Iraq. But there was unease and nervousness that it's kind of hard to get together in a setting like that without somebody wanting to talk about the issue du jour.

And so if you look at what happened that day, everybody talked about terrorism. Everybody stayed on the farm. The only one who slipped off the farm was my German colleague Joschka Fischer, who made a comment about Iraq and terrorism. And if you look at the tape, you'll see me coming out of my prepared remarks on terrorism and responding to Joschka directly, an audible response to Joschka, because I couldn't let it sit there.

The conference ended and we thought, well, we've got through that. But, unbeknownst to any of us, Dominique had gone out and given a press conference which, one way or the other, maybe it was the questions that were asked, maybe it was premeditated, but it was all Iraq. So Iraq led the whole thing the next day, nobody even knew we had a terrorism conference. And it kind of soured the atmosphere and it kind of got everybody charging in this direction, and then Blix a week later.

Now, much has been made of that event. But, in retrospect, it was going to happen either the 20th or the 27th, so I don't know that it makes a whole hell of a lot of difference in the grand sweep of history.

Q. But did the French reaction harden your position in any way, in a sense? Or did it weaken the case of [*inaudible*], the idea that having a united international community, Saddam might have gotten the message quicker and maybe there would have been a coup or something. Did the French undermine you in that way with that kind of—

Secretary Powell. Let me just say that I think it would have been much more constructive—if the French had not decided to make it an Iraq event. Now, whether it was intended or not, you know, it doesn't make any difference now. But it certainly reduced the room to maneuver, because we were all immediately defending our positions, as opposed to defending the common position.

Q. Vice President Cheney mentioned in August that in that speech it could turn into a quagmire, fool's errand, lull people into a false sense of security. Have there been any criticisms that maybe it's ended up like that? Have people said to you, well, look, you got us into the quagmire?

Secretary Powell. No, no one has said that to me. I don't think there was any choice but to go to the international community. And, you know, there are alternative quagmires out there. And you only see the one that's actually holding as you make choices.

But the President believes it was the right thing to do. We all were supportive of it. I'm not sure what others tell you, but nobody disagreed. Nobody dissented on going to the U.N. once the argument was presented and we discussed it and debated it. And for us to undertake something like this, it was important for us to try to carry as much international legitimacy as possible.

Now, could I have predicted that it would have ended up [*inaudible*] an issue, I don't know.

Q. This really is last one.
Some comments. You said you've been careful to stick to your track, your expertise. Secretary Rumsfeld has made some comments that have possibly complicated

the diplomacy [*inaudible*] Europe, British involvement. Have you had reason to say, please limit your activities?

Secretary Powell. Don and I speak candidly every day.

Remarks by President Bush, March 15, 2003

President Bush delivered the following radio address to the nation.

Good morning. This weekend marks a bitter anniversary for the people of Iraq. Fifteen years ago, Saddam Hussein's regime ordered a chemical weapons attack on a village in Iraq called Halabja. With that single order, the regime killed thousands of Iraq's Kurdish citizens. Whole families died while trying to flee clouds of nerve and mustard agents descending from the sky. Many who managed to survive still suffer from cancer, blindness, respiratory diseases, miscarriages, and severe birth defects among their children.

The chemical attack on Halabja—just one of 40 targeted at Iraq's own people—provided a glimpse of the crimes Saddam Hussein is willing to commit, and the kind of threat he now presents to the entire world. He is among history's cruelest dictators, and he is arming himself with the world's most terrible weapons.

Recognizing this threat, the United Nations Security Council demanded that Saddam Hussein give up all his weapons of mass destruction as a condition for ending the Gulf War 12 years ago. The Security Council has repeated this demand numerous times and warned that Iraq faces serious consequences if it fails to comply. Iraq has responded with defiance, delay and deception.

The United States, Great Britain and Spain continue to work with fellow members of the U.N. Security Council to confront this common danger. We have seen far too many instances in the past decade—from Bosnia, to Rwanda, to Kosovo—where the failure of the Security Council to act decisively has led to tragedy. And we must recognize that some threats are so grave—and their potential consequences so terrible—that they must be removed, even if it requires military force.

As diplomatic efforts continue, we must never lose sight of the basic facts about the regime of Baghdad.

We know from recent history that Saddam Hussein is a reckless dictator who has twice invaded his neighbors without provocation—wars that led to death and suffering on a massive scale. We know from human rights groups that dissidents in Iraq are tortured, imprisoned and sometimes just disappear; their hands, feet and tongues are cut off; their eyes are gouged out; and female relatives are raped in their presence.

As the Nobel laureate and Holocaust survivor, Elie Wiesel, said this week, "We have a moral obligation to intervene where evil is in control. Today, that place is Iraq."

We know from prior weapons inspections that Saddam has failed to account for vast quantities of biological and chemical agents, including mustard agent, botulinum toxin and sarin, capable of killing millions of people. We know the Iraqi regime finances and sponsors terror. And we know the regime has plans to place innocent people around military installations to act as human shields.

There is little reason to hope that Saddam Hussein will disarm. If force is required to disarm him, the American people can know that our armed forces have been given every tool and every resource to achieve victory. The people of Iraq can know that every effort will be made to spare innocent life, and to help Iraq recover from three decades of totalitarian rule. And plans are in place to provide Iraqis with massive amounts of food, as well as medicine and other essential supplies, in the event of hostilities.

Crucial days lie ahead for the free nations of the world. Governments are now showing whether their stated commitments to liberty and security are words alone— or convictions they're prepared to act upon. And for the government of the United States and the coalition we lead, there is no doubt: we will confront a growing danger, to protect ourselves, to remove a patron and protector of terror, and to keep the peace of the world.

Remarks by French President Chirac, March 16, 2003

President Jacques Chirac was interviewed by Christiane Amanpour of CNN.

Q. First, thank you very much indeed for joining us. I want to ask you first ... there is a summit going ahead on the Azores between the United States, Britain and Spain. Do you think now [that] war is inevitable?

President Chirac. I hope it isn't. I hope that this summit that brings together President Bush, [Spanish] Prime Minister [Jose Maria] Aznar, and [British] Prime Minister [Tony] Blair... I hope that it can be serene in its atmosphere. And I hope that it will not ignore the sentiments of the majority of the nations across the world, countries that are hoping that inspections will work, especially as they are working.

Q. What do you realistically think will come out of this summit?

President Chirac. I can't [predict] the result of the summit. I hope that reason will prevail and that this effective system, the system that is bringing us to the common goal that we have, i.e. disarmament of Iraq; the elimination and destruction of the weapons of mass destruction ... I hope that all this can be done through inspections. Indeed, inspections have proven their effectiveness to reach this goal.

Q. Mr. President, what is your bottom-line compromise? You haven't yet articulated [it], but you've said you would be willing to offer a compromise. What is your compromise to reunite the Security Council and to go ahead as a united Security Council? How many days would you be willing to grant inspections?

President Chirac. Well, I am not the one to say. The inspectors themselves have to tell us. But I have noticed a few things. First of all, that the Security Council was unanimous—and I repeat, unanimous; and it is noteworthy, especially on such an important issue—the Security Council was unanimous in adopting Security Council [Resolution] 1441, and through the resolution decided to disarm Iraq through peaceful means, through inspections, for as long as the inspectors will tell us that that is feasible. That is the first point I wanted to make.

We have also noticed, in listening to and reading the inspectors' reports, that a lot of progress has been achieved, that weapons are being destroyed every day. Of course, we haven't reached the full goal yet, but the inspectors are telling us—and they will say that again on Tuesday [in their report to the Security Council], I am sure—that we are within reach of our goal, and that we can do that without war. That is precisely my goal, my objective.

I am ready to accept any practical modalities that the inspectors will suggest in that respect, especially as for deadlines. The inspectors, I will remind you, have told us that it wasn't a question of years, it wasn't really either a question of days, but it was a question of months. Are we talking one, two months? I don't know. But we are ready, I am ready, to find an agreement on these issues if it has the endorsement of the inspectors.

Q. So you are saying you would be prepared to do a 30-day or a 60-day deadline?

President Chirac. Whatever the inspectors propose and suggest in that respect will be accepted. It has to be accepted, I think. We have given the inspectors a mission, and we have a moral obligation, and a political one, to follow their advice or else to explain why we are not following them. But if we don't follow their advice, then only the Security Council can decide not to.

That is precisely why Germany, Russia, France said yesterday, and China supported us today, that after the report the inspectors will be giving on Tuesday, and they will be outlining their work program and the possible speeding up of the work program, which, incidentally, will increase the pressure on Iraq. So as I said, we suggested that as soon as the report has been given on the program and the deadlines that there should be a meeting of the Security Council at ministerial level, either to approve or modify, or reject even, if need be, the report. But I suppose approving it or modifying it would be more likely. But again, the goal is a common goal. A goal shared by all members of the Security Council, all 15 of us. And it is indeed the goal of the international community as a whole. We have to disarm Iraq.

We can't just leave that Iraqi dictator in a position where he can hold weapons that he could use, and we don't know what he could use. Or rather we have too clear an understanding of what he might do with them. That is clear, I think. But we have to do that in the most reasonable conditions, the most normal conditions, and I think today, as I have said, we have to go through with inspections.

Q. You have said that inspections were working in great part because of the massive U.S. and British force that is arrayed outside Saddam Hussein's doorstep. Wouldn't it be even more effective if France had sent troops also to double and triple the threat?

President Chirac. I have said already, and I am very sure of what I am saying, I have said that it is indeed thanks to the pressure of British and American troops that the Iraqi authorities and Saddam Hussein himself have changed, have shifted their position and have had to agree to cooperate with the inspectors. First of all they were not too cooperative, but you have increased their level of cooperation, as the inspectors themselves have told us. So I would say that the Americans have already won. They have won, and they haven't even shot one bullet. Without their presence on the ground, of course it is very likely that nothing would have changed and that we wouldn't have been in a position to reach our goal of disarming, through inspections, Iraq, and finding and destroying these weapons.

So indeed, I feel that the Americans have had a very important role to play, and we should acknowledge that and be thankful for exercising that effective pressure. Now, that doesn't mean that we have to wage war if it isn't necessary. And as I said, I don't think that it is necessary.

Q. And yet the inspectors have said yes, things are going much better than they had in the past, but it's not perfect and active cooperation from Saddam Hussein. Wouldn't it have been a much more serious signal had France also sent troops to keep that pressure on?

President Chirac. France, from the very beginning, had agreed to a process that we felt could be successful, the process outlined by Resolution 1441. There wasn't the hypothesis of war in that resolution. France has stuck to its logic, to its understanding of things, and that was to say that we could achieve disarmament of Iraq through inspectors and through inspections. That is why we now hold the position we hold. That is also why we are also refusing today, in the current circumstances, the prospect of war. And we will go to the full consequences of our understanding. We feel indeed that there is another option, through inspections.

Now, if the inspectors were to [say]: "Look, it's not working. Not enough cooperation. There's no way in which we can scrutinize and monitor and inspect. It's just not working..." Now, if Saddam Hussein were to do something that he has already shown that he was able to do, for instance, taking a preposterous initiative, one of these wonderful initiatives he has the secret of, then of course France would change its position. If we were to see that our strategy, inspections, was failing, we would consider all the options, including war. But it isn't the case and it isn't the situation today. I think we can today still play one card, the card of peace, and it always is the most reasonable card to play.

Q. Britain and the United States have accused France of poisoning the process by saying that you would use your veto under any circumstances. Even in Iraq, newspapers loyal to Saddam Hussein are hailing, are praising, the division in the world community, calling it a great victory for Saddam Hussein. Do you not think that your repeated vow to veto has emboldened Saddam Hussein?

President Chirac. I don't not think so, no. It really isn't a topical issue. It isn't a question in the news, really. You will notice that there isn't today a majority in the Security Council supporting. There just isn't one. So veto isn't an issue, because there is no majority to start war.

Of course it is obvious that France has convictions and beliefs, that we feel war is always the worst solution. It can only be used if there is no other option. And we are true to our principles. We are not refusing or rejecting war outright. If we have to wage war... we are not pacifists. We are not anti-American either. We are not just going to use our veto to nag and annoy the U.S.. But we just feel that there is another option, another way, another more normal way, a less dramatic way than acting, than war, and that we have to go through that path. Until we realize that we have come to a dead end, but that isn't the case.

Q. And what is, for you, a dead end? I would like to know what your "red line" is.

President Chirac. Our red line is the inspector's report. For as long that the inspectors are telling us that there is cooperation, that it can be improved but that there is sufficient cooperation and that they can go on securing the disarmament of Iraq, that it isn't a question of years but a question of a couple of months ... for as long as the inspectors go on telling us that, there is no reason why we should change.

Q. So why is it that you have been unable to reach a compromise with the United States and Britain and Spain, let's say, to say, "Let's talk about what the inspectors have said—a month, two months, three months—and come to an agreement?" rather than see this Security Council completely divided and chaos on the world stage now?

President Chirac. Well, I do hope that we can have that discussion, that debate. We are ready to do so. I even suggested that there be a summit meeting of the Security Council with heads of state and government so that we can discuss and debate these issues without difficulties to see what we can do, what is in the interest of security, of peace. What is the in the interest of the common ideals and actions we need, the fight against terrorism, the fight against proliferation. See what our common interest is.

But you will no doubt have noticed that my proposal to discuss these issues in serenity was made clearly, especially as it was done on the basis of a unanimous Security Council resolution. But nobody has taken up my proposal. And I do hope, to answer your previous question, I do hope that in the Azores the three heads of state and government that seem to lean toward war will bear in mind the unanimity of the Security Council.

Q. Do you believe that Saddam Hussein has weapons of mass destruction; for instance, chemical or biological weapons?

President Chirac. Well, I don't know. I have no evidence to support that. But what we can say today, listening to what [International Atomic Energy Agency Director General Mohamed] ElBaradei is saying and his expert team, it seems that there are no nuclear weapons or no nuclear programs that would lead to the construction of nuclear weapons. That is something that the inspectors seem to be sure of.

As for weapons of mass destruction, bacteriological, biological, chemical, we don't know. And that is precisely what the inspectors' mandate is all about. They have to go with their work to find these weapon if there are any and then destroy them. And the inspectors are telling us that they can do that work. So when at one point or another they tell us that they can't or can't anymore go on doing so, then we will have to consider other options, including war. But it just isn't the case today.

So rushing into war, rushing into battle today is clearly disproportionate and inadequate given our goals. As I said, that goal is to disarm Iraq, and everybody agrees on that.

Q. The fact is, Mr. President, that in America many people think it's just because you are a friend, a pal of Saddam Hussein. That you have had long contacts with him, that you help build the nuclear reactor there, that there are the oil deals. You invited Saddam Hussein to France. There is a famous picture of you toasting him. They think it is about a personal and a business relationship.

President Chirac. That's myth, so to speak. Or controversy, if you will. I did indeed meet President Saddam Hussein when he was vice president in 1974 and '75, or '75 and '76. Never since. But in those days everybody had excellent relations with Saddam Hussein and with the Baath party. In those days it was seen as a modern party. Everybody had contacts with them.

I have not had any contacts ever since, and that is not something that everybody can say. Some important figures of the current U.S. administration had contacts with Saddam Hussein as late as 1983. I haven't. So we should not delve into controversy.

As for our interests, let us be clear about it. The trade of France with Iraq accounts for 0.2 percent of total French trade. So basically we have no economic interests in Iraq. Iraq isn't even in the list of the 60 largest trading partners of France. Not even the 60 largest.

As for oil import, they only account for 8 percent of Iraqi exports. The U.S. is importing five or six times more Iraqi petrol and Iraqi oil than we are importing. So these alleged motivations are clearly not serious motivations.

Q. There have also been persistent allegations that Saddam Hussein put money into one of your electoral campaigns. How do you respond to that?

President Chirac. It's preposterous, really ... Anything can be said about anyone. As we say in French, "The larger it is, the more likely people will believe in it." I think really that is what we are talking about.

Q. The New York Times has reported that there is evidence that French companies [are involved] in transferring materials for use in long-range Iraqi missiles. Are you aware of any French companies being involved in such an effort, and if so, what would you do to them?

President Chirac. The New York Times is a serious newspaper, so as soon as I read this I led an inquiry into it. I will confirm the official statement, as published after this inquiry by the French foreign ministry. France and French companies have never endorsed or even provided such material to Iraq. So I am clearly dispelling this allegation. This too is insecure information. Or again, maybe controversial.

Q. Can I ask you again about the nuclear reactor [built by Iraq with French assistance and destroyed in an Israeli air raid in 1981] at Osirak? You know, a lot of people called it "Os-Chirac", as you know. In retrospect, do you regret that it was destroyed, given that it could have been used to form nuclear weapons?

President Chirac. Well, this reactor was a civilian reactor. It was a civilian power plant and it was only going to produce energy. I don't think it could have been the link or the basis for nuclear technology or a military nuclear program. This being said, events such as we know them, it was destroyed, so the issue is no longer.

But in those days, all of the major democracies, all of them, each and every one of them, had contacts and trade and exchanges with Iraq, including on weapons. Even weapons of mass destruction sometimes, including bacteriological, biological weapons.

So we shouldn't come back to the past on these issues. But we shouldn't either pinpoint France or point the finger toward France, that had limited its actions to helping Iraq to produce the energy it needed to light the country.

Q. Which countries are you specifically talking about?

President Chirac. All the major democracies. Each and every one of them.

Q. Mr. President, you know that since you have taken the position you have there has been a massive backlash in the United States at almost every level of society. From the leader of the House of Representatives, who is talking about initiating sanctions against France in some form or another, to restaurants in the Congress which have renamed their frites. Their french fries are now being called "freedom fries." People feel ... they are asking, "What happened to our friendship? Does France remember who liberated them? Why is France betraying us?"

President Chirac. Two things: First of all, we shouldn't think that some excesses, either in the media or in the political world, are the same as facts on the ground. We have not noticed any kind of bad will from U.S. consumers vis-a-vis French products.

I really do think that, apart from the froth we can see for the moment, the Americans know that deep down, and they know it well, that the French, even before the 19th century, that the French have always been their friends. Always. Whenever there were difficult circumstances the French were side-by-side with the Americans.

The French don't either forget what was done in both world wars by the Americans. It is really in their minds and also deep down in their hearts. I think that the relationship between the French and the Americans, the human relationship, is a relationship of friendship. Of love even, I would say.

So really, it isn't going to change because of the current events, because it is so deeply felt by our peoples. It is a common understanding of man, the freedom of democracy, of esteem, and of acknowledgement for one another also.

So in this respect, I am not worried. I have regular contacts with many Americans, and I haven't felt, despite the intensity of the media campaign, I have not felt in them a rift or a breach in this feeling of friendship between our two countries.

I don't think either that France or Europe are calling into question an essential basis of our multiplied world of tomorrow, the trans-Atlantic link. We are all deeply committed to this trans-Atlantic relationship. It is all the more important in our view because it clearly fits into our understanding of tomorrow's world, a multi-poled world.

So really there is nothing that should bring us to confront one another, culturally, politically or in our understanding of the world. There is one specific issue on which we disagree and on which the American administration had to be very forceful and firm, and we just feel that it is going too far.

When there are people that I am just not interested in, I won't really worry. But if there is a friend or somebody I dearly love, and if you see that they are going down the wrong path, and if you feel, at least, that that is the case, then friendship demands that we tell that friend, that we warn him.

I have some experience on the international political stage, and I am telling my American friends: beware. Be careful. Think it over seriously before you make an act that is not necessary and that can be very dangerous, especially in the fight against international terrorism that we are really working hard on together.

Q. Mr. President, you talk about friendship. You talk about a relationship almost based on love. Yet some of your own commentators here are saying that this story has entered the realm of psychodrama of divorce. They say that you feel that you can challenge the United States at no cost, even when [Secretary of State Colin] Powell is saying that the threat of a veto is an unfriendly, even hostile, act, and that it could have serious consequences, long-term consequences for your relations. Do you accept that it is a potential problem for the future, and what do you think you can do to repair the damage?

President Chirac. I do not think it will be really an issue in the future. As you have rightly pointed out in citing other sources, it indeed a psychodrama. And psychodrama is all about theatre and drama. It is very superficial. It isn't deep-rooted. And I have said, for all the reasons I mentioned earlier, the relationship between both our countries will not really be affected by all these knee-jerk reactions. So I am not worried.

Q. If war starts, if diplomacy totally collapses, what will your posture be? What will France's posture be then? Will you wish British and U.S. troops speedy victory?

President Chirac. Of course. Of course. The speedier the victory, the smaller the damage is, both human damages and material damages. So of course we wish for speed of victory. But what I hope for is a comprehensive victory, and hope that that can be secured without firing one shot. And I think we can do that. We can do that through inspectors, because inspections are working. Inspections can bring about the victory; that is to say the completely elimination of weapons of mass destruction in Iraq without firing one shot and using war.

Q. What material support will France give to this war, if it happens, to the United States and Britain?

President Chirac. I can't tell yet. I don't know what Britain or the U.S. might ask of us. For the moment the U.S. have only asked for authorization to fly over the French territory. That is something that I have indeed granted, because we are friends and allies, as I have said. Even though we disagree and I disapprove of—seriously disapprove of—war today.

Q. If it should come to a point where more allied troops are needed, would France consider sending troops?

President Chirac. It isn't a topical issue, really.

Q. You have studied in the United States, you have worked briefly in the United States. You profess to love the United States. As I said, many Americans feel betrayed. Do you have anything to say in English, which I know you speak, to Americans tonight?

President Chirac. Unfortunately, my English has become very rusty. In front of such a large audience I wouldn't want to dent the language of Shakespeare and mispronounce it.

But what I can say, from the bottom of my heart, to the American people is that we have to go beyond and overcome the passions of the day. We have to have an understanding, a view of the world, have a historical understanding and knowledge also.

I think that the two problems that mankind has to deal with today at the beginning of the 21st century have to be given very clear consideration. We shouldn't react superficially or have knee-jerk reactions to it. We have indeed to refuse and reject confrontations, useless confrontations. War, or the shock of civilization or the shock of religions is worse than anything. It is only through dialogue and respect for one another, debate and discussion, that we can have a serene world, a more balanced world, a less war-like world.

The second issue, which is also a very serious issue that we have to consider, although it is not often mentioned, that is the serious and soon-to-be irreversible depletion of our planet's resources if we go on exploiting it as we are. That indeed is a very real problem that we should discuss together on the basis of scientific evidence and scientific forecasts, to try and amend the situation and put things right. To make amends for our past madness.

That is what I want to tell the American people. That we have to work together on these issues to bring about peace, dialogue and respect for one another across the world, and at the same time make sure that we have a sustainable use of our planet's resources so that our children can also benefit from it and live in serenity.

And I just want to tell them also, because you want absolutely me to say a few words in English... I want to tell them also that France and I have always been friends of the United States, and this will not change. We are very, very attached to this situation where 200 [years] of common life with great help given to us by the Americans, and before by us to the Americans, this cannot be hidden by a problem of a few weeks and different views on a specific problem. We have the same goal, the same will, but we have not the same way to go to that goal.

Q. On the eve of what looks like war, what do you have to say to President Bush, who you call a friend?

President Chirac. I just want to tell him I don't share his views, that I don't approve of his initiative, and of course I hope that things run as smoothly as possible… peaceful disarmament … if we have to have war there are as few dramas as possible.

Q. There is a notion being floated right now that the Americans might give a week deadline for Saddam Hussein to leave Iraq, and thus end this crisis. Would you accept that?

President Chirac. I said a long time ago that the best service Saddam Hussein could give his people—and I'm sure that as a leader he loves his people—was to just disappear from the scene. And that we could discuss, of course, the ways in which he could leave, even in the Security Council. But I think that given the current situation, a few attempts have been made to secure his departure, but that was unfortunately unsuccessful. I'm sorry to see that it was unsuccessful.

Q. Mr. President, is this as much about France trying to restrain American power?

President Chirac. Why are we always coming back to these old myths? Why would France want to restrain American power? And even if France wanted to do so, how could we? It's an absurd line of reasoning. It is absolutely not reasonable [or] realistic. I am trying to be more serious and more honest of our assessment of things and world affairs today. It is ridiculous, really.

Q. Here, many commentators, many newspapers have been hailing you as a hero. They have even said your position should make you qualify for a Nobel Peace Prize. Of course, in America, in Britain, they call you an appeaser. That you are appeasing this terrible dictator who may have weapons of mass destruction.

President Chirac. You know, about Saddam Hussein, I feel the same as George Bush or Tony Blair and even many other heads of government, whatever their position in the current situation. So really it is not a question of passing a judgment on an individual, on a regime, on his dictatorship. Indeed it is a dictatorship, one of the worst dictatorships, but it is not the only dictatorship. There is a rather long list of countries where there are dictatorships, and if we were going to wage war without using all the possible options to get rid of these dictatorships, then we are going to have a lot of work.

But really I don't think we are appeasing this dictator. I think the more we threaten him the more he will react as a wounded animal.

Again, every day there one more step toward cooperation done by Iraq. Maybe it is insufficient. Maybe we should go faster to secure disarmament by inspections. But I think we have to go along with the inspectors and follow that for as long as the inspectors can work, and until they tell us, "Look, we can't go any further," or "We've done it." And I think we can.

Q. Just one last question so that I fully understand here. At one point you said the presence of so many troops is what has brought him this far—and it is further than where he has been for many years. So why didn't you send troops to join that threat, and perhaps this would have been over much quicker?

President Chirac. Once again, I think that, given the current situation, the Americans do not need any assistance. Those who can help, the British, for instanced, are just making an additional contribution. But the strength, the might of the U.S., the land forces, the aerial might and the navy was enough to exercise pressure by itself.

But as I said, France considered that there was another path that we could down that was more in line with the interests and was more likely to reach this goal we wanted to have, but also which is more in line with our understanding of the world that I mentioned earlier. As I said, this objective is to limit as much as possible ... we shouldn't start a war if it isn't completely necessary ... France is the first contributor of troops abroad in NATO ... we have not come to that point.

Remarks by President Bush, British Prime Minister Blair, Spanish Prime Minister Aznar, and Portuguese Prime Minister Barroso, March 16, 2003

President Bush, Prime Minister Blair, Prime Minister Aznar and Prime Minister Barroso made their remarks at a press conference during their summit in the Azores, Portugal.

Prime Minister Barroso. Good afternoon, ladies and gentlemen. I am very pleased to welcome here in the Azores the leaders of three friends and allied countries, the United States, Spain and United Kingdom. President Bush, Prime Minister Aznar, and Prime Minister Tony Blair.

This meeting in the Azores also shows the importance of transatlantic relations, and also shows the solidarity among our countries. Actually, these agreements have approved two statements, one statement on transatlantic relations, and a declarative statement on Iraq.

We have joined this initiative and we organized it here in the Azores because we thought this was the last opportunity for a political solution—and this is how we see it, this is the last possibility for a political solution to the problem. Maybe it's a small chance, a small possibility, but even if it's one in one million, it's always worthwhile fighting for a political solution. And I think this is the message that we can get from this Atlantic summit.

As I was saying, for my English-speaking guests, I'll speak English now. First of all, let me say, welcome, George Bush, to Europe. I think it's important that we meet here, in a European country, in Portugal, but in this territory of Azores that is halfway between the continent of Europe and the continent of America. I think it's not only logistically convenient, it has a special political meaning—the beautiful meaning of our friendship and our commitment to our shared values.

So welcome to all of you. Welcome to you. And I now give the floor to President George Bush.

President Bush. Jose, thank you very much for your hospitality. You've done a great job on such short notice. And I'm honored to be standing to here with you and two other friends as we work toward a great cause, and that is peace and security in this world.

We've had a really good discussion. We've been doing a lot of phone talking and it was good to get together and to visit and to talk. And we concluded that tomorrow is a moment of truth for the world. Many nations have voiced a commitment to peace and security. And now they must demonstrate that commitment to peace and security in the only effective way, by supporting the immediate and unconditional disarmament of Saddam Hussein.

The dictator of Iraq and his weapons of mass destruction are a threat to the security of free nations. He is a danger to his neighbors. He's a sponsor of terrorism. He's an obstacle to progress in the Middle East. For decades he has been the cruel, cruel oppressor of the Iraq people.

On this very day 15 years ago, Saddam Hussein launched a chemical weapons attack on the Iraqi village of Halabja. With a single order the Iraqi regime killed thousands of men and women and children, without mercy or without shame. Saddam Hussein has proven he is capable of any crime. We must not permit his crimes to reach across the world.

Saddam Hussein has a history of mass murder. He possesses the weapons of mass murder. He agrees—he agreed to disarm Iraq of these weapons as a condition for ending the Gulf War over a decade ago. The United Nations Security Council, in Resolution 1441, has declared Iraq in material breach of its longstanding obligations, demanding once again Iraq's full and immediate disarmament, and promised serious consequences if the regime refused to comply. That resolution was passed unanimously and its logic is inescapable; the Iraqi regime will disarm itself, or the Iraqi regime will be disarmed by force. And the regime has not disarmed itself.

Action to remove the threat from Iraq would also allow the Iraqi people to build a better future for their society. And Iraq's liberation would be the beginning, not the end, of our commitment to its people. We will supply humanitarian relief, bring economic sanctions to a swift close, and work for the long-term recovery of Iraq's economy. We'll make sure that Iraq's natural resources are used for the benefit of their owners, the Iraqi people.

Iraq has the potential to be a great nation. Iraq's people are skilled and educated. We'll push as quickly as possible for an Iraqi interim authority to draw upon the talents of Iraq's people to rebuild their nation. We're committed to the goal of a unified Iraq, with democratic institutions of which members of all ethnic and religious groups are treated with dignity and respect.

To achieve this vision, we will work closely with the international community, including the United Nations and our coalition partners. If military force is required, we'll quickly seek new Security Council resolutions to encourage broad participation in the process of helping the Iraqi people to build a free Iraq.

Crucial days lie ahead for the world. I want to thank the leaders here today, and many others, for stepping forward and taking leadership, and showing their resolve in the cause of peace and the cause of security.

Jose Maria.

Prime Minister Aznar. Good evening everyone. I would firstly like to thank the Prime Minister, Jose Durao, for his hospitality and welcome, which I particularly am grateful for. And I'm very pleased to be in the Azores once again.

I have short remarks on our debate on this situation and on the documents we've agreed on during today's meeting. I'd first like to refer to our document on Atlantic solidarity. We have renewed Atlantic commitment on our common values and principles, in favor of democracy, freedom and the rule of law.

We understand that the expression of this commitment is essential, by way of guarantee of peace, security and international freedom. And I honestly believe that there is no other alternative to the expression of the Atlantic commitment in terms of security. We are committed on a day-to-day fight against new threats, such as terrorism, weapons of mass destruction, and tyrannic regimes that do not comply with international law. They threaten all of us, and we must all act, consequently.

This transatlantic link, this transatlantic solidarity has always been, is, and should continue to be, in my opinion, a great European commitment, and as such, amongst other things, we express it this way—without this commitment, today's Europe could not be understood. And without that commitment, it would be very difficult to picture the Europe of tomorrow.

So I would like to invite our friends, our allies, to leave aside any circumstantial differences and to work together seriously for that commitment of democracy, freedom and peace, so that this becomes a commitment of us all.

We've agreed on launching, on boosting the Middle East peace process, and on our vision that that peace process has to accommodate with all necessary security guarantees and putting an end to terrorism. And this should end with the peaceful coexistence of two states, an independent Palestinian state and the Israeli state.

In view of the situation created by Iraq, with their continued non-compliance of international law, I would like to remind you that we all said before we came here that we were not coming to the Azores to make a declaration of war, that we were coming after having made every possible effort, after having made this effort, continuing to make this effort, to working to achieve the greatest possible agreement, and for international law to be respected and for U.N. resolutions to be respected.

And we would like to say that we are aware of the fact that this is the last opportunity—the last opportunity expressed in Resolution 1441, adopted unanimously by the Security Council, and that being aware that this is the last opportunity, we are also making the last effort. And we are ready to make this last effort of the very many efforts we've been making throughout these last weeks and months.

We are well aware of the international world public opinion, of its concern. And we are also very well aware of our responsibilities and obligations. If Saddam Hussein wants to disarm and avoid the serious consequences that he has been warned about by the United Nations, he can do so. And nothing in our document, nor in our statement, can prevent him from doing so, if he wants to. So his is the sole responsibility.

Prime Minister Blair. Thank you, Jose Maria. Thank you, Jose, for hosting us today. And I think it's just worth returning to the key point, which is our responsibility to uphold the will of the United Nations set out in Resolution 1441 last November. And for four and a half months, now, we've worked hard to get Saddam to cooperate fully, unconditionally, as that resolution demanded.

Even some days ago we were prepared to set out clear tests that allowed us to conclude whether he was cooperating fully or not, with a clear ultimatum to him if he refused to do so. And the reason we approached it in that is that that is what we agreed in Resolution 1441. This was his final opportunity; he had to disarm unconditionally. Serious consequences would follow if he failed to do so.

And this is really the impasse that we have, because some say there should be no ultimatum, no authorization of force in any new U.N. resolution; instead, more discussion in the event of noncompliance. But the truth is that without a credible ultimatum authorizing force in the event of noncompliance, then more discussion is just more delay, with Saddam remaining armed with weapons of mass destruction and continuing a brutal, murderous regime in Iraq.

And this game that he is playing is, frankly, a game that he has played over the last 12 years. Disarmament never happens. But instead, the international community is drawn into some perpetual negotiation, gestures designed to divide the international community, but never real and concrete cooperation leading to disarmament.

And there's not a single person on the Security Council that doubts the fact he is not fully cooperating today. Nobody, even those who disagree with the position that we have outlined, is prepared to say there is full cooperation, as 1441 demanded.

Not a single interview has taken place outside of Iraq, even though 1441 provided for it. Still, no proper production or evidence of the destruction, or, for example,—just to take one example, the 10,000 liters of anthrax that the inspectors just a week ago said was unaccounted for. And that is why it is so important that the international community, at this time, gives a strong and unified message.

And I have to say that I really believe that had we given that strong message sometime ago, Saddam might have realized that the games had to stop. So now we have reached the point of decision, and we make a final appeal for there to be that strong, unified message on behalf of the international community that lays down a clear ultimatum to Saddam that authorizes force if he continues to defy the will of the whole of the international community set out in 1441.

We will do all we can in the short time that remains to make a final round of contacts, to see whether there is a way through this impasse. But we are in the final stages, because, after 12 years of failing to disarm him, now is the time when we have to decide.

Two other points, briefly, on the documents that we've put before you. The first is the—President Aznar was just saying to you a moment ago on the transatlantic alliance is, I think, very important. Some of you will have heard me say this before, but let me just repeat it. I believe that Europe and America should stand together on the big issues of the day. I think it is a tragedy when we don't. And that transatlantic alliance is strong and we need to strengthen it still further.

And secondly, we've set out for you that should it come to conflict, we make a pledge to the people of Iraq. As President Bush was just saying to you a moment or two ago, it is the people of Iraq who are the primary victims of Saddam: the thousands of children that die needlessly every year; the people locked up in his prisons or executed simply for showing disagreement with the regime; a country that is potentially prosperous reduced to poverty; 60 percent of the population reliant on food aid.

And what we say is that we will protect Iraq's territorial integrity; we will support representative government that unites Iraq on the democratic basis of human rights and the rule of law; that we will help Iraq rebuild—and not rebuild because of the problems of conflict, where if it comes to that, we will do everything we can to minimize the suffering of the Iraqi people, but rebuild Iraq because of the appalling legacy that the rule of Saddam has left the Iraqi people—and in particular, Iraq's natural resources remain the property of the people of Iraq. And that wealth should be used for the Iraqi people. It is theirs, and will remain so, administered by the U.N. in the way we set out.

Finally, on the Middle East peace process, I welcome very much the statement that President Bush made the other day. I think it's important now. He said he wanted a partner on the Palestinian side. I think the coming appointment of Abu Mazen is so important there. It allows us to take this process forward. The road map give us the way forward. The appointment of Abu Mazen gives us the right partner to take this forward. And I believe that that will demonstrate, and it's important to demonstrate, in particular at this time, that our approach to people in the Middle East, in that troubled region is indeed even-handed. And all of us will work to make sure that that vision of the Middle East, two states, Israel confident of its security, a Palestinian state that is viable, comes about and is made reality.

Q. I was asking the Portuguese Prime Minister, how does he see the result of this summit. Does the Prime Minister think that starting now, Portugal has more responsibilities with this war that seems to be inevitable?

Prime Minister Barroso. The results of the summit, as I described them and as all the other heads of state and government said it, too, this summit is—this is the last opportunity for a political solution to this very serious problem for the international community. This has been said here. It's been said here that tomorrow—tomorrow we'll start with these last initiatives towards a political solution. And it's for that reason I am very, very happy with the results of this summit.

Now, coming to our responsibility in case there is a conflict, I must say that the responsibility falls entirely on the dictator Saddam Hussein. He bears the entire responsibility because he has not respected for all of these years international law and consistently violated the U.N. resolutions. And in that case, if there is a conflict, I want to repeat it once more, Portugal will be next—side by side with his allies. And the fact that we are here today in the Azores with the United States, with Spain and with the U.K., this is very significant.

As it's been said here before, the transatlantic relationship is very, very important, not only for Europe and for the U.S., but it's very important for the whole world. I remember a few days ago, Kofi Annan in the European conference in Brussels, said the same thing—he said this is very important. It's very important for Europe and the U.S. to remain united and not separate, because the world needs the U.S. and Europe working together towards the same direction, in the same sense—not only about the security, but also fighting under-development and all the other tasks that fall to the international community.

Q. When you say tomorrow is the moment of truth, does that mean tomorrow is the last day that the resolution can be voted up or down, and at the end of the day tomorrow, one way or another the diplomatic window has close?

President Bush. That's what I'm saying.

Q. Thank you, sir. And now for the question—

President Bush. And now for your question?

Q. That being the case, regardless—

President Bush. That being my answer—

Q. Regardless of whether the resolution goes up or down or gets withdrawn, it seems to me you're going to be facing a moment of truth. And given that you've already said you don't think there's very much chance Saddam Hussein is going to disarm, and given that you say you don't think there's very much chance he's going to go to go into exile, aren't we going to war?

President Bush. Tomorrow is the day that we will determine whether or not diplomacy can work. And we sat and visited about this issue, about how best to spend our time between now and tomorrow. And as Prime Minister Blair said, we'll be working the phones and talking to our partners and talking to those who may now clearly understand the objective, and we'll see how it goes tomorrow.

Saddam Hussein can leave the country, if he's interested in peace. You see, the decision is his to make. And it's been his to make all along as to whether or not there's the use of the military. He got to decide whether he was going to disarm, and he didn't. He can decide whether he wants to leave the country. These are his decisions to make. And thus far he has made bad decisions.

Q. I understand that if tomorrow is the day for taking the final decision, that means that you consider that there's no possible way out through the United Nations because a majority does not support a war action. I would like to know, Mr. Blair, Mr. Bush, whether in that military offensive you count on many countries, whether it's going to be the U.K. and the U.S. carrying out the military offensive? I understand from what Mr. Blair that you're counting on the U.N. for the reconstruction. Are you going to look for other countries through the United Nations?

And for Mr. Aznar, what is Spain's participation in that military offensive, in addition to your political support?

President Bush. Resolution 1441, which was unanimously approved, that said Saddam Hussein would unconditionally disarm, and if he didn't, there would be serious consequences. The United Nations Security Council looked at the issue four and a half months ago and voted unanimously to say: Disarm immediately and unconditionally, and if you don't, there are going to be serious consequences. The world has spoken. And it did it in a unified voice.

Prime Minister Blair. The issue is very simply this, that we cannot have a situation where what happens through the United Nations, having agreed to 1441, having said there would be serious consequences if he does not cooperate fully and unconditionally, what we cannot have is a situation where we simply go back for endless discussion.

Now, we have provided the right diplomatic way through this, which is to lay down a clear ultimatum to Saddam: Cooperate or face disarmament by force. And that is entirely within the logic, the letter, the spirit of 1441. And that is why—all the way through we have tried to provide a diplomatic solution. After over four and a half months since we passed Resolution 1441, we're now three months on from the declaration that Saddam on the 8th of December that not a single person in the international community—not one—believes was an honest declaration of what he had. And yet, 1441 said, the first step of cooperation was to make an honest declaration.

So when people say haven't we exhausted all the diplomatic avenues, we tried exhausting. But understand from our perspective and from the perspective of the security of the world, we cannot simply go back to the Security Council, for this discussion to be superseded by that discussion, to be superseded by another discussion. That's what's happened for 12 years. That's why he's still got the weapons of mass destruction. We have to come to the point of decision. And that really is what the next period of time is going to be about.

Prime Minister Aznar. Well, I would like to say that this statement we're making today, as we've all said, it's a last chance, one last attempt to reach the greatest possible consensus amongst ourselves. And I can assure all of you that we've made—we have all made—enormous efforts, and we're going to continue making these efforts in order to try to reach an agreement, to reach a solution.

We have our own worry, our own responsibility to make U.N. resolutions be abided by. If the Security Council unanimously adopts a resolution—Resolution 1441—giving one last opportunity to disarm to someone who has weapons of mass destruction and we know he has used them, the Security Council cannot, one year after the other, wait for its resolutions to be implemented. That would be the best way to do away with it altogether. And it could do away with all the United Nations' credibility. And we honestly don't want that to happen.

To me, there is no—you cannot have the same distance between illegality and impunity. And neither Saddam Hussein, nor any other tyrant with weapons of mass destruction can set the rules for international law and the international community.

Q. I'm from the BBC. Can I ask, first of all, Prime Minister Blair—you said that you want a second resolution to be put down and voted on. Could we be clear; is that what's going to happen tomorrow, under all circumstances?

And either way—also, if I may, for President Bush—if you don't get that second resolution, what is the future for the United Nations? You talked about Saddam Hussein dividing world community. Surely, he succeeded.

Prime Minister Blair. Well, on your last point, I think this is one of the things that is tragic about this situation, that Saddam plays these games and we carry on allowing him to play them. Now, we will do, in the next period of time, with respect to the resolution, what we believe to be in the interest of the U.N.

But I would say why I think it is so important that even now, at this late stage, we try to get the United Nations to be the root of resolving this—because the threat is there and everyone accepts it: the threat of weapons of mass destruction, the threat of weapons of mass destruction in the hands of terrorists who will cause maximum damage to our people. Everybody accepts the disarmament of Saddam has to happen. Everybody accepts that he was supposed to cooperate fully with the inspectors. Everybody accepts that he is not doing so.

So, whatever the tactics within the U.N.—and that's something we can decide— whatever those tactics, the key point of principle is this: that when we came together last November and laid down Resolution 1441, now is the moment when we decide whether we meant it and it was his final opportunity to disarm, or face serious consequences—or whether, alternatively, we're simply going to drag out the diplomatic process forever. And that's why I say it's the point of decision.

Q. Vote or not?

President Bush. I was the guy that said they ought to vote. And one country voted—at least showed their cards, I believe. It's an old Texas expression, show your cards, when you're playing poker. France showed their cards. After I said what I said, they said they were going to veto anything that held Saddam to account. So cards have been played. And we'll just have to take an assessment after tomorrow to determine what that card meant.

Let me say something about the U.N. It's a very important organization. That's why I went there on September the 12th, 2002, to give the speech, the speech that called the U.N. into account, that said if you're going to pass resolutions, let's make sure your words mean something. Because I understand the wars of the 21st century are going to require incredible international cooperation. We're going to have to cooperate to cut the money of the terrorists, and the ability for nations, dictators who have weapons of mass destruction to provide training and perhaps weapons to terrorist organizations. We need to cooperate, and we are. Our countries up here are cooperating incredibly well.

And the U.N. must mean something. Remember Rwanda, or Kosovo. The U.N. didn't do its job. And we hope tomorrow the U.N. will do its job. If not, all of us need to step back and try to figure out how to make the U.N. work better as we head into the 21st century. Perhaps one way will be, if we use military force, in the post-Saddam

Iraq the U.N. will definitely need to have a role. And that way it can begin to get its legs, legs of responsibility back.

But it's important for the U.N. to be able to function well if we're going to keep the peace. And I will work hard to see to it that at least from our perspective, that the U.N. is able to be—able to be a responsibility body, and when it says something, it means it, for the sake of peace and for the sake of the security, for the capacity to win the war of—the first war of the 21st century, which is the war against terrorism and weapons of mass destruction in the hands of dictators.

Joint Statement of the Atlantic Summit, March 16, 2003

The following statement was released by the leaders attending the Atlantic Summit in the Azores, Portugal.

Iraq's talented people, rich culture, and tremendous potential have been hijacked by Saddam Hussein. His brutal regime has reduced a country with a long and proud history to an international pariah that oppresses its citizens, started two wars of aggression against its neighbors, and still poses a grave threat to the security of its region and the world.

Saddam's defiance of United Nations Security Council resolutions demanding the disarmament of his nuclear, chemical, biological, and long-range missile capacity has led to sanctions on Iraq and has undermined the authority of the U.N. For 12 years, the international community has tried to persuade him to disarm and thereby avoid military conflict, most recently through the unanimous adoption of UNSCR 1441. The responsibility is his. If Saddam refuses even now to cooperate fully with the United Nations, he brings on himself the serious consequences foreseen in UNSCR 1441 and previous resolutions.

In these circumstances, we would undertake a solemn obligation to help the Iraqi people build a new Iraq at peace with itself and its neighbors. The Iraqi people deserve to be lifted from insecurity and tyranny, and freed to determine for themselves the future of their country. We envisage a unified Iraq with its territorial integrity respected. All the Iraqi people—its rich mix of Sunni and Shiite Arabs, Kurds, Turkomen, Assyrians, Chaldeans, and all others—should enjoy freedom, prosperity, and equality in a united country. We will support the Iraqi people's aspirations for a representative government that upholds human rights and the rule of law as cornerstones of democracy.

We will work to prevent and repair damage by Saddam Hussein's regime to the natural resources of Iraq and pledge to protect them as a national asset of and for the Iraqi people. All Iraqis should share the wealth generated by their national economy. We will seek a swift end to international sanctions, and support an international reconstruction program to help Iraq achieve real prosperity and reintegrate into the global community.

We will fight terrorism in all its forms. Iraq must never again be a haven for terrorists of any kind.

In achieving this vision, we plan to work in close partnership with international institutions, including the United Nations; our Allies and partners; and bilateral donors. If conflict occurs, we plan to seek the adoption, on an urgent basis, of new

United Nations Security Council resolutions that would affirm Iraq's territorial integrity, ensure rapid delivery of humanitarian relief, and endorse an appropriate post-conflict administration for Iraq. We will also propose that the Secretary General be given authority, on an interim basis, to ensure that the humanitarian needs of the Iraqi people continue to be met through the Oil for Food program.

Any military presence, should it be necessary, will be temporary and intended to promote security and elimination of weapons of mass destruction; the delivery of humanitarian aid; and the conditions for the reconstruction of Iraq. Our commitment to support the people of Iraq will be for the long term.

We call upon the international community to join with us in helping to realize a better future for the Iraqi people.

Remarks by Secretary of State Powell, March 16, 2003

Q. Mr. Secretary, why are you not in the Azores?

Secretary Powell. The President is meeting with his fellow leaders in the Azores. Jack Straw the British Foreign Secretary and I, and Ana Palacio the Spanish Foreign Minister and I, are staying in touch with the situation in the U.N. in New York.

We've got new proposals coming in from the French, the Germans and the Russians that we have to deal with. I have already spoken to Foreign Secretary Straw early this morning and so it's a distribution of effort.

We're well aware of what's going on in the Azores and the President and I had good conversations on Friday of what we should expect just after the meetings.

Q. Mr. Secretary, with the French and Russian threat to veto a second resolution on Iraq, do you think there is still room for diplomacy at the Azores summit?

Secretary Powell. Well, that's why the three leaders decided to gather in the Azores with the Portuguese Prime Minister serving as host for them. The leaders will be talking about this issue. And they will have to make a judgment as to whether or not Turkey is coming down to the talks here as well as [*inaudible*] can be done.

But with the French, certainly, and the Russians to some extent, they asked not to be counted. The French have said they would veto any of the resolutions that might bring a solution to this crisis, that they would veto the resolution that is before the Council now, and when the United Kingdom tried to modify that resolution to make it more acceptable, the French said they would veto that, too. So we know where they stand [*inaudible*], so we'll see what comes out of the meeting in the Azores.

Q. Mr. Secretary, apparently out of France and Germany two suggestions today, first, on Tuesday the Council will meet in New York on a ministerial-level. Could you comment on that? And a second, President Chirac as a compromise suggested a 30-day delay.

Secretary Powell. On the ministerial meeting, I received the statement that the three nations issued yesterday. To the best of my knowledge, the Council and the President and the Permanent Representative of Guinea have not decided whether or not there would be a ministerial-level meeting or when Dr. Blix will be providing his report. It could be Tuesday and I will just have to wait and see what is on the schedule and make a judgment as to whether or not I will be attending or whether or not to attend.

With respect to the report that I've just heard that President Chirac has suggested a 30-day period of time, I can say nothing about it because I haven't had it confirmed and I don't know exactly whether President Chirac has or not.

Q. Mr. Secretary, if I could ask you to put your general's stars on again for a moment, the conditions over in the Gulf right now—and much is being made of the conditions over there right now—what kind of problems do they pose for the fighting forces as they get ready?

Secretary Powell. I think too much is being made about whether or not it's getting too hot or not. Troops from the United States armed forces and the armed forces of the United Kingdom are well trained, well conditioned and obviously if it gets very hot it may affect how you conduct operations, but it doesn't mean operations aren't conducted. The last I heard, it still gets rather cool at night.

Remarks by Secretary of State Powell, March 16, 2003

Secretary Colin Powell was interviewed on Fox News Sunday by Tony Snow.

Q. Secretary Powell, if the President issues an ultimatum, what sort of ultimatum would it be?

Secretary Powell. Well, let's wait and see what the ultimatum would be if there's going to be an ultimatum. Right now we're focusing on these leaders getting together in Lajes just to talk about the diplomatic situation and to make a judgment as to whether the diplomatic window is closing. And that's a refocusing on, it's not a war council and ultimatums are not the issue today. The issue today is has the diplomatic track run its course?

Q. One diplomatic effort apparently the United States has tried is to get word to Iraq that if Saddam Hussein and certain members of his inner circle were to leave the country, they could still avert war. Are we still trying to transmit such a message to Baghdad?

Secretary Powell. I think that's a fair statement. If Saddam Hussein, his sons and a number of other top leaders were to leave and a more responsible leadership come in, a leadership that is determined to get rid of its weapons of mass destruction as they are supposed to and start to provide a better life for the Iraqi people, then a war certainly could be averted.

Q. Are nations—do we know of nations that are willing, right now, to take on Saddam Hussein and that inner circle?

Secretary Powell. In terms of "take on," do you mean provide a haven for them?

Q. In other words—correct.

Secretary Powell. I think there are nations that would be willing to do that as their contribution to avoiding a war.

Q. And are we in ongoing discussions with those nations?

Secretary Powell. No, I wouldn't comment on what those diplomatic efforts might be like.

Q. Now, there's also talk, obviously, of a second resolution. The British were going to table one this week. On the other hand, it looks like the votes are not there. With the promise of a French veto, is there any chance that resolution is going to see the light of day?

Secretary Powell. Well, as you know, there—a resolution was tabled Friday before last by the United Kingdom with Spain and the United States co-sponsoring it. That's why these gentlemen are assembling in Lajes. They are the co-sponsors of this resolution.

Unfortunately, the French said they would veto such a resolution. Last week the British tried to modify it in order to deal with some of the concerns raised by France and other members of the Security Council, and France immediately said they would veto that. They said they would veto anything that might lead to the use of force. But without that possibility of the use of force, you won't get anything out of Saddam Hussein.

The steps we are seeing, which are simply not enough from Saddam Hussein are as a result, not of the inspectors, not of the French, but as a result of the possibility of force. He's trying to avoid that use of force. He is trying to divide the Council, and he's having some success because some Council members are saying, under no circumstances would we use force.

Q. He has turned over a 25-page document to Hans Blix that purports to document the destruction of VX. Do we think that is a, we, the United States Government, do you think that is a legitimate document?

Secretary Powell. I have no idea. We haven't seen it. I don't know what Dr. Blix has made of it. I know that this is a document he was supposed to have turned over in 1991. Eleven times over the last 12 years, he has provided declarations that were supposed to be full, complete and accurate.

We gave him another chance with 1441 to declare all that he knew about these weapons, to turn it all in; and he chose not to. And suddenly, here comes another 25-page document. It's part of a continuing effort on his part to break the Council up, to deceive us, and it is a game we have been watching for 12 years. It's a game that must come to an end.

Q. It's the administration's position that Resolution 1441, which called for immediate disarmament, immediate actions and serious consequences is sufficient to go ahead and use force. In hindsight, has it been a mistake to return to the United Nations and to reopen a debate we now say was settled last year?

Secretary Powell. First of all, we do believe that 1441 gives you more than enough authority, and I think the British believe that and so does Spain and a number of other countries.

Q. Spain does.

Secretary Powell. There was no question about it when it was passed that it was sufficient authority. Now we went back for a second resolution, which we didn't think we needed because a number of our friends and allies said, we really do need another second resolution for our political purposes or to reaffirm 1441.

We didn't think 1441 needed any reaffirmation, but nevertheless, we gave it a shot. And so far we've had difficulty with it because France and Russia, as well, have indicated that they would veto any second resolution.

Q. Isn't it safe to say, as a result of this debate over the second resolution that our relations with France, Germany and Russia are, in fact, more strained than they were before?

Secretary Powell. This clearly has put strains on our relations. We have had some difficulty with Germany on this issue since last summer when it became a campaign issue for Chancellor Schroeder's reelection. And it certainly has put a strain on our relationship with France because France has, frankly, not played a very helpful role in our judgment in keeping the focus on Saddam Hussein and not the focus on inspectors and new resolutions and anything but use of force.

I don't think that's been helpful in putting the pressure where it belongs on Saddam Hussein. With respect to Russia, we do have some strains as a result of this issue, but I think that with Russia we will be able to deal with this and it won't be any kind of even short-term damage in the relationship.

Q. But there will be damage with the French relationship?

Secretary Powell. I think we're going to have to see how this plays out in the future. I think there have been some issues here that we're going to have to work out. I think, in the short-term, we have damaged our relationship with France. But we have to remember France is a long-time ally. We have been together for over 225 years and we're going to be together for a long time in the future.

Q. Do you think the administration underestimated the depth of the relationship between Jacques Chirac and Saddam Hussein and the Governments of France and Iraq?

Secretary Powell. I don't think we underestimated it. We knew that there was various commercial relationships and France had been a business—had business relationships with Iraq over the years. I don't think we underestimated it. We knew from going back to 1988 when we—1998 when we saw how France dealt with the last resolution on U.N. inspections: how they watered it down for a period of seven months and even then, when a compromise was reached, France abstained on inspections; and also Russia and China abstained. So we were under no illusions about French views of this matter.

Q. Do you believe the French are trying to protect Saddam Hussein?

Secretary Powell. I wouldn't go that far, but I do know that as a result of the manner in which this has been handled in recent months, it hasn't been useful in applying maximum pressure to Saddam Hussein to do what the international community called on him to do: to comply and to cooperate fully with inspectors in compliance. That is what he has not done. And no amount of discussion about more time for inspectors, more inspectors, let's give it more time, let's come up with a new idea, let's modify the proposals on the table, all of these are interesting ideas but they don't deal with the basic problem and that is Saddam Hussein is not complying with 1441 and all the resolutions that go back for 12 years.

Q. We've talked about the French. Let me read a few quotes from Dominique de Villepin right after the passage of U.N. Security Council Resolution 1441. First he said, "If Saddam Hussein doesn't comply, doesn't fulfill his obligations, the recourse to force will be triggered." A second quote, and then we'll talk about both of them: "We think," that is the French, "that he might use the chemical-biological weapons, and I want to repeat here that we also suspect there's an embryonic nuclear element. We can't run that risk."

That was Dominique de Villepin just back in November—just a few months ago. Now all of sudden France is saying it's going to veto everything. Why do you think that's happened?

Secretary Powell. I'm not entirely sure because those are excellent quotes that you pulled up, Tony. It shows that there was no doubt, no question, about what 1441 was all about: compliance or the use of force if necessary. That's what the serious consequences meant in 1441. And also, you see an acknowledgment by the French Foreign Minister that this capability existed within Iraq for weapons of mass destruction.

1441 was premised on the reality that such weapons of mass destruction programs existed. It wasn't a figment of anyone's imagination, and all 15 members agreed. Now, in the months after that, France decided for its own purposes to just keep trying to avoid the inevitable conclusion that Saddam Hussein was not complying: keep inspections going, give them more time, let's have 120 days, let's do this, let's do that. And they did not want to face up to the reality that it is now time to consider whether or not the diplomatic track has run its course and it's time to use military force.

Q. If the French came along and said, we would like to have a longer window, whether it would two weeks or 30 days, and then at that point force would be triggered, would the United States say okay?

Secretary Powell. Two weeks or 30 days for what? All we need is two hours to decide whether or not Saddam Hussein has made the decision that he's been called on to make for the last 12 years, and that is a good way for him to manifest that he really wants to solve this problem is for him and his sons to pick up and leave town.

Q. Dominique de Villepin, again, the French Foreign Minister, has called for a ministerial meeting: foreign ministers, secretaries of state, to gather again at the U.N. Security Council on Tuesday. Do you intend to attend?

Secretary Powell. Well, right now, a meeting has not been scheduled by the President of the Council, which is the Guinean Permanent Representative, so we'll wait and see what actually is called for by the Council and I will make a judgment then. Right now, I don't know that there's any purpose to be served by yet another meeting when the disagreement is so fundamental: more inspections, more time for inspections, or full compliance right away, immediately, unconditionally, as called for in 1441 on the part of Saddam Hussein.

Q. Will the President make a call this week?

Secretary Powell. The President will consult with Mr. Aznar and Mr. Blair in the next few hours and those three gentlemen will issue statements as to what they discussed and then we'll see what the President decides to do after that, but I think the moment of truth is arriving with respect to diplomacy and what comes next.

Q. Everybody seems to believe war is imminent. The Germans are now pulling all of their ambassadorial employees out of Baghdad, the insurance company that insures U.N. helicopters, it's pulled the insurance, they are taking the helicopters out, a number of other legations are getting out. Are they wrong to do so?

Secretary Powell. I think these are expected and prudent actions. We will also be trimming down our presence in the region. We're at a moment of, where a moment of decision is coming up and the next step in this process is for the three leaders, the four leaders with the Portuguese serving as host for this meeting with the three co-sponsors taking a look at where we are diplomatically this afternoon and making a judgment about the way forward.

Q. Will you be surprised if there's no war this time next week?

Secretary Powell. I would not wish to speculate on my level of surprise or lack of surprise on events that are in the future.

Q. All right. We have talked now about our allies. There's been this conception that Tony Blair's under political stress. Do you think that's true?

Secretary Powell. Yes. He is. I mean there's no question about it. I mean Tony Blair has taken a strong leadership position. He would not walk away from this challenge, and it has cost him politically. But I hope that he will be able to persuade his cabinet, the Parliament, all the other constituencies that he has to deal with in the United Kingdom that it was the right thing to do, it was absolutely the noble thing to do and he stood tall—not just standing tall with George Bush, but standing tall for freedom, standing tall for the destruction of these kinds of weapons of mass destruction, standing tall for the United Nations Security Council to impose its will correctly on a dictatorial, evil regime like Saddam Hussein's.

Q. Which raises a critical question. The President had said if the U.N. Security Council and the U.N. failed to act on their own resolutions that they will become irrelevant.

Secretary Powell. I think on this issue, if the U.N. fails to act it will seriously the damage the Security Council and its ability to impose its will. The U.N. will still be with us for the next 50 years as it was for the last 50 years. But for these kinds of issues, the U.N. has to demonstrate its relevancy to deal with this type of problems.

Q. And if it does not do so, will the United States and others be ready to come up with some sort of alternative?

Secretary Powell. I don't know what an alternative is. I mean we have demonstrated over the years that there are different alternatives for different situations. For example, just a few years ago when the previous administration was facing the crisis in Kosovo, the U.N. didn't act at that point. The administration knew that Russia would veto a resolution put before the Security Council so it didn't call for a vote. And then a coalition of the willing went and dealt with Kosovo.

So very often, the U.N. is not the organization of choice when it comes to the use of military force and then you put together a coalition of the willing. And this has been done a number of times, most recently in Kosovo that comes to mind.

Q. We had hoped that Turkey would be part of the coalition of the willing. All deals with Turkey off the table now?

Secretary Powell. Well, Turkey is a good friend. And let's remember that Mr. Erdogan, who is now the Prime Minister, when he was not yet the Prime Minister at the beginning of this month, he and the prime minister at that time, Mr. Gul, were willing to take this issue to their parliament. And for a moment there, we thought that parliament had passed it, but as a result of second counts and parliamentary maneuvers, it was not passed. So he was willing to stand with us and take the package to his parliament.

Now he is the prime minister and we're in close touch with him. And I have met with him, I have met with the former prime minister, I've met with the minister of foreign affairs, and they are positioning themselves to take the package back to their parliament. Whether it will be in a timely manner or not remains to be seen.

Q. There's a possibility, then, that U.S. troops still might be deployed through Turkey?

Secretary Powell. I wouldn't eliminate any of the options that are on the table right now. A lot depends on what Mr. Erdogan feels he can get through his parliament, and he has to make that political judgment. And we're—you know—Turkey is a great friend. They'll be a friend in the future, and we are in the closest touch with them right now.

Q. Will the administration, quickly switching topics, final question, invite Abu Mazen to Washington to consult with the President should he become prime minister of the Palestinian Authority?

Secretary Powell. We're hoping that he will be confirmed next week as prime minister of the Palestinian Authority and we hope that he will be invested with power, real power. And that is why the President made his statement Friday with respect to the roadmap.

When he is confirmed, we will present that roadmap to him. And I'm sure that at some point in the future, I don't know when we would schedule such a visit, but when it's time we could do so, he would be welcomed in Washington.

Remarks by Secretary of State Powell, March 16, 2003

Secretary Colin Powell was interviewed on ABC's This Week by George Stephanopoulos.

Q. If this summit today is really the last chance for diplomacy, why aren't you there?

Secretary Powell. I'm staying here in Washington in order to stay in touch with my colleagues in London and in Spain, in Madrid. There's a lot going on in the U.N.. There are proposals being made, there are statements being made. We worked all day yesterday on the statements that will be examined at the summit in the Azores and so it's a distribution of labor, and that's fine.

Q. So are you actually formulating a proposal, a new proposal to bridge the gap in the Security Council?

Secretary Powell. What's going to happen in the Azores today is the three leaders will get together and review the diplomatic situation and while they are doing that, I and Foreign Secretary Jack Straw of the United Kingdom and Ana Palacio, who was on your show earlier in Madrid, we are staying in constant touch so that we can provide any advice on late-breaking developments at the U.N.. And as you know, there are a number of initiatives that other nations are taking: the French and the Germans and the Russians put forward a paper yesterday. There are things that are going to be happening in the U.N. this week; and it is for that reason we thought it would be best for the three of us to stay in touch.

Q. One of the new developments—

Secretary Powell. I'm not expecting, really, a new proposal. There is a good, solid proposal on the table now. It is a resolution that these three nations, the United States, the United Kingdom and Spain tabled Friday before last. But France has said it will veto it and every adjustment we have tried to make to that resolution during the course of last week, France said it would veto.

Q. Well, there may be a change, though, in the French position. French President Jacques Chirac gave an interview today in which he said he would be willing to consider a 30-day timeline for inspections. That's a big concession coming back off 120 days.

Secretary Powell. I don't know that it's that big a concession. I don't know exactly what President Chirac is proposing. All I know is that when the United Kingdom came forward with an adjustment to the resolution that was on the table last week, the instant response from the French Government was, "We'll veto it. We'll veto anything that leads to the serious consequences intended by resolution 1441 for Iraqi noncompliance.

Q. But is 30-day, is a 30-day timeline acceptable to the United States?

Secretary Powell. We have had timelines, we have had deadlines, and we have had benchmarks. The problem is Iraq is not complying. Iraq is playing the United Nations and playing some of our friends in the permanent membership of the Security Council like a fiddle.

They dribble out at a little of this and then over the weekend we hear they are going to let some more people come forward to be interviewed, they are going to bring forward some more documents. These are documents that were supposed to have been brought forward in 1991. These are documents Iraq said they don't have any longer, but suddenly they discover them. It's a game, George. It's a game and the problem is strictly on the shoulders of Saddam Hussein who is not complying with the simple instructions of 1441 and all the previous resolutions. And we cannot get ourselves confused about what the problem is. The problem is Iraqi noncompliance and noncooperation with the inspectors and with the will of the United Nations.

Q. And time has run out for Saddam Hussein?

Secretary Powell. I think time is clearly running out. I think a moment of truth is arriving and what's happening in the Azores today—the three co-sponsors of the resolution that is before the Council now are meeting to assess the diplomatic prospects for that resolution and to come to some conclusions as to the way forward in the week ahead.

Q. So have you given up hope on getting a U.N. resolution?

Secretary Powell. Well, right now, that's what the leaders will be talking about. Is it time to bring the curtain down on this or is there some hope? They are not going there for a war council. They are going there to examine the diplomatic situation to see if there is any hope for a peaceful solution.

But I will tell you what, Saddam Hussein has done nothing to assist in finding that peaceful solution, and some members of the Council, frankly, have not been that helpful in applying maximum pressure to Saddam Hussein for him to do so.

Let's keep in mind, the reason that we are seeing even these tentative process moves on the part of Saddam Hussein is not because of resolutions, it's not because of diplomacy, it's because of the presence of a strong U.S.-United Kingdom-and other nations participating military force in the region that is applying that kind of pressure, and if Saddam Hussein ultimately decides not to comply, and it doesn't look like he will, then he will face the serious consequences 1441 called for.

Q. But as you know, as you know, other members of the Security Council have said a little bit more time would help them. Yesterday I spoke with the Pakistani Ambassador to the United Nations and here's what he had to say about what he'd like to see from the Azores:

"What we would like to hear is that the U.S. and the sponsors are prepared to evolve a compromise, that perhaps they are prepared to wait and give a chance for peaceful disarmament of Iraq and that we can work together in the Council and bridge the gaps and reach, reach a consensus for further action."

"We definitely would need more time if a consensus is to be reached."

So what's wrong with giving a little more time to get the support of a country like Pakistan?

Secretary Powell. Because we have been waiting for 12 years. We gave a little more time when the President gave his speech. We gave a little more time when 1441 was passed. It is now four months since 1441 and we have seen nothing with respect to Iraqi performance and behavior that suggests that Saddam Hussein has made a decision to comply with the resolution and to cooperate.

Let there be no doubt, if it wasn't the threat of military force, if those military forces were not assembled in the Gulf right now, you would be seeing no cooperation from Iraq. You'd be seeing the same kind of games they have played for the last 12 years. So how much more time is necessary in order to make a judgment that Iraq is not complying and does not intend to cooperate?

Q. Well, but that's the question that your colleagues on the Security Council are asking as well. And if they need a month, what's the harm? It's—the Vice Chairman—

Secretary Powell. Do you really think that the French who have made it clear from the very beginning, have made it clear for years—since the last resolution in 1998, which they worked hard on and then finally abstained. They didn't even support the resolution that they worked on for seven months. Do you really think that 30 more days would persuade the French that if Iraq did not comply at that point they would then be willing to support the use of military force?

Q. Well, that's—

Secretary Powell. No. The French have made it clear and they made it clear again this week. They see no logic that would lead to the use of military force.

Q. Well then let me ask you about that—

Secretary Powell. But in the absence of the use of military force, it's not clear that you will get Iraq to understand the seriousness of the situation that it has put itself in.

Q. Well then, let me ask you about that because you worked very hard with the French. You worked very hard with Dominique de Villepin in negotiating 1441.

Secretary Powell. Yes.

Q. Looking back now, do you feel like they sandbagged you?

Secretary Powell. No, because 1441 was a clear statement, and we made it clear to the French at that time, 1441 was a powerful resolution that put the burden squarely on Iraq and it said that if there is not compliance this time there would be serious consequences. There was no confusion in my mind or in Foreign Minister de Villepin's mind or anyone else's mind that serious consequences meant the use of force.
Now, we have, we have—

Q. But now you're saying they are never going to accept the use of force.

Secretary Powell. Well, they—that's what they are saying. It's not what I'm saying.

Q. You're saying that's your belief about France.

Secretary Powell. No, that's what they are saying. It's not my belief about France. It's what the French keep saying. It's what they keep saying, they do not see the logic to the use of force and they keep saying, well, that's only in this context, but they keep repeating it. But the fact of the matter is, 1441 by a vote of 15—0 provided the international basis for any action that might be taken in the future; and that especially includes military action if it's necessary in the presence of continued Iraqi noncompliance. And we have now met over the last several weeks in New York some four times to evaluate Iraqi compliance or noncompliance.

Some people thing they are complying merely because they give you something the day before one of these meetings takes place. But the only reason they are complying is to try to divide the Council. And the only reason they are doing anything at all is because of the pressure that's being put on them militarily. They are trying to get rid of that pressure. They are trying to escape, once again, from their obligations not only under 1441, but for 12 years of resolutions. This goes back to 1991. They have given 11 declarations over that period of time that they said were full, complete and accurate. And we know they were not full, complete and accurate.

For years they said, we have given you a full, complete, accurate declaration that we have no biological weapons. Voila. In 1995 it became clear they did have biological weapons. They had to admit it.

Q. So time is running out.

Secretary Powell. Time is running out.

Q. The French proposal is not acceptable at this point?

Secretary Powell. I don't even know what the French proposal is.

Q. Thirty more days.

Secretary Powell. That's a statement that President Chirac apparently gave to a newscaster. I have not seen that. There is a letter that is in from the French and the Germans and the Russians that there should be some sort of meeting this week and I will just examine that letter—that's one reason I stayed behind—to deal with these kinds of issues as they are going to come up in the course of today—

Q. So given all that, do you now agree with British Foreign Minister Jack Straw that war is much more probable?

Secretary Powell. I would say that the President's and prime ministers' meeting this afternoon in the Azores will have to look very carefully at the situation we find ourselves in and make a judgment as to whether or not there is a diplomatic way ahead. And if there's not a diplomatic way ahead, then what should come next? But I will leave that to those leaders in the Azores to make a judgment on.

Q. Is the President still committed to calling for a vote on the U.S.-U.K. resolution?

Secretary Powell. The President will be discussing with Prime Minister Blair and Prime Minister Aznar the way forward, and I would leave it at that.

Q. But he was very unequivocal in his press conference two weeks ago. And last week on this program, I want to show you: this is what Condi Rice said about calling the votes.

"President Bush believes that it's time for people to stand up and be counted."
"He's going to call the vote."

Secretary Powell. The point of it is that we have seen them stand up to be counted. In the case of the French, they have stood up and said, "We'll veto anything."

Q. So there's not going to be a vote, necessarily?

Secretary Powell. I didn't say that, George. I said that's what they'll be discussing at the Azores meeting this afternoon: how to move forward diplomatically.

Q. But what changed? Why would the President no longer call for a vote?
Secretary Powell. George, I didn't say he would not call for a vote. You keep saying it. What I'm saying is—

Q. But is it an option?

Secretary Powell. What I'm saying, George—yeah, of course it's an option. They are all—everything is an option.

Q. But he didn't say it was an option before.

Secretary Powell. Everything is an option, George, and what they are doing this afternoon in the Azores is these three leaders who are the co-sponsors of that resolution, the resolution that is before the Council, they will be discussing the diplomatic way forward. And in the course of time, when they have finished their meeting, I'm sure they will make a statement as to what they have discussed and what they've agreed upon and we'll see what happens in the days ahead.

Q. Let me switch now to the issue of Turkey. Are you now under the assumption that Turkey will not allow U.S. forces to be based?

Secretary Powell. No. I'm very pleased that Mr. Erdogan was willing, even before he became Prime Minister, to send the request to the Turkish parliament in the hope that it would be passed. But it was not passed the first time in. And now that he is the prime minister, we are in constant touch with him; we are on the phones with him all the time. As you may recall, I had the foreign minister and the minister of economics in my home until midnight one night working on that economic package. I met with Mr. Erdogan and Prime Minister Gul in Davos a few weeks ago, and I know that they are trying to do everything they can to get that package through.
Now when they will resubmit the package is a matter that's up to—

Q. They said it could be as long as a week.

Secretary Powell. It could be as long as a week. I've heard different reports.

Q. Isn't that too late?

Secretary Powell. Well, we would rather it had been a couple of weeks ago, but this is an interesting political situation for Mr. Erdogan because he just became the Prime Minister, he's just putting the government together, getting his vote of confidence in place, and so it hit them at a rather difficult political time, but Turkey is a great friend of ours, a great ally of ours, we are very sensitive to their concerns about their relationship with the situation in northern Iraq and we're working very closely. We're in constant touch with the Turks.

Q. On northern Iraq, have they given you a commitment not to put Turkish forces into northern Iraq?

Secretary Powell. We have made it clear that the situation there is volatile and it would be better if there were no Turkish forces in, as part of any military operation that might take place. They are concerned about that area, but they also know that we don't want to see anything happen that would precipitate a crisis between Turkey and the Kurdish populations in northern Iraq.

Q. On the prospects of military action, Newsweek reported this morning that you objected to the original war plans put forward by Tommy Franks, and obviously you have some standing, you were Chairman of the Joint Chiefs in the last Gulf War. Is that true and are you satisfied now?

Secretary Powell. I don't know what they are talking about. I discuss options with my colleagues when we are having our principals meetings, but it is not my—you know, I didn't object to a war plan. To the extent that I could contribute to the debate on war plans a need the discussion on war plans, I did so. But this business that somehow I am in some kind of fight with Tommy Franks over his war plan is just nonsense.

Q. But you were concerned that the original plans provided for much too small of an invading force?

Secretary Powell. That was a matter for Secretary Rumsfeld to deal with General Franks on. It was not something that I got involved in. I watched as the plan developed. It was a matter of discussion between Secretary Rumsfeld and his commanders. And as the plan evolved, Don asked me for my views or I was in meetings where the plans were discussed. It was a very deliberative process and so this business of Powell arguing with Franks or Rumsfeld on the nature of the war plans is just simply not accurate.

Q. But you are satisfied now?

Secretary Powell. I'm not going to talk about war plans. That's Don's job to do. I am confident in his ability, the ability of his team, the ability of the Joint Staff and the ability of General Franks to come up with a war plan that will deal with whatever is ahead. And if military force is going to be used to resolve this matter, I am absolutely confident in General Franks' and all of our commanders' ability to handle this matter.

Q. How do you—

Secretary Powell. They were my younger officers at one point.

Q. How do you define success in this operation? If, for example, American troops do not find large caches of biological-chemical weapons, will that be a failure in your mind?

Secretary Powell. I'm quite confident they will find evidence of the presence of chemical and biological weapons and some elements of a nuclear infrastructure. And I think that that's—there's no question about that in my mind. Success, if it comes to a military action, will be a better Iraq, a better life for the Iraqi people, the use of the treasure of Iraq, its oil, for the benefit of its people and not to threaten its neighbors and develop weapons of mass destruction.

Everybody is worried about the conflict. You should worry about a potential conflict. It is always a time of high anxiety. But if it's done well, and I'm confident our military commanders, if they are told to do it by the President, if it has to come to this, will do it well. And we have quite a bit of experience in not only conducting successful military operations but rebuilding a better society afterwards where the Iraqi people can be free of fear, free of torture, free of the kinds of crimes that Saddam Hussein has committed against his own people. And there is a possibility, a strong possibility which we will go after and hopefully seize, to put in place a country that is stable, living in peace with its neighbors and no longer a threat to the regions of the world or the United States.

Q. Finally, sir, the diplomatic effort has come under a lot of criticism here in the States and around the world. We just heard the foreign minister of Spain suggest that a lot of Secretary of Defense Rumsfeld's rhetoric has not been helpful in this effort. But, you, last fall, convinced the President; it's been widely reported, over the objections of Secretary of Defense Rumsfeld and Vice President Cheney to go to the United Nations.

They warned that Saddam Hussein would stall, that the French would stall, that it would come to nothing. Looking back, do you now believe they were right?

Secretary Powell. No. They didn't disagree. They agreed with the proposition that we had to take it to the United Nations. When we finally sat around in August and had a meeting with the President about this issue, all of us agreed. Vice President—

Q. But they were reluctant.

Secretary Powell. All of us agreed: the Vice President, Secretary Rumsfeld, myself, Dr. Rice, the President, the Vice President. We all were together on this. Now, there was a degree of skepticism, a correct degree of skepticism in my mind, as to whether or not the inspection process would work. The test was to put it before Saddam Hussein as a test of him. Is he going to comply this time? Is he going to cooperate? If he were to comply, if he was to cooperate, if he was going to change the nature of his regime, the nature of his politics, his strategy—then there was a chance for a peaceful solution. But we said at that time that we're giving him one last chance to comply. And that's what 1441 was all about: one last chance to get on the right side of the international community. And we were unified going into that as a team in the administration.

Were there degrees of skepticism? Yes. Of course there were.

Q. But do you feel like you were undercut by hawks in the administration? That's also been widely reported.

Secretary Powell. Lots of things get widely reported. We went forward under the President's leadership to take it to the U.N.. We went as a team to the United Nations and we have—we fought hard for seven weeks to get a powerful resolution. And that resolution reaffirms the basis in international law to take military action if it's required. And it was 15-0. Whether people now like it or not, it was 15-0. And that remains the basis for any further action we might take.

Now, would I like to have seen others come to the same conclusion that we did— that there is a total lack of compliance on the part of Saddam Hussein, that all we are seeing is games? Of course. Would I have liked to have seen a second resolution because it would have helped our friends with some of their political difficulties? Yes. Do we need a second resolution? No. And that's what our leaders will be talking about in the Azores this afternoon: what is the next step with respect to diplomacy or other actions that might be required?

Remarks by Secretary of State Powell, March 17, 2003

Good morning, ladies and gentlemen. As you know, last fall, in an act of unanimity the Security Council came together following President Bush's historic speech to the United Nations on the 12th of September and on the 8th of November, after long negotiations, passed U.N. Resolution 1441 by unanimous vote, 15 to zero, not one member failing to raise a hand in support of that resolution.

In the months after the passage of U.N. Resolution 1441, we watched as the inspectors began their work, and we were immediately concerned that Iraq was not going to understand the intention of 1441 when Iraq submitted 30 days later, a declaration that can only be said to be false, not complete, rather, incomplete, not truthful, untruthful and nowhere near meeting the spirit intended in 1441. We called that out to the international community at that time.

We said we believed that that false declaration was a material breach. We continued to support the inspectors, we continued to watch, and although we have seen some process improvements and some grudging movement on the part of Saddam Hussein's regime to provide some information and provide some equipment to the inspectors, it certainly wasn't the kind of compliance and total cooperation that 1441 required and that we were hoping but had no illusions about Iraq being able to accept and respond to.

As a result of this and as a result of a number of briefings that we received from UNMOVIC and IAEA, a week and a half ago, the United Kingdom, the United States and Spain put forward a resolution that would once again give Saddam Hussein one last chance to act or face the serious consequences that were authorized and clearly intended in U.N. Resolution 1441.

Unfortunately, over the last roughly two weeks or thereabouts, a little less than two weeks that we have been debating this particular draft resolution, and despite best efforts to see whether or not language could be adjusted to make it more acceptable to Council members, it is clear that there are some permanent members of the Council that would veto any such resolution or any resolution resembling the one that the British tabled Friday before last at the United Nations.

As a result of this, the United Kingdom, the United States and Spain decided to not call for a vote on this resolution. We spent a great deal of time overnight and early this morning talking to friends and colleagues around the world about the resolution and it was our judgment, reached by the United States, the United Kingdom and Spain that no further purpose would be served by pushing this resolution. So we are not going to ask for a vote on the resolution. The resolution will die anyway, because it had a built-in date of 17 March within the resolution, which has not been modified.

As you heard the President and the other leaders who assembled in the Azores yesterday for the Atlantic Summit say, the window on diplomacy is closing. The moment of truth is arriving. And you will hear a speech from the President of the United States this evening. President Bush will address the nation and the world on the situation as we now see it. In his speech, he clearly will issue an ultimatum to Saddam Hussein that the only way to avoid the serious consequences that were built into 1441 is for Saddam Hussein and his immediate cohorts to leave the country and to allow this matter to be resolved through the peaceful entry of force and not a conflict. Nevertheless, the President's determination will be made clear tonight that this matter cannot continue indefinitely, that Saddam Hussein is guilty of the charges that have been brought against him previously through these many resolutions which acknowledged that he had weapons of mass destruction and he has failed to disarm himself as required by the various resolutions.

We believe and I think you've also heard an opinion from British legal authorities within the last 24 hours that there is sufficient authority in 1441, 678 and 687, earlier resolutions, for whatever military action might be required.

I'm very, very pleased that the Council did come together last November 8th for 1441, of course disappointed that we were unable to get a subsequent resolution, but we believe that our actions now are supported by international law, whatever actions we might take in the future, and the President will talk to this issue tonight.

I won't say anymore about the President's speech because the President, of course, will have the opportunity to speak for himself and make the points perfectly clear to the American people and to the international community.

You will also notice that in their statements yesterday at the Atlantic Summit, all of the leaders spoke to a future for Iraq that will be brighter if it comes to the use of military force, where this dictator will no longer be able to oppress his own people, no longer able to threaten his neighbors, and no longer able to develop these horrible weapons which could be used against his neighbors as they have been used in the past, or, of greater concern to us, and spread and be acquired by terrorist organizations which might use them against us, our friends or our interests.

I think it was also important to note in the President's statement yesterday his commitment to the U.N. and the role that we believe the U.N. will play in the aftermath of any conflict should it come and our continued support for the U.N.. And with that, I will take a couple of questions and then I have to go.

Q. Mr. Secretary, on the allies—

Secretary Powell. Yes.

Q. Back in November, when several of them tried to dilute the resolution, and they did accomplish some word changes, would it be fair to say that they understood at the end that force was possible? Because they seem to give the impression they had succeeded in sidetracking force. And could you say if you think there will be permanent damage to the alliance with what the French have done with support from Germany and Russia?

Secretary Powell. On your first question, Barry, there can be no confusion on this point. If you remember the debate that we were having before 1441 was passed, there were some nations who insisted that a second resolution would be required. And we insisted that a second resolution would not be required. And as we negotiated our way through that, we made it absolutely clear that we did not believe that the resolution as it finally passed would require a second resolution. And, in fact, the resolution that we are not taking to a vote today is not a resolution that we believe was necessary. It was a resolution we're supporting along with the United Kingdom, who tabled it, and Spain. It was a resolution that would help some of our friends to show to their publics and to the world that we had taken one last step, we had made one last effort to see if Saddam Hussein would come into compliance.

The burden of this problem rests squarely on Saddam Hussein and his continuing efforts to deceive, to deny, to do everything to divide the Council, to take advantage of every meeting we have had over the last several months, to do something just before that meeting to suggest that he is complying when he really isn't. And the world should know that this crisis is before us because of this regime and its flagrant violation of obligations that it entered into over the last 12 years. That's where the burden lies.

Q. And is there permanent damage—excuse me.

Secretary Powell. Is there permanent damage?

Q. To the alliance?

Secretary Powell. The U.N. is an important institution and it will survive, and the United States will continue to be an important member of the United Nations and its various organizations. But, clearly, this is a test, in my judgment, that the Security Council did not meet.

We all knew what we were doing last fall. The very reason that we went into a prolonged negotiation on 1441 was so that it did not become the same kind of resolution that we had seen so many times in the past, that had a lot of words, a lot of rhetoric, and Saddam Hussein can simply ignore and thumb his nose at. This was a resolution that every person who voted for it, every permanent representative who was there on the 8th of November and voted for this resolution knew that it was different, that serious consequences would flow, and those serious consequences meant the use of force to disarm Saddam Hussein if he did not comply with that resolution and cooperate fully with the inspectors to disarm that regime.

Q. Mr. Secretary, how long a period of time do you think is appropriate for Saddam Hussein to be allowed to get out? And who—who else besides him would have to leave if they want to avert war?

Secretary Powell. I won't speak to a time limit. The President may do that in his speech this evening, and I'll leave that to him.

But clearly, we would want to see Saddam Hussein depart, as well as immediate members of his family who are in positions of control and authority over the armed forces of Iraq. And there are a number of other individuals we would also like to see depart, some of them were mentioned in the weekend press. But it's not just one individual to solve the problem.

Q. Do you have a number, though?

Secretary Powell. I don't have a number at hand. There are a variety of numbers and ideas floating around. And if somebody in Baghdad wishes to know the names, I'm sure we'd be able to provide them.

Q. Mr. Secretary, can you give us some things like what has happened over the last 24 hours since the meeting in the Azores? Who were the problems, what kind of conversations did you have, who did you reach out to, and what were the responses?

Secretary Powell. The United Kingdom, obviously, reached out to a number of their colleagues and I can't speak for them; I'll let them cover their own calls and consultations. Similarly, Spain and others. Richard will give you the list of my calls for this morning, but it's about, oh, 12 or 15. I've spoken to the French. I just spoke to Foreign Minister de Villepin. I spoke to Foreign Minister Joschka Fischer of Germany. I've spoken to Foreign Minister Igor Ivanov of the Russian Federation. I've spoken to the new Chinese Foreign Minister, Foreign Minister Li. I've spoken to President Musharraf. I have spoken to Kofi Annan. I have spoken to Foreign Minister George Papandreou of Greece, who is also in the Greek Presidency for this period. I have spoken to Foreign

Secretary Straw. I've spoken to Foreign Minister Palacios of Spain. And there is a very long list waiting when I get back upstairs.

The response was, you know, this is where we are. Does anybody see any prospects for movement on this particular resolution? And, frankly, everybody pretty much accepted that this resolution was not going to be a successful one, because there was one nation, France, that had indicated that it would veto it under any set of circumstances, or any similar resolution as modified that would leave a path open to conflict. But we always knew, from the very beginning, that such a path had to be kept open. And this is what "serious consequences" meant. And without that path, Saddam Hussein would never comply.

And what he was trying to do was just stretch it out, more inspections, more time, let's delay, let's give a little here, give a little there, let's see if we can break this consensus. And with the certainty of a French veto and possibly other vetoes, this was not the time to have further division within the Council by taking this to a vote.

Q. Mr. Secretary, you seemed to imply yesterday in one of the shows that you believe French commercial interests helped drive the position. I am wondering if you can elaborate on that. And how firm a guarantee do you have that Turkey won't send its troops well into northern Iraq and cause problems with the Kurds there?

Secretary Powell. I made the point that there—in response to a question, that of course there are commercial interests that everybody has to consider. And the French have for years had difficulties with the inspection regime. And I pointed out in one of the shows yesterday that when you go back to 1998 and early 1999, when the current inspection regime was being developed, when UNMOVIC was being created after the collapse of the previous inspection regime, France worked actively for a number of months, in our judgment, to try to weaken that inspection regime. And, at the end of the day, when compromises had been made and everybody thought we had a good outcome before our time, the previous administration, even then France abstained from voting for it. And so that is a concern to us.

But, in 1441, France was solidly on board. And when you look at the statements that were made by French officials right after the passage of 1441, it was absolutely clear that they understood that Saddam Hussein and the Iraqi regime had weapons of mass destruction. It was not something just known to American intelligence; it's known to all the major intelligence agencies in the world. And France acknowledged that, everybody acknowledged that when they signed on to 1441, because that's what it says. It said, Iraq is in material breach, has been in material breach, and now has the opportunity to get out of the problem or get into further material breach. And what they did was get into further material breach. And that's our judgment and we believe that the test of the resolution has been met with respect to the appropriateness of the application of serious consequences.

Q. And the Turks and the Kurds?

Secretary Powell. Barbara—I'm sorry. On the Turks and the situation in northern Iraq, we are in the closest consultation with the Turks and let me say that we are very sensitive to Turkish concerns. We appreciate the fact that the Turkish Government did take our request for deployments into their Parliament at a difficult time for them, with a Prime Minister who was still coming in, so to speak. Mr. Erdogan was not the Prime Minister at that time. And we are in the closest touch with them now on a number of issues. One, the possibility of resubmission and he has committed to do that at a time that he believes is appropriate; and secondly, we don't think it would be useful right now to create any additional tension on the border between Turkey and northern Iraq and we are in discussions with them as to how to make sure that tensions can be kept at the lowest point and not to have difficulty in northern Iraq of a kind that concerns them.

And we have also assured the Turks that in anything that the future might hold, we are committed to the territorial integrity of Iraq.

Q. I wanted to ask, yeah, I wanted to ask just some personal reflections. After 1441 was passed, you were a very, very happy man and certainly it was quite a triumph. How have you been feeling the last few weeks? When did you realize that this was not going to happen? Do you wish you'd done anything differently? Do you wish you'd traveled more? Changed your tactics in any way?

Secretary Powell. Well, you know, this legend that is out there now that Colin Powell one, he—the first variation of it was, he doesn't travel; and the next variation was, he hates to travel; and the third variation was, he will never travel and doesn't want to travel.

You do your job by personal contacts, by contact, by travel and by the use of modern technology so that you can get more bang for the time. And so in the last six weeks, I have had four, personal, one-on-one meetings, direct meetings, with the French Foreign Minister, with the British Foreign Minister, with the Russian Foreign Minister, five such meetings with the Chinese Foreign Minister. I have gone to Davos in Switzerland, where I addressed an international setting and at that meeting I met with the Turkish Prime Minister for almost two hours and the incoming Turkish Prime Minister, Mr. Erdogan.

I have had the Turkish, a Turkish delegation here in the Department, a full delegation, the Foreign Minister, the Finance Minister; and they came to my home until midnight as we worked on the economic package. And so I believe that I have used my time properly.

At the same time, I went to Asia a few weeks ago, so I travel when I believe travel is appropriate. I'd like to travel more, but you know, the Secretary of State has many responsibilities that he or she has to deal with and one has to balance it all.

But I assure you that I do not shrink back from traveling and I will be traveling again soon.

Q. But any regrets? Anything you'd have done differently?

Secretary Powell. No. I mean you can always look and say you should have done this, should have done that, but the fact of the matter is, we came up with a good resolution and we got a solid vote for it, 15-0, and then for a period of four months after that we worked hard with the inspectors, we provided them intelligence. The focus, really, was at the U.N. in New York, not, you know, a lot of other places. That's where we had to concentrate our effort. And we did everything we could to try to persuade the Council that what they were seeing was not compliance. What they were seeing was passive cooperation that didn't get to the heart of the matter, which was a strategic decision by Saddam Hussein to comply. And that's what we weren't able to get and that's what we weren't able to convince some members of the Council is what was needed in order for us to believe that Saddam Hussein was a changed regime, was leading a changed regime that was willing now to cooperate with the international community and comply with its obligations.

Q. Mr. Secretary, you said that the ultimatum would be for Saddam Hussein to leave Iraq. Is there any form of disarmament or cooperation at this stage which could save his skin?

Secretary Powell. I think the time for diplomacy has passed. I think that's pretty clear. That's what the leaders were saying in the Azores yesterday. And we used last evening and this morning to consult broadly around the world. We did, the British did, the Spanish did. A lot of people have been talking to each other this morning and overnight, and it became clear that it would be best at this time to withdraw the resolution, and I can think of nothing that Saddam Hussein could do diplomatically. I think that time is now over. He had his chance. He's had many chances over the last 12 years, and he has blown every one of those chances.

Remarks by United Nations Secretary-General Annan, March 17, 2003

I've just come out of a [Security] Council meeting where we discussed the situation in Iraq. Obviously the members of the Council who had hoped for a long time that it ought to be possible to disarm Iraq peacefully and had hoped to be able to come up with a common position, are today disappointed and frustrated and are worried that they were not able to muster the collective will to find a common basis to move ahead. And obviously, we seem to be at the end of the road here.

Yesterday UNMOVIC, the [International] Atomic [Energy] Agency and myself got information from the United States authorities that it would be prudent not to leave our staff in the region. I have just informed the Council that we will withdraw the UNMOVIC and Atomic Agency inspectors, we will withdraw the U.N. humanitarian workers, we will withdraw the UNIKOM troops on the Iraqi-Kuwaiti border who are also not able to operate. The implication of these withdrawals will mean that the mandates will be suspended because it will be inoperable. We can not, for example, handle the Oil for Food when we do not have inspectors to monitor the imports, we do not have oil inspectors who will monitor exports of oil, and we don't have the humanitarian personnel who will monitor the distribution, receipt and distribution of the food supply. So, I have informed the Council of these suspensions.

This does not mean that, should war come to Iraq, the U.N. will sit back and not do anything to help the Iraqi population. We will find a way of resuming our humanitarian activities to help the Iraqi people who have suffered for so long and do whatever we can to give them assistance and support. And as you know we have undertaken major contingency planning to be able to move forward as soon as we can.

Q. Did you get an authorization from the Security Council to withdraw these inspectors or did you use the measures you have available to you, temporary relocation of the inspectors?

Secretary-General Annan. It is relocation of the inspectors, and the Council has taken note of my decision.

Q. Should the United States go ahead and its allies and use military action against Iraq without U.N. Security Council authorization, would that be in violation of international law according to you?

Secretary-General Annan. I think my position on that is very clear. The Council will have to discuss that also.

Q. Do you believe part of 1441, is it legal or not legal?

Secretary-General Annan. I think I have made my position very clear on that and I have indicated to you that if ... let's have a bit of order and calm here....I have made it very clear that in my judgement if the Council were to be able to manage this process successfully and most of the collective will to handle this operation, its own reputation and credibility would have been enhanced. And I have also said if the action is to take place without the support of the Council, its legitimacy will be questioned and the support for it will be diminished.

Q. Is today a very sad day for the U.N. and for the world?

Secretary-General Annan. I think almost every government and peoples around the world had hoped that this issue can be resolved peacefully. In the sense that we are not able to do it peacefully, obviously it is a disappointment and a sad day for everybody. War is always a catastrophe—it leads to major human tragedy, lots of people are going to be uprooted, displaced from their homes and nobody wanted that. And this is why we had hoped that the Iraqi leadership would have cooperated fully and would have been able to do this without resort to use of force. But the little window that we seem to have, seems to be closing very, very fast. I'm not sure at this stage the Council can do anything in the next couple of hours.

Q. Dr Blix and [El] Baradei have also been invited, would you fly to Baghdad?

Secretary-General Annan. I have no plans to fly to Baghdad today.

Q. If there is military action, then what happens?

Secretary-General Annan. Well if there is military action, the Council of course will have to meet to discuss what happens after that. I think I have made it clear that regardless of how this current issue is resolved, the Security Council is going to have a role to play. And I think that was also implied in the communique that came out of the Azores. That the U.N. has an important role to play in the post-conflict Iraq and the Council will have to discuss that. The Council will have to give me a mandate for some of the activities that we will need to undertake. And so this does not mean an end of involvement of the U.N. in the Iraqi situation.

Remarks by President Bush, March 17, 2003

President Bush delivered the following address to the nation.

My fellow citizens, events in Iraq have now reached the final days of decision. For more than a decade, the United States and other nations have pursued patient and honorable efforts to disarm the Iraqi regime without war. That regime pledged to reveal and destroy all its weapons of mass destruction as a condition for ending the Persian Gulf War in 1991.

Since then, the world has engaged in 12 years of diplomacy. We have passed more than a dozen resolutions in the United Nations Security Council. We have sent hundreds of weapons inspectors to oversee the disarmament of Iraq. Our good faith has not been returned.

The Iraqi regime has used diplomacy as a ploy to gain time and advantage. It has uniformly defied Security Council resolutions demanding full disarmament. Over the years, U.N. weapon inspectors have been threatened by Iraqi officials, electronically bugged, and systematically deceived. Peaceful efforts to disarm the Iraqi regime have failed again and again—because we are not dealing with peaceful men.

Intelligence gathered by this and other governments leaves no doubt that the Iraq regime continues to possess and conceal some of the most lethal weapons ever devised. This regime has already used weapons of mass destruction against Iraq's neighbors and against Iraq's people.

The regime has a history of reckless aggression in the Middle East. It has a deep hatred of America and our friends. And it has aided, trained and harbored terrorists, including operatives of al Qaeda.

The danger is clear: using chemical, biological or, one day, nuclear weapons, obtained with the help of Iraq, the terrorists could fulfill their stated ambitions and kill thousands or hundreds of thousands of innocent people in our country, or any other.

The United States and other nations did nothing to deserve or invite this threat. But we will do everything to defeat it. Instead of drifting along toward tragedy, we will set a course toward safety. Before the day of horror can come, before it is too late to act, this danger will be removed.

The United States of America has the sovereign authority to use force in assuring its own national security. That duty falls to me, as Commander-in-Chief, by the oath I have sworn, by the oath I will keep.

Recognizing the threat to our country, the United States Congress voted overwhelmingly last year to support the use of force against Iraq. America tried to work with the United Nations to address this threat because we wanted to resolve the issue peacefully. We believe in the mission of the United Nations. One reason the U.N. was founded after the second world war was to confront aggressive dictators, actively and early, before they can attack the innocent and destroy the peace.

In the case of Iraq, the Security Council did act, in the early 1990s. Under Resolutions 678 and 687—both still in effect—the United States and our allies are authorized to use force in ridding Iraq of weapons of mass destruction. This is not a question of authority, it is a question of will.

Last September, I went to the U.N. General Assembly and urged the nations of the world to unite and bring an end to this danger. On November 8th, the Security Council unanimously passed Resolution 1441, finding Iraq in material breach of its obligations, and vowing serious consequences if Iraq did not fully and immediately disarm.

Today, no nation can possibly claim that Iraq has disarmed. And it will not disarm so long as Saddam Hussein holds power. For the last four-and-a-half months, the United States and our allies have worked within the Security Council to enforce that Council's long-standing demands. Yet, some permanent members of the Security Council have publicly announced they will veto any resolution that compels the disarmament of Iraq. These governments share our assessment of the danger, but not our resolve to meet it. Many nations, however, do have the resolve and fortitude to act against this threat to peace, and a broad coalition is now gathering to enforce the just demands of the world. The United Nations Security Council has not lived up to its responsibilities, so we will rise to ours.

In recent days, some governments in the Middle East have been doing their part. They have delivered public and private messages urging the dictator to leave Iraq, so that disarmament can proceed peacefully. He has thus far refused. All the decades of deceit and cruelty have now reached an end. Saddam Hussein and his sons must leave Iraq within 48 hours. Their refusal to do so will result in military conflict, commenced at a time of our choosing. For their own safety, all foreign nationals—including journalists and inspectors—should leave Iraq immediately.

Many Iraqis can hear me tonight in a translated radio broadcast, and I have a message for them. If we must begin a military campaign, it will be directed against the lawless men who rule your country and not against you. As our coalition takes away their power, we will deliver the food and medicine you need. We will tear down the apparatus of terror and we will help you to build a new Iraq that is prosperous and free. In a free Iraq, there will be no more wars of aggression against your neighbors, no more poison factories, no more executions of dissidents, no more torture chambers and rape rooms. The tyrant will soon be gone. The day of your liberation is near.

It is too late for Saddam Hussein to remain in power. It is not too late for the Iraqi military to act with honor and protect your country by permitting the peaceful entry of coalition forces to eliminate weapons of mass destruction. Our forces will give Iraqi military units clear instructions on actions they can take to avoid being attacked and destroyed. I urge every member of the Iraqi military and intelligence services, if war comes, do not fight for a dying regime that is not worth your own life.

And all Iraqi military and civilian personnel should listen carefully to this warning. In any conflict, your fate will depend on your action. Do not destroy oil wells, a source of wealth that belongs to the Iraqi people. Do not obey any command to use weapons of mass destruction against anyone, including the Iraqi people. War crimes will be prosecuted. War criminals will be punished. And it will be no defense to say, "I was just following orders."

Should Saddam Hussein choose confrontation, the American people can know that every measure has been taken to avoid war, and every measure will be taken to win it. Americans understand the costs of conflict because we have paid them in the past. War has no certainty, except the certainty of sacrifice.

Yet, the only way to reduce the harm and duration of war is to apply the full force and might of our military, and we are prepared to do so. If Saddam Hussein attempts to cling to power, he will remain a deadly foe until the end. In desperation, he and terrorists groups might try to conduct terrorist operations against the American people and our friends. These attacks are not inevitable. They are, however, possible. And this very fact underscores the reason we cannot live under the threat of blackmail. The terrorist threat to America and the world will be diminished the moment that Saddam Hussein is disarmed.

Our government is on heightened watch against these dangers. Just as we are preparing to ensure victory in Iraq, we are taking further actions to protect our homeland. In recent days, American authorities have expelled from the country certain individuals with ties to Iraqi intelligence services. Among other measures, I have directed additional security of our airports, and increased Coast Guard patrols of major seaports. The Department of Homeland Security is working closely with the nation's governors to increase armed security at critical facilities across America.

Should enemies strike our country, they would be attempting to shift our attention with panic and weaken our morale with fear. In this, they would fail. No act of theirs can alter the course or shake the resolve of this country. We are a peaceful people—yet we're not a fragile people, and we will not be intimidated by thugs and killers. If our enemies dare to strike us, they and all who have aided them, will face fearful consequences.

We are now acting because the risks of inaction would be far greater. In one year, or five years, the power of Iraq to inflict harm on all free nations would be multiplied many times over. With these capabilities, Saddam Hussein and his terrorist allies could choose the moment of deadly conflict when they are strongest. We choose to meet that threat now, where it arises, before it can appear suddenly in our skies and cities.

The cause of peace requires all free nations to recognize new and undeniable realities. In the 20th century, some chose to appease murderous dictators, whose threats were allowed to grow into genocide and global war. In this century, when evil men plot chemical, biological and nuclear terror, a policy of appeasement could bring destruction of a kind never before seen on this earth.

Terrorists and terror states do not reveal these threats with fair notice, in formal declarations—and responding to such enemies only after they have struck first is not self-defense, it is suicide. The security of the world requires disarming Saddam Hussein now.

As we enforce the just demands of the world, we will also honor the deepest commitments of our country. Unlike Saddam Hussein, we believe the Iraqi people are deserving and capable of human liberty. And when the dictator has departed, they can set an example to all the Middle East of a vital and peaceful and self-governing nation.

The United States, with other countries, will work to advance liberty and peace in that region. Our goal will not be achieved overnight, but it can come over time. The power and appeal of human liberty is felt in every life and every land. And the greatest power of freedom is to overcome hatred and violence, and turn the creative gifts of men and women to the pursuits of peace.

That is the future we choose. Free nations have a duty to defend our people by uniting against the violent. And tonight, as we have done before, America and our allies accept that responsibility.

Good night, and may God continue to bless America.

Statement by French President Chirac, March 18, 2003

Ever since the beginning of the Iraq crisis, France has endeavored to make possible the necessary disarmament of Iraq under United Nations authority. This disarmament is under way, as the inspectors have been demonstrating.

France has acted in the name of the primacy of the law and in accordance with her conception of relations between peoples and between nations.

True to the spirit of the United Nations Charter, which is our common law, France considers that recourse to force is the last resort, when all other options have been exhausted.

France's position is shared by the great majority of the international community. The most recent debates have clearly shown that the Security Council was not prepared, under present circumstances, to approve a precipitate march to war.

The United States has just issued an ultimatum to Iraq. Whether, I repeat, it's a matter of the necessary disarmament of Iraq or of the desirable change of regime in that country, there no justification for a unilateral decision to resort to war.

Regardless of the forthcoming developments, this ultimatum is calling into question our idea of international relations. It affects the future of a people, the future of a region, world stability.

It is a grave decision, at a time when Iraq's disarmament is under way and the inspections have proved to be a credible alternative method of disarming that country.

It is also a decision which jeopardizes future use of methods to resolve peacefully crises linked to the proliferation of weapons of mass destruction.

Iraq does not today present an immediate threat warranting an immediate war. France appeals to everyone to act responsibly to ensure the respect of international legality. It appeals to them to maintain the Security Council's unity by staying within the framework set by UNSCR 1441.

To act outside the authority of the United Nations, to prefer the use of force to compliance with the law, would incur a heavy responsibility.

Remarks by British Prime Minister Blair, March 18, 2003

Prime Minister Tony Blair delivered his remarks to the British Parliament.

At the outset I say: it is right that this House debate this issue and pass judgement. That is the democracy that is our right but that others struggle for in vain.

And again I say: I do not disrespect the views of those in opposition to mine.

This is a tough choice. But it is also a stark one: to stand British troops down and turn back; or to hold firm to the course we have set.

I believe we must hold firm.

The question most often posed is not why does it matter? But: why does it matter so much? Here we are: the Government with its most serious test, its majority at risk, the first Cabinet resignation over an issue of policy. The main parties divided.

People who agree on everything else, disagree on this and likewise, those who never agree on anything, finding common cause.

The country and Parliament reflect each other: a debate that, as time has gone on has become less bitter but not less grave.

So: why does it matter so much?

Because the outcome of this issue will now determine more than the fate of the Iraqi regime and more than the future of the Iraqi people, for so long brutalized by Saddam. It will determine the way Britain and the world confront the central security threat of the 21st Century; the development of the U.N.; the relationship between Europe and the U.S.; the relations within the EU and the way the U.S. engages with the rest of the world.

It will determine the pattern of international politics for the next generation.

But first, Iraq and its WMD.

In April 1991, after the Gulf War Iraq was given 15 days to provide a full and final declaration of all its WMD.

Saddam had used the weapons against Iran, against his own people, causing thousands of deaths. He had had plans to use them against allied forces. It became clear after the Gulf War that the WMD ambitions of Iraq were far more extensive than hitherto thought. This issue was identified by the U.N. as one for urgent remedy. UNSCOM, the weapons inspection team, was set up. They were expected to complete their task following the declaration at the end of April 1991.

The declaration when it came was false—a blanket denial of the program, other than in a very tentative form. So the 12 year game began.

The inspectors probed. Finally in March 1992, Iraq admitted it had previously undeclared WMD but said it had destroyed them.

It gave another full and final declaration.

Again the inspectors probed but found little.

In October 1994, Iraq stopped co-operating with UNSCOM altogether. Military action was threatened. Inspections resumed.

In March 1995, in an effort to rid Iraq of the inspectors, a further full and final declaration of WMD was made. By July 1995, Iraq was forced to admit that too was false.

In August they provided yet another full and final declaration.

Then, a week later, Saddam's son-in-law, Hussein Kamal defected to Jordan. He disclosed a far more extensive BW program and for the first time said Iraq had weaponised the program; something Saddam had always strenuously denied. All this had been happening whilst the inspectors were in Iraq. Kamal also revealed Iraq's crash program to produce a nuclear weapon in 1990.

Iraq was forced then to release documents which showed just how extensive those programs were.

In November 1995, Jordan intercepted prohibited components for missiles that could be used for WMD.

In June 1996, a further full and final declaration was made.

That too turned out to be false.

In June 1997, inspectors were barred from specific sites.

In September 1997, another full and final declaration was made. Also false. Meanwhile the inspectors discovered VX nerve agent production equipment, something always denied by the Iraqis.

In October 1997, the U.S. and the U.K. threatened military action if Iraq refused to comply with the inspectors. But obstruction continued.

Finally, under threat of action, in February 1998, Kofi Annan went to Baghdad and negotiated a memorandum with Saddam to allow inspections to continue.

They did.

For a few months.

In August, co-operation was suspended.

In December the inspectors left. Their final report is a withering indictment of Saddam's lies, deception and obstruction, with large quantities of WMD remained unaccounted for.

The U.S. and the U.K. then, in December 1998, undertook Desert Fox, a targeted bombing campaign to degrade as much of the Iraqi WMD facilities as we could.

In 1999, a new inspections team, UNMOVIC, was set up. But Saddam refused to allow them to enter Iraq.

So there they stayed, in limbo, until after Resolution 1441 when last November they were allowed to return.

What is the claim of Saddam today?

Why exactly the same claim as before: that he has no WMD.

Indeed we are asked to believe that after seven years of obstruction and non-compliance finally resulting in the inspectors leaving in 1998, seven years in which he hid his program, built it up even whilst inspection teams were in Iraq, that after they left he then voluntarily decided to do what he had consistently refused to do under coercion.

When the inspectors left in 1998, they left unaccounted for:

10 thousand liters of anthrax a far reaching VX nerve agent program up to 6,500 chemical munitions at least 80 tonnes of mustard gas, possibly more than ten times that amount unquantifiable amounts of sarin, botulinum toxin and a host of other biological poisons an entire Scud missile program We are now seriously asked to accept that in the last few years, contrary to all history, contrary to all intelligence, he decided unilaterally to destroy the weapons. Such a claim is palpably absurd.

1441 is a very clear Resolution. It lays down a final opportunity for Saddam to disarm. It rehearses the fact that he has been, for years in material breach of 17 separate U.N. Resolutions.

It says that this time compliance must be full, unconditional and immediate. The first step is a full and final declaration of all WMD to be given on 8 December.

I won't to go through all the events since then—the House is familiar with them—but this much is accepted by all members of the UNSC.

The 8 December declaration is false. That in itself is a material breach.

Iraq has made some concessions to co-operation but no-one disputes it is not fully co-operating.

Iraq continues to deny it has any WMD, though no serious intelligence service anywhere in the world believes them.

On 7 March, the inspectors published a remarkable document. It is 173 pages long, detailing all the unanswered questions about Iraq's WMD. It lists 29 different areas where they have been unable to obtain information.

For example, on VX it says: "Documentation available to UNMOVIC suggests that Iraq at least had had far reaching plans to weaponise VX ...

"Mustard constituted an important part (about 70%) of Iraq's CW arsenal ... 550 mustard filled shells and up to 450 mustard filled aerial bombs unaccounted for ... additional uncertainty with respect of 6526 aerial bombs, corresponding to approximately 1000 tonnes of agent, predominantly mustard."

"Based on unaccounted for growth media, Iraq's potential production of anthrax could have been in the range of about 15,000 to 25,000 liters ... Based on all the available evidence, the strong presumption is that about 10,000 liters of anthrax was not destroyed and may still exist."

On this basis, had we meant what we said in Resolution 1441, the Security Council should have convened and condemned Iraq as in material breach.

What is perfectly clear is that Saddam is playing the same old games in the same old way. Yes there are concessions. But no fundamental change of heart or mind.

But the inspectors indicated there was at least some co-operation; and the world rightly hesitated over war. We therefore approached a second Resolution in this way.

We laid down an ultimatum calling upon Saddam to come into line with Resolution 1441 or be in material breach.

Not an unreasonable proposition, given the history.

But still countries hesitated: how do we know how to judge full co-operation?

We then worked on a further compromise. We consulted the inspectors and drew up five tests based on the document they published on 7 March. Tests like interviews with 30 scientists outside of Iraq; production of the anthrax or documentation showing its destruction.

The inspectors added another test: that Saddam should publicly call on Iraqis to co-operate with them.

So we constructed this framework: that Saddam should be given a specified time to fulfill all six tests to show full co-operation; that if he did so the inspectors could then set out a forward work program and that if he failed to do so, action would follow.

So clear benchmarks; plus a clear ultimatum.

I defy anyone to describe that as an unreasonable position.

Last Monday, we were getting somewhere with it. We very nearly had majority agreement and I thank the Chilean President particularly for the constructive way he approached the issue.

There were debates about the length of the ultimatum. But the basic construct was gathering support.

Then, on Monday night, France said it would veto a second Resolution whatever the circumstances.

Then France denounced the six tests. Later that day, Iraq rejected them.

Still, we continued to negotiate.

Last Friday, France said they could not accept any ultimatum. On Monday, we made final efforts to secure agreement. But they remain utterly opposed to anything which lays down an ultimatum authorizing action in the event of non-compliance by Saddam.

Just consider the position we are asked to adopt. Those on the Security Council opposed to us say they want Saddam to disarm but will not countenance any new Resolution that authorizes force in the event of non-compliance.

That is their position. No to any ultimatum; no to any Resolution that stipulates that failure to comply will lead to military action.

So we must demand he disarm but relinquish any concept of a threat if he doesn't. From December 1998 to December 2002, no U.N. inspector was allowed to inspect anything in Iraq. For four years, not a thing. What changed his mind? The threat of force. From December to January and then from January through to February, concessions were made. What changed his mind?

The threat of force.

And what makes him now issue invitations to the inspectors, discover documents he said he never had, produce evidence of weapons supposed to be non-existent, destroy missiles he said he would keep? The imminence of force.

The only persuasive power to which he responds is 250,000 allied troops on his doorstep.

And yet when that fact is so obvious that it is staring us in the face, we are told that any Resolution that authorizes force will be vetoed.

Not just opposed. Vetoed. Blocked.

The way ahead was so clear. It was for the U.N. to pass a second Resolution setting out benchmarks for compliance; with an ultimatum that if they were ignored, action would follow.

The tragedy is that had such a Resolution issued, he might just have complied. Because the only route to peace with someone like Saddam Hussein is diplomacy backed by force.

Yet the moment we proposed the benchmarks, canvassed support for an ultimatum, there was an immediate recourse to the language of the veto.

And now the world has to learn the lesson all over again that weakness in the face of a threat from a tyrant, is the surest way not to peace but to war.

Looking back over 12 years, we have been victims of our own desire to placate the implacable, to persuade towards reason the utterly unreasonable, to hope that there was some genuine intent to do good in a regime whose mind is in fact evil. Now the very length of time counts against us. You've waited 12 years. Why not wait a little longer?

And indeed we have.

1441 gave a final opportunity. The first test was the 8th of December. He failed it.

But still we waited. Until the 27th of January, the first inspection report that showed the absence of full co-operation. Another breach. And still we waited.

Until the 14th of February and then the 28th of February with concessions, according to the old familiar routine, tossed to us to whet our appetite for hope and further waiting. But still no-one, not the inspectors nor any member of the Security Council, not any half-way rational observer, believes Saddam is co-operating fully or unconditionally or immediately.

Our fault has not been impatience.

The truth is our patience should have been exhausted weeks and months and years ago. Even now, when if the world united and gave him an ultimatum: comply or face forcible disarmament, he might just do it, the world hesitates and in that hesitation he senses the weakness and therefore continues to defy.

What would any tyrannical regime possessing WMD think viewing the history of the world's diplomatic dance with Saddam? That our capacity to pass firm resolutions is only matched by our feebleness in implementing them.

That is why this indulgence has to stop. Because it is dangerous. It is dangerous if such regimes disbelieve us. Dangerous if they think they can use our weakness, our hesitation, even the natural urges of our democracy towards peace, against us. Dangerous because one day they will mistake our innate revulsion against war for permanent incapacity; when in fact, pushed to the limit, we will act. But then when we act, after years of pretense, the action will have to be harder, bigger, more total in its impact. Iraq is not the only regime with WMD. But back away now from this confrontation and future conflicts will be infinitely worse and more devastating.

But, of course, in a sense, any fair observer does not really dispute that Iraq is in breach and that 1441 implies action in such circumstances. The real problem is that, underneath, people dispute that Iraq is a threat; dispute the link between terrorism and WMD; dispute the whole basis of our assertion that the two together constitute a fundamental assault on our way of life.

There are glib and sometimes foolish comparisons with the 1930s. No-one here is an appeaser. But the only relevant point of analogy is that with history, we know what happened. We can look back and say: there's the time; that was the moment; for example, when Czechoslovakia was swallowed up by the Nazis—that's when we should have acted.

But it wasn't clear at the time. In fact at the time, many people thought such a fear fanciful. Worse, put forward in bad faith by warmongers. Listen to this editorial—from a paper I'm pleased to say with a different position today—but written in late 1938 after Munich when by now, you would have thought the world was tumultuous in its desire to act.

"Be glad in your hearts. Give thanks to your God. People of Britain, your children are safe. Your husbands and your sons will not march to war. Peace is a victory for all mankind. And now let us go back to our own affairs. We have had enough of those menaces, conjured up from the Continent to confuse us."

Naturally should Hitler appear again in the same form, we would know what to do. But the point is that history doesn't declare the future to us so plainly. Each time is different and the present must be judged without the benefit of hindsight.

So let me explain the nature of this threat as I see it.

The threat today is not that of the 1930s. It's not big powers going to war with each other.

The ravages which fundamentalist political ideology inflicted on the 20th century are memories.

The Cold War is over.

Europe is at peace, if not always diplomatically.

But the world is ever more interdependent. Stock markets and economies rise and fall together.

Confidence is the key to prosperity.

Insecurity spreads like contagion.

So people crave stability and order.

The threat is chaos.

And there are two begetters of chaos.

Tyrannical regimes with WMD and extreme terrorist groups who profess a perverted and false view of Islam.

Let me tell the House what I know.

I know that there are some countries or groups within countries that are proliferating and trading in WMD, especially nuclear weapons technology.

I know there are companies, individuals, some former scientists on nuclear weapons programs, selling their equipment or expertise.

I know there are several countries—mostly dictatorships with highly repressive regimes—desperately trying to acquire chemical weapons, biological weapons or, in particular, nuclear weapons capability. Some of these countries are now a short time away from having a serviceable nuclear weapon. This activity is not diminishing. It is increasing.

We all know that there are terrorist cells now operating in most major countries. Just as in the last two years, around 20 different nations have suffered serious terrorist outrages. Thousands have died in them.

The purpose of terrorism lies not just in the violent act itself. It is in producing terror. It sets out to inflame, to divide, to produce consequences which they then use to justify further terror.

Round the world it now poisons the chances of political progress: in the Middle East; in Kashmir; in Chechnya; in Africa.

The removal of the Taliban in Afghanistan dealt it a blow. But it has not gone away.

And these two threats have different motives and different origins but they share one basic common view: they detest the freedom, democracy and tolerance that are the hallmarks of our way of life.

At the moment, I accept that association between them is loose. But it is hardening.

And the possibility of the two coming together—of terrorist groups in possession of WMD, even of a so-called dirty radiological bomb is now, in my judgement, a real and present danger.

And let us recall: what was shocking about 11 September was not just the slaughter of the innocent; but the knowledge that had the terrorists been able to, there would have been not 3,000 innocent dead, but 30,000 or 300,000 and the more the suffering, the greater the terrorists' rejoicing.

3 kilograms of VX from a rocket launcher would contaminate a quarter of a square kilometer of a city.

Millions of lethal doses are contained in one litre of Anthrax. 10,000 liters are unaccounted for.

11 September has changed the psychology of America. It should have changed the psychology of the world.

Of course Iraq is not the only part of this threat. But it is the test of whether we treat the threat seriously.

Faced with it, the world should unite. The U.N. should be the focus, both of diplomacy and of action. That is what 1441 said. That was the deal. And I say to you to break it now, to will the ends but not the means that would do more damage in the long term to the U.N. than any other course.

To fall back into the lassitude of the last 12 years, to talk, to discuss, to debate but never act; to declare our will but not enforce it; to combine strong language with weak intentions, a worse outcome than never speaking at all.

And then, when the threat returns from Iraq or elsewhere, who will believe us? What price our credibility with the next tyrant? No wonder Japan and South Korea, next to North Korea, has issued such strong statements of support.

I have come to the conclusion after much reluctance that the greater danger to the U.N. is inaction: that to pass Resolution 1441 and then refuse to enforce it would do the most deadly damage to the U.N.'s future strength, confirming it as an instrument of diplomacy but not of action, forcing nations down the very unilateralist path we wish to avoid.

But there will be, in any event, no sound future for the U.N., no guarantee against the repetition of these events, unless we recognize the urgent need for a political agenda we can unite upon.

What we have witnessed is indeed the consequence of Europe and the United States dividing from each other. Not all of Europe—Spain, Italy, Holland, Denmark, Portugal—have all strongly supported us. And not a majority of Europe if we include, as we should, Europe's new members who will accede next year, all 10 of whom have been in our support.

But the paralysis of the U.N. has been born out of the division there is. And at the heart of it has been the concept of a world in which there are rival poles of power. The U.S. and its allies in one corner. France, Germany, Russia and its allies in the other. I do not believe that all of these nations intend such an outcome. But that is what now faces us.

I believe such a vision to be misguided and profoundly dangerous. I know why it arises. There is resentment of U.S. predominance. There is fear of U.S. unilateralism. People ask: do the U.S. listen to us and our preoccupations? And there is perhaps a lack of full understanding of U.S. preoccupations after 11th September. I know all of this.

But the way to deal with it is not rivalry but partnership. Partners are not servants but neither are they rivals. I tell you what Europe should have said last September to the U.S.. With one voice it should have said: we understand your strategic anxiety over terrorism and WMD and we will help you meet it. We will mean what we say in any U.N. Resolution we pass and will back it with action if Saddam fails to disarm voluntarily; but in return we ask two things of you: that the U.S. should choose the U.N. path and you should recognize the fundamental overriding importance of re-starting the MEPP, which we will hold you to.

I do not believe there is any other issue with the same power to re-unite the world community than progress on the issues of Israel and Palestine. Of course there is cynicism about recent announcements. But the U.S. is now committed, and, I believe genuinely, to the Roadmap for peace, designed in consultation with the U.N.. It will now be presented to the parties as Abu Mazen is confirmed in office, hopefully today.

All of us are now signed up to its vision: a state of Israel, recognized and accepted by all the world, and a viable Palestininan state.

And that should be part of a larger global agenda. On poverty and sustainable development. On democracy and human rights. On the good governance of nations.

That is why what happens after any conflict in Iraq is of such critical significance.

Here again there is a chance to unify around the U.N.. Let me make it clear.

There should be a new U.N. Resolution following any conflict providing not just for humanitarian help but also for the administration and governance of Iraq. That must now be done under proper U.N. authorization.

It should protect totally the territorial integrity of Iraq.

And let the oil revenues—which people falsely claim we want to seize—be put in a Trust fund for the Iraqi people administered through the U.N..

And let the future government of Iraq be given the chance to begin the process of uniting the nation's disparate groups, on a democratic basis, respecting human rights, as indeed the fledgling democracy in Northern Iraq—protected from Saddam for 12 years by British and American pilots in the No Fly Zone—has done so remarkably.

And the moment that a new government is in place—willing to disarm Iraq of WMD—for which its people have no need or purpose—then let sanctions be lifted in their entirety.

I have never put our justification for action as regime change. We have to act within the terms set out in Resolution 1441. That is our legal base.

But it is the reason, I say frankly, why if we do act we should do so with a clear conscience and strong heart.

I accept fully that those opposed to this course of action share my detestation of Saddam. Who could not? Iraq is a wealthy country that in 1978, the year before Saddam seized power, was richer than Portugal or Malaysia.

Today it is impoverished, 60% of its population dependent on Food Aid.

Thousands of children die needlessly every year from lack of food and medicine.

Four million people out of a population of just over 20 million are in exile.

The brutality of the repression—the death and torture camps, the barbaric prisons for political opponents, the routine beatings for anyone or their families suspected of disloyalty are well documented.

Just last week, someone slandering Saddam was tied to a lamp post in a street in Baghdad, his tongue cut out, mutilated and left to bleed to death, as a warning to others.

I recall a few weeks ago talking to an Iraqi exile and saying to her that I understood how grim it must be under the lash of Saddam.

"But you don't", she replied. "You cannot. You do not know what it is like to live in perpetual fear." And she is right. We take our freedom for granted. But imagine not to be able to speak or discuss or debate or even question the society you live in. To see friends and family taken away and never daring to complain. To suffer the humility of failing courage in face of pitiless terror. That is how the Iraqi people live. Leave Saddam in place and that is how they will continue to live.

We must face the consequences of the actions we advocate. For me, that means all the dangers of war. But for others, opposed to this course, it means—let us be clear—that the Iraqi people, whose only true hope of liberation lies in the removal of Saddam, for them, the darkness will close back over them again; and he will be free to take his revenge upon those he must know wish him gone.

And if this House now demands that at this moment, faced with this threat from this regime, that British troops are pulled back, that we turn away at the point of reckoning, and that is what it means—what then?

What will Saddam feel? Strengthened beyond measure. What will the other states who tyrannize their people, the terrorists who threaten our existence, what will they take from that? That the will confronting them is decaying and feeble.

Who will celebrate and who will weep?

And if our plea is for America to work with others, to be good as well as powerful allies, will our retreat make them multilateralist? Or will it not rather be the biggest impulse to unilateralism there could ever be. And what of the U.N. and the future of Iraq and the MEPP, devoid of our influence, stripped of our insistence?

This House wanted this decision. Well it has it. Those are the choices. And in this dilemma, no choice is perfect, no cause ideal.

But on this decision hangs the fate of many things.

I can think of many things, of whether we summon the strength to recognize the global challenge of the 21st century and beat it, of the Iraqi people groaning under years of dictatorship, of our armed forces—brave men and women of whom we can feel proud, whose morale is high and whose purpose is clear—of the institutions and alliances that shape our world for years to come.

To retreat now, I believe, would put at hazard all that we hold dearest, turn the United Nations back into a talking shop, stifle the first steps of progress in the Middle East; leave the Iraqi people to the mercy of events on which we would have relinquished all power to influence for the better.

Tell our allies that at the very moment of action, at the very moment when they need our determination that Britain faltered. I will not be party to such a course. This is not the time to falter. This is the time for this House, not just this government or indeed this Prime Minister, but for this House to give a lead, to show that we will stand up for what we know to be right, to show that we will confront the tyrannies and dictatorships and terrorists who put our way of life at risk, to show at the moment of decision that we have the courage to do the right thing. I beg to move the motion.

Remarks by Secretary of State Powell, March 18, 2003

Secretary Colin Powell was interviewed by International Wire Services.

Q. Sure. I'd love to begin. I'm wondering about, you know, the offer well, order to get out of the country. Is anybody helping the U.S. with this? Is there anything active going on? You know, we know the UAE showed some interest in it. I don't imagine you have any state secrets you want to give away, but is there an active campaign to persuade him to leave?

Secretary Powell. There are a number of channels that have been used to communicate the message previously such as the UAE channel, which is a rather public one, frankly, and, you know, privately. But there are other nations that, and leaders we have been in touch with who have been delivering that message to him. And I've also seen some public statements from some countries that suggest he should comply and leave. I think I saw a couple of reports this morning.

But the answer to the question is, yes, we believe a message is being delivered through a number of channels, but he has essentially dismissed the message in whatever channel that it has gone in so far to include the President's channel last night.

Q. There was some talk about Amr Musa going. And then he canceled his—

Secretary Powell. I heard that, but he—

Q. Was that what he was—is that—was that, do you know?

Secretary Powell. He was one of many who was talking about this, but I can't tell you what he was planning to say when he got there.

Q. So to mind the technical before you go into substantial stuff, first, when does the war start and how long does it last? Second, I will go into—

Secretary Powell. The ultimatum expires 48 hours after it was issued, which is tomorrow night and that's really all I think I need to say about it, I mean, a window, a window opens after that. Because that window closed, another one opened.

With respect to if there is a conflict, how long it would last; I learned many, many years ago not to make predictions of that kind. Not being the learned think-tanker, I don't know. But being somebody with considerable experience in this matter, I can assure that plans have been developed to try to do it as quickly as possible and with minimum destruction to infrastructure, to the resources and assets of the Iraqi people and with an emphasis on protecting the assets of the Iraqi people with high emphasis on avoiding collateral loss of life and with efforts to warn the population and to also advise Iraqi military units and military leaders on how they should respond to the onset of the hostilities.

Q. And for the record, you are not going to the Security Council on Wednesday?

Secretary Powell. I have no plans, no. I have no plans to go to the Security Council, but I understand there will be a session where Dr. Blix will present information on the unresolved tasks, and I know that, at least I've heard this morning, that some ministers are planning to attend.

Q. Do you have a message for them? Are they wasting their time?

Secretary Powell. I just—you know, everybody can decide what to attend, but it seems to me that, you know, it's a meeting that can be handled more than adequately by my permanent representative, our permanent representative, which is what he's there for. So I don't know that this is something that demands the attention of foreign ministers but I leave that up to each foreign minister to make an individual judgment on that. I don't think it's of the nature of the kind we've had over the last month or two where we were desperately trying to see whether or not Iraq was or was not complying. And we came to a difference of opinion on that issue.

We believe that the evidence was clear from those meetings that Iraq was not complying and was in violation, further violation of its obligations and that 1441 laid out a clear path forward. Some of our friends wanted to see another resolution and as you know, we did not go forward with another resolution, but we believe the case was clear. Some of our colleagues on the Council did not believe the case was clear and tomorrow's meeting doesn't seem to further that debate one way or the other any longer, obviously, so I don't see any particular need for me to go.

Q. Are you sending a message to the Security Council by not going tomorrow? And over the last few months, I mean you have said repeatedly that it would be irrelevant if it hadn't acted on Iraq and now that it hasn't, are you prepared to say it's irrelevant?

Secretary Powell. Absolutely not. The Security Council remains relevant. There's not reason in my judgment to go tomorrow. We'll be represented. We'll be represented by one of most distinguished ambassadors and somebody you know I have great confidence in. It's not a question of the United States boycotting the meeting, it's just that I don't see a particular need for me to go and I think most members of the Security Council will be represented at the permanent representative level, not at the foreign minister level. And so it's a judgment that, I think, the majority of the members will make that there's no particular need to go at ministerial level.

I don't recall, frankly, the president of the Council calling for it to be at ministerial level. This is an individual decision being made by some Council members that they wish to be represented at that level.

The Council remains relevant. I think it was irrelevant on this particular issue. It lost relevancy on this particular issue because it didn't deal with it forthrightly at the end of the day even though it had dealt forthrightly with it on the 8th of November when it passed 1441. But we will need the Security Council in the future as we develop new resolutions that will deal with the aftermath of a conflict if a conflict comes.

There are a number of resolutions in effect that will have to be adjusted and we want to make sure that we are acting with the support of the international community as we help Iraq build a better life for the nation and for its people.

1441 was a great achievement of the Council. I don't think you should underestimate it. It took a lot of hard work and lot of negotiation on the part of all the foreign ministers and permanent representatives. And it forms the basis for the action that might be necessary if the ultimatum is not acted upon by Saddam Hussein and conflict comes. There are some who disagree with that, but I think that the prevailing of international law says 1441 and its underlying resolutions 678 and 687 will give the international community whatever authority it needs. And as we have said repeatedly, you know, the absence of the U.N.'s willingness to come together again, the United States is prepared to lead a coalition of the willing. And we have been asking people. We now have a coalition of the willing that includes some 30 nations who have publicly said they could be included in such a listing. Richard can provide the names to you later. And there are 15 other nations, who, for one reason or another do not wish to be publicly named but will be supporting the coalition.

Q. This war against Iraq will be the "Bush Doctrine," the new preemptive attack, that you will attack—

Secretary Powell. No, no, no. This conflict, if it comes, with Iraq, will be because Iraq has been developing weapons of mass destruction and has possessed them for 12 years in violation of its international obligations. And the President took this problem to the international community. So we have to do something about it. It's a danger. The President's overall National Security Strategy remains one of working with friends and allies and helping with the crises in the world that include HIV/AIDS, read the whole document. But in that document there is also a reference to the use of preemptive action. It's higher in our list of things one can do to defend oneself, but it is not something that is brand new. We have had preemption as something one could do all along. In this case, we believe we will be acting with the authority of the international community as well as our own obligation to defend ourselves under our Constitution and the President's authority as Commander in Chief.

And so I would not, I don't want you to go down the path, well, here, new doctrine started, that one's first, that one's next, and then that one. If that was all we were about, we wouldn't have gone to the U.N. in the first place.

Q. Mr. Secretary, while the second resolution was being considered, there were countries that said they could support the U.S. only if there was a second resolution. It was clear you went back. You said you have on coalition, 15 silent additions—are there others who you have lost because of the French strategy—because of the resolution being withdrawn, and are any of them significant? Will there be a strategic or a tactical shift necessary? Your most valuable, not necessarily allies, but supporters or collaborators, whatever?

Secretary Powell. I would have to look, you know, I don't know if I could answer your question, I would like to—

Q. Well, there's—Turkey's first in my mind, but—

Secretary Powell. Turkey? The cabinet is meeting right now to see what support they'll be able to provide for this. And I got to talk again to the Turkish Foreign Minister, Deputy Prime Minister Mr. Gul. I don't remember—let's keep in mind, Turkey took it to their parliament at a time of very high tension and turmoil with a government changing. They were going to do that to support us and they didn't succeed. And they are going to take it back to their parliament and they are trying to figure out the best way to do that. It may or may not fit in with our own timing is the issue. And what exactly they are going to parliament is also an issue we're working on through them.

Sure, there are countries that we wish would have thought it possible to support our position and support our efforts but a situation like this where you have these kinds of disagreements, people make their choices, we do what we think is necessary or we believe is right and then we will regroup for the next phase.

Some of the nations who did not support us in the second, I hope they will find the way clear once we have been successful if war comes to see if there's a role they can play in the future on that issue, subsequent phases of this issue or another issue.

Q. You specified Germany, I think at a hearing, and I've asked Richard and he seems to think France would be part of it, do you think France will adjust after the war and become part of a reconstruction effort?

Secretary Powell. Well, let me not speak for France at this point. I'm not sure what position they will take and I'm not sure exactly what opportunities—

Q. I don't mean he said that he would, I'm just—he thought that having not supported the resolution doesn't exclude supporting reconstruction.

Secretary Powell. I don't know what's—I have a hard time answering that. A lot will depend on how this unfolds. You know, I think the Iraqi people will see who has been there for them; I mean who brought about their liberation and who was for them and who was not for them. And let's not fight and be nave that might affect things in the future. But at the same time, I think there's going to be enough work to do that anybody who wants to contribute in some way will be able to.

Q. Things with Turkey seem a little bit better than they were just a week ago in terms of getting a deal in there. At what point is it too late, though? I mean it looks like we're close to military action. Once military action begins, is it still possible to [*inaudible*], as well?

Secretary Powell. Yeah. We think they'll be—in the next couple of days, there are things that Turkey could do in the matter of military action in their future. And that's what I talked to the Foreign Minister about yesterday, the things that are foremost in our minds. And my colleagues at the Defense Department still feel that there are things Turkey can do some distance in the future. You know, I don't want to be precise, but we would not shut down in the near future, our opportunities to get greater cooperation from Turkey.

Q. Is this a priority on airspace right now, just getting the airspace?

Secretary Powell. Overflights.

Q. What about the APEC? Can they still get the $6 billion? Or is it going to be less now because—

Secretary Powell. The $6 billion was linked to a specific package and when that package was not able to move forward, then the $6 billion essentially was, let me just say put off to the side; taken off the table is an expression I've used, but it's not fair in the absence of that original package.

Now we'll wait to see what the Turkish Government is able to do and what the parliament is able to do and then we can respond to what's on the table or not.

Q. Assuming that Saddam does not take this opportunity to leave and assuming that conflict followed and at some point that's over and you have 220-odd thousand troops sitting in Iraq, assuming all that, what have you—have you made any outreach at all or any approach to Iran to kind of tell them that, "Look, even though these people are going to be on your doorstep and even though we have deep, deep concerns about your nuclear program, we're not going to be crossing the border? We have the next leg of the axis?

Secretary Powell. Yeah, we have ways of communicating with Iran but I don't want to go into any details on those means or what particular messages are being conveyed.

Q. So, what? You don't want me to say that there's been an assurance that whatever this operation, when it's finished in Iraq it's not going to be continued over?

Secretary Powell. I don't know why the Iranians would feel that, but we haven't been in, the dialogue that we've been having with them is not one for assurance or no assurances. It hasn't been—we haven't been discussing anything.

Q. Sir, in Russia the people, the government and the people are very concerned about the coming war that President Putin has called a mistake. They are also very concerned about our bilateral relations and the possible fallout of that relations. So what are you willing to do? What do you expect the Russians to do to keep that relationship on an even keel?

Secretary Powell. We do have a disagreement on this issue and I know that President Putin and my colleague Igor Ivanov spoke strongly that they think that war is a mistake. President Putin and President Bush spoke this morning and I think they have a clear understanding between them of their differences.

I think Russian-U.S. bilateral relations will survive this disagreement and will continue to thrive because there is much that pulls us together: our common cause against terrorism, our desire to help the Russian economy, our desire to move forward with the Treaty of Moscow reductions and I know there has been a delay before the Duma in ratifying the treaty, but we got it ratified last week. (Inaudible) 95-0 vote. And we hope the Duma will see that it is in the interest of the Russian Federation and in our bilateral relationship. And we always have chicken exports that we have to deal with. So there's so much that pulls us together. And I think we will deal with this disagreement and move on.

We have had other disagreements with the Russian Federation in the two years that this administration has been here and we've been able to find a way to deal with those and move on, whether it's the ABM Treaty, Missile Defense and how we're cooperating and discussing with each other ways of cooperating with respect to missile defense. These disagreements will come along and as long as everybody realized that we have mutual interests, we can get through them and keep the relationship growing.

* * * *

Q. Do you think the G7 and G8 will be some sort of favorite or the vehicle to rebuild the Iraqi aftermath? And what do you precisely, actually ask these governments to donate to the area.

Secretary Powell. I don't know if the G7 or G8 will really be the right model for it or whether it will be the coalition of the willing underneath some [*inaudible*] U.N. umbrella. Iraq has a source of revenue. It's a wealthy country as I heard Mr. Blair remind us all this morning. A couple of decades ago it has the Gross, GDP of Portugal. Well, this is not a destitute country; it's just a country that has misused its resources. But there are other nations that are ready to help. The European Union has expressed an interest in helping; the United Nations and its subsidiary agencies are willing to help. Japan has said that it wants to be part of the rebuilding and reconstruction efforts and they are analyzing how best they can help and that help will be welcomed, whether it's funneled directly in under international, some international [*inaudible*] or whether, ultimately the G7 and G8 decides to engage itself in the matter.

Right now we're really working with the EEU individual countries such as Japan, and now it's trying to coordinate more closely with the U.N..

Excerpts from United Nations Security Council Ministerial Meeting on Iraq, March 19, 2003

UNMOVIC Chairman Hans Blix. The United Nations Monitoring, Verification and Inspection Commission (UNMOVIC) was established by Security Council resolution 1284 (1999) and was enabled to enter Iraq and carry out its inspection work almost three years later.

It might seem strange that we are presenting a draft work program only after having already performed the inspections for three and a half months. However, there were good reasons why the Council wanted to give us some time after the start of inspections to prepare this program. During the months of the build-up of our resources in Iraq, Larnaca and New York and of inspections in Iraq we have—as was indeed the purpose—learned a great deal that has been useful to know for the drafting of our work program and for the selection of key remaining disarmament tasks. It would have been difficult to draft it without this knowledge and practical experience.

The time lines established in resolution 1284 (1999) have been understood to mean that the work program was to be presented for the approval of the Council at the latest on 27 March. In order to meet the wishes of members of the Council we made the draft work program available already on Monday this week. I note that on the very same day we were constrained together with other United Nations units to order the withdrawal of all our inspectors and other international staff from Iraq.

I naturally feel sadness that three and a half months of work carried out in Iraq have not brought the assurances needed about the absence of weapons of mass destruction or other proscribed items in Iraq, that no more time is available for our inspections and that armed action now seems imminent.

At the same time I feel a sense of relief that it was possible to withdraw yesterday all United Nations international staff, including that of UNMOVIC and the International Atomic Energy Agency. I note that the Iraqi authorities gave full cooperation to achieve this and that our withdrawal to Larnaca took place in a safe and orderly manner. Some sensitive equipment was also taken to Larnaca, while other equipment was left, and our offices in Baghdad have been sealed. Some inspection staff will now remain for a short time in Larnaca to prepare inspection reports. Others who have come from our roster of trained staff, will go home to their previous positions and could be available again, if the need arises.

I would like to make some specific comments that relate to the draft program. I am aware of ideas that have been advanced that specific groups of disarmament issues could be tackled and solved within specific time lines. The program does not propose such an approach, in which, say, we would aim at addressing and resolving the issues of anthrax and VX in March and unmanned aerial vehicles and remotely piloted vehicles in April. In the work we have pursued until now, we have worked broadly and did not neglect any identified disarmament issues. However, it is evidently possible for the Council to single out a few issues for resolution within a specific time, just as the draft program before members select 12 key tasks, progress on which could have an impact on the Council's assessment of cooperation of Iraq under resolution 1284 (1999). Whatever approach is followed, results will depend on Iraq's active cooperation on substance.

May I add that, in my last report, I commented on the information provided by Iraq on a number of unresolved issues. Since then, Iraq has sent several more letters on such issues. These efforts by Iraq should be acknowledged, but, as I noted in this Council on 7 March, the value of the information thus provided must be soberly judged. Our experts have found so far that, in substance, only limited new information has been provided that will help to resolve remaining questions.

Under resolution 1284 (1999), UNMOVIC's work program is to be submitted to the Council for approval. I note, however, that what was drafted and prepared for implementation by a large staff of UNMOVIC inspectors and other resources deployed to Iraq would seem to have only limited practical relevance in the current situation.

UNMOVIC is a subsidiary organ of the Security Council. Until the Council takes a new decision regarding the role and functions of the Commission, the previous resolutions remain valid to the extent this is practicable. It is evidently for the Council to consider the next steps.

In its further deliberations, I hope the Council will be aware that it has in UNMOVIC staff a unique body of international experts who owe their allegiance to the United Nations and who are trained as inspectors in the field of weapons of mass destruction. While the International Atomic Energy Agency (IAEA) has a large department of skilled nuclear inspectors and the Organization for the Prohibition of Chemical Weapons has a large staff of skilled chemical weapons inspectors, no other international organization has trained inspectors in the field of biological weapons and missiles. There is also in the secretariat of UNMOVIC staff familiar with and trained in the analysis of both discipline-specific issues and the broad questions of proliferation of weapons of mass destruction. With increasing attention being devoted to the proliferation of these weapons, this capability may be valuable to the Council.

* * * *

German Foreign Minister Joschka Fischer. The Security Council is meeting here today in a dramatic situation. At this moment, the world is facing an imminent war in Iraq.

The Security Council cannot remain silent in this situation. Today more than ever, our task must be to safeguard its function and to preserve its relevance. We have come together once more in New York today to emphasize that.

The developments of the last few hours have radically changed the international situation and brought the work of the United Nations on the ground to a standstill. Those developments are cause for the deepest concern.

Nevertheless, I would like to thank Mr. Blix for his briefing on the work program. Germany fully supports his approach, even under the current circumstances. The work program with its realistic description of unresolved disarmament issues now lies before us. It provides clear and convincing guidelines on how to disarm Iraq peacefully within a short space of time.

I want to stress this fact, particularly today. It is possible to disarm Iraq peacefully by upholding those demands with tight deadlines. Peaceful means have therefore not been exhausted. Also for that reason, Germany emphatically rejects the impending war.

We deeply regret that our considerable efforts to disarm Iraq using peaceful means in accordance with Security Council resolution 1441 (2002) seem to have no chance of success. Time and again during the last few weeks, we have collaborated with France and Russia to put forward proposals for a more efficient inspections regime consisting of clear disarmament steps with deadlines, most recently on 15 March.

Other members also submitted constructive proposals until the final hours of the negotiations. We are grateful to them for their efforts.

During the last few days, we have moved significantly closer to our common objective: that of effectively countering the risk posed by Iraqi weapons of mass destruction with complete and comprehensive arms control. Especially in recent weeks, substantial progress was made in disarmament. The scrapping of the Al Samoud missiles made headway: 70 of them have now been destroyed. And the regime in Baghdad is beginning, under pressure, to clear up the unanswered questions on VX and anthrax.

Iraq's readiness to cooperate was unsatisfactory. It was hesitant and slow. The Council agrees on that. But can this seriously be regarded as grounds for war with all its terrible consequences?

There is no doubt that, particularly in recent weeks, Baghdad has begun to cooperate more. The information Iraq has provided to UNMOVIC and the IAEA are steps in the right direction. Baghdad is meeting more and more of the demands contained in the Security Council resolutions. But why should we now—especially now—abandon our plan to disarm Iraq by peaceful means?

The majority of Security Council members believe that there are no grounds now for breaking off the disarmament process carried out under the supervision of the United Nations.

In this connection, I would like to make the following three points. First, the Security Council has not failed. We must counter that myth. The Security Council has made available the instruments to disarm Iraq peacefully. The Security Council is not responsible for what is happening outside the United Nations.

Secondly, we have to state clearly, under the current circumstances the policy of military intervention has no credibility. It does not have the support of our people. It would not have taken much to safeguard the unity of the Security Council. There is no basis in the United Nations Charter for regime change by military means.

Thirdly, we have to preserve the inspection regime and to endorse the working program because we need both after the end of military action. Resolutions 1284 (1999) and 1441 (2002) are still in force, even if some adjustments are needed.

Germany is convinced that the United Nations and the Security Council must continue to play the central role in the Iraq conflict. This is crucial to world order and must continue to be the case in future. The United Nations is the key institution for the preservation of peace and stability and for the peaceful reconciliation of interests in the world of today and of tomorrow. There is no substitute for its functions as a guardian of peace.

The Security Council bears the primary responsibility for world peace and international security. The negotiations on the Iraq crisis, which were followed by millions of people worldwide during the last few weeks and months, have shown how relevant and how indispensable the peacemaking role of the Security Council is. There is no alternative to this.

We continue to need an effective international non-proliferation and disarmament regime. This can eliminate the risk of the proliferation of weapons of mass destruction, using the instruments developed in this process to make the world a safer place. The United Nations is the only appropriate framework for this. No one can seriously believe that disarmament wars are the way forward.

We are deeply concerned about the humanitarian consequences of a war in Iraq. Our task now is to do everything we possibly can to avert a humanitarian disaster. The Secretary-General is to present proposals on this. Yesterday, the Security Council declared its readiness to take up these proposals. Through the oil for food program, the United Nations has provided 60 per cent of the Iraqi population with essential supplies. This experience must be used in the future.

A very large majority of people in Germany and Europe are greatly troubled by the impending war in Iraq. Our continent has experienced the horrors of war too often. Those who know our European history understand that we do not live on Venus but, rather, that we are the survivors of Mars. War is terrible. It is a great tragedy for those affected and for us all. It can only be the very last resort when all peaceful alternatives really have been exhausted.

Nevertheless, Germany has accepted the necessity of war on two occasions during the last few years because all peaceful alternatives had proved unsuccessful.

Germany fought side by side with its allies in Kosovo to prevent the mass deportation of the Albanian population and to avert an impending genocide. It did likewise in Afghanistan to combat the brutal and dangerous terrorism of the Taliban and Al Qaeda after the terrible and criminal attacks on the Government and the people of the United States. And we will stick to our commitment in this war against terror.

Today, however, we in Germany do not believe that there is no alternative to military force as a last resort. To the contrary, we feel that Iraq can be disarmed using peaceful means. We will, therefore, seize any opportunity, no matter how small, to bring about a peaceful solution.

French Foreign Minister de Villepin. We are meeting here today, just a few hours before hostilities begin, to exchange our opinions once again in observance of our respective commitments, but also to outline together the path that must allow us to recover the spirit of unity.

I wish to reiterate here that for France, war can only be a last resort, while collective responsibility remains the rule. However much we may dislike Saddam Hussein cruel regime, that holds true for Iraq and for every crisis that we will have to confront together.

To Mr. Blix, who introduced his work program, and to Mr. ElBaradei, who was represented today, I wish to say thank you for the sustained efforts and the results achieved. Their program reminds us that there is still a clear and credible prospect for disarming Iraq peacefully. It proposes and prioritizes the tasks involved in disarmament and presents a realistic timetable for their implementation.

In so doing, the report confirms what we knew all along. Yes, the inspections are producing tangible results. Yes, they offer the prospect of effective disarmament through peaceful means and in shorter time frames.

The path that we mapped out together in the context of resolution 1441 (2002) still exists. Although it is being interrupted today, we know that it will have to be resumed as soon as possible.

Two days ago, the Council took note of the Secretary-General's decision to withdraw the inspectors and all United Nations personnel from Iraq. The discharge of their mandates has therefore been suspended. It will be necessary, when the time comes, to complete our knowledge about Iraq's programs and achieve the disarmament of Iraq. The inspectors' contribution at that time will be decisive.

Make no mistake about it—the choice before us is between two visions of the world. To those who choose to use force and think that they can resolve the world's complexity through swift preventive action, we, in contrast, choose resolute action and a long-term approach, for in today's world, to ensure our security, we must take into account the manifold crises and their many dimensions, including the cultural and religious ones. Nothing enduring in international relations can be built without dialogue and respect for the other, without strictly abiding by principles, especially for the democracies that must set the example. To ignore that is to run the risk of misunderstanding, radicalization and spiraling violence. That is especially true in the Middle East, an area of fractures and ancient conflicts, where stability must be a major objective for us.

To those who hope to eliminate the dangers of proliferation through armed intervention in Iraq, I would like to say that we regret the fact that they are depriving themselves of a key tool for resolving other similar crises. The Iraqi crisis has allowed us to craft an instrument, through the inspection regime, that is unprecedented and can serve as an example. Why not envision, on that basis, establishing an innovative, permanent structure—a disarmament body under the aegis of the United Nations?

To those who think that the scourge of terrorism will be eradicated through what is done in Iraq, we say that they run the risk of failing in their objectives. An outbreak of force in such an unstable area can only exacerbate the tensions and fractures on which terrorists feed.

Over and above our differences, we share a collective responsibility, in the face of these threats, to restore the unity of the international community. The United Nations must remain mobilized in Iraq to aid in that objective. In that regard, there are duties that we must assume together.

First, we must dress the wounds of war. As always, war brings its share of victims, suffering and displaced people. So it is a matter of urgency to prepare now to provide the required humanitarian assistance. This imperative must prevail over our differences. The Secretary-General has already begun to mobilize the various United Nations agencies. France will take part fully in the collective effort to assist the Iraqi people. The oil for food program must be continued under the authority of the Security Council, with the necessary adjustments. We are awaiting the Secretary-General's proposals.

Next, it will be necessary to build peace. No single country has the means to build Iraq's future. Above all, no State can claim the necessary legitimacy. The legal and moral authority for such an undertaking can stem only from the United Nations. Two principles must guide our action: respect for the unity and territorial integrity of Iraq, and the preservation of its sovereignty.

Similarly, it will be up to the United Nations to establish a framework for the country's economic reconstruction—a framework that will have to affirm two complementary principles: transparency and the development of the country's resources for the benefit of the Iraqi people themselves.

Our mobilization must also extend to the other threats that we must address together.

Given the very nature of those threats, it is no longer possible today to address them in a casual order. To give an example, terrorism is fueled by organized crime networks; it cleaves to the contours of lawless areas; it thrives on regional crises; it garners support from the divisions in the world; and it uses all available resources, from the most rudimentary to the most sophisticated, from a knife to whatever weapons of mass destruction it can manage to acquire.

To deal with that reality, we must act in a united way and on all fronts at the same time. Therefore, we must remain constantly mobilized.

In that spirit, France renews its call for heads of State and Government to meet here in the Security Council to respond to the major challenges that we are confronting today.

Let us intensify our fight against terrorism. Let us fight mercilessly against its networks, with all the economic, legal and political weapons available to us.

Let us give new impetus to the fight against the proliferation of weapons of mass destruction. France has already proposed that our heads of State and Government meet on the sidelines during the next General Assembly to define together the new priorities for action.

Let us recover the initiative in the regional conflicts that are destabilizing entire regions; I am thinking in particular of the Israeli-Palestinian conflict. How much suffering must the peoples of the region continue to endure before we force open the doors of peace? Let us not resign ourselves to an irreparable situation.

In a world where the threats are asymmetrical, where the weak defy the strong, the power of conviction, the capacity to persuade and the ability to change hearts count as much as the number of military divisions. They cannot replace them, but they are the indispensable elements of a State's influence.

Given this new world, it is imperative that the international community's action be guided by principles.

The first is respect for law. The keystone of international order, it must apply under all circumstances, but even more so when it is a question of taking the gravest decision: to use force. Only on that condition can force be legitimate, and only on that condition can it restore order and peace.

Next is the defense of freedom and justice. We must not compromise on what is at the core of our values. We shall be listened to and heeded only if we are inspired by the very ideals of the United Nations.

Last is the spirit of dialogue and tolerance. Never before have the peoples of the world aspired so fervently to its respect. We must hear their appeal.

We see this clearly. Never has the United Nations been so necessary. It is up to this body to muster the resolve to meet these challenges, because the United Nations is the place where international law and legitimacy are founded and because it speaks on behalf of peoples.

To the clash of arms, a single upwelling of the spirit of responsibility—the voices and action of the international community gathered here in New York in the Security Council—must respond. That is in the interests of all: the countries engaged in the conflict, the States and the peoples of the region, the international community as a whole. Confronted by a world in crisis, we have the moral and political obligation to restore the lifelines of hope and unity.

The judgement of future generations will depend on our capacity to meet this great challenge, at the service of our values, at the service of our common destiny, at the service of peace.

Russian Foreign Minister Igor Ivanov. The Security Council, by unanimously adopting resolution 1441 (2002), took upon itself the serious responsibility of completing the process of Iraq's disarmament. Today, members have before them the reports of the heads of the United Nations Monitoring, Verification and Inspection Commission (UNMOVIC) and of the International Atomic Energy Agency (IAEA) on the work accomplished and, in particular, their proposals as to what must be done in order to finally solve the problem of weapons of mass destruction in Iraq. We have no doubt that UNMOVIC and the IAEA, which have deployed an effectively functioning inspection mechanism in Iraq, are in a position to carry out their tasks within a realistic time frame.

The reports submitted by Mr. Blix and by Mr. ElBaradei show convincingly that the international inspectors have succeeded in achieving tangible results. I shall not dwell on specific examples; they are well known. It is of fundamental importance that, thanks to the unity of the international community and to the joint pressure brought to bear on the Iraqi authorities—including a military presence in the region—Baghdad has fulfilled virtually every condition set by the inspectors and has not put up any kind of serious obstacle to their activities. Thus, we are in a position to state that the international inspectors—if they are given the opportunity to continue their work—have everything they need to complete the process of Baghdad's peaceful disarmament.

Therefore, the Security Council, as the body that bears primary responsibility for the maintenance of international peace and security, has fully shouldered its obligations by ensuring the deployment of international inspectors to Iraq and by establishing the conditions necessary for their activities. It is not by chance that even those who today cast doubt on the Council's role in an Iraqi settlement are forced to admit that they will have no other choice but to return this issue to the Council, which alone is authorized to deal with its comprehensive settlement.

Bearing all these considerations in mind, we believe that first, on behalf of the Security Council, we should express our highest regard for the activities of the international inspectors and should extend to them—as well as to the heads of UNMOVIC and of the IAEA, Mr. Blix and Mr. ElBaradei—our support and our gratitude for the excellent work that they have accomplished.

Secondly, we should approve the reports submitted, which clearly set forth the current status of prohibited arms programs in Iraq.

Thirdly, because of the difficult situation prevailing with regard to Iraq, we should take note of the Secretary-General's decision to withdraw the inspectors from Iraq because of the threat to their safety.

Fourthly, since the mandates of UNMOVIC and of the IAEA have not been fully implemented, the inspectors' work in Iraq has not been concluded but merely suspended. With a view to the further development of the situation, the Security Council must return to the issue of continuing this work, pursuant to resolutions 1284 (1999) and 1441 (2002).

We can only express regret that, at precisely the time when the prospect for Iraq's disarmament through inspections had become more than real, problems were put forward that have no direct bearing on resolution 1441 (2002) or on other United Nations decisions concerning Iraq. Not one of those decisions authorizes the right to use force against Iraq outside the Charter of the United Nations; not one of them authorizes the violent overthrow of the leadership of a sovereign State. Such actions, if they are undertaken, will not help to strengthen the unity of the international community at a time when the world sorely needs solidarity and united efforts, first and foremost, to repel such a real and universally shared threat as international terrorism.

Russia is convinced of the need to do everything possible, as soon as possible, in order to overcome the present crisis situation and to keep the Iraq problem within the framework of a political settlement, based solidly on the United Nations Charter and international law. Only in that way will we be able to ensure conditions for the continued, effective and multilateral cooperation needed to combat global threats and challenges, while retaining the central role of the United Nations Security Council.

On 11 September 2001, when the American people suffered a horrible tragedy, the President of Russia, Vladimir Putin, was the first person to phone the United States President, George Bush, to extend solidarity and support to him. These were sincere feelings expressed by the entire Russian people.

If today we really had indisputable facts demonstrating that there was a direct threat from the territory of Iraq to the security of the United States of America, then Russia, without any hesitation, would be prepared to use the entire arsenal of measures provided under the United Nations Charter to eliminate such a threat. However, the Security Council today is not in possession of such facts. That is why we prefer a political settlement, relying on the activities of UNMOVIC and the IAEA, which enjoy the full trust of the international community.

List of Documents

A description of the varied sources for these documents is provided at the end of volume III of this collection.

Chapter 3. August 26-October 10, 2002:
"The Danger to Our Country is Grave...":
The Bush Administration Presses Congress to
Authorize Use of Force in Iraq 221

Chapter 8. March 6-19, 2003:
The U.S. and U.K. Put Forth, Then Withdraw, a
Draft U.N. Security Council Resolution Authorizing War;
Bush Issues a 48-Hour Ultimatum 1197

Index

Name Index

Subject Index